5

THE BRITISH EMPIRE IN THE MIDDLE EAST

1945–1951

ARAB NATIONALISM, THE UNITED STATES, AND POSTWAR IMPERIALISM

Other Books by the same Author

Ruanda–Urundi, 1884–1919 (1963)

Great Britain and Germany's Lost Colonies, 1914–1919 (1967)

(with Jean Stengers) *E. D. Morel's History of the Congo Reform Movement* (1968)

British Strategy in the Far East, 1919–1939 (1971)

Imperialism at Bay 1941–1945: The United States and the Decolonization of the British Empire (1977)

Books edited by Wm. Roger Louis

Ed. (with Prosser Gifford) *Britain and Germany in Africa: Imperial Rivalry and Colonial Rule* (1967)

Ed. (with Prosser Gifford) *France and Britain in Africa: Imperial Rivalry and Colonial Rule* (1971)

Ed. *National Security and International Trusteeship in the Pacific* (1972)

Ed. (with William S. Livingston) *Australia, New Zealand and the Pacific Islands since the First World War* (1979)

Ed. *The Origins of the Second World War: A. J. P. Taylor and his Critics* (1972)

Ed. *Imperialism: The Robinson and Gallagher Controversy* (1976)

Ed. (with Prosser Gifford) *The Transfer of Power in Africa* (1982)

The British Empire in the Middle East

1945–1951

ARAB NATIONALISM,
THE UNITED STATES, AND
POSTWAR IMPERIALISM

by

Wm. Roger Louis

CLARENDON PRESS · OXFORD
1984

Oxford University Press, Walton Street, Oxford OX2 6DP

London Glasgow New York Toronto
Delhi Bombay Calcutta Madras Karachi
Kuala Lumpur Singapore Hong Kong Tokyo
Nairobi Dar es Salaam Cape Town
Melbourne Auckland
and associated companies in
Beirut Berlin Ibadan Mexico City Nicosia

Oxford is a trade mark of Oxford University Press

Published in the United States
by Oxford University Press, New York

British Library Cataloguing in Publication Data

Louis, William Roger
  The British Empire in the Middle East, 1945–1951.
  1. Great Britain—Foreign relations—Near East
  2. Great Britain—Foreign relations—20th century
  3. Near East—Foreign relations—Great Britain
  I. Title
  327.41056   DA47.9.N2
  ISBN 0–19–822489–3

Library of Congress Cataloging in Publication Data

Louis, Wm. Roger.
  The British Empire in the Middle East, 1945–1951.
  Includes index.
  1. Near East—Foreign relations—Great Britain.
  2. Great Britain—Foreign relations—Near East.
  3. Great Britain—Foreign relations—1945–
  I. Title.
  DS63.2.G7L68   1984   327.41056   83–19345
  ISBN 0–19–822489–3

Typeset by Joshua Associates, Oxford
Printed in Great Britain
at the University Press, Oxford

FOR

Andy and Cathy

PREFACE

THIS book is about British disengagement in the Middle East during the period of the Labour government 1945-51. Labour's 'grand strategy' was to refrain from direct intervention and to conciliate the 'moderate' nationalists. My purpose is to delineate the changing nature of British influence in the Middle East. The history of the period may be interpreted as the unsuccessful attempt to transform the system of domination, whether in the form of alliances, concessions, or direct rule, into a relationship of equal partners. The aim was to prevent the initiative from passing to 'anti-British extremists', and to sustain British influence by economic and social reform, in order to maintain Britain's position as a 'world power' with a predominant place in the Middle East. Non-intervention and 'partnership' thus may be regarded as an alternative means of preserving British power.

The actual withdrawal (aside from the evacuation of parts of the 'northern tier' and the former Italian colonial empire) was limited to Palestine, where the British had to cut losses in 1948, and to Iran, where they were evicted from the oilfields in 1951. The Palestine problem is the major disruptive element in the story. Arab nationalism, frustrated in Palestine, could not be appeased. In a large sense the book is a comment on the British response not only to Arab nationalism but also to Jewish and Iranian nationalism. Anglo-American efforts to resolve the Palestine problem form a major part of the volume. Another part concerns the revolution brought about in the economic affairs of the Middle East by the American innovation of the fifty–fifty split in oil profits, and the Iranian as well as the British reaction. Above all the book deals with the perpetual source of friction between the British and the Egyptians: the Canal Zone and the question of British evacuation.

The book does not systematically examine the Middle Eastern policy of the United States, but sometimes the focus shifts to the American side because otherwise the dilemmas facing the British cannot be fully understood. This is especially true in the case of Zionism. On the question of establishing a Jewish state in Palestine the Americans and the British were fundamentally divided, no less on the ethical issues than on those of power politics. To some extent in the United States there was a fusion of the Zionist movement and the American anti-colonial tradition. On almost all other Middle Eastern questions the British and American governments were basically in agreement, though Americans in general remained sceptical about British imperialism being transformed into an enlightened instrument of economic and social progress. Even in the period before the Korean war the United States increasingly regarded the British Empire as a bulwark against Communism and the Soviet Union's expansionism, but the controversy over the Canal Zone prevented the creation of a British 'Middle East Command' backed by American military and economic power. American policy at that time demonstrated a wariness towards Middle Eastern nationalism as well as an appreciation of the strategic assets of the British Empire.

The period was one of hardship for the British people. These were six gloomy years. The economic troubles were accentuated by the necessity of a $3.75 billion loan from the United States in 1945 (and with it a troubled awareness of British dependency). As if in a two-year rhythm there followed the convertibility crisis of 1947, the devaluation of 1949, and the balance of payments crisis of 1951. During this time there was prolonged public debate about the proper use of Britain's economic and military resources. The Labour government, committed to the liquidation of the old British Empire, became dedicated to the development of the Middle East and Africa as a replacement for India. This aim could be achieved in the long run only by dealing with the peoples of the Middle East as equals, not by prodding them with bayonets. This was the vision of the Labour government, particularly of the statesman who dominates much of this book, Ernest Bevin. In retrospect it may appear that the goal was an illusion, but the attempt to halt the decline and collapse of the British Empire, and to put it on a new basis, must rank, even to critics of British imperialism, as a remarkable if not a heroic episode.

The book is based on archival sources and private papers listed on pp. xv–xvii. I wish to thank the archivists and librarians of those collections for their assistance as well as the holders of copyright for permission to publish material in their possession.

It is a genuine pleasure to acknowledge the help I have received along the way. The research for the book was begun in 1979–80 when I was a Visiting Fellow at All Souls College, Oxford. At All Souls and St. Antony's I am indebted in various ways to Raymond Carr, Tony Honoré, Michael Howard, Kenneth Kirkwood, Denis Mack Smith, Roger Owen, Christopher Platt, John Sparrow—and especially Lord Beloff, who inspired certain parts of the book and then gave me the benefit of his critical views on all of it (those whose work has been subjected to his scrutiny will be aware of the anguish). Kenneth Robinson also holds a special place in these acknowledgements because of his sustained, detailed, far-reaching, and often disconcerting criticism. In a similar way I have also consistently profited from suggestions by Sir Harold Beeley, David Fieldhouse, Paul Kennedy, J. D. B. Miller, and Sir Denis Wright. With Lord Bullock I have enjoyed many fruitful discussions, and I am grateful for having been able to read the last instalment of his biography of Ernest Bevin in typescript. I also wish to thank Brian Bond, Sally Chilver, Sir Keith Hancock, Elie Kedourie, Sir John Martin, Kenneth Morgan, Sir Frank Roberts, Lord St. Brides, Zara Steiner, A. P. Thornton, D. C. Watt (whose recent book, *Succeeding John Bull*, I was able to read in typescript), and C. M. Woodhouse. Alaine Low, Keith and Simone Panter-Brick, and Alison Smith will know that mere words are insufficient acknowledgement. The same is true of that quintessential Clarendonian, Peter Sutcliffe.

My research was facilitated at different times by the John Simon Guggenheim Memorial Foundation, the Advanced Research Program of the United States Naval War College, the Rockefeller center at Bellagio, the University Research Institute of the University of Texas at Austin, and the Dora Bonham Fund of the U. T. History Department. I wish to thank my Texan colleagues in the Department of History, the Humanities Research Center, the Center for Middle Eastern Studies, and the Faculty Seminar on British Studies, not least Carlton Lake and William S. Livingston, and above all, from beginning to end and page by page, Carl Leiden and Walt Rostow. I am indebted in different ways to James Bill, Robert Divine, Hafez Farmayan, Robert and Elizabeth Fernea, Peter Green, Clarence Lasby, Malcolm Macdonald, Standish Meacham, Sidney Monas, James Roach, Michael Stoff, and Decherd Turner. Robert Stookey will know that any words of thanks would be entirely insufficient. The whole book in various ways inadequately reflects his knowledge of the Middle East.

My views on Arab nationalism and Zionism, and on the United States and the Middle East, have been influenced by the sensitive and dead-on-the-mark observations of J. C. Hurewitz. On questions of strategy and generally on the postwar era I have an enduring sense of gratitude to James E. King for guidance as well as unvarnished and fundamental criticism. To Evan Wilson I am especially grateful for assistance on the Palestine problem. On Anglo-American relations and American foreign policy I have benefited from the suggestions of John Lewis Gaddis. Michael Cohen, whose own book was being completed roughly at the same time, has helped me to try to deal both realistically and sympathetically with the question of Zionism, and parts of the book have been much improved by his comments. For various other kinds of advice and assistance I am grateful to Prosser Gifford, Peter Gran, Joseph Hamburger, Joseph Heller, Malcolm Kerr, Stephen Koss, Stephen McFarland, Ernest May, and Robin Winks. Jean Stengers will recognize his influence on the book.

Acknowledgements usually end with a disclaimer. These will not entirely conform with that tradition. Whatever the shortcomings of the book may be in the realm of the theory of imperialism, I will be glad to share them with Ronald Robinson. I am aware that the 'Imperialism of Free Trade' is inadequately pounded into each chapter, verse, and note, though it is certainly there in spirit. With such a friend, who needs critics? His sense of humour and unswerving quest for the ultimate meaning of imperialism have been an inspiration. He has been an unfailing source of support. I also wish to mention that at least certain parts of this book have managed to sustain the interest of A. J. P. Taylor, and I have benefited from his reaction. 'The affair is highly discreditable to the majority of the Labour cabinet', he wrote to me after reading the chapter on Persian oil. 'Clem as usual is the only one who comes out with his reputation enhanced—the best leader Labour ever had.'

Last and above all I wish to thank Albert Hourani. Without him this book might not have been written, and certainly not in its present form and general argument. Here the pen falters in search for appropriate words. Albert Hourani speaks with the moral passion of his generation, yet his understanding of the Middle East is not only incisive but also humane and judicious towards the Americans as well as the British, and the Jews as well as the Arabs. Working with him through these tangled problems has been an intellectual adventure of the highest order. I can only hope that the book fulfils some of his expectations.

CONTENTS

MAPS

ABBREVIATIONS AND LOCATION
OF MANUSCRIPT SOURCES

Public Record Office, London:
CAB	Cabinet Office
CO	Colonial Office
COS	Chiefs of Staff records (in the CAB and DEFE series)
DEFE	Ministry of Defence
FO	Foreign Office
PREM	Prime Minister's Office
WO	War Office

National Archives, Washington:
USSD	State Department
USJCS	Joint Chiefs of Staff

Harry S. Truman Presidential Library, Independence, Missouri: Truman Library

Israel:
CZA	Central Zionist Archives, Jerusalem
ISA	Israel State Archives, Jerusalem
WA	Weizmann Archives, Rehovot

Acheson Papers. Papers of Dean Acheson, Truman Library.

Alexander Papers. Papers of A. V. Alexander, Churchill College, Cambridge.

Alsop Papers. Papers of Joseph and Stewart Alsop, Library of Congress, Washington DC.

Attlee Papers. Papers of Clement Attlee, Bodleian Library, Oxford, and Churchill College, Cambridge.

Austin Papers. Papers of Warren Austin, University of Vermont Library, Burlington, Vermont.

Aydelotte Papers. Papers and Diary of Frank Aydelotte, Friends Historical Library, Swarthmore College, Swarthmore, Pennsylvania.

Bunche Papers. Papers of Ralph Bunche, U. C. L. A. Library, Los Angeles.

Cadogan Diaries. Diaries of Sir Alexander Cadogan, Churchill College, Cambridge.

Clifford Papers. Papers of Clark Clifford, Truman Library.

Creech Jones Papers. Papers of Arthur Creech Jones, Rhodes House, Oxford.

Crossman Papers. Papers of Richard Crossman, Middle East Centre, St. Antony's College, Oxford.

Cunningham Papers. Papers of Sir Alan Cunningham, Middle East Centre, St. Antony's College, Oxford.

Dalton Diaries. Diaries of Hugh Dalton, London School of Economics.

Fabian Colonial Bureau Papers. Rhodes House, Oxford.

Forrestal Papers. Papers and Diary of James Forrestal, Firestone Library, Princeton University.

Frankfurter Papers. Papers of Felix Frankfurter, Library of Congress, Washington D.C.

Grady Papers. Papers of Henry F. Grady, Truman Library.

Harvey Papers. Diaries and Papers of Lord (Sir Oliver) Harvey, British Library, London.

Hurley Papers. Papers of Patrick J. Hurley, University of Oklahoma Library, Norman, Oklahoma.

Hutcheson Papers. Papers of Joseph Hutcheson, Humanities Research Center, University of Texas, Austin, Texas.

Killearn Diaries. Diaries of Lord Killearn (Sir Miles Lampson), Middle East Centre, St. Antony's College, Oxford.

MacDonald Papers. Papers of James G. MacDonald, Columbia University, New York.

Sir John Martin Papers (privately held).

Kingsley Martin Papers. Papers of Kingsley Martin, University of Sussex Library, Brighton.

Mitchell Papers. Papers of Sir Philip Mitchell, Rhodes House, Oxford.

Monroe Papers. Papers of Elizabeth Monroe, Middle East Centre, St. Antony's College, Oxford.

Phillips Papers. Papers and Diary of William Phillips, Houghton Library, Harvard University.

Quilliam Papers. Papers of C. D. Quilliam, *The Times* Archive, London.

Robertson Papers. Papers of Sir James Robertson, Sudan Archive, University of Durham.

Rosenman Papers. Papers of Samuel Rosenman, Truman Library.

RIIA. Papers of the 'Middle East Group' Royal Institute of International Affairs, Chatham House, London.

Shone Papers. Papers of Sir Terence Shone, Middle East Centre, St. Antony's College, Oxford.

Spears Papers. Papers of Sir Edward Spears, Middle East Centre, St. Antony's College, Oxford.

Stansgate Papers. Papers of Lord Stansgate, House of Lords Record Office, London.

Stokes Papers. Papers of Richard Stokes, Bodleian Library, Oxford.

Truman Papers. Papers of Harry S. Truman, Truman Library.

Weizmann Papers. Papers of Chaim Weizmann, Weizmann Archives.

Foreign Relations.   *Foreign Relations of the United States* (Government Printing Office, Washington, DC).

Israel Documents.   *Political and Diplomatic Documents* (Israel State Archives and Central Zionist Archives, Jerusalem).

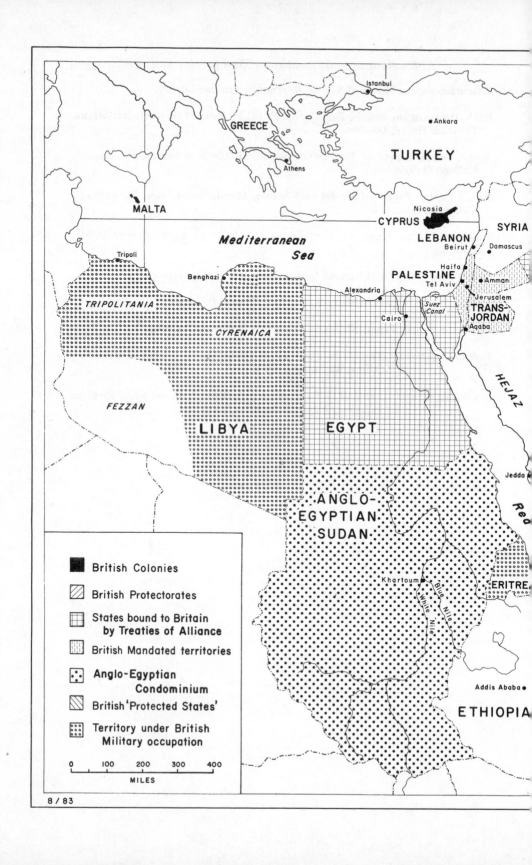

British Colonies

British Protectorates

States bound to Britain
by Treaties of Alliance

British Mandated territories

Anglo-Egyptian
Condominium

British 'Protected States'

Territory under British
Military occupation

0   100   200   300   400
         MILES

8 / 83

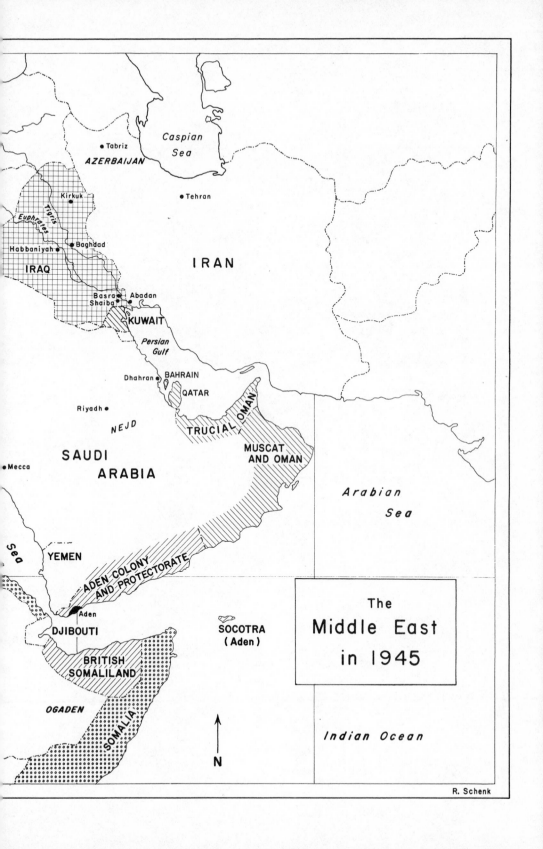

Caspian Sea

• Tabriz

AZERBAIJAN

• Tehran

• Kirkuk

Euphrates
Tigris

Habbaniyah •   • Baghdad

IRAQ

IRAN

Basra •   • Abadan
Shaiba •

KUWAIT

Persian Gulf

Dhahran •   • BAHRAIN

QATAR

Riyadh •

NEJD

TRUCIAL OMAN

MUSCAT AND OMAN

SAUDI ARABIA

• Mecca

Arabian Sea

Sea

YEMEN

ADEN COLONY AND PROTECTORATE

Aden

DJIBOUTI

SOCOTRA (Aden)

BRITISH SOMALILAND

OGADEN

SOMALIA

N

The
Middle East
in 1945

Indian Ocean

R. Schenk

PART I

INTRODUCTION

IN ALL of the complexity of Middle Eastern issues facing the British Labour government in the postwar era, there is one individual and one theme of paramount significance: Ernest Bevin and his policy of non-intervention. Otherwise all might have been different. During his tenure as Foreign Secretary from July 1945 until March 1951, Bevin, when confronted with the choice, refrained from toppling kings and unseating prime ministers. It has always been known that the Labour government claimed not to have interfered in the internal politics of the countries of the Middle East. What has not been revealed until the opening of the archives is that the policy of non-intervention was a matter of principle espoused in secret discussions above all by Bevin and endorsed by his colleagues. It was not by accident that there was nothing comparable to forcing King Farouk to accept a Wafd government in 1942 or the adventure at Suez in 1956. What distinguished the postwar Labour government was the conscious affirmation of the belief that intervention would ultimately undermine rather than sustain British influence in the Middle East. Labour's 'grand strategy' (in the sense of underlying principle and sustained aspiration) may be summed up in the phrases 'non-intervention' and 'conciliation'.

Bevin dominated the Cabinet and restrained the interventionist tendencies of the permanent officials. He presided over foreign and 'Imperial' affairs with a grasp of detail as well as a command of general policy in a manner unparalleled since Lord Curzon at the end of the First World War. The achievements of the Bevin years of postwar reconstruction and reorientation in world affairs have now been recorded in magisterial history by Lord Bullock.[1] It will not be the purpose of these introductory remarks to follow in the footsteps of his biography, but it is necessary to draw the contrast between the success of Bevin's European policies and the frustration he encountered in the Middle East. In Europe and throughout most of the rest of the world Bevin managed to bring British aims into alignment with those of the United States. The creation of the North Atlantic Treaty Organization in 1949 was a landmark in the history of the postwar world. In the Middle

[1] Alan Bullock, *The Life and Times of Ernest Bevin: Foreign Secretary 1945–51* (London, 1983). The two preceding volumes are: *Trade Union Leader 1881–1940* (London, 1960); and *Minister of Labour 1940–1945* (London, 1967). Subsequent references will be to the recent volume covering his career as Foreign Secretary and will be abbreviated as Bullock, *Bevin*. The indispensable works of reference on the Middle East for the period are the two volumes by George Kirk, *The Middle East in the War* (London, 1952), and *The Middle East: 1945–1950* (London, 1954); and Howard M. Sachar, *Europe Leaves the Middle East 1936–1954* (New York, 1972). For the themes with which the present volume is concerned the fundamental point of departure is Elizabeth Monroe, *Britain's Moment in the Middle East, 1914–1956* (London, 1963).

East however the United States and Britain stood divided on the future of Palestine.

Bevin believed that the answer to the problem of Jewish refugees and displaced persons should be sought in Europe rather than in Palestine, which he regarded as a predominantly Arab country. He found himself caught between Jewish nationalism supercharged by the emotions of the holocaust, and the anti-Zionism of the Arabs, without whose goodwill the British Empire in the Middle East would be doomed. The British could not support a Jewish state without alienating the Arabs. Nor could the British impose a settlement acceptable to the Arab countries without antagonizing the United States. The Middle East in Bevin's view was second in importance only to Europe; but, in order for Britain to remain the dominant regional power, both Arab co-operation and the support of the United States were vital. Without them Britain's influence would decline, and not only in the Middle East. Britain would sink into the status of a second-class European power like the Netherlands. That apprehension helps to explain the emotional and creative energy that Bevin and other British leaders expended on the re-generation of the British presence in the Middle East. Palestine in this larger context represented the principal stumbling block. In view of the overriding priorities of Arab collaboration and American assistance, the accusations against Bevin—for example that he was callous to Jewish suffering—become more comprehensible. In short he was pursuing a grand Imperial strategy in which Palestine played only a small but most irritating part.

Churchill once described Bevin as 'a working class John Bull'. Like all good caricatures, this contained an element of truth. With his working-class background and his concern for the welfare of common people, Bevin saw no contradiction between the development of the oil and other resources of the Middle East and what he hoped would be the future prosperity of the British Commonwealth. He believed, as did many Englishmen of his generation, that the British Empire was a beneficent force in world affairs, though the word 'Empire' would have to be replaced in the Middle East with something that suggested less of exploitation and more of equal partnership. The British and the Arabs could work together to develop the region to mutual advantage. Economically the Middle East together with Africa offered just as alluring a prospect as India had in the past. Militarily the countries of the Middle East could be brought into a system of defence that would help to offset the manpower and military potential of the Soviet Union. Such in brief was Bevin's vision, which will be discussed throughout this book in relation to the views of others who shared it or dissented from it. With imagination and tireless energy (and only rarely with lapses into pessimism and discouragement), he wove political, economic, and military strands of thought into a coherent general policy that sought to preserve Britain as a great power. The Middle East was the principal pillar of Britain's position in the world.

The strength of Bevin's personality usually enabled him to prevail in discussions on these subjects within the government. The power of his intellect as well as his domineering manner is well conveyed by Roy Jenkins:

> Towards the end of a morning in the middle years of the 1945 Government Bevin arrived late at a meeting of the Defence Committee of the Cabinet, and waddled round the table to his seat. Attlee was just beginning his summing up. This terse exercise was not allowed to continue to its rapid conclusion. As soon as he caught the drift, Bevin interrupted. 'That won't do, Prime Minister', he said. 'That won't do at all. It don't fit in with my policy.' Attlee allowed Bevin his way, as he would have allowed no other member of the Government. The discussion began again and reached the opposite conclusion. . . . Bevin on this occasion . . . simply stopped the engine in its tracks, lifted it up, and put it back facing in the other direction.[2]

Until the outbreak of the Second World War, Bevin had distinguished himself primarily as the most powerful labour leader in Britain in his capacity as head of the Transport and General Workers' Union. He had also visited the United States during the First World War, had participated in the economic and political work of the International Labour Organization, and in 1938 had attended the Commonwealth Relations Conference in Sydney. In 1940, at the age of fifty-nine, he became Minister of Labour and a member of the War Cabinet. When he was appointed Foreign Secretary in July 1945 and went to the Potsdam Conference at short notice, he immediately demonstrated a grasp of the essential issues. In Middle Eastern affairs from the beginning until near the end, there was never any doubt that Bevin was the moving force behind British policy.

He could not systematically have pursued his Middle Eastern aims without the effective partnership of the Prime Minister, Clement Attlee. Bevin was careful to square his ideas with Attlee's before Cabinet meetings. Together the two of them often made an unbreakable combination. In the first two years of the Labour government, when Attlee remained at the centre of deliberations on India, Bevin usually took the initiative in the Middle East. They held similar outlooks. Attlee adhered to the principle of non-intervention just as firmly as Bevin (as was proved in the case of the Persian oil crisis in

[2] Roy Jenkins, *Nine Men of Power* (London, 1974), p. 63.

the summer of 1951 after Bevin's death). At the same time there were important differences of temperament as well as a clash of ideas between the two men about the purpose and nature of Britain's presence in the Middle East. If there was truth in the view that Bevin pursued a Churchillian line in Imperial affairs, it was also true that Attlee was closer to the tradition of 'Little England'.

'Little Englander' was a label that could be applied with some accuracy to Attlee's outlook on the Middle East (though not, even in the eyes of his critics, on India and other parts of the world). He was much more sceptical than Bevin about Britain's economic and military capacity to remain a 'great power' in the Middle East. He questioned the value of the occupation of the former Italian colonies of Libya, Eritrea, and Somalia just as keenly as Sir William Harcourt had doubted the wisdom of the reconquest of the Sudan in the 1890s. 'Deficit areas', was the phrase Attlee used contemptuously. He furthermore believed that the development of air power during the Second World War and the potential of atomic weapons had irrevocably weakened Britain's traditional mastery of the Mediterranean based on sea power. To a far greater extent than Bevin, Attlee was willing to acknowledge the diminution of British power and to contemplate British withdrawal from the Middle East.[3]

There is one more individual who requires special introduction. He is far less of a significant historical personage, but he is nevertheless of critical importance in parts of this book. This is Arthur Creech Jones, who was Parliamentary Under-Secretary for the Colonies from July 1945 until October 1946, and then Colonial Secretary until his defeat in the general election of February 1950. Both Attlee and Bevin respected Creech Jones and listened to his advice, though Attlee lamented his political ineffectiveness and came to regard his appointment as a mistake. 'Creech Jones despite much hard work and devotion', Attlee wrote in 1950, 'had not appeared to have a real grip of administration in the Colonial Office.'[4] 'Creech' (as he was known to his friends) was sympathetic to the aims of the moderate Zionists, in other words, those who wished

---

[3] The recent biography of *Attlee* by Kenneth Harris (London, 1982), though less good on Palestine than on India, is entirely accurate in stressing the balance, moderation, and scepticism that Attlee brought to bear on Middle Eastern affairs.

[4] Attlee's notes, 1950, ATLE 1/17, Attlee Papers (Cambridge). For Labour's colonial policy see especially Partha Sarathi Gupta, *Imperialism and the British Labour Movement, 1914-1964* (London, 1975); for reappraisal of the financial and military issues in the post-war period, see his 'Imperialism and the Labour Government of 1945-51' in Jay Winter (ed.), *The Working Class in Modern British History* (Cambridge, 1983). Two older works that continue to have a lasting value for the themes of the present volume are M. A. Fitz-simmons, *The Foreign Policy of the British Labour Government: 1945-1951* (University of Notre Dame Press, 1953); and Leon D. Epstein, *Britain: Uneasy Ally* (Chicago, 1954).

to see the partition of Palestine and the creation of a Jewish state (though he himself never endorsed the idea of so large a state as the one that came into existence in 1948). It was the ability of Creech Jones and Bevin to work harmoniously together that helps to explain why the Palestine issue within the Labour government remained relatively non-controversial. The Colonial Office and the Foreign Office, the two offices of state mainly concerned with Palestine, often clashed over many issues, but when ministerial policy was agreed upon by Creech Jones and Bevin as well as Attlee, then it was virtually invulnerable to challenge by other members of the Cabinet or by the Chiefs of Staff.

Creech Jones was in fact overshadowed by Bevin and consumed by the Palestine issue. Throughout his career he was associated with Bevin, first in the Transport and General Workers' Union and later as Bevin's Parliamentary Under-Secretary at the Ministry of Labour during the war. The facts of that connection however fail to do justice to Creech Jones's passionate and long-standing interest in colonial affairs. In 1940 with Rita Hinden he founded the Fabian Colonial Bureau. In terms of knowledge about the colonies, especially the ones in Africa, he came to his position as Colonial Secretary with thorough preparation. He was responsible for endorsing the Labour government's new direction in colonial policy that later culminated in the transfer of power in Africa. He is remembered as the epitome of British decency and goodwill towards 'colonial' peoples. It is therefore ironic that he had to devote so much of his time to Palestine, which was by no means a typical colonial dependency. At first he was not unoptimistic, but eventually he came to believe that it was impossible realistically to come to terms with the Zionists. He later took pains to emphasize that he and Bevin were ultimately at one on Palestine. In the realm of economic development of the Middle East and Africa, Creech Jones's outlook was virtually identical with Bevin's.

Amongst the three of them, Attlee, Bevin, and Creech Jones possessed a wide-ranging grasp over Asian and African affairs. Attlee's participation in the Simon Commission on India in 1927–30 was critical in preparing him to take decisive action in 1945-7.[5] During the war, when he had been Deputy Prime Minister, he chaired the Armistice and Post War Committee, of which Bevin was also a member. As Lord Bullock has pointed out, there could have been no better apprenticeship for a future Prime Minister and Foreign Secretary. The same may be said of Creech Jones's experience in

[5] See R. J. Moore, *Escape from Empire: The Attlee Government and the Indian Problem* (Oxford, 1983).

the Fabian Colonial Bureau as preparation for his service as Colonial Secretary. For Attlee and Bevin the extensive committee work during the war was probably crucial in shaping their views about specific problems of the postwar world. It was the hour-after-hour deliberation in committee, for example, that gave Bevin the knowledge and the overall grip on world affairs that enabled him to move forward with such confidence in the Middle East. In these discussions, both during and after the war, he often demonstrated a fascination with Africa as well. The exploitation of the oil of the Middle East was vital to the prosperity and defence of the Empire and Commonwealth, but it was the development of the African continent that would prove to be the ultimate challenge.

The goals of the Labour government could be achieved only by dealing with the peoples of the Middle East and Asia, and eventually those of Africa, on an equal footing. The belief in the necessity for this revolution in Imperial attitude was a vital part of the ethos of the postwar Labour era. The transformation of the Empire into a multiracial Commonwealth—and the informal equivalent in the Middle East—was an article of faith. Whether the end of the old system would break the dependency relationship was another question.

Quite apart from Labour idealism, would a Conservative government under Churchill's leadership have pursued a different course in attempting to resolve the specific problems of the postwar period? The question may be answered with certainty in the affirmative, though Bevin and Churchill saw eye to eye on many issues. If anything Churchill would have evacuated Palestine earlier, and he would assuredly have done it with better grace than Bevin. Nevertheless there were substantial and divisive differences between the Tory and the Labour outlooks, in particular on the questions of the Canal Zone and the refinery at Abadan in Iran. Churchill believed that Suez should continue to provide Britain with a commanding bastion in the Middle East regardless of the loss of India. Suez in his view remained the geographical keystone of the Middle East and indeed one of the supreme geopolitical positions in all of the world. He never forgave the Labour government for offering to withdraw British troops from Egypt in the spring of 1946. He also used the word 'scuttle' in reference to the evacuation from Abadan in 1951. The differences in Tory and Labour modes of thought were real and not imagined.

The phrase 'Suez base' was misleading, as was the term 'Abadan refinery'. The two were gigantic enclaves, the one military and the other industrial. The refinery at Abadan was the largest in the world.

Its importance for the British economy, which will be discussed in the chapter on the Persian oil crisis, may be conveyed here by the fact that in 1945 Iran produced more oil than all of the Arab countries combined. The British community of 4,500 lived as a separate and self-contained cultural unit. The oil fields in southern Iran and the refinery at Abadan functioned independently from the Iranian economy. The Anglo-Iranian Oil Company possessed its own fleet, its own hospitals, and its own schools. Members of the Gymkhana Club in Abadan read the airmail edition of *The Times*. The refinery itself was a tribute to British technology. Between 1945 and 1950 the production of Arab and Persian oil increased from 13 to 18 per cent of the world's total. In 1950–2 the world's oil production rose from 535 million tons to 637 million, of which Iran produced 30 million. After the Iranian nationalization and the British evacuation in 1951, production fell to less than one million. Clearly there was a lesson here that might have been anticipated, but in this instance the men of the Labour government had drawn the wrong conclusion: if left to themselves, the Persians would come to their senses and recognize that the oil industry could not be run without British assistance. The alternative to halting the operations of the Abadan refinery in 1951, however, was military intervention. One of the last major acts of the Labour government was the decision in favour of restraint.

The Suez enclave stretched not only from the Mediterranean to the Red Sea but also westwards three-quarters of the way to Cairo. In the west it included the supply ordnance depot at Tel-el-Kabir, the site of the defeat of the Egyptians in 1882 that signalled the beginning of the British occupation. The enclave's physical structure consisted of a network of roads, railways, harbours, ports, military garrisons, airfields, and a flying-boat station. There were ammunition dumps and extensive repair facilities that were irreplaceable. In short it was a vast arsenal. The region of hills and scrub in the south as well as the barren desert areas provided splendid grounds for manœuvres and training. The canal from Cairo provided fresh water. Egyptian goods and services were available. By military standards the barracks were comfortable and the officers' mess at General Headquarters at Fayid was first-class. Life in the Canal Zone was by no means a hardship. Before 1947 Suez was the largest reservoir of British military strength outside India. Estimates of the actual numbers of British troops varied widely because many of them were posted only temporarily or were in transit, but at the close of the war there were over 200,000. By 1951 the Labour government, for statistical purposes at least, had managed to reduce the number to 38,000, which was still nearly four times the figure of 10,000 allowed by the Anglo-Egyptian Treaty of 1936.

For purposes of these introductory remarks it is the figure of 100,000, or about five divisions, that is useful to bear in mind. The number 100,000 was a figure itself that captured the public imagination. It was a magic number. 100,000 was the optimal number that the Chiefs of Staff believed to be a good military strength for Suez. 100,000 was also the number of Jewish refugees that President Truman pressed the British to admit into Palestine. 100,000 was the number of British troops at the height of the emergency in Palestine before evacuation in 1948. 100,000 was the number of Israeli troops in the 1948 war (an exaggerated figure, but one which symbolized the mobilization of a nation at war). To an Egyptian nationalist, the presence of 100,000 British troops on Egyptian soil, or even 10,000, was a constant reminder of the occupation and an endless source of rancour.

There was truth in the view that the Middle East could be regarded as a region honeycombed with British military installations. Apart from those in Egypt and Palestine, among the more important were the two air bases at Habbaniyah and Shaiba in Iraq; the military garrison of the Arab Legion at Amman in Transjordan; the airfield and military bases at Khartoum in the Sudan; and the naval bases at Bahrain and Aden.[6] Cyrenaica (the eastern province of Libya) held the greatest potential as an alternative to the military installations in Egypt and Palestine (though Kenya was also a possibility, as will be seen). This was an alternative that the British military mind contemplated only with greatest reluctance. Until the spring of 1946 the Canal Zone and Palestine together were usually regarded as the heart of a vast British military preserve. Troops could easily be transferred back and forth by road, rail, and air, and the two combined territories provided ample facilities for all three fighting services. British military strength would continue to predominate in the eastern Mediterranean, according to one school of thought, as long as Palestine remained under British sway as a fallback position from the Canal Zone. Not only was the equable Palestine climate conducive to the permanent garrisoning of troops but also the air base at

---

[6] Aden and the problems of the Persian gulf fall beyond the scope of the present book. In general see the works by J. B. Kelly, e.g. *Arabia, the Gulf, and the West* (London, 1980); and Robert W. Stookey, e.g. *The Arabian Peninsula* (Hoover Institution Press, 1984). On British policy in an earlier period in this region (and the Middle East generally) see especially Briton Cooper Busch, *Britain, India, and the Arabs, 1914–1921* (Berkeley, 1971), the themes of which connect with those of the present volume. Marian Kent, *Oil and Empire: British Policy and Mesopotamian Oil, 1900–1920* (London, 1976), is essential for the question of oil.

Lydda and the naval installations at Haifa had a strategic value that might help to offset, if necessary, an eventual withdrawal from Egypt. (Haifa was also a terminus of the pipeline from the Iraqi oil fields of Kirkuk and the location of a British refinery about one-quarter the size of the one at Abadan.) The report of the Anglo-American Committee of Inquiry on Palestine in April 1946, however, suggested that Britain might not have an indefinite future in Palestine. In the following month the Labour government offered to withdraw troops from Egypt. These developments came as profoundly disagreeable jolts to military planners. Within a year after the end of the war in Europe, the British military presence in these two key areas of the Middle East appeared uncertain. The loss of Palestine in 1948 explains the hardening of determination to stay on in the Canal Zone, and the uncertainty of the long-range British future in Suez in turn helps to make clear the reasons for the increasing importance attributed to military installations in places of lesser strategic significance such as Cyprus.

The question of maintaining a standing army in Egypt and Palestine aroused controversy in England as well as in the Middle East. 'Nearly 100,000 British soldiers had been kept in Palestine', Churchill declared in attacking the Labour government in August 1947, 'and £30,000,000 or £40,000,000 a year of our hard-earned money had been cast away there.'[7] He made that statement during the sterling convertibility crisis and at the beginning of a new period of economic austerity in August 1947. At a time when there appeared to be no limit to the amount of British money going down the drain in Palestine, the meat ration in England was being cut by one-sixth, a restriction was placed on the private use of petrol, and a ban was imposed on holidays abroad. Bread, dairy products, and sugar were already under restriction. The Middle East drama unfolded against a background of chronic economic crisis in the United Kingdom.

The Attlee government was elected with a mandate to pursue social and economic programmes at home that seemed to be at variance with the general policy of supporting the reactionary and corrupt governments of the Arab states, above all in Egypt. King Farouk was a symbol of everything with which the Labour government did not wish to be associated. The ethical aversion of the British to Farouk and the Egyptian ruling class will be discussed in the 'prelude' to Part III. Here the main point to be established is the limited amount of financial resources and the way in which the post-war economic crisis forced the British to establish priorities.

[7] Quoted in Michael J. Cohen, *Palestine and the Great Powers 1945–1948* (Princeton, 1982), p. 246.

In the course of financing the war, Britain had liquidated over £1 billion of overseas investments and at the same time had brought the general foreign debt to more than £3 billion.[8] The £3 billion debt hung over the postwar British Isles like a black cloud. It cast a shadow over the euphoric plans of the Labour government. After the abrupt termination of lend-lease in August 1945, the United States negotiated a loan with the British government for $3.75 billion. One of the conditions was that sterling would be made convertible one year after ratification, which turned out to be July 1947. These adverse economic circumstances instilled in British officials a sense of dependency on the United States. Some of them believed that the loan amounted to an ungracious attempt to take advantage of Britain's economic weakness, and to reduce the British Empire to the status of an American satellite. In any case nothing was written off except the lend-lease debt, though the architects of the settlement hoped that other countries would scale down their sterling balances in a concerted attempt to set Britain on the road to economic recovery. In Asia and the Middle East the principal creditors holding favourable sterling balances were India (£1,100 million), Egypt (£400 million), and Iraq (£70 million).[9]

The Egyptian reaction to the British economic plight reflected some of the more hostile sentiment of Arab nationalism. The plea that the sterling balances should be scaled down, possibly by about one-third, fell on deaf ears. The Egyptian nationalists were not responsive to the argument that the British army had defended them against Italian and German aggression. Nor were they moved by the predicament of the postwar British economy: the decline in overseas investments, the loss of over half of the previous shipping tonnage, the sluggish recovery of agricultural and industrial production (both of which in 1946 remained below the 1938 level), and the dollar shortage—none of these roused sympathy in the hearts of Egyptian nationalists. Egypt had provisioned the British army in the Middle East and had helped it to emerge from the war victorious.

---

[8] The best discussion of the 'costs of the war' remains W. K. Hancock and M. M. Gowing, *British War Economy* (London, 1949), chap. XIX. See also especially Richard N. Gardner, *Sterling–Dollar Diplomacy* (Oxford, 1956); and a recent work that is helpful in illuminating some of these themes, Sir Richard Clarke (edited by Sir Alec Cairncross), *Anglo-American Economic Collaboration in War and Peace 1942–1949* (Oxford, 1982). The figures followed here are those of *Sterling* (New York, 1956) by Judd Polk, an economist sensitive to the Middle Eastern dimension of the problem.

[9] For India see B. R. Tomlinson, *The Political Economy of the Raj 1914–1947: The Economics of Decolonization in India* (London, 1979). Unfortunately there is nothing comparable on the Middle East. There is however valuable work in progress on the dependent Empire: e.g. N. J. Westcott, 'Sterling and Empire: The British Imperial Economy, 1939–1951' (seminar paper, Institute of Commonwealth Studies, University of London, 1983).

Egypt was a demonstrably poorer country than Britain, however much the British might feel the pinch of postwar austerity. As for Britain's debt, it might be all right for a rich country such as the United States to cancel, but the £400 million sterling balances (which the Egyptians calculated as closer to £440 million) represented one of the few Egyptian assets. The Egyptians in short had no intention of scaling down their sterling balances. They refused to cancel any part of the debt. As for the plea that the British had saved Egypt from Nazi tyranny, one economist who lived in Egypt during the war summed up the nationalist reaction in this way: 'to extreme anti-British elements this moral argument was close to a claim that Egypt had been saved from paradise'.[10]

The critical developments that shaped the immediate future of Egypt and Palestine as well as Greece and Turkey—and, it should be added, India and Burma—became apparent in late 1946, at the beginning of the worst winter in the twentieth century. The following excerpt from a classic Zionist account well conveys the circumstances in which Middle Eastern affairs were conducted in London during the abysmal weather of early 1947:

> On February 2nd, 1947, the sun was seen over the British Isles for the last time for four weeks. On the 3rd the Austin Motor Works, and many others, closed down; unemployment was increasing; potatoes disappeared from the shops. On the same day the United States Ambassador in Athens reported to the State Department that there were strong rumours that the British were about to withdraw their troops from Greece. On the next day the Cadbury Chocolate Works stopped work because of the lack of fuel, and on February 6th a snow blizzard isolated parts of northern England from the rest of the country. It was announced that food and milk supplies were in danger, and by the 7th coal stocks were declared to be 'critically short'. Severe cuts in the supply of electricity were imposed over the whole of southern England.
>
> In this setting, in the midst of an electricity cut which plunged the entire Foreign Office into darkness, the Foreign Secretary communicated the last word of the British Government to the Jewish Agency delegation, and later also to that of the Arab States [at the London Conference of 1946–7]. . . . As the lights went out at the meeting, Bevin joked with his brute trade unionist humour that there was no need for candles as they had the Israe*lites* present.[11]

The Jews did not share Bevin's sense of humour. Here however the main point is that the winter of 1946–7 dramatized the British economic plight. There were three months of snow on the ground. Coal supplies were exhausted. Rations were tighter than during the war. In the first quarter of 1947 the British economy suffered

[10] Polk, *Sterling*, pp. 68–9.
[11] Jon and David Kimche, *Both Sides of the Hill: Britain and the Palestine War* (London, 1960), pp. 21–2.

a sharp setback.[12] During this time the sheer expense of maintaining a British presence in the Middle East weighed on the minds of statesmen and permanent officials. 'For some time to come . . .', Bevin told his Middle East hands in the following May, he would have 'to bluff his way through in foreign policy, given the financial weakness of this country'.[13]

In some of the American as well as British literature dealing with the postwar economic crisis and its consequences in the Middle East, there runs the theme that the decline of British power might have been prevented if there had been greater determination on the part of the British or more resolute support of Britain by the United States. The failure of this 'act of will' is an alluring interpretation to those seeking the causes of the decline and fall of the British Empire in the Middle East, or indeed throughout the world. Here is an example of the way in which an American writer, Theodore H. White, brings this idea to bear on the devaluation crisis of September 1949. The implications are at variance with the arguments of this book. He relates a conversation with Sir Edmund Hall-Patch, one of the principal economic authorities of the Foreign Office:

[H]is task humiliated him. Begging for the American buck was not his style. . . . [he] was talking from the heart. America must move to save and take over the British economy . . . or Britain would fade from world power. . . . He doubted whether England had the stomach to go the rough road it must go if it went alone—to cut the Empire adrift, to repudiate its distant and inner obligations, to hold on only to military command of the oil resources of the Middle East. . . .

It scarcely occurred to me then. . . . that, ultimately, we would drive the British from the Middle East . . . and leave all of America's economy and civilization in debt to, and uncertainly dependent on, the oil of the Middle East sheikhs and strong men, whom the British had previously policed for us.[14]

Guilt is thus fused with self-recrimination for failure to rescue the British Empire in the Middle East. This is a grotesque lament. But it is noteworthy because it represents one prominent school of historical interpretation, and because it throws into perspective the arguments of this book as they will be developed in later chapters.

There was no failure of an act of will, either American or British, and not much sentimentality. The allegation that the Americans intended to drive the British from the Middle East, as will be seen, was more controversial. In general the Americans of the era held that

---

[12] See the tables and discussion in W. W. Rostow, *The Division of Europe after World War II: 1946* (University of Texas Press, 1981), chap. 2, entitled a 'Disastrous Year'.

[13] As recorded in a Foreign Office minute of 6 May 1947, FO 371/62971/J2102/G.

[14] Theodore H. White, *In Search of History* (New York, 1978), pp. 291-4.

the British were responsible for their own financial predicament, and that any attempt to prolong the dependency relationship with the Arabs and Iranians would hasten rather than reverse the process of British economic decline. The British for their part indignantly denied that they intended to perpetuate a system of economic exploitation, but there was no question of infirmity of the will. The historical evidence suggests the contrary. The British, above all Ernest Bevin, persistently pursued their goals with great determination.

Here there is a paradox. If the men of the Labour government were as resolute as the historical records seem to reveal, why then did the British Empire collapse while the Russian empire, or for that matter the Portuguese empire, continued to endure? Was there, after all, ultimately a failure of British will? Those of course were large questions, but part of the answer, at least during the time of the Labour government, lies in the reluctance to endorse political or economic settlements that might have required British bayonets. That is a theme that runs through Bevin's minutes. Quite apart from his perception of the economic crisis and the scarcity of resources, he judged that the British public would not tolerate colonial war or even prolonged suppression of resistance. To paraphrase both Burke and Tocqueville, he was fully aware that democracies and empires went ill together, and that the British system, if it were to succeed at all, would have to be dismantled and then reconstructed. The history of the British Empire in the Middle East during this period may be read as the unsuccessful attempt at conversion from formal rule and alliances to an informal basis of equal partnership and influence. Here there is a final paradox. The purpose of this transformation was the perpetuation of Britain as a great 'world power'. Non-intervention thus becomes intervention by other means.

The Continuity of British Political and Economic Aims

'In peace and war', the Foreign Secretary stated in a memorandum circulated to his colleagues in the Cabinet in 1949, 'the Middle East is an area of cardinal importance to the United Kingdom, second only to the United Kingdom itself.' It is significant that Bevin could so emphatically endorse that view two years after India had become independent, and that his reasons for the British presence in the Middle East seemed to be no less compelling than when the protection of the route to India had been the ultimate justification. According to this major reassessment of British aims, the heart of the matter could be expressed in strategic and economic terms:

'Strategically the Middle East is a focal point of communications, a source of oil, a shield to Africa and the Indian Ocean, and an irreplaceable offensive base. Economically it is, owing to oil and cotton, essential to United Kingdom recovery.' The remarkable feature of Bevin's exuberant acceptance of that assessment lies in his emphasis that it did not contain 'any striking innovation'. 'It is mainly a reaffirmation of the policy pursued hitherto, which is itself the result of a progressive development since this Government took office.'[15]

The continuity of the Labour government's attitude to the Middle East consisted not only in the recognition of the region as a centre of communications between Europe and Asia, and its obvious importance as a source of oil, but above all in its relation to Africa. That view, as Bevin stressed, had progressively developed during the years of the Labour government in office. By 1950 the full potential of Africa's development seemed more and more to be linked with Britain's economic recovery. There were military as well as economic reasons. Bevin stated to his colleagues in December 1950 in a Cabinet meeting in which the late Victorians would have felt quite at home:

> There was a population of 25 million in Egypt and the Sudan, and with the assistance of the water power in Uganda it should be possible, if the friendly co-operation of these peoples was secured, to develop industries in the Nile Valley which would raise the standard of living in peace and provide a valuable industrial potential for war.[16]

In the late 1940s Africa gradually superseded India as one of the ultimate justifications of the British Empire. The Middle East, which itself held incalculable potential of wealth in oil, was its defence. Africa, where the British Empire might be maintained indefinitely, became the mystique.

It was Bevin who provided the coherence in outlook and the driving force behind the schemes for Middle Eastern economic development and defence. He recognized the imperative necessity of securing British access to Middle East oil and he also had in mind the unlimited potential 'in the belt stretching from West Africa to East Africa [which] could offset the cost of retaining the small defence commitment in the Mediterranean'.[17] The phrase 'small defence commitment' demands comment because it brought him into conflict with the Chiefs of Staff. Bevin wanted to reduce as far as possible the number of British troops concentrated in the Middle

[15] Memorandum by Bevin, 'Middle East Policy', 25 Aug. 1949, CP (49) 183, CAB 129/36. The preoccupation with Africa confirms one of the themes of John Gallagher, *The Decline, Revival and Fall of the British Empire* (Cambridge, 1982).

[16] Cabinet Minutes (50) 86, 14 Dec. 1950, CAB 128/18.

[17] Defence Committee DO (46) 10, 5 Apr. 1946, CAB 131/1.

East, especially in Egypt, in order to avoid political tension. He kept an open mind on the question where best to locate the principal British base. A good answer eluded even his ingenuity. Despite exhaustive consideration given to alternatives—Palestine, Cyprus, Cyrenaica, or a combination that would include bases in those territories as well as in Iraq and Transjordan—the conclusion invariably turned on Suez. In December 1949 the Secretary of State for War, Emmanuel Shinwell, summed up the British dilemma: 'The Canal Zone of Egypt remains our main base in the Middle East. There is no other suitable location for that base. . . . if we have to abandon Egypt we must abandon our status in the Middle East altogether.'[18] Shinwell's comment represents a major strain of British thought, in contrast with Bevin's. Bevin did not regard Suez as a point to be held at any cost. He hoped from the beginning to resolve the problem of the Suez base by conciliating the Egyptians, but this approach, as will be seen, broke down in late 1946. After that time the history of British defence schemes in the Middle East may be read as his search for a satisfactory alternative base. On this point as on others, Bevin's outlook on economic development interlocked with his ideas about defence.

No sooner did Bevin become Foreign Secretary than he began to develop proposals for transforming the unequal relationship with the Arabs into an effective partnership. His imagination became captured by the economic and military advantages of an enduring British presence. In September 1945 he held a meeting at the Foreign Office with the British representatives in the Middle East, whom he had summoned to London for a thorough discussion of all aspects of British policy. Lord Killearn, the Ambassador in Cairo, held views about British power and prestige that resembled Churchill's. He was astonished that Bevin had 'progressive ideas', in this case, those that complemented rather than contradicted the Tory view of the Middle East. There was a marriage of Socialist conviction and Tory apprehension that the only way to preserve British influence would be through measures of economic development which would raise the standards of living of ordinary people—peasants and not pashas, in Bevin's famous phrase. Bevin's idea in essence was a partnership with Middle Eastern countries whereby the British would provide technical assistance in projects of agricultural development, irrigation, education, and many other measures of economic and social welfare. He wished to put the whole matter on a 'public utility' basis, and not on one of imperialist exploitation, he said at one of the meetings.[19] There would be mutual benefits by the British and

[18] Memorandum by Shinwell, Top Secret, 9 Dec. 1949, PREM 8/1230.
[19] Minutes of F.O. meeting, 5 Sept. 1945, FO 371/45252. Diary entry by Killearn,

Middle Eastern peoples working together. The British records reveal quite clearly what Bevin believed would be one of the principal gains. It is a continuous theme in the secret discussions with his advisers. The British would eventually benefit militarily as well as economically. On one occasion he spoke of 'our peace and wartime economy, trade, and manpower'. Defence measures and economic development went hand in hand. 'We must seriously endeavour', he told the Defence Committee of the Cabinet in April 1946, 'to ensure that the regional defence scheme [in the Middle East] would function efficiently and to do all in our power to train the armed forces of countries such as Egypt, Iraq, and Saudi Arabia to a standard capable of meeting the needs of modern warfare'.[20]

With the benefit of perspective nearly four decades later, it is probably accurate to say that Bevin's grand design was not capable of fulfilment essentially for two reasons. He himself was fully conscious of them. The first was the scarcity of British resources. There was not only a shortage of funds for large-scale development plans along the lines Bevin had in mind but there was also a lack of experts willing to go to the Middle East for long-term commitments necessary to bring about the raising of standards of living and educational progress. Bevin on more than one occasion wrote that he was 'disappointed' in recruitment prospects and the time-lag necessary to see tangible results from economic planning.[21] The second reason could be found in the nature of the 'partnership'. During the prolonged Foreign Office discussions about the Arab League and its leaders, one official ruefully remarked that the British unfortunately found themselves more often than not allied with the forces of reaction rather than reform. The following minute by one of the Middle East hands of the Foreign Office admitted that there might even be an element of truth in Russian propaganda about the British Empire in the Middle East. The British were dependent on what was known as the 'old gang' in each of the Arab countries and collectively in the League of Arab States:

The trouble with the Arab League is that the Russians are to a great extent right. It *is* run at present by a lot of reactionary Pashas & Effendis, and it will never really develop into the progressive, educative and cultural force

5 Sept. 1945, Killearn Papers; Trefor E. Evans, ed., *The Killearn Diaries 1934–1946* (London, 1972), p. 347.

[20] Defence Committee, DO (46) 10, 5 Apr. 1946, CAB 131/1.

[21] See e.g. FO 371/52318, a key file on economic development, for Bevin's revelations of the difficulties in bringing about an economic revolution in the Middle East. Part of the problem with recruiting 'experts' was the difficulty in arranging long-term or even short-term assignments that would not jeopardize their permanent careers.

which it should unless an alliance is made between the Rulers & the rising generation.

If we do not fairly quickly promote such an alliance & do not so put ourselves on the side of 'the common man' in the M. E. the Russians will take the lead, and we shall be saddled with a group of old men with cast iron ideas and will go down to defeat with them.

We have a short time to influence the development of the M. E. and to push ideas towards evolution rather than revolution.[22]

Bevin himself was aware of the struggle against immense odds and the limited amount of time in which to put things on 'a new basis' and to treat the Arabs as 'genuine partners'. However much he might be criticized for regarding the manpower of the Middle East as a sort of potential cannon fodder, and however much he might have been misguided in his neo-imperialist schemes to sustain British power, Bevin during his tenure as Foreign Secretary demonstrated from beginning to end an urge 'to better the fellahin', or, in other words, the common people.[23]

How would the ruling classes of the Arab countries respond to British proposals for economic and social development? Bevin addressed himself to that question in reaction to criticism that the 'Pashas' or overlords of Egypt would regard economic reform as an attempt to dominate by non-military means:

I can well believe that the rulers and Pashas of Egypt are made to feel uncomfortable when the rotten conditions of the working people of their country are published to the world. I doubt, however, whether the people themselves feel similar resentment.

Pashadom is jealous of its power and frightened of any exposure of its shortcomings. But I do not believe that the Pashas will maintain for ever undisputed sway over Egypt. As Foreign Secretary of a Labour Government I look beyond the present Egyptian rulers, who deflect towards us the social discontent that should really be directed against them. . . . I cannot help thinking that they [the fellahin] would feel profound gratitude for anyone who helped them out of their miserably unhealthy and pauperous plight.[24]

In Bevin's view, economic and social development would prove to be the vital element in transforming the old imperial order into a new and equal partnership with the *peoples* of the Middle East.

The Labour government was committed to the gradual liquidation of the old British Empire that implied political subjugation and economic exploitation. At first sight it may therefore appear to be

[22] Minute by J. Thyne Henderson, 30 Mar. 1946, FO 371/52312.

[23] On these points and on Bevin's policy generally see Elizabeth Monroe, 'Mr Bevin's "Arab Policy" ', *St. Antony's Papers*, 11, 2 (London, 1961), a seminal article.

[24] Bevin to Campbell, 21 June 1946, FO 800/457/EG/46/32. The 'Bevin Papers' in the FO 800 series often help to throw into relief Bevin's own assumptions that he brought to bear on such matters of fundamental importance.

paradoxical that Bevin and his colleagues became increasingly intent on the achievement of economic goals within the informal as well as formal Empire. 'Development' was part of the ethos of the Labour era, and it was affirmed with conviction in the Middle East as elsewhere. The spirit of the new course, despite jarring setbacks, on the whole was supremely confident. Forebodings of collapse and anarchy were allayed by hope of economic progress and political stability through alliances between Britain and each of the important Middle Eastern countries. There was no loss of imperial nerve. Palestine may be regarded as the disastrous exception that proved the general rule. The Labour government not only believed in the benefits of development but also cherished the hope that the ideals of social democracy could be eventually carried out in the Middle East and Africa as well as in the British Isles.

This Labour idealism amounted to more than mere postwar euphoria. It was essential that Britain's Middle Eastern policy be changed, if only for reasons of economic survival in the postwar world. The aspirations of Middle Eastern nationalism had to be accommodated. The unacceptable face of 'capitalist exploitation', which the Labour party had criticized in opposition, would have to be exchanged for a new programme of economic development and plans for social welfare. All this would take time. As the British began to export to the Middle East the ideas of the welfare state designed for home consumption—above all, in Bevin's straightforward words, the raising of standards of living of ordinary people —the members of the Labour government persuaded themselves that they were prolonging the British presence, not ending it. In that view lies the resolution of the paradox of attempting to liquidate the British Empire precisely when the economic stakes were highest. The British hoped to persuade Arab leaders to co-operate in plans for economic and social development. Britain would acknowledge and confirm the political independence of each of the Middle Eastern states as a prelude to economic progress, which in turn would avert the dangers of extreme nationalism.[25] This was the formula of the Labour government. Progressive measures would be taken in concert with the moderate nationalists in order to prevent the initiative

[25] The semantic controversy about the meaning of true 'independence' did not go unnoticed by those in the Foreign Office who observed that the Americans applied the term to the nations of Latin America but attacked British 'imperialism' in the Middle East. The same official who had noted the ironic truth of Russian comments on the British Empire and its Middle Eastern allies, J. Thyne Henderson, also wrote about the phrases 'pan-Americanism' and 'Empire': 'the word pan-Americanism makes Bolivia independent, whereas empire makes Egypt dependent. There is little difference in status really between Cuba & Transjordan, between Venezuela and Saudi Arabia.' Minute of 25 Oct. 1945, FO 371/45254/E7946.

from passing to the extremists. British influence would be sustained indirectly rather than through the formal trappings of the old imperial system. The pattern of economic dependence would not be broken, though this was not the way in which British politicians and officials at the time would have viewed the essence of the problem. Those who believed in 'development' in the 1940s, at least in Britain, regarded this potential relationship as mutual self-help freely entered into. The new order would benefit the peoples of the Middle East as well as the British themselves. There was a corollary assumption that was often left unstated. The preponderant influence of Britain in the Middle East would be reconsolidated.

The Evolution of British Stategic Aims

'Xenophobia', according to the British Commander-in-Chief in the Middle East, Major-General Sir Bernard Paget, writing in October 1945, might cause the British considerable trouble after the war if care were not taken to respect Arab 'sovereign rights'.[26] The word 'xenophobia' was often used by Paget and other British officials when they wished to describe Arab nationalism as unreasonable or Arab opposition to the presence of British troops as irrational. In the transitional period between war and peace, Paget's views commanded respect. An officer of robust optimism and acknowledged organizational skill, he believed that Arab 'xenophobia' could be allayed by dealing with the Middle East as a region rather than in fragments. He proposed treating all of the Middle East (minus Turkey and Iran, where the Russians were a complication) as a single political and economic unit, an idea which resembled the Arab concept of a 'greater' or geographical Syria. He had in mind in fact the territories of all the members of the Arab League (plus Palestine). As will be discussed later in the chapter on that subject, the British distrusted this 'newly constructed facade of Arab States' (a Colonial Office description), even though they had encouraged its formation.[27] Paget was examining the defence side of the coin, which he hoped might be less controversial than the political. He proposed a 'Confederacy' of Arab states which, under British leadership, might provide for the security of the Middle East on a regional basis. His proposal became the basis of far-reaching discussion and reassessment

[26] Memorandum by Paget, COS (45) 616, 13 Oct. 1945, CAB 80/97.

[27] The phrase is Sir Arthur Dawe's in a minute of 3 Apr. 1945, CO 732/88/79238. For reasons that defy rational explanation, the Colonial Office file on the proposal for a 'Confederacy' (CO 537/1243) is closed for 75 years, though the subject received full discussion in collateral files. This is but one example not of scores but of hundreds of files on the Middle East that are still closed for a variety of official reasons.

within the British government. 'A Middle Eastern Confederacy' was the watchword at the end of the war.

The Chiefs of Staff (and the Joint Planning Staff of the C. O. S.) played a central part in the 1945 discussions not only because of the obvious military importance of the Middle East but also because the Foreign Office and Colonial Office attempted to win the sanction of the military experts in order to pursue particular Imperial causes that had to be fought out within the bureaucracy. In the case of Cyprus for example the Colonial Office and the Chiefs of Staff effectively blocked the Foreign Office's tentative plans to hand over the island to Greece, while in the case of Palestine the Foreign Office and the Chiefs of Staff worked as allies against partition. The combination of two against the other could be decisive in Cabinet discussions. In the case of 'Confederacy' both the Foreign Office and the Colonial Office were sceptical, though both saw good reasons in the abstract for hoping that a regional defence scheme might be a workable proposition. Sir Orme Sargent, Permanent Under-Secretary at the Foreign Office, confirmed that regional planning might help to palliate the Arab 'psychosis' about the alleged British tradition of divide and rule: 'a multilateral system would offer the Arab States a kind of psychological set-off to the dominant partnership represented by His Majesty's Government'. In other words Britain and any individual Arab country would be an unequal partnership, but the Arab states collectively could stand as an equal. Sargent gave a variety of other reasons for favouring the scheme of regional defence, but perhaps the most important one concerned Egypt. If the British could convince the Arabs that the old pattern of dominance would be replaced with a regional arrangement, then even Egyptian nationalism might be mollified: 'a regional approach might calm popular agitation in Egypt for treaty revision'.[28]

To the British military mind there was no strategic territory in the Middle East comparable by any stretch of the imagination to Egypt. Given the ascendancy of Egypt in all discussions of strategic aims, it is important to note that each territory in the eastern Mediterranean possessed certain strategic virtues depending on the time and circumstance of the assessment. If there was one predictable feature about these calculations, it was that, when faced with occupation, the military experts would find insuperable obstacles but, once in, any territory would quickly become strategically indispensable for the security of the British Empire. This was an old story, and the men of the Labour government despaired of military retrenchment except

[28] Memorandum by Sargent, 1 Dec. 1945, COS (45) 678, CAB 80/98; minutes in FO 371/45254.

on compelling economic grounds or the threat of imminent political collapse. 'The Chiefs of Staff will always object to evacuating anything where they have been for some time', Sir Oliver Harvey (Assistant, and then Deputy, Under-Secretary at the Foreign Office) once wrote, 'just as they will always object to occupying anything where they have not hitherto been.'[29] When the Cabinet finally decided to evacuate Palestine, Bevin observed that the Royal Air Force would continue to claim strategic rights from an 'elicopter' if they were so allowed.[30]

At the close of the war the Chiefs of Staff surveyed the Middle East as a landowner might gaze over his estates with an eye towards more or less desirable places of accommodation (Egypt and Palestine) and those more suitable merely for outdoor relief (Cyrenaica). It was important that the natives be kept friendly. Paget recommended that Jewish immigration 'be stopped at [its] source' and he made it clear that 'partition was most undesirable from a military point of view' because it would stir up both Jews and Arabs. He warned that there would be 'trouble' if the Italians were allowed to return to Libya. He waxed enthusiastic about a 'strategic reserve' in Kenya 'near Nairobi where good training facilities existed'.[31] The Foreign Office observed that the military authorities even appeared to have their eyes on Syria and Lebanon, where the favourable climate would allow opportunity for manœuvres in healthy weather and spacious accommodation in permanent brick barracks. 'Our military . . . on occasion let slip the significant remark that Syria and the Lebanon had a better climate than other countries in the Middle East', observed R. M. A. Hankey of the Foreign Office. When it became unbearable 'in the hotter areas (Iraq, Canal zone, etc.)', he went on, troops could be rotated to 'the relatively cool climate of Syria and Palestine'.[32] The Prime Minister's reaction to this expansive military exuberance could be summed up, in his own ejaculation, as 'nonsense'.[33] Attlee wished to reduce the number of British troops throughout the Middle East and especially in Egypt. 'The perfect plague in my life was to get those numbers down', he later recalled.[34]

The civilian and military mentalities clashed as much on the distribution of troops as on the number. In the last stage of the war the Minister Resident in the Middle East, Sir Edward Grigg (Lord

[29] Minute by Harvey, 3 Nov. 1947, FO 371/67084. See below p. 225.
[30] Hugh Dalton (Chancellor of the Exchequer), diary entry for 20 Sept. 1947, Dalton Papers. See below p. 475.
[31] COS (45) 214, 4 Sept. 1945, CAB 79/38.
[32] Minutes by Hankey, 5 and 22 May 1945, FO 371/45565 and 45570.
[33] As recounted in notation by Harvey on Hankey's minute of 5 May, ibid.
[34] Francis Williams, *A Prime Minister Remembers* (London, 1961), p. 177.

Altrincham) had proposed that seven divisions should be permanently stationed in the Middle East. Two of these divisions would occupy Palestine—considerably less than half of the approximate level of 100,000 at the height of the postwar crisis. He wished to diversify troop strength so that one division would occupy Cyprus and only one would be assigned to Egypt, with the rest distributed in Transjordan, Cyrenaica, and East Africa. The War Office did not accept this calculation and aimed at what would amount to permanent occupation of Egypt and Palestine by two and three divisions respectively. In other words there would be a concentration of troops in Palestine and Egypt and less emphasis on distribution. The War Office also had in mind an extensive 'building programme' in Iraq which the Foreign Office regarded as contradictory with the need to reduce troops in Iraq to peacetime requirements.[35] The only point of near agreement, which is startling in retrospect, was the indefinite occupation of Palestine by somewhere between two and three divisions. The point to bear in mind is that the military authorities were gradually forced to accept reductions because of the economic austerities of postwar Britain and the pressures of Arab nationalism. In Egypt Attlee and Bevin were determined to withdraw British troops into the Canal Zone and eventually to maintain a combatant force of only 5,000 men. Arab nationalism and the realities of postwar Britain quickly punctured the bubbles of military fantasy about permanent occupation in choice parts of the Middle East.

'Confederacy' also died a quick death, at least in its immediate postwar incarnation. The purpose was regional defence. There was a subsidiary motive, which was the wish to allay Arab suspicions about British interference with 'sovereign rights' by replacing all of the bilateral agreements with a collective arrangement. Superficially this was an idea with which everyone could agree in principle, but it did not stand up under political scrutiny. C. W. Baxter of the Eastern Department of the Foreign Office—an official who was as anxious as anyone to replace the old treaty system with a new arrangement that would suggest less British dominance—did not believe that 'confederacy' had any precise meaning. 'The advocates of a "Middle Eastern Confederacy" are sometimes not quite clear what they mean', he wrote in November 1945.[36] What countries would be included? Of course Egypt and Iraq would be, but this would involve the scrapping of the existing treaties and in the case of Iraq it was by no means clear that a new arrangement would be more beneficial for

[35] The controversy is summarized in a minute by the head of the Eastern Department of the Foreign Office, C. W. Baxter, 25 Aug. 1945, FO 371/45252.
[36] Minute by Baxter, 15 Nov. 1945, FO 371/45254/E8930/G.

the British. Palestine and Transjordan would also be included, but in those territories the British already possessed all of the military facilities they required. On the other hand Syria and Lebanon could not be expected to join a 'confederacy' because of French suspicions that the British intended to take over all of the Middle East, including the former French part of it. The inclusion of Saudi Arabia would raise similar difficulties with the Americans, who in their own way were just as suspicious of British imperialism as the French. The real problem however was with Egypt, where British military and strategic stakes were highest. At the close of the war the Egyptians had already made it clear they they expected a basic revision of their treaty relations with Britain. There was no way to escape a bilateral approach. A 'regional' solution to British defence problems of the Middle East thus was caught up in the acrimonious discussions about how to readjust Britain's relations with Egypt, which the Labour government discovered was one of the insoluble problems of the postwar era.

The more sophisticated military estimates recognized that political collaboration would be at the heart of any lasting defence arrangement. Militarily the members of the Joint Planning Staff of the Chiefs of Staff were alarmed at both the scope and the substance of Arab participation in Paget's scheme. The military experts saw no reason at all to introduce Arab political influence into East Africa, even indirectly by connecting that region to the Middle East as a sort of 'strategic reserve'. In the Middle East itself they feared that too friendly an arrangement with the Arab states might involve sharing 'access to our latest secret equipment'.[37] The Chiefs of Staff themselves recognized the political danger of a military 'confederacy' on a broad scale because the Russians would regard it as encirclement. Lord Cunningham, the First Sea Lord and Chief of Naval Staff, had vigorous opinions on the subject. He believed that it was obviously desirable to have as much co-operation as possible between the Arab states, but that the political difficulties appeared to be almost insuperable. 'Palestine would occupy a very uneasy place in such a Confederacy', he stated at a meeting of the Chiefs of Staff in November 1945. And what of France and the Levant? Or the United States and Saudi Arabia? Pitching the conclusion in highest political terms Cunningham preferred to emphasize the importance of American rather than Arab collaboration: 'More important than all the Arab States thrown together was co-operation with the United States whose economic stake in the area was already considerable.'[38]

[37] JP (45) 276, 'Middle East Policy', 6 Nov. 1945, CAB 84/76.
[38] COS (45) 269, 9 Nov. 1945, CAB 79/41.

That line of logic led the Chiefs of Staff to conclude that the British strategic position in the Middle East would best be secured through bilateral agreements reached individually with each of the Arab states and, perhaps later, through a more ambitious collective arrangement in which even the United States might participate.

The attempt to create lasting political and military alliances will be analysed in detail in the chapters of Part III. The argument of that section will be summarized here because it is critical for the book as a whole. The British remained uncertain whether the Arab League would serve British purposes or would turn against them, in the words of the head of the Egyptian Department, as a sort of 'Frankenstein's monster'. Syria and Lebanon were excluded from any possible political and military 'confederacy' because of the ever-lasting enmity of the French, who had become embittered in the final climax of Anglo-French imperial rivalry during the spring of 1945. The Syrians and the Lebanese skilfully managed to maintain their independence, and the precedent was of incalculable importance for the other Arab states. Saudi Arabia, as Lord Cunningham had hoped, became increasingly an American economic preserve and thus strengthened the American commitment in the Middle East, though in Saudi Arabia itself the British hoped to sustain their political influence with King Ibn Saud. During all of these discussions Cyprus increased in strategic significance in proportion to the growing uncertainty regarding other territories. In Egypt the British faced their most important and exasperating task. At different times and for slightly different reasons, negotiations to adjust Britain's relations with Egypt and to maintain control over the Canal Zone ended in stalemate, but from the beginning to the end the Labour government held out hope that Egyptian nationalism could be conciliated. At the same time Cyrenaica's importance as an alternative Middle Eastern base continued to burgeon. This protracted story (which involved the fate of Somalia and Eritrea as well as Libya) eventually ended satisfactorily for the British in 1949-51 with the creation of Libya as an independent state, though by that time the creative energy of the Labour government had been spent, at least in terms of Bevin's overarching design. The turning point occurred in early 1948, when plans for a new Anglo-Iraqi treaty foundered on the shoals of Iraqi nationalism. In the end the most satisfactory outcome of Bevin's Arab defence plans was a treaty with Britain's client state, Transjordan, but this carried with it certain disadvantages because King Abdullah was almost universally condemned as a British stooge.

At the same time that the British were trying to put their relations with the Arab world on a better footing, the Palestine crisis came to a head. A few words here will also be said about the argument in Part IV because it too has a general bearing on the book as a whole. Not until January 1947 did the military experts cease to regard Palestine as a 'strategic reserve'. Though a few authorities, notably Field-Marshal Montgomery, believed that a *Pax Britannica* could be maintained by bayonets, British morale deteriorated. By the summer of 1947 the British were ready to quit. They responded to a combination of international, local, and domestic pressures. From the United States and in the United Nations they were subjected to demands for the creation of a Jewish state. In Palestine itself they faced a skilful campaign of Zionist terrorism. In England a certain current of public protest guided by Richard Crossman, a Member of Parliament and assistant editor of the *New Statesman*, expressed revulsion against suppressing a people who had suffered unspeakable atrocities under the Nazis.[39] All of this was occurring at a time when the British feared the impending collapse of their economy. Underlying economic anxiety thus provides a key to the crisis of September 1947. By then the British had concluded that the only way to resolve the international, local, and metropolitan tensions was to evacuate Palestine. The same interaction of similar forces in other circumstances in Asia and Africa triggered transfers of power. In the case of Palestine the Labour government decided that the crisis could be resolved only by evacuation pure and simple.

The Chiefs of Staff and the Possibility of Atomic Warfare in the Middle East

One further dimension of British strategic calculation must be briefly examined because it overclouded all debate on the subject until it was decided not to let it interfere with traditional principles. The possibly that atomic warfare might engulf the Middle East, as well as the rest of the world, preoccupied Attlee, Bevin, and others of the 'inner ring' of the Cabinet. None of them had been privy to atomic secrets before the Labour government came to power.[40] The revolution in modern warfare weighed heavily on their minds as they attempted to establish priorities in the Middle East. The Prime Minister in particular doubted Britain's capacity to defend the Middle East, or even the Mediterranean. Furthermore there were

[39] See Khalid Kishtainy, *The New Statesman and the Middle East* (Palestine Research Center, Beirut, 1972). The private papers of the editor, Kingsley Martin (at the University of Sussex Library) are helpful in understanding this aspect of Crossman's career.

[40] See Margaret Gowing, *Independence and Deterrence: Britain and Atomic Energy, 1945-1952* (New York, 1974), I, chaps. 1 and 2.

parts of the Middle East, 'deficit areas' in his emphatic phrase, which he thought not worth defending. Attlee's challenge to the strategic tradition of the British Empire is so important that it will be discussed further in these introductory remarks and again in the chapter on the Italian colonies. His remarks were directed specifically towards the fate of the Italian colonial empire, and the question was debated in the highest level of the British Commonwealth at the Prime Ministers' Conference of 1946. Here the discussion will focus on Attlee's inquisition of the Chiefs of Staff. Without even pursuing the argument into its ramifications of atomic warfare, he held that the British had only a 'precarious' hold over the Middle East and that the situation would become worse rather than better because of Russian strength and Arab nationalism. In March 1946 Attlee, who occupied the office of Minister of Defence as well as Prime Minister, instructed the Chiefs of Staff to prepare an 'appreciation' of the strategic position of the British Commonwealth 'in the light of our resources and of modern conditions of warfare'.[41]

The Chiefs of Staff met the issue head-on: should the British cut their commitments in parts of the world where there might be potential conflict with Russia?[42] It probably came as no surprise to critics of the military mind that the Chiefs of Staff argued that, if the British moved out, the Russians would move in. 'If we move out in peace-time, Russia will move in, pursuing her policy of extending her influence by all means short of major war to further strategic areas.' Here was their main conclusion about Egypt and Palestine:

> Control of the area Egypt-Palestine would provide the Russians with a ready-made base area which could be built up by short sea route from Russia itself and which then would enable them to extend their influence both westward and southward into Africa. Such an extension would prejudice our position both in North-West Africa . . . and in the Indian Ocean. It would be the first step in a direct threat to our main support area of Southern Africa.[43]

They further held it to be imperative to continue the British presence in the Mediterranean not only to protect British access to Middle Eastern oil but also to preserve political influence in southern Europe. In this intricate and powerfully argued defence of the traditional British

[41] Memorandum by Attlee, 'Future of the Italian Colonies', DO (46) 27, 2 Mar. 1946, CAB 131/2.

[42] For the general subject of British response to the cold war, and an assessment of the question of responsibility, see especially Victor Rothwell, *Britain and the Cold War 1941–1947* (London, 1982). See also Barry Rubin, *The Great Powers in the Middle East 1941–1947* (London, 1980). A work of basic importance for its reflective analysis of these issues is D. C. Watt, *Succeeding John Bull: America in Britain's Place, 1900–1975* (Cambridge, 1984).

[43] Chiefs of Staff, 'Strategic Position of the British Commonwealth', DO (46) 47, 2 Apr. 1946, CAB 131/2.

position, the Chiefs of Staff arrived at a fundamental conclusion that enabled them to cope with the question of revolution in modern warfare, atomic and otherwise. It is so important that it deserves emphasis:

Our main strategic requirements are based principally upon facts of geography and the distribution of man-power and natural resources which do not change. We consider therefore that the basic principles of our strategy . . . will not be radically altered by new developments in methods or weapons of warfare.[44]

With that ingenious argument the Chiefs of Staff could carry on almost as if the atomic bomb had never been invented. It enabled them to uphold traditional principles until the assumptions could be proved false. Ultimately it was probably the weakness of the British economy and the decolonizing ethic of postwar Britain that undermined the strategic position in the Middle East as much as any intrinsic imbalance that arose from a bipolar world and possession of atomic bombs.

It has already been mentioned that the support of the Chiefs of Staff could often prove decisive in Cabinet discussion. In this case it was the Foreign Office that came to the aid of the Chiefs of Staff. Bevin believed that the motive behind the Russian demand for a Mediterranean port in Tripolitania, a claim put forward in September 1945, was no less than a bid for the mineral resources of tropical Africa. 'Uranium' was a word frequently on his lips in the autumn of that year. During the time of the preparation of the strategic appreciation, Bevin expressed the hope that the Chiefs of Staff would not only pay attention to particular parts of the Middle East such as Cyprus (which he hoped might be handed over to Greece) and Palestine (about which he was keeping an open mind) but also the Middle East generally as a protective shield for Africa: 'He would also like them [the Chiefs of Staff] to bear in mind the advantages of his proposals for the economic, etc. development of East and West Africa with particular regard to the uranium wealth in the Belgian Congo.'[45] After the Chiefs of Staff delivered their judgement, Bevin came down decisively on their side:

The Foreign Secretary said that he agreed with the Chiefs of Staff that we must maintain our influence in the Mediterranean. It was impossible to retain the necessary diplomatic strength if military support was withdrawn, and in his view, Russia only respected nations which had the power to command respect. At the same time, our presence in the Mediterranean served a purpose other than

---

[44] Ibid.
[45] Defence Committee DO (46) 8, 18 Mar. 1946, CAB 131/1.

military, which was very important to our position as a great power. . . . abandoning this area would mean a great loss to both our peace and wartime economy, trade and manpower.[46]

By this time the 'belt' stretching from east to west across the African continent, and not least the uranium, formed an integral part of Bevin's vision of the development of the Middle East and tropical Africa.

Within the Foreign Office it was Gladwyn Jebb, at that time an Assistant Under-Secretary, who attempted to reduce the Prime Minister's argument to its logical absurdity. Retreat from the Middle East in his view would in effect lead to withdrawal into the British Isles, with the British placing all of their hopes for the postwar world in the deterrent force of American atomic power.

> As I understand it, the Prime Minister's suggestion is that we should abandon all attempt to defend our communications in the whole of the Mediterranean and Middle Eastern areas. This would presumably entail the withdrawal of all our forces from the Middle East, and presumably in the long run from Malta, Gibraltar and Aden also.[47]

Jebb also assumed that British troops would withdraw from Greece, and that Ceylon, Burma, and Malaya would be 'written off' along with India. He further assumed that 'pro-Russian' governments might be established throughout the Middle East, Greece, Italy, and Spain. What then of France?

> I may be wrong, but it seems to me that, if a pro-Russian and anti-British Government were established in the Iberian Peninsula, the position of France would become quite untenable, and she also would join some Soviet *bloc*. It is rather difficult to see how, in such circumstances, we should be able to defend these islands and communications . . . even if we could depend entirely on the U. S. A.[48]

Jebb, and no doubt most of his colleagues, did not relish the humiliating circumstances of being dependent on the Americans, and he had little faith in the deterrent of the atomic bomb working to British advantage. He pressed the argument that Attlee's line of retreat would not only jeopardize the security of the British Isles but British civilization itself:

> Of course it may well be the Prime Minister's intention to resist Russian penetration into the areas referred to, but, if this is his intention, then we should, I suppose, simply have to rely on the deterrent effect of atomic bombs

---

[46] Defence Committee DO (46) 10, 5 Apr. 1946, CAB 131/1.
[47] Minute by Jebb, 8 Mar. 1946, FO 371/57173.
[48] Ibid.

produced in the U. S. A., and we should have to beware lest in the circumstances the U. S. A. should no longer consider these islands to be of sufficient importance to be worth protecting.

In other words, there would be every chance of our being forced into the position of being, not a client state of America, but a client state of Russia. In either case the idea of 'Social Democracy', which represents our own 'way of life', would be snuffed out between the rival forces of Capitalism and Communism, and our only role would merely be that of the grain (or perhaps chaff?) between the millstone.[49]

Sir Orme Sargent, the Permanent Under-Secretary, concurred in Jebb's views. Sargent believed that if the British Empire were to remain a 'World Power' it must hold its position in the Middle East and Mediterranean.[50] Bevin pursued the same line of argument. Quite independently of his permanent advisers he was determined, in his own words, to preserve 'our position as a great Power'.[51]

The Defence Committee of the Cabinet reached a consensus that Britain's position as a 'World Power' should be maintained just as events were reaching a climax in the two critical areas of Egypt and Palestine. In both cases Attlee and Bevin were guided by a political purpose over which the Chiefs of Staff had but little control. In the spring of 1946 Bevin offered troop withdrawal as a means of accommodating moderate Egyptian nationalism. At about the same time the Anglo-American Committee of Inquiry recommended that 100,000 certificates for Jewish immigration be issued immediately. It seemed probable that the international basis of British rule in Palestine would be altered, perhaps into an international trusteeship regime, so that the Chiefs of Staff could no longer regard Palestine as a sort of permanent military preserve. In May 1946 the Chiefs of Staff took stock of the situation. This was a critical time. It is useful to bear in mind the military inventory as background for the more detailed developments which will be traced in later chapters. To the Chiefs of Staff the alarming element in the general situation could be summed up in the word *uncertainty*:

(a) *Egypt*. His Majesty's Government has agreed to evacuate all our forces in peace-time. The terms of any future alliance which we may be able to negotiate with Egypt are not yet quite clear.

(b) *Palestine*. As a result of the report of the Anglo-American Commission, the question of Palestine may be brought before U. N. O. This may lead to

---

[49] Ibid. The end of the British 'way of life' appears to have distressed Lord Gladwyn in these years. See *The Memoirs of Lord Gladwyn* (London, 1972), p. 211, for his views on 'The Threat to Western Civilization', in a note which he dates as February 1947; it should be compared with a memorandum with the same title circulated to the Cabinet under Bevin's signature, 3 Mar. 1948, CP (48) 72, CAB 129/25.

[50] Minute by Sargent, 12 Mar. 1946, FO 371/57173.

[51] Defence Committee, DO (46) 10, 5 Apr. 1946, CAB 131/1.

the relinquishment of our present mandate and its substitution by a joint or collective trusteeship. . . .

(c) *Cyrenaica.* There seems to be no certainty that we shall obtain trustee-ship of this area, in which we have at present certain facilities by virtue of our occupation.

(d) *Tripolitania.* The future position of this area, in which we also have certain facilities, is uncertain. If we concur in Italy securing a trusteeship of this area, it will lead to a deterioration of our relations with the Arab world as a whole.

(e) *Sudan.* Our position may well be weakened as a result of the present negotiations with Egypt.

(f) *Italian East Africa.* The future of this area, which we are at present occupy-ing, is uncertain.

(g) *Iraq.* We have only limited rights under the present treaty. A demand for revision of this treaty in the near future appears possible.

(h) *Syria and Lebanon.* We have evacuated Syria and are in process of with-drawal from Lebanon. We shall shortly have no forces or rights in either territory.

(i) *Transjordan.* We have recently concluded a satisfactory alliance with Transjordan and enjoy considerable good will in that country. Its military poten-tialities are, however, very limited.[52]

Thus the only territory in the Middle East which seemed to offer the prospect of a permanent British military presence was Transjordan. It must have been a sobering thought to those who believed that the war had been fought at least in part for the preservation of the British Empire as well as the British 'way of life'.

Despite the determination of Attlee and Bevin to withdraw troops from Egypt in order to reduce political tension, the military authorities resisted the attempt to deploy the army in desert areas. Attlee reflected later: 'There was . . . a tendency to cling to Egypt, because it was a pleasant place to live in. "Probably get shoved out to Aden or some other God-forsaken place if we go from here." '[53] The contemporary military statistics bear out his complaint. At the time of the height of the crisis in the spring of 1948, there were approximately 100,000 troops in Palestine. The remainder of British forces were distributed as follows in major units up to brigade strength of about 6,000 men:

Egypt	Six
Sudan	Two
Greece	Three
Cyprus	Three
Malta	One
Aden	One
Tripolitania	Four

[52] Chiefs of Staff, 'Strategic Requirements in the Middle East', DO (46) 67, 25 May 1946, CAB 131/2.
[53] Williams, *A Prime Minister Remembers*, p. 178.

Cyrenaica	Three
Eritrea	Two
Somalia	Three[54]

One solution to the problem of troop concentration in Egypt might have been to develop a strategic base in Kenya. That project indeed developed as a rival strategy to the Suez base, but, as will be seen below, it gradually foundered along with Bevin's plans for the development of tropical Africa, for reasons of expense. When all was said there was no equivalent of Egypt, and nothing could persuade the military authorities otherwise. Here was the epitome of the Chiefs of Staff's argument for General Headquarters at Suez:

> The CHIEFS OF STAFF said that a central Headquarters had been found essential in the last war and it would be essential in any future war in order to control a major conflict. Such a Headquarters must in peace be located as near as possible to the centre of communications. . . . Egypt was the Middle East focus for all communications and political activities. . . . In this connection a Head-quarters located far to the South of Egypt [in Kenya] would find it impossible to conduct naval operations in the Mediterranean.[55]

No matter how often the question was raised, the answer was always the same. 'In the event of attack on the British Isles', the Permanent Under-Secretary's Committee of the Foreign Office concluded in April 1949, 'it [the Middle East] is one of the principal areas from which offensive air action can be taken against the aggressor. The strategic key to this area is Egypt, to which there is no practical alternative as a main base.'[56]

What if war did break out? The planning and speculation on the subject is beyond the scope of this book, but it is illuminating to dwell briefly on the apprehension that existed in the spring of 1948 when the Czechoslovakian crisis developed concurrently with the one in Palestine. Fear of a general war—that might erupt into the Third World War—was in everyone's mind. Brigadier J. R. C. Hamilton of MO4 wrote to Daniel Lascelles, the head of the Egyptian Department of the Foreign Office, that war appeared to be 'imminent'. If worst came to worst the British would have to 'neutralize' or destroy the oil fields and perhaps withdraw from Egypt itself, with the hope of recapture from the 'support areas' of East and South Africa. The letter is revealing because it indicates the ways in which the British calculated that the Russians would attempt to seize Egypt and, conversely, the Egyptian attitude. The Egyptians, Hamilton wrote, 'cannot conceivably look for any benefit from a Russian occupation

---

[54] Minute by Shinwell, 20 Apr. 1948, copy in FO 371/69333.
[55] Defence Committee, DO (46) 17, 27 May 1946, CAB 131/1.
[56] Permanent Under-Secretary's Committee (19), 30 Apr. 1949, FO 371/73502.

of the Delta and must fundamentally hope that we and the Americans will protect them from it'. What if the Russians tried to bomb the British out of Egypt, perhaps with atomic bombs? 'First of all to deny a vast expanse of territory by air attack even when using weapons of mass destruction has yet to be proved practicable, though I agree that the delta area is very vulnerable especially to B. W. Agents.'[57] The phrase 'B. W. Agents' referred to bacterial warfare.

As if that prospect did not seem to be a sufficiently hair-raising possibility, the Russians at some future time might have the following plans:

> The Russians would wish to occupy Egypt with the object of (a) stopping our long range strategic air bombing which might be launched from air bases as far south as Khartoum with refuelling airfields further North say Egypt. (b) denying us a base from which to launch our offensive to recapture the Middle East oilfields. (c) penetrating into Africa, especially through the Arab states along the shores of the Mediterranean and thereby driving us out of the Mediterranean. (d) opening up sea communications through the Mediterranean and thereby avoiding the difficult overland routes Turkey and Persia. . . . I personally feel sure the Russians would give the capture of Egypt a high priority.[58]

The extravagance of such speculation perhaps confirms the shrewdness of the Chiefs of Staff strategic assessment of April 1946 which has been discussed as the basis of British postwar planning. The strategic planners might prepare for certain contingencies in the event of the world being blown apart by atomic bombs, but in the meantime it was best to assume that the world would go on much the same as it had in the past. In the postwar era, at least, it was Arab nationalism rather than atomic holocaust that proved to be the real threat to the British Empire in the Middle East.

One psychological moment of truth for the British as a 'Great Power' in the Middle East probably did come when the Russians exploded an atomic bomb in September 1949, three years before the first British test. In any case, during the last two years of the Labour government there by no means existed the exuberant self-assurance that had characterized the military, economic, and political planning of the years 1946–7. To be sure, since the end of the war there had been no doubt that it would be extremely difficult, if indeed possible at all, to sustain the British Empire as a 'Great Power'. One of the fascinations of the candid British documentation of the era is the sense of men struggling against overwhelming odds

---

[57] Hamilton to Lascelles, BM/2266(MO4), Top Secret, 6 May 1948, FO 371/69193/J3206/G.
[58] Ibid.

with an acute awareness of moral purpose. Sir Orme Sargent wrote in October 1945 in a minute that perhaps catches the spirit of the postwar British Empire in competition with American imperialism as well as with the Russian system of political and military expansion:

> The position is no easy one and it seems doubtful whether we shall get much support from the Dominions in the uphill task of maintaining ourselves as a world power in the face of the United States, who now for the first time is prepared to assume this position with the help of the almighty dollar, export surpluses (in other words the swamping of foreign markets with dumped U. S. goods), civil aviation, and all the other instruments which they can if necessary use in order to 'penetrate' the world.
>
> If this is so it behoves us all the more to strengthen our own world position *vis-à-vis* of our two great allied rivals by building up ourselves as *the* great European Power. This brings us back to the policy of collaboration with France with a view to our two countries establishing themselves politically as the leaders of all the Western European Powers and morally as the standard-bearers of European civilisation.[59]

Despite the revolution in modern warfare and the economic threat of American imperialism, the British would persevere. They would not retreat merely because of 'the changes of modern warfare'.[60] As Sargent's minutes make clear, the sense of the moral justification of the British Empire, if not British self-righteousness, sharpened as power waned and as new justifications had to be found to counter American scepticism.

American Anti-Colonialism, Zionism, and Arab Nationalism

'It would help', President Truman once remarked, 'if, figuratively, both the Mufti and Rabbi Silver were thrown into the Red Sea.' 'Tied together', responded his conversationalist.[61] The Mufti was Haj Amin el Husseini, the anti-British extremist leader of the Palestinian Arabs who represented unyielding opposition to Zionism. Abba Hillel Silver was the American Zionist who championed the creation of a Jewish state in all of Palestine, in other words, the opposite extremist aim. The remark reveals Truman's perception of

---

[59] Minute by Sargent, 1 Oct. 1945, FO 371/44557.

[60] Minute by Sargent, 12 Mar. 1946, FO 371/57173.

[61] Truman was discussing these points with George Wadsworth (at that time Ambassador to Iraq), who was once more or less accurately described by one of the representatives of the Jewish Agency as 'a bitter resourceful and inveterate enemy of the Zionist cause' (Arthur Lourie to Sumner Welles, 25 Sept. 1947, ISA 93.03/2270/9). Wadsworth's interview with Truman is published in *Foreign Relations 1948* (V, pp. 592-5) but the lines quoted above were deleted on grounds that the remarks were, in the editor's words, 'personal observations' (see memorandum by Wadsworth, 4 Feb. 1948, USSD 711.90G/ 2448 Box C-49).

Arab and Jewish extremism as the heart of the problem in Palestine as well as his sense of humour. In his one extensive conversation with Ernest Bevin on the subject, Truman in December 1946 said about the Jews:

> They somehow expect one to fulfil all the prophecies of all the prophets. I tell them sometimes that I can no more fulfil all the prophecies of Ezekiel than I can those of that other great Jew, Karl Marx. . . .
> Mr. Truman then went out of his way to explain how difficult it had been with so many Jews in New York.[62]

Truman and Bevin shared a similar outlook on the difficulties of dealing with the Jews on the Palestine question, and it found expression in Truman's jokes no less than in Bevin's. Despite the common ground here and in other areas, the relations between the two men were uneasy. One may speculate that Anglo-American relations at this time might have been better if the Prime Minister had been Churchill, for whom Truman had great respect.[63] For the men of Britain's socialist government, Truman restrained his admiration. In fact he disliked Bevin, in part because the Foreign Secretary reminded him of the leader of the United Mine Workers of America, John L. Lewis.[64]

To those Americans who were sympathetic to the Zionist cause, Truman's response to the question of a Jewish state left much to be desired. His method as well as his stature of course invited comparison with Roosevelt's, almost always to Truman's disadvantage. Roosevelt had managed to leave the impression that he favoured Zionist goals but would not endorse a settlement unacceptable to the Arabs.[65] To the American public his pro-Jewish ideas were better known than his desire to accommodate the Arabs.[66] 'Except for Woodrow Wilson', according to Sumner Welles, 'no President of the United States has

[62] Record of conversation marked 'Top Secret' and 'No Circulation', 8 Dec. 1946, FO 800/513. There is an excerpt in FO 371/61762/E221.

[63] For an assessment of Anglo-American relations during this critical period, see especially Robert M. Hathaway, *Ambiguous Partnership: Britain and America, 1944–1947* (New York, 1981).

[64] Robert J. Donovan, *Conflict and Crisis: The Presidency of Harry S. Truman, 1945–1948* (New York, 1977), p. 323. The sequel is *Tumultuous Years: The Presidency of Harry S. Truman, 1949–1953* (New York, 1982).

[65] On this important point see especially Evan M. Wilson, *Decision on Palestine: How the U. S. Came to Recognize Israel* (Hoover Institution Press, 1979), pp. 34–5. In a formula approved by Roosevelt himself in 1943 and subsequently, the State Department was committed to a policy of 'full consultation' with the Arabs as well as the Jews. When Bevin in his conversation with Truman on 8 Dec. 1946 mentioned that the British unfortunately had given 'conflicting pledges', Truman interrupted to say 'So have we'.

[66] One of the first revelations of Roosevelt's secret diplomacy with the Arabs appeared in Elliott Roosevelt's *As He Saw It* (New York, 1946), p. 245, which relates a conversation of F. D. R. with King Ibn Saud of Saudi Arabia during the President's return journey after the Yalta conference in February 1945: 'It had been Father's hope', Elliott Roosevelt wrote, 'that he would be able to convince Ibn Saud on the equity of the settlement in

shown greater sympathy for Zionism than Franklin Roosevelt.'[67] Welles, like others, probably exaggerated Roosevelt's enthusiasm for the Zionist cause.

Welles was the foremost non-Jewish champion of Zionism in America. Until 1943 he had served in the State Department as Under Secretary. He was thus able to speak with authority on the ways in which the Truman administration was proving itself to be deficient in working towards Roosevelt's goal, as Welles interpreted it, of creating a Jewish state. Welles regarded himself as in the Wilsonian tradition of attempting to build a new world order that would, in his own words, protect 'the small and the weak', not least the Jewish people who had been ravaged by the Nazis. He believed that Roosevelt's successor had failed to meet the political and moral challenge, in part because of the influence of the British. 'The policy of the United States in the case of Palestine has been devoid of vision and devoid of principle', he wrote in *We Need Not Fail* (a book published at a critical time, June 1948, in the early stage of the Arab–Israeli war). Welles not only carried the torch of Wilsonian idealism but also nurtured the Rooseveltian flame of anti-colonialism. He harboured an abiding animosity (as had Roosevelt) for the British Empire. He is a representative figure in this book because he fused the crusade of Zionism with the tradition of American anti-colonialism.

The ethical sentiments of Loy Henderson may be drawn in contrast. Henderson was the Director of the Office of Near Eastern and African Affairs who bore the immediate responsibility for the Palestine question in the State Department. He was a career officer in the Foreign Service whose first post after the First World War had been in Dublin (which he believed gave him certain insights into problems facing the British after the Second World War in the Middle East). Most of his other assignments had been in Eastern Europe and the Soviet Union. He brought to the Middle East a first-hand knowledge of Russian aims in Europe, and a belief that the

---

Palestine of the tens of thousands of Jews driven from their European homes, persecuted, wandering. . . . Of all the men he had talked to in his life, he had got least satisfaction from this iron-willed Arab monarch. Father ended by promising Ibn Saud that he would sanction no American move hostile to the Arab people.' Elliott Roosevelt's book was one of the most widely read accounts of Anglo-American relations during the war. He was distinctly un-charitable to the British, portraying Churchill as a hard-drinking Tory buffoon with diehard ideas about the British Empire. The book was thus a delicate subject of conversation. Bevin thought it 'the height of meanness for one who has been treated as a confidant by his Father to proceed to publish all his secrets' (as recorded in a note by J. N. Henderson, 31 July 1946, FO 800/573). For the theme of American anti-colonialism see Wm. Roger Louis, *Imperialism at Bay 1941–1945: the United States and the Decolonization of the British Empire* (Oxford, 1977).

[67] Sumner Welles, *We Need Not Fail* (Boston, 1948), p. 28.

United States would have to work closely with the British in order to prevent the countries of the eastern Mediterranean and Middle East from disintegrating into revolution and Communism. On the whole he was favourably disposed towards the British.[68] He held in short that the British Empire was a stabilizing force in most parts of the world.

Henderson acknowledged Wilsonian inspiration in attempting to create a stable postwar order based on principles of liberty and self-determination. No less than Welles he espoused Roosevelt's ideas about the necessity to liquidate the European colonial empires, though Henderson believed that this process should take place over a much longer period of time than most American anti-colonialists were willing to concede. Henderson, in contrast with Welles, emphasized the importance of the other side of Roosevelt's general formula for the Middle East—that the Arabs as well as the Jews should be fully consulted about the future of Palestine. In short he believed that the establishment of a Jewish state in a predominantly Arab country would violate the principle of self-determination. The partition of Palestine against the wishes of the majority of the indigenous inhabitants would also, in Henderson's judgement, jeopardize the moral as well as the political, economic, and strategic basis of the American presence in the Middle East. He wrote in October 1946:

> Our cultural position, built up with painstaking effort over the past 100 years, as well as our commercial and economic interests, including oil concessions and aviation and telecommunications rights, would be seriously threatened [if the United States supported the partition of Palestine]. Already the almost child-like confidence which these [Arab] peoples have hitherto displayed toward the United States is giving way to suspicions and dislike, a development which may lead the Arab and Moslem World to look elsewhere than toward the West for support.[69]

More than any other official within the American government, Henderson has been vilified as anti-Jewish and even as anti-Semitic for holding such views. He himself drew the distinction (which is an important one) of not being anti-Jewish but anti-Zionist. He was neither anti-Jewish nor anti-Semitic.[70] But he believed that the Zionist goal of establishing a Jewish state in Palestine would be

---

[68] 'I feel we . . . have a very loyal friend', wrote the British Minister of Defence, A. V. Alexander, after a conversation with Henderson in 1949, '. . . and one with very sane views from our point of view' (Note by Alexander, 12 Oct. 1949, FO 371/74174/AN 3282). From the British perspective this was an accurate assessment.

[69] Memorandum by Henderson, 21 Oct. 1946, *Foreign Relations 1946*, VII, pp. 710–13.

[70] See Allen H. Podet, 'Anti-Zionism in a Key U. S. Diplomat: Loy Henderson at the End of World War II', *American Jewish Archives*, 30 (Nov. 1978).

a permanent cause of instability in the Middle East. He held with
unwavering conviction that the best solution would be some form
of a binational state in which the political and religious rights of the
Jewish minority would be guaranteed.

Welles and Henderson may be taken as representative of the two
opposing currents of thought about the future of Palestine. Such was
the ambiguity of the moral and historical issues that men of good
will towards both Jew and Arab could draw diametrically opposed
conclusions about the justification as well as the wisdom of establishing a Jewish state. One major source of controversy was the Balfour
declaration of 1917, which will be referred to so often in this book
that it is quoted here:

His Majesty's Government view with favour the establishment in Palestine
of a national home for the Jewish people, and will use their best endeavours to
facilitate the achievement of this object, it being clearly understood that nothing
shall be done which may prejudice the civil and religious rights of existing non-
Jewish communities in Palestine, or the rights and political status enjoyed by
Jews in any other country.[71]

Using the Balfour declaration as a historical premiss, it was intellectually defensible to develop an argument going in either direction,
either for a Jewish *state* (as opposed to a 'national home') or against
it. This is a matter of cardinal importance. It would do an injustice
to the protagonists in this historical drama, Arab, Jewish, American,
and British, to minimize the passionate honesty and intellectual
integrity with which those positions were upheld. This is certainly
true of the principal subjects of this book, the British, who among
themselves were sharply divided about the meaning of the Balfour
declaration and the nature of British trusteeship in Palestine.

'I will say straight out', the historian Arnold Toynbee once stated:
'Balfour was a wicked man.'[72] Toynbee believed that Balfour and his
colleagues knew the catastrophic implications for the Arabs of
fostering the equivalent of a white settler community, and nevertheless decided to support the Jews as a means of sustaining British
influence in the eastern Mediterranean. The opposite interpretation
was publicly emphasized above all by Richard Crossman, who held

---

[71] The most illuminating study of the Balfour declaration for purposes of the themes of
the present book is Mayir Vereté, 'The Balfour Declaration and its Makers', *Middle Eastern
Studies*, 6, 1 (Jan. 1970), in which there is one especially revealing sentence: 'Lloyd George
wanted Britain to gain some material benefit while assisting God's will.' Ernest Bevin would
probably have agreed with that comment (and indeed with Vereté's general interpretation).
'It was a unilateral declaration', Bevin once wrote, which 'did not take into account the
Arabs & was really a Power Politics declaration.' Minute by Bevin c.1 Feb. 1946, FO 371/
52509/E1413/G.

[72] 'Arnold Toynbee on the Arab-Israeli Conflict', *Journal of Palestine Studies*, II,
3 (Spring 1973).

that Balfour and the other British statesmen of the First World War had selflessly acted to relieve the oppression of European Jews. 'Other motives', Crossman once wrote, '—the strategic calculations, the influence on American Jewry, the effect on Russian Jewish morale—were, I believe, at most secondary factors.'[73] To Crossman the murder of six million Jews during the Second World War had dramatized the humanitarian need for a Jewish state. He admired the Jewish people, and he regarded the building of a Zionist state as one of the pioneering experiments in postwar socialism. Crossman will figure prominently in this book as the foremost public critic of British Palestine policy. He served on the Anglo-American Committee of Inquiry in 1945-6. The experience inspired a permanent commitment to the Zionist cause. 'Dear Comrade Myerson', he wrote to the future Prime Minister of Israel, Golda Meir, after his return to England in June 1946, 'I think of you all a very great deal. It looks as though Palestine for me was not merely a matter of 120 days, but has become a life-long obligation.'[74]

The public comments and debates in both Britain and the United States usually contained scathing remarks about British colonial policy. 'Trusteeship', the justification of British rule, implied the development of dependent territories for the benefit of all concerned. But in Palestine the colonial administration often appeared to interpret this doctrine in a negative sense. Colonial policy acted as a check on both Jew and Arab. Zionists not only believed that the British government prevented economic development by severely limiting Jewish immigration but also held that the colonial administration was an instrument of oppression. The following excerpt from an economic study may be taken as representative of restrained Zionist comment in America:

> When the British Treasury was dominated by the economics of Keynes, most of the senior officials of the colonial service were still struggling for an acquaintance with the economics of Ricardo and Mill. Any broad conception of a constructive, initiating role for Government, in economic and social development, was beyond their reach. . . . The project of adapting the activities of Government to the building of a Jewish national home in Palestine did not evoke their enthusiasm. . . . The design of the Mandate was a Welfare State. Its reality was a nineteenth century Police State.[75]

When Crossman examined that indictment, he concluded in the *New Statesman* that the British administration had been content merely

---

[73] Richard Crossman, *A Nation Reborn* (London, 1960), p. 32.

[74] Crossman to Myerson, 24 June 1946, CZA S25/6447.

[75] Robert R. Nathan, Oscar Gass, Daniel Creamer, *Palestine: Problem and Promise* (Washington, 1946), pp. 64-5.

to 'tolerate' Jewish development and 'to "protect" the Arab peasant from its effects, by keeping them in their conditions of squalor and illiteracy'.[76]

The secret records of the Colonial Office reveal that Crossman was close to the mark. Colonial Office officials did indeed believe that the Arabs needed to be protected from the Jews. The intention however was not to keep the Arabs in 'squalor and illiteracy' but to guard against the danger of the Jews creating a settler community such as the one in Algeria. That was the analogy used by J. S. Bennett, one of the most pro-Arab of the Colonial Office officials. In order to indicate the intensity of the internal debate, the ideas of Sir Douglas Harris may be quoted briefly in contrast. Harris had long experience in Palestine itself. He was more disposed to the view that development of the Jewish national home could benefit the Arabs as well. In any case he emphasized the *obligation* imposed on the British by the Balfour declaration (which had subsequently been endorsed by the League of Nations) to foster the national home. It is not possible to examine here the issue in its complexity, but this excerpt from one of Harris's minutes indicates the passion aroused within official circles. Harris himself was normally a somewhat unimaginative and unruffled official.

I disagree fundamentally with . . . Mr. Bennett's diagnosis of the case. He states that it is important that, in approaching the practical study of trustee-ship for Palestine, we should keep in mind what he terms the 'essential weakness of our moral and political positon'. In his view, this weakness derives from the fact that we have implemented the Balfour Declaration. . . . I would not assent for a moment to this proposition. . . . The Balfour Declaration is . . . not the policy of Great Britain but of the world [by virtue of its endorsement by the League of Nations].[77]

The controversy led Harris to examine a central issue. Should the British, in view of increasing Arab objections to the 'national home', now attempt to deprive the Balfour declaration 'of its present dynamic character'? In his judgement the British could not repudiate such a solemn commitment. They would have to work as best they could in difficult circumstances to pursue an even-handed policy towards both Jew and Arab. Harris's view reflected the consensus of official thought. Thus there was some justification in regarding

---

[76] *New Statesman*, 29 June 1946.

[77] Minute by Harris, 7 Feb. 1946. This and other extensive minutes in the CO 537 series. For Bennett's view on the question of 'trusteeship' see his letter to J. A. Majoribanks, 'Top Secret and Personal', 15 June 1946, FO 371/67181. The best study of British 'trustee-ship' remains Kenneth Robinson, *The Dilemmas of Trusteeship* (London, 1965). For the issue of self-determination see Michla Pomerance, *Self-Determination in Law and Practice* (The Hague, 1982).

postwar British policy as negative in character. Otherwise the balance would be tilted in favour of one side or the other.

American as well as British officials recoiled from the tactics of the Zionist extremists, but the State Department and the Foreign Office drew different conclusions about the political consequences of establishing a Jewish state. Neither the Americans nor the British who were reporting in secret dispatches from Palestine doubted that fanaticism motivated the militant Zionists. For example the American Consul General in Jerusalem, Robert B. Macatee, reported after the Irgun Zvai Leumi (the 'National Military Organization') hanged two British sergeants in July 1947:

> It is often noted that sufferers of mental aberration seek shelter and privilege in their own delusions, while leaning heavily on the sanity of others for the help which they need and which they invariably take for granted as their natural right. During the time of the Nazis it was a commonplace to hear the opinion that Hitler and his followers were deluded to the point where their sanity was questionable. If such generalizations are permissible, it may be well to question whether the Zionists, in their present emotional state, can be dealt with as rational human beings.[78]

Comparisons between the Jewish extremists and the Nazis, as will be seen, was a common theme in British political analysis as well. In general, however, Americans of this era believed that the Jews would recover from the trauma of the holocaust. The main thrust of American thought (but by no means one on which there was a consensus) held that a Jewish state would guarantee the political and religious rights of the Arab inhabitants, that it would help to stabilize the Middle East, and that it would align itself with the western powers against the Soviet Union.

That strain of interpretation could also be found in England among those who deplored the antagonism that had developed between the British and Jewish peoples. Some Englishmen lamented the loss of Jewish Palestine as a potential member of the British Commonwealth.[79] After the end of the Second World War that vision of the future appeared more and more improbable. 'Something has definitely snapped', Chaim Weizmann, the leader of the Zionist movement, wrote in 1946 about the deteriorating relationship between the two peoples.[80] Within British official circles there

---

[78] Macatee to Merriam, 4 Aug. 1947, enclosing memorandum dated 3 Aug., USSD 867N.01/8–447 Box 6760. Macatee's letter and memorandum were circulated in the Division of Near Eastern Affairs and the classification consequently was upgraded from 'Secret' to 'Top Secret'.

[79] For this tradition see N. A. Rose, *The Gentile Zionists* (London, 1973).

[80] Weizmann to Isaac Herzog, 21 July 1946, in Joseph Heller, ed., *The Letters and Papers of Chaim Weizmann*, XXII, Series A (Israel Universities Press, 1979), p. 172.

developed a view that was entirely at variance with the one upheld by those who hoped for a revival of Anglo-Jewish friendship, and with the optimistic American forecast. This British outlook held that the Jews would drift away from the British traditions established during the mandate period, that they would never be able to live at peace with the Arabs whose land they had appropriated, and that they would turn Jewish Palestine into a Communist state.

British apprehension about the Jews and Communism can be traced to the time of the Russian revolution in 1917. The world of the early twentieth century abounded in conspiracy theories about Freemasons, Papists, international financiers, and not least Jews. Revolutionary Jews were believed to have been decisive in the overthrow of the Czar. There later appeared to be a similarity between the collective farms in the Soviet Union and the kibbutzim in Palestine. Stereotyped ideas, absurd as they may seem in retrospect, help to explain British attitudes at the time of the beginning of the cold war. Ernest Bevin himself used the phrase 'international Jewry', with its connotation of conspiracy, as an explanation of the outcome of the 1948 war between the Arabs and the Jews.[81] If he did not subscribe to the equivalent of a latter-day conspiracy theory, at least he believed that the Jews might be fitting into Stalin's plan for eventually absorbing Jewish Palestine into the system of Soviet satellites. Bevin wrote to Hector McNeil (Minister of State at the Foreign Office) in 1947 after the Soviet decision to support the Jews in the partition proposal before the United Nations:

> I was not surprised when the Russians supported partition.... There are two things operating in the Russian mind. First of all, Palestine. I am sure they are convinced that by immigration they can pour in sufficient indoctrinated Jews to turn it into a Communist state in a very short time. The New York Jews have been doing their work for them.
> Secondly, I shall not be surprised if Russia, to consolidate her position in Eastern Europe, does not break up all her satellite States into smaller provinces, reaching down to the Adriatic. Thus partition would suit them as a principle.
> ... You must study very carefully Stalin's work on nationalities to realise how his mind works, and then you will learn that he would have no compunction at all in exploiting these nationalities to achieve his object by means of a whole series which Russia could control.[82]

During the 1948 war Czechoslovakia supplied arms and ammunition to the Jews. British intelligence reports indicated that refugees from Eastern Europe included indoctrinated Communists.[83] In 1948–9

---

[81] See minutes of F. O. Middle East conference, 21 July 1949, FO 371/75072.

[82] 'Please burn it [this letter] after you have read it', Bevin instructed McNeil. Fortunately the carbon copy was not destroyed. Bevin to McNeil, 'Confidential and Personal', 15 Oct. 1947, FO 800/509.

[83] This point is established by Bullock, *Bevin*, chap. 16 sect. 6. See below p. 481.

the British believed that they had good reason to warn the United States that the new state of Israel might become Communist.

Just as there was a tendency on the British side to attribute disagreeable developments to 'conspiracy', so also with the Zionists there was a belief that certain individuals within the American government conspired with the officials of the Arabian-American Oil Company (Aramco) against the Jews in order to remain on good terms with the Arabs. Much of this comment focused on James Forrestal (Secretary of the Navy, and, after September 1947, Secretary of Defense). A Zionist writer has accurately commented:

> [I]n some Jewish quarters he [Forrestal] earned a reputation as an anti-Semite second only to Ernest Bevin. Hatred for this strange, intense, and ultimately tragic man . . . runs high among Zionists. But the nature of his conduct indicates that his anti-Zionism stemmed from no hatred of Jews nor love of Arabs, only from his dedication to the welfare and security of the United States. . . . Forrestal was worried about oil.[84]

Forrestal was alarmed that American support of the Jews might incur 'the permanent enmity of the Moslem world' and would jeopardize 'the very core of our position in the Middle East'.[85] But there was no 'conspiracy'. The reality was quite different, with Aramco protesting that the government appeared to be impotent in the face of the Zionist lobby. In fact the representatives of Aramco themselves, though they certainly shared Forrestal's anxiety, did not see any immediate threat to the oil concession. James Terry Duce, a Vice-President of Aramco, in January 1948 wrote confidently of the Arab ability to wage sustained warfare against the Jews.[86] A year later the events of the war itself had dramatically altered many American attitudes, including Forrestal's.[87] The Israelis had vindicated themselves as gallant and able soldiers. Even anti-Zionist sceptics in the

[84] Robert Silverberg, *If I Forget Thee O Jerusalem: American Jews and the State of Israel* (New York, 1970), pp. 346–7.

[85] Forrestal Diary, 28 Jan. 1948, Forrestal Papers; see the editorial comment in Walter Millis, ed., *The Forrestal Diaries* (New York, 1951), pp. 364–5.

[86] Duce was more concerned with the long-range consequences of setting up a Jewish state. 'The resentment [of the Arabs] against partition', he wrote, 'is deep rooted in the peoples of the area and is not the result of agitation of a few fanatics.' Memorandum by Duce, 15 Jan. 1948, USSD 867N.01/1–2948. For discussion of Aramco and Zionism see especially Cohen, *Palestine and the Great Powers*, p. 168; and Aaron David Miller, *Search for Security: Saudi Arabian Oil and American Foreign Policy, 1939–1949* (University of North Carolina Press, 1980), pp. 184–91. Two other essential works are Michael B. Stoff, *Oil, War, and American Security: The Search for a National Policy on Foreign Oil, 1941–1947* (Yale University Press, 1980); and Irving H. Anderson, *Aramco, the United States and Saudi Arabia: A Study of the Dynamics of Foreign Oil Policy 1933–1950* (Princeton, 1981).

[87] Eliahu Epstein (Elath), in a revealing indication of Forrestal's changed outlook, wrote that the Secretary of Defense was now 'most cordial'. Elath to Shertok, 24 Jan. 1949, ISA 91.01/2180/32.

State Department now believed that the new Jewish state could prove to be a source of stability and a bulwark against Communism and Soviet penetration into the Middle East.

The British withdrawal from Palestine took place nine months after the transfer of power in India. To most Americans the British Empire appeared to be in a state of dissolution. When the British in early 1947 announced that they had neither the economic resources nor the manpower to continue the military occupation of Greece, the crisis of British imperialism throughout the world could be seen in dismal perspective. Walter Lippmann, the most widely read of American political commentators, wrote at that time:

> The fact is that in the whole region of the Middle East and Southern Asia from the Eastern Mediterranean to Malaya, the British authority is insufficient. It is unable to induce, and certainly it is unable to impose, solutions for the historic transition from empire to independence.[88]

Many intelligent observers believed that the impending collapse of the British Empire had some connection with the victory of socialism in England. It is a theme that characterizes the mainstream of American comment both public and private. For example Judge Joseph Hutcheson, the American Chairman of the Anglo-American Committee of Inquiry on Palestine, wrote in June 1947 in a letter that lamented the British plight:

> I am particularly impressed with . . . the British being discouraged about the present and uncertain about the future. . . . I feel that the trouble is that the British have abandoned their ancient traditions and feeling for England as England in exchange for a sorry mess of pottage, a socialist theory and a labor government.
>
> I have always regarded myself as a liberal, that is a person who believed in freedom of thought and freedom of action, to move always in the right direction for a better world. I repudiate utterly the idea that this world can come through a socialistic or communistic form of government. I think Britain's experience with the lassitude and apathy which have followed their taking over of strange and alien ideas and government which now control them is the best proof of the rightness of my instinct.[89]

This was a common American response to the problems of postwar Britain. It was expressed less politely but more succinctly by the pro-Zionist Congressman Emmanuel Celler: 'too damned much Socialism at home and too much damned Imperialism abroad'.[90]

Those typical American views would have seemed entirely misguided to the statesmen of the Labour government, but Attlee and

---

[88] *Washington Post*, 27 Feb. 1947.
[89] Hutcheson to James McDonald, 9 June 1947, McDonald Papers.
[90] Quoted in Gardner, *Sterling–Dollar Diplomacy*, p. 237.

Bevin would have recognized the paradox of socialism and imperialism. The tension between the two men about such basic issues was especially pronounced in late 1946 and early 1947. Then as always Attlee was more inclined to liquidate the empire while Bevin hoped to transform the imperial system into a new order that would benefit the peoples of the Middle East as well as those of the British Isles. 'I do not think', Attlee wrote to Bevin in December 1946, 'that the countries bordering on Soviet Russia's zone viz Greece, Turkey, Iraq and Persia can be made strong enough to form an effective barrier. We do not command the resources to make them so.'[91] When the two of them agreed that British troops should be withdrawn from Greece, Attlee viewed this problem above all as one of economic and military retrenchment.[92] As will be seen in Part II of this book, Bevin by contrast regarded the crisis in the eastern Mediterranean as an opportunity to win American commitment to a 'northern tier' that would provide a shield to enable the British to carry on with the development of the 'British' Middle East. Far from a humiliation of having to cut losses, the outcome of the drama in Greece was thus a triumph for British statecraft. To Bevin the critical part of the world was the same as the one identified by British statesmen at the close of the First World War—in Lord Milner's words, 'that great sphere of British influence extending from the centre of East Africa, through the Sudan, Egypt, Arabia and the Persian Gulf to India, which is the real British "Empire" apart from the Dominions'.[93] Bevin probably would have gone even further and would have emphasized Libya, Transjordan, and Iraq as well, though he was not obsessed with territorial control as were his predecessors. Nevertheless his ideas flowed exuberantly from the tradition of 'enlightened' British imperialism. Bevin's vision was far removed from the common American assumption of an empire in dissolution.

Whether or not Bevin could realize his aim of consolidating the 'British' Middle East depended entirely on the collaboration of the moderate nationalists. The accommodation of moderate nationalism

[91] Attlee to Bevin, 'Private & Personal', 1 Dec. 1946, FO 800/475.
[92] See the note by J. N. Henderson dated 28 December 1946, FO 800/475. The records of this file are most important in establishing the chronology of the 1946–7 crisis. This particular note for example records that two days after Christmas 1946 Attlee and Bevin not only agreed on the question of withdrawal from Greece but also on the issue of submitting the Palestine question to the United Nations. There was moreover significant agreement on Cyrenaica: 'The Prime Minister agreed [with Bevin] that if we had Cyrenaica, there would be no need to stay in either Egypt or Palestine.'
[93] Quoted in John Darwin, *Britain, Egypt and the Middle East: Imperial Policy in the Aftermath of War 1918–1922* (London, 1981), p. 21. For an assessment of this and other works that are relevant to the themes of the present book see Keith Jeffery, 'Great Power Rivalry in the Middle East', *Historical Journal*, 25, 4 (1982).

in order to prevent political extremism was the axiom of the Labour government. It is a key theme of this book. The formula itself had crystallized during the war in the assessment of the major problems to be faced after the peace. For example R. M. A. Hankey of the Eastern Department of the Foreign Office (an official who will figure prominently in discussions about British policy at the close of the war) reflected on the ways the British might best prevent a 'pan-Arab revolution' or, still worse, a 'fanatical' religious and military movement directed against Europeans comparable to the Mahdist rising (which the British before the turn of the century had finally suppressed only by military invasion of the Sudan). He wrote in November 1943:

> If we are not to produce a Mahdist or pan-Arab revolution, which will spread from wherever it breaks out to the whole Arab world, we must co-operate with the Nationalists in each country, even if they are difficult, in helping them along the road of constitutional progress towards independence and towards cultural, economic and also possibly political unity of the Middle East.[94]

This was the line of thought that lay behind the ambivalent British support of the Arab League which was formally established in March 1945.[95] The encouragement was ambivalent because the British were aware that a pan-Arab political organization might turn against them. The fostering of moderate Arab nationalism along the lines suggested by Hankey entailed a risk, but one that the British had to take.

Hankey was writing in response to a study of Arab nationalism prepared for the Research Department of the Foreign Office by H. A. R. Gibb, the Arabic scholar. The ideas in Hankey's minute thus reflected, to a degree unusual in official thought, an academic awareness of some of the more theoretical issues. Hankey himself had spent considerable time mastering the principles of Marxism in order to forecast the impact of the Soviet Union on the postwar Middle East. Here was his diagnosis:

> Hitherto, of course, the Arabs have not been attracted towards Russia. The rationalist, collectivist, and materialist outlook of Marxism is even more foreign to Moslem thought than nineteenth and twentieth century liberal rationalism has been. . . . If, however, the Russians start to allow the practice of religion by Mohammedans, this may somewhat alter the picture. . . .
> The untrammelled and outrageous exploitation of the workers by the capitalists throughout the Middle East area makes anyone from Europe astonished that the

---

[94] Minute by Hankey, 29 Nov. 1943, FO 371/39988.
[95] See especially Ahmed M. Gomaa, *The Foundation of the League of Arab States: Wartime Diplomacy and Inter-Arab Politics 1941 to 1945* (London, 1977).

whole working class is not Communist, or at least actively revolutionary, already.[96]

Hankey was uneasy about the growth of the oil industry. Unless the British government could convince the Anglo-Iranian Oil Company, for example, to pursue social as well as economic policies designed to raise the general standard of living and the quality of life, then there would eventually be a Middle Eastern explosion against the capitalist system. In the last part of this book it will be seen that Mohammed Musaddiq presented the challenge that Hankey had anticipated during the war.

If the Iranian ill-will generated by the exploitation of the Anglo-Iranian Oil Company was one major problem that eventually had to be faced, the Egyptian resentment at the British occupation of the Canal Zone was another. The latter as well as the former issue came to a head in the last months of the Labour government with the nationalists in Iran, so the British believed, giving inspiration to the Egyptians to abrogate the Anglo-Egyptian Treaty of 1936 and the Sudan Agreement of 1899. If the Iranians could get away with nationalizing the oil industry, what might the Egyptians have in mind for the Suez Canal Company? If the British failed through rational argument and moderation with the Iranians, would not greater firmness yield more satisfactory results with the Egyptians? Those were questions that divided the British public as well as those within the Labour government. C. D. Quilliam, the correspondent of *The Times* who had an intimate knowledge of Egypt, believed that good relations would depend on the British giving up long-held attitudes of 'superiority, condescension, victoriousness, and any suggestion of "time-you-came-to-your-senses" '.[97] Unfortunately those attitudes had lingered on into the postwar period. Indeed many contemporary observers believed them to be virtually personified by the Ambassador in Egypt until March 1946, Lord Killearn.

Despite the short period that he remained in Cairo after the war, Killearn casts a long shadow in this book. In the Egyptian chapters in Parts III and V the lasting consequences of his humiliation of King Farouk in 1942 will be discussed. Here a few words will be said about what Killearn represented. In some ways it was the opposite of Bevin's stand on the Middle East, though both of them shared such a similar outlook on economic development as the panacea for the problems of the Middle East that Killearn at first believed that the

[96] Minute by Hankey, 29 Nov. 1943, FO 371/39988.
[97] Quilliam to Ralph Deakin (Imperial and Foreign editor of *The Times*), 26 Nov. 1951, Quilliam Papers.

two of them had 'clicked'.[98] Bevin himself respected Killearn and, after Egypt, appointed him as Special Commissioner in South-East Asia. It was the climax of an illustrious career that had included the renegotiating of the 'unequal treaties' with China as well as the cementing of the cornerstone of Britain's position in Egypt, the treaty of 1936. Malcolm Macdonald (the former Colonial Secretary and a postwar Governor-General of Malaya) wrote of him in 1947:

> I have come to admire his energy, drive, experience and wisdom. Of course, he has his faults. He is too much concerned with his and his family's material well-being. But he is built on a grand scale, and if his vices sometimes appear large his virtues are colossal. . . . Though 67 years old, he has the physical vigour and mental freshness of a man in his prime. He is still a sort of human dynamo.[99]

That was a balanced assessment. In Egypt Killearn had discharged his duties with august authority. As one historian has written, he was 'an old-fashioned, straightforward, robustly patriotic imperialist'.[1] He was in short one of the last great Proconsuls.

Killearn believed in the British Empire as a permanent institution in world affairs. One of his maxims was 'firmness'. The dependent peoples of the Empire would respect British overlordship as long as the British themselves demonstrated the determination to preserve their position as a great power—if necessary, by force. The Egyptians were well aware of this attitude. Killearn himself was a man of imposing physical presence, six feet five inches tall and 250 pounds in weight. He was not only paternalistic but also, at times, a bully. It was common knowledge that he relished the pomp and oriental circumstance of his office, the dinners and parties, and the easy relations with many Tory leaders including Churchill. One of his colleagues, Sir Laurence Grafftey-Smith, wrote later of him: 'He was physically and temperamentally incapable of giving any convincing impression of change, and this had unhappy consequences.'[2] This was an astute remark. The Egyptians failed to believe that Killearn would or could adjust himself to a new relationship of equality rather than dominance. He would continue the occupation of the Canal Zone by bayonets if necessary. Bevin's decision to end the 'Killearn era' in March 1946 was thus symbolic of the Labour government's determination to put Britain's relations with the peoples of the Middle

---

[98] This was the word Killearn used to describe his first meeting with Bevin in September 1945 (Killearn Diary, 13 Sept. 1945). The 'clicking' definitely stopped when Killearn began to haggle over the salary and perquisites of his post in South-East Asia. 'Very trying', Bevin scrawled. See Killearn to Bevin, 9 Feb. 1946, FO 800/461.

[99] Macdonald to Creech Jones, 'Personal & Secret', 26 Sept. 1947, Creech Jones Papers.

[1] James Morris, *Farewell the Trumpets* (London, 1978), p. 439.

[2] Laurence Grafftey-Smith, *Bright Levant* (London, 1970), p. 138.

East on a new footing. Bevin did not take the view that the Egyptians could be sat upon indefinitely. Nor did he think that they could be manipulated. He believed in treating the Egyptians as equals.

With the benefit of over three decades' hindsight, it is a fair question to ask whether a complete change of attitude, even if possible, would have made any difference, and whether Middle Eastern nationalism could have been accommodated in any circumstance. In retrospect Bevin's policy indeed may be regarded as an invitation to frustration and failure. Attlee's inclination to cut losses and adjust to 'Little England'—perhaps with an eye more towards Europe—might well have been more realistic. The instability of the Middle East as a region, the volatile nature of the nationalist movements, and the resentment at the British military and commercial presence, seemed to preclude any long-range plans for economic and social development from the outset. The eviction of the Anglo-Iranian Oil Company and the unrest in Egypt at the end of the period certainly confirmed the sceptics' attitude that there was little hope for a lasting and mutually beneficial connection between Britain and the Middle East. Those issues however did not seem so clear-cut at the time. The men of this era knew that they were pitted against immense odds, but they nevertheless believed that they had a chance. The contemporary belief that the British were engaged in a heroic struggle, and that things might work out well after all, makes the story all the more fascinating.

PART II

THE NORTHERN TIER:
IRAN, TURKEY, AND GREECE,
1945–1947

THE phrase 'northern tier' is usually associated with John Foster Dulles and the 1950s, but as a geopolitical concept it has a relevance to the themes of this book. 'Nuri Pasha', wrote Harold Beeley of the Foreign Office in August 1945 recording a conversation with the Iraqi leader, '. . . talked for half an hour continuously about Russian expansion. He was particularly insistent on the importance of a firm British policy in Greece, Turkey, and Persia. There can be no doubt that most politically-minded persons in the Arab States feel some such anxiety, and are watching intently to see how strong a shield H. M. G. is likely to be.'[1] Geographically, culturally, politically, and economically, the northern tier of Greece, Turkey, and Persia (and Afghanistan, which lies beyond the scope of the present discussion) possessed little in common. Collectively the three countries formed a bulwark against Russian expansion into the eastern Mediterranean and Middle East. Greece, Turkey, and Iran (the terms 'Persia' and 'Iran' were still used interchangeably) individually proved to be the test cases of British, and eventually American, response to the question of Communism and the related issue of the aims of the Soviet Union.

For the British the problem was how to deter Russian expansion without an economically unbearable, and politically undesirable, indefinite British military occupation in Greece and Iran; and how to prevent economic and political deterioration in the three countries that might make Communism a compelling solution. It is arguable that the cold war had part of its beginnings in the collision of Soviet and British aims in the northern tier. In any case it was the British who bore the initial brunt of the hazard of Russian expansion and who had to assess the probable danger of Communist regimes in Persia, Turkey, and Greece in relation to the Middle East as a whole. In 1947 the United States government intervened decisively in Greece, while in the same year the American approach to the problem of Palestine in contrast could at best be described as schizophrenic. In the case of Turkey the future of the Straits and the

[1] Minute by Beeley, 26 Aug. 1945, FO 371/48773/411226/G. There is an excellent recent work which deals extensively with the American dimension of the subject: Bruce Robellet Kuniholm: *The Origins of the Cold War in the Near East: Great Power Conflict and Diplomacy in Iran, Turkey, and Greece* (Princeton, 1980); but see the severe comments by D. C. Watt on the weakness of it on the British side in *Middle Eastern Studies*, 18, 2 (Apr. 1982). For Iran the two key works are Rouhollah Ramazani, *Iran's Foreign Policy 1941–1973* (Charlottesville, 1975); and George Lenczowski, *Russia and the West in Iran, 1918–1948* (Ithaca, 1949). See also Hossein Amirsadeghi, ed., *Twentieth-Century Iran* (New York, 1977), especially the chapters by Rose L. Greaves and Ronald W. Ferrier; and the important essay based on Persian and Russian as well as English sources by Stephen L. McFarland, 'A Peripheral View of the Origins of the Cold War: The Crisis in Iran, 1941–47', *Diplomatic History*, 4, 4 (1980).

possible expansion of the Soviet Union into the Mediterranean had a fundamental bearing on postwar geopolitics. In Iran, at this time the largest oil producer in the Middle East and one vital to British postwar economic recovery, the British perceived the danger of Iranian nationalization of the oil industry. Six years later the Labour government ended in the midst of the crisis of the Iranian takeover. In general the British response to the challenge of Communism and Russian expansion, as well as to the specific peril that Persian oil would be cut off, was to bolster the moderate nationalists and to introduce economic measures that would raise the standards of living. The goal was to enable the Greeks, Turks, and Iranians to fend for themselves while weaning them away from political extremism in order to preserve British influence. This was the answer of the Labour government to nationalist movements throughout the world. In the countries of the northern tier it soon became clear that British aims could not be achieved without American assistance, but in 1945-6 it was by no means certain that aid would be forthcoming.

Iran

Ernest Bevin speculated in March 1946, as the Iranian crisis neared its peak, 'that the explanation of recent Soviet activities in Persia was to be sought in their oil interest, rather than a desire to acquire fresh water territory or an outlet to warm-water ports'.[2] There was in fact no consensus about Russian motives. It was just as possible to argue that the Russians had much less of a vital interest in Persian oil than did Britain and sought an oil concession less because of its importance to the Soviet economy than because they aimed at transforming Iran into a Soviet satellite, with perhaps the ancillary goal of disrupting the British economy. The Czarist drive to the Indian ocean, inherited and invigorated by the Bolsheviks, also figured prominently in British assessments. Moreover the clash could be regarded as ideological. According to C. F. A. Warner, who as head of the Northern Department of the Foreign Office had been charged with Russian affairs during the war: 'It seemed clear that the Russians were engaged in a general offensive against this country which they regarded as the weak limb in the Anglo-American capitalist bloc.'[3] Warner's successor, R. M. A. Hankey (who before becoming head of the Northern Department in 1946 had closely followed events in Iran as a member of the Eastern Department) was inclined to emphasize old-fashioned

[2] CM 25 (46) 18 Mar. 1946, CAB 128/5.
[3] See FO 371/52673/3459. In general for the Russian preoccupation of the Foreign Office, see Victor Rothwell, *Britain and the Cold War 1941-1947* (London, 1982).

earth hunger: 'I do not consider that Russian opposition to British interests in Persia (or elsewhere) is mainly due to considerations of oil policy nor do I believe that if [the] U. S. S. R. had all the oil she could possibly need, Russian policy would be more conciliatory to British interests (Possibly indeed the contrary).'[4] Hankey's views may be taken as representative of the hard line: Russian expansion was implacable and should be faced resolutely in the conviction that the British should not withdraw from the wartime occupation of Iran except on the condition of Russian retreat at exactly the same pace. 'I am personally against our evacuating a square yard unless we secure some Russian evacuation also', Hankey once wrote.[5]

The British records make it clear that Ernest Bevin and other members of the Cabinet were prepared to risk British lives in order 'to safeguard our vital Middle Eastern supplies of oil'.[6] There was unanimity on the importance of Iranian oil for British postwar recovery and future war potential. According to the Chiefs of Staff:

The supply of Middle East oil, in particular from the Persian oilfields, was essential to us in securing the peace-time economy and financial position of this country, and to sustain our effort in war. Without access to these supplies, neither the United States nor the United Kingdom could again provide supplies comparable with that forthcoming in the last war. . . . The Southern Persian and Kuwait oilfields possessed the largest and most prolific sources of oil supply in the world.[7]

In 1938 Iran had produced 4.4 per cent of the non-communist world's total oil supply, and by the late 1940s the figure had increased to 6.8 per cent with infinite promise for the future. The Anglo-Iranian Oil Company possessed its own fleet, airport, housing, hospitals, and schools. The refinery at Abadan, the largest in the world, produced a complete range of petroleum products that included gasoline, lubricating and fuel oils, and bitumen. In a striking comparison the Ministry of Fuel and Power estimated that the replacement of the British plant at Abadan would cost £120 million—'not much less than the estimated cost of retooling and modernising the coal industry in this country'.[8] On the surface there might seem to be every reason for the accomplishments of the Anglo-Iranian Oil Company to be a source of British pride and an indication of the healthy state of British capitalism. In fact there was considerable tension between the company and the Labour government. The

---

[4] Minute by Hankey, 10 Sept. 1946, FO 371/52729/E9459.

[5] Minute by Hankey, 29 May 1945, FO 371/45464/E3435/G.

[6] Bevin's words at a Cabinet meeting, CM 68 (46) 68, 15 July 1946, CAB 128/6.

[7] Defence Committee minutes, DO (46) 22, 19 July 1946, CAB 131/1.

[8] Memorandum by K. L. Stock (Ministry of Fuel and Power), 17 Sept. 1946, FO 371/52343.

uneasiness about the company was especially pronounced in the minutes of the Foreign Secretary himself.

Bevin was acutely aware that the aims of the Anglo-Iranian Oil Company did not coincide with those of the Labour government. As a socialist he believed that British companies in the Middle East should be held responsible for the economic and social welfare of their employees. It simply was not good enough for the company to fulfil minimal contractual obligations that had been agreed upon with the Iranian government during the heyday of twentieth-century British capitalism. Before the First World War, when the fleet had converted from coal to oil, the British government had bought into the company. It owned fifty-one per cent of the company shares. The government possessed a veto power over company policies, but it could be used only in extraordinary circumstances such as a crisis in which the flow of oil might be stopped. To Bevin, who had inquiries made into the government's control over the company, this was an unsatisfactory and indeed intolerable situation. He made the following observations in a dictated minute of July 1946. It makes extremely interesting reading in view of the nationalization crisis of 1951.

> [The] company itself . . . is virtually a private company with state capital and anything it does reacts upon the relationships between the British Government and Persia. As Foreign Secretary I have no power or influence, in spite of this great holding by the Government, to do anything at all. As far as I know, no other Department has. Although we have a Socialist Government in this country there is no reflection of that fact in the social conditions in connexion with this great oil production in Persia.
>
> On the other hand, what argument can I advance against anyone claiming the right to nationalise the resources of their country? We are doing the same thing here with our power in the shape of coal, electricity, railways, transport and steel.[9]

Bevin was clearly troubled over the contradiction between socialism in England and British capitalism in Iran. He wanted an answer to the accusation, which he felt compelled to admit as justified, 'that the workpeople are really working for private capitalists'.

Bevin got no satisfaction from the chairman of the company, Sir William Fraser. He pointed out to Fraser that 'we really want to be good employers'. Fraser replied that the company's wages were as good as anyone else's in Persia. 'I feel that this attitude of mind is not good enough', Bevin stated. 'A British company ought to be a model employer and should go out of their way to improve upon . . . [minimum conditions] and establish every possible relationship with the people in order to develop confidence between them and

---

[9] Minute by Bevin, 20 July 1946, FO 371/52735.

the company.' Bevin was not at all convinced that the company's policies were 'sufficiently progressive'. His socialist conscience was outraged that British capitalism appeared to be carrying on as if oblivious to developments in England. 'Here we have a company in a country where the standard of life is low and it is not saying much for us that we are a little above the average.'[10] These are themes that will be discussed further in the chapter which deals with the Persian oil crisis of 1951.

Such was Bevin's confidence in human nature that he did not take 'too tragic a view' of reports that the Communist Party in Iran, the Tudeh, had made inroads into the southern as well as the northern part of the country. 'I am hopeful', he wrote in a memorandum circulated to the Cabinet, 'that, given time, it may prove possible to wean the Tudeh Party or at least some part of its adherents, from extremist or Communist courses.' He had in mind economically progressive measures in the concession such as more 'enlightened' attitudes towards wage claims and welfare benefits. 'I am convinced that much can be done by means of sympathetic treatment of labour and social welfare in the oilfields.' This would take time, but the Iranians would become convinced of the honesty of British intentions and would prefer to develop the oil resources with the British rather than to jeopardize their liberty as well as their economy with the Russians. In a sense Bevin was affirming the ebullient British motto that had served so well in the nineteenth century, 'a fair field and no favour'. He apprehended however that the Russians would not play the game fairly. He perceived the danger of northern Persia being turned into a sort of Soviet 'showplace'. He intended to counter Russian propaganda with straightforward facts about the Anglo-Iranian Oil Company's 'amenities and conditions which they offered to their local employees' and 'pension facilities'.[11] Unfortunately for the Foreign Secretary, his imagination worked at a faster pace than the company's desire to implement a more 'enlightened' policy towards its employees. Others in the Foreign Office, and in Iran, were far more sceptical about the Anglo-Iranian Oil Company's ability to compete with a Russian monopoly, which would in effect be an arm of the Soviet government.

Was it to British advantage to encourage a Russian oil concession under 'fair' conditions? There was a powerful current of Foreign Office thought during the war which held that Anglo-Soviet relations could be improved if it could be demonstrated to the Russians that the British did not intend to corner all of the Persian oil resources. Geographically the mountainous area of nothern Iran

[10] Ibid.   [11] Minutes of FO meeting, 18 Apr. 1946, FO 371/52673.

(especially the region of the oil reserves on the Caspian side of the Zagros mountains) was not one that the British in any case could hope to exploit. 'I cannot help wondering', the head of the Northern Department of the Foreign Office had written at the time of the Russian demand for a concession in October 1944, whether 'the course of practical wisdom' might not be to look at the problem from the angle of 'long-term Anglo-Soviet relations' rather than from the point of view of the feckless Persians. Warner continued in a minute that may be taken as representative of Foreign Office opinion in favour of conciliating the Russians:

> Even supposing the Russians do not frighten the Persians into giving them the oil concession, can they not achieve complete domination of the northern Persian provinces at any time they like in other ways? . . . The Russians are bound to have an economic stranglehold on the northern provinces and certainly after the war, it seems to me, can achieve a political and strategic stranglehold on those provinces whenever they like. . . . *Vis-à-vis* of the Russians, it seems to me that our obstruction would be the more difficult to explain in that we have the oil-fields in South Persia.[12]

Warner in other words did not favour a dog-in-the-manger attitude in a region where the Russians probably would predominate in any case. He believed that the Ambassador in Tehran, Sir Reader Bullard, was pursuing a dangerous course by encouraging Persian defiance—in his own words summing up Bullard's policy, 'inciting them to resist'. Here lay a major area of controversy.

Sir Reader Bullard holds a place of particular interest in Anglo-American relations in the Middle East as well as in the origins of the cold war. Loy Henderson, the postwar director of the Office of Middle Eastern and African Affairs of the State Department, who usually took a sympathetic view towards British officials, believed that the Iranian crisis of 1946 could be traced directly to Bullard's policy in 1944–5. 'Those of us who have been following developments in the Middle East', Henderson wrote in 1946, 'are inclined to agree that Bullard . . . is to a large extent personally responsible for present developments because he laid the groundwork for present Soviet activity.'[13] Henderson in short believed that Bullard had pursued a policy of appeasement. The judgement was dramatically and entirely wrong. Bullard thought that British troops should be withdrawn from Iran as soon as possible (from that outlook may be traced the source of Henderson's misjudgement) but his motives in urging that course were exactly the opposite of believing that the Russians should or could be 'appeased'. It is difficult to think of

---

[12] Minute by Warner, 12 Oct. 1944, FO 371/40241/E6191/G.
[13] Henderson to Acheson, 30 July 1946, USSD 891.00/7-3046.

anyone, even R. M. A. Hankey or Sir Maurice Peterson, who in Middle Eastern affairs took a more severe line towards the Russians. Such was the breadth of Bullard's thought, especially in its psychological dimension and in its bold religious analogies, that it is reminiscent of the analysis of Russian behaviour by George Kennan. Bullard's ideas thus deserve to be briefly elucidated in their Middle Eastern context. His thought on the whole is of considerable interest in regard to Iran because it represents a British response, sophisticated yet blunt, to the question of Soviet expansion and the danger of Communism based on long experience in the Middle East.

Bullard had entered the Levant Consular Service and served in his first post at Beirut in 1909. By the time of the outbreak of the Second World War three decades later he had an almost uninterrupted record of service in the Middle East and the Balkans (Russia's 'security belt' in his phrase) and four years in Russia itself in Moscow and Leningrad. His first hand experience in the Soviet Union gave him insight, he believed, into Russian 'modes of thought'. He had no illusion about the nature of the Soviet regime, which in its 'Hitler technique' was as unscrupulous as Nazi Germany. In the realm of ideology he believed that the assumptions of Soviet Communism bore comparison with the tenets of Islam. Here is the way in which Iran fitted into the Russian cosmos in 1946:

> The attitude of the rulers of Russia, whoever they may be, towards the rest of the world resembles that of the early Moslem lawyers, who named it the Dar al Harb, or Region of War, as opposed to their own Region of Islam. The Region of War comprised all lands where Islam was not dominant, and it was legitimate to make war on any of them, the only criterion being the prospects of success. The Soviet Government seem to have decided that this is a favourable moment to effect the virtual inclusion of part of Persia in the Dar al Soviet and to establish indirect control over the rest of the country.[14]

As if the humane aims of the British Empire could be regarded as being in a state of rivalry with the perverted ideals of the Soviet

---

[14] Bullard to Bevin, No. 76 Secret, 15 Mar. 1946, FO 371/52670/E2813. In this and in a companion dispatch (No. 65 Secret, 3 Mar. 1946, FO 371/52667/E2318) Bullard attempted to distil his accumulated historical and philosophical knowledge of Soviet Russia and Iran. See also his autobiography, *The Camels Must Go* (London, 1961), and his survey, *Britain and the Middle East* (London, 1951). The description of him by an American official in retrospect quoted by Kuniholm, *Origins*, p. 155, is of interest and is essentially accurate: 'a real old-school British Middle Eastern specialist, with the virtues and the faults that characterized that breed. He looked upon the Iranians as grown-up children, not to be trusted very far but to be protected against themselves and guided in the way they should go. Needless to say, they should also be guided in ways that would protect British interests; that, after all, was what he was paid for. He was not averse to exerting pressures, through the British occupation troops or Britain's control of trade with the outside world, nor was he averse to the traditional methods of oriental intrigue, but he preferred the velvet glove approach when possible, rather than the Russian-style bludgeon. . . .'

Union, Bullard continued to develop his religious analogy. In Iran, in competition with Soviet propaganda, the British faced the same disadvantages encountered by the Christian missionaries competing with Islam in tropical Africa. 'A religion which demands above all self-sacrifice of its followers would be difficult enough to accept even if it were not presented differently by different exponents, and a primitive mind finds it easier to embrace Islam with its five simple duties, one of which offers the fun and excitement and community feeling of the pilgrimage.' In this apparently uneven match the moral weakness of the Iranians further played into Soviet hands. Bullard in fact had a contempt for the Iranians:

> It is regrettable, but a fact, that the Persians are ideal Stalin-fodder. They are untruthful, backbiters, undisciplined, incapable of unity, without a plan. The Soviet system is equipped with a complete theoretical scheme for everything from God to goloshes, and power to impose discipline and unity; and the Soviet authorities do not require from their followers the impossible feat of refraining from lying and backbiting, but only that these qualities shall be canalised according to the orders of the day.[15]

Bullard could identify no Iranian 'civil virtues'. They did not exist. The Iranian masses were simply subjected to 'the mercy of a selfish, ineducable ruling class'.

The uncomfortable part of the British position in Iran was the identification with the ruling class which Bullard despised. He lamented: 'the Tudeh never cease to label us as reactionaries trying to keep the masses in ignorance, and the claims of the Right to be our friends unfortunately gives support to the thesis'. The purpose of the British occupation was to secure the supply route to Russia, not social reform. But, once there, the British were attacked by 'young Persian intellectuals' and the followers of the Tudeh who wished to end the old regime. 'What . . . vitiates our policy in the eyes of some of the young intellectuals is that it leaves Persia as it was; and they don't want that.' How different it might be, Bullard continued in an exclamatory vein, if the wealth could be redistributed and the ownership of the land broken up so that the Persian people could realize their potentialities! 'How different, the Soviet Government would say, is the situation in Russia, where every minority is encouraged to use its own language and to develop its culture and opportunities for education and self-development are open to all individuals without discrimination.' In Bullard's despatches there is a tone of indignation at the 'Persian intellectuals' who failed to distinguish between Soviet propaganda and the Russian reality, and, at the same time, a note of resignation

[15] Bullard to Bevin, 15 Mar. 1946.

in regard to the 'ruling class' of Iran which he regarded as 'too selfish and slothful ever to take action for the benefit of the people'.[16]

On the question of minorities and the separatist movements in Iran which the Russians were attempting to support (or to use his word, 'exploit'), Bullard drew distinctions between ethnic nationalism and fissiparous elements within the Persian state. The centre of activity was the northern province of Azerbaijan, where the Kurdish nationalists and 'Azerbaijan Democrats' were attempting to break away from the central authority of Tehran. The latter had established a 'national government' at Tabriz. Quite apart from Russian sponsorship, Azerbaijan had its own secessionist sentiments, more so according to Bullard than any other province of Iran and for good historical reasons. 'Cowardice and lack of public spirit' of the Iranian administration at Tabriz had caused the Azerbaijan people to greet the Russians in 1941 as liberators. Even the Russians appeared to be preferable to the corrupt and oppressive Persians. As a consequence Bullard judged that there would be a tendency 'to gravitate more and more towards union with Soviet Azerbaijan'. As for Kurdish nationalism, the Russians were attempting to turn it to their advantage by weakening the neighbouring states. 'Russian influence in the northern part of Persian Kurdistan may leaven not only the southern part of Persian Kurdistan, but the Kurdish territories of Iraq and Turkey, too', Bullard concluded.[17]

It was important to comprehend Russian treatment of minorities, Bullard believed, in order to understand the probable fate of the Azerbaijan and Kurdish peoples. In one of his dispatches he made his point by attacking the 'sentimental' American view affirmed by Henry Wallace. 'Mr. Wallace, when he was Vice-President of the United States, stated in a speech about the Soviet Union that America could learn much from Russia in the matter of the treatment of minorities.'[18] The Americans had not yet discovered, Bullard continued, an answer to 'the coloured problem' in the United States, but if they were to apply the Soviet solution they would find it unpalatable. It would be the achievement of equality by the reduction of the two elements of white and black 'to a common subservience'. He emphasized the Iranian possibility of the Soviet formula in its application to the Kurds:

[16] Ibid.

[17] Bullard to Bevin, 3 Mar. 1946.

[18] Bullard to Bevin, 15 Mar. 1946. For Wallace's views see John Morton Blum, ed., *The Price of Vision: The Diary of Henry A. Wallace 1942–1946* (Boston, 1973), which is valuable for insight into American ideas about British motives, e.g. p. 519 where Wallace reports Byrnes as saying that 'the British were as bad as the Russians in wanting to hold their troops in Iran'.

There is a great deal of humbug about the Soviet treatment of minorities. It may be too strong to say that it consists of folk-songs tempered by executions, but it is true that the uniformity of opinion imposed by the Soviet system is a high price to pay for social reforms and the permission to use one's mother tongue. . . .

The feudal chiefs who are being used by the Soviet Government as their instruments would soon be liquidated, but the rank and file of Kurds might well be better off materially, they would have wide educational opportunities, and their nationalist feelings, hostile alike to Turk and Arab and Persian, would be flattered by the union of the three territories in which they live, and by the encouragement of their language, even if it was used in the main to fill them with the chaffy propaganda of Soviet Government.[19]

Bullard anticipated that Soviet assimilation of the Kurdish and Azerbaijan peoples would produce 'a sort of performing dog rather than a nobler human being'. It is a remarkable indication of his paternalistic attitude towards the Iranians that he believed that the Kurds, the Azerbaijanis, and other minorities would nevertheless be better off under Russian despotism than Persian tyranny. This is a theme that characterizes the British political reporting of the era, and it is one useful to bear in mind when considering the general problem of Communism in the Middle East. The British consul in Tabriz, J. W. Wall, wrote in July 1946, when the international crisis over Iran had reached its peak: 'the ordinary people of Azerbaijan . . . are materially somewhat better off than they were seven months ago under direct Persian rule, for the local Democrats are, on the whole, honester'.[20]

The immediate origin of the Iranian crisis of 1946 was the Soviet demand for an oil concession in October 1944. It was at that time when Bullard found himself at the centre of controversy about 'inciting the Persians to resist'. Though he did not have much faith in the 'national vitality' of the Persians he recognized a certain cunning in their strategy of 'equilibrium', or to put it in his more mundane language, of playing off the British against the Russians, or the Americans against both. He also clearly saw what he believed to be the Russian design in demanding an oil concession. He took it as a premiss (which some of his colleagues did not) that the Soviet Union was and would be self-sufficient in oil and therefore had no internal need of the reserves in northern Iran. He based this assessment on his reading of consular reports as well as his years of service in Russia, and on the opinion of oil experts in the Anglo-Iranian Oil Company. The purpose of the Russian demand, he believed, was eventually to use an Iranian surplus of oil as an economic weapon

[19] Bullard to Bevin, 15 Mar. 1946.
[20] Wall to Le Rougetel, No. 23 Secret, 16 July 1946, FO 371/52679/E7243.

on the international market, to add to Soviet war potential, and, most important, to deny it to others, especially the British. The Russians would furthermore use the control of the oil in northern Iran as a means of undermining the Anglo-Iranian Oil Company:

> They could introduce labour conditions which would drain the Anglo-Iranian Oil Company's labour market in a very short time. Moreover the mere presence of an enormous Soviet State-controlled company operating in Persia would provide them with a first-class political lever for use in inducing the Persian authorities to harass the Anglo-Iranian Company—if indeed it did not become the *de facto* government of northern Persia and consequently to a large extent of the whole country.[21]

He was insistent on the point of Russian intervention in northern Iran as the crux of the entire situation: 'on what the Russians do in North Persia depends the fate of Persia as a whole—including, in the last analysis, the fate of our vital oil supplies in the South'.[22]

Bullard made a further basic assumption (again one that some of his colleagues did not share). On the basis of his own political assessment and his discussions with British military authorities, he held that the British military occupation of Iran was more of a liability than an asset. Strategically the British troops were useless, if only because there was a 'practical impossibility of going to war with Russia' in Iran. He acknowledged the force of the argument (put forward for example by R. M. A. Hankey) that British troops should be withdrawn only at equal pace with the Russian troops, but he attached greater importance to the propaganda value of the Atlantic Charter. He believed that the British should emphasize to the Russians and especially to the Americans that the Persians should have the right to determine their own form of government without foreign interference in accordance with that solemn declaration of wartime idealism. To sum up the thrust of his thought, 'the Atlantic Charter is one weapon in our admittedly ill-stocked diplomatic armoury. . . . It is not a large-calibred weapon, but it is perhaps the best we have.'[23]

Bullard's assessment as a whole was shrewd because the Iranians, in keeping with the strategy of the 'equilibrium' and its corollary of preventing domination by any single power, refused to grant further oil concessions until after the war.[24] Bullard also accurately detected the strong Iranian sentiment in favour of the evacuation of all foreign troops. The desire for troop withdrawal, he wrote, 'is

[21] Notes by Bullard on a W. O. memorandum dated 25 May 1945, Top Secret, FO 371/45464.

[22] Ibid.   [23] Ibid.

[24] On this point see especially McFarland, 'A Peripheral View of the Origins of the Cold War'.

perfectly genuine and deeply felt by the great bulk of the politically-minded classes in Persia'.[25] He furthermore probably had insight into the Soviet psychological makeup. It would be an error to assume, he pointed out, that the Russians lacked a sense of caution. Their methods might be brutal but their timing was calculated (on this point his thought flowed in the same direction as George Kennan's). The Russians, he wrote, 'with all their cynicism', were by no means insensitive to 'world opinion':

> Russia will only get what she wanted in North Persia (i.e. a controlling influence in the first place, but much more than that ultimately) if she wants it more than she dislikes the disadvantages which it would entail from the point of view of her world publicity. . . . It is for us to exploit the potentiality, and also if need be the actuality, of these disadvantages by every means in our power before accepting the defeat which the realisation of her Persian ambitions would inflict upon us. Any other attitude savours to my mind of defeatism masquerading as realism—an even more serious fault than a predilection for 'appeasement'![26]

Bullard was sensitive to the charge that he endorsed 'appeasement' because of his stand on troop withdrawal. 'I yield to no one', he stated emphatically, 'in my appreciation of the cynical opportunism of Russian policy, and I have always realised that the only way of handling the Russians is to coerce them.' In this case he believed that the Russians could be forced to evacuate by the British 'recruiting world opinion in support of Persian independence'. He thus proposed 'to beat the Atlantic Charter drum in regard to Persia'.[27]

The American panjandrum of the Atlantic Charter and its application to Iran was Major-General Patrick Hurley. In 1943 as President Roosevelt's envoy, Hurley had written that the fulfilment of the 'benevolent principles of the Atlantic Charter' would lead to 'the American pattern of self-government and free enterprise' in Iran. Roosevelt's own imagination was fired by these ideas. He wrote in response to Hurley' report:

> Iran is definitely a very, very backward nation. It consists really of a series of tribes and 99% of the population is, in effect, in bondage to the other 1%. The 99% do not own their land and cannot keep their own production or convert it into money or property.
>
> I was rather thrilled with the idea of using Iran as an example of what we could do by an unselfish American policy. We could not take on a more difficult nation than Iran. I would, however, like to have a try at it. . . . [28]

---

[25] Bullard to Sir Olaf Caroe, Top Secret and Personal, 8 June 1945, FO 371/45464.
[26] Notes by Bullard . . . 25 May 1945.
[27] Ibid.
[28] *Foreign Relations 1943*, IV, p. 420; copy in the Hurley Papers. The Hurley Papers at the University of Oklahoma are a revealing source for the study of American anti-colonialism.

This is not the place to dwell upon the celebrated American wartime enthusiasm for the development and liberation of the European colonies and backward areas, but it should be noted in passing that in such effervescence can be found the inspiration for regarding Iran as a 'model' of an undeveloped and corrupt country which nevertheless had great potential. Under American sponsorship, the Iranian people would acquire, in Hurley's words, 'health, happiness and general welfare'. Not everyone in Washington regarded this euphoric possibility with the same enthusiasm as Roosevelt. One of Dean Acheson's assistants at the time, Eugene Rostow, referred to Hurley's ideas as 'messianic globaloney' (as will be seen below, Eugene Rostow later had some acute observations about Greece and Palestine as well).[29] It was a neologism that probably would have brought a groan from Sir Reader Bullard, who had a strict sense of linguistic purity as well as a realistic outlook on the chances for Iranian reform and prosperity. In any case Bullard believed that there might be a positive American response to the beating of the 'Atlantic Charter drum'.

In order to understand the postwar Iranian crisis in relation to the significance of the Atlantic Charter—which became identified with the principles of the United Nations—it is important to bear in mind the wartime chronology. After the Anglo-Soviet invasion of 1941, the British, Iranian, and Soviet governments concluded an agreement in January 1942 by which troops would be withdrawn six months after the end of the war (after Japan's defeat, the date was indelibly inscribed on the next year's calendar as the 2nd of March 1946). At Tehran in late 1943 Roosevelt, Churchill, and Stalin guaranteed Iran's sovereignty and territorial integrity. At Yalta in early 1945 the Russians refused to discuss troop withdrawal. Here was an important source of propaganda. The British could now claim that by refusing to discuss early evacuation of Iran the Russians had violated 'the spirit of Yalta'.[30] At Potsdam in the following July the British pursued the issue, this time putting forward a proposal for withdrawal in stages. Stalin agreed to evacuate Tehran, and to discuss further withdrawal at the London Conference of Foreign Ministers in September 1945. The question was now whether the Russians would respect the deadline of the 2nd of March 1946. As long as Soviet troops remained in northern Iran, according to a memorandum by the Eastern Department of the Foreign Office in August 1945, 'it leaves the Soviet military authorities . . . [with] what

[29] Dean Acheson, *Present at the Creation* (New York, 1969), pp. 133–4; Kuniholm, *Origins*, p. 170.
[30] Minute by Nevile Butler, 5 Mar. 1945, FO 371/45463/E1473.

amounts to the Soviet stranglehold on Persia'.[31] At the London Conference Ernest Bevin obtained Molotov's reaffirmation of the date of withdrawal. In November 1945 however there were large-scale uprisings in the province of Azerbaijan. The British now feared that the self-determination clause of the Atlantic Charter could be turned to Russian advantage. The Russians could argue that the Azerbaijan 'Democrats' and the Kurdish nationalists had the right to secede from the reactionary Persian state. With this unfolding of events the crisis could be described as becoming acute. 'This is a menacing development', wrote the head of the Eastern Department in November 1945. 'It has for some time become evident that the next four months, preceding the withdrawal of the Russian troops, are going to be a very critical period in Persian Azerbaijan.'[32]

It seemed clear to the British that to get the Russians out of Iran, if not to prevent the creation of Soviet satellites in Azerbaijan and Kurdistan, the Americans would have to be rallied to exert pressure on the Soviet government. Nevile Butler, an Assistant Under-Secretary who had served during most of the war as head of the North American Department of the Foreign Office, spoke of the 'apathy' of the American government as one of the intractable elements in the situation. There was a further dimension which again is revealed in the despatches of Sir Reader Bullard. The British feared that the more the Americans became acquainted with the Persians the less alluring would be the Atlantic Charter. The American Ambassador in Tehran was the former director of the Office of Near Eastern and African Affairs in the State Department, Wallace Murray. Butler once described him as a 'truculent nationalist'.[33] Murray had the reputation within the Foreign Office as being one of the most anti-British of all American officials. His passions in the latter part of 1945 seemed to be turning against the Iranians. *Ingratitude* was the word he used to sum up the Iranian attitude towards American assistance. Bullard described Murray's reaction to the realities of Persian politics as 'disillusioned sentimentality'.[34]

Murray was extremely irritated that the Iranians now not only criticized the Americans but also seemed to regard the United States

[31] Memorandum dated 4 Aug. 1945, FO 371/45467.

[32] Minute by Baxter, 7 Nov. 1945, FO 371/45435/E8514.

[33] Minute by Butler, 10 Apr. 1944, FO 371/39985/E2683.

[34] Bullard to Baxter, Confidential, 1 Oct. 1945, FO 371/45487/E7835. In the Foreign Office one official made this comment which was probably true in a general way for other American officials and the non-western world: 'Mr. Wallace Murray . . . from the safer distance of Washington was always prepared to believe the best of the Persians.' Minute by Sir George Young, 18 Oct. 1945, ibid. For Murray's background and general outlook see Phillip J. Baram, *The Department of State in the Middle East 1919–1945* (University of Pennsylvania Press, 1978), pp. 67–8 *et passim*).

as in the same imperialist class as the British Empire. Murray had had a large hand in shaping American policy towards Iran on such weighty issues as the Atlantic Charter and the Tehran Conference declaration, and to him this attitude seemed both preposterous and intolerable. Bullard, with a mixture of amusement and apprehension, wrote to the head of the Eastern Department about Murray's response to articles in the Iranian press about American 'imperialism':

> Wallace Murray . . . reproached the Persians for their ingratitude—to *him*, who for so many years had defended them—the man who when President Roosevelt was in Tehran drafted the declaration about Persia. . . . Knowing that Mr. Murray used to be the great opponent of British imperialism in Persia . . . I could not but feel some inward amusement at the ferocious reproaches and threats against Persia which now poured from him. He would show them! This was their gratitude for help and protection! . . . That this should happen to *him* . . . Mr. Murray said the Persians would see. He would show them! The British might be obliged to put up with abuse . . . but the Americans weren't. They didn't care what happened. They could pull right out . . . and leave the Persians to stew in their own juice.[35]

Leaving the Persians stewing in their own juice was an impulse which British officials also occasionally shared, but in the autumn and winter of 1945 it seemed to be singularly ill-timed. The point here is that from the British vantage point it was difficult to judge how the Americans would respond to 'the beating of the Atlantic Charter drum'.

British scepticism about the Americans taking a robust stand on Iran led Bevin in December 1945 at the Moscow Conference of Foreign Ministers to urge the appointment of an Anglo-Soviet-American commission to investigate the problems of Azerbaijan. He actually discouraged Iranian initiatives to submit the issue to the United Nations, which he referred to as 'their half-formed plan'.[36] No one wished to see the United Nations wrecked at the outset by controversies which might be resolved quickly and with less public friction by the British, the Americans, and the Russians themselves. The British calculation was that their influence would be greater in a commission than in the untested forum of the United Nations, and that if worst came to worst the recognition of an 'independent' Azerbaijan might at least shore up Iranian authority in the rest of the country. It was not a coincidence that the phrase 'iron curtain' gained currency at this time.[37]

[35] Bullard to Baxter, Confidential, 1 Oct. 1945, FO 371/45487/E7835.

[36] As recorded in Bullard to Bevin, No. 65, 3 Mar. 1946, FO 371/52667/E2318.

[37] Churchill delivered his 'iron curtain' speech on 5 Mar. 1946, one day before Soviet troop movements in Azerbaijan began to create general alarm (see *Foreign Relations 1946*, VII, pp. 346-7). He commented later in the month that the Russians 'might confront the world with a fait accompli of the establishment of a quisling regime. . . . this is a very

The American Ambassador in Tehran denounced the British scheme as calculated appeasement. The British, Murray wrote, were preparing a 'tacit deal leaving Soviets free hand in north while they consolidate British position in south'. In his view the British had decided that they had nothing to gain in a public controversy with the Russians 'in a cause already lost' and would now concentrate 'on making sure of their own sphere of influence in [the] Persian gulf'.[38] Stalin, after initial concurrence with Bevin's proposal for a commission, refused to go along with the scheme. The Iranian crisis now moved from local confrontation into what appeared to be a Russian challenge to the postwar order. Truman in January 1946 in a famous line wrote that he was 'tired of babying the Soviets'. The Secretary of State, James Byrnes, in response to Russian troop movements in Azerbaijan, declared that he would give the Russians 'both barrels'.[39] The Iranian government took the case to the United Nations. The British had little influence in these dramatic developments. It was the Americans themselves who decided 'to beat the drum of the Atlantic Charter'. When faced with a crisis in which there appeared to be clear-cut aggression and an issue of principle—in this case one which might determine the survival of the United Nations—the Americans proved capable of resolute action quite independent of British inspiration.

To anticipate a major theme that will emerge towards the end of this book, Iranian nationalism was anti-British as well as anti-Russian. One of the keys to the crisis of 1946 was the politician referred to by Bullard as 'the demagogue', Mohammed Musaddig. In December 1944 Musaddig had been instrumental in the enactment of petroleum legislation by the Iranian Parliament, the Majlis. This bill was aimed at preventing foreign exploitation of Iranian oil. In it may be found the seeds of Musaddig's 'nationalization' programme of 1951. It is important to bear in mind those two landmarks in Iranian history in relation to the events of 1946. In April of that year the Prime Minister, Qavam al-Saltana, signed an oil agreement with the Soviet government which granted a concession in northern Iran in return for withdrawal of Soviet troops. The link between oil and Soviet

important test for the United Nations Organization at the beginning of its career'. *New York Times*, 22 Mar. 1946. For a good analysis of the significance of the Fulton speech and its reception, especially in official British circles, see Henry B. Ryan, 'A New Look at Churchill's "Iron Curtain" Speech', *Historical Journal*, 22, 4 (1979).

[38] Murray to Byrnes, 10 Jan. 1946, *Foreign Relations 1946*, VII, pp. 299-301.

[39] Ibid., p. 347. For Byrnes's account of the Iranian crisis see James F. Byrnes, *Speaking Frankly* (New York, 1947), chap. 6. For an understanding of the Byrnes era at the State Department, Robert L. Messer, *The End of an Alliance: James F. Byrnes, Roosevelt, Truman, and the Origins of the Cold War* (Chapel Hill, 1982), is most helpful.

evacuation was crucial. Stalin won the oil concession but Qavam gained Soviet withdrawal. Qavam was passionately denounced by Musaddig in the Majlis. A year and a half later, in October 1947, the Majlis by a vote of 102 to 2 declared that the oil agreement with the Soviet Union was 'null and void'.[40] Musaddig was the driving force behind nationalist sentiment against foreign exploitation, whether Russian or British. His part in the oil controversies of 1944 and 1946 is critical in understanding his 'nationalization' policies of 1951, when he turned against the British. The Iranian crisis of 1946 is usually depicted in the mythology of the cold war as an important victory for the United States, a triumph of the principles of the United Nations, and a setback for the Soviet Union. It is also a remarkable indication of the force of Musaddig's 'negative equilibrium', which the British interpreted as a skilful manipulation of the great powers, not least themselves, against each other.

What is of interest here from the British vantage point is not so much the conflict as an episode in the cold war, but the trends of British thought during the 1946 crisis that had significance for the rest of the Middle East. The first point of importance, which may be made briefly, is the development in Bevin's attitude towards the Anglo-Iranian Oil Company after the successful demand by the Russians for an oil concession in Azerbaijan. At the time it appeared that the Russians and the Iranians would agree on a fifty–fifty basis on which to share the petroleum resources and profits. From Bevin's point of view the salient feature of this arrangement would be 'Persian state employment' in the Russian concession:

> The more I have studied the question the more I have come to the conclusion that instead of anything on a basis of royalties it would be preferable to examine the question of whether Great Britain and Persia should not now enter into an arrangement for a joint company on similar lines, and so establish the relationship between the Abadan Oilfield and the Persian Government on a basis which is mutually advantageous. . . .[41]

The British could repudiate charges of exploitative capitalism if the workers were employed by the Iranian government. Though he thought it was too early to predict the exact profit sharing in the Russian–Iranian venture, Bevin apparently anticipated something in the nature of an equal division. The idea of the fifty–fifty split therefore had its origins in the abortive Russian oil concession of 1946 as well as in the Aramco arrangement of 1950, which is generally

---

[40] For these developments see especially Ramazani, *Iran's Foreign Policy*, chaps. 6 and 7. See also Daniel Yergin, *Shattered Peace* (Boston, 1977), pp. 179–92, which emphasizes oil in American calculations during the crisis.
[41] Minute by Bevin, 20 July 1946, FO 371/52735/E7357.

regarded as sparking the nationalization crisis of 1951. This is a theme which will be developed in a later chapter.

One of the principles of the Atlantic Charter was the equality of access to raw material. From the British vantage point it was American determination not to be cut out of the Iranian oil market as much as the threat of a Soviet satellite in Azerbaijan that would guarantee a continuity of American interest in Iran. Here as in Saudi Arabia the British goal was to encourage American concessions rather than, as some officials in the American government suspected, to try to seal off as much as possible of the petroleum reserves into a British sphere. 'With regard to South Eastern Persian oil', Bevin is recorded as saying in April 1946, 'he did not want to see the United States kept out by British oil interests.'[42] The greater the American investment in the Iranian oil industry, the greater would be the chances of a sustained American political commitment. American critics tended to attribute to British imperialism a lingering appetite, waning but still voracious, which is comprehensible only in view of past suspicions. In Iran the official British outlook held that there was sufficient oil to go around, and that in view of the magnitude of the Russian threat it was imperative to have American participation.

A military showdown between the British and the Russians would have been disastrous because of the overwhelming Russian dominance. In December 1945 there were 5,000 British troops in southern Iran versus 30,000 Russian troops in Azerbaijan alone (there were estimates of over double that figure for the entire area of Russian occupation). The figures made painfully clear that the British troops were, in Bullard's phrase, 'strategically useless' and more a liability than a military asset, even in the sense of policing the oilfields. There was no question of a prolonged military occupation. A British garrison would arouse Iranian nationalism, an unnecessary provocation since the oilfields and the Abadan refinery could be protected by forces stationed in Iraq. In Iran—as in Greece and Egypt—Bevin set troop withdrawal as one of his priorities. It was based on political calculation as well as the economic reality of postwar Britain. The Labour government wanted to prove the honesty of British intentions to evacuate—to the Egyptians as well as the Iranians—and in the case of Iran to demonstrate that the British had no intention of threatening Russian security. 'The Treaty date for the completion of the withdrawal of our forces from Persia is the 2nd March', Bevin had written to Attlee in February 1946, 'and I want to be in a position to state . . . that all

[42] Minutes of F.O. meeting, 18 Apr. 1946, FO 371/52673.

British forces have in fact left Persia.'[43] British withdrawal from Iran, Bevin hoped, would indicate a willingness to meet the demands of Middle Eastern nationalists who insisted on the evacuation of all foreign troops.

The British on the whole were sceptical of American staying power unless it rested on economic commitment rather than on what they suspected might be ephemeral enthusiasm for the principles of the United Nations.[44] The Russian interest in Iran, by contrast and for historical and geographical as well as for immediate postwar military and political reasons, would remain constant and menacing. There were other ways to cope with the Russian danger to the British position in the Persian gulf. Instead of relying on the United States and the hope that the ideals of the United Nations would continue to flourish, should not the British plan eventually try to defeat the Russians at their own game? A discussion of that point took place in the Foreign Office in April 1946 after the conclusion of the Soviet–Iranian agreement on the oil concession and the evacuation of Russian troops. The immediate crisis had been resolved as well as could have been expected because of the vigorous American stand. But how could the situation in Iran be dealt with over the long haul? The arguments for and against a more aggressive stand are especially revealing for general British Middle Eastern policy.

The paper used as the basis for discussion was prepared by Robert Howe, an Assistant Under-Secretary of particular importance in this book because of his later involvement in similar issues in the Sudan as Governor-General. The danger in Iran according to Howe was that the Russians would eventually secure 'a Russian stooge Parliament and Government'. It should be noted that at this time, as in other discussions, the British were more preoccupied with the pro-Soviet proclivities of Iranian politicians and the corrupt Iranian government than with the Shah as a leader who might exert a counterforce.[45] With their 'stooges' in government and parliament,

---

[43] Bevin to Attlee, 22 Feb. 1946, PREM 8/285.

[44] The British view bears a certain similarity to the Russian outlook: 'Throughout this period . . . Soviet diplomacy often seemed to have operated on the assumption that, confronted with protracted and apparently fruitless negotiations, Americans would simply "give up" out of sheer exhaustion, out of the inability of a democratic nation to keep attention and energies focused on a subject so peripheral to the interests of a vast majority of its citizens.' Adam B. Ulam, *Expansion and Coexistence: Soviet Foreign Policy, 1917–1973* (New York, 1974), p. 410.

[45] For the Shah in British calculations see Rose L. Greaves, 'The Reign of Mohammad Riza Shah', in Amirsadeghi, *Twentieth-Century Iran*; for American assessments of the Shah at this time see especially Richard Pfau, 'Containment in Iran, 1946: The Shift to an Active Policy', *Diplomatic History*, 1, 4 (1977).

the Russians 'will be in a fair way to controlling the whole of Persia with possible far-reaching effects on our position generally in Persia and in the Middle East generally and particularly as regards the Anglo-Iranian Oil Company'. The Russians would probably even incite the Persians to cancel the British concession. How could the British respond to this threat? They could continue to hope for the best; or they could conclude that 'Persian independence is already a thing of the past' and that to protect the British oil concession 'we can adopt Russian tactics and encourage an autonomy movement in South-West Persia'. Howe acknowledged that this course of action would violate traditional British policy of respecting the independence of small countries and refusing to interfere in their internal affairs. But the postwar world had created new and dangerous circumstances in which such intervention might be necessary. What Howe was proposing in other words was to foster a breakaway nationalist movement which would form the British equivalent of a Soviet satellite. He was explicit in the suggestion of initial tactics: 'to organize and finance an opposition party or parties to keep the Tudeh out of power'. He went on to emphasize that this was 'a dangerous policy' which would probably involve the British in taking sides in a civil war. There would probably be adverse reaction 'from British public opinion and in the United States', Such was the magnitude of British dependence on Iranian oil for postwar recovery that such a course of action had to be seriously considered.[46]

Bevin's response is of utmost importance in understanding British policy not only in Iran but throughout the Middle East. It was consistent with his attitude towards Greece and Egypt. He drew the line at intervention in 'Cabinet making' and 'unseating' kings as well as at attempting to manipulate political movements. In Greece he refused to strengthen the monarch. In Egypt he stopped short of toppling the Prime Minister, Nokrashi, or King Farouk. He consistently held that the only wise course was to abstain from political intervention. Interventionist schemes would backfire with unforeseeable consequences. The British did not always stay clear of internal entanglements in the postwar Middle East, but it was a danger that Bevin attempted to guard against with remarkable persistence. There was an element of pragmatism in his outlook. In the case of Iran he said decisively: 'With regard to the possibility of organising an anti-Tudeh Party on a national scale . . . this was a very dangerous policy.' The minutes continued to record a reservation of considerable interest: it was a policy 'which he was not

[46] Memorandum by Howe, 16 Apr. 1946, FO 371/52673.

prepared to countenance at present'.[47] He was not prepared to intervene in part because he did not believe it would work, at least at
that time. Perhaps pragmatism proved to be the better part of
political wisdom, but, looking back at postwar Middle Eastern
history, Bevin's non-interventionist course was indeed political
wisdom.

Turkey

'It is no exaggeration to say', Sir Maurice Peterson wrote in July
1945, 'that in every sphere of Turkey's activities—internal as well
as external and over the whole range of commerce and industry—
the dominating factor at the moment is the uneasy state of Russo-
Turkish relations.'[48] Peterson was an old Middle Eastern hand. He
had served in Egypt and Iraq and was now Ambassador in Turkey.
In British circles he had the reputation of being a strong man. He
was anti-Zionist, more so even than most of his colleagues in the
Foreign Office. He stood up to Americans as well as Russians.
During the war as an Assistant Under-Secretary he had taken a stiff but
friendly line with an American delegation (the section of the
Stettinius mission led by Wallace Murray) which had drawn the
American and British governments closer together on Middle Eastern
questions in 1944. He believed that Americans respected 'firmness',
one of his watchwords. 'Wallace Murray and others of his ilk',
Peterson wrote in characteristic vein, should not be confused about
British purpose in the Middle East.[49] He was critical of 'Tory
Imperialists' such as Lord Lloyd (under whom he had served in
Egypt), but he believed that the British should hold their own.
Peterson later served as Ambassador in the Soviet Union, 1946–9,
an indication of the Labour government's respect for his toughness
and ability. His political reporting reflected shrewdness and historical
insight. At the close of the war Peterson wrote that the key to the
situation in Turkey could be summed up in these words: 'The

[47] Minutes of F. O. meeting, 18 Apr. 1946, FO 371/52673.
[48] Peterson to Bevin, Secret, 28 July 1946, FO 371/48774/R13467. For a competent
and detailed account of the Turkish question 1943–6, see David J. Alvarez, *Bureaucracy and
Cold War Diplomacy: The United States and Turkey* (Thessaloniki, 1980). The definitive
work on American policy towards the Straits is Harry N. Howard, *Turkey, the Straits and
U. S. Policy* (Baltimore, 1974). See also Ferenc A. Váli, *Bridge across the Bosporus* (Baltimore, 1971); and George S. Harris, *Troubled Alliance: Turkish–American Problems in
Historical Perspective, 1945–1971* (Stanford, 1972). For the Turkish problem in relation to
the broader themes of this chapter, the relevant parts of Kuniholm, *Origins of the Cold War
in the Near East* are helpful. See also especially Rothwell, *Britain and the Cold War*,
pp. 395–405.
[49] Minute by Peterson, 25 Feb. 1944, FO 371/39984/E1580.

attitude of Turkey . . . is . . . that nothing will induce her to concede to Russia military bases in the Straits . . . [and] that Turkey would fight rather than make these concessions which she would regard as tantamount to the surrender of her independence.'[50]

Peterson believed that Turkey should be regarded more as a Balkan state preoccupied with problems of eastern Europe and the Soviet Union than as a Middle Eastern state sharing common goals with the Arab states and the British Empire. The founding of the Arab League did not arouse much interest in Turkish leaders. In searching for an explanation of the bitter relations between the Soviet Union and Turkey, Peterson confessed that he could find no clear-cut answer other than the revival of Russian ambition to dominate the Straits. 'A little more than twenty years ago', he wrote, 'a real sympathy existed between the Russia of Lenin and the Turkey of Mustafa Kemal.' The mutual sentiment could now only be described as deep-seated enmity. He believed that the Russians had justification in being displeased with Turkey's behaviour during the war. Turkish neutrality had acted as a buffer helping to prevent German penetration into the Middle East. The Russians would now see it as working against their own ambitions. Beyond the specific complaint of impeding the traditional Russian drive towards the Mediterranean, there was a general resentment towards the Turks because of the wartime experience. 'When the Russians had their backs to the wall at Stalingrad', Peterson reflected, the Turks had massed their troops on the frontier, as if ready to take advantage of Nazi victory.[51] Only in the last months of the war had the Turks entered the struggle against the Germans, and only then in order to secure a seat in the United Nations. Peterson described his own attitude in his autobiography. It is euphemistically representative of British thought:

> Turkey's attitude during the war I had regarded as frankly disappointing. . . . acting on instructions which resulted from the Yalta Conference . . . I was able to . . . secure a declaration of war against Germany. It was Turkey's last chance to enter the new Organisation of the United Nations on the footing of an Ally and I remember that I used the metaphor of a club which had a few unexpected vacancies for new members who would not be required to pay the entrance fee of 'blood, sweat and tears'.[52]

However compelling the reason for the lack of 'blood, sweat and tears', Turkish coolness towards the Allied cause helps to explain the British attitude towards Turkey at the close of the war. The British reaction to postwar Greece was profoundly different, and

---

[50] Peterson to Bevin, 28 July 1946.
[51] Ibid.
[52] Maurice Peterson, *Both Sides of the Curtain* (London, 1950), p. 241.

different still from the paternalistic solicitude towards the Iranians. The British respected Turkish determination to stand up to the Russians, but Peterson, for one, understood, though he did not condone, the Russian attitude towards 'the cur yelping in the gutter'.[53]

It is revealing to contrast briefly the American attitude towards the Turks. Laurence Steinhardt, the American Ambassador, whose views were just as incisive as Peterson's, believed that if a conflict broke out between the Russians and the British then the Turks would throw in their lot with the British 'with enthusiasm'. The 'meekness' of the Turks during the war could be explained by the husbanding of resources for the inevitable showdown with the Russians. The proper analogy was not with Iran or Greece but with Finland: 'The dividends now being received by the Finns on their 5-year investment in uncompromising resistance to threatened Soviet domination as distinguished from present conditions in Poland, Rumania and Bulgaria is not being overlooked by the Turks with a population five times that of Finland, only two cities of any importance, little industry, a largely self-sufficient peasant population and a mountainous country with extensive areas suitable for guerrilla warfare.'[54] These ideas may be traced further into what might be described as a dominant American impression of the stalwart Turks. The journalist Stewart Alsop for example wrote later, at the time when the crisis over Greece and Turkey came to a head in early 1947, that to understand Turkish stamina one had to comprehend the inspiration of the historic figure Kemal Ataturk—whom Alsop described for the benefit of his American audience as an 'astonishing renaissance figure . . . drunkard, lecher, and great political figure':

No country, not even the Soviet Union, has undergone such vast changes in its whole way of life as has Turkey in one generation. For all these changes Ataturk alone was responsible. Ataturk has been dead more than eight years, but his memory lives on together with the revolution which he created single-handed from the inexhaustible reserves of his energy. . . . A new revolution in Turkish politics . . . is now being attempted. . . . It can only be understood in terms of Kemal Ataturk's astonishing feat in wrenching Turkey out of Asia and into the Western world and, above all, in terms of the fear of the Soviet Union, the fear which colors and affects all Turkish life.[55]

---

[53] Ibid. Anti-Turkish sentiment of British officials is also conspicuous in unpublished, private wartime writings, e.g. Oliver Harvey's diary of 19 Feb. 1943: '[The] Turks look less and less like coming into the war. I'm glad. They have no lot or part in what we are fighting for. They are backward and barbarous.' Harvey Diaries Add. MSS, 56400.

[54] Steinhardt to Secretary of State, 26 Mar. 1945, *Foreign Relations 1945*, VIII, pp. 1225–8.

[55] *Washington Post*, 16 Feb. 1947.

Thus from the American vantage point the picture was rosier and perhaps more heroic than from the British angle of vision, but essentially the impression was the same: the Turks would stand up to the Russians—or, to put it in the words of a British report, 'it is really taken for granted that a communist in Turkey must be a venal and conscious traitor'.[56]

Maintaining the independence of Turkey was one of the foundations of British foreign policy in the postwar era. Bevin was consistently clear on this point in his statements in the House of Commons and in his conversations with Stalin. The crux of the matter was epitomized in a memorandum by the Research Department·of the Foreign Office which was given wide distribution within the government and British embassies:

> The Russians regard as intolerable the armed custodianship of a Turkey in whom they see a British catspaw. They therefore seek a base to give them physical control of the Bosphorus and Dardanelles. But such a base would inevitably turn Turkey into a Russian satellite and lead to the supersession of Britain by Russia in the Middle East.[57]

The possible causation might be disputed, but in British circles there was no doubt of the validity of the argument's premiss: a weakening of Turkey might undermine the British position in the Middle East. It should be noted in passing that there were two other ways, apart from a possible frontal assault on the Dardanelles, in which the Russians appeared to be disrupting the Turkish regime. The first was the claim to the eastern provinces of Kars and Ardahan, where there was an attempt to create secessionist states comparable to the neighbouring one of Azerbaijan.[58] In eastern Turkey the Russians claimed to champion the cause of Georgian and Armenian nationalists.[59] The other way was by the 'war of nerves' by which the Russians kept the Turks in a state of tension and forced them to anticipate

[56] Sir David Kelly to Bevin, Secret, 21 Jan. 1947, FO 371/67273.

[57] Foreign Office Research Department memorandum, 6 Jan. 1947, FO 371/59231/R17969.

[58] Peterson repeatedly warned that the 'eastern frontier' would be 'the place where any trouble is likely to begin', in part because it was less obvious than the Straits (Peterson to Sargent, 'Secret & Personal', 1 Aug. 1945, FO 371/48774). Geoffrey McDermott, the expert on Turkey in the Southern Department of the Foreign Office, believed that Peterson's ideas about Soviet aggression in eastern Turkey were 'far-fetched'. He also took issue with Peterson on the importance of Turkey to the British economy: 'Turkey has few products of interest to us and their prices are still preposterously high.' Minute by McDermott, 16 Aug. 1945, FO 371/48774/R13427/G.

[59] 'To say that the areas claimed are peopled by Georgians or Armenians', wrote M. S. Williams of the Southern Department, 'is nonsense. They have all been massacred long since by the Turks.' Minute of 23 Dec. 1945, FO 371/48775/R21419. For discussion of the Soviet Union and the question of minorities in Turkey and elsewhere see especially Hugh Seton-Watson, *Neither War Nor Peace: the Struggle for Power in the Postwar World* (New York, 1950), pp. 69–70 *et passim*.

a crisis either in eastern Turkey or at the Straits. The Turks in the postwar years maintained a standing army of 600,000. It had disastrous effects on the economy. The possible collapse of the Turkish state because of inflation and the disproportionate amount spent on military upkeep explains one of the currents of British eastern Mediterranean anxiety at the time. By early 1947 as the British themselves entered into prolonged economic crisis, a British solution to the problems of the Turkish economy was all but unthinkable.

The issue of the Straits (meaning the entire waterway stretching from the Black Sea to the Aegean) is one of great historical complexity and it will be the purpose of these comments to examine the subject essentially in the Middle Eastern rather than its broader context. In short the British aimed at preserving the status quo. They attempted to restrict the scope of discussion about possible demilitarization and internationalization, which was the American solution to be applied throughout the world. They wished to limit the postwar negotiations to the Straits themselves because otherwise they might be forced to discuss Suez (or Gibraltar, or both), which they wished to avoid at any cost. The immediate point of historical departure was the Montreux convention of 1936, which had bestowed the guardianship of the Straits upon the Turks. It was a compromise arrangement between the Russian desire to have free passage for Russian warships while excluding others, and the British aim to prevent the Black Sea from being solely a Russian lake. During the war Churchill told Stalin that the British would agree to liberalize the Montreux convention by allowing free passage of Russian warships and merchant ships (by lifting for example the restrictions that the Turks could impose during wartime). As late as the Potsdam Conference of July 1945 the question was still moot.[60] In a briefing paper for the conference the British Chiefs of Staff defined their aims at that time:

> From our strategic point of view, the best solution would be the maintenance of the status quo regarding bases covering sea gateways, particularly in view of the effect that any change may have on our position in Gibraltar and the Suez Canal.[61]

At Potsdam Stalin finally defined the Soviet aim. It was no less than a base at the Dardanelles. It was a goal that acquired symbolic

---

[60] The Russians had already begun to demand from the Turks the cession of the provinces of Kars and Ardahan as well as a base in the Straits. There is a full analysis of these points and the Potsdam discussions in Kuniholm, *Origins*, pp. 255-70.

[61] 'Montreux Convention and Security of the Baltic', COS (45) 459, 12 July 1945, CAB 80/95; minutes in FO 371/48697.

significance. According to Truman as he reflected in his memoirs, 'What Stalin wanted was control of the Black Sea Straits and the Danube. The Russians were planning world conquest.'[62] At the time, to the British military experts, the Soviet bid appeared perhaps less earth-shaking but nevertheless menacing enough: 'It may be a first step to Russian expansion into the Eastern Mediterranean and Middle East.'[63]

Bevin was much more flexible on the question of Soviet ambitions in the Mediterranean than his Foreign Office advisers or the military authorities. Like Churchill, he sympathized with the Russian desire for a warm water port, provided it would not in some way jeopardize British 'security' (when it came to the point, there was no port the Russians might acquire anywhere in the world which would not threaten British 'security'). As will be seen in the chapter on the Italian colonies, Bevin was prepared to consider Soviet trusteeship over part of Libya as part of a general settlement. On the other hand he was firm in resisting Russian demands on the Turks. Like his advisers and the military experts he believed that a Russian base on the Dardanelles would have dangerous implications for the Middle East generally as well as for Turkey and Greece. At the Moscow Conference in December 1945 he took care to make sure that Stalin knew exactly the British attitude towards Turkey: 'I was anxious not to destroy Turkey's free and independent position', he emphasized to Stalin.[64]

There is a bracing candour to the British minutes which contrasts glaringly with the published polemics of the cold war. One official of particular interest (he later became ambassador in Turkey, Greece, and Iraq) who studied the question of Anglo-Soviet rivalry in Turkey, Roger Allen, wrote of 'our' countries and 'their' countries. He believed that Russian domination of their satellites was 'far more "extreme" ' than the corresponding British sway, but that it was important to recognize that the British as well as the Russians aimed at 'control'.[65] This theme of political realism was also pronounced in the despatches of Sir Maurice Peterson. 'Having got hold of Turkey we have not the least intention of letting her go', he once wrote.[66] It obfuscated the issue to try to insist that principles of

---

[62] Harry S. Truman, *Memoirs: Year of Decisions*, I, p. 412.

[63] COS Joint Planning Staff, JP (45) 233, 4 Sept. 1945, CAB 84/75; minutes in FO 371/48698.

[64] Bevin to Attlee, Top Secret, 21 Dec. 1945, FO 371/48775. Bevin subsequently stated: 'I do not want Turkey converted into a satellite State. What I want her to be is really independent.' *Parliamentary Debates* (Commons), 21 Feb. 1946, col. 1357.

[65] Minute by Allen, 1 Sept. 1945, FO 371/48775/R14773/G.

[66] Peterson to Sargent, 'Secret & Personal', 1 Aug. 1945, FO 371/48774/R13427.

political freedom and democracy were being upheld in Turkey. By preventing the collapse of Turkey the British (and eventually the Americans) might be holding the line against Communism, but in Turkey itself democracy was more of a façade than a reality and to induce the Turks to reform their system of government into more of a democracy would be, in the phrase of the expert on Turkey in the Southern Department, Geoffrey McDermott, a matter 'of utmost delicacy'. The British had no doubt whatsoever that the long-term aim was above all 'to keep Turkey (and Greece) in our orbit'.[67] The Americans shared that sense of priority. The visit of the USS *Missouri* to Istanbul in April 1946 (ostensibly to return the remains of the Turkish Ambassador who had died in Washington during the war) served as a symbol of American political and strategic vigilance at the Straits.

To keep long-range goals clearly in mind, British planners believed it was desirable to strip the symbolism of naval power and the mythology of the Straits down to postwar military reality. Roger Allen, for one, thought that it was extremely difficult to assess the ways in which the atomic bomb might alter traditional calculations, but that in any case the Straits now appeared to have lost much of their historic significance. Developments in air power would enable the Russians to wage war without the use of the Straits (just as in time of war the denial value of the Suez canal had been of greater importance to the British than its continued use), and in any event the Russians, in Allen's words, 'are likely to be able to seize the Straits, fortifications or no fortifications'.

Allen's views about strategic planning are important because he represented the Foreign Office on the Joint Intelligence Sub-Committee of the Chiefs of Staff. The point that he tried to impress on his military colleagues was that the principal threat to Turkey lay in '*political* penetration in the neighboring countries'.[68] The minutes of the Chiefs of Staff committees reflect this political judgement, as well as the assessment that the Russians, for reasons of their own, did not wish to bring about a collapse of the United Nations by a takeover of the Dardanelles.[69] They might continue to press the

---

[67] Minute by McDermott, 16 Aug. 1945, FO 371/48774/R13646/G.

[68] Minute by Allen, 1 Sept. 1945, FO 371/48775/R14773/G.

[69] Allen emphasized to the Chiefs of Staff that the Joint Intelligence Sub-Committee considered that the Russians 'had not yet decided on aggressive action against Turkey which would entail withdrawing from the World Security Organization'. COS (45) 244, 9 Oct. 1945, CAB 79/40; minutes in FO 371/48775. This interpretation also characterized American analysis: 'To embark on war against Turkey would mean that Soviet rulers have taken fundamental decision to break with policy of cooperation with Western democracies. This would be very grave decision fraught with heavy risks.' Wilson to Byrnes, 18 Mar. 1946, *Foreign Relations 1946*, VII, pp. 818–19.

demand for a military base in the Dardanelles against the Turks as part of the 'war of nerves', but, as Allen explained in the Chiefs of Staff deliberations, the immediate danger lay in Iran and Greece, not in Turkey. In Soviet eyes Turkey would appear too difficult to assimilate, and the corresponding temptations in the other countries would appear much greater. In the year after the end of the war the continuing assessments of the Joint Intelligence Sub-Committee confirmed that judgement. Soviet troop movement in the Balkans, according to British intelligence reports, indicated that the Russians had higher or more immediate priorities than Turkey.

In contrast with most of the Middle Eastern countries with which this book is concerned, Turkey represented a favourable situation in the sense that the British did not have to preach the danger of Russian aggression. In Egypt the message fell on deaf ears. In Turkey it was the Turks themselves who valued the battered but still intact Anglo-Turkish alliance of 1939. 'The *British Alliance*' according to the Research Department of the Foreign Office, despite wartime mistrust, had remained 'the sheet anchor of Turkish policy'.[70] Bevin could argue that the Turks needed the British in the long run more than vice versa. He told the Turkish ambassador that 'while Turkey may depend on us for security, we did not depend on Turkey. . . . our strategic position was not necessarily dependent on maintaining communication through the Eastern Mediterranean'.[71] It was the strength of Turkish nationalism and the need for an ally against the Soviet Union that paradoxically placed Turkey near the bottom of the British list of priorities for economic and military assistance. The list was growing shorter. By the time of the crisis in early 1947 Bevin merely endorsed the conclusion of the Chiefs of Staff: 'Although the Chiefs of Staff emphasize the very great strategic importance of maintaining the strength of Turkey they point out that there is little practical help that we can give.' Bevin's concluding words in this memorandum written for the members of the Defence Committee of the Cabinet were full of pregnant Middle Eastern significance: 'I recommend that we should . . . proceed to discuss the matter with the Americans.'[72]

It is the British response to the American reaction of August 1946, as well as the clarion sounding of the dangers of Soviet aggression, which is of interest. In an attempt to exploit the victory and to

[70] F.O.R.D. memorandum, 24 July 1946, FO 371/59316.

[71] Record of Bevin's conversation with the Turkish ambassador, 18 April 1946, FO 371/59232; Rothwell, *Britain and the Cold War*, p. 399.

[72] Memorandum by Bevin, DO (47), 2, 2 Jan. 1947, CAB 131/4; Report by COS, DO (47) 1, 1 Jan. 1947, ibid.

settle old accounts with the Turks, the Russians decided at that time to press the demand for a change in the regime at the Straits that might have allowed the establishment of a Soviet military base. Six months after the crisis in Iran, President Truman declared that he might as well discover whether the Russians were bent on 'world conquest' then as in ten years time.[73] He was now prepared to endorse 'to the end' these propositions put forward by the Secretaries of State, War, and Navy:

> In our opinion, the primary objective of the Soviet Union is to obtain control of Turkey. . . . If the Soviet Union succeeds in its objective [of] obtaining control over Turkey it will be extremely difficult, if not impossible, to prevent the Soviet Union from obtaining control over Greece and over the whole Near and Middle East.[74]

The United States Navy reinforced the presence of the USS *Missouri*, the battleship of the signing of the Japanese peace treaty now paying a courtesy visit to Istanbul, with a task force in the eastern Mediterranean that included the aircraft carrier *Franklin D. Roosevelt*. From the British angle it is important to grasp that the British themselves had nothing to do with this robust response. It was entirely and distinctively American. 'Gratifying', remarked M. S. Williams of the Southern Department of the Foreign Office.[75] Here is the way in which F. B. A. Rundall of the North American Department analysed the significance of the 'Dardanelles scare'. It is important as a British assessment of the American response to the cold war in relation to the Middle East as of August 1946:

> It is very doubtful if the [American] public realises that war is possible or is psychologically prepared for it. . . . If the U. S. S. R. can put enough pressure on the Turkish Government to make them willing to compromise, we may expect the United States to protest loudly and to bring the matter before the United Nations, but I doubt they would send an ultimatum. Flagrant aggression might provoke one, but I do not think that we should count on it.[76]

Christopher Warner, the former head of the Northern Department and now an Assistant Under-Secretary, believed that the Soviet probe was part of the process of 'hotting up the atmosphere in the Balkans'.[77] The problem of Turkey's defence was thus a Balkan question linked with the issues of Yugoslavia and Greece, but at the same time, most significantly in British eyes, the Americans had connected it directly with the general defence of the Middle East.

[73] Walter Millis, ed., *The Forrestal Diaries* (New York, 1951), p. 192.
[74] Acheson to Byrnes, 15 Aug. 1946, *Foreign Relations 1946*, VII, p. 840.
[75] Minute by M. S. Williams, 23 Aug. 1946, FO 371/59227/R12306.
[76] Minute by Rundall, 26 Aug. 1946, ibid.
[77] Minute by Warner, 24 Aug. 1946, ibid.

The key to understanding the co-ordination of American and British policy in the Middle East lies in Greece, but it is important to bear in mind what the British believed they had learned from the experience in Turkey in 1945-6. In the words of Sir David Kelly, 'though the American character was apt to be mercurial . . . their attitude was fundamentally quite firm'.[78] The Dardenelles scare of August 1946 demonstrated American resolution in standing up to possible Soviet aggression. Its aftermath indicated, to British eyes at least, that the Russians would probably now concentrate on Iran or Greece rather than Turkey itself. According to Christopher Warner, Russian policy 'is not to invade Turkey by force of arms, at this stage, or even . . . to press claims . . . to a base near Constantinople. . . . [but] to keep Turkey mobilised, and gradually to ruin her economically'.[79] This was a dominant theme of British thought. The Greek door was ajar and much more easily kicked open. Or, to change the metaphor into one which frequently came to mind in discussions about Russian aims, 'Turkey is the toughest nut they have to crack in the Middle East.'[80]

Greece

Sometimes in considering large and complex problems, such as the British Empire in the Middle East, it is helpful to take a step back from the centre in order to see in perspective other parts of the landscape. The question of Greece offers such an opportunity. To contemporary observers Greece was not part of the Middle East, yet the decisions taken about the future of Greece might determine the future of the British in the Middle East, or for that matter western civilization itself. In Greece there were principles of liberty and freedom at stake which symbolized, in British eyes, the justification of the Second World War. It is useful to bear in mind these large questions, in relation to the specific purpose of examining the connection between Greece and the Middle East, because in the post-war controversy about Greece may be found an indication of the vitality of the British Empire and Commonwealth and the sense of British purpose not only in the Middle East but throughout the world.

The British Ambassador in Greece, Sir Reginald Leeper, who did not quail before such momentously broad issues, addressed himself

[78] Kelly to Bevin, No. 253 Confidential, 18 May 1946, FO 371/59233/R7996.
[79] Warner to Balfour, Secret, 19 Aug. 1947, FO 371/67308/R9489/G.
[80] F. K. Roberts to Bevin, Top Secret, 'Light' (Special Distribution), 3 Sept. 1947, FO 371/67309/R12139/G.

to two questions about the future of Greece: '(a) Is an independent Greece possible? and (b) If not, how can Greece be kept on our side of the fence?'[81] 'Rex' Leeper, as he was known to his friends and colleagues, offered quite provoking answers that had gradually been taking shape in his mind in February 1946, six months after the close of the war and one year before the crisis of Greece and Turkey came to a head in 1947. He was an Australian who had entered the Foreign Office during the First World War and had long experience with eastern Europe. His strong anti-appeasement sentiments resembled those of the Permanent Under-Secretary at the time of the rise of Nazi Germany, Sir Robert Vansittart. At the beginning of the war Leeper had served as director of the British propaganda office ('Political Warfare', as it was called) by which he earned the distinction of being labelled by Joseph Goebbels as his 'most dangerous opponent in the Foreign Office'. In 1943 Leeper was appointed as Ambassador to the Greek government, first in Cairo and eventually in Athens. He was bearing in mind, as he wrote in 1946, that Greece was 'our first fighting ally'. In that single phrase he summed up a basic distinction in the British mind between Greece and Turkey, and one that usually carried emotional commitment to the Greek cause.[82]

In Leeper's judgement it was impossible for Greece to be truly

[81] Leeper to Sargent, 27 Feb. 1946, FO 371/58678/R3496. There is a comprehensive treatment of the Greek question on the American side: Lawrence S. Wittner, *American Intervention in Greece, 1943-1949* (New York, 1982). For the British perspective see G. M. Alexander, *The Prelude to the Truman Doctrine: British Policy in Greece 1944-1947* (Oxford, 1982). See also John O. Iatrides, *Revolt in Athens* (Princeton, 1972), and his edited work, *Greece in the 1940s* (University Press of New England, 1981); and especially Stephen G. Xydis, *Greece and the Great Powers 1944-1947* (Thessaloniki, 1963). There are valuable chapters on the Greek-Turkish crisis of 1946-7 in Kuniholm, *Origins*; see also Barry Rubin, *The Great Powers in the Middle East, 1941-1947* (London, 1980); Terry H. Anderson, *The United States, Great Britain, and the Cold War, 1944-1947* (University of Missouri Press, 1981); and Robert M. Hathaway, *Ambiguous Partnership: Britain and America, 1944-1947* (New York, 1981). The older and indispensable accounts of the Greek crisis are William Hardy McNeill, *The Greek Dilemma: War and Aftermath* (New York, 1947); and William Reitzel, *The Mediterranean: Its Role in America's Foreign Policy* (New York, 1948). Leeper's own book, basic to the present discussion, is *When Greek Meets Greek* (London, 1950). C. M. Woodhouse's *Apple of Discord* (London, 1948); *The Struggle for Greece, 1941-1949* (London, 1976); and his recent autobiography, *Something Ventured* (London, 1982), are also fundamental.

[82] McNeill, *Greek Dilemma*, described Leeper as 'a clever man, rather austere and forbidding in manner, . . . [who] sometimes offended the Greeks by an air of haughtiness' (p. 160). The American Ambassador, Lincoln MacVeagh, wrote in 1944 that Leeper 'has some un-English qualities, like a love for bargaining and indirection, which make . . . me think he may very well have some Jewish blood' (Wittner, *American Intervention in Greece*, p. 319 n. 66). Bevin once remarked to Leeper after a discourse on Greek politics: 'You sound to me like 'Erb Morrison trying to fix an election.' Sir William Hayter, *A Double Life* (London, 1974), p. 77. Alexander Cadogan noted in his diary: 'Leeper . . . the trouble with him—he's too clever by half and never plays quite straight.' Diary entry for 24 Nov. 1945, Cadogan Papers.

'independent' in the economic and political conditions of the post-war world. One of two things, he wrote, would happen to Greece: 'either she must be kept as a satellite in our own orbit, at the cost to us of military in lieu of financial and economic assistance; or she must inevitably gravitate into the Russian orbit for lack of such assistance from us'. There is no need to elaborate here the reasons why Leeper believed that Greece should be kept under British sway. His arguments included Greece as 'a vital link in our system of Imperial communication and defence', and the British lives and resources already expended in the Greek cause. He had no sympathy with the 'Treasury people' who wanted 'to cut our losses'. There were far greater issues at stake, which may be summed up as 'the permanent loss to Greece of her independence'. To prevent Greece from drifting into the Russian orbit, Leeper examined two possibilities: an indefinite occupation of Greece by British troops, which he feared would be uneconomic and politically dangerous; or the running of Greece 'more or less on the Cromer model', by which he meant the establishment of financial responsibility and political order by using as a model the British experience in Egypt before the First World War.[83] One might pause to reflect how long was the shadow, and how unexpected its nuances, of the British occupation of Egypt.

Leeper rejected those possibilities in favour of a third solution that he believed to be more creative and ultimately more satisfactory. It is just as startling in retrospect as the proposal to apply the 'Cromer model'. Leeper believed that Greece should become a member of the *British Commonwealth*:

Nobody of good faith can deny that the Dominions (unlike the component republics of the Soviet Union) are voluntary members of the group to which they belong and have not only the theoretical right, but also the practical possibility, of seceding from the Commonwealth whenever they choose.

Objections would no doubt be raised to the incorporation of a very foreign, very Mediterranean element from the other end of Europe in a predominantly Anglo-Saxon group. But . . . are we not hoping that before long the utterly foreign peoples of India will enjoy that status?[84]

With his Australian background Leeper could see many mutual advantages to Greece prospering in the Commonwealth. 'Incidentally', he added, 'the Cyprus question would solve itself.' It is a reminder of the power of the Commonwealth idea that in 1946 it appeared that even the economic and political problems of Greece might be overcome in the tradition of Dominion status. 'The alternative of

[83] Leeper to Sargent, 27 Feb. 1946.
[84] Ibid.

letting Greece go', he concluded, 'would be a clear indication that we had lost the will to maintain our position in the world. Have we lost it?'[85]

Leeper's ideas about Greece as a British Dominion are striking not least because they went against the current of Foreign Office thought. 'What he perhaps means', wrote William Hayter, the head of the Southern Department, 'is that Greece should become part of the Empire and that we should assume responsibility for controlling and defending her.' As a pragmatist Hayter simply did not believe it would work, either in theory or in practice: 'this would turn Greece not into a Dominion but into a Crown Colony, which would be much more indefensible internationally and would be quite unacceptable to the Greeks themselves'. Hayter in fact was sceptical about Greek motives. What the Greeks wanted, he continued, 'was that they should govern the country themselves and that we should pay for it and defend it'.[86] Christopher Warner was more sympathetic to Leeper's scheme, above all because it would help to solve the defence problem. 'We could hardly be criticized for stationing troops in a Dominion', Warner wrote. But he too had reservations: 'I fear that neither the British nor American public wd. stand for the Dominion solution & it would not get over the financial difficulty —which is the terrible snag in the course we are trying to pursue.'[87] Warner had identified the two salient elements of the problem, the occupation by British troops and financial insolvency. Hector McNeil, the Parliamentary Under-Secretary whose minutes frequently appeared in discussions about Greece, emphasized another theme, which might be best described as British exasperation at the Greek national character. McNeil, like Leeper, believed that Greece should be viewed as a sort of colony, though not one on its way to Dominion status:

I . . . think that Colonial treatment . . . is the only method which offers any hope of nursing Greece towards solvency and political stability. 'Dominion status' is meantime impossible because as Mr. Hayter infers Greece is a backward, extravagant and irresponsible country whose vanities are made greater and whose

---

[85] Ibid.

[86] Minute by Hayter, 8 Mar. 1946, FO 371/58678/R3496.

[87] Minute by Warner, 11 Mar. 1946, ibid. Into these discussions Sir Orme Sargent injected a comment which deserves to be recorded in the annals of British constitutional history as an example of the way in which a Permanent Under-Secretary viewed the practical aspects of Dominion status. Sargent believed that 'it was a *sine qua non* that a Dominion should be self-supporting and able to stand on her own feet. So long as any territory fails to fulfil this requirement it either does not acquire Dominion status, e.g. India, or, having already got it, is in danger of being deprived of it, e.g. Newfoundland.' Minute by Sargent, 12 Mar. 1946, ibid.

difficulties are therefore accentuated because for both us and the U. S. S. R. Greece has strategic importance.[88]

'Backward', 'extravagant', and 'irresponsible' were words that recurred in various combinations in British minutes of 1945–7.

Greece did not become a British colony, but it could well be argued that the British dealt with the Greeks as if Greece were all but part of the British Empire. 'Up to 1947', C. M. Woodhouse has written, 'the British Government appointed and dismissed Greek Prime Ministers with the barest attention to constitutional formalities.'[89] There was nevertheless an important difference between the Churchill wartime era and the postwar years of Attlee and Bevin. The Labour government had little sympathy with a right-wing Royalist regime. In Greece, in contrast for example with Egypt (where there was also a strong British tradition of 'Cabinet-making') Bevin was perhaps less successful in restraining British interference, but the impulse was consistent. The Secretary of State, noted Warner in December 1946, 'has often expressed himself against intervention in Cabinet-making in Greece'.[90] Hector McNeil, who acted as Bevin's lieutenant in Greek affairs, observed emphatically that 'we should not have any part in Cabinet-making at this stage and at no stage have any part in urging the King to be otherwise than a constitutional monarch'.[91] Bevin and McNeil were attempting to check the interventionist inclinations of the Embassy in Athens. Leeper was candid in describing the extent of British interference. 'Since the civil war ended in January 1945', he had written at the end of his tour of duty in February 1946, 'I have done everything in my power to prevent political opinion swinging too far to the Right and to encourage and strengthen a moderate Centre.'[92] As if in symbolic succession, Lord Killearn relinquished his duties as Ambassador in Cairo in the same month as Leeper's departure from Athens, thus signifying the Labour government's wish to end the era of intervention.

It is not the purpose here even to broach the complicated questions of Anglo-Greek relations at the close of the war, but it is important to note the wartime legacy, especially as perceived by the Americans.[93] Lincoln MacVeagh, the American Ambassador, wrote

[88] Minute by McNeil, 29 Mar. 1946, FO 371/58678/R3496.
[89] Woodhouse, *Struggle for Greece*, p. 149.
[90] Minute by Warner, 14 Dec. 1946, FO 371/58717/R17830.
[91] Minute by McNeil, 17 Dec. 1946, ibid.
[92] Leeper to Bevin, No. 53 Confidential, 22 Feb. 1946, FO 371/58677/R3388.
[93] For discussion of Anglo-Greek relations based on wartime Foreign Office files see Phyllis Auty and Richard Clogg, eds., *British Policy Towards Wartime Resistance in Yugoslavia and Greece* (London, 1975), chap. 7.

to President Roosevelt that the heart of the problem in Greece was the British treatment of the Greeks as if they were recalcitrant natives: 'at bottom, the handling of this fanatically freedom-loving country (which has never yet taken dictation quietly) as if it were composed of natives under the British Raj, is what is the trouble'.[94] MacVeagh's wartime analysis of British weakness is also of considerable interest, not only in regard to Greece but all of the Middle East. He wrote in October 1944, while still based in Cairo:

> Every day brings its evidence of [British] weakness and dispersion, or consequent opportunism, and dependence on America's nucleated strength. No one, I feel, can keep his eyes and ears open here and fail to believe that the future maintenance of the Empire depends on how far England consents to frame her foreign policy in agreement with Washington, and how far we in our turn realize where that Empire, so important to our own security, is most immediately menaced.
>
> British fumbling in the Balkans, fears of what may happen in Palestine, uneasiness as to Syria, doubts regarding Turkey, and alarm over growing Soviet interest in Iran, Saudi Arabia, Egypt and the whole North African coast, together with the fact that it was only through America's productive strength being thrown into the balance that Rommel's threat to this region was defeated, all seem to me to teach the same lesson in their varying degrees.[95]

The 'lesson' could be summed up by stating that the British Empire would become increasingly dependent, economically and militarily, on the United States.

The British could not depend on American assistance. So weak did the position seem to the Prime Minister that he considered the possibility of cutting British losses and turning the Balkans and Middle East into a sort of no man's land. This idea played a prominent part in the strategic debate of March 1946 that has been emphasized in the introduction of this book. Bevin's response merits attention here because it clearly reveals the connection between Greece and the Middle East as well as the importance of maintaining 'our position as a Great Power' in the eastern Mediterranean and throughout the world. At the beginning of the Labour government, Bevin had stated that British policy in the Middle East would remain the same, in other words, that he would pursue Churchill's aims. His remarks in March 1946 indeed had a Churchillian ring to them:

> The Mediterranean is the area through which we bring influence to bear on Southern Europe, the soft underbelly of France, Italy, Yugoslavia, Greece and Turkey. Without our physical presence in the Mediterranean, we

---

[94] MacVeagh to Roosevelt, 8 Dec. 1944, in John O. Iatrides, ed., *Ambassador MacVeagh Reports* (Princeton, 1980), p. 660.
[95] MacVeagh to Roosevelt, 15 Oct. 1944, ibid., pp. 627–8.

should cut little ice with those States which would fall, like Eastern Europe, under the totalitarian yoke. We should also lose our position in the Middle East. . . .[96]

Bevin thought it 'essential' for Greece to remain 'with us politically'. The mention of the word Greece evoked thoughts of liberty and independence. Bevin believed that by protecting the eastern Mediterranean the British would be defending social democracy and ultimately the British 'way of life'. The following statement was perhaps one of his most eloquent on the subject:

> In the European scene . . . we are the last bastion of social democracy. It may be said that this now represents our way of life as against the red tooth and claw of American capitalism and the Communist dictatorship of Soviet Russia. Any weakening of our position in the Mediterranean area will, in my view, lead to the end of social democracy there and submit us to a pressure which would make our position untenable.[97]

In March 1946, when Bevin made that impassioned plea, assistance from the United States still appeared to be remote, though indications of future American aid may be traced to the same month.[98] The spring of 1946 was a time of precarious balance in the Middle East. March was the same month as the Iranian crisis. It was also the same time that the British decided to press ahead with treaty revision and troop withdrawal in Egypt. The Anglo-American Committee on Palestine was now in the third month of its deliberations. March 1946 was also the month of the Greek elections, an event of cardinal importance to the British as well as the Greeks.

'My policy has been', Bevin had written in early November 1945, 'that the Greeks must form their own Government without my intervention.'[99] In order to 'consolidate' the situation so that elections might be held, Bevin despatched his Parliamentary Under-Secretary to Athens to 'advise' the Greeks. The details of Hector McNeil's mission are beyond the scope of the present discussion but in short he felt compelled to intervene in order to carry out the Labour government's policy of non-intervention. In the words of a contemporary American account, which incisively describes the paradox, McNeil wanted 'a reorganization of the [Greek] Cabinet to make it representative of a coalition of political parties. . . . Such high-handed intervention in the affairs of the "sovereign" state of Greece was reminiscent of the methods Churchill had used. . . .'[1] McNeil's

---

[96] Memorandum by Bevin, DO (46) 40, 13 Mar. 1947, CAB 131/2.
[97] Ibid.
[98] See Woodhouse, *Struggle for Greece*, p. 195.
[99] Memorandum by Bevin, CP (45) 266, 3 Nov. 1945, CAB 129/4.
[1] McNeill, *Greek Dilemma*, pp. 220–1.

'colonial treatment' (his phrase, by which in his own mind he associated British political and economic control over the Egyptians), helped to reduce Greece, in the words of the same American historian, to the status of 'a client state'. Ernest Bevin and his colleagues had not intended to create a British satellite, but by mid-1946 both Russians and Americans could agree that it seemed to be the result of British 'colonial treatment'. This raises a fundamental question, which has Middle Eastern ramifications. What type of state and society were the British attempting to reconstruct?

A clear answer at the straightforward political level may be traced in the minutes of the head of the Southern Department as he pondered the problems of the Greek elections. 'What would suit us best', Hayter wrote in February 1946, would be a left-of-centre coalition 'with enough strength to hold the balance of power.' What would suit the British least, he continued, would be a victory of the Communist-dominated National Liberation Front, the E. A. M., 'which would mean the end of British influence in Greece and the rapid conversion of that country into another Yugoslavia'.[2] Hayter in any case was pessimistic about the prospects of the Greek elections because whatever the result it probably would not stabilize the country. He believed that the British would have to learn to live with Greek politics, even if they were to lead to a repressive or 'reactionary' regime distasteful to the British. In Hayter's view the 'professional defenders of Greek democracy' in the House of Commons had obscured the issue because it was unrealistic to expect democracy of the British variety to function in Greece. The British aim should merely be independence, as in the case of Turkey, where the British found the regime even more 'unpalatable' but nevertheless necessary as a buffer against Russian expansion. Hayter was lucid in defining the British goal that he believed should be kept clearly in mind at all times: 'This is to bolster up Greece financially as far as we can, to ´relieve her as far as possible of the expense of armed forces which are beyond her means, and to make it plain that we regard her independence as essential to our security.'[3]

In view of the tone and substance of the minutes written by Hayter and others in 1946, the judgement rendered at the same time by the American historian, William Hardy McNeill, in *The Greek Dilemma* strikes one as remarkably fair-minded about the type of state the British were attempting to create. He wrote as

[2] Minute by Hayter, 21 Feb. 1946, FO 371/58676/R3032.
[3] Minute by Hayter, 8 Mar. 1946, FO 371/58678/R3496; and other minutes by Hayter in FO 371/58676-79.

an observer of the wartime and postwar experience up to the autumn of 1946:

> The British, I believe, would have liked to see a liberal society and government emerge from this welter [of wartime politics and civil war]. Their first and principal concern was that the Government of Greece should always be friendly toward them; and the men who shaped British policy for Greece were by this time firmly convinced that an EAM Government would not be friendly.[4]

Precisely what 'friendly' meant, McNeill continued, was not entirely clear, but his impressions are confirmed by the secret files. British policy was less sinister or Machiavellian than was commonly supposed and more or less in line with McNeill's contemporary estimate:

> Probably it [a 'friendly' government] meant in part the reestablishment of economic concessions to British-owned public utility and other companies; but in last analysis and far more important, it meant a Government in Greece that would side with Great Britain in case of another war. . . . With serious doubts of the King and even deeper distrust of a republic, the British policy in practice was little more than one of wait and see, meanwhile keeping the Left from exclusive power.[5]

After the elections of March 1946 the British could at least congratulate themselves that an international mission of observers had attested that the results had not been, in Bevin's phrase, unduly 'cooked'. After the plebiscite and on the eve of King George II's return to Greece in late September, Bevin 'impressed' on the King 'how important it was that he should keep on the "constitutional rails" '.[6] What type of state were the British attempting to reconstruct? The British preferred for it to have the constitutional trappings of a democracy. But neither Bevin nor his advisers were under any illusion that democracy in a British sense would flourish in Greece. Sir Clifford Norton (Leeper's successor) in December 1946 expressed a sentiment with which everyone could agree: 'We are wrong if we try to impose British standards or methods on this mercurial and semi-Oriental people.'[7]

---

[4] McNeill, *Greek Dilemma*, p. 162.   [5] Ibid.

[6] Bevin to Norton, No. 624 Secret, 26 September 1946, FO 371/58609/R14393. In the following month the American Ambassador reported that the Labour government appeared to be succeeding in pursuing its 'hands off' or non-interventionist policy. In fact MacVeagh observed that the Foreign Office was perhaps imposing too much restraint on the Embassy in Athens: 'The British [in Athens] hampered by the leftist affiliations of their [Labour] Government, and wanting to maintain their control while fearing to take the steps necessary to that end, seem to be pursuing a dangerously "hands off" policy. I say "dangerously" because, if left to themselves, the King and the politicians are only too likely to repeat their old non-cooperation of 1935–1936 and to run into a similar impasse to that which produced the dictatorship.' *MacVeagh Reports*, p. 704. For British policy in the earlier period see the first-class work by John S. Koliopoulos, *Greece and the British Connection, 1935–1941* (London, 1977).

[7] Norton to Bevin, No. 361 Confidential, 28 Dec. 1946, FO 371/66994/R143.

What type of state, to rephrase the question, were the British attempting to create after it became apparent in the spring and summer of 1946 that the civil war had again broken out? In mid-1946 the Foreign Office began to draw up a balance sheet. Hector McNeil's 'colonial treatment' showed few political or economic indications of progress. Despite British 'advisers' in every part of the Greek government—'army, police, finance, railways, roads, and distribution and supplies', to use Bevin's shorthand summation—the Greek economy showed no sign of long-term recovery. British resources seemed to be flowing into 'a bottomless well', or to use another phrase that recurred in British minutes, into a political system that was 'irremediably corrupt'. Which was the anvil and which was the hammer? British 'assistance' was being pounded into Greek forms. Critics of British 'imperialism' might denounce the creation of a satellite but to the British themselves it appeared that they were being mulcted by the Greeks. By the summer of 1946 the uneasiness about the use of British manpower and financial aid was developing into a sense of outrage. After the March election there had been a marked increase in banditry in northern Greece. It was accompanied by murders of non-communist leaders and a general breakdown of law and order. Who was responsible for public order in Greece—the British or the Greek government? Should British troops suppress the bandits and restore order—in other words risk involvement in the Greek civil war? This was a matter on which Hector McNeil, in his own words, held 'the strongest views'. The Greek government, not the British troops, should be held accountable for public order in Greece, and in particular for the disarming of the bandits. 'It is just one other example of political cowardice on the part of the Greeks', he wrote. 'Any job involving ordeal is handed on to us.' Quite significantly, Bevin noted 'I agree'.[8] The type of state the British were attempting to reconstruct was definitely not one in which the British would be indefinitely held responsible for the maintenance of public order.

In drawing up the balance sheet in mid-1946 it became increasingly obvious that a clear-cut decision would have to be made on the financial versus security priorities of the Labour government. British economic resources could not continue to flow indefinitely into a 'bottomless well'. The Chancellor of the Exchequer, Hugh Dalton, held as a premiss that financial assistance to foreign countries, even those of 'semi-colonial' status, should not be extended unless it were 'absolutely vital for the defence and security of this country'. During these discussions Dalton expressed scepticism about the wisdom as

[8] Minutes by McNeil and Bevin, 20 May 1946, FO 371/58695.

well as the efficacy of British aid. He wrote later, in a comment that sums up his attitude throughout, 'I regard the Greeks as a very poor investment for the British tax payer.'[9] He had only reluctantly agreed to subsidizing the Greek army—which the Chiefs of Staff wished to build into a permanent force of 100,000—and emphasized repeatedly that this could not be a long-range commitment. Nor did he view with favour the prolonged occupation by British troops. 'It seemed most undesirable', Dalton said in March 1946, 'to allow the Greeks to believe that we would continue to pay for an army of this size as a long-term policy.'[10] The cost to the British Treasury for maintaining the Greek army amounted to £13,000,000 in 1945 and Dalton estimated that it would be £15,000,000 in 1946. If any one thing were certain, it was that the Greeks themselves could not pay for the upkeep. Dalton wished to withdraw British troops by the 1st of September and severely curtail assistance to the Greek army.

Within the Foreign Office that formula was referred to as 'chronic Daltonism'. British losses could be cut, but at what price? 'We will have spent over £50,000,000 in 1945 and 1946 in keeping the Communists out of Greece', noted Ralph Selby of the Southern Department. In the spring and summer of 1946 the British faced increasing revolutionary activity on the left and the threat of violent repression on the right. Should logic be thrown to the wind, asked the same official, 'and let Greece sink?'[11] If so would it not make an absurd ending to the loss of British blood and treasure? Would not the immense political and strategic loss be greater than the short-term economic relief? The head of the department answered those dire questions with a comment that is chronologically significant. 'I do not think that the time has yet come to consider cutting our losses in Greece', Hayter wrote in June 1946.[12]

July 1946 marked a turning point for the British in several different ways. First of all the Foreign Office now devoted considerable attention to defining the nature and the necessity of military and economic assistance. This critical time is made clear in an agonized minute by Hayter dated the 20th of that month. The time had come, he wrote, '*to grasp this nettle and make up our minds that the Greek army are our mercenaries*'.[13] Hayter based his argument on the premiss shared by Bevin and all others that British troops could not remain indefinitely in Greece. It was therefore best

[9] Minute by Dalton, 18 Apr. 1947, FO 371/67040.
[10] Defence Committee minutes, DO (46) 9, 27 Mar. 1946, CAB 131/1.
[11] Minute by Selby, 5 May 1946, FO 371/58694/R8332.
[12] Minute by Hayter, 13 June 1946, ibid.
[13] Minute by Hayter, 20 July 1946, FO 371/58701/R11542/G. Emphasis added.

realistically to recognize the function of the Greek army. Apart from attempting to maintain internal order, the Greek army guarded the northern frontiers. Without it British forces would have to intervene in case of attack. Hayter's minute is revealing because of its preoccupation with possible invasion from the north in mid-1946.

> It is hard to believe that we would sit back and allow a Yugoslav or Bulgarian invasion of Greece. The effect on our strategic situation of a Communist control of Greece would be bad enough in itself, and its repercussions elsewhere would be incalculable. . . .
> A collapse of our position in Greece would probably mean that the Turks would give in too. The reaction of this on our situation in the Middle East can well be imagined.[14]

Hayter was clarifying the military and strategic realities in such brutal fashion because the Greek Prime Minister had requested the extension of the British subsidy to the army to the end of March 1947 (the end of the fiscal year, which incidentally explains the prominence of the date in the shaping of the Truman doctrine). Here it is important to bear in mind the central question. What type of state were the British attempting to reconstruct? It was a state that the British would continue to support economically within their capabilities for their own strategic purposes, but one in which British troops would be withdrawn in measured pace as quickly as possible. Greek forces would take their place, in Hayter's phrase, as British 'mercenaries'.

Why were the British so intent on troop withdrawal in Greece when in contrast the Middle East as a whole appeared to resemble a permanent British fortress? The answer may be grasped in Bevin's ideas on the subject. On the 22nd of June 1946 (at the very time that Hayter and his colleagues independently were grasping the nettle of a mercenary force), the Defence Committee of the Cabinet agreed to extend British assistance to the Greek army until the end of March 1947 and to maintain a British division of 20,000 men in northern Greece until the end of 1946. Bevin was flexible, as will be seen, on the timing of the withdrawal of British troops, but he was adamant on the necessity to get them out 'at the earliest possible moment'.[15] In January at the United Nations the Russians had protested the presence of British forces in Greece (and Indonesia) in retaliation against the Iranian complaint about Russian forces in Azerbaijan. Bevin was sensitive to criticism in the United Nations, especially at a time when he was trying to prove to the Egyptians the honesty of British intention to withdraw troops from Egypt proper into the Canal Zone.

[14] Ibid.   [15] See minute by Dixon, 5 Apr. 1946, FO 371/58687.

Bevin also believed that the Russians had genuine anxieties about their security. He wished to remove all grounds for legitimate Russian complaint. He probably thought that the Russians would respect Greece as a British sphere of influence, as Churchill and Stalin had agreed in October 1944, just as the British respected Bulgaria as a Russian sphere of influence. He hoped that the Russians would withdraw their troops from the Balkans at the same time that the British would pull out of Greece, in accordance with the terms of the peace treaties. In late May 1946 Bevin wrote:

> I do not anticipate a direct Russian attack on Greece, but I cannot put out of my mind the possibility of encouragement being given by Russia to these other [Balkan] powers to create trouble with Greece. . . .
> It would be unwise to commit ourselves to withdrawing British forces from Greece until the international situation is clearer and at least until we know what we can obtain about the withdrawal of Russian troops from South East Europe, and until the Greek Army is strong enough to defend its frontiers against Yugoslav and Bulgarian aggression.[16]

Later in the year he became more insistent. He increasingly held the view that British troops should be withdrawn despite the presence of Russian forces in the Balkans. He wrote to Attlee in November 1946:

> There is no doubt in my mind that the withdrawal of our forces at an early date would both deprive the Soviet Government of a source of grievance and suspicion against us and would also strengthen the position of Greece internationally for the United Nations Organisation. . . . In my view, the question of the withdrawal of British forces in Greece should not be affected by the question whether there are or are not Soviet troops in Bulgaria.[17]

Bevin had dictated that minute while in New York at a time when he was preoccupied with United Nations affairs. There were other reasons that demand elucidation.

In mid-1946 British intelligence reports began to reflect alarming developments in the activities of the Greek communists. The plan of action was guerilla warfare 'against the Right Wing, and, to a considerable extent, against the British forces'. The British had no evidence of Russian aid, but they knew from 'most secret sources' that the K. K. E., the Greek communist party, anticipated Russian help: 'in the event of civil war all aid short of armed assistance will be extended to the Left Wing from the U. S. S. R.'.[18] Hector McNeil's

---

[16] Memorandum by Bevin, C. P. (46) 213, 30 May 1946. The best assessment of Greece and the beginning of the cold war, in this writer's judgement, is Woodhouse, *Struggle for Greece*, chapters 6 and 7, which takes into balanced account 'revisionist' interpretations.

[17] Minute by Bevin, 16 Nov. 1946, FO 371/58715/R16951.

[18] One arresting aspect of this information was that the K. K. E. believed that they would have no difficulty in buying equipment 'from members of the British forces'. Minute by D. J. McCarthy, 2 July 1946, FO 371/58698.

response to this intelligence warning was immediate and firm. 'The two points to my mind are: (1) British troops must not be used; (2) The Greek Government must proceed against Right and Left with determination.'[19] McNeil apprehended a backlash of violence on the right against the left. Thus he emphasized the need for the Greek government to move resolutely against both sides. He had little confidence that the Greek government could effectively maintain middle ground. What he feared was the British being caught between the two sides. Thus the problem of northern Greece amounted to much more than mere 'banditry'. Greece was moving towards the resumption of full-scale civil war. In the coming months, according to Hayter, the K. K. E. would probably encourage 'criminal violence on a large scale'.[20] So alarming did this prospect seem that it brought to mind Palestine. In fact at this time the Ambassador in Athens reported that in his judgement the situation in northern Greece was beginning to resemble the one in Palestine. Sir Clifford Norton's secret despatches independently confirmed the intelligence reports. He believed that if British forces remained in Greece they would be confronted with problems just as intractable as the ones in Palestine. Here the answer to the question of British aims may be summed up emphatically and negatively. The dangers of drifting into a hopeless situation haunted the official mind. The British wished to avoid at almost any cost getting trapped as they had in Palestine.

There was a further and even more intangible element in the British outlook. In drawing up the balance sheet in 1946 the ministers of the Labour government did not believe the Greeks to be a sound investment for the scarce resources of postwar Britain. The Chancellor of the Exchequer held that view with stentorian insistence. The Foreign Secretary shared it. 'The trouble about this', Bevin wrote in September 1946, 'is that the Greeks will not put out a reconstruction programme to rally the people & so isolate the Communists.'[21] The Greeks did not have the 'political courage' to introduce the unpopular economic measures necessary to prevent the economy from collapsing. 'No Greek Government of the eight we have had in fifteen months', Hector McNeil wrote in November 1946, 'has shown the guts for this complex and unpalatable task.'[22] This view

[19] Minute by McNeil, 2 July 1946, ibid. 'The Right . . .', Hayter observed, 'for the present at any rate . . . is a far less serious phenomenon.' Minute by Hayter, 24 July 1946, FO 371/58698.

[20] Ibid.

[21] Minute by Bevin, 17 Sept. 1946, FO 371/58708/R13858. The quotation follows the deciphered version of his handwriting.

[22] Minute by McNeil, 29 Nov. 1946, FO 371/58716.

of Greek fecklessness played an important part in the assessments of the latter part of 1946 when the British agonized whether to cut their losses. The exasperation may be summed up in McNeil's arresting words when he wrote of 'cowardly, unreal & therefore ineffective Greek politics'.[23]

The catalyst in the debate about troop withdrawal was the visit of the Chief of the Imperial General Staff in November 1946. Lord Montgomery's quick and trenchant analysis warned of imperial disaster. Here too Palestine had a bearing on the situation, at least indirectly. Montgomery viewed the situation in Greece, as in Palestine, as essentially one of terrorism. He believed that Jewish terrorism could be quelled by determined military action by the British ('smoking them out', in his phrase). He detected a danger of far greater magnitude in Greece. He believed that the Greeks themselves could cope with terrorism in northern Greece by bold and resolute acts of courage (will power and valour were essential parts of Montgomery's mental make-up). But he was sceptical of Greek tenacity. British forces in any case should not take part in the suppression of the terrorists. The Greek situation in this respect differed fundamentally from the one in Palestine. The British in Greece faced the prospect of being drawn into a civil war.

Montgomery's assessment, in short, caused the Chiefs of Staff to become more aware of how quickly the situation was deteriorating. They shifted towards greater emphasis on getting the Greeks to develop mobile counter-guerilla 'frontier' forces rather than to continue to build up a conventional army. The military experts believed that the coming winter months might be decisive. As for British troops, the Chiefs of Staff wrote in December 1946 after Montgomery's return:

> The presence of British troops in Greece is symbolic. Even if retained at their present strength they would be totally inadequate to deal with external aggression. It is essential that British troops should not become involved in action against the bandits, whose activity is increasing, or that the Greeks should think that we would assist them actively in maintaining law and order. The fewer the number of British troops in Greece, the less likely are they to come into armed conflict with the bandits.[24]

For slightly different reasons the logic of the Chiefs of Staff marched in the same direction as Bevin's. By early 1947 the Cabinet had decided to reduce British troops to one brigade of four battalions

---

[23] Minute by McNeil, 1 Feb. 1947, FO 371/66998.

[24] COS (46) 288, 10 Dec. 1946, CAB 80/103; minutes in FO 371/58718. For a detailed examination of the British documents at this time see Alexander, *Prelude to the Truman Doctrine*, chap. 6.

(about 11,000 men)—down from the figure of two divisions of 41,000 a half year earlier. At the same time (to keep the perspective) British troops in Palestine were approaching four divisions and would grow close to 100,000 men.

When did the British believe that eventual American assistance could be regarded as a probability rather than as a remote possibility? The time can be established with certainty. It was mid-October 1946. In that month the British learned, 'under strictest injunctions to complete secrecy', that the Americans were working on 'a new policy' towards Greece.[25] It was indeed on the 11th of October that the American Ambassador in Greece, Lincoln MacVeagh, had talked to King George about the necessity to pursue a plan 'of widespread tolerance, justice and mercy similar to the program of Lincoln after the American civil war'.[26] The State Department endorsed those ideas as 'the finest kind [of] US advice' to the head of a friendly government 'whose future is of extreme concern [to] this Govt.'[27] In Greece as in Iran and Turkey the Americans were responding in a way that far surpassed British expectations. Earlier in this chapter attention has been called to the British hope that the Americans might rally to the beating of 'the drum of the Atlantic Charter', in other words, the idealism of the Second World War. The British now fully recognized that this response had to be a genuine American sentiment. It was not one that the British could in any way induce. In late 1946 and early 1947 Americans did regard the future of Greece in the same way that they had viewed the fate of the western democracies during the war. Greece was the only Balkan country still free from communist domination. When General Marshall became Secretary of State in early 1947 he took the position that 'the world has arrived at a point in its history that has not been paralleled since ancient history'.[28]

It is important to keep the focus on the connection (and lack of it) between Greece and the Middle East because this book is about the British Empire in the Middle East and only peripherally about the United States and the origins of the cold war. Attlee later reflected: 'By giving America notice at the right moment that we couldn't afford to stay and intended to pull out we made the Americans face up to the facts in the eastern Mediterranean.'[29]

[25] See minutes by Selby, 16 Oct. 1946, FO 371/58710/E14984; and Warner, 20 Oct. 1946, FO 371/58712/R15733.

[26] Iatrides, *MacVeagh Reports*, p. 701; *Foreign Relations 1946*, VII, p. 234.

[27] *Foreign Relations 1946*, VII, p. 235 n. 98.

[28] *Foreign Relations 1947*, V, p. 66.

[29] Francis Williams, *A Prime Minister Remembers* (London, 1961), p. 172. The turning point in Attlee's thought may be traced to a letter he wrote to Bevin on 3 Dec. 1946:

The timing was all-important. Hector McNeil, who played a central part in the Foreign Office discussions, as late as the end of November 1946 believed that no confidence could be placed in the Americans' coming to the rescue and that whatever form American assistance might take 'we will still be left to carry the political stigma of maintaining our troops in Greece'.[30] What he and his colleagues in the Foreign Office were much more certain about was the impending emergency in Greece. By late 1946 the Greek state was on the verge of collapse. The catastrophic conditions of Greek finances seemed to indicate that the entire economy would disintegrate. Famine was imminent. There was general agreement that Greece was on the verge of all-out civil war. *Now* the time had come to cut British losses. There was no way in which British economic resources and manpower could be used to save Greece from revolution. The Middle East was a different matter.

The famous British communication to the State Department of the 21st of February 1947 took most American officials by surprise. To those not directly concerned with Greek affairs, it was the abruptness of the intended British departure as well as the emergency itself that came as a revelation. The British in short stated that economic assistance to Greece (and Turkey) would cease at the end of March. To General Marshall, in the words of a frequently quoted passage, 'this dumped in our lap another most serious problem— that it was tantamount to British abdication from the Middle East with obvious implications as to their successor'.[31] The British documents do not sustain such an interpretation. As will be seen in later chapters, it certainly was not the British intention to evacuate the Middle East, and still less to calculate an American takeover. The British hoped rather to adjust relations with the Arab states, as with colonies and countries throughout the world, so that British influence would be strengthened, not liquidated. Yet the American records convey the dominant impression that the British Empire was in a state of dissolution. Again to quote from Marshall, from

'I am beginning to doubt whether the Greek game is worth the candle.' See Bullock, *Bevin*, chap. 8, which discusses the differences in assessment by Attlee and Bevin on this critical issue.

[30] Minute by McNeil, 29 Nov. 1946, FO 371/58716. It is of interest that in these discussions McNeil and his colleagues regarded Turkey as a relevant issue only 'because strategically they [Greece and Turkey] are complementary areas'. Ibid. From the British vantage point the American lumping together of Greece and Turkey in 1947 bears out the contemporary comment quoted by Lloyd Gardner that when 'the new dish was being prepared for American consumption, Turkey was slipped into the oven with Greece because that seemed to be the surest way to cook a tough bird'. Lloyd Gardner, *Architects of Illusion* (Chicago, 1972), p. 224.

[31] Millis, *Forrestal Diaries*, p. 245.

a summary of remarks he made to Congressional leaders in a meeting in the President's office: 'They are liquidating their positions in Burma, India, Palestine and Egypt. There is no reasonable basis for doubting that the same considerations are operating to terminate their expenditures in Greece and Turkey.'[32] Marshall also mentioned the circumstances of the savage winter of 1946–7 in England, the coal crisis, and the 'extreme economic distress' in which the British found themselves.

The blizzard of January 1947, the coal shortage, and the cuts in fuel and electricity (which plunged one of the Anglo-Jewish meetings on Palestine into further darkness) added to the drama of the situation. But the decisions on Greece were not taken because of the weather, or even because of Dalton's persistent complaint about 'our endless dribble of British taxpayers' money to the Greeks'.[33] It is perhaps important to bear in mind that Bevin together with Attlee, not Dalton, dominated the Cabinet. Bevin was inclined to give way on the issue of Greek aid—an issue on which he would have eventually been forced by economic circumstances to yield anyway—because in his words, 'we get no help from the Greeks'.[34] He was in no particular hurry to tell the Americans that all economic assistance to Greece would be cut off; but he did regard it as 'most urgent' that the Americans 'should make up their minds what economic help they will give Greece and what form it will take'.[35] He agreed to increasingly strong language in the communications to the State Department in order to precipitate an American decision.[36]

[32] *Foreign Relations 1947*, V, p. 61.

[33] Hugh Dalton, *High Tide and After* (London, 1962), p. 206.

[34] Minute by Bevin, 18 Feb. 1947, quoted in Anderson, *The United States, Great Britain, and the Cold War*, p. 168. For full discussion of these issues see Alexander, *Prelude to the Truman Doctrine*, chap. 7.

[35] Bevin's draft telegram to Washington, *c*.5 Feb. 1947, FO 371/67032. The catalytic stage in Bevin's mind appears to have been early 1947, when he wrote to members of the Defence Committee that 'in view of the very marked increase in American interest in Greece, I have hopes that she will be prepared to contribute not only towards Greece's economic requirements . . . but also to her military needs'. Memorandum by Bevin, DO (47), 2 Jan. 1947, CAB 131/4.

[36] E.g. 'I agreed . . . that we should put up a strong telegram to the United States asking them what they were going to do and on the other hand telling the Greeks that we could not continue for the sole purpose of bringing matters to a head.' (Minute by Bevin, 18 Feb. 1947, FO 371/68032/R2442/G.) Dalton's diary entry of 14 Mar. 1947 is of great interest as a Treasury counterpoint to the F.O. version. According to Dalton the stiff line of the Treasury brought matters to a head. In this entry he clarified the 'deal' made between him and Bevin. The Americans would be told that economic support to the Greeks would cease; but the Greeks themselves would not yet be told because of the possibility of bringing about the fall of the Greek government. 'E. B. said, not perhaps quite realizing what he was agreeing to, "Well, that's quite fair".' In view of Bevin's other preoccupations the remark is probably an accurate statement. The rest of the entry reads as follows (it should be borne in mind that Dalton was writing slightly after the event): 'The Americans took fright lest

As Attlee reflected later, to re-emphasize the importance of his insight, it was a question of giving the Americans 'notice at the right moment'.

Were the British 'sincere'? The question merits attention merely because it so agitated American sceptics and enemies of British imperialism in early 1947. The inquiry would be a red herring. Sincerity can be an inexpensive virtue, as American officials at the time were well aware, and the British were obviously sincere about their economic distress. The key answer to the question of motive, which is different, was carefully summed up by the committee chaired by Loy Henderson to study the crisis: 'we are inclined to believe that the British Government is really convinced that it is unable any longer to expend funds, supplies and manpower in the Near East in the future as it has in the past; and that it hopes that the United States, realizing how important it is that the independence of Turkey and Greece be maintained, will undertake to relieve Great Britain of these financial responsibilities. . . .'[37] That conclusion was entirely true as far as it went. What was much more clear from the British side was its corollary. It is of paramount importance in comprehending the British position in the Middle East in the postwar era. By assuming responsibility for Greece and Turkey, the United States not only provided enormous economic relief to the British. The Americans also found themselves generally (with the exception of Palestine) underwriting the British Empire in the Middle East. Gladwyn Jebb (Lord Gladwyn) by no means understated the case when he later wrote that when the United States decided to extend aid to Greece and Turkey it was 'a red letter day' for the British.[38]

Russia should overrun the whole of the Balkans and the Eastern Mediterranean. The Treasury officials told me afterwards that they never thought that the effect would be so quick and so volcanic. I had insisted on this line being taken and they now admitted that I had been right.' Apart from the self-congratulatory tone, Dalton's remarks serve as a reminder that the economic extremity of the British government ultimately determined policy towards Greece, even though some members of the Cabinet, notably Bevin and even Attlee, acted as if the British Empire were in a state of reversible decline and not imminent collapse. The entry is perhaps even more revealing about the confused and haphazard origins of the 'Truman Doctrine'.

[37] *Foreign Relations 1947*, V, p. 51. On the question of manpower the representative of the Jewish Agency in Washington, Eliahu Epstein, made this incisive comment to Henderson: 'if the British are feeling the burden of keeping 10,000 in Greece, they certainly feel the burden that much more in keeping 100,000 troops in Palestine'. Memorandum by Epstein, 1 Mar. 1947, CZA S25/6623.

[38] *The Memoirs of Lord Gladwyn* (London, 1972), p. 202. Gladwyn Jebb is a personality of particular interest in this regard because as head of the Economic and Reconstruction Department of the Foreign Office during the war he had been one of the most incisive critics of muddled American idealism (see the discussion of his attack on Sumner Welles and

The British Ambassador in Greece, Sir Clifford Norton, wrote in early February 1947, before the Americans had come to the rescue:

British troops are being reduced and may be withdrawn this year. But unless some solution to [the] economic and financial problem can be found it seems absolutely certain that all efforts of His Majesty's Government—expressed in terms of British lives and British resources—to preserve Greece as an independent democratic state will have been in vain.

Economic collapse would lead inevitably to political collapse and thence through a period of civil war and great suffering to incorporation in the Soviet system of buffer police states controlled by Communist minorities. . . .

It may seem out of place to mention [the] debt of the West to Greece as [the] main source of our civilisation and culture. But the more recent incurred obligation as an Ally who gallantly fought alongside us when our fortunes were at their lowest ebb should not be forgotten.[39]

He thus put into clear perspective the broad meaning of the crisis for the British. The basic British response was the same as the American. Greece was a touchstone of western civilization. It is important to bear in mind the common cause because British and American aims in the Middle East ultimately had much in common, despite the bitter divisiveness in Palestine. British troops in Greece became, in American eyes, 'symbolical of the determination of the Western democracies to insure the continued independence of the Greek state'.[40]

The divisive issue was Palestine, which evoked a dramatically

'colonial liberation' in Louis, *Imperialism at Bay*, pp. 498-9). As an Assistant Under-Secretary he now viewed the 'Truman Doctrine' and the possibility of an open-ended commitment 'to help *all free peoples*' in the struggle against Communism as 'a badly thought out and impetuous gesture' (*Memoirs*, pp. 200-2). Nevertheless at the time of Truman's speech in March 1947 he along with most other British officials was 'delighted with it' and commented that it was 'the most important statement of American policy probably since the first World War'. The American Embassy in London had selected Jebb as a weather vane of British official reaction. 'The British had been considerably surprised', according to Jebb, 'at the character of Mr. Truman's action and the extent to which he had gone.' Memorandum of 17 Mar. 1947 enclosed in Robert Coe to Secretary of State, Secret, 28 Mar. 1947, USSD 868.00/3-2847 Box 6785.

[39] Norton to Bevin, No. 285 Top Secret 'Light', 5 Feb. 1947, FO 371/67032.

[40] Marshall to Douglas, 8 Sept. 1947, *Foreign Relations 1947*, V, p. 331. The withdrawal of British troops remained a point of controversy. Once the Americans were committed, Bevin only reluctantly agreed to continue a token presence of British forces. A Foreign Office minute of August 1947 records his views at the time when the economic crisis in England had hit with full force: 'The Secretary of State feels that we must now realise that America has taken on from us responsibility for Greece. Having done this she must also take on the responsibility of providing manpower to carry out her obligations. . . . At present they [the Americans] do not wish to use a man overseas, but to protect their interests by use of dollars. We must disabuse them of any idea of using us to man their outposts overseas, and we shall bring them up against this by removing our troops from Greece. At the present moment, though we have not sufficient troops to do anything in Greece if trouble blows up, they are sufficient to allow the Americans to feel that they can still evade their responsibilities.' Minute by J. P. S. Henniker, 16 Aug. 1947, FO 371/67045.

different American response. Eugene Rostow has written with great insight on the connection between the Greek and Palestine crises and the American reaction. In the case of Greece the American people generally as well as those in official circles, in his view, identified 'our absolute bed-rock national interest in assuring the independence and the democratic character of Western Europe'. The firm and steady American reaction had a direct historical explanation. 'That, of course, was why we fought in both World Wars. Against the background of Soviet behavior in the Middle East and Eastern Europe . . . the Soviet thrust for Greece touched this vital nerve. Our response was electric.' There was in contrast, in Eugene Rostow's interpretation, a basically different American reaction to the crisis in Palestine:

> While the British quandary in Greece triggered an American response of remarkable dimensions, the British quandary in Palestine resulted only in American hand-wringing, dithering, ineffectiveness, and indeed irresponsibility. For the Middle East, unlike Greece or Turkey, or Iran for that matter, our motto remained the old isolationist battle-cry, 'Let the British do it.'[41]

The argument that the Americans usually depended on the British to hold the line does not provide an entirely adequate explanation, as will be seen in later chapters, but on the whole the unpublished records sustain it to a remarkable degree. The United States supported the British Empire as the predominant regional power. The Greek crisis of 1947 greatly worked to British advantage throughout the Middle East.

---

[41] Eugene V. Rostow, 'Israel in the Evolution of American Foreign Policy', in Clark M. Clifford, Eugene V. Rostow, and Barbara W. Tuchman, *The Palestine Question in American History* (New York, 1978), pp. 56–8.

PART III

BRITISH DEFENCE OF THE MIDDLE EAST

PRELUDE:
TURNING POINTS AND CONTROVERSIES

THE turning point in the revolution in Britain's postwar relations with the Arab states occurred in the winter and spring of 1948. 'The political situation was boiling up', the Secretary of State for Foreign Affairs said to his Middle Eastern advisers in January of that year, and he 'did not agree that we should wait'. With an impatience egged on by intuition, Ernest Bevin believed that the time was opportune to resolve all major Middle Eastern problems in Britain's favour: Egypt, Cyrenaica (the eastern province of Libya), Iraq, Transjordan —everything in other words except Palestine, and even there Bevin hoped that British influence might still prevail. 'We might not get Cyrenaica', he commented in regard to the dispute over the ex-Italian colonies, and the British might 'lose Egypt' if they waited. 'He would like to have the bird in the hand *and* the bird in the bush.'[1]

To clarify the goals that Bevin had in mind, it is illuminating to speculate how a realization of his grand imperial design might have re-established a Pax Britannica in the Middle East and how the forces of Middle Eastern nationalism might have aided the phoenix of the British Empire to live on into a different era as a major world power. In that same discussion about the Cyrenaican bird in the bush and the Egyptian bird nearer to hand (by virtue of the Anglo-Egyptian treaty of 1936), the Permanent Under-Secretary, Sir Orme Sargent, changing the metaphor, commented that Cyrenaica 'was undoubtedly the best "aircraft carrier" in Africa—though admittedly the territory lacked the necessary manpower and other resources'. That remark prompted Bevin to reveal his thoughts about the harnessing of Egyptian nationalism for use as a positive force to strengthen the British Empire. He believed that Egyptian manpower could be utilized to offset the military power of the Soviet Union if the Egyptians were treated on an equal footing:

The Secretary of State spoke of the value to us of Egyptian manpower during the last war, especially as ground personnel for our airfields. He would far rather have properly and technically trained Egyptians at our disposal in the

[1] Minutes of a meeting entitled 'Egypt & Sudan', 10 Jan. 1948, including Bevin, Sir Orme Sargent, Sir Ronald Campbell, Sir Robert Howe, E. Hall-Patch, Michael Wright, Frank Roberts, and Daniel Lascelles, FO 371/69192/J255.

event of war than 10,000 British troops occupying an unwilling country. In the past we had made the mistake of neglecting the potentialities of the Middle East reserve of military manpower.

At this point Bevin affirmed his socialist's belief in racial equality, which was not inconsistent with his emphasis on military potential:

The Russians treated all the different races of the Soviet Union, from the Pacific to the Baltic, on exactly the same footing . . . and the result was that they had at their disposal one vast and homogeneous force. We should do the same. We must exploit the manpower resources of the Middle East by means of joint defence boards set up under treaties between H. M. G. and each of the states concerned. . . . Thus we should have one great Middle Eastern Army. This was the more necessary now that we could no longer count on India as a man-power reserve.[2]

There lay the bare bones of Bevin's Middle Eastern strategy. Treaties would be concluded with Egypt, Iraq, and Transjordan in which those countries would be recognized as entirely independent and sovereign nations. The mutually advantageous ties that bound them together would be tantamount to military alliances and would consolidate British power from the eastern Mediterranean to the Indian Ocean.

The daring breadth and imaginative scope of this grand design was worthy of Lord Curzon and Imperial architects of an earlier era. If it could be achieved, then Palestine could be written off as a minor loss. 'The Jews had always laughed at him', meaning himself, Bevin said, 'when he had told them that we might clear out of Palestine, and had maintained that we never could do so since Palestine was strategically essential to us.' On the contrary, Bevin, like Churchill, believed that Palestine was expendable, though not to be lost without a struggle to maintain British influence. Bevin did not intend to lose focus on the geographical point of greatest Imperial importance, Egypt and the Suez canal; but even Egypt was not indispensable if a strategic fortress could be built in Cyrenaica. 'We must get it out of the heads of the Egyptians', Bevin said, 'that the Canal Zone was essential to us, and that we are consequently dependent on them in all circumstances.'[3]

Bevin had an irrepressible optimism, but he knew that he would not achieve all that he desired even in the best of circumstances. His logic prepared him for an unfavourable outcome as well. If the worst came to the worst the British, failing Egypt, would fall back on Cyrenaica. If international circumstances blocked the building of

[2] 'Egypt & Sudan', 10 Jan. 1948, FO 371/69192/J255.
[3] Ibid.

a strategic base in Cyrenaica, the gravity of Middle Eastern defence would shift to Iraq. If, God forbid, Iraqi nationalism should prevent Iraq from becoming a permanent part of the British defence network, then British imperial defence would ultimately rest in Transjordan. 'Thank God for King Abdullah!'—or, in a more humiliating phrase, 'Mr. Bevin's Little King'. Those phrases summed up the story as it actually could be told by mid-1948. Within a few months it had proved to be as impossible as ever to come to terms with the Egyptians; the base in Cyrenaica remained only a long-range possibility; and Iraqi nationalists aborted new defence arrangements. Only Transjordan stood a steadfast friend. The birth of the state of Israel in May 1948 plunged the Middle East into a war that further undermined British influence. Britain remained the dominant western power in the Middle East, but hardly along the lines of Bevin's heady hopes only a few months earlier. Cyprus appeared to be the only secure Imperial pillar in the eastern Mediterranean (and it too would be severely shaken within a few years).

So barren was the fruit of Bevin's general Middle Eastern policy that critics then and later believed that it would have been decidedly better to have vigorously cultivated the tradition of 'Little England'. In the postwar era the opponents of Imperial expansion found their champion in no less a personage than the Prime Minister. In March 1946 Attlee had challenged the tenets of British imperialism in that part of the world on grounds of economy and the changing nature of British power. He did not believe that Britain's resources could maintain a strategic position in countries of the Middle East, or that the Mediterranean or Red Sea could be defended. The defence of the British Empire now rested on air power as well as on its traditional base of sea power:

> The advent of air power means that instead, as in the era of navalism, of being able to maintain the route by the possession of Malta and Gibraltar and by a friendly attitude on the part of Egypt, we must now provide very large air forces in North Africa, large military forces in Egypt and Palestine and also large sums of money for the deficit areas, such as Cyrenaica and Libya, if we wish to occupy them as air force bases.
>
> In the Red Sea, where formerly we had only to maintain Aden, we have now to keep on good terms with Ibn Saud, and also apparently to occupy Eritrea and Somaliland, which are also deficit areas.[4]

The phrase 'deficit areas' found itself increasingly on the lips of Labour statesmen during the economic crisis of 1946-7. Not with

[4] Memorandum by Attlee, 2 Mar. 1946, DO (46) 27, CAB 131/2; COS (46) 54, CAB 80/100.

a sense of despair but of reality the Chancellor of the Exchequer, Hugh Dalton, wrote in his diary about retrenchment:

C. R. A[ttlee] is inclined to think that it is no good pretending any more that we can keep open the Mediterranean route in time of war. If this is so it means that we could pull troops out from Egypt, and the rest of the Middle East, as well as Greece. Nor could we hope to defend Turkey, Iraq, or Persia against a steady pressure of the Russian land masses. And if India 'goes her own way' before long, as she must, there will be still less point in thinking of Imperial communications through the Suez Canal. We should be prepared to work round the Cape to Australia and New Zealand. If, however, the U. S. A. were to become interested in Middle Eastern oil the whole thing would look different.[5]

Nevertheless Attlee and his colleagues did not yield to the temptation of ruthless imperial liquidation. As Dalton later noted in his memoirs, Attlee's search for 'disengagement and large economies' became 'much toned down'.[6] The reasons lay in the British hope that moderate Arab nationalists would co-operate in preserving British influence, and that the United States would share in the overall defence of the Middle East and contribute to its economic development, as Dalton had anticipated. The British were under no illusion about American motives. If the Americans came to the aid of the British Empire it would not be because of love for British imperialism, but because of the lure of Middle Eastern oil and the fear of Communism and Russian expansion.

The clash between the 'Little Englander' and 'Imperial' ideas about the Middle East should be seen in relation to another sweeping strategic scheme that interested both Attlee and Bevin and other Labour statesmen who now began to see the military as well as economic value of tropical Africa. Its tenet held that Kenya, not Cyrenaica, should be the strategic linchpin in the eastern hemisphere. The bitterness of the controversy that developed on this issue may be inferred from a comment made by the Governor of Kenya, Sir Philip Mitchell, who wrote in June 1948: 'I suppose that the nation that built Singapore could hardly be expected to refrain from building another one in Cyrenaica.'[7] The opponents of a British fortress in the eastern Mediterranean believed, along the lines of Attlee's argument, that the canal and the bases in northern Africa or the Levant could not be held in the event of war and that in any event military, air, or naval bases could not be permanently maintained because of Arab nationalism. In tropical Africa, where the dangers of nationalism

[5] Dalton Diary, 18 Feb. 1946, Dalton Papers.
[6] Hugh Dalton, *High Tide and After* (London, 1962), p. 101.
[7] Mitchell to Poynton, 29 June 1948, CO 537/3514.

seemed remote, a permanent line of British defence could and should be decisively drawn.

With overtones of the scramble for Africa of the 1880s and 1890s, the map of tropical Africa would be painted a new shade of British red from Mombasa to Lagos, with the vital centre in the Sudan. In the Sudan rail or air links could be provided, if the Egyptians were amenable, to Cairo and Cape Town. Cecil Rhodes and Sir Harry Johnston would have cheered from their graves. The proponent of this grandiose plan was again Ernest Bevin. A Lagos–Mombasa axis did not cancel his Suez–Cyrenaica strategy—he wanted both. Dalton's diary is revealing about Bevin's fertile Imperial imagination:

> E. B. is rather fascinated by the Middle East. . . . On the other hand, he is very much attracted by the Lagos–Kenya idea and wants to build a road linking them right across Africa passing through the top of French Equatorial Africa and enabling us, if need be to protect the deposits in the Belgian Congo. He also thinks great trade developments might come between East Africa (including Natal), India and Australia. This would be a triangular ocean trade.[8]

The bubbles of euphoric imperial fantasies soon burst on economic realities such as the cost of road-building in the swamps of the southern Sudan, but it is important to bear in mind that throughout that era the Labour government regarded tropical Africa as a possible fallback position from the Middle East.[9] Retrenchment in the direction of the Sudan and Kenya did not necessarily contradict the withdrawal from the Middle East sometimes acerbically advocated by the Prime Minister.

The 'Kenya Road' and the Sudan played an important part in the Anglo-American political and military conversations of October–November 1947 which have become known as the 'Pentagon Talks'.[10] The British emphasized the question of the Sudan because they believed, correctly, that the Americans insufficiently recognized the strategic importance which British planners attached to the Sudan and because the State Department appeared not to see the difficulties arising from the demands of the Egyptians for 'unity of the Nile

[8] Dalton Diary, 22 Mar. 1946.

[9] See CO 537/1230 ff. The epitaph to the Labour government's Kenya road project was perhaps best inscribed by the *Johannesburg Star*'s reporting of the results of an official mission of inspection in 1951: 'stores were lying in the open, rusted and unusable, and . . . road rollers and electric motors were covered by thick vegetation'. Phillip Darby, *British Defence Policy East of Suez 1947–1968* (London, 1973), p. 38.

[10] For the 'Pentagon Talks' see *Foreign Relations 1947*, V, pp. 485–626; for the American assessment of the 'Central African Road', pp. 528–9: 'Kenya is a Crown Colony and is, therefore, reasonably secure from political complications such as nationalist disturbances.' For the Sudan, pp. 590–1: 'the maintenance of British military facilities in the Sudan is essential to the security of the Middle East and would be in the interest of the maintenance of world peace'. Previously regarded by the Americans as a colonial backwater, the Sudan at British insistence now received recognition as a critical link in world security.

Valley', which would include the Sudan under Egyptian sovereignty. The issue of Egypt and the Sudan even more than the question of British troop withdrawal from Egypt prevented Anglo-Egyptian accord in late 1946 and again in early 1948. 'Whatever suggestions he put to the Egyptians' about the Sudan, Bevin noted later in disgust, 'they turned down' and, in his view, the persistent Egyptian insistence on 'unity' with the Sudan was 'unhelpful', 'hopeless', and 'unfriendly'. 'The Egyptian government had recently behaved almost like an enemy government', Bevin once said.[11] The persistent, post-war Egyptian attitude was an example of the sort of problem the British wished the Americans knew more about in order to acquire a keener understanding of British perplexities in the eastern Mediterranean. On the Sudan and on an array of other problems the British found a sympathetic American ear in the autumn of 1947.

The 'Pentagon Talks' are important for a general understanding of British imperialism in the postwar years because the Americans essentially endorsed British aims. They did so because of the emergency in Greece. It created, in Bevin's frank words, the opportunity to present to the Americans 'for their education' the historic part the British had played in that part of the world as a guardian against Bolshevism. The British could emphasize the importance of the defence of the British Empire as a means of stopping further Russian expansion. For example an official who figured prominently in many of these discussions, R. M. A. Hankey, wrote in May 1947, in lines that expressed British apprehension at Russian ambitions not only in the 'northern tier' of the Middle East but also in the ex-Italian colonies:

> Under no circumstances should we allow the Soviets any foothold beyond the barrier represented by Greece, Turkey and Persia. Their long-term objective is to smash our position with our friends and dependencies overseas and we should, on no account, help them to do so. The Soviet Union has gained a quarter of Roumania, 48% of Poland, all three Baltic States and a fair percentage of Finland to say nothing of exclusive influence in the whole of Eastern Europe beyond the Elbe and the Adriatic. . . .
>
> Even the United States has got a new empire in the Pacific. I suggest that it is now our turn, and that if we are going to hold our own in the Middle East notwithstanding events in Palestine and Egypt (which will eventually have grave repercussions in Iraq) we should think of our own interests [in Cyrenaica] at this point.[12]

The crisis in Greece thus enabled the British to connect the danger of expansion on the periphery of the Middle East with problems that directly confronted them in specific Arab countries.

[11] Minutes of a meeting on Egypt and the Sudan, 12 Mar. 1948, FO 371/69193/J1872.

[12] Minute by R. M. A. Hankey, now head of the Northern Department, 29 May 1947, FO 371/63195.

The Eastern Department of the Foreign Office drew this sharp division of responsibilities on the eve of the Anglo-American talks:

Greece and Turkey are, politically and strategically, the North Western bastions of the Middle East: Greece is under severe politico/military pressure and if it falls under Communist domination the position of Turkey will be seriously weakened. . . .

As primary responsibility for aid to those countries now lies with the United States Government, it is perhaps proper for them to raise issues and for us to concentrate on those Middle East points which are our primary interest.[13]

To use a comparison of Harold Macmillan that has a peculiar relevance to the general crisis of 1947, the British were reacting to the Americans as the Greeks had to the Romans.[14] The British willingly gave advice on problems of Greece, where they wished to become more 'idle', and on the Middle East, where they put forward their more 'advanced' ideas on joint defence, economic development, dollar loans, the Arab League, possible American military missions, supply of military equipment, and many other topics pertinent to British and Arab 'partnership'. The Americans for their part were quite aware of the British aim: 'the British realize their inability to implement their political and economic policy in the Middle East without American help but they hope that such cooperation on our part will not preclude their retention of a certain special position in the area'.[15] The British for their part regarded the talks as an unqualified success. They were glad to be assured, for example, that the Americans did not intend to replace them in Iraq or 'to profit there at our expense', and above all they were pleased to have more explicit reassurances that the State Department would support them in claims to Cyrenaica. One of the leaders of the British delegation, Michael Wright (Assistant Under-Secretary at the Foreign Office) wrote in January 1948: 'The principal result of the Washington talks is that for the first time American policy has crystalised on the line of supporting British policy. It is not the Americans who have altered our policy, but we who have secured American support for our position.'[16]

[13] For this and other 'steering briefs' for the conference see FO 371/61557-59.

[14] See Joseph Frankel, *British Foreign Policy 1945-1973* (London, 1975), pp. 163 and 207, where he develops the imperial analogy with 'the United States . . . assuming British responsibilities and . . . one might say absorbing the imperial ethos'.

[15] See *Foreign Relations 1947*, V, pp. 511-21 for this and other American assessments.

[16] Minute by Michael Wright, 20 Jan. 1948, FO 371/68041. The other British representatives were John Balfour (Minister at the British Embassy); W. D. Allen (Counsellor); T. E. Bromley (First Secretary); and three members of the British Joint Staff Mission, Admiral Sir Henry Moore, Air Chief Marshal Sir Guy Garrod, and General Sir William Morgan. The American representatives were Loy W. Henderson (Director, Office of Near Eastern and African Affairs); John D. Hickerson (Director, Office of European Affairs);

The partnership of the British and the Americans defending the Arabs against Communism and the Russians fuelled the myth of a 'special relationship'. There certainly was a consorting of sorts, but hardly one of the sentimental variety. The British needed American economic and military support, and they wished to preserve as much freedom of action as possible. Bevin stated flatly to his advisers 'that he wanted to keep the Middle East predominantly a British sphere and to exclude the United States militarily from the area'.[17] Sir Orme Sargent distrusted the use to which American military missions might be put in such places as Egypt. Contemplating the lamentable possibility of British withdrawal, he wrote: 'if we pull out of Egypt the Americans should not go in and train and organise the Egyptian Army for use against us in the Sudan and Cyrenaica'.[18] The British generally were suspicious that the Americans might use military and economic influence to the detriment of the British Empire in other parts of the world as well. They refused to discuss further regional agreements.[19] In the British view, the Americans, for reasons of expediency saw benefits that would derive from buoying up the British Empire in the Middle East, but what if they were to press the British to go along with half-baked ideas on, for example, China? There was moreover the question of who and what represented American 'policy' and the extent to which the Americans would prove to be reliable. Michael Wright wrote in reviewing the outcome of the Pentagon talks:

> American decisions are still apt to be taken piecemeal; it is often the case that various Divisions and various levels of the State Department have different and uncorrelated views on policy, and that the American Service Departments hold different opinions from the State Department (if the State Department has a single view). In the background is the White House where pressure from party managers (e.g. over Palestine) may cut across the advice of the State Department and the Service Departments.[20]

The emergency in Greece had driven the British and the Americans into general accord on the Middle East; but the crisis in Palestine in the spring of 1948 came within a hairsbreadth of wrecking it, not least because of the sporadic intervention of the White House.

George F. Kennan (Director, Policy Planning Staff); Raymond A. Hare (Chief, Division of South Asian Affairs); Edward T. Wailes (Chief, Division of British Commonwealth Affairs); Vice Admiral Forrest Sherman (Deputy Chief of Naval Operations); Lieutenant General Lauris Norstad (Director of Plans and Operations, General Staff, US Air Force); and Major General A. M. Gruenther (US Army).

[17] Minutes of a meeting of 8 Oct. 1947, FO 371/61558.

[18] Minute by Sargent, 12 Sept. 1947, FO 371/62984.

[19] See minutes by departmental heads in FO 371/61559 in which it was generally agreed that discussion with the Americans on most other regions would produce friction.

[20] Minute by Wright, 14 Nov. 1947, FO 371/61559.

'Truman's double-cross came as a shattering surprise to everyone here', the British Ambassador in Baghdad wrote three days after the President's recognition of the state of Israel on 14 May 1948.[21] The reasons for the accusation of treachery on the part of Britain's ally in the Middle East will be explained later in the section on Palestine. At this stage for purposes of general comment it is important to emphasize the broader implications of the creation of the state of Israel as they were seen by the British in the aftermath of American recognition. In a 'Green' (highly secret) 'Strategic Appreciation' prepared by the Foreign Office a week and a half after American recognition, Bevin and his advisers attempted to estimate the worldwide as well as the Middle Eastern implications of the new Jewish state. They believed that the conflict itself at best might result in stalemate and at worst in the defeat of Transjordan. Even assuming that the Arab Legion might hold its own, Zionism triumphant would have a catastrophic impact on Arab morale which in turn would affect the Middle Eastern balance of power. The Arabs would know that the United States and the British Empire were divided. 'They see Great Britain and the United States, their natural friends, in conflict. . . . The Arabs may well conclude in despair that there is no clear choice between the West and Communism, and embark on desperate or defeatist courses.' Here is the way in which the Foreign Office judged that the Soviet Union might benefit from the Anglo-American rift:

> There are tremendous material resources especially oil, involved. This may sound mercenary, but our experience of Russian pressure on Persia indicated a desire on her part to get into the Middle East and the Persian Gulf. If she could detach the Eastern world from the West she would gobble up Iraq and make Turkey a satellite, and oil, one of the great resources essential for the material and political recovery not only of Europe but of other parts of the world, will be gone, and enormous power will be placed in the hands of Russia.[22]

In the same spring and summer the British witnessed the fall of Czechoslovakia and experienced the emergency in Berlin. Bevin himself circulated a memorandum to the Cabinet on 'The Threat to Western Civilisation'. Without believing that he expressed undue alarm, Bevin concluded that events in the Middle East as well had taken 'a most unfortunate turn'.

There was a further dimension of the Middle Eastern crisis that particularly affected the British Empire and Commonwealth. The British had to take into account the pro-Muslim sentiment that extended throughout the eastern hemisphere.

[21] Henry Mack to Wright, 17 May 1948, FO 371/68556.
[22] F.O. 'Strategic Appreciation', 24 May 1948, FO 371/68650/E7032/G.

The Arabs are largely Moslems, and . . . there is a closer affinity, from a religious point of view, between them than between almost any other peoples in the world. This religious or communal feeling extends from Morocco, Egypt and the Lebanon as far as Pakistan and Indonesia.

Bevin and his advisers believed that the crystallizing of the Zionist issue brought about by the actual establishment of a Jewish state might unify the entire Muslim world.

Moslems are a fanatical people when roused. It has been the object of British and United States policy to keep Pakistan and India in the Commonwealth, or at least to arrange defence and trade agreements which will keep them within our orbits. But the attitude now adopted by the United Nations on Palestine must sooner or later have the opposite effect . . .

It may well be that, in spite of the present apparent state of disorganisation, the Moslems will under provocation produce a leader or a general, or someone who will bring them together, in which case we may find ourselves faced with a tremendous anti-European movement embracing the whole Arab and Moslem world.[23]

The worldwide consequences of militant and triumphant Zionism might not be immediately apparent, but the Arab experts of the Foreign Office thought there would be a consolidation of Arab forces in the Middle East. 'The Arabs have been divided since 1918 into separate States', Bevin continued. 'They have often quarrelled. There has been a lack of cohesion, but the pressure of the Palestine question, together with what is to them the apparent hostility of a great Power like the United States . . . is having the effect of bringing about cohesion in the Arab . . . world.'[24]

The myth of Arab unity persisted despite the outcome of the Palestine war, but it momentarily was eclipsed by revelations of Arab inefficiency, corruption, and military ineptness. The war of 1948 gave vitality to the corresponding myth of an omnipotent, expansionist, and ruthlessly organized Zionist state that would dominate the Middle East, in words attributed to Ben-Gurion, from the Euphrates to the Nile.[25] The British official who most persistently warned the Foreign Office of the long-range dangers of militant Zionism was Sir John Troutbeck, the head of the British Middle East Office in Cairo. Troutbeck's job was to co-ordinate regional policy. He held passionate views about the rights and wrongs of the Jewish–Arab struggle. His ideas illuminate British thought at one end of the spectrum. Though he was wrong about certain points such as the

[23] FO 'Strategic Appreciation', 24 May 1948, FO 371/68650/E7032/G. After the phrase 'tremendous anti-European' Bevin added, in his own handwriting, '& anti-Western'.

[24] Ibid.

[25] These are the themes of Jon and David Kimche, *A Clash of Destinies: The Arab–Jewish War and the Founding of the State of Israel* (New York, 1960).

influence of Communist immigrants, he identified other problems that critics of Israel believe persist to the present day. According to a Foreign Office minute that reflected Troutbeck's views:

> The Americans are unduly optimistic about the re-establishment of good relations between the Jews and the Arabs even after a peace settlement is reached. The Israeli State will be expansionist. Such immigrants as may reach Israel from behind the Iron Curtain will probably be picked communists. The State of Israel will not be viable and American funds will begin to dry up once 'the drama is taken out of the Palestine question'. Are the United States prepared to maintain Israel as a pensioner in order to avoid the growth of communism in conditions of financial and economic collapse? Such conditions would moreover exacerbate the Jewish urge to expand.[26]

Troutbeck was unabashedly pro-Arab and specifically pro-Egyptian —for moral as well as strategic reasons. On the last point he believed that no other country, not even brave little Jordan, could ever replace Egypt in the defence of the British Empire:

> If we were to lose Egypt, Transjordan's value as an ally would be nil. Is the Arab Legion expected to put the Red Army to rout with no support from us? And where could our support come from except through Egypt, using Egyptian ports, airfields, railways, roads, workshops and labour?[27]

British strategic dependence on Egypt remained, as in the late nineteenth century, inescapable because of geographical circumstances.

Troutbeck's views are important not only because of his position as head of the Middle East Office but also because they represented those of many other Englishmen who believed that a great moral injustice had been done to the Arabs. In his view those who poured scorn on 'the myth of Arab unity' were shortsighted and usually biased. He thought that British sympathy should properly rest with the Arabs. In his reports to the Foreign Office Troutbeck frequently dwelt on the Arab League and its Secretary-General, Azzam Pasha. The Arab League since its founding in the Second World War had not fulfilled the hopes of the Foreign Office Arab experts who thought that it might provide a framework of Arab unity in harmony with British aims. Instead Azzam Pasha had often been denounced as a wild visionary and the goals of the Arab League as 'unrealistic', 'unfriendly', 'childish', and even 'imbecile'. In a secret and personal letter written in March 1949 to Michael Wright, Troutbeck explained why, though he understood the reason for those emotional words, he stood by the Arabs:

---

[26] Minute by J. G. S. Beith, 22 Mar. 1949, FO 371/75064.
[27] Troutbeck to Wright, 3 Mar. 1949, FO 371/75064.

I am very conscious of the moral principles involved in the Palestine question and it was with pain and grief that I saw how little ice they cut in the world at large and even in our own country. For there is no gainsaying the fact that there *is* a moral case in this business and, though I can claim very little affinity with the Arabs whose language I do not understand and whose way of life is utterly strange to me, I feel strongly that the way they have been pushed out of one morally impregnable position after another is a very grave reflection on our western civilisation.[28]

Giving expression to his own feeling about injustice to the Arabs and British moral responsibility, Troutbeck concluded his lament by writing that 'I think it is because Azzam for all his wildness has the same kind of feeling about it [the moral issue] . . . that my sympathies tend to go out to the childish and imbecile Arab League.'

Troutbeck's point of view of course was one of many that had to be taken into account. If there was such a thing as the official mind of British imperialism, it took it a considerable time to reconcile the divergent interpretations, the conflicting emotions, and the lessons of the Palestine war in order to judge the best course for the future. Perhaps as balanced as any other contemporary judgement on the consequences of the 1948 war can be found in a report written by Sir William Strang who, on his assumption of responsibilities as Permanent Under-Secretary at the Foreign Office (on the retirement of Sargent in 1949) toured the Middle East a year after the creation of the state of Israel. In violation of chronological sequence (since Sargent's ideas will be discussed as well), here is an extract from Strang's report that helps to explain the pro-Arab outlook of the Foreign Office:

Sir J. Troutbeck and I visited Azzam Pasha, secretary-general of the Arab League, at his small, plainly furnished flat in Cairo. Except Sir J. Troutbeck, hardly anyone, British or Arab, had a really good word to say for him. Yet he was perhaps the one Arab I had any talk with who was able to look at the Arab world as a whole and not merely in the light of his own personal or local interests or ambitions or jealousies. He may be a dreamer; and the Arab League has broken in his hands. But he seemed to me to have some saving qualities . . .

He understands our economic objectives. . . . But we think too much of treaties and bases. The Middle East is a place where people live, not merely a place to which troops should be sent. . . . The British can have any facilities they want, anywhere. But they must treat the Arabs as friends and gain their trust and confidence, and not seem to care more for bases than for their good will.[29]

[28] Troutbeck to Wright, 3 Mar. 1949, FO 371/75064.
[29] 'Sir William Strang's Tour in the Middle East (21st May–18 June, 1949)', FO 371/75067.

Strang himself did not discount the vitality of the Arab League or its possible chances of a less ignominious future:

In spite of disillusion, sentiment for Arab unity is still strong. The unity of the Arab world is favoured by religion, language and political interest and a common anti-Communist outlook. It is frustrated by dynastic and personal jealousies. . . . In Arab Palestine, there is much opposition to the incorporation of Arab Palestine in Jordan. In other Arab countries, it is seen as no better than a regrettable necessity, in view of the exasperating personality of King Abdullah.[30]

In the aftermath of the Palestine war, Abdullah proved himself as an ally and indeed as the personification of a British protégé; but as a 'landgrabber' he was a source of embarrassment. He made no secret of his desire not only to incorporate Arab Palestine into Transjordan but also to unite his kingdom with Syria under the Hashemite crown. On his return to England, Strang resolved, among other things, to try 'to keep Abdullah from talking too much'.

'No Arab is at heart reconciled to the existence of Israel', Strang wrote. In the Arab view, 'Israel is a canker which unless checked will spread from the Nile to the Euphrates. . . . Even if territorial expansion is averted there is the danger of economic domination of the Arab States by Israel with American assistance.' While taking the Arab view sympathetically into account Strang nevertheless could not help but admire the Jewish achievement:

For all their European culture, they remain an Eastern people, at home in Palestine. When one remembers that Zionism was distilled from the miseries of the ghettoes of Eastern Europe and brought to fruition by the Nazi savageries, it strikes a sympathetic chord to see the Israelis walk as free men in a land of their own, however unjustly acquired.[31]

British sympathy for the plight of the Jews during the Hitler era could not expunge from the official mind the contradictions of the Balfour Declaration. The Jews now had a national home, but one at the expense of the Arab inhabitants. 'The presence of this disruptive alien civilisation', Strang noted, 'is viewed with horror.' Nor would the Arabs find any solution in the foreseeable future. Strang's general assessment presupposed Jewish superiority, an assumption that characterized British and American thought at the time; the Arabs, he wrote, 'face an incalculable new challenge in the dynamic and expansionist State of Israel, vastly superior to them in intelligence, tenacity and purpose, planted among them by superior force

---

[30] Ibid.
[31] Ibid.

and skill, against a futile resistance on their part, the defeat of which has left them humiliated and resentful'.[32]

Writing less than a year after Ernest Bevin had expressed concern about the possible end of the British era in the Middle East because of the imminent intervention of the Russians and the Americans into the Palestine war, which then might erupt into global holocaust, Strang judged that, on the whole, the British had managed to muddle through. 'In spite of everything', he wrote, 'the Arab States have not lost faith in Great Britain.' With unextinguishable British optimism he concluded: 'They have, in truth, no one else to turn to. We are the best of a bad lot.'[33]

The 'official mind of British imperialism', like most mythical creatures, had good moods as well as bad, fits of optimism and pessimism, memories pleasant and ill-boding. Its relevance here is the complex British reaction to Middle Eastern dilemmas. The bureaucratic mind simultaneously responded to diverse international, colonial, and metropolitan influences. In the 1945–8 era in the Middle East, forces of erratic American Palestine policy and super-charged Jewish nationalism were so vibrant that it is perhaps easy to underestimate the less dramatic but no less important dimension of domestic restraint on British imperialism. The mood of the British public would not tolerate a prolonged colonial war in Palestine, no matter the amount of terrorist provocation, against a people savaged by the Nazis. In a period of imperial retrenchment and economic austerity the British public and Parliament also questioned the bolstering of corrupt and reactionary Middle Eastern governments. A mention of the Middle East would immediately bring to mind King Farouk's regime, not least because of the wartime experience of British soldiers who had travelled through the Suez Canal.

On the specific problem of the canal, and on the question of the eastern Mediterranean generally, the British public and those who shaped British policy shared a common set of ideas. Jewish terrorism and Arab recalcitrance in Palestine might cause the British to reflect whether the game was worth the British candle. Egyptian corruption might cause those who supported the Labour government as well as ministers themselves to ponder the discrepancy between the welfare state in England and the gap between rich and poor in Egypt. Yet the Suez Canal remained vital to all British calculations. One of its principal justifications in imperial defence, the protection of the Indian empire, might no longer exist, but it remained the principal

[32] 'Sir William Strang's Tour in the Middle East (21st May–18th June, 1949)', FO 371/75067.   [33] Ibid.

route to the East and a symbol of Imperial power. Substitute bases such as one in Cyrenaica might be planned, but there was no substitute for control over the canal itself. In Strang's words, 'The Middle East is important strategically because it shields Africa. . . . The strategic key to this area is Egypt, to which there is no practical alternative as a main base.'[34] Yet the Foreign Office and Chiefs of Staff could make plans for the defence of Egypt and the canal only if the Egyptians wished British protection and—no less important—only if the British public and Parliament thought the Egyptians worth defending.

The Egyptian problem, and the domestic restraints on solving it, held a prominent place in the mind of Sir Orme Sargent, Strang's predecessor, in the months before his retirement in early 1949. Sargent's thought, like Strang's, may be taken as representative of the 'official mind' disagreeably forced into generalization on diverse and often paradoxical problems, in this case on the unsatisfactory resolution of Egyptian issues at the time of succeeding generations of Egyptian nationalists, Arabi, Zaghlul, and now Sidky and Nokrashi. Sargent himself could reflect on nearly three decades of unhappy Anglo-Egyptian relations, including the time when they had to be resolved forcibly, as Lord Killearn had done in 1942 by surrounding the Royal Palace with British tanks in order to persuade Farouk to adopt a more enthusiastic pro-British attitude. Sargent had pondered the 'irrational' demands of the Egyptian nationalists for withdrawal of British troops and he believed that the 'fickle' Egyptians would not prove to be reliable allies even if a new treaty of friendship could be negotiated. In February 1949 he wrote a lengthy letter to the British Ambassador in Cairo reminding him that the Foreign Office had only a limited amount of sympathy for the Egyptians because of wariness in Parliament. In general the British public held the Egyptians in low esteem. The letter is an unusual and trenchant example of the 'official mind' taking into account the sentiment of British 'public opinion'.

There was one point, according to Sargent, that had a fundamental bearing on Britain's position in the Middle East which was probably easier to gauge in London than in Cairo. 'I am referring', he wrote, 'to the unpopularity of Egypt among Ministers and in Parliament, and among the general public.' Time and again the Foreign Office and Chiefs of Staff in a spirit of goodwill had tried to adjust the relations of the two countries on the basis of a 'partnership' and mutual defence, but what had been the result? To Sargent it could be summed up in the phrases 'Egyptian sabotage' and 'scurrilous abuse'.

[34] Memorandum by Strang, 30 Apr. 1949, FO 371/73502.

He went on to emphasize the profound aversion of the British public towards the Egyptians that had been shaped as a result of unfortunate wartime experience of British soldiers.

If opinion in higher circles towards Egypt is bad, it is just the same, if not worse, among the general public whose views have been largely influenced by the hundreds of thousands of soldiers who passed through Egypt at some stage or other during the war. They now form a large element in what constitutes public opinion, and their views on Egypt and the Egyptians are almost consistently unfavourable. The recollection of the average soldier is of a corrupt ruling class with a King who was credibly believed to be plotting with the Axis powers. His recollection of the Egyptian people is that they profiteered, swindled him, and if they could, robbed him.

Above all he remembers that the Egyptians did not fight. The returned soldier then compares the Egyptians as he remembers him with the Arab. He may not have had much to do with the genuine Arab but his Pecksniffian notion of the Arab is, however, a favourable one for he has heard a lot of stories of how the Bedouin Arab helped our Commandos. . . . He also sharply differentiates the Arab from the Egyptian whom he does not regard as an Arab at all. All this may be incorrect, unjust or sloppily romantic, but the fact is that myths are much more powerful than realities, and the myth of the despicable Egyptian and the stout-hearted Arab is one which is propagated throughout the country by these hundreds of thousands of returned soldiers, and is a fundamental element in British public opinion on the Middle East.[35]

Giving reign to his own indignation, Sargent lamented that since the return of British troops the Egyptians had done virtually nothing to promote good feeling between the two countries: 'Since their return to this country, nothing has happened in Egypt to correct the possibly false impressions of these soldiers. On the contrary, the riots, assassinations, outrages against British soldiers etc., are to them only additional proof of the general beastliness of the Egyptian.'[36]

Sargent now turned to the question of the corrupt Egyptian monarchy. It seemed to symbolize everything with which the Labour government in England did not wish to be associated. It could not be said, he continued, 'that the personality and conduct of King Farouk . . . which are naturally popular features in the Press have done anything to create the slightest respect for Egypt among the rest of the British public who, already infected by the tales of the returned soldier traveller, have come to regard him as the epitome of all Egyptians'. The British in short regarded Farouk's regime as weak and corrupt. It would be a mistake, concluded another official, the

---

[35] Sargent to Campbell, Confidential, 2 Feb. 1949, FO 371/73502/J768.

[36] Ibid. For Campbell's response see his letter to Strang of 26 Feb. 1949, Personal, FO 371/73502/J1952: 'Egypt is an *essential* factor in our strategic problem. . . . We cannot afford the lunacy of being angry with Egypt.'

head of the Egyptian Department, 'to hitch our wagon' to Farouk's chariot because it might be likely 'to collapse in the very near future'.[37]

How could the British place themselves on the side of moderate reform? It was a dilemma by no means confined to Egypt. On occasion the situation in Iraq seemed just as bad if not worse: 'Corruption and inefficiency are unfortunately to be found at all levels and among all classes of Arabs in general and Iraqis in particular.'[38] To pose the question in its bluntest form, as Sir Stafford Cripps did after he became Chancellor of the Exchequer, 'why do we', a Labour government, 'support reactionary selfish and corrupt governments in the Middle East instead of leaders who have interests of their people at heart?' The general answer of the Foreign Office should perhaps be borne in mind while studying the more detailed problems of British imperialism in the postwar era. The short reply, according to Michael Wright, was that 'we have never deliberately done so'. The British tried to promote self-government, which was not necessarily good government; indeed it often meant that government 'in these countries tends to fall into the hands of unscrupulous and self-seeking politicians'. The British could only exert political and economic pressure as discreetly as possible in the hope 'of social progress and the raising of the standards of living of the population'. Here was the general line of the 'official mind of British imperialism' candidly expressed by Michael Wright, who wrote from a background of Egyptian experience as well as from his position as Assistant Under-Secretary supervising Middle Eastern policy:

> The moral is, I suggest, that we must maintain our friendly pressure in the interests of good government, being prepared hand in hand with financial assistance and the provision of technical experts to push the case for social reform very hard when necessary, and being also prepared to give considerable backing to the best elements. This may at times bring us very near to the border of internal interference, or even across it.[39]

To the British public, Egypt might remain, in the popular phrase, 'the land of dirty postcards', but the Labour government would attempt to clean up Eygpt and other reactionary countries, provide economic and social development, and preserve the Middle East as part of Britain's informal empire.

The Egyptians rightly inferred that the condescending British attitude held them to be deficient in 'national character'. They also detected more than cultural arrogance. The British might talk about

[37] Minute by G. L. Clutton, 30 July 1948, FO 371/69193/J5239.

[38] Minute by Michael Wright, 19 Mar. 1949, FO 371/75064.

[39] Minute by Wright, 19 Mar. 1949, FO 371/75064, with notation by Bevin that the Prime Minister should see the minute.

'inefficiency' and 'corruption', but in effect were they not rational-
izing the continued occupation? Was it indeed true that the
Egyptians were so lacking in technological sophistication that there
could be no question of their managing the Suez base, at least
in the near future? In the Sudan was not the historic Egyptian
presence in the Nile valley as much of a 'civilizing mission' as the
more recent and spectacular advent of the British? Did not the
'defence of the West' in fact mean the preserving of the British
Empire? Those were questions that troubled American critics of
British imperialism as well as Egyptians favourably disposed to the
British cause.

In the following chapters of this section, no attempt will be made
systematically to examine the less conspicuous and tacit side of the
American 'partnership' in the Middle East. Ultimately the support
given by the Americans to the British is perhaps best understood
negatively as an attempt to prevent the 'vacuum' that might occur
if the British Empire were to collapse. It is thus important to bear in
mind the American anti-colonial tradition which in this period was
more dormant than previously but nevertheless to the British a
potent force. Part of the purpose of economic development and
social reform was to justify the British Empire in the eyes of the
Americans as well as the British public. The British in this period
were keenly aware that they still held dominant power in the Middle
East, and that the immediate future would tell whether the British
Empire would revive or become a spent force. If it were again to
flourish there needed to be no less than a moral regeneration of the
Imperial mission. The British took the initiative in issues of *realpolitik* as well. One of the keys to the era is an understanding of the
way in which they attempted to sustain their regional hegemony by
gaining American assistance (as in the 'Pentagon Talks') and by
cutting losses (as in the case of Greece and eventually Palestine). In
short they aimed to consolidate their position, if possible, in the
'Central' (i.e. British) 'Arab World' of Egypt, Cyrenaica, Iraq, and
Transjordan.

　　The chapters in this section will trace the major developments in
the Arab states as the British attempted to implement their policies
up to the summer of 1948. Many of the issues of substance had
nothing to do with Zionism, but the war of 1948 should be regarded
as a turning point in Britain's postwar Middle Eastern fortunes. As
Strang suggested in his report that has been quoted at length, there
are basically two ways in which the general significance of this watershed can be assessed. The one is the optimistic view that Strang

emphasized. The British had managed to muddle through and could now devote full energies to economic development and social reform —and even finally to the reconciliation of Jew and Arab. The other more sceptical view holds that the British Empire, which had reached an unprecedented peak of military and territorial dominion during the Second World War, had now suffered a major defeat and was on its way to expulsion from the Middle East. The following summary will comment briefly on the major events that suggest such ambiguous yet complementary themes.

One of the central ambiguities of the postwar period lies in the British attitude towards the question of Arab unity. This is the theme of the second chapter. On the 22nd of March 1945 the heads of delegations from the Arab states signed a pact that created the League of Arab states. Publicly the British government welcomed this development. Secretly the official mind was much more ambivalent. This tension between wishing the Arabs well and the apprehension that Arab unity might not be compatible with British overlordship had existed at least since the time of the military campaigns of 1941 (almost as if the history of the First World War was grotesquely repeating itself). It is important to grasp the connection between British statements that encouraged Arab aspirations, on the one hand, and, on the other, the British occupation of Iraq of May 1941. For the British this was the time of their darkest hour. They not only faced Rommel's armies in the Western Desert but also a pro-axis government in Baghdad and the possibility of a German breakthrough into the Fertile Crescent that would mean the loss of the oil of Iraq. The legacy of the brief regime of Rashid Ali and the four colonels of the 'Golden Square', who harboured anti-British sentiments and pan-Arab ambitions, will be discussed in the chapter on Iraq. Here the significant point is the statement made by the Foreign Secretary, Anthony Eden, on 29 May 1941:

> This country has a long tradition of friendship with the Arabs, a friendship that has been proved by deeds, not words alone. . . . The Arab world has made great strides since the settlement reached at the end of the last War, and many Arab thinkers desire for the Arab peoples a greater degree of unity than they now enjoy. In reaching out towards this unity they hope for our support. No such appeal from our friends should go unanswered. It seems to me both natural and right that the cultural and economic ties between the Arab countries, and the political ties too, should be strengthened. His Majesty's Government for their part will give their full support to any scheme that commands general approval.[40]

Eden's words helped to emphasize that Britain's presence in the Middle East served a higher purpose than mere military occupation.

[40] Kirk, *The Middle East in the War*, p. 334.

They were spoken at a time of military extremity and dire need for Arab friendship. Once recorded, they could not be expunged. Like other wartime promises, the pledges in support of Arab unity stood to be redeemed.

During the Syrian campaign of June–July 1941, the British consistently upheld the principle that Syria and Lebanon should become independent states at the end of the war. 'Syria shall be handed back to the Syrians', in Churchill's words. At the same time he assured the French that they would have 'the dominant superior position in Syria'. Chapter three deals with the crisis in the Levant in May 1945, at which time those commitments had to be met. The British were caught between the irreconcilable attempts by the Syrians and Lebanese to achieve complete independence, and by the French to re-establish their former position. Why had the war been fought? Not for territorial aggrandizement or 'imperialism', especially of the French variety. The issue of independence in the Levant became a test case of whether or not the British would fulfil their wartime promises. It had profound implications for all of the Arab world. Once Syria and Lebanon gained unfettered independence, none of the other Arab countries would settle for anything less.

The question of Libyan independence also had its origins in British wartime pledges. On the 8th of January 1942 the Foreign Secretary promised the Senusi of Cyrenaica that they would never again be subjected to Italian domination. Chapter seven may be read as a study in which the British attempted to resolve the perplexities of self-determination in Libya, Eritrea, and Somalia—with one over-riding consideration: Cyrenaica would provide an alternative strategic base if they were forced to withdraw from Suez. This is the key to the puzzle of Libya and it helps to answer many other complicated questions during the whole of the postwar era.

Of the critical periods associated with wartime antecedents of postwar problems, the date of the 4th of February 1942 deserves special emphasis. At that time Sir Miles Lampson (Lord Killearn) presented an ultimatum to King Farouk to abdicate or install a Wafd nationalist regime under Nahas Pasha (who in the event successfully collaborated with the British during the rest of the war). The ultimatum was presented with a blatant show of force. British tanks surrounded the Royal Palace and Lampson did not disguise his pleasure in humiliating the young King. It was a demonstration of British power that rankled not only with Farouk but also the younger nationalists, not least Gamal Abdel Nasser. Anthony Eden wrote shortly afterwards: 'The fact that *we* put Wafd in will be known to all Cairo, tanks troops etc. Yet I remain convinced that on main lines our policy was right.'[41] Intervention was justified on grounds of wartime exigency. The major way in which the postwar Labour government attempted to break with this imperialist tradition was in its pursuit of a non-interventionist policy. The end of the Killearn era on the 9th of March 1946 may be taken as a symbol of Ernest Bevin's determination to turn a page in Anglo-Egyptian history.

At the close of the war there was passionate hope within the Labour government that relations with Egypt could be placed on a new and equal footing. As the intractable nature of the Suez problem became more apparent, the question of the Canal Zone cast a shadow over all of the eastern Mediterranean. The failure to come to terms with the Egyptians caused the British to take a hard look at alternative sites for a strategic base, notably in Cyrenaica but also Cyprus. According to critics of the Labour government, the problem of Cyprus might have been decisively resolved by the cession of the island to Greece after the end of the Second World War. Chapter five is devoted to the attention given to this question by the Labour government in 1945–7. Rightly or wrongly the opportunity was not seized. As the talks with the Egyptians became more and more difficult and as Cyprus became a point of discussion in the beginning of the cold war, the Greek solution faded irrevocably.

At the close of the war there were over 250,000 British troops in Egypt. The Labour government aimed to reduce this number to the 10,000 specified by the Anglo-Egyptian treaty of 1936 for peace-time garrisoning of the Canal Zone. This was one of the two fundamental issues in Anglo-Egyptian relations. The other was in the Sudan. Chapter six deals with the British attempt to find a solution in the critical year following the end of the war. On the 7th of May 1946 Attlee announced that British troops would be withdrawn if a satisfactory alternative could be found. In other words, if the British indicated their good faith by announcing their intention to evacuate, then presumably the Egyptians would be reasonable enough to conclude a defence agreement. That was the logic of the Labour government, and with it Bevin actually reached tentative accord with the Egyptian Prime Minister, Sidky Pasha, in October. The 'Sidky-Bevin Protocol' specified stages of troop withdrawal (but with the right of British re-entry) and acknowledged Egyptian symbolic sovereignty in the Sudan (but with the right of the Sudanese to self-determination). The Sudan, not evacuation, proved to be, in Bevin's reiterated phrase, the 'stone wall' that blocked agreement between the British and the Egyptians throughout the period of the Labour government. The breakdown in late 1946 ultimately proved to be irreparable.

[41] Minute by Eden, 8 Feb. 1942, FO 371/31567.

'Palestine' was not an issue that aroused the same intensity of emotion in Egypt as the slogans of 'evacuation' and 'unity of the Nile valley'. Nevertheless the anti-Zionist campaign complemented the anti-British movement in Egypt. Egyptian leaders rose to the occasion to prove themselves no less anti-Zionist, in rhetoric at least, than the other Arab comrades-in-arms. These interlocking causes worked to British disadvantage. The Egyptians took their complaint about the British occupation to the United Nations in August 1947. They lost their case, but they were able to champion the anti-colonial as well as the anti-Zionist movement.

The enigma was the King of Saudi Arabia. Though Ibn Saud denounced the Jews as passionately as any Arab nationalist, the question was whether he would cancel the American oil concession as a tangible protest against the support given to the Zionist cause by the United States government. Chapter four deals with this question as it came to a head in late 1947 and early 1948. It also traces the evolution of the British attitude towards the American presence in Saudi Arabia from the time of the war years. Far from viewing the Americans as having cornered the potentially most valuable part of the Arabian peninsula, the British regarded the exploitation of oil as the only possible way for the Americans to become committed to the development and defence of the region. The British nevertheless anticipated that Ibn Saud would follow their lead in planning for regional pacts in the winter and spring of 1948. The collapse of the plans to include Saudi Arabia in a network of British alliances proved to be only one of many disappointments during that tumultuous year.

The beginning of British misfortune in 1948 was the abortive treaty with Iraq signed at Portsmouth on the 15th of January. The reasons for this débâcle have already been touched on in these introductory remarks and will be developed further in chapter eight. The British miscalculated the temper of Iraqi nationalism. The only Arab state to conclude a new treaty of alliance was Transjordan on the 15th of March. At that time the Arabs and the Jews were already in fact at war for the possession of Palestine, though the mandate did not terminate until the 15th of May. The last chapter discusses the possible ways in which the struggle might have ended favourably for King Abdullah as well as for the British themselves. Most of Arab Palestine would have been absorbed by Transjordan. On the eve of the Arab–Israeli war the British were apprehensive about its outcome, but virtually no one anticipated the extent of the Arab collapse and the Zionist victory. This reflection is somewhat to anticipate another part of the book, but one of the themes that runs through these chapters is the essential British commitment to the Arab cause as one ultimately compatible with their own sense of mission in the Middle East, and the growing conviction that a grave injustice was being perpetrated because of American support for the Zionists.

2

THE ARAB LEAGUE

IN ONE of the most astute contemporary assessments of the founding of the Arab League in March 1945, the British Ambassador in Cairo, Lord Killearn, observed that 'the influence of Egypt is a determining factor in the present evolution of Arab States'. He believed that Arab union had been achieved 'only on paper', and that the 'Egypto-Arab *bloc*' would preserve their previous conflicting rivalries.[1] Without British 'good offices' the Arab League might disintegrate. Some might argue, Killearn continued, that a return to the tried and true principle of 'divide and rule' might best promote long-range British security in the Middle East. Killearn, and most of the Middle East experts of the Foreign Office, did not agree with that view. As has been emphasized in the previous chapter, in 1941 Anthony Eden, in a celebrated statement that had become the axiom of British policy, had sympathetically though vaguely endorsed the goal of Arab unity. In 1943 he further encouraged the political and economic co-operation of the Arab states. In 1945 the Foreign Office reaffirmed the wisdom of not impeding Arab union. In Killearn's words, 'we have a long-term interest in promoting through Arab co-operation the material welfare and the satisfaction of the sentimental aspirations of these countries as far as our Imperial interests permit'. There was a *realpolitik* that underlay this circumspect sanction of a 'sentimental' venture. To perpetuate 'the balkanisation of the Arab world', Killearn concluded, would lead 'to material retrogression which militates to

---

[1] Killearn to Eden, No. 80, 23 Mar. 1945, FO 371/45237/E2091. In the Colonial Office the official who most attentively followed developments in the Arab world at this time, Sir Arthur Dawe (Deputy Under-Secretary), used almost identical language to express the same sentiment. In particular he commended Killearn, a kindred soul, for giving 'a realistic assessment' (Minute by Dawe, 3 Apr. 1945, CO 732/88/79238). The wartime years and the founding of the Arab League are examined fully and perceptively by Ahmed M. Gomaa, *The Foundation of the League of Arab States* (London, 1977). See also especially two essays by Elie Kedourie, 'Pan-Arabism and British Policy', in *The Chatham House Version* (London, 1970); and 'Arab Unity Then and Now', in *Islam in the Modern World* (London, 1980). Robert W. Macdonald, *The League of Arab States* (Princeton, 1965), is concerned with the organization and function of the League. It has a useful bibliography which should be used in conjunction with Gomaa's. Ralph M. Coury, 'Who "Invented" Egyptian Arab Nationalism?', *International Journal of Middle East Studies*, 14 (1982), is an important reassessment both of the history of the founding of the Arab League and the development of Egyptian nationalism at a critical stage.

provoke discontent in a large area lying across our lines of communications and containing our vital oil interests'.[2]

It is important to grasp the significance of Egyptian participation in the Arab League in order to understand the British response to the problems of the Middle East in the closing months of the war. Killearn described Egypt as a 'new element'. The pan-Arab movement associated with the Hashemites and Nuri al-Said since the time of the First World War had become transformed by 1945 into an association of Arab states under Egyptian leadership. Nuri, who more than anyone else could be described as the architect of the Arab League, had persuaded the Egyptian Prime Minister, Nahas Pasha, to take the initiative. Nuri's ideas will be discussed in more detail in the chapter below on Iraq. Here the main point is that he had hoped that Egypt might neutralize the hostility of the Hashemites and the Saudis. Instead there developed a rivalry between Egypt and Iraq for the League's leadership. Again Killearn's analysis is of considerable interest because it reflects the views of a latter-day proconsul in Egypt at the critical time of the Arab League's establishment:

> The Hashemites and Nuri, so intimately associated with the Arab Movement from its early stages, were not unnaturally piqued at being ousted by a newcomer [i.e. Egypt] from the major rôle. By a natural process Ibn Saud aligned himself with Egypt against his old enemies, the Hashemites and Nuri. The Lebanon, which was fearful of domination by a still uneuropeanised Moslem hinterland, naturally followed suit, regarding Egypt as more modernised and less fanatical than Syria and Iraq. . . .

Killearn went on, with not too delicate a brush, to paint the contrasting tones of rivalry between the Hashemites and most of the rest of the Arab world, which could now be limned as the Egyptian 'bloc':

> Syria, which at the beginning was not enthusiastically pro-Egypt, has gradually evolved towards Egypt owing to the desire of the present governing elements in Syria to preserve the republican régime and their apprehension of Hashemite designs on Syria. King Farouk has always treated the Emir Abdullah very superciliously and there is no love lost between them. Moreover, inevitably a Hashemite Emir, with his dreams of a Syrian throne, would find himself in the opposite camp to that of the present Syrian ruler. It was equally inevitable that, in spite of rivalries between Abdallah and the Iraqi Royal family over Syria, the two Hashemite Powers should find themselves standing together against the Egyptian *bloc*.[3]

---

[2] Killearn to Eden, No. 80, 23 Mar. 1945, FO 371/45237/E2091.

[3] Ibid. An official in the Eastern Department, Victor Holt, noted in regard to Egyptian leadership: 'Once Egypt was persuaded to join the Arab Unity Movement, her wealth and advanced civilisation naturally gave her the leadership. It would be ridiculous for Iraq to

In short the Egyptians had succeeded in isolating the Hashemites within the Arab League.

Killearn was a past master at portraying prominent personalities and the shaping of events. He continued his pastiche of recent Arab history:

> Nahas Pasha wished to strengthen his internal prestige by posing as a leader of the Arab world, and King Farouk wished to strengthen his throne by assuming a similar rôle. King Ibn Saud was, from the beginning, opposed to the idea of Arab Union because he feared it would mean a Hashemite domination of the Fertile Crescent with the consequent danger to his own position in the Hejaz. Hence his determination to *saboter* any northern combination. . . . Ibn Saud . . . [was] kept within the League largely by the influence of Egypt.[4]

Despite his colourful discourse on Arab rivalries, Killearn believed that the aspiration for Arab unity would be a 'permanent factor' with which the British would be well advised to come to grips if they wished to see stability in the Middle East. Above all there would be a solidarity of Arab effort to get rid of the French in the Levant and to prevent the Zionist domination of Palestine. In that sense the Arab League was anti-imperialist. Whether or not the Arabs could unite on positive measures of political integration was the subject of controversial speculation.

Before going on further to examine the quite mixed and contradictory British reactions to the birth of the Arab League, it is helpful to look briefly at the Arab side of the question. In the spring of 1947, two years after the founding of the League and at a time when the Palestine controversy entered its penultimate stage, an article appeared in the *Middle East Journal* entitled 'The Arab League in Perspective'. Its author was Cecil Hourani, at that time secretary of the Arab Office in Washington. His purpose was to explain Arab nationalism to the American audience. It remains perhaps the clearest contemporary exposition of the nature and purpose of the Arab League published in English, and thus is useful in comparing western ideas at the time. Cecil Hourani dwelt on 'the spirit of popular Pan-Arabism' rather than on the controversies among Arabs themselves (though his account did not contradict Killearn's secret analysis). He argued against the French accusation that the Arab League was merely a British 'trick' to oust France from the Levant, and also against the Zionist interpretation prevalent in the United States that the Arab League had been invented by the British in

---

compete for this position. Neither Egypt nor Syria (which regards herself as a far more advanced State than Iraq) could be expected to permit Iraq to play a leading rôle.' Minute of 29 Mar. 1945, FO 371/45237/E2091.

[4] Killearn to Eden, 23 Mar. 1945, ibid.

order to frustrate the establishment of a Jewish state. He held that the Arab League represented a victory for moderate Arab nationalists and for 'secular liberalism' in Arab thought:

> The League is sometimes accused by ill-wishers of being reactionary, xeno-phobic, Pan-Islamic. An examination both of the actions of the League and of the personalities who created it is a sufficient refutation of these charges. The framers of the League were men brought up in the tradition of 19th century liberalism, not in the tradition of the Pan-Islamic movement which has long ceased to be an effective force in Arab politics, if indeed it ever was, nor in the tradition of 20th century totalitarian movements. The ideas of Mazzini express perhaps better than any others the dominant concepts of the Arab nationalist spirit incorporated into the League.[5]

The ideas and motivation of Arab nationalism thus bore certain similarities with European nationalism.

Though the ideas of Arab nationalism were not recondite, Cecil Hourani warned against the danger of drawing direct parallels. Pan-Arabism was not comparable with pan-Slavism. There was a funda-mental difference between Arab and European ideologies. European nationalism derived from the idea of the state inherited from the traditions of Roman law and society, and from the concept of 'a homogeneous racial group'. Arab nationalism by contrast was not built on the concept of a strong sovereign state, nor was Arab society 'exclusively racial' but rather composed of 'heterogeneous groups bound together by a common Arab culture and world of thought'. Cecil Hourani believed that western observers made their most funda-mental error by failing to grasp the heterogeneous character of Arab society which nevertheless shared common ideas and cultural values. From his concluding comment one may still infer today that Arab 'unity' may never come about along the lines of European develop-ment, but that the idea of a real union among the Arabs is deeply rooted in the minds of the Arab people.

There are three points of Cecil Hourani's analysis which are especially relevant to an examination of the British official mind of 1945. The first is how the British perceived the strength of sentiment in favour of Arab unity in relation to the heterogeneous nature of Arab society. The second is the question whether the issue of Palestine

---

[5] Cecil A. Hourani, 'The Arab League in Perspective', *Middle East Journal*, I, 2 (April 1947), p. 134. Eliahu Epstein, the representative of the Jewish Agency in Washington, had written in January 1947 in a memorandum that reveals Jewish perceptions of the Anglo-Arab connection: 'Cecil Hourani . . . together with his older brother Albert . . . became one of the active promoters of the Arab National Cause and, as a member of the inner circle established during the war by Brigadier Clayton in Cairo, had a share in formulating the broad lines of Foreign Office policy in the Arab world.' Memorandum by Epstein, 6 Jan. 1947, CZA S25/6618.

would foster an effective Arab unity in action or merely a united but ineffective sentiment against the Jews and perhaps against the British as well. The third is the extent to which the Arab League was a British 'invention'. As will already have been gathered, the British had made official pronouncements in favour of Arab unity and had observed the creation of the Arab League with considerable scepticism and suspicion. By the time that Cecil Hourani wrote his essay in the spring of 1947, the words 'Frankenstein's monster' were a recurrent phrase in the secret minutes of the Foreign Office.

The minutes of R. M. A. Hankey provide insight into British assessments of Arab nationalism. Hankey served in the Eastern Department of the Foreign Office before he became head of the Northern Department in 1945, and his views are thus of particular interest then and later in regard to Russia as well as Palestine. He had spent part of the war in Cairo and Teheran (and had some knowledge of Persian). He held informed opinions which were bluff and quintessentially British. He believed that the divisive forces in the Arab world would prevail, though he recognized a certain sentiment in favour of unity:

> There is a unity about the Middle East which all Arabs feel but it is very easy to overstate the practical applications of this feeling. Egypt with its semi-African population and peculiar traditions, Syria so much the intellectual centre of Arabia, the Lebanon with its Christian population, Palestine with its Jews, the fanatical Nejdis in Saudi Arabia, and the population of Iraq scattered over such a colossal area and having such different problems that even though they feel in a similar way about a number of subjects, one cannot for purposes of Government easily treat them on a parallel basis.[6]

In Hankey's view it would be best to encourage the Arabs 'gently' in the direction of some sort of union without holding out much hope for eventual success. He believed it would definitely be a mistake for the British themselves to try to take the lead in promoting Arab unity because the Arabs then would regard British guidance as 'a new and devilish interference with their independence and a crafty imperialistic way of creating a new dominion'. There were other and better ways, Hankey concluded, 'to get something useful'.[7]

[6] Minute by Hankey, 28 Jan. 1945, FO 371/45250. Hankey wrote in response to an article in *The Economist* entitled 'Middle Eastern Unity' (27 Jan. 1945) which had criticized the Foreign Office for a 'policy of drift'. 'Except as regards Palestine', Hankey retorted, 'where we are all at sixes and sevens, it is incorrect to taunt [the Foreign Office] . . . with not having a policy in the Middle East. . . . It should be obvious to anybody that what we are aiming at in the Middle East is the creation of a number of respectable independent States which will rely upon the Western powers for advice and help in coping with their very difficult and intricate technical problems.'

[7] Ibid.

At the time of the birth of the Arab League, Hankey wrote an important minute epitomizing general British policy. Hankey's views about the Arabs were unvarnished to the point of being artless; but his colleagues found his ideas persuasive. 'I agree with everything Mr. Hankey has written', wrote the head of the Egyptian Department. 'So do I', noted the head of the Eastern Department: '. . . it is the policy which we have been pursuing for a long time now.'[8] Hankey's synoptic minute therefore may be taken as representative of inner-Foreign Office thought, and, because of his ingenuousness, revealing. His main point was that the Arab League should be looked upon as a means to promote British policy in the future and that his colleagues might pause to benefit from the lessons of the recent past:

> *Divide et impera* may be a risky motto for us in the future, for others may well profit by the divisions for their own ends. The Balkans are a lesson of what is liable to happen when the Great Powers compete in creating divisions and in backing rival blocs; but whereas we failed to create any local solidarity in the Balkans in spite of many attempts, the local States have done it themselves with relatively small encouragement in the Middle East. I suggest that there will be real advantages in the future in promoting solidarity among the Arab States and in encouraging them to look to us for leadership and help, as there is a strong tendency for them to do.[9]

Hankey's ingenious idea was to let the Arabs themselves sustain British influence. If the British were to sponsor a regional organization for defence purposes, for example, then the Americans, the Russians, the French, and everyone else, including even the Turks and the Persians, would have to be included. 'We should be in a great minority among the outside Powers and this would diminish our prestige and influence in the Arab States of the Middle East.' Thus to Hankey's mind there were great advantages to an Arab League which would look to the British for 'leadership'. 'We should be able to influence its activities much more than any other Power can.' Taking a broad look over the Middle East horizon, he re-emphasized that 'the Arab League is not bad from our point of view'. He did inject one note of doubt, which indeed he identified as 'the principal danger'. Abdul Rahman Azzam, an Egyptian, had been appointed Secretary-General of the Arab League. Hankey feared that, instead of working with the British on problems of economic and social development, Azzam might 'concentrate instead on the more showy but more dangerous and useless task of stirring up the Arabs'.[10]

---

[8] Minutes by Patrick Scrivener and Charles Baxter, 6 and 8 Apr. 1945, FO 371/45237/E2091.

[9] Minute by Hankey, 30 Mar. 1945, FO 371/45237/E2091.

[10] Ibid.

British forebodings about Azzam proved to be well founded. In the postwar years Azzam's name became virtually synonymous with the Arab League and its anti-British, pro-Egyptian thrust. His critics denounced him for usurping the power of the League and creating a sort of personal dictatorship. Zionists saw in him the 'fanatical' traits of their Arab adversaries; Nuri regarded him as an 'unbalanced' rival; and the Foreign Office, in a phrase with which everyone could agree, looked upon him as a 'volatile' personality. There was truth in each outlook, though even his enemies granted him an unfeigned earnestness of purpose which transcended personal ambition and narrow nationalism. Azzam had shaped his ideas about pan-Arabism against the background of his struggle against the Italians in Libya since the time of the First World War.[11] The scope of his ideas about pan-Arabism had a northern Africa dimension to them which the British, not to mention the French, wished he would restrict to the central Arab world. Azzam himself was unabashedly an Egyptian nationalist as well as one of the foremost exponents of pan-Arab idealism. He did not believe that Egyptian nationalism and pan-Arabism were in the least contradictory, and consistently held that Egypt would be the natural leader of the Arab League—perhaps because of his belief in the superior quality of the Egyptian national character. 'I do not deny, and no one denies', he once stated, 'that Egypt is the first nursery of mankind. God singled it out above all other nations. This is a characteristic of Egypt, and this is what always made of Egypt the shining place of the world.'[12]

Azzam had a philosophical and poetic twist of mind that sometimes found expression in eulogies of Arab unity and military prowess. David Horowitz, whose book *State in the Making* contains sensitive Zionist impressions of the protagonists of the postwar era, recounted a dramatic encounter with Azzam after the release of the report by the United Nations Special Committee on Palestine in September 1947. The committee recommended the partition of Palestine. Azzam defiantly rejected the possibility. The conversation is revealing because of Azzam's insistence on Arab solidarity. Less than a year later during the Arab–Israeli war he was widely blamed for having helped to create a popular myth rather than a political and military reality. 'The Arab world regards you', the

[11] For the development of Azzam as both an Egyptian and a pan-Arab nationalist, see Coury, 'Who "Invented" Egyptian Arab Nationalism?', for full discussion. For present purposes the essay is significant in demonstrating that Azzam was essentially moderate and pro-British, and that he acquired the reputation as an anti-British fanatic when the British became increasingly frustrated with the Arab League.

[12] Quoted by Anwar G. Chejne, 'Egyptian Attitudes toward Pan-Arabism', *Middle East Journal*, 11, 3 (Summer 1957), p. 260.

Zionists, he told Horowitz, 'as invaders and is ready to fight you.' Azzam described the Arabs as imbued with a 'new spirit'. He emphasized nationalism as the driving and uniting force behind Arab aspirations. He spoke in such a manner as to seem to endorse force and violence as the best means to achieve Arab goals. To Horowitz, writing with recent memory of Nazi oppression of the Jews, Azzam appeared to be expressing a 'Fascist' *Weltanschauung*:

> Azzam Pasha's forcefulness and fanaticism impressed us deeply. His world-outlook had something of the biological determinism of racial theory. The realistic picture he painted was a fatalistic one of objective, almost blind forces erupting and spilling over unchecked on the stage of history. . . . We saw looming up before us latent, powerful forces pushing us irresistibly and inescapably toward the brink of a sanguinary war, the outcome of which none could prophesy.[13]

The theme of Arab destiny in Azzam's thought was similar to the ponderous refrain of fatalistic acceptance of an impending *Götter-dämerung* which Richard Crossman identified in the ideas of Jemal Husseini, one of the leaders of the Palestinian Arabs and a cousin of the Mufti of Jerusalem.[14] Azzam usually spoke so passionately, in Horowitz's phrase, 'with dark, piercing eyes', on the subject of Arab fate that he seldom left his listeners in doubt about the intensity of his conviction.

Brigadier I. N. Clayton, the expert on Arab affairs in the British Middle East Office and the most perceptive local observer of the Arab League, at least on one occasion made a direct comparison between Azzam and Nuri. It was at the time of the meeting of the representatives of the Arab League in May 1946. The date is of interest because of its mid-way mark between the creation of the Arab League a year previously and the time when the Palestine issue moved to the fore of international attention in the United Nations a year later. In May 1946 the British were still trying to determine which way the wind would blow in the aftermath of the Anglo-American Committee of Inquiry. British officials on the whole were uncertain how to gauge Azzam's influence. Clayton regarded Nuri, by contrast, as a stabilizing element in the general affairs of the Middle East as well as a reliable pro-British stalwart. He was now forming an opposite opinion of Azzam. According to Clayton, Nuri spoke bitterly of Azzam, who, as Secretary-General of the Arab League, seemed to regard himself 'as a sort of super-head of all [Arab] States'. Nuri believed that Azzam had usurped the authority of the Arab League and had used it for Egyptian purposes. In effect

---

[13] David Horowitz, *State in the Making* (New York, 1953), pp. 234–5.
[14] Richard Crossman, *Palestine Mission* (London, 1946), p. 130.

the Arab League had degenerated into little more than an instrument of Egyptian nationalism, and Azzam served as its mouthpiece. In Clayton's words, 'Nuri was depressed about the whole situation and angry with the Egyptians, who he says, are trying to get 100% and not giving 1%.' Nuri judged Azzam to be, quite bluntly, a malignant force—'not' according to Nuri, 'from malice but because he is stupid, unbalanced and vain'. In reporting this conversation Clayton made allowance for Nuri's dislike of Azzam. He nevertheless basically agreed with the assessment. Clayton did not write lightly about such matters. Azzam, he concluded, was 'a dangerous influence'.[15]

In September 1946 Ernest Bevin had a conversation with Azzam. The Foreign Secretary regarded most of the Secretary-General's comments as so doctrinaire that he did not bother to record them. 'I listened to his story', Bevin wrote. It amounted to a 'repetition' of Egyptian complaints about British troops in Egypt and the refusal to recognize Egyptian sovereignty in the Sudan.[16] This controversy will be discussed below in the chapter on Egypt. Here the point of interest is that Azzam alarmed Bevin on one particular point. Azzam told him that the Arab League had now gained sufficient strength to unite, for example in the United Nations, on specific issues. If the French had not agreed to evacuate their troops from the Levant, Azzam said, then Egypt would have broken off relations with France. The other members of the Arab League would have followed. In short he suggested that international chaos in the Middle East might be a real possibility. To the British this veiled threat cast a shadow over the Palestine controversy as well as the future relations between Britain and Egypt. The Arab states feared Zionist expansion to the extent that they would support the Egyptians against the British in return for assurance of a united Arab front under Egyptian leadership in Palestine. The Egyptians held the hand of an anti-British whip, in part because of Azzam's grip over the Arab League. To summarize the course of events in which Azzam's influence became painfully obvious to the British, in late 1946 the Anglo-Egyptian negotiations on troop withdrawal and the Sudan reached deadlock. In 1947 the Egyptians decided to take their case to the United Nations.[17] There was a bitter upsurge of anti-British

---

[15] Minutes by Clayton of 28 and 29 May 1946, FO 371/52313–14. Clayton also noted that Nuri himself was partly responsible for creating the unsatisfactory state of affairs: 'he conveniently forgot that he had himself played a large part in bringing Egypt in, in the belief that he could use the Egyptians'.

[16] Bevin to Campbell, Secret, No. 671, 17 Sept. 1946, FO 371/52315/J3922/G.

[17] For the Egyptian case before the UN see especially L. A. Fabunmi, *The Sudan in Anglo-Egyptian Relations* (London, 1960), chap. 11.

sentiment in Egypt. British resentment at the Egyptians in turn reached new heights in the spring and summer of 1947. The Foreign Office generally believed that much of the trouble could be traced to Azzam and his exploitation of the Arab League for anti-British purposes.

No one, not even the Egyptians, believed that the legal case against the British had much merit in international law. The Egyptians sought abrogation of a treaty in an organization whose purpose it was to uphold the sanctity of treaties. They brought the case before the Security Council, whose purpose was to keep the peace. Probably even the most implacable foes of British imperialism doubted whether the presence of British troops in Egypt, where they had been since 1882, constituted an immediate threat to world peace. But, to the everlasting annoyance of the British, the Egyptians appeared to be winning a sort of moral victory even before they submitted the case.[18] Though most members of the United Nations did not think highly of the legal argument, there was a substantial amount of sympathy for the Egyptians. And Azzam's 'blackmail' appeared to be working. The Arab states pursued an anti-British line because of Egyptian support on Palestine. According to Sir Hugh Stonehewer Bird, the Ambassador in Baghdad, the Iraqis disliked Azzam 'for his arrogance, his irresponsible actions, and his tendency to exploit the Arab League for personal ends'; but they nevertheless followed his leadership.[19] Stonehewer Bird wrote in April 1947 in a letter which reflects British resentment at Azzam and the Egyptians in general:

> The Iraqis . . . feel themselves forced to follow the Egyptians' lead lest they forfeit the support of Egypt over the Palestine question. Egypt is not naturally interested in Palestine. Egyptians not only are not Arabs but they have not the same to [sic] fear as have the Iraqis and the Syrians that a Jewish state would be a menace to their own countries. Egypt shows interest in Palestine because Palestine is the one question on which all Arab States are agreed and if Egypt is to continue to dominate the League she must take the lead in this question.[20]

Stonehewer Bird reflected that the situation from the British point of view was 'most unsatisfactory'. The Iraqis in general thought that

[18] In the end the British even failed to obtain a clear-cut, adverse decision against the Egyptians which would have reaffirmed the validity of the treaty of 1936. The question was not withdrawn from the UN's agenda, thus implying that there might be some validity in the Egyptian position. On the other side of the question the Security Council unanimously supported, to British satisfaction, the right of the Sudanese to self-determination. The Egyptians for their part failed to achieve their goal of a UN ultimatum to the British to evacuate, but they gained worldwide sympathy as a victim of British imperialism. There is a clear discussion of these points by Fabunmi, *The Sudan in Anglo-Egyptian Relations*, p.260.

[19] Stonehewer Bird to Bevin, 3 Mar. 1947, FO 371/61523/E2687.

[20] Stonehewer Bird to Sir David Kelly, 21 Apr. 1947, FO 371/61524/E3682.

the Egyptian case for overlordship in the Sudan was 'immoral': 'it was ridiculous for Egyptians who could not govern themselves to wish to govern others'. Yet the Arabs supported the Egyptians against the British because of Palestine. 'I should say that every Arab State', Stonehewer Bird concluded, '. . . felt that Egypt had a rotten case' but did not want to risk Egyptian goodwill and the solidarity of the Arab League.[21]

What could be done about Azzam and the Arab League? It was a question that provoked heated comment in the Foreign Office. It aroused controversy between individual officials as well as the two principal departments, the Egyptian and the Eastern. It is a measure of Egypt's importance in British official eyes that Egypt, together with the Sudan, in the postwar years continued to be worthy of a domain of its own, while most of the rest of the Middle Eastern territories and problems were dealt with individually and collectively by the Eastern Department. The Arab League usually fell under the jurisdiction of the latter, even though the members of the Egyptian Department, according to the head, Daniel Lascelles, 'are the main sufferers from the Arab League, and suffer quite a lot'.[22] There developed a major division of judgement on the Arab League, specifically on what to do about Azzam, between the two departments. The controversy resembled the debate, discussed below in the chapter on Egypt, on whether or not to unseat Farouk. The general question of British intervention will be emphasized here (rather than a detailed description of Britain's relations with the Arab League) because the discussions about it illuminate the calculations of how best to preserve British influence in the Middle East as well as the contemporary assessments of the pan-Arab movement. British doubts about the wisdom of intervention usually prevailed in the era of the Labour government, as in the case of Azzam and the Arab League in 1947.

Azzam found a defender, virtually a solitary champion, in Harold Beeley, whose moderate voice sounded as if in counterpoint to the general anti-Azzam tenor of the Foreign Office. Beeley, who in a later era became Ambassador to Egypt, at that time was regarded within the Foreign Office as the expert on Palestine. He thus found himself at the vortex of many of Britain's postwar Middle Eastern problems. Part of his concern of course was to secure as much general Arab co-operation as possible in resolving the Palestine controversy. In this regard he did not believe that Azzam was necessarily anti-British. In a different area however Azzam had to be

---

[21] Stonehewer Bird to Sir David Kelly, 21 Apr. 1947, FO 371/61524/E3682.
[22] Minute by Lascelles, 17 Jan. 1948, FO 371/61530.

regarded as anti-Italian. On one occasion Beeley reminded his colleagues of Azzam's formative years in Libya and an important fact which distinguished him from most other Egyptians: 'It should be remembered that Azzam Pasha is one of the few Egyptians who have in fact fought in a war. It was, furthermore, a war against the Italians, for whom he retains a cordial and well-known dislike.' Beeley affirmed that Azzam was not embittered towards the British because of his anti-colonial campaign against the Italians, and that he sometimes revealed a co-operative frame of mind. He based his judgement of Azzam in part on personal acquaintance with him at the United Nations' discussions. Azzam in person did not give, at least not always, the impression of the inflexible ideologue that he sometimes gave in print. 'It seems to me', Beeley wrote, 'that he might, if carefully handled, be helpful to us.'[23]

The discussions about possible intervention took place in the spring and summer of 1947, at which time some of Beeley's colleagues urged the ousting of Azzam by bringing pressure to bear on the individual Arab states. Beeley believed that such action, whether it succeeded or failed, would make things worse rather than better. 'If the move succeeded', he speculated, 'the Arab League would at once become labelled as an instrument of British policy. This would provide an additional theme of anti-British propaganda in the Arab countries, and would undermine the League and probably lead to its disintegration.' Perhaps the collapse of the League in its present form might eventually be a good thing, but Beeley thought it unwise to bring it about without full consideration of the consequences. In any case he believed that an attempt to get rid of Azzam would misfire:

It is much more likely . . . that the attempt would fail. In that event, we should have stirred up so much hostility to ourselves, and suspicion of our motives in relationship to the Arab League, that we might not in future be in a position to exercise any influence at all over its deliberations.[24]

Not least, Beeley urged his colleagues to take into consideration the effect on Azzam himself: 'Azzam Pasha is an impulsive and volatile character, and I am not convinced that his mind is, at present, set in any anti-British mould. But if we tried and failed to dislodge him, there is grave risk that we should turn him into a confirmed enemy.'[25]

The foremost advocate of ousting Azzam was the head of the Egyptian Department. Lascelles used the phrase 'Frankenstein's

---

[23] Minute by Beeley, 20 June 1946, FO 371/61503/E5247.
[24] Minute by Beeley, 14 Apr. 1947, FO 371/61523/E2883.
[25] Ibid.

monster' to describe the Arab League. He had been educated at the
Royal Naval College at Dartmouth, and his further experience at
Balliol must have added only a few embellishments to a truculent
style that left no doubt about his sentiments. He wrote in the
military idiom of showing a tooth. In the case of Azzam and the
Egyptians in general he believed it would be salutary to let them
know that the British lion could bite back. 'We have never bared
a fang', he lamented in May 1947:

> Why shouldn't we? Why shouldn't we intimate quite plainly to . . . Nuri and
> the Regent, to Abdullah, Ibn Saud . . . if the League persists in supporting these
> pseudo-Arab Egyptians before the United Nations, we shall be obliged to take
> up, henceforth and irrevocably, a definitely hostile stand against it—with all
> the implications that that will have for the interest of the Arab world in
> general?[26]

Lascelles thought that the Arabs wished to follow the British lead
but had been intimidated by the Egyptians, whom he described,
perhaps paradoxically, as a 'cowardly' race which had only a 'pseudo'
or 'spurious' claim for membership in the Arab League.

> Can we do anything about this Frankenstein of ours [i.e. the Arab League]
> beyond trying to get rid of Azzam or put him in his place? . . . . the Egyptians
> have very little real title to call themselves Arabs at all. . . . If the upshot [of
> British intervention] were the disruption of the League, how much would we
> care? Has the League been so useful to *us* hitherto . . .? Egypt is never likely to
> be a friend of ours; and, to the extent to which the other members of the League
> fall foul of her through being induced to support us against her, they will
> become more dependent upon us.[27]

Lascelles in short believed that the British should break the Arab
League and return to sounder principles of an earlier day. '*Divide
et impera* is still a good maxim, though much blown upon of late.'
    The British sometimes believed that the 'oriental mind' harboured
poisonous anti-western thoughts. There was enough venom in the
pen of Daniel Lascelles to match that of his Egyptian adversaries.
'Of course', Lascelles wrote, the Arab League's hostility to the
British was 'due to the fact that the League is in the pocket of Egypt
and Azzam'. Egypt's wealth and power relative to the Arab states
would explain Azzam's 'natural ascendancy', but what might account
for the underlying and undiminishing Egyptian hostility towards the
British? Lascelles believed that the explanation had to be psychological. The springs of Egyptian behaviour could be found in:

[26] Minute by Lascelles, 5 May 1947, FO 371/61524/E4697.
[27] Ibid.

(a) the acute inferiority complex of an essentially cowardly and underbred race which we have had to sit on in the past,

(b) incipient imperialist ambitions—quite a normal symptom of an inferiority complex—directed towards objectives, e.g. control of the Upper Nile and of North Africa generally, the attainment of which we could in no circumstances tolerate.[28]

Lascelles did not think that Egyptian animosity could be placated. It flowed from irrational emotions of jealousy and hatred. The Egyptian inferiority complex was beyond British treatment. It would not change regardless of the outcome of the controversies over the Sudan or Palestine. The League's hostility would therefore also remain the same because of Egyptian domination. 'Given the League's Egyptian colouring', Lascelles continued, the animosity of the Arab League itself 'will neither fade nor be appreciably less anti-British after the removal of such present troubles as the Palestine and Egyptian disputes'. Lascelles therefore favoured the reconstitution of 'a real Arab League'—in other words, one without Egypt.[29]

Harold Beeley challenged Lascelles' interpretation of the founts of the Arab League's hostility. In temperate and careful language he wrote that 'Mr. Lascelles may perhaps not have put his finger exactly on the reasons for the undoubted fact that the existence of the League does create certain difficulties'. How could one account for the individual attitudes of the Arab states, which on the whole were friendly and satisfactory, and the collective and hostile sentiment of the League?

This should be accounted for, it seems to me, not by any antithesis between the Arab States on the one hand and the League on the other, but by the contrast between the attitudes of Arab politicians in their own capitals, and the attitudes of the same politicians at the meetings of the League Council.

When they get together, each is afraid of appearing less ready than his colleague to assert and defend any of the claims of Arab Nationalism. The result is that there is a tendency for the most intransigent opinion to prevail on all issues.[30]

If Beeley's interpretation was correct, then the anti-imperialist stance of the League should not be attributed entirely to Egyptian dominance

[28] Minute by Lascelles, 27 June 1947, FO 371/66527/E6465.

[29] Ibid. Lascelles continued to argue that one of the major purposes of the Arab League, at least in British eyes, was regional defence, which could never be achieved while the Egyptians remained members: 'the Egyptians would be glad to see their fighting done for them by others if it came to a war involving the Middle East. They would, however, have strong objections to an arrangement which would in their view increase the chances of bringing the war in their direction. (They are short-sighted and provincial enough to believe that they can best keep out of trouble by avoiding all military commitments and appearing to be completely neutral as between Russia and the West.)'

[30] Minute by Beeley, 31 June 1947, FO 371/61527/E6465.

or the influence of Azzam. And even if the Arab League were dissolved, the problems would persist. It probably would be reconstructed, with or without Egypt, and with or without British guidance, because to the Arabs themselves the Arab League served some of the same functions of the old Ottoman Empire. Here Beeley made an incisive comment on the nature of Middle Eastern and British power politics: 'The Arab League (or alternatively an Asiatic Arab bloc) seems to be the natural successor of the Ottoman Empire in British Commonwealth strategy, fulfilling the same role of a buffer zone insulating the Indian Ocean from the influence of European land powers.'[31] In a similar way Albert Hourani has commented on the significance of the analogy. The point may be taken as fundamental in comprehending the inspiration of the Arab League in the postwar years: 'At the meetings which founded the Arab League in 1944–5, many observers must have been struck by the Ottoman as well as the Arab links between those who spoke for the various Arab states east of Egypt: they had been at school together in Istanbul, they had been in the same army or served the same government, they had a common way of looking at the world; behind the vision of Arab unity lay memories of a lost imperial grandeur.'[32]

The question remained, what should be done about the Arab League and its 'unsatisfactory' anti-British attitude? Should the British encourage the tendency for the Arab states to break away from Egypt, or to drive Egypt out of the League? Beeley put these questions to the Egyptian Department. They were answered by Lascelles.

Beeley	*Lascelles*
(i) if facilities in Cyrenaica form an essential part of our strategic planning in this region, can we afford to write off the possibility of including Egypt in our plans for regional military co-operation?	It is not a question of excluding the Egyptians if they *want* to participate, but of getting along without them if they don't. . . .
(ii) if we renew or conclude alliances with a group of Arab States from which Egypt is excluded, what is likely to be the future orientation of Egypt's foreign policy?	Anti-British—in this and all other circumstances!

Those points remained controversial, but no one disagreed with Beeley's major conclusion: 'The Arab League is kept in being, not by British policy, but by the still rising tide of Pan-Arab feeling.'[33]

---

[31] Minute by Beeley, 31 June 1947, FO 371/61527/E6465.
[32] Albert Hourani, *The Emergence of the Middle East* (London, 1981), p. 18.

The minutes by Lascelles and Beeley were adjudicated by Peter Garran, an official in the Eastern Department senior to Beeley. Garran wrote such a lucid and compelling synthesis that it in turn received endorsement, through the rank of Assistant Under-Secretary, without dissent. The main point made by Garran merely summarized Beeley's explanation of the League's anti-British attitude: 'competitive Arab nationalism dominates their deliberations'.[34] An anti-imperialist attitude would therefore continue to dominate the League. The British should not react by trying to drive Egypt out of the League, or, at the other extreme, by attempting to appease the League. Gladwyn Jebb, at this time Assistant Under-Secretary supervising United Nations affairs, held the view that the Arab League might agree to a 'deal' over Palestine in return for support in Cyrenaica. 'I certainly feel that the moment is coming', Jebb wrote, 'when we ought to make a pretty firm approach to the Arab League, and if we can bring ourselves to say that we are fed up with Palestine and will evacuate it by a given date, provided only that they will support us in a British Commonwealth plus Egypt [and] trusteeship for Cyrenaica, I think there might be the makings of a deal.'[35] The minutes by Lascelles and Beeley made it lamentably clear that the British could not rely on the Arab League for any such 'deal'. Garran agreed with Lascelles that the Arab League needed to be dealt with firmly and without any false hopes.

On the other hand Garran disagreed with Lascelles that active steps should be taken to break up the League. 'The Arab States need some centralising element', Garran wrote, 'to counteract their internal divisions, and the Arab League provides that element, for all its disadvantages.' There was no real disagreement between the Egyptian and Eastern departments about the desirability of an Arab League to provide a political and economic unity to the Middle East that had lapsed since the demise of the Ottoman Empire. The substantive point of disagreement between the two departments was whether or not the Arab League as then constituted could function compatibly with British interests, particularly in view of Azzam's leadership. Here Garran tended to be sceptical of Beeley's assessment, but no one could dissent from the conclusion: 'As for Azzam Pasha', Garran wrote, 'I am not convinced that he can be trusted as genuinely friendly, but I agree that he is going to play an important part in Arab affairs in the years to come and we should therefore

---

[33] Minutes by Beeley and Lascelles, 31 June 1947, FO 371/61527/E6465.
[34] Minute by Garran, 2 July 1947, FO 371/61527/E6465.
[35] Minute by Jebb, 25 June 1947, FO 371/61526/E5890.

be very careful to ensure so far as possible that he is with us and not against us.'[36]

The resolution of the internal debate in the Foreign Office about the Arab League had taken place in the spring and summer of 1947, at a time when emotions ran high because of Egyptian denunciation at the United Nations of British imperialism. In the end the British braced themselves with the philosophic outlook that whatever might replace the Arab League might be worse. Until the time of the explosion of the Arab–Israeli war of 1948, British policy in fact remained substantially the same as it had since the founding of the Arab League in 1945. In part because of its hot air about British imperialism, the League seemed to function as a sort of safety-valve releasing forces that otherwise might fuel extremist organizations such as the Muslim Brethren. British policy would continue, as in the past, in Garran's words, 'to give unobtrusive but steady encouragement to the League as a cohesive and co-ordinating force among the Arab States'. Garran, like his colleagues, saw Azzam personally as the principal impediment in achieving that goal:

> The League is being perverted and used for the furthering of Egyptian national aims, owing to the restless ambition and extremist national feeling of the Secretary-General, Azzam Pasha. As the League is constituted at present, Azzam Pasha seems to have a pretty free hand to do and say exactly what he likes, although his activities are disapproved of and frowned upon by the Iraqi, Lebanese and Transjordan Governments.

Garran went on to emphasize the useful purposes of the League, again returning to the central problem of Azzam:

> It would seem a pity that there should be any weakening of the Arab League, which, besides serving as a binding element serves also as a convenient safety-valve for Arab nationalist sentiment. If the League were to break up, or become discredited, there would seem to be a danger that such nationalist sentiment would find other outlets, for example in the development of Arab nationalist movements such as the Moslem Brethren. What seems needed therefore, is to control the ambitions and extravagances of Azzam Pasha. . . .[37]

The British did not find a satisfactory means of controlling Azzam, but at least he was a known quantity and easier to live with than 'the more extreme and xenophobe elements' which might have replaced him.[38]

Although Azzam continued to be Secretary-General of the Arab League until 1952, his star quickly waned after the outbreak of the

[36] Minute by Garran, 2 July 1947, FO 371/61527/E6465.

[37] Minute by Garran, 2 May 1947, FO 371/61524.

[38] These were the words used in a memorandum entitled 'The Arab League—F. O. Attitude', which summarized the various points discussed above, 17 Sept. 1947, FO 371/61529.

Arab-Israeli war in May 1948. The Arab unity which he championed in the realm of ideas now broke on the realities of Arab disarray. To give but one example of the collapse of Azzam's influence, the Embassy in Cairo reported a conversation with King Farouk in July 1948 (which is difficult to believe was not written tongue in cheek):

King Farouk . . . was disgusted to find that the Arab League States were actuated purely by selfishness. He found that the dreams that Azzam had put into his head of leading the Arab States united in generous concern for the promotion of the interest of the Arab world as a whole were empty, and based on nothing but the thin air into which they had vanished. He was disgusted to find that he had been misled, that selfish sectionism reigned instead of unity, and that the fine rôle for which Azzam had led him to cast Egypt had no basis in reality and no material to work with.[39]

Azzam no doubt served as a convenient scapegoat, but in 1948-9 there seemed to be one point on which most British officials could agree. In the words of Sir Hugh Dow, the Consul-General in Jerusalem: 'the recent policy of the Arab League under Azzam's direction . . . has been uniformly calamitous for the Arabs'.[40]

It was a harsh judgement, and it is perhaps important in assessing Azzam's influence in the postwar years to bear in mind that he seemed to represent, to western observers at least, more than the political leadership of the Arab League. When he spoke before the Anglo-American Committee of Inquiry in February 1946, Richard Crossman recorded in his diary that he had no doubt that Azzam had spoken 'for the whole Arab world'. Perhaps more than any other Arab leader of the era he conveyed the Arab moral case against the Jews. Crossman, who was himself a philosopher, described Azzam's argument as one which, if accepted, 'cut away at a single stroke the whole Jewish case'. It is for this statement that Azzam will perhaps be remembered as well as for his leadership of the Arab League. Crossman described him almost as if a poet, tall and melancholy, tossed into the realm of politics. Azzam spoke of 'brothers' and 'cousins' who had become transformed into Zionists:

Our Brother has gone to Europe and to the West and come back something else. He has come back a Russified Jew, a Polish Jew, a German Jew, an English Jew. He has come back with a totally different conception of things, Western and not Eastern. That does not mean that we are necessarily quarrelling with anyone who comes from the West. But the Jew, our old cousin, coming back with imperialistic ideas, with materialistic ideas, with reactionary or revolutionary ideas and trying to implement them first by British pressure and then by American pressure, and then by terrorism on his own part—he is not the old cousin and

[39] Memorandum of 27 July 1948, enclosed in Campbell to Wright, Personal and Secret, 26 July 1948, FO 371/69193.
[40] Dow to Wright, Secret, 15 Mar. 1949, FO 371/75064.

we do not extend to him a very good welcome. The Zionist, the new Jew, wants to dominate and he pretends that he has got a particular civilizing mission with which he returns to a backward, degenerate race in order to put the elements of progress into an area which has no progress. Well, that has been the pretension of every power that wanted to colonize and aimed at domination. The excuse has always been that the people are backward and that he has got a human mission to put them forward . . . the Arabs simply stand and say 'NO'. We are not reactionary and we are not backward. Even if we are ignorant, the difference between ignorance and knowledge is ten years in school. We are a living, vitally strong nation, we are in our renaissance; we are producing as many children as any nation in the world. We still have our brains. We have a heritage of civilization and of spiritual life. We are not going to allow ourselves to be controlled either by great nations or small nations or dispersed nations.[41]

One further observation on the part of Azzam may serve as a conclusive comment about Britain and the Arab states from the Arab perspective. It is a judgement that is useful to bear in mind in relation to themes of other chapters of this book. Azzam's thoughts were confidentially recorded by C. D. Quilliam of *The Times* after the shattering experience of the Arab–Israeli war of 1948: 'He thinks Britain has tried, weakly, to secure the Arabs a fair deal and believes the British would have taken a quite strong anti-Zionist stand had they not been bullied by the Americans.'[42]

[41] Crossman Diary, 'February 1946', Crossman Papers; *Palestine Mission*, pp. 109–10.
[42] Quilliam to Deakin, Confidential, 3 Dec. 1948, Quilliam Papers.

3

INDEPENDENCE IN SYRIA AND LEBANON: THE SIGNIFICANCE OF THE CRISIS OF 1945

'THE Syrian frontier', wrote R. M. A. Hankey in May 1945, 'is only twenty miles from Haifa, the principal source of oil for the British forces in the Mediterranean.' Hankey was the official in the Foreign Office who directly dealt with the crisis in the Levant. Uppermost in his mind was the need to conciliate the Syrians with the French, and above all to preserve British influence. In this particular minute he was describing the workings of the British military mind. He concurred in the arguments about the strategic imperatives of the British Empire. If Charles de Gaulle had been able to read the secret minutes of the Eastern Department of the Foreign Office, he would have confirmed his abiding conviction that the British intended to exploit French weakness in order to entrench themselves in French territory. 'We ought', Hankey continued, 'to be able to establish air defences and use the communications of Syria and the Lebanon in the event of another war.' 'Exactly', Oliver Harvey (Assistant Under-Secretary) noted in sardonic affirmation. 'This is what the French suspect we are after. How right they are!'[1]

The discussion about the future of the Levant took place against the background of rising tension. In May 1945 the drama of French imperialism and Arab nationalism appeared to be entering its denouement. At the end of the month, the British Foreign Secretary, Anthony Eden, announced to the House of Commons that fighting had broken out between Syrians and French troops. When he described the French bombing of Damascus, cries of 'Shame' could be heard from both sides of the House. The disturbances were spreading throughout Syria and

---

[1] Minute by Hankey and notation by Harvey, 5 May 1945, FO 371/45565. In his private diary Harvey wrote of 'the stupid military mind' and recorded Churchill's irritation: 'We discovered that [the] British army is using Syria as a training ground and building semi-permanent barracks there. This annoyed even [the] P. M. who said it was [a] gross waste of money to build in other people's country, apart from feeding French suspicions of our intentions.' Entries of 20 Oct. 1944 and 10 June 1945, Harvey Diaries Add. MSS 56400.

might, Eden said, threaten 'the security of the whole Middle East'.[2] The British Commander-in-Chief was instructed to restore order, to impose a cease-fire, and to demand that French troops withdraw to their barracks. The weak military position of the French gave them no choice but to comply. The humiliating circumstances, in the phrase that was used by the French at the time, were worse than those of Fashoda.[3] 'We are not . . .', de Gaulle told the British Ambassador, 'in a position to open hostilities against you at the present time. But you have insulted France and betrayed the West. This cannot be forgotten.'[4] According to Duff Cooper, the Ambassador, de Gaulle was 'genuinely convinced that the whole incident has been arranged by the British so as to carry out their long-planned policy of driving the French out of the Levant in order to take their place'.[5]

The purpose of this chapter will be to study the well-known events that led to the crisis of 1945, and to examine the dilemmas that faced the British in the closing months of the war and the way in which the decisions made at that time helped to determine the subsequent course of events in the Middle East. There were three choices that faced the British in 1945: going to the aid of the French; standing aside and allowing the French and the Syrians to fight it out; or throwing their weight behind the independence of Syria and Lebanon. In the event, the British chose the last course, even though it meant extremely bitter Anglo-French relations in Europe as well as in the Middle East. The crisis of 1945 is revealing as a concluding chapter in the history of Anglo-French rivalry in the Middle East.

There were two further dimensions of the problem which also had far-reaching significance. In May 1945 the Americans, in particular the officials in the Office of Near Eastern and African

[2] *Parliamentary Debates* (Commons), 31 May 1945, cols. 378–9.

[3] Duff Cooper, British Ambassador in Paris, noted in late May 1945 that General Bernard Paget, the Commander-in-Chief, Middle East, 'has issued a statement that seems designed to humiliate the French, and which I am sure was quite unnecessary. They say it is worse than Fashoda.' Duff Cooper, *Old Men Forget* (London, 1953), p. 354. See Martin L. Mickelsen, 'Another Fashoda: The Anglo-Free French Conflict Over the Levant, May–September 1941', *Revue française d'histoire d'Outre-Mer*, LXIII, 230 (1976), which is an interesting examination of the British archives of 1941. Christopher M. Andrew and A. S. Kanya-Forstner, *France Overseas: The Great War and the Climax of French Imperial Expansion* (London, 1981), chap. X, develops the theme against the background of the experience of the First World War. The book itself is a historical breakthrough without which it would be difficult to comprehend the issues of the later period.

[4] *The War Memoirs of Charles de Gaulle*, III (New York, 1960), p. 221, to be compared with Winston S. Churchill, *Triumph and Tragedy* (Boston, 1953), pp. 561–8. The high political drama of de Gaulle and Churchill, including the clash over the Levant, is related with verve by François Kersaudy, *Churchill and De Gaulle* (London, 1981). See also Geoffrey Warner, *Iraq and Syria 1941* (London, 1974).

[5] Cooper, *Old Men Forget*, p. 354.

Affairs of the State Department, viewed French actions with profound mistrust. At the very time that the international conference in San Francisco was laying the foundations of the world's peace by the creation of the United Nations, the French were committing an act of aggression that could only be compared with the Japanese takeover of Manchuria which had helped to destroy the League of Nations. American anti-colonialism was a powerful force in the Levant settlement of 1945. The last dimension of the crisis was the one of paramount importance to the Syrians and Lebanese themselves. It was the question of national independence. By skilfully exploiting Anglo-French rivalries, the Syrians and Lebanese managed to obtain complete independence. Once they had achieved that status, none of the other Arab states would settle for an inferior position.

After the Allied invasion of the Levant in 1941, the British as well as the French had pledged themselves to the independence of Syria and Lebanon. The British guarantee served to underwrite the French commitment made in a time of political and military adversity. Since the British held military control, they were well aware that the Arabs throughout the Middle East would look to them to prevent French reneging. But there was another important part of the British undertaking. The British had also recognized the paramount position of France in the Levant. Churchill's authoritative statement in Parliament in September 1941 was made in part to make clear both aspects of the British commitment and to prevent lamentable misunderstandings such as those that had arisen during similar circumstances of the First World War:

> We have no ambitions in Syria. We do not seek to replace or supplant France, or substitute British for French interests in any part of Syria. . . . Syria shall be handed back to the Syrians, who will assume at the earliest possible moment their independent sovereign rights. . . . On the other hand, we recognize that among all the nations of Europe the position of France in Syria is one of special privilege, and that in as far as any European countries have influence in Syria, that of France will be pre-eminent. . . . The independence of Syria is a prime feature in our policy.[6]

Unfortunately for the British, the principles of independence and French paramountcy did not prove easy to reconcile. The Syrians and Lebanese had no desire to recognize a French position of privilege. They were not easily persuaded of the desirability of a relationship with the French similar to the one between Iraq and

---

[6] Quoted in A. H. Hourani, *Syria and Lebanon: A Political Essay* (London, 1946), pp. 245-6. Hourani's book remains indispendable for all aspects of the problem. See also esp. Patrick Seale, *The Struggle for Syria* (London, 1965) for Middle Eastern perspective.

Britain. In short they insisted on complete independence. The French for their part demanded that the British fulfil the part of the agreement about a privileged position. The tension persisted throughout the war.

In the closing months of the war the British, with a crescendo of alarm, anticipated an inevitable collision of the Syrians and the Lebanese, on the one hand, and the French on the other—with the British themselves unhappily in the middle. In speculating on that uncomfortable probability, R. M. A. Hankey believed that the situation would become so dangerous that the British would ultimately have to intervene on the side of the French. Hankey wrote in the humanitarian and self-assured tradition of British imperialism that could in different circumstances just as well have been penned in the days of Lord Palmerston:

> English and American people in the Levant States tend to talk rather loosely, but with pleasurable anticipation, of the French being thrown into the sea, but my own impression, after consulting the Army Commander and other people, is that the French would maintain themselves, though with difficulty, until reinforced; and that we should probably have to support the French in order to prevent Europeans and Christians being murdered, when it came to the point.[7]

Hankey was entirely willing to place the responsibility for this distressing state of affairs on the Syrians and Lebanese as well as on the French. Anglo-French relations were not good, he wrote, and 'the Syrians and Lebanese do everything they can to make them bad'. With the 'locals' provoking the French, and the French not possessing the virtues of balanced and impartial colonial rulers, Hankey concurred in the judgement that the Levant resembled a 'madhouse' in which the British presence provided the only hope of sanity. The explanation for this aberrant colonial situation lay in part in French inability to deal with the 'locals' other than as 'stooges':

> The French only see their own stooges, which is bad for them. Everyone . . . without exception, hates the French like poison and denounces them, lock stock and barrel, often quite unreasonably—but the French have a very bad record. The locals certainly behave as provocatively to the French as they dare and an outburst of Gallic impatience is always possible.[8]

There is a refreshing candour to Hankey's minutes, from which one would gather that the stoic virtues of the British in the Middle

---

[7] Minute by Hankey, 3 Mar. 1945, FO 371/45575.

[8] Minute by Hankey, 28 Feb. 1945, FO 371/45561/E1776. Hankey's views about Syrian antipathy to the French were representative of British official thought. Oliver Harvey's comments in his diary thus stand out as unusually unorthodox and acute: 'The Syrians hate us as much as they hate the French, but they think they can use us. Our long term interests and those of the French are identical.' 4 Dec. 1943, Harvey Diaries Add. MSS 56400.

East remained one of the few constants in a changing and perplexing era.

Even the most phlegmatic of British officials could not but admit the legitimacy of certain French complaints against the British in Syria. Though he would never confess it to de Gaulle, Duff Cooper wrote from Paris, during the war the British had given all appearances of pursuing a 'policy to oust the French from the Levant [and to have us] take their place'. Cooper was raising an extremely sore point between the British and the French. No one could deny, he continued, that 'His Majesty's Government appointed as head of a special mission to Syria in July 1941 a General who openly pursued that very policy and continued to do so until he was withdrawn in December 1944'.[9] Cooper referred to Major-General Sir Edward Spears.[10] In fact the accusation was at best only partly correct because Spears had attempted to accommodate the nationalists and at the same time to make life as difficult as possible for the French without actually rupturing relations with the Free French movement in the Levant.[11] It was no secret to either the French or the nationalists that he was a close and staunch friend of the Prime Minister himself. He acted exactly as Churchill expected. One result was the shackling of the Foreign Office. Even after the end of his mission, Spears, to the great annoyance of the Foreign Office, continued to speak out on Middle Eastern issues in Parliament and in the press.[12]

[9] Cooper to Eden, No. 868, 5 June 1945, FO 371/45569/E3823.

[10] See Sir Edward Spears, *Fulfilment of a Mission* (London, 1977). The other British memoirs of particular importance, which are necessary to restore a balance to Spears's account, are: *The Memoirs of Lord Chandos* (London, 1962); and Lord Casey, *Personal Experience 1939-1946* (New York, 1962). For the French side see Général Catroux, *Dans la bataille de Méditerranée* (Paris, 1949), esp. chap. XXIII, 'Sur le Général Sir Edward Spears'. For critical comment on Spears see the review essay by Elie Kedourie in the *Times Literary Supplement*, 27 Oct. 1978.

[11] On this point see especially Kersaudy, *Churchill and De Gaulle*, e.g. p. 195: Spears 'was not only instructed to foster the independence of the Levant States; he was also . . . to "back the Free French wholeheartedly". Wholeheartedly or not, this instruction too was carried out to the letter. Hence we find Spears refusing to back a Syrian nationalist and anti-French movement at the beginning of 1942. . . . The Free French would probably have rubbed their eyes had they seen telegrams such as these. To them, the name of Spears was the very synonym of anti-French agitation in the Levant.' Spears became such a champion of Lebanese and Syrian independence that he was made a 'Citizen of the Lebanon' by the Lebanese Parliament as well as a 'Citizen of Damascus' by the Syrian Parliament. He wrote in his memoirs, in a highly revealing passage: 'I was somewhat abashed when a few years later the same honour was conferred on Nehru—not one of my favourite characters—but as I knew of no means of foregoing my citizenship, I had to let it pass.' *Fulfilment of a Mission*, p. 297.

[12] The American Embassy in London compiled careful political reports on Spears's speeches and writings. See for example the perceptive evaluations by Raymond Hare, who on one occasion wrote that Spears's attitude towards the Levant resembled Lord Palmerston's: 'any other attitude', according to Spears, 'would have been as foolish as for a man with an estate in the North of England and a residence in the South to wish to own all the

'Spears again!', Eden once wrote in exasperation.[13] Hankey observed that Spears's belligerent anti-French line had raised Anglo-French relations to a 'quite shocking pitch'.[14] To be as honest as possible in dealing with the French, Hankey wrote, all that could be said was that the British had 'played very straight indeed' after Spears's departure.[15] After that time the Foreign Office had more latitude to pursue a course of conciliation between the Syrians and the French rather than to act as the Prime Minister's mouthpiece. Sir Alexander Cadogan wrote to Eden about the end of the Spears mission and the beginning of a new era:

> He has already mis-managed the situation badly, and is obviously out of sympathy with any policy except throwing the French out. It is true enough that he has great influence, but he will not use it in the way we require. . . . As you know, his very capable successor, who has won elsewhere the confidence of the Arabs and of the French, is now available.[16]

Spears's successor was Terence Shone, who most recently had served as Minister in Cairo under Lord Killearn.

In London in the 'post-Spears' period the official who played the criticial part in assessing the dangers of the collision course between the French and the Syrians and the Lebanese was R. M. A. Hankey, who, as the acting head of the Eastern Department, carried considerable influence during the crisis of 1945. Hankey's minutes are of interest for the light that they throw on the decisions made in the spring of 1945, and for other reasons as well. He wrote with such unrestrained honesty and clarity that his views may be taken as an exceptional example of the official mind methodically attempting to cope with the countervailing influences of French imperialism, American anti-colonialism, and Arab nationalism. Hankey had an unsceptical confidence in the British Imperial mission. He was not any more anti-French than others of his generation. He merely took it for granted that the French could not be trusted. 'The plain fact is', he once wrote, 'that the French have never taken a single step to carry out their (& our) promises of independence except under strongest pressure from us. . . . This is no

---

inns on the Great North Road, when all that was needed was that "the inns should be well kept, always accessible, and furnishing him, when he came, with mutton chops and post horses" ' (Raymond A. Hare, First Secretary of Embassy, to Secretary of State, 17 Feb. 1945, USSD 741.90/2-1745 Box 3981). Hare also noted that Spears was waging 'a campaign for recognition as top-flight British spokesman on matters Middle Eastern'. 5 Mar. 1945, USSD 741.90/3-545 Box 3981.

[13] Minute by Eden, 28 June 1945, FO 371/45575/E4709.
[14] Minute by Hankey, 28 Feb. 1945, FO 371/45561/E1776.
[15] Minute by Hankey, 5 June 1945, FO 371/45569/E3823.
[16] Cadogan to Eden, 16 Oct. 1944, FO 371/40318.

exaggeration at all!'[17] He also noted that the French army was a particular source of trouble: 'the French Army cannot be trusted not to interfere in internal affairs, e.g. by intriguing with the minorities against the Syrian Government, if they have the chance'. He drew the distinction between the principles on which the French and British conducted their affairs in the Middle East:

French policy in the Levant States is not to help the local Governments, as we do in Egypt and Iraq, but generally to intrigue with the opposition against them, and it is impracticable in my view . . . to hope that the French could pursue a policy of government by guidance, as we do in Iraq.[18]

What then could be the solution if the French refused to withdraw? 'The only answer I can find is that their "special position" must be too inferior for them to be able to interfere much.'[19]

Hankey did not want the French to be entirely kicked out of the Levant because the British themselves required bases in Syria. If the British moved in as the French moved out, how could the British sincerely maintain that they had no imperialistic aims? Hankey's solution would be to allow the French to remain in the Levant with a hand on their collar, and at the same time to fetch the Americans to the general cause of defence. He wrote in the closing months of the war, at a time when it appeared that the Allied powers would establish bases throughout the world as the best means to safeguard the peace after the defeat of Germany and Japan. Here was Hankey's inspiration in selling the idea to the Syrians and the Lebanese as well as to the French. He took it for granted that most of the French colonial empire would be placed under some form of international trusteeship and would thus be available for bases.

The only hope that I can see of getting the acquiescence of the Levant States in the continued presence of French forces is . . . [to] say to them that in the post-war world the principal United Nations will have bases everywhere. America will have bases in the West Indies and in Indo-China. We already have bases all over the world. The French will participate in the maintenance of security in the Eastern Mediterranean and will have to have a base in Syria.[20]

The actual area occupied by the French would be strictly circumscribed, and thus would not be a cause of alarm to the 'locals'. The French for their part would have the chance to perfect the art of desert warfare:

The French base should not be near any centre of population . . . the troops would be confined to the base and would not be able to go elsewhere except

[17] Minute by Hankey, 5 June 1945, FO 371/45569/E3823.
[18] Minute by Hankey, 3 Mar. 1945, FO 371/45575.
[19] Ibid.
[20] Ibid.

for training in the surrounding desert. The number of troops would be limited to a low figure. . . . We should aim at keeping French troops away from the places where they can be used to intimidate Governments and Parliaments.[21]

To Hankey's logical way of thinking the Syrians, despite those guarantees, would probably be reluctant to grant military facilities to the French unless the British themselves would accept military responsibilities, which would serve to check French ambitions: 'The Syrian Government will of course not wish to give these rights to the French alone, but, in view of the development of air warfare during the war, we ourselves seem likely to need radar and aerodrome facilities in Syria & I now suggest that we should be prepared to come in on a joint agreement [between the Syrians and the French] which would provide us with these.'[22] Hankey thus systematically proposed to remove the causes of anxiety of the Syrians and at the same time to make sure that the French would not suffer a loss of 'prestige'.

The next step would be to devise a general defence scheme in the eastern Mediterranean in which the United States would wish to participate. Hankey wrote of 'squaring' the Americans and he candidly admitted that his suggestions would probably violate the British pledges of 1941. 'I cannot believe', he continued, 'that we can afford a military vacuum in Syria and the Lebanon, which would be the case if both French and British troops withdrew.' To allay American suspicions of British imperialism Hankey proposed the bold step of placing the Levant under international trusteeship. He knew however that the Syrians and the Lebanese might not like the ingenious idea of returning to the disguised chains of the mandate:

[Trusteeship] might . . . make the idea more palatable to the Americans, but we shall have to be careful how we do this, as we have promised to wind the Mandate up and the Syrians will be sensitive about not being left in any sort of tutelary position which would be inferior to that of Egypt or Iraq.

The Americans, in any case, will not be in a very good position to object to the scheme . . . because they seem likely to want bases themselves all over the place. If any sort of application of the principle of colonial trusteeship would make it look more respectable, that no doubt would help with the Americans.[23]

Hankey thus found a way, in his own phrase, 'to square' the Americans and assure the Syrians, but he nevertheless had a pang of conscience. 'I realise that this scheme is going back on our statements of 1941', he lamented. But he thought that the plan had a good chance of acceptance by the Americans as well as by the Syrians because 'we

---

[21] Minute by Hankey, 3 Mar. 1945, FO 371/45569.
[22] Ibid.   [23] Ibid.

seek nothing for ourselves' other than legitimate defence arrangements.[24]

What if the French proved to be obstinate, as Hankey suspected that they would be? Then, in his judgement, the British should insist on French withdrawal, even if in consequence it meant forfeiting the chance for British bases. With or without the French, the British would aim at a 'sensible' settlement in the Levant which would contribute to the general stability of the Middle East. Though Hankey emphasized the possible importance of British radar installations and airfields in Syria, he by no means believed that British defence arrangements should override political considerations. He also did not think that the propositions of defence and political freedom were necessarily contradictory. In turning these problems over in his mind he began to develop the idea of an 'Arab Confederation'. With British guidance, the Arab states might create a regional defence organization. For geographical as well as for general political reasons, Hankey believed that it would be imperative for the Syrians and the Lebanese to participate. For that reason the French problem was one of grave delicacy. An unwanted French military presence would undermine the development of an 'Arab Confederation'. And if the French continued to 'squat' without the acquiescence of the Syrians and the Lebanese, he foresaw other grave consequences for the British:

They [French troops] would be a perpetual reminder to the peoples of the Middle East that our undertaking that the Levant States would be granted independence had not been made entirely effective and that, in spite of it, there was a major question outstanding in Syria. Unless the French are able to reach an amicable agreement with the Levant States, they will never be anything but a very disturbing factor in the Middle East for which we shall be blamed.[25]

Hankey was writing only a couple of weeks before the actual founding of the Arab League. It was by no means certain that the Arab states would work together for defence purposes in a way that would harmonize with British aims. Irrespective of the French, it was impossible to predict the Arab side of the problem. Hankey was quite certain however about French suspicions: 'They are very much afraid that we shall use the Arab League . . . to turn the whole Egypto-Arab world into an area looking to Great Britain for help and almost a new sort of dominion.'[26]

[24] Ibid.

[25] Minute by Hankey, 16 Mar. 1945, FO 371/45561/E1726.

[26] Ibid. Hankey also took into account the arguments in favour of siding with the French: 'it could be argued that we should only help the French to remain in Syria if we could be sure that they would use their influence there in a useful way—e.g. to help us keep the Arabs quiet in the event of trouble in Palestine or not to oppose our policy as

Though Hankey was primarily interested in Syria and Lebanon only 'in so far as they affect our relations with the rest of the Middle East', it must not be assumed that his searching minutes neglected the welfare of the Syrians and the Lebanese themselves. On the contrary he was keenly sympathetic, if in a paternalistic sort of way, with their political aspirations. For one thing, they needed to be protected from Russian influence, about which, in his view, they were certainly naïve. And one could not help but sympathize with their pro-British sentiments:

> We may well have trouble if we leave them entirely unencumbered with any obligation or ties with West European Powers, either because of the effect on other Middle Eastern countries where we have a special position, or because of the possibility that Soviet influence will replace British and French influence.
>
> These struggling smaller States certainly deserve our sympathy and help. They are very conscious of their own difficulties and shortcomings and are relying on us rather pathetically to help them.[27]

What sort of 'help' did the British have in mind? During the Second World War the Syrians and the Lebanese were hurled, with British assistance, into an independence for which, according to one strain of historical interpretation, they were ill-prepared. The historian is ineluctably drawn to the question, how far did the British of the postwar era contemplate measures that might have averted the tragedy or, as Elie Kedourie has put it, 'the perils of independence', in the Levant?[28]

Terence Shone's Estimate of the 'Viability' of Syria and Lebanon, April 1945

In February 1945 the Foreign Office had instructed the British Minister in the Levant to address himself to a question of pregnant significance: 'to what extent . . . have [we] been justified in regarding Syria and the Lebanon as viable States reasonably mature and capable of maintaining a healthy national existence on their own?'[29] The general answer to that question has long been known. In *Syria and Lebanon: A Political Essay*, published in 1946, Albert Hourani fully examined the question of national independence in all of its

---

regards Arab unity'. He did not however believe that the argument of supporting the French outweighed the dangers of Arab hostility. 'In any case I feel sure that the French will only secure in Syria a position which will not give them very much influence there any way.'

[27] Minute by Hankey, 3 Mar. 1945, FO 371/45575.

[28] See Elie Kedourie, 'Lebanon: The Perils of Independence', in *Islam in the Modern World* (London, 1980).

[29] Quoted in Shone to Eden, No. 63, Secret, 19 Apr. 1945, FO 371/65563/E2780.

political, religious, ethnic, and economic complexity. Hourani's analysis of the problem will probably not be surpassed. What is of interest here is the secret assessment within the British government. It is of considerable general interest because Syria and Lebanon were the first states to achieve independence from the European colonial system as a result of the Second World War. The author of the assessment, Terence Shone, attempted to generalize about the problems of independence as well as to explain the unique challenges to it in Syria and Lebanon. His report was written in April 1945, shortly before the major crisis in the Levant in the following month, and during the time that 'colonial independence' was being intensely discussed by the delegates at the San Francisco Conference who were establishing the trusteeship system of the United Nations. Shone's assessment and the official minutes about it thus provide insight into the workings of the official mind on the question of national independence at a critical time.

Shone brought to bear a gift for political and economic analysis which was recognized within the Foreign Office as exceptional. He had the confidence of that arch-defender of the British Empire, Lord Killearn, who valued his discriminating judgement. Hankey referred to Shone's 'admirable balance' and on one occasion noted that if it had not been for his 'strenuous efforts' the situation in the Levant 'would have got a lot worse'.[30] The Minister Resident in the Middle East, Sir Edward Grigg, believed that Shone's ability was so great that if it were humanly possible he would have reconciled the irreconcilable forces of the Arab desire for independence and the French determination to preserve their influence—'but no man can reconcile the irreconcilable' and Grigg detected a certain 'anxiety' in attempting to do so that perhaps contributed to Shone's early retirement after equally successful tours of duty in which he distinguished himself as the first High Commissioner in India.[31] Shone was anxious to be fair minded to the French as well as to the Syrians and Lebanese, but he had to admit that the French in the Levant did not make it an easy task. 'I am as fond of France as anyone', he wrote during the May crisis, '. . . but as an Englishman *here* . . . and with the experience I have had of French personnel and methods here', the French contribution to 'independence' could only be deplored.[32]

Shone began his analysis of the viability of Syria and Lebanon by calling attention to the thrust of French policy, which was in the

[30] Minutes by Hankey, 28 Feb. and 29 May 1945, FO 371/45561 and 45566.

[31] Grigg to Eden, Private and Personal, 23 Jan. 1945, FO 371/45559; Shone's obituary in *The Times*, 30 Oct. 1965.

[32] Shone to Campbell, No. 364, Top Secret and Personal, 18 May 1946, FO 371/45564/E3179/G.

opposite direction from independence. The French, wrote Shone, 'have not merely failed to help the Governments further on the path to independence, but have sought to maintain in various ways what remains of their former position here and even to instil the belief amongst the local populations that their position will be strengthened'.[33] Any estimate of the prospects of Syrian and Lebanese independence, in other words, would be clouded with controversy about the given fact that French influence existed. Even if the French factor were eliminated, was it desirable for Syria and Lebanon to have full independence? It was a question that is as controversial now as then.[34] Shone did not attempt to answer it directly but rather assumed that the two states should have the right to independence, even though it might amount to no more than the independence of the corrupt and unstable states of Latin America. Shone in fact believed that Syria and Lebanon had better prospects:

> In so far as other Middle Eastern countries are concerned—and it is pre-sumably by their standards that we should seek to judge the Levant States, experience shows that States can continue to exist even though their Admini-strations are riddled with corruption and nepotism and are inefficient to a point which we ourselves would regard as intolerable. It seems, in fact, essential to avoid setting the standard of 'viability' too high and, above all, not to be influenced unduly by preconceived notions of what constitutes good govern-ment.[35]

Those were words of unusual tolerance in an era in which there was a common belief that good colonial administration should constitute the best preparation for independence.

Both Syria and Lebanon shared the common defect of lacking a competent civil service. Perhaps no other point, Shone wrote, so clearly revealed the difference in the traditions of the French and British empires: 'The French . . . did nothing to train up a civil service, as we did in Egypt before that country became independent.' On the basis of discussions with various colleagues, Shone had developed a fairly high regard for the Syrians in comparison with

[33] Shone to Eden, No. 63, Secret, 19 Apr. 1945, FO 371/45563/E2780.
[34] See e.g. Elie Kedourie in the *Times Literary Supplement*, 27 Oct. 1978. For con-trasting interpretation, see Albert Hourani, 'Lebanon: the Development of a Political Society', in *The Emergence of the Modern Middle East* (London, 1981), e.g. p. 140: 'Arab nationalists saw in the [Second World] War, the weakness of France, and the temporary presence of England, an opportunity to rid themselves of the Mandate, and they were now prepared to pay the price . . . the old rivalry of England and France in the Middle East played itself out, perhaps for the last time, through the struggles of local political groups, and some of these groups exploited it with skill.'
[35] Shone to Eden, No. 63, Secret, 19 Apr. 1945, FO 371/45563/E2780; material of related interest in the Shone Papers.

other Middle Eastern peoples, but he regarded the legacy of Ottoman administration as one of mixed blessings. On the whole he was not unoptimistic about the future of public administration in Syria:

> The Syrians are more intelligent and potentially more capable than the Iraqis or the Persians. There is a residue of Turkish-trained senior officials, who have some notion of administration but also the usual Turkish faults. The country lacks competent junior officials, there is no tradition of public life amongst her leading families. . . . But if foreign advisers and technicians are made available and properly used, and a better sense of public duty is developed amongst the younger generations, there is hope for the future.[36]

In Shone's view the Lebanese were even more intelligent and capable but their administration functioned less well than the Syrian:

> The Lebanese are widely regarded as the most intelligent of all Middle-Eastern peoples, and have some officials and politicians of a relatively high standard. In general, the competence of the administration is lower than in Syria, but it manages to keep going somehow in present conditions.[37]

In both Syria and Lebanon the police force and gendarmerie were sufficient to keep order and to enforce justice and the collection of taxes. Probably only a severe economic or political crisis would bring about a breakdown of administration. In sum the governmental machinery of Syria and Lebanon, 'creaking but turning', would probably grind along in normal times. It was important to bear in mind that the two states had to overcome the handicap of French colonial tutelage. The standards of 'viability' should not be set too high, he re-emphasized.

Shone was much less optimistic about the prospects of democracy:

> Democracy in Syria works no better than in other Arab States; democracy combined with republicanism is still more unsuited to the fickle, self-seeking, hypocritical Syrians. The feudal organisation of the country and the ignorance and illiteracy of the masses are at present effective bars to any real popular representation; the Chamber of Deputies is ranged according to personalities, not policies, and the manifest lack of civic spirit amongst even the more enlightened leaders will always form a serious obstacle to the promulgation of legislation calling for sacrifices from the population.[38]

In Shone's judgement Syria would probably be better off under a 'benevolent autocracy', but barring an economic blizzard or a similar crisis he believed that the political system 'could probably rub along much as at present in normal times'. His prognosis for democracy in Lebanon was still more gloomy:

> Republican democracy is even less successful in the Lebanon than in Syria: the country is too small, the ruling classes too level in calibre and too much inter-related. Chamber debates, and politics in general, are squabbles between

[36] Ibid.   [37] Ibid.   [38] Ibid.

cliques. Centuries of domination or protection, and a common consciousness of minority status, have deprived all but a few Lebanese of any civic spirit or true nationalist feeling. The Lebanon, even more than Syria, requires to be ruled, but it is difficult to conceive what type of ruler could impose his authority on these conflicting elements.[39]

Lebanon could not yet be properly regarded as a nation, in Shone's judgement, because the religious and cultural divisions had prevented the growth of a national consciousness. He could not hold out much hope for the development of a 'true' nation, but on the other hand the government would probably keep functioning under normal circumstances.

It was the religious and ethnic dimension of the problem which most troubled Shone. In Syria the question was less acute than in Lebanon, but it nevertheless found reflection in what he called 'Damascus-mindedness' at the expense of the tribes and provinces. 'Although comparatively homogeneous in race, religion and language, Syria has still far to go before becoming a nation.' The sense of ethnic identities impeded the development of a 'Syrian' consciousness. On the other hand, Shone did not believe that the possible persecution of ethnic minorities would be as problematical as in other parts of the Middle East:

Persecution of minorities appears improbable, for the Syrians, though their religious sheikhs are amongst the most reactionary and bigoted of Islam, are not themselves fanatical, and will have too great a need of foreign Powers to risk thus alienating them. . . . Provided that they [the minorities] could . . . consider themselves first and foremost as Syrians, they should have little or nothing to fear.[40]

Syria in the future would face many domestic problems, but in comparison with Lebanon it could be said that at least the basis of the Syrian 'nation' existed. 'Lebanon', Shone wrote, 'is so much less a nation even than Syria.'

In contrasting Lebanon with Syria, Shone emphasized Lebanese confessional fissures. 'Christian–Moslem hostility, resulting partly from history and partly from the clash between their respective Occidental and Oriental cultures, is not always outwardly apparent, but smoulders beneath the surface and breaks out on occasion.' Here there was nothing especially original in Shone's analysis, but the following passage had an important bearing on his later conclusion:

The more enlightened Christian families intermarry to some extent; Christians with Moslems seldom or never. The Maronite Patriarch and other Christian prelates jealously guard their communities' real or fancied interests, and still

[39] Shone to Eden, No. 63, Secret, 19 Apr. 1945, FO 371/45563/E2680.
[40] Ibid.

wield more power than any Government have up to the present felt able to defy. The provision in the Constitution that all communities must be equitably represented in the administration has by tradition been carried to such lengths that nowadays not only Ministers but judges and even gendarmes must be so chosen as to preserve the proportional distribution of such posts amongst the communities. A more formidable obstacle to the emergence of a true national consciousness or an efficient administration can hardly be imagined.[41]

Even more than in Syria, Shone concluded, French attempts at continued control in Lebanon 'sooner or later' would lead to an internal explosion, especially if the French attempted to carve out a Christian enclave where French influence would remain predominant.

The economic part of Shone's assessment was less substantial than the political, in part because the economic future of the two states would be determined by political imponderables. In the 1930s both Syria and Lebanon had an unfavourable balance of trade, but both had built up budget surpluses during the war. Syria had no major source of wealth, such as the oil of Iraq or the cotton of Egypt. Lebanon possessed one good port. There was little confidence in the local currency, which presumably would have to be backed by the French. Here the uncertainties of the world's economy defied prognostication. In a word everything would depend on the future relations with France. Even with France granting full independence on amicable terms, without rupturing commercial relations, it was by no means certain that Syria and Lebanon would continue to function as an economic unit for customs and other economic purposes: 'there is a bitter mutual rivalry between Syrian and Lebanese commercial interests, which is at present generally being subordinated to the desire of the two Governments to form a common front against the French but which in normal times might easily result in serious differences on such issues as tariffs'. Nor could it be said that the other Arab states would help Syria and Lebanon economically: 'Unfortunately, it seems more likely that the chief preoccupations of the League will be political rather than economic.' In the end all that could be said, politically as well as economically, was that 'nationalist fervour' would blind the Syrians and the Lebanese from seeing how much foreign assistance they needed, and would reinforce their tendency 'to muddle along in their own way'.[42]

On the whole Shone provided a fascinating and realistic estimate of the first two states of the European colonial world to achieve independence during the era of the Second World War. In concluding his report Shone offered one prediction, and one warning. The

[41] Ibid.   [42] Shone to Eden, 19 Apr. 1945.

prediction was that the Syrians and the Lebanese, if they turned away from France, 'would prefer to look to us or to the United States of America; but . . . Syria at least would hotly resent any attempt to force help upon her or to impose any form of "trustee-ship" '. The warning was about the French: 'it is impossible to exclude the possibility that the French, if they failed to secure their desiderata in Syria or the present Lebanon, might try, by hook or by crook, to ensure for themselves a predominant position in a small, mainly Christian, Lebanon'.[43]

Within the Foreign Office Hankey wrote the principal comment on Shone's report. By this time events in the Levant had moved into crisis, and Hankey directed his remarks to Shone's warning about the French:

> The result of the present crisis will undoubtedly be the elimination of French influence from Syria but it may quite possibly not be the elimination of French influence from the Lebanon. This will produce a rift between Lebanon and Syria, which will regard a Lebanon under French influence as a dagger aimed at the heart of the Arab world.[44]

That train of thought led Hankey to conclude that if the French were expelled from Syria they should be pushed out of Lebanon as well. Otherwise, as Shone had emphasized, there probably would be 'a rift inside Lebanon itself between the Moslems and Christians'. Connecting his argument with Shone's analysis of 'viability', Hankey wrote in a manner that is revealing about the way in which Franco-phobia could be reconciled with native welfare:

> It will be from every point of view better if a solution of the Levant States is a general one and not purely a Syrian one i.e., if France loses her special position in Syria she had better lose it also in Lebanon in which case the two states can probably rub along much as they are at present with some foreign assistance which they can get wherever it is best available. If necessary they could arrange a further fusion of the two states as they are fused at present for currency, customs, public monopolies and other financial questions.[45]

Events had overtaken Shone's report, but it still gave invaluable guidance into the question of future viability of the two states. It was clear to Hankey that Syrian and Lebanese antipathy to the French was now so great that the British could have nothing to do with a privileged French position. 'Our power to help the French in these countries', he concluded, '. . . has come to an end and . . . we should cease to talk about a special position for France in the Levant.'[46]

[43] Shone to Eden, 19 Apr. 1945.
[44] Minute by Hankey, 6 June 1945, FO 371/45563.
[45] Ibid.   [46] Ibid.

The May Crisis and Its Significance

On the 30th of May 1945 the President of Syria, Shukri al-Quwatli, sent the following message to the American Secretary of State:

> Where now is the Atlantic Charter and the Four Freedoms? What can we think of San Francisco? I would that President Truman re-read and confirm to us Mr. Roosevelt's last letter (December 7 [1944]) assuring us of his support of our independence; if ever the principles voiced in its last paragraph were applicable, it is today; your country has encouraged us in our stand to refuse special privilege to France or any other country but you have permitted France to block the adequate arming of our *gendarmerie*; now the French are bombing us and destroying our cities and towns with Lend-Leased munitions which were given for use against our common enemies.[47]

It was a plea well calculated to stir up American indignation at French imperialism. With a mixture of outrage and suspicion—of the British as well as the French—the Office of Near Eastern and African Affairs of the State Department had watched the crisis develop as if the clock had been turned back, in the words of the director, Loy W. Henderson, 'to the practices which, from 1931 to 1939, resulted in the present war'.[48]

It is necessary to comprehend the general American attitude towards the Levant in order to understand the British dilemma. To the American public the Levant ranked almost along with China as a field for missionary and educational opportunity. American goodwill and good work were manifest in missions, schools, and hospitals. The American University of Beirut by anyone's book had played an important part in the spread of western ideas in the Middle East. A determination not to allow the European powers an exclusive commercial advantage had formed the main theme of American economic relations with the mandates. For those reasons the Levant had a special place in the minds of the officials responsible for protecting American commercial, missionary, educational, and philanthropic interests. 'We regard our policy towards the independent Levant States', Henderson wrote, 'as entirely distinct and separate from our policy toward France and the French Empire.'[49] The question was 'distinct and separate' because Henderson and his

[47] *Foreign Relations 1945*, VIII, p. 1118. For Roosevelt's letter see ibid., 1944, V, p. 812: 'The American people have recently recorded overwhelmingly their determination that the United States shall assume its full share of the responsibility, in cooperation with other nations of like mind, in creating a future world of peace, prosperity and justice for all.'

[48] Memorandum by Henderson, 23 May 1945, USSD 890D.01/5-2345 Box 6942; *Foreign Relations 1945*, VIII, pp. 1093-5.

[49] Memorandum by Henderson, 16 Feb. 1945, USSD 890D.01/2-145 Box 1642. For discussion of the contradictory American wartime policies towards the French colonial empire, see Louis, *Imperialism at Bay*, chap. 2.

colleagues did not intend to lose sight of it in the morass of other problems which they would face in trying to liquidate the French colonial empire. American officials in short distrusted de Gaulle and the Free French who, they suspected, would pursue an unbridled course of exploitation unless checked. The French colonies held a special place in the American demonology of European imperialism as sinks of iniquity and corruption. In September 1944 the United States had recognized Syria and Lebanon as independent nations. The officials of the State Department, galvanized in particular by Loy Henderson, were prepared to take stringent measures to prevent the reassertion of French control.

George Wadsworth, the American representative in the Levant who became the first Minister to Syria and Lebanon, also held forceful views about the necessity for the United States to 'play politics in the Big League' in the Middle East. He had confidence in what he referred to as the American 'moral leadership in the Near East'.[50] Before he had entered the Foreign Service, Wadsworth had taught at the American University at Beirut. He regarded the Atlantic Charter as the lodestar of American policy in the Levant. In his view the Syrians and the Lebanese should have the right to determine their own form of government without any French interference whatsoever. To the French he presented such an outrageous interpretation of the Atlantic Charter—as 'the new international gospel' and 'the Tables of the Law'—that his motives were called into question. A French journalist for example believed that he regarded the French presence in the Levant as 'the incarnation of the most diabolical "papistry" and Latin Jesuitry'.[51] Wadsworth in fact was no more anti-French or anti-Catholic than his colleagues in the State Department (though he was more anti-Zionist). He was merely pro-American, pro-Syrian, and pro-Lebanese (and thus suspicious of the British as well as the French). Loy Henderson defended him against French charges by stating that he had represented the views of the American government 'with great clarity' during the crisis of 1945. William Phillips, Special Assistant to the Secretary of State, agreed that Wadsworth had 'maintained exactly the right approach'.[52] It is therefore illuminating briefly to dwell on the crux of American wartime policy towards the Levant from Wadsworth's perspective.

'We have based policy on the Atlantic Charter and talked of the four freedoms', Wadsworth wrote, 'while Arab leaders here continued

[50] Memorandum by Wadsworth dated 'December–January 1946', USSD 890D.00/3-46.

[51] See Kirk, *The Middle East in the War*, p. 273 n. 1.

[52] Memorandum by Henderson with a notation by Phillips, 9 June 1945, USSD 711.90E/6-945.

to nurse four fears—of French imperialism, British insincerity, American isolationism, and Zionist expansionism.'[53] The catalyst of those conflicting elements was the Lebanese crisis of November 1943. Wadsworth at that time had reported to Washington that the French response to Lebanese nationalist aspirations had been made clear by the arrest of the President and members of the Cabinet, the suspension of the constitution, and the seizure of public buildings by French marines and Senegalese troops. This is not the place to comment on this wartime turning point in the affairs of the Levant, but it is important to stress that Wadsworth believed he had witnessed historic events. After the British presented an ultimatum to restore civil order—or face the alternative of a complete British takeover— the French commander told him that 'the whole affair reminded him of Fashoda'.[54] The experience left a profound impact on Wadsworth, who described French policy in terms of 'unblushing hypocrisy'. He—and his superiors including Roosevelt himself—drew the conclusion that the French simply could not be trusted to fulfil the pledges of independence. The November 1943 crisis united the Lebanese nationalists against the French. And, Wadsworth reported, it had an equally important consequence for the British. It was clear, to him at least, that the divergent strains of British policy—supporting the French in a privileged position while encouraging Lebanese and Syrian independence—could not be reconciled. From that time on Wadsworth took an unbending and unyielding stand against the French claim to a pre-eminent position. He was almost as critical of the British for acquiescing in the French pretension as he was of the French themselves for failing to take steps to implement a transfer of power. To the Americans the Levant in the last two years of the war was on its way to becoming a test case for postwar colonial independence.

The United States extended recognition to Syria and Lebanon in September 1944 on grounds of 'the accelerated transfer of governmental powers' (as a consequence of the Lebanese crisis). The real test of independence was the issue of troop withdrawal.[55] It proved to be a volatile subject of discussion in a meeting between the Syrian President and the British Prime Minister in February 1945, when the two met in Cairo on the latter's return from the Yalta Conference. Quwatli told Churchill that the issue of troops was the 'vital' question.

[53] Wadsworth to Hull, 23 Mar. 1943, USSD 890D.00/948 Box 5169; *Foreign Relations 1943*, IV, pp. 963-5.
[54] Wadsworth to Hull, 22 Nov. 1943, USSD 890E.00/255 Box 5173; *Foreign Relations 1943*, IV, pp. 1040-3.
[55] Hull to Wadsworth, 5 Sept. 1944, USSD 890D.01/8-944 Box 5170; *Foreign Relations 1944*, V, p. 774.

When would the French transfer authority over the 25,000 *Troupes Spéciales* to the Syrians, he asked? 'They were Syrians', he told Churchill, 'and it was intolerable that the Syrians were liable to be attacked by their own children.' Though Churchill attempted to shift the topics, Quwatli would revert to the *Troupes Spéciales*. Churchill for example expostulated that the French simply could not be kicked out. 'The French must have a position of some sort', he told the Syrian leader. Quwatli rejoined that they could have 'most-favoured-nation' treatment and reiterated that the *Troupes Spéciales* must be placed under Syrian authority as soon as possible. Churchill stressed the point, as if it should matter to the Syrians, that 'constant rows with the French were very annoying to His Majesty's Government'. De Gaulle, he emphasized to Quwatli, was 'a dangerous man'. Quwatli was entirely unmoved. 'It was essential', he said, returning to the charge, '. . . that the transfer of the *Troupes Spéciales* should be settled before British troops left.'[56] Churchill thus made little headway. He was perhaps beginning to comprehend the reasons for the wide regard for Quwatli as the champion of Syrian nationalism, the man whom the British Minister Resident in the Middle East had described as the only 'outstanding' man in the Levant.[57] Quwatli knew his own mind, and he pointedly told Churchill that the Syrians would not under any circumstances settle for a relationship with the French similar to the one between the Iraqis and the British. The solution that the British had preferred throughout the war was thus dismissed out of hand—and with finality.[58] By early 1945 the British knew that there would be little hope of conciliation between the French and the Syrians, especially not, in Quwatli's phrase, on the 'burning issue' of the *Troupes Spéciales*.

On different occasions, and to all parties concerned, Quwatli spoke out passionately on the issues of freedom and independence. On one occasion he said that he would rather see Syria become 'a Soviet Republic' than continue a relationship dependent on the French.[59] Another time he said that he would 'cut off his right hand rather than sign a treaty with the French'.[60] He stressed repeatedly that he liked to believe, injecting a note of scepticism, that the principles of the Atlantic Charter would be applied. His statements about independence and freedom of course appealed to the Americans,

[56] 'Cairo Conversations, February 1945', Top Secret, FO 371/45560.

[57] Grigg to Eden, Private and Personal, 23 Jan. 1945, FO 371/45559. Churchill later described Quwatli in his memoirs as 'a sensible and competent man'. *Triumph and Tragedy*, p. 565.

[58] 'Cairo Conversations, February 1945.'

[59] Wadsworth to Secretary of State, 15 Sept. 1944, USSD, 890E.01/9–1544.

[60] Shone to Eden, 30 Apr. 1945, quoted in Kersaudy, *Churchill and De Gaulle*, p. 398.

especially within the context of French colonial exploitation. He even evoked a sympathy of sorts from the Eastern Department of the Foreign Office. Hankey noted that the Syrians 'rather pathetically' were depending on the British to save them from the French.[61] Shone also wrote in almost identical language that Quwatli was 'pathetically anxious to be friendly and have close relations with us'.[62] At the same time there was a tone of lament that can be detected in British minutes. The more Quwatli publicized Syrian rights to choose their own form of government and their own friends, as they claimed from the idealistic heritage of the war, the less room the British had to manœuvre. *'The whole Arab world is watching the situation closely and our widest interests, strategic and political, are too closely affected'*, Hankey noted.[63] And in another minute Hankey carefully concluded on a note of anguish: 'we cannot, I am sure, afford not to carry out fully the promises of independence which we have made to the Levant States because the effect on our position in the rest of the Middle East would be disastrous'.[64]

Quwatli proved himself a consummate politician in exploiting the international awareness of the British guarantee of independence. It is probable that until early 1945 he remained sceptical of British intent. After his interview with Churchill in February he had appeared to Terence Shone, who talked with him afterwards, to be very pleased with himself. He had good reason to be. By vehemently proclaiming that the Syrians would never be a party to an arrangement similar to the one between the British and the Iraqis, he had gained Churchill's admission that the Syrians would not be forced to accept such a treaty.[65] It was a moment of truth for Quwatli. He had suspected, as did the Americans, that the British and the French had concluded a secret arrangement which the British would now be obliged to honour.[66] In fact there was no secret agreement. There was no 'Sykes-Picot', the phrase he used with Shone. The settlement in the Levant would be based on the principles of the Atlantic Charter after all. At the same time he had left no doubt in Churchill's mind about the danger of a nationalist uprising against the French if the question of the *Troupes Spéciales* could not be resolved. Quwatli

[61] Minute by Hankey, 3 Mar. 1945, FO 371/45575.
[62] Shone to Campbell, Top Secret and Personal, 18 May 1945, FO 371/45564/E3179/G.
[63] Minute by Hankey, 16 Mar. 1945, FO 371/45561/E1726, emphasis added.
[64] Minute by Hankey, 3 Mar. 1945, FO 371/45575.
[65] Minute by Shone, 18 Feb. 1945, FO 371/45560.
[66] 'There is a possibility that the British have already given certain commitments, unknown to us, to the French with regard to French demands upon the Levant States.' Memorandum by Henderson, 21 May 1945, USSD 890D.01/5-2145; *Foreign Relations 1945*, VIII, pp. 1085-7.

might talk about a 'Soviet Republic' or of cutting off his hand before
he would sign an agreement with the French, but in fact what he
had in mind was a Syrian republic whose independence would be
backed by the Soviet Union as well as the United States and one that
would be free so far as possible from British as well as French interference.

Churchill of course saw Quwatli's game of playing the British off
against the French, and he did not like it. 'It is not for us alone to
defend by force either Syrian or Lebanese independence or French
privilege', he stated in the House of Commons.[67] Churchill pursued
that line persistently, and on the very day of the beginning of the
crisis, the 28th of May, he telegraphed a personal message to General
Bernard Paget, the Commander-in-Chief, 'to maintain a strictly
impartial and negative attitude to both sides'.[68] Three days later he
ordered British troops to intervene. It was a momentous decision
reached only after searching and frantic reappraisal.

It is an amusing commentary on the way in which events overpass
long-range plans that on the eve of the crisis Hankey and his colleagues
in the Eastern Department were still debating the abstract issues of
'viability' (based on Shone's report), and the advantages of the
Syrian weather for the possible permanent occupation of British
troops. 'Our military . . . on occasion let slip the significant remark
that Syria and the Lebanon had a better climate than other countries
in the Middle East', Hankey noted.[69] On the 17th of May, little over
a week after VE day, French troops landed at Beirut. Far from yielding on the question of the *Troupes Spéciales*, the French had decided
that reinforcements and, if necessary, force itself, would be the only
guarantee of a 'privileged position'. In London the Foreign Secretary
himself was among the first to scent the immediate danger. Eden
lamented that British troops had not been withdrawn before being
exposed to the predicament of being caught in the crossfire. He
wrote on the 20th of May: 'I consider that we have got ourselves into
a bad position by maintaining these troops here for so long. They are
of course quite useless strategically, & we should have brought them
out during the lull a month or two back.' Eden was writing in
response to an appraisal by Hankey, who characteristically had
identified the presence of British troops as a guarantee of native
welfare. If the British now withdrew, he wrote, the Syrians would
be left 'entirely at the mercy of the French'. Eden had no patience
for that sentiment.

[67] *Parliamentary Debates* (Commons), 27 Feb. 1945, col. 1290.
[68] Minute by Churchill, 28 May 1946, FO 371/45565/E3407/G.
[69] Minute by Hankey, 22 May 1945, FO 371/44570/E3829/G.

As regards Mr. Hankey's point . . . I can assure him that this is *not* . . . how we shall appear in world opinion. We are really too naive if we believe that anyone will accept . . . [Hankey's argument] in this wicked world. On the contrary many will accept the French story that this is a struggle between France & ourselves for the control of the Levant States in which we have made use of France's weakness to entrench ourselves. . . .[70]

Despite those strongly held views, Eden, like Churchill, was eventually brought round to the advisability of intervention.

Eden was receptive to a series of rigorous assessments by Hankey and Sir Ronald Campbell (Assistant Under-Secretary). They wrote together on the 25th of May: 'Direct military action by us in the Levant States would almost certainly result in the ultimate elimination of the French from the Levant States altogether, or at any rate in our being saddled with the full responsibility for devising any other settlement that had to be arranged or imposed.' There thus was no doubt about the seriousness of the issues at stake for the French. Eden noted, 'I agree'.[71] Hankey and Campbell also pointed out that if the British stood aside the consequences would be just as serious, not least for the British themselves. In the end it was this assessment by Campbell that carried Eden's concurrence in favour of intervention:

Reports from our Middle Eastern posts make it clear that if the British troops do not intervene, and if H. M. G. do nothing to stop the fighting, this country will be held to have let the Arab world down, and to have gone back on the obligations they are regarded as having undertaken when they endorsed the French declaration of Syrian and Lebanese independence. It is the view in the Arab world in spite of the Prime Minister's statement in Parliament that it was not for this country alone to enforce the French promise.[72]

Eden again noted, 'I agree'. He wrote elsewhere, as if resigning himself for the worst, 'I think that now we must leave our troops where they are until this storm blows itself out or bursts on our devoted heads.'[73] That evening, on the 29th, fierce fighting broke out between the French and the Syrians in Damascus.

In the Cabinet discussions Churchill addressed himself to the painful dilemma of taking up arms against an ally or, in his own words, doing 'nothing to assist Syria and the Lebanon against French aggression'. He deplored the situation in which the British had been manœuvred into assuming sole responsibility of restoring order. If at all possible he wished the Americans to assist with 'a token force'.[74]

[70] Minutes by Hankey and Eden, 20-1 May 1945, FO 371/45570/E3829/G.
[71] Minute by Eden, 25 May 1945, on 'Note for the Secretary of State', FO 371/45569/E3826.
[72] Minute by Campbell, 28 May 1945, FO 371/45569/E3802.
[73] Minute by Eden, 29 May 1945, FO 371/45570.
[74] Cabinet Conclusions CM 2 (45), 30 May 1945, CAB 65/53.

Events would not wait. Before assessments could be made of the pros and cons of inviting the Americans to help uphold the principle of 'independence' in the Levant, the situation further deteriorated. On the next day, the 31st, Churchill initialled the telegram to General Paget instructing him to impose a cease-fire and restrict French troops to their barracks. After that message had already been sent, he received a telegram from Quwatli passionately denouncing the French attack:

> Every part of Syria is being destroyed. French bombs pitilessly poured on to peaceful defenceless towns. Homs, Hama and Aleppo are subjected to unprecedented bombardment. For three days Damascus, historic and holy town of Arab and Mohammedan world, has undergone savage bombardment by aircraft, artillery and tanks. Fires resulting from the bombardments are breaking out everywhere. Whole streets and districts ravaged by fire bombs and destruction. Several thousand killed and wounded in streets and under ruins. Bombing and machine gun fire continues, wiping out peaceful men, women and children. All this slaughter is only justified by our having refused to grant France special privileges incompatible with our sovereignty and independence. Our country is being destroyed despite the assurances given by the Allies recognising our independence.[75]

Quwatli's telegram gave consolation that the right decision had been made, but nothing could be done to mitigate the fury and the humiliation of the French. De Gaulle saw the British action as no less than the fulfilment of a long-calculated plan 'to oust the French from the Levant and take their place'.[76]

The French (and the British) did not finally withdraw from the Levant until the 15th of April 1946, but the May crisis of 1945 effectively marked the end of the French era in the Middle East. American suspicions of French motives lingered on. At the Potsdam Conference in July President Truman was sufficiently briefed on the subject to be able to snap to Churchill and Stalin that the United States 'stood for equal rights for all, and special privileges for none'.[77] In December Loy Henderson, who kept a vigilant eye on French imperialism, concluded that French policy in the Levant remained so 'cynical' that there was no hope that France would play a 'con-

---

[75] Quwatli to Churchill, 1 June 1945, FO 371/45567/E3614.

[76] Cooper to Eden, No. 836, 5 June 1945, FO 371/45569/E3823. Churchill had telegraphed to Paget on 3 June 1945: 'As soon as you are master of the situation, you should show full consideration to the French. We are very intimately linked with France in Europe and your greatest triumph will be to produce a peace without rancour.' FO 371/45569/E3825. *Triumph and Tragedy*, p. 565.

[77] British minutes, 23 July 1945, FO 371/45578/E5483. Stalin said that he shared the President's view on that point, and according to the American minutes, added that the Syrians in any case were reluctant to give any privileges to the French. At that point Truman, Stalin, and Churchill had a good laugh at French expense. See memorandum by George Allen, 24 July 1945, USSD 890D.00/7-2445.

structive role' in the Middle East.[78] In February 1946, in the last stage of kicking out the French (and the British too), the Syrians and Lebanese brought a complaint before the Security Council of the United Nations. Ernest Bevin, who had assumed the mantle of Churchill and Eden as the guardian of independence in the Levant, perhaps learned an important lesson about nationalism from this episode. He could not get the Syrians and the Lebanese to acknowledge that the British had come to their aid and had stayed on only in their defence. Indeed they seemed to be implying that the British because of their own continued occupation were now a party to the dispute on the side of the French! According to an American observer, 'This had a profoundly disturbing effect on Bevin'.[79] Nationalists could be fickle friends.

It is easy to detect a note of *schadenfreude* in the British minutes about the troubles of the French in the Levant at the close of the war. The French, their old colonial rivals, had, in the words of Terence Shone, 'now finally cooked their own goose'.[80] But it was not the outcome the British would have preferred. A 'privileged position' for France in Syria and Lebanon comparable to Britain's in Iraq would have strengthened the general British position in the Middle East, whereas the independent status of Syria and Lebanon gave the other Arab states the incentive to accelerate their own drive to unfettered independence.[81] And there was a further reason for British dissatisfaction at the outcome of the crisis in the Levant. Any move that the British might make to associate Syria and Lebanon with a regional organization ('Greater Syria' or an 'Arab Federation'), whether for economic or defence purposes, would, in Oliver Harvey's words, 'appear to the logical and suspicious French mind as deliberate and perfidious'.[82] As will be seen in the chapters below,

---

[78] Memorandum by Henderson, 28 Dec. 1945, USSD 890.00/12-2845.

[79] Memorandum by Benjamin V. Cohen to Henderson, 1 Mar. 1945, USSD 890D.01/3-146; *Foreign Relations 1946*, VII, p. 775 n. 42. For the Security Council debate see *Official Records of the Security Council*, First Year, No. 1. The Russians on this occasion took the opportunity to exercise the veto, the first time in the history of the United Nations. They expressed disapproval that the French would not agree to evacuate immediately.

[80] Shone to Campbell, Top Secret and Personal, 27 Aug. 1945, FO 371/45582. For Shone's comprehensive account see his dispatch to Bevin of 25 Aug. 1945, Shone Papers.

[81] The negative side of this point is a repeated theme in the diary of Oliver Harvey, e.g. 20 Oct. 1944: 'If we weaken the French in Syria, we weaken our own position.' Add. MSS 56400.

[82] Minute by Harvey, 3 Oct. 1945, FO 371/45583. On that point there arose controversy about priorities in British policy—Europe versus the Middle East. Harvey (who later became Ambassador to France) believed it essential to 'convince the French that we do not intend to take advantage of their absence to bring the Levant directly or indirectly into the British system' (ibid.). His view won out, but Robert Howe (who later became Governor-General in the Sudan) lamented that 'a self-denying ordinance on our part . . . not to provide

the project for a 'Greater Syria' continued to be debated among Arab leaders and theorists of the pan-Arab movement, but the crisis in the Levant effectively killed any British sponsorship of it. The bitter legacy of the dispute with France served as a check against integrating Syria and Lebanon into the 'British' Middle East.

From the American vantage point the outcome was much more satisfactory, though a warning by the first Minister to Syria and Lebanon, serves to indicate the general sense of unease with which American officials were watching events in the Levant in relation to the general affairs of the Middle East. Wadsworth believed that Zionism would be a greater danger in the future than French imperialism had been in the past. He wrote in regard to Syria and Lebanon, but he believed that Zionism would continue to be a disruptive force in other countries as well. He described 'a growing Arab belief' that the United States supported the basic aim of the Zionists: 'the conversion of Palestine, with its Arab majority, into a Jewish state'. He himself believed that endorsement of Zionism would contradict the basic American principle of self-determination, and he knew for certain that the Arabs would view it in that way. To them it would seem 'a denial of our principles that no basic politico-territorial change should be made in any country without the consent of the inhabitants and that peoples may choose the form of government they desire'. Wadsworth was unabashedly anti-Zionist. Making allowance for that outlook, it is illuminating to read his conclusion as one written not only by the first American Minister to Syria and Lebanon but also by a former teacher at the American University at Beirut: 'If we use our influence to make Palestine a Jewish state, all our building and most of that of a century of earnestly creative Americans before us will, I fear with them, become as writing on water, and our economic and cultural interests may well look forward to folding their tents among the Arabs.'[83]

these States with . . . assistance . . . would cut at the root of our proposed Middle East policy of treating the area as a single region' (minute by Howe, 3 Oct. 1945, FO 371/45583). Terence Shone also wrote in October 1945: 'I fully appreciate the reason for . . . the importance of ridding the French mind of suspicions that we are supplanting them in the Levant States. But there is another side to the picture. It is . . . that the Levant Governments have been begging us to give them advice of every kind, to help them to set their houses in order (which the French have signally failed to do). . . . If the States felt that we were washing our hands of them or taking the French part, and if the Americans failed them, I would not exclude the possibility of Russian influence being increasingly established in the States' (minute by Shone, 8 Oct. 1945, FO 371/45584/E7740).

[83] Memorandum by Wadsworth dated 'December–January 1945-6', USSD 890D.00/3-46.

4

SAUDIA ARABIA: THE QUESTION OF OIL AND THE ACCOMMODATION OF THE UNITED STATES

THE British Minister in Saudi Arabia, Laurence Grafftey-Smith, wrote in 1945: 'We are dealing in Saudi Arabia with a museum-piece Oriental potentate in a desert setting.'[1] That assessment of Abdul Aziz Ibn Saud is fundamental in understanding British reactions to American economic and strategic aims as well as contemporary assessments of Saudi Arabia's future political orientation. Ibn Saud himself held a unique position in the Arab world. Though his international influence was still modest, his personal stature surpassed that of all other Arab leaders. His kingdom stretched over a desert territory one-quarter the size of the United States. By 1945 the oil reserves had already begun to transform Saudi Arabia into a critical area of American enterprise and strategic defence. That trend, so stark in retrospect, did not at the time appear to British observers to be a matter of certainty or, so far as that goes, an entirely desirable development. During the crucial period of the mid-1940s the British continued to regard Ibn Saud as an exceptionally shrewd and courageous Arab leader whose benevolence towards them played an important and perhaps decisive part during the wartime years. 'If Ibn Saud had not been favourable to us', R. M. A. Hankey noted, 'we should have had endless trouble in the Middle East, given the chances of making trouble there, and in fact it is probable that this would have made the difference between holding the Middle East or just losing it, given the internal security commitment which the Army would probably have had to take on.'[2] Hankey's line of reasoning provides the key to British thought of the latter part of the 1940s. Anglo-Saudi friendship had survived the test of the war. The economic exploitation of Saudi Arabia by American oil companies, which had begun by the eve of the war, ought to be encouraged rather than resisted by the British in order to anchor the involvement

---

[1] 'Annual Report on Saudi Arabia for 1945', enclosed in Grafftey-Smith to Bevin, No. 31, Confidential, 23 Feb. 1946, FO 371/52823/E2249.

[2] Minute by Hankey, 22 Sept. 1944, FO 371/40266. For an assessment of the reasons for Ibn Saud's decision 'to cleave to the Allies . . . even in the darkest days of 1942' see D. C. Watt, 'The Foreign Policy of Ibn Saud 1936–39', *Journal of the Royal Asian Society*, L, II (April 1963).

of the United States in the Middle East. While yielding the economic field to the Americans, the British would sustain a predominant political and military influence through close ties with Ibn Saud.

The note of British gratitude is important as a wartime theme spilling over into the postwar era. It is reflected in Churchill's account of the famous meeting with Ibn Saud after the Yalta Conference in February 1945. Churchill, unlike Roosevelt, had not made the mistake of asking Ibn Saud to sympathize with Zionist aims in Palestine. Churchill's comment is in line with the secret assessments of the Foreign Office and is important in grasping the general British impression of Ibn Saud. It was not disingenuous:

> King Ibn Saud made a striking impression. My admiration for him was deep, because of his unfailing loyalty to us. He was always at his best in the darkest hours. He was now over seventy but had lost none of his warrior vigour. He still lived the existence of a patriarchal king of the Arabian desert, with his forty living sons and the seventy ladies of the harem, and three or four official wives, as prescribed by the Prophet, one vacancy being kept.[3]

In similar vein Grafftey-Smith could also write in 1945, on the basis of long years of experience in the Middle East: 'A lifetime of friendly relations with the British is not easily forgotten, and Ibn Saud is not a man to forget or revile his friends.'[4] The virtues of loyalty and friendship moreover formed the theme of minutes within the Foreign Office. According to Nevile Butler (Assistant Under-Secretary): 'Ibn Saud is far and away our most influential friend among the Arabs: his favourable influence is almost certain to be required in connexion with the Levant, Palestine, and in economic questions in his own country where the Americans are running us hard.'[5] Butler, like his colleagues, was confident that Ibn Saud would continue to be conciliatory and pro-British on all major issues except Palestine, a point on which the King stood intractably against Zionism.

It is certain that the Foreign Office officials who wrote such minutes were well aware that gratitude between nations could prove to be a cheap virtue, just as past friendship could prove to be a fickle guide to the future. What then was the source of their optimism? In part their assessment was based on the conviction that Britain in the postwar period would remain the dominant power in the Middle East despite her weakened economic position. In Saudi Arabia the Americans, if kept under control, could actually come to the aid of the British by helping to put Ibn Saud's finances on a sounder basis. It is important not to let the facts of the postwar

---

[3] Winston S. Churchill, *Triumph and Tragedy* (Boston, 1953), p. 398.
[4] Grafftey-Smith, 'Annual Report on Saudi Arabia for 1945'.
[5] Minute by Butler, 21 Feb. 1945, FO 371/45523.

oil boom obscure the way in which the British regarded Saudi Arabia at the close of the war. It was an immense, sparsely populated, and desperately poor country where Ibn Saud depended on foreign assistance for the revenues needed to maintain internal order. There is not only a tone of confidence but also one of condescension as the British observed the growth of American influence. According to Sir Maurice Peterson, who had served as Ambassador in Iraq and played a key part in the wartime discussions with the Americans about Saudi Arabia: 'The crux of the matter is that, however accommodating we may show ourselves to the Americans over Saudi Arabia (and we are anxious to be accommodating) we cannot make over to them any part of the "good-will" we have accumulated in that country which must inevitably secure, for our representative and over many years to come, the edge over the American.'[6]

Into those discussions Grafftey-Smith injected a note of scepticism. He did not question Ibn Saud's goodwill so much as he doubted the vitality of the British response to the economic challenge of the Americans and the religious and political transformation of the Arabian peninsula. Grafftey-Smith himself had witnessed the creation of the modern state of Saudi Arabia within the scope of his own official career. He had entered the Levant Consular Service as a student-interpreter in 1914. In 1920 he began a tour of duty at Jedda, with the Hejaz as his consular district, during the era of King Hussein. Hashemite hatred of Ibn Saud left an indelible impression on Grafftey-Smith's mind. Four years later Hussein was an exile and Ibn Saud had added the holy cities of Mecca and Medina to his central Arabian domains. Grafftey-Smith's analysis of the forces behind those events, which he later related as a sort of epic, provides insight into the British response to the rise of Ibn Saud's political and religious, and, later, economic power. 'Grafftey', as he was known to his friends, is rightly regarded as one of the great *raconteurs* of the history of the British Empire in the Middle East.[7] If one scratches beneath the anecdotes, one finds an exceptionally astute observer of Middle Eastern affairs. As an introduction to the problems

[6] Peterson to Campbell, Personal and Confidential, 13 June 1944, FO 371/40266.
[7] See his autobiography, *Bright Levant* (London, 1970). On Ibn Saud the accounts which Grafftey-Smith himself valued were: H. C. Armstrong, *Lord of Arabia* (London, 1934); Gerald De Gaury, *Arabia Phoenix* (London, 1946); H. St. John Philby, *Arabian Jubilee* (New York, 1952); Jacques Benoist-Mechin, *Arabian Destiny* (London, 1957); D. Van der Meulen, *The Wells of Ibn Sa'ud* (London, 1957); and, the best of the biographies, David A. Howarth, *The Desert King: Ibn Saud and His Arabia* (New York, 1964). For bibliographical comment see Derek Hopwood, 'Some Western Studies of Saudi Arabia, Yemen and Aden', in Derek Hopwood, ed., *The Arabian Peninsula: Society and Politics* (London, 1972). See also Robert Lacey, *The Kingdom* (New York, 1981); and David Holden and Richard Johns, *The House of Saud* (New York, 1981).

of the 1940s, the following comments will emphasize Grafftey-Smith's perception of Ibn Saud's forging of Saudi Arabia into a modern state.

The sword with which Ibn Saud carved his dominion was the militantly religious organization called the *Ikhwan*, or 'Brethren'. The *Ikhwan* drew inspiration from Muhammad ibn Abdul Wahhab, an eighteenth-century religious leader who taught that the Koran was literally the word of God. Wahhabism was a fundamentalist or 'puritan' Muslim revival which Grafftey-Smith, and most other British observers, regarded as close to religious fanaticism. Strict Muslim principles guided Ibn Saud's personal life and his style of rule. He attempted to enforce Wahhabism as a code of individual conduct among his subjects. Nevertheless he was receptive to alien technology when it could be used to strengthen his government's reach. Thus he not only introduced motor vehicles but also radio communication. He shrewdly neutralized some of the protests of his religious counsellors by broadcasting passages from the Koran. The legend of Ibn Saud began when he and a handful of followers had captured Riyadh, the Saudi capital held by one of his powerful rivals, Ibn Rashid, in 1902. At that time Ibn Saud emerged as a leader of great personal magnetism and courage. But it was his decision in the years before the outbreak of the First World War to revive his dynasty's support of Wahhabism that created, in Grafftey-Smith's words, a 'fiery organisation in which all tribal loyalties vanished' and gave him 'an invincible weapon of expansion'. The religious fervour of the *Ikhwan* served his political ambition. By the early 1920s Ibn Saud had consolidated his hold over central Arabia. When the *Ikhwan* drove Hussein out of the Hejaz in 1924, Ibn Saud was at the height of his powers.

Grafftey-Smith, in his accounts of the rise of Ibn Saud, identified a crucial element that he believed brought the *Ikhwan* to a halt. He thought that Iraq and Transjordan might also have fallen to Ibn Saud and the advance of the *Ikhwan* had it not been 'for the genius of John Glubb', the British officer whose name later became synonymous with the leadership of the Arab Legion of Transjordan.[8] The frontiers between Nejd and Iraq, and between the Hejaz and Transjordan, were drawn by Ibn Saud in part in recognition of British military strength behind the two Hashemite states. Ibn Saud in other words proved to be a shrewd judge of his own capacities; but in 1928 the *Ikhwan* rebelled. Having used the *Ikhwan* to conquer his Arab rivals, Ibn Saud now stood accused of being less of a true Muslim than his militant followers. He refused to carry the Wahhabi crusade

[8] *Bright Levant*, p. 266. See Sir John Bagot Glubb, *War in the Desert* (London, 1960).

into Iraq. The *Ikhwan* conducted raids against Iraqi tribes without his approval. At this turning point in modern Arabian history, Ibn Saud crushed the *Ikwhan* in the battle of Sibilla in April 1929, thus averting civil war and liquidating the movement which had become, in the words of the famous explorer-scholar Harry St. John Philby, 'the Frankenstein of his own creation'.[9] Grafftey-Smith's point was this. When the *Ikhwan* came into contact with Glubb's detachments of the Iraqi army and the Royal Air Force, the British indirectly helped Ibn Saud to secure his throne. The British response to the *Ikhwan* had been defensive, but the bombs dropped by the aircraft of the RAF and the firepower of the Lewis guns of the Iraqi Desert Camel Corps demonstrated the danger of prolonged war with the British as well as the vulnerability of a religiously fervent but technologically inferior Wahhabi force. Against the Arabian tribes, to re-emphasize Grafftey-Smith's phrase, the *Ikhwan* had been 'an invincible weapon of expansion', but against the British it was not invincible. Glubb went so far as to conclude that British forces thus were largely instrumental in 'saving' Ibn Saud.[10] The 'gratitude' which characterized Ibn Saud's attitude towards the British was based on proven military capability. The events of the last months of the Second World War provided a similar lesson for the postwar period. The ousting of the French in the Levant made it clear that Britain remained dominant in the Middle East and could still intervene with decisive consequences.

In the era after the crushing of the *Ikhwan*, in Grafftey-Smith's judgement at least, Ibn Saud's greatest achievement was the ending of desert warfare and plundering. The King now drew his strength from a tempered Wahhabi movement which created a sense of unity throughout Saudi Arabia. The 'puritanical and iconoclastic Wahhabi zeal' was now directed to the restraint of 'highly intractable nomad freebooters' and the imposition of peace 'even among the wildest elements of the desert'.[11] So great was the unprecedented phenomena of public security and tribal peace that even cynics gasped with astonishment. The key to Ibn Saud's success lay, in Grafftey-Smith's unvarnished language, in bribing the chiefs and providing a dole to the nomadic tribesmen who now had to depend on his largesse rather than the rewards of plundering. In the 1930s the poverty of the

---

[9] H. St. John Philby, *Sa'udi Arabia* (London, 1955), p. 313. This book remains the most substantial of the general histories. For the critical period of the creation of the modern state, see Gary Troeller, *The Birth of Saudi Arabia: Britain and the Rise of the House of Sa'ud* (London, 1976). For the drawing of the frontiers, see especially Christine Moss Helms, *The Cohesion of Saudi Arabia* (London, 1981).

[10] Glubb, *War in the Desert*, preface.

[11] The phrases are from Grafftey-Smith's annual report for 1946, FO 371/62095B.

Bedouin posed to Ibn Saud the severest test in holding together his domain of 'Saudi Arabia' (as the country was renamed in 1934). 'Great hordes of pauperised Bedouin', according to this mundane and vigorous interpretation, 'lived in idleness on his charity outside the town of Riyadh.' At the same time there were increasing demands on Ibn Saud's purse from his family. At one time Grafftey-Smith calculated that Ibn Saud had thirty-seven living sons, who, as they reached their years of indiscretion, expected palaces, wives, and Cadillacs.[12] In the 1930s the beginnings of the oil revenues were mortgaged against ever-increasing demands of the tribes living in penury and malnutrition, and what Grafftey-Smith described as 'the large extravagances of the Palace and of Ibn Saud's pullulating brood of princelings'. In the decade before the war Ibn Saud's finances had a twofold basis: the revenues from the annual pilgrimage, and the beginnings of the oil income. Neither was adequate. His large ideas of his functions and obligations as a King always surpassed his available cash. The economic depression of the 1930s caused a decline in the revenue from the pilgrimages, which further declined after the outbreak of the war. The production of oil, which was severely curtailed during the war, did not prevent the deterioration of Ibn Saud's finances into a state of distress. Here follows a brief comment on the British response to the financial crisis, again from Grafftey-Smith's vantage point. He referred to it as the development of 'an Arabian Nightmare'.[13]

Grafftey-Smith frequently complained that the chaos of Saudi finances defied description, but on one occasion he suggested that the following observation at least clarified the political source of the confusion:

> It is not easy for a Bedouin Arab ruler to refuse any favour; and Ibn Saud's generosity to tribal leaders and others, though carefully calculated, is so natural to his conception of his rôle as it is assumed to be natural by the recipients. His Majesty, whose personal tastes are simple, will spend anything he gets.[14]

Ibn Saud merely compensated the tribes for the lack of 'excitement and profits of raiding' by subsidies which, together with the funds exploited by the 'parasites' of the court, drained the government's financial resources. To Grafftey-Smith's everlasting irritation, there was no sense whatever of British fiscal responsibility. What concerned him was not only misuse of the King's own funds but also profligate abuse of British subsidies. After 1940 Ibn Saud's revenues from

[12] See *Bright Levant*, pp. 265–6.
[13] Grafftey-Smith to Baxter, Top Secret, 28 Apr. 1945, FO 371/45525/E2942.
[14] 'Annual Report' for 1945.

pilgrimage fees had dwindled so drastically because of wartime conditions that the British had begun to offset his lack of income by subsidies. By 1943 the amount came to £4 million, which the American government shared on a fifty-fifty basis. The Saudi official who controlled these funds was the Sheikh Abdullah Sulaiman, the Finance Minister, who found his duties so overwhelming that he frequently felt compelled 'to drink both methylated spirits and scent'.[15] Grafftey-Smith summarized the 'vicious circle' of Saudi finances in April 1945:

> Thanks to our subsidy, Ibn Saud is able to play up to the Beduin Arab conception of Kingship and distributes bounty on an almost national scale in his home Province of Nejd. Thanks to his royal prodigality, the Nejdis are relatively well-supplied with funds, and the Exchequer is heavily in debt. . . . There is no doubt that the incalculable provision which Abdullah Sulaiman has to make . . . for the lavish extravagance of royal bounty not only to the tribal elements but also to a multitudinous horde of male and female relatives and other dependants, make any estimate of local budgetary expenditure an Arabian Nightmare.[16]

Despite his frequently expressed exasperation at Saudi fiscal irresponsibility, Grafftey-Smith believed that the subsidy was a good political investment. It enabled Ibn Saud to keep peace on the frontiers, to maintain public order throughout the country, and, not least, it helped to sustain Anglo-Saudi friendship. 'I think that present conditions of peace and good will in a territory one-quarter the size of the United States, in which we are imperially interested, are well worth £2 million a year to His Majesty's Government.'[17]

By the phrase 'imperially interested', Grafftey-Smith did not mean the economic exploitation of Saudi Arabia. In a lament that echoed traditional Foreign Office regret about the passive nature of British overseas capitalism, he observed that the London financiers had been indifferent to attractive opportunities in the Arabian peninsula. 'British capital has not hitherto displayed any marked interest in the potentialities of Saudi Arabia', he once wrote, and the British lack of initiative 'contrasted painfully' with the American spirit of enterprise.[18] By 'imperially interested' Grafftey-Smith rather had in mind the British Empire as the ultimate guardian of British Muslim subjects. During the mid-1940s the British witnessed what they believed to be the American economic take-over of Saudi Arabia.

---

[15] This was one of Grafftey's favourite anecdotes about Saudi Arabia, which he repeated in his autobiography: 'He was the only Finance Minister I ever met who drank methylated spirit.' *Bright Levant*, p. 267.

[16] Grafftey-Smith to Baxter, 28 Apr. 1945.

[17] Ibid.

[18] Grafftey-Smith to Eden, 25 July 1945, FO 371/45545/E5774.

They could not remain indifferent, Grafftey-Smith warned, to 'American economic imperialism' in 'the spiritual metropolis of hundreds of millions of British Moslems'.[19] The archives reveal that the British at this time were beginning to be uncomfortably aware of the consequences for Saudi Arabia of American economic exploitation. One of the fascinations of the historical documents of the era is the revelation of clash in outlook over how best to 'develop' Saudi Arabia along lines that would be compatible with the defence of the British Empire as well as the strategic and economic aims of the United States.

In the robust and representative British views of Grafftey-Smith, Ibn Saud's regime on the eve of great economic and social change could be summed up as primitive, ramshackle, and resilient. It is an illuminating point of view. Ibn Saud had followed up his desert campaigns by 'statesmanlike clemency' which nevertheless kept his former rivals under close supervision, and by marriage alignments 'not lacking in political expediency'. The families of Ibn Saud and Mohammed Abdul Wahhab, the eighteenth-century founder of the Wahhabi movement, remained closely linked, 'and all Arabia knows it'. Ibn Saud depended on the *ulama*, or religious counsellors, to endorse his administrative and other innovations, of which Grafftey-Smith's favourite example was the broadcasting of passages of the Koran over the radio. Ibn Saud brought to the twentieth century a religious philosophy of the seventh century, and in making adjustments he obtained the consent of the *ulama* 'just enough to avoid trouble'.[20] His political advisory council, the *diwan*, consisted of 'an assortment of alien advisors', mainly Syrian, but which included Harry St. John Philby—scholar, linguist, Ford motor company agent, disillusioned administrator, Muslim convert, and, most important, Ibn Saud's 'trusted adviser'. It is an indication of Grafftey-Smith's broad-mindedness that he acknowledged the central and creative importance of this erratic personality who possessed such an 'obsessive antipathy' towards the British government that in Saudi Arabia he caused 'more of a problem than all the other Britannics put together'.[21] Philby perhaps is best understood as an old-fashioned

---

[19] Grafftey-Smith to Campbell, 17 Mar. 1945, FO 371/45543/E1995.

[20] *Bright Levant*, pp. 247–73. For Wahhabism as a reform movement responsive to change, see George Rentz, 'Wahhabism and Saudi Arabia', in Hopwood, *Arabian Peninsula*: under Ibn Saud after the suppression of the *Ikhwan*, 'a moderate form of Wahhabism would rule the state, and changes that did not conflict with the fundamental principles of Islam would be accepted in Wahhabite society'.

[21] *Bright Levant*, p. 262. For Philby, see Elizabeth Monroe, *Philby of Arabia* (London, 1973). An Arab comment quoted in the prelude to her book is perhaps worth bearing in mind in relation to the way in which Grafftey-Smith generally agreed with Philby's analysis of issues in Saudi society: Philby 'came nearer to understanding our mind than did any other Englishman'.

Englishman, and, in his own eccentric fashion, a patriot. He did not disguise his outrage at what he believed to be misguided British policies in the Middle East. He gave Ibn Saud full exposure to currents of western thought and corrected misapprehensions about both the British and the Americans. Philby's and Grafftey-Smith's accounts of Saudi Arabia at the beginning of the great economic revolution reinforce each other and convey the impression of the oil story, in Philby's words, as 'surpassing the most improbable tales of the *Arabian Nights*'.[22] Both Grafftey-Smith and Philby, in a pessimistic vein that characterizes the minutes of the Foreign Office as well, had grave apprehensions about the way in which the new wealth would be used.

In perhaps the single most incisive wartime comment on the danger of American economic penetration in Saudi Arabia, the British Minister Resident in the Middle East, Lord Moyne, in September 1944 assessed the conflicting British and American ideas about 'development'. He wrote only a few months before his assassination. His views are of particular interest because he held the office of Colonial Secretary in the early wartime period shortly after the enactment of the Colonial Development and Welfare Act of 1940. To that act he, like all other British officials concerned with colonial affairs, attached cardinal importance. It renewed in practical and fiscal terms the British commitment, in his own words, of 'improving conditions among backward peoples by indirect means and long-term planning'.[23] He emphasized that to Saudi Arabia the British had no such commitment. But the Americans did have such a responsibility, whether they recognized it or not, in a particular moral sense. The Americans were the ones depleting the only resource of the country while also benefiting from the resulting conservation of their own oil reserves. A certain indignant note of inequity runs through British comment at this time.

Moyne stressed the point about trusteeship because he believed it to be at the heart of Anglo-American 'serious friction' in Saudi Arabia. He wished to make it clear that the British had no commitment to 'CD&W' in Saudi Arabia and that the Americans should be made more fully aware of the responsibilities of 'development' (which critics of British and American imperialism, putting it in less lofty language, would call exploitation pure and simple). The British wartime subsidy was a relief measure designed to meet wartime needs and was not aimed at long-range projects such as the building of roads, the conservation of water, or the provision of wells. The

[22] Philby, *Sa'udi Arabia*, p. 331.
[23] Moyne to Eden, 29 Sept. 1944, FO 371/40266/E16177.

Americans in 1943–4 had begun to talk in terms of raising the
standards of living in Saudi Arabia. Moyne wished them well, though
he was sceptical whether they would do so effectively and might
make things worse by paying a sort of conscience money. He re-
emphasized his point that, even if the British had the money, Saudi
Arabia, fortunately or unfortunately, was not a British colony. 'We
have . . . no moral obligation to the Saudis which would justify the
continuance of our financial assistance after the war emergency.' On
the other hand:

> The U. S. is in a very different position. When the Ras Tanura Refinery is
> completed, they will be dealing daily there and at Bahrein with 90,000 barrels
> of oil. . . . A pipe-line is also in contemplation which I am informed might deal
> with further amounts up to 300,000 barrels per day. These supplies will enable
> the Americans to conserve their home reserves and it seems right that they
> should recognise their great moral obligations to the Saudi population on
> account of the exhaustion of the oil deposits which are the only considerable
> asset of that desert country. It can however be no reproach to us that as we have
> no part in the U. S. advantage, we do not share in the corresponding obliga-
> tion.[24]

Moyne's argument was based on the unfounded assumption, as will
be seen, that the American government might take responsibility for
Saudi welfare. Here the point is that he anticipated the main development in British policy: 'I would . . . recommend that we limit our
assistance to Saudi Arabia . . . leaving to them the field of development and welfare.' He was uneasily aware that American assistance
might be misguided, in part because the Americans, unlike the
British, did not have long experience in dealing with the Arabs:
'there is a serious risk of their adopting an excessively paternal and
patronising attitude to Saudi Arabia from a failure to understand
that a fanatical Moslem population does not take the same view of
the blessings of American civilisation as they do themselves'. Moyne
ended this pessimistic analysis with a clear warning, which may be
taken as representative of British official thought at the close of the
war: 'If the results of misguided American benevolence should be
to undermine the independence of the country and make it a satellite
of the U.S.A., it would have serious reactions throughout the Moslem
world and gravely prejudice British interests.'[25]

---

[24] Moyne to Eden, 29 Sept. 1944, FO 371/40266/E16177.
[25] Ibid. Eden minuted, 'This seems pretty serious to me.'

The American 'Stranglehold'[26]

If there ever was such a thing as mutual and total misapprehension about wartime aims between the British and the Americans, the case of Saudi Arabia might serve as an example. The American point of view, in direct contrast with Moyne's lament, was well expressed by Alexander Kirk, the Minister in Egypt:

Saudi Arabia is rapidly becoming an active battle ground in the implementation of two systems of foreign policy—the British which in the past has aimed to make countries in which they are interested dependent in perpetuity . . . economically upon the Empire, and the American system which is based on the intent to help backward countries to help themselves in order that they may lay the foundation for real self dependence. Needless to say a stable world order can be achieved only under the American system.[27]

Lord Moyne, along with most other British officials, would probably have regarded that statement as not only naïve but fatuous. Kirk, who along with other American officials suspected that the war would bring out expansionist tendencies of the British Empire, would have defended it to the hilt. From the American vantage point it represented almost an article of faith. So great was the gap during the wartime years between British ideas of 'colonial development and welfare' and American conceptions of 'independence' that genuine suspicion existed on both sides. Kirk's comment is particularly valuable to bear in mind as an example of the way in which Saudi Arabia could be regarded as a microcosm in which the economic and political aims of the United States vied with those of the British Empire.

It is beyond the scope of this chapter to trace in detail the wartime controversy or to re-examine the material covered by recent scholarship, but the main features must be delineated in order to understand the situation at the close of the war.[28] If the financial stakes had not been so great the story might resemble farce rather than political drama. In 1933 the Standard Oil Company of California had acquired a concession from Ibn Saud, assigning it to an *ad hoc* subsidiary (later named Aramco) to which the Texas Company

[26] Grafftey-Smith's word, in a telegram to Bevin, No. 605, 27 Dec. 1945, FO 371/45543/E10148.

[27] Kirk to Hull, 25 Apr. 1944, *Foreign Relations 1944*, V, p. 690.

[28] There are three complementary works: Michael B. Stoff, *Oil, War, and American Security: The Search for a National Policy on Foreign Oil, 1941–1947* (New Haven, 1980), incisive on personalitites and intellectual trends of the 1940s; Aaron David Miller, *Search for Security: Saudi Arabian Oil and American Foreign Policy, 1939–1949* (Chapel Hill, 1980), especially perceptive on the bureaucratic collisions within the American government; and Irving H. Anderson, *Aramco, the United States and Saudi Arabia: A Study of the Dynamics of Foreign Oil Policy 1933–1950* (Princeton, 1981), an outstanding contribution to the corporate dimension of the problem.

was admitted as equal partner in 1936. Production began in 1938 and reached 30,000 barrels per day in 1940, netting Ibn Saud royalties at the rate of £200,000 annually.[29] When the United States entered the war, however, Aramco found itself far down the priority list for allocation of equipment essential to its day-to-day operations. Its output slowed to a trickle, and Ibn Saud's revenues shrank proportionally. The company reluctantly advanced him royalties of $3 million against future production but felt unable to meet his further demands. Fearing the loss of its concession, Aramco looked to the American government for help, which was not immediately forthcoming. 'I hope they', the British, 'can take care of the King of Saudi-Arabia', Roosevelt noted in 1941: 'This is a little far afield for us!'[30] The British government initiated the subsidy to Ibn Saud to offset the loss of revenue from the pilgrimage. A chain reaction of suspicion now set in. Though they welcomed the financial relief, the Americans believed that the British were out to steal the concession. The American government now came to the aid of the company. In February 1943 Roosevelt determined that Saudi Arabia was vital in the strategic defence of the United States and therefore could qualify for lend-lease. The Americans and the British would participate in a fifty–fifty subsidy to Ibn Saud. Though the British now welcomed the financial relief, they had no doubt about American motives. In blunt language, Sir Maurice Peterson (Assistant Under-Secretary) wrote in 1944: 'The Americans are out to bribe, or buy, Ibn Saud.'[31]

It must not be assumed that the naked spirit of economic imperialism exclusively motivated the American quest for oil. Indeed the flowering of American wartime idealism cross-fertilized the budding economic ambition, and vice versa. Economic aspiration happened to coincide with national defence and a moral obligation to raise the standard of living of primitive peoples throughout the world, not least in Saudi Arabia. In this regard Harold L. Ickes, Secretary of the Interior and Petroleum Administrator, played a central part. 'This was more than a business venture', he later testified before a Senate committee. 'This involved the defense and safety of the country.'[32] Ickes's authority carried with it a reputation of crusty integrity and fierce determination to get his own

[29] These developments are clearly discussed by Benjamin Shwadran, *The Middle East, Oil, and the Great Powers* (New York, 1959 edn.), section 4; and George W. Stocking, *Middle East Oil: A Study in Political and Economic Controversy* (Vanderbilt University Press, 1970), chap. 3.

[30] *Foreign Relations 1941*, III, p. 643.

[31] Minute by Peterson, 25 May 1944, FO 371/40265/E3105.

[32] US Congress, Senate, Special Committee Investigating the National Defense Program, *Hearings*, pt. 41, *Petroleum Arrangements with Saudi Arabia*, 80th Cong., First Sess. (Washington, 1948), p. 25240.

way.[33] He described his battle with the oil industry during the war as
one of the toughest he ever fought in Washington. The more he
studied the problem of depletion of American resources and the
potential of Arabian oil, the more he saw one vista open up after
another. He perceived the chance to curb the excesses of the oil
industry and, by serving as a watchdog of oil production in the
Middle East, to protect a legitimate field of American enterprise
from British encroachment. Ickes, like other prominent American
statesmen of this era, had a habitual dislike of British imperialism. He
also distrusted American oilmen who, he believed, let their incentive
for a profit get the better of their sense of ethical business conduct.
Ickes in short thought that the business of Middle Eastern oil was too
important to be left to American businessmen, and he did not want
Saudi Arabia treated as if it were a British Protectorate.

In 1943 President Roosevelt created the Petroleum Reserves
Corporation with Ickes as its head. Ickes intended for the federal
government to buy out Aramco, lock, stock, and Arabian barrel, or
at least to obtain a controlling interest in the concession. He wanted
federal control over Arabian oil in order to ensure a strategic reserve.
Never again would the United States have to face the possibility of
oil crises that would cripple American military strength or paralyse
the domestic economy. Nor did Ickes's ideas stop with the possibility
of a government oil monopoly. When he encountered resistance from
the oil companies, he developed an alternative plan for the construction of a government-owned pipeline stretching across Saudi Arabia
from the Persian Gulf to the Mediterranean. In Ickes's fertile mind
the pipeline project would work out even better than a government-
owned concession. The federal government then could not be
accused of entering the oil business and the companies, in return
for use of the pipeline, would be compelled to grant the government
a twenty-five per cent reduction from commercial prices. These
schemes in retrospect strike one as bizarre in the extreme, or at least
as excessively optimistic, and it is difficult to believe that such
a departure from traditional American practice could have got as far
as it did without Ickes as the driving force behind it.

A caricature of Ickes's 'mental processes' entitled 'Mr. Ickes'
Arabian Nights' that appeared in the American magazine *Fortune*
had a hard element of truth in it which is revealing about his attitude
towards the British:

What drew Ickes into the scheme in the first place? . . . His reformer's side
rejoiced in the pleasure of luring them [the oil companies] into the trap of

---

[33] For discussion of Ickes see esp. Stoff, *Oil, War, and American Security.*

government control. Was this all? A man who followed Mr. Ickes' mental processes during this deal is convinced that the Secretary was plotting an ambush on the distant and storied desert. He has the Midwesterner's abiding suspicion of Britain; he mistrusts British domination of the Middle East oil not just because —by his definition—it is a monopoly but because it is a British monopoly. He thought he was striking at the British oil companies.[34]

Ickes did indeed believe that he was striking out against British imperialism. On one occasion he wrote to Roosevelt that it was imperative 'to counteract certain known activities of a foreign power which presently are jeopardizing American interests in Arabian oil reserves'—by which he meant the British.[35] Ickes suffered under the common American illusion that the British were attempting to take over Saudi Arabia. It was in fact the British who felt threatened, and this sense of economic anxiety became acute when Ickes entered the field with the threat not merely of an oil corporation owned by the American government but also of a pipeline extending from the Persian Gulf to the Mediterranean. For the present discussion the point is that American assumptions were based on an entirely erroneous suspicion of British motives. There is no evidence in the British archives of any attempt to persuade or coerce Ibn Saud to abandon the Americans in favour of the British. Grafftey-Smith again believed he had insight into the psychological dimension of the problem: 'for reasons familiar to psychiatrists, the very processes of American penetration generate in American minds the darkest suspicions of British jealousies and intrigue'.[36]

The year 1943 was critical in the development of American enthusiasm for Saudi oil. The significance for postwar problems is perhaps best understood by grasping the ideas of Ickes's rival, Cordell Hull, the Secretary of State, and Herbert Feis, the principal official who attempted in this context to give Hull's ideas a precise application. Feis, the Economic Adviser in the State Department, found 'scant or no evidence that either the British government or the British oil companies would exert themselves deliberately to oust or gravely injure their American rivals'.[37] Hull himself believed in the 'Open Door', a cliché of such magnitude that British officials usually

---

[34] *Fortune* (June 1944).

[35] *Petroleum Arrangements with Saudi Arabia*, p. 25238.

[36] Annual report for 1945. It could also be argued that there was a comparable British psychosis about the American entry into the Middle East, e.g. Oliver Harvey's diary, 19 Feb. 1943: 'Roosevelt is jumping us into a conference on oil in the Middle East—rather outrageously. We hate it, though we should welcome it. We cannot bear anyone to touch us in that part of the world—even our friends. As though we had made such a success of it!' Harvey Diaries Add. MSS 56400.

[37] Herbert Feis, *Seen From E. A.: Three International Episodes* (New York, 1947), p. 111. See also *The Memoirs of Cordell Hull* (New York, 1948), chap. 110.

dismissed it as meaningless or regarded it as veiled ambition to 'open' the British Empire to American trade which, in wartime circumstances, meant that the American economic system would predominate. What is of interest here is Feis's outlook. He believed that the British and the Americans could reach agreement on Arabian oil because the British saw good reason for a postwar American commitment in the Middle East. The Atlantic Charter's principle of equal access to raw materials made sense in the Middle East because British as well as American oil companies wished to remain competitive for further concessions and future advantages. Hull was just as concerned as Ickes about the depletion of American domestic reserves and the indications that the United States would become a net importer rather than exporter of oil (as it did from 1948 on). Hull, and Feis in a more particular way, believed that rational agreement with the British was not only possible but desirable in the planning of the region's economic development. They agreed with those concerned with the military dimension of the problem that the United States had to be prepared 'to oil another war'. On that point there was a general consensus within the American government perhaps best expressed by the Secretary of War, Henry L. Stimson: 'No one doubts about the need of getting the reserves of oil, but the question was what method and means to be used in pursuing them.'[38] Here Ickes and Hull were poles apart. Ickes, as has been seen, believed, in the words of his critics, in 'getting the government into the oil business', at least in the sense of owning the vital pipeline. Nothing could have been more calculated to raise, in British eyes, the spectre of American economic imperialism. Hull, true to liberal principles given meaningful expression by Feis, wished to secure the Arabian oil reserves in a way 'which could not be construed either by the Arab world or by our war allies as unfair or threatening'. Such was the principal division within the American government on the eve of the Anglo-American oil talks of 1944.

There are certain intangibles in the atmosphere of those wartime discussions which are important in understanding the postwar period. The British had by no means forgotten that Roosevelt's sudden discovery of lend-lease as an instrument of economic aid to Saudi Arabia (a country not even at war) had occurred only shortly after the turn of the military tide in the Middle East after the British victory at El Alamein. Did the Americans plan to take over the Middle East by economic means? Suspicion existed on the British side as well as on the American. The British could also perceive a change of American mood in 1943-4. It was the feeling that

[38] Quoted in Stoff, *Oil, War, and American Security*, p. 77.

accompanied the discovery of great potential wealth, the excitement of getting a share of the treasure. In those two years the size of the potential treasure seemed to increase almost beyond imagination. In January 1944 a distinguished geologist, Everett Lee De Goyler, confirmed that the centre of gravity of the world's oil production was shifting from the Caribbean to the Persian Gulf with 'reserves of great magnitude' still to be discovered. The vision of wealth caused great excitement among the American participants. It opened vistas of lofty opportunity as well as the chance for profit.

In February 1944 Churchill sent Roosevelt a telegram warning him that a 'wrangle' might occur because of the rivalry for oil. 'There is apprehension in some quarters here', Churchill emphasized, 'that the United States has a desire to deprive us of our oil assets in the Middle East' and that the British were being 'hustled'.[39] Roosevelt responded in earthy but brilliant words assuring the British that 'we are not making sheep's eyes at your oil fields in Iraq or Iran'.[40] In similar vein Churchill at once tried to dispel American suspicion by assuring Roosevelt, in equally mundane words that amounted to no less of a brilliant stroke, that the British had 'no thought of trying to horn in upon your interests or property in Saudi Arabia'.[41] Those exchanges, blunt as they may seem, formed the implicit basis of the 1944 agreement and the tacit postwar understanding about Saudi Arabia as an American economic preserve.

The Anglo-American oil agreement of 1944 raised issues of such complexity that its significance is perhaps best understood in the negative sense of Churchill and Roosevelt wishing to keep the question of Middle Eastern oil subordinate to the larger political problems of the war. Lord Beaverbrook (Lord Privy Seal) led a British delegation to Washington in the summer of that year. He believed that after the war Middle Eastern oil would be one of the few remaining British assets. He was determined to stand firm in the cause of imperial unity and self-sufficiency, of which he was the self-proclaimed champion. He insisted on one point in particular which is the underlying theme of British official thought from 1944 until the time when the agreement died a protracted and unlamented death at the hands of the United States Senate in 1947. It was the question of oil and the sterling area. Beaverbrook was sensitive to the possible postwar foreign exchange shortages. He insisted on the British right to restrict imports and to pay for oil in sterling rather than dollars. On other points he proved to be more agreeable. On the large

[39] Churchill to Roosevelt, 20 Feb. 1944, PREM 3/332/6.
[40] Roosevelt to Churchill, 3 Mar. 1944, *Foreign Relations 1944*, III, p. 103.
[41] Churchill to Roosevelt, 4 Mar. 1944, ibid.

issue of equal access to raw material, both sides reaffirmed the idealism of the Atlantic Charter in order to prevent the exclusive rights of the other. Those involved in these discussions of 1944 hoped for the creation of an effective Anglo-American petroleum commission which might have provided the basis for rational planning as well as some measure of government control over the oil industry. This proved to be one of the lost hopes of the Second World War. It was now becoming clear, as the military threat in the Middle East diminished and the British proved to be less aggressive than had been anticipated, that the oil companies wanted protection and not partnership in their Middle Eastern ventures. The phrase 'socialization of the oil industry' proved to be deadly to Ickes's schemes. For the purpose of the present discussion, the main point is that the 1944 talks and their sequel in the next year helped to dispel American suspicions of British imperialism in Saudi Arabia. On the British side there ran a current of thought that there was plenty of oil to go around anyway. For political purposes of removing Saudi Arabia as an irritant between the two governments, the British in 1944 made it clear that the Americans would have a free economic hand in Saudi Arabia.[42]

The British hoped that their political influence would be sustained by the annual subsidy to Ibn Saud, which the American government had shared since 1944 on a fifty–fifty basis. Towards the end of the war American beneficence continued to increase while the economic restraints on British policy began to be more sharply felt. One British official noted some of the dilemmas: 'our subsidy to Saudi Arabia, which started as a comparatively modest figure, has now grown to three or four millions and it seems likely that the Saudi Arabian appetite will grow as time goes on'. Extravagance and corruption by 1944 had become conspicuously noticeable. 'While we are perfectly willing to supply Saudi Arabia with her essential requirements', the same official went on, 'we can see no justification for pouring in supplies and coin which are not really necessary.'[43] To R. M. A. Hankey the answer appeared to be to continue the subsidy as long as possible and tell the King that, for the British, economically the times were not as good as they used to be. As usual Hankey wrote with exceptional candour:

[42] Stoff, *Oil, War, and American Security*, Miller, *Search for Security*, and Anderson, *Aramco, the United States and Saudi Arabia*, each in its own way makes a distinctive contribution to an understanding of the 1944 agreement. For distillation of controversial points on the American side see Burton I. Kaufman, 'Oil, Security, and America's Involvement in the Mideast in the 1940s', *Reviews in American History* (March 1981).

[43] Minute by H. M. Eyres, 23 May 1944, FO 371/40265/E3105.

We are not on a good wicket if we try to stand in the way of the Americans giving when the Saudi Arabians wish to receive. . . . If the Americans wish to insist on giving a great deal more to Ibn Saud, we should try to get them to make their gifts in different forms, so as not to affect the fifty-fifty basis [of the subsidy]. . . . If after all the fifty-fifty basis cannot even so be maintained, because the Americans want to put the amount of assistance up to such a pitch that we cannot afford our half of it, we should maintain our subsidy at its present level, irrespective of the amount given by America, explaining to Ibn Saud that we wish him well, do not wish to stand in his way, but have a compelling need for economy, etc. etc.[44]

In early 1945 the Treasury compelled the Foreign Office to reduce the share of the subsidy by one-half, from £2½ million ($10 million at that time) to £1¼ million. The economic facts of the situation were bluntly summarized by the economic adviser at the Foreign Office, Edmund Hall-Patch, whose words may be taken as a sort of ringing anticipation of the problems facing postwar Britain. He wrote two weeks after VE day in May 1945, as if composing an epitaph to an era of Imperial greatness:

In our present impoverished position . . . we are no longer able to use finance as one of the ordinary weapons in our diplomatic armoury. Subsidies and the like can only be used in the most exceptional circumstances. We are now the greatest debtor nation, and are at present dependent on others for a good deal of the food we eat. With the end of lease lend food, subsidies to foreign countries can only be made at the expense of the subsistence levels of the U.K. population.[45]

The British might console themselves that Ibn Saud would continue to recognize past friendship and experience, and that the Americans had only one advantage. The one weapon they held, however, as one Foreign Office official observed, 'is admittedly a good one—notably, money'.[46]

Grafftey-Smith protested the economic accommodation of the United States for political reasons of 'higher policy'. He referred to it as an abnegation of Imperial responsibilities. In this case he may be said to represent the conscience of British imperialism. In a stream of telegrams and letters in 1945, he denounced British 'appeasement' of the Americans and the 'racket' of Saudi corruption. His language carried a particular sting because of his acknowledged authority on Middle Eastern affairs. As one who had first observed the politics of the Hejaz and other parts of Arabia since the days of the First World War, the spectre of 'American economic imperialism' could not but be highly disturbing in a region where the British had

---

[44] Minute by Hankey, 22 Sept. 1944, FO 371/40466/E5672.
[45] Minute by Hall-Patch, 23 May 1945, FO 371/45525/E3008.
[46] Minute by Thomas Wikeley, 22 Mar. 1945, FO 371/45524.

held supreme political power. Grafftey-Smith did not regard himself as anti-American, nor would anyone who knew him well so have regarded him. But the picture he painted of the Americans in Saudi Arabia was unflattering. He referred to them as no less than 'gold diggers' and 'gold brick merchants' who would 'ruthlessly' pursue economic aims camouflaged in language of philanthropy or military security. Apart from problems of oil, he called particular attention to the American plans to build a military air base at Dhahran. It might have a strategic justification but it would also benefit TWA and Pan American airlines on its eventual conversion to a civilian base. The communications system which would accompany it would damage British commercial companies such as Cable and Wireless. In short American business would profit at the expense of British enterprise because of the economic aid of the American government. The extension of lend-lease to Saudi Arabia past the cut-off date in 1945 made Grafftey-Smith sardonically comment that it was too bad that an American oil company did not hold an oil concession in the United Kingdom.[47]

Grafftey-Smith was also genuinely alarmed at the effect of American money pouring into Saudi society. At the close of the war one could already observe the 'haemorrhage of income' and the creation of 'a rich and idle class'. He could admire individual Americans for their ingenuity, industry, and efficiency, but he lodged a heartfelt complaint against the impact of the American economic system. It was all the more distasteful to British observers because American economic imperialism was couched in rhetoric that the Americans themselves appeared to believe. In crudest terms, what was good for America would be good for Saudi Arabia. Grafftey-Smith for one doubted whether the benefits of American civilization would be so pure and simple as the representatives of Aramco seemed to think. He—and most other Englishmen in the Middle East—also resented the high-handed manner in which the Americans were establishing themselves in Saudi Arabia without recognizing that the Arabian peninsula was a long-standing sphere of British influence. 'This is not Panama or San Salvador', Grafftey emphatically protested.[48]

The British did acquiesce in American treatment of Saudi Arabia almost as if it were a Latin-American country. Partly in response to Grafftey-Smith's protests, the Foreign Office in late 1945 made

---

[47] Grafftey-Smith to Baxter, 17 Mar. 1945, FO 371/44543/E1995; see also esp. Grafftey-Smith to Bevin, No. 554, 30 Nov. 1945, FO 371/45543/E9324; and Grafftey-Smith to Bevin, No. 605, 27 Dec. 1945, FO 371/45543/E10148.

[48] Ibid., 17 Mar. 1945.

a critical inventory of British and American commitments and objectives. The principal author of this inquiry was Thomas Wikeley, the official directly in charge of Saudi affairs who had served in Jedda during the war. The word 'inevitable' recurs in his minutes. He believed that the Americans would 'dominate' economically 'whether we like it or not'.[49] Wikeley and his colleagues nevertheless thought that British political influence would and should continue to be paramount. Here is an excerpt from Wikeley's assessment entitled 'Anglo-American Relations in Saudi Arabia' written in November 1945. It has an importance that transcends the immediate issue because it spells out British assumptions that often remained implicit, and because it clearly states the British interpretation of Ibn Saud's motives:

> Ibn Saud's influence in the Middle East is very great, and it has been used consistently for a number of years in support of our policy. This happy position has come about principally because Ibn Saud is convinced that we are the only great Power who has the real interests of the Arabs at heart, and the only great Power who can be trusted not to abuse its strength where weak States are concerned. . . .
>
> He realizes of course that our motives are not purely altruistic, although he gives us credit for a considerable measure of altruism, but that the friendship of the Arabs is an essential requirement of our foreign policy. He therefore regards us as the only Power to which the Arabs can safely look for help and guidance until such time as they are strong enough to stand by themselves. This is the cardinal point of Ibn Saud's policy.[50]

The British therefore should not be unduly alarmed that they could no longer hope to influence Ibn Saud through economic means such as the subsidy.

Since the British had 'abandoned' the opportunities of oil to the Americans, according to the Wikeley assessment, there was no real clash of economic policies. Grafftey-Smith's complaints were mainly those of local 'political friction'. From a local point of view Anglo-American rivalry might seem intense but, when viewed against the background of political and strategic problems of the Middle East as a whole, it diminished in significance. It helped to bear in mind that Saudi Arabia was a glaring exception to the general pattern of British predominance. In Wikeley's estimation the British should be prepared to be more tolerant of 'obnoxious' American behaviour and ungentlemanly trade practices, if only because complaints would irritate rather than remove the causes of friction. 'Saudi Arabia is the only country in a very wide area (including Africa, the Middle East and India) where they have a position not inferior to our own

[49] Minute by Wikeley, 28 Dec. 1945, FO 371/45543/E10148.
[50] Memorandum by Wikeley, 30 Nov. 1945, FO 371/45543/E9331.

and where they may therefore be able to attain their objectives in spite of our opposition.' The oil revenues would increasingly bind Ibn Saud 'irrevocably to the American orbit', which was an unfortunate but unavoidable fact. It was one that need not cause dismay, Wikeley continued, because of the political and strategic gain of having an American commitment in the Middle East, and because of Ibn Saud's character and sense of loyalty. 'We must remember that he is by nature and training of a ruggedly independent character, that he rules over a people the majority of whom are intolerant of Western ways and jealous of foreign interference, and that he is already committed to extensive cooperation with us.' Wikeley's train of thought was leading to a conclusion of supreme importance. It preoccupied both the British and the Americans in the postwar era. If the American hold over Saudi Arabia grew too tight, or if the American attitude towards Zionism became too indulgent, Ibn Saud could always cancel the oil concession and turn to the British. It was a heady and a problematical thought. 'He holds a trump card against them in the shape of the possible cancellation of the oil concession.' Ibn Saud's 'trump card' will be discussed in the next section of this chapter. Here the main point to be grasped is Wikeley's conclusion, which governed the British attitude during all of the postwar era for larger political and strategic purposes: 'we should allow, and even encourage, the Americans to "penetrate" Saudi Arabia to their heart's content'.[51]

Ibn Saud and Zionism

Any comment about Saudi Arabia and the Palestine controversy must come to grips with what Elie Kedourie has called the 'sentimental effusions about Ibn Sa'aud's readiness to shed tears and [the] simple-minded belief in his good faith'.[52] From beginning to end Ibn Saud spoke of the Jews with an emotion that revealed extreme hatred. Towards the creation of a Jewish state he expressed the unyielding hostility of his subjects. The historical evidence is filled with his bitterness. But as the tears flowed the oil revenues increased. He made no anti-American, or anti-British, move in the Palestine controversy. He had a talent for appearing to be all things to all men.[53] The charm and the magnetism of his personality was undeniable. It would have come as no surprise to officials such as

---

[51] Ibid. See also minutes of inter-departmental meeting, 11 Dec. 1945, ibid.

[52] Elie Kedourie, *Islam in the Modern World* (New York, 1980), p. 155.

[53] For his earlier success in conveying his apprehension of 'the threatening and alien hand of Britain' to the Germans and the Italians, see Watt, 'The Foreign Policy of Ibn Saud'.

Grafftey-Smith, who regarded him with a decidedly realistic eye, that the secret records of the American government transcribed professions of friendship equally as warm as the loyalty he proclaimed for the British. It pleased the Americans to hear that Ibn Saud harboured a distrust of British imperialism. It pleased the British, on the whole, that the Americans were there to please him. To the British the key to Ibn Saud's piece of the Palestine puzzle was, as had been stated in the Wikeley assessment, the possible cancellation of the oil concession. But the more this idea was examined, the more it took a new twist. Those who knew Ibn Saud well, Grafftey-Smith for example, did not believe for a moment that his devotion to the Arab cause in Palestine ('second to none' in Philby's phrase) would be allowed to interfere with his income.

The question was how Ibn Saud would play his hand, especially in view of increasing tension after the war. In late 1945 Grafftey-Smith detected a change in Saudi mood:

> There is evidence that the local climate is changing with the growing conviction that America is the main protagonist of Zionist claims. Public opinion seems to be restive at the successive manifestations of American influence here. Various delegations of pilgrims are said to have congratulated Ibn Saud on his threat (apocryphal but widely publicized in the Middle East) to cancel American oil concessions if the United States Government continued pro-Zionist activity, and this and similar evidence of present American unpopularity amongst the Moslems is said to have shaken Ibn Saud considerably.[54]

The more apprehensive Ibn Saud appeared to be, the more the American oil concession seemed to be in jeopardy. 'He is not blind to the danger of a position of complete financial dependence on the Americans', Grafftey-Smith reported.[55] Here was the way in which the 'trump card' more and more figured in British calculations. The American investment, political as well as economic, might create a lobby within the United States, in Congress as well as within the military and diplomatic branches of the government, to offset the Zionist lobby. Ibn Saud's 'trump card' might galvanize the American government into tempering its pro-Zionist attitude. 'I had every reason to welcome American involvement in Arab affairs', Grafftey-Smith wrote later, 'and the creation of an oil-lobby in Washington potentially offsetting the hitherto unchallenged lobby influencing attitudes on Palestine.'[56]

The American 'lobby' could perhaps better be described as a tacit and uneasy alliance between certain officials within the American

---

[54] Grafftey-Smith to Bevin, No. 554, 30 Nov. 1945, FO 371/45543/E9324.
[55] Ibid.
[56] *Bright Levant*, p. 258.

government and the businessmen of Aramco. Ultimately they proved to be unsuccessful against their foes, the Zionists, but they did manage to keep the concession in the hands of the company. It is illuminating to examine briefly the response of William A. Eddy to Ibn Saud's 'trump card' because he was associated with both the government and the company, first as Minister in Jedda, 1944-6, and later as a consultant to Aramco. Eddy was a man of stern purpose and considerable ability. He was born of missionary parents in Beirut and spoke Arabic so fluently that even Grafftey-Smith acknowledged his proficiency. He served as Roosevelt's interpreter at the meeting with Ibn Saud at Great Bitter Lake in 1945. He held the rank of Colonel in the United States Marine Corps, and he brought to his duties in Jedda a brutal honesty more typical of a military officer than a diplomat (as when he described his British counterpart, S. A. Jordan, Grafftey-Smith's predecessor, as suffering from 'incipient insanity' while as far as the British could see the only defect was a commendable 'breezy' attitude towards the Americans).[57] According to a confidential British assessment: 'He is hard-headed . . . obeys orders implicitly, and . . . he is not an intriguer.'[58] Eddy believed that the alliance being forged between the United States and Saudi Arabia was 'more than a bank transaction' and would be a 'political commitment of long standing'.[59] He was in short one of the principal figures in what Philby later described as 'the cementing of an American political link with Arabia [as] . . . the outstanding development of these war years: with far-reaching results which have completely transformed the social and economic structure of the country within a single decade'.[60] Eddy's significance is that he was aware of this transformation because of his missionary background and his experience as an educator at the American University in Cairo. His telegrams and despatches reveal an acute uneasiness at the way in which the fragile 'link' could be broken by those within the American government who wished to pursue a pro-Zionist course.

There is a revealing analogy that runs through some of Eddy's writings. Before the war he had taught at the American University in Cairo, where he had served as the head of the English Department. He had helped to introduce the game of basketball to Egyptian students (and indeed translated a basketball manual into Arabic). In Saudi Arabia he believed that the political struggle was in the

[57] See minutes in FO 371/40265.
[58] Eastern Department to Chancery, Confidential, 1 July 1944, FO 371/40266/E3779.
[59] Eddy to Secretary of State, 28 Dec. 1945, USSD 890F.51/12-2845; *Foreign Relations 1945*, VIII, p. 995.
[60] Philby, *Sa'udi Arabia*, pp. 337-8.

nature of a game, with the British trying to regain the initiative from the American challengers. On the question of Zionism he believed it to be a game of deadly stakes which might consume even the greatest of the protagonists. 'The King', Eddy reported in January 1945, 'stated he would be honored to die on [the] battlefield himself, a champion of Palestine Arabs.'[61] Shortly after the Anglo-American Committee of Inquiry issued its report, Eddy wrote in May 1946: Ibn Saud 'said that he and his sons will die in battle before they will permit Palestine to receive major increments of Jewish immigration'.[62] Eddy believed that Ibn Saud spoke the truth and saw him as a figure of heroic stature. Eddy himself took a stand as one of the staunch anti-Zionist officials of the era. He holds a particular place in the history of the United States and the Middle East. He was the only official who actually resigned in protest at American policy.[63] For the present discussion he may be taken to represent the strain of American thought which held that Ibn Saud would play his trump card and cancel the oil concession unless American policy determined against Zionist expansion in Palestine.

The ideas of Eddy's successor as Minister in Saudi Arabia, J. Rives Childs, are also worth emphasis because, like Grafftey-Smith, Childs was sceptical. He shared the calculation that Ibn Saud would stop short of severing American connections and endorsed it just as strongly as Eddy did his more pessimistic assessment. For purposes of looking briefly into corporate as well as official thought, the following comments will also deal succinctly with the ideas of the most articulate of the Aramco officials, Terry Duce. It is ironic that those in the 1946–8 period who were well acquainted with Ibn Saud and Saudi Arabia made essentially the same prediction as the pro-Zionist advisers of President Truman, notably Clark Clifford, who based his guess on nothing more than optimistic ignorance but whose judgement nevertheless appears shrewd in retrospect. They all held that Ibn Saud would not break with the company.

Before pursuing the nuances of American response to Ibn Saud's 'trump card', it is important to note the constraints under which State Department officials worked after Ickes's retirement in early 1946, when the State Department attempted to reassert its natural weight against the American oil industry in Saudi Arabia without

---

[61] Eddy to Secretary of State, 5 Jan. 1945, USSD 890B.00/1–545; *Foreign Relations 1945*, VIII, p. 679.

[62] Eddy to Secretary of State, Secret, 10 May 1945, USSD 711.90F/5–1046 Box 3494.

[63] See Evan M. Wilson, *Decision on Palestine* Stanford, 1979), p. 147. For an assessment of Eddy's career, including his service in the Office of Strategic Services, see Phillip J. Baram, *The Department of State in the Middle East* (University of Pennsylvania Press, 1978), p. 76.

the aberration of interference from the Department of Interior. The State Department believed that the foreign operations of the oil companies needed to be controlled, but there were certain limitations of action. After the evaporation of wartime exuberance and the passing of the wartime scare of exhausting domestic oil reserves, any scheme to provide subsidies to foreign governments and an American company abroad was bound to encounter Congressional opposition, not to mention the hostility of the American taxpayer. At the same time it was clearly desirable to develop Arabian oil, not only for strategic advantages in the event of another war but also to fuel European recovery by Middle Eastern oil rather than depleting oil reserves in the western hemisphere.

One of the most incisive intellects grappling with the question of oil resources was that of William L. Clayton, the Assistant Secretary for Economic Affairs who played a large part in shaping postwar economic policy. Clayton fully recognized the importance of Arabian oil, but he was also conscious of the 'popular antipathy' against 'the government's getting into the oil business'. If the Navy were to attempt to acquire a strategic reserve in Saudi Arabia (along the lines Ickes had proposed, for example), there would be cries of 'American imperialism' abroad; moreover, if the government continued beyond the wartime emergency to finance budgetary deficits of foreign countries in which Americans did business, there would be an outcry from the taxpayer at home. Clayton believed in other words that Aramco would have to stand on its own feet.[64] The re-endorsement of a *laissez-faire* economic philosophy at the close of the war had a powerful bearing on the offical postwar American position in Saudi Arabia. By assuming as far as possible a hands off policy towards Aramco, the American government limited its influence on Ibn Saud. At the same time the State Department was placed in the position of having to rely on the company to carry out American aims.

The philosophy of *laissez-faire* economics at first sight might seem to be academically removed from the realities of Ibn Saud's response to militant Zionism and American capitalism, but to the American Minister in Jedda some of the results were acutely obvious. The company attempted to dissociate itself from the Zionist influences reputedly at work within the American government, and locally it reigned economically supreme. By 1947 according to Childs it had even established an intelligence network 'comparable in some respects to the Central Intelligence Group of the United States' (the forerunner of the CIA) and demonstrated 'a scarcely veiled

[64] Memorandum by Clayton, 7 Apr. 1945, *Foreign Relations 1945*, VIII, pp. 869–71.

indifference' to the official American Legation. Left unchecked, Childs wrote, Aramco might turn into a sort of 'octopus' mutation of malignant capitalism:

> We can, of course, make a fetish of the free enterprise system, and in its name avoid any attempt to exercise a control over the octopus represented by Aramco. The longer we delay [to impose a regulatory control], however, the deeper its tentacles will be spread and in the end the policy of the Government of the United States in Saudi Arabia and in the Middle East may be dominated and perhaps even dictated by that private commercial company. That to me is not a pleasant prospect. . . .[65]

What was Ibn Saud's response to this creature of economic imperialism, to continue Childs's extended metaphor, this 'octopus whose tentacles have extended into almost every domain and phase of the economic life of Saudi Arabia'? The answer, according to this southern gentleman who espoused the lofty idea that American policy in Saudi Arabia should represent the American people and not 'a tiny fragment of the American people composing the Company's stockholders', was that the company suited Ibn Saud's purposes. Above all it was not British. Ibn Saud also liked the company precisely because it did seem to be beyond the control of the American government and therefore did not seem to pose a political threat. Childs himself praised the officials of Aramco for demonstrating 'great vision in the administration of its trust as the concessionary company'. The American government could be grateful that the company's representatives on the whole were patriotic Americans. They were, in Childs's judgement, imperceptive of the larger social and economic problems of trying to mould Saudi Arabia in America's image, but they could not be accused of being cutthroat capitalists.

Childs's point was that the American economic system had produced in this instance one of the better specimens of capitalist exploitation. He warned that it should be kept under surveillance, and urged that some form of control should be imposed, but despite its tentacles it was not yet a malevolent creature. Childs nevertheless was uneasy. Taking a purely hypothetical example, what if an American oil company with less ethical motives were to move into Yemen? What if the American government objected to unscrupulous exploitation and caused the surrender of the concession to a European company or government? Childs's answer to his own question is a striking example of the continuing power of Wilsonian idealism:

[65] Childs to Marshall, No. 186, Secret, 11 Mar. 1947, USSD 711.90F/3-1147 Box 3494. For his general views see J. Rives Childs, *Foreign Service Farewell: My Years in the Near East* (University of Virginia Press, 1969).

'it would be better from the point of view of our long range interests that we lose that area to another nation rather than suffer in prestige from the operation of an unworthy American company'.[66] In the case of Saudi Arabia, Childs did not think that such an extreme conflict would ever occur. There was a strong element of sheer luck in having Aramco as a healthy and indeed unique product of the American economic system. Childs and his colleagues in the State Department believed that it was important to keep Saudi oil in the hands of an American company, and that the officials of the company on the whole would not be unresponsive to Saudi welfare.

Another important theme that runs through Childs's despatches and telegrams is Ibn Saud's perception of the reasons for the fluctuation of official American policy. It is important to bear in mind that at the time when the Palestine crisis began to come to a head in the winter of 1947–8 American strategic planners still regarded the Middle East to be of 'critical importance' rather than 'vital' to the security of the United States.[67] The airfield at Dhahran never did acquire a definite place, still less a symbolic significance, in the defensive arc around the Soviet Union. Ibn Saud was aware of the domestic American pressures for fiscal restraint, and he also knew that the American government seemed to be at war with itself whether to pursue a pro-Zionist or a pro-Arab policy. After the United Nations vote in favour of partition in November 1947, it was an open secret in the Middle East that the American government, at least indirectly, had tilted the outcome in favour of the Jews. It was at this stage that Ibn Saud asked Childs a direct question: 'What was the attitude of the United States Government towards the Government of Saudi Arabia?' Ibn Saud furthermore specifically wished to know whether the United States had any secret agreement with the British which, by leaving Palestine as an American problem, might have strengthened the British hand over the rest of the Middle East. It is important to clarify this political dimension of the problem at the time of the Palestine crisis in 1948 before the economic part of it can be fully comprehended in regard to Saudi Arabia. Ibn Saud was playing his 'trump card' with extreme caution. During this same interview with Childs, he said that he hoped not to be drawn into conflict with either Britain or the United States. His

[66] Childs to Marshall, No. 111, Confidential, 4 Jan. 1947, USSD 890.6363/1-447 Box 6785.

[67] US JCS CCS 381 (11-19-47) Section 1. David Alan Rosenberg discusses this important point in 'The U. S. Navy and the Problem of Oil in a Future War: The Outline of a Strategic Dilemma, 1945-1950', *Naval War College Review*, XXIX, 1 (Summer 1976). For extensive and critical analysis of the assessments of the Joint Chiefs of Staff and the State Department, see Miller, *Search for Security*, chaps. 7 and 8.

assurance on that point is clear and precise: 'Although the other Arab states may bring pressure to bear on me I do not anticipate that a situation will arise whereby I shall be drawn into conflict with friendly western powers over this question.'[68] Ibn Saud had anxieties besides Jewish, and he rightly detected an overarching British design.

As will be discussed in detail in the chapters on Iraq and Transjordan, Ernest Bevin in the aftermath of the partition vote of the United Nations made a bold move to recapture the British political initiative in the Middle East. His goal was a system of defensive alliances to be concluded individually with each of the important Arab states. The first steps would be taken with Iraq and Jordan and would eventually encompass Saudi Arabia as well. On the basis of successful treaties with those countries Bevin hoped to bring even Egypt back into the British fold. The underlying rationale was that the Arab states would now look to the British for leadership because the British had avoided a pro-Zionist line at the United Nations. Unfortunately for the British, the Arabs did not respond with a sense of gratitude. For reasons not directly related to the present discussion, the whole ingenious scheme collapsed because of Iraqi nationalist protest. For Ibn Saud the British initiative aroused old apprehensions of British imperialism, and, even more important, deep fears about the expansionist ambitions of the ruling dynasties in Iraq and Transjordan, his ancient rivals the Hashemites.

The American records—in contrast with the British—are extremely revealing about British imperialism and Ibn Saud in early 1948. At first Childs had feared that American support of the Jews would 'throw' Ibn Saud into the hands of the British. Palestine however was not the principal cause of the King's agitation. In discussing the Anglo-Iraqi treaty he reflected on the 'dependent status' which the British were, he believed, trying to impose on the Arab countries. He thought it would be 'humiliating' for Saudi Arabia to adhere to a similar agreement. That was strong language, but the real key to Ibn Saud's attitude towards the British at this critical time lay in his statement that 'the British themselves will not harm me' but he was certain that the Hashemites would if they could. Ibn Saud emphasized that he felt 'strongly' about his old friendship with the British but 'they could not always be trusted'. He feared that the British might attempt to 'egg on Hashemites to adventures in western Saudi Arabia'. Childs rose more than once to the occasion. His response explains in part why the British grand design of 1948, as far as Saudi Arabia was concerned, fell flat. Childs

[68] Childs to Marshall, Top Secret, 4 Dec. 1947, USSD 890F.00/12-447; *Foreign Relations 1947*, V, pp. 133-38.

assured Ibn Saud 'of my government's unqualified support of
territorial integrity and political independence [of] Saudi Arabia'. He
reported Ibn Saud's response in detail. 'His Majesty's eyes sparkled.'
Childs had rarely seen him in 'so pleasant a mood'.[69] With American
assurances of his territorial integrity and political independence, Ibn
Saud did not need a further, and in his view, humiliating, treaty with
the British.[70] For Childs the episode revealed that the Hashemites
rather than the Jews remained Ibn Saud's main external anxiety.

How then did Ibn Saud's 'trump card' fit into these tangled
American–Saudi–Anglo–Hashemite relations? Did the American
officials and businessmen believe that Arab sentiment ultimately
would force him to cancel the concession? Childs never excluded
the possibility; but the imminent danger appeared to be the abandonment by the King of any lasting political tie between the two governments. This too had economic overtones. The oil royalties by 1948
still by no means matched Ibn Saud's requirements. He wished the
United States to provide a military mission to train Saudi forces for
modern warfare against the Hashemites and to provide the weapons,
armoured vehicles, and aircraft. The Joint Chiefs of Staff, preoccupied
in 1948 with the European crisis, not surprisingly balked at this
request, though they offered $1,500,000 to recondition the Dhahran
airfield. 'Truly and actually, I never believed', Ibn Saud said, that
the 'US Government would give me this kind of reply to my request
for aid.'[71] The King now had specific financial reasons to be annoyed
with the American government. Childs anticipated rough political
relations, but he knew that Ibn Saud's financial well-being was tied
to the fortunes of the company. The King, despite the assurances
about territorial integrity and political independence against the
British and the Hashemites, most certainly did distrust the American
government because of its support of Zionism. The company was
a different matter. If worst came to worst in Palestine, Childs concluded, Aramco could merely become incorporated in Canada and
thereby dissociate itself further from American Zionism.[72] In the

[69] Childs to Marshall, Top Secret, 21 Feb. 1948, USSD 741.90F/2-2148; *Foreign Relations 1948*, V, pp. 222–3; and 24 Apr. 1948, 890F.7962/4-2448, ibid., pp. 235–7.

[70] A few days later Ibn Saud told the British Minister that he could not consent to an
arrangement that his subjects would regard as a surrender of sovereignty. The British
detected that his real objection was that he was being asked to accept a treaty similar to
the one which had met with disastrous opposition in Iraq, but there is none of the violent
language that appears in the American documents. See e.g. Trott to Bevin, No. 39, Confidential, 26 Feb. 1948, FO 371/68766/E3155.

[71] Childs to Marshall, Top Secret, 24 Apr. 1948, USSD 890F.7962/4-2448; *Foreign
Relations 1948*, V, pp. 235–7; J.C.S. Memorandum, 10 Aug. 1948, ibid., for strategic
assessment of Saudi Arabia at that time.

[72] Childs to Marshall, No. 171, Confidential, 24 June 1948, USSD 711.90F/6-2448
Box 3494.

event, the company did not have to suffer even the transmogrifica-
tion of Canadianization.

By 1948 Aramco had invested $80 million in Saudi Arabia and
faced the financing of a further $100 million for the construction of
the Trans-Arabian Pipeline (TAPLINE) stretching over 1,000 miles
from the Persian Gulf to the Mediterranean.[73] What of the risk in
view of Ibn Saud's 'trump card'? James Terry Duce, Vice-President
and Director of Aramco, from November 1947 to January 1948
travelled to the Middle East with precisely that question in mind.
He visited not only Saudi Arabia but also Lebanon, Syria, Egypt,
and Palestine. He concluded that there would be a protracted and
bitter Arab war against the Jews fought in a tradition reminiscent
of the war against the crusaders. He foresaw nothing other than
immense destruction of life and property in Palestine and the
possible massacre of Jewish communities in Iraq, Syria, Lebanon,
and Egypt. He believed that 'the anti-Zionist war in these countries
will be a cruel and a bloody one'. On the specific question of Ibn
Saud's 'trump card', Duce wrote in January 1948:

> Should the Palestine fighting continue for a long period of time and should
> American troops be ultimately involved in that fighting, then it is possible that
> the rulers in the Arab countries may have their hands forced by the population
> and have to take steps to revoke the concessions granted to American nationals
> and possibly to others or commit political suicide. To those who say that the
> Arabian stake in oil is so great that there is no possibility of the concessions
> being cancelled, the reply is a simple one—such people have not considered
> the passions to which such populaces are subject.[74]

No one who knew anything about the Middle East at that time
would have discounted that long-range possibility, though it was
perhaps less true for Saudi Arabia and other Arab states not so
directly involved as Jordan or Iraq. Duce's optimism however
triumphed over his forebodings. In the short run he believed that
the American company probably would not be endangered. He
even thought that the negotiations with the Arab governments for
TAPLINE could be successfully concluded, though he doubted that
the actual construction in Jordan and Syria could be completed
while hostilities were taking place in Palestine. He believed in other
words that the struggle would be resolved in favour of the Arabs
before Ibn Saud would feel compelled to take measures that might
adversely affect Aramco.

Duce's optimism reflected the general Arab sentiment before the
spring of 1948 that the Jews would be defeated. In particular he had

---

[73] Anderson, *Aramco*, p. 122 *et passim*, which is an excellent analysis.
[74] Memorandum by Duce, 22 Jan. 1948, USSD 867N.01/1-2948 Box 6762.

been influenced by lengthy conversations with Azzam Pasha, and he called attention to Azzam's success as a leader in the guerrilla war against the Italians in Tripoli, which seemed to augur well for a campaign against the Jews in Palestine. Duce's views were in line with other judgements he expressed both before and after the actual outbreak of the Arab–Israeli war. He emphasized of course the danger to American access to Middle Eastern oil.[75] As for Aramco, he was buoyant. When he testified before a US Senate committee in October 1947, shortly before his trip to the Middle East, Duce had spoken with unfeigned exuberance and pride about the bringing into production of four Saudi oilfields, the building of a refinery at Ras Tanura, the construction of a deep-water port on the Persian Gulf, and the network of highways, power lines, and public utilities. The company employed 'native labor' and the Saudi Arab could be trained to be 'an excellent worker'. Not only had the company developed irrigation and agricultural projects but it had also provided electricity, sanitation, and hospitals. An American visitor could even arrive in Dhahran on an American airline, and enjoy an all-American breakfast of ham and eggs, coffee, orange juice, and hot cakes in an air conditioned room.[76] It would be easy to caricature the export of American civilization to Saudi Arabia, but that would be to miss the point of American ingenuity, efficiency, and hard work in transforming a desert into one of the leading oil-producing regions in the entire world. It is quite accurate to argue that the concession was kept in American hands because of the initiative of American private enterprise.[77] Aramco was entering its golden age.

Even accounts exceedingly hostile to the corruption of Saudi society by American capitalism, Philby's for example, acknowledge Ibn Saud's admiration of 'American technology, financial and economic cooperation in the development of all the natural resources of the land'.[78] At the time of the Palestine crisis of 1948, A. C. Trott, the British Minister who succeeded Grafftey-Smith, believed that Ibn Saud himself still did not fully comprehend the magnitude of the riches of the 'Black Eldorado'. He wrote in the British confidential annual report for that year that 'luxurious cars' were now conspicuous, but that 'it is doubtful whether the importance, to his potential enemies as well as to his friends, of the Saudi Arabian oil wells is yet fully appreciated by King Ibn Saud himself'.[79] In any

[75] Ibid.

[76] *Petroleum Arrangements with Saudi Arabia*, pp. 24924–25012.

[77] This is one of the main themes of Anderson, *Aramco*, which waxes rather enthusiastic on the subject.

[78] Philby, *Sa'udi Arabia*, p. 343.

[79] 'Annual Review for 1948', FO 371/75505.

case Ibn Saud made a clear distinction between the company, which provided the wealth, and the American government, which had recognized the Jewish state. During the Arab-Israeli war the King began to receive criticism from Egypt and Iraq, as reported by Childs, that he had become 'a virtual satellite of the United States' and that he should cancel the oil concession in order to prove his faith in the Arab cause by retaliating against the United States. Ibn Saud replied to such advice by stating that the oil royalties helped to make Saudi Arabia 'a stronger and more powerful nation, better to assist her neighboring Arab states in resisting Jewish pretensions'.[80] He thus refused to play his 'trump card'.

Philby once remarked that Ibn Saud's attitude towards the Palestine struggle remained 'Platonic'.[81] He stayed aloof, but no one who knew him well doubted his passion for the Arab cause in Palestine, or his bitterness towards the American government. In more mundane terms Childs summed it up in December 1948: 'The King has not permitted his feelings toward the United States Government to interfere with his friendly relations with the Arabian American Oil Company.'[82]

[80] Childs to Marshall, No. 264, Secret, 9 Dec. 1948, USSD 711.90F/12-948 Box 3494.
[81] Philby, *Sa'udi Arabia*, p. 348.
[82] Childs to Marshall, 9 Dec. 1948, n. 80 above.

5

CYPRUS: SELF-DETERMINATION
VERSUS STRATEGIC SECURITY IN
THE EASTERN MEDITERRANEAN

'THE current of Enosis' flowing towards union with Greece, Sir Arthur Dawe wrote in early 1945, 'always runs strongly under the surface' of Cyprus politics.[1] He added that it would be 'a mistake' to attach much importance 'to these ephemeral ups-and-downs' of the nationalist movement, which he believed could be permanently checked by a 'full-blooded statement' that Cyprus would forever remain an integral part of the British Empire. The movement for union with Greece expressed in the slogan 'Enosis' in short could be defeated by steadfast resolution of British purpose. That belief may be taken as a brand of official doctrine. Sir Arthur Dawe was its high priest.

Dawe was the Deputy Under-Secretary at the Colonial Office. Among other responsibilities he superintended the Mediterranean Department. In a Conservative rather than a Labour government he probably would have achieved the rank of Permanent Under-Secretary (a post that went in 1947 to an official of far more flexible and liberal inclination, Sir Thomas Lloyd). In 1945–7 he still possessed vivid memories of the nationalists' burning of Government House in Nicosia a quarter of a century earlier in 1931. He believed that the 'fires' of Enosis were merely 'fanned by the political agitators who are out for union with Greece'.[2] His comment represents secret,

---

[1] Minute by Dawe, 2 Feb. 1945, CO 67/327/16. At this time the discussion by the Colonial Office and Foreign Office about the future of Cyprus was sparked by reports in the *New York Times* by C. L. Sulzberger. He based his accounts on inside information of the State Department's postwar planning staff to the effect that the United States would favour the cession of Cyprus to Greece as part of the peace settlement. Sulzberger's ideas about Cyprus, Palestine, and Egypt may be followed through the occasional entries in his diaries, published as *A Long Row of Candles* (New York, 1969). George Kirk described him as 'a consistent propagandist for *Enosis*' (*The Middle East 1945–1950*, p. 176 n. 1). For detailed comment on the British and Enosis from the nineteenth century to 1948, see Sir George Hill, *A History of Cyprus* (4 vols., Cambridge, 1940–52), IV, chap. XIII. Two other works that are important for the postwar years are H. D. Purcell, *Cyprus* (London, 1969), and Robert Stephens, *Cyprus: A Place of Arms* (London, 1966). See also Nancy Crawshaw, *The Cyprus Revolt* (London, 1978).

[2] Minute by Dawe, 2 Feb. 1945, CO 67/327/16. On this and related issues Dawe persistently took a severe line. On the question for example of allowing political exiles to return after the war, he wrote: 'A policy of appeasement may only encourage agitation.' Minute of 10 May 1945, CO 67/327/16.

true-blue Tory thought in 1945 that found public expression nearly a decade later in 1954 in the famous Parliamentary statement that Cyprus would 'never' be independent.[3] Dawe brought to colonial administration large ideas of imperial destiny and a determination not to see the British Empire of the mid-twentieth century suffer a fate like the one in the American colonies or Ireland. His outlook is important in grasping the reasons why the British found themselves, as Nicholas Mansergh has written in a slightly different way, on 'the wrong side of history'.[4] Ireland was the prominent analogy in the British official mind. The determination not to repeat the experience of Ireland, where the question of 'union' had proven disastrous to stalwarts of the British Empire, led to perhaps lesser but equally disastrous consequences in Cyprus. The seminal period of controversy was the postwar era, when the question of nationalism in Cyprus had to be kept steadily in mind not only in relation to events in Greece but also those in Egypt and Palestine.

The fires of Greek nationalism, Dawe believed, could be permanently extinguished by the quelling of economic discontent. He argued vigorously for full employment and closer economic ties between British and Cypriot merchants as well as projects for irrigation that would, it was hoped, bring about agricultural prosperity. Economic development in the postwar years would be the means by which the British would wean nationalists from the unwholesome hankering after Greek union. Making a solemn pronouncement on the question of the permanence of Cyprus within the British Empire, the Colonial Office maintained, would clear the way for economic progress. Dawe wrote in August 1945:

> Having made our position clear on the question of union with Greece we shall be better able to go forward with a policy of economic improvement, social welfare and constitutional advance. But before we can start on this policy with any hope of eliciting an adequate amount of local goodwill and support, we must make it clear that we are not playing with any idea of handing the Island over to a foreign power.[5]

In some Colonial Office circles there was an emotional attachment to Cyprus which helps to explain the determination to hang on to the island. Cyprus constitutionally was a Crown Colony, the only British 'possession' in the eastern Mediterranean. 'I find it almost impossible to believe', Dawe commented, 'that any British Government, particularly after what this country has been through during the last six

---

[3] See David Goldsworthy, *Colonial Issues in British Politics 1945–1961* (Oxford, 1971), pp. 310–11.

[4] For his comment on the Irish connection with Cyprus in Tory colonial thought, see Nicholas Mansergh, *Commonwealth Experience* (New York, 1969), p. 196.

[5] Minute by Dawe, 6 Sept. 1945, CO 67/327/16.

years, would seriously contemplate handing over Cyprus to Greece, or that if they did contemplate it, public opinion would stand for it.'[6]

With considerable gifts of persuasion and logic, Dawe pounded home the arguments of permanence to all those who crossed the Colonial Office's Cypriot path. He especially emphasized them to those in the Foreign Office who wished to pursue a different course. The Foreign Office appeared not to recognize that a pusillanimous stand on Cyprus could be catastrophic for the unity of the Empire itself. The officials of the Colonial Office, as they had feared in the aftermath of the signing of the Atlantic Charter, now at the close of the war had to confront the principle of self-determination. If the Cypriots were allowed to go their own way, they might set an example for other ethnic or national groups who would cause the Empire to split into fragments.[7] In the case of Cyprus the Colonial Office argued that the island had never been politically united with Greece. 'The Cypriots were not real Greeks', Dawe explained to Christopher Warner of the Foreign Office. It may have been a weak argument, but such was the alarm about the future of the island that Colonial Office officials minimized the sentiment of Enosis and described it as a superficial movement. What they most feared was precedent. The cession of Cyprus to Greece would create a dangerous example for other British colonial possessions. According to Dawe: 'if we handed over Cyprus it would result in a clamour for the handing over of other colonial territory, e.g. the Falkland Islands, Hong Kong, etc.'[8] There was one further consideration that the Colonial Office believed should be decisive in the controversy about Enosis. In an island of 520,000 the population was divided along ethnic and religious lines, eighty per cent Greek Orthodox, nineteen per cent Turkish Muslim. The handing over of Cyprus to Greece would entail the abandoning of the loyal Turkish Cypriots 'who have stood by us for nearly seventy years'.[9]

The Colonial Office doctrine of a 'British' Cyprus met with powerful dissent. The officials of the Foreign Office, in particular Sir Oliver Harvey (Deputy Under-Secretary) and W. G. Hayter (head of the Southern Department), were inclined to recognize Enosis as a genuine passion felt by the majority of the population. 'Sooner or later H. M. G. must face the issue of self-determination there', Harvey once noted.[10] The British Hellenic tradition associated with

[6] Minute by Dawe, 13 Sept. 1945, CO 67/327/16.
[7] For the wartime controversy about self-determination and the future of the colonies, see Louis, *Imperialism at Bay*, chap. 6.
[8] As recorded in a minute by Warner, 12 Sept. 1946, FO 371/55761.
[9] Memorandum by Hall (drafted by Dawe), CP (46) 260, 5 July 1946, CAB 129/11.
[10] Minute by Harvey, 9 June 1947, FO 371/67083.

Gladstone and nineteenth-century liberalism continued to flourish in the postwar Foreign Office. A writer in the *Contemporary Review* expressed the ideas of this tradition in regard to Cyprus in robust language that found echoes in official minutes:

> It will be a pity if a British Socialist Government cannot rise to the degree of magnanimity of the Government which in 1864, in accordance with the wishes of their inhabitants, restored the Ionian Isles to Greece. We do not regret . . . that Corfu and Ithaca are under the Greek instead of the British flag to-day. What is there different about Cyprus, even judged from its new strategic importance? Nowhere among British possessions . . . is the moral case for retention weaker . . . The British Socialist Government will make a tragic mistake if it imagines that the Greeks of Cyprus will readily suppress their patriotic sentiments and the spiritual thirst for reunion in return for belated economic wellbeing and a more tolerant régime. . . .
>
> Mr. Attlee should dwell on what Mr. Gladstone had to say about Cyprus. The Grand Old Man expressed a fervent desire to see . . . 'the population of that Hellenic island placed by a friendly arrangement in organic union with their brethren in the Kingdom of Greece and Crete'. Sooner or later 'organic union' must come.[11]

In the months following the close of the Second World War the Foreign Office actively contemplated the cession of Cyprus to Greece. It seemed to be within the realm of political possibility because the Dodecanese islands would be transferred under the terms of the Italian peace treaty. 'In the autumn of 1945', Hayter reflected in 1947, 'our relations with Russia were much better than they are now and . . . the prospects of Communist control of Greece were far more remote.'[12] The British could still count on bases in Egypt and Palestine, compared with which Cyprus paled in strategic significance. Above all the cession of Cyprus would, as Sir Oliver Harvey remarked later, 'be the greatest possible contribution to Greek morale and British influence'. Harvey concluded on a note which strikes one in retrospect as acute: the transfer might take place, he noted (in a comment given in full below), '*before* the Cypriot campaign is embittered by violence and *before* cession can be represented as yielding to force'.[13]

Here the historian faces one of the significant 'might have beens'

[11] Thomas Anthem, 'The Cyprus Farce', *Contemporary Review* (June 1947). For F. O. comment on the legacy of Britain and Greece in the nineteenth century, see e.g. minute by Harvey, 26 Sept. 1947, FO 371/67084: 'We are still living in Greece on the credit of Mr. Gladstone's retrocession of the Ionian Isles.'

[12] Minute by Hayter, 24 Oct. 1947, FO 371/67084. The basis of Hayter's thought in regard to Greece and Cyprus may be traced to a minute of 19 Mar. 1945: 'It is possible to conceive of circumstances in which the cession of Cyprus to Greece, possibly in exchange for bases in Cyprus itself and in other Greek territory, might be very much to our advantage.' Similar minutes by Sir Orme Sargent and others are in the same file.

[13] Minute by Harvey, 26 Sept. 1947, FO 371/67084/R13462/G. Emphasis added.

in postwar history. It is similar to the speculative proposition that a binational state of Arabs and Jews in Palestine might have succeeded as late as the close of the Second World War if both Britain and the United States had acted resolutely to establish it. In the case of Cyprus the chances for a peaceful unification with Greece might have been greater than the prospects of a binational state in Palestine. In Cyprus there was no comparable problem of immigration. The Turkish minority was smaller than the Jewish minority in Palestine. At the end of the war Turkey was in no position to intervene. Constitutional guarantees for the Turkish Cypriots and military assurances to the Turkish government had a better chance of acceptance then than later.[14] Historical speculation is usually barren, but in this case the proposition is important to bear in mind because the project of a British-sponsored Enosis held out momentary hope as a workable alternative to what in retrospect appears as a historical tragedy of the 'emergency' of 1955–60 and eventual communal war.

To the Colonial Office the question of Cyprus could best be approached by drawing inspiration from Disraeli rather than Gladstone, and from Curzon rather than Grey. Here is a minute which reveals the dubious way in which lessons of the past could be applied to contemporary crises. It is a romp through Imperial history with the purpose of demonstrating the danger of Foreign Office intervention in the larger affairs of the British Empire:

In the 1870's British policy, not for the last time . . . was deeply concerned in preventing Russian penetration into the valleys of the Tigris and Euphrates. Lord Beaconsfield called for a base from which further Russian expansion could be stopped, that base was Cyprus and it secured both the overland and canal routes to India, the Far East and Australasia. . . .

In 1915 Lord [sic] Grey at the Foreign Office, without the knowledge of the Cabinet, offered Cyprus to Greece as a bribe to enter the war in fulfilment of her Treaty obligations, and was severely criticised by Lord Curzon for his unconstitutional and unilateral action in a Cabinet paper of 1919 in which he likened the proposal to the cession of Heligoland; and we must hope that the Foreign Office will not be so blind to every British and Cypriot interest, or so maladroit in the affairs of another Department, in 1945.[15]

This historical reconstruction was sufficiently loose to cause another official to comment 'Rubbish', but the general argument was the important point. The Foreign Office, 'flouting history and Greek character', wished to sacrifice 'our sovereignty over the only British

---

[14] The point has been stressed in a perceptive study of the contemporary history of Cyprus, Robert Stephens, *Cyprus: A Place of Arms*, p. 206: 'Turkey's record in the war gave her little ground for complaint. . . . It would, of course, have been incumbent on Greece to do everything in her power to convince Turkey of her good intentions by a generous treatment of the Turkish minority and the demilitarisation of the island. . . .'

[15] Minute by Juxon Barton, 4 Oct. 1945, CO 67/327/16.

possession in the Eastern Mediterranean'.[16] No one endorsed that
view more strongly than Sir Arthur Dawe, who even denied any
particular Greek connection with the island. To him the main
historical facts were clear and compelling:

> The Colonial Office have always strongly held that Greece has no kind of
> historical claim to Cyprus. We took over the administration of the Island from
> Turkey in 1878 and we subsequently annexed it when Turkey joined our
> enemies in November, 1914. Since the end of the last war, all British Govern-
> ments of whatever party colour have stood firm on the question and have
> refused to consider the cession of the Island to Greece.[17]

Dawe was certain that the Chiefs of Staff would agree on the necessity
of retaining Cyprus within the British Empire. In Cyprus as in
Palestine the concurrence of the Chiefs of Staff would enable either
the Colonial Office or the Foreign Office to carry the issue in the
Cabinet. In the case of Cyprus the assessments by the Chiefs of
Staff worked in favour of the Colonial Office. 'As was expected',
Dawe wrote in September 1945, the Chiefs of Staff 'pronounced in
favour of retaining Cyprus on strategical grounds'.[18]

The Chiefs of Staff reports of September 1945 are extremely
important because they established Cyprus as a fixed designation in
British calculations. Further assessments about Egypt and Palestine
always took the Cyprus estimate into account. The first report, produced within a month following the dropping of atomic bombs
in Japan, noted by way of preface that the planners did not attempt
to assess 'changes to our strategy likely to be caused by the advent
of new weapons'. To readers in September 1945 it therefore conveyed a sense of being slightly removed from reality. In the words of
John Martin of the Colonial Office, 'the appearance of the atomic
bomb, as an instrument of war, has for the moment imported a certain
unreality into discussion of strategic situations'.[19] The report in fact
could just as well have been written almost as if in the days of Lord
Curzon. There was perhaps one all-important difference. Cyprus was
now the only British 'possession' in the Middle East where the British
could make plans 'unfettered by treaties'. It helped to bear in mind
that the island was the third largest in the Mediterranean after
Sardinia and Sicily. It possessed over twenty airfield sites, two of
which were all-weather and could serve as bases for transport and other
aircraft. The airport near Nicosia had potential as a communication

[16] Minute by Juxon Barton, 4 Oct. 1945, CO 67/327/16.
[17] Minute by Dawe, 15 Aug. 1945, CO 67/327/16.
[18] Minute by Dawe, 6 Sept. 1945, CO 67/327/16.
[19] Minute by Martin, 10 Sept. 1945, CO 67/327/16. Dawe brusquely commented on
Martin's remark: 'We must look to the Chiefs of Staff to say how far these new developments are to be taken into account.'

link with other parts of the Middle East. Unfortunately for the military planners, the only harbour, Famagusta, 'is small and can only accommodate one cruiser and four destroyers'. The development of a Cyprus air base might nevertheless contribute 'to the defence of Egypt and Palestine'. The island was within fighter distance of the Suez canal. Moreover Cyprus had a certain denial value. 'Its control by any other power, even if friendly, might prove to be a very considerable embarrassment since we cannot be certain that its territorial integrity can be guaranteed.' The advantages in war and peace could be summed up:

> In war, the island is strategically placed to assist in the defence of our interests in the Middle East.
> In peace, it provides us with alternative air staging bases, and naval and air facilities for the security control of the Eastern Mediterranean.

The Chiefs of Staff had hardly produced a masterpiece of strategic planning, but it went down well in the Colonial Office because it firmly recommended 'the retention of Cyprus and British rule'.[20]

Shortly after the Colonial Office received the good news from the Chiefs of Staff, Dawe and his colleagues learned to their consternation that Bevin, as if in grotesque aping of Sir Edward Grey, had responded not unsympathetically to a suggestion by the Greek Regent that Cyprus be transferred to Greece in return for British military rights in the Aegean. Bevin was non-commital, but his mind clearly was working in that direction. He did not like the report by the Chiefs of Staff. The Foreign Office now requested another one, this time asking for a different type of assessment. What military rights should the British demand of the Greeks in return for giving up Cyprus? On this occasion the military mind found inspiration. In an ingenious reply the Joint Planners pointed out that the cession of Cyprus would probably jeopardize rather than secure the British military position. There could be no guarantee that the promises of the present Greek government would be honoured by successor governments. 'There is plenty of evidence to show that the present Greek Government is just as unstable as its predecessors. There is, therefore, a danger that some future Greek Government with communistic leanings might extend the offer of facilities to the Russians.' The military experts were leery of accepting Greek gifts, even though the offer might at first sight seem strategically attractive. They stated the hidden dangers in unyielding terms:

> By accepting bases in Crete and the Aegean Islands, we should strengthen the present Russian case for bases in the Black Sea Straits and encourage the Russians

[20] COS (45) 215, 5 Sept. 1945, CAB 79/39; minutes in CO 67/323/5 and FO 371/ 58760-1.

to argue that they were as much entitled to bases in the Aegean and in Crete as we were. . . .

We are faced . . . with acquiring, not necessarily permanently, the right to potentially valuable bases but at the risk of accelerating Russian infiltration around Turkey, Greece, and the Greek islands, and permanently sacrificing our sovereignty over the only British possession in the Eastern Mediterranean.[21]

The military planners therefore concluded that British sovereignty should be maintained in Cyprus—'even at the risk of increased agitation in the island and of unfavourable reactions in Greece'.

The Colonial Office now pressed the Foreign Office to acquiesce in a 'full-blooded' reaffirmation of British sovereignty in Cyprus. The point is of considerable interest because of the way in which the 'sovereignty' later became a fixation of the Tory governments of the 1950s. The Colonial Secretary, Hall, whose views merely reflected those of Dawe and Martin, wrote to Bevin that he was 'greatly disturbed' to hear that the Foreign Office had considered 'giving away' Cyprus. Public opinion in England, he emphasized, would not stand for it. The Greeks would get reward enough for their war effort by the 'compensation' of the Dodecanese. 'I cannot exaggerate', Hall wrote, 'the effect which the cession of this British Colony would have upon the public confidence in other British territories, particularly those held under mandate.'[22] Nothing less than a stalwart statement of British sovereignty would steady nerves in the colony itself and prepare the way for urgently needed economic development. Bevin replied curtly to this entreaty of Imperial exigency. 'I am not persuaded that the arguments in favour of the retention of Cyprus are sound', he wrote to Hall. 'Nor do I find the paper produced by the Chiefs of Staff a convincing one.' Bevin insisted on postponing the question, but the combined effort by the Colonial Office and the Chiefs of Staff in September 1945 successfully checked the Foreign Office's initiative in the direction of Enosis.[23]

---

[21] JP (45) 247, 12 Sept. 1945, CAB 84/75; COS (45) 574, CAB 80/97; CO 67/327/6. This report is probably the basis of the comment by Sulzberger of the *New York Times* in *A Long Row of Candles*, pp. 311-12.

[22] Minutes by Martin and Dawe, 13 Sept. 1945, CO 67/327/16; Hall to Bevin, 'Top Secret and Personal', 18 Sept. 1945, FO 371/48360. The reference to mandates was probably to the mandated territories of tropical Africa rather than to Palestine. Dawe hoped to transform Tanganyika from a mandate into a 'permanent' Crown Colony. See Louis, *Imperialism at Bay*, p. 401.

[23] Bevin to Hall, 'Top Secret and Personal', 21 Sept. 1945, CO 67/327/16; FO 371/ 48360. C. M. Woodhouse, a protagonist in the liberation of Greece and a participant in the discussions about Cyprus in Athens, has commented on the Turkish dimension of the problem in 1945: 'Fear of a Turkish reaction played no part at that date, for the Turks had neither the legal right nor the moral standing nor even the inclination to object. Nevertheless the decision [taken by the British government] was negative.' In his autobiography, *Something Ventured* (London, 1982), p. 100.

The Foreign Office in turn managed to block the Colonial Office's move towards a proclamation of absolute and indefinite sovereignty.

Cyprus in a sense could be taken as a microcosm of British colonial affairs which reflected nationalist and strategic dilemmas as well as the ethical tribulations of the Labour government. In the clash over the future of the colony the officials of the Colonial Office who advocated permanent union with Britain found themselves more in the mainstream of postwar British thought than did the sceptics of the Foreign Office. In October 1945 the Fabian Colonial Bureau published an important and widely read pamphlet entitled *Strategic Colonies*. It argued that the economic and political destiny of certain colonies, including Cyprus, Malta, Gibraltar, Aden, and Hong Kong, lay in association with Britain. A key passage of the argument read:

> As Cyprus is not self-supporting and will have to lean for protection and security on a larger state, the best chance of economic recovery and a higher standard of living may, in spite of suspicion, rather lie in association with Britain which is now actively pursuing schemes of economic, political and educational development, and has already given in earnest in other territories of a new, progressive orientation in her colonial policy.[24]

Intelligent Englishmen who gave thought to colonial problems probably generally agreed that a rational colonial policy should above all be aimed at the raising of Cypriot standards of living rather than indulging in hopes of union with Greece. At the same time there was considerable doubt that Enosis could be eradicated. The following sections will deal with the Colonial Office's political and economic solution for the problems of Cyprus and the Foreign Office's warning that, however rational and desirable the goal might be, the examples of Ireland, India, and Palestine did not hold out much hope for a united and 'British' Cyprus.

'Colonial Development and Welfare' (CD&W)

Shortly after the close of the war, Arthur Creech Jones, who suddenly found himself transformed from a principal Parliamentary critic of wartime colonial policy into Parliamentary Under-Secretary at the Colonial Office, wrote that 'the whole unhappy problem of Cyprus' would have to be taken in hand at an early date.[25] The long-range weapon to be used in a potentially violent situation would be the

[24] Fabian Colonial Bureau, *Strategic Colonies and Their Future* (London, Fabian Publications and Gollancz, 1945), p. 36.

[25] Minute by Creech Jones, 28 Aug. 1945, CO 67/323/5. Creech Jones wrote in regard to a conflict involving Enosis, AKEL, and the Cyprus newspapers which had been suppressed at the time of Greek liberation. (See Kirk, *The Middle East 1945-1950*, pp. 165-6.) In the House of Commons he had stringently criticized the police. In the Colonial Office it did not

Colonial Development and Welfare Act of 1945. From the CD&W Fund the Colonial Office would allocate £6 million for a ten-year development programme that would deal 'with every aspect of the island's life and economy'—agriculture and irrigation, the forests, medical and educational services, expansion of the ports, and the development of tourist facilities.[26] In the autumn of 1945 the Colonial Office developed these plans with a sense of urgency. In part the motivation may be traced to the need to dispel the 'false' hopes aroused by the Atlantic Charter. The Colonial Office also aimed at averting the danger of the local Communist party, AKEL, linking the cause of Communism with the goals of Enosis.

The recurrent nationalist name in Colonial Office files at this time was Ploutis Servas, the Communist mayor of Limassol. He had spent the years 1929-34 in Russia. Subsequently he had been deported from Greece. According to the District Commissioner in Cyprus, Servas was 'not at all a bad fellow' but 'with a lazy, cynical charm, he talked with a sweet Liberal reasonableness which might reflect either his genuine personal convictions or the latest tactical directive from Moscow'.[27] Officials in the Colonial Office took a less sympathetic view. Servas dominated Enosis as well as the Communist movement, a combination which might prove deadly to the British. According to one account that provided the basis of much discussion in the Colonial Office:

> While this intensification of [Enosis] feeling may be ascribed in part to natural sympathy with the successful resistance of Greece to Italian aggression, the more recent deliverance from German bondage and to hopes based on the Atlantic Charter, it is due also to a deliberate fanning of the flames by the Akel party which seeks to employ Enosis as a smoke-screen for its own ends and these are purely anarchical.
>
> Herein lies the immediate danger for Akel . . . can bring to the movement a direction and a discipline which it has hitherto lacked. Servas and his associates will stop at little to achieve their purpose and require the firmest of handling.[28]

take him long to become convinced of the wisdom of the official line of combating Communist propaganda, though his minute reveals the lingering pangs of the conscience of the colonial reformer: 'There is much agitation in this country about this trial and it succeeds in its purpose because of our past unfortunate record. The facts as stated in these [secret] papers are not known here [in England]. Though while not wishing to condone propaganda with intent to create a violent situation we must have some regard to the economic background, political aspirations & "colonial" background of the language used'.

[26] For the Colonial Secretary's explanation of the purpose of CD&W as applicable to Cyprus, see his memorandum of 5 July 1946, 'Proposed New Policy for Cyprus', CP (46) 260, CAB 129/11.

[27] Patrick Balfour, *The Orphaned Realm* (London, 1951), p. 189.

[28] Note by Miles Clifford, 8 Sept. 1945, CO 67/327/16. In another passage Clifford wrote: ' "Enosis" is an idée fixe and its attainment the natural aspiration of a people who,

In November 1945 the Governor of Cyprus, Sir Charles Woolley, during a visit to London emphasized similar points to the Colonial Secretary and other high-ranking officials, including Creech Jones, Dawe, Martin, and Stephen Luke. They addressed themselves to the question of 'external' sources of Enosis. According to Woolley, whose assessment of Communism and Russian influence is revealing:

> The AKEL, or Communist, Party was most numerous in the towns of Cyprus, but the villages were more moderate in their sympathies; the villages would however, soon succumb to an active electoral campaign by the Akelists. There were close relations between AKEL and the Communists in Greece and in Palestine, but since the war there was no trace of Russian propaganda in Cyprus —though Servas, the leader of the Enosist movement, had spent some years in Russia and was a devout Communist.[29]

Woolley spoke forcefully of the need to make it clear in Cyprus and throughout the world that 'no change in the sovereignty of Cyprus is contemplated'. A month later Sir Douglas Harris, the Palestine expert of the Colonial Office, arrived back in London after a brief visit to Cyprus and confirmed 'most emphatically' the tension and 'acute feeling of uncertainty' that existed because of the Colonial Office's paralysis of policy.[30] Servas and other 'agitators' would exploit rumours that Britain might cede Cyprus to Greece. 'The Cypriots are notoriously inflammable', Dawe wrote, 'and any lack of reasonable firmness on the part of the Government in present conditions may lead to serious consequences.'[31]

It is a measure of Ernest Bevin's influence in imperial affairs that he could frustrate Colonial Office action on a matter that seemed to those directly concerned with the future of the British Empire to be a matter of cardinal and urgent importance. The permanent officials of the Colonial Office believed that they could not move the Colony forward in economic development, constitutional progress, and reconciliation with the Greek Orthodox Church until the mood of uncertainty was dissipated. After prolonged and acrimonious bureaucratic controversy, Bevin finally in September 1946 wrote that if the Colonial Office continued to insist on a declaration of

Greek as they are in language as in mentality and culture, have lived for centuries under foreign domination; though nothing is likely to eradicate their desire for union with Greece a good deal might be done to moderate it.' Dawe, in a corrective comment that reveals one of his fixations, wrote: 'This is not correct in suggesting that Cyprus was Greek once.'

[29] Notes of a meeting of 23 Nov. 1945, CO 67/323/5.

[30] See minute by Luke, 19 Dec. 1945, CO 67/327/16.

[31] Dawe added: 'I was in the Island just before the outbreak in 1931, when Government House was burnt down by rioters, and it looks to me as if we may be drifting into rather similar conditions now.' Minute of 19 Dec. 1945, CO 67/327/16.

sovereignty then there would be a showdown in the Cabinet. He
summarized his position in a letter to the Colonial Secretary:

Generally speaking, my feeling as regard Cyprus is to let sleeping dogs lie and
not to say anything at all about the island at this particular moment. From the
foreign affairs point of view I obviously do not want to complicate the already
difficult situation in the Balkans and the Middle East by starting a controversy
about the future of Cyprus. . . . You can imagine the play which the Russians
and their Communist agents in Greece will be able to make with any statement
to the effect that H. M. Government have definitely decided to hold on to
Cyprus indefinitely.

The matter so far as Bevin was concerned boiled down to a question
of what was more important, 'the local aspect of the question or the
foreign affairs aspect'.[32] In ominous language he stated that if the
Colonial Secretary persisted, then 'I can see nothing . . . but for you
to raise the matter at the Cabinet.' This was an intolerable situation
for the permanent officials of the Colonial Office. They knew that
Bevin, basing his case on the international emergency of the eastern
Mediterranean, would defeat the Colonial Office argument, despite
the backing of the Chiefs of Staff and support in the Cabinet
Office.[33] The Colonial Secretary acquiesced. But he succeeded in
getting Bevin's agreement to the formula '*no change is contemplated*'.[34] It by no means satisfied Sir Arthur Dawe, but at least it
provided an anchor against the drift towards Enosis. It was against
this background that Creech Jones assumed control of the Colonial
Office in October 1946. He at least could embark on a detailed
programme of political and economic development with the
assurance that, if asked in Parliament or elsewhere about sovereignty
in Cyprus, he could reply with the stock answer 'no change is
contemplated'. He was under constraint however not to mention
the bugbear of sovereignty itself.

In the same month in which Creech Jones became Colonial
Secretary, Lord Winster was appointed as the new Governor of
Cyprus. Winster, formerly Reginald Fletcher, after a naval and Parliamentary career had served in the Labour government since 1945
as Minister of Civil Aviation. He was an acknowledged authority
on naval and defence affairs, but he had no experience in the
Colonial Empire. Though he had impeccable Labour credentials,
temperamentally he found it difficult to export the benefits of the

---

[32] Bevin to Hall, 17 Sept. 1946, FO 371/53761.

[33] The official of the Cabinet Office who advised Attlee on colonial problems in 1945–6,
T. L. Rowan, believed that 'although it may be old-fashioned . . . there is more for the
people of Cyprus within the British Commonwealth and Empire than there would be for
them under Greece'. Minute of 18 Jan. 1946, PREM 8/740.

[34] See Bevin's minute on Hall's letter of 28 Sept. 1946, FO 371/58761.

welfare state to a colonial society in which a majority preferred the simplicities of Greek civilization to the austerities of British colonial rule. His real passion was the internal politics of the Labour government. He did not for example believe that Bevin was as inflexible on Cyprus as the Colonial Office made him out to be, or that other members of the Cabinet were beyond persuasion on the question of sovereignty. In February 1947 he wrote a letter to his friend Creech Jones that establishes the connection at that time between the debate on the British economy, the strategic issue of Cyprus, and the larger question of colonial independence:

> Dalton sees no reason why . . . we should spend in the island money which we need sorely at home. Attlee thinks there is a possibility that such talk [about Enosis] is all froth and may die away when the Cypriots find there is nothing doing. Alexander is for holding on to the island for strategical grounds. The Chiefs of Staff are also for holding on. Bevin is somewhat torn in two, dislikes giving anything more away and largely sympathizes with the views held by you and myself. But believing as he does that a plebiscite in Cyprus would show a vote in favour of union with Greece, he feels difficulty in making the statement [on sovereignty] we want when (a) we have just granted independence to India and Burma [and] (b) he has lost a Treaty with Egypt through standing firm for self-determination for the Sudanese.[35]

As Governor of Cyprus, Winster proved to be an unhappy choice. Though he developed an enthusiasm for Cyprus politics of the parish pump variety, he remained aloof from the political leaders who disagreed with his view that Cyprus should remain a permanent part of the British Empire. In the Creech Jones papers there is a damning minute by Sir John Martin about Winster's fitness as a Colonial Governor. Martin was a fair-minded, able official with broad experience. He identified a signal weakness in the postwar British era in Cyprus:

> It must be stated that Lord Winster was much criticized for shutting himself up in an ivory castle at Government House, where the only Greeks he saw were a few officials and the two (very unrepresentative) Greek members of his Executive Council. . . . Lord Winster made a great point of meeting the village Mukhtars [headmen], but he was out of touch with the educated-professional and mercantile class.[36]

Martin's assessment was a just summary of the Cyprus career of the man selected by the Labour government to implement a far-reaching programme of constitutional and economic development.

Martin made a further perceptive comment about the postwar years in Cyprus. He noted that the Colonial Secretary at Nicosia,

---

[35] Winster to Creech Jones, 14 Feb. 1947, Creech Jones Papers Box 59.
[36] Minute by Martin, 9 Feb. 1949, Creech Jones Papers Box 59.

Roland Turnbull, 'has been much more open to Cypriot society'.[37] Turnbull served as Acting Governor before and after Winster. Dawe described him as 'a young but very competent man'.[38] He was a career officer in the colonial service who later became Governor of North Borneo. He possessed a dramatically different temperament from Winster's. The clash of personalities caused friction in Nicosia. Turnbull passionately threw himself into the debate about Enosis. He canvassed opinions, Turkish as well as Greek, and reported at great length on the nuances of the political climate in Cyprus as he perceived them in football matches and religious services as well as in political assemblies. It is therefore remarkable that Winster, disdainfully aloof from Cyprus politics, and Turnbull, ardently involved, should arrive at basically the same assessment of Enosis.

Winster and Turnbull, whose ideas represented a wide current of British postwar thought on Cyprus, believed that only a minority of Greek Cypriots favoured Enosis. The percentage appeared greater than it actually was because of intimidation by the clergy and the Communists, who in common had a hatred of the British. There was a third and vitally important element—the politicians, lawyers, journalists, and 'intellectuals' who opportunistically seized on the issue but who at heart did not believe in it. Accordingly it was a false assumption to think that Enosis was an 'authentic' movement.

Turnbull gave a full evaluation of the superficial nature of Enosis in a letter to Martin in March 1947. It went on record as the considered estimate by Government House in Nicosia. Turnbull acknowledged the 'sentimental affection' of the Greek Cypriots 'for Greece and things Greek'; but at bottom Enosis was an 'artificial' phenomenon. The peasants regarded the agitation for union with Greece 'with sceptical disinterest'. They knew that prosperity would decline in the event of political amalgamation. The Communist party, AKEL, according to Turnbull, merely followed the Greek Communist party 'and ultimately Russia'. In the Church he admitted that one could find something that 'more nearly approaches a real wish for Enosis for its own sake'; but the 'intellectuals', lawyers, and journalists merely used it for their own purposes. Here was Turnbull's major conclusion:

> Until . . . we have succeeded in associating the local Greeks with our government, and they have attained political maturity, enosis will always recur as a political slogan, but we should at suitable intervals rap their knuckles, *as they expect us to do*, before it becomes an issue as it has done now . . . without the

---

[37] Minute by Martin, 9 Feb. 1949, Creech Jones Papers Box 59.
[38] Minute by Dawe, 19 Dec. 1945, CO 67/327/16.

rap, the campaign takes on the character of a snowball and grows beyond the control and the intentions of its instigators, who yet cannot with dignity desert it—which is what has happened now. Our reluctance to deliver the rap is causing grave anxiety, and I foresee that in the end the issue, even to our best friends, will become one of 'Govern or get out'.[39]

Two years later Turnbull made a slight revision of his estimate, in which, among other things, he accused Winster (who had resigned in February 1949) of failing to grasp the essence of Cyprus politics by 'refusing contact with the political leaders and more intellectual members of Greek society'.[40] The essential theme was the same as both he and Winster had persistently reported to the Colonial Office. Enosis was not an authentic movement. In 1949 Turnbull believed it now could be attributed more to 'the persistent irredentist propaganda from Athens'. But the basic interpretation remained remarkably constant. Enosis was not a genuine movement endorsed by the majority of Cypriots.

The Foreign Office officials who dealt with Cyprus were extremely sceptical of Turnbull's evaluation of Enosis in 1947. 'Colonial Office efforts to explain away the agitation over "Enosis" take peculiar forms', wrote D. J. McCarthy. Usually the Colonial Office argued that local sentiment did not favour the idea of union with Greece but, at the same time, that widespread riots would break out if it were not made thunderously clear that Cyprus would remain permanently within the British Empire. Sceptics might doubt that the two arguments were compatible. Now Turnbull's train of logic introduced the additional idea that the Greek Cypriots periodically should be scolded for expressing an urge for union that they did not

[39] Turnbull to Martin, Top Secret, 3 Mar. 1947, copy in FO 371/67082. Winster's views, which flowed in the same direction, may be traced in the candid, private letters he wrote to Creech Jones. At one time Winster added an additional dimension of the Enosis controversy caused by the distortion of the British press, notably *The Economist* and the *New Statesman*. 'I am really astonished at the change which has come over *The Economist*', he wrote to Creech. 'It was at one time balanced, impartial, and above all, devoted to getting at the facts. Now, under the influence I imagine of Barbara Ward, it is beginning to develop the loose criticism and thin, acidulated tone which, under Kingsley Martin, has ruined the *New Stateman* and deprived it of influence.' Winster to Creech Jones, 26 July 1947, Creech Jones Papers Box 57.

[40] Turnbull to Martin, Top Secret, 27 June 1949, CO 537/4979. It would do an injustice to such a knowledgeable and humane an authority as Sir Harry Luke to put him in the same intellectual camp as Winster and Turnbull, but nevertheless there was a similarity of general argument. Luke raised it to a higher plateau: 'A Frankenstein's monster greater than even terrorism is Enosis itself. The villagers have had to pay lip-service to it when all that most of them have wanted is to be left alone. No one dares to say he is against for fear of being branded as a traitor, a dangerous thing when the organization that imposes the deterrent is, as in Cyprus, the Church and terrorists are on the pounce for "traitors". . . . People who talk of self-determination for Cyprus should reflect that, were a plebiscite on this issue to be held there, it would be a regimented one and therefore meaningless.' Sir Harry Luke, *Cyprus* (London, 1957), p. 180.

genuinely feel in the first place. McCarthy examined this 'new claim':

> It is that no-one wants enosis but that everyone feels themselves bound to say that they do. They say so in the expectation that they will be comfortingly rapped over the knuckles for making a claim for union with Greece and are now seriously disturbed because we are not rapping them over the knuckles. It all seems very roundabout to me.[41]

J. R. Colville, who had served as one of Churchill's secretaries during the war and followed Greek affairs with particular interest, remarked that 'The C. O. are supreme wishful thinkers.'[42]

The Foreign Office suspected that the Colonial Office denied the authenticity of Enosis because of pangs of remorse over the unsatisfactory nature of colonial rule in Cyprus since 1931. 'I can only suggest', McCarthy wrote, that the assessments of Cyprus politics 'are based on consciousness in the Colonial Office that their arbitrary means of government in Cyprus and their panic-stricken abolition of the Assembly in 1931 have caused genuine discontent.'[43] There was an element of truth in the speculation. Colonial rule in Cyprus was out of line with the general policy of the gradual introduction of representative institutions. In comparable colonies, Ceylon for example, the development of Legislative Councils would lead to preparation for independence within the Commonwealth. In 1931 the Colonial Office had suspended the Legislative Assembly because of Enosist riots and Cyprus had remained, for all intents and purposes, a bureaucratic autocracy. Along with economic development, the relaunching of Cyprus upon a sound constitutional course became a colonial priority of the Labour government.

It is illuminating to examine the minutes of Stephen Luke on the question of constitutional reform in Cyprus. In 1947 Luke was seconded from the Colonial Office to the Cabinet Office, where he advised the Prime Minister on colonial questions. Luke himself had a long and distinguished career in colonial affairs, including service in Palestine. His views are important here because they provide the basis of Attlee's intervention when the matter came to a head in late 1947. Luke believed it essential to provide the Cypriots with a constitution that would give them increasing responsibility in the central government. He also recognized the difficulty of making concessions that would satisfy them in view of British determination to retain control, for strategic reasons, over external affairs and defence matters. Whatever the British might yield would probably be scorned

---

[41] Minute by McCarthy, 27 Mar. 1947, FO 371/67082.
[42] Minute by Colville, 28 Mar. 1947, FO 371/67082.
[43] Minute by McCarthy, 27 Mar. 1947, FO 371/67082.

by the Cypriots as inadequate. Specifically the Greek Cypriots would probably reject any constitutional proposals that did not provide the basis for eventual union with Greece. Luke confronted these difficulties in a minute to Attlee of December 1947:

> The Cypriots are an intelligent and civilised Levantine people, who should be as capable of making a success of responsible Government as, for instance, the Maltese. That the present administration in Cyprus is an unqualified bureaucracy is due, not to any reluctance to associate the local population with the Government, but to the fact that all the Cypriot political parties have hitherto concentrated their attention almost exclusively on the aim of securing union with Greece. They have not been granted a liberal constitution, because they were not interested in participating in any form of Government which involved the continuance of Cyprus within the British Commonwealth.[44]

In late 1947 the Greek Cypriots had indicated a change of heart. Their representatives were divided, but some of them seemed disposed to accept proposals which had been worked out with great patience and perseverance by Lord Winster. Luke pointed out that the Communists supported Winster's constitutional plans. At this stage the Prime Minister wrote an opinion on the subject. It is highly revealing about Attlee's thought on colonial affairs, at a time when Burma was about to decline membership in the Commonwealth, and Ceylon was about to achieve independence within the Commonwealth. What was to become of the Cypriots, who could probably manage their own affairs as well as the Ceylonese and the Burmese not to mention the neighbouring Lebanese and the Syrians?

Attlee was suspicious of the Communists' support of a British liberal constitution. 'They probably hope that Greece is going to become a Soviet satellite and therefore want to get as much power as they can in anticipation', he wrote. Attlee also expressed caution for an entirely different reason. On the basis of his experience with constitutional reform in India, he was wary of 'dyarchy', which had raised its head in the discussion about Cyprus in the Cabinet's Committee on Commonwealth Affairs. In its application in the case of Cyprus, 'dyarchy' would mean the designation of certain posts with only partial responsibility for them. Attlee wished to have clearcut lines of authority and to avoid the fault, as he believed experience had demonstrated in India, 'of giving opportunity for criticism without real responsibility'. Here is the way in which Attlee summed up his attitude to the question of the future of Cyprus, and his answer to Enosis:

> If we are to move in the matter, I would . . . say firmly that we intend to retain control of Foreign Policy and Defence, but that in all other spheres we

---

[44] Minute by Luke, 19 Dec. 1947, PREM 8/740.

will concede fully responsible government with any safeguards necessary for minorities. Our aim should be to get the Cypriots to form Parties based on internal policies economic and social and thus wean them from the delusion of Greek nationalism.[45]

In the event, Greek nationalism did not prove amenable to a British solution that would have left the island as a permanent strategic out-post of the British Empire and Commonwealth. As for economic development, Roland Turnbull probably expressed the main point when he observed that 'their emotions draw them to Greece . . . with wild disregard of their pockets'.[46]

The 'Winster Constitution' foundered on the shoals of Enosis. The Archbishop of Cyprus issued encyclicals forbidding members of the Greek Orthodox Church to support or take part in the establish-ing of the proposed constitution. It would have moved the colony along the classic path of self-government, though with the all-important reservation of British control of foreign and defence affairs. Lord Winster returned to London to explain the nature of the stalemate. In July 1948 he explained to members of the Cabinet's Committee on Commonwealth Affairs that in the three large towns there was some support for Enosis, but—in line with his persistent interpretation—'this did not mean that . . . there was in fact any genuine desire for union with Greece'.[47] Four-fifths of the population, Winster believed, were indifferent to Enosis, which had been whipped up by the Church and the Communists, and by propaganda from Greece. To his credit Winster did not believe that a British constitution should be forced on a people who would not accept it. In early 1949 he retired, a disappointed and bitter man. The constitution remained in abeyance. The Cyprus question entered into a new and substantially different phase when Makarios III became Archbishop in 1950.

The Foreign Office Warning: Sir Oliver Harvey and the Principle of Self-determination

Enosis would have stood a better chance of British aquiescence in the postwar years if the political situation in Greece had not deteriorated. There was a current of sympathy among high officials of the Foreign Office that ran in favour of cession of the island as late as 1947. In February of that year the Permanent Under-Secretary,

[45] Minute by Attlee, 22 Dec. 1947, PREM 8/740. For the discussions about the consti-tutional provisions see the minutes and memoranda of the Commonwealth Affairs Committee, CAB 134/54–56.
[46] Turnbull to Martin, 3 Mar. 1947, copy in FO 371/67082.
[47] CA (48) 7th Meeting, 26 July 1948, CAB 134/55.

Sir Orme Sargent, still argued that nothing should be done about Cyprus in the hope that eventual Greek stability would bring about conditions favourable for an exchange of the island in return for 'facilities in the way of bases etc. which we would want'. Sargent had his eye on the broader political aspects of the problem as well as on strategic security in the eastern Mediterranean. He was sceptical of pursuing, for opportunistic anti-Egyptian reasons, a policy of self-determination in the Sudan and denying it in Cyprus. 'The day will come', he wrote, 'when a less friendly Government in Greece will stir up agitation, both in Cyprus and elsewhere, with a view to forcing us to allow the Cypriots to decide their future status— in other words, to vote themselves into Greece.'[48] The political instability and economic bankruptcy of the Greek government, however, made the prospect of cession appear less and less feasible. Christopher Warner wrote in April 1947:

The Greeks . . . are utterly insolvent and incapable, without outside support, of running their existing territory. Nor can they maintain internal security in their existing territory without large subsidies from abroad. They have a thoroughly inefficient Government and Governmental machine. In these circumstances no unbiassed authority could imagine that Greece could give a decent administration. . . .[49]

By the spring of 1947 advocates of eventual cession admitted that nothing should be done because of the possibility that Greece might fall to the Communists. 'Cyprus is considered vital as a potential strategic base', Warner concluded, 'and nothing must be done to reduce the chances of its being held in friendly hands in an emergency.'[50]

The crisis in Palestine and the collapse of the Anglo-Egyptian negotiations over the withdrawal of troops from Egypt greatly contributed to the hardening of British attitudes. In February 1947 the British decided to hand over the issue of Palestine to the United Nations. In September they decided to evacuate. At both times the British grip over Cyprus tightened. The official who acted as liaison with the Chiefs of Staff, M. J. Creswell, wrote in February: 'Developments in Egypt and in Palestine in the last three weeks are likely to make . . . views harden still more on the strategic importance to us of retaining full sovereignty over Cyprus.'[51] Members of the Cabinet in the same month, even though they refrained from making a declaration on sovereignty, went on record as giving 'strong expression'

[48] Minutes by Sargent, 3 and 12 Feb. 1947, FO 371/67081.
[49] Warner to Norton, Confidential, 17 Apr. 1947, FO 371/67082.
[50] Ibid.
[51] Minute by Creswell, 7 Feb. 1947, FO 371/67081.

that Cyprus 'should remain within the Commonwealth'.[52] In September Sir Orme Sargent virtually closed the discussion about possible cession by writing that there were now 'insuperable arguments' against it.[53] At both times in 1947 when the Palestine issue came to a head, in February and late in the year, the Prime Minister steadied the debate on Cyprus on the side of retention. In February he emphasized to Bevin the strong sentiment in the Cabinet in favour of keeping the island within the Empire.[54] In December Attlee wrote: 'the position in Palestine and Egypt has deteriorated and it is now more than ever necessary from the strategic aspect to keep our foothold in the Eastern Mediterranean in Cyprus'.[55]

There was one official who continued to favour the union of Cyprus with Greece. Though history did not turn out precisely the way he foresaw, his lone dissent sounded out like a trumpet about the future troubles of the next decade. Sir Oliver Harvey, the Deputy Under-Secretary, believed that the transfers of power in India, Burma, and Ceylon, and now the withdrawal from Palestine, should be followed by a graceful cession of Cyprus to Greece. He wrote in September 1947:

> The action of H. M. Government in India and Burma has enormously impressed opinion throughout the world. Our proposed evacuation policy in Palestine and the possibility that we may propose independence for Cyrenaica, when coupled with what we have done in India and Burma, makes our continued presence in Cyprus indefensible. . . .
> British administration in the island is meeting difficulties owing to increasing Cypriot non-co-operation. Hitherto, serious violence has been avoided but with the examples of Palestine, Egypt and Greece itself, we cannot hope that this will last long. . . .
> I would strongly advocate that consideration be given to the very early cession of Cyprus to Greece, before the Cypriot campaign is embittered by violence and before cession can be represented as yielding to force.[56]

In this eloquent plea for cession, Harvey made the additional points that the Greeks governed Crete effectively, and had now been given the Dodecanese. Britain could no longer give material aid to Greece, but at least Anglo-Greek friendship might be maintained and Greek morale stiffened. He believed that in the long run the Cypriots would be just as well off under Greek dominion as under British rule.

Harvey's advocacy of yielding Cyprus met with unanimous opposition. C. H. Johnston of the Southern Department emphasized

[52] See draft minute by Attlee, 11 Feb. 1947, PREM 8/740.
[53] Minute by Sargent, 30 Oct. 1947, FO 371/67084.
[54] Minute by Attlee, 12 Feb. 1947, FO 371/67081.
[55] Memorandum by Attlee, 22 Dec. 1947, Prem 8/740; CA (47) 21; CAB 134/54.
[56] Minute by Harvey, 26 Sept. 1947, FO 371/67084.

that 'Cyprus is in fact the only bit of firm ground in the Middle East that is left to our strategic planners'. He dwelt on the Palestine connection:

Assuming a worst but by no means impossible case, with the Russians possessing a foothold in Palestine as a result of their efforts in the United Nations, and with Cyprus ceded to Greece which had subsequently gone Communist, we should . . . not only have created a vacuum in the Middle East, we should have gone halfway towards letting the Russians fill it.[57]

Christopher Warner noted that Johnston's and other minutes made it 'crystal clear' that there could be no question of handing over Cyprus to the Greeks. 'Nor, in point of fact', Warner wrote, 'am I particularly impressed by the arguments that to do so would stiffen Greek morale against the bandits, and that it would be in the interest of the Cypriots.'[58]

Sir Oliver Harvey made a bitter concluding comment. 'The Chiefs of Staff will always object', he wrote, 'to evacuating anything where they have been for some time, just as they will always object to occupying anything where they have not hitherto been.' He further observed, perhaps slightly unfairly, that the Colonial Office case could be dismissed because of narrowness of outlook. 'The views of the Colonial Office are, of course, not worth having on the subject, which is essentially foreign affairs.' He ended with a prophecy which no one ventured to rebut: 'When the Greeks in despair turn to the methods of the Irish, the Jews, the Hindus and the Egyptians, then, I suspect, the British people will rise and compel the Government to evacuate.'[59]

[57] Minute by Johnston, 24 Oct. 1947, FO 371/67084.
[58] Minute by Warner, 30 Oct. 1947, FO 371/67084.
[59] Minute by Harvey, 3 Nov. 1947, FO 371/67084.

6

EGYPT: BRITISH 'EVACUATION' AND THE 'UNITY OF THE NILE VALLEY'

IN MARCH 1946 Lord Killearn sang his Egyptian swan-song. It made an invaluable historical recording that summarized a crucial decade of the British era in Egypt in comparative perspective. Surveying his twelve years of service—as if moving from rhapsody to history—he looked further back to his seven years as head of the British Legation in China. As departing Ambassador in Egypt he saw a similarity of problems. When he had arrived in China in 1926 there had been an intense nationalist drive directed against the British. When he left in 1934, 'common sense' had prevailed and Britain again occupied an unchallenged position as the pre-eminent foreign power. 'We were on terms of marked amity with the Kuomintang, the Nationalist party, which by that time ruled the land and which had been specially violent against us.' This period had provided an invaluable lesson, Killearn wrote, a lesson of how to get on good terms with a strong nationalist movement. The problem was the same in Egypt, where there also existed anti-British nationalism. But unfortunately for the British, the lesson of China could not be directly applied. There was a fundamental difference. British interests in Egypt were of a more compelling nature because of geographical circumstance. Egypt lay athwart British lines of communication. 'In China one had been a spectator, interested, but in a sense passive. In Egypt Fate had decreed that such passivity was not feasible. Egypt was an essential link in British world security.' In traditional British terms, Killearn summed up the nature of the problem and its solution: 'The Egyptians are essentially a docile and friendly people, but they are like children in many respects. They need a strong but essentially a fair and helpful hand to guide them: "firmness and justice" is the motto for Egypt, just as it used to be for the Chinese.'[1]

---

[1] Killearn to Bevin, 6 Mar. 1946, FO 371/53288/J1135. Robert Howe, the Asssistant Under-Secretary superintending Middle Eastern affairs and himself an old China hand, took issue with Killearn's comparison between Egypt and China. 'In China in the 1920's we were faced with a Nationalism which represented the whole of articulate China—there was no opposing party of any power or consequence. In Egypt we have a very powerful other party, the King, & the balance of power is probably still on the side of the King. Both sides are trying to get us into the arena against the other. I submit that wisdom lies in our not becoming involved in these domestic issues as long as British vital interests are not

In dealing with these 'children' one major difficulty was that they constantly quarrelled among themselves, which placed the British in the position of 'arbiter'. In fact the political forces in Egypt consisted broadly of the King and his coalition government; the Wafd or principal nationalist party led by Nahas Pasha, who had supported the British during the war; and the British themselves. There might be added the independent politicians, who did not succeed in forming a solid party after the 1920s but who were never negligible, and who were not British or palace stooges. The King, Farouk, had followed a pro-Axis line early in the war in the belief that the Germans might grant independence sooner than the British. When it appeared that the Germans might occupy Egypt he was of course determined to remain King; but his sympathies lay with the Italians rather than with the Nazis. In February 1942, in a confrontation that was seared into Egyptian memory, Killearn (then Sir Miles Lampson) had issued an ultimatum. 'I arrived at the Palace', he recorded in his diary, 'accompanied by . . . an impressive array of specially picked stalwart military officers armed to the teeth. . . . Whilst we waited upstairs I could hear the rumble of tanks and armoured cars taking up their positions around the Palace. . . . So much for the events . . . which I confess I could not have more enjoyed.'[2] Killearn had given Farouk the choice between abdicating or purging the court of Axis influences in order to bring to power a pro-British Wafd government under Nahas Pasha. The Wafd leaders remained loyal to the British. In the words of a prominent British historian of Egypt which reflect a consensus of British opinion at the time as well as after the war: 'It is to the eternal credit of the Wafdist Government and the Egyptian people that they stood firm at this grim moment. Nahas

endangered.' (Minute by Howe, 16 Mar. 1946, ibid.) The only comment by the Permanent Under-Secretary, Sir Orme Sargent, was an instruction to circulate Killearn's message to the Cabinet.

As a preface to the main themes of this chapter, John Darwin, *Britain, Egypt and the Middle East: Imperial Policy in the Aftermath of War 1918–1922* (London, 1981), is especially useful. For the interwar background see especially Afaf Lutfi al-Sayyid-Marsot, *Egypt's Liberal Experiment: 1922–1938* (Berkeley, 1977), which is based on Arab as well as British archival sources and thus serves as a corrective to Anglocentric accounts. Two other works are also especially important for the general Egyptian response to British imperialism in the present context: Jacques Berque, *Egypt: Imperialism and Revolution* (Engl. trans. London, 1972); and Alexander Schölch, *Ägypten den Ägyptern!* (Zurich, 1972). In the foreword to the latter work Albert Hourani calls attention to the importance of financial influences on British imperialism (in relation to the political and strategic motives stressed by Robinson and Gallagher) that are also relevant to the post-Second World War period. See also Janice Terry, *The Wafd 1919–1952* (London, 1982).

[2] Killearn Diary, 4 Feb. 1942, Middle East Centre, St. Antony's College; Trefor E. Evans, *The Killearn Diaries 1934–1946* (London, 1972), pp. 213–15. For the ultimatum as 'a landmark in Egypt's political history', see Gabriel Warburg, 'Lampson's Ultimatum to Faruq, 4 February, 1942', *Middle Eastern Studies*, 11, 1 (Jan. 1975).

and his colleagues had made their choice, and they stood to it like men.'[3]

The Wafd leaders bore the legacy of the famous patriot Zaghlul Pasha who in 1919 had championed Egyptian independence at the time of the Paris Peace Conference. They claimed to be 'representatives' of the Egyptian people and denounced the King as a corrupt reactionary. The British were sceptical on both accounts. According to the head of the Egyptian Department of the Foreign Office, Patrick Scrivener:

We should not fall into the over-simplification of thinking that the King is a reactionary autocrat and the Wafd the torch-bearers of a liberal democracy. The King has autocratic tendencies, admittedly, but the Wafd's autocratic tendencies have been shown to be equally destructive of decent government. . . . In fact democracy as understood in this country and America is still non-existent in Egypt.[4]

Sir Walter Smart, the Oriental Minister at the Embassy who possessed an unrivalled British knowledge of Egyptian politics, remarked in similar vein:

It is, I think, essential that we should no longer be associated with the Wafd as we were inevitably from 1942 to 1944 owing to the exigencies of war. The Governments of the Wafd are more corrupt and inefficient than other Governments in Egypt. . . .

We do not want . . . to be in the position of appearing to the Egyptian people to be directly responsible for the maintenance in power of a sort of Tammany Hall like the Wafd. Moreover, it must be remembered that . . . King Farouk, though no longer perhaps so popular as before, still appears to the popular imagination as a future *vedette*. We cannot afford to antagonize King Farouk at this moment.[5]

---

[3] John Marlowe, *A History of Modern Egypt and Anglo-Egyptian Relations 1800–1953* (New York, 1954), p. 319. For an important interpretation of the long-term significance, P. J. Vatikiotis, *The Modern History of Egypt* (New York, 1969), p. 349: 'The King had been humiliated. More widely, the Wafd's standing with its more extremist followers went into serious and continuous decline. The extent of this decline became clear in 1950–1.'

[4] Minute by Scrivener, 13 Aug. 1945, FO 371/45923. Scrivener also wrote in the same minute in regard to Nahas: 'We owed Nahas Pasha a debt for his support in 1942, but we have most amply discharged it by (a) maintaining him in power for many months against attacks by all comers, and (b) protecting him, after he fell, from the consequences of his family's . . . racketeering which made history—even in Egypt.'

[5] Memorandum by Smart, 5 Nov. 1945, FO 371/45928/J3947. For Smart see *Walter Smart by some of his friends* (Chichester, n.d., copy in the St. Antony's Middle East Centre). I write this note on the morrow of the funeral of Anwar Sadat. In one of his recent recollections he mentioned the significance of the 'Oriental Secretary' at the British Embassy. His comment is perhaps more revealing about the psychology of Egyptian nationalists than about individuals such as Smart, though there is no doubt that Smart himself was a personality to be reckoned with: 'in 1956 the British evacuated this country and at last ended the shameful era when the secretary for oriental affairs at their embassy in Cairo was the real ruler of Egypt, fawned upon by the pashas and the party leaders'.

Whatever the interpretation of Egyptian politics, there were two points on which the King, the leaders of the Wafd, and virtually all other Egyptians could agree. The first was the evacuation of British troops. The second was 'the unity of the Nile valley', or in other words the restoration or assertion of Egyptian sovereignty over the Sudan.

The Sudan question had caused the breakdown of efforts to forge an Anglo-Egyptian alliance in 1930. At that time the Egyptians had insisted on the right of unrestricted immigration into the Sudan. The British adamantly refused to give way to anything that might increase Egyptian influence. Six years later, at the time of the Ethiopian crisis, they yielded on the question of immigration (which some Foreign Office officials believed to be academic in any case) in return for military concessions in Egypt. The Egyptians for their part of course tried to use Mussolini's East African adventure to their advantage in bargaining with the British, and pro-Italian sentiment was substantial; but there was genuine fear of Italian expansion. The geographical proximity of Ethiopia instilled in Egyptian nationalists an apprehension that was not replaced, to British regret, a decade later by Russian expansion in eastern Europe.

The Anglo-Egyptian treaty of August 1936 represented a landmark in the history of British imperialism. It was concluded fifty-four years after the British occupation. It gave full recognition to Egypt as an independent and sovereign nation. And it marked for Anthony Eden, Foreign Secretary at the time, the beginning of an association with Egyptian affairs that ended disastrously twenty years later.[6] According to Eden himself the treaty was 'defensive' in the sense that Britain would come to Egypt's aid in the event of an emergency. Egypt in return would grant Britain the military facilities to protect lines of communication. In time of peace British troops would be restricted to the Canal Zone. But there were further provisions that deeply troubled Egyptian nationalists. These were the military clauses, which stipulated that in case of emergency British

Interview with Sadat by Frank Gibney of the *Encyclopaedia Britannica, Austin American-Statesman*, 11 Oct. 1981.

[6] For Eden and the 1936 treaty see *The Eden Memoirs: Facing the Dictators* (London, 1962), pp. 390–4. 'This Treaty', Eden wrote in retrospect, 'was one of the very few worthwhile settlements negotiated in that time of international lawlessness.' For perspective see David Carlton, *Anthony Eden* (London, 1981), chap. 3. For balanced and sardonic interpretation see al-Sayyid-Marsot, *Egypt's Liberal Experiment*, chap. 6. See also especially Marlowe, *Egypt and Anglo-Egyptian Relations*, chap. 13; and Mahmud Y. Zayid, *Egypt's Struggle for Independence* (Beirut, 1965), which has a valuable map indicating military installations. For analysis of the British strategic issues see especially Brian Bond, *British Military Policy between the Two World Wars* (Oxford, 1980), pp. 265–8.

forces would have free use of Egyptian land, water, and air. One
point later proved to be especially sensitive. The withdrawal of
troops to the canal did not apply to the Royal Air Force's right to
range freely over Egyptian air space and to maintain airbases. On
another portentous subject, the question of the Sudan's sovereignty,
the treaty was silent. These two issues—the presence of British
troops (even the maintenance of airbases by skeleton crews) and the
problem of the Sudan—later became particular objects of Egyptian
resentment. 'Egypt for the Egyptians', the slogan of 1882, could
never be realized until such issues were resolved.

To the British in the postwar era their military presence appeared
to be one thing, the 'unity of the Nile Valley' quite another. They
were publicly committed to self-government in the Sudan. 'The
Sudanese are becoming more and more politically conscious and
ambitious' as a result of the war, the Governor-General wrote in
September 1945. They were beginning to think ahead in terms of
nationhood—an ambition in direct conflict with Egyptian designs
of absorption. British sympathy lay with the Sudanese, who, it was
hoped, would in some way remain permanently associated with the
Empire and Commonwealth. To preserve the Anglo-Sudanese
'connection' much more would have to be done than to provide the
Sudanese with an English-type administration. There would have
to be large-scale economic assistance as well as social and educational
development. This was the tenet of British policy in the Sudan.
There was no room for false optimism. The Governor-General
commented:

> 45 years of British administration have not turned the Sudanese into African
> Englishmen, nor will another 20 years of it. Their form of self-government and
> standards of public life will be fundamentally oriental and their national outlook
> will be Arab and Middle Eastern. The ties of common origin, common outlook
> and tradition, which play so large a part in binding together the British
> Commonwealth, cannot influence the Sudanese nation of the future.[7]

The British could at least hope for Sudanese friendship, provided
they made clear that they supported Sudanese nationalism rather
than Egyptian expansionism. There were opportunistic anti-Egyptian
reasons for British support of the Sudanese. Critics then and later
rightly detected a disingenuous note of Foreign Office solicitude for
Sudanese self-determination. Those in the Sudan Political Service
more clearly perceived the division of nationalist sentiment towards
the Egyptians, but they too projected on to the Sudanese their own
anti-Egyptian views and foresaw the evolution of the Sudan's political
development in terms of decades rather than years. In general the

[7] Memorandum dated 12 Sept. 1945, FO 371/45985.

British viewed the Sudan's future as separate from Egypt's. The question of 'colonial independence' for the Sudan did not come to a head until the 1950s, but it should be borne in mind that, despite the large public controversy about British troops leaving Egypt, it was the Sudan that proved to be the 'stone wall' (Bevin's repeated phrase) in the Anglo-Egyptian discussions of the 1940s.

The question of military withdrawal from Egypt, even in a limited sense to the Canal Zone, raised fundamental questions. Within the British government, officials pondered issues of military security and the possibility of future political intervention. In Parliament, members reviewed the merits of British rule since the days of Lord Cromer. In the press, opinion split between those who viewed the prospect as 'scuttle and run' and those who regarded Imperial retreat as an act of 'magnanimity and wisdom'—with American commentary agreeing almost entirely with the latter proposition.

Of the protagonists, Lord Killearn perhaps held the strongest views. He lamented the lack of a clear-cut policy towards Egypt and he regretted that long ago the British government had not declared a 'sphere of influence' in the Middle East. 'I often wished', he wrote in August 1945, 'that in years gone by we had followed America's wise example and established a sort of Monroe doctrine in this area.'[8] Such determined action would have enabled the British to deal much more firmly with the Egyptians, who well understood the strength of the British Empire. 'With powder in the gun', according to this staunch British imperialist, '. . . in the East it is usually unnecessary to discharge it. The knowledge we mean business is enough.'[9] Such a view, by no means restricted to Killearn, gravely underestimated the intensity of nationalist feeling in the younger generation of Arabs not only in Egypt but throughout the Middle East. And in any case postwar Britain did not have the money to keep the powder in the gun, even if there had been the will to do so. On the whole the predisposition of the Labour government was to move ahead cautiously with the moderate nationalists, for reasons well expressed by Sir Walter Smart in November 1945: 'we have been stalling on Treaty revision. . . . I am of the opinion that this stalling is no longer in our interest politically. The effect of the stalling is that a free field is being left to every kind of extremist and vociferous, half-baked politician, and nationalist claims tend to become more and more unrestrained.'[10]

[8] Killearn to Bevin, 1 Aug. 1945, FO 371/45923/J2614.

[9] Killearn to Bevin, 6 Mar. 1946, FO 371/53288.

[10] Memorandum by Smart, 5 Nov. 1945, FO 371/45928/J3947. Scrivener noted in response that 'It is not our fault that we are stalling.' The head of the Eastern Department, C. W. Baxter, wrote about Smart's general comments: 'We shall not get an entirely pro-Arab

The Debate within the British Government

The head of the Egyptian Department of the Foreign Office, Patrick Scrivener, in contrast to Lord Killearn, believed in a distinctly moderate line sympathetic to the King. Anticipating the Egyptian demand for evacuation, he wrote that the only way to get a good bargain with the Egyptians would be to collaborate with Farouk. In return for strategic assurances, the British would guarantee that they would remain mere 'spectators' in Egypt, provided the King did not 'victimize' the leaders of the Wafd. Scrivener believed that co-operation with the King would be the best way not only to achieve an acceptable revision of the treaty but also to bring about genuine economic and social reform:

> If there is to be serious social reform in Egypt the King seems the only available instrument for its realisation. For reforms mean money which in turn can only come from taxation of the rich. And such taxation can probably only be imposed by the will of the King. . . . The Monarchy has prestige and it has continuity. Let us give it a run.[11]

Such recommendations ran against Ernest Bevin's instincts as a socialist Foreign Secretary. He commented, 'I am very doubtful about this', and noted elsewhere that the military position should be secured before speculating about social reform in collaboration with the King.

On the 20th of December 1945 the Egyptians formally requested the revision of treaty relations. Bevin now formulated his views for the Cabinet. With a combination of misguided confidence and false optimism, he believed that the Egyptians would accept a treaty that reproduced 'the essential features of the old' treaty of 1936. Britain would withdraw troops to the Canal Zone, but would retain the right to reoccupy Egypt in the event of war. This was a fairly accurate assessment of what the nationalists under the best of circumstances might accept, but it underestimated Egyptian resentment of British

solution of either the Palestine or the Levant problems: but we must try to secure a just and reasonable compromise which will not permanently alienate the Arabs.' Minute by Baxter, 24 Nov. 1945, FO 371/45928.

[11] Memorandum by Scrivener, 17 Oct. 1945, FO 371/45927. Lewis Jones, the Middle East expert at the American Embassy, once commented that Scrivener was 'more Foreign Office' than anyone else he had met there and that he could not imagine him putting forward any imaginative solution to the Egyptian problem (Jones to Tuck, 24 Dec. 1946, USSD 741.83/12-2246). Scrivener's memorandum about collaboration with the King is one example that confirms Jones's judgement; but it should be noted that other officials listened with an open mind to the argument that the King should be given the benefit of the doubt. Recording a conversation with the Egyptian Ambassador, Robert Howe wrote that Farouk 'is all out for a programme of social reform and for the gradual education of the Egyptian nation for real and not faked democracy'. Minute by Howe, 10 Sept. 1945, FO 371/45925/J3216.

troops in Suez as well as in Cairo. The British moreover tended to be inflexible on the question of the Sudan, about which the Egyptians had passionate feelings. British control over the Sudan and the presence of troops in Egypt, according to the formal Egyptian communication to the British government, wounded 'the national dignity'. Bevin's proposal to revise the 1936 treaty in its 'essential form' offered little to salve the wound.[12]

A few substantial concessions would be made. Under the 1936 treaty the British had the right to maintain 10,000 troops (and 500 pilots) in the Canal Zone. The Chiefs of Staff were prepared to reduce this number to 5,000. But on the whole the military authorities argued that the defence arrangements of the 1936 treaty should remain inviolate, the major revision being political—in other words, the impression should be removed that British 'imperialism' existed in Egypt. Bevin agreed. Speaking to the Defence Committee (the inner circle of the Cabinet dealing with these problems), he said: 'our object must be to clear right out of Cairo as soon as practicable . . . it was important that we should as soon as possible remove all grounds for a charge that Egypt was "an occupied country" '. He hoped that agreement in principle to withdraw would induce the Egyptians to ask the British to stay on indefinitely, at least in the Canal Zone. In any case he recommended, following the American example, that the Suez base be held as a 99-year lease rather than as an occupied territory with absolute rights for shorter periods. The Egyptians would thus be persuaded that they were 'equal partners' in the defence of the Middle East and not a subservient race.[13]

It was publicly announced on the 2nd of April 1946 that the Cabinet had decided to send a delegation to Egypt. This was a move in the Middle East which some compared with the decision to send the Cabinet mission to India.[14] In drawing up their estimate for the delegation's guidance, the Chiefs of Staff fully considered the political as well as the military aspects of withdrawal. In mid-April they reported that they substantially agreed with the Foreign Secretary's recommendations. 'We realize that if our delegation tries

[12] Memorandum by Bevin, 18 Jan. 1946, CP (46) 17, CAB 129/6; see also minutes in FO 371/53282. The key interpretation by Bullock, *Bevin* (chap. 6 sect. 5) is that it required the Foreign Secretary's own driving energy and concentration finally to launch the Anglo-Egyptian negotiations on a steady course.

[13] Defence Committee DO (46) 8th Meeting, 18 Mar. 1946, CAB 131/1; see also minutes in FO 371/53289 which are also important for issues such as Mombasa and Cyrenaica.

[14] Especially in the American press, e.g. the *New York Times*, 6 Apr. 1946, which commented that the decision would give the discussions 'the same rank and dignity of those now under way between the British Cabinet Mission and leaders of the various Indian factions'.

to stand out for demands which the Egyptian Government are unable to accept, the consequences are likely to be, at the worst, bloodshed, and at the best, non co-operation and ill will on the part of the Egyptians.' The Egyptians might even take their case to the United Nations. The Chiefs of Staff thus saw the need to compromise. They were prepared to yield on the maintenance of combatant troops in the Canal Zone. But they stood firm on an issue of fundamental importance, as they thought proved by the Second World War—fighter squadrons and bomber bases. The Chiefs of Staff did not think that 'complete withdrawal' included the fighter defence system in Egypt itself. 'Although eventually the Egyptian Air Force might be able to undertake this commitment, it is totally inadequate to do so at present.' Nor did evacuation mean the abandoning of potential bomber bases. 'To maintain these bases adequately they would have to be supervised in peace by British staffs and be available for periodical visits by bomber units.'[15] Bevin, who agreed that anything less than a minimal defence system would be 'unacceptable', assumed the leadership of the delegation, though he himself did not go to Egypt. Pressing business at the Council of Foreign Ministers (and also the possibility of assassination by Zionists) caused him to pass the responsibility to one of his colleagues. In view of the implications for air defence and bomber bases, it is not surprising that the job fell to the Minister for Air, Lord Stansgate (father of the Labour politician, Tony Wedgwood Benn).

The Stansgate mission, the departure of Lord Killearn, and the advent of his successor, Sir Ronald Campbell, seemed to contemporary observers to offer the hope for a far-reaching change in Anglo-Egyptian relations. C. D. Quilliam, the correspondent of *The Times*, wrote confidentially: 'The arrival in March of Sir Ronald Campbell at once produced an almost magical change in the political atmosphere in Egypt and the equally obvious sincerity and sympathetic personality of Lord Stansgate reinforced the belief that a fundamental change in relationships between the two countries was at hand.' This basic altering of attitude, Quilliam believed, would be based 'on Mr. Attlee's policy of friendship and mutual trust'.[16] The Egyptian crisis, in other words, would be one of the first major tests of the Labour government in coming to grips with postwar nationalism in the Middle East on the basis of 'equality'.

The Egyptian Prime Minister with whom Stansgate had to deal was Ismail Sidky—described by the Chargé d'Affaires in Cairo, R. J.

---

[15] Defence Committee DO (46), 15 Apr. 1946, CAB 131/2; minutes in FO 371/53292; Ministry of Defence to Foreign Office, 18 Apr. 1946, FO 371/53293.

[16] Quilliam to Deakin, Confidential, 11 Aug. 1946, Quilliam Papers.

Bowker, as 'the symbol of political and capitalist reaction and also of financial corruption'. Bowker added that most Egyptians also regarded him as 'the ablest administrator and financier in Egypt and the strongest man in Egypt'.[17] According to John Marlowe:

He was the last survivor of the 'old guard' of Egyptian nationalists who had formed the original Wafd. He had soon broken away from Zaghlul, and for over twenty years had played a genuinely independent role in Egyptian public life. A Turk by race, an autocrat by temperament, and a realist by instinct, he had nothing in common with the raucous demagogy of the Wafd. After his term of office as Prime Minister from 1930 to 1933, he had devoted himself mainly to big business, in which he amassed a large fortune. In politics he played the part of a detached elder statesman, observing, encouraging, criticizing. During the war he had been an outspoken critic of British policy in Egypt.[18]

The British faced a formidable and shrewd Egyptian nationalist. In the judgement of Grafftey-Smith, which confirms Marlowe's, he was 'The most astute operator of them all. . . . He was *capable de tout*, which in Egypt means a lot.'[19]

Upon Stansgate's arrival in Egypt on the 15th of April 1946, Sidky stated in categorical terms that the Egyptians demanded *complete* evacuation, including fighter squadrons and bomber bases. To the British this was a devastating start to the negotiations. How could the Egyptians expect the British to defend them unless military bases were at their disposal? Could the Egyptians not see the lesson of 1939? The Egyptians after all (so the Foreign Office assumed) were glad enough to have British troops present in 1942 when Rommel battered at the gate. The Permanent Under-Secretary, Sir Orme Sargent, noted with indignation:

The Egyptians cannot have it both ways. They cannot expect us to ensure the safety and independence of Egypt unless they give us the facilities which will enable us when the time comes to take the necessary action.

The futility, under modern conditions of warfare, of our undertaking to defend a country without being on the spot to carry out our obligation, was demonstrated once and for all when we guaranteed Poland in 1939.[20]

With such an attitude on the part of the Egyptians, Sargent, for one, became increasingly sceptical whether the Egyptians were worth saving, treaty or no treaty.

Officials in London were aghast when Stansgate seemed to cave

---

[17] Bowker to Bevin, 18 Feb. 1946, FO 371/53284.

[18] Marlowe, *Egypt and Anglo-Egyptian Relations*, p. 338.

[19] Laurence Grafftey-Smith, *Bright Levant* (London, 1970), p. 28. 'Something about the cut of his moustache made the creamy smile with which he greeted bad news or good a little feline. He was one of the rare Egyptian politicians whose conversation was an intellectual excitement.' Ibid.

[20] Minute by Sargent, 24 Apr. 1946, FO 371/53292.

in to Sidky's demands during the preliminary discussions. Stansgate took issue with the Chiefs of Staff on the issue of 'qualified withdrawal'. Unless the British left—fighters, bombers and all—it would make nonsense of the proposition that the British could protect the Middle East (a somewhat confused thought, as officials in the Foreign Office were quick to note). Unless the British left bag and baggage, he wrote in mixed metaphor, it would damage 'our prestige'. He insisted that the British government should deal with the Egyptians on a basis of unequivocal equality. Why could the British not withdraw from Egypt as they had from Persia? Did they want to give the impression of being 'kicked out'?[21]

Stansgate's message drew a furious response from the Foreign Secretary. The Cabinet, Bevin telegraphed, had agreed to evacuation only with gravest misgivings. Britain's capacity to repel aggression in the Middle East consequently had been weakened and it would be weakened catastrophically if bases could not be maintained in Egypt. There was no analogy at all between withdrawal from Persia and Egypt since the latter was at the heart of the British defence system. 'If we are not being "kicked out" we are none the less evacuating against our better judgement and in pursuance of our undertaking to treat Egypt as an Ally and an equal.' Britain after all would defend Egypt against aggression. On this subject Bevin, like Sargent, reflected on one of the causes of the Second World War. He felt so strongly about the point that he scrawled in his own hand: 'We will never do again what we did over Poland in 1939 when we undertook to come to a country's assistance in war without possessing any organisation to enable us effectively to take the necessary action when the time came.'[22]

At the same time that Bevin wrestled with the Egyptian question, he also grappled with the problem of the Italian colonies with the Russians and Americans in Paris. The Council of Foreign Ministers indirectly brought the Egyptian crisis to a head. The discussions in Paris, Attlee announced to the Cabinet, were narrowing down to 'the strategic position in the Mediterranean'. Stansgate's warnings about the weakness of the British position in Cairo were now accentuated by broader considerations of Britain's delicate international position. After summarizing the pros and cons of making the announcement of 'withdrawal' at the beginning of the negotiations— rather than saving it as an ace to be played later—the Cabinet

---

[21] Stansgate to Bevin, 28 Apr. 1946, FO 371/53293/J1854/G. Stansgate himself was shocked by the degree of Egyptian intransigence. 'I hope you won't be too disappointed at the results of five weeks of very hard work', he wrote to Bevin privately in May. 'The Egyptians are in an extraordinary state of morbidity.' Stansgate to Bevin, 24 May 1946, FO 800/457.

[22] Draft by Bevin; Bevin to Stansgate, 29 Apr. 1946, FO 371/53293.

reached the controversial conclusion that it should be made at the outset in order to create 'a more favourable atmosphere'.[23]

Stansgate, for one, held strong opinions about the 'myth' that the British threw away the decisive card by announcing that they ultimately intended to evacuate. In fact there was no other realistic basis for an agreement. 'We have many thousands of British troops here without any Treaty right at all', he wrote to a colleague in the Cabinet. 'We had, therefore, really no card at all in our hand. The talk about throwing away the ace is nonsense.'[24] The discussions of the Cabinet and Defence Committee in April–May 1946 were based on the realistic assumption that, unless the British began with the premiss of withdrawal, then there could be no hope for a settlement with the Egyptians. This was a point that was perceived by Bevin and Attlee as well as others within the Cabinet, but not by their critics, notably Churchill, who held that the 1936 treaty should be maintained at whatever the cost until there was a satisfactory replacement.

The decision *publicly* to announce the decision stirred up further controversy. From published as well as unpublished records it is a matter of certainty that this was an issue on which a Tory government under Churchill would have followed different tactics. As will be seen in a later chapter, the Labour government itself eventually regretted the move. Once the British became publicly committed to withdrawal, the Egyptian leaders were left with no room for manœuvre. From that time onwards no Egyptian nationalist could accept anything less than complete evacuation. In view of Britain's later determination to stay on in Suez, one must ask why the Labour government in the spring of 1946 so easily came to the conclusion that withdrawal was the proper course. The answer can be found in part in the early exuberance of the Labour leaders. They had not yet discovered that alternative bases in Cyrenaica and Kenya or even Palestine were not feasible possibilities. Churchill's instinctive response at this time is a matter of great historical interest. He did

---

[23] Cabinet Conclusions 42 (46), 6 May 1946, CAB 128/5; minutes in FO 371/53294.

[24] Stansgate to Lord Addison, 27 May 1946, Stansgate Papers. The Stansgate Papers and the Robertson Papers (in the Sudan Archive at the University of Durham) confirm the impression of the Foreign Office records that Stansgate must have agonized over conflicting impulses to be fair to both the Egyptians and the Sudanese. Before Stansgate left for Egypt, the agent of the Sudan government in London told him 'that the Sudanese had an inborn contempt for Egyptians as a less manly race, rather than a hatred of them, founded on their misrule in the Sudan. This contempt was reinforced by what Sudanese visiting Egypt saw of inefficiency and corruption in Government officers, and of the dishonesty of party politics' (K. Haselden to Robertson, 28 Apr. 1946, Robertson Papers 523/10/1). Despite his 'great admiration' for the British administration in the Sudan, Stansgate became increasingly pro-Egyptian.

not make the assumption of a strategic alternative. When Attlee announced to the House of Commons on the 7th of May 1946 that all British forces would be withdrawn from Egypt, he rose immediately to say that this was 'a very grave statement, one of the most momentous I have ever heard in this House'.

The Parliamentary Debates on Egypt, May 1946

Attlee's announcement caught the House of Commons off guard, but it provoked a heated debate. Since the speakers were unprepared, the debate of the 7th of May is less significant than the one later in the month, but several remarks are noteworthy. Anthony Eden, recalling his negotiation of the 1936 treaty, was outraged in his urbane way that his work should be tossed overboard without any apparent thought given to Britain's 'Imperial duty' to safeguard the Suez canal. Richard Crossman congratulated the Prime Minister on 'a really bold and imaginative move'. He provoked the Tories by suggesting that the Labour government was genuinely trying to promote racial equality in the Middle East. Crossman was speaking immediately upon his return from Palestine as a member of the Anglo-American Committee of Inquiry:

> I am convinced that through the Middle East and the Arab world there will be, at last, a feeling that there is a Government which intends to do something about equality. [Laughter.] Hon. Members on the other side laugh at that idea, but it is not a laughing matter.

Unless the British grasped the overwhelming importance of the growth of Arab nationalism and the significance of equality in race relations, Crossman said, then the British Empire would not survive.[25] In winding up the debate Herbert Morrison taunted Churchill with one of his own quotations (of October 1945):

> There are no more enemies to conquer; no more fronts to hold. . . . All our foreign foes have been beaten down into unconditional surrender. Now is the time to bring home the men who have conquered, and bring them back to their families and productive work.

Could the Labour government be blamed for demobilizing in a peaceful world and attempting to put Anglo-Egyptian relations on a solid footing of equality, goodwill, and mutual defence?[26]

In answering that question it seemed as if everyone who had ever had anything to do with Egypt took pen in hand and entered the controversy. In May 1946 the Egyptian issue attracted the public's

[25] *Parliamentary Debates* (Commons), 7 May 1946, cols. 883–6.
[26] Ibid., cols. 896–902.

attention in a way reminiscent of General Gordon's death some sixty years earlier. Lord Beaverbrook thundered in the *Daily Express* that it should be 'clearly understood that there can be no compromise so far as the Suez Canal is concerned'. The *Express* went on: 'If Britain parted with it an essential part of the Empire would be gone. The Suez Canal is as much a part of the Empire as the homeland itself.' The *Daily Mail* took an extreme Tory line and criticized the 'philosophy of retreat and mood of apology', not only on Egypt but also on India and the issue of imperial preference. Some organs of the British press such as *The Economist* commented with moderation that the debate was 'over dramatized' and correctly observed that the Labour government appeared to be giving away much more than was the actual case. On the whole however the commentary was passionate. In a leading article in the *New Statesman* Richard Crossman again developed the theme that 'at long last a British Government is not merely paying lip service to the equality and independence of a Middle Eastern nation'. The *Daily Herald* seemed to take a perverse pleasure in the controversy because it refuted critics who charged that no difference existed between Tory and Labour policies. The Egyptian question was quickly becoming a party issue.[27]

The split between the parties on an imperial issue—the first since the advent of the Labour government—became sharply apparent during the Parliamentary debate of the 24th of May. Instead of responding to the Tory attack, Bevin sat tight-lipped and grim-faced. According to Raymond A. Hare of the American Embassy, who provided a sensitive first-hand account, Attlee cocked his feet on a table and fixed his eyes on the ceiling. Churchill's style seemed to resemble that of a heavyweight boxer, while Eden's reminded one of a less aggressive but accomplished sparring partner. All in all, Hare wrote, there was a 'dramatic atmosphere'.[28]

Eden's comments again are of interest, especially because of the great Suez crisis a decade later (the years 1936, 1946, and 1956 have a peculiar Egyptian rhythm to them, not least for Eden). He denied that the 1936 treaty humiliated the Egyptians any more than the British were humiliated by allowing the Americans to use British bases in the West Indies. He argued that in a 'troubled world we have need of Egypt's friendship, and Egypt also has the need of the friendship of the British Empire'. Eden urged the government

---

[27] All press commentary cited above 8–11 May 1946. There were many bizarre comments (at least from today's perspective), e.g. Lord Altrincham (Sir Edward Grigg, former Minister of State Resident in the Middle East) argued in the *Sunday Times* that 'there is a fundamental affinity between the British type of democracy and modern Islamic culture' (19 May 1946).

[28] Report by Hare, Confidential, 31 May 1946, USSD 741.83/5–3146.

to carry out the purpose of the 1936 treaty—mutual defence and co-operation.[29]

Churchill took a much more belligerent line. He repeatedly interrupted the debate. He heckled his opponents who responded in kind. The participants raised far-reaching questions. A Labour MP, Major Lyall Wilkes, for example stated that the problem with the Egyptians was psychological. They knew that the British regarded them as 'wogs'. 'We have sat on Shepheard's veranda too long with the wrong kind of people.' Unlike most of his colleagues, he pleaded for greater co-operation through the United Nations. Later in the debate, Patrick Gordon-Walker (later a Labour Dominions Secretary) charged that if Churchill's attitude towards Egypt were adopted 'our country and the Government would be repeating the mistakes made by George III who threw away our first Empire'. A Tory MP, Douglas Dodds-Parker (formerly of the Sudan Political Service), responded by saying that such fallacies could only have been picked up from Victor Gollancz and the Left Book Club. Further in the debate a Labour member objected to Churchill's interventions, telling him to stop behaving like a schoolboy. Another quipped that Churchill's voice reminded him of what Matthew Arnold said of Byron's, 'like the thunder's roll'. He added that Churchill's merely had a deafening effect. By the time Churchill finally rose to speak in his own right, the House was tense.

On this occasion Churchill's speech was more notable for its invective than for its substance. He denounced Lord Stansgate as a 'lightweight'. He accused Bevin of having 'undue apprehension about leaving his tail uncovered'. He hoped that the Foreign Secretary would not escape from the debate under 'the blether and blare' of majority cheering. Churchill felt strongly that the Egyptians should not permit themselves suspicion but gratitude—'gratitude, I might say, such as two nations have ever owed to another'. He covered many points, none of which were especially new. He repeated that he had suffered a great shock. And he concluded: 'What has been gained with enormous effort and sacrifice, prodigious and superb acts of valour, slips away almost unnoticed when the struggle is over.'[30]

Bevin now rose to reply. He was one of the few people in the House of Commons who could stand up to Churchill and he did so successfully on this occasion. With powerful oratory Bevin traced the history of the 1936 treaty in relation to the frustrated goals of the League of Nations. He pointed out that the United Nations now

---

[29] *Parliamentary Debates* (Commons), 24 May 1946, cols. 701–8.
[30] Ibid., cols. 766–79.

existed. 'Countries assume that through that organisation there is to be a new era of regional defence, and that their great salvation lies in that, rather than in supporting solely one State. . . . Every State which I have had to deal with as Foreign Secretary has really pinned its faith on that basis.' They thus lived in a new era. Bevin acknowledged the work of Lord Cromer and other distinguished Englishmen associated with Egypt; 'but we cannot live in the past'. He went on: 'Here is a new age, and we are trying to meet it with advice on education, social services, health, training and all the rest of it.' Though he did not say so explicitly, that programme amounted in fact to an export of the welfare state to places such as Egypt. Once the Egyptians and others acquired those benefits, he optimistically suggested, Anglo-Arab friendship would spread from Egypt through the Muslim world into India. Looking at Churchill, he said 'I do not think the Poona mentality suits today.' Lest he leave any doubt that he saw the power politics of the Egyptian situation, he concluded with a sentence that became perhaps the most famous of the debate: 'I will be no party to leaving a vacuum.'[31] Bevin thus demonstrated that he had his own sense of Imperial responsibility, both as a socialist and as a protector of Britain's strategic position in the eastern Mediterranean.

The Stansgate Mission and the Attitude of the United States

When Lord Stansgate accepted the leadership of the delegation to Egypt, he was sixty-nine years old and had a reputation as a prominent Parliamentarian and as Ramsay Macdonald's liberal but undistinguished Secretary of State for India (1929–31). As Secretary for Air he was expected to persuade the Egyptians to accept the crucial clauses about fighter squadrons and bomber bases. Not all of the members of the Cabinet thought it a wise appointment. 'Wedgy' was 'too old', 'losing his grip', 'not knowledgeable about Egyptian affairs'—though it was commonly granted that he was a 'fighter'. Attlee himself eventually regarded the appointment as a mistake. Stansgate was 'asked' to retire in October 1946.[32] Earlier in the year, Attlee, Bevin, and other members of the Cabinet had

[31] Ibid., cols. 779–90. By referring to Churchill's outlook on India he thus wound up as rough and tumble a debate as he had intended. His private secretary had written two days previously: 'E. B. is determined to go for Winston, and is rolling vituperative phrases round his mouth (swollen from the extraction of 3 teeth, making him almost indistinguishable from a bloodhound).' Piers Dixon, *Double Diploma* (London, 1968), p. 214.

[32] Attlee Papers (Cambridge) 1/17. Bevin had written in August: 'I think Stansgate is too ready to give in when bargaining with Arabs who invariably pitch their demands too high and expect, as in the market place, that they will meet considerable resistance from the other side.' Bevin to Attlee, 4 Aug. 1946, FO 800/457.

been perturbed to see Stansgate reveal a certain radicalism in his negotiations with the Egyptians. He arrived in Egypt to find deplorable conditions. According to an American report, 'he was shocked immeasurably at what he found here as a result of some sixty years of British occupation'.[33] He tended to take the view that the British had accomplished virtually nothing during their occupation and that the best course would be total evacuation. In a conversation with the American Ambassador 'he referred bitterly to Britain's past relationship with Egypt during the "imperialistic era" and concluded by saying "we must not only get out of Egypt but we must get out quick"'.[34] Stansgate is not usually regarded as holding a distinguished place in the history of the dissolution of the British Empire, but on this point he should be remembered as the statesman who perhaps more than any other believed that the remnants of British imperialism in Egypt should be unequivocally liquidated.

There was close collaboration between the Stansgate mission and the American Embassy in Cairo, a collaboration ordered from high quarters. In the recess during the debate on the 24th of May, Bevin had summoned the American Ambassador in London, Averell Harriman, to the House of Commons. He told Harriman that he was 'on a hot spot over Egypt'. Bevin explained that the British wished to lease bases from the Egyptians in the way the British had granted the Americans bases in Bermuda and the West Indies. He further described to Harriman the ways in which he hoped to improve health standards in Egypt by purifying the Nile and eliminating debilitating diseases. Harriman gained the impression that Bevin genuinely wanted to improve living conditions in the Middle East as well as to provide a defence system. On the latter point he telegraphed to Washington: 'I was impressed with Bevin's sincerity in attempting to forward the moral issue of full respect for Egypt's sovereignty in the withdrawal of British troops and at the same time realistically dealing with the security needs of the Canal and the Middle East.'[35]

The Americans in Cairo consequently from time to time took an active part in attempting to resolve the question of security. The American Ambassador, S. Pinkney Tuck, like Lord Stansgate, became preoccupied—perhaps obsessed would not be too strong

---

[33] Memorandum by Cecil B. Lyon (Chargé d'Affaires), 13 Aug. 1946, USSD 741.83/8-1346.

[34] Tuck to Byrnes, Secret, 27 May 1946, USSD 741.83/5-2746.

[35] Harriman to Byrnes, 24 May 1946, USSD 741.83/5-2446. In Bevin's account of the conversation he emphasized to Harriman the danger of the 'vacuum' if Egypt were left alone: Egypt 'would become a magnet of attraction to any expansionist country. The Egyptians were far too weak to defend the Zone or even to hold it.' Bevin to Campbell, Top Secret, 26 May 1946, FO 371/53298.

a word—with the need for immediate troop withdrawal. He predicted that if the British protracted the retreat over a period of years —for example the five years required by the British Chiefs of Staff —then Anglo-Egyptian relations would be further poisoned and there would be no treaty revision. Under instructions from Secretary of State Byrnes, Tuck informed the King that the United States had a 'deep interest in the welfare of all peoples of the Middle East'. The Secretary of State hoped that the Egyptians and British would find a satisfactory solution to defence problems that were also of 'fundamental importance' to American security. Tuck believed privately that American professions of concern for Arab welfare would merely make the United States vulnerable to charges of hypocrisy since President Truman at the same time was pressing for the admission of 100,000 Jews into Palestine. Far from helping to resolve 'ancient' controversies between the British and the Egyptians about defence and the Sudan, American intervention, Tuck believed, would merely antagonize Egyptian nationalists who would be quick to recognize empty rhetoric.[36]

Tuck and his colleagues sympathized with Lord Stansgate. They viewed him and the new Ambassador, Sir Ronald Campbell, as representing the enlightened impulses of British imperialism in contrast with the reactionary tendencies of Lord Killearn. Nevertheless the Americans criticized the way in which Stansgate dealt with the Egyptians and they regarded Campbell as weak and ineffectual, perhaps again in part because of the contrast of the overbearing personality of his predecessor. One American official wrote that the British conducted the negotiations 'in a somewhat amateurish manner' and seemed once again to be 'muddling through'. As they watched this *'opéra bouffe'* the Americans found it difficult to believe Egyptian charges of nefarious British plots. Indeed the casual British attitude seemed to refute 'the reputation which has been built up of Perfidious Albion carefully plotting and scheming in intricate detail for Empire control and world domination'. The British in Egypt appeared on the contrary to have a profoundly pessimistic attitude. The same American official who wrote of the British 'muddling through' had another insight, he believed, into the postwar British imperial mentality. If an average ('lower class') British subject were asked, should Britain dominate Egypt against the will of the people?—the following answer would probably have been forthcoming: 'Why should we? . . . Let 'em 'av their blinkin' country, eye say.'[37] That comment might

---

[36] See the series of telegrams and letters by Tuck to the Secretary of State written in 1946-7 in USSD 741.83.

[37] Memorandum by Lyon, 13 Aug. 1946, USSD 741.83/8-1346.

have sounded like an American caricature to those in the Labour government, but it probably represented the exasperated and disillusioned attitude of many men of the occupying army.

Bevin and Sidky: Agreement and Breakdown

With a mixture of combativeness and conciliation, Bevin continued to press the Egyptians for concessions. Having failed to persuade them to lease bases on the analogy of British bases in the West Indies, he now proposed the creation of a Joint Defence Board similar to the United States–Canada Defence Board. Its purpose would be 'to keep under review the international situation and to consult .·. upon all events which may threaten the security of the Middle East'.[38] The Chiefs of Staff did not like this proposal because the 'Board' would be merely consultative and could not empower the British to reoccupy in the event of war. In the words of the Chief of the Imperial General Staff, 'We had hoped to obtain complete freedom to return in an apprehended emergency.'[39] Even the Chiefs of Staff however recognized the delicacy of the question of reoccupation. They wrote:

> We are . . . on the horns of a dilemma. On the one hand, the political effect of pressing for our full requirements involves the risk, which the local advisers regard as a practical certainty, of
> (a) Disorders necessitating the despatch of considerable reinforcements to Egypt to restore and maintain order:
> (b) Permanently ruining our relations with Egypt: and
> (c) Being pilloried in the Security Council.
> On the other hand, we stand to secure the friendly co-operation of Egypt, but by a definite sacrifice to our military position. Of the two, we consider the latter to be the lesser of the two evils.[40]

In Bevin's slightly different language, 'The real choice . . . was a new Treaty freely negotiated with the Egyptian Government or the maintenance of our position in Egypt by force.' Friendship with Egypt should take precedence over military precaution. Conciliation ('appeasement' according to critics) was the persistent line taken by Bevin, Attlee, and the Cabinet.

By the summer of 1946 the project of a possible Anglo-Egyptian combination now seemed to resemble a watered-down 'goodwill treaty' rather than an effective military alliance. Even the Egyptian

[38] Memorandum by Bevin, 5 June 1946, CP (46) 219, CAB 129/10; minutes in FO 371/53301.
[39] Cabinet Conclusions 57 (46), 6 June 1946, CAB 128/5; minutes in FO 371/53301.
[40] Ibid., appendix; see also Defence Committee (46) 84, 2 July 1946, CAB 131/3; and COS (46) 158, CAB 80/101; and minutes in FO 371/53305.

response to the pre-eminent British requirement, the defence of the canal, could only be described, in Bevin's view, as 'slight and grudging'.[41] Bevin continued to hold firm that he would not be a party to creating a 'vacuum' in Egypt. He—and even the Chiefs of Staff—would be willing to sanction an orderly retreat over a period of three years and would even yield on the issue of fighter and bomber bases. But in return he wanted at least a 'goodwill treaty' of substance that would save face and indicate to the world at large that Egypt remained a British preserve, though an entirely 'independent' one.

Lord Stansgate on the other hand believed that only immediate withdrawal would salvage the alliance. He warned Bevin of the dangers of prolonged occupation, drawing on the lesson of the post-First World War era:

> In 1919 Egypt was a Protectorate. We controlled [the] whole administrative machinery and we committed large numbers of troops. There was trouble then. We deported Zaghlul twice and General [Sir Edward] Bulfin was given subsequently some six divisions to clean up the country which he did very thoroughly with the loss of many Egyptian lives. There never was a better example of firmness.

Stansgate now told the moral of the story. Repression brought about the opposite of the intended effect:

> Within less than three years the British Government was driven to a policy of scuttle. [The] Protectorate was abandoned and Zaghlul [was] moved from his prison cell to be Prime Minister and Master of Egypt and he gave us plenty of trouble thereafter. If that was forced on Lloyd George who had no scruples how would we do better?[42]

Bevin did not like moral lectures, at least in his direction. He must have been piqued at Stansgate's injunction, 'we ought not to be afraid to do the right thing'. There was a clash of temperament as well as a difference of opinion and tactics. In retrospect it seems clear that Stansgate had a more realistic impression of Egyptian nationalism than Bevin and his advisers were willing to acknowledge in 1946. It would be a mistake, Stansgate thought, to minimize the anti-British and ultimately irrational quality of a nationalist movement that bore comparison with its Irish counterpart. Sidky Pasha and his friends, he noted, were the 'Redmonds and Dillons' of Egypt.[43]

---

[41] Bevin to Campbell, Secret, 5 Aug. 1946, FO 371/53308/J3333.

[42] Stansgate to Bevin, Personal, 12 Aug. 1946, FO 371/53309/J3498.

[43] Ibid. The Irish analogy was prevalent in the Egyptian press. For example one newspaper recounted an imaginary conversation with Eamon de Valera, who told his Egyptian friends that 'Ireland although a weak country won her cause by struggle, whereas Egypt had spent 25 years negotiating with inconclusive results'. As recounted in Bowker to Bevin, 9 Nov. 1946, FO 371/53317/J4678. The Stansgate Papers contain a large and revealing collection of cuttings from the Egyptian as well as the British press.

Stansgate nevertheless endorsed the view shared by Sir Walter Smart and other experts that Sidky could secure the King's support and the approval by the Egyptian Parliament of a treaty between the two countries. In Stansgate's judgement Sidky was not only 'the cleverest statesman in Egypt' but also 'Egypt's most able administrator' who wished 'to crown his life by securing evacuation'.[44] Bevin and the Foreign Office as well as Attlee and the Cabinet continued to hope that Sidky himself would be able to consolidate nationalist support behind a renewed Anglo-Egyptian alliance. Sir Walter Smart summarized the balanced reasoning: 'the present Government of Egypt was a minority one, and opposed by the Wafd and by certain independent personalities of influence. Nevertheless, Sidky should be able, with King Farouk's support, to secure Parliamentary approval in any treaty which he . . . concluded with us.'[45] Bevin thus had reason to be optimistically anxious when Sidky Pasha arrived in London in October 1946, after months of delay and exasperation, to see if the issues of controversy could be resolved personally and directly. It was a time of tension when all members of the Labour government were preoccupied with the crises in India and Palestine as well. Bevin's private secretary, Pierson Dixon, noted afterwards that the arduous discussion with the Egyptians constituted 'the worst ten days I remember'. Throughout there was underlying tension. Again in Dixon's words, 'The real worry is whether Sidky can put these arrangements through.'[46]

Bevin and Sidky had five meetings between the 18th and 25th of October. Sidky made it clear at the outset that any agreement would have to be approved by the Egyptian King, Cabinet, and Parliament. Both Bevin and Sidky genuinely wanted an understanding, and the discussion about the first point of controversy, evacuation, was conspicuously marked by hard bargaining and an effort to

[44] Stansgate to Bevin, Personal, 8 and 26 Aug. 1946, FO 371/53310.

[45] See minutes of meetings of 4 and 5 Oct. 1946 which included Bevin, Stansgate, and Campbell, FO 371/53314/J4213. Stansgate continued to participate in the discussions but at the end of October Attlee forced his retirement on grounds of defence reorganization; in fact it probably was the Egyptian issue that provided the main motivation. Stansgate himself confessed to disappointment in dealing with the Egyptians and in clarifying some of the major issues. 'I myself feel very confused', he wrote in January 1947. 'The Egyptians have been pig-headed in their failure to understand the growth of [Sudanese] national feeling.' Stansgate to Campbell, 31 Jan. 1947, Stansgate Papers.

[46] Dixon, *Double Diploma* (London, 1968), p. 233. The original Egyptian delegation consisted of Sidky and two other leaders of political parties, Nokrashi Pasha and Heikal Pasha. Their refusal to participate at the last moment dealt a blow to Sidky's hopes for successful negotiations. They were replaced by the Minister for Foreign Affairs and staff members who could not of course command the same political support in Egypt. It is a measure of Sidky's self-confidence that he believed he could secure the treaty without the participation of the leaders of two important nationalist parties, not to mention the Wafd.

resolve mutual misapprehension. They agreed that all British troops would be withdrawn in stages—from Cairo, Alexandria and the Delta by the 31st of March 1947 and from the rest of Egypt by the 1st of September 1949. As evidence of sincerity of British intent, Bevin and Sidky could point to the British handing over of the British headquarters in Cairo, the Citadel, that had taken place, (to the amusement of the Americans) on the 4th of July 1946. There was agreement that all British troops should be withdrawn as soon as possible from bases in the vicinity of Cairo and Alexandria in order to remove, in Sir Orme Sargent's words, 'one of the things that particularly irritate the Egyptian public'.[47] In a sense the British military evacuation of Cairo represented one of the first transfers of power of the postwar era. It had a symbolic significance, as Sidky emphasized to Bevin: 'Egyptians had seen the King of Egypt take over the Citadel . . . for sixty years Egypt had wanted her soil to be free of British troops.'[48]

Egypt refused to be treated as if still a part of the British Empire, formal or informal. Here lay the difficulty in agreeing upon the terms of a quasi-military alliance. In the event of war, would Egypt declare on the side of Britain? In 1939 it was a question that, even with the Dominions, had depended on good faith rather than on the letter of a military agreement. In 1946 with the Egyptians, the British had to settle for informal assurance, in Sidky's words, that 'Egypt would not fail' and that 'once war had broken out Egypt would enter'.[49] In the formal language of a treaty, 'action' would be substituted for 'war' and 'consultation' would replace unilateral decision on the part of the British. Thus Bevin readjusted British defence requirements to meet the changed conditions of the postwar era. Pierson Dixon, who participated in the discussions, recorded the result as a success:

The essence is that we and Egypt are jointly responsible for the defence of the area, and we agree to take action (i.e. British forces move back into Egypt) if war breaks out in the adjacent territories, and to consult (i.e. it is up to us to convince the Egyptians that action is required) if war breaks out further afield. We couldn't have done better than this. The days are past when we could treat

---

[47] Minute by Sargent, 18 May 1946, FO 371/53295. Sargent had written about the necessity of evacuation after a meeting between Attlee, Bevin, and others at Chequers. Attlee believed it imperative to reduce the number of troops in Cairo in order to succeed in the negotiations and to avoid the danger of a 'revolutionary movement' with British bases as the target. Bevin gave instructions to press the issue with the Chiefs of Staff. Robert Howe noted that as long as British headquarters remained in Cairo it would be 'a standing reminder to every Egyptian of the British occupation'. See minutes in PREM 8/1388; and in FO 371/53295 and 53300.

[48] Minutes of meeting of 18 Oct. 1946, FO 371/53315.

[49] Ibid.

Egypt *de haut en bas*, and act as a great Power using a little Power's territory for our own purposes as and when judged our interests required it.[50]

In sum the defence arrangements with Egypt provided for calculated probability of British reoccupation in the event of war. But it was not an automatic right of re-entry.

The sticking point was the Sudan. This was the cause ultimately of the breakdown of the Bevin–Sidky arrangement. There was a real element of mutual misunderstanding. It is instructive to examine some of the details because they reveal the extent of the Labour government's commitment to the Sudanese as well as conflicting interpretations of self-determination. Sidky from the outset demanded British recognition of Egyptian 'sovereignty' in the Sudan. He defined sovereignty as 'an emblem of unity'. Egypt hoped for the development of the Sudan as a self-governing country, to use British parlance, in the same way as a trustee wished to see a ward develop and prosper. It is ironic to find the British on the receiving end and having to listen to such language: 'Egypt wanted to regard the Sudan as a smaller and weaker brother.' Bevin recognized the sentiment; he found it difficult to reconcile it with the publicly declared goal of the Labour government to work towards self-government and self-determination in the Sudan. He said to Sidky that 'he had tried and failed to understand the Egyptian point of view'. There followed lengthy and exhausting discussions about the 'historical nature' of sovereignty, 'symbolic' sovereignty, sovereignty under a 'common' Egyptian crown, and the extent of 'British' sovereignty in the Sudan. British participants in the discussions actually read Cromer on the Anglo-Egyptian agreement of 1899. Bevin finally called for the opinion of the Lord Chancellor, who began his reply by stating what everyone suspected: 'no one has suceeded in defining the conception underlying sovereignty'. His opinion was extremely useful to Bevin because it concluded that 'we are not the sovereign' (a fact that Bevin of course did not reveal to Sidky). It would be legitimate in international law to support the Egyptian claim since Ottoman sovereignty presumably now resided in the Egyptian crown.[51] Bevin therefore could logically acknowledge that a 'union' existed between the Sudan and Egypt in the form of a common crown if at the same time he could secure the political guarantees of Sudanese self-determination. That in short was what he attempted to do.

The crucial point in the discussions between Bevin and Sidky was the insistence of the British that the Sudanese had the right of self-

---

[50] Dixon, *Double Diploma*, p. 232.

[51] See memorandum by the Lord Chancellor, 'Egypt and the Sudan', Secret, 24 Oct. 1946, FO 371/53316.

determination. If the Sudan, Bevin said in language reminiscent of Gladstone, 'struggling for independence' wished to be free of Eygptian control then the Egyptians would have to grant independence. He wished to make it 'quite clear', he said to Sidky, that nothing would be done 'to prejudice the right of self-determination'. Sidky found no difficulty in accepting Bevin's demand. Since this became an explosive issue, one might ask why there could be such mutual mis-understanding in the face of such explicit comment. The answer is that Sidky, like most Egyptians, believed that in time, when Britain would withdraw from all of the Nile valley including the Sudan, self-determination simply would not arise as an issue, at least in the immediate future. Sidky stated in regard to that specific point: 'the question . . . was a matter for our children to decide . . . if the Sudanese reached a certain point of development they would surely become independent'. The Egyptians as well as the British pressed the issue of self-determination. Each party was as guilty as the other of wishful thinking about 'colonial independence'. Each believed that some future generation of Sudanese would make essentially a pro-Egyptian or pro-British decision (whereas in fact the Sudanese achieved independence within a decade according to their own criteria). Even though the transcripts reveal 'sharp disagreement' between Bevin and Sidky on the Sudan, both of them in good faith could think that the problem would peacefully and satisfactorily resolve itself. Bevin believed that he had stated the guarantees in iron-clad language. He could accept 'symbolic sovereignty' without betraying the Sudanese. For the near future the existing British administration of the Sudan would continue and the agreement 'would in no way affect British military dispositions in the Sudan'. Sidky for his part secured British acquiescence in the Egyptian claim of unity of Egypt and the Sudan under the common crown of Egypt.[52] Agreement on the Sudan thus formed the heart of the 'Bevin–Sidky Protocol' of October 1946.

As soon as Sidky arrived back in Cairo reports began to appear in the press that he had succeeded 'in bringing the Sudan to Egypt' and that 'it has definitely been decided to achieve unity between Egypt and the Sudan under the Egyptian crown'.[53] The press reports did

[52] See the lengthy printed memorandum by the Egyptian Department of 12 Mar. 1947, which summarizes the negotiations, in FO 371/62962.

[53] A writer in the *Round Table* subsequently recalled that Sidky, 'an old, sick and exhausted man, but glowing with pleasure at his success, made an incautious and probably misrepresented statement to an Egyptian journalist as he stumbled from his aircraft late in the night' in Cairo on the 26th of October 1946 (Mar. 1951, p. 115). This was about the time of Bevin's departure for the meeting of the Council of Foreign Ministers in New York, where he had to continue the Egyptian business indirectly.

not mention British insistence on the right to self-government and self-determination. On the 28th of October Attlee stated unequivocally in the House of Commons that there would be no change in the politicial status or administration of the Sudan.[54] He thus seemed publicly to repudiate Sidky. The Sudanese would decide their own future, even though in theory the Egyptian crown might be sovereign. He thus hoped to reassure the Sudanese. To the public he succeeded in rebuffing the former without conciliating the latter. The Sudan administration had expected, as Bevin had explained to the Cabinet, 'considerable political tension . . . and the possibility of disorder'— but not to the extent that actually occurred.[55] An extra battalion of troops from Palestine had to be flown to Khartoum to restore order. Members of the independence party, the Umma, destroyed the headquarters of the rival Ashigga who favoured union with Egypt. The Umma's newspaper called for no less than a holy war against both the British and the Egyptians. Demonstrators flew the red, black, and green tricolour of the Mahdist Sudan. In early November the Governor-General, Major-General Sir Hubert Huddleston, flew to London to warn that if Egyptian sovereignty over the Sudan were formally recognized then Sudanese good faith in the British would be destroyed and there would be bloodletting unknown since the days of the Mahdi. The leader of the Umma was in fact the son of the Mahdi. It must have caused a disturbing sense of *déjà vu* to those in the Labour government who identified themselves with the tradition of 'Little England' and who sympathized with Gladstone's statement, which now seemed much less misguided than half a century earlier, about peoples rightly struggling to be free.[56]

Huddleston reported directly to the Prime Minister who himself assessed the danger of Sudanese nationalist reaction. Attlee wrote to members of the Cabinet: 'It appears that the powerful Nationalist (as opposed to the pro-Egyptian) party in the Sudan, which is led by (posthumous) son of the Mahdi, have been thrown into a mood of bitter and dangerous fanaticism, [and] that they accuse His Majesty's

[54] *Parliamentary Debates* (Commons), 28 Oct. 1946, cols. 295-6.
[55] Memorandum by Bevin, Top Secret, 23 Oct. 1946, DO (46) 124, FO 371/53315.
[56] For the continuity in Sudanese nationalism since the time of the Mahdi see Peter Woodward, *Condominium and Sudanese Nationalism* (London, 1979); and another principal work on the subject, Mohamed Omer Beshir, *Revolution and Nationalism in the Sudan* (London, 1974), e.g. p. 152: 'by 1946 Mahdism was no longer in the eyes of many Sudanese that bogy which the British administration had tried to make it since the reconquest. It had become another political party. Neo-Mahdism in this way fulfilled [Sir Stewart] Symes' prophecy of 1917 when he wrote: "It would be in the natural order of things if the Mahdists of today became the nationalists of tomorrow".' For further references see the bibliographical essay in P. M. Holt and M. W. Daly, *The History of the Sudan* (third edn. London 1979).

Government and the Sudan Government of betraying them to Egypt.' Attlee in fact sympathized with the Sudanese and regarded the Egyptians as guilty of 'deliberate duplicity'. He nevertheless believed that the Bevin–Sidky 'protocol' should be upheld. Otherwise the entire British position in the Middle East would be adversely affected:

If we now repudiate the Sudan Protocol we shall lose the whole treaty, for Sidky Pasha's Government would be swept away. Our relations with Egypt and our defence arrangements in the Middle East would again be in the melting pot, and we might face the international complications of an Egyptian reference to the United Nations organisation.[57]

Attlee hoped to save the Egyptian arrangement by not yielding to Sudanese protest, even if it meant the use of force. At the same time the British would continue to make two points clear to all parties concerned, above all to the Sudanese: 'that the Sudanese shall, when the time comes, be free to choose complete independence, and that the United Kingdom has an unconditional right to maintain what troops she wishes in the territory'. In the balanced mind of the Prime Minister there was no contradiction between self-determination and imperial defence. To Attlee there was a proper time and place for everything, and the coming to terms with the Egyptians was more important at that particular time than dealing with the more remote problem of the Sudan's independence. Like Bevin, he believed the Sudan question could be dealt with later, and without ethical sacrifice, by endorsing the principle of self-determination.

Bevin, now attending the meeting of the Council of Foreign Ministers in New York, began to send Sidky some stiff advice. The protocol did not change the status of the Sudan; the Sudanese, when ready for self-government, would have free choice of status, including independence; the British had military freedom of action in the Sudan; and, ominously, the 1936 treaty remained intact. The Sudanese were taking Egyptian 'sovereignty' to mean 'domination' or 'mastery'. Unless Sidky repudiated that perverted meaning, Bevin warned, there would be a full statement in the House of Commons. Bevin would explain how the 'phrase' about the Sudan and Egypt being under a 'common crown' had actually been used. It was a recognition of symbolic sovereignty, and 'was never intended as a brake on the wheel of Sudanese progress towards independence'.[58] Unfortunately Sidky could not comply. 'Sidky seems to have committed himself up to the hilt', the Embassy in Cairo reported to

---

[57] Memorandum by Attlee, Secret, 18 Nov. 1946, FO 371/53318. For Attlee's views on all of these problems, which he followed carefully, see PREM 8/1388.

[58] See the memorandum by the Egyptian Department, 12 Mar. 1947, FO 371/62962.

the Foreign Office, to a diametrically opposed interpretation of the protocol—meaning that full Egyptian sovereignty in the Sudan had been restored—because there was no other way to save the draft treaty.[59] The more Sidky bore the protest of having caved in to British imperialism, the more he emphasized his success in securing Egyptian sovereignty in the Sudan. He finally reached the breaking point, in terms of politics and his own health, little over a month after his return to Cairo. On the 9th of December 1946 Sidky Pasha resigned as Prime Minister.

The breakdown of the Bevin–Sidky protocol ended a chapter in Anglo-Egyptian history. From that time on the British were never able to find another Egyptian leader willing or capable of resolving the two issues of evacuation and the Sudan to the satisfaction of both sides. It is illuminating to examine the reactions of the two principals in the immediate aftermath. Sidky saw himself as the victim of a Wafd vendetta. He thought, probably correctly, that the Wafd leaders themselves would have come to the same terms. It was therefore unfortunate for the British that Farouk's feud with Nahas Pasha prevented the collaboration of the Wafd when the British needed it almost as badly as in 1942. Sidky bore no particular grudge against Bevin, whom he regarded as a 'great statesman'. He thought that Bevin had genuinely attempted to understand the Egyptian point of view. He criticized him however for being more concerned with *formulas* (such as self-determination) rather than *principles* (such as sovereignty). His attitude towards self-determination as a mere formula or 'formality' becomes comprehensible in view of the Egyptian belief that about eighty per cent of the Sudanese would 'self-determine' in favour of union with Egypt (and that most of the remaining twenty per cent, the 'savages' of the south, could not be expected to have an informed opinion). So far as there was a set of principles in the negotiations, Sidky believed that he had triumphed. He had secured the abolition of the hated 1936 treaty, which had, in his eyes, continued Egypt's status as a British sphere of influence. He had achieved the recognition of the union of the Sudan under the Egyptian crown. Thus from Sidky's point of view the 1946 'Bevin-Sidky Protocol' represented a bitterly unfulfilled victory.[60]

Bevin of course was angry that so much British goodwill, an

---

[59] Bowker to Scrivener, 21 Nov. 1946, FO 371/53319/J4994.

[60] In addition to Foreign Office files this passage is based on a memorandum by Sidky himself dated 18 Nov. 1946 in the St. Antony's College Middle East Centre Archives. For a valuable commentary on the Egyptian belief that the Sudanese overwhelmingly wished to unite with Egypt, see the memorandum by Philip W. Ireland (First Secretary at the American Embassy and a sensitive observer of Egyptian politics), 23 Dec. 1946, USSD 741.83/12-2646.

inordinate amount of time, and considerable emotional energy had all come to nothing. He continued to explore possible ways of coming to terms with the Egyptians, and his optimistic temperament allowed him to hope that Britain and Egypt could resolve the issues of evacuation and the Sudan. In late 1950, as will be seen in a later chapter, he again entered into discussions with the Egyptians only to arrive at an even more hopeless stalemate. Then as in 1946 he ultimately had to fall back on the basis of the British position in the eastern Mediterranean that had been secured before the Second World War. In a moment of self-consolation and determination he groaned: 'I shall stick to 1936.'[61]

Nokrashi, the United Nations, and Anglo-Egyptian Deadlock

Sidky's successor was Nokrashi Pasha. From the Foreign Office point of view there could have been none worse (though there was qualified dissent on that point). Like Sidky he led a minority party at odds with the Wafd. The key to his political power lay in his good relations with the King and in his ability to rally anti-British Egyptian nationalism. Most British officials believed that in 1924 he had been involved in the murder of Sir Lee Stack (Governor-General of the Sudan and Sirdar of the Egyptian Army). He probably was not. At that time he had not yet seceded from the Wafd, and neither his nor the party's fortunes stood to prosper by implication. But the popular belief of his involvement is important because in his career as national leader the British regarded him generally as a political assassin now appearing 'in a different uniform'.[62] Official reports (especially those written by Killearn, who disliked him) depicted him as a rigid and unbending nationalist, the captive of such slogans as 'total evacuation', 'unity of the Nile Valley', and 'One River, One Valley, One Land'. Reports from the American Embassy tended to emphasize by contrast that he was a shrewd politician, well aware of the limits within which he could manœuvre, and more inventive and humane than the British made him out to be. Having left the Wafd, Nokrashi was always careful to demonstrate that his nationalist credentials were as good as his political opponents'. In any case his stand on the two major issues, the timing of evacuation and self-determination in the Sudan, led the Foreign Office to believe that further negotiation was hopeless. Nokrashi demanded total

[61] Minute by Bevin, *c.*20 Feb. 1947, FO 371/62965.

[62] Grafftey-Smith, *Bright Levant*, p. 128. Quilliam of *The Times* would have warmly contested that judgement: 'Nobody who knows Nokrashy well can believe that he is a murderer or that he would organize or condone murder.' Quilliam to Deakin, 29 Mar. 1948, Quilliam Papers.

evacuation *at once* and proclaimed *absolute* Egyptian sovereignty in the Sudan. In an epitome of British estimates of this 'unbending' and 'dangerous' nationalist, Sir Ronald Campbell wrote:

> Nokrashi is narrow, stubborn and inelastic. It is fashionable when applying these epithets to recall that he began as a school master. . . . As regards the darker passages in his career . . . he firmly denies . . . any complicity, at any rate, in the murder of Sir Lee Stack, but he knows that British people remember his extremist activities and that they consider he was implicated in many of the murders [of the post-First World War era], and, moreover, that many English people do not acquit him of complicity in the Lee Stack crime. . . .
> He can be bloody-minded and extremely petty when annoyed with us and anxious to take it out on us. . . . In negotiation he is unimaginative, and conspicuously lacking in any suppleness. . . . I would say that he was capable of a dour vindictiveness.

Campbell also noted that Nokrashi was personally 'honest', which appeared to be one of his few redeeming attributes.[63] The British— and the Americans—had no difficulty in accepting his words at face value. He had become Prime Minister with one driving ambition. As reported by the American Ambassador in Cairo, 'his motivating ambition is to go down in history as [the] man who got [the] British out of Egypt'.[64]

The Foreign Office found Nokrashi so objectionable that Bevin's highest advisers debated whether steps should be taken to 'unseat' him. These discussions took place in the winter and spring of 1947 between Robert Howe and Sir Orme Sargent, and finally included Bevin himself. The British, in peace time, now contemplated intervention in the domestic affairs not merely of a foreign but of an allied state. The moving spirit was Howe, who, at Sargent's instruction, looked into 'our old habits of Cabinet making' in Cairo.[65] In April Howe left to become Governor-General of the Sudan. In view of that appointment, which might fairly be described as among the most delicate in the Empire and Commonwealth at that time, it is important to note the axiom of his position, which remained constant before his departure and during his lengthy tour of duty

[63] Campbell to Butler, Secret, 5 June 1947, FO 371/62975. Nokrashi's 'honesty' is a salient theme in contemporary British assessments. In Sargent's judgement Nokrashi could at least be taken at his word and the British might do worse with the 'devious' type of Egyptian politician. 'At any rate he is honest and we know where we are with him.' (Minute by Sargent, 29 Nov. 1948, FO 371/69195/J4511). The theme of integrity was also prominent in the private letters of C. D. Quilliam: 'Like most Egyptian politicians, he is only second-rate. He is not brilliant, he is slow and he is schoolmasterish. . . . But he is honest and a man of principle and strength of character.' Quilliam to Deakin, Confidential, 27 Nov. 1945, Quilliam Papers.

[64] Tuck to Marshall, Secret, 7 May 1947, USSD 501.BB/5-747 Box 2181; *Foreign Relations 1947*, V, pp. 772-4.

[65] See Sargent to Campbell (draft), Top Secret and 'Personal & Private', 27 Jan. 1947, FO 371/62961.

at Khartoum. He would not barter the right of the Sudanese to self-determination in order to achieve strategic security with the Egyptians; and he believed that Nahas Pasha might be more reasonable about these problems that Nokrashi. Farouk, Howe noted, 'was not really our friend' whereas the Wafd in contrast 'stood loyally by us during the war'. Howe continued:

> The Wafd is undoubtedly still the majority party in Egypt. In fact it is the only party which rests on popular support. It ostensibly stands for democracy as opposed to the reactionary policies of the present Palace governments of Pashas which succeed one another at the behest of the King. If the Wafd came into power as the result of our intervention there is a good prospect that we could soon get our Treaty through.[66]

He was confronting a problem that went far beyond a mere treaty, though the scope of that treaty, since it dealt with evacuation from Egypt as well as the future of the Sudan, seemed vital at the time. Howe was also addressing himself to the question of *possible revolution in Egypt*. He wrote in March:

> As long as Nokrashi is in power there is little likelihood of an improvement in our relations with Egypt or in the prospects of resuming the treaty negotiations. It may well be that as long as a Palace minority government is in power the same situation will hold and that our only hope is to work for a return of the Wafd. The return of the Wafd may in fact be the only means of avoiding a revolution in Egypt which will inevitably bring down the King.[67]

Here was a test of the Labour government's boldness. Should an ultimatum be given to Farouk to bring in a Wafd government, as in 1942?

Bevin followed the issue as closely as he could, but he had to do so indirectly. Having returned from New York and having thrown the Palestine controversy to the United Nations, he was now in Moscow for another meeting of the Council of Foreign Ministers. He received from Sargent a telegram, which Attlee endorsed, giving the following estimate of Farouk and the domestic situation in Egypt:

> As for the King, I [Sargent and the F. O. staff] must confess that I feel very suspicious of him especially as regards the Sudan. He is no friend of ours and bears a grudge against us. His attitude over the Sudan is and always has been inspired by self-glorification and personal prestige. . . . His only reason for working in with us at all is because he is unsure of his own future. His dynasty may be in danger in the event of a popular movement led by the Wafd and exploited by the Communists when we might, he thinks, be the only Power to come to his help.[68]

---

[66] Minute by Howe, 17 Jan. 1947, FO 371/62961.

[67] Minute by Howe, 18 Mar. 1947, FO 371/62967.

[68] Sargent minute to Attlee, 3 Apr. 1947; Sargent to Bevin, Top Secret, 8 Apr. 1947, FO 371/62969.

Bevin agreed. He did not like King Farouk:

I fully share your views about the King and base no hopes whatsoever on his being friendly towards us except in so far as he feels this to coincide with his narrow and rather sordid interpretation of what he considers the interests of himself and his dynasty to be.[69]

Nevertheless Bevin drew the line at direct intervention. He did not follow the lead of the Permanent Under-Secretary in the direction of what would have been, in effect, an ultimatum to bring to power a pro-British Wafd government which might have been more favourably disposed to social reform. In retrospect it seems clear that the Wafd could not have been relied upon to introduce the reforms the British thought desirable, or even to resolve to British satisfaction the issues of evacuation and the Sudan.

The evidence about Bevin's overruling his permanent officials is extremely important. It is also revealing about his inner thoughts. He did not believe that Egyptian politicians or parties could be manipulated. He thought that intervention would probably backfire. Here is an excerpt of minutes of a meeting that took place, after his return from Moscow, with his advisers in early May 1947:

Sir O. Sargent said that the main question was whether or not an attempt should be made to unseat Nokrashi.

The S[ecretary]/S[tate] thought it would be a mistake to try to do so. If we did and it proved a flop we should be in a very bad situation. If we pressed for free elections etc he would find himself in the same position as in e.g. Poland. He had followed the Americans and their policy had led to no useful result at all.[70]

Bevin had no confidence at all in the intentions of Nokrashi or Farouk; but he stopped short of intervention in part for the pragmatic reason that it would not produce the desired results and might place him in a vulnerable international position. He did not want to bear criticism of the kind the Russians were receiving in eastern Europe. On the other hand, if the Egyptians requested the United Nations to demand British evacuation he might later change his mind. He instructed his permanent officials to pursue a temperate line. 'We had kept cool so far and there had been no serious incidents.'[71] There was indeed a contrast between Bevin's policy in 1946-7 and Eden's belligerent line during the Suez crisis a decade later.

---

[69] Bevin to Sargent, Top Secret, Personal, 11 Apr. 1947, FO 371/62969.

[70] Minutes of a meeting of 6 May 1947, FO 371/62971.

[71] There is evidence that the Egyptians knew of Bevin's resistance to his advisers. Reporting a conversation with the Egyptian Ambassador who had returned briefly to Cairo, Quilliam wrote confidentially to one of the editors at *The Times*: 'he [the Ambassador] found keen appreciation here (as I myself have found) of the fact that for over two years Mr. Bevin has refused to attempt any interference in Egyptian internal affairs'. Quilliam to Deakin, 29 Mar. 1948, Quilliam Papers.

On the 11th of July 1947 the Egyptians submitted the case to the United Nations. It will not be the purpose here to examine in detail the heated and emotional issues debated in New York but rather to connect them with the broader and related ones facing the British at the time.[72] The cause of greatest anxiety was, of course, Palestine. During the summer of 1947, when the Egyptians argued their case before the Security Council, the United Nations Special Committee on Palestine conducted an investigation in Palestine that resulted in a majority report recommending partition. In September the members of the Security Council found themselves unable to reach agreement about the Egyptian case despite intense British pressure to make a clear-cut decision in favour of the sanctity of treaties and the principle of self-determination. Here the British believed that they rested their case on the side of the angels, but the Egyptian plea against troops on foreign soil had a powerful anti-colonial appeal.

The British had feared an adverse outcome on both issues, Egyptian as well as Palestinian. They could find consolation in the Egyptian failure to achieve a United Nations ultimatum demanding British evacuation. The British in fact had won a modest victory, one of their few at the United Nations in the realm of colonial affairs. They were not, in the words of an official in the Egyptian Department, D. M. H. Riches, being 'pushed out of Eygpt without a treaty' or forced to retreat on the issue of the Sudan. There had moreover been a further underlying anxiety about the internal situation in Egypt. An Egyptian victory would have strengthened Nokrashi and Farouk and would have, the Foreign Office believed, further cancelled any hopes for social reform. The issue of possible revolution preoccupied the British. In Riches' judgement, endorsed by Howe and others, if Britain had been forced to accept an unfavourable United Nations decision then there might have been adverse consequences throughout the Middle East and particularly in Egypt:

Our declared policy in the Middle East is to raise the standard of life of the people of Arab countries, to promote stability and democracy, and not to interfere in the internal government of the countries concerned. If Nokrashy & the King triumph it will mean that a Palace régime of a wholly anti-democratic character will be riveted on Egypt indefinitely. It will do nothing for the fellahin or the industrial workers while it exists, and it will be brought to an end by revolution.[73]

In the summer of 1947 when Farouk made public appearances his subjects cheered him as the King of Egypt and the Sudan. It by

[72] For Egypt's appeal to the Security Council, see L. A. Fabunmi, *The Sudan in Anglo-Egyptian Relations* (London, 1960), chap. 11.
[73] Minute by Riches, 14 Mar. 1947, FO 371/62967.

no means went unnoticed both in London and in Washington that he wore a fragile crown.

The principal American official who, more than anyone else, shaped American policy towards Egypt at this time was Loy Henderson, the head of the Office of Near Eastern and African Affairs. With a sense of dismay shared by his colleagues in Washington (notably Gordon Merriam, the head of Near Eastern Affairs in the same office) and in Cairo (especially the Ambassador, Tuck), Henderson foresaw nothing other than bitter recrimination between the British and the Egyptians until the former decided finally and forever more to end the occupation of Egypt. 'The presence of our troops in Egypt', John Balfour of the British Embassy reported after a conversation with Henderson, appeared to the Americans as ' "a splinter in the thumb" affecting generally our position in the Middle East'.[74] Henderson nevertheless believed that the British had a 'cast-iron' case before the Security Council. The Americans, in perhaps an unprecedented gesture of postwar support of the British Empire, championed the British case '100 per cent' against the Egyptians.[75] The United States upheld the sanctity of the treaty of 1936 and the principle of self-determination in the Sudan. Henderson and his colleagues thought, in short, that the Egyptians were being unreasonable about the question of evacuation, which the British were willing to concede, and preposterous in their argument that the Sudan formed a part of Egypt. Like the British the Americans foresaw a lengthy period of gestation of Sudanese nationhood—'the minimum period is usually put at twenty years', Merriam wrote.[76] On the question of gradual colonial independence the Americans found themselves generally in agreement with the British. There was moreover a consensus about the defensive position of the United States in relation to Britain. It had been well expressed earlier by the *New York Times*: the American position in the Mediterranean, as the history of the Second World War clearly revealed, indicated 'that the British Empire is our first line of

[74] Balfour to Wright, Secret, 22 Aug. 1947, FO 371/62983/J4141.

[75] The phrase used by Cadogan in a telegram to Bevin, Secret, 18 Aug. 1947, FO 371/62980/J3892. Despite this categorical and highly unusual endorsement of British imperialism by the State Department, the Foreign Office continued to regard the American UN delegates as 'deplorable'. (Minute by Riches, 8 Aug. 1947, FO 371/62979.) In particular Herschel Johnson, the leader of the American delegation, was too pro-Zionist, pro-Egyptian and anti-imperialist to British taste.

[76] Memorandum by Merriam, 28 Mar. 1947, USSD 741.83/3-2847 Box 3981. In this memorandum, which is perhaps the most incisive American analysis of the time, Merriam also commented on the 'delicate' issue of British administration of the southern Sudan as almost a separate territory and further remarked that the larger question of the unity of the Sudan with Egypt was extremely sensitive 'in view of the modern trend toward nationalistic fragmentation'.

defence'. In sum it is entirely possible to conclude that the Americans closed ranks with the British against the Egyptians. Such was certainly the deduction of the Egyptian Prime Minister. Nokrashi himself had flown to America to present the Egyptian case at the United Nations.[77] He returned to Cairo 'disillusioned' at the general anti-Egyptian American attitude.[78]

It is also possible to conclude that beneath expressons of distress about the 'splinter in the thumb' there was a sense of deep alarm at the mutual mistrust between the British and the Egyptians as well as a desire to remain friendly with the Egyptians in the anti-colonial American tradition. Henderson expanded on his comment about the danger of British troops in Egypt:

> Their presence is poisoning the atmosphere of the whole Near and Middle East rapidly and to such an extent that unless some indication is given in the near future that British troops are to be withdrawn from Egypt unconditionally . . . the relations of the Arab world with the Western world may be seriously impaired for many years to come.[79]

Though he had no doubt about the 'cast-iron' legal case before the United Nations, Henderson also thought that the highly emotional and moral arguments of Egyptian nationalism would prevail. He urged the British to give the Egyptians 'as soft an answer as circumstances permit'.[80] He pressed on them, as the British understood it, 'a policy of the appeasement vis-a-vis the Egyptians'.[81] The United States thus acted as a mediator, though to the Egyptians a pro-British one. Henderson also cautioned the British to make alternative strategic arrangements as soon as possible. He was moreover well aware of the 'Little England' sentiment:

[77] *New York Times*, 6 Apr. 1946. For assessment of Nokrashi's mission see Tuck to Marshall, Secret, 1 Oct. 1947, *Foreign Relations 1947*, V, pp. 811–12. In a meeting with the Secretary of State in Washington, Nokrashi had explained that 'the Moslem religion was opposed to the concept of communism' but that the continued presence of British troops would cause popular discontent and thus would 'afford a fertile field for communist infiltration'. Unless the United States treated Egypt as 'an equal and independent nation', Nokrashi continued, 'Egyptian support for the democracies would not be forthcoming'. After these uncompromising statements about Egyptian nationalism Marshall merely expressed his 'personal pleasure' at having had the opportunity to meet the Egyptian Prime Minister. Neither succeeded in penetrating the formal reserve of the other. See memorandum by Marshall, 1 Aug. 1947, *Foreign Relations 1947*, V, pp. 785–6.

[78] Quilliam wrote confidentially after Nokrashi's return to Cairo: 'I am certain he feels that his mission was a complete failure. . . . Nokrashi feels that the world is against him and it may take time before he recovers his balance.' Quilliam to Deakin, Confidential, 7 Oct. 1947, Quilliam Papers.

[79] Memorandum by Henderson, Top Secret, 28 Aug. 1947, USSD 841.2383/8-2847; *Foreign Relations 1947*, V, pp. 800–2.

[80] Henderson to Marshall, 9 July 1947, USSD 741.83/7-947.

[81] Minute by Scott-Fox, 10 Sept. 1947, FO 371/62984.

There is already a tendency in certain British circles to withdraw entirely from the Near and Middle East leaving no great power established in that area, and thus exposing it to Russian aggression or infiltration. It is essential that this British tendency be discouraged. The question therefore arises as to where the British forces might be sent.[82]

His answer may be summed up in one word: Cyrenaica. It was the same answer that Bevin himself emphasized to Henderson and the American Ambassador in September 1947: 'In case we withdrew from Suez, we must have some base to fall back upon. We consider Cyrenaica as that base.'[83]

The difficulty with a base in Cyrenaica, as the next chapter will make clear, was that it required the endorsement of the United Nations. Until Libya's independence in 1951 the British faced constantly changing political configurations that might or might not favour British strategic requirements at any particular time. There was only one certainty in the international background: the unswerving Egyptian hostility to British troops in Suez and to any effort to separate the Sudan from Egypt. Until an alternative base could be secured, the British would stay in Suez; the longer the British stayed, the greater the Egyptian resentment. In 1947-8 and in 1950-1 the British hoped to break that chain of circumstances. The narrative in the present chapter, as in its companions, will end in relation to the Palestine question in 1948. But it is important to note the link between the British initiatives because it connects the question of the canal's security with the issue of nationalism in the Sudan— two questions, which, when combined, the Labour government found irresolvable in the 1945-51 era.

In the winter of 1947-8 the Egyptians seemed, to western observers, shaken and isolated by the outcome of the Security Council's inability to present the British an ultimatum. Events in Europe caused general fear of the outbreak of a global war and the possibility of the British drawn back into Egypt proper for another indefinite occupation. The Egyptians were moreover apprehensive that Iraq might take the lead in treaty revision with the British and thus challenge Eygptian leadership in the Arab world. In those circumstances the British had hopes of reaching a defence

[82] Memorandum by Henderson, Top Secret, 28 Aug. 1947, USSD 841.2383/8-2847; *Foreign Relations 1947*, V, pp. 800-2.

[83] Quoted in memorandum by Henderson, Top Secret, 9 Sept. 1947, USSD 741.90/ 9-947. 'If only we were sure of being able to establish our base in Cyrenaica', Sir Orme Sargent lamented, 'there would be a great deal to be said for cancelling the 1936 Treaty, withdrawing our troops from Egypt and refusing to make any further Treaty with Egypt while maintaining intact our rights of possession in the Sudan under the 1899 Protocol.' Minute by Sargent, 12 Sept. 1947, FO 371/62984.

arrangement with the Egyptians by using 'stages of evacuation' as the basis of agreement. The question of the Sudan would be postponed. In view of the manifest strength of Sudanese nationalism, the British now could not yield even on the question of 'symbolic' unity. Nokrashi however was constrained by the powerful cries of Egyptian nationalism—immediate evacuation and unity with the Sudan. The British could not yield on an issue that Egyptian nationalists regarded as the fundamental prerequisite. Bevin's optimism now temporarily evaporated. 'Nokrashi was hopeless', he concluded with a tone of resignation in March 1948.[84]

Nine months later, on the 28th of December 1948, Nokrashi was assassinated by a member of the Muslim Brotherhood. A Foreign Office official 'in a mood of deep gloom' commented to an American colleague that 'from the way things are going from bad to worse in Egypt it seems to me that a revolution there is inevitable'.[85] The British had believed that the situation would be static or worse as long as Nokrashi remained in power. After his death there followed a period of uncertainty in Egyptian public life. No coalition of parties without the Wafd, even with the full support of the King, had sufficient strength to conclude the agreement with the British about such volatile issues as evacuation and the Sudan. This period also coincided with the creation of the North Atlantic Treaty Organization and a general tightening of defence arrangements which the British hoped would indicate to the Egyptians the necessity of security in the eastern Mediterranean. It is necessary to say a few words about this later era in order to make comprehensible the end of the episode dealt with in this chapter. In January 1950 Nahas Pasha and the Wafd returned to power. British hopes revived. 'It must be remembered', Michael Wright had written earlier, 'that Nahas has a past record of friendship with us (he alone held Egypt steady at the time of Alamein).'[86] The British now put forward schemes for the defence of Egypt, again in Wright's words, 'on an ad hoc working basis'—in other words, separate and individually 'modest' agreements—that they hoped would remove the psychological bugbear of the 1936 treaty.[87] They would again postpone the question of the Sudan and deal with it separately. The Egyptians

[84] Minutes of a meeting of 12 Mar. 1948, Top Secret, FO 371/69193.

[85] Holmes to Acheson, Secret, 7 Jan. 1949, USSD 883.00/1-749 Box 6903; *Foreign Relations 1949*, VI, p. 187. Perhaps the ultimate British assessment of Nokrashi may be summed up in the words of James Robertson, the Civil Secretary of the Sudan administration, after the assassination: ' "Nokkers" was an honest if misguided patriot.' Robertson to Myall, 'Personal and Secret', 30 Dec. 1948, Robertson Papers 533/3/60.

[86] Minute by Wright, 29 Aug. 1947, FO 371/62984/J4331/G.

[87] See memorandum by Wright, Secret, 22 May 1950, FO 371/80382.

once more refused to divide the issues. The slogans of 'evacuation' and 'unity of the Nile valley' had so powerful a grip over the Egyptian nationalist psyche that it required a statesman of greater stature than Nahas Pasha to defuse the emotional resentment against the seven decades of British occupation.[88]

The positions of the British and Egyptians had polarized. Even if the two parties had been able to reach agreement about evacuation of Suez, about which the British, as will be seen, were increasingly disinclined, there was absolute disagreement over the Sudan. The Sudan administration had contributed to the hardening of attitude. The Foreign Office had contemplated giving the Egyptians a larger voice in the Sudan's administration. It would have been a major concession. British administrators in the Sudan adamantly and successfully opposed it. They had nothing but contempt for Egyptian influence. According to R. W. Bailey of the Egyptian Department: 'British officials in the Sudan, who are rightly proud of the way in which they have run the country, look upon Egypt as the nigger in the woodpile and as having been all the way through the disturbing influence.'[89] The reasons for deadlock over the Sudan were becoming much more clear-cut than they had been in 1946. The Ambassador in Cairo, Sir Ralph Stevenson, wrote in May 1950: 'The Sudanese have evolved very rapidly in the last three or four years and their feet are now firmly set on the path towards independence. They will allow nothing to deflect them.'[90] Within a few years Sudanese nationalism had developed to the extent that it now had to be considered in an African as well as an Egyptian context. In the view of R. H. G. Edmonds of the African Department:

The Sudan has progressed so far towards independence that, in the present state of African nationalism as a whole, it is impossible to imagine either Codominus imposing upon the Sudan a policy resisted by the majority of the Sudanese.[91]

Thus Bevin's statement that the Sudan was the 'stone wall' that could not be surmounted by the British and the Egyptians proved to be even more true in 1950–1 than it had in 1946. To anticipate the story that will be told in a later chapter, in October 1951 the Egyptians denounced the Treaty of 1936 and the Sudan Agreement

---

[88] For example C. D. Quilliam of *The Times* wrote confidentially in June 1949: 'Nahas [fears] the disintegration of the Wafd. The present state of the party is a striking example of the complete subordination of the general interest to the pride and megalomania of one man . . . Nahas.' Quilliam to Deakin, 2 June 1949, Quilliam Papers.

[89] Minute by Bailey, 6 Jan. 1949, FO 371/69195.

[90] Minute by Stevenson, 31 May 1950, FO 371/80382.

[91] Minute by Edmonds, 5 Dec. 1950, FO 371/80388.

of 1899. The rift was finally complete. The British refused to recognize the unilateral denunciation. The British government, in the racy words of John Marlowe, now assumed 'the position of a husband imposing his marital rights on a reluctant wife'.[92]

At least until the end of 1948 the deteriorating situation in Palestine had a direct bearing on the general British outlook on Egypt, and vice versa. According to Sir Ronald Campbell, in Egyptian eyes the pusillanimity of British troops in Palestine lowered British 'prestige' throughout the Middle East and in Egypt itself British restraint was viewed as British weakness:

> One kind of British prestige, i.e. that which rests on physical considerations, has been much lowered by events in Palestine where we do, as we must, bear with patience and without retaliation, the worst possible outrages and humiliations.
>
> This kind of prestige is also lowered by the position in Egypt where, circumscribed by the charter of U. N. O. and . . . by the principle of non-interference in the internal affairs of another country . . . we see ourselves the object of attack and unfriendly policy while being precluded from reacting in the way in which . . . Egyptians would expect us to react.[93]

On several occasions, as has been seen, the British did consider intervention in order to reassert the strength and prestige of the British Empire. They stopped short because of justified scepticism about the reliability of Nahas and the Wafd, on the one hand, and the danger of collaborating with Farouk on the other. 'I do not at all like the idea of our negotiating a hole-and-corner settlement with the King', Sir Orme Sargent wrote in October 1947. 'The trick might come off to the greater glorification of the King, but if it failed and if, for instance, the Wafd attacked it and stirred up public opinion against it, what would our position be as fellow-conspirators of the King?'[94]

The inclination of the official mind, especially as it found expression in the minutes of the Permanent Under-Secretary, was to let the Egyptians stew in their own juice, even at the risk of it bubbling into revolution. Sargent wrote in the summer of 1948, after the collapse of Egyptian forces during the Arab–Israeli war, that it would be best to go 'very slowly' on the matter of pressing the Egyptians for an agreement about Suez:

> We do not know yet how Egyptian policy is going to crystallize as a result of the [Egyptian] failure in Palestine and how the King's personal position is going to be affected. Meanwhile we must not give the impression of running after the King. It is by no means certain that it is in our interests to strengthen his position.[95]

[92] Marlowe, *Anglo-Egyptian Relations*, p. 370.
[93] Campbell to Wright, Top Secret, 9 Aug. 1947, FO 371/62980/J3810.
[94] Minute by Sargent, 29 Oct. 1947, FO 371/62988.
[95] Minute by Sargent, 31 July 1948, FO 371/69193/J5239.

Toward the end of the year Michael Wright made a comment in similar vein that serves to summarize British Egyptian policy and the Palestine question as well as the British answer to possible revolution in the Middle East:

> It has been evident for a long time past that until Egyptian and other Arab Nationalist leaders, and especially the Arab League, received an extremely severe jolt of some sort and were shaken out of their pretentious and arrogant frame of mind, matters in the Middle East would continue to go from bad to worse. They have now received such a jolt over Palestine. There is of course the grave risk that the effects of the jolt may prove too severe, and that economies or even régimes may crumble.
>
> Our own policy should not be to run after the Arabs, but to show them that we are still their friend—perhaps their only friend—and that hand in hand with us they can, if they will follow a sensible policy, achieve stability, make economic and social progress, and become partners in sensible defence arrangements.[96]

So far as Egypt was concerned, in Sargent's words, 'we are sitting pretty with the 1936 Treaty'.[97]

---

[96] Minute by Wright, 10 Dec. 1948, FO 371/69211.
[97] Minute by Sargent, 31 July 1948, FO 371/69193/J5239.

7

THE ITALIAN COLONIES AND BRITISH STRATEGIC RIGHTS IN CYRENAICA

THE controversy about British troop withdrawal from Egypt caused 'something like consternation' in the minds of high American officials.[1] That perplexity helps to throw into relief the clear-cut and persistent nature of British aims. There was general confusion of American thought about the future of the Middle East and the eastern Mediterranean, and, in particular, the fate of the Italian colonies. Sumner Welles, an attentive observer of British colonial affairs, commented publicly in June 1947 that American policy towards Libya, the most important of the territories at issue, could only be described as 'both timid and wavering'.[2] It was an accurate remark. The attitude of the United States vacillated between the idealism of self-determination in Libya and the more realistic urge to deny the Soviet Union access to northern Africa. Nevertheless there was a continuity in American thought. The former Italian colonies should be granted 'independence' as soon as they were prepared for it, and they should be guided to self-government by United Nations trusteeship. British policy also fluctuated but the goal remained always the same: strategic rights in Cyrenaica, or the eastern part of Libya, in order to safeguard the eastern Mediterranean.

The case of Libya reveals the classic themes of British imperialism recast in a postwar mould: the search for indigenous collaboration and the reconstruction of an administrative framework; the drain on British resources by the continued military occupation; and the attempt to gain the co-operation of the United States in order to secure British strategic rights. Although this chapter emphasizes the international dimension of the problem, it is vital to bear in mind the British efforts to harness Arab nationalism and to palliate the economic dilemmas of the Labour government. The interaction of the postwar crises contributed to the birth of the state of Libya in 1951 as the first 'international' dependency to achieve colonial independence—with the British at last securing the military rights they had sought since the end of the war.

[1] The phrase is Bevin's in a draft telegram of 27 Apr. 1946, FO 371/57176/U4539.
[2] *Washington Post*, 4 June 1947.

There were three ex-Italian colonies.[3] The principal territory was
Libya, which the British preferred to regard as two colonies, Tripolitania (including the Fezzan) in the west and Cyrenaica in the
east. Here to the British there was a great contrast. In the sparsely-
populated desert region of Cyrenaica they had secured the wartime
co-operation of the Senusi, while Italian and French influences
continued in the more populated and more economically developed
provinces in the west. The other two Italian colonies were Eritrea
and Somalia, both on the Red Sea bordering Ethiopia. They were
divided by the Somali territories of the British and the French, the
latter possessing the strategic rail entrance to Addis Ababa. In
addition to these colonies there should also be mentioned the
Ogaden area, or the south-eastern part of present-day Ethiopia south
of Italian Somaliland which Britain held on a wartime lease from the
Emperor. Italy had seized the three colonies before the First World
War and the Ogaden during the Italian–Ethiopian war. By 1939 there
was a substantial settler community in Libya. Fascist statistics are
notoriously unreliable, and, in the Libyan case for example, the prewar figures range from 30,000 to well over 100,000 (part of the
discrepancy depends on whether army personnel are included in the
estimate). Official British statistics, based on the 1946 military
census, established the Italian community in Tripolitania at 50,000
and, because of the civilian evacuation of 1942, a virtually non-
existent Italian population in Cyrenaica.[4] The Italian government
disputed British estimates, but in any case the territory in which
Britain staked a claim, Cyrenaica, had a negligible Italian population. The Arab population of Libya was estimated at over one
million. There was still a politically significant Jewish population
of over 30,000. In Eritrea, according to a War Office report of March

[3] For Libya see especially Majid Khadduri, *Modern Libya: A Study in Political Develop-
ment* (Baltimore, 1963); and the monumental work by the United Nations architect of
Libyan independence, Adrian Pelt, *Libyan Independence and the United Nations* (New
Haven, 1970). John Wright, *Libya* (New York, 1969) is also helpful. For Somalia see I. M.
Lewis, *The Modern History of Somaliland* (London, 1965); and Saadia Touval, *Somali
Nationalism* (Harvard University Press, 1963). The best work on Eritrea is by G. K. N.
Trevaskis, *Eritrea: A Colony in Transition 1941-52* (Oxford, 1960). For the Italian era see
Claudio G. Segrè, *Fourth Shore: The Italian Colonization of Libya* (Chicago, 1974); and
Robert L. Hess, *Italian Colonialism in Somalia* (Chicago, 1967). A full discussion of the
Italian dimension of the problem is beyond the scope of this chapter, but attention should
be called to one of the most important recent works on the subject, Renzo De Felice,
Ebrei in un Paese Arabo (Bologna, 1978). The essay by Benjamin Rivlin, *The United
Nations and the Italian Colonies* (New York, 1950) is still an essential guide to the
complexity of the problem at the United Nations. Philip C. Jessup, *The Birth of Nations*
(New York, 1974), chap. 6, is helpful in understanding the later stage of the controversy
in 1949-50.

[4] For the British population estimates see CP (46) 165, 18 Apr. 1946, CAB 129/9;
and minutes in FO 371/57173.

1946, there were 37,000 Italians and a mixed indigenous population of less than 800,000. After the war there were some 5,000 Italians left in ex-Italian Somaliland, but in that territory the paramount question was self-determination, or denial of it, to the Somali-speaking peoples there and in British and French Somalia as well as in the Ogaden area. The Somalis of northern Kenya seldom figured into British considerations of a 'Greater Somalia'. With that exception, a 'Greater Somalia' was conceived as a possible nation based on ethnic and linguistic frontiers and the principle of self-determination.

According to contemporary views in 1945-6, Libya might be ready for independence in approximately ten years, while Eritrea and Somaliland would remain indefinitely under European or Ethiopian control. In September 1945 the United States put forward the proposal that Libya should be administered under 'collective trusteeship'. There arose considerable confusion about what that phrase actually meant.[5] Did it mean the control of Libya by the major powers—the United States, Britain, the Soviet Union and, perhaps, France? Was Italy to be included? Or did it mean administration by the Trusteeship Council of the United Nations—or, the worst possibility in British eyes, the conglomeration of nations of the General Assembly? There were further perplexing questions. The Americans in 1946 stated that, if the United Nations refused to acknowledge a United States 'strategic trust' territory of Micronesia, then they would stay in the islands by right of conquest. Could not Britain make the same claim to the Italian colonies? If so would not South African (and also Australian) claims have also to be acknowledged? In January 1942 Anthony Eden as Foreign Secretary had pledged in the House of Commons that the Senusi would never again be subjected to Italian domination. Was there then not a moral issue involved? Ivor Thomas, Parliamentary Under-Secretary for the Colonies, asked similar questions in the secret deliberations of the Colonial Office in a way that sums up the complexity in finding the central issue:

What do we mainly want? Is it strategic rights in Cyrenaica? Or the exclusion of Russian influence from Africa? Or the friendship of the Arabs of Tripolitania and Cyrenaica? Or the restoration of good Anglo-Italian relations? Or the maintenance of the *Entente Cordiale* with France?[6]

Answering his own questions some time later, against the background of the Egyptian complaint against the British in the Security Council and the decision to withdraw from Palestine, Thomas

[5] See memorandum of 14 Sept. 1945, *Foreign Relations 1945*, II, pp. 179-81.
[6] Minute by Thomas, 24 July 1947, CO 537/2087.

wrote: 'Our policy must aim primarily at preserving military rights in Cyrenaica.'[7]

The priority of Cyrenaica defines the overriding aim of British policy, and it explains the coincidental and undesirable outcome, at least in Colonial Office eyes, of the collapse of the 'Greater Somalia' project. In the words of another Colonial Office official, British military facilities in Cyrenaica had to be maintained *'whatever the cost'*.[8] This extreme necessity is revealed by Ernest Bevin's willingness to reverse traditional British strategic priorities by yielding in the eastern part of the continent, in other words in Somalia, in order to gain concessions in the west, and at one stage by his willingness even to tolerate a Soviet presence in Tripolitania. The reasons for the British obsession with Cyrenaica will become clear by an examination of the documents that reveal the thoughts of Bevin, Attlee, Smuts, and others who shaped imperial strategy in highest councils of the Empire and Commonwealth.

The aims are clearer than the means by which the British achieved them. The British were in fact presiding over the birth of a state, though this was not obvious to many contemporary observers and sometimes not even to those directly involved. The historical process of the creation of the modern Libyan state within half-a-dozen years of the end of the war is an elusive theme in the British documents and even more so in the American. Fortunately for the historian, one of the foremost British anthropologists of the twentieth century provided firsthand explanation of the collaboration between the British and the Senusi that came to unexpectedly rapid fruition. It is one of the remarkable British short-term success stories of the postwar era.

In the same year that the United Nations resolved that Libya should be granted independence within two years, E. E. Evans-Pritchard published *The Sanusi of Cyrenaica* in 1949. He had served as a political officer in the British military administration of Cyrenaica. Part of the purpose of his book was to explain the historical development of the Cyrenaican nationalist movement. In the words of Michael Brett, who has translated the anthropological essence into the idiom of African history: 'The warfare of the Cyrenaicans against the Italians . . . appears [to be] the perfect example of the ability of a stateless society, that of the beduin, to generate the rudiments of a state in the face of external attack, and by the same token, of a primary resistance to colonial penetration which became a move-

[7] Minute by Thomas, 26 Sept. 1947, CO 537/2088.
[8] A. W. Galsworthy in a minute taking account of the views of the Chiefs of Staff, 24 Sept. 1947, CO 537/2088.

ment for independence.'⁹ Nationalism in Libya thus had roots in the colonial era rather than merely the shallow subsoil of postwar power politics.

Though Cyrenaican nationalism did not command prewar loyalty in Tripolitania or the Fezzan, after 1945 it generated a movement that extended over all of Libya and could gain common acceptance because of the Sayyid Idris, the spiritual and temporal head of the Senusi and later the first King of Libya. Idris had worked in both active and latent partnership with the British against the Italians since the time of the First World War. During his years of exile in Cairo in the interwar years he remained head of the nascent Cyrenaican nationalist movement. It was thus fortunate for the British that they could throw their support behind him in 1942 in the Parliamentary pledge to the Senusi against the common Italian enemy. Evans-Pritchard gave this sketch of Idris in 1949:

> Sayyid Idris did not return to Cyrenaica till the third British occupation of the country during the late war (1943), though he continued in Egypt to represent the forces of resistance. . . . At the time of his flight [in 1923 to Cairo in exile] he was 33 years of age. He gave the impression of being tall and rather portly, very unlike the slight and delicate figure he presents to-day.
> Nurtured, as were all the Sanusi family, in piety and learning in oasis retreats and accustomed to a refined and sedentary life, he has never been a man of action. . . . That he is vacillating and evasive cannot be denied, and though these characteristics may sometimes have been a wise response of the weak negotiating with the strong . . . they seem to be weaknesses to which he is temperamentally prone and to have become an aversion to directness in either thought or action . . . he is intelligent, religious, and gifted with a profound moral sense and political intuition. He is firm in decisions once he has taken them and keeps his promises.¹⁰

In 1946 the British elevated Idris to the status of 'Amir' (critics quickly pointed out Abdullah's progression from 'Amir' to 'King' in the same year). They awarded him official recognition of his leadership 'of the anti-Italian resistance movement . . . during the war'. According to J. S. Bennett of the Colonial Office the leadership of Idris of the nationalist movement in Libya 'has the sympathy of the Arab League' and, generally, the British believed that a trusteeship regime 'with independence after a short period' would be agreeable to the Arab states.¹¹

For the sake of clarity it is useful to set out in schematic form the

⁹ Michael Brett, 'The U. N. and Libya', *Journal of African History*, XIII, 1 (1972), pp. 168–70.

¹⁰ E. E. Evans-Pritchard, *The Sanusi of Cyrenaica* (Oxford, 1949), pp. 155–6. See Pelt, *Libyan Independence*, p. 6 n. 3 for the importance of the book in the minds of those who established the Libyan state.

¹¹ Minute by Bennett, 25 Apr. 1946, CO 537/1474.

optimal British and American objectives at the outset of the controversy. Though tactics changed, there did exist a certain coherence, especially on the British side.

British objectives:

 (a) Cyrenaica placed under international trusteeship with Britain as the administering authority. The security of essential British military facilities.

 (b) Tripolitania and the Fezzan placed under international trusteeship, possibly with Italy as the administering authority in the former and France in the latter, but with the Sayyid Idris acknowledged as the supreme ruler.

 (c) The creation of a 'Greater Somalia' composed of Italian and British Somalilands and the Ogaden area.

 (d) The splitting up of Eritrea between Ethiopia and the Sudan.[12]

American objectives:

 (a) Libya placed under the 'collective trusteeship' of the United Nations and granted independence in ten years. Responsibility would rest with an administrator appointed by the Trusteeship Council and advised by representatives from the United States, the Soviet Union, Britain, France, and Italy.

 (b) Similar provisions for Eritrea under international trusteeship but with a territorial concession to Ethiopia for access to the Red Sea.

 (c) Somaliland placed under international trusteeship but with no fixed date for independence.[13]

In the autumn of 1945 the British had been prepared to modify their proposals and to support the American plan in its essential form, provided they secured strategic rights in Cyrenaica. The situation became transformed however when the Russians on the 14th of September demanded trusteeship over Tripolitania.

It is important to catch the tone of the British response to the danger of Russian expansion in order to comprehend the temper of the time in which the discussions about the Italian colonies took

[12] See e.g. minute by J. G. Ward, 6 Feb. 1946, FO 371/57170; F. O. memorandum, 21 Feb. 1946, FO 371/57171; memorandum by Bevin, CP (46) 165, 18 Apr. 1946 CAB 129/9, and minutes in FO 371/57176.

[13] See memorandum of 14 Sept. 1945, *Foreign Relations 1945*, II, pp. 179–81. There is a good indication of the initial British response to the controversy in the diary entry by Alexander Cadogan: 'Cabinet . . . decided, wisely, that [the] ridiculous American plan of a collective trusteeship was better than any *Soviet* trusteeship.' Cadogan Diary, 15 Sept. 1945.

place. Bevin and his colleagues in the Cabinet—notably G. H. Hall (Colonial Secretary), A. V. Alexander (First Lord of the Admiralty), and Hugh Dalton (Chancellor of the Exchequer)—viewed the possibility of Russia in Africa with utmost alarm. Bevin thought that the Russians wanted a part of Libya only as a stepping-stone to the Congo. 'E. B. is convinced', Dalton wrote in his diary in October 1945, 'that what the Russians really wanted was Uranium.' In retrospect it seems clear that the Russians put forward their African claim to a large extent as bargaining power, but the British in 1945-6 looked upon it as a grave omen. Dalton described the motives of the Soviet Foreign Minister:

He [V. M. Molotov] had gone on to say that Russia wanted a Colony somewhere in Africa, that they considered they had earned the right to one of the Italian Colonies, since ten Italian Divisions had fought against them and since they had had great success in civilizing backward nations within the U. S. S. R.

Dalton further explained Molotov's ulterior reason for an interest in Africa:

'But' M went on 'if you won't give us one of the Italian Colonies, we should be quite content to have the Belgian Congo.' This, of course, is where all the radioactive stuff is mined. The Russians, no doubt with their terrible inclination to suspicion, believe that Britain and America have cornered the material for the Atom Bomb and are preparing to use it against the U. S. S. R.[14]

With such cataclysmic thoughts in mind, the British pondered the future of the Italian colonies.

The Logic of Imperial Defence

During the winter and spring of 1946 British statesmen discussed the issue of the Italian colonies as a question that might determine the future shape of the Empire and Commonwealth. The same theme of Imperial lines of communication in Africa preoccupied Dominion Prime Ministers, members of the Cabinet, and permanent officials as it had twenty-five years earlier in the aftermath of the First World War. Then as in 1946 these issues were debated in broadest context by the representatives of the white Dominions who, with the exception

---

[14] Dalton Diary, 5 Oct. 1945; cf. Hugh Dalton, *High Tide and After: Memoirs 1945-1960* (London, 1962), pp. 56-7. The idea was also discussed by high American officials. Byrnes, at a meeting with the Secretaries of War and Navy, 'remarked that in his opinion the principal reason Russia wants Libya has to do with uranium. He pointed to the map how a Soviet base in Libya would facilitate their access right down to the Belgian Congo.' (Minutes of meeting of 16 Oct. 1945, *Foreign Relations 1945*, II, p. 60.) This was one of the few occasions on which Byrnes demonstrated any interest at all in the Italian colonies. See Robert L. Messer, *The End of an Alliance* (Chapel Hill, NC, 1982), pp. 139-40.

of the Canadian, viewed the question of the eastern Mediterranean as directly affecting the security of their countries. General Smuts brought to bear his firsthand experience in the shaping of the post-First World War settlement. His outlook serves as a good point of departure from which to examine the ramifications of the controversy as viewed by Attlee and of course Bevin as he prepared for his confrontation with the Russians.

Looking at the British position as a world power, Smuts viewed the crisis in the Mediterranean as the most severe test facing the Commonwealth as a whole. He hoped that the Empire–Commonwealth would hold the balance between Russia and the United States. He believed that a strategic base in Cyrenaica capable of delivering atomic bombs would forestall Russian aggression or American retaliation and would help to preserve the peace of the world. He watched with dismay the erosion of Anglo-Egyptian goodwill and the consequent threat to the Canal. He viewed Russian expansion into the Mediterranean with gravest apprehension. The behaviour of the Soviet Union in the half-year following the end of the war alarmed him. As the Chiefs of Staff recorded Smuts's anxiety, 'mistrust of Russian intentions is the dominating factor in his mind'.[15] He believed that the British would have to be 'on our guard as regards any arrangements which may lead to a situation where our vital communications are virtually at the disposal of the Soviet Union'. He emphasized the ominous consequences of Russian expansion:

> It is necessary only to point to Balkan developments, to Russia's attitude in Iran, her attitude towards Turkey and indications of her policy towards Arab States. With the Balkan States as virtual Soviet satellites she will have the free use of the Adriatic and soon she will also acquire the free use of the Straits. Across a weakened and dependent Iran she may be looking towards the Persian Gulf with all its oil and other values.[16]

In Smuts's warnings to the British government in early 1946 can thus be found some of the early currents of the cold war. He stated them repeatedly in regard to the Italian colonies.

He connected the future of Italy's former possessions with large geopolitical problems:

> Our routes through the Mediterranean towards the Indian Ocean are vital to Commonwealth communications and to the status of Great Britain as a great power and may be seriously affected by the contemplated arrangements for

---

[15] Memorandum by Chiefs of Staff Committee, 13 Feb. 1946, COS (46) 43, CAB 80/99; minutes in FO 371/57173.

[16] Smuts to High Commissioner, London, 26 Jan. 1946, DO 116/90/27; minutes in FO 371/57171; see also Smuts's other letters and telegrams in the same files and in FO 371/57173; and minutes in FO 371/57176.

the disposal of the Italian Colonies. An international trusteeship administration in which Russia would claim a major share might place her in a commanding position in the Mediterranean.[17]

Nor should the Soviet Union be allowed into the Red Sea. In Smuts's view it would be 'reckless folly' to allow the Russians near a British colony or territory under British control. He contrasted the positions of the United States in the Pacific and Britain in the Mediterranean:

> America will hold on to necessary territory conquered by her as long as it is in her interest. Why should we make free of the Italian Colonies conquered by us at fearful risk and cost? Russia has surrendered nothing. If Tripolitania is lost we must hold on to Cyrenaica at all costs, at least for the present. We must above all play for time and delay the distribution of these Colonies until we see more of the shape of the future.[18]

Smuts thus urged tactics of delay in order to thwart Russian advance and to safeguard British lines of communication.

He judged the resuscitation of Italy to be vital to the well-being of the Empire and Commonwealth and to European peace. 'Italy is necessary to Western Europe', Smuts wrote, 'and we must help to restore her to the comity and community of the west.' Italy belonged to western civilization. The British Commonwealth had no quarrel with the Italian people. In that sense the war against Italy had been a tragic mistake, fought against a tyrant rather than against the Italian nation. Smuts believed that Britain should take the lead in bringing Italy back into the western community, perhaps by giving back one of her colonies.

> Restore her honour and self-respect and make her our friend, whom we may much need in the future. . . . A fine gesture would be to restore to Italy one or two of the African Colonies as trusteeships while depriving her of their sovereignty. Tripolitania is the one she would most covet and whose trusteeship would help to restore her self-respect.[19]

With Italy as the trusteeship power in Tripolitania, Britain would be in a better position to claim Cyrenaica, the key point, in Smuts's view, for the defence of the Mediterranean. And by taking a generous attitude towards Italy, President Truman, who was sensitive to the response of the Italian-American community in the United States, would be more inclined to co-operate with the British. There was in fact no real reason for the United States not to take a sympathetic attitude. 'Britain is most helpful to the United States of America over her interests in the Pacific and Atlantic', Smuts concluded, 'and there should be the same generous response to Britain from the United States of America.'

[17] Ibid.   [18] Ibid.   [19] Ibid.

As Smuts developed his argument that Russia as a trusteeship power would be a 'Trojan horse' in the British defence system, he drew vigorous support from the Chiefs of Staff. To the military mind the problem could be summed up by stating that British paramountcy in the Mediterranean should be maintained at any cost. To the Chiefs of Staff, as to Smuts, the most urgent requirement was the acquisition of strategic rights in Cyrenaica. The British thus would be able to dominate the eastern Mediterranean as well as the western desert and thus would be able to prevent any threat to Egypt such as had occurred in 1942. Italy, though in military eyes 'never likely to be a reliable ally', should be given Tripolitania as a trust territory in order to keep her on friendly terms. The Chiefs of Staff were content with Smuts's suggestion that the Italian colonies on the Red Sea should be held under British or Italian trusteeship—or possibly even American trusteeship in order to strengthen the defence commitment of the United States. 'Under no circumstances', the Chiefs of Staff emphasized, 'would sole Russian trusteeship of the Italian colonies be acceptable.'[20]

The principal sceptic of the strategic view propounded by Smuts and the Chiefs of Staff was the Prime Minister himself. Attlee also held the office of Minister of Defence. He wrote in March 1946, as has been emphasized in the introductory chapter, that it did not seem 'self-evident' to him that the Mediterranean should be held for reasons of strategic security. Indeed it could well prove impossible for Britain to defend the Mediterranean. The British Empire, he wrote, had been built up during the era of sea power. They had now entered an epoch in which air and sea power were interlinked. Attlee, for one, did not comprehend how a Mediterranean fleet could be defended from attack by a powerful land-based enemy controlling for example Spain, or Italy, or the Balkans, or the Levant. It also appeared clear to Attlee that Britain could not rely on the permanent friendship of Egypt—as Bevin painfully learned during the course of the year. And if the classic 'lines of communication' argument boiled down to the defence of India, who could predict whether India would remain in the Commonwealth? If not, was it self-evident that India should be defended?

Attlee also repeatedly underlined another point. It is especially important not only in regard to his inclination to take a 'Little England' stand but also in regard to the economic constraints of the Labour government. The Italian colonies were *deficit areas*. Britain could by no means afford further territorial responsibilities, especially

[20] Memorandum by Chiefs of Staff Committee, 13 Feb. 1946, COS (46) 43, CAB 80/99; minutes in FO 371/57173.

in areas such as Somaliland which from the beginning had been 'a dead loss'. Attlee urged his colleagues not to make costly military and administrative commitments 'for sentimental reasons based on the past'.[21]

The Prime Minister's permanent officials greeted his analysis of the decline of British power with little enthusiasm. A sense of reality and not sentimentality motivated the Colonial Office to dissent. In general the Colonial Office agreed with General Smuts and the Chiefs of Staff; but there was an important difference in outlook. The Colonial Office did not disagree about the *objective*—the exclusion of Russia from northern Africa and the Red Sea area—but the *method*. Smuts believed that 'delaying tactics' or obstruction at the United Nations would benefit the British in Africa in the same way the Russians had profited in eastern Europe and Germany through obstinacy and endless wrangles with the western powers. 'Let us', Smuts urged, 'like Russia in Iran, play for time and not make concessions.'[22] The Colonial Office on the other hand worked towards an immediate settlement, above all because of Somaliland. Colonial Office officials wanted to alleviate the problems of this 'deficit area' (they used the same phrase as Attlee) and at the same time they felt a sense of responsibility. They believed that the only chance of making the territory viable would be to create a 'Greater Somalia' ('United Somalia' was a synonymous phrase) composed of British and Italian Somaliland and the Ogaden area of Ethiopia inhabited by Somali people. The British administered the Ogaden under a wartime agreement with the Emperor due to expire in March 1947—hence the need for urgency and not delay. The only way the Emperor could be persuaded to yield the Ogaden region would be to offer him a slice of Eritrea, which was another reason for immediate action. The problems were interlocked.

In Libya the Colonial Office had only an indirect concern, though it was an important one. Colonial Office officials feared that the restoration of Italian rule in Tripolitania, even under the supervision of the United Nations, would provoke the Senusi into armed resistance. The British would find themselves embroiled in a colonial war. In consequence there would be a worsening of Britain's position throughout the Middle East. More specifically from the Colonial Office's point of view, an Italian reoccupation of Tripolitania would have indirect and adverse repercussions in Palestine.[23]

[21] Memorandum by Attlee, 2 Mar. 1946, Defence Committee DO (46) 27, CAB 131/2; minutes in FO 371/57173.
[22] Smuts to High Commissioner, London, 16 Apr. 1946, copy in FO 371/57176.
[23] See minutes in CO 537/1468-74.

The Mediterranean controversy also stirred up far-reaching discussions in the Foreign Office. The debate centred on the future of the British Empire itself. If the Prime Minister's line of reasoning were followed, might the British not face a line of retreat extending from the Canal through Palestine, Cyprus, and Malta, to Gibraltar? Where would the final line be drawn? If the Mediterranean were to become 'a second Black Sea' (a recurrent phrase) and Italy were to fall under Soviet influence, would not France be in jeopardy? Oliver Harvey (Assistant Under-Secretary) commented:

> If we went out, the Russians would go in and the Mediterranean would become a second Black Sea sealed at either end. Russian influence would not stop at Europe, it would of course spread into Africa, with all the political, economic and strategic consequences involved. These are far weightier reasons than the route to India argument for our making heavy sacrifices to hold on in the Mediterranean.[24]

Sir Orme Sargent also emphatically endorsed the position of General Smuts:

> Our position as a World Power and therefore as a Great Power depends surely on our maintaining our position in the Mediterranean, and this not for strategic reasons but on political grounds. In other words, the Mediterranean is of vital importance to us not so much because it is our direct link with the East but because if we abandon it in present circumstances the Russians will take our place there, with incalculable results not only on the Middle East but also on Italy, France, Spain, and Africa.[25]

Only by the tenacious entrenchment of British forces in northern Africa—specifically in Cyrenaica—could western decline be halted.

In April 1946 the Prime Ministers of the Commonwealth met in London. On Smuts's arrival on the 28th of April they discussed the Italian colonies. Bevin took a line much closer to Smuts's than Attlee's. He linked the question of the Italian colonies with the larger issue of 'Imperial Defence'. His outlook can be described as almost Churchillian. He wrote for the benefit of the Dominion Prime Ministers: 'In my view it is essential that we should maintain our position in the Mediterranean and Red Sea. It is not only a question of preserving this life-line in time of war, but also the vital importance of acting in peace-time on the soft under-belly of Europe from the Mediterranean.'[26] At the meeting itself Bevin implicitly supported Smuts but attempted to give the impression of having an open mind. He knew that the Dominion Prime Ministers would have conflicting

---

[24] Minute by Harvey, 11 Mar. 1946, FO 371/57173.
[25] Minute by Sargent, 12 Mar. 1946, FO 371/57173.
[26] Memorandum by Bevin, 18 Apr. 1946, CP (46) 165, CAB 129/9; minutes in FO 371/57178.

views. Smuts expressed his ideas at length, emphasizing the need to rejuvenate Italy and the necessity of keeping Russia out of Africa. He put forward his solution of delaying tactics. 'Let us play for time', he urged his colleagues.

The Australian Prime Minister, Ben Chifley, did not agree. He argued that the colonies should be administered as trusteeship territories under the administration of a single colonial power—the United Kingdom, or, in the case of Somaliland, perhaps South Africa. Walter Nash of New Zealand believed that the Russians were bluffing. They claimed Tripolitania, he thought, in order to strengthen possible demands for a base elsewhere, perhaps in the Dodecanese. 'If the British Commonwealth could not obtain the trusteeship of Libya', Nash said, 'it might be given to the United States.'[27] Bevin no doubt listened to these proposals with mixed emotions. Though he did not disfavour an American base on the Red Sea, his primary objective remained a British fortress in Cyrenaica. But if the British gained Cyrenaica as a trust territory, it would give the Russians better reason to claim Tripolitania. There was one point of consensus. All of the Dominion Prime Ministers entirely agreed that Russia should be excluded from Africa whatever the cost. Attlee, the only one active in the discussion who sympathized with the 'Little England' tradition, was entirely consistent. Whenever the question of 'cost' arose he reiterated that the Italian colonies were 'deficit areas'.[28]

The Council of Foreign Ministers discussed the Italian colonies in Paris at the same time that the Dominion Prime Ministers vented their views in London. Bevin, coming and going, to and from London, with Egypt and Palestine on his mind as well as the Italian colonies, was an intensely busy Foreign Secretary (described in Dalton's diary as often being on the verge of collapse). He collided head-on with Molotov, who now proposed that the Soviet Union should become along with *Italy* the co-trustee of Tripolitania. Since both Britain and the United States feared a communist take-over in Italy, the suggestion did not fall on favourable ears. Bevin listened incredulously, according to his own account, as Molotov impugned the motives of the British Empire. It seemed quite clear, Molotov said, that Britain had an appetite for all of the Italian colonies and even more voraciously wished to have a piece of Ethiopia (a reference to the Ogaden region). Molotov thought that 'it would be difficult for England to digest these additional colonies'. He chided Bevin for

[27] Cabinet Office transcript of Dominion Prime Ministers Meeting, 28 Apr. 1948, copy in FO 371/57178.

[28] Ibid.

putting forward 'selfish' proposals. Bevin responded 'with some heat', in the watered-down language of the official transcript. He said that those words sounded very strange coming from someone whose country covered one-seventh of the earth's surface. When Molotov replied that all Soviet territory had been legally acquired, Bevin spoke of Poland and denounced the Russians for 'sitting' on the Kurile islands. Perhaps it had been a mistake, he said in full-blooded indignation, for Britain not to have concluded secret treaties in the Russian fashion to dispose of the Italian colonies.[29]

To counter the Russian proposal for joint trusteeship with Italy, Bevin now recommended immediate independence for Libya. He moved in advance of official thought in London. His advisers feared that Britain would be denounced for creating another Arab puppet. But there was an obvious logic to his scheme. It fitted into his general Arab policy and might, he thought, help to win over the Egyptians (which it did not). A treaty with an independent Libya might secure strategic rights in Cyrenaica. Bevin clearly did not believe that the Russians would swallow this classic British solution —hence his astonishment when, on the 10th of May 1946, the Russians yielded their claim to Tripolitania. Molotov did so by backing the motion of the French Foreign Minister that all of the colonies should be placed under Italian trusteeship. Bevin quickly put in a claim for Cyrenaica under British trusteeship.

Bevin telegraphed to Attlee (recounting a conversation that does not appear in the American records):

> Molotov took us all by surprise by definitely dropping his claim to be in the African continent and backing the French proposal that all the Italian colonies should be returned to Italy.
> Byrnes immediately showed signs of weakening and it was at once obvious to me that, from the moment that Russia was ready to withdraw her claim to be in Africa, American interest in collective trusteeship would drop to zero. . . .
> With the Egyptian situation and Palestine in my mind I felt it imperative that I should at once spring a claim for Cyrenaica.[30]

Bevin suspected that Byrnes might stop supporting him and throw his hand in with the French and the Russians—for a curious and statistically quite inaccurate reason: Bevin believed that Byrnes had 'an eye on the seven million Italian votes in New York'.[31]

---

[29] Records of the April–May meetings of the Council of Foreign Ministers in FO 371/57177–9; cf. *Foreign Relations 1946*, II, e.g. the meeting of 2 May, pp. 221–2.

[30] Bevin to Attlee, 11 May 1946, FO 371/57179/U5196. Oliver Harvey in his diary described Bevin's presentation of the British case as 'a really masterly performance. . . . Mr. Bevin [was] very quiet and spoke in simple unhurried language without a note, a really impressive performance', 29 Apr. 1946, Harvey Diaries Add. MSS 56400.

[31] A Foreign Office official had commented a few days earlier, in a remark that sums up

American Responses to the Controversy

Bevin and Molotov to Jimmy Byrnes must have resembled two blind giants at odds with each other in the same room. Neither could see the other, but of course even two blind men can damage each other, not to mention the room. Byrnes saw himself as a statesman in the Wilsonian tradition who attempted to keep the peace between two such antagonists. He once remarked that the President in 1919 had tried to arrive at fair settlements equitable to both small and large powers, colonial subjects and Europeans alike. He added that Wilson had been thwarted because of American domestic politics—a remark that must have reminded Bevin that American 'public opinion' had constantly to be taken into account. Like Bevin, Byrnes aimed to keep the Russians out of Africa. But Bevin accurately observed that once Molotov dropped the Russian claim to Tripolitania, Byrnes began to waver. The more Russian attention focused on Italy, the less Byrnes gave support to the British in Cyrenaica. Nevertheless Byrnes was sensitive to the charge of 'appeasing' the Russians. On the question of the Italian colonies he stood firm. He persistently held that they should be placed under the direct supervision of the United Nations and that the Trusteeship Council should be charged with finding 'neutral' administrators. He believed that Libya should be prepared for independence within ten years. He opposed the return of the Italians, who he believed would cause 'disorder and violence'.[32] He gradually modified his position in the hope of reaching agreement with the other parties. Instead of ten years he proposed a 'review' after that time to see whether the Libyans were ready for independence. When the Communist movement in Italy proved to be less strong than had been anticipated, he began to listen more sympathetically to the idea of Italian trusteeship. When the Council of Foreign Ministers reached deadlock in May 1946, Byrnes with considerable exasperation stated that he would throw the entire matter 'open to the public so that world opinion can see just what the situation is and just where stumbling blocks lie'.[33]

The Mediterranean controversy was in fact already public knowledge. In mid-May 1946 Walter Lippmann attempted to put the

the British official estimate of the American Secretary of State: 'One begins to fear for Mr Byrnes as soon as Molotov begins to coo: he can always be caught by the Russians.' Minute by J. G. Ward, 30 Apr. 1946, FO 371/57177/U4652. Alexander Cadogan had written earlier in his diary: 'Byrnes is a light weight, an erratic amateur and, I am afraid a slippery customer.' Cadogan Diary, 25 Nov. 1945.

[32] Byrnes's views are amply documented in *Foreign Relations 1946*, II, e.g. pp. 155-6 and pp. 558-9.

[33] Ibid., p. 204.

problem of the Italian colonies in broadest geopolitical perspective. In doing so he managed to define the essence of the British problem. The Russians, he wrote, aimed at no less than a breakup of the British Empire. They hoped first of all to dominate the eastern Mediterranean. 'This would disrupt the British Empire by separating Great Britain from the Middle East, from Africa, and from South Asia.' The Russians further looked westward, perhaps towards Trieste, perhaps towards northern Africa. 'This is a blatantly crude plan to settle the Mediterranean problem by taking possession of the Mediterranean.'[34] The Soviet Union in short hoped to transform the Mediterranean from a British lake into a Russian lake. They could not do so, Lippmann believed, without bringing about another world war. But they might be tempted. With France weakened and Italy defeated, Britain's power rested on fragile foundations. The British were over-extended—not only in the Mediterranean but also in adjacent areas such as the Red Sea. And in Somalia the British appeared to be expanding their military position rather than consolidating it.

The Death of the 'Greater Somalia' Project

As far as the British Chiefs of Staff were concerned, Italian Somaliland was expendable provided it could be neutralized. The distinctions between a Somaliland dominated by the Italians, the British, the Ethiopians, or even the Somalis themselves did not escape the military mind, but in general the principal preoccupation was the possibility of a colonial war that might be precipitated by the return of the Italians. That danger of course was also perceived by officials of the Colonial Office and Foreign Office, all of whom shared a common assumption. It was stated clearly in retrospect by the Chief Civil Affairs officer, Major-General D. C. Cumming: 'no one in his right mind could suppose that we should want to add yet another area of light sandy soil to the Empire's already long list of liabilities'. The scheme for a 'Greater Somalia', in Cumming's words, 'was quite genuinely conceived in a spirit of helpfulness to the Somali peoples'.[35] When Bevin proposed it to his colleagues in the Council of Foreign Ministers, however, he was greeted with scepticism. What seemed to him to be a matter of 'common sense' and the chance for a better

---

[34] *Washington Post*, 16 May 1946.

[35] D. C. Cumming, 'British Stewardship of the Italian Colonies', *International Affairs*, XXIX, 1 (Jan. 1953). Somalia as a financial liability was a recurrent theme in official minutes. 'We do not want to collect deserts any more than Mussolini', Robert Howe wrote in July 1946. The minutes in the Ethiopian files are especially revealing on the question of the Ogaden and 'Greater Somalia'. See e.g. minute by Howe, 10 July 1946, FO 371/53467.

economic life for the Somalis appeared to Molotov, as it did even to Byrnes, to be the military expansion of the British Empire. It is important to note the exchange between Bevin and Molotov on the subject of Somaliland in May 1946 because it foredoomed the project of a 'Greater Somalia' from the beginning, despite the perseverance of the Colonial Office.

> Mr. Bevin . . . said that Great Britain had set a good example in asking for no new territory. He had merely wished to help the natives in that area, which in the past had been split up between British and Italian Somaliland. In fact, if he could be given credit for an honest motive, it would seem that he was merely trying to remedy some Nineteenth Century wrongs. . . . He concluded with the statement that Nineteenth Century imperialism was dead in England, which was no longer an expansionist country.[36]

Bevin made it clear that he wished to see Italian Somaliland 'demilitarized', but his remarks drew a thunderous rebuke:

> M. Molotov said [that] . . . when M. Bevin said that Nineteenth Century imperialism was dead, he forgot that there were Twentieth Century imperialist tendencies in the world, including in Great Britain. . . . It is sufficient to say that England has troops and military bases in Greece, Denmark, Egypt, Iraq, Indonesia and elsewhere. The Soviet Union has no bases beyond its borders, and this shows the difference between expansion and security.[37]

There was no way that the British could convince the world at large, especially the Russians, of the purity of British motives in Somalia. Molotov's words stultified further discussion. It seemed clear that the more the British insisted on 'Greater Somalia' the less they would get in Libya. Bevin decided, at least tentatively, to 'kill' the scheme.[38] Much to the dismay of the Colonial Office, he withdrew his proposal for a 'Greater Somalia' on the 20th of June 1946.[39]

The Colonial Office had anticipated criticism of 'Greater Somalia' and did not accept the Foreign Secretary's retreat as a final outcome.[40] Andrew Cohen (the head of the East African Department) and J. S. Bennett (head of the International Relations Department) together elaborated the philosophical as well as the concrete and local reasons why the British should press ahead with the project despite Russian intransigence. They had the support of Creech Jones, who from October 1946 could argue in favour of the project in the

---

[36] *Foreign Relations 1946*, II, pp. 254–5.
[37] Ibid., p. 255.
[38] Bevin to F. O., 21 June 1945, FO 371/57182/U6039.
[39] See *Foreign Relations 1946*, II, p. 558.
[40] See CP (46) 243, 22 June 1946, CAB 129/10; minutes in FO 371/57182; and CO 537/1468 ff. After considering the C. O.'s protest, the Cabinet decided that the question of a 'United Somalia' should be 'postponed and not abandoned'. CM 61 (46), 24 June 1946, CAB 128/5.

Cabinet.[41] The Somali question in fact did not die, in part because of
the possibility of oil in Italian Somaliland which the British became
aware of as a realistic prospect only after Bevin's encounter with
Molotov. The question of oil served to refuel the Foreign Office's
interest in Somali trusteeship.[42]

Cohen and Bennett countered the accusation of British 'land
hunger' by putting forward rational arguments about the irration-
ality of Somali boundaries. Italian Somaliland, like Eritrea, was an
'artificial creation', the by-product of the scramble for Africa half a
century earlier. The Europeans who partitioned Africa had arbitrarily
split up the Somali peoples into three European colonies while still
others lived in southern Ethiopia (the heartland of the Somali
nationalist movement) and northern Kenya (which Cohen tended to
leave out of the discussions because the region at that time was
peaceful and the problem already sufficiently complicated). Without
any hope at all of bringing in the French, Cohen and Bennett
believed that the Ethiopians could be persuaded to yield the Ogaden
in return for support for the Ethiopian claim to Eritrea. Acquisition
of the Ogaden had long preoccupied the East African Department
because without it the Somalis in British territory were cut off from
grazing lands thought to be vital to their existence. For those reasons
Cohen and Bennett were prepared to indulge in a pastime highly
repugnant to them—in Bennett's phrase, the 'horse-trading' of
African colonies.[43] They wanted 'to rectify the mistakes of the
nineteenth century'. To them the *only* (their emphasis) solution to
the Somali problem was the unification of the Somali peoples. To
effect this they were prepared to take extreme (in Bennett's
emphatic word, *radical*) measures—collective trusteeship.

The Colonial Office fell back on the solution of joint trusteeship
merely because international circumstances would not permit the
establishment of a British regime. An international solution would

---

[41] Creech Jones had noted after the C. O. learned of Bevin's proposal in May to the
Council of Foreign Ministers to create a 'Greater Somalia' under British trusteeship: 'I
should imagine that a British mandate over a United Somalia will strengthen the demand of
the Russians for one themselves. It may also involve us in criticism because obviously the
Ogaden should be included & it looks superficially as if Britain is benefiting by taking
a part of Ethiopia. But it involves us in a heavy liability. We can only wait.' Minute of 3 May
1946, CO 537/1468.

[42] See e.g. minutes in CO 537/1472 and 2084; and FO 371/53467.

[43] Minute by Bennett, 19 July 1946, CO 537/1472. As an example of their joint views
see the Cabinet paper prepared by them for the Colonial Secretary, CP (46) 243, 22 June
1946, CAB 129/10. Bennett had noted after the Bevin–Molotov exchange about the nature
of twentieth-century imperialism: 'There is a lot of paper being generated now at New York
about human rights. Here is a practical test case [Somalia], worth any amount of paper.
And it is being dealt with entirely in terms of power-politics.' (Minute of 30 May 1946,
CO 537/1474).

at least have had the advantage of alleviating the financial burden, which was a major consideration in view of a 'deficit area'. The evolution of Colonial Office thought went through three distinct phases: the consideration of administration by the United Nations, which was quickly rejected because of the danger of Russian participation; study of a prospective 'federal' administration of the Ogaden, Italian Somaliland, and British Somaliland under international trusteeship; and, finally, the Colonial Office's reluctant conclusion that the Italians should be allowed to administer the former Italian colony as a trusteeship territory and that the Ogaden should revert to Ethiopia. The guiding hand was Andrew Cohen's. It is illuminating to examine the flow of his ideas because his analysis encompassed the international, colonial, and economic dimensions of the problem, and because he anticipated the thrust of Somali nationalism in relation to, in his phrase, 'advanced African opinion and negro world opinion'.[44]

Cohen above all did not want to repeat the tragedy of the era of the partition of Africa. Here is the way in which he viewed the problem in historical perspective:

We ought, if we can, to avoid making the same mistakes which were made after the last war, when slices of territory were handed to European powers as part of the squaring up of accounts between these powers with little regard for the interests of the inhabitants. The first incident in the struggle between Italy and Ethiopia was the clash at Walwal in 1934, which arose directly out of the most unsatisfactory frontier arrangements settled by diplomats fifty years ago without regard for the realities of North East Africa.

It would be a tragic conclusion of all the events since 1934 if we simply reverted to the status quo in this area, the Somalis being divided between ourselves, Ethiopia and Italy, with no hope of being built up ultimately into a nation of their own. Such a conclusion would be utterly contrary to all the principles of Colonial progress to which we and other nations are committed to the hilt.[45]

To Cohen far and away the most satisfactory solution to the problem of Somalia would be a British trusteeship regime that would prepare the Somalis for independence; but he knew that such a solution would never be accepted by the United Nations and in any case he thought it highly unlikely that the British Treasury would acquiesce in the enlargement of a 'deficit area' which would further drain British resources. He therefore studied the possibility of 'collective' trusteeship by various powers of the United Nations (including those of

---

[44] 'I do not want to give too much weight to the latter consideration, but I suggest that it is one which we in the Colonial Office ought to take seriously.' Minute by Cohen, 20 Mar. 1947, CO 537/2081.

[45] Ibid.

Scandinavia), but he became more sceptical of its practicality the more he observed the politics of the Trusteeship Council. 'I fear that until the United Nations has made considerably more progress', he wrote in March 1947, 'such an arrangement would merely lead to friction and would be contrary to the interests of the inhabitants.'[46]

Unless the British and the Americans came up with a workable alternative, Italian Somaliland would revert to Italy. It was not a prospect, Cohen wrote, to be regarded 'with any equanimity'. After long and intense thought he endorsed the idea of 'joint British, Italian and Ethiopian Trusteeship' over a united Somalia:

> This would have the advantage of providing for the ultimate independence of the whole area. In the immediate future it would solve, without territorial adjustments, the vital problem of the grazing areas. It would not involve us in appreciable additional financial commitments over and above what we must in any case spend on British Somaliland. It would be acceptable strategically. It would meet Italian aspirations and would indicate our willingness to co-operate with the Italian Government on a friendly basis.[47]

Cohen thus attempted to provide the basis of a Somali national state and at the same time to reconcile Italian and Ethiopian ambitions. 'A United Somalia', he concluded, 'constitutes the only satisfactory solution for the horn of Africa. Only in this way can the Somali territories be built up towards a self-governing state in the future.'[48]

Cohen and his colleagues found themselves frustrated in every direction. The vital importance attached by the Chiefs of Staff to Cyrenaica indirectly reduced British bargaining power in Somalia. The Foreign Office apprehended that Italian alienation over the colonial issue might strengthen the Communist party in Italy and perhaps even contribute to a Communist take-over. The Ethiopian side of the problem proved to be no less difficult. The Ethiopians would probably refuse to participate in a trusteeship regime which included the Italians. The Colonial Office nevertheless hoped that the Ethiopians might be willing to bargain even if they refused to place the Ogaden under trusteeship. The British could offer the port of Zeila in British Somaliland in return for the grazing lands of the Ogaden. Even this modest attempt to rectify arbitrary boundaries came to nothing. The Ethiopians' interest in the 'Zeila corridor' lessened as their chances of success in Eritrea increased.[49] So far as the fate of Italian Somaliland itself was concerned, the Colonial Office acknowledged the Italian factor as decisive. Another comment

[46] Minute by Cohen, 20 Mar. 1947, CO 537/2081.
[47] Ibid.
[48] Minute by Cohen, 8 Sept. 1947, CO 537/2086.
[49] For the discussions about the 'Zeila corridor' see e.g. CO 537/1472 and CO 537/2084; and, in the FO Ethiopian files, FO 371/53467, FO 371/69290B, and FO 371/69291.

by Cohen indicates the way in which the broader issues of inter-national politics determined the particular question of Somalia. It was necessary, he said, to take a long-term view of Italy as a European power as well as the long-range future of the horn of Africa. To put it 'bluntly', the fate of Europe was more important: it was essential that Italy 'be retained on the right side of the iron curtain'.[50]

The Colonial Office yielded on the 'Greater Somalia' issue only under great pressure from the Foreign Office. A minute by Cohen reveals the anguish:

> We have worked very hard on this plan and it is painful to have to give it up; but I think that it would be wrong to continue to press it when there seems no means of bringing it to fruition. If, moreover, Italian Somaliland is going to be given back to the Italians under trusteeship, we had better do this with a good grace and get the maximum benefit out of it in the shape not only of friendly feelings from Italy but also satisfactory arrangements over the British Somaliland–Italian frontier.[51]

In the end Cohen believed that Italian trusteeship would not neces-sarily be a setback for Somali nationalism. The British would attempt to channel the energies of the Somali Youth League, the political party of the nationalist movement, in the constructive direction 'of not too distant independence'—a goal established indirectly by the United Nations resolution of 1949 which set the date of indepen-dence for ex-Italian Somaliland in a timetable of ten years. Cohen's shaping of British policy on the question of Somali nationalism, despite the disappointment of 'Greater Somalia', was consistent with the broader conception of British goals as he stated them subse-quently: 'co-operation with nationalism is our greatest bulwark against communism in Africa'.[52]

The British decision to support Italian trusteeship in Somalia took place against the background of the Italian elections of April 1948, when the fate of western Europe as well as Italy seemed to hang in the balance. In May a fact-finding commission of the United Nations reported after a seven-month investigation in the former Italian colonies that the majority of the inhabitants of Italian Somali-land did not favour the return of the Italians and that the Somalis would go to any length to prevent Ethiopian control. The British representative on the commission, Brigadier F. E. Stafford (a member of the Egyptian Department of the Foreign Office with extensive African experience) presented a balanced evaluation in

[50] Comment by Cohen in an inter-departmental meeting of 24 Jan. 1947, minutes in CO 537/2083.
[51] Minute by Cohen, 8 Sept. 1947, CO 537/2086.
[52] Andrew Cohen, *British Policy in Changing Africa* (London, 1959), p. 61.

International Affairs less than a year later, when the general issue of the Italian colonies was still being publicly debated:

The strongest political force was the Somali Youth League, which . . . aimed at breaking down tribal differences, and uniting all Somalis and the lands in which they live. The League campaigned for trusteeship by the Four Powers for a period of ten years in preparation for independence and the union of all the Somalilands. It was strongly opposed to Italian rule, and also to Ethiopian rule. The movement was well organized and had competent leadership, and had obtained support throughout the country, embracing all the educated people, most of the urban classes, and, through the influence of chiefs and elders, almost all the tribes. . . .[53]

There was no essential discrepancy between Stafford's public assessment and the conclusions reached in the Colonial Office by Cohen and his colleagues. They had hoped for a 'Greater Somalia' and had yielded to Italian trusteeship in order not to make the mistake of 1919 when Germany had been stripped of her colonies and subsequently had nurtured a colonial grievance. What remained obscure until the archives of the Colonial Office disgorged their secrets was the extent to which the East African Department held firm against the advice offered insistently by the Governor of Kenya, Sir Philip Mitchell, whose robust views serve to put the entire issue, including the strategic importance of the Kenya base, into relief.

Mitchell had distinct views about the Somalis and their historic leader, Sayyid Mohammed Abdille Hassan, who is doomed to live forever in the pages of British Imperial history as the 'Mad Mullah of Somaliland'. The British campaigns against the Somali 'dervishes' had come to a close only in 1920 after two decades of desert warfare by the British Camel Constabulary Corps and in the last stage by the Royal Air Force bombing the Somalis into submission. In the post-war period Sayyid Mohammed was remembered as a national hero and patriot, the forerunner of modern Somali nationalism.[54] To Sir Philip Mitchell he remained merely another dangerous Muslim fanatic. Mitchell regarded the Somalis in the same vein as had his predecessors twenty years earlier. The 'fanatical Moslem population', he warned the Colonial Office in April 1948, would fight to the death any Italian troops foolish enough to set foot again in Somalia. Mitchell predicted no less than a jihad in which the Ethiopians would join the Somalis to expel all western influence. The British Empire would inevitably become involved:

[53] F. E. Stafford, 'The Ex-Italian Colonies', *International Affairs*, XXV, 1 (Jan. 1949), p. 50.
[54] See Lewis, *Somaliland*, chap. 4.

If the Ethiopian regulars and patriot forces intervened to help the Somalis (as they almost certainly would) an Italian defeat would be probable and hostilities might well spread, not only throughout the Horn of Africa, but into Kenya, Uganda and Tanganyika. Opportunity for political adventurers in Sudan would be created. Our position on Suez Canal while the Italian convoys passed through to a colonial war in which Egypt would be hotly on the side of Moslem victims of aggression would be interesting.[55]

By abandoning the Somalis to the Italians, the British, Mitchell believed, would be guilty of 'a betrayal which coloured and Colonial people would regard as worse than Munich'.

When the members of the Defence Committee of the Cabinet on the 30th of April 1948 decided to support Italian trusteeship in Somalia, they thought sufficiently of Mitchell's warning that they authorized the Chief of the Imperial General Staff to draw on the battalion stationed in Aden to deal with Somali disturbances. To leap ahead of the story at hand, the Ogaden reverted to Ethiopian control in September 1948.[56] The Italians assumed trusteeship responsibility in their former colony in April 1950. Mitchell proved to be a false prophet. There were no disturbances. The long-term significance of the return of the Italians, according to the foremost authority on the subject, I. M. Lewis, was that Somali nationalists through United Nations trusteeship 'gathered fresh access of support'.[57]

At the time, the officials in the Colonial Office felt that they owed Mitchell an explanation. A. H. Poynton in a 'Top Secret & Personal' letter explained to him that the problem 'bristles with every conceivable sort of difficulty'. To acquire 'support *internationally*', Poynton wrote, the British had to support the Italians in Somalia in order to solidify American, French, and Italian backing of British strategic rights in Cyrenaica.[58] The decision in favour of Italian trusteeship was the only one possible in deplorable circumstances. Mitchell found this information 'exceedingly disturbing'. His views may be taken as representative of the true-blue Tory tradition of protest against 'international' interference in the affairs of the British Empire. 'I fear that "international opinion" in these matters', he wrote to Poynton, 'means no more than the Chicago Tribune, the Central American Republics, and Russia.' Mitchell was even more disconcerted to learn that the Chiefs of Staff had by the spring of 1948 virtually

---

[55] Mitchell to Creech Jones, Top Secret, 2 Apr. 1948, CO 537/3514; see also FO 371/69330 and 69336.

[56] Bevin had noted in regard to the cession of the Ogaden: 'Better do what we are going to do & not prolong the agony.' Minute by Bevin, c.23 Apr. 1948, FO 371/69292/J2889.

[57] *Somaliland*, p. 129.

[58] Poynton to Mitchell, Top Secret and Personal, 5 June 1948, CO 537/3514.

abandoned the plan for the development of a strategic base in Kenya:

> I have the greatest personal regard for both Montgomery and Tedder and know them both personally, the latter well. I find it all the more inexplicable to understand how they have contrived to convince themselves that Cyrenaica, which has no port and nothing that could be made into a port, no technical resources and almost every believable disadvantage, can really be of the slightest use to us situated where it is.[59]

It was in this letter that Mitchell made the caustic remark, already mentioned in the introductory chapter, that the nation that built the Singapore base could hardly be expected not to repeat the same mistake in Cyrenaica.

The response within the Colonial Office to Mitchell's lament assessed the 'international' element in British colonial policy as well as the overriding importance of Cyrenaica. A. N. Galsworthy wrote in July 1948:

> His views are interesting, but I am sure he underestimates the strength of international opinion in regard to the disposal of the Italian colonies. . . . That section of international opinion which is able to command a two-thirds majority of the votes of the General Assembly will . . . be a real force—in fact the deciding factor.
>
> Sir P. Mitchell's views on the strategic importance of Cyrenaica are, I am afraid, a complete heresy. In all their recent planning the Chiefs of Staff have been absolutely categorical about the overriding necessity of retaining strategic facilities in Cyrenaica, and in fact this is the key-stone to the whole of our policy regarding the former Italian colonies.[60]

Officials in the Colonial Office deplored the collapse of the 'Greater Somalia' project, but they generally concurred in the necessity of strategic rights in Cyrenacia and the need to keep on friendly terms with Italy—even, in Ivor Thomas's words, if it meant being 'a little unkind' to the Somalis. 'Somaliland is pretty worthless territory', he once wrote.[61]

---

[59] Mitchell to Poynton, Top Secret and Personal, 29 June 1948, CO 537/3514.

[60] Minute by Galsworthy, 7 July 1948, CO 537/3514. Cohen had anticipated that Mitchell would find the decision 'profoundly disappointing and disturbing'. Minute of 10 Aug. 1948, ibid.

[61] Thomas to Mayhew, 25 Aug. 1947, FO 371/63190/J4057. The same line of reasoning was pungently expressed by F. R. (Derick) Hoyer-Millar of the Foreign Office: 'It might well pay us to be a little less susceptible to the wishes of the native inhabitants, if thereby we could secure the friendship of Italy—which may be very important to us during the next 25 years. I am afraid I am sufficiently cynical to prefer having a friend in the Mediterranean even at the cost of being rather unkind to the Somalis at the other end of the Red Sea.' Minute of 10 Mar. 1947, FO 371/63188.

'Self-Determination' and 'Realpolitik' in Eritrea

'Cynical as it might seem', noted the head of the Egyptian Department of the Foreign Office in June 1948, 'the question of Eritrea and Somaliland must not be allowed to interfere with the achievement of our aims.'[62] In the case of Eritrea the deliberate subordination of the conflicting aims of Italy and Ethiopia to the greater problem of Cyrenaica proved to be much more difficult than in Somalia. The principle of 'independence' for the Somalis could at least be reconciled with Italian trusteeship, and, the British hoped, the Ethiopians could be placated by being given part of Eritrea. By satisfying Italian aspirations in Somalia, the British nevertheless had to provide an answer to the Italian demand for restitution of Eritrea, which had a much more substantial Italian population (37,000 versus 5,000 in Somalia) and a particular place in the national psyche as the oldest Italian colony. To the Ethiopians the territory of Eritrea represented, above all, the historic route of invasion. It was an indispensable key to Ethiopian security.[63] In the winter and spring of 1948 public sentiment in Italy reached a crescendo demanding the return of the colonies while in Addis Ababa the future of Eritrea became 'a burning question'.[64] The British—and the American—inclination was to remain as quiet as possible about Eritrea until after the outcome of the Italian elections in April. But some action was necessary. The Italian peace treaty that had been signed on the 10th of February 1947 came into force on the 15th of September. Unless the Council of Foreign Ministers could agree on the fate of the Italian colonies within a year, the entire issue would be placed before the General Assembly of the United Nations in mid-September 1948. As that danger approached, British policy shifted from an essentially pro-Italian stand in Eritrea to a stance that took more into account the general anti-colonial attitude of the United Nations and the tendency of the United States to support the Ethiopians. Bevin deliberately remained flexible in order to keep firm on Cyrenaica.

In Somalia there was a recognizable nascent Somali nation. In Eritrea by contrast regional identity had only been carved, in Margery Perham's phrase, by the sword of Italian imperialism. Eritrea was an artificial creation. 'It has neither historical, racial nor cultural unity.'[65] The opposite view, pressed intently on the British public

---

[62] Minute by G. L. Clutton, 24 June 1948, FO 371/69337.

[63] 'Strategically, Eritrea was as vital to Ethiopia as the Low Countries had traditionally been to Britain.' Trevaskis, *Eritrea*, p. 58.

[64] Stafford to Scott-Fox, Top Secret, 28 Apr. 1948, FO 371/69334/J3333.

[65] In a letter to *The Times*, 12 Mar. 1946; Margery Perham, *Colonial Sequence 1930 to 1949* (London, 1967), pp. 278-9. The problems of national unity in Eritrea identified

in the 1940s by the champions of Ethiopia led by Sylvia Pankhurst,
held that Eritrea both ethnically and traditionally formed a part of
the 'Ethiopian motherland from which it was torn by Italian conquest'.[66] Ivor Thomas referred to the writings of these enthusiasts
as 'baths of romanticism about the Ethiopians which have no sound
basis in fact'.[67] To British officials Eritrea appeared to be an artificial territory divided between the Christian highlands and the
Muslim lowlands. Reduced to simplest terms, the Coptic Christians
demanded union with Ethiopia while the Muslims of the north-
western part of the territory worked towards independence. 'The
Unionist Party wants all Eritrea to go to Ethiopia; the opposition
wants the whole country, plus part of Ethiopia and the Sudan, to be
an independent Eritrea.'[68] Geographically and linguistically a good
case could be made for the incorporation of the Muslim and 'pagan'
north-western part into the Sudan.

The debate within the British government to some extent divided
the officials of the Foreign Office and Colonial Office on the issue
of trusteeship.[69] But in general the complex issue of Eritrea cut
across departmental lines and evoked a variety of passionate
memories of Ethiopia and Italian aggression as well as emotional
responses of 'fair play' to Italy as a former colonial power. Robert
Howe wrote shortly before his departure to the Sudan as Governor-
General:

> For us to support the return of Eritrea to Italy would quite rightly be regarded
> as a blatant exhibition of international selfishness and power politics. Any such
> attitude on our part would arouse the bitterest resentment in Ethiopia, who does
> not forget that Italy attacked her twice from Eritrea, once in 1896, long before
> the Fascist era, when the Italians suffered a resounding defeat by Menelik.

incisively by Miss Perham have continued to preoccupy historians of a later era. Basil
Davidson has recently written: 'I am one of those Englishmen who thought and think it
very just and right that England should give up her colonies. Yet the English, as a matter of
historical fact, held India, for example, for almost twice as long as the Ethiopians have held
the Ogaden. If the English should leave India, for example, what can justify the Ethiopians
in not leaving the Ogaden? . . . the same arguments can be applied with force to the case of
Eritrea. A colony is no more justified in natural right because it is a new one than because
it is an old one.' In a foreword to Richard Sherman, *Eritrea: The Unfinished Revolution*
(New York, 1980).

[66] E. Sylvia Pankhurst, *Ethiopia and Eritrea* (London, 1953), p. 13. 'Dedicated to the
gallant people of Ethiopia who throughout the ages have never surrendered their freedom.'

[67] Thomas to Mayhew, Personal and Confidential, 4 June 1947, FO 371/63192/J2518.

[68] Stafford, 'The Ex-Italian Colonies', whose views and statistics here reflect sanitized
Foreign Office thought for the benefit of the public.

[69] For example Bennett wrote of one of the members of the Egyptian Department of
the Foreign Office, R. D. Scott-Fox: 'he makes no secret of his contempt for all "colonial"
peoples, and is the kind of man who would always put the interests of diplomatic con-
venience first'. Minute by Bennett, 17 Apr. 1947, CO 537/2087.

It may be unpalatable to a great many people to visualize the handing over of Eritrea to a backward country like Ethiopia and there is no doubt that Eritrea would be found to suffer for a time under Ethiopian administration, but there is no doubt that a large part of the Eritrean plateau should, on racial, religious and economic grounds, be part of Ethiopia.[70]

F. E. Stafford, who served as the British representative on the commission of inquiry of the United Nations, wrote confidentially in perhaps more balanced vein than Howe: 'One cannot but have some sympathy with the Italians in the loss of their territories, but there is no doubt that . . . in East Africa they did little deliberately to improve the lot of the inhabitants, and made themselves a belligerent nuisance to their neighbours.'[71]

Ivor Thomas, in contrast to Howe and Stafford (and certainly in contrast with most of his colleagues in the Colonial Office as well), took a distinctly anti-Ethiopian line. 'What have the Eritreans done to suffer the fate of being included in Ethiopia?' He believed that almost anyone could hope for better treatment. His line of questioning carried him into areas of controversy that persist to the present day. 'If the argument is that Eritrea is not a natural entity, can this be used as an argument for including portions of it in Ethiopia, when Ethiopia is just as little a natural entity?' Should Eritrea therefore be divided between Ethiopia and the Sudan? If so then a dangerous precedent might be established. 'If it is argued that every State which consists of heterogenous elements should be split up, is not this going to have far-reaching consequences through the British Empire?'[72] Thomas in short thought that Eritrea should be restored to Italy. Otherwise irreparable harm would be done to Anglo-Italian relations. 'There is strong feeling in Italy that all their sacrifices on the Allies side were in vain', he wrote, 'and that a democratic Italy has received in this matter exactly the same treatment as a defeated Fascist Italy would have received.' He moreover regarded Italy's colonial record as much better than commonly acknowledged, and certainly better than Ethiopia's might be:

I could wish to see the greater part of Eritrea return in trust to Italy. . . . It was very well administered, and so far as I know . . . the Italians are not unpopular there. . . .

---

[70] Howe continued in regard to Somalia: 'The return of Italian Somaliland to Italy would also be resented in Ethiopia, although not so bitterly as the return of Eritrea. We have a better claim for trusteeship for Italian Somaliland than anyone else and the Russians, with their immense acquisitions of territory in Europe as a result of the War, have least of all people the right to criticise us on these grounds.' Minute of 6 Mar. 1947, FO 371/63190/J1627.

[71] Minute by Stafford, 28 Apr. 1947, FO 371/63190.

[72] Minute by Thomas, 6 May 1947, CO 537/2081.

The Red Sea coast has not belonged to Ethiopia since the shadowy days of the sixteenth century, and there is no affinity of race or religion which would justify absorption of the coast in Ethiopia. . . . It was her [Italy's] first colony and for that reason it has a special place in Italian affections, it was well-administered by the Italians, who are liked there, and Arab hostility need not be anticipated.[73]

The most powerful part of Thomas's argument was that Italy would be compelled to divest herself of her colonies not under duress but in the enlightened tradition of British trusteeship—'not as a punitive measure imposed on a former enemy, but as an act of justice corresponding to our own actions in India, Burma and so on'.[74]

There was an essential reservation in the mind of the Foreign Secretary as the problem of Eritrea became refined through departmental minutes and inter-departmental discussion. Bevin doubted whether the Italians could be restored to colonial power without the use of force. 'We are not going to use B[ritish] Bayonets for this purpose & that is the real issue', he noted in response to the mounting Italian campaign for the return of the colonies.[75] With that *obiter dictum* in mind (it recurred in his minutes), Bevin nevertheless demonstrated a solicitude for the Italians. He knew that it was slightly out of line with his general pro-Arab policy and that it ran the risk of African resistance. It was the approaching Italian elections that caused his deflection. 'We must somehow allow Italy to have a show with some special arrangement', he wrote in January 1948, 'or we shall lose the Italian scene because with the Election coming in Italy a blank turn-down of the Italian [colonial] position . . . will be disastrous.'[76]

Bevin thought that Eritrea as well as Somalia and perhaps Tripolitania might be placed under Italian trusteeship. In that way 'justice' might be meted out to Italy if the risk of colonial war in the horn of Africa did not prove to be too great. But his generous attitude towards the Italians waned after the election setback for the Communists. Throughout the entire period he remained consistent on the overriding necessity of British rights in Cyrenaica. With sufficient guarantees of military neutralization, he was prepared to see the Italians, Ethiopians, Americans, or the French in other parts of the former Italian colonial empire. 'I have a little departed from a Policy to meet an election position', he minuted in early April. He concluded that it had been an unwise move and implicity lamented the

---

[73] Memorandum by Thomas, 31 Mar. 1947, FO 371/63190; Thomas to Mayhew, 25 Aug. 1947, FO 371/63196.

[74] Thomas to Mayhew, Personal and Confidential, 4 June 1947, FO 371/63192/J2518.

[75] Minute by Bevin, *c*.17 Feb. 1948, FO 371/69328.

[76] Minute by Bevin, 28 Jan. 1948, FO 371/69327.

aberration of appeasing the Italians at the expense of general Arab goodwill. He now wanted to get back 'on the rails' of an overall Middle Eastern policy.[77]

During the rest of the year Bevin continued to receive reports, some of them perceptive, on the danger of driving Italy into the communist camp unless some colonial compensation could be given to restore her prestige.[78] In December 1948 the Ambassador to Italy, Sir Victor Mallet, warned in a hair-raising telegram that an Eritrean award to Ethiopia rather than Italy would contribute to the creation of another Soviet satellite: 'by giving Eritrea to Negus we may end by finding that we are also helping to hand Italy to Stalin'. This alarmist speculation proved to be too much for the Foreign Secretary, who in any case had a limited amount of sympathy for the Italians. He was distinctly irritated, as his rebuke indicates:

While I recognize that Mallet must give me the Italian point of view, I see little evidence of real appreciation by him of our position as the administering power vis-à-vis the United States, Russia and France. We have the responsibility. It is our soldiers who are there; we had the task of fighting; we have to maintain law and order. He takes no account of native views but seems to swallow the whole Italian case. I should like to see more vigour in putting our case over, instead of trying to make our flesh creep.[79]

Sir Orme Sargent accordingly chastised Mallet. 'Is it really true', Sargent asked, 'to say that by giving Eritrea to the Negus we shall be helping to hand Italy to Stalin?' He pointed out that an Italian colonial war in Eritrea would 'saddle Italy with a commitment which would drain her resources and create a situation in which Communism can best flourish'.[80]

The fate of Eritrea, in the short term at least, was determined in July 1948. Despite the war in Palestine the Americans and the British drew closer together on certain general issues that had specific ramifications. Eritrea was one of them. The Americans favoured the Ethiopian claim to Eritrea, with the exception of the north-western Muslim part which they hoped would be incorporated into the Sudan. With

[77] Minute by Bevin, c.7 Apr. 1948 on memorandum by Noel Charles pointing out the advantages of supporting 'independence' for Libya: 'we would earn the esteem of the local inhabitants and the Arabs as a whole. It would be the "juster" course to pursue, but we would earn the enmity of Italy and the opposition of the French.' 7 Apr. 1949, FO 371/69331.

[78] For example John Ward wrote in May 1948: 'It seems very important to get the business over this year as every month that goes by the Italian lobby gets stronger and they work themselves into an evermore emotional condition. It is sad how almost all the mistakes made after 1918 are repeating themselves, and particularly the delay in disposing of these wretched colonies.' Ward to Scott-Fox, Personal and Confidential, 21 May 1948, FO 371/69335/J3782/G.

[79] Minute by Bevin, 29 Dec. 1948, FO 371/69350/8158/G.

[80] Sargent to Mallet, Secret, 11 Jan. 1949, FO 371/69350/J8158/6/G.

the anxiety of the Italian elections now past, Bevin yielded to the Americans. In any case he found no support in the Defence Committee of the Cabinet for his proposal of Italian trusteeship. The Colonial Office and Chiefs of Staff combined to endorse the view of Sir Philip Mitchell about the hazard of another Italian–Ethiopian war. Bevin himself fully recognized the danger, in words he had used before, of re-establishing 'Italian rule with British bayonets'.[81] At this time he began to emphasize the importance of securing Ethiopian support for economic development projects, notably the one of water resources of Lake Tsana and the Nile valley. There was the further powerful argument stated by Sir Philip Mitchell, which struck all parties involved, including the Foreign Office, as persuasive: 'an anti-colonial campaign with a base in Addis Ababa might have very grave and far-reaching effects'.[82]

The Eritrean settlement dragged on for another four years. When the General Assembly failed to reach agreement on the Italian colonies in November 1949, another commission of inquiry was dispatched. It produced a divided report, two members favouring Eritrean independence and two favouring incorporation with Ethiopia. In September 1950 the British threw their weight behind a compromise solution of 'federation', thereby securing guarantees for the Italian settlers and a measure of autonomy. With a tone of resignation and relief that the end finally was in sight, Bevin wrote to members of the Cabinet: 'While there are grave practical difficulties in the way of federating two such entities as Ethiopia and Eritrea, I am satisfied that a compromise of this kind is the only one which is likely to secure the necessary majority in the General Assembly of the United Nations and thus to settle the future of Eritrea'.[83]

In September 1952 Eritrea became 'an autonomous state federated with Ethiopia under the sovereignty of the Ethiopian Crown'.[84] In the seven years since the close of the war Eritrea had not been a large issue in British imperial affairs, but the withdrawal of British troops evoked thoughts about imperial destiny. Major-General D. C. Cumming pondered the paradoxes of the decline and fall of empires: 'When the

---

[81] Defence Committee DO (48), 14th Meeting, Top Secret, 30 July 1948, CAB 131/5. Bevin also emphasized the unpopularity of the issue of handing over Eritrea in addition to the historical danger to Ethiopia. He stated subsequently: 'The whole Labour party would vote against the proposal. Nor would it be fair to put Ethiopia between the two pincers of the Italians in both Somaliland and Eritrea.' (Minutes of a meeting at the Quai d'Orsay, 26 Oct. 1948, FO 371/69347.) The American documents reveal the same concern about the revival of Italian imperialism and the disinclination to restore a position of Italian 'pincers' against Ethiopia.

[82] Mitchell to Creech Jones, No. 236, Secret, 2 Apr. 1948, CO 537/3514.

[83] Memorandum by Bevin, Confidential, 2 Sept. 1950, CP (50) 202, CAB 129/42.

[84] Trevaskis, *Eritrea: A Colony in Transition*, provides the best analysis.

last of the British garrison was withdrawing from Eritrea, we heard doubts expressed about the future stability of the country. One could not help reflecting that the officers of the Roman legions leaving our own shores, fifteen hundred years ago, probably shook their heads over the preposterous notion that the ancient Britons could manage the affairs of their islands. But further reflection persuaded one that it was not a line of speculation which gave much comfort.'[85]

The Evolution of American Policy and the Anglo-American Creation of the State of Libya

'After all', Michael Wright remarked in the summer of 1947, 'you Americans started this trusteeship business and should be able to think of a way out of the present box into which we seem to be placed.'[86] The remark was only partly humorous. The British had to rely on American support in order to resolve any and all parts of the turgid controversy about the Italian colonies. The American side of the story, though perhaps an unrivalled yarn of bureaucratic verbosity, may be told briefly because the documentation on the subject has been fully published in the *Foreign Relations* volumes and because the United Nations aspect has been exhaustively recounted by Adrian Pelt in *Libyan Independence*. There were four phases. In the first, which has been described in the beginning of this chapter, James Byrnes presided sporadically over American policy with a suspicion of British motive and indifference towards the fate of the ex-Italian colonies except so far as American security might be involved.[87] In 1947 the crisis in Greece drew the British and the Americans into general agreement on problems of the eastern Mediterranean and the horn of Africa. In the third phase, roughly the first half of 1948, Palestine and the uncertainty of the outcome of the Italian elections caused a hiatus in the planning of a general settlement. In the last phase, from the summer of 1948 until the birth of the state of Libya in the winter of 1951-2, the British and the Americans worked together in bringing about the general consensus of the United Nations. It was a long and arduous path, frequently filled with obstacles that caused frustration, but generally

---

[85] Cumming, 'British Stewardship of the Italian Colonies', p. 21.

[86] As recounted in Clark to Marshall, Top Secret, 19 Aug. 1947, USSD 865.014/8-1947 Box 6682; *Foreign Relations 1947*, III, p. 599.

[87] 'Mr. Byrnes was not particularly interested in the Italian Colonies', Bevin told his advisers. (F. O. memorandum, 26 Aug. 1946, FO 371/57187/U6951.) The point was entirely accurate. See above, n. 14.

the British and the Americans avoided pitfalls of mutual suspicion and recrimination. Part of their success may be attributed to the relative unimportance of the issue to the United States (but not to Britain) which enabled the career officials of the State Department patiently and methodically to plod along without White House interference.

The key figures were Loy Henderson (head of the Office of Near Eastern and African Affairs); John Utter (African Affairs Division and the Department's representative on the United Nations commission of inquiry); Joseph Palmer (also in the African Affairs Division); and, in the last phase, George C. McGhee (Assistant Secretary for Near Eastern and African Affairs). Their work was characterized by competence and, on the whole, good humour. The following exchange between McGhee and the British Ambassador, Sir Oliver Franks, is an example which the historian seizes on like a jug of water in a Somali desert, so arid is the documentation. After an ill-tempered remark by Franks that the Americans themselves should assume administrative responsibility in the horn of Africa, since they had so many ideas about the subject, McGhee retorted that the British were much more experienced in such matters and therefore could do a better job. 'The proof of this is in their administration of the United States when it was still a colonial area.'[88] The first part of the remark, as in Michael Wright's gibe about American responsibility for the trusteeship system, could be taken seriously. The Americans relied on the British to provide a stable administration of the Italian colonies. They discovered that their aims were complementary. The case of Libya in particular may be regarded as a microcosm of the postwar American experience in colonial affairs. The Americans entered the controversy with a still buoyant anti-colonial attitude. They examined the principles of self-determination and strategic security, and they increasingly supported the British Empire as a means of securing both principles simultaneously. One final anecdote gives emphasis to the point. At a Ramadan dinner party in 1951, a Libyan addressed the following question to the American commissioner, Lewis Clark. 'Less than two hundred years ago the United States were a British colony. They fought hard to free themselves. Today they appear on friendly terms with the British, yet nevertheless I still feel in Mr. Clark something of the anticolonialist. How do you explain this, and is he sincere?'[89] Clark tried, on this occasion apparently without success, to reconcile old-fashioned

[88] Memorandum by Moose, Secret, 20 Oct. 1949, USSD 865.014/10-2049; *Foreign Relations 1949*, IV, p. 598.
[89] Pelt, *Libyan Independence*, p. 209 n. 4.

anti-colonialism with his new friendship for the British Empire. Such was the American tension in the question of the Italian colonies.

The evolution of American policy towards Somalia and Eritrea reflects a delicate balancing of Wilsonian doctrine and a gradual strengthening of the strategic element. In the first phase of the controversy, 1945–6, 'international trusteeship' was applied as a general formula. It proved to be more applicable to Somalia than to Eritrea. Italian trusteeship resolved the problem of self-determination for at least part of Somalia and at the same time gratified the Italians. It also limited the period of their direct control. The timetable of ten years could not but have far-reaching implications for the colonial regimes of British and French Somalia, but the British, who in this case were extremely sceptical whether 'independence' would have any real meaning, could reconcile themselves without anguish to a neutral buffer zone that might eventually be united with British Somaliland and might ameliorate the problems of a 'deficit area'. The Foreign Office, but not the Colonial Office, easily yielded on the question of 'Greater Somalia' that would have included the Ogaden. 'In broad political settlements it is almost always necessary to outrage the pawns in the game', noted a Foreign Office official about the expendable Somalis in relation to the Cyrenaicans.[90]

One of the principal revelations of the State Department's archives is the extent to which Ethiopian influence on the Americans contributed to the defeat of the 'Greater Somalia' project. The Ethiopians emphasized that the 'literate classes' in Ethiopia would regard 'Greater Somalia' as a 'national calamity'.[91] Apparently Loy Henderson found the argument persuasive. The State Department did not object to the possible unification of the British and Italian territories, he wrote in October 1947, but 'we see no justification for including the Ogaden'.[92] The State Department also responded to Italian sentiment. The American Ambassador in Rome reported in June 1948: 'With [the] exception of Trieste there is no other single issue upon which Italian people are so completely united. . . . The almost pathological Italian attitude towards Italian Colonies must be regarded as a deep seated fixation and not a temporary phase of emotional development subject to change or palliation.'[93] The State Department endorsed the solution of Italian trusteeship in the summer of 1948. At that time the policies of the United States and Britain converged. Though the general problem of the Italian colonies

[90] Minute by J. G. Ward, 20 June 1946, FO 371/57181/U5952.

[91] See USSD 844.014/5–1146; *Foreign Relations 1946*, II, p. 159, n. 69.

[92] Memorandum by Henderson, 1 Oct. 1947; *Foreign Relations 1947*, III, pp. 601–5.

[93] Dunn to Marshall, Top Secret, 28 June 1948, USSD 865.014/6-2848 Box 768; *Foreign Relations 1948*, III, pp. 916–18.

caused further delay, the fate of Italian Somaliland was in effect determined in favour of independence. The United Nations set the timetable of ten years in the next year. The initiative for the ten-year limitation came from the 'anti-colonial' nations, not the United States.

The case of Eritrea proved to be much more complex. There the State Department moved from a position favouring trusteeship to one recommending incorporation into Ethiopia—with the exception of the north-western Muslim part, which, in accordance with the Wilsonian principle of adjustments in favour of the inhabitants, would have been united with the Sudan. Here the State Department met with unexpected opposition from the Foreign Office. Bevin wished to avoid the boundary adjustment because it would give the Egyptians opportunity to fish in the troubled waters of Sudanese sovereignty.[94] Nevertheless the British were prepared to go along with the division of Eritrea in order to smooth the way in Cyrenaica. Once Bevin passed through the 'aberration' of wanting to restore Eritrea to Italy for Italian political reasons in the early months of 1948, the Foreign Office and State Department could easily endorse the proposition that most of Eritrea should revert to Ethiopia. The summer of 1948, as with Somalia, was the crucial period in determining the future of Eritrea. Once the British and the Americans had reached firm agreement it was only a matter of time until they pulled the other powers along with them towards a definite settlement. The effort to apply the principle of self-determination in the north-western Muslim province proved to be abortive not because of American or British efforts to buy off the Ethiopians but because of the power politics of the United Nations. When the General Assembly failed to reach agreement on Eritrea in November 1949, the smaller issue of ethnic and linguistic frontiers became lost in the larger controversy of Eritrean 'independence' or 'unification' with Ethiopia. 'Federation' finally proved to be a solution that the Americans, like the British, could accept with a sense of relief that the matter finally seemed to be resolved—which of course it was not.

In a sense the State Department in the case of Eritrea could be

---

[94] 'As regards the American suggestion that the western Moslem lowlands should go to the Sudan, we know that the Sudan Government are not keen to receive this very poor slice of territory and there is the further difficulty that such a transfer would require joint action by Egypt and ourselves which might raise the fundamental question of Sudan sovereignty.' Minute by D. Scott-Fox, 21 July 1948, FO 371/69340/J5231. Bevin further explained to the Defence Committee of the Cabinet: 'as the Sudan was an Anglo-Egyptian condominium, the incorporation of Eritrea would entail *prima facie* admission of the Egyptian claim to part of that territory'. DO (48) 13th Meeting, Top Secret, 6 Aug. 1948, CAB 131/5.

found guilty of betraying the anti-colonial tradition of the United States. One of the stakes at issue was trusteeship. When the British and the Americans in the summer of 1948 decided that Eritrea's political future lay with Ethiopia, one reason for not moving in the direction of trusteeship and eventual 'independence' was the reluctance to see Ethiopia admitted to the Trusteeship Council of the United Nations. The Ethiopians would vote with the anti-colonial bloc. Here is a key minute that summarizes the British attitude:

> The Ethiopians are hardly able to govern themselves. . . . If Ethiopia were given trusteeship of Eritrea, she would become a member of the Trusteeship Council. She would certainly vote in its deliberations with the anti-colonial powers, and thereby the whole balance of the Trusteeship Council (which is already giving us enough trouble) would be upset.[95]

The State Department quite independently came to the same conclusion: 'Ethiopia's membership in [the] Trusteeship Council might upset [the] balance between present administering and non-administering powers because of Ethiopia's sympathy for so-called "colonial peoples".'[96] There were further reasons for the failure to establish a trusteeship regime in Eritrea (and both the British and the Americans shifted their positions) but it is a historical fact that Ethiopia did not become a trusteeship power and that Eritrea eventually became 'federated' in part because of calculations about Ethiopia's 'anti-colonial' attitude. If Eritrea had been placed under international trusteeship it is virtually certain that independence in some form would have been achieved since even the most 'backward' of the trusteeship territories, New Guinea, gained independence in 1975. Instead the State Department unwittingly participated in the beginning of Eritrea's *Unfinished Revolution*.[97]

American enthusiasm for out-and-out trusteeship began to wane at the same time that strategic calculations continued to wax. The Joint Chiefs of Staff and the State Department began to give specific attention to the question of Eritrea in the autumn of 1947, in other words, when the coming into force of the Italian peace treaty meant that the problem could no longer continue to drift. The political assessment of the State Department held that the failure by Ethiopia to acquire Eritrea might have profound consequences in Ethiopia itself: 'one of two courses appears to be likely: (1) Ethiopia will fall into the hands of reactionaries and be set back many years politically, economically, and socially; or (2) Ethiopia may turn

---

[95] Minute by Clutton, 11 Aug. 1948, FO 371/69341/J5376.
[96] Marshall to Douglas, Top Secret, 6 Aug. 1948, USSD 865.014/8–648 Box 6684; *Foreign Relations 1948*, III, pp. 934–6.
[97] The title of the book published in 1980 by Richard Sherman.

towards the Soviets'.[98] The strategic assessment by the Joint Chiefs of Staff held that the problems of Eritrea and Ethiopia should be viewed within the context of the British Empire:

> From a strategic standpoint, Ethiopia is becoming increasingly important to British Empire security and, therefore, to our own security. An increase in Soviet influence in Ethiopia would constitute a direct threat to British control of the strategically important southern entrance to the Red Sea.[99]

The defence of the British Empire in eastern Africa, with the corollary of Ethiopia as a vital indirect part of it, thus by October 1947 had become a strategic aim of the United States. Within a year later the Joint Chiefs of Staff specified that Eritrea itself had acquired a certain strategic potential: Asmara might be developed as 'a tele-communications base facility' and, in the event of an emergency, Massawa as 'an air and naval base facility'. The Joint Chiefs of Staff estimated that the 'telecommunications' facilities 'categorically' were so advantageous to both the United States and Britain that they surpassed those of all other locations 'in the entire Middle Eastern Mediterranean area'.[1] The Ethiopians would be willing to co-operate fully in the development of American bases. By happy chance the interpretation of Eritrean self-determination in favour of Ethiopia worked to the advantage of American strategic security.[2] And fortunately for the British as well, the security of the British Empire in eastern Africa had now been identified with the security of the United States.

Strategic considerations had been paramount in the case of Libya since the end of the war, but it was the European crisis in the spring of 1948 that galvanized Anglo-American defence plans. In May of that year Bevin mentioned as a 'new factor' the American base in Tripolitania at Mallaha. It would be of 'no use' to the Americans, he continued, 'if Tripolitania were plunged into disorder'.[3] By that remark he meant the chaos or bloodshed that might accompany the return of the Italians, if they were allowed the chance. And the

---

[98] Memorandum by Henderson, Top Secret, 1 Oct. 1947; *Foreign Relations 1947*, III, pp. 601–05.

[99] Ibid. Memorandum by State–War–Navy Coordinating Committee, Top Secret, 8 July 1947, SWN-5543; *Foreign Relations 1947*, III, pp. 592–4.

[1] Marshall to Douglas, Top Secret, 23 July 1948, USSD 865.014/7–2248 Box 768; *Foreign Relations 1948*, III, pp. 923–4; memorandum by Joint Chiefs of Staff, Top Secret, NSC 19/3, 5 Aug. 1948, full copy in Modern Military Branch, National Archives; *Foreign Relations 1948*, III, pp. 933–4.

[2] The irony did not escape the National Security Council: 'it is fortunate that in this case an act of justice (the granting of Ethiopia's legitimate claim in Eritrea) and U. S. national interest (the use of military facilities) coincide in the policy supported by this Government'. NSC 19/4, 19 July 1949; *Foreign Relations 1949*, IV, p. 575 n. 6.

[3] Minutes of a meeting between Bevin and F. O. officials, 7 May 1948, FO 371/69334.

comment was pregnant with further meaning. Mallaha, known better to the world as Wheelus Air Force Base, was a 'new factor' only in the sense that the United States, jolted into a sense of emergency, might be persuaded to step in to assume trusteeship responsibility over Tripolitania. Bevin never really believed that the Americans would agree, but he seriously discussed the possibility with his advisers. John Utter, who represented the State Department on the United Nations commission of inquiry of November 1947–May 1948, reported from London after his return from Africa that the British hoped for an Anglo-American partnership in Libya that would stabilize the situation in the Mediterranean: 'From indications which British have given us', he wrote, 'we are convinced this is [the] controlling factor.' He detected mutual anxiety. 'It is our opinion that [the] British probably fear possibility [of] US withdrawal from Mediterranean as much or more than we fear possibility [of] British withdrawal.'[4] Wheelus Field had in fact been virtually demobilized in 1947. Plans for its revitalization as a major postwar base took place in mid-1948 at the same time that the Americans and the British reached agreement on the future of Eritrea and Somalia.[5] As if written in sand, all plans for Libya itself remained indefinite because of the campaign gaining momentum in Italy for the return of the colonies and because of the shifting background of international politics.

The situation in Libya was so complex, Michael Wright wrote shortly after the conclusion of the Anglo-American 'Pentagon Talks' of 1947–8, that 'it is important to keep the fundamentals of the problem clearly in mind'.[6] His caveat is especially true in grasping the international, British, and Libyan influences that brought about the creation of the Libyan state. The essential element to bear in

[4] Douglas to Marshall, Top Secret, 28 July 1948, USSD 865.014/7-2848 Box 769; *Foreign Relations 1948*, III, pp. 928–9. In July 1948 Joseph Palmer together with Utter disillusioned the Foreign Office officials of any possibility of American trusteeship in Libya. Palmer said with considerable understatement: 'In view of the Palestine crisis it was felt that this would not be the time for the U. S. to take on territorial responsibilities in the Arab world.' Minute by Scott-Fox, 21 July 1948, FO 371/69340/J5231.

[5] For previous discussion about the American base see e.g. FO 371/63187. The British identified Lt. Col. Charles E. Bonesteel as the moving spirit on the American side. His general outlook was 'extremely close to the British views'. Memorandum by A. S. Cope, 27 Nov. 1946, ibid. The first American Ambassador in Libya, Henry S. Villard (formerly of the Division of African Affairs) later reflected that 'as late as 1947 there was no disposition on the part of the United States to expand, or even to continue, its interest in the place'. Henry S. Villard, *Libya* (Ithaca, 1956), p. 137.

[6] Minute by Wright, 26 Feb. 1948, FO 371/69328/J1278/G. His comment illuminates the importance of the Italian elections in the American assessment of the colonial problem: 'as regards the future of Somaliland, Eritrea and Tripolitania they [the Americans] do not wish to take any final decision at least until after the Italian elections. They have taken this line quite consistently since we first talked the matter over with them.'

mind is that by the beginning of 1948 the Americans had committed themselves fully to back British claims to Cyrenaica.[7] The overriding goal, which had remained constant since the war, was the establishing of British strategic rights in Cyrenaica, and, after the summer of 1948, the development of a major American base at Mallaha. The aims of the two powers thus interlocked. To achieve British security, Bevin was prepared to sacrifice Somalia, Eritrea, and almost everything else. As late as June 1947 he had even toyed with the idea of allowing the Russians into Tripolitania if they in turn would guarantee a British Cyrenaica.[8] The point serves to emphasize the fluidity of the situation until the European crisis of 1948 created a catalyst for American aims.

For economic and domestic reasons the British wished to end the military occupation of Tripolitania. They hoped if possible to avoid the burden of its future administration. The Foreign Office therefore weighed the advantages of the return of the Italians in a trusteeship capacity, which would cut expenditure in a 'deficit area' and improve Anglo-Italian relations, against a possible colonial war and the general loss of Arab goodwill. There thus was a superficial similarity with the problem of Somalia. In Tripolitania however there was an Italian population of some 50,000, which could be expected to increase under an Italian regime. This was a distinction of magnitude. It raised the question of the future of settler communities in northern Africa. To what extent did this long-range issue figure in British calculations?

This chapter, like its counterparts, will draw to a close by examining briefly the question of Libya in relation to the conflict in Palestine, where the similar issue of Jewish settlement proved to be irresolvable with the Arabs. It is illuminating in this regard to turn again to the records of the Colonial Office because there the question was studied closely in relation to ethical responsibility of the administering authority to the indigenous inhabitants as well as in the military and economic aspects. This theme is particularly salient in the minutes of J. S. Bennett, the head of the International Relations Department. During the war Bennett had served on the staff of the Minister Resident in the Middle East and thus brought to bear certain general insights about British purpose and responsibility for

[7] The 'Pentagon Talks' of late 1947, which have been discussed in the prelude to this section, were crucial in that regard: 'the Americans, whose attitude will probably prove the key to the problem . . . have told us they will help us over retaining strategic facilities in Cyrenaica.' Minute by Wright, 26 Feb. 1948, FO 371/69328/J1278/G.

[8] 'The Secy. of State's view is that if it is essential for us to get strategic facilities in Cyrenaica, then we can hardly avoid making some kind of concession to Russia in Tripolitania.' Minute by Scott-Fox, 10 June 1947, FO 371/63195/J3634.

the future course of events. His views may be taken as representative of Colonial Office officials and those in the Foreign Office who gave special attention to the question of trusteeship.[9]

Bennett believed that Libya was first and foremost an *Arab* country. He thought that the return of Italian settlers would inflame Arab nationalism and would be 'a perpetual cause of friction in that part of the world'. If a resuscitated Italy were to 'peel off' a strip of the Mediterranean coast or be given the opportunity to reoccupy all of Tripolitania, then there would be nothing but 'incessant friction and frequent disturbances'. He anticipated in other words a repetition of the British experience in Palestine, where one could see the direct collision between a 'settler' and an 'Arab' policy. Bennett wrote in June 1946, immediately after the publication of the report by the Anglo-American Committee of Inquiry: 'Palestine agitates the whole Middle East today because it appears that the Arab majority of the inhabitants are deprived of self-government and self-determination in the interests of a European settler minority.' He applied the lessons of Palestine to the Middle East generally, with specific implications about a 'bridgehead' policy in Libya:

For the European powers, I believe it is now a choice between treating the Arab world as a whole (in which case we can look for good relations with it), or having a series of 'bridgeheads' along the Mediterranean coast into a hostile Arab interior. You can't play both policies at once. The French and the Zionists (and previously the Italians) frankly go for the 'bridgehead' policy. I don't believe that, with our wide Middle Eastern interests, we can afford to.[10]

In Bennett's view Libya would quickly rank along with Palestine as one of Britain's major Middle Eastern problems if the Italians were allowed to return. Above all, British attempts to gain strategic rights in Cyrenaica would 'go sour'.

It would be tempting to suppose that ethical motives of protecting the Arabs from Italian colonization governed British efforts to resolve the Libyan entanglement. In fact Bevin was quite prepared to yield Tripolitania to the Italians and for that matter the Fezzan to the French. For strategic rights to Cyrenaica he would stop short of nothing save protecting the Italians 'with British bayonets', a danger that he believed the Colonial Office and the War Office exaggerated.

---

[9] For the views of F. E. Stafford, whose ideas ran parallel with Bennett's, see especially minutes in FO 371/63178, 63187; 63188, 63190, and 69334.

[10] Bennett to J. S. Majoribanks, 15 June 1946, FO 371/57181. Bennett wrote that his letter was TOP SECRET AND PERSONAL because technically from the Colonial Office's point of view he had no official interest in Libya; but he clearly thought that the Libyan problem would profoundly affect the formal dependencies of the Colonial Office. His similar views run throughout the CO 537 series.

He took a calculated risk which brilliantly resolved the problem of trusteeship by eliminating the Italian factor. He was quite aware of the strong anti-Italian sentiment on the part of the 'anti-colonial' powers at the United Nations. Having secured a firm American promise to back a British bid for Cyrenaica, the British, with the Americans reluctantly in tow, in May 1948 sponsored a proposal that would have placed the British in Cyrenaica, the Italians in Tripolitania, and the French in the Fezzan. The section of the proposal dealing with Italian trusteeship failed to secure the necessary two-thirds majority of the General Assembly and thus the entire plan was defeated.[11] But Bevin had managed to restore a measure of Anglo-Italian goodwill. And he had removed the danger of throwing Tripolitania into 'disorder' by the return of the Italians. The Libyan controversy now entered into a phase in which 'independence', scarcely credible two years earlier, appeared to be the only proposition on which all parties could agree.

The British made the critical decision in July 1949. 'We are coming to the conclusion', Bevin wrote, 'that the solution for Libya must be independence.' The Sayyid Idris had developed into a national leader of sufficient stature to hold together a Libyan state on the model of Transjordan (the recurrent British analogy in the 1949–51 period).[12] The proposal for Italian trusteeship in Tripolitania had succeeded in uniting both the Libyans and the 'anti-colonial' nations of the United Nations against trusteeship of any kind and had created a momentum towards independence. 'Nothing short of independence is likely to acquire the support of the Arab–Moslem–Asiatic bloc', reasoned Bevin and his advisers, and anything less than independence would now not be acceptable to Idris.[13] The American Ambassador in London reported to the State Department that the Foreign Office regarded independence as 'inevitable' and that it

[11] These developments are clearly summarized in *Foreign Relations 1949*, IV, pp. 542–3. See also especially Pelt, *Libyan Independence*, pp. 79 ff. The Americans had agreed to follow the British initiative because of the importance of the Cyrenaican issue. Joseph Palmer especially regretted the result of being dragged behind the British Imperial chariot: 'the U. S. . . . found itself in the position of supporting a proposal which was against the clear wishes of the inhabitants of the territories and, in my opinion, served to dissipate—temporarily at least—a large amount of the reserve of good will which we enjoy among the Asiatics as the result of our treatment of the Philippines'. Memorandum by Palmer, Secret, 27 May 1949, USSD 865.014/5–2749 Box 770; *Foreign Relations 1949*, IV, pp. 558–61.

[12] The situation in Libya was in fact much more complex because of the issue of a unitary versus a federal state. The Tripolitanians (and for example the Egyptians) favoured a unitary state because they were less destitute and numerically stronger and would tend to dominate in a unitary state. They would also be more immune to foreign influences. The Senusi (and the British) favoured a federal state in which a measure of Cyrenaican autonomy would be preserved. On the evolution of the complex federal system see especially Khadduri, *Modern Libya*.

[13] Bevin to Franks, No. 7222, Secret, 20 July 1949, PREM 8/921.

would be to the advantage of the United States 'to climb on [the] bandwagon and thereby gain good will of [the] Arabs'.[14]

The general conclusions of officials in Washington were similar in tone and content with those of the British. According to a National Security Council report, the British investment in cultivating Idris would now pay off:

> The British have spent a great deal of time, money and effort in successfully establishing close relations with Sayed Idriss. . . . The Emir is the only accepted leader of the people of Cyrenaica, and, in addition, is the only figure in Libya who has wide support among the Tripolitanians as a leader. Therefore, one means of assuring U. K. and U. S. influence throughout the area is the creation of a united and independent Libya in which Sayed Idriss would be Chief of State.[15]

Any other course, according to the National Security Council, would jeopardize 'our military facilities, particularly Wheelus Field'. The British and the Americans therefore took the plunge into what theorists of 'dependency' might term an unblushing venture of military and economic imperialism. The British and American records are explicit on the nature of the bargain which had to win the concurrence of Adrian Pelt, the Libyan High Commissioner of the United Nations. Economic support for the new state would be reciprocated with strategic rights. According to Michael Wright in May 1950, Pelt's co-operation in securing strategic facilities was entirely contingent 'on economic assistance to Libya'.[16] In 1953 Britain signed a twenty-year Treaty of Alliance with Libya, at last securing the air and military bases in Cyrenaica that had been the paramount aim since the end of the war.[17] As if to underscore the analogy between Libya and Jordan, the treaty was signed by the former Ambassador in Jordan, now the first British Ambassador in Libya, Sir Alec Kirkbride.

With Gallic wit the French Foreign Minister, Robert Schuman, summed up the situation in the spring of 1949. His observation puts the Libyan question in the broader perspective of the British and French experience in Egypt. 'The British' in Libya, Schuman remarked, 'if they were there for two or three years more, would never get out except perhaps as part of an independence scheme,

[14] Douglas to Acheson, Top Secret, 14 July 1949, USSD 865.014/7-1449 Box 770; *Foreign Relations 1949*, IV, pp. 566-7.

[15] National Security Council report, 4 Aug. 1949; *Foreign Relations 1949*, IV, pp. 571-8.

[16] See *Foreign Relations 1950*, III, p. 1031.

[17] A further agreement between the United States and Libya was signed in 1954. The British economic support amounted to £2,750,000 a year in comparison with the American sum of $42 million over the period 1954-71. See Wright, *Libya*, pp. 232-3; and Khadduri, *Modern Libya*, pp. 226-31 and 252-8. The treaties are reproduced in ibid., appendices IV and V.

like that of Trans-Jordan, which would give the British a continuing special position.' In Libya as elsewhere there was a certain continuity, Schuman continued, in the history of British imperialism. 'He referred to the British history in Egypt. The British had a quality, for which he did not reproach them, of looking out for themselves.'[18]

[18] As recounted in a memorandum by John Foster Dulles, Secret, 12 Apr. 1949, *Foreign Relations 1949*, IV, p. 545.

8

IRAQ: 'THE VITAL IMPERIAL CONNECTION' AND QUESTIONS OF IRAQI NATIONALISM

'NURI PASHA', reflected the British Ambassador to Iraq in 1949, 'is as keen as ever on closer relations between Syria & Iraq, which he would like to see established on the lines of the old Austria-Hungary.'[1] More than any other Arab statesman, Nuri al-Said for over three decades had vigorously pursued the goal of Arab unity essentially in harmony with British aims in the Middle East. In the latter part of the 1940s the British regarded him as 'the elder statesman' of the Arab world and spoke of his 'statecraft, long experience and breadth of vision'.[2] The 'Fertile Crescent' scheme of Arab unity, perhaps under Hashemite leadership, formed an important part of that vision. From the British vantage point Nuri's ascendancy in Iraqi domestic affairs constituted another vital element in the general spectrum of Middle Eastern politics. Nuri could be regarded as holding the balance between extreme Iraqi nationalists who had associated themselves with the Axis powers during the war and those who believed that Communism would prove to be the political instrument to free Iraq from British imperialism. The distance between the

[1] Minute by Sir Henry Mack, n.d. but Jan. 1948, FO 371/75077/E1152. The allusion to European unification is recurrent in both British and Arab historical literature of the 1940s. 'For a long while, Arab thinkers have been hoping that an Arab Prussia would arise and unify us.' Musa al-Alami, quoted by Majid Khadduri, 'The Scheme of Fertile Crescent Unity', in Richard N. Frye, ed., *The Near East and the Great Powers* (Cambridge, Mass., 1951). Khadduri's *Independent Iraq 1932–1958* (London, 1960) is indispensable for an understanding of the British era in Iraq. The same is true of the terse and incisive essay by Elie Kedourie, 'The Kingdom of Iraq: A Retrospect', in his *The Chatham House Version and other Middle-Eastern Studies* (New York, 1970). See also especially S. H. Longrigg, *Iraq 1900 to 1950* (London, 1953). Edith and E. F. Penrose, *Iraq: International Relations and National Development* (London, 1978) is especially good on the economic causes of political discontent. Hanna Batatu, *The Old Social Classes and the Revolutionary Movements of Iraq* (Princeton, 1978) is an exhaustive study of communism in Iraq that throws much light on all aspects of Iraqi society and serves as a corrective to accounts based on British sources. Peter Slugett, *Britain in Iraq 1914–1932* (London, 1976) is an exemplary study of British aims and methods of control, and the Iraqi response. Mohammad A. Tarbush, *The Role of the Military in Politics: A Case Study of Iraq to 1941* (London, 1982), provides a valuable account of the military coups 1936–41 that are prelude to the political developments dealt with in this chapter.
[2] Stonehewer Bird to Bevin, 9 Jan. 1947, FO 371/61568. The standard biography is by Lord Birdwood, *Nuri As-Said: A Study in Arab Leadership* (London, 1959). Penrose, *Iraq*, develops the theme of Nuri as a corrupt politician who buttressed the old regime.

two extremes was not as great as it might appear at first sight. One of the Middle Eastern experts of the Foreign Office, M. T. Walker, wrote at a time of crisis, in February 1948: 'action should be taken to encourage the moderates under Nuri Pasha . . . to oppose the erstwhile Nazis, who are clearly prepared at a few hours notice to become communists and, as in 1941, to sell their country to a dictatorship for the pleasure of being rid of the British'.[3]

Nuri's ubiquitous presence was inseparable from all major British initiatives in both the external and internal affairs of Iraq. It is therefore imperative to assess, if only briefly, his limitations and handicaps as well as his political virtues. Nuri aspired to be a pre-eminent pan-Arab statesman. But the basis of his political strength, the Hashemite dynasty, placed him at odds with the head of the major dynastic power in the Arabian peninsula, King Ibn Saud, as well as with Azzam Pasha, whose leadership of the Arab League gave it an Egyptian and anti-Hashemite thrust. Nuri, according to the Embassy in Baghdad, 'is suspect in Egypt as an opponent of Egypt's leadership of the Arab World, and in Syria and Saudi Arabia as a Hashimite henchman'.[4] Nor did Nuri's absorption in pan-Arab affairs always work to his advantage in Iraq. His pan-Arab ambitions in fact stirred up suspicion. His peers regarded him as a schemer. 'It is a pity', noted one Foreign Office official, 'that Nuri Pasha is not trusted by his own Govt., is so fanatically Hashimite, & so hostile to Azzam Pasha. These facts colour his ideas, & the knowledge of this tends to make these ideas suspect. He talks a lot. . . .'—too much, in the Foreign Office view, on general pan-Arab questions and not enough about more pressing domestic Iraqi problems.[5]

Though Nuri could be relied upon to speak knowledgeably on general affairs ranging from the Euphrates to the Nile, on specific topics of, for example, local irrigation projects, the names of his political cronies would appear as sponsors. Foreign Office officials did not expect Nuri to be innocent of 'oriental' vices of bribery and corruption, but they lamented his lack of dynamism in genuine political and economic reform. Unfortunately for the British, Nuri, their arch-collaborator, was simply not the man to count on for the 'peasants not Pashas' goals of the Labour government. In a balanced assessment of his position in Iraqi politics in the early postwar era, the political arm of the Embassy in Baghdad, the Chancery, judged his influence to be on the decline.

[3] Minute by Walker, 26 Feb. 1948, FO 371/68447/E4099.
[4] Chancery to Eastern Department, 16 July 1946, FO 371/52315.
[5] Minute by J. T. Henderson, 24 June 1946, FO 371/52314/E5695.

He is still without doubt the most influential man in Iraqi political circles. He is the one Iraqi who is known outside the restricted circle of Arab countries; he stands well above any other Iraqi politician in both knowledge and ability and his skill in negotiation and in intrigue is very great. In spite of these outstanding qualities, it is, we think, arguable that in internal Iraqi affairs the day of the skilful combiner of cabinets, such as Nuri, is drawing towards it close.[6]

The future of Iraq, if it were not to fall into the hands of the communists, would depend on 'moderate progressive elements'. Here the British could not rely on Nuri, yet 'one of our most pressing and difficult tasks' would be encouragement of economic and social reform:

> We doubt if Nuri can be of much help here for he is not really interested in internal affairs, in rooting out bribery from the administration, in embarking on schemes of social reform. Nor can he ever forget a political friend: if he is asked a favour by one of his old associates he will not hesitate to grant it, and with the old gang in power this country cannot hope to progress very far.[7]

The phrase 'old gang' recurs in British commentary on the postwar situation in Iraq. The British hoped that the 'old gang', meaning in general the circles of the 'rich and corrupt' who ruled Iraq (which included a miscellany of former Ottoman officials, lawyers, and army officers), would yield in influence to younger and more representative politicians who wished to reform and modernize. The Chancery's estimate continued:

> Nuri's influence . . . though at present paramount particularly in Palace, tribal and what may be called 'old political' circles is destined, we feel, to decrease eventually. . . . Nuri's reputation as a staunch supporter of Britain does not increase his influence.[8]

The Foreign Office perhaps misjudged Nuri's tenacious capacity for political survival for another dozen years, but the theme that he was becoming less suitable for British purposes was persistent: 'Within Iraq Nuri's influence, at present paramount in ruling circles, will eventually decrease, and . . . it will be no bad thing even though we lose a staunch friend of Britain. Nuri is not the man to recruit a moderate progressive party, carry through schemes of social reform and root out bribery & nepotism from the administration.'[9]

It is easy to emphasize the prominent theme of scepticism in official thought towards Nuri, but in fairness to Nuri himself it is perhaps equally important to recognize the disingenuous tone of Foreign Office minutes, which might be read as if the forces of British imperialism were on the side of social reform, the distribution

[6] Chancery to Eastern Department, 16 July 1946, FO 371/52315/E7045.
[7] Ibid.   [8] Ibid.
[9] Minute by G. H. Baker, 29 July 1946, FO 371/57315/E7045.

of economic benefits to all parts of Iraqi society, and the eventual
abolition of the 'old gang'. Such an interpretation would be a distortion. Bevin might express such hopes, but they found expression
in the felicity of official thought rather than action. The acuteness
of some of the British political writing on Iraq in this period (as well
as some of the obtuse reporting on the causes of the trouble of 1948,
as will be seen) must not be confused with the underlying sympathy
of the British for the 'old guard'. British officials could genuinely
hope for the reform of the old regime, which in Iraq was not so
corrupt or removed from the people as the one in Egypt. Nuri
himself, as virtually all sympathetic British observers of the era
recognized, was by no means devoid of social conscience or of
interest in economic development. Even by British standards he was
honest (though some members of his family were not). The British
might lament his political associates and his ineffectiveness in taking
immediate steps towards a comprehensive economic development
plan, but in fact the basic British as well as Iraqi calculation during
this era was that social discontent could be held down for ten or
twenty years until the effects of development would be felt in all
parts of Iraqi society. Nuri may have been shortsighted, but no more
so than the British. His pro-British attitudes may have made it
difficult for the Foreign Office to convince critics of British imperialism of the sincerity of the hope for a new era in Iraq. Nevertheless
Nuri stood on the side of economic and social reform, and when all
is said he was a pillar of British strength in the Middle East.

If Nuri's pro-British inclinations sometimes seemed to be an
impediment in persuading Iraqi nationalists that the British wished to
break the influence of the 'old gang', the pro-British attitude of the
Regent, Abdul Ilah, was an actual embarrassment. The Regent ruled
on behalf of Faisal II, who was three years old at the time of his
accession in 1939. British commentators on Iraqi politics referred
euphemistically to the Regent as a mild-mannered man who
courteously listened to all those who spoke to him, meaning, in fact,
that he caved in to the advice of those who last talked to him. He
was the son of Ali, the eldest son of Hussein I, King of the Hejaz.
If the Hashemites had not been driven out, Abdul Ilah would have
been King of the Hejaz. It is perhaps also important to note that
he was the nephew of Abdullah, since Abdullah always thought that
he would have been more appropriately placed in Iraq or Syria rather
than relegated to the small and artificially created territory of Transjordan. Unfortunately for the British, the Regent had none of the
outstanding political abilities of Faisal I, who had ruled Iraq until his
death in 1933. Faisal had held nationalist aspirations in check by

keeping a certain distance from British overlordship, or, perhaps more accurately, he had cultivated moderate anti-British nationalism in order to offset the dangers of British support. The Regent by contrast did not possess sufficient strength of character even to be compared favourably with Faisal's successor King Ghazi, who ruled until his accidental death in 1939. In the judgement of Air Commodore K. C. Buss, long an observer of Iraqi politics and now attached to the Research Department of the Foreign Office:

He [the Regent] is the antithesis of his cousin, Ghazi, and he has failed entirely to follow the example of his uncle, Feisal I, who successfully built up a fair amount of popularity for himself on a foundation of nationalistic fervour while at the same time, in his relations with H. M. G., showing that he appreciated the identity of Iraqi with British interests. . . .

[The Regent's] troubles are due to his friendship with us and to internal conditions for which he is only in a small degree responsible. His cousin, Ghazi, was incompetent, lazy and debauched but was popular because he hated us. . . .

[The Regent] has failed completely to fulfil the high promise which he gave in 1941 and by his interference in Cabinet making, insistence on other unpopular appointments, frequent long absences from the country, extravagance and, in general, his play-boy attitude to his responsibilities has gone far, I am afraid, to undermine the position of the Royal House.[10]

Buss emphasized the year 1941 as a juncture in the relations between Britain and Iraq because at that time the British had forcibly restored the Hashemite monarchy and attempted to quell the type of Iraqi nationalism that allied itself with the Mufti, Hitler, and other mortal enemies of the British Empire.

The Legacy of 1941

The Rashid Ali revolt of 1941 left a permanent imprint on the British memory of recent history.[11] If the official mind of the postwar era had known that Nuri Pasha had hedged his bets by making secret overtures to the Nazis, the perplexities of Iraqi nationalism would probably have appeared in an entirely different light. As Elie Kedourie has pointed out, the allied victories of 1941 probably offered a better guarantee of the loyalty of the Arabs than their

[10] Minute by Buss, 23 Feb. 1948, FO 371/68385/E3471/G. For an important and much more favourable account of the Regent than can be found in F. O. files, see the book by a latter-day British adventurer, Gerald de Gaury, *Three Kings in Baghdad, 1921–1958* (London, 1961). De Gaury was the Regent's confidant and adviser. According to the head of the Eastern Department: 'Col. de Gaury is not always a very reliable informant but he has a wide range of contacts in Iraq and undoubtedly has a large measure of the Regent's confidence.' (Minute by Bernard Burrows, 2 Mar. 1948, FO 371/68446/E2693/G.)

[11] For example Oliver Harvey in his diary recorded Churchill's reaction: 'The Arabs have done nothing for us except to revolt against us in Iraq.' Harvey Diaries, Add. MSS 56400, 20 Oct. 1944.

professions of friendship of 1939–40.[12] Then as later Nuri believed that British unwillingness or inability to solve the Palestine problem undermined his position in Iraq as well as his effectiveness as a pan-Arab leader. As events transpired the Mufti had rejected Nuri's offer of collaboration. Nuri sustained his pro-British reputation. He played a key part in the suppression of the revolt, the restoration of the Regent, and the hobbling of the Iraqi army.

In the 1945–8 era, when Iraqi preoccupation with Palestine was even greater than in the early period of the war, British officials reflected on the causes of the 1941 uprising. They identified the presence of the Mufti in Baghdad (where he had fled from Jerusalem) as a catalyst of Iraqi nationalism that found extreme expression in the revolt of Rashid Ali and the four colonels. Again the remarks of Air Commodore Buss are of particular interest because he brought to bear his military expertise in assessing the military element of the revolt, and because he wrote in another time of nationalist crisis, February 1948. Military interference in Iraqi politics was a constant source of British anxiety. In 1941 the 'dictatorship' of the army by the four colonels had been 'disposed of' by the British with relative ease, but the effectiveness of British intervention in wartime had not solved the larger problem of how to prevent a military take-over in the time of peace. As if addressing himself to the problems of the late 1950s, Commodore Buss, ten years before Nuri's assassination in 1958, examined the reasons for political extremism in the army of the 1940s. He commented on the Mufti's appeal to the half-baked ideas of the Iraqi élite, including army officers, who were 'easily inspired' by the Mufti 'or Hitler or Stalin' or, in other words, authoritarian figures 'who epitomize the ruthless anti-foreign leader each of them would like to be'. He explained Iraqi nationalism and the revolt of 1941 in relation to the Zionist movement since the time of the First World War:

> The interest shown in Iraq [in the Palestine controversy] is a result not only of the presence of the Mufti there in 1939 but also of the doctrine carefully instilled into the minds of school boys and girls since 1921 or thereabout that H. M. G. had let down the Arabs, and particularly the Hashimites, in the Peace Settlement of 1919 of which the mandates for Iraq and Palestine and the foundation of the Jewish National home were a part. Denunciation of H. M. G. for the part which they continued to play in Iraq and Palestine formed two variations of one theme.[13]

---

[12] See Majid Khadduri, 'General Nuri's Flirtations with the Axis Powers', *Middle East Journal*, 16, 3 (Summer 1962). On the more general subject of Germany and Iraq see Lukasz Hirszowicz, *The Third Reich and the Arab East* (London, 1966); see also especially Francis Nicosia, 'Arab Nationalism and National Socialist Germany, 1933–1939', *International Journal of Middle East Studies*, 12, 3 (Nov. 1980). For Kedourie's views see Elie Kedourie, 'How . . . to Seek Peace in the Middle East', *Encounter* (May 1978), p. 46.

[13] Minute by Buss, 23 Feb. 1948, FO 371/68385/E4371/G.

Unfortunately for the British, the Palestine controversy continued to feed extreme Iraqi nationalism which in turn made it more difficult for the British to accommodate American policy, and moderate Zionism, in Palestine. Buss in short concluded that there was a correlation between the intensity of the struggle in Palestine and the tide of nationalism in Iraq that worked to Britain's general disadvantage in the Middle East.

The year 1941 represents a watershed in the history of the British era in Iraq, and its significance is essential in understanding the nationalist rejection of the treaty of alliance with the British in 1948 and the end of the Hashemite dynasty ten years later.[14] The British at the time denounced the uprising as a revolt, and by no means thought of it as a 'war of liberation', as the nationalist movement claimed it to be. They regarded Rashid Ali and his supporters as renegades, but as the official mind refined its views the coup of 1941 came to represent a much more intractable problem than mere wartime opportunism. The pan-Arab nationalists of 1941 hoped to destroy French rule in Syria and Lebanon, and to annihilate the Jewish national home in Palestine. The extreme aim did not diminish. During and after the war its exponents continued to press for the creation of a unitary Arab state incorporating Iraq, Syria, Lebanon, Transjordan, and Palestine. In the eyes of the extreme nationalists the Hashemites could not be trusted to bring about this unification. The Hashemites had lost nationalist confidence.[15] King Abdullah was universally regarded as a British puppet. The Regent had been restored by British bayonets. In this sense the events of 1941 created an irreconcilable breach between the British and the extreme nationalists. There was no room for compromise. The question of the 1940s was whether Nuri's moderate brand of Arab nationalism could prevail.

The Fertile Crescent

Nuri's pan-Arab or 'Fertile Crescent' scheme attempted to achieve the basic aims of the pan-Arabs in harmony with the British rather than in inevitable conflict with them as the extremists anticipated. The British themselves had no general reason to resist pan-Arab ambitions. If the Arabs themselves could agree on the creation of a pro-British Arab state based on the geographical and historical dimension of 'Greater Syria' then it would make much better political

[14] For important comment on the Arab interpretation of 'the revolution of 1941' see Ayad Al-Qazzaz, 'The Iraqi–British War of 1941', *International Journal of Middle East Studies*, 7 (1976), which is a review of accounts based on Arabic sources.

[15] This point is emphasized by Patrick Seale, *The Struggle for Syria: A Study of Post-War Arab Politics 1945–1958* (Oxford, 1965), p. 8.

and economic sense than the artificial creations of the post-First World War settlement. By endorsing the desirability of pan-Arab schemes in 1941 the British merely placed the onus of responsibility for failure on the Arabs rather than on themselves. But any British support for any particular scheme, whether for Nuri's 'Fertile Crescent' or Abdullah's 'Greater Syria', would immediately raise suspicions of another façade of British imperialism. The Saudis and Egyptians regarded Hashemite unity schemes as an attempt to dominate the Middle East. Nuri's plan therefore attempted, in part by its flexibility, to offer the Arabs themselves the opportunity to unite in a 'Greater Syria' (Syria, Lebanon, Palestine, and Trans-jordan) which would be joined by Iraq. The type of government might be federal or unitary, monarchical or republican, but it would be created with the consensus of Arab nationalists. There would be international guarantees for minorities, including Jews in Palestine and Christians in Lebanon. Nuri further proposed that other Arab states, notably Saudi Arabia and Egypt, could be associated together in a greater Arab League.[16] He thus had ambitions that stretched far beyond the 'Fertile Crescent' and hoped to reconcile eventually the Egyptians and the Saudis with the Hashemites.

Nuri's staunch support of the Hashemites since the time of the Arab revolt provided him with the credentials and the general mystique of a pan-Arab nationalist. But he did not necessarily predicate his plan on Hashemite leadership. He thus perhaps offset some suspicion of Hashemite expansionism, but at the same time he created tension between himself and the Regent, on the one hand, and Abdullah on the other.[17] Abdullah's own plan for a 'Greater Syria' (which will be discussed in the next chapter) was more modest than Nuri's—Abdullah merely wanted to see himself enthroned as the monarch of Transjordan, Syria, Lebanon, Palestine, and perhaps eventually Iraq as well—but he pressed so vigorously that the Foreign Office in mid-1947 had to contrive a Parliamentary statement of neutrality in order to offset Saudi and Egyptian suspicion of British complicity in a Hashemite bid for a take-over of the Middle East.[18] So far as the British are concerned, there is little point in pursuing the intricacies of the various pan-Arab schemes of the 1940s, but it should be emphasized that 'Greater Syria' continued

[16] See Nuri's famous pamphlet published in 1943, *Arab Independence and Unity*.

[17] See especially Reeva S. Simon, 'The Hashemite "Conspiracy": Hashemite Unity Attempts, 1921–1958', *International Journal of Middle East Studies*, 5 (1974).

[18] See the statement by Hector McNeil, *Parliamentary Debates* (Commons), 14 July 1947, col. 9, which denied 'most strongly' that the British government supported plans for a 'Greater Syria'. 'The attitude of His Majesty's Government on the subject is . . . one of strict neutrality.'

to preoccupy both British and Arab leaders. The following comment by the head of the Arab Legion, Glubb Pasha, indicates the vitality of the issue at the end of the decade. He wrote of course with Transjordan's interests in mind, but his thoughts illuminate the kaleidoscopic complexity of possible solutions.

> Syria . . . seems ripe for disintegration. Iraq–Syrian union is at present being canvassed but it is extremely doubtful whether it will actually take place (or if it takes place whether it will subsequently 'come unstuck'). If Greater Syria is unattainable, a Fertile Crescent Federation of Iraq, Syria and Jordan would be more satisfactory than Iraqo-Syrian union with Jordan excluded.[19]

At every twist and turn in these developments and possibilities, the British could see the hand of Nuri Pasha. He probably appeared to some of the more cynical observers in the Foreign Office to confirm Lord Cranborne's comment in 1938: 'a devious intriguer with a passion for having his finger in every pie'.[20]

Postwar Iraqi Politics

In the postwar period the 'Oriental Counsellor', or in other words the Arab expert of the Embassy in Baghdad, Stewart Perowne, described Nuri as 'the most able statesman in the country' whose success in domestic as well as external affairs could be attributed to the Regent's support. The Regent, according to Perowne, trusted Nuri: 'The only Iraqi statesman in whom he has real confidence is Nuri Pasha, and in this he shows wise judgement.' On several occasions Perowne developed the next stage of the argument: the happy circumstances of postwar Iraq could ultimately be traced to the Regent's love of England as well as his faith in Nuri.

> The credit for this state of affairs must in large measure be assigned to the Regent. . . . There is no doubt that His Royal Highness has a great admiration and liking for Britain and for British methods and persons. His cars, his aircraft, his clothes, his hunters, his fox-hounds, even his swans, are British, and so are many of his closest friends.[21]

---

[19] Memorandum by Glubb, 25 Oct. 1949, FO 371/75279.

[20] Quoted in Ahmed M. Gomaa, *The Foundation of the League of Arab States* (London, 1977), p. 67. The assessment is not incompatible with Elie Kedourie's in regard to the critical importance of the year 1941: 'The British occupation of the country in 1941 enabled him to discredit his enemies, weaken his rivals, and reign supreme for nearly two decades, presenting to the world the picture of an old statesman full of wisdom and up-rightness, dedicated to progress and reform. This is not at all how the matter looked to his opponents, who considered him a cunning and dangerous enemy, an autocrat in power and an intriguer out of it; and his very skill in manipulating power, unmatched by any other politicians of his day in Iraq, served but to increase the hate and envy to which, in the end, he fell victim.' Kedourie, 'The Kingdom of Iraq', p. 281.

[21] Memorandum by Perowne in Stonehewer Bird to Bevin, 6 Jan. 1947, FO 371/61588.

What many observers of the postwar Arab world would have taken as a cause for alarm filled Perowne with a feeling that approached optimistic complacency. In any case he believed the Regent to be a more influential political personality than did most contemporary observers, though he did note deficiencies of character:

> The influence he exerts on politics and administration in Iraq is all-pervading, if often unseen. He is still shy, and suffers from the introspective melancholia of his house; but he had made strenuous and largely successful efforts to overcome this defect. He often carries procrastination and indecision to almost Elizabethan lengths but . . .[22]

At the phrase 'Elizabethan lengths' one must pause to comment on its author and his extraordinary reports to the Foreign Office on Iraqi society and politics.

The Foreign Office depended on the oriental counsellors of the embassies in the Middle East to provide insights into contemporary affairs as perceived from the Arab as opposed to the European point of view. The cumulative effect of Perowne's reports achieved just the opposite aim of imposing a striking and indeed eccentric English interpretation of Iraqi behaviour. The point is important because the quality of political reporting from Baghdad in the postwar period helps to explain British misapprehensions and unanticipated developments. From Baghdad the Eastern Department received reports with such literary and fastidious English flair that they must strike the historian, as they did contemporaries, as bizarre. Perowne had a passion for English history.[23] One finds statements of Iraqi politicians, as reported to London, that echoed the thoughts of Queen Anne and the Duke of Marlborough, that dwelt on parallels of corruption in eighteenth-century England and twentieth-century Iraq, and that emphasized a march of nineteenth-century progress that Perowne hoped had now reached Baghdad. It was from Perowne that the Foreign Office learned of the Regent's similarities with the young George III, of Nuri's strengths and weaknesses in comparison with Disraeli's, of Iraqi political parties interpreted as Tory and Whig, and of the fundamental religious tension in the country between Sunni and Shia Muslims described in the language of great historical literature: the 'Sunni–Shia fission [has] . . . revealed once again the basic weakness of the country', Perowne wrote at the close of 1946: 'now, as one thousand years ago, "in every profession which allowed

---

[22] Memorandum by Perowne in Stonehewer Bird to Bevin, 6 Jan. 1947, FO 371/61588.

[23] Along with an ebullient interest in both ancient and modern history, archaeology, and horses, Perowne had a reputation as a noted philatelist. He designed issues of postage stamps and currency notes for Malta, Aden, Barbados, Libya, and the West Indies Federation.

room for two persons, the one was a votary, the other an antagonist"
... (Gibbon)'.[24]

In the Foreign Office the state of Iraqi politics appeared to be
much less 'stagnant' than Perowne seemed to suggest, except perhaps
in a dangerous sense. The British found themselves allied with the
'old gang' of Iraqi politicians who, in British eyes, personified reaction and corruption. The officials in the Eastern Department
believed that the Regent held only a tenuous religious, political, and
military sway. They doubted that he could, even with the versatile
aid of Nuri Pasha, hold together the fractious society of Iraq. The
fiercely independent disposition of the Kurds, who formed one-fifth
of the population, was but one specific example of future trouble.
There existed uneasy relations between the politically dominant
Sunni and the Shia majority, between rural, tribal, and urban
elements, between pro-Arab military officers and pro-British politicians, and, not least, generally between the nationalists and the
British. Antipathy to the British can be found at every level of Iraqi
society, but there was also strong pro-British sentiment, especially
among the older generation of political leaders. The Regent himself
endorsed the 'reactionary' and 'oppressive' policies of the 'old gang'
who surrounded him. In the words of G. H. Baker of the Eastern
Department, these Iraqi political leaders were 'extremely conservative and see in repression the only way of dealing with the demands
and propaganda of the left-wing parties'.[25] The British in general
sympathized with the reformers who demanded, among other things,
social justice, educational programmes, and agricultural development. Unless such requests were met, the intelligentsia might swing
to the left and the Communist faction would be buttressed. If the
situation deteriorated the British would find themselves aligned with
the corrupt ruling class with the political extremes of the far right
and far left combined against them. They thus faced a dilemma. On
the one hand the British favoured reforms; on the other they wished
to retain the friendship of those ruling Iraq. Again according to
G. H. Baker, who at this time was one of the principal analysts of
Iraqi politics, the problem of whether to continue backing an ultra-
conservative regime could be summed up in these words: 'we should
not continue to be associated with reactionary political elements.
But we should have to be careful not to alienate the good will of
the government in power, who might retaliate by adopting an

---

[24] Ibid. He added: 'On the Euphrates the fires of fanaticism still smoulder behind the
black veils of Najaf and Kerbala, whose sterile and greedy hierophants are ever ready to
exploit religious antipathy and racial hatred.'

[25] Minute by Baker, 26 Sept. 1946, FO 371/52402.

anti-British tone in the hope of securing cheap kudos from the vocal left-wing elements.'[26]

The Foreign Secretary himself held vigorous opinions about the failure of the 'old gang' to introduce reforms. Bevin pressed the Regent, during a visit to London, to hold free elections, to reduce the censorship of the press, and to raise the standard of living of the working classes, 'particularly in the oil fields'.[27] Bevin also told the Iraqi Minister for Foreign Affairs, Fadhil al-Jamali:

> I thought to deal with Communism by means of repression alone was not the best method. Many of these young men and women in all probability were really anxious that their country should develop an energetic social policy and they found an outlet for their energies in supporting that line of action. Would it not be wise therefore to have a definite policy devised and put it before the country, then rally the bulk of the people?[28]

In particular Bevin attached importance to development schemes for irrigation that would 'capture a large acreage of land cultivation'.[29] He urged the Iraqis to pursue 'a bold development plan . . . on the line of the T. V. A.'[30] He thus hoped to remove the justified grievances of the reformers and at the same time, by demonstrating the benefits of economic development, to keep on good terms with the governing circles of Iraq.

Two dates of critical importance for the domestic situation in Iraq, from the British point of view, were December 1945, when the Regent promised eventual free elections, and March 1947, when the elections at last were actually held. The Regent assured political freedom, encouraged the development of political parties, and hoped that the achievement in Iraq of genuine parliamentary democracy would lead to economic and social reform.[31] The policies pursued by the Regent in fact remained repressive. The British supported the Iraqi monarchy; the Regent upheld the authoritarian policies of his ministers; ministers suppressed the newspapers and took no initiative in land reform or agricultural or educational matters; and the cumulative result came full circle to the British: 'British policy will be held responsible for the present reactionary trend of the Iraqi

---

[26] Minute by Baker, 19 Aug. 1947, FO 371/52402.

[27] See Bevin to Stonehewer Bird, 19 July 1946, FO 371/52402/E6928.

[28] Bevin to Stonehewer Bird, 18 Sept. 1946, FO 371/52402/E9355.

[29] Bevin to Campbell, 13 June 1947, FO 371/61591/E4853.

[30] Ibid.

[31] For significance of the Regent's speech of 27 Dec. 1945, see Khadduri, *Independent Iraq*, p. 253, and, for British analysis, Stonehewer Bird to Bevin, 31 Dec. 1945, FO 371/52401, which commented that 'some cynics, chiefly the older generation, have adopted the attitude that the more the situation changes the more will it remain the same; but among the younger generation there is no doubt that the Regent's initiative has been welcomed'.

Government', Baker noted in September 1946.[32] Phrases such as 'unhealthy' and 'disquieting' recurred in the comments of the officials of the Eastern Department.[33] It was therefore with a sense of anxiety that they awaited the results of the election. They hoped that the Shias might find more effective representation, and that 'younger men' with 'new blood' and 'new ideas' might replace some of the 'old gang' in the Iraqi Parliament. They were on the lookout in particular for the fortunes of Saleh Jabr, a Shia leader, whom they regarded as the 'coming young man' in Iraqi politics.

Stewart Perowne reported the results of the election with literary gusto and a political verve that reflected 'great credit on the humanity, no less than on the sagacity, of Nuri al Said'. The long-awaited elections, Perowne wrote, took place in tranquil circumstances in March 1947. He noted with satisfaction that the new Chamber of Representatives would include 68 Sunnis, 57 Shias, 6 Christians, and 6 Jews. Perowne then analysed the general circumstances of the election, the historical evolution of Iraqi democracy, and the tension between 'oriental' politics and the British tradition of public service. There were those in the Foreign Office who had little patience with Perowne's excessively English interpretation of Iraqi politics, but his reports received the endorsement of the Ambassador, Stonehewer Bird, and other independent confirmation. His account of the 1947 election is of particular interest because it reveals assumptions about 'oriental' politics that were seldom so clearly expressed. Most British officials, if pressed intellectually, would probably have agreed with him even if they might have regarded some of his literary and historical allusions as frivolous.

'Were the elections free?' Perowne asked, as if to reassure those who perhaps suspected that they had been rigged by Nuri.

If by 'free' is implied freedom from physical interference or menace, the answer is 'yes'. Neither the Government, nor, so far as I know, any other individual or association, has used force, or threatened to use it. There have been no arrests, no interrogations. . . . Coercion and intimidation, such as have become the melancholy and humiliating routine in so many States of Europe and America, were entirely absent.[34]

---

[32] Minute by Baker, 26 Sept. 1946, FO 371/52402/E9585.

[33] See e.g. minutes by Baxter, 30 Sept. 1946: 'the government is run by a limited circle of politicians who do not represent the country as a whole. . . . Free elections . . . may be the best remedy for the present situation'; and by Howe, 4 Oct. 1946: 'The Regent is, unfortunately, not a strong character and is inclined to take the advice of the last person he listens to. . . . elections . . . will be one step at least in the right direction.' FO 371/52402/9585.

[34] Memorandum by Perowne enclosed in Stonehewer Bird to Bevin, 13 Mar. 1947, FO 371/61589/E2695.

Truly the Iraqis had made progress from only recent times when merely a change of government would create an atmosphere of 'turmoil, resentment and indignation'. On a long-range scale a keen eye for historical trends could also detect Assyrian, Babylonian, Roman, Persian, Arab, Turkish, and, especially, British antecedents of Iraqi parliamentary democracy down to the year 1924, when the Iraqi Parliament had met for the first time. 'Democracy had arrived', Perowne wrote. 'But it was hardly to be expected', he continued in one of his more lighthearted allusions, 'that it would be the democracy which (in Mr. Shaw's phrase) "substitutes election by the incompetent many for appointment by the corrupt few".' He explained the way in which the Foreign Office might best interpret the recent history of Iraq:

> King Feisal I dominated his Parliament. . . . After [his] death [in 1933] the royal primacy waned. The constitution, and the spirit of our age, were invoked against it. But latterly, as in the England of King George the Third, 'the power of the Crown, almost dead and rotten as prerogative, has grown up anew [because of the Regent], with far more strength and far less odium, under the name of influence.'

Perowne did not wish to imply that the Iraqis would demonstrate anything that approached British standards of public honesty and integrity. Indeed he lamented the lack of genuine parliamentary democracy and statesmanship, and regretfully concluded that Iraqi politics appeared to be of the Italian variety. On this occasion he wrote with real insight:

> The selfless dedication to a principle, the acquiescence in obloquy, neglect and disappointment, the indifference to personal advancement and the stubborn confidence in the eventual vindication of a cause, such as invigorated and ennobled a Wilberforce, a Shaftesbury or a Webb—these are not to be sought in an oriental political party. Its prototype is rather the Italian 'combinazione', a transient association of a few interested individuals for a transient material end.[35]

Despite the 'oriental' or 'Italian' flavour of the election, Perowne concluded that the British had good reason to be pleased. As he had expected it had not ousted the 'old gang' but it did constitute a 'victory' for Britain's two best friends in Iraq, the Regent and Nuri. 'In broad terms, the old régime has received a new mandate. What it will do with it remains to be seen.' Among other things the new mandate would probably include the social and economic reforms urged by Saleh Jabr, whom Perowne described as 'an able administrator and an astute politician', one who aspired 'to become Iraq's first Shia Prime Minister'.

---

[35] Memorandum by Perowne enclosed in Stonehewer Bird to Bevin, 13 Mar. 1947, FO 371/61589/E2695.

Saleh Jabr's political fortunes had also been fully assessed by another official in the Embassy in Baghdad, Douglas Busk. During the critical period of late 1947 and early 1948 Busk found himself, because of the illness of the Ambassador, virtually in charge of the Baghdad side of delicate Iraqi business. The Foreign Office valued his political estimates. It was from Busk that the Eastern Department received full reports in the autumn of 1946 on the question of revising the treaty of 1930. Though Busk's reports did not contradict Perowne's, they dealt much more critically with both Nuri and Saleh Jabr. Busk commented on the latter in September 1946:

I am much impressed by his ideas and forcefulness. He strikes me moreover as being capable not only of making plans but of carrying them through. His past record in this respect is outstanding in Iraq. . . . He is a staunch patriot and a hard bargainer. Moreover he will be under great pressure to revise the Treaty [of 1930] and he will inevitably have to bow to public opinion. . . . undoubtedly there will be difficulties because he is a Shia.[36]

In March 1947 Saleh Jabr became the first Shia Prime Minister in the history of Iraq.

Saleh Jabr introduced a programme of such sweeping economic and social scope that it made the goals of the Labour government in England seem modest in comparison. Parts of it, especially the plans for economic development, clearly were Utopian, but as a manifesto it appeared to the Eastern Department of the Foreign Office to be 'balanced . . . progressive and enterprising'. Saleh Jabr had a reputation as Nuri's protégé (he had served, for example, as Nuri's Minister of Justice during the war, when he had sentenced nationalists who later helped to bring about his fall). He now had come of age, in fact he was 47, as Iraq's foremost young politician who, the British hoped, would 'meet the growing demand from left wing circles for more radical change'.[37] Saleh Jabr's significance for the history of British imperialism in Iraq at this juncture was that of a moderate and strong nationalist who, it was hoped, would co-operate with the British in both domestic and foreign affairs. He would accomplish internally what Nuri merely talked about. The British did not doubt that Nuri possessed a social conscience; but they thought that he became so absorbed in pan-Arab affairs that he could not be relied upon to force the pace of social change on

---

[36] Busk to Bevin, 19 Sept. 1946, FO 371/52402/E9585. On another occasion Busk had commented ominously on Jabr's wife, 'who forces him into intrigues of the most disreputable sort in the interests of her rapacious family'. (Busk to Bevin, 6 Sept. 1946, FO 371/52402/E9318.) The theme of pernicious 'petticoat influence' runs through Busk's despatches, especially in regard to the Regent.

[37] Minute by Garran, 28 Apr. 1947, FO 371/61589, which contains extensive correspondence and minutes on Saleh Jabr's programme.

his friends in the 'old gang'. They therefore welcomed his ascendancy to the Presidency of the Iraqi Senate, where he would continue as usual to manipulate behind the scenes. Saleh Jabr, by contrast with his mentor, had the reputation of being a straightforward, tough-minded, honest nationalist with whom the British could do business. If the basis of Anglo-Iraqi friendship—critics would say the formal instrument of British imperialism—the treaty of 1930, needed to be adjusted, then Saleh Jabr appeared to be the best man in sight to reaffirm it in only slightly modified form.

The Foundation of 1930 and Postwar Defence

Nationalists on the right as well as 'Left Wing agitators' shared similar sentiments about the Treaty of Alliance of 1930, which governed Anglo-Iraqi relations. The main points of that arrangement may be summed up by stating that it terminated the mandate and recognized Iraq's independence. It paved the way for admission to the League of Nations in 1932. The League welcomed Iraq's entry into the comity of nations with no dissenting votes. To the generation of Iraqis who regarded mandated status as a stigma of international inferiority, acceptance into the League symbolized Iraq's accession to international equality; but to the next generation the continued existence of the bilateral treaty represented as great a servitude as the mandate had seemed to the previous generation.

The treaty of 1930 contained certain military clauses that were as offensive to Iraqi nationalists as were the provisions in the Egyptian treaty of 1936 to Egyptian nationalists. The British acquired two air bases and secured 'the permanent maintenance and protection in all circumstances' of 'essential' communications. They retained the right to move armed forces 'in transit' across Iraq and in case of war to have access to 'all facilities and assistance including the use of railways, rivers, ports, aerodromes, and means of communication'. Of those military clauses the occupation of the air bases rankled most in the minds of Iraqi nationalists.

The two air bases were Habbaniyah, sixty miles to the west of Baghdad, and Shaiba in the south, twelve miles from Basra. They differed geographically from the air bases in Egypt because of relative remoteness from major cities. Nevertheless by mid-1946 it became increasingly clear to the British that the Iraqis would not indefinitely tolerate foreign 'enclaves' and that an alternative defence system would eventually have to be found.

Legally the treaty of 1930 should not have expired until 1957; but the British, anticipating Iraqi resistance, agreed to discuss treaty revision in 1946-7. In return for this concession the Regent and other Iraqi leaders agreed not to force the pace until the Egyptian situation became clarified (which it did when the British and Egyptians reached deadlock in December 1946). The British believed that goodwill on their part, reciprocated by Iraqi leaders, had prevented agitation on the Egyptian scale. In analysing Iraqi motives, Foreign Office officials saw no clear driving force other than a desire not to be left in an inferior position to the Egyptians. According to Robert Howe in November 1946:

> The Iraqis themselves do not seem to have any very clear idea of what they want. . . . The real urge, such as it is, for treaty revision is partly due to the knowledge that the Anglo-Egyptian Treaty is being revised.[38]

Preoccupied with Egypt and Palestine, Bevin and his advisers in 1945-6 played for time in Iraq, hoping for a less conservative regime and a stabilization of Iraqi politics. The auspicious moment arrived when Nuri yielded the Prime Ministership to Saleh Jabr in March 1947. The British now believed that they would be less vulnerable to charges of conniving with the 'old gang'.

In assessing the military and political risks of upsetting the splendid arrangement of 1930—which one author from an Iraqi point of view has described as having reduced Iraq 'into an appendage of the British Empire'[39]—the British official mind pondered the significance of the revolt of 1941. A key issue in the discussion with the Iraqis would be the restructuring of the Iraqi army, which, with Nuri's aid, had been kept in a state of suppression because of its support of Rashid Ali. The army was essential to the British as an instrument of internal security as well as an arm of Middle East defence, and thus was vital to the question of the future of both Iraq and the British Empire. The British now hoped to improve the army's fitness as well as its loyalty. At any cost they wished to avert a recurrence of an army coup such as the one of 1941.

The head of the British military mission in Baghdad, General J. M. L. Renton, recorded his thought on the events of 1941 in a way that casts invaluable light on their significance in military calculations of 1946-7. Renton in fact reconstructed the episode of 1941 as a prelude to answering questions about the future function of the army in Iraqi politics and, in a wider sense, British imperialism. The army had been created in 1931. The rearmament programme against Germany and the financial crisis of the 1930s had prevented the British from providing the Iraqi army with adequate arms (which in

---

[38] Howe to Dixon, Secret and Personal, 29 Nov. 1946, FO 371/52403/E11727.
[39] Batatu, *Old Social Classes and the Revolutionary Movements*, p. 545.

any case they feared might be used against them in Palestine). That neglect inflamed Iraqi nationalism. In 1941 the army rebelled. Here follow excerpts from Renton's historical comment on sensitive aspects of the army up to the time of his arrival as head of the military mission in 1944:

After 1935 . . . the British failure to supply equipment exasperated nationalist feeling in the Army and was universally attributed to the British fear of Iraqi armed forces intervening on the Arab side in Palestine. This feeling was of course fanned by the Mufti (at that time in exile in Iraq), and was a godsend to the German Minister and to all the pro-Germans in the country. . . . As the feeling on the subject became more and more intense it culminated in the Rashid Ali Revolt of 1941, when the Army, although somewhat half-heartedly, went into open rebellion.

After the collapse of the Revolt and the entry of British troops into Baghdad, the British authorities decided that although it was not possible to disband the Iraqi Army, a policy of weakening it indirectly should be adopted, mainly through the agency of Nuri Pasha who combined the offices of Prime Minister and Minister of Defence. Rations were cut down by 1,000 calories a day below what was considered necessary by the medical authorities for Eastern troops, no clothing or equipment were purchased and by the Spring of 1944 the Army was in rags, with no equipment and no morale. For this Nuri Pasha under British guidance was considered responsible in the eyes of almost all the officers, although even they admit that the policy had the support of the Iraqis as a whole, among whom the Army was at this time most unpopular.[40]

In 1947 Renton still continued to report that the fitness of the army remained lamentable. For purposes of internal security, it would be mandatory to retrain officers and troops and supply them with new equipment. Otherwise when the British eventually withdrew the country would collapse into anarchy. In Renton's considered judgement: 'while it is extremely improbable that at least during the next ten years the Iraqi Army will be of the slightest value in delaying actions against a major enemy, it is essential in our own interests that the Army should be able to maintain internal security in the country'.[41] Rejuvenation of the army became one of the principal British aims in postwar Iraq.

The British had a paramount strategic goal as well. It could be defined in the phrase 'air defence system', the purpose of which would be to secure 'lines of communication' and air transit from Transjordan to the Persian Gulf as well as to protect the oilfields.

---

[40] Memorandum by Renton, 4 Aug. 1947, FO 371/61593/E7401/G.

[41] Other members of the Baghdad Embassy emphatically agreed with that point. Douglas Busk wrote: 'while it is extremely improbable that at least during the next ten years, the Iraqi Army will be of the slightest value in fighting delaying actions against a major enemy, it is essential in our own interests that the Army should be able to maintain internal security in the country. With this thesis I entirely agree.' Busk to Bevin, 'Most Secret Light', 23 May 1947, FO 371/61591/E4770.

Habbaniyah fulfilled this requirement for northern Iraq while Shaiba protected the southern oil fields and the head of the Persian Gulf. Both bases were within striking distance of southern Russia, though British plans at this time were primarily defensive in the grand Imperial tradition: 'Our requirements in this area consist of airfields linking Palestine/Trans-Jordan and Bahrein on the Persian Gulf.'[42] When the Chief of the Air Staff, Lord Tedder, visited Baghdad in November 1946 and began preliminary discussions about these matters, he was relieved to find that the Regent and Nuri Pasha concurred in general British defence plans.[43] The geographical proximity of the Soviet Union instilled a fear of Russian expansion in some Iraqi nationalists that most Egyptian nationalists never shared.

The Iraqis, like the Egyptians, believed that they were more capable of self-defence than the British seemed to assume. The issue of control of the two air bases was certain to be a major point of controversy. The Iraqis also put forward an awkward military request. They wished to modernize the army with new military vehicles and equipment and to have the British send a military mission to Iraq to train a nucleus of officers in the use of modern weaponry. Though the War Office and Air Ministry could easily send a mission for such training purposes, the demand for modern equipment raised a set of peculiar difficulties. Tanks, jeeps, and transport vehicles were not being produced in quantity in postwar Britain. 'It is simply not possible for us to supply this equipment', lamented the head of the Eastern Department, C. W. Baxter.[44] When the British broached the idea of handing over a few Sherman tanks from the Canal Zone, the Iraqis refused to be foisted off with used Second World War equipment. They suspected that the British saw advantages in Iraqi military inferiority which would perpetuate the client relationship. In May 1947 the Air Vice-Marshal, Sir Brian Baker, and Brigadier F. C. Curtis flew to Baghdad to discuss these issues. Their report was not encouraging: 'The Iraqi representatives were frankly incredulous about our inability to supply the Iraqi Army with new equipment. All efforts to persuade them that no such new equipment was at the moment being manufactured in the United Kingdom failed.'[45] The question of providing military equipment was quickly becoming one of British good faith. It was a deficiency the British made good within the next six months, perhaps proving one of Lord Killearn's axioms: where Imperial will existed, the wherewithal

---

[42] See JP (46) 178, 25 Oct. 1946, CAB 84/84; minutes in FO 371/52403.
[43] Stonehewer Bird to Bevin, 22 Nov. 1946, FO 371/52403/E11445.
[44] Minute by Baxter, 11 Apr. 1947, FO 371/61589.
[45] Busk to Bevin, 23 May 1947, FO 371/61591.

would be forthcoming. There was a logic to British assistance. The more equipment and advisers the Iraqis accepted, the greater would be the British control. 'The presence . . . of British Advisers', an official in the Eastern Department once noted, 'is one of our most potent means of maintaining our influence in Iraq.'[46]

British assessments of military collaboration acquired a tone of urgency in the summer of 1947, after the preliminary military discussions in Baghdad and before the denouement of the Palestine question, which the British correctly anticipated would come in the autumn. The Eastern Department now knew for certain that the issue of the two air bases could prove to be a symbol of nationalist protest against British imperialism unless handled with great care and with an eye towards the future rather than the standing of the 1930 treaty in international law. C. W. Baxter summarized the results of the May discussions:

> The Iraqis evidently felt that it was unfair and unreasonable that they should provide us with bases in Iraq for Middle-Eastern defence while the Syrians and Lebanese and other Arab States made no such contribution. Indeed, Iraq is incurring odium in the other Arab States as being too pro-British.[47]

The Eastern Department continued to hope that the Iraqis would prove amenable to a continued British presence and at least a 'shared' control of the two bases, but Baxter and other officials now began to consider the possibility of evacuation from Iraq in favour of more permanent bases in Transjordan and the Persian Gulf. During this time Douglas Busk sent a number of telegrams and despatches to London that proved decisive in the swing towards dealing with Iraqi strategic questions within the broader spectrum of Arab nationalism.[48] He argued in brief that it would still be possible to come to terms with Iraqi nationalists while Saleh Jabr headed the government (with Nuri in the background), but that the British would have to act now or make alternative plans. 'The tide of nationalism is rising in the Middle East', Busk wrote, 'though perhaps slower in Iraq than elsewhere.'[49] The officials of the Eastern Department by the summer of 1947 thus had definite warning of a possible wave of Iraqi nationalism, though it probably would be unfair to blame them for not foreseeing its future tidal proportion that arose a few months later

---

[46] Minute by L. F. L. Pyman, 9 Mar. 1946, FO 371/52401/E1947.

[47] Minute by Baxter, 17 June 1947, FO 371/61591/E4770/G.

[48] See especially his 'Most Secret' and 'Light' (special distribution) despatch of 23 May 1947, FO 371/61591, his 'Most Secret and Personal' letter to Peter Garran of 27 June 1947, FO 371/61592, and his 'Immediate' 'Light' and 'Top Secret' telegram given Cabinet distribution of 1 Aug. 1947, ibid., which Baxter noted was 'most important and valuable'.

[49] Busk to Bevin, 1 Aug. 1947, FO 371/61592.

because of the crisis in Palestine and other circumstances within Iraq itself.

The aim of indirectly controlling the Persian Gulf (as well as all of Iraq) involved the establishment of a series of 'police stations' from which the British would be able to intervene against internal disturbances or external aggression. Busk wrote in June 1947:

> It seems to me that our strategic and security interests throughout the world will be best safeguarded by the establishment in suitable spots of 'police stations' fully equipped to deal with emergencies within a large radius. Kuwait is one such spot from which Iraq, South Persia, Saudi Arabia and the Persian Gulf could be controlled. It will be well worth while to go to considerable trouble and expense to establish and man a 'police station' there.[50]

Busk anticipated Iraqi demands for total evacuation of Habbaniyah and Shaiba, if not in the immediate future then within the next few years. He proposed a two-part scheme to prepare for British withdrawal. First, the British would 'share' the two bases with the Iraqis, thus providing time for training and transition. The second step would be at some unspecified date to hand over the two air bases in full sovereignty. To maintain British sway, Busk wrote, 'I should start *now* to establish a new base in Kuwait where we can reasonably count on security of tenure for a great many years.'[51]

Busk believed it essential immediately to adopt a conciliatory attitude towards the nationalists on the issue of the two air bases in order to secure their collaboration both in Iraq and in the more general aims. He reiterated that the sharing and eventual cession of the bases would be the only way 'to meet Iraqi amour propre'. General Renton, whose views the Eastern Department also particularly valued, reinforced the point about 'amour propre' in his assessment of the attitude of the Iraqi military officers:

> From the Iraqi officers' point of view the retention of bases of a foreign power in their country is humiliating and this is being continually rubbed into them by all other Arab countries as an instance of incomplete independence. Everywhere in the Middle East the cry is for the evacuation of foreign troops, but as the latter are less conspicuous in Iraq than elsewhere, the cry is not so acute. At the same time, any attempt to bind Iraq to provide bases for a further period would be bitterly resented in the Army as a whole as humiliating and unnecessary. . . .
>
> The majority of officers . . . would like . . . some form of sharing to save their amour propre with a scheme of definite training in the maintenance and upkeep of bases. This would be extremely popular throughout the Army as it would give a promise of the bases being eventually under Iraqi control.[52]

[50] Busk to Garran, 27 June 1947, FO 371/61592.
[51] Ibid.
[52] Memorandum by Renton, 4 Aug. 1947, FO 371/61593.

The Eastern Department concurred in the estimates by Busk and Renton. Michael Wright commented on the virtual certainty of having to abandon Egypt and Palestine and the necessity of cultivating Transjordan, Bahrain, Kuwait, and above all Iraq. He supported Busk's judgement on the need to make concessions: 'Better a compromise now in Iraq which has a better chance of lasting, than to hang on a short time longer there on a wicket which will soon become altogether unplayable.'[53] Bevin noted 'I agree', thus setting in train the candid Anglo-Iraq conversations that took place in the latter part of 1947.

In October of that year Bevin put the Iraqi problem before the Cabinet. He argued a powerful case for the Labour government to move decisively in imperial affairs. Unless Britain acted now, the initiative would pass to the Iraqi extremists. 'It would be wiser to avoid fighting a diplomatic rearguard action', he wrote, 'to defend a position which we are bound to give up in the end, and so arouse the maximum of nationalist fervour and anti-British feeling in the process.'[54] Later in the month he discussed the business of treaty revision with the Regent, who had come to London in part for personal pastimes, in part to prepare the way for negotiations. Bevin told the Regent that Britain had made 'immense strides' in air development 'and we were anxious to make all these new facilities available to the Iraqis as members of the family'.[55] With a slight streak of exaggeration he stated that he hoped to make Habbaniyah and Shaiba 'the best bases in the world'—though he warned that in doing so Iraq would have to help foot the bill. Changing the metaphor, he emphasized that 'Iraq and Great Britain must sink or swim together'. In late 1947 he had good reason to think that the two countries would not only keep afloat but would pull together towards the common goal of defence of the Middle East against possible Soviet aggression.

Bevin pressed forward insistently with the Iraqis at a time when the Palestine struggle was reaching a critical stage. On the 25th of September the Colonial Secretary announced in the United Nations that Britain would withdraw. Little over two months later the United Nations voted in favour of partition. The question therefore arises, how clearly did the officials of the Foreign Office see the connection between the Palestine issue and anti-British nationalism in Iraq? It

[53] Memorandum by Wright, 30 July 1947, FO 371/61592.
[54] Memorandum by Bevin, CP (47), 277, 3 Oct. 1947, CAB 129/21; minutes in FO 371/61594.
[55] Batatu, *Old Social Classes and the Revolutionary Movements*, p. 550, remarks that Bevin made this remark 'tongue in cheek' but it is entirely consistent with Bevin's socialist conception of the Empire and Commonwealth.

is an easy question to ask in retrospect, and the striking point to the historian is the clear answer in the files of the Eastern Department. G. H. Baker wrote in October 1947:

The extreme Right [in Iraqi politics] are . . . the champions of Iraqi nationalism in particular, and of Arab nationalism in the wider field. . . . the Left also plug the nationalist line in order to win the support of the masses. The extreme Right and the extreme Left are at one in vociferating against British 'imperialism' *with particular reference to Palestine.*[56]

Peter Garran commented that 'the symptoms are present in Iraq of an increase in extreme or violent nationalism'. The new head of the Eastern Department, Bernard Burrows, merely added 'very interesting' and noted in a separate minute that the Secretary of State wished to move forward with 'a series of bilateral treaties' that would include Transjordan and perhaps Saudi Arabia.

There lay the key to Bevin's thought. He hoped to 'stabilize' (Burrows's word) the situation in Palestine by separate agreements with the Arab states. The agreements would not be about Palestine *per se*, but would reaffirm British and Arab friendship in various degrees of political and military alliance. If the worst came to the worst, militant Zionism would prove the benefits of an alliance with Britain (which, it could be argued, proved to be the case with Jordan). Whatever happened in Palestine, Bevin would attempt to turn it to British advantage or at least cut British losses by simultaneously strengthening Anglo-Arab ties. Such was his underlying motive as far as it can be deduced from his cursory minutes. He also bore in mind the failure of the Egyptian negotiations, which still rankled. By dealing successfully with the Iraqis, King Abdullah, and perhaps King Ibn Saud, Bevin hoped to bring even the Egyptians into line.[57] No one could accuse Ernest Bevin of lacking political imagination. In mid-November 1947 he noted that he wished the Iraqi business to be settled 'at once'.[58]

In plunging ahead into the agreement with the Iraqis, Bevin assumed that the Iraqis themselves would back away if they saw

---

[56] Minute by Baker, 1 Oct. 1947, FO 371/61594/E8789, emphasis added. He continued in an incisive summary of British policy and the class structure of Iraq: 'Of·the two sets of extremists, the Iraqi Government is most in fear of the Left, who are seen to threaten the existing social structure from which the governing classes draw their incomes. Our policy has been to try to allay these fears and to urge the Iraqi Government to adopt social and economic reforms which would help to remove some of the legitimate grievances of the under-privileged classes and so weaken the appeal of the Left Wing agitators.'

[57] His hope in the Egyptian direction lay in the British perception of the vanity of Egyptian nationalism which, as reported from Cairo, manifested a 'jealousy that British policy [might be] . . . built up round an Iraqi treaty and not an Egyptian one'. Chapman Andrews to Bevin, 31 Jan. 1948, FO 371/68444/E1332.

[58] Minute by Bevin on Busk to Bevin, 11 Nov. 1947, FO 371/61596.

difficulties ahead because of Palestine. This was an important assumption and its background must be examined in detail. In mid-October Peter Garran had written: 'although our own attitude over Palestine should serve to retain the goodwill of the Arabs, it may well become impracticable to proceed with the informal talks in Baghdad leading up to Treaty revision'. Burrows then noted that the initiative *to refuse* to go further or to postpone the negotiation should come from the Iraqis. Otherwise Iraq would be left in the lurch as a jilted Arab suitor (a dilemma that the British also faced with King Abdullah). Bevin noted, 'I agree with Burrows'.[59] At the time that Bevin made that comment, the Regent was still in London. The British tried to draw him out specifically on the danger of Palestine and anti-British Iraqi nationalism. Lord Tedder told him explicitly that the Arabs had 'a great deal of trouble in their part of the world'. 'This did not produce any reaction.' Busk then asked a blunt question. Did the Iraqi government *really* want an agreement—if so 'we would set the machine in motion at once'. The Regent replied that 'his Government did want it'.[60]

It should be noted that the Eastern Department chose to rely on the judgement of the Regent rather than on other informed opinion about the Iraqi response to the Palestine question. From New York, Harold Beeley, the Palestine expert of the Foreign Office, reported that in the view of the Iraqi Foreign Minister, Fadhil al-Jamali, Iraq faced three problems in this order of importance: 'Palestine, economic development and Treaty revision'.[61] It is perhaps not surprising that the Eastern Department did not attach any particular significance to Jamali's ranking of the Palestine question as the foremost problem facing Iraq since he made his judgement from the vantage point of the United Nations. What is perhaps more noteworthy is Nuri's response during his visit to London on his return journey to Baghdad in the aftermath of the partition vote in New York. Nuri, like all Arab leaders, was furious with the Americans: 'It would take a long time for the United States to live down the intense resentment they had now aroused in the Arab countries.'[62] When Bevin asked him about treaty revision, the Foreign Secretary's private secretary had

[59] Minutes by Garran, Burrows, and Bevin, 14 Oct. 1947, FO 371/61596/E10298.

[60] See minute by Busk, 16 Oct. 1947, FO 371/61596.

[61] Beeley to Burrows, 1 Nov. 1947, FO 371/61596/E10118.

[62] Nuri added a point of considerable interest that confirms the general impression of contemporary observers about the part played by the White House in the last-minute lobbying for votes in favour of partition. He told Bevin: 'Mr. Marshall had assured representatives of the Arab countries when the Assembly opened that the United States Government would refrain from exercising . . . pressure. There had been no signs of their doing so until after 19th November. . . . in the interval before the next meeting the United States Government had intervened behind the scenes. He cited China, Haiti the Philippines and others as instances.

to record that Nuri 'was clearly unaware of recent developments in detail'. In retrospect the officials of the Eastern Department could only lament Nuri's absence from Baghdad, their acceptance of the assurances of the Regent, and their failure sufficiently to note Beeley's warning from New York: 'the internal situation in Iraq', he wrote, was 'dangerous'.

The Treaty of Portsmouth

Ernest Bevin recognized that nothing other than a basis of 'equality', in his own emphatic words, and 'complete independence' would satisfy nationalist demands. He emphasized 'complete independence', a phrase he repeated, in part because of socialist conviction and in part because of his estimate of the Iraqi Prime Minister. Saleh Jabr from the outset of his career as Prime Minister had staked his reputation on successful negotiations with the British. His aims included military equipment and a general assurance that Britain would not 'abandon' the Arabs in Palestine. On the latter issue American Zionist policy worked to British advantage. On the question of modernization of the Iraqi army the Foreign Office had successfully importuned the Ministry of Defence to provide the equipment.[63] The critical issue was the control of the two air bases. On that point the British between the spring and winter of 1947 moved substantially to meet Iraqi wishes. They knew that, unless they relinquished real control as well as theoretical 'sovereignty' of the bases, Saleh Jabr would resign and leave them to face demands of evacuation rather than of 'sharing'. Here Bevin preferred to gamble with moderate Iraqi leaders rather than risk the initiative passing to the extremists. The British recognized Saleh Jabr's political courage in being willing to consummate an alliance. What they did not fully perceive was his only tepid support by prominent political leaders in all parts of Iraqi society, and the general discontent caused by famine. During the time that their leaders talked high politics the Iraqi people suffered from inflation, locust plagues, bad harvests, and bread shortages. Though the British were not unaware of the fragile political and popular foundation of Saleh Jabr's government, they judged him to be a statesman of sufficient stature to weather political storms and to anchor the Anglo-Iraqi alliance lest it drift into misunderstanding and futility.

The British had hopes that the negotiations with the Iraqis would

He believed there had been direct action by the White House.' Memorandum by Bevin, 11 Dec. 1947, FO 371/61600/E11793/G.

[63] See e.g. minutes and correspondence in FO 371/61593.

prove to be so successful that the treaty could be used as a 'model' for 'defensive alliances with all of the states of the Arab League'.[64] It fell to Douglas Busk to work out the complicated details as well as to convey in Baghdad the general thrust of British policy. Though still relatively young for an acting head of mission (he was only age 41 in 1947), he had the confidence of Sir Orme Sargent and Michael Wright that he was well placed to conclude this sensitive business. Since the summer of 1947 he had urged the Foreign Office to accelerate plans for the eventual handing over of the two air bases. During the autumn he continued to warn that events were moving faster than anticipated, and that unless the British convinced Saleh Jabr of their genuine intent to relinquish the bases then they would feel the lash of nationalist sentiment. To the Iraqis Busk elaborated the meaning of 'sharing bases' and to the Foreign Office he emphasized how British generosity in that direction would conciliate the nationalists. 'All existing facilities at Habbaniyah should be shared between the two forces. That is to say workshops, hangars and installations of all kinds and of course accommodation for officers and personnel and facilities for recreation etc.' By 'sharing' the British would maintain a military presence, to which Busk and his colleagues in London attached highest importance. In explaining the fundamental reason for the necessity of the British retaining at least partial control of the bases he drew upon the lessons of the Second World War. Here Busk put British policy into the larger perspective of the past and future survival of the British Empire:

> It will be recalled . . . that Allied forces were pushed back from Norway largely because all suitable bases had been seized or destroyed by the Germans in the first few days of the campaign. Without properly maintained bases it would be impossible for His Majesty's Government to fly assistance in time to Iraq in the event of war or threat of war.[65]

The lessons of wartime experience were thus applied directly to Iraq. The British were determined not to let it happen again.

In December Busk obtained Iraqi acquiescence on two difficult points. First, Royal Air Force personnel at the bases would be required to wear uniforms, and, second, be in 'formed units in sufficient number' to operate the bases 'efficiently' (and, it should be added, if necessary without Iraqi assistance). Another important matter was the creation of a 'Joint Defence Board', which in the Iraqi context can be best understood as a sort of senior staff college as well as a high-ranking military body to co-ordinate defence plans. The head of the military mission, General Renton, wrote:

---

[64] Minute by Walker, 14 Jan. 1948, FO 371/68441/E324.
[65] Busk to Bevin, 3 Nov. 1947, FO 371/61596/E10295.

I know that the leading officers of the younger generation of the Army will expect great things from a Joint Defence Board. No one knows better then they do how much requires to be studied. Plans for the air defence of the country . . . for the construction of Military roads, for the organisation of civil defence, and even a thorough reconnaissance of the frontier are all among the many problems which they know have so far been ignored.

To serve on the Joint Defence Board would be the ambition of all the best officers of the Army, especially of those who had graduated at British Staff Colleges.[66]

When Busk obtained satisfactory assurances from the Iraqis on final points such as those of the Joint Defence Board, the path lay open to a meeting between Bevin and Saleh Jabr.

Before Saleh Jabr left for London, the Regent summoned him and other prominent political figures to discuss the future of Iraq and Britain. The participants in this élite group were mainly those of the 'old gang', elder politicians who did not inspire confidence in the leaders of the political parties or most of the press. Those in attendance agreed that it would be desirable for Iraq to have a new treaty. They endorsed the proposal to give the British the right to 'share' the bases and to use them in the event of war.[67] Saleh Jabr arrived in London on the 6th of January 1948 together with some of the strongest members of the government.[68] The Regent remained in Baghdad, surrounded by weak ministers and indirectly facing the opposition of leaders of the hostile nationalist movements on both the far left and far right.

The ground had been so thoroughly laid that the meetings in London were pensive and sometimes almost festive occasions rather than sessions of hard bargaining. Bevin welcomed the Iraqi delegation by saying simply that he wished to have a treaty 'on a basis of perfect equality'. He emphasized that both Britain and Iraq 'had learned much from the wars of 1914 and 1939' and stated to the Iraqis that 'Great Britain would emerge from her present troubles and would take her place as one of the leading powers in the world'. To those sentiments the Iraqi Prime Minister responded with confidence 'in the future of Great Britain as a great power assuring the peace of the world, in which task Iraq hoped to assist according to capacity'.[69] Critics of these exchanges, then as later, charged that Bevin had merely found a collaborator willing to whitewash the treaty of 1930 and bring it up to date with 'new-fashioned

[66] Renton to Busk, 17 Dec. 1947, FO 371/68441.

[67] For the Regent's meeting see Khadduri, *Independent Iraq*, p. 264; and Batatu, *Old Social Classes*, p. 547.

[68] The other members of the delegation were Nuri Pasha, Fadhil al-Jamali, Taufiq al-Suwaidi (a former Prime Minister), and Shakir al-Wadi (Minister of Defence).

[69] Minutes of meeting with the Iraqi Delegation, 7 Jan. 1948, FO 371/68442.

terminology'.[70] Such was not the intention of Saleh Jabr, who wished to be recorded in history as the nationalist who delivered Iraq from the British on a basis of complete equality. And whatever one might think of Bevin's pursuit of a generally Churchillian line in Imperial affairs, his words in the Iraqi negotiations ring with a sense of historic conviction that he had now reached a landmark in Middle Eastern affairs in the tradition reminiscent of the settlement in India: 'he wished to emphasize that this Treaty was to be in spirit and in heart a Treaty of complete equality in all respects. He thought that from the record of the Labour Government since it had come into power in its dealings with countries like India and Burma complete equality was the main basis of foreign affairs'.[71]

In the course of the discussions Lord Tedder 'frankly and in confidence' expanded on the importance the British attached 'to maintaining a really strong and efficient air base in Iraq which would be ready at a moment's notice day and night'.

> He said that in modern war, time is of the essence—hours not days—and he did sincerely trust that Iraq and [the] U. K. would work together in common defence measures in the closest possible co-operation. Only so was there hope of an effective defence of Iraq which would be ready in an emergency.[72]

The Iraqi delegation did not dissent, but such phrases as 'common defence measures' and 'closest possible co-operation' within a few days provoked strong nationalist protest in Iraq. When the terms of the treaty were published, the world at large learned that the new arrangements provided for the 'sharing' of the two air bases, a Joint Defence Board, British rights of transit, and general British assistance. The circumstances of publicity for this new era of British imperialism, or perhaps the end of it so far as Iraq was concerned, were inauspicious. The Foreign Secretary had been so pleased with the results of the Iraqi visit to England that he and the Minister of Defence invited the delegation to be guests of the Royal Navy at Portsmouth—hence the name of the treaty. After a luncheon that hardly conformed with the austerity of postwar Britain—not to mention the circumstances of famine in Iraq—the Treaty of Portsmouth was signed aboard Nelson's *Victory* on the 15th of January 1948. With phrases that resounded of 'principles of liberty and social justice', Bevin concluded with a remark about the weather: 'the sun is shining upon us, which I think is a good augury, an augury that we have done right'.

Bevin had been intent on avoiding the mistakes he had made with

---

[70] See Batatu, *Old Social Classes*, chap. 22.
[71] Minutes of meeting of 10 Jan. 1948, FO 371/68442.
[72] Ibid., 9 Jan. 1948.

the Egyptians. He had now made new ones with the Iraqis. He had averted prolonged negotiations. But the speed with which he concluded the treaty aroused explosive suspicion in Baghdad. Within three days a student strike led to general rioting. The extreme nationalists on both the right and left protested against the government for caving in to British imperialism. They maintained, among other things, that the Joint Defence Board tied Iraq's hands more completely than did the old treaty; that Britain had extorted a pledge of defence in event of war; and that the new treaty did not limit British 'aid' whereas the old treaty limited British assistance to railway, river, and air communication.[73] The nationalists who wished to scrutinize the precise meaning of the terms had to read them in English, not Arabic. When journalists in Baghdad asked for a translation, they learned to their astonishment that none existed. The leaders of the opposition parties next revealed that they had not been consulted. Neglect developed into insult—at a time when economic distress, including bread shortages, contributed to internal unrest. The delegates in London remained so far out of touch with these developments that they dallied in London to celebrate the conclusion of the historic treaty. Ernest Bevin and Saleh Jabr might have noticed that the sun was shining in England, but in Iraq severe thunderclouds were gathering. A violent political storm burst upon the exposed Regent.[74] He wobbled, then collapsed. Faced with intense nationalist protest and consequent 'hysteria' of his family (according to British reports), he issued a statement on the 21st of January that he would not ratify a treaty that did not fulfil the 'national aspirations' of the Iraqi people. His proclamation was in fact a repudiation. Within a week after Portsmouth, Bevin's Iraqi policy lay in shambles.

'I am sorry to hear that there should have been disturbances in Baghdad because of misunderstandings', Bevin telegraphed to the Regent.[75] The Foreign Office and the Embassy in Baghdad did not succeed in clearing up these 'misunderstandings'. Bevin lamented to Attlee, 'It seems clear that the members of the Government in Baghdad and the Regent himself lost their nerve in the face of disturbances and allowed themselves to be rushed into issuing this

[73] For the negative interpretation of the treaty see Batatu, *Old Social Classes*, p. 550.

[74] Here, as in Bevin's remark about the sun, the weather appears to have been on the official mind—sometimes in connection with Palestine: 'the whole of the Middle East is involved in the Palestine earthquake and Iraq in addition is undergoing a severe local thunderstorm'. Memorandum by Busk, 13 May 1948, FO 371/68386.

[75] Bevin to Busk, 22 Jan. 1948, FO 371/68443. Bevin referred to the beginning of the demonstrations in which two students had been killed. Four days later, on the 26th, between 300 and 400 protesters were killed in the streets of Baghdad. The riots are given detailed and vivid treatment in Batatu, *Old Social Classes*, chap. 22.

unfortunate statement.'[76] According to a report from Baghdad, the Regent's ministers 'were gibbering with fear' and the Regent had broken down under the pressure of rumours of impending revolution.[77] Douglas Busk pithily expressed the British distress after his return to Baghdad: 'I have always known the Regent to be weak, but I hardly think one could have expected such utter disintegration.'[78]

The Iraqi débâcle did not increase the Foreign Office's faith in alliances with Arab governments. 'As you may guess', Michael Wright wrote to Busk, 'one of the results at this end was to arouse or increase doubts in many quarters of the wisdom of ever placing any reliance whatever on anything that Arab countries say or do, and to induce a general feeling of "a plague on all your houses".'[79] Bevin now took the same line as he had with the Egyptians: the existing treaty remained in effect. When the Regent became more 'calm' after the return of the delegation and began to speak of taking the treaty out of 'cold storage', Bevin growled: 'I do not propose to do anything until they ask. We should show no anxiety.'[80] Bevin thus held a stiff Imperial upper lip, but in fact his entire Middle Eastern strategy had been dealt a severe blow. Beginning with the assumption that the Iraqi treaty would serve as a 'model' for alliances with all other major Arab states, he could now hope to salvage only Transjordan.

Post Mortem on Iraqi Nationalism

Where lay the responsibility for the fiasco? Why had the British been so caught off guard? Why did they entirely fail to anticipate that the crisis would force the resignation of Saleh Jabr? Those are important questions because the Labour government had drastically misread the temper of Iraqi nationalism at a time when the date of the 15th of May had already been set on the formal time-charge for the explosion of Jewish and Arab nationalism in Palestine. The Foreign Office pinned the blame on the Regent for not having enough backbone to take a firm stand. There was however sharp disagreement in British circles. General Renton in Baghdad thought that the quick action of the Regent had prevented nothing less than a revolution.

It is the opinion of every responsible unofficial British resident—who was here at the time—and of all the Iraqis I have spoken to—that it was only the

---

[76] Bevin to Attlee, 26 Jan. 1948, FO 371/68444.
[77] Pelham to Attlee, 25 Jan. 1948, FO 371/68446.
[78] Busk to Bevin, 28 Jan. 1948, FO 371/68444/E1242.
[79] Wright to Busk, draft letter dated March 1948, FO 371/68446/EE2254.
[80] Minute by Bevin on Mack to Bevin, 16 Feb. 1948, FO 371/68446/E2182.

Regent's prompt actions in issuing this statement and eventually forcing the resignation of Ministers that saved the country from Revolution and anarchy. The alternative would have been to declare Martial Law, and to use the Army to shoot down the rioters in Baghdad and other large towns.[81]

Renton further believed that British officials themselves no less than the Regent had misinterpreted the springs of Iraqi nationalism.

> There is no doubt that there has been a complete breakdown of political intelligence—both British and Iraqi. The Regent and the members of the Saleh Jabr Government all under-estimated the depth of feeling among the population before the delegation left for London—and the Embassy were equally in the dark. . . . In addition to this the whole method of presentation of the Treaty was amateurish. There was no adequate Arabic translation, and the hurry with which the whole thing was done excited the deepest suspicion and alarm.
>
> In a country where you take six months bargaining to buy a rug, a Treaty concluded in five days is simply not understood. Finally, the delay of the Ministers and British Chargé d'Affaires [Busk] in returning to Baghdad was the last straw. It was just as if a British Prime Minister had gone off to Moscow, signed a Treaty in Russian without an English text, and then gone off for a week's rest to the Crimea.[82]

Busk, by contrast, emphasized the 'almost incomprehensible' methods of Saleh Jabr, Nuri, and the 'old gang'. Here then were two dramatically different interpretations within the British official mind. Renton struck some sensitive nerves. Busk and the officials of the Eastern Department gave expansive reasons in explanation of the disaster.

In telegrams, despatches, and private letters, Busk first emphasized the spinelessness of the Regent and then the peculiar circumstances that had united the forces of Iraqi nationalism against the British. To some extent he understandably was trying to exculpate himself by implying that Iraqi actions were unreasonable and to some extent irrational, but it is important to follow his interpretation because it is representative of the British official response to the troubles of 1948. He was entirely disillusioned with the Regent. 'Nationalism has come to stay', he wrote in his most mature reassessment, but

[81] Renton to Charteris (War Office) 5 Feb. 1948, FO 371/68446. M. T. Walker, after studying the Arabic press, concluded that political opinion in Baghdad supported Renton's interpretation. Minute of 27 Feb. 1948, ibid.

[82] Ibid. Renton was so disenchanted with the Embassy's handling of the negotiations and the riots that he entrusted this letter to the War Office to his former military colleague, Colonel Gerald de Gaury, the Regent's confidant, rather than the diplomatic pouch. The Embassy staff of course took offence and the incident did not improve relations between the War Office and Foreign Office (see Mack to Wright, 'Personal and Secret', 9 Feb. 1948, and minutes in FO 371/68446). De Gaury later in *Three Kings in Baghdad* was sharply critical of the Foreign Office, the Embassy, and in particular Busk, whom he viewed as an incompetent official with 'little or no experience of the Arab world' (p. 155). See also Renton's confidential talk to the Middle East Group of the Royal Institute of International Affairs, 10 June 1948, RIIA.

'the Regent is not the man to lead it'.[83] He could be summed up as 'a notoriously weak man', Busk wrote in another full-length reconstruction of the events of January.[84] He also had nothing good to say about Nuri. 'I have . . . found it a most stimulating mental exercise to try and fathom Nuri Pasha's mind. A few months later it becomes clear what he has been working for, but at the time obscurity is intense.'[85] Busk lamented that Nuri had been chosen as a member of the delegation because of his reputation as 'a pro-British puppet'. Nuri the master-intriguer had failed to warn Saleh Jabr of the intrigues in Baghdad. If the delegation had returned immediately to Baghdad they could successfully have seen the treaty through.[86] Saleh Jabr and his colleagues had not adequately gauged their unpopularity and lack of support, or the nature of the riots:

> The demonstrations began mildly as student outbursts. As always in the past these fed on success and on the second and later days hooligans and professional agitators, seeing their chance, took it. I do not however think that even the most evilly intentioned agitator could have hoped in his wildest dreams to meet such disunity and weakness in responsible quarters.[87]

In so far as the riots had any purpose, they were, in Busk's judgement, directed against Saleh Jabr and not against the British. Here Busk was in solid agreement with the rest of the Embassy staff in Baghdad. In the words of the new ambassador, Sir Henry Mack, who arrived shortly after the tumult: 'Dislike of Saleh Jabr by the old gang and of the apparent rapidity with which the Treaty of Portsmouth was concluded, combined with the bad economic situation, were the chief causes of the January disturbances. The treaty itself was merely the excuse.'[88] Busk himself, perhaps because of nervousness about his central involvement, concluded jocularly in German that the situation was hopeless but not serious ('*Die Lage is hoffnungslos,*

---

[83] Memorandum by Busk, 13 May 1948, FO 371/68386.

[84] Busk to Bevin, 6 Feb. 1948, FO 371/68446.

[85] Busk judged that Nuri's devious mentality was identical with the 'oriental' intellect of the 'old gang' in general and could not easily be comprehended by Europeans: 'their methods are almost incomprehensible to Europeans except those with very long experience of the country'. Ibid.

[86] They had not returned, in Busk's judgement, because of Saleh Jabr's wife, who wished to linger in London: 'She is accustomed to having her own way and, as events proved, no mere man could prevail against her.' Busk also related disastrous circumstances of the women in the Regent's family: 'Here . . . more petticoat influence appears. The Regent was certainly worked upon by his mother and sisters and I have reliable information that they were profoundly influenced by hysterical telephone messages from ladies in Bagdad.' Ibid.

[87] Ibid.

[88] Mack to Bevin, 29 Mar. 1948, FO 371/68448/E4291.

aber nicht ernst').[89] In the aftermath of the riots the situation never-theless must have looked bleak enough to the Foreign Office, where the officials of the Eastern Department found little consolation in Busk's witticisms.[90]

The most perceptive interpretation written from Baghdad was composed in the heat of the moment on the 25th of January, by G. C. Pelham, the Chargé d'Affaires while Busk was in London. Pelham went to the heart of the matter by stating that the Hashe-mites had 'never succeeded in establishing themselves firmly in the heart of the people'.[91] In this sense the mutual mistrust between the government and the people could be viewed as an unfortunate legacy of the First World War era, and it became especially apparent in times of tension. In this case Pelham emphasized the economic distress caused by the failure of the grain crops during the last year and the consequent bread shortages in the towns. 'When Saleh Jabr brushed aside a debate on the bread situation in the Majlis just before his departure for London, he did little to improve the chances of the Treaty.' Pelham continued with a third and final reason for the riots against the Portsmouth treaty. Less than two months previously, the United Nations had voted in favour of the partition of Palestine.

Iraqi opinion, in common with other Arab opinion, has grown steadily more and more concerned with what seems to them the manifest injustice of the National Home policy in Palestine. This conviction of injustice is rendered sour and bitter in the minds of the better-informed Iraqis by their realisation that the Arabs are relatively powerless to right this wrong and that one of the reasons for their impotence is the unwillingness of the Arab Governments, including their own, to sink their own differences and combine whole-heartedly in defence of Arab Palestine.

The man in the street and the coffee house has been excited by the successive outrages in Palestine since the partition decision and Palestine has formed one of the subjects of slogans shouted in all the recent demonstrations in Baghdad.[92]

As if pursuing the logic of the Palestine argument to its ultimate conclusion, another official, P. M. Broadmead (Minister in Damascus)

---

[89] Memorandum by Busk, 13 May 1948, FO 371/68386.

[90] For summary of extensive Eastern Department analysis see memorandum entitled 'Arab Politics and British Policy in the Middle East', 24 June 1948, FO 371/68386. It was characteristic of Bevin that he wrote to Busk: 'Don't fret. You did your best and none can do more'. Quoted in an unpublished memoir by Busk on 'The Treaty of Porstmouth' (courtesy of D. C. Watt).

[91] Pelham to Attlee, Confidential, 25 Jan. 1948, FO 371/68446/E2217. This is a theme pursued by Elie Kedourie: 'there was this nagging feeling that it was a make-believe kingdom, built on false pretences and kept going by a British design and for a British purpose. This is the origin and explanation of the rabid anti-British feelings of large sections of the ruling classes of Iraq, a feeling which persisted until the end, and which occasionally exploded in bursts of hatred and violence.' 'The Kingdom of Iraq', p. 278.

[92] Pelham to Attlee, 25 Jan. 1948, FO 371/68446.

wrote that 'If it had not been for Palestine, we should have seen the treaty ratified.'[93]

'Save our brothers in Palestine!' But that was only one of several powerful slogans shouted from the roofs of Baghdad coffee houses in early 1948. 'Down with black bread!' 'Provide Bread to the People!' 'Saleh Jabr and Nuri Said to the Gallows!' 'We want Rashid Ali Back!' 'Long Live the Republic!' 'Long Live the Communist Party!' The slogans themselves revealed the confused nature of the protest, and they raised certain questions that were not easy to answer. Had the rioting and opposition to the treaty been orchestrated, for example, by the Communists? Could the treaty have been put through if the Regent had not lost his nerve? Was Saleh Jabr's lack of popularity with the 'old guard' an important contributing problem? What of Nuri's miscalculation? The questions in turn made it clear that Palestine was only part of the problem, and that the explanation of the underlying causes of the crisis would have to be found in the tensions within Iraqi society. The emotional response to the events building up to a climax in Palestine contributed to the desperate mood.

This chapter will close by establishing the connection that the British saw between the impending full-scale civil war in Palestine, the continuing deadlock with the Egyptians, and the possibility of social revolution in Iraq. First however it is necessary to explain some of the reasons for the lack of effective British political intelligence. Otherwise the explanations of the pressing forward with the treaty in the face of heavy odds, and the rationalizations of some of the post mortems, would be as inexplicable as the 'inscrutable' reasoning which the British diagnosed in the Iraqi mentality. There was a shift in British personnel at this time that cumulatively was no less than dramatic. Gerald de Gaury later made an acute analysis of this unprecedented turnover:

> The wheels of administration turn come what may and in this case their rhythm was off beat with events. Owing to the illness of the British Ambassador [Stonehewer Bird], and his consequent absence for some ten months, the burden of conducting the negotiations with the Iraqis and interpreting them to the Foreign Office had fallen on a Counsellor, as Chargé d'Affairs [Busk]. . . . The Oriental Counsellor had been sent as Colonial Secretary to Barbados [Perowne]. He was replaced by a man who was an archaeologist of distinction and a genuine Arab scholar with knowledge of tribes [John Richmond]. Unfortunately this officer had no friends or even acquaintances among either Government or opposition leaders in Baghdad. . . .
>
> In London the Foreign Office department conducting the negotiations went through almost similar changes. A senior official who had visited Baghdad to

[93] Broadmead to Bevin, 1 June 1948, FO 371/68386/E7801.

make the acquaintance of the leading personalities was sent as Ambassador to Rio de Janeiro [Sir Nevile Butler]. The head of the Eastern Department was sent as Minister to Iceland [Charles Baxter]. The distinguished official who was in charge of the actual negotiations and who even came to Baghdad to assist in conducting them in November was posted to the Berlin Control Commission in December [Garran]. Even the junior official in charge of the Iraq Section was sent as Head of Chancery to Rangoon [Baker].[94]

Bernard Burrows had assumed his responsibilities as head of the Eastern Department on the eve of the crisis in November 1947. After the collapse of the Portsmouth treaty he drew up a reassessment of British policy in the Middle East. He queried, among other things, the extent to which the Palestine issue was responsible for British troubles in Iraq.[95]

One of the most incisive comments came from the Middle East Office in Cairo, where the pen of Brigadier Clayton flowed with a continuity that marked a contrast with the piecemeal responses elsewhere. Clayton believed that the Palestine demonstrations taking place throughout the Middle East at this time were not 'manufactured' by the Communists or the extreme nationalists but rather reflected genuine Arab anxiety about developments in Palestine. On the other hand he did not think that the Palestine question itself lay at the centre of British difficulties in Iraq. There as elsewhere he detected a 'frustration' among Arab nationalists that found constant expression in the demand for 'complete and final evacuation of all foreign troops from the soil of Arab countries'.[96] In other words he saw a similarity of Iraqi and Egyptian response. That assessment went to the heart of the matter. The problem of anti-British sentiment in Iraq because of the two military bases and because of the connection between the British and the 'old gang' would ultimately prove to be just as intractable as in Egypt. This revelation came as a blow to the Foreign Secretary. According to an official of the American embassy, who gave independent confirmation of the importance of the parallel between Egypt and Iraq, Bevin 'has taken rejection particularly hard and sees in Iraqi developments [a] repetition of his experience with [the] Bevin–Sidky agreement'.[97]

[94] De Gaury, *Three Kings in Baghdad*, pp. 154–5.

[95] For the result of this inquiry see the Eastern Department's memorandum on 'The Failure of the Iraq Treaty and Arab Nationalist Movements', 7 Apr. 1948, FO 371/68385/E4371/G.

[96] Memorandum by Clayton, 'Factors affecting the Situation in the Middle East', 17 Feb. 1948, FO 371/68385.

[97] The telegram continues: 'Since rejection Burrows said "we can hardly get Bevin to listen to anything re Arabs" ' (Gallman to Marshall, 6 Feb. 1948, USSD 741.90G/2–648). For Bevin's reaction to the setback in Iraq see Bullock, *Bevin* (chap. 12 section 7), which emphasizes his persistence in the face of adverse Arab circumstances.

In the aftermath of the collapse of the Portsmouth treaty, there was much speculation in British circles about the spinelessness of the Regent, the antagonism between Saleh Jabr and the 'old gang', and Nuri's failure to keep abreast of developments in Iraqi politics because of his involvement in the Palestine issue at the United Nations. As the dust settled, there was a consensus that firmer 'guidance' might have won acceptance of the treaty, but on the other hand the British would have found themselves accused of the 'interventionist' tactics they were attempting to abandon. 'We relied on the Iraqi representatives who came here being the best judges of how to handle their own political situation', Bernard Burrows wrote in the principal post mortem. 'We were clearly quite wrong to do so and should in future rely more on our own judgement and make greater efforts to obtain material on which to base it.'[98] The main deficiency in intelligence could be attributed to the narrow political reporting by the Embassy (particularly by Busk). In their search for an explanation of what went wrong, the officials of the Eastern Department found that they had precious little reliable information on the activities of the far right and especially the far left of Iraqi politics.[99] It was the interaction of the supporters of the 'Istiqlal' or 'Independence' party at the one extreme and the Communists at the other that the Middle East experts of the Foreign Office ultimately found to be the most alarming part of the problem.

Minutes written in the midst of rapidly moving events are often the most revealing about essential issues. The Iraqi crisis of early 1948 occurred during a period of economic and political discontent in Baghdad, at a time when Palestine was about to erupt into fullscale war, and at a critical stage of the cold war. The following two minutes indicate the anxieties as well as the priorities of those concerned with Middle Eastern affairs at the Foreign Office. They were written by Malcolm Walker, at that time a junior official but one who revealed perception and power of analysis. He had served from the mid-war years until October 1947 in Baghdad. The rest of his career was not distinguished.

[98] Burrows continued on the theme of the paradoxical British position in Iraq: 'We have in fact to adopt a dual attitude. We must negotiate as though we were dealing with an equal and sovereign power, but we must also take our own measures and precautions as though we were dealing with a protectorate.' Eastern Department memorandum, 7 Apr. 1948, FO 371/68385.

[99] There is virtually no indication in the files that have been made publicly accessible that the British were aware of the extent to which the leader of the Communist Party, Yusuf Salman Yusuf (Fahd), had been able to organize the Communists from behind prison bars in Kut (see Batatu, *Old Social Classes*, chaps. 21 and 22). There is much more revealing comment on the 'Istiqlal' party, but mostly of an indirect nature. The leader of the party, Mohammad Mahdi Kubba, wrote Sir Henry Mack in a typical remark, 'looks sinister, is probably able and, from our point of view, dangerous' (Mack to Bevin, 29 Mar. 1948, FO 371/68448/E4291).

It is perhaps ironic that one of the best minds of the 'Arab experts' of the Foreign Office, Charles Baxter's, now found leisure to reflect on Icelandic fisheries and that Walker's own Middle Eastern expertise eventually flowered in Liberia. The gift of political insight so valued by historians often had no relation to official success.

Walker was a keen reader of the Arabic press, which helps to explain the incisiveness of his views. He wrote in late February 1948 about the key issue of Saleh Jabr's political abrasiveness:

> There can be no doubt that the unpopularity of Saleh Jabr and his Government was in very large measure due to the mounting cost of living and that the deterioration of bread, even though it did not begin until after September last year, was the last straw. . . . At the same time Saleh Jabr succeeded in alienating all of his friends—not that he had many. . . .[1]

In his other minute Walker made the connection between the Palestine issue and Iraqi nationalism. It is a striking example of British awareness of the way in which Arab nationalists viewed 'Zionism' and 'British Imperialism' as complementary if not identical forces. No less is it remarkable for the perception of the danger of a 'sellout' by the 'Istiqlal' party to the Communists. He wrote on the day after the Communist coup in Czechoslovakia:

> The most violently hostile section of the politically conscious class in Iraq is that represented by the Istiqlal Party. . . . A large number of its members were imprisoned during the war by the Iraqi Government under Nuri Pasha for being supporters of Rashid Ali and the Nazis. Doubtless they were led to welcome the Germans as a means of getting rid of the British and now . . . it is becoming clear that they will not hesitate to welcome the communists if by that means they will have another chance to turn the British out.
>
> On December 30th [1947] . . . their chief newspaper 'Liwa Al Istikalal' said 'We resist the communists today because we not only abhor . . . [communist] principles but also because we have no desire to become [one of] a group of nations lost among the satellites dominated by dictatorship. We shall never on the other hand tolerate or surrender to Zionist imperialism but rather than accept Jews as rulers of our countries *we would hand ourselves over to communism.*' [Walker's emphasis.]
>
> This is a frank admission that communism is preferable to Zionism, which in the opinion of the Istiqlal Party is merely a part of the British connection. . . . if the Istiqlal Party obtains power in Iraq there is every possibility that Iraq will go the same way as Hungary, Roumania, Bulgaria and Czechoslovakia. . . . It seems to me, in view of recent events in Central Europe that the danger of the communists obtaining control in Middle Eastern countries, among which Iraq would doubtless be one of the first, cannot by any means be ruled out.[2]

It was at this stage that Walker made the comment, quoted at the beginning of this chapter, that the British should act to encourage

---

[1] Minute by Walker, 27 Feb. 1948, FO 371/68446/E2693/G.
[2] Minute by Walker, 26 Feb. 1948, FO 371/68447/E4099.

the moderates under Nuri and Saleh Jabr to oppose the nationalists on the far right. Otherwise the supporters of the 'Istiqlal' party might, if they continued to gain strength, have the political opportunity to sell their country to the Communists 'for the pleasure of being rid of the British'. In retrospect the danger may have been exaggerated, but the explanation of the anti-Zionist issue in the Iraqi context helps to make the crisis of early 1948 more comprehensible. In any event Iraq proved to be a classic case of the British attempting to preserve their influence by buoying up the moderate nationalists in order to fend off the extremists from both ends of the political spectrum.

9

TRANSJORDAN AND
'MR. BEVIN'S LITTLE KING'

THERE existed a certain temptation, Sir John Troutbeck once objected, to 'hold fast to Transjordan which is our only reliable ally, and let the rest [of the Arab states] go hang'.[1] The reason for that exasperated statement may be attributed, in the British view, to incessant and difficult Arab demands from all quarters to put Britain's relations with Middle Eastern states on a new and different footing. In 1948 even Transjordan insisted on treaty revision—despite a treaty of alliance concluded less than two years earlier in March 1946. Sir Orme Sargent, in the aftermath of the Iraqi collapse, diagnosed the case of Transjordan as part of the general Middle Eastern malaise. 'This craving for new treaties seems to be infectious in the Middle East and I do not think it is a healthy sign.' He continued to reflect on the British predicament in Transjordan in regard to Arab nationalism in general:

Although we can easily make new Treaties with certain friendly politicians or the local King or Regent, when we try to get them ratified we run up against a new force which the ruling classes can no longer control, namely a new Arab nationalism which has come into existence since the war and which it would be foolish to try to ignore. It is not primarily anti-British but it might easily become so if we play our cards clumsily.

Sargent's comment clearly reveals the reluctance of the official mind to acknowledge that even Transjordan, like the other Arab states, would settle for anything less than the independence achieved by Syria and Lebanon. He continued, as if grudgingly recognizing that Arab nationalism might have to be regarded as an unpleasant but permanent fact of life:

This nationalism may if it has nothing to feed on calm down gradually in the face of the complexities and dangers which the 'independent' states of the Middle East have now got to confront for the first time in their short history.

[1] Troutbeck (Head of the Middle East Office) to Michael Wright, 3 Mar. 1949, FO 371/75064. There is no satisfactory historical survey of the relations between Britain and Jordan, but see Anne Sinai and Allen Pollack, eds., *The Hashemite Kingdom of Jordan and the West Bank* (New York, 1977), which has a good bibliography of standard sources. The most useful, and perceptive, single work, though with a particular focus, is by P. J. Vatikiotis, *Politics and the Military in Jordan: A Study of the Arab Legion 1921–1957* (London, 1967).

But there is no sign of this at present. It is bound to be a slow process and the important thing is that we should do nothing meanwhile which would give the nationalists further material for agitation and might enable the Russians and Communists to represent themselves as the defenders of Arab independence against British imperialism.[2]

Bevin shared the foreboding that Arab nationalism in Transjordan might turn against the British as it had elsewhere. He did not wish to add Transjordan to a list of disasters that now included Egypt and Iraq. Nevertheless he calculated that Abdullah would be worth the gamble. 'I have taken every precaution', Bevin noted in late February 1948.[3] With those words he reaffirmed the continuity of relations in the 1940s between Britain and her most reliable ally in the Middle East.

With considerable circumspection the official British mind pondered the broader international as well as the more immediate Middle Eastern dangers of 'dressing up' King Abdullah to make him appear to be less of a British 'stooge' (a word used within the Foreign Office as if in slightly humourous acknowledgement of an uncomfortable fact). Transjordan was a client state, denounced as such by American Zionists and Arab nationalists. As a potential inheritor of Arab Palestine, Abdullah proved to be more responsive to partition plans than did the Egyptians, Iraqis, and Palestinian Arabs. British support of Abdullah aroused suspicion above all in his arch-rival, Ibn Saud, who feared Hashemite irredentism. Arab denunciation of Abdullah as a puppet of British imperialism found repercussions as well in England, where critics scathingly referred to him as 'Mr. Bevin's Little King'.[4] On the whole however Abdullah sustained his reputation, at least in England, as a desert prince of the Arab revolt who, with the help of an annual British subsidy of £2 million, had provided Transjordan with a rudimentary administration. The economic and social state of affairs was unsatisfactory, expecially if measured against the aspirations of the Labour government. The British were well aware that Abdullah needed to be prodded.

In a sort of symbiotic relationship stretching over a quarter of a century, Abdullah had remained a steadfast friend of the British Empire and the British had remained faithful to him. Abdullah was the son of Hussein I, Sharif of Mecca and King of the Hejaz, and the brother of Faisal I of Iraq. Faisal's death in 1933 had not

[2] Memorandum by Sargent, 2 Feb. 1948, FO 371/68817/E1758.
[3] Minute by Bevin, 21 Feb. 1948, FO 371/68819/E2526.
[4] See FO 371/68821 as an example of discussion of this point. The phrase was unwittingly ironic in view of Abdullah's robust and imposing presence, though it clearly was intended to convey his minor but irritating importance in the Arab world as a 'lackey' of British imperialism.

stopped the comparisons made between him as the 'warrior' son of Hussein and Abdullah as the more sophisticated and somewhat devious 'diplomat'. Abdullah in his own right had played a prominent part both before and after 1916 in the Arab revolt against the Turks. He had the reputation among the British as a vivacious, mercurial personality with an impish sense of humour and a quaint devotion to falconry (or so he liked to have the British believe). There was a tendency in some British circles to take a romantic view of Abdullah, of which the following *Observer* 'Profile' in 1948 is an example:

Abdullah is 67 this year. He belongs, therefore, to a generation in which Kings were hardy souls, capable of riding all day, fasting if need be, and feasting with zest whenever opportunity arose. He possesses many of the royal attributes of this epoch: complete self-reliance; a capacity for listening to advice, but nevertheless doing what he thinks; an intolerance of insubordination. . . . Most important of all, he possesses the habit of decision. He is thus in a class apart from the average Arab politician.

The *Observer* also described Abdullah's 'love of intrigue' and his difficulties with his Syrian, Egyptian, and Saudi Arabian neighbours:

Territorial ambitions and a somewhat incautious tongue have earned him many enemies. Syrian republicans hate his 'Greater Syria' plan for combining their lands with his own. Egyptians too, dislike the thought of a bigger and better Hashimite family kingdom. King Ibn Saud dislikes him (the dislike is returned) not only because of dynastic rivalries but for some garrulous and ill-pruned memoirs which he published two years ago.[5]

The *Observer*'s frank comment implied that Abdullah generally felt more at home with the British than with fellow Arabs. To his enemies he was no more than a creature of British imperialism. In bluntest language which caused anguish in the Foreign Office, 'King Abdullah is regarded as a Quisling by many Arabs'.

In fact Abdullah was not entirely a puppet but he was also not a statesman of the calibre the British would have preferred. His regime from its beginning bore the stamp of British authority. At the close of the First World War the British designated Abdullah as Amir of 'Transjordan'—literally, the region across the River Jordan, and administered the territory in loose association with Palestine as a mandate under the League of Nations. According to the British, Abdullah ruled as a benevolent autocrat, though his critics would have described him at best as an indifferent autocrat and historians will probably ultimately judge that he was obsessed

[5] Observer, 2 May 1948. The English translation of the book is *Memoirs of King Abdullah of Transjordan* (New York, 1950).

with his own ambitions and negligent of his subjects' welfare.[6]
Though the British preserved the façade of indigenous administration, 'advisers' worked closely with the 'Resident' who represented
the High Commissioner for Palestine and Transjordan in Jerusalem.
In return for providing a rudimentary administration and obviating
the need for a British military occupation, Abdullah in March 1921
gained an assurance from Churchill, then Colonial Secretary, that
no Jews would be allowed to settle in Transjordan. That guarantee
effectively created Transjordan as an Arab country apart from
Palestine, where the British commitment to a 'national home'
remained a delicate problem between Abdullah and the British.
Abdullah like all Arab leaders opposed the creation of a sovereign
Jewish state, but he eventually did prove to be more compliant than
his Arab counterparts in its accommodation.

To the Middle Eastern experts of the Foreign Office, Abdullah in
sum personified the 'better type' of Arab potentate despite his
defects of character. He could be obstinate but he could also be
relied upon. The British Resident, Sir Alec Kirkbride, later recalled
that he was the only Arab ruler who had the 'moral courage' to voice
fears about the general outcome of a war with the Jews. 'All that
his frankness brought him were accusations of being a traitor to the
Arab cause and, ultimately, a violent death' in 1951.[7] Above all,
in view of his self-interests, he was reliable, a virtue that made a
permanent imprint on the official British mind. During the Second
World War the Arab Legion had assisted the British in suppressing
the Iraqi uprising of 1941 and had fought against the Vichy French
in Syria. When the question of the abolition of the mandate and the
future of Transjordan arose at the end of the war, the British Cabinet
bore in mind Abdullah's 'unswerving loyalty'.[8]

The value of the Arab Legion as a small and efficient military unit
and the strategic circumstances of Transjordan gave the British good
reason to keep on good terms with Abdullah. According to the
principal assessment of the Chiefs of Staff: 'The strategic importance
of Trans-Jordan lies in its central position in relation to the Middle
East area as a whole and in the fact that direct communications

---

[6] 'The rule of King Abdullah is, in a sense, autocratic but it is a benevolent form of
patriarchal autocracy which serves to control the democratic side of the administration,
a control sadly lacking in some adjacent Arab countries.' (Kirkbride to Bevin, 26 Apr.
1948, FO 371/68386/E5468). That was the official line. For the historian's view, one awaits
the work in progress of Mary Wilson of St. Antony's College, Oxford.

[7] Sir Alec Kirkbride, *From the Wings: Amman Memoirs 1947–1951* (London, 1976),
p. 2. His other memoir is *A Crackle of Thorns: Experiences in the Middle East* (London,
1956).

[8] See especially the memorandum by the Colonial Secretary, G. H. Hall, 18 Feb. 1946,
C. (46) 3, CAB 134/52; minutes in CO 537/1842 and FO 371/52573.

between the oil producing areas of Iraq and Persia and our main base and supply areas in Palestine and Egypt traverse the country.'[9] If Abdullah had had his way, the strategic and political signficance of Jordan would have been greatly enhanced. He hoped to remedy his kingdom's lack of a corridor to the Mediterranean and to make more secure the precarious outlet to the Red Sea through the Gulf of Aqaba. Aqaba itself, so highly regarded a quarter of a century earlier as a prize of war, appeared to the Chiefs of Staff as well as Abdullah to be a port of great potential military and naval importance, despite high winds, steep shores, and the general unsatisfactory physical conditions as a remote supply port and depot. One possibility of developing ·the southern region of Jordan was the construction of a pipeline that would enable oil brought by tanker from the Gulf to Aqaba to be pumped to Gaza (in other words from the Red Sea to the Mediterranean), thereby avoiding Suez Canal duties and providing another outlet for Persian and Arabian oil. In the event another pipeline for Saudi oil was constructed across a two hundred mile stretch in northern Jordan, but, like the projected base in Kenya, the possibility of a pipeline from Aqaba played an important part in general British strategic calculation.

Abdullah's enemies, above all Ibn Saud, suspected him of bargaining with the Zionists in the hope that they might be agreeable to extending Jordan's boundaries to the Mediterranean in return for acquiescing in the establishment of a Jewish state. Abdullah's inclination to accommodate Zionism created resentment among the Palestinian Arabs, who regarded his 'appeasement' as undercutting their opposition. There were ties of kinship and common traditions between Arabs of both banks. The Arabs of Palestine and Jordan— and everyone else—believed that Transjordan was entirely an artificial creation. It was the most contrived of all the Middle Eastern states. The river Jordan no more demarcated a natural boundary separating differing peoples and geographical areas than the Nile or the Niger (or, to use the comparison frequently employed by American Zionists, the Mississippi). Transjordan proper consisted of a few arable highlands and a bizarrely designed hinterland of arid desert. It was among the poorest territories of the Middle East. The population in 1946 was less than one-half million. There were uneasy relations between the Bedouin, the village farmers, the settled townspeople, and the educated élite who regarded themselves more as 'southern Syrians' than as Tranjordanians. For the 'southern Syrians' as well as for Abdullah, Transjordan was an 'unnatural'

[9] JP (46) 27, 18 Feb. 1946, CAB 84/78; minutes in CO 537/1842-45 and FO 371/52572.

national territory, in any case one that was much too small. Here lay a major source of tension. Abdullah hoped to extend his domain not only in the south and west but also in the north to include Syria. Indeed he aspired to become sovereign over a vast Hashemite unitary state that together with Iraq would dominate the Middle East.

Abdullah's 'Greater Syria' Project and the Clash with Saudi Arabia

Abdullah's plan for a 'greater Syria' essentially was an aspiration of the 1940s, though he had persistently developed his ideas on the subject since the time of the First World War. It appeared to become more within the realm of possibility, at least to Abdullah, after the Peel Commission recommended the partition of Palestine in 1937 and after the erosion of French authority in Syria and Lebanon during and after the Second World War. He espoused Pan-Arabism and emphasized the Islamic element in Arab nationalism, though not entirely for nationalistic or religious reasons. To Abdullah the restoration of Damascus as the centre of the Arab world would fulfil the goal of the Arab revolt, and, it should be added, his personal ambition. His father the Sharif of Mecca and his two brothers (Ali and Feisal), he once wrote, in 1916 had come 'out of the Hejaz for the sake of Syria, Transjordan, Palestine and Lebanon, which are one entity—Greater Syria'.[10] Iraq, Abdullah hoped, would eventually be united with 'Greater Syria' in a 'Federal Union' to achieve Hashemite supremacy in the Middle East. His ambitions, in short, were grandiose.

Though passionately committed to the idea of some sort of Hashemite state stretching across the northern Arab world from the Mediterranean to Iraq, Abdullah was not an inflexible ideologue. He took a pragmatic approach to complex problems such as ethnic and religious minorities and even Zionism. He was usually willing to negotiate on the basis of the status quo. These attributes together with a professed desire for the public welfare of his subjects enabled him to get on with Ernest Bevin. The Foreign Secretary however let Abdullah know in no uncertain words that the scheme for a greater Syria would not carry British endorsement. 'Dangerous' Bevin once

[10] Quoted by Israel Gershuni, 'King Abdallah's Concept of a "Greater Syria" ', in *The Hashemite Kingdom*. For an exhaustive historical analysis of the project see the memorandum by the Research Department of the Foreign Office in FO 371/61497, the conclusions of which endorse Albert Hourani, *Syria and Lebanon* (London, 1946), pp. 269–74. For comment on the significance of the plan as it appeared shortly after Abdullah's assassination, see Esmond Wright, 'Abdallah's Jordan: 1947–1951', *Middle East Journal*, V (1951).

noted.[11] The Foreign Office could not support Abdullah's ambition because of Saudi and Egyptian antagonism; but on the other hand Bevin and several of his advisers (including the head of the Eastern Department) believed that the answer to many of the problems of the Middle East, including those of Palestine, might ultimately lie in regional amalgamation.[12] Circumstances of contradictory Arab ambitions compelled Bevin to take a genuinely neutral line on the question of 'Greater Syria'.

Abdullah was willing to recognize semi-autonomous Jewish communities under the sovereignty of Transjordan or a 'Greater Syria'. He wished his kingdom to be 'Muslim' in the sense that Muslim social values would be respected, but he saw himself as the heir of the Ottoman tradition of flexibility and tolerance for non-Muslims provided they did not ally with the enemy. Thus he would have been willing to accept Jewish communities, just as the Ottomans had accepted privileged or autonomous Christian districts. The Saudis and the Egyptians however denounced him as a traitor to the Arab cause, not so much because of his tolerance of Jewish settlements but rather because they knew that he had been in touch with the Zionists and feared that he might allow them to spread and eventually establish a Jewish state on both sides of the Jordan. Abdullah for his part maintained to the end that Zionism would be 'swallowed up' by a 'Greater Syria'.

The Jews of course had no intention of being digested by the Arabs, under the 'benevolent' despotism of Abdullah or any other Arab despotism. Nor did Abdullah's 'Greater Syria' project find substantial support elsewhere in the Middle East. It is true that the scheme stirred the interest of some Middle East experts of the Foreign Office who believed that the only way to make Transjordan and other Middle Eastern states economically viable would be to create larger political units along the lines of 'Greater Syria'. But on the whole the reaction to Abdullah's project was hostile. The leader of the Palestinian Arabs, Haj Amin el-Husseini, violently opposed the scheme. The republicans in Damascus who ruled Syria regarded Abdullah's ambition as a menace to Syrian independence. In Egypt pan-Arabism did not become an obsession until the advent of Nasser, but the Egyptians leaders such as Azzam Pasha who laid the basis of Egypt's leadership in Middle Eastern affairs regarded 'Greater Syria' as a veiled manifestation of British imperialism. In

---

[11] Minute by Bevin, *c*.6 Mar. 1946, FO 371/52573. The minute is significant because it probably indicates Bevin's first awareness of the extent of Abdullah's ambition. 'Have we encouraged this?' Bevin asked.

[12] See e.g. minute by C. W. Baxter, 29 Aug. 1945, FO 371/45379.

Iraq, Nuri Pasha promoted his own 'Fertile Crescent' scheme to unite Iraq in a 'federal union' with Syria, Transjordan, Lebanon, and Palestine—with a much greater weight given to Iraq than Abdullah had in mind. The fiercest antagonist was King Ibn Saud. His hostility towards 'Greater Syria' reflected the enmity between the Wahhabi dynasty in the Arabian peninsula and the Hashemite family.[13] As has been related in an earlier chapter, in the wars of the 1920s the Wahhabis, a fundamentalist Muslim sect, had driven Hussein out of Mecca. Ibn Saud consolidated his hold over the Hejaz and created the present-day state of Saudi Arabia. Two decades later the Saudis feared *revanchisme*. Abdullah, if he had possessed a base of power in 'Greater Syria', might indeed have attempted revenge. Whichever way they turned, Bevin and his Middle Eastern advisers saw the wisdom of playing the part of an 'impartial arbiter' and keeping a foot on the skirt of King Abdullah's robe.[14]

After the close of the Second World War, Abdullah demanded from the British that he be elevated from Amir to King. He expected no less as a reward for his service, in H. St. John Philby's sarcastic phrase, as 'a loyal and faithful servant of the British crown'. The British had no grounds to resist Abdullah's 'Kingship'. But they were apprehensive about the repercussions in the Arabian peninsula. The Saudis in particular regarded Abdullah's enthronement as ominous. 'Ibn Saud will dislike the Amir's rise in status', wrote the head of the Eastern Department, C. W. Baxter. 'He . . . [Ibn Saud] regards the Amir Abdullah, the head of the Hashemite family, as his greatest enemy. But it is difficult to see how he can reasonably object to his becoming King. After all, Ibn Saud himself is a self-made King.'[15] If Abdullah realized his ambition of a 'Greater Syria' then eventually he might attempt to recapture the Hejaz. If he became King of Syria as well as Jordan, then the future of Palestine might be, from the Saudi vantage point, adversely affected. Baxter summed up the problem in these words:

If the Amir Abdullah's hopes are fulfilled and he becomes the ruler of Syria as well as of Transjordan, this may have a very important bearing upon a future Palestine settlement. This would be, in fact, a step towards the 'Greater Syria' scheme. . . . Palestine might then become a part of this 'Greater Syria', or alternatively, if Palestine were partitioned, the Arab part might become a part of the Greater Syria under 'King' Abdullah.[16]

On the other hand if events developed adversely to Abdullah and a Jewish state were created, then Jordan might lose access to Haifa

---

[13] For the background of Ibn Saud's attitude see Gary Troeller, *The Birth of Saudi Arabia: Britain and the Rise of the House of Sa'ud* (London, 1976).

[14] The phrase is I. N. Clayton's in a letter to Burrows, 27 Sept. 1947, FO 371/61497.

[15] Minute by Baxter, 6 Mar. 1946, FO 371/52573.

[16] Ibid.

and Jaffa (a right enjoyed during the mandate era) and become completely cut off from the Mediterranean.

Less speculatively, in 1946, Abdullah's 'Kingship' had ramifications in the south. Ibn Saud claimed as part of Saudi Arabia the port of Aqaba and the major town in southern Jordan, Maan, the head of the Hejaz railway. He refused to recognize the annexation by Abdullah two decades earlier in 1925. Since this region had traditionally been ruled as part of the Hejaz under the Sharifs of Mecca, it had acquired a special meaning in Hashemite memory. So long as Britain held Transjordan as a mandate, Ibn Saud had agreed not to press the claim. If the mandate were terminated, however, according to the British representative in Jedda, Ibn Saud would reassert his rights over what he claimed to be Saudi territory. All the British could do was to adopt, in the phrase of Robert Howe (Assistant Under-Secretary), an attitude that Abdullah was 'clearly right', and hope that they would not be dragged into a dispute characterized by 'Bedouin desert methods of settling international relations'.[17]

In planning for the termination of the mandate the British first took the necessary precaution of gaining the approval of the United Nations. The Colonial Secretary reported to the Cabinet in February 1946: 'our intention to terminate the mandate for Trans-Jordan had been warmly welcomed by the First General Assembly of the United Nations Organisation and had received the unanimous approval of the Trusteeship Council'.[18] Since most of the members of the United Nations believed that 'independence' should be the outcome of trusteeship, they easily endorsed the general proposition of ending the British era. It was less easy to convince critics of British imperialism that there would be *real* independence. The sceptics were entirely right. If they had been given access to the secret files of the Colonial Office and Foreign Office they would have verified that the British, in the words of the High Commissioner for Palestine and Transjordan, intended to give Transjordan only *'the outward semblance of sovereignty'*.[19] Such was the basic design when the Amir Abdullah arrived in London in January 1946.

The Resident accompanied Abdullah. Kirkbride had been associated with the affairs of Transjordan since 1921. His Middle Eastern career included a tour of duty on the Jerusalem Secretariat and he had served as District Commissioner in Galilee as well as on the mandatory staff in Transjordan. He observed in his memoirs that

---

[17] Minute by Howe, 1 Apr. 1946, FO 371/52574/E2705.

[18] Cabinet Conclusions, 25 Feb. 1946, 18 (46) CAB 128/5; minutes in CO 537/1843 and FO 371/52573.

[19] General Sir A. G. Cunningham to Hall, 26 Dec. 1946, copy in FO 371/52572; emphasis added.

the British government had allowed the Resident a relatively free hand because of preoccupation with Palestinian affairs and refusal to be bothered 'about the remote and undeveloped areas which lay to the east of the river'.[20] It seemed to him that British policy should aim at developing Transjordan as an exclusively Arab territory that would eventually be able to absorb Palestinian Arabs dislocated by the Jewish 'National Home'. He respected Abdullah, who might not possess the stature of other Arab leaders but was nevertheless blessed with 'streaks of shrewd intuition'. In his capacity as Resident, Kirkbride controlled the budget and all other aspects of the mandate's administration. In a dour manner he saw his duties as getting on as well as possible with Abdullah and ensuring that the Foreign Office did not regard Jordan as a second-rate Arab state (a delicate point to him as well as Abdullah). Respected by both Abdullah and the officials of the Colonial Office for his reliable political instinct (and despite his veiled contempt for Arabs in general), Kirkbride had acquired the reputation of a solid if somewhat unimaginative latter-day proconsul. In the slightly exaggerated words of one friend of Jordan who wrote a popular history of the country in the late 1950s, he had 'an unrivalled knowledge of the country . . . [and] he forged with the Amir Abdullah a British–Arab connection that perhaps was the most rewarding in all British Mandatory history'.[21] Kirkbride in short was a person of consequence in the Anglo-Arab world, certainly the most important British political figure in Transjordan in a crucial decade. It is therefore especially relevant to note, in his own words, the difference that 'independence' made in his duties. The passage is revealing about the distinction between British 'formal' and 'informal' empire: 'When Jordan became independent in 1946, my title changed [from Resident to Minister] . . . without causing any drastic modification in my activities. . . .'[22] The nomenclature of the British Empire might change, but to Kirkbride it would be business as usual. Such was his attitude when he helped to conclude the treaty of 1946 which terminated the mandate and launched Jordan into a new era of 'independence'.

The Treaty of 1946

The Colonial Office, Foreign Office, and Chiefs of Staff intended the treaty with Jordan to confirm both a political and a military alliance. The political part, which would last for twenty-five years, posed

[20] Kirkbride, *Crackle of Thorns*, p. 19.
[21] Ann Dearden, *Jordan* (London, 1958), p. 55.
[22] *Crackle of Thorns*, p. 2.

few problems. Britain would grant Transjordan 'full independence'. There would be 'perpetual peace and friendship' between the two countries. There would also be 'full and frank discussions' about foreign policy. An all-important ingredient of the understanding was the annual subsidy. In the interwar period the British Treasury had provided, mainly for military purposes, one-fourth of Transjordan's budget. The subsidy during the war and afterwards remained roughly on the same scale, but between 1939 and 1945 the Arab Legion had grown from a strength of 1,600 to 8,000 (and by 1956 to 25,000 officers and men). The British hoped eventually to reduce the size of the Legion; but in the meantime they would continue the annual subsidy of about £2 million. Fortunately for the British the amount could be sustained even by the impoverished Exchequer. Transjordan was the only Middle Eastern state satisfied with the amount of British 'aid'.

The strictly military part of the treaty consisted of a military 'convention' renewable at intervals of five years. Here the British trod on dangerous ground. In euphemistic language they tried to reconcile a straightforward old-fashioned military treaty with the charter of the United Nations. They emphasized 'mutual defence' but clearly to all observers this phrase meant that, if Jordan were attacked, Britain would defend Jordan and vice versa. The danger point lay in the Aqaba–Maan controversy. If Ibn Saud occupied either the port or the railhead, Britain might be automatically at war with Saudi Arabia, a prospect not relished in official circles in London. Nevertheless, after intense debate among the Chiefs of Staff, Colonial Office, and Foreign Office, the risk seemed worth taking. Ibn Saud would never grant the military privileges at Aqaba and elsewhere conceded by Abdullah. The Chiefs of Staff in particular attached importance to the potential value of Aqaba as a major port. They also believed it imperative to continue a generous subsidy to Abdullah that would enable the Arab Legion to fulfil the following British requirements:

(1) to maintain law and order in Trans-Jordan and to safeguard the pipe-line;
(2) to deter neighbouring States from attacking Trans-Jordan and
(3) to prevent smuggling [of war matériel] into Palestine.[23]

The Chiefs of Staff valued the Legion's service in keeping the peace in Palestine. But they recognized that after the granting of

---

[23] Memorandum by Chiefs of Staff Joint Planning Committee, JP (46) 27, 15 Feb. 1946, CAB 84/78; see also COS (46) 31, 1 Feb. 1946, CAB 80/88; and minutes in CO 537/1842 and FO 371/52572.

'independence' it would be difficult to justify the garrisoning of Legion troops outside the borders of Jordan. Therefore the Chiefs of Staff insisted that Britain should have the right to station troops *in* Jordan to deal with whatever emergencies might arise in the Middle East. With an uncertain future in Egypt, Cyrenaica, and Palestine, the Chiefs of Staff required a secure base in Jordan.

The right to station and train troops became one of the most controversial aspects of the treaty. To Arab critics the bugles of British soldiers on the soil of an 'independent' Middle Eastern country sounded like an echo from the days of General Allenby. But, if the troop issue appeared in Arab (and Jewish) eyes as the most objectionable part of the bargain, other aspects of the treaty seemed also to personify the hydra-head of British imperialism. The British acquired the right to 'develop' the port of Aqaba; to move troops across the territory with 'complete right of transit'; to establish 'a signal communication system'; and to maintain two air bases at Amman and Mafrak.

Abdullah did not merely acquiesce in those demands. He enthusiastically agreed to them. The head of the International Relations Department of the Colonial Office, J. S. Bennett, commented that the other members of the Arab League would excoriate Abdullah's 'over-eagerness' to fall in with British requirements, but that Transjordan needed to be 'levelled up' with Egypt and Iraq. It was almost certain, he added, that the terms of the alliance would have been the same regardless of the line taken by Abdullah.[24] Abdullah himself was not ingratiating; he was merely polite in giving way to British demands and securing his part of the bargain, which above all consisted of the annual subsidy and the support of British troops. There was a logic to his concessions: the greater the British involvement in Jordan, the greater their commitment to the Hashemite Kingdom. The symbiotic relationship had developed into one of Siamese twins.

When Abdullah met with Attlee in mid-March 1946, he told him that his visit to England had been a 'complete success'. With the charm and presence of an Arab prince, Abdullah mentioned the fulfilment of his personal ambition to meet the British Prime Minister. He emphasized the 'Arab cause'. 'It is a pity', he said, 'that the movement is not united under the influence of a single personality'— an oblique comment on his ambition to become ruler of 'Greater Syria'. He then dwelt on the threat of Russian expansion. 'Russia is playing a dangerous game in the Middle East', he told Attlee.

----

[24] Minute by Bennett, 11 Apr. 1946, CO 537/1849.

He went on to say, in words remarkable for anticipating western anxiety about defence problems of later decades as well as in the postwar period:

Russia is following a forward policy in Iran and Kurdistan, a policy which may well aim at expansion to the Persian Gulf and the Mediterranean. Against this, it is desirable that a defensive front should be built up covering Turkey, Iran and Afghanistan by the 'fertile crescent' of Arab countries stretching from Basra to Aqaba.[25]

Abdullah next gave Attlee an explicit comment on the problem of Zionism. The Jews had overrun Palestine, he said, 'and are indulging in acts of violence which no one would have dreamt they would dare to commit'. In words that must have impressed even the impassive Attlee; Abdullah warned: 'If, God forbid, matters pass the endurable limit, there will be an explosion of terrible violence on the part of the Arabs.'[26]

Abdullah had a conclusive talk with Bevin on the 22nd of March 1946, the date of the signing of the treaty. He drove home to the Foreign Secretary the point of inexperienced 'native politicians' usurping control of Syria. Syria, he said, was 'the really weak spot' in the Middle East—again an indirect reference to his ambition of transforming Syria into a bastion of Hashemite strength. Abdullah made it clear to Bevin the extent to which he valued the British military presence. 'He was quite sure that the maintenance of some [British] divisions in Iraq and Transjordan would have a salutary effect', especially on Egypt. When Bevin asked whether Transjordan might leave the Arab League because of ill will between Egypt and Transjordan, Abdullah replied: 'there were some grounds for a suspicion that a close connexion existed between Ibn Saud and King Farouk, whose idea was to run the whole of the League'. But, Abdullah continued, Transjordan would not leave the League abruptly or without full consultation with Britain. Bevin was much relieved. He replied that if Transjordan abandoned the League after the signing of the treaty, 'it would be assumed by all other countries that this was due to British inspiration; it would be a fatal step to take'.[27] The remark is revealing. Britain's place in the Arab world now depended not only on her own military power but also on the political calculations of such collaborators as Abdullah.

The signing of the solemn commitment between Britain and Jordan took place little over twenty-five years after Abdullah had sat

---

[25] Memorandum by Kirkbride transcribing Abdullah's remarks, 14 Mar. 1946, CO 537/1847.
[26] Ibid.
[27] F.O. to C.O., 22 Mar. 1946, CO 537/1845.

with Churchill and gained the concession that Transjordan would be administered apart from Palestine as an Arab territory. The date of the 22nd of March was also almost twenty-five years to the day when he had formally become Amir of Transjordan. In 1946 he became King. It was in every sense, as H. St. John Philby pointed out sardonically from the Saudi vantage point, a 'silver jubilee'.[28] To critics of the British Empire there was an element of self-evident farce in Abdullah's enthronement.

The ceremonies in Amman took place on the 25th of May 1946, at which time the Legislative Council declared Jordan a completely independent state with Abdullah Ibn Hussein as King. A salute of 101 guns marked the reading of the proclamation. Afterwards in the 'Throne Room' of the Palace, members of the government presented Abdullah with a scroll of the Koran in a gold box. Iraq, the Lebanon, and Yemen sent representatives to take part in the celebrations. The other Arab countries boycotted the enthronement. Privately Abdullah spoke bitterly about Syria not only refusing to send a delegation but also preventing invited guests from crossing the frontier. The British delegation included the High Commissioner for Palestine; the Commander-in-Chief, Middle East; and the highest ranking officers of the Royal Navy and Royal Air Force in that part of the world. The festivities drew to a close with King Abdullah and the Regent of Iraq reviewing a parade of Mounted Desert Camel Police and the Arab Legion. Military bands played the Jordan national anthem followed by the national anthem of Iraq. Despite the heat and the dust the parade was, in the words of the High Commissioner for Palestine, 'an unqualified success'——one that probably had few equals in British pomp and Arab circumstance in the postwar era. Speaking on behalf of the people of Jordan, King Abdullah closed the celebration with words of gratitude to Great Britain 'for having raised them within twenty-five years from an unknown corner of the Ottoman Empire to the status of an independent Kingdom'.[29]

The International Protest

Middle Eastern reaction to the alliance ranged from lukewarm approval in Iraq to condemnation in Egypt. In Baghdad newspaper editors who usually supported the British expressed unenthusiastic approval of the treaty. On the whole the Iraqi press that represented moderate nationalist opinion held that Jordan had not been granted

    [28] Philby's article, 'Akaba——Test for Arab Diplomacy', *Egyptian Gazette*, 28 Mar. 1946, clipping in FO 371/52575.
    [29] Cunningham to Hall, 18 June 1946, copy in FO 371/52935/E6403.

'full' independence and that as long as British forces remained in Arab countries there would always be Anglo-Arab misunderstanding. In Damascus newspapers denounced the military part of the treaty as symbolizing a prolonged British military occupation of Transjordan, though some Syrian officials thought that Abdullah had overplayed his hand and that the 'alliance' would be a 'fatal blow' to his ambition of a 'Greater Syria'. In Lebanon the reaction of the press was milder, though one editorial urged that the status of Jordan be brought before the Security Council because the British 'strategic bases' constituted a threat to world peace. In Saudi Arabia the newspaper comment was restrained but Ibn Saud made it clear to the British that he greatly disliked the treaty and that he was moreover alarmed at continuing Jewish immigration. The treaty with Transjordan and the increasing influx of Jews caused a deterioration in Anglo-Saudi relations. In Egypt the general sentiment could be summed up in the newspaper caption 'Transjordan—a Lackey of British Imperialism'. Abdullah had cemented his friendship with the British but as a result he had become more and more isolated in the Arab world.[30]

Zionists and their sympathizers in the United States also responded bitterly to 'British perfidy and Arab intrigue', most notably in the Senate and House of Representatives. On the 1st of April 1946 Representative Emmanuel Celler, a Democrat from New York (whom a Foreign Office official described as 'unbridled and irresponsible') denounced Abdullah as 'a mere sycophant of Great Britain in the pay of the British Government'. This 'new perfidy' of the British, he stated, worked to the detriment of both Jews and Arabs. 'In Transjordan there is uttermost poverty as contrasted with the industry and high standard of living, the fine insitutions of education, and hospitals, the sanitation, and the culture of Palestine'. Representative Celler believed that the separation of Palestine and Transjordan was both 'ungeographical' and uneconomic:

Palestine and Transjordan present one economic and geographic unit as the writers of the mandate meant it to be. This unit must be kept intact if 300,000 half-starved inhabitants of Transjordan are to have a happier prospect open to them. Without the benefits of Jewish settlement therein the progress of Transjordan is doomed. Britain's, not the people's, interests are served.[31]

Senator Claude R. Pepper of Florida attacked the claim that British troops occupied Jordan for purposes of 'freedom' and mutual defence. 'Sanctimonious pretence', he said. Representative Gordon L.

---

[30] See telegrams, reports of press reaction, and press cuttings in CO 537/1849.
[31] *Congressional Record*, vol. 92, pt. 10, A1817–18, 1 Apr. 1946. For British reaction see minutes in FO 371/52575.

McDonough of California spoke of the 'heroic and creative Hebrew people' who would be 'infinitely better as the guarantors of western peace and freedom in the Near East than can illiterate nomadic Bedouins'. Other disparaging remarks were made about nomadic life and lack of sanitation. Many Senators and Representatives unabashedly endorsed the American stereotype of the 'dirty Arab'.

The rhetorical heights of anti-Arab and pro-Zionist remarks were probably reached in an eloquent way of sorts by Representative Augustus W. Bennet of New York. Bennet dwelt on the historical and religious significance of the River Jordan:

> There is one river, gentlemen, a small river, in a small country, which flows . . . intimately through the history, the geography, and the traditions of its land. . . . Indeed, it flows through the traditions of the whole of the civilized world. The river is the Jordan, and its country is Palestine. From Moses, to Jesus, to the present day, they have never been separated. Never, until just recently, have men ever entertained the slightest notion of splitting Palestine at the Jordan. Neither the east nor the west of the country could survive without it.[32]

It was just as unthinkable to separate Palestine and Transjordan by an artificial boundary of the River Jordan as it would be to divide the United States at the Mississippi:

> The Mississippi is not a boundary, not a moat which separates and divides us; it is our main artery, through which much of the life of our great nation flows from all its parts, east and west. The Father of Waters is, furthermore, the center of much of our great tradition, renowned and revered in our memories of the great heritage of this nation. From Pere Marquette to Tom Sawyer, to the people who live along its banks to-day the Mississippi is America.[33]

The Mississippi symbolized the American flag just as the River Jordan had forever been associated with the Bible. So ran the flow of anti-Arab Congressional oration. Now in 1946 Great Britain, 'a power thousands of miles from Palestine, holding it not as a possession, but as a sacred trust for civilization . . . has dared to sunder what God has made a Holy Land'. The British, it appeared to Representative Augustus Bennet, had profaned sacred soil and had deliberately 'slapped the face' of the great nation of Tom Sawyer.

Many of the pro-Zionist speakers in Congress urged non-recognition of the new state. In February 1946, about a month before the signing of the treaty, Loy Henderson (Director of the Office of Near Eastern and African Affairs) informed British officials that the State Department had received 'numerous protests' from organizations such as the American Zionist Emergency Council and the Jewish Agency. Such Zionist groups denounced the British granting of

---

[32] *Congressional Record*, vol. 92, pt. 10, A1897–98, 4 Apr. 1946.
[33] Ibid.

Jordan's independence as 'illegal' and in violation of an Anglo-American treaty of 1924 that required consultation in the event of any change in Transjordan's international status. These protests created a predicament for State Department officials. On the one hand they could not ignore the Zionist lobby in Congress. On the other hand it would prove embarrassing for the American government to deny recognition to a newly independent state, especially one that had been a mandate. The Anglo-Jordan treaty did not formally grant the British explicit economic or other special privileges; and the State Department and War Department believed that continued military assistance by the British would be necessary for the stability of Jordan and the security of the eastern Mediterranean. 'Our position in general', Henderson explained, 'was that in the absence of an understanding, freely entered into, voluntarily given, foreign troops should not remain in the territory of an independent country against the will of that country.'[34] Since Abdullah, with the support of the Jordan government, had freely entered into a military alliance, the treaty did not conflict with American requirements. Nevertheless the unpopularity of the treaty and the strength of the protest in both the United States and the Middle East caused the State Department to regard the question of recognition as 'premature'. Not until January 1949 did the United States finally extend *de jure* recognition. And the opposition to the new state on the part of the Arab countries and the Russian bloc remained so strong that the United Nations denied Jordan's admission until 1955.

Political Tension in 1947

To the consternation, or at least the annoyance, of officials in the Foreign Office, Abdullah used the treaty of alliance as a basis to promote his political and territorial ambition. The British, he implied directly and indirectly to anyone willing to listen, supported his scheme for a 'Greater Syria'. In the words of the head of the Eastern Department, Charles Baxter, 'the King is . . . prepared to give the *impression*, whenever it suits him, that he has our backing'.[35] From secret reports as well as general rumours the Foreign Office in the spring of 1947 had reason to believe that Abdullah might be implicated in plans for a *coup d'état* in Syria. Those who knew him well, for example Kirkbride, tended to discount his influence beyond the borders of Transjordan, but they recognized an element of danger. The important point, Kirkbride wrote, was to prevent Abdullah from

---

[34] *Foreign Relations 1946*, VII, p. 795.
[35] Minute by Baxter, 25 Apr. 1947, FO 371/61492.

'taking any positive action such as an act of aggression by the Arab Legion or the fomentation of a rebellion in Syria against the present régime'.[36] Abdullah appeared psychologically to be preparing himself for illusions of Syrian grandeur when in May 1947 he published a 'White Paper' on 'Greater Syria' which discussed at length the geographical and historical basis of Transjordan and Syria as one country.[37] 'Very wild and unbalanced' noted Garran on Abdullah's general views. 'Ridiculous', observed Baxter in reaction to Abdullah's opinion that 'Communist agents' had infiltrated into the government of Syria. Nevertheless the British had to take Abdullah seriously if only because his utterances about 'Greater Syria' made Ibn Saud 'speechless with rage' and, even more seriously, because Abdullah might actually participate in an attempt to overthrow the Syrian government by 'using a part of the Arab Legion' in order to bring to power politicians sympathetic to his aims.[38]

At this point British officials had to confront one of the classic problems of imperial expansion as it had appeared in extreme form in the nineteenth century: the question of 'sub-imperialism'. How could the 'agents' or 'collaborators' of British imperialism be controlled? Abdullah might appear to be a bizarre reincarnation of a Gordon or a Rhodes, but the dilemmas he presented were similar. Sir Orme Sargent, who regarded Abdullah's machinations as both dangerous and irritating, asked whether the deadliest weapon available might be used to bring him into line: 'are we prepared . . . to tell King Abdullah that he must stop his intrigues and propaganda for a Greater Syria or else we shall cut off his subsidy?'[39]

Sargent had little patience for 'oriental intrigue' but he found reasons to be tolerant in the powerful logic of the head of the Eastern Department. The British needed to continue to support the Arab Legion specifically, Baxter argued, and Abdullah generally. The Hashemites offset anti-British Egyptian influence, and, increasingly important in 1947, the Legion was necessary to keep the peace in Palestine.

It would be very difficult to threaten King Abdullah with cutting off his subsidy. We pay him that subsidy as much in our own interests as in his own, in order that there may be in Transjordan a small, but efficient military force

[36] Minute by Kirkbride, 'Greater Syria', 9 Sept. 1947, FO 371/61497.
[37] For lengthy F. O. analysis see FO 371/61497. Foreign Office officials tried to take the line with the Saudis and others alarmed at the publication of the 'White Paper' that 'it is not deserving of any particular attention' (minute by Butler, 5 June 1947, FO 371/61493). It provoked considerable comment in the British press. '294 pages of wishful thought do not make a kingdom' remarked *The Economist* (10 May 1947).
[38] See minutes by Garran and Baxter in FO 371/61492-94.
[39] Minute by Sargent, 17 Apr. 1947, FO 371/61492.

which would be at our disposal in case of trouble. At present, indeed, the force is somewhat inflated in size and some two thirds of it are stationed in Palestine and rendering us invaluable assistance in the maintenance of order there. In the present man-power shortage we could ill-afford to do without these units of the Arab Legion.[40]

The Eastern Department persistently took the line that Abdullah's ambitions should not be taken 'too seriously' (sometimes implying that there were ludicrous implications) and that the King, as Peter Garran explained to Lewis Jones of the American Embassy, 'had been a good friend of ours in the past'.[41]

In a balanced assessment that at once affirmed the benefits of Abdullah's friendship and the need to keep grandiose ambitions in check, Sir Alec Kirkbride pointed out that Abdullah in the past had responded to British guidance. Frank criticism might throw the King into fits of depression, but he recognized his vulnerability. The trouble, according to Kirkbride, was that he had become obsessed with the idea of 'Greater Syria' and various self-seekers egged him on. Abdullah's psychological make-up and his slightly bent sense of humour unfortunately made things more difficult:

> King Abdullah no longer seems to be capable of appreciating that the majority of the inhabitants of Syria do not appear to have any desire to place themselves under his rule and he lends too willing an ear to the Syrian malcontents and seekers of profit who visit Amman periodically and encourage his dreams, to their own gain. . . .
> The irritable public reactions of the Saudis and Syrians to King Abdullah's periodical pronouncements on the subject of Greater Syria fill King Abdullah with impish satisfaction and do much to sustain his activities in this matter.[42]

Kirkbride agreed with Baxter and Garran that Abdullah needed to be bridled, but that if the reins were drawn too tight he might bolt. Kirkbride again emphasized the psychology of the situation:

> I would . . . urge the importance of any discouragement to the King being kept entirely confidential. His enemies would make great play of his being checked by H. M. G. and might well drive him in sheer exasperation to defy H. M. G. and embark on some course of direct action. . . . care must be taken not to drive him to some act of folly on the spur of a moment of irritation.[43]

[40] Minute by Baxter, 25 Apr. 1947, FO 371/61492.

[41] Minute by Garran, 12 May 1947, FO 371/61493. The State Department had made inquiries not only because of American concern about Abdullah's expansionism but also because of prompting on the part of Ibn Saud. See *Foreign Relations 1947*, V, pp. 738–59. 'Each successive public indiscretion of King Abdullah's', Garran noted later, 'has thrown King Ibn Saud into a greater state of agitation.' Minute by Garran, 3 Sept. 1947, FO 371/61495/E8245.

[42] Minute by Kirkbride, 9 Sept. 1947, FO 371/61497.

[43] Ibid.

Kirkbride, who knew Abdullah as well as any Englishman, thus believed that frank talk and firm advice would 'check King Abdullah's eloquence on the subject of Greater Syria'. Abdullah, though unfortunately a braggart, was not a fool.

In September 1947, when the movement for a 'Greater Syria' appeared to be reaching a crescendo, King Abdullah also preoccupied the thoughts of Brigadier I. N. Clayton, who connected the problems of Transjordan with larger political and military issues. He identified two danger points. The first was the breakaway tendency of the Druzes of southern Syria (along the Transjordan frontier) who, he believed, were attempting to play off Abdullah against the government in Damascus. The second was the Aqaba–Maan controversy between Abdullah and Ibn Saud, which might eventually draw in the Iraqis. According to Clayton:

> There is the possibility that trouble in the Jebel Druze, always a likelihood, might tempt Abdullah to intervene either directly or indirectly. An extremely probable sequel to this would be intervention on the Syrian side by Ibn Saud which intervention might take the form of occupying Aqaba and Maan. The Regent of Iraq would be tempted by family ties to support Abdullah unless restrained by his Government and the Arab World would be hopelessly split.[44]

If the situation deteriorated, Egypt and Syria might attempt to expel Transjordan from the Arab League: 'the action would certainly be construed by our enemies everywhere as an attack on our position in the Middle East'.

Clayton, who had a reputation as the éminence grise of British imperialism in the Middle East, paid King Abdullah a visit. 'And you have come!' exclaimed the King, as if recognizing a moment of crisis.[45] In fact Clayton arrived in Amman only two days after the British announcement at the United Nations of the intention to withdraw from Palestine. His report on his talks with Abdullah is therefore of considerable interest. At this time, in late September 1947, talk of 'Greater Syria' continued to wax while speculation about the future of Palestine also became much more intense. 'This question of Greater Syria is mounting', Clayton wrote, to the extent that it predominated over all other subjects in discussion with Abdullah. 'The impression created on me is of a man who is completely obsessed by an idée fixe to the extent almost of monomania.' It took the momentous turn of events in Palestine to jar Abdullah out of

---

[44] Clayton to Garran, 4 Sept. 1947, FO 371/61496/E8358. In regard to Abdullah and the 'pro-Hashimite Jabal Druze' see Patrick Seale, *The Struggle for Syria* (London, 1965), p. 14, *et passim* for a valuable account of Abdullah and Syria.

[45] 'Whether this was intended as a compliment or an expression of his disappointment, at seeing only me [rather than someone of the stature of Ernest Bevin] I am not sure!' Clayton to Burrows, 27 Sept. 1947, FO 371/61497.

his fixation and turn his attention to the future of the Arabs and Jews. Clayton's comments—in a letter to the Foreign Office so 'Secret' that only one other copy was sent to Kirkbride—illuminate the vital position held by King Abdullah at this time:

> The King's attitude over Palestine . . . left little doubt that he personally would be prepared to accept any solution of the Palestine question short of giving the whole of Palestine to the Jews. The latter, certainly, are convinced that this is the case. Such an attitude might, obviously, be of considerable value to us in certain circumstances, but his constant campaign to aggrandise his Kingdom will lay him open to the charges already made, that he is prepared to sell Palestine for his own ends.[46]

Coming almost immediately after the announcement of withdrawal from Palestine, those words record the almost instantaneous reaction of one of the most knowledgeable British officials. Abdullah in this judgement would provide the key to the eventual settlement in Palestine if he could curb his 'Greater Syria' ambitions and appear as a peacemaker rather than an annexationist in the west.

In the winter of 1947–8 events in the Middle East broke with a lightning-like rapidity. To the British the United Nations' resolution of the 29th of November in favour of the creation of a Jewish state struck like a thunderbolt. It had not been unanticipated, but its explosion lit the landscape of the Middle East in ominous perspective. Ernest Bevin prepared not only to weather the storm but to seize the initiative. He hoped to forge a formal and informal system of alliances with the Arab states that would help to bring about the partition of Palestine as smoothly as possible. King Abdullah played a key, indeed delicate, part in this overarching scheme, but his role must be seen in the overall complexity of international politics, military calculation in the Middle East, and, in England, the extent to which Bevin could bear the brunt of accusations of 'collusion' with the Arabs against the Jews. Britain of stark necessity needed to preserve American goodwill at a time of economic extremity and international peril, which meant in some way the accommodation of a Jewish state. At the same time Bevin aimed to prevent the deterioration of Britain's position as the predominant power in the Middle East, which necessitated the striking of a balance between Egypt and Saudi Arabia at one extreme and Transjordan at the other. The treaty with Iraq would be the particular case in which Britain would prove to the other Arab countries and the world at large that the British wished to end once and for all the old system of imperial domination and work as equal partners towards a stable and peaceful Middle East. The collapse of the Iraqi treaty in early

[46] Clayton to Burrows, 27 Sept. 1947, FO 371/61497.

1948 was a devastating blow to Bevin's general plans. He then had to calculate the advantages of a renewed formal bond of friendship between Britain and Transjordan against the disadvantage of international protest against Abdullah as a solitary British 'stooge'.

The Treaty of 1948 and the Question of Palestine

Against the background of unprecedented general tension in the Middle East, there is a recurrent theme in the historical literature of Abdullah's rule that represents the late 1940s as the most happy years of the 'Siamese twin' relationship between Transjordan and Britain. That interpretation can be sustained because of the effectiveness of the military arrangements. In early 1948 Transjordan, alone among the Arab powers, agreed to continue a military as well as a political alliance. Transjordan appeared as a friendly Hashemite island of stability in a hostile sea of Middle Eastern unrest. With British leadership the Arab Legion served as a breakwater against internal violence and revolution as well as a stabilizing force in Palestine. During the Arab–Israeli war the Legion became the only Arab military unit to acquit itself honourably. Its leader was John Glubb, 'Glubb Pasha', whose name at that time was synonymous with the Legion itself.

Glubb had assumed command of the Arab Legion in 1938. During the Second World War and in the following years he galvanized the Legion into such an effective force that these words could be found in an Israeli military handbook of 1948: 'In Jordan there is an army which owns a state.'[47] The Legion kept the peace between tribal chiefs and generally provided them with security, status, and subsidies, which were repaid by loyalty to Glubb and Abdullah. Through long-term enlistment the Legion gave Bedouin tribesmen economic and educational opportunities that otherwise probably would not have existed. The Bedouin too responded with loyalty. It is no exaggeration to say, in the words of P. J. Vatikiotis, that the Legion virtually created and sustained the state of Jordan.[48] Internally it held the territory's fractious society together and externally it deterred aggression from hostile tribes across the frontiers.

Glubb Pasha was always under the command of a civilian government headed by a Hashemite monarch. Glubb respected that authority. He was not a schemer. He was a genuinely modest man. 'I have spent all my life in Government service', he wrote in 1946, 'as did my father and grand-father before me. I have no higher ambition

---

[47] Vatikiotis, *Politics and the Military in Jordan*, p. 5 note 5.
[48] This is Vatikiotis's major theme in his book, ibid.

than to serve my country as they did.' Contemporary acquaintances could well have added that he had a military competence which, in combination with a shrewd but unsophisticated sense of Arab politics, enabled him to survive as one of the famous military figures in Anglo-Arab history. He was under no illusion about the permanence of his position as commander of the Legion. He wrote after the conclusion of the 1946 treaty:

> Our position in Trans-Jordan is still good, and the local Government expresses its anxiety to retain our services. It seems to be doubtful, however, how long it will continue to do so. The appetite for independence increases with indulgence. . . . Even if the Trans-Jordan Government wishes to retain our services, it is quite possible that it might get rid of us in a year or two, as a result of the taunts of other Arab States. It is, in any case, unlikely that the Trans-Jordan Government will wish to retain a British officer in command of its armed forces for another 15 years.[49]

When he was abruptly dismissed in 1956, five years before his optimistic estimate of fifteen years, he had witnessed a calamitous increase in Jordan's population (by the annexation of the west bank in 1948), and the expansion of the Legion by more than threefold, from 8,000 to about 25,000 officers and men. The year 1948 in this regard was a juncture in the Legion's history, and it is important to emphasize its size and nature at that time in order not to allow its subsequent transformation to obscure its limited but effective capacity on the eve of the Israeli–Arab war. Under Glubb's command between 1948 and 1956 the Legion's officer corps became 'Arabized' and expanded from a *corps d'élite* into a national mass army composed mainly of conscripts. In 1948 the Legion was still a long-enlistment, volunteer, regular force whose efficiency rested on mobile strike capacity over long frontiers. 'A treaty with Britain', Glubb wrote in 1948 about the treaty concluded two years earlier, 'resulted in making the weakest Arab country into militarily the most effective.'[50] It was the Legion's proven military capacity that the British had to weigh against the more nebulous capability of militant Zionism in 1948.

The treaty of 1946 lasted only two years rather than its life expectancy of twenty-five. Its revision in 1948 was a calculated gamble in public relations. Neither side wished substantially to alter the terms agreed upon two years earlier, in other words those of a slightly disguised old-fashioned military alliance, but both wished to make Transjordan appear to be less of a puppet and more of an ally on an equal footing. If the treaty with Iraq had not collapsed, the one with

[49] Memorandum by Glubb, 27 May 1946, FO 371/52931/E10014.
[50] Memorandum by Glubb, 12 Aug. 1948, FO 371/68822/11049/G.

Transjordan might have been recognized as a part of a new and less domineering regional arrangement between Britain and the Arab states; as events transpired, Transjordan was exposed to the full glare of international attention as an unrepentant beneficiary of British imperialism.

The terms of the treaty itself, agreed upon quickly and without controversy in January and February 1948, may be briefly summarized.[51] The British merely succeeded in getting from Abdullah what they failed to obtain from the Egyptians and Iraqis. Abdullah, to use his own words, obtained 'higher status in the eyes of the Arab world'.[52] British military commitment was reduced to the maintenance of two air bases at Amman and Mafraq. The treaty created a 'joint Defence Board' responsible for external defence and strategic planning. The British would continue to subsidize the Arab Legion at £2 million per annum plus £½ million for military equipment. Lieutenant-General Gerald Templer at one stage of the discussions stated that he had 'no comment' about the slightly revised military arrangements because in the opinion of the Chiefs of Staff the military arrangements remained essentially unaltered. By 1948 the strategic requirements of the Chiefs of Staff could be met by the maintenance of the Arab Legion as 'an efficient and well organized force' and by the strategic rights at Mafraq.[53] The subject of the Joint Defence Board, however, agitated the collective mind of the Chiefs of Staff. In Templer's words the board's 'members would have little to do' and indeed might prove to be a nuisance by meddling in the affairs of the Arab Legion. Kirkbride gave reassurances from Amman that the Joint Defence Board could be kept under control by the appointment of a 'tame' senior Arab officer. 'This is bad', Bevin noted in one of the few episodes of explosive disagreement in the 1948 proceedings. His words recorded a genuine conviction of the need for a change in Anglo-Arab relations: 'It is just the way I do not want to treat the Arabs.'[54]

General Glubb accompanied the Jordan Prime Minister, Taufiq Pasha Abul-Huda, to London for the discussions with the Foreign Office and Chiefs of Staff. Taufiq was a modest, competent, and loyal lieutenant of Abdullah. There is nothing remarkable about the exchange of views between the British officials, headed by Michael Wright, and the Jordan delegation led by Taufiq. The transcripts

---

[51] See FO 371/68817-22 for the main files of minutes and correspondence.

[52] Kirkbride to Bevin, 5 Feb. 1948, FO 371/68817.

[53] The Chiefs of Staff now attached less importance to the base at Amman because of its unsuitability 'for use by modern aircraft'. For the views of the C. O. S. see especially COS (48) 24, 29 Jan. 1948, DEFE 5/10; and F. O. Minutes in FO 371/68817-19.

[54] Minute by Bevin on Kirkbride to Bevin, 21 Feb. 1948, FO 371/68819.

strike the reader as perfunctory, as if recorded while events of greater magnitude preoccupied the participants. Like the meaning of Sherlock Holmes's observation about the dog that did not bark in the night, the significance of the conversations lies in what was not said as much as in the recorded agreement.

The key point at issue of course was Palestine. The British as well as Abdullah found themselves in an excruciating political and geographical dilemma. To the British by early 1948 the best solution would be simply for Jordan to annex Arab Palestine. Kirkbride had repeatedly urged the wisdom of this course of action and had made it clear that Abdullah would agree to the creation of a Jewish state:

> Transjordan has [the] best claim to inherit [the] residue of Palestine . . . occupation of Arab areas by Transjordan would counteract chances of an armed conflict between a Jewish State and other Arab States. . . . King Abdullah would be prepared to acquiesce in [the] formation of a Jewish State provided Transjordan obtained the rest of Palestine.[55]

This solution would carry with it the strategic bonus of providing Transjordan access to the Mediterranean.[56] But the British could not encourage Abdullah to occupy areas of Palestine not designated 'Arab' by the United Nations. These provisional Arab and Jewish 'boundaries' were entirely 'artificial', in the view of both the Foreign Office and Colonial Office, but they nevertheless existed because they had been drawn up and submitted by the United Nations Special Committee on Palestine in the summer of 1947. In the arresting description of George Kirk, these hastily drawn up delimitations cut the two potential states into segments 'entwined in an inimical embrace like two fighting serpents'.[57] Despite the preposterous nature of these boundaries the British had to respect them. To collude in their violation would strain American relations to the breaking point and would undermine the basic premiss of British foreign policy, the upholding of the principles of the United Nations. On the other hand the British feared that restraining Abdullah, and so allowing Zionists to occupy Arab areas of Palestine, would bring denunciation from the other Arab states and might even cause him to lose his throne.

What then was said on the question of Palestine? The head of the Eastern Department, Bernard Burrows, wished to say so little that Bevin himself complained that the general position of the Foreign Office was 'too indefinite'.[58] For his part Burrows may have been

---

[55] Kirkbride to Bevin, 29 Oct. 1947, FO 371/62226.
[56] Minute by Burrows, 9 Feb. 1948, FO 371/68368.
[57] George Kirk, *The Middle East 1945–1950* (London, 1954), p. 246.
[58] Minute by Bevin on memorandum by Burrows, 24 Jan. 1948, FO 371/68817.

deliberately vague, but he had precise ideas about the dilemma. At the time of the termination of the mandate in mid-May Abdullah would face two choices:

(a) to occupy those areas which have been awarded to the Arabs by the United Nations;

(b) to disregard the frontier drawn by the United Nations, and to occupy, if not the whole country, at least those areas which are permanently Arab in population.[59]

If he pursued the second choice, he would find himself in defiance of the United Nations and would run the risk of sanctions. To choose the other option of restraint would be much more disastrous: 'he would in effect be helping the United Nations to implement their plan, against which the whole Arab world has protested'. Abdullah would be condemned by all other Arab countries 'as a quisling' and his acquiescence in a solution imposed by the United Nations 'might even cost him his throne in Transjordan'.[60] Bevin was thus apprised of the vital issues at stake, which he preferred to discuss in private with Taufiq rather than in the formal meetings between the representatives of the two countries.

How far and in what circumstances would Britain support her ally? Could King Abdullah count on British loyalty or would the British in the tradition of *perfide Albion* leave him in the lurch? The answer to those questions, at least in the form of prologue, came in response to the unanticipated and disastrous circumstances of the nationalist rejection of the Iraqi treaty. Abdullah had often claimed to be Britain's only true friend in the Middle East, and in late January 1948 it became painfully true that he was right. Sir Orme Sargent, who had never been convinced that Arab governments would prove to be reliable allies, wrote that he was sufficiently disillusioned to doubt the wisdom of consummating the new Anglo-Jordan treaty. In the reasoned and slightly bitter memorandum quoted at the beginning of this chapter, Sargent commented generally on Arab nationalism in relation to the particular problems of Jordan. He also emphasized that whatever new treaty might be concluded with a local king or regent—clearly he was addressing himself indirectly to the Iraqi crisis—nothing could prevent its repudiation by the 'new Arab nationalism'.

No doubt King Abdullah and his present Ministers will be ready to sign a new Treaty on the model of the Iraq Treaty. Also there is no organised opposition in Transjordan to stir up demonstrations as in Iraq, nor would ratification of the

[59] Memorandum by Burrows, 23 Jan. 1948, FO 371/68817.
[60] Ibid.

Treaty by the Transjordan Parliament be necessary. Nevertheless what guarantee have we that the King would not subsequently be bullied by his local Nationalists and by the Iraqi and Egyptian Governments into refusing to ratify it? If this were to happen so soon after the rejection of the Iraqi Treaty the victory of the Nationalists throughout the Middle East would be complete and it might be very difficult for us to maintain our position and prestige in the face of this further rebuff.[61]

Sargent believed that the new treaty with Transjordan would merely fuel the engine of anti-British nationalism. He proposed in short 'to scrap' it. 'Even though this would be very disappointing to King Abdullah the Treasury are enabling us to gild the pill by being very generous about our subsidy for the maintenance and equipment of the Arab Legion.'

Bevin, understandably enough, revealed considerable anxiety. 'Events in Iraq', he instructed Kirkbride to tell Abdullah, had been 'a severe blow to British prestige throughout the Middle East and we could not risk another experience of the same kind.'[62] A week later he conveyed another personal message to Abdullah in the same anxious vein: 'After what has happened in Iraq and the propaganda in other Arab countries, the signature by Your Majesty of a new treaty at this moment may expose Transjordan to criticism and pressure from neighbouring countries.'[63] Abdullah assured him that 'the people of Transjordan' were 'solidly behind' the treaty. It was in response to that communication that Bevin did not retreat from his general stand on the Middle East and decided, against the advice of his Permanent Under-Secretary, to sign the treaty with King Abdullah.[64]

What, again, had been said of Palestine during those tumultuous days? Very little, except in the last meeting between Bevin and Taufiq.[65] Glubb accompanied Taufiq to act as interpreter. Taufiq told Bevin that Abdullah had received many requests from Arabs on the west bank requesting protection by the Arab Legion as soon as British troops withdrew from Palestine. Taufiq said that the Transjordan government 'accordingly proposed to send the Arab Legion across the Jordan when the British mandate ended, and to occupy that part of Palestine awarded to the Arabs which was contiguous with the Frontier of Transjordan'. Glubb recalled, 'I can to this day

---

[61] Memorandum by Sargent, 2 Feb. 1948, FO 371/68817/E1758.

[62] Bevin to Kirkbride, draft of 3 Feb. 1948, FO 371/68817.

[63] Bevin to Kirkbride, 10 Feb. 1948, FO 371/68817.

[64] Minute by Bevin on Kirkbride to Bevin, 21 Feb. 1948, FO 371/68819/E2526.

[65] For example Michael Wright gave the following instructions to the British representatives: 'Nothing should be said at this meeting about Palestine as the Transjordan Prime Minister wishes to have a private meeting with the Secretary of State on this subject.' Memorandum by Wright, 2 Feb. 1948, FO 371/68817/E1758.

almost see Mr. Bevin sitting at his table in that splendid room' at the Foreign Office. Bevin's response to Taufiq's statement reveals his disposition towards Palestine shortly before the birth of the state of Israel and the outbreak of the war between the Arabs and Jews. Commenting on Transjordan's intention to occupy the west bank, Bevin said 'It seems the obvious thing to do', and then repeated, 'It seems the obvious thing to do . . . but do not go and invade the areas allotted to the Jews.'[66]

The British, Abdullah, and the Theory of the 'Rump Jewish State'

It is clear from the Foreign Office records as well as from Glubb's published account that certain things were of such a sensitive and secret nature that Bevin did not wish to have them recorded. Glubb later referred to a Transjordan 'plan' of which British officials were fully aware. To pose the question bluntly, did this 'plan' amount to collusion? Did the British aim at reducing the Jewish part of Palestine to a 'rump state'? The accusation has been rife since 1948. It was given publicity in a book entitled *Both Sides of the Hill* by Jon and David Kimche, and endorsed by Richard Crossman, who gave it intellectual vogue. According to the Kimches, the agreement between Bevin and Taufiq went further than the occupation by the Arab Legion of the parts of Palestine not occupied by the Jews.

> It was understood by Bevin's advisers that an agreement had been reached with King Abdullah which provided that some areas allotted to the Jews would be occupied by the Arab Legion and that, as a result of any fighting, there would be a much smaller Jewish State than the United Nations had recommended.
> This rump of a state would then probably seek the protection of the British for an arrangement with its Arab neighbours.[67]

Crossman found this interpretation so engaging that he speculated on the decisions made within the government:

> Once it had been decided . . . to end the Mandate, Bevin's aim, apparently, was to ensure that Abdullah's Arab Legion should over-run most of Palestine, leaving a rump Jewish State, so weak that it would have to throw itself on the mercy of the British Government. This aim was so shameful that it was never revealed to the Cabinet and so could not be expressed in clear directives to the men on the spot. Hence that dreadful impression of weakness and indecision, combined with malignant anti-Jewish prejudice which characterized British policy throughout.[68]

[66] Lieutenant-General Sir John Bagot Glubb, KCB, CMG, DSO, OBE, MC, *A Soldier with the Arabs* (London, 1957), pp. 63–6.

[67] Jon and David Kimche, *Both Sides of the Hill* (London, 1960), p. 39.

[68] Crossman in the *New Statesman*, 23 July 1960.

Crossman also in retrospect paid Abdullah the compliment of being 'the one Arab who was a match, in statemanship as well as in strategy, for the Israeli Premier', David Ben-Gurion. As will be seen, from a Zionist point of view Crossman's outlook was entirely consistent.

In view of the far-reaching consequences of the part played by the Arab Legion in the 1948 war, it is of paramount historical importance to establish whether or not the conspiracy theory holds true. The following concluding comment will anticipate themes to be developed in later chapters, but it will also attempt to clarify the way in which the Middle East hands of the Foreign Office appraised Abdullah in 1948 and the way he fitted into their ideas about the possibility of a successful outcome of the war.

The Kimches and Crossman smelt the blood of British imperialism, but the scent led them to conclusions that cannot be sustained by the evidence. Abdullah's 'plan' as conveyed by Glubb (and Kirkbride) to the Foreign Office was quite compatible with the main principle of agreement arrived at by Bevin and Taufiq. According to Glubb in August 1948:

> The original Trans-Jordan plan was based on the supposition that, at the end of the British Mandate, the Jews would proclaim a Jewish state within the boundaries laid down by the U. N. O. partition scheme. The Arab areas of Palestine would remain vacant, except possibly for bands of irregulars. The Arab Legion would march in and occupy these areas, pending a decision on their final disposal. There would be no conflict between the Arab Legion and the Jewish forces. The proposed occupation was to be no more than a police operation.[69]

Glubb of course was describing the most optimistic outcome. He was by no means naïve enough to think that there would be no clashes between the Jewish forces and the Arab Legion, nor did he believe that Abdullah would or could accept the boundaries prescribed by the United Nations. The 'portrait by Picasso', as the proposed United Nations settlement was sarcastically described by both sides, would have to be touched up. Here the Kimches and Crossman were on to something. Abdullah's territorial ambitions were well known. How far, if possible, would the British allow him to realize them? What were the British motives?

The answer to those questions will not please critics of British imperialism, though some of the evidence does provide the basis for speculating about missed opportunities. The governing British motives were to make the frontiers between the Jewish state and the neighbouring Arab countries more ethnically rational, and to achieve a settlement that would satisfy minimal Arab aspirations. Those two themes may be traced through the major chronological developments.

[69] Memorandum by Glubb, 12 Aug. 1948, FO 371/68822/E11049/14/G.

It was not a question of revenge against the Jews but how best to perpetuate British influence in the Middle East that provides the key to the official mind.

For purposes of the present discussion there are two periods that need to be distinguished: (1) the time of the United Nations vote on the 29th of November 1947 until the end of the mandate on the 14th of May 1948; and (2) the outbreak of full-scale war in May 1948 until the armistice in early 1949. During the first period Abdullah secretly met twice with Jewish representatives—the first time in order to prepare the ground for the settlement that he and Taufiq as well as Bevin and Glubb all had in mind. Rumours of these meetings did not inspire Arab confidence that he was not, as Brigadier Clayton put it, 'selling Palestine', and it is certainly true that the contacts with the Jews have to be taken into account in explaining the reasons for the assassination of the 'Rabbi Abdullah' in 1951. Golda Myerson (Golda Meir) gave this account of their first meeting in November 1947:

> We drank the usual ceremonial cups of coffee and then we began to talk. Abdullah was a small, very poised man with great charm. He soon made the heart of the matter clear: he would not join in any Arab attack on us. He would always remain our friend, he said, and like us, he wanted peace more than anything else. After all, we had a common foe, the mufti of Jerusalem, Haj Amin el-Husseini.[70]

Abdullah was prepared to partition Palestine along lines that were shortly to be reaffirmed in the conversation between Bevin and Taufiq—in other words, Transjordan would absorb most of Arab Palestine. At his second meeting with Golda Myerson in May 1948, however, Abdullah adopted an entirely different attitude. By all accounts he was close to nervous exhaustion.[71] According to Myerson he looked 'worried' and 'harassed'. He did not entirely repudiate the previous understanding that he would annex only Arab territory and attempt to live in peace with the Jews, but he said that he now had 'no choice' but to fight because he was 'no longer alone'.[72]

The Jewish military victories in the spring of 1948—before the end of the mandate—were decisive in shaping the Arab reaction

---

[70] *My Life by Golda Meir* (London, 1975), p. 176.

[71] 'He spends his days, and some of his nights', Kirkbride reported from Amman, 'in alternate moods of lucidity and something approaching a complete nervous breakdown.' Quoted in Cohen, *Palestine and the Great Powers*, p. 333. In this part of his book, which is an important interpretation of Abdullah, Cohen draws upon a work in Hebrew by Y. Nevo, *Abdulla and Palestine* (Tel Aviv, 1975). In English see Nevo's summary, 'Abdallah and the Arabs of Palestine', *Weiner Library Bulletin*, XXXI (1978), which gives insight into Abdullah's policies as well as Zionist assessments.

[72] Shertok to Goldman, 13 May 1948, *Israel Documents* (December 1947–May 1948), p. 791.

throughout the Middle East. In April Jewish forces penetrated into Arab areas. Within a single week several important 'mixed towns' fell from Arab control. The conquest of Haifa on the 22nd was perhaps the crucial event that appeared in Arab eyes to represent the Jewish bid for all of Palestine. Four days later Abdullah declared that, unless the Jews accepted citizenship in an Arab state, then he would take the lead in an Arab war of liberation. This was a dramatic change of tactics. It was not a change of heart. It was not the course he would have preferred.

Nor was it for the British. For purposes of the present discussion the critical question is whether, in anticipating these developments, the British entertained the idea of the 'rump state'. Harold Beeley, Bevin's principal adviser on Palestine, had written in March:

> Arabs and Jews alike are very nearly helpless in the face of their own extremists. The Zionist leaders would not dare to return from Lake Success [the United Nations] to Palestine having committed themselves to any form of compromise which appreciably modified the Assembly's resolution to their disadvantage.
>
> On the other side, the Arab Governments (with the exception of Transjordan) are probably anxious not to become too deeply involved in Palestine. None of them, however, will wish to lag behind the others, and the Iraqi and Syrian Governments have a violent public opinion in their own countries to consider. The pace of the Arab League is, therefore, set by the public opinion of Bagdad and Damascus, worked upon by the Mufti of Jerusalem with his agents.[73]

Later in the same month Beeley elaborated on Arab internal rivalries:

> The Mufti of Jerusalem aims at personal control over an independent Arab State occupying the whole of Palestine. King Abdullah wishes to incorporate as much Palestinian territory as possible in the Kingdom of Transjordan, and would be prepared if it furthered his purpose to accept the establishment of a Jewish State in other parts of the country. It is possible that the Syrian Government have territorial ambitions in Palestine. . . . Finally both the Syrians and Ibn Saud would view with hostility any proposal for the aggrandizement of Transjordan.[74]

Those appraisals were written in the weeks following the conclusion of the new treaty of alliance between Britain and Jordan. The minutes by Beeley and others make it clear that the Foreign Office foresaw the danger of Abdullah being caught up in a jihad against the Jews. Whatever the result might be, British influence would be less than if there were a partition between the Jews and Abdullah. Far from speculating on the possibility of a 'rump state', the Middle Eastern experts of the Foreign Office, as will be seen in a later chapter, began to doubt whether even the Arab Legion could withstand Jewish forces. In any case the decisions taken in late April by

[73] Minute by Beeley, 1 Mar. 1948, FO 371/68536/E3048.
[74] Minute by Beeley, 16 Mar. 1948, FO 371/68538/E3549.

the other Arab states to intervene militarily ended the prospect that Transjordan might merely absorb Arab Palestine as Bevin had hoped only a few months earlier.

It was the question of the frontiers that caused Bevin to act with such secrecy and caution in early 1948 in his conversations with Taufiq. By working together with Abdullah to achieve anything other than the boundaries endorsed by the United Nations, the British would find themselves accused of undermining the principles of the U. N. Charter. They would come into head-on collision with the policy of the United States, which upheld the United Nations boundaries as the basis of the new Jewish state. The boundaries included the desert area of the Negev, or what is known today as most of southern Israel. When the controversy entered into the next stage—after the outbreak of full-scale war in May 1948—British policy aimed at detaching the Negev in order to provide a common frontier between Transjordan and Egypt. In this sense there was truth in the charge that the British intended to reduce the new Jewish state to a 'rump'. Here however there is a question of semantics. In this larger context Zionist usage of the word 'rump' was the equivalent of British usage of the phrase 'compact state'. There is no question that the British were working towards a settlement that would not have satisfied Zionist ambitions. The British consistently held that, the more 'compact' the Jewish state, the greater would be the chances of Arab acquiescence. On the other hand there is no basis for Crossman's indictment of Bevin's 'shameful' policy that reputedly would have unleashed the Arabs and would have forced the Jews to throw themselves on British mercy. Harold Beeley, for example, described the Arab collective aim, as far as it could be comprehensively defined, as containing the Jews in the coastal plain, not driving them into the sea.[75] In any event the British never encouraged the aims of the Arab extremists. By March 1948 it was clear that ultimately the size of the Jewish state would be determined by force of arms, and that the British could best influence the eventual settlement by continuing to support Abdullah's quest for most of Arab Palestine.

In re-examining these questions with the benefit of some thirty-five years' hindsight, it is tempting to ask whether the British backed the wrong Arab horse. Rather than Abdullah might it not have been better to have created an independent state out of Arab Palestine? At first sight this is an alluring question because it suggests an easier answer to the problems of the refugees and Palestinian Arab irrendentism than the one provided by Jordan's—or Israel's—annexation

[75] Minute by Beeley, 16 Mar. 1948, FO 371/68538/E3549.

of the West Bank. But it overlooks the dilemmas that the British faced in 1948. The alternative to Abdullah was the Mufti, Haj Amin el-Husseini—who in British eyes was less of an Arab nationalist than a renegade who had cast his lot with Hitler and who was dedicated to the destruction of the British Empire in the Middle East. That view no doubt distorts Haj Amin's actual significance in the history of Arab nationalism, but it was an article of British faith in the post-war era. The official minutes are emphatic on the consequences of an 'independent Arab state' under Haj Amin. 'The disadvantages of a separate Arab state under the Mufti', wrote Bernard Burrows in August 1948, 'are too obvious to need elaboration.' He went ahead to elaborate them:

It would be a hotbed of ineffectual Arab fanaticism and after causing maximum disturbance to our relations with the Arabs would very likely fall in the end under Jewish influence and be finally absorbed in the Jewish state, thereby increasing the area of possible Russian influence and excluding the possibility of our obtaining strategic requirements in any part of Palestine.[76]

Burrows wrote that minute at a time when arms from eastern Europe had begun to turn the military tide decisively in favour of the Jews and when the Arab Legion was virtually exhausted of ammunition. Nevertheless the Legion held its own. In retrospect one of the salient features of the 1948 war is that the Arab Legion did not collapse and that Abdullah maintained his political alliances on the West Bank with the Nashashibis in opposition to the Husseinis.[77] 'Mr. Bevin's Little King' proved to be an effective British ally.

After the assassination in 1951, Richard Crossman stated in the House of Commons that Abdullah had been murdered because he desired peace with Israel.[78] From a pro-Zionist perspective Crossman saw the wisdom of statesmanship. To those who followed these issues from an Arab point of view Abdullah's reputation was vulnerable to more sceptical interpretation. Within official circles there had been a running debate about his merit as a British ally, and these secret discussions make a striking contrast with the public comment about the 'shameful' British policy of reducing Israel to a 'rump state'. A point of honour was being discussed by British officials that had quite different implications from the Zionist accusation. At the time of the armistice discussions in early 1949, Sir John Troutbeck had denounced Abdullah for exploiting the conflict with the Jews in order to pursue territorial aggrandizement.

[76] Minute by Burrows, 17 Aug. 1948, FO 371/68822/E11049/G.
[77] See Y. Porath, *The Palestinian Arab National Movement* (London, 1977), vol. II, chap. 3; and Ann Mosely Lesch, *Arab Politics in Palestine, 1917–1939* (Ithaca, 1979), chap. 10.
[78] *Parliamentary Debates* (Commons), 30 July 1951, c. 1002.

'The important fact', Troutbeck wrote, 'surely is that Abdulla for all his qualities is a born land-grabber.' Troutbeck sympathized with the outlook of Azzam Pasha and the nationalists who believed that Abdullah should be viewed in the same way as those who had collaborated with Hitler. This of course was an explosive sentiment, and it reveals the way in which one element in British official opinion about Abdullah had polarized by the end of the 1948 war:

> Abdullah . . . was never very interested in the question [of Palestine] except as means of getting more land for himself, and of course . . . he was in pretty close touch with the Jews all the time he was proclaiming his determination to hurl them into the sea. He told the Jews himself . . . that he had been dragged into the conflict against his better judgement by the other Arab states, which is the kind of thing that Laval would have said to Hitler but does not exactly go down with one's allies if they get to hear of it.[79]

Troutbeck's indictment may be summed up by stating that he believed Abdullah to be motivated more by territorial and personal ambition than by a moral commitment to the Arab cause.

The most full-blooded rejoinder to Troutbeck came from Sir Hugh Dow, the Consul-General in Jerusalem. Dow was almost as anti-Zionist as Troutbeck, but he saw the benefits of the alliance with Abdullah in down-to-earth terms of the future of Palestine. 'What is the practical alternative', Dow asked, 'to handing over to Transjordan the major part of Arab Palestine?'

> We should be thrown back on an independent Arab state, which would not be and could not be made viable, and which would almost certainly be dominated by the Mufti, an implacable enemy both to us and to the Jews. We ought to be thankful that Abdullah is a land grabber.[80]

Michael Wright, in arbitrating this lacerating anti-Zionist controversy, decided to give the benefit of the doubt to King Abdullah: 'The idea that there is any deep plot between King Abdullah and the Jews, of which we have knowledge, is mistaken. He is doing his best in difficult circumstances. . . .'[81] The motives of 'Mr. Bevin's Little King' might be controversial, but there was no way to escape the conclusion that

---

[79] Troutbeck went on to sum up his ideas about the difficulties of collaborating with the Arabs in general and particularly Abdullah: 'Of course one does not expect from Arabs the same kind of loyalty to each other that one expects but does not always get from Europeans, and it would probably not be difficult to show that many of the Arab leaders are the most perfidious double-crossers. All I wish to suggest here is that the other Arab leaders do in fact have a case against Abdulla which cannot be written off as mere anti-British sentiment, and that he as well as they need to be worked on if we are to succeed in preventing him from being permanently isolated in the Arab world. And, as he is everywhere regarded as our protégé, everything he does is naturally reflected upon ourselves.' Troutbeck to Wright, 3 Mar. 1949, FO 371/75064.

[80] Dow to Wright, 15 Mar. 1949, FO 371/75064.

[81] Wright to Campbell, 30 Mar. 1949, FO 371/75064.

he usually acted so deftly that, whatever he did, it was bound to be regarded as the fulfilment of British policy. With one hand on his collar and no hope, in Wright's phrase, of changing his 'habits of mind', the British thus chose to make the best of their oldest and most reliable ally in the Middle East, and to assist him in saving 'what he can from the dismal wreck of Arab Palestine'.[82]

[82] Ibid.

PART IV

PALESTINE

PRELUDE: ERNEST BEVIN AND
THE LEGACY OF THE
BALFOUR DECLARATION

'BALFOUR is dead', Ernest Bevin remarked in February 1947 in his most comprehensive review of the Palestine problem in the House of Commons.[1] Both the implication and the date are important for an understanding of the last years of the British mandate. He meant that further debate about the meaning of the Balfour declaration of 1917 would be of little help in resolving post-1945 Palestinian dilemmas. Even A. J. Balfour might have been perplexed if asked to give a definition of a Jewish national home in Palestine in the light of fundamentally altered circumstances following the Arab revolt of 1936–9 and the extermination of European Jews during the Second World War.[2] The date of February 1947 is significant because it represents a watershed in British attitude. Less than two years after the close of the war and little more than a year before the creation of the state of Israel, a British solution to the Palestine problem now seemed impossible, even to the supremely confident Ernest Bevin, unless it could be achieved through the auspices of the United Nations and with the support of the United States.

Bevin himself was the architect of Britain's Palestine policy. From the British vantage point it is illuminating to regard him as the central figure responding to pressures exerted by the Americans, the Jews, the Arabs, and more specifically by individuals who influenced him

[1] *Parliamentary Debates* (Commons), 25 Feb. 1947, cols. 1901–19. In general Bullock, *Bevin*, is an essential companion for this section.

[2] For this background see J. C. Hurewitz, *The Struggle for Palestine* (New York, 1950), which for lucidity and scope remains indispensable. The most important recent scholarly work based on comprehensive archival sources is by Michael J. Cohen, *Palestine and the Great Powers 1945–1948* (Princeton, 1982), which is a sequel to his *Palestine: Retreat from the Mandate* (New York, 1978). See also Nicholas Bethell, *The Palestine Triangle: The Struggle between the Jews and the Arabs 1935–48* (London, 1979); and two articles by Ritchie Ovendale, 'The Palestine Policy of the British Labour Government 1945–1946' and '1947: the Decision to Withdraw', *International Affairs*, 55, 3, and 56, 1 (July 1979 and Jan. 1980). Joseph Gorny, *The British Labour Movement and Zionism* (London, 1983), is valuable for Zionist perceptions of British leaders as well as an account of Labour policy. For the refugees see Leonard Dinnerstein, *America and the Survivors of the Holocaust* (New York, 1982); and Yehuda Bauer, *Flight and Rescue: Brichah* (New York, 1970). Christopher Sykes, *Crossroads to Israel* (London, 1965) deserves particular mention as a sensitive Zionist account which is sympathetic to the Arabs. The classic Arab perspective is George Antonius, *The Arab Awakening* (London, 1938).

in Parliament and within the government. It is also useful to examine Bevin's initiatives in relation to the inclination of the Foreign Office (which was pro-Arab), the strategic aims of the Chiefs of Staff (also pro-Arab), and the tradition of trusteeship of the Colonial Office (which if not less anti-Jewish was at least less pro-Arab). Bevin was portrayed by extreme Zionist propaganda as possessed with a demonic anti-Jewish prejudice as irrational as the one that had driven Hitler. In the diabolical interpretation upheld by such American critics as the playwright Ben Hecht and the editors of the New York newspaper *P. M.*, Bevin's racism was reinforced by a Gestapo: the permanent officials of the Foreign Office. Even the moderate leader of the Zionist movement, Chaim Weizmann, who denounced comparisons of the British with the Nazis, described Bevin's first major Parliamentary speech on Palestine as 'brutal, vulgar and anti-semitic'.[3]

As will be seen in the following chapters, Bevin was not anti-Semitic but his pro-Arab and anti-Zionist sentiments made him vulnerable to charges of pursuing an anti-Jewish course. He believed that the solution to the problems arising from the Holocaust should be resolved by reintegrating the Jews into European society rather than encouraging mass immigration into Palestine. He identified the question of Jewish immigration into a predominantly Arab country as the critical issue. In the end he refused to countenance the creation of a Jewish state because of its disruptive impact on the Arab world and, in turn, on the British Empire. For that consistent outlook he earned himself, quite unfairly but understandably in view of his rough sense of humour and uncompromising temperament, an enduring anti-Semitic reputation.

In getting a bearing on Bevin's spoken and tacit assumptions as well as the general nature of the Palestine problem in the postwar years, it is helpful to begin with the position of the Colonial Office and Bevin's closest ministerial associate, Arthur Creech Jones. Since 1922 Palestine had been a Colonial Office responsibility. In the late 1930s its minor mandatory importance became transformed into one of international and strategic concern on the part of the Foreign Office and Chiefs of Staff. In 1945–8 the Foreign Office and Colonial Office shared responsibility for Palestine, the former for the international dimension of the problem, the latter for the mandate's administration. Both departments responded to the strategic demands of the Chiefs of Staff, the Colonial Office in relation to Palestine as a strategic base and fallback position from Egypt, the Foreign Office in regard to broader aspects of the defence of the Middle East and

---

[3] *The Letters and Papers of Chaim Weizmann* (Universities of Israel Press), hereafter *Weizmann Letters*, XXII, p. 72.

global security of the Empire and Commonwealth. When Creech Jones became Parliamentary Under-Secretary at the time of the formation of the Labour Government his principal interests lay in tropical Africa, but his Parliamentary duties immersed him into the strategic, administrative, and ethical depths of the Palestine mandate. When he succeeded G. L. Hall as Colonial Secretary in October 1946, Palestine became his main concern until mid-May 1948. Creech Jones sympathized with the moderate Zionists who hoped to establish a Jewish state in Palestine (but not with the 'revisionists' or extreme Zionists whose idea of a Jewish state included Transjordan). During his tenure as Colonial Secretary he favoured partition as a solution, but on this and other important issues he eventually yielded and followed Bevin's lead. On the whole Bevin found in Creech Jones a supporter as faithful as he could have expected in the head of another major, and in some senses rival, government department.[4]

In Parliament Bevin confronted Churchill, who was not only his most powerful and persistent adversay in Imperial and foreign affairs but also his principal critic on the tactics and timing of withdrawal from Palestine. Churchill was particularly important in the background of the Labour government's policy towards Palestine because after the First World War he himself as Colonial Secretary had penned the official elaboration of the Balfour Declaration. The declaration of 1922 established Transjordan as an Arab territory distinct from Palestine. Palestine itself, in words that followed the Balfour Declaration's phraseology, was not to be a Jewish 'National Home' but there was to be a 'National Home' *in* Palestine. Jewish immigration would be allowed, in Churchill's own phrase, up to the limit of 'economic absorptive capacity', which was to be judged by the mandatory power. The declaration of 1922 served as the basis of British policy for nearly two decades. When the White Paper of 1939 attempted to curtail and stabilize the Jewish population of Palestine at one-third of the Arab majority (with further immigration after five years dependent on Arab consent), Churchill denounced

---

[4] The single most revealing document on Creech Jones and Bevin is a letter written by the former to Elizabeth Monroe of 23 Oct. 1961 (Creech Jones Papers). He wrote in response to her 'Mr Bevin's "Arab Policy" ', *St. Antony's Papers*, 11, 2 (London, 1961; the argument is condensed in *Britain's Moment in the Middle East 1914–1956*, London, 1963, chap. 7). The letter is a detailed critique of Miss Monroe's assessment of Bevin's Jewish and Arab policy (which makes the essay itself a matter of historical interest). The detailed drafts of the letter indicate that he intended it as an explanation of his own as well as Bevin's attitude towards Palestine while in office. Like all documents written *ex post facto* it must be used with caution, but nevertheless it is invaluable in understanding Creech Jones and Bevin, neither of whom was inclined to expand on his inner thoughts in official minutes. The Monroe Papers at St. Antony's College are also an important source.

it as a breach of faith with the Jews.[5] Throughout his career Churchill, with varying degrees of enthusiasm and scepticism, remained a moderate Zionist. As Prime Minister during the war he became the moving spirit behind the solution of partition and its possible corollary of an independent Jewish state. But he always kept his Zionism subordinate to his Imperial priorities. In A. P. Thornton's phrase he never 'calloused his hands for the cause'.[6] He never became a convert to the idea that strategically Palestine might be substituted for Egypt. And he always believed that a relatively minor conflict or 'wars of mice' between Arabs and Jews should never disrupt the Anglo-American 'alliance'. After the war he excoriated the extravagance of so large a military and economic commitment in so small and Imperially insignificant a territory. In August 1946 he summarized a point he had frequently made before: 'it is our duty . . . to offer to lay down the Mandate. We should . . . as soon as the war stopped, have made it clear to the United States that, unless they came in and bore their share, we would lay the whole care and burden at the foot of the United Nations organisation.'[7]

Anglo-American co-operation over Palestine proved to be the single most frustrating and elusive goal of the Labour government in Imperial and colonial affairs. A major disagreement developed in August 1945 when President Truman requested the admission of 100,000 Jewish refugees into Palestine. The number 100,000 recurred endlessly in the discussions, and it is useful to note that the figure 100,000 also roughly represented the British occupying army and police force at its zenith. Bevin reflected in May 1948 after the dramatic and—to the British—astounding American recognition of the state of Israel that he did not wish to feel recriminative but that 'had it not been for a succession of unfortunate actions on the part of the United States' that followed Truman's demand for the 100,000 the question 'would have been settled long ago'. In Bevin's eyes the 100,000 seemed to be the only consistent aim in American policy. It was the Palestinian King Charles's head about which everyone concerned wrote memoranda. It would arise in any discussion. On almost all else the British could not detect or predict a leitmotiv. To Bevin the only certainty apart from the 100,000 was that American

[5] For the 1939 White Paper see especially Michael J. Cohen, 'Appeasement in the Middle East: The White Paper on Palestine, May 1939', *Historical Journal*, 16, 3 (1973); and 'Part II: The Testing of a Policy, 1942–1945', ibid. 19, 3 (1976).

[6] A. P. Thornton, *Imperialism in the Twentieth Century* (Minneapolis, 1977), p. 122. For an important comment on the consistency of Churchill's pro-Zionist attitude in the face of Foreign Office opposition during the war, see Ronald W. Zweig, 'The Palestine Mandate', *Historical Journal*, 24, 1 (1981).

[7] *Parliamentary Debates* (Commons), 1 Aug. 1946, c. 1253.

behaviour in Palestine would turn out to be the opposite of what he might guess. He wrote in summarizing the British reaction to the American twists and turns in Palestine: 'These changes of policy and surprise initiatives had left us bewildered and frustrated.'[8]

To British observers of the Truman administration who were closer to American politics than Bevin, the President demonstrated a remarkable tendency to favour partition as a solution, at least after the autumn of 1946. In another *post mortem* analysis, John Balfour, then serving with the rank of Minister in Washington, wrote in May 1948:

> It is clear that the President himself has always supported partition. Although there is no reason to doubt his personal sincerity, it is also true that he has been under very great pressure from his campaign managers, who have all along been terrified of incurring the ill-will of the very powerful Zionist lobby and of its loyal blocs of voters in key states.
>
> Even when the United States Government was officially maintaining that partition could not be implemented and that some other interim solution must therefore be sought, Mr. Truman made it evident that he continued to hope for partition as the ultimate solution. This was also the hope of most Americans, who tend to see the partisans of a Jewish State as following in the footsteps of the United States founding fathers and the Arabs as the modern equivalent of George III.[9]

Balfour also dwelt on the issue of the 100,000, which over time acquired an almost symbolic significance. To most Americans as to the President himself the admission of the 100,000 Jewish refugees was a sincere act of humanitarian statesmanship and, in time, a tangible and not unreasonable step towards the creation of a Jewish state.[10]

Truman's *idée fixe* of the 100,000 originated in a report on displaced persons in Europe by Earl G. Harrison, the American representative on the Inter-Governmental Committee on Refugees. Harrison

[8] Bevin to Inverchapel, 22 May 1948, FO 371/68749.

[9] Balfour to Bevin, 24 May 1948, FO 371/68650.

[10] See *Memoirs by Harry S. Truman: Years of Trial and Hope* (New York, 1956), chaps. 10–12, where there is a slightly different emphasis: 'In my own mind, the aims and goals of the Zionists at this stage to set up a Jewish state were secondary to the more immediate problem of finding means to relieve the human misery of the displaced persons' (pp. 144–5). For Truman and the Palestine question see especially the balanced biography by Robert J. Donovan, *Conflict and Crisis: The Presidency of Harry S. Truman, 1945–1948* (New York, 1977), chaps. 34 and 39. There are two recent and complementary studies on the Truman administration and Palestine: Kenneth Ray Bain, *The March to Zion: United States Policy and the Founding of Israel* (Texas A & M Press, 1979); and Zvi Ganin, *Truman, American Jewry, and Israel, 1945–1948* (New York, 1979). See also John Snetsinger, *Truman, the Jewish Vote and the Creation of Israel* (Stanford, 1974). There is one further important work in a special category because of the author's former official position as the Palestine desk officer in the State Department who served as one of the secretaries to the Anglo-American Committee of Inquiry: Evan M. Wilson, *Decision on Palestine: How the U. S. Came to Recognize Israel* (Stanford, 1979).

was Dean of the University of Pennsylvania Law School and a former Commissioner of Immigration and Nationalization. His word carried authority when the *New York Times* on the 30th of September 1945 summarized his report on the appalling conditions of the displaced-person camps. He related that the refugees found themselves in circumstances of armed guards and barbed wire that differed little from those of the German concentration camps: 'we appear to be treating the Jews as the Nazis treated them except that we do not exterminate them. They are in concentration camps in large numbers under our military guard instead of S.S. troops.' By all accounts Harrison's report stirred Truman's sympathy for the Jews and alerted him to an issue that would arouse the political as well as the humanitarian emotions of the American public. Truman wrote to Attlee that the granting of 100,000 certificates of immigration to Palestine would contribute to the solution of the future of the European Jews.[11] He thus joined two issues of profound importance which the British government wished to keep separate. He linked the problem of the refugees with that of Palestine. To the Americans it seemed to be the obvious answer.

To the British the issue of the 100,000 had immediate and disturbing implications, which seemed even more alarming to the statesmen of the Labour government after their election. In May 1945 Hugh Dalton had nailed a declaration on Palestine to the masthead of Labour's policy with these memorable words: 'It is morally wrong and politically indefensible to impose obstacles to the entry into Palestine now of any Jews who desire to go there.' In office Labour politicians now reacted with caution and with a perception of imminent danger. They feared that the 100,000 would open the floodgates of Palestine to unlimited Jewish immigration.[12] Such

[11] *Foreign Relations of the United States 1945*, VIII, pp. 727–9; see also USSD 867N.01/10–145 Boxes 6751 and 6752; for British reaction see especially PREM 8/627; CAB 128/1; FO 371/45380 ff.; and CO 537/1754. The dismay of Harold Beeley, who became Bevin's principal adviser on Palestine, may be taken as representative of Foreign Office response: 'The Zionists have been deplorably successful in selling the idea that, even after the Allied victory, emigration to Palestine represents for many Jews "their only hope of survival".' Minute of 27 July 1945, FO 371/45378. The report by Harrison had been influenced by Zionist officials. For this and other points of detail as well as for an important reassessment, see Joseph Heller, 'The Anglo-American Commission of Inquiry on Palestine (1945–46): The Zionist Reaction Reconsidered', in eds. Elie Kedourie and Sylvia G. Haim, *Zionism and Arabism in Palestine and Israel* (London, 1982).

[12] Yehuda Bauer points out that in August 1945 there were only 50,000 Jews in the western European occupied zones. In other words, in 1945, before the 'Brichah' or 'flight' from eastern Europe, the Jewish Agency could not have fulfilled a quota of 100,000. 'It seems that Britain committed a grave political mistake in her refusal to accept the 100,000. . . . the Jewish Agency. . . . soon came to regard its proposal of the 100,000 as rather less than wise and was very much afraid that the British might accept it' (*Flight and Rescue*, p. 79). The point is of considerable importance because it could be argued that British

a deluge would in effect repudiate the basis of British policy, the White Paper of 1939, and would cancel the hope of Jews and Arabs being able to create a binational state. It would reverse the current of British policy from pro-Arab to pro-Jewish. For those reasons the Labour government responded with such alarm to the President's request.

Bevin approached the problem with a confidence in his proven skill as a Trade Union negotiator and with an earthy sense of humour that Jewish leaders failed to find amusing. If necessary he would bang together a few heads to reach agreement. At the beginning of his involvement in the Palestine controversy he probably possessed no more of an anti-Jewish prejudice than many others of his working-class background and experience; but his seemingly insensitive approach to the problem and to Jewish suffering in general caused Chaim Weizmann to doubt a lifelong faith in England as 'the good and free country which will help the Jews to establish their own state'.[13] If the Jews wanted a fight, Bevin said, they could have one. Another time he stated at a press conference in November 1945 that the Jewish overemphasis on the racial issue caused him anxiety: 'if the Jews, with all their sufferings, want to get too much at the head of the queue, you have the danger of another anti-Semitic reaction through it all.'[14] What he probably meant to stress was the

rigidity on the question of the 100,000 proved to be the most serious tactical error in the controversy with the Americans. It was however extremely difficult to predict Jewish immigration trends in 1945. There was not only a question of how many Jews might be entering Palestine but also one of how many might be leaving. The American Consul-General in Jerusalem, Lowell C. Pinkerton, who was regarded by British as well as American officials as one of the most knowledgeable authorities on Palestine, wrote in September 1945: 'I have been expecting an exodus from Palestine; but so far, it hasn't happened. Judging from the interest taken in visas for the United States, a great many will leave as soon as travel across the Atlantic opens up. My guess is that as many as ten to fifteen thousand will want to go to the United States as soon as they can. German, Austrian, Czechoslovak and other western European Jews have failed to settle here in a permanent way, and they will become migrants. Many of them have not learned Hebrew, and one can still hear as much German on the streets as Hebrew. The Eastern Jews are intolerant of the German-speaking Jews, and employment for non-Hebrew-speaking persons is very difficult. . . . So, the Jews themselves are not having too easy a time, and settlement of their external problem with England will not take care of their internal problems.' Pinkerton to Merriam, Personal and Secret, 5 Sept. 1945, USSD 867N.01/9-545.

[13] Isaiah Berlin, *Personal Impressions* (New York, 1981), p. 53.

[14] Weizmann responded on several occasions, e.g. when he said to a meeting of American Zionists in November 1945 that there had been a time when 'the Jews had the highest priority in the queues which led to the crematoria of Auschwitz and Treblinka'. *Weizmann Letters*, XXII, p. 73. On these points see especially Sykes, *Crossroads*, particularly p. 284 n. 29: 'The offense caused by this remark may have been through a fancied reference to American anti-Semitic witticisms to the effect that Jews behave unfairly in queues. The joke is not known in England and Bevin was certainly alluding on this occasion, and in a good-humored way, to the distressing amount of queueing necessitated by shortages in England.'

danger of a resurgence of anti-Semitism which would make it more difficult to persuade the refugees to resettle in Europe. A new wave of anti-Semitism would prove Hitler's point that the Jewish problem could not be solved in Europe. It would aggravate the immigration problem in Palestine. In any case Bevin's famous statement about the Jews wishing to get to the head of the queue, like others he made, contributed to his reputation as a bigot.

In response to Truman's request about the 100,000 the British government, on Bevin's initiative, proposed the creation of a joint commission to study the question of displaced persons and the 'absorptive capacity' of Palestine, among other places, to alleviate the problem. Truman accepted in a manner that struck the British as dictatorial if not arrogant. He made it clear that he believed that the British merely wished to 'shelve the issue' by appointing a public committee, and he demanded speedy results. In agreeing to the terms of reference of the committee Bevin yielded on two important points. He accepted Palestine as the geographical focus of the study of a solution for the refugee problem; and he concurred with Truman's insistence that the committee report within one hundred and twenty days. Bevin later faced considerable criticism that he had caved in too quickly on those vital issues, but at the time he merely followed his inclination to subordinate smaller issues such as Palestine to the larger one of sustaining Anglo-American friendship. He had not yet fully grasped the intractable nature of the Palestine problem. He believed that men of common sense investigating the problem would quickly conclude that a small territory such as Palestine could not possibly provide a solution to the Jewish refugee problem and that in any event his skill as a negotiator would see him through. On the 13th of November 1945 Bevin announced the committee's appointment in the House of Commons. So great was his self-confidence that he concluded with a statement which later gave Churchill the opportunity to say that 'no more rash a bet has ever been recorded in the annals of the British turf'.[15] Bevin said, 'I will stake my political future on solving the problem.'[16]

[15] *Parliamentary Debates* (Commons), 29 Jan. 1949, c. 948. Bevin rejoined: 'May I ask whether it was greater than that which the right hon. Gentleman undertook when he went after Denikin and Koltchak?' Churchill retorted: 'I certainly did not stake my political reputation upon the successes which those generals would have, but I think the day will come when it will be recognised without doubt, not only on one side of the House but throughout the civilised world, that the strangling of Bolshevism at its birth would have been an untold blessing to the human race. . . . Let me return to the more peaceful paths of Palestine . . . and leave these furious controversies of a bygone period.' The exchange indicates Bevin's general grasp over foreign affairs and puts the 'peaceful' Palestine question into historical perspective, at least as Churchill saw it.

[16] Ibid., 13 Nov. 1945, c. 1934.

The tone of optimism may seem peculiar in view of subsequent events and the special place which Bevin occupies in Zionist demonology. One common Jewish accusation against him is that he was callous to Jewish suffering. He espoused the 'infamous' White Paper of 1939 as a guide to the solution of the problems of postwar Palestine. And he thus became a captive of the permanent officials of the Foreign Office who had designed the White Paper as part of a comprehensive policy of 'appeasement' towards both the Nazis and the Arabs. There is an element of truth in those charges, but it is important to distinguish the views attributed to him by Zionists and his actual outlook at the time. Bevin relied upon his permanent officials for expert advice, but he was not their pawn. He himself decided on the wisdom of a joint committee of inquiry, which alarmed his advisers. They were much more sceptical about co-ordinating policies on an issue that aroused political passions in America. In retrospect it seems clear that he could have paid greater attention to the danger signals given by James F. Byrnes, the American Secretary of State, in October 1945 about the need to take New York elections into account. The postponing of Jewish immigration into Palestine, Byrnes told the British Ambassador, 'would inflame the million or so Jewish voters as also their sympathies and altogether destroy the prospects of the Democratic candidate whose Republican rival for Mayor was, he reminded me, a Jew'.[17] At this early stage in the controversy Bevin tended to yield to American entreaties about election difficulties. He optimistically believed that the President would eventually act on the obvious merits of the case and the need to align British and American policies in the Middle East rather than in direct response to American politics. Bevin moreover assumed that there would be a correlation between the position adopted by the President and the line pursued by the State Department. Those assumptions proved to be false.

As will be discussed in the chapter on the United Nations Special Committee on Palestine, individual cases of anti-Semitism persisted in the British civil service (as in American official circles). It is difficult however to sustain the argument that anti-Semitism explains British policy towards the immigration question. Bevin was fully aware, in his own words, that 'the plight of the victims of Nazi persecution, among whom were a large number of Jews, is unprecedented in the history of the world'.[18] But neither he nor his advisers drew the conclusion that the future of the Jews lay in Palestine. Bevin and other British leaders, including Churchill, consistently

---

[17] Halifax to Bevin, No. 7157, Top Secret, 27 Oct. 1945, PREM 8/627/1.
[18] *Parliamentary Debates* (Commons), 13 Nov. 1945, c. 1927.

advocated the revival of Jewish society on a basis of equality with
other Europeans within Europe itself. The Foreign Office was indeed
anti-Zionist, but not for reasons that were necessarily anti-Semitic.
Paul Mason, who supervised the refugee question, wrote in October
1945:

> We insistently deny that it is right to segregate persons of Jewish race as such
> or to classify persons in any displaced persons category as at this stage as 'non
> repatriable'. . . . It has been a cardinal policy hitherto that we regard the
> nationality factor as the determining one as regards persons of Jewish race just
> as in the case of other racial or religious peoples. Once abandon that, and the
> door is open for discrimination in favour of Jews as such which will ultimately
> become discrimination *against* Jews as such.
>
> To the Zionists, all weapons are good ones and instead of trying to help us
> produce conditions in which persons of Jewish race can live side by side with
> their fellow nationals of other groups, they exploit (it is the only word) all
> examples of ill treatment to prove the case for Zionism. . . . It is a safe bet that
> the largest proportion of those Jews who opt for Palestine versus repatriation do
> so under Zionist pressure.[19]

In this analysis of the refugee question, Mason drew attention to the
overcrowded conditions and other deplorable circumstances of the
displaced-person camps. But he refused to recognize the immediate
postwar conditions of the Jews in Europe as so irremediable as to
necessitate mass emigration to Palestine: 'that is not an argument
for saying that there is no future for persons of Jewish race in
Europe'. Mason in particular deprecated the implications of Earl
Harrison's report which gave fuel to the Zionists: 'it is entirely lacking in proportion for Mr Harrison to suggest that the displaced persons of Jewish race are no better off (other than that they are not
now exterminated), now than [when] they were under the Nazis'.[20]
    As far as the Foreign Office was concerned, the purpose of the
Anglo-American Committee of Inquiry would be to educate the
Americans and get them to act responsibly both on Palestine and
the refugee issue. Robert Howe, the Assistant Under-Secretary who
supervised these questions, wrote at the time of the framing of the
committee's terms of reference that 'the United States, who now
criticise us irresponsibly, should assume a share in the responsibility
for the settlement of the Palestine problem, and . . . steps should
be taken without delay to ameliorate the situation of the Jews in
Europe'.[21] The British intended to demonstrate to the Americans
that the refugee problem was so great that its solution could not be
found in Palestine alone but rather in the acceptance of Jewish

---

[19] Minute by Mason, 2 Oct. 1945, FO 371/45380.
[20] Ibid.
[21] Memorandum by Howe, 6 Oct. 1945, FO 371/45380.

displaced persons in other countries, not least the United States. Nevertheless the British would be prepared to admit into Palestine 1,500 refugees a month as the calculated figure representing 'the present absorptive capacity of Palestine'. The White Paper of 1939 continued to govern Foreign Office thought.

Bevin's basic aim was the creation of a binational state. It may be taken as a common British aspiration of the era, though endorsed by others with greater degrees of scepticism. Creech Jones and the Colonial Office for example, bearing the brunt of local antagonism between the Jews and the Arabs, urged 'autonomy' of the two communities on a federal basis that might have led either to a binational state or to the establishing of two separate states. Bevin himself, in his last dramatic bid to achieve a binational solution, reaffirmed the right of self-determination if the destiny of Palestine were to be partition by peaceful means.[22] A letter written by President Truman at the time of American recognition of the state of Israel suggests that he all along might have preferred the binational solution rather than partition.[23] 'Binationalism' was the recommendation of the Committee of Inquiry. Yet one cannot but agree with one of the first authorities who wrote on the subject dispassionately, J. C. Hurewitz, that by 1946 it was too late.[24] By then the forces of Jewish and Arab nationalism had foredoomed a binational solution to failure. For that reason the episode of the Committee of Inquiry and subsequent events convey a sense of tragedy that is thrown into only slightly comic relief by the blunders of the American and British governments.

In the following chapters it is important to bear in mind that immigration was the key to the Palestine question. In 1945 the respective Jewish and Arab populations were 560,000 and 1,200,000. At the close of the war the question of Jewish refugees was linked with Palestine as a possible answer. In the United States there was great sympathy for the plight of Jewish displaced persons but also resistance

[22] See the notes in preparation for his speech of 27 Jan. 1947 in FO 371/61747.

[23] In a letter to Bartley Crum of 15 May 1948, Truman Papers, Official File 204D, Box 776. He wrote that 'eventually we are going to get it worked out just that way', i.e. along the lines of the Committee of Inquiry's recommendation of a binational solution. Several writers have commented that the remark is puzzling in view of his endorsement of partition (e.g. Ganin, *Truman, American Jewry, and Israel*, p. 188, and Wilson, *Decision on Palestine*, p. 204 n. 16). It is indeed contradictory, but one possibility is that Truman was expressing the hope, consistent with his ideas from the beginning, that the Jews and Arabs would be able to work out things peacefully together. Other interpretations might be that he merely wrote in great haste, or that he had only a tenuous grasp of the Palestine problem. The three possibilities are not necessarily contradictory.

[24] Hurewitz, *Struggle for Palestine*, p. 246.

to a change in the immigration laws that might have made possible an American solution. During the next year public interest in the refugees diminished. The British felt less pressure to admit displaced persons into Palestine. The Zionist leaders confronted the problem of how to partition Palestine in order to create a state in which the Jewish population would be numerically preponderant. The more refugees, the stronger would be the Zionist position; but ultimately the question of a Jewish state could be resolved only by force of arms and population upheavals. In the 1948 war 700,000 Arabs fled from the parts of Palestine under Jewish control. Between 1948 and 1950 the population of the state of Israel increased from 650,000 to over 1,000,000.

In this section the problems of the partition of Palestine and the creation of the Jewish state will be examined in the context of Anglo-American relations. The British were compelled to rely on the United States in attempting to find a viable solution, and co-operation was impeded because of the American anti-colonial tradition. Truman did not have a fixation, as had Roosevelt, with British colonialism as an underlying cause of war and oppression; but Truman no less than Roosevelt had a powerful mistrust of the British bureaucracy. And unlike Roosevelt, Truman was not inclined to strike up a close political partnership with British politicians. By temperament and with a sense of equity, Truman, in the beginning stages of the controversy, favoured the solution urged by the Anglo-American Committee of Inquiry in April 1946. This was the answer of a binational state in which neither Jew nor Arab would predominate. After the collapse of the plans to implement the committee's recommendations, Truman's policy increasingly supported the Zionist cause. As will be explained later, his advisers had an eye on the Jewish vote and he himself was well aware of an opportunity that would serve a political purpose as well as gratify his own humanitarian impulses. The point of these introductory remarks, however, is to clarify his response within the framework of Anglo-American relations. The turning point was his 'Yom Kippur statement' of October 1946. In it Truman called for a bridging of the gap between the British and Zionist positions, but his words were widely misinterpreted as an endorsement of the Zionist programme. His advisers on the White House staff did not contradict the Zionist version that the President of the United States now supported the proposal to create a Jewish state in Palestine. Truman himself eventually endorsed this solution.

The tension between the officials of the State Department and the Foreign Office revealed a sophisticated variant on the theme of American anti-colonialism. The career officers of the State Department worked towards the goal of the gradual and peaceful liquidation of the British Empire, in Palestine as throughout the world. On the specific problem of Palestine, however, there was much more of an anti-Zionist consensus between American and British officials than there was conflict about the optimal solution of a binational state. The head of the Office of Near Eastern and African Affairs, Loy Henderson, believed that partition benefiting the Jewish minority would be a caricature of the principle of self-determination. He persistently worked towards the solution of a binational state under the auspices of an international trusteeship regime. His ideas were not incompatible with those of the British Foreign Office. The critical juncture here was the British decision in February 1947 to refer the Palestine issue to the United Nations. This move was not intended as an abandonment of the mandate but rather as an attempt to win international endorsement for a binational solution. Both the State Department and the Foreign Office underestimated the resourcefulness of the Zionists. One way of interpreting the sequence of these complex events would be to maintain that it was the Zionists' year for a miracle. Their campaign ended victoriously in the United Nations vote of November 1947 in favour of partition.

A more mundane interpretation might hold that the struggle for the Jewish state was fuelled not only by a sense of guilt of the Holocaust and genuine humanitarian sentiment but also by a worldwide animosity against the British Empire. Anti-colonialism, as it has been traditionally understood, was a conspicuous force in the summer and autumn of 1947. The opportunity to disrupt the British Empire in the Middle East certainly helps to explain Russian motivation and the tacit alliance between the United States and the Soviet Union in favour of the Jews. The anti-colonial movement found vociferous representation on the United Nations Special Committee on Palestine which, the British could later sadly reflect, was the first of many United Nations bodies dedicated to the exposure of the evils of colonialism. Not least the Zionist archives reveal the part played by Sumner Welles. Welles was a former Under Secretary of State who virtually embodied, in British eyes, the more virulent tradition of American anti-colonialism, which in this case he combined with a passionate belief in the justice of the Zionist cause. Welles gave the Jews invaluable advice about the politics of the United Nations. The part he played in the establishing of the Jewish state represents a remarkable example of the fusion of the principles of the anti-colonial and Zionist movements.

The last two chapters of this section deal with the liquidation of Palestine as a British responsibility. To Americans who took an interest in colonial affairs, this episode was perceived as the British Empire in a state of dissolution. The preoccupation with what might replace British rule helps to explain the divergent attitudes during the war of 1948. At that time Jewish efficiency, determination, and valour contributed to diminishing American political and ethical doubts about the wisdom of creating a Jewish state. The Jews appeared to be emerging as a stabilizing and democratic force in the Middle East. The Americans of this era on the whole were not inclined to question the proposition that the expansionist tendencies of militant Zionism would naturally subside, or the assumption, after the conclusion of the 1948 war, that the state of Israel could peacefully coexist with its Arab neighbours if the latter would refrain from aggression.

From the British perspective the Empire was not in a state of dissolution but rather of transformation. Formal rule would be replaced with more modest informal influence, but Britain would remain the dominant regional power. The men of the Labour government were responding not only to the Zionist campaign in the United States and the United Nations but also to terrorism in Palestine and demands from Tory as well as Labour politicians to cut losses. To those who shaped British policy, however, the decision in September 1947 to evacuate merely marked a change in tactics. The salient feature of this period was the persistent effort on the part of the British, especially Ernest Bevin, to support the Arabs and thereby to sustain British power in the Middle East. As a case study in decolonization, Palestine demonstrates the convergence of ethical sympathy for the Arabs and political calculation of how best to maintain British influence. There is one further point of general historical importance. It seemed clear to the British of this time that, whatever the historic justice of the Jewish cause, militant Zionism could only be curtailed by the United States. The British failed to convince the Americans of the need to intervene in order to mitigate Arab irredentism. This exchange of views about the United States and the future of the Jewish state forms one of the themes in the last chapter in this section.

2

THE ANGLO-AMERICAN
COMMITTEE OF INQUIRY

FROM New Year until Easter 1946 six British and six American members of the 'Committee of Inquiry' pondered the problem of Palestine.[1] At the end of their deliberations, to the general surprise of all concerned, not least themselves, they submitted a unanimous report to Attlee and Truman that recommended the immediate admission of the 100,000 refugees into Palestine and the solution of a binational state in which neither Arab nor Jew would predominate. One of the American committee members wrote in his diary that it was no less than a 'miracle' that 'twelve such different individuals from two countries should have made an agreed report and that that report should be as good as it is'.[2]

The American part of the committee consisted of Judge Joseph 'Texas Joe' Hutcheson (the American Chairman, who described himself as a Jeffersonian Democrat); Frank Aydelotte (American Secretary of the Rhodes Trust and Director of the Institute of Advanced Study at Princeton); William Phillips (Roosevelt's envoy to India and a former Under Secretary of State regarded by the Zionists as a 'conventional diplomat'); Frank Buxton (pro-Zionist editor of the *Boston Herald* and winner of a Pulitzer Prize who held deep suspicions of British imperialism); James G. McDonald (former High Commissioner on Refugees for the League of Nations, later first Ambassador to Israel); and Bartley Crum (a San Francisco lawyer committed to the Zionist cause). All of the Americans were sympathetic to the case for the 100,000. Throughout the proceedings Crum and McDonald consistently took pro-Zionist positions. Judge Hutcheson, the dominant personality of the group, waged a successful battle against political Zionism and became the champion of the binational solution. Buxton supported him almost as a henchman. Aydelotte attempted to find common cause with the British. Phillips, though less Anglophile than Aydelotte, also worked

[1] For detailed assessment of the committee's work based on full use of archival sources, see Amikam Nachmani, 'British Policy in Palestine after World War II: The Anglo-American Committee of Inquiry' (Oxford D.Phil. thesis, 1980). See also especially Cohen, *Palestine and the Great Powers*, chap. 5; Dinnerstein, *America and the Survivors of the Holocaust*, chap. 3; and Wilson, *Decision on Palestine*, chap. 6.
[2] Frank Aydelotte's Diary entry of 20 Apr. 1946, Aydelotte Papers.

towards conciliation and proved to be the most politically perceptive of the Americans.

The British group was composed of Sir John Singleton (the British Chairman and a High Court Judge, referred to by some of the American members as 'the John Bull amongst us'); Lord (Robert) Morrison (a Labour work-horse not to be confused, as Truman did, with Herbert Morrison); Sir Frederick Leggett (British representative at the International Labour Office and one of Bevin's personal friends); Wilfrid Crick (a rather narrow-minded economic adviser to the Midland Bank who devoted much of his attention to Palestine's economy); Reginald Manningham Buller (a Tory MP described by an American member of the committee as 'devoted to the Kipling idea of empire'); and Richard Crossman (a Labour MP and assistant editor of the *New Statesman*).[3]

Singleton and Manningham Buller resisted the arguments in favour of the 100,000 and pursued a line that coincided with the policy of the British government. Crick generally agreed with them but his British as well as American colleagues found him obstinate and querulous. Morrison and Leggett were compatible with the Americans holding middle ground, notably Aydelotte and Phillips. Crossman, acknowledged by almost all contemporaries to be the most brilliant member of the committee, played a key part in bringing about a consensus. After the conclusion of the committee's work, Crossman published a short book entitled *Palestine Mission*. In it he described the American chairman:

[3] Of the unpublished diaries of the committee members, James McDonald's contains the sharpest descriptions, which on the whole are remarkably fair-minded: '*Sir John*: able, dependable, but likely to follow the governmental line; *Lord Morrison*: the most British of the group; even more sensitive than Sir John about any possible questioning of "the infallability" of British officialdom; *Crossman*: brilliant, sparkling with ideas, wanting to be liberal in foreign affairs but likely to consider such liberality less vital than success of the Labor program in Britain; *Crick*: financial technician, cold and precise; *Leggett*: the professional conciliator but very British; *Manningham-Buller*: quiet, searching, precise and perhaps the ablest intellect in the British group. Though a Conservative, I doubt if he will be more imperialist than his colleagues. As to the *Americans*. The *Judge* [Hutcheson] is shrewd, very honest, determined to find if possible, a "just solution". . . . He is . . . a tremendous worker, with an extremely keen mind, who will probably end up with a surprising comprehension of the whole problem; *Aydelotte* is romantic and Anglophile; *Phillips* is inevitably somewhat traditional but on points where the rest of us are obtuse, he has been quite discerning . . .; *Crum*: an amazingly energetic and keen student . . .; *Buxton*: though dry and restrained, has strong convictions and holds to them tenaciously' (Diary, 14 Jan. 1946, McDonald Papers). As for McDonald himself, there is a revealing entry in his diary about an exchange between him and Judge Hutcheson, who asked him if he knew how the British regarded him: 'It . . . became evident that I have been condemned out of hand as a Zionist propagandist and that nothing objective is to be expected from me' (ibid. 30 Mar. 1946). McDonald consistently pleaded the case for the displaced persons, but he proved to be more flexible on the question of a Jewish state than his colleagues anticipated.

'Texas Joe' was a 'character'—and he knew it. He was nearly seventy, an appeal judge of a circuit court. . . . He . . . was in fact a conservative Texan who regarded Roosevelt and the New Deal as the ruin of the Democratic party. He rarely admitted, except under pressure, that he had been a valiant opponent of the Ku Klux Klan, and a friend of the Negro, when such attitudes were deeply unpopular. . . . He had a real love of language and could use it more explosively than any other member of the committee. . . . He could exhibit prejudice without undermining our confidence in his integrity.[4]

Crossman described the British chairman as Hutcheson's antithesis:

[Singleton] always dressed in exquisitely cut clothes. . . . A man of intense and simple patriotism, he showed himself throughout our investigations intensely loyal to what he conceived to be the interests of the government, and sometimes exhibited a sensitiveness to criticisms of British policy or British officialdom which irritated our American friends. He had had no previous experience in international work of this sort. His belief in the necessity for maintaining law and order was simple and rigid, and his natural horror of terrorism had been sharpened by his experiences during the Irish troubles.[5]

The work of the committee may be comprehended as the clash between Hutcheson and Singleton with the former ultimately prevailing. Singleton was anti-Zionist. He favoured doing whatever possible to assist the British administration in maintaining law and order. He would have preferred the disarming of the Jewish defence force (the Haganah) and the reduction of functions of the incipient Jewish government (the Jewish Agency); and he would have made the admission of the 100,000 dependent on such conditions. Hutcheson favoured the 100,000 and insisted on a clear-cut formula of a unitary state in which Jew and Arab would live and work together as equals.

According to the unpublished diary of William Phillips (which is in implicit agreement with Crossman's and other accounts), Singleton's rigid legal habits and bias interfered with his objectivity. Phillips

---

[4] Richard Crossman, *Palestine Mission: A Personal Record* (London, 1947), p. 21. The other contemporary work about the investigation by another committee member is Bartley C. Crum, *Behind the Silken Curtain* (New York, 1947), which, as will be discussed later, was concocted as self-serving Zionist propaganda. The contemporary authority on Palestine, J. C. Hurewitz (who had detailed knowledge of the historical evolution of the problem because of his wartime work in the Office of Strategic Services), observed that Crossman 'wrote as if he were lecturing on logic at Oxford [and] Crum as if he were exposing international intrigue'. *Saturday Review*, 6 Nov. 1948. The fullest published exposé of Crum's book is Wilson, *Decision on Palestine*, p. 202, which describes it as 'ghostwritten', 'written in haste', and filled with 'many inaccuracies'. Crossman commented that Crum 'reads nothing, drinks too much and changes his mind according to the last newspaper he receives from the States'. Crossman Diary, 8 Apr. 1946, Crossman Papers.

[5] Crossman, *Palestine Mission*, p. 15.

wrote of Singleton's chairing of the committee during one of the sessions in London:

> Having formed the attitude of 20 years of judgeship, he spoke to some of them [the witnesses] as if they were criminals before the bar, while to others, such as Lord Samuel, Leopold Amery, and such ilk, he was a sweet as honey.

Phillips also wrote towards the end of the committee's work:

> In looking back . . . Judge Hutcheson, in my opinion, stands out as the one who has done most to achieve our success. . . . Sir John has also been very helpful but the Judge is his intellectual superior, with the result that matters have drifted more and more in the direction of the Judge.[6]

Phillips made it clear that Crossman was instrumental in Hutcheson's success: 'I think Crossman deserves perhaps the highest praise of all. He . . . has been a most helpful medium between the American and British viewpoints, usually taking the American side.'[7]

Crossman's published and unpublished writings hold a place of unique importance in the Palestine controversy. For perception of the Arab as well as the Jewish side of the case, *Palestine Mission* stands above all other contemporary writings on the committee. Crossman's insights were penetrating and imaginative. During the course of the investigation he became a convinced Zionist for intellectual as well as humanitarian reasons, and his ideas about socialism played an important part in the transformation of his attitude. He passionately hoped for the success of a Jewish socialist state. He described himself at the time as intellectually arrogant. Bevin, who later lamented his appointment, certainly so regarded him. Crossman eventually became 'the leading opponent of Mr. Bevin's Palestine policy'.[8] For those reasons the following account will draw especially from Crossman's writings in order briefly to narrate the history of the committee and to clarify the clash of the American and British points of view that Crossman helped to resolve. It should be borne in mind that Crossman was pleading the Zionist case, and that his book, contrary to the fair-minded impression which it attempts to convey, is a subjective and skilfully argued dialectic. Therein lies part of its fascination.

For Crossman the first two weeks of the commission's work in Washington was significant not only for the evidence, presented largely

---

[6] Phillip's Diary entries, 7 Feb. and 14–18 Apr. 1946.

[7] Ibid. 14–18 Apr. 1946.

[8] As Crossman described himself in the book he edited on Communism, *The God that Failed* (New York, 1949). The reasons for Crossman's appointment to the committee in the first place are not entirely clear, but apparently it was Attlee's idea, subsequently endorsed by Bevin as an opportunity for Crossman to prove himself. There are valuable details about the appointments in FO 371/45384.

by Zionists, but also for the sorting out of his own ideas. He left London recalling that in 1939 he had 'reacted violently' against the White Paper but now almost unconsciously accepted its premiss that Jews and Arabs should live harmoniously within a single state. Why the change in attitude?

Why was the White Paper so indignantly received in 1939? . . . Was it that we were all on the lookout in 1939 for *appeasement* and saw the Arabs as a Fascist force to which Jewish liberty was being sacrificed? Partly, perhaps. But I suspect that six years of this war have fundamentally changed our *emotions*. We were pro-Jew emotionally in 1939 as part of 'anti-fascism'. . . . Now, most of us are not *emotionally* pro-Jew, but only rationally 'anti-anti-Semitic' which is a very different thing.[9]

Intellectually he acknowledged the force of the Arab argument as he understood it in part from *The Arab Awakening* by George Antonius.[10] In Washington he became disgusted when the Arab case went by default in the face of strong Zionist propaganda.[11] He frequently became exasperated with the lack of precision in discussions about Zionism. 'Any gentile who is compelled to study Zionism for weeks on end reaches a point when he feels inclined to bang on the table and walk out of the room.'[12] He disliked the 'smooth' legalistic approach of many of the Zionist spokesmen and preferred the voice of the 'real rabbis'. The only witness appearing before the committee who won Crossman's intellectual respect was Reinhold Neibuhr. To Crossman he represented 'a voice in the wilderness' by urging Anglo-American co-operation rather than merely attacking British imperialism. Crossman's general reaction to the witnesses in Washington led him to a conclusion remarkably similar to one of Ernest Bevin's more notorious judgements of American motives. The average American supported immigration to Palestine simply because he did not want any more Jews in America. 'By shouting for a Jewish state, Americans satisfy many motives', Crossman wrote in his diary. 'They are attacking the Empire and British imperialism, they are espousing

---

[9] Crossman, *Palestine Mission*, pp. 18–19.

[10] Crossman had read Antonius's book while crossing on the Atlantic. He described it as 'a brilliant survey of Arab history, far superior as a piece of writing to any Zionist publication I had read. . . . *The Arab Awakening* has been standard reading for the British members of the committee, but we found in Washington that the State Department had not got a copy.' *Palestine Mission*, pp. 41 and 123. His remark may be revealing about the State Department's library, but the implication is false; American officials were familiar with Antonius's work.

[11] On this point William Phillips noted in his diary that the hearings in Washington were mainly useful 'as a means of blowing off the steam of the Zionist cause. We had only one or two representatives of the Arab world—the majority of witnesses were political and cultural Zionists.' Phillips Diary, 24 Jan. 1946. For Phillips's later reflections on the committee, see his book, *Ventures in Diplomacy* (Boston, 1952).

[12] *Palestine Mission*, pp. 64–5.

a moral cause, the fulfilment for which they will take no responsibility, and, most important of all, they are diverting attention from the fact that their own immigration laws are one of the causes of the problem.'[13]

On the whole Crossman found the witnesses' testimony depressing. After a day of verbal onslaught against the British Empire he wrote:

> Why should these people from a safe position across the Atlantic lambast my country for its failure to go to war with the Arabs on behalf of the Jews? America was not prepared either to receive the Jews from Europe or to risk a single American soldier to protect them in Palestine. And the American Jews were just exploiting traditional anti-British feeling and egging the Americans on. I felt sore and full of self-pity.[14]

He pulled himself out of his depression through an intense conversation with David Horowitz, recently arrived from Palestine as a representative of the Jewish Agency. Horowitz regarded the meeting as so fateful that he later entitled a chapter in his own book (*State in the Making*) 'An Evening with Crossman'. He thought that Crossman immediately and accurately pierced to the heart of the Palestine problem by asking such questions as 'What about the principle of Jewish employment? Are you ready to admit Arabs into your trade union?' Crossman told Horowitz that he found Marxist analysis useful in answering such questions. Horowitz replied that he was familiar with the dialectical method of analysis. According to Horowitz's account, which is of interest because of the light it throws on two 'intellectuals' influencing the outcome of a momentous issue in world politics:

> I went on to describe, from the dialectical standpoint, the influence wielded by Jewish settlement in the Middle East and the prospects of the Zionist enterprise in the light of prevailing regional conditions. I alluded to the social revolution brought about by Zionism in the Jewish world, the metamorphosis of the social and professional class structure, and the impulses stirring the movement. He showed rapt interest.[15]

In the course of the conversation Crossman became convinced that the Jews would welcome Arab assistance in the financing and management of labour in development projects such as irrigation. They would share the benefits with the Arabs. Crossman and Horowitz went on to discuss problems such as immigration and 'economic absorptive capacity'. The lengthy conversation marked a turning point in the mind of Bevin's principal critic on Palestine. 'You must

---

[13] *Palestine Mission*, p. 38.
[14] Ibid., pp. 39–40.
[15] David Horowitz, *State in the Making* (New York, 1953), p. 45.

inspire us with the moral power of your effort, as you have done
with me this evening', Crossman told Horowitz in his parting words.
He had resolved a fundamental doubt—that the Jews would not be
fair to the Arabs. Horowitz for his part believed that a powerful
intellectual and moral force had been won over to the Zionist cause.
'Dick Crossman had a warm heart as well as a clear mind', he concluded.[16]

As a result of his visit to Washington Crossman believed that he
gained an insight into the nature of the American Zionist movement.
Like most Englishmen, he wrote, in the past he held simplistic ideas.
'I had assumed that support for Zionism was limited to American
Jews and to those isolationist groups which saw in it a useful stick
with which to beat the British. Zionism, I supposed, was simply a
well-organized pressure group which could swing elections in New
York State and could therefore dictate governmental policy.'[17]
He found on closer examination that Zionism had to be compre-
hended in relation to a conception basic to American expansion—
the 'frontier mentality'.

> Zionism after all is merely the attempt by the European Jew to rebuild his
> national life on the soil of Palestine in much the same way as the American
> settler developed the West. So the American will give the Jewish settler in
> Palestine the benefit of the doubt, and regard the Arab as the aboriginal who
> must go down before the march of progress. After all he only achieved his own
> freedom by a war of independence against George III and if the Jew in Palestine
> comes into conflict with George III's successors in colonial administration he is
> bound to win an instinctive American sympathy.[18]

Crossman in short believed that such insights into the American
'mentality' now gave him 'the *feel* of the [Zionist] movement'. The
lessons of the American revolution fuelled anti-British sentiment;
and the history of the American west seemed to explain, to most
Americans, the problems facing the Jews in Palestine. These analogies
troubled Crossman. He saw that the Arab perception of Zionism
could be compared with the reaction of the American Indian to the
white man's conquest of the frontier. For a man of a generation
which usually assumed without question both the benefits and the
inevitability of western domination of ethnic groups such as the
American Indians, this was a remarkable revelation.

Crossman had touched on a central issue. Could the Arabs and
Jews live together as equals within a unitary state, or would the
Jewish immigrants, bringing with them the advantages of western

---

[16] Ibid., p. 47.
[17] Crossman, *Palestine Mission*, p. 32.
[18] Ibid., p. 33.

technology, subject the Arabs to political and economic domination? What of the question of land alienation? The members of the committee made up their minds about those questions as they were being influenced by humanitarian concern for the refugees and arguments of 'economic development' that might benefit the Arab as well as the Jew. It is helpful to identify the views about immigration and development with some of the personalities. The British members of the committee were inclined to accept the proposal for the 100,000 and further increases in the immigration quota only on conditions that would make the Jewish influx as minimal a disruption as possible for the administration. Singleton held the staunchest views about the dangers of a Jewish rebellion (along the lines of the Irish troubles) that might be abetted by further immigration. Leggett's ideas should be mentioned as representative of a more flexible British approach. He demonstrated considerable insight into possible compromises such as accepting the 100,000 and curtailing immigration thereafter, and planning for economic development that would raise the Arab standard of living up to the Jewish level.

On the American side Frank Buxton espoused the crude Darwinist outlook that the Jewish march of progress would inexorably result in economic and cultural victory (on the analogy of the white men in the American west). According to James McDonald's diary, Buxton 'developed the idea of "eminent domain" citing as examples the United States' conquest of Mexico, the American conquest of the Indians and the inevitable giving way of a backward people before a more modern and practical one. He thought that strong people would naturally replace weaker ones.'[19] McDonald and Crum believed that Jewish development of Palestine would benefit the Arabs as well. Aydelotte and especially Phillips were more sensitive to the need for guarantees for the Arabs. Hutcheson's views stand out as a singular warning against the dangers of political Zionism, which he regarded as a threat to a predominantly Arab country. He held that ultimately the only peaceful solution would be a Palestinian state in which the constructive energies of both Arab and Jew, in his own words, would 'bring out the best in each people for the good of the [Palestinian] state'.[20]

Crossman, though he increasingly favoured partition, was prepared to go along with Hutcheson's binational solution. With this flexible outlook he was able to act as a conciliator between the British and

[19] McDonald Diary, 1 Apr. 1946, McDonald Papers.
[20] Memorandum by Hutcheson entitled 'Purely Tentative Thoughts on our Terms of Reference' (n.d. but written towards the end of the committee's deliberations), which is perhaps the most revealing document about Hutcheson's views. Hutcheson Papers.

American groups and between divergent ideological positions. It is important to grasp the steps in the evolution of his attitude because he attempted to resolve the contradiction between the principle of self-determination and the partition of a preponderantly Arab country. Admission of the 100,000 would help to solve the immediate problem of the refugees, but further immigration would have to be measured against the formula of economic absorptive capacity and the need to safeguard Arab land tenure. Crossman was not in fact much worried about the Arabs being subjected to the economic and cultural domination of the Jews. Like most members of the committee, he believed that immigration schemes and economic development could work to the advantage of both parties. He was prepared to test the solution of the binational state within a unitary framework that would provide political and religious safeguards for both parts of the community. If eventually the binational experiment failed—in other words if after all the Jew and Arab simply could not live together—then partition would be the next and ultimate step.

During the hearings in Washington, the committee members studied various plans for the development of Palestine. Such experts as Walter Clay Lowdermilk presented maps and charts of a Jordan Valley Authority (modelled on the Tennessee Valley Authority) and Robert Nathan, the author of a widely quoted economic study on Palestine, outlined, in Crossman's words, 'the most remarkable blueprint for Palestine's development'.[21] According to Bartley Crum:

> Nathan reported that in the last twenty-five years the population of Palestine had trebled, manufacturing production had increased sixfold, changing from handicrafts to modern mass production, and electrical consumption—always an index of development—had increased eightyfold. The country, he concluded, could absorb 100,000 refugees within six to nine months: and, depending upon conditions, could absorb from 615,000 to 1,125,000 immigrants within the next ten years.[22]

A good deal of this testimony implied that the only stumbling block to Palestinian progress and prosperity was the narrow-minded and anti-Jewish attitude of the British administration. This assumption outraged the British, particularly Singleton. 'I was anxious lest Sir John Singleton would explode', Crossman wrote. 'He was used to being dictator in his own court. . . . Now he had to sit quietly while, in defiance of the proprieties of British legal procedure, his country was held up to scorn, and each British member of the committee

---

[21] Crossman, *Palestine Mission*, p. 36. See Walter Clay Lowdermilk, *Palestine: Land of Promise* (New York, 1944); and Robert R. Nathan (with Oscar Gass and Daniel Creamer), *Palestine: Problem and Promise: An Economic Study* (Washington, 1946).

[22] Crum, *Silken Curtain*, p. 15.

was made to feel that he was held personally responsible for the death of six million Jews.'[23]

The testimony of Albert Einstein distilled the reasons for racial animosity and lack of economic development in Palestine. Einstein believed that the sinister hand of the British Colonial Office lurked behind the appointment of the committee. He had not only mastered the secrets of the universe but also the recondite nature of British imperialism:

I find that the British rule is based on the native. . . . I find that everywhere there are big landowners who are exploiters of that race of people. These big landowners, of course, are in a precarious situation because they are always afraid they will be gotten rid of. The British are always in a passive alliance with those land-possessing owners who exploit the work of the people of the different trades. It is my impression . . . that Palestine is a kind of small model of India. There is an attempt to dominate, with the help of a few officials, the people of Palestine, and it seems to me that the English rule in Palestine is absolutely of this kind.[24]

Einstein went on to state emphatically that the committee was a 'waste of time' since in the long run 'the Colonial Office would impose its own policies'. He denounced the committee as a mere 'smoke screen'. Crossman was quite disgusted with this performance. His diary recorded:

Professor Einstein came to the stand with adoring women gazing up at him like Gandhi, flashlights, movie cameras and so on. It was to be the high point. He delivered the expected attack on British imperialism. The British had deliberately instigated the unreal conflicts of Jews and Arabs in order to prolong their rule in the Middle East. The audience purred contentedly. Then under questioning, the old man said that a Jewish majority in Palestine was 'unimportant' and he disapproved of nationalism. The audience nearly jumped out of their seats.[25]

Einstein's comments, delivered in the full-blooded tradition of American anti-colonialism, more than any other testimony annoyed the British members of the committee who were otherwise favourably inclined towards both the Americans and the Jews. Crossman perceptively observed that the extreme Zionist case also perturbed the

[23] Crossman, *Palestine Mission*, p. 36.

[24] Crum, *Silken Curtain*, pp. 25–6.

[25] Crossman, *Palestine Mission*, p. 39. Though Einstein struck some of his audience, especially Crossman, as naïve, the transcript of the testimony conveys a consistent impression of profound scepticism about the British and pessimism about the creation of a Jewish state (transcript dated 11 Jan. 1946, USSD 867N.01/1–1146 Box 6753). After the completion of the committee's work, Einstein wrote to Crossman congratulating him on his book, *Plato Today*. He added: 'The report of the Commission on Palestine has shown to me that the members have tried their best to achieve justice under precarious conditions. On the other hand you will now agree that my remark was not quite unjustified; I mean the remark that in the eyes of the British Government the Commission was looked upon only as a smoke-screen.' Einstein to Crossman, 3 June 1946, Crossman Papers.

moderate American members of the committee (at this stage he was mistaken about Crum): 'By overstating their case and revealing their real aims, the Zionists don't irritate merely the British. They have really worried our Texan judge and fair-minded men like Crum and Aydelotte and Phillips, who support Jewish immigration into Palestine, but are beginning to react against the totalitarian claims of the Zionists. As democrats they are shocked.'[26]

To Crossman the notable experience of the committee's next stage of investigation, in London in late January, occurred at a luncheon when Bevin made his one and only appearance before the committee. 'Mr. Bevin's speech, though obviously impromptu, made an enormous impression on all of us, especially on my American colleagues.' The Foreign Secretary tried to dispel the idea that the committee amounted to 'only a stalling device'. He told the committee members that he would accept their report if it were 'unanimous'. He emphasized that point. He would follow the unanimous recommendation of the committee. Those words were both reassuring and consequential. 'We were all convinced', Crossman wrote in *Palestine Mission*, 'that he really had an "open mind" and was relying on us to make it up for him.'[27] In his private thoughts however Crossman was less certain. 'The Labour Party's Zionism', he confided in his diary, was 'about as half-baked and ill thought out a policy as I could conceive.' Bevin himself must have already suspected Crossman's pro-Jewish conversion. In a three-minute conversation about Palestine (the only one Crossman ever had with Bevin on the subject), Bevin 'confined himself to asking me whether I had been circumcised'.[28]

Crossman had swung over to a pro-Jewish position while in the United States, but he refused to support the proposal for the immigration of the 100,000 refugees until he himself investigated conditions in Europe and Palestine. From London the commission split into groups to tour the displaced person camps. Crossman, who fell ill in London and rejoined his part of the mission ten days later, surveyed the problem of the refugees mainly from Vienna, but he vicariously could experience the ordeal of his colleagues because of a visit to Dachau eight months earlier. When he met Crum and Leggett in Vienna he noted in his diary that 'they had smelled the

[26] Crossman, *Palestine Mission*, p. 39.

[27] Ibid., p. 57. Bevin's statement that he would accept a unanimous report played an important part in motivating the committee members actually to achieve unanimity. He later must surely have rued his incautious words. William Phillips noted in his diary at the time: 'Bevin went so far as almost to commit himself and the British Government to follow the advice of our Committee, whatever its final report might be, which was gratifying, but I thought, a bit injudicious.' Phillips Diary; cf. *Ventures*, p. 426.

[28] Crossman Diary entry dated January 1946.

unique and unforgettable smell of huddled, homeless humanity. They had seen and heard for themselves what it means to be the isolated survivor of a family deported to German concentration camp or slave labour.'[29] In this part of the investigation Crossman's principal revelation, which he shared with other members of the committee, was the impossibility of refugee repatriation. 'They had no countries of their own. Their roots had been torn up by the Nazis and they could not be replanted in their native soil. Nor was it possible to resettle them in Germany or anywhere else in Europe. The urge to get away was far too strong.' On this point Crossman resolved in his own mind the important and contentious point of how many refugees actually wished to immigrate to Palestine. He estimated that the approximate number would be seventy out of every hundred. He did not believe that Palestine by any means could absorb all of the Jews who wished to go there. But the 'abstract arguments' about Zionism now seemed to him 'curiously remote after this experience of human degradation'.[30] There clearly was a need for immediate action. At one stage Crossman optimistically calculated that if the report of the commission were completed on time at the end of April then the actual moving of some 100,000 Jews could be accomplished by the end of the following August.

The next leg of the committee's journey was Cairo. Here it is instructive to contrast Crossman's impressions with Bartley Crum's because the latter's views of Egyptian life may be taken as representative of those of many other Americans who found themselves travelling in the non-European world following the Second World War. In Egypt Crum quickly learned from Egyptians that 'Britain is our problem'. He heard for the first time slogans that echoed from the days of Mr. Gladstone and the British occupation: 'Egypt for the Egyptians' and not for the British. Crum felt 'the danger, the explosiveness of the political situation'. He discovered that the streets of Cairo 'swarmed with humanity'. 'I saw Arabs sprawled sleeping in doorways and in the shadow of buildings, and Arab women crouched with their young, munching bread undisturbed while flies clustered in seething masses on the abscessed eyes of their infants, and I was sickened.'[31] By contrast he noted in the British haunt of Shepheard's Hotel that around him 'sat the upper-class Cairenes, languidly brushing away the flies with horsehair switches; with their Western clothes, their red fezzes, their air of well-fed imperviousness, it was impossible not to sense their remoteness from the squalor about them'. Crum in

[29] Crossman, *Palestine Mission*, p. 75.
[30] Ibid., p. 75.
[31] Crum, *Silken Curtain*, p. 147.

short found Cairo noisy, intolerable, and oppressive—'a city whose human degradation I could not put out of my mind, and in which I could not free myself from the impression that disease stalked me as I walked'.[32] He could not but think that the Jews in comparison sought dignity and the chance for a decent life as free as possible from squalor, disease, corruption, and exploitation. The less advanced common man in Egypt would also seem the virtues of progress, Crum believed, if the Egyptians were introduced to the principles of western idealism, specifically, 'life, liberty, and the pursuit of happiness'. More to the point of his mission, Crum noted that in Cairo no Jews were allowed to testify before the committee.[33] In the discussion with Arab leaders about Palestine he observed that the only motivation seemed to be the preservation of the status quo. 'In that desire, I concluded reluctantly, they were joined by the British Colonial Office and its staff throughout the Middle East.'[34]

Crossman also denounced British imperialism, above all in its diplomatic mutation. 'A week in Egypt', he wrote in early March 1946, 'makes you so mad with the British Embassy that you want to blow up. They are all exquisite professional diplomatists, strutting about in high society, and treating the Egyptians like niggers.'[35] Those sentiments, which from time to time he voiced more politely in the House of Commons, no doubt influenced his general outlook on the British future in the Middle East, but they did not seem to impinge on his analysis of the problem of Arab nationalism and Zionism. In Cairo Crossman's examination of the Arab case led him to admit that it was as strong as the Jewish. The Arabs undercut the historical and humanitarian appeal for a Jewish national home by the

---

[32] Ibid., p. 147.

[33] On this point Crum's account is slightly misleading because other members of the committee had extensive conversations with some of the Egyptian Jews. For example James McDonald wrote in his diary: 'unlike British, American or French Jews, Egyptian Jews (and this . . . applied to nearly all Oriental Jews) had never really become parts of the countries in which they lived. On the contrary, they had remained aloof, had had a certain sense of superiority and had been treated with rather special consideration. Now, however, their position [in] Egypt and elsewhere in the Orient was seriously shaken and they are indeed in danger.' McDonald Diary, 2 Mar. 1946.

[34] Crum, *Silken Curtain*, p. 155.

[35] Deleted entry of Crossman's diary, 6 Mar. 1946, Crossman Papers. 'The only man I liked', Crossman continued, 'was the man responsible for all the trouble—Lord Killearn —who at least is a man of character, and would probably be excellent in Tanganyika.' The analogy of Tanganyika was recurrent in Middle Eastern commentary by British officials. It seemed to represent the opposite end of the British Empire, and Crossman also employed it in his criticism of British administration in Palestine: 'it is quite obvious that this administration, schooled in the autocratic habits of Tanganyika or Nigeria, and dependent on London for every major decision of policy, cannot possibly run a modern, self-assertive, self-consciously democratic community like the Jews of Palestine'. *Palestine Mission*, pp. 154–5.

simple argument that 'western civilization, with its enormous un-developed areas and its colonial territories, has no right to impose the solution of the Jewish problem . . . on the Arab world'. From the Arab point of view Jewish colonial settlement in Palestine merely varied the aggression of western imperialism. 'How can the Arab nationalists who are determined to end the British regime and to clear the British troops out of Egypt, possibly consent to the slow conquest of Palestine by settlers, who may be Semitic by origin, but behave exactly like European colonists?'[36] Crossman despaired of an answer to that question. When he considered partition as a possi-bility from the Arab vantage point it became clear to him that no one in the Middle East, including the British and American represen-tatives in the Arab states, supported a compromise solution. No one was concerned with the fate of the Jews. Everyone saw the issues in black and white, the White Paper versus unlimited Jewish immigra-tion, and Arab versus Jewish civilization.[37] Crossman nevertheless continued to hope that the issue of the national home might be reduced from the scale of Armageddon to its true proportions of a local issue that might be resolved between Jews and Arabs in Palestine itself.

From Cairo the committee travelled by train to Palestine for the last three weeks of the Middle Eastern tour (6–28 March). Here again it is revealing to dwell briefly on the impressions of Bartley Crum, not only because of the contrast between his ideas and Crossman's but also because of his part in the Palestine controversy after the conclusion of the committee's investigation. Such is Crum's significance that it is useful to bear in mind his background. He was a friend of one of Truman's advisers on Palestine, David Niles. Zionists welcomed Crum, a non-Jewish Zionist, into their ranks. He had the reputation of being a successful and ambitious civil rights lawyer in the tradition of Clarence Darrow. In 1948 he became co-owner of *P. M.*, the New York tabloid the most vehemently anti-British and pro-Jewish of all American newspapers. In the same year Sumner Welles praised him for 'his passionate faith in the justice of the Zionist cause', which is a measure of his esteem among non-Jewish Zionists.[38] He was also a political opportunist as well as a champion of the Zionist cause. 'Indeed', Crossman wrote, 'he was the only American with us who had a political career in front of him which could be made or marred by the attitude he adopted toward the Jewish question.'[39] In one

[36] *Palestine Mission*, p. 111.
[37] Ibid., p. 114.
[38] Sumner Welles, *We Need Not Fail* (Boston, 1948), p. 38.
[39] Crossman, *Palestine Mission*, p. 22.

sense Crum is an important figure because he combined the sentiments of American anti-colonialism with the fervour of a non-Jewish
Zionist convert. He is also remembered because of his book, *Behind
the Silken Curtain*. It is a biased, dishonest, and indeed ghost-written
account. Therein lies its interest, as an unabashed piece of Zionist
propaganda.

To Bartley Crum the journey from Egypt to Palestine passed from
lifeless Egyptian mud houses and faceless children to the green fields
and smiling children's faces of the Holy Land. He noted that the
women wore bright peasant blouses with colourful embroidered
designs in contrast with the drab black robes of Egyptian women.
'For the first time, too, I became conscious of the British military.
Barracks built of corrugated iron stood near the [Gaza] station, and
hundreds of Tommies were about.'[40] Tommy guns and armoured
cars are recurrent in Crum's narrative and perhaps his dominant
impression of the British in Palestine can best be conveyed by his
comment that the police station on the hill, rather than the school
house, symbolized the British presence. In the days of testimony
Crum along with the other members of the committee listened to the
principal Jewish and Arab leaders in Palestine. He found individual
British administrators such as the High Commissioner, General Sir
Alan Cunningham, to be humane officials inclined to a generous
settlement in favour of the Jews. But on the whole he did not believe
that British policy would deviate from 'the alliance with reactionary
Arab chiefs', even under the long-range direction of a Labour government. The reason he summed up in a single sentence: 'the Middle
East was crucially important to Britain's existence as a great power'.
On this point he thought that the British misjudged their power
indefinitely to control the Arabs. He believed that the outcome
would not be determined by ephemeral British military strength or
by fictitious Arab unity but by the Jewish sense of destiny in creating
a national home. He held that belief as passionately as any Jewish
Zionist. In Jerusalem Crum along with the other members of the
committee listened to hour upon hour of testimony by Jewish and
Arab leaders in Palestine. But it is difficult to detect any progression of thought other than towards the establishment of an independent Jewish state. His mind, like James McDonald's, was already
made up.

Although Crossman also persistently argued the case for partition,
he rigorously examined all aspects of the controversy and posed
difficult questions to the witnesses regardless of their political
position. With David Ben-Gurion he sallied into the byways of Oxford

[40] Crum, *Silken Curtain*, p. 160.

philosophy and tried to convince him that Plato was not a 'fascist'. In print he described Ben-Gurion as a 'Pickwickian cherub'; but privately he referred to the future Prime Minister of Israel as the 'Lenin' of the Jewish community in Palestine.[41] Ben-Gurion made an unfavourable impression before the committee. He even went so far as to profess ignorance of the Haganah, yet he made it clear that the Jews would fight. If the Jews failed to achieve a Zionist state by peaceful methods then they would resort to violence. 'In deciding our destiny', he told Crossman, 'don't make the mistake of thinking of us as Jews like the Jews you have in London. Imagine that we're Englishmen fighting for our national existence, and calculate that we shall behave as you would behave if you were in our situation. . . . Make up your minds, one way or the other, and remember that either way, we shall fight our Dunkirk.'[42]

When Weizmann appeared before the committee he made a similar point about the danger of not recognizing the need for deliberate, agonizing, and clear-cut decision. Crossman was greatly impressed with Weizmann's candour:

> He spoke for two hours with a magnificent mixture of passion and scientific detachment. Here is a Jew who frankly admits that every Jew carries the virus of anti-Semitism with him and founds his case for a Jewish commonwealth on that fact. He is the first witness who has frankly and openly admitted that the issue is not between right and wrong but between the greater and the lesser injustice. Injustice is unavoidable and we have to decide whether it is better to be unjust to the Arabs of Palestine or to the Jews.[43]

In private conversation Crossman and Weizmann discussed the possibility of partition. Weizmann recalled how Churchill had supported the plan of partition during the war (which came as news to Crossman) and how he himself had worked towards this goal since the late 1930s. Weizmann preferred partition rather than the various solutions of a unitary or binational state because it would be clear-cut and final. He believed that even the extremists would accept the solution of an independent Jewish state in part of Palestine rather than attempt to create a Zionist state in *all* of Palestine. 'Weizmann specifically mentioned that Ben-Gurion, whatever he may say, would accept it as he personally knew.' Like others who spoke with him, Crossman was impressed with Weizmann's wisdom, moderation, and quiet determination.[44]

----

[41] Crossman explained his use of the word 'Lenin' as 'the dictator who runs the Jews in Palestine, including the illegal army' (Crossman Diary, 26 Mar. 1946). For discussion of Crossman's impressions of Ben-Gurion and Weizmann see Cohen, *Palestine and the Great Powers*, pp. 102 ff.

[42] Crossman, *Palestine Mission*, p. 163.   [43] Ibid., p. 123.

[44] Crossman Diary, 26 Mar. 1946.

From the Arab leaders Crossman learned nothing that he did not already know. Jemal Husseini, the cousin of the Mufti and the spokesman of the Palestinian Arabs, gave him the impression of speaking with 'fatalistic acceptance' of impending conflict. On this point Crossman's interest in philosophy perhaps blunted his perceptions. Husseini and other Arab leaders were less concerned about political ideology than Crossman believed. They certainly had no reason to convey the impression of upholding Nazi principles. They were however intent on maintaining public unity against the Jews. The comment of William Phillips in his diary is of interest because of his more favourable impression of Husseini than most of his colleagues: 'he elaborated his remarks with firmness, and even though he was adamant in the position which he took against the Jews I had the feeling that he was a reasonable man at heart and might privately hold a less rigid position'.[45] Crossman, by contrast, was more intent on exposing Husseini's pro-Nazi sentiments. In an unexpected demonstration that some of the members of the committee suspected as an effort to steal the spotlight, Crossman produced wartime photographs in Berlin of the Mufti saluting Hitler, as if indicating Arab allegiance to the Nazis. The Arab delegates were thrown into disarray.

Crossman and other members of the commission were unexpectedly and favourably struck with the testimony of a representative of the Arab Office in Jerusalem, Albert Hourani. Even to Crum he 'made an extremely competent summation of the Arab case'.[46] Hourani analysed the possible solutions to the Palestine problem and the probable Arab reaction to them: the establishment of a Jewish state; a binational state; and a compromise short-term solution in which a substantial but limited number of Jews, for example 100,000, might be allowed to immigrate. In each of these solutions he saw insurmountable conflict because of probable Zionist insistence on increases in immigration which the Arabs would resist tooth and nail. He believed that the only solution lay in a Palestinian state with an Arab majority who would guarantee equal rights of Jewish

---

[45] Phillips Diary, 12 Mar. 1946.

[46] Crum, *Silken Curtain*, p. 254. The Jews recognized Hourani as their most relentless intellectural adversary: 'His testimony was ably and brilliantly presented. He analyzed the problem with merciless logic and consistency and tried by precept and example to show that any solution was liable to provoke a conflict.' Horowitz, *State in the Making*, p. 67. This assessment is confirmed by reports in the Central Zionist Archives by Arthur Laurie (another representative of the Jewish Agency following the work of the committee), e.g. 30 Mar. 1946, CZA Z6/18/1: 'Hourani . . . seems to have made a most able and intelligent analysis (from the Arab point of view but with an air of detachment). . . . Hourani is apparently the natural successor to the late George Antonius; and friend and enemy alike were loud in their praises of charm and the distinction of his presentation.'

citizenship. The immigration quota would be determined by the majority of the population. He held that the Arabs would be 'unalterably opposed' to the creation of a Jewish state in Palestine. Ultimately he rested his case on the argument that Crossman earlier had granted as undercutting the entire Zionist position: neither the Jews nor the great powers had the right to impose the burden of the Jewish refugees on Palestine or to create a new state in a predominantly Arab territory. Hourani in fact made a ringing reaffirmation of the premiss of George Antonius, who had written in 1939: 'the logic of facts is inexorable. It shows that no room can be made in Palestine for a second nation except by dislodging or exterminating the nation in possession.'[47]

The committee spent its last few weeks in seclusion in Switzerland as they attempted to reach a consensus. They pondered the philosophic admonition of Chaim Weizmann that the committee would have to decide whether injustice should be done to the Jew or the Arab. Individual members sank their personal differences because they believed that their governments urgently needed a unanimous recommendation. Crossman at the end of the deliberations correctly wrote that the report was 'a compromise document' arrived at after intense disagreement.[48] The committee submitted ten complicated recommendations designed to meet the crisis of the refugees in Europe and the Arab–Jewish conflict in Palestine. In essence there were two major points which might be fairly deduced:

1. The immediate entry into Palestine of 100,000 Jewish victims of Nazi persecution.

2. The eventual solution of a binational state in which neither Jew nor Arab would dominate. There would be equal representation. The mandate would be converted into a United Nations trusteeship territory. The Arabs would be raised to economic and cultural equality with the Jews.

The bitterest controversy in the committee had arisen over the issue of how to prevent immediate conflict in Palestine. Sir John Singleton made his agreement to the admission of the 100,000 refugees dependent on the disarmament of the Jewish defence force, the Haganah. Manningham-Buller supported him. They pursued the same line of thought as Attlee and Bevin as well as the officials of the Foreign Office. The British believed that the disarming of the Jews was

[47] Antonius, *Arab Awakening*, p. 412. For Hourani's later reflections, see '*The Arab Awakening* Forty Years After', in Albert Hourani, *The Emergence of the Modern Middle East* (London, 1981).

[48] Memorandum by Crossman, 'Notes on Palestine Report', 22 Apr. 1946, Crossman Papers; PREM 8/302.

necessary not only to prevent further terrorism but also to avert an outbreak of general hostilities between the Jews and Arabs. Singleton and Manningham-Buller acquiesced in the majority view only because of the pressure to issue a unanimous report and because the other members of the commission yielded to their insistence on having a section of the report devoted to Jewish terrorism and the 'illegal' Jewish army. Once they had reached agreement on the Haganah, the members of the committee found unexpected consensus on other controversial issues such as control of immigration and land. Long-term immigration would be linked with development projects such as the Jordan Water Authority, and there would be provisions for the protection of small Arab land-holders.

The admission of the 100,000 and the change in the regulations of land transfers (which would be possible 'irrespective of race, community or creed') would have fundamentally altered, if it would not have destroyed, the basis of British policy, in other words, the White Paper of 1939. Immigration, as Albert Hourani pointed out after the report's publication, would now ultimately be determined 'by the pressure which the Jews and Arabs are able to bring in London'.[49] On the other hand the committee denied the Jews the basis of the Zionist programme. There would be no Jewish state. 'It may be', William Phillips recorded in his diary, 'that the recommendation for the issuance of 100,000 certificates may calm the troubled waters and lessen the bitter disappointment of our recommendation against the establishment of a Jewish state.'[50] This proved to be a false hope, but the optimism about the 100,000 is important in comprehending the nature of the agreement in which all members of the committee were able to acquiesce.

The two bases of the report, the 100,000 and the binational solution, may be regarded as a victory for Judge Hutcheson and a defeat for Sir John Singleton. Such was the robust quality of Hutcheson's leadership and the incisiveness of his legal mind that he was able to carry with him the Zionists on the American side. McDonald and Crum for tactical reasons were willing to go along with the binational state in order to reach agreement on the 100,000. Buxton followed Hutcheson's lead. Phillips and Aydelotte, both anti-Zionists, believed in the binational solution as a principle of justice. So also did all of the members of the British side except Crossman, who, like McDonald, yielded on the question of partition in order to achieve consensus on the 100,000. Singleton proved to be maladroit in his handling of specific issues such as guarantees against terrorism (for example the

[49] 'Middle East Study Group', 17 May 1946, RIIA.
[50] Phillips Diary, 14–18 Apr. 1946.

disarming of the Haganah) and generally as a chairman. His resentment towards Hutcheson flared up at one of the concluding dinners
of the committee in Lausanne. All of these details were well known
to the Zionists monitoring the committee because of the accounts
given to them by Buxton (and also McDonald and Crum). According to a Zionist report using the code names 'Singer' for Singleton,
'Dolly' for Hutcheson, and 'Harvey' for Buxton:

> The key man in all this business . . . was Hutcheson, Singer remained un-
> regenerate, and having had a good deal too much to drink on Friday night . . .
> let himself go with great profanity about Dolly whom he regarded as having
> betrayed him, and Harvey whom he regarded as Dolly's 'evil genius'. . . . The
> defeat of Singleton was also a defeat for Beeley who remains strongly pro-
> Arab.[51]

Harold Beeley, as will become apparent in the following chapters,
was the Foreign Office official who acted as Bevin's right-hand man
on the Palestine issue and who at this time was serving as one of the
committee's secretaries.

The word 'binational' was not actually used in the report. The
committee members could not agree on a precise definition. The
limited amount of time in which they had to draw up the report
helps to explain the vagueness of the constitutional proposals. The
officials of the Foreign Office and Colonial Office, who were expected
to implement the committee's recommendations, found these
obscure ideas to be most unsatisfactory. The stalemate between the
Zionist and anti-Zionist outlook had produced little more than a
formula expressed in Hutcheson's phrase, 'No Arab, No Jewish State'.
James McDonald noted the rationale in his diary: 'Neither an Arab
nor a Jewish state should be organized because neither people can
justly claim the whole country.'[52] The point is of particular interest
in regard to McDonald because, by virtue of his long experience with
the refugee question, he could claim to be the staunchest pro-Zionist
of all of the committee members. At a critical point in the discussions
(when he threatened to submit a minority report of one), he yielded
on the issue of partition in order to receive assurances on the other
issue of even greater importance to him, the 100,000. Along with
Buxton, Crum, and Crossman, McDonald believed that the tangible
resolution of the refugee question was an immediate imperative, and
that the increase of Jewish population in Palestine would ultimately
help to tip the balance in favour of a Jewish state. This was a basic
Zionist assumption (though not one that commanded universal agreement). Eliahu Epstein, the representative of the Jewish Agency in

---

[51] Report by Arthur Lourie, 21 Apr. 1946, CZA Z6/18/1.
[52] See especially the entry for 1 Apr. 1946, McDonald Diary.

Washington, wrote that everything would depend on 'the successful transfer of a maximum number of Jews to Palestine within a minimum of time'.[53] The pro-Zionists within the committee endorsed that line of thought. The more metaphysical concept of a Jewish state would be realized in due course.

Ben-Gurion, for one, believed that the creation of a Jewish state was even more important than the 100,000. This point is significant for the present discussion because Crossman, who played such an important part as conciliator in the clash between the British and American points of view, worked on the false assumption that the binational solution might help to buoy up Weizmann's influence and what Crossman considered to be a less extreme outlook. Albert Hourani proved to be a much more astute contemporary analyst when he pointed out that the initiative within the Zionist movement had already passed to Ben-Gurion and that 'the "moderates" and "extremists" do not [now] really differ in anything but tactics'.[54] As Michael Cohen has written, Crossman's ideas reflected 'the naïveté of a recent convert to the cause'.[55] Crossman was also misguided in believing that Attlee and Bevin would sympathize with his intellectual acrobatic performance that had, after all, done much to produce a unanimous recommendation. They were well aware that he was responsible for the drafting of the Palestine part of the report, and that the proposals for the Americans to accept specific responsibilities remained vague in the extreme.

Crossman commended the report to Attlee as a fair-minded compromise that did not jeopardize British interests and that would clear the way to a permanent settlement.

> I cannot help seeing this report, if adopted by you, as a useful, indeed necessary, step to an ultimate partition. This report tells the Jews once and for all that even six Americans [biased in their favour] cannot after examining the facts recommend a Jewish State over the whole of Palestine. It knocks on the head the extreme claims of the Jews. But similarly it also disposes of the extreme demands of the Arabs for an immediate Arab State in the whole of Palestine.[56]

Though the Palestine mission had been mentally and emotionally enervating, Crossman was pleased with the result. He wrote a few months later: 'Ingenuously we believed that it was now only a matter of weeks before the displaced persons would be on the boats.'[57]

Crossman's disillusionment came quickly. On the same day as the

[53] Epstein to Shertok, 25 Jan. 1946, CZA S25/6618.
[54] 'Middle East Study Group', 17 May 1946, RIIA.
[55] Cohen, *Palestine and the Great Powers*, p. 107.
[56] Crossman, *Palestine Mission*, p. 187. He omitted the bracketed phrase in the published version.
[57] *Palestine Mission*, p. 184.

release of the report, the 30th of April 1946, President Truman announced that he accepted the committee's recommendation that the 100,000 Jewish refugees should be admitted to Palestine. But he gave no indication that the United States would help to implement the other nine-tenths of the report. Crossman was dismayed that the President had queered the entire Palestinian pitch. 'Mr. Truman precipitately welcomed the Committee's recommendation that 100,000 certificates should at once be issued', he lamented in the *New Statesman*, 'but showed no readiness to offer American assistance.'[58] Attlee was incensed that Truman, not for the first time, had taken a portentous step without consulting him. At this particular juncture renewed Jewish terrorism in Palestine also preoccupied him. The day after Truman's *obiter dictum* he stated in the House of Commons that the British government would not proceed until the 'private armies' in Palestine were disbanded. 'Jews and Arabs in Palestine alike must disarm immediately.'[59] In two strokes within two days the President and the Prime Minister cut the work of the committee into shambles.

It wounded Crossman to learn that the Prime Minister disapproved of the report. 'I was much depressed by hearing . . . that I and my colleagues had let you down so badly', he wrote to Attlee, 'and had produced a Report which was, in your view, "grossly unfair to Great Britain" .' In fact Crossman had been labouring under the illusion that the Cabinet wanted a unanimous report that would reconcile the differences between Britain and the United States.

> I cannot help feeling that you are a little unfair to us. When we were appointed no indication was given to us whatsoever that you desired us to push responsibility on to America. . . . At a lunch given to the Committee in London, the Foreign Secretary stated unequivocally that, if the Committee reached unanimity, he himself would carry the Report into effect. He made no reference whatsoever to American assistance being a *sine qua non*.

Crossman's jeremiad concluded with a moral injunction that Attlee must have found annoying. Unless a firm stand were at last taken then the British would drift into an Anglo-Jewish war as disastrous as the one that preceded the birth of the Irish Free State.

> I believe that morally we are bound to rescue those Jews in Europe, and let them go to the only place which will welcome them, the National Home. I believe that militarily this can be done with the minimum risk of bloodshed if we are firm and show the Arabs that we mean business. But equally I am convinced that the Labour Government which has consistently supported Zionism and denounced

[58] 11 May 1946. For the American side of the controversy at this time, see USSD 867N.01 Box 6754. For the extensive British Cabinet papers, see CAB 129/9 and CAB 133/83.

[59] *Parliamentary Debates* (Commons), 1 May 1946, c. 197.

the White Paper, cannot go back on its word in the face of this unanimous Report without causing the very bloodshed you are so anxious to avoid, and also performing what must be a deeply dishonourable action.[60]

Attlee did not respond in kind. He merely summarized for Crossman the reason for his anger. 'I am sorry if I appeared to you to be unfair to the Commission. . . . My annoyance is with the Americans who forever lay heavy burdens on us without lifting a little finger to help.'[61]

[60] Crossman to Attlee, 7 and 9 May, Crossman Papers; PREM 8/302.

[61] Attlee to Crossman, 9 May 1946, Crossman Papers. It should perhaps be added that Crossman's part in the committee and his outspoken criticism of British policy infuriated Bevin. He refused to talk to Crossman about the publication of *Palestine Mission*. 'Nothing I can say will make him alter his ideas about Palestine which derive from his lack of judgement and his intellectual arrogance', Bevin wrote to Attlee. 'I will, however, get [Harold] Beeley in my Department who was one of the Secretaries of the Anglo-American Committee to see Crossman informally. He may be able to get him to add certain sobering facts to the book but I have no hope of anyone persuading Crossman to alter his line of argument or to omit any passages he is bent on inserting however damaging they may be to H. M. G.' (27 Sept. 1946, PREM 8/302. For Foreign Office criticism of Crossman and his explanations of various parts of the report see FO 371/52524.) Crossman's obituary in *The Times* (6 Apr. 1974) noted Attlee's 'profound distrust of him'. His involvement in Palestine certainly did not inspire the Prime Minister's confidence or launch his Parliamentary career on a stable course.

3

THE EVOLUTION OF AMERICAN
POLICY AND THE QUEST FOR
A BINATIONAL STATE

TRUMAN may have been unsophisticated in international affairs, but he quickly adopted an approach to the Palestine question that enabled him ultimately to steer, from his point of view, a successful though tempestuous course between the whirlpools of Zionism and British imperialism. To his domestic Jewish constituency he persistently expressed compassion for the refugees. At the same time he resisted commitments that might alienate the Arabs and jeopardize the supply of Middle Eastern oil. To the British he revealed a characteristic American suspicion of imperialism and the usual British 'stunt' of deviousness and delay. If any one thing was clear in his mind it was the necessity to avoid being sucked into Middle Eastern troubles that would involve American troops. To Zionist leaders he publicly indicated a willingness to resolve simultaneously the problems of the displaced persons and the Jewish national home, but in fact he offered tangible American assistance only in the form of transport for the 100,000 to Palestine. He resented Zionist pressure, but he never forgot that the three million Jews of New York constituted the largest metropolitan Jewish population in the entire world and that their vote might be decisive in a national election. Like Bevin, Truman had a remarkable capacity for occasional indiscreet and honest comment. When asked for an explanation of his pro-Jewish policy he once replied: 'I have to answer to hundreds of thousands who are anxious for the success of Zionism; I do not have hundreds of thousands of Arabs in my constituents.'[1]

Truman wanted to be the master of his own Palestine policy, but

---

[1] William A. Eddy, *F. D. R. Meets Ibn Saud* (New York, American Friends of the Middle East, 1954), p. 37. For an evaluation of the importance of the New York vote see Ganin, *Truman, American Jewry*, pp. 179–80, and Snetsinger, *Truman, the Jewish Vote, passim.* Beyond the question of the Jewish vote, there can be no doubt that Truman was influenced by intimates who held Zionist views. His former business associate in Kansas City, Eddie Jacobson, was a Jew. Jacobson on one occasion wrote to him: 'Again I am appealing to you in behalf of my People. The future of one and one-half million Jews in Europe depends on what happens at the present. . . . In all this World, there is only one place where they can go —and that is Palestine. You and I know only too well this is the only answer' (Jacobson to Truman, 3 Oct. 1947, President's Secretary's Files, Truman Library). Truman had a warm heart that could sometimes be stirred by such personal appeals of old friends.

he faced not only conflicting demands within his administration but also the contradictory pledges given by his inimitable predecessor. F. D. R.'s right hand had promised sympathy for the Jewish national home while his left hand conveyed assurances that he would take no action 'which might prove hostile to the Arab people'. In his famous conversation with King Ibn Saud on the return from Yalta, Roosevelt had confirmed a growing impression that the Arabs would not yield on the question of Jewish immigration. In Ibn Saud's words, the United States would be compelled to choose between 'an Arab land of peace and quiet or a Jewish land drenched in blood'.[2] Roosevelt perhaps had a postgrave laugh. As a legacy to Truman he had left probably the most irresolvable dilemma of the 1940s. Perhaps it would have baffled even his own political ingenuity. It is arguable that he would have responded basically as Truman did, though his actions would have been characterized by an effervescent self-confidence and with a command over the bureaucracy that his successor lacked. Truman acted precipitately yet consistently. He did not systematically follow the same advice, nor did he develop a coherent set of ideas. The theme of continuity may be found in his concern for the Jewish vote and his reluctance to commit American troops. To Truman's critics he appeared to lunge from crisis to crisis, and in the spring of 1948 he did in effect lose control of American policy towards Palestine; but when he regained it he acted decisively in favour of partition with results comparable to F. D. R.'s great triumphs in world politics.

Truman by no means had a grasp comparable to Attlee's over rival bureaucratic factions or over general policy. Attlee sometimes disagreed with Bevin but he relied on him to master the complexities of the Palestine issues in conjunction with the Colonial Office and the Chiefs of Staff. The committee system functioned; the Cabinet made the major decisions; Members of Parliament in both Houses in turn gave full expression of their views. Half of the British delegation on the Anglo-American Committee of Inquiry were Members of Parliament. By contrast on the American side there was no major political figure.[3] Within the American government there existed no standing inter-departmental committee to give sustained attention to Palestine, nor did the President delegate responsibility to co-ordinate the views of the State Department and the Joint Chiefs of Staff. In 1945–6 the State-Navy-War Coordinating Committee gave

[2] *Foreign Relations 1945*, VIII, p. 687.

[3] For an explanation of the American appointments see Dinnerstein, *Survivors of the Holocaust*, p. 83. Byrnes wrote to Truman: 'It really is not a friendly service to a Senator or Congressman to appoint him to this Commission.'

the problem only perfunctory attention. Intelligence reports contained information that could be gleaned from major newspapers. The Secretary of State took only an erratic interest in the matter. Dean Acheson as Under Secretary in effect presided over American Palestine policy and attempted to reconcile the views of the White House staff and the area specialists of the Foreign Service. In London a Foreign Office official reflected on Acheson's uncomfortable position: 'The State Department seems to be caught between its own Middle East representatives and the President's political advisers.'[4]

Given the lack of sustained political control, the power of the American bureaucracy asserted itself. A coherent response to the Palestine problem could be found in the State Department's Office of Near Eastern and African Affairs. The Director of that office was Loy W. Henderson. His general Wilsonian outlook on the Middle East, which Acheson endorsed, can be conveyed in the following sentence written in August 1945: 'the active support by the Government of the United States of a policy favoring the setting up of a Jewish State in Palestine would be contrary to the policy which the United States has always followed of respecting the wishes of a large majority of the local inhabitants with respect to their form of government'.[5] Acheson depended on Henderson for the basic formulation of Middle Eastern policy and described him as an 'entirely loyal and competent officer'.[6] George Kennan wrote of him in his memoirs as a 'man of so active an intelligence, such deep seriousness and impressive sincerity, and such unbending conscientiousness . . . that he left his impression on everyone who was associated with him'.[7] Those estimates were not perfunctory and are important to bear in mind when evaluating the attacks of American Zionists on Henderson as the *éminence grise* responsible for the pro-Arab undertow of the State Department.

   [4] Minute by Beeley, 23 May 1946, FO 371/52525.
   [5] Memorandum by Henderson, Secret, 24 Aug. 1945, USSD 767N.01/8-2445 Box 6731; *Foreign Relations 1945*, VIII, pp. 727-30. For Henderson and other officials of the Office of Near Eastern and African Affairs, see especially Evan Wilson, 'The Palestine Papers, 1943-47', *Journal of Palestine Studies*, II, 4 (Summer 1973). Wilson's service as Palestine desk officer and Assistant Chief of Near Eastern Affairs as well as American Secretary on the Anglo-American Committee placed him in a unique position to comment. He wrote of Henderson: 'His background, prior to going to Iraq [as Minister] had been in Eastern European affairs, and his approach to the problems of the Near East showed a broader perspective than that of many who had concentrated on that one area. He was completely objective and fair in his attitude towards the Palestine question and sincerely interested in finding a solution. In view of this it is ironic, though perhaps inevitable, that he was later so sharply attacked by the Zionists.'
   [6] Dean Acheson, *Present at the Creation* (New York, 1969), p. 170.
   [7] George F. Kennan, *Memoirs 1925-1950* (Boston, 1967), p. 61.

Like the Eastern Department of the Foreign Office, the Office of Near Eastern Affairs reflected the views of official representatives in the Middle East. The Foreign Service officers who served there believed that the 100,000 refugees might lead to unlimited immigration which in turn would transform the Middle East into a violent bloc of anti-American Arab states. Even though motivated by purely humanitarian reasons, Jewish immigration schemes would result in bloodshed and, to recall Roosevelt's ungodly phrase (as he himself used it), 'a Holy Gehad'. Beyond those momentous issues lay the question of American power, which in the Middle East ultimately depended on Arab willingness to co-operate. 'Prestige' and good faith counted for the Americans as well as for the British in the non-European world, and in the Middle East the reputation of the United States, in Henderson's view, had been undermined by promises reminiscent of British pledges during the First World War. 'We feel that our good name is at stake in the Near East', he wrote in October 1945.[8]

During the time of the work of the Committee of Inquiry, Bartley Crum identified Henderson as the key official in the State Department who wished to resolve the Palestine question on the basis of power politics rather than on the overwhelming need to accommodate the Jewish refugees.[9] Henderson, according to Crum, wished to support the Arab cause rather than the legitimate Zionist quest for a national home. He suspected that Henderson had been proselytized by the British Foreign Office and that therefore he held exaggerated fears of Russian expansion in the Middle East.[10] In the course of his

[8] Memorandum by Henderson, 1 Oct. 1945, USSD 867.01/10-145 Box 6752; *Foreign Relations 1945*, VIII, pp. 751-3.

[9] Crum accurately described Henderson as the moving anti-Zionist spirit in the State Department's 'middle level', but he also bore him a grudge for attempting to block his appointment to the committee. Henderson later recalled: 'Crum seemed to me to be a type of left-leaning lawyer who was almost tireless in his search for publicity. He was a member of several "united front" organizations, and was noted for his demagogic speeches. He seemed to me to be the kind of person who would use his membership in a commission of this kind for gaining personal publicity and acclaim rather than for achieving the extremely serious purposes for which the commission had been created. . . . I later learned that Dave Niles and Crum were close friends, and that Niles had suggested Crum's appointment to the President. . . . He was able to get the President's support and Crum was appointed.' Henderson 'Oral History Interview', Truman Library.

[10] 'Some State Department officials', Crum said, 'are captives of the British social lobby in the capital.' They believed the British line that if the gates of Palestine were opened to the Jews then 'the Arabs would flock to the Soviet banner'. Crum emphasized that 'King Ibn Saud of Saudi Arabia, King Farouk of Egypt, and other Arab leaders were as likely to join Premier Stalin as . . . John D. Rockefeller should ask Joe Stalin that he use his good offices with John Snyder to get him a reduction in his income tax'. For Foreign Office evaluation of Crum's comments to the press see FO 371/52548 and 52554. British officials distrusted Crum and therefore were not surprised. The head of the Eastern Department noted merely that he had become 'rather an extreme type of Zionist'.

work on the committee Crum, like other members, had access to a confidential file that contained the contradictory assurances to Arab and Jewish leaders. In August 1946 he publicly admonished the State Department to reveal these 'shocking things' in the American record in the Middle East. At the same time he demanded Henderson's resignation. He failed in his effort to get Henderson fired, but he believed that at least he had focused the public's attention on the source of the trouble in American policy towards Palestine. It was a mistaken judgement. Henderson and his colleagues, for better or worse, did not carry the weight that Crum imagined. One official writing to Henderson in September 1945 gave an accurate description of the fluctuating influence of the Office of Near Eastern Affairs: 'It seems apparent to me that the President (and perhaps Mr. Byrnes as well) have decided to have a go at Palestine negotiations without bringing NEA into the picture for the time being. . . . I see nothing further we can appropriately do for the moment except carry on our current work, answering letters and telegrams, receiving callers, etc., as best we can, pending the time (which will come soon) when the whole thing will be dumped back in our laps.'[11] Another official with a long-standing experience in Middle Eastern affairs, Gordon P. Merriam, later summed up the problem of the State Department in the 1945–8 period: 'We have no long-term Palestine policy. We do have a short-term, open-ended policy which is set from time to time by White House directives.'[12]

The centre of Palestine activity in the White House was the office of David Niles, who served as the President's adviser on minority affairs. With a sense of the historic significance of the possible creation of a Jewish state, Niles in the first years of the Truman administration became increasingly committed to the Zionist cause. Though he was hardly discreet in his dealings with Jewish spokesmen or in his monitoring of the State Department's Palestine business on behalf of the President, he won Truman's trust in part because he kept the more fire-eating Zionists at bay. Judge Samuel I. Rosenman, who along with Niles had been inherited by Truman from Roosevelt, also acted as an important contact with Jewish leaders. Rosenman served as Special Counsel to the President until mid-1946 when he was succeeded by Clark M. Clifford, a young lawyer and former naval officer from Missouri. Rosenman continued to serve as Truman's intermediary (notably with Weizmann), but after that time Clifford's

[11] Comment by the Deputy Director of the Office of Near Eastern and African Affairs, George V. Allen, on memorandum of 26 Sept. 1945, USSD 867N.01/9-2645 Box 6792; *Foreign Relations 1945*, VIII, pp. 745–6 note 42. For Crum's bogus charges about the 'secret file', see Wilson, *Decision on Palestine*, p. 202.

[12] Memorandum by Meriam, 15 July 1948, *Foreign Relations 1948*, V, pp. 1221–2.

star ascended on the Palestine horizon. That particular stellar phenomenon can best be viewed by keeping bearings on the elections of
1948. Niles was another matter. He became so absorbed in the
Zionist cause that Truman himself feared for his emotional stability;
but there was a bond of affection. Niles was among the first whom
the President notified of Israeli recognition in May 1948. Two years
earlier, after the conclusion of the work of the Committee of Inquiry,
Niles had played an instrumental part in Truman's unilateral acceptance of the committee's recommendation of admitting the 100,000
Jewish refugees into Palestine, and in urging the President to postpone action on the rest of the report.

It is important to note some of the details of the Niles–Crum
connection in order to understand the furious British response to
Truman's re-emphasis on the 100,000. In the last days of the committee's work in Switzerland, Crum telephoned the White House to
tell Niles that, though he could not speak freely because 'his wires
were being tapped' by the British secret service, the committee
would probably recommend unanimously the admittance of the
100,000 to Palestine. Niles then prepared a telegram to be sent to
the committee by Truman again reiterating the importance of the
refugees. The American chairman used it to advantage in bringing
the committee to a unanimous conclusion and establishing the
100,000 as the foremost recommendation. Crum, on his return to
the United States in late April, together with James McDonald met
Rabbi Abba Hillel Silver, who commanded the activist leadership of
the American Zionist movement. Silver intended to denounce the
report because it failed to endorse a Jewish state. Crum and McDonald
warned Silver that such an attack would merely stir up Truman's
wrath against Zionism. They persuaded Silver that the best way of
dealing with the report would be to persuade Truman to accept the
part dealing with the 100,000 and postpone decision on the other
points. Crum took a draft along those lines to David Niles at the
White House. Truman then made the declaration that irritated the
British, agitated the Arabs, and mollified the American Jews.[13]

The British, in particular Bevin, became all the more infuriated
when they learned of Truman's slapdash procedure. Bevin had given
forewarning that he would not be dictated to on the subject of the
100,000. Two days before Truman's announcement, in a conversation with H. Freeman Matthews (the Director of the Office of European Affairs in the State Department), he stated that he would go
along with the recommendation about the refugees but that, of

[13] See Niles to Connelly, 16 Apr. 1946, Truman Library; Ganin, *Truman, American
Jewry*, pp. 60-4, which is based on the Silver Papers. Cf. Crum, *Silken Curtain*, chap. 20.

course, they could not all be admitted to Palestine at the same time. His remarks revealed his increasing irritation at the Jews. What worried him most, Bevin said, 'was the fact that the Jews are acquiring large supplies of arms, most of them with money furnished by American Jews, and are in a very aggressive frame of mind'. He went on to emphasize the British military burden in Palestine and the danger of Russian intervention:

> At present he is forced to retain four Divisions there and this cannot go on indefinitely. He realizes that after British withdrawal there might be Russian penetration in the area and that it would weaken the whole situation in the Middle East, but he sees little hope of any improvement unless we accept a share of the responsibility.[14]

Above all Bevin complained about the belligerent attitude of the Jews and the consequent damage to Anglo-American relations. 'The Jews through their aggressive attitude were "poisoning relations between our two peoples".' To American ears, at least, Bevin's remarks had a distinct anti-Jewish ring. In any case even before the publication of the committee's report, Bevin generously distributed the blame for its shortcomings between the Jews and the Americans.

Although it is not in chronological sequence it is important to grasp a development in Bevin's anti-Jewish outlook from the time of the debate about the 100,000 in the summer of 1946. It cast an increasing shadow over the controversy from then onwards. Bevin later claimed that Truman, not he, had rejected the magnificent opportunity offered by the Anglo-American report. His version of the story differed entirely from the American. The divergent accounts are in fact so blatant that one cannot but be reminded of the British and American controversy over the Manchurian crisis in the 1930s when Henry L. Stimson stated that 'the British let us down'. In the aftermath of Stimson's provocative comment, myth became mixed with historical reality; and in 1946 there developed a similar mixture of historical truth and mythical exaggeration. It reached its most pronounced form in an account by James G. McDonald, the non-Jewish Zionist who had served on the Anglo-American committee. McDonald met Bevin for the second time in London in 1948 on his way to Israel as the first American ambassador. It seemed hard to believe that the two of them could refer to the same historical episode of the committee's report with such a vastly different recollection of the facts. Bevin said:

[14] Memorandum by Matthews, 27 Apr. 1946, *Foreign Relations 1946*, VII, pp. 587–8.

I did give an unequivocal pledge that I would accept the report if it were un-animous. I gave it, and I kept it. There were ten points in your program. I accepted all ten. President Truman accepted only one.[15]

McDonald responded to Bevin's comment with powerful emotions:

I was aghast. For the moment I felt as if I had heard the echo of Hitler's words about telling a big lie. For the truth in this matter was exactly the con-trary. If any fact was beyond dispute, it was the fact that Bevin had rejected virtually all of them.[16]

Bevin's anger mounted as he recalled that 'the fault was all President Truman's':

Facing Bevin across his broad table, I had to tell myself that this was not Hitler seated before me, but His Majesty's Principal Secretary of State for Foreign Affairs. . . . By this time he was in full swing and turned his attack upon the Jews. What extraordinary demagoguery! Banging his fist on the table, at times almost shouting, he charged that the Jews were ungrateful for what Britain had done for them in Palestine, that they had wantonly shot British police and soldiers, hanged sergeants, and now were alienating British opinion by their attitude toward Arab refugees.[17]

McDonald's later reflections on Bevin may be taken as the extreme indictment against him as the demagogue responsible for Britain's failure in Palestine. 'Did he believe his own diatribe? It is impossible to be certain; but I am almost sure that he had genuinely talked him-self into the belief that his failure was the fault of President Truman. His bitterness against Mr. Truman was almost pathological: it found its match only in his blazing hatred for his other scapegoats—the Jews.'[18] McDonald's account in short represents the demonological

[15] James G. McDonald, *My Mission in Israel 1948–1951* (New York, 1951), pp. 24–6.

[16] Ibid. Bevin was technically correct in maintaining that he never formally rejected the committee's report, but there is telling evidence from unimpeachable sources that he committed himself unequivocally at the luncheon with the members of the committee to acceptance of the report if it were unanimous. For example Sir Douglas Harris recorded: 'The Foreign Secretary in his speech at the lunch given by him to the Committee, announced that he intended to accept the Committee's recommendations. . . .' (Minute by Harris, 7 Feb. 1946, CO 537/1759.) Writers from the American vantage point have emphasized Bevin's rejection of the report as a turning point in the Zionist movement. For example: 'A furious Bevin refused to accept the report, and in so doing profoundly affected Jewish history. By reneging on his word, he alienated an American President, wiped out the last traces of moderation within the Zionist leadership, and created a set of circum-stances that made the establishment of Israel possible.' Melvin I. Urofsky, *We Are One! American Jewry and Israel* (Garden City, NY 1978), p. 112.

[17] McDonald, *Mission in Israel*, pp. 24–6.

[18] Ibid. McDonald told the Israeli Ambassador in London, I. J. Linton, that he had failed to have any real exchange of ideas with Bevin but that 'the interview had been useful, because it had given him an insight into the atmosphere of the Foreign Office'. (Linton to Shertok, Secret, 4 Aug. 1948, ISA 93.04/37/12.) The Foreign Office record of this conversa-tion is much subdued in comparison, though it does emphasize Bevin making the point 'that the Jews were treating them [the Arab refugees] as they themselves had been treated by the Nazis'. (F. O. minute, 3 Aug. 1948, FO 371/68578).

interpretation of Bevin and Britain in Middle Eastern history. It
gained increasing American acceptance during and after the summer
of 1946.

Bevin's contemporary biographer, who knew his moods, wrote
that Truman's reiterated demand for the 100,000 threw him into one
of his 'blackest rages'.[19] In the aftermath of the Anglo-American
Committee of Inquiry, his American and Zionist critics branded his
remarks at the Labour Party conference at Bournemouth in June
1946 as an example of unbridled bigotry. 'There has been the agitation', Bevin said on that notable occasion, 'and particularly in New
York, for 100,000 Jews to be put into Palestine.' He stressed New
York at the risk of making a racial slur on the domestic troubles of
another country. These remarks in particular acquired lasting
notoriety: 'I hope I will not be misunderstood in America if I say
that this [100,000] was proposed with the purest of motives. They
did not want too many Jews in New York.' Lest his message be misunderstood, Bevin a few days later initialled a cautionary statement
by the Foreign Office emphasizing that his remarks about the New
York Jews should not be taken out of the context of 'an exceedingly
delicate and complex problem'. He had after all made a number of
positive points as well. He had urged Jew and Arab to 'please put
your guns away'. He had admonished the Jews not 'to blow up the
British Tommy, who is quite innocent in this matter'. In another
remark aimed directly at the Jews he said that anti-British violence
in Palestine merely stirred up 'another phase of anti-Semitic feeling'.
He also said emphatically that 'if we put 100,000 Jews into Palestine
tomorrow I will have to put another division of British troops there.
I am not prepared to do it.'[20] When the Foreign Office circulated his
Bournemouth remarks so that they could be read in 'context', Bevin
did not mean to retract. He meant what he said, and his warning was
clear. 'Your criticism of New York', the British Ambassador reported,
'has, of course, not only hit the nail on the head but driven it
woundingly deep.' In Bevin's own words, 'We have made our position
clear.'[21]

[19] Francis Williams, *Ernest Bevin* (London, 1952), p. 260.

[20] Bevin consistently took the line that, if the 100,000 were sent to Palestine, he would
request up to four divisions of American troops to assist in keeping order. His estimate was
calculated to shock the Americans but was not out of line with British military estimates
or for that matter the figure of over 100,000 troops estimated by the American Joint Chiefs
of Staff as the number necessary to enforce the peace (*Foreign Relations 1948*, V, p. 800).
For an incisive comment on the military problem see Sir John Bagot Glubb, *A Soldier with
the Arabs* (London, 1957), p. 58: 'It was a question of how many divisions of troops would
have been necessary to fight a three-cornered civil war against Jews and Arabs simultaneously.'

[21] Inverchapel to Bevin, 13 June 1946; minute by Bevin, 14 June 1946, FO 371/52529.

Bevin delivered his Bournemouth speech after he had presided over British Palestine policy for nearly a year. During that time he had become exasperated at Jewish lack of co-operation with what he believed to be reasonable plans for compromise. His frustration had now reached new heights. Bevin's critics pointed out that his style of politics frequently combined fertile expediency with obstinate bullying. In any case his domineering personality often enabled him to get his way, but in the instance of Palestine the Zionists refused to be cowed. From his point of view, if the Jews succeeded in establishing an independent state it would destroy the chance of a lasting peace in the Middle East and thus would wreck his plans, in the phrase he used at Bournemouth, for a 'not quite Churchillian' *Pax Britannica* based on alliances with the Arab states. There was a further dimension to Jewish interference with his long-range calculations. To preserve British overlordship in the Middle East, Bevin needed the economic underwriting, and, if necessary, military support of the United States. The Jews in his eyes now threatened to poison his relations with the Americans, not to mention the Arabs.

Truman understood Bevin's aims. He refused to be drawn into far-reaching economic and military commitments in Palestine that in his view did not have an immediate bearing on the security of the United States. He noted Bevin's anger at the New York Zionists' promotion of illegal immigration and the supply of arms to terrorist groups. So long as Bevin did not bring him personally into the fray or insult the office of the Presidency, Truman had a politican's respect for Bevin's tactics and a sympathy with his frustration. He told a group of Zionists shortly after the Bournemouth speech that he 'did not regard the Bevin statement about New York agitation as being an insult to him or to the American people. He said he understands Bevin having "blown up" because he is often tempted "to blow up" himself because of the pressure and the agitation from New York.'[22]

Bevin's implicit but nevertheless blatant criticism of the United States for refusing to increase the Jewish immigration quota did not fall on deaf ears. Truman tried to provide more flexibility. He unsuccessfully broached the possibility of a change in immigration legislation with Congressional leaders. He also took immediate steps to implement the report of the Anglo-American committee by appointing a Cabinet committee consisting of the Secretaries of State, Treasury, and War, with 'alternates' who would conduct

---

[22] Ganin, *Truman, American Jewry*, p. 75, quoting a letter that conveyed the results of the interview to Rabbi Silver.

negotiations with the British. In London Attlee and Bevin were prepared to make concessions if at last the Americans would agree to definite points of co-operation. The timing was inauspicious. Following the publication of the committee's report, renewed terrorism broke out in Palestine. On the 22nd of July the Irgun Zvai Leumi blew up the British military headquarters at the King David Hotel in Jerusalem, with heavy loss of British, Arab, and Jewish life.

The explosion at the King David may be described as an atrocity or historical necessity, depending on one's attitude towards 'terrorists' or 'freedom-fighters'. The controversy here, and in a larger sense about the legitimate motives of terrorists, will never be resolved. But it can be understood. The extreme Zionists believed that violence was the only effective means to force British evacuation. Others hoped that a peaceful solution might still be possible. President Truman expressed the outrage of those who believed in the principle of non-violence when he made a dubious prediction: 'such acts of terrorism will not advance, but, on the contrary, might well retard the efforts that are being made . . . to bring about a peaceful solution of this difficult [problem].'[23] It is however a melancholy fact that the blowing up of the British military headquarters polarized the Palestine conflict. Everyone in the British civil administration or army had a friend or acquaintance who had been killed at the King David. For the Zionists it became a symbol of effective, if lamentable, political violence. Among the British it stirred up powerful and conflicting emotions that terrorism should be repressed and, at the same time, that they should quit Palestine because of Jewish ingratitude. The Chief of the Imperial General Staff, Field Marshal Bernard Montgomery, wrote two days after the incident: 'We shall show the world and the Jews that we are not going to submit tamely to violence.'[24] Churchill, on the other hand, represented a wide current of public thought when he questioned the wisdom of further loss of British life in Palestine. The blowing up of the King David explains much about the public mood about Palestine in the summer of 1946. Emotions were running high.

When the House of Commons met to debate Palestine on the 31st of July–1st August, Attlee was in Paris and Bevin was ill. Herbert Morrison opened the debate. Though he only hinted at it in his speech, he had learned only that morning that Truman had

---

[23] See Byrnes to Harriman, 23 July 1946, USSD 867N.01/7–2346 Box 6756; *Foreign Relations 1946*, VII, p. 651. For the event itself see Thurston Clarke, *By Blood and Fire: The Attack on the King David Hotel* (New York, 1981). For full discussion of the Jewish side and the tension in the Yishuv between the terrorist organizations, the Haganah, and the Jewish leaders, see Cohen, *Palestine and the Great Powers*, chap. 4.

[24] Montgomery to Dempsey, 'Personal and Top Secret', 24 July 1946, WO 216/194.

again stultified the most recent—and, as it turned out, the last—effort to resolve the Palestine problem by joint action of Britain and the United States. The debate therefore reads as if most of the participants had a grasp of the essentials at least one step removed from reality. It is nevertheless useful to study the general discussion before delving into the complex negotiations. The debate distilled with simple clarity what most observers regarded as the bewildering circumstances of British withdrawal from Palestine. Churchill attacked the Labour government but he also rose above party politics to meditate on the significance of Palestine and the destiny of the British Empire. Richard Crossman wrote that Churchill indeed 'made one of the most remarkable speeches of his career'.[25]

Churchill's oration stands as a noteworthy postwar commentary on the impending collapse of the British Empire as well as the problems of the Middle East. He analysed the problem of Palestine in relation to Egypt and India. He conveyed a wealth of personal and historical knowledge. He spoke of his commitment to Zionism since the time of the First World War. He made distinctions between mandatory responsibility in Palestine, treaty rights in Egypt, and sovereign power in India. And, not least, he brought clarity to the general confusion of thought about Palestine and the problem of displaced persons in Europe. It is important to bear in mind the chronological circumstances. At the time that Churchill spoke the '100,000' were still interned in displaced-person camps. He still reeled from the 'great personal shock' of Attlee's announcement of withdrawal from Egypt proper into the Canal Zone. He had not yet reconciled himself to the loss of India, and the great political acceleration towards the transfer of power in India had not yet occurred.

Churchill held common ground with Bevin that Palestine would not provide a solution to the problem of Jewish refugees. He spoke without danger of being denounced as an anti-Jewish bigot. His comments defied basic Zionist doctrine. The principal solution to the problem of displaced persons, he said, would have to be found in Europe, not Palestine. The 100,000 merely symbolized a humanitarian gesture (and Churchill well knew its use for political purposes in the United States). The point is important because many people at the time believed that the 100,000 at one stroke would solve the refugee problem. Churchill contemptuously dismissed that possibility.

No one can imagine that there is room in Palestine for the great masses of Jews who wish to leave Europe, or that they could be absorbed in any period which it is now useful to contemplate. The idea that the Jewish problem could

[25] Crossman, *Palestine Mission*, p. 197.

be solved or even helped by a vast dumping of the Jews of Europe into Palestine is really too silly to consume our time in the House this afternoon.

I am not absolutely sure that we should be in too great a hurry to give up the idea that European Jews may live in the countries where they belong. . . . It is quite clear . . . that this crude idea of letting all the Jews of Europe to go into Palestine has no relation either to the problem of Europe or to the problem which arises in Palestine.[26]

Churchill emphasized the unfair position of Britain bearing the brunt of Zionist attacks while 'the United States . . . sat on the sidelines and criticised our shortcomings with all the freedom of perfect detachment and irresponsibility'. His logic led him to conclude, as he had previously, that, if the United States would not share the administrative and military burden of the Palestine mandate, Britain should hand it over to the United Nations. If he had refined that point he would probably have been entirely in agreement with the Prime Minister, the Foreign Secretary, and the Colonial Secretary. The British did not want actual American interference in administrative and military affairs in Palestine, but as a matter of urgency they needed economic assistance and the guarantee of military support if the Palestine conflict spread to other areas of the Middle East.

Churchill dwelt on the insignificance of Palestine within the British Empire. It was, he stated, a 'country with which we have no connection or tradition and where we have no sovereignty as in India and no treaty as in Egypt'. By the 'precipitate abandonment' of Egypt the Labour government had infused a strategic importance into the Palestine issue that Churchill regarded as a calamitous blunder. By contemplating Palestine as a strategic base to protect the Suez Canal, the British would merely revive profound suspicions of British imperialism throughout the world.

What the Government have done in Egypt . . . has greatly weakened our moral position in Palestine by stripping us of our disinterestedness in that country. . . . the moment [we become] . . . dependent upon Palestine for a base from which to defend the Suez Canal, we should greatly hamper all possibility of obtaining American co-operation.[27]

Churchill wanted to avoid the accusation of 'a national strategic motive' for staying on in Palestine that would undermine Britain's moral support of moderate Zionism. He also believed that there had

---

[26] *Parliamentary Debates* (Commons), 1 Aug. 1946, cols. 1246–57. In the course of his remarks in that regard Churchill made one comment that will continue to provoke historical controversy: 'I must say that I had no idea, when the war came to an end, of the horrible massacres which had occurred; the millions and millions that had been slaughtered. That dawned on us gradually after the struggle was over.'

[27] Ibid.

been a grave miscalculation: a strategic base in Palestine would provide only ephemeral security.

Churchill concluded with a general assessment of the state of the British Empire. His comments revealed a sense of Imperial priorities and the crisis of mid-1946:

Take stock round the world at the present moment; after all we are entitled to survey the whole field. We declare ourselves ready to abandon the mighty Empire and Continent of India with all the work we have done in the last 200 years, territory over which we possess unimpeachable sovereignty. The Government are, apparently, ready to leave the 400 million Indians to fall into all the horrors of sanguinary civil war—civil war compared to which anything that could happen in Palestine would be microscopic; wars of elephants compared with wars of mice.

Indeed we place the independence of India in hostile and feeble hands, heedless of the dark carnage and confusion which will follow. We scuttle from Egypt which we twice successfully defended from foreign massacre and pillage. We scuttle from it, we abandon the Canal zone about which our treaty rights were and still are indefeasible; but now, apparently, the one place where we are at all costs and at all inconveniences to hold on and fight it out to the death is Palestine, and we are to be at war with the Jews of Palestine, and, if necessary, with the Arabs of Palestine. For what reason? Not, all the world will say, for the faithful discharge of our long mission but because we have need, having been driven out of Egypt, to secure a satisfactory strategic base from which to pursue our Imperial aims.[28]

Churchill hoped that the newspaper reports of yet another Anglo-American impasse over Palestine were not true. If the United States would not co-operate, then he believed that the British government should make a clear-cut decision: 'we should now give notice that we will return our Mandate to U. N. O. and that we will evacuate Palestine within a specified period'. He made a final point that is vital in understanding the Palestine crisis in the summer of 1946. It was one of his insistent arguments: 'It is far more important that there should be agreement [between Britain and the United States] than that there should be this or that variant of the . . . various schemes of partition or cantonisation which have been put forward.'[29]

The belief in the need for an Anglo-American consensus on Palestine was shared by the President's delegation, who represented the Cabinet committee, as well as by the British Cabinet, the Colonial Office, and the Foreign Office. There was a sense of urgency to the negotiations of mid-1946. Truman attached such importance to the success of the mission that he arranged for its members to be flown to London in his private airplane, the *Sacred Cow*. They had arrived on the 12th of July. The head of the delegation was Henry F. Grady, who had no previous Palestine experience but was regarded as an

[28] Ibid.   [29] Ibid.

experienced negotiator. He had served on the mission to observe the Greek elections. He was well aware of the military and economic dilemmas facing the British. His two colleagues, Goldthwaite Dorr (War Department) and Herbert Gaston (Treasury) also did not possess any expertise on Palestine. They conceived of their mission as gaining British acquiescence in the 100,000 and, if possible, agreement on the future government of Palestine. They would implement, in other words, the general recommendations of the Anglo-American committee. They found the British in a conciliatory mood, ready, as Churchill hoped, to reach an understanding rather than quarrel about details.

Both the American delegation and the Zionists had ideas about partition versus a binational state, but neither had plans that had any remote chance of being accepted by all parties concerned. The Colonial Office did. Its principal author was Sir Douglas Harris (regarded by the Zionists as a *bête noire*), who had refined his ideas during his years of service in Palestine and in London at the Colonial Office as the principal Palestine expert. It had been presented to the members of the Anglo-American Committee in January 1946 and had been rejected by them as an unacceptable compromise because it fell far short of Zionist aspirations. Six months later it received attention because it appeared to be (as indeed it was) the last chance for the British and Americans to reach agreement. It became known as the Morrison–Grady plan (after Herbert Morrison, who introduced it in the House of Commons, and Henry Grady, whose name was associated with it as leader of the American delegation).

The central element of the Morrison–Grady plan was ambiguity. It could be read as a step towards partition or a binational state. Its principal features were reminiscent of constitutional dyarchy in India, but it was a classic Colonial Office solution applied to the unique problem of Palestine. There would be provincial autonomy with certain powers reserved to the central administering authority (Britain as the trusteeship power would be the 'administering authority' for an indefinite period). As Herbert Morrison explained it in simple terms to the House of Commons, there would be a Jewish province and an Arab province, together with a district of Jerusalem and a district of the largely uninhabited desert territory of the Negev. The central government would have reserved powers over foreign relations, defence, justice, and taxation. There would be development of representative institutions that would lead to self-government in the grand Colonial Office tradition. Final control over immigration would rest with the central government which would authorize provincial requests for immigrants up to absorptive economic capacity. The government of the Arab province would be able to exclude Jewish immigrants and the Jewish province would have the power to accept them. The existing land regulations would be repealed. The Arab province would have the authority to permit or refuse the purchase of land by Jews. In the Jewish province opportunities for land purchase by Jews would be increased. There would be guarantees for the protection of minorities and for the safeguarding of the Holy Places. The Colonial Office thus offered an immensely complicated prospect of a binational state not far removed from the traditions of Canada and South Africa. At the same time it laid the basis for possible partition.[30]

It is important to note the constraints under which the American delegates responded to the Colonial Office scheme. On the 21st of June the Joint Chiefs of Staff advised Truman that no American troops should be involved in Palestine.[31] Truman so instructed Grady. The President also categorically rejected any possibility of joint-trusteeship. Truman consistently refused to be drawn into military or administrative commitments in Palestine. On the other hand he offered economic aid and a willingness to recommend to Congress the admission of 50,000 refugees into the United States.[32] The political leverage of the American experts was thus slight. Grady was relieved to learn that the British did not insist on military aid or participation in the trusteeship administration. They would on the other hand give wholehearted assistance in the moving of the 100,000 Jews to Palestine. The British, Grady wrote to Henderson, 'have been most reasonable and completely cooperative'.[33] The American delegation, two weeks after arrival in London, reached unanimous agreement with their British colleagues on the 24th of July. Attlee telegraphed to Truman commending the American delegates for 'their energy and co-operative spirit'.[34]

[30] See Colonial Office memorandum, 'Long-Term Policy in Palestine', 8 July 1946, CP (46) 259 CAB 129/11; minutes in FO 371/52537.

[31] Memorandum by the Joint Chiefs of Staff to the State-War-Navy Co-ordinating Committee, 21 June 1946, *Foreign Relations 1946*, VII, pp. 631-3: 'We urge that no U.S. armed forces be involved in carrying out the Committee's recommendations. . . . Such contingents might in theory be of a size to contribute to pacifying the situation *in Palestine*, but we believe that the political shock attending the reappearance of U.S. armed forces in the Middle East would unnecessarily risk such serious disturbances throughout the area as to dwarf any local Palestine difficulties. Such a condition would, among other effects, invalidate entirely any current estimates of required strengths of the Army and Navy. Further, the Middle East could well fall into anarchy and become a breeding ground for world war.'

[32] See 'Memorandum on Matters Regarding Palestine to be Considered Before the London Conference', *Foreign Relations 1946*, VII, pp. 644-5, and Acheson to Harriman, 15 Aug. 1946, ibid., pp. 684-5.

[33] Grady to Henderson, 24 July 1946, USSD 867N.01/7-2446 Box 6756; ibid., p. 652.

[34] Attlee to Truman, 25 July 1946, USSD 867N.01/7-2646 Box 6756; ibid., p. 669; PREM 8/627/3.

Truman was inclined to accept the Morrison–Grady proposal. It is clear that he himself did not master the details of 'cantonization', but generally the scheme struck him as a fair interim solution in the direction of a binational state. (The solution of partition had not yet crystallized in his mind.) Grady however made a fatal mistake. He acquiesced in the British insistence that the 100,000 be linked with the acceptance of the constitutional proposals. The State Department immediately responded that the transfer of the 100,000 would have to begin 'at once' and not depend on the inevitable and exasperating delays of implementing a metaphysical constitution. Truman moreover had begun to feel the political heat of the proposal. Senator Robert A. Taft as the leading Republican with an interest in the subject denounced the plan as a sellout to the British. Even more important, Truman became apprehensive about the New York Democrats who feared political setback in the November elections. In one particularly incendiary interview with James McDonald and the two New York Senators, Truman learned with great irritation that he would go down in history as the co-creator along with Ernest Bevin of a 'ghetto' in Palestine if he followed the advice of his delegates. Truman began to lose patience. When he discussed Palestine with the Cabinet on the 30th of July, he made a remark which in a Bevinesque sort of way revealed his exasperation with the Zionist lobby. He said that he was 'put out' with the Jews: 'Jesus Christ couldn't please them when he was here on earth, so how could anyone expect that I would have any luck?.'[35]

There are conflicting reports of the Cabinet discussions of the 30th of July, to which might be added the following because it captures the drama of the debate and poses one of the great 'might have beens' if the United States had accepted the plan for provincial autonomy in Palestine. It is based on a British account that relates the recollection of Acheson. That morning Truman discussed the various issues with the Cabinet committee consisting of Robert P. Patterson (Secretary of War), John W. Snyder (Secretary of the Treasury), and Acheson (who represented the State Department).

They came to the conclusion that the proposals were sensible, and . . . Acheson represented . . . that the proposals amounted to a viable solution of the problem, and that Jewish and Arab agreement should be obtained by the British and American Governments. He admitted that there would be an outcry from the Zionists in this country, but contended that as there were still two years to run before the 1948 elections, the outcry could be ignored, since the whole business would be forgotten by 1948 if a solution could be obtained right away.

[35] John Morton Blum, ed., *The Price of Vision: The Diary of Henry A. Wallace 1942–1946* (Boston, 1973), p. 607.

After further discussion the President 'acquiesced', but then a message was brought to him. Truman 'emitted an expletive'. He read aloud a telegram from Byrnes, who was discussing the issue in Paris with Attlee.

In it Mr. Byrnes urged that acceptance of the Morrison–Grady proposals would have serious domestic repercussions, asked the President to ignore all telegrams on the subject from Paris which had so far been sent over his signature, and ended by begging the President to make up his mind on his own as to the right course of action.

In spite of Byrnes's telegram the meeting broke up with the understanding that the President would still support the Morrison–Grady plan. There was still hope for a binational state.

After lunch the full Cabinet met to reach a final decision.

Acheson again spoke strongly in favour of the Morrison–Grady proposals, and the Cabinet seemed quite prepared to give them their approval. Just at the end, the President said that he ought perhaps to round off the proceedings by reading Mr. Byrnes's telegram. As soon as he had done so, signs of cold feet became apparent among the more politically minded members of the Cabinet. Mr. Anderson began to express doubts and then Mr. Henry Wallace urged that the Jews should be given the Negeb, since it was a vital factor in the scheme for a Jordan Valley authority. . . .

When a vote was taken, Acheson found himself alone in his support of the Morrison–Grady proposals. . . . if Mr. Byrnes's telegram had arrived only a couple of hours later the Cabinet would almost certainly have approved the Morrison–Grady proposals, in which case the history of the Palestine problem during the last two years would have been far different and much happier.[36]

When Bevin read the account he noted angrily that Byrnes was a 'double crosser'.

The American nails in the Palestinian coffin of provincial autonomy had been hammered in by the members of the Committee of Inquiry when they met with Grady and his colleagues in early August 1946. Bartley Crum set the tone of the discussion when he greeted Grady —'Hello, sucker!'.[37] The members of the committee were generally disappointed, indeed offended, that their report had not been

---

[36] Bromley to Burrows, 'Personal and Secret', 10 June 1948, FO 371/68650. The account of the meeting should be compared with Blum, *Price of Vision*, pp. 606–7; and the reasons given for the decision in Walter Millis, ed., *The Forrestal Diaries* (New York, 1951), pp. 346–7.

[37] Ganin, *Truman, American Jewry*, p. 92. Grady's disillusionment with the entire affair is revealed in his unpublished autobiography, 'Adventures in Diplomacy' (Truman Library.) Judge Hutcheson had prepared the members of the Committee for the meeting with these lines about Henderson and other State Department officials: 'It looks to me as though they have slipped and fallen on their faces. . . .[They assured] me that they would take [our] . . . report as their Bible and insist on its being carried out as a whole. . . . it appears like another case of Satan quoting Scripture to his purpose.' Hutcheson to members of the Committee, 2 Aug. 1946, McDonald Papers.

re-endorsed and resubmitted to the President. They denounced the
Grady delegation as dupes of British imperialism. They found the
delegation guilty of 'ghettoizing' Palestine and surrendering indefinite
political and economic control to the British.[38] The delegation had
failed in their foremost task of the immediate transfer of the 100,000.
They had appeased Bevin.[39] So ended the history of the plan for provincial autonomy, which, if it had been implemented decisively by
the two countries at the end of the Second World War might have
either created a binational state or, perhaps, brought about a more
peaceful partition.

[38] E.g. in the words of James McDonald: 'The stupidity of an American committee
getting itself involved in this sort of ghettoizing of the Jewish community in Palestine is
nearly incomprehensible.' McDonald to Lola Hohn, 30 July 1946, CZA Z4/15440.

[39] The details of the confrontation were leaked to the press, probably by Crum. Drew
Pearson wrote in his column 'Washington Merry-Go-Round' that before the end of the
meeting Acheson 'received one more merciless jab from sharp-tongued, quick-witted Bart
Crum of San Francisco. "Mr. Secretary," said Crum calmly, "I have one question to ask
you. . . . after all you've seen and heard, do you have any faith whatsoever in any promises
the British Foreign Office makes on any subject at any time?" ' According to Pearson,
Acheson did not reply. *Washington Post*, 16 Aug. 1946. In the aftermath of the Morrison–
Grady episode, Truman appears to have taken a philosophical attitude: 'Of course, the
British control Palestine and there is no way of getting the Hundred Thousand Jews in there
unless they want them in. I have done my best to get them in but I don't believe there is
any possible way of pleasing our Jewish friends.' Truman to Edward J. Flynn, 2 Aug. 1946,
President's Secretary's Files Box 184, Truman Papers.

4

FROM YOM KIPPUR 1946 TO BRITISH ATONEMENT IN THE UNITED NATIONS 1947

A FEW weeks after the collapse of the project for a binational state, Truman's statement on the eve of Yom Kippur signified a major change in the direction of his thought. The 4th of October 1946 represented an important date in the history of the Zionist movement and British imperialism in the Middle East. In the summer and autumn of 1946 the breeze of 'partition' developed into what the British Ambassador in Washington, Lord Inverchapel, referred to as a 'whirlwind'. It gained great momentum when Truman on the eve of Congressional elections appeared to give support to 'the creation of a viable Jewish state in control of its own immigration and economic policies in an adequate area of Palestine instead of the whole of Palestine'. The significance of Truman's statement must not be exaggerated because the British government and the Arab states for another year and a half continued to withstand the gale blowing in the direction of a separate state, and Truman himself blew hot and cold. But from that time on the wind of partition could be felt in all major discussions.

The President probably did not grasp all of the nuances of his own statement. If read carefully it could be understood as more in the nature of a plea for compromise than as a full-blown endorsement of partition. To the dismay of the Zionists, who, as will be seen, prepared the statement, the Office of Near Eastern and African Affairs of the State Department had managed to insert the idea that the United States hoped to see a *bridging of the gap* between the British and the Zionist proposals. Nevertheless the American press unanimously emphasized the part about partition, as if this represented the President's stand. 'I must say', wrote Eliahu Epstein, the Jewish Agency representative in Washington, '. . . that not a single newspaper has pointed up this part of the statement [the "bridging of the gap"] and all the headlines carried by the papers read "Truman's Support of a Jewish State".'[1]

Truman's apparent endorsement of a Jewish state occurred at the time of a transformation within the Zionist movement. His shift

[1] Epstein to Goldmann, 9 Oct. 1946, WA.

in attitude was linked with the Goldmann mission of August 1946. Nahum Goldmann, one of the most effective representatives of the Jewish Agency, believed that Zionism faced a military, moral, and diplomatic crisis. In his estimate the tension in Palestine between the British authorities and the Jewish population could erupt into a war that would prove devastating to the Zionist cause. He and other moderate Zionists broke with the extremist aim of establishing a Jewish state in all of Palestine because of the simple statistical fact that the Jews did not constitute a majority. He was sceptical, in the aftermath of the wartime holocaust, about the amount of land the Jews could effectively colonize. He espoused a solution of a Jewish state extending over only part of Palestine that would not, he hoped, be inequitable to the Arabs. Probably no one else could have so effectively argued these ideas other than Weizmann himself. To key figures in the Truman administration Goldmann appeared to be reasonable, practical, and relatively moderate. He was also extremely energetic and persuasive. He offered a way out of the cul-de-sac of American policy in Palestine.

Some of the details of Goldmann's success in attempting to reorient American policy contradict traditional British explanations that Truman's actions were governed by the expediency of domestic politics. Goldmann, through Bartley Crum and David Niles, made contact with Acheson. Goldmann calmly and rationally argued that if the drift in Palestine continued then the terrorists would get the upper hand. There would be war between the British and the Jews. It would have disastrous consequences for the United States as well as Britain. For the United States there would be profound inter-national repercussions as well as the denunciation by the American public of a war against the Jews fought only a few years after the Nazi attempt at extermination. Goldmann believed that this disaster, which seemed well within the realm of possibility to Americans with ambivalent feelings about British imperialism, could be averted by partition. A peaceful solution might be found through the United Nations with the assistance of the United States.

Acheson accepted the basic logic of Goldmann's argument. He put him in touch with the other two members of the Cabinet committee on Palestine, John Snyder and Robert Patterson, and with consider-able persuasion and ingenuity Goldmann also won them over. Gold-mann left it to David Niles and Acheson to put the case before the President. Truman, though well aware of Niles's commitment to Zionism, had basic confidence in him. He believed that Niles had sound political and humanitarian judgement. He also knew that Niles had shielded him from extremists. On this question Truman also relied on Acheson, who was not known for evangelical enthusiasm. Goldmann's solution made sense to Niles and Acheson, and to Truman, because it seemed equitable, because its chances appeared to be as good as any other, and because the creation of a Jewish state would appeal to the American people. Truman accepted it on the 9th of August. Niles for one believed he had witnessed a historic occasion. Afterwards he went to Goldmann's hotel room, threw himself on the bed and shouted in Yiddish, 'If my mother could hear that we are going to have a Jewish state.'[2] Although the Zionists were disappointed with the watered-down version of the President's statement on the eve of Yom Kippur, Niles's emotional outburst had captured a historical moment.

It is helpful to study the British response to Truman's Yom Kippur statement from the vantage point of Attlee and Bevin. Their basic hope had been to close ranks with the Americans by persuading them to agree to a workable and concrete plan of action, in other words provincial autonomy. They were prepared to implement, gradually, the admission of the 100,000, which they thought might have at least a remote chance of Arab acceptance if it could be put forward as a basis of permanent settlement backed by both Britain and the United States. Truman had dealt this general scheme a crippling blow by the refusal to endorse the Morrison–Grady plan. Attlee and Bevin nevertheless went ahead with plans for a major conference to be held with the Jews and the Arabs in the autumn of 1946. The work of the London conference will be discussed later in this chapter. Here the purpose is to illuminate the attitude of Attlee and Bevin towards American policy. They correctly believed that the Zionists were in disarray, at odds over the extremist demand for a Jewish state in all of Palestine. They hoped that the moderates might be brought to negotiate a peaceful settlement if the Americans would hold firm to the solution of a binational state (with the possibility of eventual peaceful partition). The Jews in fact refused to attend the London conference unless granted the acknowledged premiss of a Jewish state. In September at the conference itself the Arabs put forward proposals for a 'democratic' and 'unitary' state that would provide constitutional safeguards for the Jews. The British asked for an adjournment of the conference in order to study the proposals and to persuade the Jews to offer counter-proposals. Then came news of Truman's 'Yom Kippur' speech. Attlee had

---

[2] Ganin, *Truman, American Jewry*, p. 93. The basic story is related in *The Autobiography of Nahum Goldmann: Sixty Years of Jewish Life* (New York, 1969), chap. 20. It is confirmed and supplemented by Ganin, chap. VI, which is based on extensive use of Zionist archival sources. For the key American documents see USSD 867N.01 Boxes 6755-7.

requested that the President delay his speech in order to confer urgently with Bevin, who was away from London. Truman replied that unfortunately he could not wait. His speech drew a rebuke from Attlee that must rank high in memorable exchanges between British Prime Ministers and American Presidents.

'Dear Mr. President', Attlee telegraphed Truman. 'When just on midnight last night I received the text of your proposed statement on Palestine, I asked you at least to postpone its issue for a few hours in order that I might communicate with Mr. Bevin in Paris.' Attlee's commnication conveys not only extreme anger at the lack of American sensitivity to British responsibilities in Palestine but also a sense of exasperation of failing to obtain American co-operation.

> I have received with great regret your letter refusing even a few hours' grace to the Prime Minister of the country which has the actual responsibility for the government of Palestine in order that he might acquaint you with the actual situation and the probable results of your action.
>
> These may well include the frustration of the patient efforts to achieve a settlement and the loss of still more lives in Palestine.
>
> I am astonished that you did not wait to acquaint yourself with the reasons for the suspension of the Conference with the Arabs. You do not seem to have been informed that so far from negotiations having been broken off, conversations with leading Zionists with a view to their entering the Conference were proceeding with good prospects of success.
>
> I shall await with interest to learn what were the imperative reasons which compelled this precipitancy.[3]

It did not amuse Attlee and Bevin to learn that Truman made the statement on the eve of Yom Kippur (with no mention of the Congressional elections) for the reason that the Jewish people on their

---

[3] The flawless handwritten draft of Attlee's letter, which still radiates white-heat anger, is in PREM 8/627/5. *Foreign Relations 1946*, VII, pp. 704–5. The State Department archives confirm the pro-Zionist attitude of the British Ambassador, Lord Inverchapel (Clark-Kerr), who on the occasion of the Yom Kippur speech told Acheson 'quite confidentially . . . that, while the statement would probably make London very angry, he believed that in the long run it might be beneficial to the solution of the whole question'. Memorandum by Acheson, 3 Oct. 1946, USSD 867N.01/10–346. A comment written privately by Joseph Alsop a year and a half later is remarkable for its perception of the British reaction: 'in 1946 . . . I think the British were sincere in believing they could bring the Jews and Arabs to agree, if the Jewish claims were not raised too high by confidence in all-out American interest. . . . At that time, after all, the Palestine responsibility was British, and we were simply in a position of giving advice from the sidelines. . . . Whether or not Mr. Attlee was right about the prospect for a settlement, it seems to me that Truman's action was utterly inexcusable. For he issued a quite unnecessary statement, for pure purposes of political advantage, in the face of a warning from an Allied chief of state, who was actually responsible for solving the problem, that this statement would torpedo all hope of settlement. . . . the British were really more flicked on the raw by the self-righteousness of the American government (since this was combined with a constant refusal to assume any direct responsibility for the Palestine problem) than they were by the actions of the Jewish terrorists.' Alsop to Frances Gunther, 17 Feb. 1948, Alsop Papers Box 3.

day of atonement 'are accustomed to give contemplation to the lot of the Jewish people' and therefore that he hoped to relieve 'their feeling of depression and frustration'.[4] The officials of the Near Eastern Division of the State Department, who had been hard pressed to find a convincing explanation, could at least congratulate themselves that it was an ingenious reply.[5]

Ernest Bevin's public reaction to the Yom Kippur statement at first was slight. Like most other British observers of American politics, he attributed Truman's apparent endorsement of partition, and the repeated emphasis on increased immigration, as a pandering to the Jews of New York and the Democratic party machine. 'Policy is being run from New York and how can I deal with American nationals?' he once exclaimed.[6] Bevin had an exaggerated view of the power of the New York Jews over Truman and a much less sensitive comprehension of the springs of American policy than did, for example, his colleague Hugh Dalton, the Chancellor of the Exchequer. Dalton visited the United States in October and had some inkling of the significance of the Goldmann mission from Felix Frankfurter. 'Truman isn't just electioneering in this endless repetition on the one hundred thousand', Dalton noted in his diary. 'This is part of the general outlook of Americans of both parties.'[7]

Bevin also visited America in the autumn of 1946 and received a quite different welcome from the hail-fellow-well-met reception of Dalton. He went to New York to attend the meeting of the Council of Foreign Ministers. The experience did not mellow his temperament. Dock workers refused to handle his luggage. He was booed at a football game by a crowd that remembered his statement about the Americans not wanting any more Jews in New York. He did however control his temper. He emphasized to Jews and Americans in general that he would receive all proposals with an open mind. 'The Jews here', he telegraphed Attlee from New York, 'have been pressing me very strongly to say that His Majesty's Government will be prepared to consider partition.' Bevin met with Rabbi Abba Hillel Silver, the bitterly anti-British leader of the American Zionist movement. Without rejecting the possibility of partition, Bevin remained silent on the question. He explained to Attlee:

Even if His Majesty's Government were to change their policy now and to seek American support for partition I am sure it would be most unwise to reveal

---

[4] Truman to Attlee, 10 Oct. 1946, enclosed in memorandum by Acheson to Truman, President's Secretary's Files Box 170, Truman Papers; *Foreign Relations 1946*, VII, pp. 706–8.
[5] Wilson, *Decision on Palestine*, p. 99.   [6] Williams, *Bevin*, p. 260.
[7] Dalton, diary entry, 7 Oct. 1946, Dalton Papers.

this now either to the Americans the Jews or anyone else. If it leaked out that we were willing to consider partition the Jews having got us to that point would undoubtedly endeavour to keep us on the run and as a means of doing so would put pressure on the United States Government demanding the whole of Palestine for themselves.[8]

In his talk with Silver, Bevin had given no encouragement about the possibility of partition. In fact he told the Rabbi that if the Jews pressed the issue then the British 'would give up the mandate' and hand it over to the United Nations. 'At this, Doctor Silver showed signs of distress.'[9]

Silver represented the leadership of American Jews who took the extreme position of demanding a Jewish state in all of Palestine. He was a figure to be reckoned with. The British Ambassador in Washington described him as 'vain . . . and something of a megalo-maniac'. 'I feel that if you turned a little of your charm on him', Inverchapel continued in a note to Bevin, 'you could get him into your pocket.'[10] Bevin did not follow the Ambassador's advice. He let Silver know in carefully measured terms that if the Jews would not attempt to come to agreement with the Arabs then the British would turn to the United Nations. Bevin thus made this point explicit to a prominent Jewish leader during the adjournment of the Palestine conference, when the British were attempting to bring the Jews into negotiations with the Arabs, and on the eve of the Zionist World Congress in Basel in December 1946. It was more than a warn-ing. It was an articulation of what might be called the British 'United Nations strategy'.[11]

As will be explained later in this chapter, the game at the United Nations was one in which the British believed they could win. In the autumn and winter of 1946, when Bevin's ideas crystallized in New York against the background of discussion in the Council of Foreign

---

[8] Bevin to Attlee, 26 Nov. 1946, FO 371/52565. Bevin was also greatly struck with the extent to which Palestine had become a political issue. The Zionist question, he wrote to Attlee, was 'so competitive here that really it is a contest for the New York votes as between Truman and Dewey'. 26 Nov. 1946, PREM 8/627/6.

[9] Memorandum of Conversation, 14 Nov. 1946, FO 371/52565.

[10] Memorandum by Inverchapel, 16 Nov. 1946, FO 371/52565.

[11] The evolution of Foreign Office thought in this direction may be traced in the minutes of Bevin's principal adviser on Palestine, Harold Beeley, who followed the issue closely in regard to developments in American policy. For example he wrote in October 1946: 'We have had . . . indications that the United States Government would like to see some transfer of responsibility for Palestine to the United Nations. In the long run this would no doubt relieve them of the domestic pressure which is now put upon them with a view to persuading them to influence our policy in Palestine. But when the issue was first presented to the United Nations they would have to take some definite line, and they might find this embarrassing. From . . . [our] point of view there is much to be said for an attempt to secure the approval of the General Assembly for the policy we eventually adopt in Palestine.' Minute of 21 Oct. 1946, FO 371/52561.

Ministers and the United Nations, it would have been a bold prophecy to have anticipated Zionist success in mobilizing two-thirds of the members of the General Assembly in support of the creation of a Jewish state. It would require the unlikely combination of the American and Russian voting blocs and what seemed to British and American officials alike to be the flouting of a fundamental principle of the organization itself—the imposition of a form of government against the wishes of the majority of the inhabitants.[12] With such thoughts in mind, Bevin and his advisers hoped that the United Nations might endorse the solution of a binational state. Bevin himself continued to be sceptical about partition because he believed that the Arab opposition would be so great that it would undermine Britain's entire position in the Middle East.[13] Nevertheless at this time he began to give serious thought to the possible military and strategic consequences of the division of Palestine as well as to a possible political solution through the United Nations. 'Partition' was generally in the wind in the British Cabinet. A meeting on the 25th of October 1946 concluded: 'several Ministers said that they were glad that the possibility of Partition was not excluded . . . and expressed the view that this would in the end be found to be the only practicable solution of the Palestine problem'.[14]

The Chiefs of Staff held that Britain could not successfully impose a solution by force if it were actively resisted by both communities. If compelled to choose between Arab and Jew, there could be no doubt whatsoever of the imperative need to preserve Arab goodwill. The Chiefs of Staff wrote in the aftermath of the publication

[12] This line of thinking was pursued in particular by Gordon P. Merriam of the Division of Near Eastern Affairs. 'U. S. support for the partition of Palestine as a solution to that problem can be justified only on the basis of Arab and Jewish consent. Otherwise we should violate the principle of self-determination which has been written into the Atlantic Charter, the Declaration of the United Nations, and the United Nations Charter—a principle that is deeply embedded in our foreign policy. Even a United Nations determination in favour of partition would be, in the absence of such consent, a stultification and violation of UN's own charter.' Acheson found the thoughts expressed in this memorandum to be so 'explosive' that he ordered it to be destroyed. Wilson, *Decision on Palestine*, pp. 99–100.

[13] Although Bevin was consistent in his opposition to partition, the records in London, Washington, and Jerusalem make it clear that he did not have a closed mind. In an especially revealing conversation with Nahum Goldmann in August 1946 he talked about partition as a 'possibility' but added that he was troubled about the prospect of a Jewish 'racial state' ('I got annoyed at that', Goldmann noted, and pointed out to Bevin that 300,000 Arabs would be included 'with equal rights'). Bevin emphasized several times that he 'never ruled out partition'. Goldmann for his part believed that he detected a more fair-minded attitude than the one usually attributed to Bevin. But he told him, 'you have treated us abominably'. Bevin responded by saying that he had always wanted to be fair to the Jews, and that 'he knew the Jewish tragedy and their sufferings'. Memorandum by Goldmann, 14 Aug. 1946, CZA Z6/17/21.

[14] Cabinet Conclusions 91 (46), 25 Oct. 1946, CAB 128/6; see minutes in FO 371/52563.

of the 'disastrous' report by the Anglo-American Committee of Inquiry:

All our defence requirements in the Middle East, including maintenance of our essential oil supplies and communications, demand that an essential feature of our policy should be to retain the co-operation of the Arab States, and to ensure that the Arab world does not gravitate towards the Russians. . . . We cannot stress too strongly the importance of Middle East oil resources to us both in peace and war.[15]

It is important to note that in mid-1946, when it became clear that British military, air, and naval forces might be withdrawn from Egypt, the Chiefs of Staff attached emphatic importance to the retention of strategic rights in Palestine. Haifa would be substituted for Alexandria as the linchpin of British defence in the eastern Mediterranean.

At that time the Chiefs of Staff believed that Jewish terrorism could be quelled. Police and military authorities attempted to break the back of Jewish resistance by searches for arm caches and internment of prominent leaders of the Jewish Agency, including the head of the Political Department, Moshe Shertok. The British army hoped at the minimum to neutralize the Jews' ability to attack. Those tactics had the opposite of the intended effect on Jewish morale, though the military effectiveness of the Haganah was weakened. Zionists in New York virulently denounced the British for 'smashing, looting, killing and maiming'.[16] After the King David Hotel explosion, the British Commanding Officer, General Sir Evelyn Barker, ordered British troops to have no 'social intercourse with any Jew' and to punish the Jews 'in a way the race dislikes as much as any, by striking at their pockets and showing our contempt for them'. He accused prominent Jews of 'hypocritical sympathy' with the terrorists. By August the Colonial Office feared that Palestine would be plunged into a bloodbath.

The Prime Minister steadied British nerves. Attlee believed that firmness against terrorism would strengthen the moderates with whom it might be possible to work out a political solution. He stuck by his maxim of trying to accommodate the more sensible of the

---

[15] CP (46) 267, 10 July 1946, CAB 129/11; minutes in FO 371/52538. The American Joint Chiefs of Staff, reporting to the President at about the same time, expressed the identical sentiment: 'for very serious consideration from a military point of view is control of the oil of the Middle East. This is probably the one large undeveloped reserve in a world which may come to the limits of its oil resources within this generation without having developed any substitute. A great part of our military strength, as well as our standard of living, is based on oil.' SWNCC 311, 21 June 1946, JCS 1684 CCS 092 Palestine (5-3-46) Sec. 2; President's Secretary's Files Box 184, Truman Papers; *Foreign Relations 1946*, VII, 631-3.

[16] E.g. *New York Post*, 21 Aug. 1946, clipping in the Creech Jones Papers, important because it indicates the Colonial Secretary's sensitivity to such attacks.

leaders of the Jewish Agency in order to prevent the extremists from precipitating, in Jewish eyes, a war of liberation. Curfews and house-to-house searches were relaxed. Barker was reprimanded for his non-fraternization order. Attlee's 'appeasement' did not please the Chief of the Imperial General Staff, Field-Marshal Montgomery, who continued to believe that military force would and should prove to be the only answer in Palestine. Montgomery stated in late 1946:

The policy of appeasement which had been adopted during the last few months had failed. Searches had been discontinued and internees had been released with no consequent improvement in the position, which in fact had deteriorated. The police and military forces were placed in a most difficult position and he cited cases in which terrorists caught red-handed and sentenced to death had been released or commuted to sentences of imprisonment. . . . He felt that what was required was a clear directive by His Majesty's Government to the High Commissioner to use all the forces at his disposal to maintain strict law and order. . . .[17]

Montgomery had a high estimate of British capability of imposing a peace with bayonets. His memoirs veil only slightly his contempt for Attlee and Bevin's caving in to the Jews, and for Creech Jones's 'spineless' handling of Palestine he reserved a special rancour. The Minister for Defence, A. V. Alexander, summed up the attitude of the Chief of the Imperial General Staff: 'Montgomery [is] anti High Commissioner, anti Secretary for the Colonies and perhaps even anti Government, for what he believes to be a lax way we are handling Palestinian affairs.'[18]

Despite the behemothic quality of some British military attitudes towards Palestine, not least those of Montgomery, British strategic thought went through searching political evaluation in the autumn and winter of 1946. The catalyst was the mind of Brigadier I. N. Clayton of the Middle East Office in Cairo. In late August 1946 he examined the ideas of the leaders of the Jewish Agency towards partition. He correctly believed that they now aimed at the creation of a Jewish state of limited but considerable size— one as large as they could get. They would be opposed by extremists who still hoped for Jewish dominion in all of Palestine, and by the terrorist groups and other irreconcilables who would remain a violent minority. British officials who analysed the problem of Palestine at this time usually shied away from historical analogies,

---

[17] COS (46) 169th Meeting, 20 Nov. 1946; see minutes in FO 371/52565. Montgomery contentiously discusses his part in the Palestine controversy in *The Memoirs of Field-Marshal the Viscount Montgomery of Alamein* (Cleveland, 1958), chap. 29. For critical assessment of the political consequences of his military policies in Palestine, see especially Cohen, *Palestine and the Great Powers*, chap. 8.

[18] Alexander to Attlee, 17 Mar. 1947, Alexander Papers.

but Clayton seized upon Ireland because of the importance the Zionists attached to it:

It is worth considering what happened in Ireland in 1921, the history of which is closely studied by the Zionists. The party which accepted the partition of Ireland included the moderates. Immediately on beginning to function as a Government it was involved in Civil War. The same is not unlikely to happen in Palestine.

What then should the British do? Clayton re-examined his own thought, which he believed to be representative of most other British observers of the Middle East:

The writer, in common with practically all British authorities in the Middle East, has always held the opinion that Partition offers no final solution of the Arab–Jew conflict and that the only solution which complies with the demand of justice and of British interests in the Middle East is the one of the White Paper of 1939. It would even, probably, in time command the support of an increasing number of Jews in Palestine as offering some prospect of finality.[19]

Clayton had previously underpinned his political thought with the premisses of the 1939 White Paper. He had rejected Zionism. He believed in a constitutional and humane solution for the Jews already in Palestine within the framework of a unitary state. He now believed that to be impossible. The forces of Zionism and Arab nationalism would collide head-on.

Clayton came to the heart of his analysis. Enlightened Arabs might accept partition. He excluded the political and spiritual head of the Palestinian Arabs, the Mufti. But other Arab leaders would probably accept partition 'if they dared':

The crux of the question lies in the words, 'if they dared'. It is probable that a considerable portion of the Arabs in the present Arab Governments do not in their hearts nourish any very deep-seated opposition to some form of partition. This is certainly the case in the Levant States, in Trans-Jordan and in Egypt; it is possibly partly true of Ibn Saud. It may be true of 'Iraq'.

Ultimately Clayton viewed partition as only a temporary solution.

Even if partition is accepted by the Jews it is most unlikely to be final. No Zionist will abandon his aim of extending Jewish dominion over the whole of both Eastern and Western Palestine. It may, however, give a breathing space and the bare possibility that a Semitic solution rather than a Jewish or Arab one may eventually be found. The omens for this are not promising but even a temporary one may be better than a continuance of the present state of affairs.[20]

---

[19] Memorandum by Clayton, 30 Aug. 1946, FO 371/52557.

[20] Ibid. The British Ambassador in Cairo, Sir Ronald Campbell, for one, preferred the traditional view. He wrote in a covering letter to Clayton's memorandum: 'I am persuaded that what all Arabs fear is that a Jewish State of limited extent in Palestine would be the thin edge of the wedge for subsequent penetration into the surrounding Arab States. For

Clayton put forward his ideas with diffidence and scepticism, but he nevertheless presented a challenge to all concerned to reconsider the consequences of partition.

The High Commissioner in Palestine, General Sir Alan Cunningham, responded to Clayton's reassessment in a letter that the Colonial Secretary circulated to the Prime Minister and the Foreign Secretary. Cunningham matched Clayton's views from Cairo with his own from Jerusalem. They were in agreement.[21] Cunningham was sympathetic to moderate Zionism. The Jewish leaders respected him as a friend of their cause, though one who would protect British interests even if he had to 'destroy half Tel Aviv'.[22] He anticipated the failure of the cantonal or provincial autonomy scheme. It might work in Switzerland, but Palestine was not Switzerland. He believed that in the last resort partition would give 'the only hope of peace in this country'.[23]

Cunningham judged that the Arab reaction to partition would depend on the political influence of the Mufti. To the Arabs he was a national and a religious hero whose leadership would and should be followed with unquestioning faithfulness. If the British were able to contain the fanatical influence of the Mufti, then the outlook would be more hopeful. Cunningham wrote to the Colonial Secretary:

> In regard to the Arabs in Palestine, the leadership . . . is at present vested in men who have repeated the same parrot cry for so long that they are completely incapable of seeing any other point of view but their own or of appreciating any changing influences which time brings. Without the Mufti their power for harm appears at present to be confined to the urban areas. The villages are enjoying a period of comparative prosperity never before known to them and the bulk of them remember too well the hardships of the Arab rebellion to show much inclination to undergo similar trials once more.[24]

Cunningham then assessed the possible political and strategic consequences of partition for the Jews. He believed that Arab, British, and American observers of the Zionist movement tended to overestimate its dynamic. If the Jewish state could be established in a limited area (for example, as recommended by the Royal Commission in 1937), then the Jews would have so much

this reason they are inclined to see no finality in the Partition solution.' Campbell to Bevin, 4 Sept. 1946, FO 371/52557.

[21] Except on the fundamentally divisive issue of the White Paper of 1939. 'I do not agree with Brigadier Clayton's remarks . . . that the White Paper of 1939 could in time command support of an increasing number of Jews in Palestine. Of this I see not the slightest hope.' Cunningham to Hall, 'Top Secret and Personal', 20 Sept. 1946, copy in FO 371/52562.

[22] *Autobiography of Nahum Goldmann*, p. 230.

[23] Cunningham to Hall, 20 Sept. 1946.

[24] Ibid.

on their hands that there would be little danger of further Zionist expansion.

The argument against partition providing a final solution arises mainly from the fear that it would merely be a step towards further Jewish expansion in the future. I feel this fear is apt to be exaggerated. Should they get their State, the Jews will surely require a period of peace in which to develop it, and the bulk of them are responsible enough to realize that a small Jewish State with expansionist ideas in the middle of the Arab States could only result in keeping the Palestine problem in the condition of a running sore. To them, as well as to the Arabs, there would seem to be every advantage in an established and guaranteed frontier which confines the Jewish immigration between limits.[25]

Like Clayton, Cunningham hesitated to say that partition would be final or ultimately satisfactory, but of all the possible solutions he judged that partition gave the greatest hope for eventual peace between Jew and Arab.[26]

American and British experts on the Middle East found themselves in general agreement that the Arab reaction to partition would probably be less violent than commonly assumed. Loy Henderson, whose judgement the British respected, passed on the following estimate to the Foreign Office:

The Arabs would oppose partition with various degrees of tenacity.

(a) Iraq . . . [Nuri's] views of the matter were not strong. Both he and the Regent would make a fuss for forms sake but would be unlikely to do more. There would be rioting in Bagdad.

(b) Transjordania. Abdullah would feign opposition and squawk but would in fact be in favour seeing in partition good chances of extending his domains.

(c) Syria. Here the opposition would be genuine, strong and noisily vocal.

(d) Lebanon. Here the Moslems would oppose and the Christians would not care.

(e) Saudi Arabia. Ibn Saud and his people would be stirred partly because of native fanaticisms and partly because they would at once perceive in partition an accretion of strength of the Hashimites. But in the face of the Anglo-American united front Ibn Saud's resistance would not be sustained.

(f) Egypt. The Egyptians would be noisy but the noise would be meaningless. There might be demonstrating and anti-Semitic riots in Cairo and Alexandria but they would not last long.[27]

Henderson foresaw the danger of terrorism but 'felt no anxiety about military actions', provided the British and the Americans showed 'a determined attitude'.[28]

---

[25] Cunningham to Hall, 20 Sept. 1946.

[26] Ibid. Bevin noted on the letter, 'Very interesting'.

[27] Inverchapel to Bevin, 26 Nov. 1946, FO 371/52565; CO 537/1787.

[28] The impending military consequences looked quite different from local perspective. Sir John Glubb wrote in December 1946 from Amman that he was above all concerned with 'speed of implementation' of partition after the decision. 'Once the Jewish State had been

One of the shrewdest minds in British Middle Eastern officialdom analysed the State Department's estimate. Sir Walter Smart, the Oriental Secretary at the British Embassy in Cairo, took issue in detail with some of Henderson's judgements. In particular Smart thought that the State Department underestimated reaction in Iraq, Christian sentiment in Lebanon, and the possible collective strength of the Arab League. On the whole however Smart agreed with Henderson. He also concurred in Cunningham's judgement of the Arab psychological apprehension of Zionist expansion: 'If it were possible to accompany the announcement of partition by a definite undertaking to admit no further immigrants pending the establishment of the Jewish state, the reactions all over the Middle East might be less violent.' Smart however added a stinger that went to the bottom of the Arab side of the problem. 'The trouble of course is that it is very difficult to make the Arabs believe that there can be anything definite about such assurances.'[29] If the Arabs could no longer believe in the White Paper of 1939, they would hardly put faith in further guarantees.

The ghost of the White Paper of 1939 haunted the London conference on the Middle East that convened sporadically, officially and unofficially, from September 1946 to February 1947. The Arabs stood by the letter and spirit of the guarantees of 1939 and would yield to nothing less than Palestine as an Arab state. The Jews boycotted the proceedings because of the denial of the opposite premiss of a Jewish state. They conducted unofficial simultaneous negotiations with the British. Bevin and Creech Jones (who became Colonial Secretary in October) provided the basis of discussion by presenting in essence the plan for provincial autonomy. It was as close as British ingenuity could come to reconciling Arab and Jew and preserving as much of British influence as possible. The Arabs proved by no means as amenable to the possibility of partition as Clayton and Cunningham had anticipated. During the winter of 1946-7 Arab and Jewish positions polarized. Within two months Clayton virtually retracted his views because circumstances had rendered them 'misleading'. His reconsideration as of late October reveals the transformation in attitudes and temperament: 'during the last two months Arab opinion has hardened against partition, which is now labelled in all Arab countries as a Zionist solution'.[30] The

set up and the Arab areas taken over by Trans-Jordan, partition would be a fait accompli.' (Glubb to Beeley, 14 Dec. 1946, FO 371/61858.) The question thus turned on how quickly the Arab Legion could twist the situation to the advantage of Jordan.

[29] Minute by Smart, 2 Dec. 1946, FO 371/52565.
[30] See memorandum by Howe, 23 Oct. 1946, FO 371/52562.

Arabs rejected the British plan for a binational state precisely because
they believed it to be a move towards partition.

For the Jews the polarization was just as extreme and was perhaps
symbolized by the fall from formal political power of Chaim Weizmann at the Zionist Congress in Basel in December. When Ben-Gurion
met with British officials shortly thereafter he stated that Weizmann
was 'still first in moral standing' but his political defeat came about
because of 'his blind trust in Britain'.[31] Those who now led the
Zionist movement did not believe that the British would leave
Palestine unless they were pushed out, though Ben-Gurion made it
clear that he hoped for a nudge as peaceful as possible. They judged
the plan for provincial autonomy in exactly the opposite way as did
the Arabs. To the Jews it was merely a step in the direction of an
Arab Palestinian state. The London Conference ended as it had
begun, in deadlock.

Within the British government the critical stages in the decisions
about Palestine began to develop in December and January of 1946-7
and reached a climax in February. The decisions took place against
the great emotional debate about India, the general deterioration of
Britain in the Middle Eastern 'northern tier', a sense of impending
economic disaster, and one of the worst winters in British history.
The two great offices of state, the Foreign Office and the Colonial
Office, clashed over the interpretation of trusteeship. Trusteeship
for whom? Arab or Jew? In another sense the story can be told of
the Foreign Office Goliath and the Colonial Office David. Lest that
description seem irrelevant or unfair to Bevin or Creech Jones, it
was the way in which Zionist leaders viewed the two men. David
Horowitz, a participant in the unofficial negotiations with the
British during the conference, gave this impression of Bevin entering
the conference room. His was perhaps the epitome of the Zionist
outlook:

> Suddenly there was a whisper and a furtive movement [among the British
> representatives] . . . and they were electrified into attention. I looked toward
> the open doorway and saw the thickset figure of the British Foreign Secretary
> coming through. We all felt that this man was the central figure among our
> hosts. He had a magnetic, almost hypnotic effect over the officials clustered
> around.
>
> Ernest Bevin's bulky person, about which he himself often spoke jocularly
> through his pursed lips, and his broad shoulders and piercing eyes were expressive
> of power, authority, influence, and a rare stormy temperament. . . . which was
> repulsive rather than attractive, oppressive rather than cordial, and as having

---

[31] 'Note of Interview with Mr. Ben Gurion at the Colonial Office', 2 Jan. 1947, copy in
FO 371/61762.

the same lack of diffidence and faculty of contemplation, which were replaced by intuition and impulsiveness.

Although it was evident that he was not in good health and his hands trembled slightly, one could sense the man's aggressive temperament and the egocentricity exuding at every pore of his being.[32]

Creech Jones by contrast impressed the Jews as 'the antithesis of Bevin: short, soft and gentle, hesitant in speech, without any sharp angularities of personality, moderate and quiet, without much influence or power'. On another occasion Horowitz recounted a joke banging around in Jewish circles: 'the difference in political weight between burly Bevin and the slight-framed Creech-Jones was the same as the disparity of their physical weight'.[33]

The savage humour of the Jews persistently identified Bevin's character with the demonic and demogogic power of Hitler. Nahum Goldmann once told Bevin after a towering rage over American Jews: ' "Well, that takes care of everything except the carpet, Mr. Bevin"—an allusion to Hitler's outbursts of rage that are said to have ended with his biting the carpet.'[34] During the course of the negotiations in the winter of 1946 Creech Jones became reduced, in the opinion of the Zionists, to the status of a sycophant before this raging megolomaniac. According to another account that related Jewish attitudes after Creech Jones 'abandoned' the cause of partition:

Creech-Jones now tries to hide when our people come to see him about something. He is not hostile, just contemptible. His officials are happily looking forward to the day when Palestine will have been taken off their necks, so that [they can] get down to organizing the Gold Coast. With the exception of the Stern Gang nobody imagines that the Colonial Office has anything to do with Palestine policy.[35]

Those Zionist perspectives on Creech Jones are perhaps distorted, vicious, and cruel, but they are important because Jewish leaders thought of His Majesty's Secretary of State for the Colonies in that vein. They also serve as a reminder that Creech Jones worked in Bevin's shadow, and that the Foreign Secretary's overpowering personality often dominated the British Cabinet.

In the clash between the Colonial Office and the Foreign Office the same issues re-emerged that had divided the British public, Parliament, Cabinet, and permanent officials in the late 1930s. The Foreign Office worked towards an Arab state that would stabilize

[32] Horowitz, *State in the Making*, pp. 130–1.
[33] Ibid., p. 127.
[34] *Autobiography of Nahum Goldmann*, p. 237.
[35] Cohen, *Palestine and the Great Powers*, p. 226.

or limit Jewish immigration and that would preserve British influence in the Middle East through Anglo-Arab friendship—in other words the goal of the 1939 White Paper. During the Second World War the Colonial Office under the leadership of Oliver Stanley had pursued the solution of partition based on the same principles as those of the Royal Commission of 1937. Creech Jones attempted to reaffirm the tradition of trusteeship by partition. On the Foreign Office side Halifax and Bevin, who possessed opposite personalities as night and day, were both accused of pursuing a policy of appeasement towards the Arabs. Appeasement in a positive sense can mean the recognition of legitimate claims and the rectification of genuine grievances. Bevin's policy at worst was denounced as the deliberate anti-Jewish manipulation of public sentiment with the intent of preserving British imperialism in the Middle East. At best it aimed at the creation of a genuine unitary or binational state. The Colonial Office policy as pursued briefly by Creech Jones recognized Arab and Jews as irreconcilables. At best it aimed at a partition of Palestine that would fulfil moderate Zionist ambitions without alienating the Arabs or jeopardizing British security in the Middle East. Negatively it could be interpreted as a 'ghettoization' of the Jews in Palestine, or, from the other point of view, as an attempt to dispossess the Arabs. Thus the issues of early 1947 resembled those of the late 1930s and the wartime period. The common ground for discussion between the Colonial Office and Foreign Office (and, both departments hoped, between the Arabs, Jews, and Americans as well) was the plan for provincial autonomy. Its ambiguity allowed it to be taken as a step in either direction.

In this sustained debate two permanent officials need to be mentioned specifically. They are Douglas Harris of the Colonial Office and a personage of far greater significance in the history of the Middle East, a young Foreign Office official named Harold Beeley. Harris, as the principal architect of the provincial autonomy scheme, worked from a set of Colonial Office principles that were applicable to dependent territories throughout the world: above all, guarantees for all segments of a 'plural society', in this case a binational one. The British would introduce economic and social measures designed to bring Arab standards up to the Jewish level, and would gradually foster representative political institutions with a legislative council and all the other trappings of an embryonic British parliamentary democracy. The difficulty with this general scheme, as its critics did not hesitate to point out, was that it assumed an indefinite period of benevolent British trusteeship which neither Arab nor Jew would tolerate. Reduced to its minimum, the provincial autonomy scheme would at least contribute to an orderly devolution of power and the preservation of social, economic, and political institutions introduced by the British. Douglas Harris brought to those problems the detailed knowledge of colonial administration he had acquired in Palestine. During that time High Commissioners had come and gone, but Harris, in David Horowitz's phrase, had remained 'the uncrowned ruler of Mandated Palestine'.

Harold Beeley was Bevin's closest adviser on Palestine. He had been thrust into the centre of the Palestine controversy in part because of sheer intellect. His approach complemented rather than contradicted Harris's, and the two of them worked together to co-ordinate British policy. Beeley's outlook may be summarized by stating that he believed that continuing Jewish immigration would ignite a powder keg of Arab hostility. A constitutional and humanitarian solution to the Jewish problem in Palestine could best be found by sticking to the principles of the 1939 White Paper. He believed that a unitary state guaranteeing Jewish rights might avert a Jewish–Arab war and the possibility of disastrous Russian intervention. Beeley had served as British Secretary to the Anglo-American Committee of Inquiry. Bartley Crum quickly identified him as the *éminence grise* of the Foreign Office who, Crum erroneously believed, arranged for the monitoring of American mail and the tapping of telephones. That opinion of Beeley's influence was shared by a person of much more discerning insight, David Horowitz, who devoted an entire chapter in his book to Beeley. Horowitz gave this description:

From the outset I found the man, with his cold, incisive intellect, to be an interesting study. He was of the type of person who, in spite of an icy temperament, develops an intensity of passion which holds him in a tight grip. He was not an anti-Semite. His grim, unyielding antagonism to Zionism arose from his assessment and appreciation of British Imperial interests in the East, and perhaps also from a modicum of romantic, and irrational, sympathy for the Arabs. He remained an uncompromising and unrelenting foe.[36]

Horowitz also acknowledged that Beeley, like Harris, was the epitome of an English gentleman who discharged his duties in the highest standards of the British civil service.

By January 1947 two elements in the Palestine problem began to

---

[36] Horowitz, *State in the Making*, p. 38. Contemporary American assessments of Beeley's unique influence confirm Horowitz's judgement. Lewis Jones, the Foreign Service officer in charge of Middle Eastern affairs at the American Embassy, wrote that the Palestine problem was so complicated that Beeley's superiors tended to give him more than ordinary scope for initiative, and that Beeley often consulted directly with Bevin. 'There is a general tendency in the Foreign Office to "leave it to Beeley" so far as possible.' Memorandum by Jones, 18 Apr. 1947, USSD 890.00/4-2247.

crystallize in the minds of the Cabinet. Neither could be turned to the advantage of the Colonial Office. The first was the urgent need for an explanation before the United Nations. The British government was committed to the charter of the United Nations and with it the necessity to transform the League of Nations mandate into a United Nations trusteeship. Not even the shrewdest analyst of international organization could predict the results of handing over any territory, especially Palestine, to the whims of a 'motley international assembly'. Yet the issue had to be faced or Britain would run the risk of following South Africa's lead and becoming an international pariah, as in the case of South West Africa. The Foreign Office on this point effectively argued that the Arab powers would enforce their rights as 'states directly concerned' and would block any solution short of a unitary state. The argument for partition nevertheless had strong advocates in the Cabinet. Hugh Dalton was among them. He recorded in his diary:

> On Palestine a number of us have been shouting for partition—Creech Jones is very good on this and much more decisive than his predecessor. E. B. and the P. M. try to tangle up the merits of various solutions with hypothetical conclusions of who would vote for this or that at U. N. O. I have been trying to keep these disentangled and have been urging that partition is the least objectionable of all policies.[37]

The general point was clear but it was also moot. Britain could not avoid discussion of Palestine in the United Nations, but as a political issue it could be argued either way—or not at all.

The second issue that became clear in early 1947 was the strategic situation in the eastern Mediterranean. The Chiefs of Staff continued to advise that British troops could impose a solution by force upon one community in Palestine but not upon both, as would in their view be the case if the plan for provincial autonomy were implemented. The more extreme solution of partition would, in bluntest terms, destroy Britain's position in the Middle East. Provincial autonomy or partition under British sponsorship would involve drawing in British troops from other parts of the Middle East and Europe, notably Germany, which had far-reaching military implications. At a time when there was great uncertainty whether there would be a peaceful transfer of power in India, this was not a risk the British Cabinet would take. Whenever Bevin felt his case for a unitary state weakened by the Colonial Office, he would call for the aid of the Chiefs of Staff, whose strategic arguments in the case of Palestine invariably buttressed those of the Foreign Office.

It could be argued that the collective responsibilities of the War

[37] Dalton Diary 17 Jan. 1947, Dalton Papers.

Office, Admiralty, and Air Ministry (merged into the new Ministry for Defence in late 1946) rivalled those of the Colonial Office and Foreign Office. The War Office in particular faced a demission of territorial power and the transfer of troops. Those problems of course touched on the general issue of the defence of the British Empire in the Middle East and indeed in the eastern hemisphere. They could be alleviated, if not permanently solved, by naval, military, and air bases guaranteed by treaty rights. A treaty with a Palestinian state similar to the one with Transjordan might also grant strategic rights for air transit of troops and the protection of pipelines. The Chiefs of Staff presented their case for these demands in a Cabinet meeting of the 15th of January 1947:

It was essential to our defence that we should be able to fight from the Middle East in war. . . . In future we should not be able to use India as a base for . . . deployment of force: it was the more essential, therefore, that we should retain other bases in the Middle East for this purpose.

Palestine was of special importance in this general scheme of defence. In war, Egypt would be our key position in the Middle East; and it was necessary that we should hold Palestine as a screen for the defence of Egypt.[38]

Far from wishing to relinquish Palestine for mere reasons of political discontent, the Chiefs of Staff wished to retain it as a permanent possession. A naval base at Haifa, a few military garrisons scattered throughout the territory, and a strategic air base in the interior would satisfy British strategic requirements. Transjordan could not alone bear the weight of British security. Partition of Palestine was anathema. The creation of two separate states among other things would produce indefensible borders. Partition would furthermore probably turn all of the Middle Eastern states (with the possible exception of Transjordan) against Britain and thus would be disastrous for the British strategic position. To the traditional British military mind treaty rights with a Palestinian Arab state would provide, under the circumstances, the best answer to the strategic problems of the British Empire in the eastern Mediterranean.

Lieutenant-General Sir Alan Cunningham, in his capacity of High Commissioner for Palestine, attempted to reverse the current of British strategic thought. His views re-enforced those of the Colonial Secretary at the decisive juncture of the controversy of mid-January 1947. Cunningham based his judgement on his knowledge of the local political as well as military crisis in Palestine. He held that neither side would accept the provincial autonomy scheme as a temporary solution. The British military situation, he argued, would worsen under an extended period of trusteeship. He urged a quick

[38] CM (47) 6th Conclusions, Minute 3, Confidential Annex, 15 Jan. 1947, CAB 128/11.

and decisive partition. With an optimism greater than most of his colleagues, he continued to believe that most of the Arab states would acquiesce in a clear-cut decision and that British military rights could be secured in the Jewish state as well as in the Arab state. In a memorandum circulated to the Cabinet by the Colonial Secretary, Cunningham argued against provincial autonomy with such ringing clarity that it virtually sounded the death-knell for the scheme and contributed to the polarization of attitudes within the government. His analysis is of interest among other reasons because it identified the vital weakness of the plan in relation to colonial nationalism as a problem within the British Empire as a whole.

The attraction of the Provincial Autonomy Plan is that it . . . is an admirable piece of administrative planning for a system of government in a country where political reasoning has any chance of success over pure nationalism. There is no chance of this in Palestine because the forces of nationalism are accompanied by the psychology of the Jew, which it is important to recognise as something quite abnormal and unresponsive to rational treatment, and because Arab politics have their raison d'etre not in the field of government or administration but in the field of religion and nationalism only.[39]

Military and strategic specifications would not meet the requirement, Cunningham concluded, of a political solution. 'It cannot be said too often', he emphasized, that the problem was 'entirely political'.

Creech Jones presented the political case for partition with the full force of Colonial Office persuasion and polemic. A policy of partition would have greater public support in both Britain and the United States than any other solution. If it were implemented quickly and decisively it might avert civil war. On the other hand a solution favouring the Arabs would precipitate the Jewish equivalent of the American revolution. Creech Jones also reminded his colleagues of the pledges of the Labour Party supporting the Zionist movement. Hugh Dalton, the moving spirit behind the 1945 declaration, wrote in his diary that partition made for sound political logic and would have wide support in England, the United States, and the United Nations. If Dalton had been Colonial Secretary in 1947 the solution of partition might have stood a better chance. Creech Jones could not withstand the political power of Bevin. Nor could he conduct skilful enough negotiations with the Jews in order to put a more persuasive case before the British Cabinet. In the end he reconciled himself to Bevin's policy as 'inevitable'.[40] Bevin for his part took care not to alienate the Colonial Secretary. He averted a rupture with Creech Jones by the argument that ultimately the case for

[39] Memorandum by Cunningham, CP (47) 31, 16 Jan. 1947, Creech Jones Papers.
[40] See Creech Jones to Elizabeth Monroe, 23 Oct. 1961, Creech Jones Papers.

partition was untenable because of overriding reasons of British security.

Bevin argued the case relentlessly in the discussions of the Cabinet. He exposed what he believed to be a fatal flaw in the Colonial Office argument. His emphasis on that point probably tilted Cabinet members towards his solution of a binational state. It was the failure to apprehend the repercussion of partition in the Arab states. The result would be no less than an estrangement of the British and Arab peoples. In the words of one of his deputies, who detected the ultimate weakness in the Colonial Office case:

> To how great an extent partition would result in an estrangement between Great Britain and the Arab peoples it is not possible to estimate. But the consequences of such an estrangement would be so grave that the risk of it should be a major consideration in the examination of partition as a possible policy. The loss of Arab good will would mean the elimination of British influence from the Middle East to the great advantage of Russia. And this in turn would greatly weaken the position of the British Commonwealth in the world.[41]

In the end that was an argument that Attlee as Prime Minister had always to bear in mind.[42]

The key to Attlee's (and Bevin's) thought lies in a statement he had made to the Cabinet in late November 1946. Though the solution of partition might have a powerful attraction as an immediate and decisive solution, Attlee said, 'His Majesty's Government should not commit themselves to support of this solution before all the alternatives had been fully discussed in the . . . proceedings of the Palestine Conference'.[43] The Jews and Arabs would be given the chance to agree or disagree to all reasonable proposals, including the extremes of partition and a unitary state. If no solution were found then they and not the British would bear the main brunt of failure. Attlee and Bevin independently arrived at the same conclusion. They did not want to be held responsible in Arab eyes for a policy of partition. If there could be no agreement, then the British government would continue to play the same hand at the United Nations where a showdown could not be avoided. The British would appear to assume an impartial position, but in fact they would allow the pro-Arab majority of the General Assembly to decide the issue for them. That calculation explains Dalton's comment in mid-January about the preoccupation of Attlee and Bevin with UN votes.

[41] Memorandum by Robert Howe, 21 Jan. 1947, FO 371/61858.

[42] One is reminded how in 1938 Chamberlain utilized a similar argument in favour of appeasement. Declaration of war against Nazi Germany might rupture the Commonwealth and end the influence of the British Empire in world affairs. See Ritchie Ovendale, *'Appeasement' and the English Speaking World* (Cardiff, 1975).

[43] Cabinet Conclusions 101 (46), 28 Nov. 1946, CAB 121/6.

The United Nations Department of the Foreign Office produced highly sophisticated minutes which Harold Beeley refined into calculations of how such enigmas as China, India, and Yugoslavia might vote on Palestine. This shrewd and deadly course of political action came as a revelation to David Horowitz during a conversation with Beeley after the Jewish leaders agreed to recourse to the United Nations:

'Why did you agreee so readily to the idea of handing over the Palestine problem to the United Nations?' Beeley asked. 'Look at the Charter of the United Nations and the list of its member nations. To get an affirmative decision, you'll need a two-thirds majority of the votes of these members. You can only win a majority if the Eastern bloc and the United States join together and support the same resolution in the same terms. That has never happened, it cannot happen, and it will never happen!'

That was it, then! Bevin's policy was now to count strongly on the clash in the world's political arena between the colossi of East and West, in which it was believed that our tiny cause would be lost in the grim struggle.[44]

Beeley and the Foreign Office generally did not have the Machiavellian self-confidence that Horowitz implied, but the analysis was sound. The United Nations would determine the issue in favour of a unitary state, which in turn would conclude a treaty securing the strategic and economic benefits of Britain's traditional informal empire in the Middle East.

In the last stages of the London conference, which still dragged on formally and informally until mid-February, Bevin continued to guide the discussions on the basis of the plan for provincial autonomy. With an ostensibly even hand he exhausted possibilities of concessions that might be interpreted as a step towards partition or towards a binational state. The more the details of partition were examined the more the problem seemed insuperable. With impending stalemate Bevin and Creech Jones then put forward last proposals in the form of a binational Arab–Jewish state. In what became known as the 'Bevin plan' there would be a five-year trusteeship regime supervised by the Trusteeship Council in which Palestine would be prepared for independence as a binational state. Instead of provincial autonomy there would be 'cantons' determined by Jewish or Arab majorities. The cantons were not necessarily contiguous and were more restricted in autonomous government than the scheme for provincial autonomy. On the other hand the 100,000 (or close to that mythical figure) would be admitted to Palestine within a period of two years. The 'Bevin plan' represented the last effort to resolve the problem of Palestine in the tradition of British trusteeship. Jewish

[44] Horowitz, *State in the Making*, p. 143.

and Arab local and self-governing institutions would be 'rooted in the lives of the people'. Jews and Arabs would share in the central government of a binational state.[45]

The results of the London conference may be briefly summed up. The Arabs refused to consider Jewish self-government in any form, or further Jewish immigration. Thus the British confronted one impasse. The Jews regarded the boundaries of the 'cantons' that the British were prepared to allocate to them as totally unacceptable and would not agree to any scheme not based on the premiss of an eventual Jewish state. Thus the British presided over final deadlock.

The painful moment of revelation for Creech Jones had finally come during his close examination of the demographic consequences of partition. He explained to the members of the Cabinet on the 7th of February 1947 that previously he had thought that partition would provide the only solution. The more he studied the details, however, the more sceptical he had become. 'It would be very difficult to establish a viable Jewish State without prejudicing the vital interests of the Palestine Arabs; and wherever the frontiers were drawn, large numbers of Arabs must inevitably be left under Jewish rule.'[46] The Jewish representatives themselves confirmed Colonial Office doubts in a meeting four days later on the 11th of February. David Horowitz again had vivid memories.

> David Ben-Gurion, Moshe Shertok, and I arrived at the Colonial Office, on the west side of Whitehall, on. . . . a typical London day, overcast and rainy.
> We were shown into a small office where Sir Norman Brook, Sir Douglas Harris, and Harold Beeley awaited us. They unfolded a map. . . . B.-G. indicated with a broad stroke of the finger the Zionist idea of a possible Partition map of Palestine.

With mixed emotions of good faith and calculated risk, the Jews had outlined their maximum territorial ambitions, which in fact more or less coincided with the frontier arrived at in the armistice agreement two years later. In February 1947 those boundaries seemed to strike the British as phantasmagoric. When pressed to reconfirm their territorial demands the Jews concurred in the cartographical detail. Horowitz believed afterwards that they had fallen into a British trap:

> It was a cunning move to evolve a hypothesis from what had only been a swift movement of the hand. It demonstrated the ostensibly absurd and fantastic nature of our demands, and showed how unreal and impracticable they looked, once put down on paper.[47]

[45] Memorandum by Bevin and Creech Jones, CP (47) 49, 6 Feb. 1947, CAB 129/16.
[46] CM (47) 18, 7 Feb. 1947, CAB 128/9.
[47] Horowitz, *State in the Making*, pp. 140-2.

If Creech Jones had any lingering doubts about the impossibility of coming to terms with the Jews, they were now removed. He now fully accepted Bevin's argument that agreement about partition was a futile quest.

Bevin and Creech Jones together in mid-February 1947 submitted to the Cabinet a report anticipating difficulties at the United Nations. They outlined complex problems of procedure in the General Assembly. They emphasized that once the British made the decision to refer the Palestine controversy to the United Nations they would have to act with all possible speed to bring about a final solution because otherwise the administration in Palestine itself would face renewed outbreaks of terrorism and possible civil war. At this stage the British considered, but rejected with a ring of self-confidence, the possibility of evacuation. They did not wish to leave the Arabs, Jews, the Americans, and the United Nations stewing in their own juice. Such an abnegation of responsibility, according to Bevin and Creech Jones, would be ignoble and would amount to a repudiation of the 'sacred trust' of the mandate: 'We do not recommend the adoption of this humiliating course.'[48] Creech Jones re-emphasized that point in the subsequent Parliamentary debate: 'We are not going to the United Nations to surrender the mandate.'[49]

In the Parliamentary debate of the 25th of February 1947 Bevin attempted once and for all to repudiate Zionism as a basis for a Palestinian settlement. He based his principal argument on the demographic fact that the Jews were a minority. In one of the few analogies he ever drew with the other major colonial crisis of 1947, Bevin stated: 'I cannot alter the balance of people in a State—that is impossible—any more than one can alter it between Nehru and Jinnah today in India.'[50] What would be the result of partition in Palestine? He said that in a fair-minded way he had looked at all possibilities and invariably came to the same fundamental conclusion. There were only two possible consequences. 'Either the Arabs in the partitioned State must always be an Arab minority, or else they must be driven out—the one thing or the other.' Though his critics pointed out that he could just as well have developed the same case for a Jewish minority in an Arab state, Bevin argued that a binational state would best secure the 'national home' promised by the Balfour Declaration.

[48] Memorandum by Bevin and Creech Jones, 13 Feb. 1947, CP (47) 59 CAB 129/17; for minutes see CO 537/2327–8.

[49] *Parliamentary Debates* (Commons), 25 Feb. 1947, col. 2007.

[50] Ibid., col. 1911.

Those Jews who have migrated there should have their liberty and freedom
—no pogroms, no persecution—and be equal citizens of the State. That makes
it a national home—[Interruption.] My national home is in England, with the
same conditions.

So went his argument. It was not new but he presented it with great
vigour.[51] Harold Beeley explained to the Americans that its purpose
was to make clear Bevin's straightforward and honest rejection of
Zionist demands for a Jewish state.[52]

Bevin also lashed out again at the United States. He wanted it
understood that the Americans would have to rise above a provincial approach if the United Nations were to succeed. He stated
that he could not allow grave issues 'with a thousand years of religious
differences' to be settled by local elections in New York. He noted
the competitive bids of 100,000, and multiples thereof, by Mr.
Truman and Mr. Dewey for the Jewish vote. For his part Truman,
to use his own words, was 'outraged' that a British Foreign Secretary
would accuse the President of the United States of a cheap political
trick.[53] Bevin, though speaking extemporaneously, had made the
remark deliberately. Immediately after the debate he sent a secret
and personal telegram to Lord Inverchapel: 'I recognize that certain
passages in this speech may give offence in the United States . . . but
it was necessary to show the House of Commons how we have striven
for American co-operation, and how the attitude of the United
States has in fact complicated our problem.'[54] With such polemics he
hurled Palestine into the arena of the United Nations.

[51] Ibid., cols. 1901-20.

[52] Gallman to Marshall, 26 Feb. 1947, *Foreign Relations 1947*, V, p. 1058-9.

[53] *Memoirs by Harry S. Truman: Years of Trial and Hope*, p. 154.

[54] Bevin to Inverchapel, 27 Feb. 1947, FO 371/61769. James McDonald, who was in
London at the time of Bevin's speech, wrote that he detected a basic change in British
attitude: 'For the first time I am beginning to believe that the British are seriously contemplating getting out of Palestine. . . . there is a startling feeling here of loss of power, and
ability to handle adequately the traditional imperial role.' McDonald to David Niles, 7 Mar.
1947, McDonald Papers.

THE UNITED NATIONS SPECIAL COMMITTEE ON PALESTINE AND THE BRITISH DECISION TO EVACUATE

THE rapid deterioration of British moral suasion and military power in Palestine took place against the background of political drama in the United Nations. It was accompanied by the rising danger of anti-Semitism in England and by increasingly virulent anti-British sentiment in New York. In Palestine Jewish 'terrorism' and British 'oppression' reached symbolic heights. In July the Irgun brutally hanged two British sergeants and placed booby traps on their bodies. They became martyrs. Bevin told Marshall that the executions 'would never be forgotten' and that as a result 'anti-Jewish feeling in England now was greater than it had been in a hundred years'.[1] The Jews also had symbolic figures, and they appealed to a much greater public conscience. In the same month British authorities turned away some 4,500 Jewish refugees aboard the *Exodus 1947*. In one of his 'black rages' Bevin decided 'to teach the Jews a lesson'. The passengers aboard the *Exodus* would be returned to their port of embarkation in France. As it transpired the Jews refused to disembark and the hapless British wound up sending these survivors of Nazi murder camps back to Germany.

The Economist described the consequences of the *Exodus* episode not only as a disaster for Britian's relations with the Jews in Palestine but also as a catastrophe for Britain's moral reputation throughout the world.

The decision to send the Exodus Jews to Hamburg, to disembark them there by force, to put them in places which retain the physical lay-out and accessories of Nazi concentration camps, and to hold them under an administration partly German, was an act of which nobody can yet measure the consequences.

It has not only produced an unprecedented hostility and resentment towards Britain among Zionists everywhere; it has also convinced most Germans that Britain is at last learning the truth of what Hitler said about the Jews, and it has thus wiped out at a stroke whatever has so far been achieved in 're-educating' Germany away from the Nazi creed; last but not least, it has given a great psychological impetus to anti-semitism in this country.[2]

[1] Marshall to Lovett, 25 Nov. 1947, USSD 867N.01/11–2547 Box 6761; *Foreign Relations 1947*, V, pp. 1287–9.
[2] 18 Oct. 1947.

In this incisive commentary *The Economist* next touched on a sensitive subject. It has been the theme of recent important and controversial historical research.[3] *The Economist* judged anti-Semitism in the British civil service to be one of the roots of trouble in Palestine.

That anti-Jewish sentiment—of a mild brand, it is true, but real enough—flourishes today, though without public expression, in high official circles in Britain is a proposition which only hypocrisy or blind-eyed complacency will deny. Its main source is to be found among those who have been concerned in civil or military administration in the Middle East; this background accounts for its strength in the Colonial Office and the War Office.

Its existence in the Foreign Office is due to a somewhat different cause: to the fact that the Foreign Office conducts diplomatic relations with a number of Arab States, and is continually informed by its mission in their capitals how disastrously these relations will be affected by any concession to the Jews whereas friendly relations with Zion form no part of foreign policy.[4]

One of the most important organs of the British press thus identified anti-Semitism within the government as well as in the public at large as an active ingredient in British attitudes during the last year of the mandate.

In order to keep perspective on the anti-Jewish sentiment, it is useful to bear in mind general attitudes towards Asians and Africans. It is also important to grasp the psychological dimension of the problem in order to comprehend the reason why Palestine was like a current flowing alongside, but distinct from, the mainstream of British decolonization. In one of the first major historical surveys of the mandate, John Marlow commented that in Palestine the British reaction to Jewish terrorism was almost pusillanimous compared with the robust and determined response in Malaya and Kenya.

As had been seen in Ireland, British public opinion, much as it disliked Sinn Fein, was unable to view the prospect of a 'firm hand' against Europeans with the same detachment as it would have viewed the prospect of a 'firm hand' employed against 'natives'—that is to say Indians, Chinese, or any people with other than a white skin.

To the ordinary English voter—however discreditable this may seem—a white man, even a German in 1945 or a Jew in 1947, was an individual in a sense that a black man or a brown man or a yellow man was not. The massacre of Jews by Germans horrified British public opinion in a way that a similar massacre of Africans would not have done.[5]

[3] Notably Bernard Wasserstein, *Britain and the Jews of Europe 1939–1945* (Oxford, 1979). For the anti-Semitic outbursts in England following the hanging of the two sergeants (which included possible arson and the smashing of the windows of Jewish shops and synagogues), see Cohen, *Palestine and the Great Powers*, p. 245.

[4] *The Economist*, 18 Oct. 1947.

[5] John Marlowe, *The Seat of Pilate* (London, 1959), p. 229. Marlowe's suggestion that the British public would have responded indifferently to an African massacre sparked a flicker of protest by the reviewer in the *Times Literary Supplement* (10 Apr. 1959).

When Jewish terrorism increased in 1947 it appeared to intelligent observers of events in Palestine that Britain stood on the brink of a racial war with the Jews, as commentators with such different views as Churchill and Crossman had already warned. They would not be fighting an all-out war against 'black barbarians' (a phrase that lingered in Tory circles), but a race already savaged by the gas chambers of the Nazis. Elements of prejudice and guilt became fused with a vague humanitarian concern not to dispossess the Arabs. The moral case for an even-handed retreat had a powerful emotional appeal.

The poetry of the playwright Ben Hecht, which he transformed into advertisements for Zionist newspapers in New York, let the British know in stinging language that Jews regarded them as no better than Nazis. In a famous piece of May 1947 he wrote 'to the Terrorists of Palestine':

My Brave Friends . . .

The Jews of America are for you. You are their champions. You are the grin they wear. You are the feather in their hats.

In the past fifteen hundred years every nation of Europe has taken a crack at the Jews. This time the British are at bat. . . .

Every time you blow up a British arsenal, or wreck a British jail, or send a British railroad train sky high, or rob a British bank, or let go with your guns and bombs at the British betrayers and invaders of your homeland, the Jews of America make a little holiday in their hearts.[6]

The British bitterly resented such diatribes—so much so that Sir Orme Sargent lectured the American Ambassador, Lewis Douglas, on the irresponsibility of the New York press inciting to violence and murder in Palestine:

I . . . asked him what would be the feeling of the United States Government if, for instance, British Communists were to publish in the British press an advertisement to the effect that 'every time you blow up an American arsenal or wreck an American gaol or send an American railroad train sky high . . . British Communists make a little holiday in their hearts'. Mr. Douglas said that the indignation of his Government would know no bounds and they would not be slow to show it.[7]

Vituperation against the British as murderers, and Bevin as a hangman, continued unabated. Ben Hecht for one believed he detected a loss of British nerve. He wrote further to the terrorists in Palestine: 'The British put the matter of who's who and what in Palestine up to the United Nations because they were frightened of you.'

In May 1947 the United Nations appointed a 'Special Committee'

⁶ Ben Hecht, *A Child of the Century* (New York, 1954), p. 615.
⁷ Memorandum by Sargent, 20 May 1947, FO 371/61754.

to report on the Palestine problem. When its members visited Jerusalem in the summer of that year, they found the British community in Palestine in a state of siege. Wives and children had been evacuated. The number of British police and military forces together with contingents of the Arab Legion now rivalled the symbolic figure of the 100,000 Jewish refugees who were still interned in European displaced person camps. The United Nations committee observed 'Bevingrads', the British redoubts in the centre of Jerusalem and other places where British personnel were bivouacked behind barbed wire. One-tenth of the armed forces of the entire British Empire now occupied a territory the size of Wales. There was one soldier for every eighteen inhabitants in the country, or, as one observer calculated, one for every city block. The drain on the economy for military upkeep alone amounted close to £40 million per annum. 'There is the manpower of at least 100,000 men in Palestine', Churchill stated in Parliament, 'who might well be at home strengthening our depleted industry. What are they doing there? What good are we getting out of it?'[8] When Britain moved into severe economic crisis in 1947, there developed a broad consensus of public, Parliamentary, and Cabinet opinion that recognized military withdrawal as an economic as well as a political and ethical imperative.

The general crystallization of British sentiment in favour of withdrawal did not necessarily contradict the Foreign Office's hope of preserving Britain's political and strategic position by relying on the probable action of the United Nations. It was a rational and indeed ingenious calculation, as the Zionists at the time recognized. It was based on the assumption that even biased or obtuse observers would not endorse partition because the creation of a Jewish state would precipitate civil war. The Foreign Office also assumed that the Soviet Union and the United States on this issue as on others would gravitate into opposite camps, and that such influences as Catholicism would militate against the Jews. The British in short hoped that the United Nations would support an independent binational state in which Jewish rights would be guaranteed and the promise of a national home more or less fulfilled. As it turned out the British merely reconfirmed that United Nations special committees as well as the General Assembly did not operate on British rational assumptions.

The political make-up of the special committee consisted of western Europe (Sweden and the Netherlands); eastern Europe (Czechoslovakia and Yugoslavia), the Commonwealth (Australia and Canada), Asia (India and Iran), and Latin America (Guatemala,

[8] Parliamentary Debates (Commons), 31 Jan. 1947, col. 1347.

Mexico, and Peru). Ralph Bunche was a member of the committee's secretariat. For ideological reasons the Foreign Office lamented the inclusion of the Yugoslavian representative, and the Colonial Office regarded the appointment of the Guatemalan, Jorge García-Granados, as a political disaster for the British Empire. He already had acquired the reputation as one of several dedicated and volatile enemies of British imperialism in the United Nations.[9] The 'travelling circus' (the phrase the Colonial Office also applied to the Visiting Missions of the United Nations) spent five weeks in Palestine, from mid-June to late July 1947. They submitted their recommendations on the 1st of September. During that time the committee, like previous committees on Palestine, developed its own personality as individuals took sides with Arab or Jew and became less or more sympathetic with the British as the investigation proceeded. It is illuminating to dwell briefly in this regard on García-Granados because he attempted relentlessly to expose British weaknesses of a moral and administrative character and because he became staunchly pro-Zionist. In his own judgement, many of his colleagues at the United Nations did not share his extreme enthusiasm but they endorsed his anti-British and pro-Zionist arguments. He was also representative of the 'Latin type' (another Colonial Office phrase) of anti-colonialist who became the bane of the Colonial Office during the era of decolonization.[10]

García-Granados had a tempestuous and tenacious temperament. He bore first-hand testimony of the evils of British imperialism in his neighbouring country, Belize (in other words, British Honduras, issues of which the Colonial Office did not wish to see injected into the Palestine controversy). He believed that he represented the Latin-American revolutionary tradition in a committee generally sympathetic with the British. He became intent on exposing British despotism in Palestine. At one session he asked the Chief Secretary, Sir Henry Gurney (whom he described as having 'a strong sense of superiority concealed under an icy courtesy'): 'How much is spent on army and police?' Gurney responded: 'We do not spend anything on the army. The amount spent on the police last year was 6,052,000 pounds and this year 7,010,000 pounds.' In other words the British army was not the fiscal concern of the Palestine administration. The amount necessary for the maintenance of the police force was sufficient to make the point García-Granados wished to stress. He noted emphatically to himself: *'in this small country, nearly*

[9] See CO 537/2336.

[10] See Jorge García-Granados, *The Birth of Israel: The Drama as I Saw It* (New York, 1948); for comment on the credibility of his testimony see Herbert Feis, *The Birth of Israel: the Tousled Diplomatic Bed* (New York, 1969), p. 77 n. 3.

$30,000,000 spent for police in one year! More than $2,000,000 a month! Could anyone deny that this was a police state?'[11] García-Granados later urged his colleagues to protest the death sentences of three Jewish terrorists. He based his case not on judicial or administrative propriety or precedent but on the cause of human freedom and justice. He said to his fellow committee members:

> Let me make my stand clear. . . . Some of you say these men are criminals. I don't know. Only history can pass judgement on the Palestine underground. History alone will state the last word on the French, the Dutch, the Polish, the German, the Yugoslav, and the British underground. These men fought Hitler in defense of their country and their principles. We applauded them because we thought they were right. These men are fighting now for similar beliefs. How, then, can you condemn what they are doing?[12]

He overwhelmingly proved that at least one member of UNSCOP was not 'a tool of the British administration in Palestine'.

García-Granados laughed off as 'idiotic' the accusations that he was anti-British. He merely denounced the tyranny of British administration in Palestine as he would despotism in Latin America. He along with his fellow committee member and friend Enrique Rodriguez Fabregat of Uruguay (who shared García-Granados's revolutionary fervour) met secretly with the champion against British imperialism, the leader of the Irgun, Menachem Begin. According to Begin's account of the meeting:

> When I [Begin] told Granados my name, he stepped back and in a loud voice said: 'So you are the man!'
> Taken aback by the ringing tone . . . I laughed. Fabregat did not laugh. He put his arms round my shoulders and hugged me as one hugs a younger brother and said something in Spanish.
> 'We are brothers in arms,' I said, when I found my voice. 'All the world's fighters for freedom are one family.'[13]

On less buoyant occasions García-Granados sometimes thought about the paradoxes of British imperialism. After an evening with the High Commissioner, he reflected:

> The British themselves really have no conception of their own rigidity and cruelty in the Palestine matter. There is a fundamental contradiction in British policy, for while their statesmen preach democracy to all the peoples of the world—and I believe they do so sincerely—at the same time they do not permit democracy to function in their own colonies, protectorates and mandates.
> One might say that the British are really cursed by their possession of the

[11] García-Granados, *Birth of Israel*, p. 46, italics in the original.
[12] Ibid., pp. 58–9.
[13] Menachem Begin, *The Revolt: Story of the Irgun* (Tel Aviv, 1964), p. 307. For incisive remarks about Begin and the British at this time see Sykes, *Crossroads to Israel*, pp. 244–5.

world's largest empire; in their desire to keep it intact they apply methods which their ethical principles certainly would prohibit them from using in private dealings.[14]

As Christopher Sykes has remarked, García-Granados's account must be read with an awareness of 'extreme and sometimes absurd bias', but it reveals the basic sentiments of the non-European world that he brought home to the British during the UNSCOP visit to Palestine.

García-Granados and two other members of the UNSCOP witnessed the expulsion of the *Exodus* from Haifa harbour.[15] In August when the members of the committee were writing their recommendations in Switzerland, word reached them in Geneva that the refugees would be forcibly deported to Germany. The committee as a whole was appalled. No doubt the particular tragedy of the *Exodus* did not change any general attitudes, but it helps to explain the eight to three vote in favour of partition.

There were other intangible influences besides that of the *Exodus* episode that were of incalculable importance. The Arabs effectively boycotted the committee. Even their staunchest friends in the Foreign Office lamented their 'exceedingly inept' diplomacy (Beeley's phrase) at the United Nations and the failure to recognize that their unyielding and dogmatic stand would create sympathy for the Jews rather than support for Arab nationalism.[16] The boycott prevented the Arabs from driving home their basic argument that the Jewish problem in Europe should not and could not be resolved in Palestine. Towards the end of the committee's deliberations in Switzerland seven of the eleven members made a tour of displaced person camps. The three members who voted against partition (the Indian, the Iranian, and the Yugoslav) did not visit the camps. More than the other committee members, they remained impervious to the lobbying of the Zionist leadership, which was of high calibre. It was an intellectual and ethical distance removed from the gutter level of the Zionist press in New York. It included men of irreproachable integrity such as Moshe Shertok and David Horowitz. The interaction of political manœuvring and random influence usually determines the membership and results of such international committees, and on this occasion the combination produced compassion for the Zionist cause, despite the steadfast pro-Arab bias that was introduced into the discussions by the Indian delegate, Sir Abdul Rahman.[17] The

[14] García-Granados, *Birth of Israel*, p. 193.

[15] For the *Exodus* affair see especially Bethell, *Palestine Triangle*, chap. 10.

[16] See e.g. Beeley's report of 7 June 1947, FO 371/61780.

[17] Rahman, a devout Muslim, appears in the pages of García-Granados's *Birth of Israel* as a caricature whose pro-Arab passions were not far removed from bigotry. García-Granados may have distorted Rahman's attitude, but in any case the theme of racial animosity runs

leaders of the Jewish Agency presented their case skilfully and indefatigably, while the case of the Arabs went mainly by default.

On the sensitive issue of frontiers the committee proposed a delimitation known derisively as the one preparing the ground for 'two
fighting serpents', which a glance at the map suggested.[18] From the
Zionist vantage point the demarcation would not prove economically
viable or militarily defensible, but at least the committee had not
recommended two non-contiguous, nominal Jewish states that would
have 'ghettoized' the Jews in Palestine. The committee's frontiers
marked the passing of the initiative for a territorial settlement from
the Colonial Office, where the proposed delineation aroused professional contempt, to the United Nations, where member nations
now had a basis of their own for cartographical speculation. On this
and other points the general international mood was perhaps best
expressed in American language of sympathy for the underdog. It
was a mood not fully comprehended at the time by Jemal Husseini,
the leader of the Palestinian Arabs, or by Arab politicians generally.
It can be related by the attitude of the Canadian representative, Ivan
Rand, who carried perhaps the greatest single influence within the
committee. David Horowitz, in discussing the possibilities of partition with him, said that the Jews were now fighting with their 'backs
to the wall'. Rand replied, 'I won't allow you to be placed in a
territorial ghetto.'[19]

'I am talking to you frankly, as I know you to be an honest man',
Rand told Horowitz. This candid exchange of ideas between the
Canadian judge and the Jewish economist reveals the principal doubts

through the important unpublished accounts of the committee's work. Racial intolerance
or tolerance knew no national boundaries. For example in one of the more ludicrous or
outrageous experiences of the committee, the members who visited the displaced person
camps encountered an American colonel in charge of the American zone in Austria. The
Colonial Office recommended the following passage to the Foreign Office for its 'entertainment value'. It was written by David MacGillivray, the British liaison officer to the
committee. 'For those who enjoy a tense situation this was the highlight of the tour. He
[the American colonel] is reported to have been complacent, conceited and very outspoken.
He began by saying that the Jewish D. P. problem was a mere nothing and he did not know
why all the fuss was being made about it. He had far bigger refugee problems on hand
created by those b—s the Soviet satellites who were persecuting their minorities and giving
him a big headache by forcing thousands of miserable refugees over their frontiers into
his camps and doing nothing to stop the flow from the east.... When asked how he would
tackle the problem of the Jewish D. P.s in his area . . . [he] said, "Well, when I was in
Palestine during the war there was a great big desert there. So far as I know it's still there." '
MacGillivray to Trafford Smith, 20 Aug. 1947, copy in FO 371/61786. The fullest accounts
of the inner-history of the committee are those by MacGillivray in the CO 537 series.

[18] On this point and other details about UNSCOP's recommendations see especially
George Kirk, *The Middle East 1945–50* (London, 1954), pp. 245–6; and Cohen, *Palestine
and the Great Powers*, pp. 260–8.

[19] Horowitz, *State in the Making*, p. 219.

of many western observers about the possibility of a Jewish state as well as the Jewish reassurances that did much to dispel the anxieties of Zionist well-wishers. Rand admired the Jewish qualities of initiative and determination:

I know that you [Horowitz] are one of those who left school and everything to work on the land and to do the real work. I was greatly impressed by Ben Gurion's statement that he ploughed the land with a rifle on his back. That required toughness and character. . . . You have to have a land which will not be a mockery, but which will be adequate for your needs, and then you have to be free in your policy.[20]

Rand nevertheless had qualms. He wished to be reassured that a Jewish state, once established, would live peacefully within its own frontiers and would not menace its neighbours. Horowitz was insistent on the peaceful aims of the Jews and emphasized the 'natural guarantee' of a hostile Arab world:

We are surrounded by 40–50 million Arabs in independent Arab States. But even so, we are prepared to give them any guarantee that we shall not commit any acts of aggression, because we really do not intend to commit such acts.[21]

The arguments put forward so earnestly and persuasively by Horowitz were decisive in swinging Rand, a key member of the committee, into solid support of the Jewish state. In a general sense Horowitz's ideas carried conviction with those who may have had apprehensions about militant Zionism. At the time of the creation of the Jewish state in 1947–8, it seemed reasonable to assume that the Jews, if only in self-defence, would wish, in Rand's words, 'not to defy the United Nations and world opinion'.[22]

The UNSCOP majority decision in favour of partition quickly came to represent the cutting of the Palestine knot. In retrospect it is possible to interpret the chain of events towards partition as inevitable after the passing of the British initiative to the United Nations in February 1947 if not before. The ineluctable tug of circumstances continued in September with the vote in favour of a Jewish state by UNSCOP. The affirmative UNSCOP vote prepared the way for the vote by the General Assembly in favour of partition on the 29th of November. Those events did not however seem inevitable at the time, especially to the British. In one of his more perceptive commentaries on the crisis, Richard Crossman wrote:

For two years Mr. Bevin has played for time, in the hope that something would turn up which would justify the retention of southern Palestine as a

[20] 'Conversation between Justice Rand and D. Horowitz', 6 Aug. 1947, ISA 93.03/2266/24.
[21] Ibid.
[22] Ibid.

British military base and enable him simultaneously to defeat the Jewish demands for statehood. Nothing has turned up; and we are now left with the choice of either clearing out, bag and baggage, or creating a Jewish state.[23]

In fact a lot had turned up, but little of it happened to be favourable to the British. On the other hand the British could still salvage Arab friendship and not alienate American and world opinion by an even-handed retreat. With that logic in mind the Colonial Secretary made an historic statement before the United Nations on the 26th of September 1947:

> *I have been instructed by His Majesty's Government to announce, with all solemnity, that they have . . . decided that in the absence of a settlement they must plan for an early withdrawal of British forces and of the British administration from Palestine.*[24]

The British would end the mandate, but they would not impose by force a solution unacceptable to either Jew or Arab.

The Decision to Quit

What inspired the decision to evacuate? There can be no doubt that the UNSCOP report triggered it, but the international annoyance only acted as a catalyst of more fundamental discontent. The minutes of the Cabinet on the 20th of September 1947 only starkly convey the sense of relief at arriving at a firm decision that marked the end of two years of frustration. 'This', Dalton wrote in his diary, 'if we stick to it, is a historic decision.'[25]

The Foreign Secretary came to the meeting armed with a memorandum that again stated the case against endorsing partition. He was not willing, Bevin re-emphasized in a remark that became his public leitmotiv in the coming months, 'to enforce a settlement which was unacceptable' to either side.[26] The Foreign Office, in particular Harold Beeley, would pursue a course of masterly inactivity.[27] The Colonial Secretary, who by now was thoroughly embittered at Jewish

---

[23] *New Statesman*, 20 Sept. 1947.

[24] Emphasis added, as perhaps Creech Jones should have done when he made the speech. His audience was sceptical. Crossman, who attended the session in New York, wrote in the *New Statesman*: 'Mr. Creech Jones' . . . speech made a thoroughly bad impression largely because, believing that Britain did not really intend to withdraw, everyone assumed that he was merely dismissing the Majority Report in order to enforce the *status quo*' (25 Oct. 1947).

[25] Dalton Diary, 20 Sept. 1947, Dalton Papers. For detailed treatment of these questions, see Cohen, *Palestine and the Great Powers*, pp. 268–76, with which the present abbreviated analysis is in agreement.

[26] Cabinet Minutes (47) 76th Conclusions, 20 Sept. 1947, CAB 128/10; PREM 8/859/1; CP (47) 259, 18 Sept. 1947, CAB 129/21..

[27] See e.g. Beeley's memorandum of 17 Aug. 1947 from which he elaborated further ideas, FO 371/61948.

terrorism, had resigned himself to 'leaving Palestine in a state of chaos'. Creech Jones would instruct the staff of the Colonial Office to begin making plans for the withdrawal of approximately 5,200 British subjects in the civil administration.[28] The Minister of Defence, Alexander, was not hopeful about maintaining law and order over the whole of Palestine for an indefinite period of time. The army could however protect the oil installations and the airfields without additional military reinforcements.[29] The Minister of Health, Bevan, hoped that British withdrawal would finally demonstrate to other powers, notably the United States, that the British 'did not wish to retain forces in Palestine for imperialist reasons'. The Labour government would at last live up to its pledges. The Minister of Fuel and Power, Shinwell, stressed the importance of an 'orderly' evacuation in order to avoid the impression of British 'weakness'. There was the apprehension that leaving Palestine in 'chaos' might not be compatible with British 'dignity'. The Chancellor of the Exchequer emphasized that the continuing presence of British troops 'merely led to a heavy drain on our financial resources and to the creation of a dangerous spirit of anti-Semitism'. Dalton also introduced the theme of a timetable. 'He . . . felt that a date for the withdrawal of the British administration and British forces should be announced as soon as possible.'[30] Here lay the key to the problem as it had also crystallized in the mind of the Prime Minister.

Attlee was determined to liquidate Palestine as an economic and military liability. In the aftermath of the transfer of power in India, he began more and more to apply the same formula to Palestine. He wrote for example three days before the decision on evacuation by the Cabinet: 'We should . . . state that we will withdraw our administrative officers and troops from Palestine by a definite date which should not be longer than six months, even if no other mandatory has been appointed and no agreement has been come to between the Arabs and the Jews.'[31] Only by imposing a definite time limit would there be any hope of forcing the Arabs and the Jews to make arrangements for their own political future, as had been proved, Attlee believed, in the analogous case of India. The minutes of the meeting of the 20th of September record Attlee's train of thought:

---

[28] The dilemmas facing the Colonial Office and other ministries are outlined in a memorandum by the Official Committee on Palestine, DO (47) 83, 5 Nov. 1947, Creech Jones Papers; CAB 134/4.

[29] See memorandum by Alexander, 'Military and Strategic Implications', 18 Sept. 1948, CP (47) 262, CAB 129/21.

[30] CM (47) 76, 20 Sept. 1947, CAB 128/10.

[31] Minute by Attlee, 17 Sept. 1947, FO 371/61878.

The Prime Minister said that in his view there was a close parallel between the position in Palestine and the recent situation in India. He did not think it reasonable to ask the British administration in Palestine to continue in present conditions, and he hoped that salutary results would be produced by a clear announcement that His Majesty's Government intended to relinquish the Mandate and, failing a peaceful settlement, to withdraw the British administration and British forces.[32]

The Indian solution thus played a prominent part in the evolution of the thought of the Prime Minister. It was duly applied to Palestine, with sanguinary results only on a smaller scale.

There are two documents in particular that give insight into the decision of the 20th of September, one written at the time, the other in retrospect. Dalton noted in his diary an exchange that does not appear in the official minutes. It indicates the extent to which the British were fed up with a thankless military occupation. During the meeting the only plea for a continued military presence was voiced by the Secretary for Air, Philip Noel-Baker. He said that the Royal Air Force wished to stay on. Bevin's response reveals the gap that frequently occurred between strategic planning and political reality: 'Tell [them] that, if they want to stay, they'll 'ave to stay up in 'elicopter.'[33]

The other document is a letter written by Creech Jones to Elizabeth Monroe some fifteen years after the event. He reflected on the decision to withdraw. He commented on the polarization of Arab and Jewish attitudes in 1947 and the British despair of any hope of reconciling them. 'The terrorism on both sides could not be abated and the drain on our limited resources was felt to be unbearable.' The British found no consolation from any quarter. 'World, American and Parliamentary opinion was intensely antagonistic and whatever considerations of strategy and bases might be, the issues of immigration, security and stateless persons in Europe were becoming irrestible so far as Britain was concerned. With accelerating speed the Cabinet was pushed to the conclusion that they could no longer support the Mandate.' He mentioned one episode in particular that left an indelible mark on the mind of the British public as well as officials at the time: 'A few weeks earlier the reprisals and hanging of the two young sergeants struck a deadly blow against British patience and pride.'[34]

The episode of the two sergeants received wide and bitter comment in the British press, perhaps most incisively in a leading article in

[32] CM (47) 76, 20 Sept. 1947, CAB 128/10.
[33] Dalton Diary, 20 Sept. 1947, Dalton Papers.
[34] Creech Jones to Elizabeth Monroe, 23 Oct. 1961, Creech Jones Papers.

The Economist. In powerful language it denounced the murder of
the two young Englishmen who had been grotesquely hanged with
booby traps on their bodies. It captured the British public sentiment
of the time:

> The time has come not to examine international or Arab or Jewish or even
> American interests in Palestine, but to write the British balance sheet. Why
> should British soldiers continue to be exposed to this kind of killing? Why
> should the British community bear the cost? ... The cost of Palestine to Britain is
> incalculable—in its material burden on the overstrained British economy, but,
> much more serious, in the moral degradation to which it exposes young men
> living under conditions which by their monotony incite them to excess and by
> their violence are likely to send them home very perfect anti-Semites.

The lure of the analogy of the Indian experience found expression in
The Economist's article just as it did in official minutes.

> In any situation of complete deadlock, the only hope is to introduce a com-
> pletely new factor—a catalyst—such as was found in India when the Govern-
> ment announced a date for the transfer of power. If the policy of the catalyst
> worked there, could it not work in Palestine?[35]

The Economist followed the argument through to the logical conclusion of partition supervised by the British, though it did not hold
out much hope for success and it based the proposal entirely on
British self-interest. The concluding words may be taken as representative of the emotions and thoughts that explain general British
support of withdrawal:

> . . . partition now is not [advocated] primarily because it is in the best
> interest of the Jews or the Arabs . . . it is simply because it is in the best interests
> of the long-suffering British, and is, indeed, their last offer before they remove
> themselves lock, stock and barrel from an area which is a drain on their resources,
> a death-trap for their soldiers and a source of degradation, both to the men who
> are sent there and to the growing number of potential anti-Semites at home.

The danger of anti-Semitism may have been overdrawn, but it was
emphasized throughout the British press. *The Times*, for example,
concluded that 'The bestialities practised by the Nazis themselves
could go no further'.[36] By such comment the British themselves
perhaps proved that no other method, however deplorable, could
have been more effective in getting them to quit Palestine.

The British decision to withdraw was irrevocable once the
announcement had been made to the United Nations, but the mood
of exasperation and defeat must be sought in the general crisis of
1947. The year 1947 of course was a landmark in the history of the
British Empire as well as a year of momentous events in the beginning

---

[35] *The Economist*, 9 Aug. 1947.
[36] *The Times*, 1 Aug. 1947.

of the cold war. Everything dwindled in importance in comparison with the transfer of power in India on the 15th of August. New limbs of the Commonwealth might flourish, but the backbone of the old British Empire had been severed. In the same month the British entered into a period of unprecedented economic austerity. Yet blood and treasure were still being drained away in Palestine. Public indignation at Jewish terrorism swelled to new proportions after the hanging of the two sergeants. A general sense of malaise pervaded the public mood in the aftermath of the *Exodus* episode. When the British government finally made the decision to quit, the British Parliament, press, and public greeted it with overwhelming approval. The British people would not tolerate a colonial war in Palestine.[37]

[37] For the author's more extensive and reflective thoughts on the British withdrawal from Palestine, see Wm. Roger Louis and Robert W. Stookey, eds., *The End of the Palestine Mandate* (University of Texas Press, in press).

6

THE UNITED STATES AND THE UNITED NATIONS VOTE OF THE 29TH OF NOVEMBER 1947

'THERE are people on the 3rd and 4th levels of the State Dept. who have always wanted to cut my throat', Truman wrote when the Palestine crisis reached its peak in the spring of 1948. He had in mind the Office of Near Eastern and African Affairs headed by Loy Henderson, and the emotional tone of this diary entry expressed more than mere exasperation at the usual tug-of-war that characterized the inner workings of the American bureaucracy. Even to sophisticated British observers the 'gyrations' (a word employed when 'tug-of-war' seemed inadequate) of American policy appeared to be almost incomprehensible. They are perhaps best understood in terms of general cultural attitudes of most Americans towards Jews and Arabs, the conflicting aims of the State Department officials and the White House staff, and the motivations. of the dominant personalities, not least the President's.

Truman, like Roosevelt, believed that on matters of supreme importance the President should be commander-in-chief of American foreign as well as military affairs. He shared Roosevelt's suspicion of British imperialism, though not with such outspoken opinions and without the confidence of a 'trusteeship' solution in Palestine. He resented the attacks by the Zionists. He was sensitive to the charge that the Jews indirectly manipulated American foreign policy. In particular he became angered at critics who impugned the integrity of the office of the Presidency by insinuating that he was a captive of the New York Jews, and he became frustrated when the bureaucratic machinery within the government seemed to contradict or thwart his purpose of relief of the displaced Jews in Europe and minimal though pro-Jewish involvement in Palestine.

It is helpful to see Truman's part in the Palestine controversy in relation to his Secretaries of State, Byrnes and Marshall, and their respective deputies. Byrnes had recognized Palestine as the President's domain. He gave the British the impression of having higher priorities, and he exasperated Bevin with vague if not contradictory assurances. The one time he took a Palestinian initiative in mid-1946 (at the time of the Morrison–Grady 'provincial autonomy' discussion) he became caught in the web of Anglo-American misunderstanding on issues that he himself clearly had not mastered. He was embarrassed by the failure of his one bid for peace in Palestine. In Forrestal's words it resulted in Byrnes's 'washing his hands of the whole Palestine matter'.[1] During the Byrnes era Truman relied on Acheson, whose judgement he trusted on the principal thrust of the Yom Kippur statement of October 1946—as it was popularly misunderstood—that partition might be the best solution.[2] Neither Truman nor Acheson gave the proposal for the creation of a Jewish state a wholehearted endorsement. The Yom Kippur declaration served to placate the New York Jewish constituency and it gave the President time to see whether the British themselves might still be able to solve the Palestine problem. The Zionists complained in 1946-7 that the President was indecisive and apparently internationally impotent, as evidenced by his failure in getting the 100,000 to Palestine. Truman himself believed that he had 'stuck his neck out' far enough on the refugee question. He responded bitterly and indignantly to the charges of making political capital on a humanitarian issue, and his touchiness helps to explain his caution.

When General Marshall became Secretary of State in January 1947, the chain of command over Palestine policy tightened. Acheson provided the link in transition. He emphasized in his talks with the British Ambassador the American preference for partition as a solution and his reluctance to see the issue thrown to the United Nations. Early in 1947 Acheson began to prepare for the worst. '1947 is going to be a bad year in Palestine and the Middle East', he wrote, and if the issue were to come before the United Nations 'it is hard to see how we can escape the responsibility for leadership'.[3] Marshall endorsed Acheson's general line that the United States should not rock the British boat. Both Marshall and Acheson worked well with Henderson, who had similar ideas. In a discursive sort of way there was a common reaction to the Palestine problem in the 'upper' and 'middle' levels of policy making. Henderson also had good working relations with Acheson's successor, Robert Lovett, whose friendship with Forrestal gave him sensitivity to the military dimension of the problem. Lovett carried forward Acheson's initiative of

[1] Forrestal Diary, 4 Sept. 1947, Forrestal Papers; Millis, *Forrestal Diaries*, p. 310.

[2] In his memoirs Acheson generously commented on Byrnes's refusal to deal with Palestine unless he could help it: 'I detected no inclination on the part of Secretary Byrnes to project himself into this issue, but rather a tendency to leave supervision of the Department's work on it more and more to me.' *Present at the Creation*, p. 169. On the partition suggestion in the Yom Kippur speech Acheson in his memoirs remained silent about the influence of the Zionist lobby.

[3] Acheson to Henderson, 15 Feb. 1947, USSD 867N.01/2-1547; *Foreign Relations 1947*, V, pp. 1048-9.

working as closely as possible with the British, and he also preferred
to do so through the American Embassy in London rather than with
Lord Inverchapel, whom State Department officials believed to be
too indulgent with the Zionists. The Secretary of State himself
sympathized with the British. In September 1947 Marshall told
Creech Jones and Inverchapel that the British 'had been the victims
of an impossible situation and considerable unjust criticism'.[4] In his
approach to the Palestine problem Marshall frequently mentioned
the word 'troops', which immediately brought to mind the shrinkage
of the American armed forces at the close of the war from three and
a half million men to less than 500,000 two years later. Perhaps no
one more than Marshall recognized the perils of committing American
troops in Palestine, yet he knew that the success of American policy
would depend on the determination to use American power, if
necessary, to enforce either partition or a binational state. Marshall
and the officials of the State Department clearly saw, or so they
believed, the British game of manœuvring them into a position the
British themselves no longer wished to play.

Shortly before he assumed office as the first Secretary of Defense in
September 1947, James Forrestal at a Cabinet meeting noted
Marshall's 'sharp resentment' at the British withdrawal of troops from
Greece and his comment that British evacuation of Palestine would
result in 'a bloody struggle between the Arabs and the Jews'.[5] Forrestal
himself held equally sharp and less neutral views. He thought it deplorable that the President allowed domestic Jewish pressures to jeopardize
American access to Middle Eastern oil. Forrestal's efforts to exert a
countervailing influence against the pressures of the President's pro-
Zionist advisers will be discussed in the next chapter. Here the point
is that he, Marshall, Lovett, and Henderson were at one. They did not
in Henderson's phrase, consider oil to be a 'dirty word' but an obvious
basis of American strategic security: 'oil . . . is not necessarily a symbol
of sinister imperialism but a vitally needed commodity like food'.[6] The
Secretary of Defense, the Under Secretary of State, and the Director
of the Office of Near Eastern Affairs held common ideas about oil
and also about the danger of Soviet intervention in the eastern Mediterranean. Their views approximated those of British ministers and
officials such as A. V. Alexander, Sir Orme Sargent, and Harold Beeley.
Such an identity of outlook did not exist between Marshall and
Bevin. Marshall disliked the 'blackmailing tactics' of the Arabs as

---

[4] Memorandum by Marshall, Secret, 25 Sept. 1947, USSD 501.BB Palestine/9–2547
Box 2182; *Foreign Relations 1947*, V, p. 1164.
[5] Millis, *Forrestal Diaries*, p. 303.
[6] Henderson, 'Oral History Interview', Truman Library, p. 57.

much as the 'ignominious' methods of the Jews. He was sceptical about the Russians being able to transform a Jewish state into a Soviet satellite, and he did not accept Bevin's view that the 'illegal' immigrants from eastern Europe were 'indoctrinated Communists'.[7] Nevertheless Marshall's basic inclination drew him to support the British in the Middle East as a stabilizing influence in the Arab World and as a bulwark against Russian expansion. Had it not been for Truman's firm instruction to support the majority report of UNSCOP, it is probable that he would have pursued a course towards a binational solution in line with the arguments so vigorously presented by Loy Henderson.

Henderson based his tenacious case against the creation of a Jewish state on the dual premiss that American support of partition would alienate the Arab world from the United States and that an Arab–Jewish war would undermine the British Empire in the Middle East. He did not believe that the Arab states would become Communist as a result of an American pro-Zionist stance, but that they would regard the United States as one of their deadliest enemies. They would turn to the Russians for assistance just as the Americans themselves had done in the search for co-operation against the Nazis. There would also be profound internal repercussions. 'If we press for a Jewish state', Henderson argued, 'we shall undoubtedly weaken the position of the moderate Arabs who are friends of the western world and strengthen that of the fanatical extremists.' In a final warning shortly before the United Nations vote in late November, Henderson wrote to Marshall:

I feel it again to be my duty to point out that it seems to me and all the members of my Office acquainted with the Middle East that the policy which we are following in New York at the present time is contrary to the interests of the United States and will eventually involve us in international difficulties of so grave a character that the reaction throughout the world, as well as in this country, will be very strong. . . . It is impossible for the British to remain a force in the Middle East unless they retain the friendship of the Arab world. By our Palestine policy, we are not only forfeiting the friendship of the Arab world, but we are incurring the long-term Arab hostility towards us.[8]

Despite the cogency of his arguments and his considerable skill at bureaucratic in-fighting, Henderson failed to reverse the drift towards American support of a Jewish state.

[7] See memorandum of conversation between Bevin and Marshall, 24 Nov. 1947, FO 371/61796. Bevin was not entirely consistent in his assessment of the Communist danger in Palestine, but he was fully aware of the possibility of infiltration according to British representatives as well as intelligence reports. See e.g. Pelham to Bevin, 20 Oct. 1947, FO 371/61883.

[8] Memorandum by Henderson, Top Secret, 24 Nov. 1947, USSD 867N.01/11-2447 Box 6761; *Foreign Relations 1947*, V, pp. 1281-2.

Henderson had a powerful opponent in a vital position. David Niles saw that the strong currents of the bureaucracy, to use the improbable language of the American Zionists who compared the Jordan with the Mississippi, would keep rolling along unless checked by the office of the President. On a matter of such intricate complexity and controversial importance as Palestine, the White House staff needed someone who could virtually keep daily surveillance over the ebbs and flows of State Department policy, and not from a pro-Arab vantage point. In July 1947 Niles learned that George Wadsworth, the American Ambassador to Syria, together with Henderson would serve as advisers to the UN delegation during the crucial Palestine proceedings. Niles wrote to the President urging that Major-General John H. Hilldring, the State Department's Assistant Under Secretary for Occupied Areas, be appointed to offset this pro-Arab influence. His memorandum reveals a sense of distrust not uncommon in the American government.

> Loy Henderson and George Wadsworth . . . are widely regarded as unsympathetic to the Jewish viewpoint . . . on the basis of their past behaviour and attitudes, I frankly doubt that they will vigorously carry out your policy. But your administration, not they, will be held responsible.
>
> It may not be feasible to oppose Henderson and Wadsworth as advisers to the Delegation. In any event, I believe it is most important that at least one of the advisers be a vigorous and well-informed individual in whom you, the members of the United States Delegation, and American Jewry have complete confidence. There is only one person I know who would fill the bill completely—General Hilldring.[9]

Truman not only appointed Hilldring but urged him 'to keep a channel of communication open directly to the White House'. Hilldring proved to be a persuasive and effective pro-Zionist spokesman. His assistant, Herbert A. Fierst, wrote later with extravagance but not without an element of truth: 'Hilldring was a tower of strength in support of the President's position. The two-thirds majority in favour of partition on November 29, 1947, might never have been achieved but for his efforts.'[10]

Hilldring had become sympathetic to the Zionist cause through his experience with the displaced person camps. As an officer responsible for 'occupied areas' his attitude towards the Jewish question was also influenced by problems he confronted with the resuscitation of the German nation. He believed that the American line in the

[9] Memorandum by Niles with covering letter by Truman to Lovett, 6 Aug. 1947, President's Secretary's Files Box 184, Truman Library.

[10] Herbert A. Fierst, 'Lest We Forget—Tribute to Hilldring', *Near East Report*, 30 Jan. 1974.

United Nations should be immediately to affirm the principle of the creation of a Jewish state. He received strong support from another member of the delegation, Eleanor Roosevelt.

Mrs Roosevelt led the attack against Henderson both before and during an important meeting of the delegates on the 15th of September when they met to discuss how best to proceed. According to Henderson:

> Mrs. Roosevelt . . . said, 'Come now, come, Mr. Henderson, I think you're exaggerating the dangers. You are too pessimistic. A few years ago Ireland was considered to be a permanent problem that could not be solved. Then the Irish Republic was established and the problem vanished. I'm confident that when a Jewish State is once set up, the Arabs will see the light; they will quiet down; and Palestine will no longer be a problem.'[11]

Mrs Roosevelt also had decided views about the attitude of the Arabs towards the Russians and vice versa. To universal astonishment the Russians in May had given encouragement to the Zionists. Four months later it appeared to all members of the American delegation except Mrs Roosevelt that the Soviet Union would nevertheless support the Arabs for obvious reasons of wishing to exploit Arab anti-western sentiment and to subvert the British Empire; and conversely it seemed clear that the Arabs, in Henderson's words, 'would work with the U. S. S. R. against the No. 1 enemy, ourselves'.[12] Mrs Roosevelt on the contrary thought 'that the Arabs were clearly more afraid of the U. S. S. R. than of us', and, as a minority of one, proved to be right about what Russians would do— though probably for the wrong reasons.[13] The Soviet delegation upset all calculations by supporting the Jews.[14] Without the endorsement of the eastern bloc the United Nations in late

[11] Henderson, 'Oral History Interview', p. 127. Henderson added, 'I'm sure that Mrs. Roosevelt didn't know that my first post in the Service was Dublin.'

[12] Minutes of US Delegation, 15 Sept. 1947, *Foreign Relations 1947*, V. pp. 1147-51.

[13] The Russian decision to support the Jews astounded contemporary observers and has continued to perplex historians. The best summary of the evidence is by Arnold Krammer, 'Soviet Motives in the Partition of Palestine, 1947-8', *Journal of Palestine Studies*, II, 2 (Winter 1973), who puts considerable emphasis on the lobbying of individual left-wing Zionists such as Moshe Sneh as well as on Russian calculations of Zionist links with revolutionary socialism and a drastic miscalculation of 'the Arab world's potential strength and anti-Western sentiment'. See also especially Yaacov Ro'i, 'Soviet-Israeli Relations, 1947–1954', in Michael Confino and Shimon Shamir eds., *The U.S.S.R. and the Middle East* (New York, 1973). The explanations have become sophisticated, but it seems clear that the overriding Russian aim was the disruption of the British Empire.

[14] It came as a great shock in particular to the British, whose basis of calculation was the improbability of the Soviet Union and the United States being able to find common ground. The unexpected Russian support of the Jews, in Beeley's words, 'gave rise to a great deal of speculation', not least among those who thought it dead certain that the Arabs would be the beneficiary of Russian magnanimity. See his memorandum enclosed in Cadogan to Bevin, 7 June 1947, FO 371/61780.

November could not have voted in favour of the creation of a Jewish State.

Marshall had carefully read the majority and minority reports of UNSCOP. He was surprised at the quality of analysis (which was an unwitting tribute to Ralph Bunche, who had drafted both parts). Though he disliked 'pussyfooting', Marshall instructed the delegates to remain as neutral as possible. If the United Nations voted in favour of partition, Marshall emphasized, then 'we will have to be ready to put troops into Palestine'. The reasons for his support of partition were straightforward. The United States would stand behind the creation of a Jewish state, if the United Nations favoured it, because it was American policy to make a success of the United Nations. Marshall and Bevin later discussed the tactics of that aim when the latter passed on a complaint from Nuri Pasha that 'American pressure' had been decisive in the vote on partition. Marshall replied that the Arabs had also brought pressure to bear, which he had tried to resist as well: 'He felt it was better in the long run not to intervene. He had given his people instructions accordingly over Palestine.'[15] Marshall was not dissimulating. Here was a paramount example of the American equivalent of a British proconsul or statesman in the highest tradition comparable to that of the British Empire attempting to fulfil the mission, in Lord Curzon's phrase, of 'imperial arbiter'.

Though cynics then and later found it difficult to believe, the element of impartiality played an important part in American attitudes towards Palestine in the winter of 1947–8. It helps to explain confusion in American policy. Fair-mindedness did not preclude general sympathy of the public for the Jewish underdog who was fighting, in a recurrent American phrase, 'the dirty A-rab'.[16] Americans in general admired Jewish culture, hygiene, and industriousness—but in Palestine and not, as Bevin had detected, in New York. They believed that the Jewish people had a moral right to create their own home in Palestine and, as Crossman had noted in his book, regarded the desert of the Negev as the equivalent of the American frontier. Those general attitudes found reflection at the highest level of American policy making. In an important interview with the President on the 19th of November, Chaim Weizmann,

[15] Memorandum on 'Anglo-American Conversations', 17 Dec. 1947, *Foreign Relations 1947*, V, pp. 1312-13.

[16] Truman had a tempered sympathy in regard to the 'underdog' theme: 'I fear very much that the Jews are like all underdogs. When they get on top they are just as intolerant and as cruel as the people were to them when they were underneath. I regret this situation very much because my sympathy has always been on their side.' Margaret Truman, *Harry S. Truman* (New York, 1973), pp. 384-5.

whom Truman would address within the next year as the President
of Israel, dwelt so persuasively on the theme of cultivating the Negev
with desalted water that Truman afterwards telephoned the American
mission at the United Nations. At that time the delegates were upholding Arab claims to the Negev, which in a rough sense encompassed
most of southern Palestine. More than a desert was at stake. It was
the strategic frontier of the future Jewish state. Truman's inverven-
tion threw the American delegation into disarray. He explained a few
hours later that he had not wished to 'upset the apple cart'. Whose
apple cart? The Zionist apple cart? His own apple cart of an impartial
American policy?[17] Truman subsequently proclaimed disgust at the
proceedings of the United Nations being reduced to the level of the
pork barrel. Yet it was his own intervention that caused a vital issue
to be resolved in favour of the Zionists.

Truman remained aloof from the seamier side of the scramble for
votes at the United Nations until the last decisive days. He probably
did not know of the extent to which David Niles became, in Henderson's words, one of the 'trump cards' held by the Zionists.[18] Through
Niles's co-ordinating efforts at the White House the Zionists were able
to launch a campaign that left the President and officials at the State
Department reeling under a bombardment of letters, telegrams, and
telephone calls. Truman wrote in his memoirs that he never 'had as
much pressure and propaganda aimed at the White House as I had in
this instance'.[19] Lovett reported after the vote that he had never
'been subject to as much pressure'.[20] Emmanuel Cellar and Sol
Bloom in the House of Representatives exerted their considerable
influence on Congressional colleagues, the executive branch, the
State Department, and in particular on the United Nations representatives from the Philippines, Liberia, and Haiti. Ten Senators
sent telegrams to the President of the Philippines, who also received
the friendly admonition of Felix Frankfurter and another Supreme
Court Justice, Frank Murphy. The Cuban Ambassador, who remained
recalcitrantly pro-Arab, complained that the Costan Rican vote had

[17] See Ganin, *Truman, American Jewry*, pp. 138–41, for a detailed treatment of this
episode. According to the representative of the Jewish Agency in Washington, Eliahu
Epstein, Weizmann, on Epstein's own advice, decided to 'take up *one point only*—Elath',
in other words, the outlet to the Red Sea. (Eliahu Epstein, *Israel and Elath: The Political
Struggle for the Inclusion of Elath in the Jewish State*, London, 1966, p. 20.) Weizmann did
indeed succeed in convincing the President of the benefits of developing the desert and of
the necessity for the Jewish state to have a port on the Gulf of Aqaba. Truman recalled
these points in 1949 when the British put forward arguments that the Negev should be
Arab.

[18] Henderson, 'Oral History Interview', p. 110.

[19] *Memoirs by Harry S. Truman: Years of Trial and Hope*, p. 158.

[20] Millis, *Forrestal Diaries*, p. 346.

been bought with a $75,000 bribe. Niles used business connections in an abortive effort to swing the Greek vote. Bernard Baruch let the representatives from China and France know that nothing less than economic assistance would be in jeopardy if they failed to vote in favour of partition. Harvey Firestone brought Liberia to heel. As Robert Donovan summed it up in an understatement in his biography of Truman, intrigue was rife.[21] So close was the vote and so intense the pressure that Truman himself finally threw his weight behind the Zionists in the last three days—but probably not to the extent conveyed by Niles to the head of the American delegation in New York. Niles said that the President wished the delegation 'to get busy and get all the votes they could, [and] that there would be hell if the voting went the wrong way'.[22] David Horowitz judged that Truman's intervention was decisive: 'the United States exerted the weight of its influence almost at the last hour, and the way the final vote turned out must be ascribed to this fact'.[23]

On the day of the vote the heart of the largest Jewish cosmopolis in the world pounded with an excitement usually reserved for the World Series.[24] Thousands of people, many of whom were New York Jews waving signs and shouting pro-Zionist slogans, lined up for admission to the United Nations General Assembly Hall in Flushing. Harold Beeley, among others, graphically described the atmosphere as that of a great sports event.[25] Throughout the city the fans at home, to modify his analogy slightly, kept score over the radio. The Jews were the home team, and to use Ben Hecht's phrase, they now had their turn at bat. According to Beeley the propaganda in the press had built up the fever of excitement to the extent that opponents of partition were regarded as enemies of the American people, or rather like the Yankees visiting at Ebbets Field. When the representative of France struck in favour of partition he received

---

[21] Donovan, *Presidency of Harry S. Truman*, p. 330.

[22] Quoted in Cohen, *The Great Powers and Palestine*, p. 296. The Zionist lobbying has been subjected to microscopic scrutiny. See also Bain, *March to Zion*, pp. 178–82; Ganin, *Truman, American Jewry*, pp. 144–6; Snetsinger, *Truman, the Jewish Vote*, pp. 66–71; and Urofsky, *We Are One!*, pp. 145–6. Fred J. Khouri, *The Arab–Israeli Dilemma* (Syracuse, 1968), chap. 3, is a balanced account that helps to restore the Arab perspective.

[23] Horowitz, *State in the Making*, p. 301.

[24] The comparison was in fact in everyone's mind because the Dodgers had been defeated by the Yankees. A writer in the *Spectator* explained to his readers that the Dodgers were 'the underdogs . . . facing a powerful and apparently unbeatable organisation'—much the same as the Jews and the Arabs at the United Nations (7 Nov. 1947, p. 587). This was the same year that Jackie Robinson played his first world series and Ralph Bunche found himself slammed into international fame because of Palestine. 'Congratulations making the Honor Role', a well-wisher wrote to Bunche. 'I hope you don't mind finishing second to Jackie Robinson.' L. Finklestein (later an authority on the United Nations) to Bunche, 11 Feb. 1948, Bunche Papers.

[25] For Beeley's report dated January 1948 see FO 371/68528/E416.

tumultuous cheers. The Greek delegate was booed when he batted against partition. As if in the ninth inning the fans made it re-soundingly clear what they thought of the great power trying to play the part of an impartial umpire, the United Kingdom. The British Commonwealth did not perform with team-like solidarity. The white Dominions pitched in favour of the Jews, and India and Pakistan in favour of the Arabs. The final score was thirty-three to thirteen with ten abstentions. Using far more serious language than that of a base-ball game, García-Granados described the outcome as a triumph for those who believed in the 'justice and historic necessity' of the creation of a Jewish state 'by the supreme authority of civilized mankind'.[26]

Postmortem Appraisal of the United Nations Game: Sumner Welles and the Zionists

'The positive attitude both of America and of Russia', Chaim Weiz-mann had written in October 1947, was almost 'tantamount to a miracle.'[27] Without the fortuitous combination of the United States and the Soviet Union, there could not have been a resolution in favour of the Jews. There are many aspects of this 'miracle' that will continue to demand attention of historians as they pursue detective work on certain key votes such as Greece (against), Haiti and Liberia (for), and China (abstention). For the purpose of illuminating one of the themes of this book—American anti-colonialism and the British Empire—there is óne particular archival revelation. It is the part played by Sumner Welles in the Jewish campaign that led to the critical international endorsement of partition on the 29th of November. Welles believed that he had contributed to an achieve-ment that ultimately would be no less significant than the Balfour Declaration. He summed it up later as 'Israel's basic title to inde-pendence'.[28] So narrow was the vote that the sense of moral victory seemed all the more keen. His part in the triumph was fully acknow-ledged by Jewish leaders at the time. 'You were the first I tried to phone after I received the news', Weizmann wrote to him the next day.'[29]

Welles holds a place of special importance in the history of Ameri-can anti-colonialism. It would be difficult to think of another indi-vidual who combined such moral outrage at the British Empire with

---

[26] García-Granados, *Birth of Israel*, pp. 268-9.
[27] *Weizmann Letters*, XXIII, p. 23.
[28] *Washington Post*, 21 Dec. 1948.
[29] *Weizmann Letters*, XXIII, p. 52.

so righteous a belief in the American cause. He had served as Under
Secretary of State from 1937 to 1943. His considerable abilities
included power of analysis of complex international controversies
(he was the most outspoken and consistent postwar critic of American
policy towards Indonesia, Indochina, and Kashmir as well as Palestine)
and grasp of detail about the structure and politics of the United
Nations. He had an unshakeable faith in the potential of American
'leadership' in world affairs. He regarded himself, in the Wilsonian
tradition, as an arbiter between the imperial powers of Europe and
the peoples of Asia and Africa who aspired to independence. His
sympathies definitely were with the latter. During the war he had
regarded Churchill as an oppressive force in colonial affairs and he
had viewed Oliver Stanley, the Colonial Secretary, as 'the most
narrow, bigoted, reactionary Tory' he had met during his official
career.[30] After the war he saw little reason to change his views
about the 'outmoded' political and economic colonial system of the
British. In contrast with Stanley, Creech Jones appeared to him to be
a nonentity and Bevin as an inept but dangerous perpetuator of
Churchill's 'imperialist' policies. Welles went so far as to denounce
Bevin 'as the worst Foreign Secretary Britain had ever had'.[31] He
expressed that view privately, but it was not far removed from his
public statements in the *Washington Post*: 'Mr. Bevin seems to have
little interest in American public opinion and no understanding of
the factors by which American sentiment is motivated. He lacks
political instinct in his conduct of foreign policy'—and, at another
time, Welles wrote of Bevin's 'narrow bias and blind obstinacy'.[32]
'Bevin-pox' was the phrase he used to sum up the plague in international affairs caused by postwar British imperialism.

After his resignation from the State Department in 1943, Welles
had written a syndicated column on foreign affairs that appeared in
many of the leading American newspapers. Latin America was his
particular domain. In the postwar period he pontificated with
authority about the danger of Communism in the western hemisphere and the need to preserve American influence throughout
Latin America. Eliahu Epstein, the representative of the Jewish
Agency in Washington, explained to Weizmann in March 1947:

[30] Louis, *Imperialism at Bay*, p. 35 and especially pp. 497–9 for his wartime ideas. See
Wilson, *Decision on Palestine*, p. 2 *et passim* for his pro-Zionist attitude during the war.
[31] Memorandum on a conversation with Welles by Eliahu Epstein, 17 Nov. 1947, WA;
ISA 93.03/2270/9.
[32] *Washington Post*, 23 Sept. and 19 Nov. 1947. Antipathy towards Bevin runs throughout his writings, e.g. ibid., 29 June 1948: 'So long as Mr. Bevin continues to be Britain's
Foreign Secretary there will be no British policy in Palestine that is marked by justice
toward the Jews.'

The influence of some of Mr. Welles' ideas has increased enormously because of an intensified United States participation in Latin-American politics due to . . . growing Communistic activities in certain of the Latin-American countries. . . . For years Mr. Welles has urged United States leadership in the western hemisphere, and of late he and other prominent supporters of this idea have been very much disturbed by the existing situation in the direct neighborhood of the United States. . . . This situation has made Mr. Welles influential today to an extent that he has not been since his association with the Department of State.[33]

In the same letter Epstein also described Welles as 'a very sincere and conscientious friend'.

The critical period of Welles's influence occurred between the time of the British decision to refer the Palestine issue to the United Nations in February 1947 and the vote in favour of partition in November. He was one of the masterminds behind the Zionist United Nations strategy. It would be a mistake to assume that without his assistance the vote would have been different, or that his influence was decisive. What can be said with certainty is that the Zionist leaders welcomed his help, that he worked indefatigably for their cause both in the press and behind the scenes, and that his creative intelligence definitely influenced the tactics of the campaign. It is important to note his fundamental assumption. It was the opposite from the British, and one on which American officials held divided opinions. Welles believed, in his own words, that the new Jewish state would 'contribute immeasurably to the maintenance of world peace and to the rapid progress of all of the Near East'.[34]

The prospect of a vote by the General Assembly of the United Nations initially had thrown the representatives of the Jewish Agency into despair. Epstein wrote to Welles in March 1947:

I am afraid that in the present set-up there is little probability of a 2/3 majority in our favour. In the Assembly there is an initial hostile bloc of 8 out of 55 which numbers virtually a Moslem unit—the 5 Arab States, Turkey, Iran, and Afghanistan. The British bloc, i.e. Great Britain and the Dominions, together with Holland, Greece, and Belgium, must be counted also to react probably negatively.[35]

If one added to a negative list most of the Latin-American states, the Soviet Union and its satellites, 'and the Asiatic and African countries like India, Ethiopia and Liberia', then the Jewish case at first sight seemed to be appalling. Welles did not agree with that analysis. Neither he nor anyone else at that stage could have predicted with certainty how the Russians would respond, but he believed that the

---

[33] Epstein to Weizmann, 21 Mar. 1947, WA.
[34] Welles to Epstein, 1 Dec. 1947, CZA S25/6618.
[35] Epstein to Welles, 14 Mar. 1947, CZA S25/6618.

white Dominions of the Commonwealth and the countries of western Europe would be favourable to the Jews. He also took a much more optimistic outlook on the critical area of Latin America. He replied to Epstein:

I see no reason to believe that there is any justification for the repeated assumption in the press here that the Latin American Republics will support the so-called Arab bloc. Nor do I feel under present conditions that we need necessarily assume that the smaller nations of Western Europe and such of the Dominions as Australia and Canada are going to follow British policy. The situation in the Assembly will not, in my opinion, be unduly favourable, but I do not think that, if proper work is done, we need anticipate so unfavourable a situation as you expect.[36]

Welles in the last years of his official duties at the State Department had played a key part in the discussions about the creation of the future United Nations, and in his newspaper column he had established himself as one of the principal analysts of UN politics. He also had many years of experience in dealing with the representatives of the Latin-American countries. He knew many of them personally. In the coming months his firsthand knowledge and acquaintances proved to be an invaluable asset in the Zionist campaign.

Welles advised the Jewish representatives to concentrate their efforts on the small or medium-size nations represented at the United Nations, and to assume that the British Dominions, with the exception of Pakistan and perhaps India, could be persuaded by moral and historical argument to vote in favour of the Jews. As he surmised, Pakistan remained staunchly pro-Arab, and, as he apprehended, India, after prolonged moral torment, voted against the Jews essentially because of the substantial Muslim community in India. He was certain that humanitarian sentiment would help to pull the white Dominions on to the Jewish side, and that H. V. Evatt, the Australian Foreign Minister, would see opportunities for his own career in the United Nations by politicking in favour of an even-handed settlement (while in private he committed himself to partition).[37] Canada, New

---

[36] Welles to Epstein, 17 Mar. 1947, CZA S25/6618.

[37] The Jewish representatives were well aware that Evatt's ego could be used to their advantage. Michael Comay, the representative of the Jewish Agency at the United Nations, related an interview in which 'Evatt did most of the talking' in May 1947: 'After I had emphasized the unique position he occupied at UNO, and our eagerness to seek his advice (I laid it on thick), he opened up. . . . He was willing to support a "liberal partition" large enough to form the basis of a possible state. . . . He added some unflattering comments on the Arabs; the British policy of kowtowing to them was disgusting.' (Michael Comay to Shertok, 2 May 1947, ISA 90.03/2266/15.) Evatt publicly attempted to give the attitude of being impartial in order to enhance his reputation as an arbiter. For his general pro-Zionist attitude see Alan D. Crown, 'The Initiatives and Influences in the Development of Australian Zionism, 1850–1948', *Jewish Social Studies*, XXXIX, 4 (Fall 1977). For Jewish

Zealand and especially South Africa supported the Zionist cause. Welles was not directly involved in these votes, but his general analysis, which helped guide the Zionist leaders, was as shrewd as any other contemporary assessment. As at the time of the San Francisco Conference, he perceived that the white Dominions would not necessarily follow a British lead. Nor would the 'smaller countries' (his particular concern) vote in any particular pattern.

It is important to see one point in perspective because the subsequent history of the United Nations might suggest otherwise. In 1947 there was not yet a solid 'anti-colonial' bloc. Welles and others detected a certain 'color consciousness' on the part of some representatives that caused China, for example, ultimately 'to wobble' into the camp of abstention. Though the Latin-American countries were usually regarded by the British and others as American puppets, they were much more recalcitrant, from the American point of view, than they sometimes appeared to be. There was in fact no Latin-American 'bloc' either. The Latin Americans could not be relied upon either to vote consistently against the British or to follow the lead of the United States. At the end of June, Welles advised the representatives of the Jewish agency that the Latin-American votes as a whole seemed to be more uncertain than any other, and that 'we should intensify our activities in Latin America during the coming months, striving for a broader understanding by the public in these countries of the Palestine problem'.[38]

Welles placed a great deal of emphasis, both negative and positive, on certain individuals. He was extremely sceptical about the value of the prominent part played by García-Granados. Welles feared that this 'clumsy and undiplomatic' assistance 'may harm rather than help us'.[39] There was in fact good cause for alarm, and not only about the diplomatic activities of García-Granados. During the visit of UNSCOP to Palestine, the American Consul General at Jerusalem reported in a 'Top Secret' communication to the State Department that García-Granados had 'developed "a beautiful friendship" with a Jewess named "Emma" in Tel-Aviv'.[40] The personal conduct of García-Granados did not in actuality become a scandal, but it might have, and it would have been a serious embarrassment to the Jews

impressions of other Commonwealth personalities, see especially Michael Comay's letter of 3 Dec. 1947, *Israel Documents (Dec. 1947–May 1948)*, pp. 3–15.

[38] Memorandum by Epstein, 30 June 1947, CZA S25/6618.

[39] Ibid.

[40] Macatee to Merriam, Top Secret, 21 July 1947, USSD 501.BB Palestine/7-2147 Box 2181. The Consul General continued: 'The Australian alternate . . . has expressed himself as being terribly annoyed by the conduct of the Guatemalan and the Uruguayan. "Can't you do something about those Banana Republics?" he asked, adding: "They're terrible!" '

if their self-proclaimed champion had been accused of corruption, even though his 'beautiful friendship' may have been quite innocent. In that sense Welles's warning was prescient.

There is a memorandum in the Weizmann Archives dated the 17th of November—less than two weeks before the vote—that reveals the continuing anxiety about the wooing of 'smaller countries' and the courting of the Latin-American votes. 'Mr. Welles said he had dined with a number of people from the UN', Epstein reported, and had been 'shocked' to find that the Luxembourg delegate believed that 'war' in the Middle East would break out if Palestine were partitioned. After an hour's conversation with the Luxembourger, Welles believed that this particular vote was securely Jewish. He was less satisfied about a point of general importance that continued to preoccupy the Zionists up to the eve of the 29th. Welles and others who talked with the Latin-American representatives were constantly reminded of the influence of the Catholic Church. It was 'very much on the alert', Welles warned, and he apprehended that the representative from El Salvador appeared to be 'dead against us' for religious reasons.[41] El Salvador eventually abstained, but there is no evidence of Welles's influence.

The winning of the United Nations' vote was a systematic and team effort, and it would be wrong to exaggerate Welles's part in it even, in its Latin-American dimension.[42] It would also be a mistake to underestimate the quality of advice that Welles gave and continued to give to the representatives of the Jewish agency. In February 1948 for example he warned that it would be misguided to believe that much influence could be effectively exerted on American military officials, and he acutely explained the part that strategic planning played in the shaping of American policy. He rightly emphasized that the issue of Palestine was essentially a political question that ultimately would have to be resolved in all probability by the President himself. This is how Welles isolated the military and strategic element for the benefit of the Zionist leaders after the partition vote:

> The problem we are up against is primarily a political problem. The policy that this Government will follow will be decided by those responsible for determining policy and, while strategic and defense considerations, of course, play a part in the picture, the final decision will depend upon the vision of those entrusted with the formulation of policy in relation to the survival of the United Nations and in its relation to the prevention of a major conflagration in the Near East.[43]

[41] Memorandum by Epstein, 17 Nov. 1947, WA.
[42] See for example a committee memorandum of 15 Mar. 1947 in ISA 93.03/2270/9 which independently addressed itself to many of the same problems that Welles anticipated.
[43] Welles to Benjamin Akzin, 7 Feb. 1948, ISA 93.03/66/4.

One pauses to reflect how State Department policy might have developed had Sumner Welles remained Under Secretary after 1943. He had a much greater belief in the potential of the Jewish state to stabilize the Middle East than did his successors. It might be added that the Israeli leaders would probably have felt the full force of his autocratic personality whenever he felt there was a lapse from idealistic principle.

In any case Welles gave the representatives of the Jewish Agency sound advice on how to influence American policy. He was sceptical about converting or even influencing individuals in the State Department or the Pentagon. The most effective pressure that could be brought to bear on the Administration, he wrote in February 1948, would be through 'outstanding Senators of both Parties'. He thought that it would be entirely possible, as indeed it was, to persuade leading members of the House of Representatives and the Senate that it would be in the best political and strategic interests of the United States 'to compel the Administration to take . . . an initiative'.[44] In the end he believed that most of the American people as well as the politicians could be convinced, as he himself had been, that the Jews deserved support in the quest for 'a transcendent ideal which has been forged by 2000 years of tragic suffering and an unsurpassed amount of sacrifice, capacity and effort'.[45]

In early 1948 Welles also forcefully advised that Weizmann personally might have a decisive influence on Truman. 'In my opinion his presence here' in the United States, Welles wrote to Epstein, 'would unquestionably be more valuable than in any other place. . . . I realize what a severe burden this imposes upon him but this year of 1948 is unquestionably a deciding moment.'[46] This again was sound advice that confirmed the views of the Zionist leaders about how best to proceed, as will be seen in the following chapters, in the spring of 1948. This was also the time that Welles began to prepare, with the assistance of the Jewish Agency, his book *We Need Not Fail*, which appeared at the critical time of the early days of the Arab–Israeli war in June 1948.[47]

The Zionists leaders were grateful for Welles's advice and support. In view of his substantial and sustained effort, both in the press and behind the scenes, it is not at all surprising that he was the first person whom Weizmann had attempted to telephone after the triumphant vote of the 29th of November.

[44] Ibid.
[45] As he later summarized the moral argument in the *Washington Post*, 21 Dec. 1948.
[46] Welles to Epstein, 4 Feb. 1948, ISA 93.03/66/4.
[47] See the correspondence about the book in ISA 93.03/66/4.

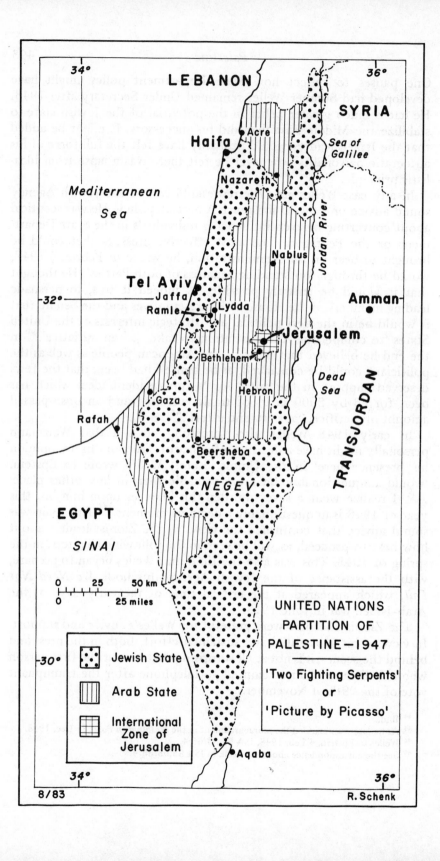

34°

LEBANON

SYRIA

Acre

Haifa

Sea of
Galilee

Mediterranean

Sea

Nazareth

Jordan River

Nablus

Tel Aviv

Jaffa

Ramle

Lydda

Amman

32°

Jerusalem

Bethlehem

Dead
Sea

Hebron

Gaza

TRANSJORDAN

Rafah

Beersheba

NEGEV

EGYPT

SINAI

0   25   50 km

0   25 miles

UNITED NATIONS
PARTITION OF
PALESTINE—1947

30°

Jewish State

Arab State

International
Zone of
Jerusalem

'Two Fighting Serpents'
or
'Picture by Picasso'

Aqaba

34°

36°

8/83

R. Schenk

7

THE WINTER OF 1947–1948:
TOWARDS PARTITION OR
TRUSTEESHIP?

THE principal British response to the partition vote of the United Nations was to set a definite date for the termination of the mandate. The pattern of a contracted timetable in India now recurred in Palestine: The pace of events had accelerated British withdrawal from an indefinite period of years under British trusteeship to the possible date of August 1948. After the vote in the United Nations the British now set the time of the transfer of power for the 15th of May 1948. The transfer of power to whom? Unlike India there would be no army, police, or civil service—only, to use the recurrent British phrase, anarchy. As in India the end of British rule would be absolute and not gradual or piecemeal. Much of the debate in the winter of 1947-8 centred on how to provide a gradual and orderly transfer of authority, possibly through the creation of a trusteeship regime in which United Nations representatives would co-operate with British officials in at least maintaining public services. One can detect an element of *schadenfreude* as the British observed the Americans now assuming the burden of finding a workable solution. As in India the British remained adamant on the date and absolute character of withdrawal. Otherwise, they feared, they would find themselves imposing *de facto* partition or presiding over the destruction of a unitary or binational state.

Jewish planning after the victory in the United Nations immediately turned to the question of implementation. It was clear that a transfer of power was imminent, though it would not follow the pattern established in India. Uncertainty of British plans, and the impossibility of predicting the American reaction, added to the suspense. This was the critical period in which the Jews began to assume informal political and effective military control in Jewish Palestine; but without the continued backing of the United States the chances of ultimate success seemed precarious. The representatives of the Jewish Agency who followed these issues were well aware of the danger of the State Department and the Pentagon reversing the decision to give American backing to partition. Bureaucratic 'inaction' in Washington, as one Jewish document described it, could be a dangerous weapon to sabotage the establishing of the new state.[1] Even worse might be the success of Loy Henderson in imposing an indefinite trusteeship regime that would kill the momentum that the vote of the 29th of November had created. The Jewish archives reveal an awareness in intricate detail of the American debate within the government as well as in public about the future of Palestine. It is the Jewish perception of the magnitude of the issue—to the Zionists a question of national life and death—that gives each stage of the American controversy both in public and in secret an additional element of historical drama.

In the United States the partition vote caused widespread comment about the direction and motive of American policy. In the press Walter Lippmann perceived a rationality that British and American officials actually involved in the issue certainly did not see. It is an analysis of interest because of its arresting generalizations at variance with official policy. Lippmann's commentary gave historical perspective to the problem in relation to the issues of the cold war. The UN vote had taken place shortly after the publication of his book *The Cold War*, which was essentially, on the one hand, an attack on the 'Truman Doctrine' of containment against Russian expansion, and, on the other hand, an endorsement of the Marshall Plan, which he interpreted as assistance to threatened states capable of helping themselves. The partition of Palestine, he wrote in his column in the *New York Herald Tribune*, was inevitable, just as the partition of Ireland and India had been inevitable. The British no longer possessed the power to hold together fundamentally diverse communities. The United Nations had wisely refrained from the attempt to provide a substitute for British colonial administration. The Arabs and the Jews would have to learn to rule themselves, 'even though the price is the blood, the sweat, and the tears which all peoples have paid who have achieved freedom'. The significance of the United Nations decision, he continued, was the implied agreement of the Soviet Union and the United States to stay out of experiments of internal administration that had not worked in Germany, Austria, or Korea. The future peace of the world would depend on the Russians and the Americans withdrawing from 'the hotspots of the globe'. The smaller nations, in this case a Jewish state and an Arab state (presumably one amalgamated with Transjordan), would themselves have to provide stability rather than having it imposed by the great powers. Here was his general point:

[1] Memorandum by Jewish Agency Office, 'Strictly Confidential', 30 Jan. 1948, ISA 93.03/126/4; *Israel Documents* (December 1947–May 1948), pp. 267–76.

Those who take this view will say that a two-power world is intolerable, and that the other states and nations, now submerged beneath the Soviet–American conflict, must be called back to redress the balance which Russia and America alone can never hope to achieve. That, however much it may be misrepresented by its enemies and even by many of its ardent but uninformed supporters, was the original purpose of the Marshall Plan.[2]

In the mind of Walter Lippmann, at least, the Marshall Plan thus found specific relevance in Palestine.

To those within the American government—with the exception of the pro-Zionists on the White House staff—the partition of Palestine did not have such a clear-cut significance except in the general sense of a Middle Eastern time bomb. The views of the Secretary of Defense represented almost the opposite of Lippmann's. Forrestal too pondered the analogy of Ireland, but to him it brought to mind dire premonition rather than optimism. Could the Jews and Arabs be regarded as 'submerged' peoples called upon to redress the balance between Russia and America? Along with Robert Lovett and the Middle East experts of the State Department, Forrestal thought that there was a general under-estimation of ferocious Arab resentment. He did not regard American support of partition as a rational policy calculated on the basis of national security but one determined by the emotions of a powerful pressure group. He deplored the injection of American domestic politics into foreign affairs. In January and February 1948 Forrestal took the initiative in trying to promote a bipartisan Palestine policy. He attempted to persuade Republican leaders such as Thomas E. Dewey and Arthur Vandenberg that the Zionist lobby for the United Nations 'bordered closely on a scandal'. He tried to convince them that American support of a Jewish state would terminate American access to Middle Eastern oil, which, in the phrase of General Alfred M. Grunther (the Chairman of the Joint Chiefs of Staff), had been

[2] *New York Herald Tribune*, 2 Dec. 1947. Lippmann's ideas perhaps commanded the attention of the American public more than any other individual writer, but, for the issues actually being debated within the government, the representatives of the Jewish Agency attached much more importance to the views expressed by James Reston in the *New York Times*. Reston wrote on the basis of inside information in the State Department. On the 29th of January 1948 for example he described the developing split between the pro-Zionists of the White House and the anti-Zionists of the Department of Defense on the question of oil reserves. His comments perturbed the Jewish representatives. For their assessment of his connections see for example memorandum by Epstein, 5 Mar. 1948, *Israel Documents* (December 1947–May 1948), pp. 425-7. The other American journalists of particular prominence who were alarmed at the pro-Zionist influences on American defence policy were Joseph and Stewart Alsop. For critique of their influence (described by the pro-Zionist New York tabloid *P. M.* as 'slick and poisonous') see the letter written by the Chancery of the British Embassy in Washington to the Eastern Department, 11 Feb. 1948, FO 371/68648.

'spiked' because of the UN vote. In view of the depletion of American oil reserves, denial of Arab oil would prove to be critical to the security of the United States and, in Forrestal's opinion, would necessitate such drastic changes in the American way of life as the conversion to four-cylinder automobiles. Forrestal sympathized with Henderson and other State Department officials who were 'seriously embarrassed and handicapped by the activities of Niles'. As a result of his foray into the American politics of Zionism, Forrestal became more aware, as he recorded in his diary, of the explosively emotional nature of the controversy. He also apprehended the reluctance of the Republicans to give the Democrats the advantage over Palestine, and the great importance that Democratic party leaders attached to Jewish funds. Here Forrestal detected misguided priorities. What difference would the loss of New York, Pennsylvania, or California make in a national election if the United States itself might be lost?[3]

The Palestine issue had now assumed such ominous importance that it merited the attention of the newly founded National Security Council.[4] The cumbersome machinery of the American bureaucracy would now forge the views of the State Department, Department of Defense, and Central Intelligence Agency into a single sword. The process of systematic review began with George Kennan, then Director of the State Department's Policy Planning Staff. He drafted a report in close consultation with Henderson, who viewed the National Security Council as the last chance to reverse the Zionist policy of the White House. Kennan, who previously had not been involved in the Palestine controvery, as usual brought to bear an incisive intellect and a fresh readiness to look into previous policy from all angles, not least the one concerning the Soviet Union. He was appalled at what he saw. He immediately anticipated these consequences of American support of partition:

(a) Arab cancellation of base rights, commercial concessions and pipeline construction;

(b) decline in strategic position because of loss of access to military facilities in the Middle East;

(c) possible deaths of American citizens in the Middle East because of Arab violence; and,

(d) a threat to the success of the Marshall Plan because of European dependence on Arab oil.

[3] Forrestal Diary, entries for Jan.–Feb. 1948, *passim*, Forrestal Papers; Millis, *Forrestal Diaries*, pp. 346–65.

[4] For the function of the National Security Council in its early years see especially Thomas H. Etzold, 'American Organization for National Security, 1945–50', in Thomas H. Etzold and John Lewis Gaddis, eds., *Containment* (New York, 1978).

The Policy Planning Staff also pointed out that the Russians would gain by the UN solution because they would have the opportunity to place Soviet troops in the Middle East to enforce partition; or on the other hand they could benefit by pursuing a hands-off policy and letting the United States 'incur the odium' of the Muslim world. The United States in Kennan's view thus faced a 'damned-if-we-do and damned-if-we-don't' situation. He concluded that the Americans in short had got themselves into a deplorable position.[5]

The logic of the Policy Planning Staff (and probably Kennan's in particular) revealed apprehension about the domestic repercussions of a pro-Zionist policy. It indicated a paternalistic concern for American Jews:

> In the U. S., the position of Jews would be gravely undermined as it becomes evident to the public that in supporting a Jewish state in Palestine we were in fact supporting the extreme objectives of political Zionism, to the detriment of overall U. S. security interests.[6]

Domestic pressures had impinged on issues of national security. The consequences would be grave, especially if the United States persevered in a policy of creating two separate states. The Policy Planning Staff concluded, as had Marshall previously, that American troops would probably be necessary to enforce partition and that there would be incalculable Arab reaction:

> Ultimately the United States might have to support the Jewish authorities by the use of naval units and military forces. It should be clearly recognized that such assistance given to the Jewish state, but withheld from the Arabs and the Arab States, would in Arab eyes be a virtual declaration of war by the U. S. against the Arab world.[7]

The Policy Planning Staff report bore the stamp of Kennan's intellect. His vigorous logic, his ability to see problems of the Middle East

---

[5] See *Foreign Relations 1948*, V, pp. 545–54.

[6] Ibid. Henderson voiced similar sentiments. Elmer Berger, the Jewish anti-Zionist leader, later recalled: 'Henderson was under savage attack from the Zionists. . . . He was labelled as "anti-Semite." . . . It was perhaps out of this deep, personal anguish that . . . he wistfully said to me, "I hope you and your associates will persevere. And my reason for wishing this is perhaps less related to what I consider American interests in the ·Middle East than what I fear I see on the domestic scene. The United States is a great power. Somehow it will surmount even its most foolish policy errors in the Middle East. But in the process there is great danger of creating divisiveness and anti-Semitism among our own people. And if this danger materializes to a serious extent, we have seen in Germany and in Europe that the ability of a nation to survive the consequences is in serious question." ' Elmer Berger, *Memoirs of an Anti-Zionist Jew* (Beirut, 1978), p. 21. For Berger's important review of the 1948 Palestine volume of *Foreign Relations*, stridently anti-Zionist in tone, see 'Genealogy of An American Tragedy', *Jewish Alternatives to Zionism*, reports 30 and 31 (Nov. 1977).

[7] *Foreign Relations 1948*, V, p. 553.

within the shifting power relations of the United States and the Soviet Union, and his fearlessness in standing firm in principle against opposing schools of thought, led him to a conclusion at once simple and direct. It bore a similarity to the British answer to the Palestine problem. It was the opposite of the solution of the White House staff. The Policy Planning Staff in mid-January 1948 recommended that the United States take 'no further initiative' in implementing partition.[8]

Kennan's entry into the Palestine controversy was like a rocket's. It illuminated the sky with a shower of strategic and ethical sparks and then faded. No one could predict when it might return or what its future course might be.[9] It left in its wake embers of controversy that had to be dealt with by a fireman of entirely different temperament, Dean Rusk.[10] Rusk at that time headed the newly created Office of United Nations Affairs. Privately he believed that enforced partition would be unwise and dangerous; but it was he who had the duty of directing American policy at the United Nations and sending specific instructions to the delegation. He saw straightaway that Kennan and Henderson were urging no less than a complete reversal of American policy. On what grounds? Rusk did not believe that the United States or any other power should dogmatically adhere to the majority opinion of the United Nations. But was there sufficient reason to overthrow the previous position? The arguments produced by the Policy Planning Staff were not new ones, however persuasively they might be presented. 'Obviously a major change in our Palestine policy', Rusk wrote, 'would require the approval of the President as well as of leading Members of Congress.' Was there now a 'new situation' in Palestine that would persuade the President of the need to change course? Kennan and Henderson gave the answer, in short, of imminent civil war. To Rusk however the armed clash of Jews and Arabs was not at all a 'new situation' but merely the confirmation of what everyone had anticipated. He realistically took the view that the United States had been responsible for the outcome of the UN vote and consequently would not be able 'to avoid responsibility for a Palestine solution'.[11]

Rusk and Kennan also disagreed about how to deal with the

---

[8] *Foreign Relations 1948*, V, p. 553.

[9] Amid the fireworks of the 'X' article and other events of 1947–8, Kennan did not find space in his *Memoirs* (Boston, 1967) to mention his Palestine trajectory, but it ignited similar controversy.

[10] For a balanced and valuable assessment of Rusk and the Palestine question see Warren I. Cohen, *Dean Rusk* (Totowa, NJ, 1980), chap. 2.

[11] Memorandum by Rusk, Top Secret, 26 Jan. 1948, USSD 867N.01/2-648 Box 6762; *Foreign Relations 1948*, V, pp. 556–62.

British. So grave was the crisis that Rusk himself had day-by-day conversations with Creech Jones, Cadogan, Beeley, and other British officials attending the Palestine debates in New York who were determined to maintain, in Beeley's phrase, the stance of masterly inactivity. Much to Rusk's irritation the Americans now bore the brunt of Arab resentment. 'Irresponsible' was the word he used to describe British neutrality (which he viewed in effect as a veiled pro-Arab policy), and to him the responsibility for it could be traced directly to 'the great personal irritation of Mr. Bevin'.[12] Rusk began to work towards a compromise solution that led him away from partition, but he did so on the basis of step-by-step possibilities of concessions from both Jews and Arabs rather than assuming a false attitude of benevolent neutrality.

Kennan disliked Rusk's attitude as well as his inclination to look for a pragmatic solution. He thought that Rusk greatly underestimated the importance of Britain's strategic assets in the Arab world, which to him were of overriding importance if considered against the broader background of Russian ambitions. Kennan wanted a solution based on principle as well as on British and Arab friendship. Everything Rusk had in mind, he wrote, 'seems to me to point toward a line of policy designed to gain for us some relief from the difficulties of our present position, but to do this at the expense of our relations with the British and Arabs and at the cost of further involvement in commitments leading toward international enforcement of the Palestine decision'. Rusk believed that the United States should pursue conciliation and perhaps take part in a commission to bring about a truce. Kennan had deep misgivings about such a course. He thought that American policy should draw a sharp line that stopped at non-involvement. Otherwise the Americans would find themselves holding 'major military and economic responsibility for the indefinite maintenance by armed force of a *status quo* in Palestine fiercely resented by the bulk of the Arab world'. Kennan recognized that his proposals to retreat into a position essentially the same as that of the British might damage the United Nations and lead to the loss of American prestige. 'But I think it will be worth it if we can thereby regain the full independence and dignity of our position in this confused and tragic question.'[13]

[12] Ibid.
[13] See memoranda by Kennan, 29 Jan. 1948, *Foreign Relations 1948*, V, pp. 573–81. A month later Kennan gave further refinement to his ominous thoughts on Palestine: 'We are now heavily and unfortunately involved in this Palestine question. We will apparently have to make certain further concessions to our past commitments and to domestic pressures.' He spoke of guidance 'not by national interest but by other considerations' and 'dissipation and confusion of effort'. 'If we do not effect a fairly radical reversal of the trend

Henderson was the sustaining force against partition. He believed that there should be a 'reconsideration of the whole question', but his attack on the problem was more subtle, pragmatic, and determined than Kennan's. Since Henderson is usually the one held responsible for almost having 'pulled the rug' from under the President (Truman's own phrase), it is edifying to survey the developments during the tumultuous days of February and March 1948 from the vantage point of the Office of Near Eastern and African Affairs. Against the background of the crisis in Czechoslovakia, the State Department received reports of armed clashes between the Jews and Arabs in Palestine. The Arabs controlled the main road to Jerusalem. The British administration was disintegrating. It seemed to be only a matter of weeks until there would be full-scale civil war. Henderson probably doubted whether the President perceived the startling pace of events. From his colleague George Wadsworth, who was about to depart on his new assignment as Ambassador to Iraq, Henderson knew that Truman continued to dwell on the old themes of 'British bullheadedness and the fanaticism of our New York Jews'.[14] He also knew that Truman would remain absolutely firm on the vital point that 'no American troops would be sent to Palestine to impose partition'. When Wadsworth had mentioned that possibility, the President had interrupted with 'a categorical ejaculation'.[15] Yet all the evidence in the possession of the Office of Near Eastern and African Affairs indicated that partition could not be enforced without American armed intervention. If, Henderson argued, events demonstrated the impossibility of a peaceful partition, the question would turn on a practicable alternative. That alternative would be an international trusteeship regime. Henderson's thoughts flowed in the same direction as Rusk's. They had in mind, in Rusk's words, 'a trusteeship for Palestine to replace the present mandate until such time as the Jews and Arabs could work out a *modus vivendi*'.[16]

of our policy to date', he concluded, 'we will end up either in the position of being ourselves militarily responsible for the protection of the Jewish population in Palestine against the declared hostility of the Arab world, or of sharing that responsibility with the Russians and thus assisting at their installation as one of the military powers in the area. In either case, the clarity and efficiency of a sound national policy for that area will be shattered.' Ibid., pp. 656–7.

[14] Wadsworth's own ideas also seemed to lack a sense of immediacy. On the eve of the Israeli–Arab war he continued to speak of 'Greater Syria' and the irrigation of the Tigris Euphrates valley. Truman offered a different interpretation of Tamerlane, ancient civilization, and the problems of modern reconstruction: 'reconstruction was the active policy of the United States'. See memorandum by Wadsworth, 4 Feb. 1948, USSD 711.90G/2–448 Box C-49; *Foreign Relations 1948*, V, pp. 592–5.

[15] Ibid.

[16] Memorandum by Rusk, 11 Feb. 1948, USSD 501.BB Palestine/2-1148 Box 2183; *Foreign Relations 1948*, V, pp. 617–18.

The goal in essence would be something along the lines of the Foreign Office's solution of a binational state. If that could not be eventually achieved, then at least the United States might avoid being forced to adopt a Zionist stance as sponsor of a Jewish state.

In mid-February 1948 the Policy Planning Staff of the State Department set forth three alternatives of American policy. The Americans, like the British, could attempt to become neutral (Kennan's solution); they could continue to support partition (the answer of the White House advisers); or they could attempt to bring about a reconsideration of the entire question by the United Nations in an effort to resuscitate the plan for a binational state (Henderson's strategy).[17] A further assessment by the staff of the National Security Council revealed that the Air Force, Army, and Navy representatives refused to endorse the proposal to continue to support partition and instead recommended a reconsideration of the entire problem.[18] When Marshall presented the three choices to the National Security Council itself, he proceeded with caution. He refused to endorse any one of the three alternatives on behalf of the State Department.[19] If the solution of partition were to fail, however, the State Department would be ready to step into the breach with a trusteeship scheme. The White House staff continued to view partition as the premiss of American policy. But the President himself remained adamant that American troops would not be sent to Palestine except as part of a peace-keeping mission. Trusteeship found its way into these discussions as the principal alternative. In view of Truman's public commitment to the United Nations vote to create a Jewish state, Henderson and his colleagues in the Office of Near Eastern and African Affairs could at least be satisfied that trusteeship would be the basis of an alternative solution. The pace of events in the United Nations would probably confront the American government with a choice between partition and trusteeship. Since agreement on the former might break down, the solution of the latter might prevail.[20]

The Central Intelligence Agency independently argued the same case as Henderson. In late February 1948 the CIA concluded that partition 'cannot be implemented'. The agency's comprehensive

[17] Memorandum by Policy Planning Staff, 11 Feb. 1948, *Foreign Relations 1948*, V, pp. 619-25.

[18] 'Draft Report Prepared by the Staff of the National Security Council', 17 Feb. 1948, *Foreign Relations 1948*, V, pp. 631-2.

[19] See the editorial note in *Foreign Relations 1948*, V, p. 625. For the National Security Council discussion see Forrestal diary entry of 12 Feb. 1948, Forrestal Papers.

[20] 'Department of State to President Truman', 23 Feb. 1948, *Foreign Relations 1948*, V, pp. 637-40.

inquiry emphasized the insuperable difficulty of creating not only two autonomous states and an international zone of Jerusalem but also, in accordance with the General Assembly's vote, an economic union of the two. The CIA's estimate perhaps grasped as clearly as any other American appraisal the Arab side of the question:

> Such a plan cannot be implemented without Arab cooperation, and it is inconceivable that the Arabs will abandon their present violent opposition to partition. To the masses, the fight has become almost a religious tenet; to the governing classes, it has become a political creed which they dare not forsake. The Arabs can never be forced to acquiesce in a Western-sponsored movement which they believe is threatening the twentieth-century renascence of their indigenous civilization.[21]

If the United States continued to back partition, what would be the outcome? The President had unequivocally ruled out unilateral intervention by American troops. Might there be a 'police force' established by the Security Council? If so the Russians would insist on having a hand in it. 'Since both the UK and the US have strong strategic reasons for refusing to allow Soviet or Soviet-controlled troops to enter Palestine', according to the CIA analysis, 'it is highly improbable that an international police force will ever be formed.'[22] The CIA also warned that intervention by the Security Council of the United Nations would cause earth-shaking tremors that would be felt throughout the world. Palestine in effect would set the precedent of how the Security Council would respond to dangers to 'international peace'.

When Senator Warren F. Austin, the Ambassador to the United Nations, addressed the Security Council on the 24th of February 1948, he followed specific instructions from the President to say 'nothing' that would represent a retreat from partition.[23] He read the verbatim text of a speech prepared by highest officials in the State Department. So important was the message that Marshall himself participated in the final drafting. It was no ordinary blast or propaganda or perfunctory endorsement of the ideals of the United Nations. In essence it defined the powers of the Security Council for intervention in Palestine. It was of momentous importance because Palestine would be established as the test case for the scope of intervention in future crises. Technically the subject was so opaque in international law that Marshall cautioned that it would require special treatment by State Department spokesmen

---

[21] 'Report by Central Intelligence Agency', 28 Feb. 1948, ibid., pp. 666–75.
[22] Ibid.
[23] Truman to Marshall, 22 Feb. 1948, ibid., p. 645. Alexander Cadogan commented in his diary in a remark that holds true for other speeches by Austin: 'Very American and woolly, but not particularly embarrassing.' 24 Feb. 1948, Cadogan Diaries.

to ensure its translation into 'plain English'. It boiled down to the 'kernel' of the constitutional position.[24] Did the United Nations possess the constitutional capacity to enforce the partition vote? Or would intervention of the Security Council in Palestine and elsewhere be limited to the maintenance of international peace? In other words, would the United Nations in Palestine have the power to enforce a political settlement or merely to keep the peace—a cease-fire? The decision on Palestine therefore would represent a landmark in American interpretation of the powers of the United Nations.[25] The State Department came down on the side of restraint. In short the partition of Palestine could not be enforced against the wishes of the inhabitants. The State Department assured the President that Austin's speech 'does not represent recession in any way' from partition, which, in a negative sense, was technically correct—but in fact those who drafted the statement well knew that it 'knocks the plan for the partition of Palestine in the head'.[26] The Security Council would have the power to enforce a cease-fire, not a political settlement. It is important to bear in mind this connection between long-range precedents in the United Nations and immediate policy in Palestine.

Less than a month later, on the 19th of March, Austin made another speech in the Security Council that caused the equivalent of an earthquake within the American government as well as in the United Nations. It was rightly interpreted throughout the world as American abandonment of partition in favour of a trusteeship regime. Austin began by stating obvious facts of 'chaos, heavy fighting and much loss of life in Palestine'. He dwelt briefly on the responsibility of the Security Council to restore peace. He then came to the explosive part of the speech:

My Government believes that a temporary trusteeship for Palestine should be established under the Trusteeship of the United Nations to maintain the peace and to afford the Jews and Arabs of Palestine, who must live together,

---

[24] *Foreign Relations 1948*, V, pp. 648–9 n. 1. There is an important discussion of various aspects of the Palestine issue in international law in Philip C. Jessup, *The Birth of Nations* (New York, 1974), chap. 7.

[25] Warren Cohen accurately catches the point at issue as Rusk perceived it: 'To Rusk, the critical point about the trusteeship idea was that it would allow the United Nations to send a peace-keeping force to Palestine which could effect a truce and then guarantee whatever arrangements . . . without outside interference. For Henderson and Kennan, the trusteeship may have been seen as requisite to a reversal of support for partition, but to Rusk it was a step to create a stronger legal basis for UN action.' *Dean Rusk*, p. 22.

[26] The phrase of Robert M. McClintock (Rusk's jaunty Special Assistant) who prepared the draft. For the extensive drafting see USSD 501.BB Palestine/2-2348.

further opportunity to reach an agreement regarding the future government of that country.[27]

The complete reversal threw the Zionists into despair. The Secretary-General of the United Nations threatened to resign.[28] This was the occasion on which Truman noted in angry frustration that the State Department had pulled the rug from under him and at the same time had attempted to cut his throat.[29]

What had happened? In heated controversy historians on the one hand have denounced Truman as pandering to the Jewish vote and on the other hand have detected Machiavellian cunning on the part of the State Department.[30] The truth is more complex than either extreme interpretation would suggest, but it is harmonious with previous attitudes and objectives. The President found himself told by the State Department, the Department of Defense, and the Central Intelligence Agency that partition could not be implemented and that the United States must prepare a trusteeship scheme as an alternative. The archival and published evidence is clear and insistent on that point. At the same time Truman also found himself being urged, notably by one of his advisers, Clark Clifford, to see partition through to the end not only for moral reasons but also because the creation of a Jewish state would be the only way to prevent Russian expansion and the possible outbreak of a major war in the Middle East. The establishment of a Jewish state would moreover appeal to the American public, not least American Jewry, who might prove to be of vital importance in the election.

[27] *Foreign Relations 1948*, V., p. 743. The Austin Papers at the University of Vermont reveal only tantalizing details about the 19 March speech, but it was in line with his consistent belief held since the 1930s that a binational state, not partition, should be the goal of American policy. (See Austin Papers Box 23.) The Jews were caught off guard. But the response was instantaneous. Rabbi Abba Hillel Silver replied in an address to the Security Council on the same day by denouncing the 'shocking reversal' and concluding that the American delegation had succumbed to Arab 'threats and intimidation'. See *Israel Documents* (December 1947–May 1948), pp. 474–8.

[28] 'I brooded the night . . . amid radio reports of United Nations depression, Arab jubilation, Zionist despair, and British self-righteousness. After lunch the next day . . . I bared . . . [to Senator Austin] my sense of shock and of almost personal grievance. Washington well knew where I had stood in the struggle over implementing partition. Its reversal was a rebuff to the United Nations and to me.' Trygve Lie, *In the Cause of Peace: Seven Years with the United Nations* (New York, 1954), pp. 170–1. The trusteeship proposal also astonished Ralph Bunche, who would have borne the responsibility of implementing the scheme. 'As you can imagine', he wrote to Benjamin Gerig, 'we in the Trusteeship Department [of the UN] received the surprise U.S. proposal on temporary Trusteeship for Palestine with mixed emotions and not a little shock. I thought you liked us.' Bunche to Gerig, 25 Mar. 1948, Bunche Papers.

[29] Margaret Truman, *Truman*, p. 388.

[30] See Michael J. Cohen, 'Truman and Palestine, 1945–1948: Revisionism, Politics and Diplomacy', *Modern Judaism*, 2 (1982), pp. 1–22.

Truman approved of trusteeship as an alternative to partition. He made this decision on the 8th of March, and Lovett, for one, reconfirmed that there was 'absolutely no question but what the President approved it'.[31] The approval bore the endorsement 'if and when necessary'; in other words, the trusteeship scheme could be announced at the State Department's discretion. It is entirely possible that, three days after General Clay's telegram about possible outbreak of war with Russia, Truman gave the matter only perfunctory attention. He probably expected the State Department to consult him again on such a controversial an issue as a major change of Palestine policy. He probably further assumed that the American delegation at the United Nations would exhaust all possibilities of implementing partition before turning to trusteeship as a temporary measure. He did not necessarily view it as a reversal of support for partition.

The State Department accordingly made plans for 'temporary' trusteeship.[32] The United States had only two months to implement a plan for trusteeship and to lay the basis of a binational state that had eluded the British during the entire mandatory period. The machinery at the UN, however, did not accelerate at the speed the State Department thought necessary. It may seem pedantic in retrospect but at the time State Department officials also attached great importance to the constitutional issues of precedent as well as those of Palestinian substance. The Security Council had to dispose of the partition question before it could address the issue of trusteeship. Here is the key passage in the State Department's deliberation, which is summarized in telegraphic staccato:

It is apparent that situation in Palestine grows daily more fraught with danger to international peace. Security Council must exercise its responsibilities for maintenance of international peace. However, once Council directs its inquiry to security situation in Palestine, if it has not already disposed of issue of partition with economic union, the two questions, although constitutionally separate, will become merged and we will find our efforts to maintain the peace made immensely more difficult because they will be construed by a majority of the people of Palestine as being a covert method of carrying out partition by force.[33]

The project of partition, in other words, had to be removed before the trusteeship scheme could take its place. The State Department, particularly Rusk and his special assistant, Robert McClintock, feared indecisive drift at a time when a clear-cut decision on trusteeship was urgent. On the 16th of March Marshall instructed Austin

---

[31] See *Foreign Relations 1948*, V, pp. 749–50.
[32] See e.g. memorandum by Marshall, 5 Mar. 1948, ibid., pp. 678–9.
[33] Marshall to Austin, 16 Mar. 1948, ibid., pp. 728–9.

that 'The time factor is imperative and [Security] Council must act without delay'.[34] If the Americans did not act immediately, the Russians might step in to seize the initiative. In the assessments of possible Soviet intervention lies the final explanation of the timing and motive of the State Department's trusteeship proposal of the 19th of March. In the words of Robert McClintock, who was a central figure in these discussions, there was the possibility 'that the Soviet Union will advocate that the Security Council implement by force, if necessary, the partition plan'.

On the eve of the trusteeship speech, Ambassador Austin had balked. He thought the matter so important that he wished to consult the President. In McClintock's words, 'Ambassador Austin did not wish to knock partition on the head at this juncture.'[35] In the end Rusk persuaded him that trusteeship would merely be a temporary solution 'without prejudice to whatever future settlement . . . arrived at by agreement between the peoples of Palestine'.[36] The matter seemed so clear-cut that apparently no one except Austin thought it necessary to 'reclear' the instructions, perhaps because of the apprehension that Niles or Clifford might interfere. Austin's speech of course represented a major victory for Henderson and others in the State Department who believed that the ultimate solution in Palestine lay in the direction of a binational state and not partition. To the Zionists it momentarily appeared to be the gravest defeat since the White Paper of 1939.

Upon cooler reflection Truman admitted that it was the timing and not the substance of the trusteeship announcement that irritated him, but at the time his anger was volcanic. He ordered Clark Clifford to conduct an investigation. He believed that the bureaucrats of the State Department had forced his hand. They had formally committed him to a reversal of policy, to trusteeship, rather than partition. He felt humiliated. How could he confess to the American public that the bureaucracy and not the President controlled foreign policy? Why had he not been informed? As it transpired the State Department officials successfully maintained that they had not acted beyond instructions, though everyone involved agreed that the

[34] Marshall to Austin, 16 Mar. 1948, *Foreign Relations 1948*, V, pp. 728-9.

[35] Memorandum by McClintock, 17 Mar. 1948, USSD 505.BB Palestine/3-1748 Box 2184; *Foreign Relations 1948*, V, pp. 729-31. Even when Austin did make the announcement he showed little enthusiasm for it. Of the organs of the American press *Newsweek* perhaps best caught the general sense of legalism and weariness reflected in Austin's presentation of the new American position: 'Obviously tired, and in a tone and manner that seemed slightly defensive, Austin expounded the legal justification for the about-face. . . . In effect, partition was dead.' (29 Mar. 1948.) These and other news cuttings in the Austin Papers, but without comment by Austin.

[36] See Memorandum by McClintock, 17 Mar. 1948, *Foreign Relations 1948*, V, pp. 729-31.

President should have been warned of the consequences so that he might have been prepared, in Marshall's phrase, for 'the blast of the press'. Clifford relentlessly argued that the State Department should definitely have let events in the Security Council run their course and that the speech in its final form should have been resubmitted to the President before its actual delivery. Marshall himself assumed full responsibility. The climax of the 'investigation' was tense. The President and the Secretary of State on the 24th of March met with those principally involved, including Henderson and Rusk on one side of the table and Niles and Clifford on the other. According to a first-hand account: 'David Niles showed his feelings towards Henderson—the atmosphere was charged with the dislike between the two as they exchanged words.'[37]

In the course of the Palestine controversy the influence of David Niles waned, perhaps because of his emotional commitment to the creation of a Jewish state. Truman commented that Niles would 'burst into tears' in discussions about Palestine.[38] The influence of Clark Clifford waxed. Within the White House staff he became the staunchest supporter of partition and his name is permanently associated with the birth of the state of Israel. Clifford was from Missouri. He held the title of 'Special Counsel to President Truman' when he was only in his early forties. Truman liked and respected him. Clifford in return expressed to the President ideas about Palestine with the robust vitality of a fellow Missourian.

In March 1948 Clifford attempted to buck up the President at a time of crisis, and to restore a sense of direction in foreign affairs. He frankly stated that the American people 'from one end of the country to the other and among all classes' suffered from a collapse of morale:

This lack of confidence is shared by Democrats, Republicans, young people and old people. There is a definite feeling that we have no foreign policy, that we do not know where we are going, that the President and the State Department are bewildered, that the United States, instead of furnishing leadership in world affairs, is drifting helplessly.[39]

Clifford believed that the drift could be stopped by taking a decisive stand in favour of the partition of Palestine. By doing so the President would restore the faith of the American people in the United Nations. He would fulfil the promises made by Woodrow Wilson,

[37] Memorandum by Charles Ross, 29 Mar. 1948, Ross Papers Box 6, Truman Library; quoted by Ganin, *Truman, American Jewry*, p. 163.

[38] 'Oral History Transcript of Oscar Ewing', p. 276, Truman Library. I am indebted to my colleague Clarence Lasby for this quotation.

[39] Memorandum by Clifford, 8 Mar. 1948, Clifford Papers, Truman Library; *Foreign Relations 1948*, V, pp. 690–6.

Franklin Roosevelt, and Truman himself. He would provide a 'high-minded, statesmanlike' solution. Clifford thought that Truman would act in accordance with 'what is best for America' even if it meant 'the defeat of the Democratic Party' in November. Such noble sentiments must have been heartening to a President who never lost sight of the American domestic side of the Palestine question.

Clifford also emphasized the way in which the creation of a Jewish state would strengthen the American position against Russia. It would provide a permanent solution and thus would limit rather than expand American military involvement in the Middle East. He minimized Arab reaction. On this point Clifford perhaps expressed the unconscious prejudice of many Americans about the inferiority of the 'desert nomads' who in any case would continue to sell oil to the United States because they needed the money. In a contemptuous remark about the Arabs, Clifford also evoked memories of British policy before the Second World War:

[T]he United States appears in the ridiculous role of trembling before threats of a few nomadic desert tribes. This has done us irreparable damage. Why should Russia or Yugoslavia, or any other nation treat us with anything but contempt in light of our shilly-shallying appeasement of the Arabs.

Clifford buttressed all of his arguments in favour of the creation of a Jewish state by reminding the President that the United States had been responsible for the majority vote of the United Nations and that he believed that Truman's own views had been influential if not decisive: 'We "crossed the Rubicon" on this matter when the partition resolution was adopted by the Assembly—largely at your insistence.'[40]

Truman was susceptible to such counsel pitched in a personal vein. Despite his resolution not to tolerate further pressure from the Zionists, he also proved willing to listen to his old friend Eddie Jacobson. In a celebrated interview in mid-March 1948 the Kansas City haberdasher pointed to a miniature reproduction of a statue of Andrew Jackson. Jacobson said that he too had a hero. He was Chaim Weizmann. Weizmann was now an old man broken in health but he was 'the greatest Jew who ever lived' and had travelled

[40] *Foreign Relations 1948*, V, pp. 690–6. Clifford's reconstruction, which he delivered as an address to the American Historical Association in 1976, was published in *American Heritage*, April 1977; (see also Clark M. Clifford, Eugene V. Rostow, and Barbara W. Tuchman, *The Palestine Question in American History*, New York, 1978). His aim was principally an attempt to vindicate Truman, 'a man who had fought ably and honorably for a humanitarian goal to which he was deeply dedicated' and to refute 'revisionist historiography' which 'argues that President Truman's Palestine policy was motivated by the purely political consideration of wooing the Jewish electoral vote'.

thousands of miles to see the President. Truman reflected and then responded, 'You win, you bald-headed son of a bitch. . . . I will see him.'[41]

Truman's meeting with Weizmann and the circumstances of the next few days help to explain the course of subsequent events. The President once again found Weizmann's arguments persuasive. Weizmann was a statesman of extraordinary charm and ability to convey faith in a Jewish state that would be economically as well as politically viable. Truman had a genuine admiration for Weizmann. He reassured him that there would be no change in the American policy of support for partition.[42]

The President's meeting with Weizmann occurred on the 18th of March. Then on the next day the American Ambassador at the United Nations made the statement that the United States would support trusteeship as a solution. The timing explains Truman's astonishment and anger. He also noted on his calendar on the 19th:

> This morning I find that the State Dept. has reversed my Palestine policy. The first I know about it is what I see in the papers! Isn't that hell? I am now in the position of a liar and a double crosser. I've never felt so in my life.[43]

Questions of personal honour aroused powerful emotions in Truman. 'I assured Chaim Weizmann that we were for partition and would stick to it. He must think I am a plain liar.'[44] He sent personal word to Weizmann that he would continue to support partition. On the other hand, as he told Marshall, he did not object to trusteeship as an alternative solution. It was the inept timing that outraged him and caused him great personal embarrassment. Far from reversing American policy the State Department had unwittingly caused the President to seize tighter control over decisions and to set a determined course towards the creation of a Jewish state.

Despite Truman's assurances, the Jews had little more than faith on which to believe that the State Department would not prevail over the White House, or for that matter that the United Nations would not take back the blessing it had given to partition the previous November. Though the actual timing of Austin's trusteeship speech had come as a surprise to the representatives of the Jewish Agency, they had known since late February that the State Department would put forward the powerful argument that a trusteeship regime should be established in order to bring about 'peace before

[41] Donovan, *Conflict and Crisis*, p. 375. On Jacobson see especially Frank J. Adler, *Roots in a Moving Stream* (Kansas City, Missouri, 1972), chap. IX.

[42] See Ganin, *Truman, American Jewry*, pp. 167–8.

[43] Margaret Truman, *Harry S. Truman*, p. 388.

[44] Donovan, *Conflict and Crisis*, p. 376.

partition'.[45] They detected a genuine anxiety among those in the American government who believed that partition might lead not only to war but also to massacres similar to the ones that had occurred in India. In Jewish circles there was general despair that little could be done to offset the growing attitude that trusteeship might be the best solution after all, at least temporarily.

The setback to the Zionist cause is poignantly reflected in the letters of Chaim Weizmann. Despite occasional encouragement—from Truman himself—the tone of Weizmann's reaction to the drift towards trusteeship in the winter and spring of 1948 was one of almost unrelieved gloom. He summarized his visit to New York as 'the most heart-breaking and futile waste of time I have ever experienced'.[46] In a letter to Felix Frankfurter he poured out his feeling of despair by recounting the story of a rabbi he had known in his youth:

> There was a venerable old rabbi . . . a pious, saintly man, and when things went hard with his flock and with the people around him he used to betake himself to the great synagogue at a time when there was nobody there and go up to the Ark, open the doors, pull the curtain and enter into a conversation with the Almighty—something of the following nature: 'God of Israel, I have come to ask you to give me an account as to why you persecute your people so much and so often . . .'[47]

The quest for a Jewish state as late as the spring of 1948 still seemed to be so elusive that Weizmann could find no solace in reflecting on the rabbi's experience: 'I am sure the great rabbi felt considerable relief after having spoken thus, and it is very unfortunate that even this sort of comfort is not given to us, and we have to carry the pain in us until the heart breaks and the moral force begins to ebb.'[48]

The Arab reaction to the American reversal was essentially sceptical and, like the Jewish response, based on moral conviction. '[T]hey were pleased with this latest turn of events, but they did not gloat', an American official wrote in summary.[49] Loy Henderson, for one, was fully aware, in his own words 'that the Arabs would be suspicious of a slanted trusteeship' which might ultimately prove to be another cloak for Jewish domination.[50] The Arabs would oppose trusteeship because it would postpone independence of a unitary Palestinian

---

[45] See e.g. Epstein to Jewish Agency Executive, 1 Mar. 1948, *Israel Documents* (December 1947–May 1948), pp. 393–4.

[46] Weizmann to Bergmann, 20 Apr. 1948, *Weizmann Letters*, XXIII, pp. 111–12.

[47] Weizmann to Frankfurter, 31 Mar. 1948, ibid., pp. 92–4.

[48] Ibid.

[49] Memorandum by S. K. Kopper, 19 Mar. 1948, USSD 501.BB Palestine/3-1948.

[50] Memorandum by Henderson, 26 Mar. 1948, USSD 867N.01/3-2648; *Foreign Relations 1948*, V, pp. 764–5.

state; and the Jews would reject trusteeship because it would rule out partition, at least in the near future. The Americans were thus confronted with the same impasse that the British had faced during the era of the mandate. There was also an identical apprehension about the outcome. 'The Arab world will face political and economic disaster', Henderson wrote, 'if the Palestine situation develops into mass fighting.' American officials who attempted to prevent the slide into civil war did so with an acute sense of foreboding. As if anticipating the course of events, Henderson warned that trusteeship, even as a quite temporary solution, would never work so long as the Palestine issue in America remained 'a football of domestic politics'.[51]

[51] Memorandum by Henderson, 22 Apr. 1948, USSD 867N.01/4-2248; *Foreign Relations 1948*, V, pp. 840-2.

8

THE UNITED STATES AND THE END
OF BRITISH RULE IN PALESTINE

BY APRIL 1948 the British may perhaps be pardoned for being slightly confused at the Arab turns and Zionist twists of American Palestine policy. To those unaware of the seething tempers in the White House and State Department it may have been tempting merely to agree with *Pravda*'s commentary, which was not without an element of truth: 'the United States policy over Palestine . . . [has] proceeded on a series of zig zags, now in favour of the Jews to satisfy the domestic role, now in favour of the Arabs at the prompting of United States oil monopolies and military circles'.[1] At first the British were relieved at what they thought to be the abandonment of partition. Trusteeship, whatever form it might take, would be, in Beeley's words, 'the end of the impracticable and dangerous Partition Plan'.[2] They were rightly sceptical about the stability of American policy and they held a guarded attitude towards the State Department's crash programme of trusteeship. They were of course unaware, as was the State Department, of the President's secret assurances to Chaim Weizmann before and after the State Department's change of policy. They also knew nothing about a further most important exchange between Weizmann and Truman.

On the 9th of April, five weeks before the termination of the mandate, Weizmann wrote Truman another eloquent and moving letter. He drew attention to the psychological effects of promising Jewish independence one moment and cancelling it the next. He warned that the clock could not be stopped. He pointed out that 'a virtual Partition is now crystallising in Palestine'. He ended with these sombre words: 'The choice for our people, Mr. President, is between Statehood and extermination.'[3] Truman again rose to historic occasion. He did not trust word to paper but communicated it through a trusted adviser, Samuel Rosenman. On the 23rd of April Weizmann was told that the President would do all in his power

[1] As paraphrased in Peterson to Bevin, 27 May 1948, FO 371/68557.
[2] Minute by Beeley, 18 Mar. 1948, FO 371/68538.
[3] Weizmann to Truman, 9 Apr. 1948, *Weizmann Letters*, XXIII, pp. 99–101; *Foreign Relations 1948*, V, pp. 807–9.

promptly to recognize the Jewish state, if the United Nations would continue to support partition.[4] Truman enjoined Weizmann to secrecy. In studying the chronology of April and May 1948 it is important to bear in mind that within the Jewish Agency, and even among Weizmann's close associates, extremely few knew of the secret. Neither the Foreign Office nor even the State Department knew that the President had committed himself to the eventual recognition of the state of Israel.

Truman was not the first and certainly not the last American President to withhold secrets from the State Department, but in this instance there were high risks. He might rationalize that he had always regarded trusteeship merely as an alternative course, but there was a conflict between his intent and his public policy. He might justify his commitment to Weizmann on grounds of high principle and personal honour, but was he not deceiving Marshall? Truman's recent biographer, Robert Donovan, makes an incisive point. Truman correctly gauged the extent of Marshall's loyalty.[5] A full revelation of his secret commitment to Weizmann on a basic issue of foreign policy would probably have strained even Marshall's allegiance. Truman also correctly estimated Weizmann, for if the latter (or more probably one of his associates) had denounced the President as a double-crosser Truman's relations with the Jews would have been ruptured irrevocably.[6] As events transpired Truman satisfied himself that Weizmann did not regard him as a liar and he was able opportunistically to reap the political benefit of intervening decisively in favour of the Jews. In the meantime he placed those who attempted to implement the trusteeship policy in a false position.[7]

---

[4] Zeev Sharef, *Three Days* (New York, 1962), p. 243; Urofsky, *We Are One!*, p. 169; Ganin, *Truman, American Jewry*, p. 179; Dan Kurzman, *Genesis 1948* (New York, 1970), pp. 211–12, adds that Weizmann was so overjoyed that he stuck a cigar in the mouth of a bronze bust of himself. For authoritative comment on the dates of the meetings between Rosenman and Weizmann, see *Weizmann Letters*, XXIII, p. 109 n. 3.

[5] Donovan, *Conflict and Crisis*, p. 387.

[6] See the editorial comment in *Israel Documents* (December 1947–May 1948), Companion Volume, p. 109, in which Eliahu Epstein is quoted: 'The President not only refrained from telling him [Weizmann, in the meeting of 18 March] about the contents of Austin's speech, but encouraged him to believe that there would be some favourable changes. . . . Weizmann was not entirely satisfied.' The Jews were thus clearly suspicious of possible duplicity on Truman's part.

[7] Truman probably would have defended himself along the line he took in his memoirs (*Years of Trial and Hope*, p. 163), which is most clearly restated by the editors of *Foreign Relations 1948*, V, pp. 744–5: 'his policy on Palestine did not mean commitment to any set of dates or circumstances but was rather a dedication to international obligations and relief of human misery. In this sense, he said, the trusteeship proposal was not contrary to his policy. He expressed his certainty, however, that some State Department officials anticipated that the Jews and Arabs would interpret the trusteeship proposal as an abandonment of the partition plan. In this sense, he stated, trusteeship was at odds with his attitude and policy.'

It was Henderson who now took the initiative in attempting to implement the trusteeship plan. From the outset he probably knew that he faced almost impossible odds. Any settlement in Palestine, whether in terms of trusteeship or merely a truce, could be achieved only in co-operation with the British. There was now less than two months to act on an extremely complicated constitutional and administrative apparatus that the British had debated for more than two decades. To the British, American assistance in arriving at a comparable solution during the last two years had been distinctly unhelpful and vacillating. Henderson noted in late March:

> The British are extremely bitter at what they consider to be our lack of consideration for their difficulties with regard to Palestine in the past and because of their belief that internal political shifts in the United States will render the American Government an unreliable partner in the carrying out of any Palestine policy.[8]

Henderson wrote those words in the aftermath of the 'investigation' conducted by Clark Clifford. The tension between the White House staff and the State Department hardly inspired British confidence in a stable American policy in the future. Yet British assistance was vital. Henderson continued to express the dilemma: 'If we are to obtain British co-operation, we must also let the British know that the Executive Branch will take all possible steps in order to see that the United States will bear its fair share of the financial and military responsibilities involved.' In the phrase 'military responsibilities' he struck the root of the problem of possible Anglo-American co-operation in Palestine. It was by no means clear the extent to which the President or the Department of Defense would be willing to back trusteeship or a truce with American force. The question became even murkier if raised in regard to the British.

What would happen, Forrestal asked Truman, if the American delegation at the United Nations were asked whether the United States would contribute its fair share of troops to a 'police force'? Truman was evasive. 'If we had to respond', he said, the United States would try to participate 'up to the limit of our ability'. Forrestal therefore conferred with the Joint Chiefs of Staff. Rusk attended the meeting in order to explain the State Department's position. He said that, if the United States did not move in, then the Russians might. Not wanting to paint too black a picture, Rusk mentioned

---

[8] Memorandum by Henderson, n.d., USSD 501.BB Palestine/3-2448 Box 2148; *Foreign Relations 1948*, V, pp. 756-7.

that the American presence 'would give us the opportunity to construct strategic bomber fields in the Middle East'.[9]

The Joint Chiefs gave Rusk a chilly response. In their view a cease-fire in Palestine would be virtually impossible to enforce. They were wary of stepping into a situation which the British as an occupying power had already found unmanageable. They concluded that a staggering number of 104,000 troops would be necessary to keep the peace—in other words, a force larger than the British army at its peak. If the truce broke down, then the prospect would be even more alarming. The Joint Chiefs of Staff calculated that the 'police force' of 104,000 might have to be doubled or even tripled. Based on the lowest figures of an American contribution, 46,800, the Department of Defense reached a most alarming conclusion. 'This number represents substantially our entire present ground reserve, both Marine and Army.' The Department of Defense would have no troops available for deployment in any other area in case of emergency. The United States consequently would have to review all policies towards Italy, Greece, Turkey, Iran, and China.[10] Such were the world-wide ramifications of sending a 'police force' to Palestine!

The Joint Chiefs of Staff based their calculations of an effective police force on these figures:

United Kingdom	45 per cent	46,800 personnel
United States	45 per cent	46,800 personnel
France	10 per cent	10,400 personnel[11]

There were three fatal flaws. The first was the blatant omission of the Russians, who would hardly agree that the British, French, and Americans had the right to be in Palestine on the basis of the peace treaties of the First World War (the legal justification). The second

[9] 4 Apr. 1948, Forrestal Diary, Forrestal Papers. Rusk's biographer, Warren Cohen, judges that Rusk was being 'outrageously disingenuous' in making this approach to the Joint Chiefs. (*Dean Rusk*, p. 24.) The point is of interest because of the similar efforts of the Foreign Office and Colonial Office to win the support of the Chiefs of Staff.

[10] Forrestal to Marshall, Top Secret, 19 Apr. 1948, USSD 501.BB Palestine/4-1948 Box 2184; *Foreign Relations 1948*, V, pp. 832-3. Lovett gave his friend Forrestal a biting official retort: 'leaving the possible use of an American contingent in the United Nations police force for Palestine out of the picture entirely, it seems clear from your letter that the forces available at present are inadequate to support fully our policies in the other areas mentioned, or elsewhere'. Lovett to Forrestal, Top Secret, 23 Apr. 1948, Box 2184; ibid., pp. 851-2.

[11] Memorandum by Joint Chiefs of Staff, 4 Apr. 1948, ibid., pp. 798-800. For discussion of the JCS and Palestine, see Kenneth W. Condit, *The History of the Joint Chiefs of Staff: The Joint Chiefs of Staff and National Policy*, II, 1947-1949 (Wilmington, Del., 1979), chap. III. For further detail on the 'police force' see the study entitled 'Force Requirements', 31 Mar. 1948, US JCS 1684/11 CCS092 Palestine (3-5-46 Sec. 3).

was the certainty of explosive Arab reaction to the reintroduction of French troops in the Middle East. The third was British determination to withdraw. The British would not consider the commitment of British troops, at least land forces, beyond the 15th of May. Regardless of how the figures might be juggled and the forces of smaller powers substituted, for example, for those of the French, it would have been virtually impossible for the Americans to produce a workable plan for a 'police force' within a period of weeks without wholehearted British co-operation, which they did not have.

To the British the trusteeship project, and the 'police force' to back it up, presented the hazard of enmeshing themselves in the situation from which they were only now being extracted. No matter how deftly the legal instrument of trusteeship might be drafted, it could not gloss over the question of Jewish immigration, which the Arabs would resist as vehemently as in the past. The Jews on the other hand would reject any solution that did not prepare the way for a Jewish state. Beeley, whose minutes provided the basis for Bevin's public statements on the subject, believed that the positions would continue to polarize before the 15th of May. The best that might be hoped for, Beeley thought, was a truce. He believed that American military intervention even as part of a 'police force' would never occur.[12] As the 15th of May drew closer, the greater grew the determination of the Jews to declare an independent state that was, in effect, already in existence.

The crux of the matter was that it would be impossible for a 'police force' indefinitely to remain neutral. The United States might in extremity authorize American troops under the command of the United Nations to prevent the extermination of the Jews in Palestine, but they would not be permitted to deter the forcible establishment of a formal Jewish state. If the British favoured benevolent military neutrality for the Arabs, the Americans favoured it for the Jews. Dean Rusk perhaps best expressed the drift of official sentiment in Washington in the final stages of the Palestine crisis:

It is not according to plan but nevertheless there is a community in existence over there [in Palestine], running its own affairs. Now that community apparently is going to get an open shot at establishing itself. We have told them that if they get in trouble don't come to us for help in a military sense. Nevertheless, I don't think the boss [Truman] will ever put himself in a position of opposing that effort when it might be that the US opposition would be the only thing that would prevent it from succeeding.[13]

[12] Beeley to Burrows, 24 Apr. 1948, FO 371/68546.
[13] Memorandum of 11 May 1948, *Foreign Relations 1948*, V, pp. 965-9.

Beeley, the shrewdest British observer of American involvement in Palestine, had detected the same decisive pro-Jewish sentiment that would govern American military non-involvement: 'I do not see', he wrote in late April, 'how the U. S. Government could possibly employ troops in Palestine to overthrow the Government of a Jewish State.'[14]

Henderson, who perceived the military polarization as keenly as anyone, made a final effort to resolve the crisis on a political basis. He thought there might be a chance to break the 'log jam' at the United Nations by calling upon 'moderate and temperate' Jewish and Arab leaders to make a last plea for peace.[15] He had in mind Azzam Pasha, the head of the Arab League, and Judah Magnes, President of the Hebrew University. Azzam Pasha declined.[16] Magnes accepted Henderson's invitation to come to Washington. Here at last moderation and a belief in racial reconciliation might prevail. Magnes had a long involvement in Jewish politics as the champion of a peaceful settlement between Jews and Arabs. He believed that the only lasting solution to the crisis in Palestine would be the creation of a binational state. In retrospect he appears as one of the tragic figures in the Palestine controversy, but at the time he was regarded as one of the few people who might be able at the last minute to prevent the situation from deteriorating into civil war.

Magnes left a highly favourable impression on Marshall when the two of them met on the 4th of May, less than two weeks before the end of the mandate. Magnes, according to Marshall himself, spoke 'with great conviction and intensity'. He believed that the Jews and Arabs alike were 'heartily sick of the situation in which they find themselves and that their burning desire is peace'. Marshall and Magnes discussed practical matters such as maintenance of the water supply in Jerusalem, municipal councils, and the Arab and Jewish police forces. They mentioned Mountbatten and General Mark Clark as possible mediators for the United Nations. Marshall told Magnes at the close of the interview that 'this was the most straightforward account on Palestine I had heard'.[17] Alas the clock

[14] Beeley to Burrows, 24 Apr. 1948, FO 371/68546.

[15] Memorandum by Henderson, 9 Apr. 1948, 501.BB Palestine/4-948 Box 2184; *Foreign Relations 1948*, V, pp. 804-5.

[16] Azzam Pasha was 'frankly and bitterly hostile' to the proposed trusteeship plan because it would replace the mandate with a regime possessing 'some handicaps, many additional defects and no redeeming features'. He believed, as did most Arabs, that trusteeship would be merely a cloak for the establishment of a Jewish state 'not merely in Palestine but . . . in all of Palestine'. The Jewish Agency on the other hand refused to discuss trusteeship because 'it does not provide for [the] establishment of a Jewish state'. Ibid., V, 832 n. 2.

[17] Memorandum by Marshall, Secret, 4 May 1948, USSD 501.BB Palestine 5-548 Box 2185.

would not be stopped. There was no time to offset the countervailing Zionist sentiment building to a climax in favour of the decisive creation of a Jewish state. Here the secret assurances conveyed by Truman to Weizmann came into play. Weizmann could not reveal the President's intent, but he placed his stature as the moral leader of the Zionist movement behind the birth of a Jewish state when the British mandate expired—then or never.

When the State Department in March had momentarily prevailed over the White House staff for the control of Palestine policy, Henderson hoped for British co-operation. The goal of a binational state after all had been Bevin's predominant aim. Instead of receiving British sympathy and aid, American officials who laboured under the deadline of the 15th of May and the pressure of the United Nations politics, received, according to Henderson's personal complaint to Beeley, 'official reticence or unofficial sneers'.[18] Henderson's words were true. It seemed preposterous to officials of the Foreign Office, who had dealt with the problem over a period of many years, that the Americans could now brew ersatz trusteeship tea palatable to all concerned. According to the head of the Eastern Department: 'it is absurd to think that it will be possible to reach agreement between the two communities on a constitutional machinery for Palestine now that tempers have become so hot, when we failed hopelessly to achieve any such agreement in far more favourable circumstances in the past'.[19]

---

[18] For Beeley's account of this important exchange of ideas see his letter to Burrows of 3 May 1948, 'Secret and Personal', FO 371/68554. Beeley did not protest Henderson's description of the British response to the American trusteeship proposals as 'cynical' but merely emphasized that the British and Americans 'were less far apart than had perhaps appeared in recent exchanges between them'. The conversation took place shortly after the announcement of a White House appointment in the State Department. The President on the 28th of April had instructed General Hilldring to assume duties as Special Assistant to the Secretary of State, with particular responsibility for Palestine. Beeley made special note that Henderson did not allude to the appointment 'or its possible consequences' during their talk, but it caused considerable speculation in British circles. Inverchapel reported that it probably indicated 'a pro-Zionist turn in United States policy' and that Forrestal 'was very worried about this appointment'. An official in the UN delegation, R. H. Hadlow, wrote to Philip Mason at the Foreign Office in a secret and personal letter (on which Bevin wrote instructions that the Prime Minister should see it): 'Loy Henderson heard the first news of Hilldring's appointment when the radio made the announcement from evidently Jewish sources. Though upset and bewildered, he feels he can carry on. . . . Forrestal and the State Department are unanimous about ascribing the appointment to the personal influence of Niles . . . over Truman. . . . Hilldring's appointment is not going to neutralise Loy Henderson, whom Forrestal greatly likes and respects and whose policy accords with that of the War Department. To sum up Hilldring's appointment is a pure piece of political juggling in the hope of reviving the waning fortunes of the Democratic party.' (2 May 1948, FO 371/68649.) Hilldring did not take up the appointment because of ill health. See *Foreign Relations 1948*, V, p. 879 note 2.

[19] Minute by Burrows, 2 Apr. 1948, FO 371/68540.

Bevin took pains to give the impression that he wished the Americans well with trusteeship, and he explained at length to the American Ambassador that he did not wish to throw 'cold water' on the plan. Ambassador Douglas reported that the Foreign Secretary, in a rare lapse from his usual ingenuity, was at 'his wit's end to know what to do'.[20] In fact his Palestinian fit of absence of mind could be largely explained by the coincidence of crises in Palestine and Berlin. Bevin found Palestine extremely annoying but tried not to let it interfere with larger problems. He and his staff were content to let trusteeship, and its dangerous ramifications of further British commitment, expire in blasts of hot air at the United Nations. The key to British policy at this time may be grasped by a minute written by the Permanent Under-Secretary, Sargent, who wrote in earthy metaphors that trusteeship would 'die of itself' and that he much preferred this natural death rather than 'our intervening to kill it'.[21] By about 1st of May even the American delegates at the United Nations acknowledged that the trusteeship plan was dead. There was now general recognition that the Jews would settle for no less than an independent Jewish state. Creech Jones, who attended the United Nations special session on Palestine in the spring of 1948 in order to preside over the liquidation of this part of the Empire, wrote to Bevin about the death of trusteeship and the striking change in general attitude towards the creation of a Jewish state:

We cannot escape the fact that since November the psychology and the shape of things in Palestine has profoundly changed. The Jewish leaders now absolutely refuse to retreat from immediate statehood. They have geared everything to the achievement of their state by May 15th. I am persuaded that no Palestine solution is possible which ignores this fact.[22]

Creech Jones held out hope for a truce in Jerusalem but not for Palestine as a whole.

Through most of the spring of 1948 the British suffered under the handicap of international incredulity. Virtually no one believed it to be in the nature of the beast of British imperialism willingly to withdraw. Only by late April could Beeley report from New York that 'the conviction that we really intend to leave is slowly spreading'. He wrote further that the consensus of informed opinion at the United Nations recognized that the future of Palestine would be settled 'by fighting between Arabs and the Jews', which in the end

[20] 'I am confident', Douglas wrote, that Bevin 'is not deliberately adopting a "Dog-in-the-manger" attitude.' Douglas to Marshall, 20 Apr. 1948, *Foreign Relations 1948*, V, p. 837.

[21] Minute by Sargent, c.29 Apr. 1948, FO 371/68545.

[22] Creech Jones to Bevin, 2 May 1948, Creech Jones Papers.

might provide the only basis for a stable peace.[23] No one could predict the outcome, but the British and the Americans, for different reasons, nervously began to anticipate that it might not be to their liking. In a revealing 'secret and personal' letter written two weeks before the end of the mandate, Beeley speculated to Bernard Burrows, the head of the Eastern Department, how some of the consequences of Jewish victory might be calamitous for the British Empire:

> You may think that I am plunging . . . into the realm of fantasy when I suggest that we ought to be considering the risk, which admittedly may be remote, that Jewish forces might in the course of the struggle succeed in invading Transjordan. After all, the Arab armies cannot be classed as formidable, the Jews may be very well armed, it appears that the relative strength of the Irgun is increasing, and we know that the Irgun . . . claim that Transjordan as well as Palestine should be included in the Jewish State. I assume that, if matters came to this pass, H. M. G. would take action to preserve the integrity of Transjordan.[24]

If Jordan suffered defeat at the hands of the Jews, Beeley concluded, 'our prestige in the Middle East would in my view be irremediably destroyed'.[25]

There were further dimensions to the problem of Jewish military prowess. Neither the British nor the Americans wished to lose control of the conflict. Both wished to localize it. The trusteeship proposal lingered on in the form of a possible truce. Should the British commit themselves to enforcing it together with the Americans? What line should the British take if it proved to be impossible to achieve a truce? Bevin in late April refused even to discuss his ideas with the Americans at a preliminary stage—'too risky', he noted in view of the erratic turns of American policy.[26] He was also concerned about the dangers of leaks in the press. British public sentiment at this juncture absolutely opposed further military involvement in Palestine. Yet Bevin had to consider the possibility not only of the licit and illicit arms flowing to the Arabs from British sources and to the Jews from American sources but also of arms supplied to the Jews from the Soviet camp. Bevin therefore began to think of means of circumscribing the war. The British in extreme circumstances might provide a blockade if land forces were provided by the Americans. The project was fraught with difficulties. Could the Americans be persuaded not only to cut off arms but also the Jewish sources of dollars? If an arms embargo were stringently

[23] Beeley to Burrows, 'Personal & Confidential' 24 Apr. 1948, FO 371/68546/E5598.
[24] Beeley to Burrows, 'Secret and Personal', 30 Apr. 1948, FO 371/68554/E6676.
[25] Ibid.
[26] Bevin to Creech Jones, 22 Apr. 1948, FO 371/68544.

applied would it be linked with general economic sanctions? How would British access to Arab oil be affected? Bernard Burrows, the head of the Eastern Department, in a 'Green' (highly secret) paper analysed some of the problems that would arise:

The most effective way of localising the conflict would be to seal the land and sea frontier, which would require the provision of large forces from outside. Here again, we should make it a firm condition that our own contribution would be limited to naval and air forces and we would of course only provide these if other Powers provided forces to seal the land frontiers.

The question whether we should go as far as this in discussion with the Americans must depend on the Service Departments' estimate of the availability of our naval and air forces and on the estimated reaction of public opinion here to the continued employment of units of these forces, but excluding British land forces and therefore almost certainly excluding the possibility of further casualties.[27]

The British in other words were groping for a solution that would localize the conflict with a minimum of involvement of British forces.[28] The constraints of public sentiment were severe.

The State Department in late April and early May still held hope of a genuine truce concluded by the two sides rather than the more drastic remedy of localization of a war. After intense discussion with Arab and Jewish representatives at the United Nations, Rusk believed that both sides had reasons for postponing a showdown, if only because of the uncertainty of the outcome. On the 29th of April he discussed the subject with Truman. He told the President that an immediate truce should now be 'our fundamental objective'. Truman firmly endorsed that principle: 'Yes, that is the thing', he said, 'We are trying to stop the fighting.' When Rusk warned that the Jews might reject a truce, Truman replied that 'if the Jews refuse to accept a truce on reasonable grounds they need not expect anything else from us'. Giving him the benefit of the doubt, he apparently saw no contradiction between that warning and his commitment to the eventual recognition in happier circumstances of a Jewish state.

[27] Minute by Burrows, 19 Apr. 1948, FO 371/68649.

[28] When the British finally broached some of these possibilities in early May, the departure from their usual attitude of 'neutrality' caused the American delegation at the United Nations to recall that in past months the British had been 'obstructive'. Now 'at the eleventh hour' they raised immensely complicated questions such as effective sanctions. At the same time Beeley 'said flatly that in the British view any attempt to apply economic sanctions against the Arab states would wreck the Marshall Plan and everything we are trying to do in Western Europe'. On the question of sanctions against the Jews, Beeley 'expressed frank doubts' whether the American government in a showdown would 'stop the flow of dollars which enabled [the] Jews to support their military potential'. (Austin to Marshall, 8 May 1948, *Foreign Relations 1948*, V, pp. 936-40.) Lovett commented later that 'our mutual task would have been easier . . . had [the] British not been extremely laggard until [the] eleventh hour in dealing with a crisis largely of their own making'. (Lovett to UK Embassy, 28 May 1948, ibid., pp. 1070-2.)

Truman's attitude towards the truce was unambivalent. He concluded the interview with Rusk:

The President said our policy will not change. We want a truce. Tell the Arabs that our policy is firm and that we are trying to head off fighting in Palestine. Remind them that we have a difficult political situation within this country. Our main purpose in this present situation is to prevent a war. He expressly stated his concern over the Russian aspect of the situation. He ended by saying 'go and get a truce. There is no other answer to this situation. Good luck to you and let me know if there is any way in which I can help.'[29]

The President's emphasis on the Arabs perhaps indicated that he thought they would be the ones responsible for the breakdown of the proposed truce, but the State Department now put both sides to the test. Arab and Jewish representatives would be flown to Jerusalem to negotiate an immediate cease-fire. The Jews immediately declined this 'spectacular process' for reasons of 'moral responsibility'. To Rusk (and his special assistant, McClintock) the 'moral' reasons were apparent. He summarized the state of affairs as he saw them a week and a half before the end of the mandate: 'the refusal of the Jewish Agency . . . to agree to our proposal for on-the-spot truce negotiations in Palestine on grounds that they could not accept the "moral obligation" to undertake such conversations rather clearly reveals the intention of the Jews to go steadily ahead with the Jewish separate state by force of arms'.[30]

Like Bevin, Marshall feared the consequences of Jewish military success, though for different reasons. He explained them to Moshe Shertok, the head of the Jewish Agency's political department. Shertok had been in New York and was on the verge of returning to Palestine to confer with his colleagues in the Agency's Executive about such fundamental issues as whether or not definitely to reject the American proposals for a truce, which would involve a delay in the creation of the Jewish state. His interview with Marshall, a week before the end of the mandate, was therefore of crucial importance because he probably represented the last chance for the Secretary of State to talk to a Jewish leader of stature who could influence decisions made by the Agency's Executive. Marshall told him that he wished to speak as a participant in the Second World War and more recently as an observer of the civil war in China. According to Shertok, he spoke with utmost sincerity and gravity. Pointing to a map of Palestine, Marshall indicated the coastal regions held by the

[29] Memorandum by Rusk, 30 Apr. 1948, USSD 501.BB Palestine/4-3048 Box 2184; *Foreign Relations 1948*, V, pp. 877–9.

[30] Memorandum by Rusk, Secret (drafted by McClintock), 4 May 1948, USSD 501.BB Palestine/5-448 Box 2185; ibid., V, pp. 894–5.

Jews and the mountain ridges occupied by the Arabs. The Jews might achieve significant initial victories, but they were surrounded by professional Arab armies trained by the British. Ultimately the Jews could not hold out.[31] Perhaps they would not face the stark fate of extermination as Weizmann had warned Truman, but in any case they would confront calamity. Shertok responded by stating that the Jews now stood at the threshold of fulfilling a hope cherished for centuries. The Jewish leaders now making these decisions would be answerable to Jewish history. He left Marshall with little hope for a truce.[32]

On the Jewish side, Shertok recorded the conversation with Marshall in perceptive detail, but the point of importance is the emphasis he placed on the momentum that had built up for the establishment of the Jewish state. Lovett and Rusk were also present, and the skill with which Shertok presented his case did much to soften their criticism. In essence the plea was that, if delayed, the opportunity for the creation of a Jewish state might be lost forever. 'The State was within our physical grasp', Shertok explained. 'To let go now might be fatal. . . . the tension around the date of May 15th was mounting daily, I might even say hourly, not only in Palestine but among Jews throughout the world.' Shertok accurately judged that Marshall, Lovett, and Rusk were not basically opposed to partition. They were all sceptical, but none of them were committed anti-Zionists. Shertok did not believe, as did some of his colleagues in the Jewish Agency, that the State Department's proposal for a truce amounted to a trap. He detected genuine anxiety about civil war in Palestine. It was therefore imperative for the Jews not to antagonize the Americans by rejecting the truce proposals without at least reassuring them that the Jews were moving forward, in Shertok's words, in full confidence that 'the process of territorial and functional taking-over was in full swing. It was impossible to break the momentum.' This was the point he repeatedly made. He successfully left the impression that an incipient state already existed. At

---

[31] Marshall's estimate was similar to Bevin's, though the latter tended towards a broader scale: 'we had always assumed the Jews might win the first battles', Bevin wrote to Creech Jones, 'but we feared that fighting might take a much wider form later on. . . . A country like Pakistan might render considerable assistance to the Arabs and the whole Moslem world might become inflamed. The real bloodshed might not come for sometime but I felt pretty certain it would come and would create a very dangerous situation.' Bevin to Creech Jones, 22 Apr. 1948, Creech Jones Papers.

[32] Memorandum by Marshall, 12 May 1948, *Foreign Relations 1948*, V, pp. 972-6; Sharef, *Three Days*, pp. 87-9; Urofsky, *We Are One!*, pp. 170-1; Larry Collins and Dominique Lapierre, *O Jerusalem!* (New York, 1972), pp. 316-17. Shertok on his departure at La Guardia airport on his way to Tel Aviv found himself paged over a loud-speaker by Weizmann, who had a message for Ben-Gurion: 'Tell B. G., tell everyone: it's now or never! Fear not, nor be dismayed.' Kurzman, *Genesis 1949*, p. 214.

least his plea made them more sympathetic to the Jewish point of view: 'to break the momentum might be fatal'. The Americans might take a more pessimistic outlook, but at least they could not believe that the Jews were flouting serious advice.[33]

Marshall in any event had to face the possibility of American intervention in Palestine in order to prevent the adverse outcome of what might develop into a major war, if not another holocaust. He suspected that American efforts to establish a truce and to delay the proclamation of a Jewish state had been undermined by the British. The archives do not reveal his emotions after the interview with Shertok, but probably he was extremely angry—at the British. In New York Shertok had talked with Creech Jones. The British Colonial Secretary, Marshall learned, was more candid than the British Foreign Secretary. Creech Jones had in effect confirmed Abdullah's plans for invasion. The Arab Legion would avoid clashes with the Haganah 'without appearing to betray the Arab cause'. At the same time, from a different source, Marshall learned that Bevin welcomed the American truce proposals.[34] What was Bevin's real policy? Was the British aim a truce or the carving up of Palestine? Marshall regarded the conflicting reports as evidence of British duplicity. 'It was generally agreed', he said four days after his talk with Shertok, 'that the British had played a lamentable, if not altogether duplicitous, role in the Palestine situation.'[35]

When the question of recognition of the Jewish state arose in early May 1948 the governing consideration was that a state already existed. A State Department official identified the transcendence of that point when he emphasized '*the inescapable fact that a Zionist State already is in being*'.[36] The crucial meeting on whether or not to recognize it took place on Wednesday the 12th of May. Truman, Marshall, Lovett, and Clifford were the protagonists. David Niles and Robert McClintock were also present. Clifford presented the case for recognition. He made these points:

[33] Memorandum by Shertok, 8 May 1948, *Israel Documents* (December 1947–May 1948), pp. 757–69.

[34] See *Foreign Relations 1948*, V, pp. 940–1. Creech Jones was actually attempting to assure the Jews that the British were attempting to prevent a scramble for Arab Palestine, but the conversation as Shertok reported it to the Americans gave the impression (as it filtered back to the Foreign Office) that the Arab Legion would not attack and therefore 'there was no need for them [the Jews] to bother about a truce'. See the unsigned letter (presumably by Sir John Balfour) to Wright, 'Secret and Personal', 25 May 1948, FO 371/68563/E7797/G. It is debatable whether Shertok intended to sow this seed of American suspicion. See his memorandum of 8 May, *Israel Documents*.

[35] Memorandum by Marshall, 12 May 1948, *Foreign Relations 1948*, V, pp. 972–6.

[36] Memorandum by John E. Horner, 4 May 1948, ibid., V, pp. 898–901. Italics in the original.

1. Recognition is consistent with U.S. policy from the beginning.

2. A separate Jewish State is inevitable. It will be set up in a few days.

3. Other nations will recognize it. We shall have to, also, in a few days.

4. It is better to recognize now—steal a march on the U.S.S.R.[37]

Clifford had also given the question of recognition particular attention in relation to the Jewish vote in the impending Presidential election. He did not say so explicitly, but in fact international expediency went hand in hand with domestic necessity. Here Marshall emphatically parted company:

> I remarked to the President that, speaking objectively, I could not help but think that the suggestions made by Mr. Clifford were wrong. I thought that to adopt these suggestions would have precisely the opposite effect from that intended by Mr. Clifford. The transparent dodge to win a few votes would not in fact achieve this purpose. The great dignity of the office of the President would be seriously diminished. The counsel offered by Mr. Clifford was based on domestic political considerations, while the problem which confronted us was international. I said bluntly that if the President were to follow Mr. Clifford's advice and if in the elections I were to vote, I would vote against the President.[38]

Clifford added afterwards, 'He said it all in a righteous God-damned Baptist tone.'[39] Marshall's caution prevailed—momentarily. Truman acquiesced in his insistence that he and Lovett look 'very carefully' into the question of recognition after the Jewish declaration of statehood.

Clifford returned to the charge. On the afternoon of the 14th he told Lovett that the President now faced 'unbearable pressure to recognize the Jewish state promptly'. Lovett replied that the United States would be 'buying a pig in a poke'. Clifford countered with an argument that on innumerable occasions had proved to be decisive in similar British crises. Intervention, in this case in the form of recognition, would prevent Palestine from lapsing into anarchy. 'At six o' clock Friday night', according to Clifford, 'there would be no government or authority of any kind in Palestine. Title would be lying about for anybody to seize and a number of people had advised the President that this should not be permitted.' Lovett continued to protest about 'indecent haste' and emphasized 'the tremendous

[37] See *Foreign Relations 1948*, V, p. 976.
[38] Memorandum by Marshall (drafted by McClintock), Top Secret, 12 May 1948, USSD 501.BB Palestine 5/1248 Box 2185; ibid., pp. 972–6.
[39] Jonathan Daniels, *The Man of Independence* (New York, 1950), p. 319. For Clifford's reflections on these critical discussions, see Clark M. Clifford, 'Recognizing Israel', *American Heritage* (Apr. 1977). The comment is important for insight into Clifford's outlook rather than accuracy of detail.

reaction which would take place in the Arab world'. He fought a losing battle. Clifford responded by saying that the time of recognition was 'of the greatest possible importance to the President from a domestic point of view'. Lovett summed up:

> My protests against the precipitate action and warnings as to consequences with the Arab world appear to have been outweighed by considerations unknown to me, but I can only conclude that the President's political advisers, having failed last Wednesday afternoon to make the President a father of the new state, have determined at least to make him the midwife.[40]

The President recognized the state of Israel at 6:11 p.m. on the 14th of May, in other words, a few minutes after expiration of the mandate at midnight time in Palestine. As his biographer notes, in view of an issue still charged with the emotions of the holocaust and one that appeared to be important in swinging votes and money in Truman's direction in the presidential campaign, it is difficult to see how any American President would have reacted differently, though perhaps not so precipitately.[41]

The sudden recognition of Israeli independence created, in Marshall's words, 'a hell of a mess' at the United Nations. Since the beginning of May the focus of American policy had shifted from trusteeship, to truce, to mediation. At the very time of the President's recognition the delegates were discussing the proposal sponsored by the United States to send a United Nations representative as 'Mediator' to Palestine. The American delegates with prodigous effort had marshalled a majority of votes in support of the proposal. Then they themselves learned of the Presidential proclamation only when news of it from the tickertape began to filter through the delegations. There was pandemonium. The Cuban delegate had to be physically restrained from seizing the speaker's podium and denouncing the Americans as double-crossers. He spoke later with only slightly less bitterness. Trafford Smith, a Colonial Office official, caught some of the drama of the occasion in a report written for the benefit of Creech Jones:

> At about 6.15 p.m., rumours began to seep through the delegations to the effect that the United States had recognized the Jewish State of Israel. Mr. [George] Ignatieff [of Canada] told the British delegation that he had himself seen it on the ticker-tape. These rumours caused the Colombian delegate, Mr. González-Fernandez, to make a formal request to the United States Delegation

[40] Memorandum by Lovett, Top Secret, 17 May 1948, USSD 501.BB Palestine/5–1748 Box 2185; *Foreign Relations 1948*, V, pp. 1005–7.

[41] Donovan, *Conflict and Crisis*, p. 387. Bevin's reaction to American recognition is also noteworthy. According to the Foreign Office file, the Foreign Secretary 'expressed his extreme displeasure'. (Minute by Michael Wright, 15 May 1948, FO 371/68665/6758.) The imagination is left to speculate what Bevin actually said.

to confirm or deny the rumour. Mr. [Francis B.] Sayre mounted the rostrum to say somewhat ignominiously that the United States Delegation had heard of the press reports but had no official information.

A few minutes later, Mr. Belt, the Cuban delegate, who had been most co-operative in furthering the Mediator resolution, intervened to make clear with some asperity that he would no longer vote for the resolution in view of the grant of recognition by the United States, which reduced the United Nations to an 'elegant international club'. Faris Bey el Khouri, the Syrian delegate, soon after made a most bitter speech in which he accused the United States delegation of deliberately playing out time until the termination of the Mandate, in order to be able to recognize the Jewish State *de facto* before the General Assembly had reached any final conclusion. . . .

An eloquent speech by Mr. [Charles] Malik of the Lebanese Delegation, expressing his sense of the futility of the United Nations organization, if the great powers themselves used it as no more than a cover for underhand dealings, concluded the debate. Mr. Malik literally wept in the course of his speech and the United States Delegation looked as though they would have been glad if the ground had opened and swallowed them up.[42]

Trafford Smith spoke afterwards to an American official, Gordon Merriam (Chief of the Office of Near Eastern Affairs). Merriam made no effort to defend American policy but 'said quite openly that it was useless to adhere to a consistent policy since they never knew what bombshells might not descend from the White House at the moment'.[43]

In Washington at the British Embassy the Minister, Sir John Balfour, regarded the United Nations débâcle as only a part of 'a melancholy story of indecision and weakness'. Balfour went on to comment on American policy in general, which he believed threw 'vivid light' on the 'inefficiency of the American governmental machine':

It is also symptomatic of a political immaturity, not yet entirely outgrown, which from time to time permits considerations of domestic policy to prevail over the demands presented by the realities of the international situation in an unstable world. It is this factor which so greatly alarms other nations who are perforce dependent upon the United States Government, with its great potential military strength and economic resources, to rescue them from the difficulties and dangers with which they are beset.[44]

[42] Memorandum by Trafford Smith, 3 June 1948, Creech Jones Papers.

[43] Ibid. For an important account by the American official who read the statement to the General Assembly see Philip C. Jessup, *The Birth of Nations* (New York, 1974), chap. 7. Another American official 'snapped' to García-Granados: 'That is White House language, not State Department.' *Birth of Israel*, p. 290. The Austin Papers do not reveal Austin's reaction to the Presidential recognition, but as leader of the American delegation it must have been an exceedingly painful experience. According to Rusk's account, 'he simply went home' as a sort of silent protest, rather than to give the impression that he had been involved in any double dealing. *Foreign Relations 1948*, V, p. 993.

[44] Balfour to Bevin, 24 May 1948, FO 371/68650.

Balfour probably like most other Englishmen believed that Palestine could hardly be ranked as a British 'Imperial' success, but at least the British formally had extricated themselves. On the other hand the Americans had entangled themselves as sponsor of a Jewish state in a way that held incalculable dangers for the future.

In Jerusalem General Sir Alan Cunningham brought to a close Britain's mandatory era in Palestine. British withdrawal lacked the pomp and splendour of the transfer of power in India but Cunningham rose to the dignity and solemnity of the occasion. On the eve of his departure he spoke briefly and honestly:

> Tomorrow, at midnight, the final page in the history of Palestine and the British Mandate in Palestine is turned. On the morrow a new chapter opens and Palestine's history goes on. . . . if it shall be that by our going we bring eventual good to the people of Palestine, none of us will cavil at our departure.[45]

The military band played 'Auld Lang Syne' as well as 'God Save the King'. At Haifa he remained in the territorial waters of Palestine aboard the aircraft carrier *HMS Ocean* until the exact moment of the termination of the mandate. Unlike any other episode in the history of the end of the British Empire, the British withdrew without designating a successor power. The United Nations had delegated an advance guard of a secretariat to go to Palestine to take over essential services but in the event only a handful of international civil servants had actually arrived. 'In the end', Cunningham wrote a few months later, 'the British were blamed for not having handed over to anyone, whereas, in point of fact, there was nobody to whom to hand over.' Cunningham had not presided over a transfer of power but a liquidation of 'Imperial' responsibilities. 'And so we left', he recounted in *International Affairs*. 'It is a melancholy business presiding over such an occasion, but I sincerely trust we can feel that we left with dignity, using all our efforts to the last for the good of Palestine.'[46]

In London the organ of the British press that had intimately followed the details of the struggle for Palestine, the *New Statesman*, viciously attacked both Truman and Bevin as the villains who would be responsible for future bloodletting. The remarks bore the stamp of Richard Crossman:

> Mr. Truman, not unnaturally, has resented receiving lectures on political morality from the Foreign Secretary of a Labour Government solemnly pledged to support Zionist claims in Palestine. A weak but very honest man, he has the

---

[45] Sharef, *Three Days*, p. 258.
[46] Sir Alan Cunningham, 'Palestine—The Last Days of the Mandate', *International Affairs* (October 1948).

typical American sympathy for the Jewish colonists struggling to achieve independence against the modern George III, and the typical American ignorance of Middle Eastern realities. . . .

Whatever the excuses, American vacillation has been almost as fatal in Palestine as British partisanship. Between them, Mr. Bevin and Mr. Truman have . . . permitted the Middle East to drift to the very edge of general war.[47]

With black premonition the *New Statesman* predicted that Bevin's 'pig-headed partisanship' would produce in Palestine a replica of the history of Ireland after the First World War.

The British Empire, like the Roman Empire, produced poets of stature who memorialized its decline and fall. Some of this poetic exuberance is less memorable for stylistic felicity than for the capturing of a historical moment—as in the case of 'Sagittarius' in the *New Statesman* singing the woes of Britannia on that fateful day, the 15th of May 1948:

> End *Pax Britannica,*
> Shield of Arabia!
> *Fiat Justitia*!
> And peace in Palestine!
>
> Strife at a word will cease,
> Force will secure the peace,
> UNO will send police
> To guard the Holy Land.
>
> Pilgrims come under Fire!
> (Who against peace conspire?)
> Pilgrims in haste retire
> From doomed Jerusalem.
>
> Forward, the Haganah!
> Forward, Arabia!
> *No Pax Britannica,*
> And war in Palestine![48]

[47] *New Statesman*, 29 May 1948.
[48] Ibid., 15 May 1948.

9

THE ARAB–ISRAELI WAR OF 1948:
POLITICAL IMPLICATIONS

SIR JOHN TROUTBECK, the fervently anti-Zionist head of the
British Middle East Office in Cairo, wrote in June 1948 that in his
judgement the new Jewish state would be run 'by an utterly
unscrupulous set of leaders'. Its size would be relatively unimportant,
he continued, but it would now be up to the British to convince the
Arabs to accept the existence of no less than a gangster state.
Troutbeck's ideas represented the extreme end of the spectrum of
British thought. His interpretation however explains much about the
British attitude in mid-1948 that otherwise might remain puzzling.
He and others believed that the Arab states now faced the dilemmas
of Czechoslovakia in 1938. Troutbeck himself had served in Prague
at the time of the Munich crisis.

> I must confess that many of the elements seem to me to be present in Pale-
> stine to-day. . . . The situation before Munich was one in which the weaker side
> with the juster cause was being cajoled and browbeaten into accepting . . . a
> solution which it knew quite well would be fatal to itself. . . . What has stuck
> in people's gorge ever since [Munich] is the cant and hypocrisy of the argument
> used in justification of our actions.

He expanded on the analogy of the Arabs and the Czechs, and by
implication the Jews and the Nazis:

> Some of their [Arab] leaders may be pretty worthless and their general out-
> look on life may leave much to be desired. Certainly they are not blameless
> in the present struggle, but nor were the Czechs in theirs. But when all is said
> and done . . . they are up against opponents who will stick at nothing.[1]

Troutbeck urged emphatically that the British not apologize for the
existence of the new state in terms of historical 'justice'. 'We should
in the long run serve our own cause in the Middle East far better by
frankly telling the Arabs, who are realists in these matters, that we

---

[1] Troutbeck to Bevin, Secret, 2 June 1948, FO 371/68559/E7376. The head of the
Eastern Department, Bernard Burrows, noted that 'the analogy with Munich . . . should
perhaps not be pressed too far but it is a timely reminder of the responsibilities which we
have undertaken'. On the subject of the war, Dan Kurzman, *Genesis 1948: The First Arab-
Israeli War* (New York, 1970), and Larry Collins and Dominique Lapierre, *O Jerusalem!*
(New York, 1972) are popular accounts, and both of considerable historical interest because
of the wealth of detail based on extensive interviews. Both have valuable bibliographies. The
most important recent scholarly analysis of political developments during the war is Joseph

have done what we can for them but that we cannot stand up against the U. S. A. plus the U. S. S. R. nor run the risk of wrecking the U. N.' The adjustment of British policy in 1948 in fact followed the suggestion of Troutbeck's assessment of the need to bow to the political pressure of the United States as well as the military reality of the Israeli victories.

For purposes of the present analysis, there were two critical phases in the war, one in mid-1948 and the other at the end of the year. In July, after the first truce, the Jews consolidated their control over the northern part of Palestine, which included the areas of eastern and western Galilee. Western Galilee had been designated as Arab by the United Nations in 1947. Towards the end of the year the Jews extended their sway over the southern part of Palestine that included the desert of the Negev. This was an area that, as has been seen, had been allocated to them by the United Nations in 1947. They had in fact secured their claim only by President Truman's intervention. Jewish leaders attached vital importance to the Negev because of its potential for settlement and agricultural development, its possible mineral and petroleum resources, and its strategic value as an outlet to Africa and Asia.[2] These regions of Galilee and the Negev assumed an almost transcendental value in the Israeli psyche. In the words of an American report, 'Weizmann and Ben-Gurion looked with mystical tenacity toward holding Negev and Galilee too.'[3] Apart from the questions of Jerusalem and the 'Arab triangle' (or what later became known as the 'West Bank'), Israeli aims essentially consisted of the incorporation of both Galilee and the Negev into the new state. To the British however this seemed to be, in the words of the head of the Eastern Department of the Foreign Office, 'manifestly [an] unjust . . . solution' for the Jews to acquire *both* Galilee and the Negev.[4] At this time the British still hoped to arrive at a compromise between the Jews and the Arabs that would be minimally acceptable to the latter. According to

Heller, 'Failure of a Mission: Bernadotte and Palestine, 1948', *Journal of Contemporary History*, 14 (1979). Shlomo Slonim, 'The 1948 American Embargo on Arms to Palestine', *Political Science Quarterly*, 94, 3 (Fall 1979) is also useful for the American side. Jon and David Kimche, *Both Sides of the Hill: Britain and the Palestine War* (London, 1960) is the Zionist historiographical point of departure for both military and political questions. The best Zionist military account is Netanel Lorch, *The Edge of the Sword: Israel's War of Independence 1947-1949* (Jerusalem, 1961).

[2] Weizmann wrote in July 1948: 'the Negeb represents a vast territory—true, empty and desolate now—but with water can be made to hold a very considerable population. In fact it is the only empty place in Palestine to-day, and we must hold on to it for dear life.' *Weizmann Letters*, XXIII, p. 178.

[3] Griffis to Marshall, Top Secret, 15 Sept. 1948, USSD 501.BB Palestine/9-1548 Box 2187; *Foreign Relations 1948*, V, p. 1398.

[4] Minute by Burrows, 5 June 1948, FO 371/68559.

Bevin's principal adviser on Palestine, Harold Beeley, the specific aims would be:

(a) To make the frontier [the UN frontiers of 1947] more rational.

(b) To remove as many as possible of the Arab objections to partition.[5]

In the end the British were frustrated in achieving those goals because of Israeli determination not to yield either Galilee or the Negev, and because of American unwillingness to force the Israelis to do so. Bevin later summed up what he believed to be the heart of the difficulty by emphasizing the American tendency to 'let there be an Israel and to hell with the consequences'.[6]

There was never any doubt on the British side that the frontiers of the Israeli state would be drawn along the lines of military control. This is a pronounced theme in the minutes of Harold Beeley, and it is illuminating to trace the evolution of his ideas. They throw much light on the Zionist assumption that the British would unleash the Arab armies in order to drive the Jews into the sea, or, at best, would attempt to reduce Jewish Palestine into a rump state dependent on British mercy.[7] Beeley had written in March 1948:

A reasonable forecast seems to be that the Jews, left to themselves, would be driven out of the entire southern area awarded to them by the United Nations [the Negev] and would also lose North-Eastern Galilee, but that they would succeed in defending the coastal plain, including the cities of Tel Aviv and Haifa.[8]

At first sight that might appear to be a misguided assessment, but about a month and a half later Beeley began to take account of a new and momentous development. He then wrote in April 1948, shortly after the Jews had received the first consignment of Czech arms:

It seems certain that the Jews will proclaim a State on the 15th of May, and that uncontrolled warfare will follow in Palestine. From the point of view of H. M. G. this situation will involve two grave risks:

(i) The Russians may intervene by supplying arms to the Jews and by facilitating the despatch of reinforcements from Black Sea Ports.

(ii) Given sufficient quantities of military material, whether from Soviet or other sources, the Zionists may win resounding victories which would result in Arab appeals to H. M. G. for assistance.[9]

[5] Minute by Beeley, 17 June 1948, FO 371/68567/E8764.
[6] Bevin to Franks (draft), 3 Feb. 1949, FO 371/75337/E1932. See below p. 567.
[7] See Kimche, *Both Sides of the Hill*, p. 39.
[8] Memorandum by Beeley, 16 Mar. 1948, FO 371/68538/E3549.
[9] Beeley to Burrows, 'Secret and Personal', 30 Apr. 1948, FO 371/68554/E6676. For the supply of arms from Eastern Europe see Arnold Krammer, *The Forgotten Friendship: Israel and the Soviet Bloc, 1947–53* (University of Illinois Press, 1974).

In the same letter Beeley warned, as has been mentioned earlier, that Jewish forces might even defeat the Arab Legion, which would have disastrous consequences for British influence and prestige in the Middle East. As late as the end of April, less than three weeks before British evacuation, Beeley also emphasized that only at that time had it begun to sink in, especially to the Arabs, that the British actually intended to evacuate, and that the future of Palestine would be settled by the Arabs and the Jews fighting it out.[10]

At the time of the end of the mandate the Israelis held the military initiative. They had already seized Haifa on the 22nd of April, a critical development both militarily and psychologically. Jaffa, the largest of the Arab cities, fell to the Jews on the 12th of May. In the third week of the month Israeli forces successfully attacked and held Acre, the only remaining Arab coastal town. The large-scale Arab evacuations alarmed the British, but the military operations themselves were more or less in line with their own predictions. On the 25th of May Attlee summoned the American Ambassador, Lewis Douglas, to attend what amounted to an informal meeting of the Defence Committee of the Cabinet to discuss these developments. Among those present were Bevin, Alexander, and the service chiefs. They hoped to impress on the Americans the serious nature of the conflict and the need to keep it localized. Lord Tedder, the Chief of the Air Staff, explained to Douglas that if the fighting continued then 'the Jews would have initial successes . . . since their armed forces outnumber the armed forces of the Arabs four to one and were better armed'. The long-range outlook however would be quite different. If the war lasted over a period of years, according to Tedder, 'the Arabs would wear the Jews down by constant opposition and guerrilla fighting'. Attlee and Bevin expressed the hope that the British and the Americans would now be able to co-operate in bringing about Arab acceptance of the Jewish state. Douglas later recorded this as a 'milestone' in the history of British thought on Palestine. Bevin specified two points on which it would be necessary for the Jews to make concessions:

(i) the inclusion of Gaza and the Negeb in the Jewish State had been a terrible mistake as there were no Jews there, and this must be righted.

(ii) Jaffa and Acre, which were purely Arab towns, should be given back to the Arabs.[11]

---

[10] Beeley to Burrows, 'Personal & Confidential', 24 Apr. 1948, FO 371/68546/E5598.

[11] F.O. record of meeting of 25 May 1948, FO 371/68650/E7024; *Foreign Relations 1948*, V, pp. 1047–50. There is a good account of the British dilemmas caused by the fall

Those points appeared to the British, as they did to Ambassador Douglas, to be reasonable demands that the Israelis could easily accept in return for Arab acquiesence in the existence of the Jewish state. There was a sense of optimism about this meeting. The spirit of hopefulness indeed lingered on into the summer. Michael Wright, the Assistant Under-Secretary who supervised these questions, wrote of Palestine as an abscess in Anglo–American relations that had needed to be lanced. Now that the mandate had ended, the British and the Americans once again could work together.[12]

In the meeting between the American Ambassador and British Ministers on the 25th of May, Lord Tedder had evoked an historical analogy that seemed to be just as compelling and more immediately relevant than the one of Munich. He spoke of the Spanish civil war. Both the Americans and the British were apprehensive that the war between the Jews and the Arabs might develop into an international conflict in which the United States and Britain might be fighting each other through surrogates. 'What Lord Tedder feared', Douglas reported, was the 'repetition of civil war in Spain during which both sides were supplied with arms by different sets of outside powers'.[13] The United States in December 1947 had imposed an arms embargo that continued to be enforced during the Arab–Israeli war.[14] The British had also curtailed military supplies to the Arab states.[15] The two embargoes interlocked. Neither side could supply arms without running the risk of the other lifting its embargo. The American Ambassador clearly caught the essence of the implied agreement as well as the force of the analogy of the Spanish civil war: 'The worst prospect I can see on horizon [of] American–British relations', he had reported on the 22nd of May, would be the 'possibility that we raise embargo on Middle East arm shipments to favor Jews. If we do so, it will be only short step until British . . . may lift embargo re arms to Arabs.' The consequences would be, he wrote in summary, 'the two great democratic partners . . . indirectly . . . ranged on opposite sides of a battle line scarcely three years after May 8, 1945'.[16]

of the coastal towns (and the friction between Bevin and Montgomery on the question of the British army's precipitate withdrawal) in Cohen, *Palestine and the Great Powers*, pp. 338–41.

[12] Minute by Wright, 23 June 1948, FO 371/68650/E8121.

[13] *Foreign Relations 1948*, V, p. 1049.

[14] See Slonim, 'The 1948 American Embargo on Arms to Palestine'.

[15] The rationale may be summed up in Bevin's own words: 'If we had not first curtailed and then stopped war material deliveries [to the Arabs] the United States embargo would inevitably have been lifted. The Jews would have gained enormous advantage from this.' Bevin to Campbell, No. 1454 Confidential, 25 Aug. 1948, FO 371/68583.

[16] Douglas to Marshall, Top Secret, 22 May 1948, USSD 867N.01/5-2248 Box 6765; *Foreign Relations 1948*, V, p. 1031.

The point about the possibility of another Spanish civil war is extremely important in understanding the British attitude in the summer of 1948. It was a time of general anxiety because of the crisis in Berlin. The Soviet blockade began in June. In the Middle East there was acute apprehension that political pressure in America might force the White House to lift the arms embargo on the Jews, thus setting off a chain of events that might lead to direct British intervention to prevent Jordan's defeat. The possibility was so real that British and American representatives confronted it directly in Washington on the 6th of June 1948. This exchange took place between Loy Henderson and Harold Beeley:

> I . . . asked Mr. Beeley what he thought the British attitude would be in the following circumstances: If warfare should continue in Palestine, it might become necessary for the United States to lift its arms embargo. With immigration and arms it was quite likely that the Jews would win. Extremists might push on into Transjordan . . . What would be the British reaction to such attacks?
> Mr. Beeley replied that the British Government would have no alternative under its treaty with Transjordan but to repulse such attacks.[17]

The dangers were thus explicitly stated. So also was the unequivocal British response.

The meeting between Beeley and Henderson (and other representatives) took place towards the end of the first phase of the formal war (the 15th of May to the 11th of June). At this time it appeared that the Arabs and Jews might be evenly drawn, and therefore this particular exchange between the British and the Americans is of considerable interest because it illuminates the prospective settlement foreseen at a critical stage of the conflict. Both Henderson and Beeley agreed that it would be in the interest of all concerned, including the Jews, if the 1947 frontiers were redrawn in order to create a small and compact Jewish state that included all of Galilee. The Negev on the other hand would be Arab. Henderson, according to Beeley, believed that 'the map would look much more tidy if they [the Jews] were given the whole of Galilee in exchange for the south [i.e. the Negev], and for similar reasons he thought they might also have Jaffa'. The point on which they differed was Jerusalem. Henderson thought that the Jewish part of the city should be part of the Jewish state. Beeley believed strongly to the contrary: 'the incorporation of any part of Jerusalem in the Jewish State would wreck all prospect of a settlement. The Arabs might perhaps agree to an international régime in Jerusalem, but in my view that

[17] Memorandum by Henderson, 6 June 1948, USSD 501.BB Palestine/6-648 Box 2185; *Foreign Relations 1948*, V, pp. 1099–101.

was the farthest limit to which they could be pushed.' Beeley possessed an analytical mind and he was especially sensitive to the Arab side of the question. In view of the central part he played on the British side it is important to note the two elements of compromise that he believed both sides would have to acknowledge as a preliminary. The first was Arab acquiescence in the existence of the Jewish state. The second was Jewish willingness to redraw the frontiers so that the Negev would be Arab.[18]

In London the officials of the Foreign Office by mid-June had finally reconciled themselves to the inescapable conclusion that there would be a Jewish state—partition. This was the revelation Lewis Douglas referred to as a 'milestone in British thinking'.[19] To obtain Arab assent however it appeared mandatory to the Foreign Office that the Jewish state must have 'boundaries smaller than those contemplated' by the United Nations plan of 1947. The best the Arabs could hope for, according to Michael Wright, 'would be that the Negeb should become Arab, and that the Jews should give back Acre, Jaffa and at least part of Western Galilee'. The revealing feature of Wright's line of analysis is the negative emphasis. A Jewish state, if not too large, would force the Jews themselves to limit immigration and thus might help to diminish its danger in the eyes of the Arabs. In retrospect there is a certain element of self-deception or wishful thinking in this outlook. Viewing partition as the least of the possible evils, Wright and others in the Foreign Office now saw the Jewish state as a stimulus to Arab unity which in turn somehow might be pro-British.

> Partition involving the setting up of a Jewish state but with boundaries smaller than those contemplated ... would avoid the danger of the Jews gradually obtaining control of a unitary state for the whole of Palestine. It might result in the Jewish authorities themselves having to limit immigration. And the existence of a Jewish State would be a source of unity among the Arabs ... If there was Partition the Arab areas would almost certainly be divided up mainly between Transjordan and Egypt.[20]

The Arabs in those circumstances would now look to the British for guidance. 'It is virtually certain that the Arab countries will seek our advice at some stage', Wright conjectured, as if the Arab League might, after all, emerge as a pro-British force in the Middle East with more unity and more gratitude after a test by fire.

British officials were convinced that the Jewish state might become

---

[18] Beeley to Burrows, 7 June 1948, FO 371/68566.

[19] Douglas to Marshall, Secret, 19 June 1948, USSD 867N.01/6-1948 Box 6765; *Foreign Relations 1948*, V, pp. 1124-5.

[20] Minute by Wright, 15 June 1948, FO 371/68650/E8409/G.

Communist. They anticipated the worst from the refugees of eastern Europe. There was fear of infiltration by Soviet agents, but there were other reasons which were recognized by the Zionists at the time as misconceptions of Jewish purpose. Weizmann and others rightly emphasized that it was misguided if not irrational to believe that the Jews fleeing from the oppressive regimes of the Russian satellites would wish to create their own Communist dictatorship in Palestine. Jewish experiments in socialism did not inspire British confidence. Richard Crossman was a remarkable exception. In official circles there was a contrast between the willingness to assume that the Arabs might be a stabilizing influence and the reluctance to grant the possibility of the Jews becoming a moderate and democratic force in Middle Eastern politics. If the Jewish state were small, however, it might be controlled. There was not a similar assumption about a Palestinian Arab state. British officials now believed that the rest of Palestine should be partitioned among the Arab states. Most of it would be absorbed by Jordan and perhaps a part by Egypt. From the outset there was no question of a separate, independent Arab state. The reason for this axiomatic pattern of thought was twofold. A Palestinian state would be too small to be viable; and if it were established it would probably fall under the control of the anti-British extremists led by the Mufti. The British hoped that partition might now actually strengthen their position in Transjordan and even Egypt.

All of these strains appeared in the minutes of the head of the Eastern Department. The discursive ideas of Bernard Burrows may be taken as a representative summary of British reaction to the war in Palestine at the end of the first phase:

Our political strategic and commercial interests demand that the settlement should be one which is reasonably acceptable to the Arabs or which at least will not create such turmoil and hatred of the West in Arab countries as to ruin our position there. . . .

A Jewish state would be a spearhead of communism. On the other hand . . . the Palestinian Arabs . . . have shown themselves to be incapable of organisation and entirely immature politically . . . The Palestinian Arabs might very likely be under the extremist and inept leadership of the Mufti. . . .

Even if the Jewish state was strongly subject to communist influence this would have its good side since the Arabs would automatically dislike communism because it is associated with the Jews. . . .

The Negeb would clearly have to be Arab. There would have to be an Arab corridor up the coast from Gaza as far as Jaffa. There would have to be a large exchange of populations . . . so that Western Galilee might become Jewish and Syria receive compensation. . . .

Jerusalem . . . should be a demilitarised city under United Nations control. . . .

The general conclusion of these thoughts . . . seems to be that the disadvan-

tages of a separate Jewish state from our point of view and that of the Arabs,
have been over-emphasized and that provided the boundaries could be very
radically altered, it might be the least of many evils.[21]

In sum the British by mid-June 1948 believed that the consequences
of partition might not be as bad as previously thought, but they held
it as essential that the territorial scope of the new state should be
small. Such a circumscribed territory would force the Jews themselves to curtail immigration and thus would make the Jewish state
more acceptable to the Arabs. Its frontiers would have to be drawn
with finality. Such was the British reaction to the war at the time
when the two sides still appeared to be evenly drawn.

The Bernadotte Proposals

The key to the success of the truce of the 11th of June 1948, as Sir
John Glubb accurately wrote in his account of the war, could be
described as a simple military stalemate in which neither side would
risk an advantage at that time.[22] Both sides seized upon the injunction of the United Nations in order to pause, plan, and reorganize,
which the Jews did more effectively than the Arabs. Contrary to
the propaganda of both sides, the numbers of troops was fairly
balanced with about 19,000 Israelis and 23,000 Arabs. The Arab
Legion held the Old City of Jerusalem and the strategic point of
Latrun, which commanded the main route from the coast to Jerusalem. The Jews held the coastal plain and a precarious corridor
to Jerusalem (the 'Burma road' south of Latrun) as well as eastern
Galilee. At this stage the general situation was more favourable to
the Arabs, at least in the eyes of the Israelis. 'It would be almost
a miracle', Michael Wright noted, if the United Nations mediator
succeeded in finding a solution acceptable to both sides.[23]

The mediator was Count Folke Bernadotte of Sweden. In Zionist
literature he is often portrayed as a catspaw of the British. He was
certainly so regarded at the time by the Israelis. 'I think I am not
mistaken', Chaim Weizmann wrote, 'if I say that he is just a stooge
of the British.'[24] Weizmann on this occasion erred in his judgement,

[21] Minute by Burrows, 9 June 1948, FO 371/68566.

[22] Sir John Bagot Glubb, *A Soldier with the Arabs* (London, 1957), p. 141. Moshe
Shertok wrote in June 1948: 'The main reason which prevailed for the truce was the military
situation. . . . All our fronts were extremely tenuously held.' Shertok to Goldmann, 15 June
1948, *Israel Documents* (May–September 1948), pp. 162–4.

[23] Minute by Wright, 15 June 1948, FO 371/68650/E8409/G.

[24] Weizmann Letters, XXIII, p. 160. For Bernadotte see Sune O. Persson, *Mediation
and Assassination: Count Bernadotte's Mission to Palestine 1948* (London, 1979), which is
based on the Bernadotte papers and other archival material.

though for reasons that had nothing to do with Palestine. In the last months of the war Bernadotte had acted as an intermediary between Nazi Germany and the Allies. Even though he had some success in saving Jewish lives, his association with Heinrich Himmler was enough to blacken his reputation among the Jews. He was energetic, garrulous, and vain. His intellect and his decisiveness inspired British and American hopes that here was a man for the occasion no less than Mountbatten had been in India. There were in fact similarities of personality and circumstances. The description of Pablo de Azcárate of the United Nations mission is both fair-minded and incisive: 'Count Bernadotte's marked predilection for the spectacular and the ostentatious, undoubtedly helped to create a propitious atmosphere in which the personal action of the Mediator . . . could produce the desired result.' Azcárate also accurately detected the dynamic and inspired element of Bernadotte's personality:

> I got the impression of a man wholly preoccupied with the idea of speed and activity, anxious to appear as someone who came to the point at once and knew his own mind. . . . But whatever the external characteristics of his personality. and methods, no one could refuse to pay a tribute of admiration and respect to the wholehearted devotion with which he flung himself into his task, or to his impartiality and his fervent desire to accomplish a work of peace and justice in Palestine.[25]

Bernadotte's impartiality, as will be seen, was tempered by a sense of justice more sympathetic to the Arabs than to the Jews. There is one further revealing remark by Azcárate that he had noted in 1948 in his diary. 'The Count gives me the impression of a man who is lost in a labyrinth, who yet continues walking with great speed and decision as if he knew exactly where he is going.'[26] Bernadotte's path led him to conclusions that were essentially the same as the British.

It is now known from Bernadotte's posthumously published account that during his first month in the Middle East, from the time of his appointment as mediator on the 20th of May, he gained the conviction that a binational or unitary state rather than partition would have been the best solution. 'The artificial frontiers given to the State of Israel', he wrote, ' . . . were bound to result in warlike complications.' Bernadotte was also struck with what he described as 'the solid resistance put up by the Arab world against the partition of Palestine and the creation of a separate Jewish State'.[27] He now

---

[25] Pablo de Azcárate, *Mission in Palestine 1948-1952* (Washington, 1966), pp. 93-5.
[26] Ibid., p. 94.
[27] Folke Bernadotte, *To Jerusalem* (London, 1951), p. 118. Persson, *Mediation and Assassination*, quotes many expurgated passages.

had to meet the challenge of a just settlement even though the military situation, in his judgement, favoured the Jews. The plan that he devised and hoped to implement quickly and decisively was to give the Negev to the Arabs and Galilee to the Jews. Haifa would become a free port and Lydda a free airport. Although there would be sophisticated guarantees for Jewish rights and representation, Jerusalem would become Arab.

Bernadotte's proposals, formally put forward on the 27th of June 1948, bore similarities to British schemes of the past. He had in mind for example, that there should be a 'union' between the Jewish state and Transjordan that would co-ordinate economic affairs and foreign policies of both countries. He also proposed to limit Jewish immigration. The Foreign Office response reveals that there was nothing at this stage that could be described as collusion between the mediator and the British. Indeed Bevin's general attitude towards Palestine at this time may be summed up in his own words of exclamation, 'I take the view that our task is over.'[28] Harold Beeley wrote in assessing Bernadotte's proposals that 'they demonstrate his sincerity and fairmindedness'.[29] The minutes however make it clear that the British were extremely sceptical of any success, and that the British, if they had been asked, probably would not have advised coming down so firmly on the control of immigration and an Arab Jerusalem. 'Speaking privately', Beeley explained to Ivor Linton, an Israeli representative in London, the British knew that the Jews would never yield on those points. The critical issue in Beeley's mind was the exchange of Galilee for the Negev. The Israeli record of this point is important because it accurately reflects an understanding of the way in which the British regarded the central problem that eventually would have to be resolved: 'the Jews would have to give up the Negev'. This is the theme that runs through Beeley's minutes as well as his conversations with the Israeli representatives: 'He thought that the Arabs could not agree to Egypt being cut off from direct land contact with the rest of the Arab states.'[30]

The idea of an Israeli Galilee and an Arab Negev figured prominently in the evolution of American thought. It was especially salient in the comments of the State Department official who within a few months played a key part in the armistice negotiations, Robert McClintock (who, as has been mentioned previously, acted as Dean

[28] Minute by Bevin on Kirkbride to Bevin, Confidential, 10 June 1948, FO 371/68570. For all stages of the Bernadotte 'plan', Persson, *Mediation and Assassination*, is an essential companion.

[29] Minute by Beeley, 2 July 1948, FO 371/68569/E9031.

[30] Memorandum by I. J. Linton, 5 July 1948, *Israel Documents* (May–September 1948), pp. 271–3.

Rusk's special assistant at the United Nations). In early July 1948 McClintock wrote of 'the sins of the Chosen People—and their equally sinful adversaries'.[31] He viewed the British with less humorous detachment. His racy comments made it clear that he held their strategy of 'masterly inactivity' responsible for the Middle Eastern crisis of 1948. Nevertheless his views were remarkably similar to the British outlook as expressed by Harold Beeley. McClintock believed that Jerusalem should be internationalized. He detected what he thought to be a ruinous flaw in Bernadotte's proposals: 'Jerusalem is as much a Jewish city as it is an Arab metropolis and it contains shrines sacred to three of the principal world religions. To permit it to be made the capital of King Abdullah would rouse Jewish passions and irredentism. . . .'[32] Most of Arab Palestine however he believed should be allocated to Transjordan. He held the same ideas as Beeley (and Bernadotte) about the exchange of Galilee for the Negev. 'If the State of Israel were thus redefined geographically', McClintock wrote, 'it would be a more homogeneous unit possessing an improved economic patrimony.' He hoped in short to clear up the map of Palestine which in its present shape in one of his favourite phrases, resembled 'a portrait by Picasso'. Once redrawn the frontiers would have to be definite and permanent. McClintock, like others in the State Department, feared the ambitions of the Zionist extremists:

If the boundaries of Israel were re-drawn and the adjustments . . . agreed to by the Arabs and Jews there should then be an international guarantee by the United Nations, and, if possible, by treaty between Israel and the Arab States, of the territorial settlement. This would be of particular advantage to the Arabs as 'freezing' the boundaries of Israel and thus affording protection to the Arab States against the wider pretensions of the Jewish revisionists and such fanatics as those of the Irgun who have pretensions to the conquest of Transjordan.[33]

The acquisitions of the moderate Zionists, in McClintock's sardonic view, presented enough problems, at least for the present: 'It might . . . be timely to recall that there is a Biblical prophesy to the effect that the world will come to its end once the Jews regain their homeland.'[34]

Both before and after the 'nine days' war' of 8–18 July, the Central

---

[31] Memorandum by McClintock, Top Secret, 1 July 1948, USSD 501.BB Palestine/7-148 Box 2186; the memorandum appears in *Foreign Relations 1948* (V, pp. 1171–9), but the quoted lines were omitted at editorial discretion.

[32] Memorandum by McClintock, Top Secret, 23 June 1948, USSD 501.BB Palestine/6-3048 Box 2185; *Foreign Relations 1948*, V, pp. 1134–7.

[33] Ibid., p. 1136.

[34] Memorandum by McClintock, 1 July 1948, with quoted lines omitted from the version in *Foreign Relations 1948*, V, pp. 1171–9.

Intelligence Agency demonstrated a keen appreciation of the essential stakes of the conflict. The point is of interest among other reasons because it indicates that the best of American military and political intelligence corresponded with British assessments, and that despite this common yet independent analysis the 'crevasse', as Bevin referred to it, between the British and the Americans continued to widen. The four weeks' truce had favoured the Jews. On the day of resumption of hostilities on the 8th of July, the CIA accurately estimated that nothing could now stop the Jewish drive to establish a sovereign state and that the Arabs would eventually be compelled to withdraw their armies.[35] It seemed clear then, as it has in retrospect, that the Arabs committed at least a tactical error by resuming full-scale hostilities. During the nine days' war the Jews gained military control of the rest of Galilee. At one stroke the Arabs lost by force of arms what the British and Americans, at least, believed to be the principal means of bargaining to acquire the Negev.

On the Jewish side of the analysis, the CIA commented that the position had been immensely strengthened:

> The truce resulted in so great an improvement in the Jewish capabilities that the Jews may now be strong enough to launch a full-scale offensive and drive the Arab forces out of Palestine. Events during the truce, and the enormous increase in Jewish strength resulting from them, considerably change the previously held estimate of the probable course of the war in Palestine.[36]

On the Arab side there had developed not only a corresponding weakening of the logistical position but also a dangerous psychological mood:

> The Arab people were confident of victory and were assured by their leaders that the truce would not be extended. Their bitterness may well erupt into violence against their governments or the Western powers or both. If their wrath is turned against their leaders, some of the Arab governments in an attempt to survive may well resume the Palestine war. Arab leaders, however, will first make every effort to turn the anger of their people against the UN, the US, and the UK, or even against one another.[37]

In London one of the more searching comments on the Arab psychology of the war was made by Harold Beeley in a remark about Azzam Pasha, the Secretary-General of the Arab League: 'Azzam believes that on a long view, the Arab revival for which he is working will be better served by military action and defeat than by capitulation and

---

[35] CIA memorandum, 8 July 1948, *Foreign Relations 1948*, V, p. 1200.
[36] CIA memorandum, 27 July 1948, *Foreign Relations 1948*, V, pp. 1240–8.
[37] Ibid., p. 1242.

compromise. He may be wrong, but I am sure he holds this opinion sincerely.'[38]

In the American as well as the British estimates the key to a lasting peace on the Arab side lay with King Abdullah. McClintock had written in May before the termination of the mandate:

> Given this intolerable situation, the wisest course of action might be for the United States and Great Britain . . . to work out a *modus vivendi* between Abdullah of Transjordan and the Jewish Agency. This *modus vivendi* would call for, in effect, a *de facto* partition. . . . Abdullah would cut across Palestine from Transjordan to the sea at Jaffa, would give Ibn Saud a port at Aqaba and appease the Syrians by some territorial adjustment in the northern part, leaving the Jews a coastal state running from Tel Aviv to Haifa.[39]

Apart from the concession of Aqaba to Ibn Saud, that proposal could just as well have been put forward in the British Foreign Office. As late as mid-July it still seemed within the realm of possibility. By that time it had become obvious to all concerned, at least in western circles, that the Arab Legion was the only effective Arab fighting force. 'It seems clear that Abdullah is the only one who has any very substantial material bargaining power', a major American assessment concluded.[40] McClintock in particular attached great importance to Abdullah's pragmatism as a virtue that should be encouraged in order to protect American petroleum interests as well as to provide a sound geo-political settlement. He continued to espouse the solution of an enlarged Transjordan. He deplored the 'mystical' reasons for which some of the other Arabs, in contrast with Abdullah, appeared to be fighting:

> As for the emotion of the Arabs, I do not care a dried camel's hump. It is, however, important to the interests of this country that these fanatical and over-wrought people do not injure our strategic interests through reprisals against our oil investments and through the recision of our air base rights in that area.[41]

By the time of the nine days' war in July the officials of the State Department entirely agreed with their counterparts in the Foreign Office that Abdullah was 'still the only Arab leader capable of retrieving the situation'. Abdullah was even referred to in these discussions between the British and the Americans as the 'trump card' to be played in order to bring about a settlement

[38] Minute by Beeley, 18 July 1948, FO 371/68572/E9433.
[39] Memorandum by Rusk (drafted by McClintock), 4 May 1948, USSD 501.BB Palestine/5-448 Box 2185; *Foreign Relations 1948*, V, pp. 894-5.
[40] Memorandum by Jessup (UN), 30 June 1948, *Foreign Relations 1948*, V, pp. 1161-71.
[41] Memorandum by McClintock, 1 July 1948, USSD 501.BB Palestine/7-148 Box 2186; *Foreign Relations 1948*, V, pp. 1171-9.

in which most of Arab Palestine would be absorbed by Trans-jordan.[42]

Abdullah held one of the central positions, but the British were acutely aware that it was precarious. 'King Abdullah would accept partition', Sir Alec Kirkbride in Transjordan had reported in mid-June, but the result 'might have a boomerang effect on ourselves'.[43] If Abdullah accepted the settlement of partition, which to the British appeared to be increasingly inevitable, he would face renewed charges of being no more than a craven stooge of the British, while the British themselves would be denounced not only for aggrandize-ment of their puppet state but also for a calculated Arab defeat. 'The fiction that we forced the almost victorious Arab States to accept the truce by withholding arms and ammunition', Kirkbride continued, 'is already in the process of formation'.[44] He had detected the genesis of a powerful mythology. It was one that Bevin himself combatted vigorously and to no avail. 'I will do my utmost to help King Abdullah', he telegraphed to Kirkbride in the first stage of the nine days' war in July, 'but I cannot repeat not do this by the supply of ammunition.'[45] To do so would not only flout the United Nations but would also bring about the lifting of the American arms embargo on the Jews. King Abdullah was a British 'trump card' only so long as there was a military stalemate. The British thus regarded the nine days' war and the loss of Galilee as a political as well as a military disaster.

Unless one took a cataclysmic view of world history—as did Azzam Pasha for example—then the Arabs seemed to be defeating their own purposes as well as undermining the British position. A telegram by Bevin in late August conveys a sense of lament as well as a recognition of the tenuous military strength of the Arab armies. It also suggests a certain indignation that the Arabs could hold the British responsible for Arab defeats:

It is quite untrue to suggest that we have let the Arabs down or failed in any obligations towards them. We did not urge them to intervene by force in Pale-stine nor did we promise them support if they did so. They went in of their own accord in most cases without telling us beforehand.

The very small measure of military successes which they achieved shows that their forces, while capable perhaps of occupying friendly territory, were not prepared for and incapable of undertaking the major military operations which would have been necessary to achieve the announced object of the Arab States,

[42] Douglas to Marshall, Top Secret, 9 July 1948, USSD 501.BB Palestine/7–948 Box 2186; *Foreign Relations 1948*, V, pp. 1203-5.

[43] Kirkbride to Bevin, Secret, 16 June 1948, FO 371/68565/E8190.

[44] Ibid.

[45] Bevin to Amman and other posts, Top Secret, 12 July 1948, FO 371/68572.

namely to drive the Jews into the sea. Being unwilling to admit this state of affairs publicly, the Arab Governments allowed their peoples to be deluded . . . into thinking that their armies were achieving all kinds of successes.[46]

Rather than advancing from victory to victory, as the Arab governments and newspapers had prophesied, the Arab armies suffered defeats at key strategic points (such as Lydda, the airfield, and Ramle, a key junction), and setbacks in the Negev. Sir John Glubb recalled the mood of the Egyptians: 'The public were expecting an early end to the war, the occupation of Tel Aviv by the Egyptian army, and the surrender of Israel. . . . The Egyptian people were incensed—they had been given to understand that complete victory was in their grasp.'[47]

The Americans as well as the British now apprehended internal instability in the Arab states. According to Joseph C. Satterthwaite, the Director of the Office of Near Eastern and African Affairs in the State Department (Henderson's successor), if the Arabs continued in the direction of total defeat—which would almost certainly occur for example if the American arms embargo on the Jews were lifted—then the consequences for both the United States and the British Empire would be incalculable:

The military setbacks which the Arabs could be expected to suffer would probably result in the overthrow of some of their governments. The attendant chaos would provide a breeding ground for communism, or a series of dictatorships might arise on a wave of anti-American and anti-British sentiment. Governments hostile to the Western powers would mean the loss of vital strategic facilities in the Near East coveted by the Soviet Union. The intensification of the disturbances might undermine our strategic position in Greece, Turkey, and Iran as well.[48]

By August 1948 the best that could be hoped for, from the perspective of the State Department and the Foreign Office, was an armistice along the lines of military control.

From the time of the second truce on the 18th of July until Bernadotte's murder in September, the conspicuous element in the effort to bring about an armistice, if not a lasting peace, was the collaboration of the mediator, the British, and the Americans. Bernadotte himself now had ample reason to believe that he alone could

[46] Bevin to Cairo and other posts, 25 Aug. 1946, FO 371/68583.
[47] Glubb, *Soldier with the Arabs*, p. 150.
[48] Memorandum by Satterthwaite, *c.*14 July 1948, USSD 867N.113/7-1448 Box 6766; *Foreign Relations 1948*, V, pp. 1217-18. Eliahu Epstein's assessment of Satterthwaite is of interest: 'Joseph Satterthwaite, who succeeded Henderson . . . is honest and loyal, but does not differ in views and attitude on Palestine from his predecessor. Less biased and aggressive than Henderson, he will probably observe more strictly instructions [from] his superiors.' Epstein to Shertok, 20 July 1948, *Israel Documents* (May-September 1948), pp. 372-3.

not reconcile the Arabs and Jews. Both sides found his terms intolerable. He also had to recognize that the second truce was much
more precarious than the first. The Israelis had greatly strengthened
their military capacity. During the nine days' war their victories
added three times as much territory as in the first month of the war.
The second cease-fire, imposed by threat of economic sanctions by
the United Nations, did not possess the virtue of military stalemate,
nor did the fatalistic attitude of the Arabs augur well for a durable
truce. If peace were to come it would have to be in the nature
of a political settlement backed by Britain and the United States.
'Bernadotte is not eager to offer suggestions', according to the
State Department in mid-August, 'until he is assured that US and UK
govts are in agreement on general lines of an equitable settlement.'[49] This was a shrewd assessment of the way in which Bernadotte would attempt to bring the British and Americans into line
with his views. It also indicated the possibility of the British and
Americans seizing the phrase 'made in Sweden' to disguise a settlement designed by the British and American governments.

Apart from the Negev, the main sticking point was Jerusalem.
Bernadotte now believed that a greater degree of internationalization
might be necessary. Though he personally continued to hold that
'justice' lay with the Arabs, he now saw the need to be more flexible
with the Jews. He had moved closer to the British position. At this
stage the Foreign Office had not ruled out the possibility of parti-
tioning the city (with a 'corridor' connecting it with the Jewish
state) but the consensus in the Eastern Department favoured internationalization. 'The Internationalisation of Jerusalem in some
form', according to Bernard Burrows, 'is one of the few things on
which there is almost universal agreement between the Powers.' He
had specifically in mind 'a neutral enclave surrounded by Arab
territory'. Expanding on his ideas about general issues, Burrows,
in a minute reminiscent of earlier ideas expressed by Harold Beeley,
wrote of a general settlement based on 'lines of force', in other
words, military control. 'The "lines of force" settlement towards
which we are moving . . . with the Americans', he continued, 'has
the great merit of reducing more or less compact areas.'[50] The
pattern of thought in the State Department progressed in the same
direction. The mediator and the American and British governments
held common ground. They might disagree on particular issues, but,

---

[49] Marshall to Douglas (drafted by McClintock), Top Secret, 13 Aug. 1948, USSD
501.BB Palestine/8-948 Box 2187; *Foreign Relations 1948*, V, pp. 1308-10. For analysis
of Bernadotte's views at this time see Persson, *Mediation and Assassination*, chap. 12.

[50] Minute by Burrows, 18 Aug. 1948, FO 371/68582.

no matter the intrinsic importance of a particular question such as Jerusalem, a solution could be found in part because of the political will of the mediator. The Americans and British were willing to follow his lead partly because they believed that Bernadotte, like Mountbatten in India, had the charisma to carry it off. According to Bernadotte himself, in Jerusalem there would be 'local autonomy for the Jewish population and with an international commission'. As for the rest, he proposed in bold strokes that 'the Jews should be given valuable lands in western Galilee which they now hold by virtue of military conquest but in return for this acquisition should permit Arabs to take over most of Negev'.[51]

Secret negotiations were held between the British, the Americans, and the mediator on the island of Rhodes during 13–15 September. The British representative was Sir John Troutbeck, whose anti-Zionist outlook has been indicated in the beginning of this chapter. The American representative was Robert McClintock. The mood was one of determination. If a workable settlement could not be agreed upon, the opportunity might be lost forever. It would be necessary not to flinch at a 'just' solution. In the course of the discussions it became clear that Bernadotte's idea of 'strict justice' would probably outrage the Jews who were fixed on including the Negev in the state of Israel. 'If the Jews were to receive all of rich Galilee', according to Bernadotte, then 'all of the Negev should be given to the Arabs', for whom 'it would ever remain a worthless desert'.[52] Bernadotte took a stiff line in opposing a suggestion put forward by McClintock that the Jews might at least be given a slice of the Negev because they attached so much 'political' and even 'mystical' importance to the desert. The suggestion was not accepted, though in retrospect it is doubtful whether a minor concession in the Negev would have made any difference. Troutbeck's account of the proceedings reveals that McClintock in fact had a realistic outlook and that he gave a warning which proved to be remarkably accurate:

McClintock throughout called attention to the strong mystical feeling now felt by the Jews for the Negev. Dr. Weizman [*sic*] in particular is obsessed by this idea. While therefore McClintock will himself recommend to State Department that they support Mediator's suggestions to give whole of Negev to the Arabs, he thinks it quite possible that White House will intervene, as it apparently did on an earlier occasion.[53]

---

[51] Marshall to Douglas, 13 Aug. 1948, *Foreign Relations 1948*, V, pp. 1308–10.

[52] Griffis to Marshall, Top Secret, 15 Sept. 1948, USSD 501.BB Palestine/9-1548 Box 2187; *Foreign Relations 1948*, V, pp. 1398–1401.

[53] Troutbeck to Bevin, Top Secret, 18 Sept. 1948, FO 371/68587/E12163.

The Bernadotte 'plan' in its final form now retained the advantage of clear simplicity. Though in many respects it was exceedingly complex, in essence it recommended that Jerusalem would be placed under international control. Galilee would become Jewish and the Negev would become Arab.[54]

McClintock's secret telegram to the State Department at the end of the meeting on the 15th of September bore eloquent testimony to the mediator's diligence and sense of duty as well as to the gravity of the historical moment:

> My overall impression . . . is that Bernadotte, who has taken an immense amount of first-hand testimony, has come from last minute talks with leaders on both sides, and who is sternly determined to advocate only a solution based on equal justice to both sides, feels that now is the optimum moment: that if not 'now' it is 'never' . . .[55]

On the 18th of September Bernadotte was assassinated by Jewish extremists.

The Israeli October Victories and the Question of a 'Middle Eastern Munich'

The Stern gang had already decided to murder Bernadotte before the details of the September plan had been made public. The assassination did not change anyone's mind. In the words of an Israeli scholar, 'the murder itself was a superfluous act of political fanaticism'.[56] If anything it made the Israeli side of the problem more difficult. Bernadotte had become a martyr in the cause of a 'just' settlement, which in the eyes of most impartial observers did not include a Jewish Negev. The assassination came as a revelation to many Americans about the nature of militant Zionism. According to the British Ambassador in Washington, Oliver Franks, the 'murder at the hands of the Stern gang came as a profound, even if transient, shock to all those in the United States who take an interest in international affairs'.[57] It came as a particular shock to Ralphe Bunche, the United Nations official who now assumed Bernadotte's mantle.[58] Bunche was a modest man of genuine goodwill. He was among the first of the postwar generation of American Negroes to achieve international

[54] More specific points included the creation of Lydda as a 'free airport', and the designation of Haifa 'including the oil refineries' as a free port. The question of refugees was also dealt with in detail. See *Foreign Relations 1948*, V, pp. 1401–6; and Persson, *Mediation and Assassination*, chaps. 13–16.

[55] Griffis to Marshall, 15 Sept. 1948, *Foreign Relations 1948*, V, pp. 1398–1401.

[56] Heller, 'Failure of a Mission', p. 525.

[57] Franks to Bevin, Confidential, 2 Oct. 1948, FO 371/68651/E13062.

[58] Bunche's principal interest lay in trusteeship affairs, and his friends, with a sense of dismay, watched him being dragged into the Palestine dispute. One of them, Huntington

prominence. He had an acute sense of the need to fulfil Bernadotte's mission. He possessed a gifted intellect, and it is appropriate to recall at this stage that Bunche himself had drafted with even hand both the minority and majority reports of the United Nations Special Committee on Palestine. It is even more important to note that he had drafted the Bernadotte report at Rhodes. His sympathies, like Bernadotte's, tended to be on the side of the Arabs, but unlike Bernadotte he was more flexible and less inclined to look for a 'just' solution.[59] He could see historical justice on both sides. Both Arabs and Jews found him perceptive—from the Israeli side too inclined to accept Arab arguments about the strategic and symbolic importance of the Negev. Bunche and other UN officials, according to Michael Comay (head of the Israeli mission at the UN but reporting from Haifa), seemed to be preoccupied with Arab fears about 'the long wedge of Jewish territory thrust down between them; and the doubts about the validity of our development claims' in the Negev.[60]

In the House of Commons, Bevin, after paying tribute to the mediator's humanitarian services, endorsed the Bernadotte plan above all because it would lead to the incorporation of most of Arab Palestine into Transjordan. The British solution in other words remained the same. Bevin was indirectly expressing anxiety about the Negev, and not merely because of the Jews. He addressed himself to the alternative solution of an independent Arab state. The matter is of interest because the creation of such a state has been regarded in retrospect as a missed opportunity of solving the Arab–Israeli conflict. The British at the time would have nothing to do with the proposition. Bevin referred to the 'infertile area' that would never form the basis of 'a viable State'.[61] What was not at first sight apparent from his speech is that he was obliquely referring to

Gilchrist (an authority on international organization) wrote to him: 'What a tough assignment you have taken on and under what depressing circumstances! I remember that you really did not want to go to Palestine at all in the first place, but from the general point of view, I am glad that the U.N. has someone with your poise, courage and readiness to handle difficult, acute problems available to take over in this most complicated political spot in international relations today.' (20 Sept. 1948, Bunche Papers.) Perhaps subconsciously, Bunche frequently referred to Palestine in his correspondence as 'a killing assignment'.

[59] Bunche had an admiration for Bernadotte and later defended him, in one instance against the innuendo of anti-Semitism. 'The attribution of anti-Semitic attitude to Folke Bernadotte is a malicious attack on the character and reputation of one of the great humanitarians of our times. I am deeply grieved to learn that such a slanderous attack has been made' (Bunche to Henrik Beer, 27 Feb. 1953, Bunche Papers). He wrote in response to an article by H. R. Trevor-Roper, 'Kersten, Himmler, and Count Bernadotte', *Atlantic Monthly* (Feb. 1953).

[60] Comay to Israeli UN Mission, 27 Sept. 1948, *Israel Documents* (May–September 1948), pp. 640–4.

[61] *Parliamentary Debates* (Commons), 22 Sept. 1948, col. 899.

Egyptian ambitions. The question of Egyptian jealousy of King Abdullah had been the subject of searching comment within the Foreign Office. The British feared the establishing of an independent Palestinian Arab state because it would fall into the hands of anti-British extremists led by the Mufti (whose influence the British continued greatly to overestimate, in this case, as an ally of the Egyptians). The weakness of an Arab state, so ran a parallel argument, would also make it prey to Jewish territorial expansion.

Sir Hugh Dow, the Consul-General at Jerusalem, spoke out in stentorian vein on that subject, in part perhaps because of his own suspicions and indeed dislike of both the Egyptians and the Jews:

> Egypt doesn't want any other Arab state to increase its relative power and importance, and an Arab Palestinian State would be a hopeless proposition and render the next step in Jewish expansion a very easy one. And it would, of course, play directly into the hands of the Mufti.[62]

Dow also explained why neither side would ever accept the Bernadotte proposals in any form. His comments conveyed certain psychological as well as political insights:

> The Jews are frankly expansionist and refuse to put forward any terms, for fear they should ask for less than changing circumstances and the inefficacy of the United Nations may enable them to grab. The Arabs see little hope of practical help, either from us or from the United Nations, and in consequence the 'in for a penny, in for a pound' school of thought tends to prevail. . . . I do not think it is true to say that the Arabs realise that the Jews cannot be driven into the sea. . . . They feel it cannot be done today, but perhaps it can be done tomorrow, and almost certainly the next day. They are wrong, of course, but that is what most of them think.[63]

The pessimistic analysis carried weight in part because of Dow's own past experience in dealing with comparable problems. He was an old Indian hand. After a career in the Indian Civil Service, he had arrived in Palestine in the spring of 1948 only to see repeated, in his view, the worst of the tragedy of the partition of India. After Bernadotte's assassination he made one particularly revealing remark about the Arab reaction. That was at a time when the newspapers throughout the world had emphasized the abomination of Jewish terrorism. According to Dow's reading of Arab opinion, the Arabs 'had much better grounds than [the] Jews for desiring elimination of [the] Mediator'—Bernadotte after all had accepted the existence of the Jewish state. The comment served as a reminder that the British were still attempting to reconcile two equally extreme forces.[64]

---

[62] Dow to Burrows, 23 Aug. 1948, FO 371/68584/E11364.
[63] Ibid.
[64] Dow to Bevin, 23 Sept. 1948, FO 371/68588/E12410.

The question of the Negev was of fundamental importance. The territorial dimension of the problem may in a rough sense be equated with the southern half of the present state of Israel. For the Jews the Negev meant an opportunity for settlement and agricultural development in the only unpopulated part of Palestine. For the Arabs the Negev under Jewish sway would mean the physical separation of Egypt from the Arab states. By the autumn of 1948 the question turned not so much on the existence of the Jewish state, or on its exact frontiers, but on the imposing of a limit to Israeli expansion. The Arab experts of the Foreign Office were not at all optimistic that this would be possible short of total Arab defeat which in turn might extinguish British influence in the Middle East. There was thus an anguish in the minutes of the Foreign Office officials at this time.

One of the more reflective British officials who dealt with such long-range implications was Air Commodore K. C. Buss, who, as has been mentioned previously, had extensive experience in Iraq and was now a member of the Research Department of the Foreign Office. Buss believed that most Arabs had reconciled themselves to the idea of a Jewish state: 'there are clear signs that, in their hearts, all but the most rabid fanatics, like Haji Amin [the Mufti], realise that the existence of the State of Israel will have to be accepted sooner or later.' What the Arabs could never agree upon among themselves would be the division of Arab Palestine. Buss regarded it as 'a waste of time' to think that the Egyptians would agree to an extension of Transjordan over most of the Negev. The thwarting of the expansion of Abdullah's kingdom had become one of the few goals on which the other Arab states could agree:

Various reasons can be assigned to this attitude—jealousy of Transjordan, antipathy to King Abdullah, mistrust of his reliability in an anti-Zionist sense, disbelief in the suitability of the Transjordan administration to the parts of Palestine to be taken over, fear of an extension of British influence—none of them objections having any foundation on a statesmanlike appreciation of the facts.[65]

It would be up to the British to try to save the Arabs from themselves. As a matter of urgency this meant the curtailing of Israeli expansion. By the autumn of 1948 the only hope left to the British was co-operation with the United States and the United Nations in imposing, in Buss's words, 'a territorial limit to the Zionists'. His phrase summed up what had become, to the British, the critical issue.

Bevin believed that he had General Marshall's concurrence in the need for a quick and decisive fixing of the frontiers. Shortly after

[65] Minute by Buss, 11 Oct. 1948, FO 371/68642/E13266.

Bernadotte's assassination the two of them had discussed it in Paris at the beginning of the third regular session of the General Assembly of the United Nations. In a statement of the 21st of September (the day before Bevin's speech in Parliament) the State Department had accepted the Bernadotte plan 'in its entirety'—an endorsement that had thrown the Israelis into consternation.[66] The Arabs, Marshall told Bevin, 'seemed to think that he, Mr. Marshall, was pro-Jewish, whereas he was under very strong attacks from Jewish elements in the United States for propounding what they considered a pro-Arab solution'. Marshall hoped that Bevin would be able to bring the Arabs 'to take a more reasonable view'. Marshall himself would try to deal with the conflicting pro-Zionist influence of the White House and the 'anti-Jewish prejudice' of the United States Congress. He warned Bevin that Weizmann was making 'a direct appeal to President Truman'.[67]

A few days later the State Department learned of the President's deep concern that the Bernadotte report had been accepted *'in its entirety'*. Robert Lovett, who had underlined that point, recorded that the mounting pressure 'from the Jewish groups' threatened to become 'as bad as the time of the trusteeship suggestion' in the previous spring—when Truman, Lovett, and all concerned had complained that they had never felt such intense public pressure.[68] The Presidential campaign was now reaching its climax. As if to dramatize the seriousness of acquiescing in all of the recommendations of the Bernadotte report, Clark Clifford conducted this business over the telephone while aboard the Presidential train in Oklahoma. President Truman, he explained, had 'ordered' him to send a telegram to General Marshall in Paris that would disavow the unconditional affirmation of the frontier proposals. Lovett replied that the President himself had endorsed the State Department's position. '[From] the freight yards at Tulsa, where the conversation was punctuated by the whistles of on-coming trains', Clifford then engaged Lovett in a dispute almost as heated as the one in the previous May about the recognition of the Jewish state.[69] The trenchant analysis of the situation as well as the picturesque language flowed from the pen of Robert McClintock, who had recorded

[66] See Eban to Shertok, 22 Sept. 1948, *Israel Documents* (May–September 1948), pp. 623-4.

[67] FO memorandum, 24 Sept. 1948, FO 371/68589/E12523/4/G. In fact Weizmann appealed to Truman through Samuel Rosenman and Eddie Jacobson. See *Weizmann Letters*, XXIII, pp. 209-12.

[68] Memorandum by Lovett, 29 Sept. 1948, USSD 501.BB Palestine/9-2948 Box 2187; *Foreign Relations 1948*, V, pp. 1430-1.

[69] Memorandum by McClintock, 30 Sept. 1948, USSD 501.BB Palestine/9-3048 Box 2187; *Foreign Relations 1948*, V, pp. 1437-8.

the conversation and who was now witnessing the rapid realization of his prediction made only two weeks previously at Rhodes. 'I was very careful to warn Bernadotte that our government would probably have to modify its views', he wrote to Dean Rusk in explanation of these new developments both in Rhodes and in Oklahoma. As if preoccupied with freight trains and whistle-blowing, McClintock noted that Lovett 'has done a magnificent job in keeping the train on the track'.[70] The compromise arrived at on this occasion between Lovett and Clifford was that 'the President's domestic political requirements' could be met by *not* insisting on 'every detail' of the Bernadotte report. Here was a loophole that could prove to be as large as the Negev.[71] By the time of the Israeli operations in the Negev of 15–22 October, the American government had already begun to back away from the insistence that all of the Negev be handed over to the Arabs in exchange for a Jewish Galilee.

The strength of Israeli claims to the desert increased in proportion to military prowess and capacity, which had developed dramatically. The Israeli armed forces now approached the legendary figure of 100,000.[72] The arms and equipment from Czechoslovakia and elsewhere (including aircraft, tanks, and artillery), had tilted the overall military balance in Palestine in favour of the Jews. The morale of the Israeli army was high because of the victories in July. In the Negev the number of Israeli troops roughly equalled the strength of the Egyptian army. On the 15th of October the Israelis commenced operations against the Egyptians on grounds of blocking convoys to Jewish settlements in the desert, though in the blunt and accurate judgement of Glubb Pasha 'They decided to take the Neqeb before UNO could decide that they could not have it.'[73] The result in short was the Israeli success in severing the Egyptian army by the capture of the strategic point of Beersheba. The Egyptians in the east were cut off from their base. In the west the Israelis broke through to the coast at Beit Hanum. In the words of Jon and David Kimche, 'The Egyptian "finger" pointing to Tel Aviv had been amputated.' This is not the place to discuss the cause of the Egyptian military collapse. The main point is that, by the time the United

---

[70] McClintock to Rusk, 30 Sept. 1948, USSD 501.BB Palestine/9–3048 Box 2187; *Foreign Relations 1948*, V, p. 1439.

[71] Memorandum by McClintock, 30 Sept. 1948, *Foreign Relations 1948*, V, pp. 1437–8.

[72] 'About 100,000 of our best young men are tied up on the various fronts', Weizmann wrote in December 1948 (*Weizmann Letters*, XXIII, p. 237). Netanel Lorch, the Israeli military historian of the war, puts the figure at 90,000, though this is a sum that includes total mobilization. (*Edge of the Sword*, p. 387.)

[73] Glubb, *Soldier with the Arabs*, p. 196.

Nations had succeeded in imposing a cease-fire on the 22nd of October, the Israelis had brilliantly succeeded in militarily strengthening their claim to the Negev.

The military developments in the Negev occurred at exactly the same time that the question of the Jewish state burst publicly into the American Presidential campaign. Less than two weeks before the election, on the day of the cease-fire, Truman's Republican opponent repudiated the Bernadotte plan. Dewey criticized Truman for 'abandoning' the plank in the Democratic platform that upheld Israeli independence and the UN boundaries. The President's reaction, Lovett cabled to Marshall in Paris, would be 'immediate and aggressive' because Dewey had challenged Truman on the breach of a campaign promise.[74] Clark Clifford, for one, was delighted. He considered Dewey's action to be 'a serious error' and 'the best thing that has happened to us to date'.[75] Clifford consequently set about drafting a major campaign statement on Palestine. For present purposes the main point of interest is how it would effect the Negev. Clifford, in a masterstroke of political invention, merely reaffirmed the original plank in the Democratic platform, which at the time had been intended to apply to the UN boundaries of November 1947. On the 25th of October, seven days before the election, Truman rebutted Dewey on Palestine. The statement contained this passage on the frontiers:

We approve the claims of the State of Israel to the boundaries set forth in the United Nations' resolution of November 29 [1947] and consider that modifications thereof should be made only if fully acceptable to the State of Israel.[76]

By simply re-endorsing the original platform, the Truman administration now stood behind Israel in the Negev. Whatever frontier adjustments might be made, they would have to be acceptable to Israel.

The reaction of the British to the Israeli victory was one of unrelieved dismay. Michael Wright wrote of the dangers of 'unlimited Jewish expansion'. Sir Orme Sargent, whose pessimism now reached new depths, predicted that the Israelis would rout the Egyptian

[74] Lovett to Marshall, Top Secret, 23 Oct. 1948, USSD 501.BB Palestine/10–2348 Box 2188; *Foreign Relations 1948*, V, pp. 1507–8.

[75] Clifford to Truman, 23 Oct. 1948, *Foreign Relations 1948*, V, p. 1509.

[76] Ibid., p. 1513. The phraseology actually followed Lovett's suggestion, which he had put forward as a means of avoiding detailed discussion about the Negev. It is debatable whether he was aware of the danger of the Zionists seizing on the words 'fully acceptable' to mean a fulfilment of virtually all of their aims. In a speech at Madison Square Garden on the 28th of October Truman gave further encouragement by stating that the Israeli state should be 'large enough, free enough, and strong enough to make its people self-supporting and secure'.

forces out of 'the whole of the Negev'. 'Cock-a-hoop' was the phrase he used to describe the attitude of the Jews.[77] Nor was the fate of the Egyptian army the only British anxiety. Bevin told Marshall in Paris that the existence of the Arab Legion was in peril. The arms embargo had worked in favour of the Jews because of the Czech arms shipments, but it had placed the Arabs at such a disadvantage that the Arab Legion faced the danger of running out of ammunition. If the worst came to the worst the British would intervene to prevent Transjordan's defeat. This would mean nothing less than war between Britain and the new Jewish state. Marshall reported the gravity of Bevin's warning:

With the defeats inflicted upon the Egyptian Army and the present position of the Jewish forces, Abdullah's Arab Legion might become exposed to annihilating attacks on the part of the Jews. . . .

He [Bevin] made it quite clear that Great Britain could not stand by and see Transjordan and the Arab Legion placed in a position where it would be unable to defend itself against possible Jewish attack. He went so far as to state categorically that if the Israel forces should attack Transjordan proper at any time, the treaty of assistance with Great Britain would be immediately operative.[78]

Bevin had thus stated the ultimate danger, as it appeared to him, in such strong language that it conveyed to Marshall, at least, that the British were not bluffing. In this and other discussions the British also emphasized that they would re-arm Transjordan and even Egypt if Israeli forces continued to expand the frontiers of the new state. As an indication of willingness to come to terms, the British would now be willing to sanction Israeli control of the northern part of the Negev (in other words the part now under Israeli occupation) if in return King Abdullah were allowed to acquire the southern half—so that Transjordan might have a corridor to the Mediterranean.[79]

The British fixation on this strategic corridor may be explained by the apprehension that a Jewish 'wedge' driven between Egypt and the Arab countries would give the Russians opportunity to exploit Arab resentment. On the American side it appeared that the British apprehended a Soviet take-over of the Middle East. Indeed the British pursued the strategic and political arguments so vigorously that it seemed evident that fundamental issues were at stake. They were relentless in driving home to the American Ambassador in London that Israel might become a Soviet satellite. The Negev

[77] Minutes by Wright and Sargent, 21 Oct. 1948, FO 371/68594/E14099.

[78] Marshall to Lovett, Top Secret, 27 Oct. 1948, USSD 501.BB Palestine/10-2748 Box 2188; *Foreign Relations 1948*, V, pp. 1520-2.

[79] See Lovett to Marshall, 10 Nov. 1948, *Foreign Relations 1948*, V, pp. 1565-7.

consequently took on a new and immediate strategic significance. Douglas needed little persuasion. The Palestine situation, he telegraphed to the State Department, 'is probably as dangerous to our national interests as is Berlin'.[80] Douglas became an eloquent spokesman for the British cause, and, as the British hoped, he took the case directly to the President. On the 6th of November he and Truman discussed Palestine at length. Douglas dwelt on the dangers of 'a real division' between Britain and the United States in the Middle East. 'The President replied . . . that this must not be allowed to happen.'[81] The conversation thus served the purpose of reassuring the British that Palestine would not cause Truman to lose sight of the overriding importance of the Anglo-American partnership.

Robert Lovett also took part in this conversation about the future of the Jewish state. A few days earlier he had cabled Marshall in Paris that 'It has been absolute hell here.' He referred to the pressures before the election. He had hoped that after the election, whatever its outcome, there might be 'a new chance to review our Palestine policy . . . and plan a consistent course of action which we can stick to honorably and resolutely'.[82] Douglas's interview with the President a few days after the election now provided the opportunity to test these new and honourable possibilities. The President was not unreceptive when Lovett pointed out that the Israelis were acquiring far more territory than had been allocated to them by the United Nations in 1947. Lovett explained the rationale of the Bernadotte plan, which still seemed to him to be a reasonable proposition. If the Israelis now wished to hold on to the Negev, Lovett argued, then they should give up part of Galilee and perhaps Jaffa, or vice versa. The President agreed that this appeared to be a sound basis for a settlement. It is important to note Truman's attitude on the 6th of November 1948:

In plain language, the President's position is that if Israel wishes to retain that part of Negev granted it under [the UN] Nov 29 resolution it will have to take the rest of Nov 29 settlement which means giving up western Galilee and Jaffa. We feel that there is room for a mutually advantageous arrangement— Israel to retain western Galilee and Jaffa in return for relinquishing part of Negev to Arab States, presumably Transjordan and Egypt.[83]

[80] Douglas to Lovett, Top Secret, 26 Oct. 1948, USSD 501.BB Palestine/10-2648 Box 2188; *Foreign Relations 1948*, V, pp. 1516-18.
[81] Douglas to Lovett, Top Secret, 12 Nov. 1948, USSD 501.BB Palestine/11-1248 Box 2189; *Foreign Relations 1948*, V, pp. 1570-2.
[82] Lovett to Marshall, Top Secret, USSD 501.BB Palestine/10-3048 Box 2188; *Foreign Relations 1948*, V, pp. 1533-4.
[83] Lovett to Marshall, Top Secret, 10 Nov. 1948, USSD 501.BB Palestine/11-1048 Box 2189; *Foreign Relations 1948*, V, pp. 1565-7.

In the judgement of the State Department, such a settlement modifying the Bernadotte plan would find British backing and Arab acquiescence. It had the ingredients of a lasting peace in the Middle East, if the frontiers could be imposed decisively. It had the President's blessing.

At this stage the British believed that they had won a minor victory. But they were not the only ones attempting to influence the President. On the 5th of November Weizmann had written to Truman. Now corresponding as one President to another, Weizmann warmly congratulated Truman on his re-election. The letter contained lofty sentiments and noble thoughts that were no doubt genuinely felt, especially the thanks on behalf of the Israeli people for 'the enlightened help which you gave to our cause in these years of our struggle'. The point of importance for the present discussion is Weizmann's emphasis on the Negev. He recalled his conversation with Truman in November 1947, and he now drew attention to the British designs of 'detaching' the Negev from Israel:

> I feel emboldened to ask for your intervention in this matter, remembering your deep sympathy and understanding which you displayed when I had the privilege of stating to you our case on the Negev and displaying to you maps showing its potentialities for settlement. It was with a deep feeling of elation that I left you on that day, and it is this which now encourages me. . . .
> Sheer necessity compels us to cling to the Negev. Our pioneers have done yeoman work in opening up this semi-arid country; they have built pipe lines through the desert, set up agricultural settlements, planted gardens and orchards in what was for centuries a barren land. They will not give up this land unless they are bodily removed from it.[84]

When Truman received the letter he wrote a note to one of his advisers asking him to 'analyze it and suggest an answer'. The recipient was a person who continued to take a passionately pro-Zionist interest in the Palestine issue. Truman had given the assignment to David Niles.[85]

Truman did not respond to Weizmann until the 29th of November. In the meantime the Israelis were challenged by a Security Council resolution of the 4th of November that called for a return to previously held positions, in other words, evacuation of the northern Negev. The Israelis justified their continued occupation on grounds that they held the Negev 'by right' (by virtue of the UN resolution of November 1947) and that their occupation of other areas (for example, western Galilee) would be 'a matter for discussion'. Robert

[84] Weizmann to Truman, 5 Nov. 1948, *Weizmann Letters*, XXIII, pp. 221-3; *Foreign Relations 1948*, V, pp. 1549-51.
[85] See *Foreign Relations 1948*, V, p. 1551.

Lovett, pursuing his goal of a course of action to which he could adhere 'honorably and resolutely', told the Jews bluntly that 'one could discuss all one wanted to, but the fact was that the retention by Israel of Western Galilee . . . could not be justified on the grounds of right and justice'.[86] Marshall was equally candid. 'Don't overplay your hand', he told Moshe Shertok.[87] In mid-November McClintock made an inquiry into how much the Jews were actually prepared to yield. He arrived at a pessimistic but accurate conclusion based on statements of the Israeli Foreign Minister. In summary, Israel:

1. Refuses to relinquish the Negev.
2. Will never accept loss of 'its share in the Dead Sea'
3. Is uncompromisingly opposed being debarred from the Gulf [of] Aqaba,
4. Claims 'permanent inclusion in Israel of modern Jerusalem', and
5. Claims all of Galilee.[88]

Despite the uncompromising stand, the Jews won widespread sympathy, especially in America among those who regarded Weizmann as a moderate and far-seeing statesman. On the issue of the Negev, according to the American representative in Tel Aviv, James McDonald, Weizmann held common ground with all Israelis. Weizmann wished all of the world to know that 'Israel will never surrender [the] Negev', and that 'every Jew there will resist to death' a forced evacuation.[89]

Truman replied to Weizmann on the anniversary of the United Nations partition vote. The letter is one of the singular documents of the Truman administration. Truman himself later judged that it so felicitously expressed his attitude to the Jews that he reproduced it in the concluding part of the Palestine section of his memoirs. In warm and gracious language he recalled how he and Weizmann had both fought for 'lost causes' and how both of them had won. He sympathized with Weizmann's concern 'to prevent the undermining of your well-earned victories' (a phrase that could be taken to

---

[86] Memorandum by Lovett, 10 Nov. 1948, USSD 501.BB Palestine/11-1048 Box 2189; *Foreign Relations 1948*, V, pp. 1562-3.

[87] Memorandum by Marshall, 13 Nov. 1948, USSD 501.BB Palestine/11-1748 Box 2189; *Foreign Relations 1948*, V, pp. 1577-80.

[88] Memorandum by McClintock, 17 Nov. 1948, USSD 501.BB Palestine/11-1748 Box 2189; *Foreign Relations 1948*, V, pp. 1598-1601.

[89] McDonald to Lovett, Secret, 17 Nov. 1948, USSD 501.BB Palestine/11-1748 Box 2189; *Foreign Relations 1948*, V, pp. 1606-7. McDonald himself attended some of the sessions of the UN General Assembly in Paris, during which time he maintained direct contact with Clark Clifford. The suspicion and ill will between the State Department and the White House that had characterized the crisis in the previous April and May was thus revived later in the year. Dean Rusk cabled to the State Department that, if telephone calls from the White House began to cut across previous instructions, then Lovett should 'reserve a wing at St. Elizabeth's' for the American delegation. Rusk referred to the mental hospital in Washington. *Foreign Relations 1948*, V, p. 1630.

mean military as well as political victories). Truman wrote of the Negev:

I remember well our conversations about the Negeb, to which you referred in your letter. I agree fully with your estimate of the importance of the area to Israel, and I deplore any attempt to take it away from Israel. . . .

Since your letter was written, we have announced in the General Assembly our firm intention to oppose any territorial changes in the November 29th Resolution which are not acceptable to the State of Israel. I am confident that the General Assembly will support us in this basic position.[90]

Truman referred to the American statement in the General Assembly on the 20th of September. It was the formal expression of the position that the British had tried and failed to bring into alignment with their own ideas. It re-emphasized the point Truman had made during the pressures of the campaign: any frontier settlement would have to be acceptable to the Jews. This statement now became much more than campaign rhetoric. It became the explicit policy of the United States government and, eventually, of the United Nations. The United States, the United Kingdom, and other members of the United Nations would be able to offer advice, but in the end it would be up to the Israelis and the Arabs to settle the issues of the frontiers.

Truman's letter to Weizmann reflected the American belief, which had crystallized during the Israeli military campaigns, that the valiant Jewish people in the face of great adversity were creating a state in a way perhaps comparable to the winning of the American west. They were entitled to the fruits of their victory. There was an equally important corollary assumption about the democratic, rational, and humane nature of Israeli leadership. These points are of basic importance in comprehending the decisive shift in American policy away from the Bernadotte plan—which would have imposed frontiers that balanced the Negev with Galilee, or vice versa— towards a settlement that the Israelis themselves would be able to dictate. Part of the reason for this shift may be explained by the President's personal identification with Weizmann, and part of it may be understood as a development that was consistent with American reluctance to embrace a military or political commitment necessary for a compromise adverse to Jewish aspirations. The moral, military, and political arguments all interlocked.

It is not the purpose here to trace in detail the complex negotiations that culminated in the powers granted to the United Nations conciliation commission as a result of the stand described in Truman's letter. The United Nations would not be empowered to enforce a political settlement. This limitation was consistent with American

[90] Truman, *Years of Trial and Hope*, pp. 168-9.

policy in the previous spring, as will be recalled from an earlier chapter. The British objected to the doctrine of restraint in this case because a 'toothless' UN commission would lead to a sellout to Israel. They viewed the willingness of both sides to 'acquiesce' as the central feature of conciliation. But how could the Jews be expected to yield if they knew that the United States would tacitly support their non-compliance? There could be no settlement unless the Jews themselves found it acceptable—in direct accord with the President's wishes. Here the corollary about the nature of Jewish leadership came into play. Within the State Department the shift in policy was not without ethical tribulation, but even among sceptics the belief prevailed that the Israelis could be relied upon not to impose an 'unjust' peace. This pro-Jewish attitude was reinforced by the quickness and the decisiveness of the Israeli victories, which seemed to indicate that in the future the Jews rather than the Arabs would be more dependable 'allies'. Most Americans believed that the Jews (the terms 'Jews' and 'Israelis' were used interchangably) were not only fighting a 'just' war but were doing so with extraordinary efficiency. Robert Lovett, who now represented the honourable tradition of a balanced Wilsonian approach of equal justice, could thus tell the British in late November that 'the State Department were convinced that the American line and not the British one was the right one'.[91]

The British believed—passionately and bitterly—that the abandonment of the Bernadotte plan was an abject and dishonourable capitulation. They felt betrayed. The exchanges of November 1948 represent a particularly revealing moment in the history of the Anglo-American partnership. Attlee, speaking uncharacteristically 'with great feeling', told Ambassador Douglas that he believed the future of the United Nations was at stake.[92] The words 'Manchuria' and 'Ethiopia' were frequently on British lips. Sir Orme Sargent's attitude may be taken as an epitome. When he learned that the Americans would stand behind the Israelis rather than behind a 'just' settlement, he reacted in the same way as Sir John Troutbeck, whose ideas about appeasement have been discussed in the beginning of this chapter. Sargent stated that 'on the horizon lies another Munich'. The analogy is of great historical interest because of the way in which the lessons of the 1930s continued to inspire the British at critical times. Sargent believed that Transjordan would be placed in the position of Czechoslovakia. The Jews now held the military initative.

[91] Franks to Bevin, Secret, 23 Nov. 1948, FO 371/68598/E15079.
[92] Douglas to Lovett, Top Secret, 15 Nov. 1948, USSD 501.BB Palestine/11-1548 Box 2189; *Foreign Relations 1948*, V, pp. 1585-9.

There was no reason to believe, so far as the British were concerned (they made the opposite assumption from the Americans), that the Jews would stop short of territorial annexations which the Arab states would find intolerable. With the acquiescence of the United Nations, Israeli ambitions would remain unchecked. What if, Sargent asked rhetorically, the United Nations were to ask the British to declare the treaty with Transjordan as null because King Abdullah refused to settle with the Jews? 'To sell Abdullah down the river for the sake of spurious peace, easy consciences, and the "greater good" would ... be', in Sargent's acute foreboding of history repeating itself, 'a re-enaction of the Czech tragedy'.[93]

That the British perceived their own power and prestige to be in jeopardy increased the dramatic tension. Hitler's quest for a *Mitteleuropa* now found a Jewish parallel in the Middle East. 'The Negev', Douglas telegraphed in summary of the British view, '. . . is like a dagger blade dividing [the] Arab world.' Lovett and other American officials regarded those interpretations as almost ludicrously exaggerated. 'We have no thought', the State Department replied in dismissing the historical analogy to which the British attached such great importance, of '. . . putting pressure on Transjordan as a victim of a Near-Eastern Munich'.[94] Lovett and his colleagues now simply worked with a premiss different from the British. The State Department, following the President's lead, presumed that the Jews would be responsive to a 'just' settlement that could, as if with a sense of relief, be left up to the conciliation commission. Some American officials personally dissented. Douglas, for one, believed that the American government had followed the easy path of appeasement. He summed up the critical question in early December by asking whether there was a point beyond which the United States would *not* back the Israelis—'a southern frontier somewhere in [the] Negev beyond which [the] US will not support Israeli claims'.[95]

[93] Douglas to Marshall, Top Secret, 17 Nov. 1948, USSD 501.BB Palestine/11–1748 Box 2189; *Foreign Relations 1948*, V, pp. 1602–3.

[94] Lovett to Douglas, Top Secret, 22 Nov. 1948, USSD 501.BB Palestine/11–2248 Box 2189; *Foreign Relations 1948*, V, pp. 1621–3.

[95] Douglas to Lovett, Top Secret, 2 Dec. 1948, USSD 501.BB Palestine/12–248; *Foreign Relations 1948*, V, pp. 1642–3. Lewis Jones, the Middle East expert in the American Embassy in London, also disagreed profoundly with the decision to allow the Israelis to set their own terms. Jones was sensitive to the Arab as well as the British side of the question because of his day-by-day contact with the officials of the Eastern Department of the Foreign Office. 'At present I am living the role of "whipping-boy" ', he wrote in a personal letter in early December. 'My friends in the Foreign Office must have someone with whom they can "speak frankly," and I hear a great many things which I would blush to report.' Jones to Satterthwaite, 8 Dec. 1948, USSD 867N.01/12–848; *Foreign Relations 1948*, V, pp. 1650–1.

The End of the War

The breaking point in American tolerance, according to the Israeli archives, nearly occurred in early January 1949. Eliahu Epstein reported that 'public and official Washington opinion [is] dangerously tense, almost hostile'.[96] Israeli military strikes across the Egyptian frontier finally provoked the answer to the question of where the line ultimately would be drawn. On the 30th of December 1948 the American representative in Tel Aviv, at the request of President Truman, had informed Ben-Gurion and Weizmann that there might be 'a substantial review' of the American attitude unless the Israelis fulfilled expectations of being 'a peace-loving state'.[97] According to James McDonald, when Moshe Shertok received this admonition 'his fingers tightened around his pen and his face was white with tension'.[98] Ben-Gurion was surprised and anguished. He said that he was not accustomed to receive communications from the American government that might just as well have been written by Ernest Bevin. Weizmann was distressed. He proceeded to write another letter to Truman, this one explaining the defensive nature of the war against the Egyptians.[99] The message that had stirred such emotions was more in the nature of a cautionary rebuke than an ultimatum; but it produced instantaneous and dramatic results. By the 2nd of January the Israelis affirmed that 'not an Israeli hoof remained in Egypt'.[1] The Jews were greatly relieved to learn that the severity of the American response to the crisis had been directed at the British rather than against them. The British appeared to be close to intervention. Nevertheless the answer to the question—where would the frontier finally be drawn—at last had come.

The defeat of the Egyptian army took place between the 22nd of December 1948 and the 8th of January 1949. The eastern flank, cut off by the October offensive and then encircled at Al Auja, capitulated to Israeli forces after a battle of more than twenty-four hours on the 27th of December. Al Auja, near the western border of the Negev, controlled the road from Jerusalem through Sinai to Cairo. The other part of the Egyptian army occupied the Gaza strip. The purpose of the Israeli strikes across the frontier had been to neutralize the garrison at El Arish, which could have led to the paralysis of the entire Egyptian army in Sinai as well as the Negev.

[96] Elath (Epstein) to Shertok, 6 Jan. 1949, ISA 130.09/2308/8.
[97] Lovett to McDonald, Top Secret, 30 Dec. 1948, USSD 501.BB Palestine/12-3048 Box 2190; *Foreign Relations 1948*, V, p. 1704.
[98] McDonald, *My Mission in Israel*, pp. 117-18.
[99] Weizmann to Truman, 2 Jan. 1949, *Weizmann Letters*, XXIII, pp. 242-5.
[1] *Foreign Relations 1949*, VI, p. 602 n. 4.

In response however the British threatened to invoke the Anglo-Egyptian treaty of 1936. This was the ultimatum that the Americans had in mind when they demanded the withdrawal of Israeli troops from Egyptian territory. The British and the Israelis were close to war. In early January the tension heightened when the Israelis shot down four Royal Air Force aircraft on a reconnaissance flight. Nevertheless the end of the conflict was in sight. The Israelis had surrounded the frontier post at Rafah, thus cutting off the Egyptian forces in Gaza. At this stage, on the 7th of January, the Egyptians announced their willingness to enter into armistice negotitions. The war came to an end.

The RAF incident on the 4th of January 1949 had come as a revelation to the British public. The shape of events and circumstances, previously vague and confused, suddenly became clear. A Jewish state now existed, and it was successfully defending its frontiers. The British government not only appeared to be on the verge of war with this new state but also had aligned itself with a dubious ally, Egypt. Why should the British wage war against the Jews in order to aid the Egyptians? That was a question which the Labour government would find difficult to explain. Bevin, who had been supervising the reconnaissance flights as a quasi-commander-in-chief, recoiled from the possible consequences of outright war.[2] The RAF incident and its aftermath signified military acquiescence in the frontiers established by the Zionist state. As long as the Israelis refrained from invading Egypt, the frontiers would have to be redrawn by diplomatic rather than military initiative.

The purpose of these concluding comments will not be to discuss the armistice and the quest for a lasting peace between the Arabs and the Jews, or the question of the refugees, or the political future of the Negev. These issues will be dealt with in the last section of the book. Here the point of central importance is the realignment of British policy in response to the military and political reality of the new Jewish state. The British at last reconciled themselves to political defeat. They cut their losses in the face of an unbreakable Israeli-American combination, though one that had begun to test American indulgence. 'It was important to know when one had to stop', Jon and David Kimche wrote later of the Israeli sense of timing.

Sir John Troutbeck played an important part in the drawing up of the balance sheet. His anti-Zionist views did not interfere with his political judgement. As head of the British Middle East Office in Cairo he took a broader view than many of his colleagues charged

---

[2] For Bevin's part in the RAF incident see minutes by J. G. S. Beith and Bernard Burrows, 3 Feb. 1949, FO 371/75402/E1967.

with more narrowly defined responsibilities. One of his own particular duties was strategic planning, which is another reason why his
ideas are of especial interest. Troutbeck believed that Israeli aims
were less expansionist than commonly assumed in British official
circles. He thought that the Jews were not dissimulating when they
disclaimed ambitions of territories of Egypt or Transjordan, at least
at that time. In a telegram of the 4th of January 1949 he also commented on the future of the Negev:

> I believe Shertok was speaking the truth when he denied any intention of
> seizing Egyptian territory. I doubt too if the Jews at the moment have any
> intention of threatening the integrity of Transjordan. That country is to fall
> into their lap later starting, no doubt, with Aqaba.
>
> What the Jews are after now is to clear the Egyptians out of Negeb and
> send Iraqi and Transjordanian armies home. . . . I dare say that for the sake of
> an early peace they would be ready to leave a portion of Palestinian territory
> nominally in Transjordanian hands for the time being.[3]

Troutbeck realistically regarded the United Nations and the Arab
armies as 'broken reeds'. What then could the British do? In his
judgement they could do little except defend the territorial integrity
of Egypt and Transjordan, which he did not believe the Israelis
would challenge. 'The key to the situation seems to lie with the
United States Government', he wrote. He did not hold out much
hope, but he believed that the Americans might now be persuaded to
force the Israelis 'to observe international decencies'.[4] He also had in
mind the retention in Arab hands of a strategic corridor in the
southern Negev that would connect Egypt with Transjordan.

The British, like the Jews, knew that the only way to alter American Palestine policy would be by influencing the President himself.
The British Ambassador in Washington, Sir Oliver Franks, armed
with lengthy instructions from Attlee and Bevin, secured an interview with Truman on the 13th of January. Though the conversation
was friendly, Franks was rebuffed on every point. He made no headway whatever. Truman was in a buoyant mood. He stated that he
now felt a 'real optimism' about the Jews and Arabs, and that he did
not think the British had any reason 'to feel alarm and anxiety'.
Franks explained that it was important for strategic reasons to
maintain an uninterrupted and compact piece of Arab territory in
the southern Negev. He broached the question of the overland route
from Egypt to Transjordan and Iraq. Truman—with words that
would have disconcerted the Israelis—said that 'he was not prepared
to make a point of the Negeb. It was a small area and not worth

---

[3] Troutbeck to Bevin, Top Secret, 4 Jan. 1949, FO 371/75334/E156/G.
[4] Ibid.

differing over.'[5] Nevertheless he made it clear that he had no intention of yielding to the British on a matter they considered to be of grave strategic significance. Nor did Franks find any consolation in his talks with Lovett and the officials of the State Department: 'They did not agree, in fact, that the placing of the roads within Arab territory is essential to our common strategic interest in the Middle East.' Indeed they gave the impression that the British demand was too 'emotional in tone', as if the creation of the Jewish state had somehow upset the rational basis of British policy.[6] In short the British were turned down flat in their last effort to bring about a change in American policy which they believed would be to the strategic advantage of both countries. 'The American attitude on Palestine', Franks wrote in a personal letter to Bevin, 'seems to me to have hardened noticeably and no amount of argument made a real impression.'[7] Bevin himself responded to this humiliating snub. As if finally resigned to Truman's pigheaded and calamitous sellout, he wrote bitterly that the American attitude appeared to be not only to 'let there be an Israel and to hell with the consequences' but also 'peace at any price, and Jewish expansion whatever the consequences'.[8]

Within the Foreign Office it was Hector McNeil who took it upon himself to advise the Foreign Secretary on the 'most unpleasant job of cutting our losses'. As Minister of State, McNeil had served as the liaison with Israeli representatives in London. Though he could hardly be described as a Zionist, he was probably as well disposed as anyone in the Foreign Office to the Jewish cause. He thought it advisable after the Egyptian defeat to face up to certain unpalatable facts. These included the subordinate and humiliating part the British now played to the Americans in world affairs. 'This is not a happy situation for us', he wrote to Bevin. 'Indeed it is so unhappy, that whenever some new offence or indignity is given to us, or some further disadvantage is imposed upon the Arabs, we are tempted to act unilaterally.' By pretending still to be the masters of the Middle East, the British tended to lose sight of the overriding importance of retaining American goodwill. 'For we admitted to ourselves that we no longer had the means nor the military resources to command this whole area by ourselves.' American collaboration had to remain the paramount consideration. 'It is essential even when the Jews are

[5] Franks to Bevin, Top Secret, 13 Jan. 1949, FO 371/75534/E615/G.

[6] Lovett to Douglas, Top Secret, 13 Jan. 1949, USSD 501.BB Palestine/1–1349 Box 2190; *Foreign Relations 1949*, VI, pp. 658–61; Franks to Bevin, Top Secret, 13 Jan. 1949, FO 371/75334/E613.

[7] Franks to Bevin, 13 Jan. 1949, FO 371/75337/E1932.

[8] Bevin to Franks (draft), 3 Feb. 1949, FO 371/75337.

most wicked and the Americans most exasperating not to lose sight
of this point.' It was no consolation to reflect that, each time the
British had attempted to work in concert with the Americans, the
President had intervened—in a phrase McNeil had used earlier, as
a 'double-crosser'.

Each time the Americans have shifted. One way of explaining this is to point
to the undoubted weakness of their President. Another way of explaining it is
that each time the Jews have been permitted too much time so that they have
been enabled to put the screw on Truman.[9]

Whatever the explanation, it always led McNeil to the same conclusion which he now pressed on Bevin: 'As long as America is a
major power, and as long as she is free of major war, anyone taking
on the Jews will indirectly be taking on America.' Since the Americans would not co-operate, the only alternative would be for the
British themselves to fight in the Negev. McNeil ruled out this possibility for a simple and compelling reason: 'Our public would not
stand for it.'[10] British policy had thus led to a dead end. There was
nothing left but to accommodate the Jews on their own terms.

Sir Orme Sargent, like McNeil, drew attention to the President's
responsibility for the outcome of the Palestine struggle. He referred
to Truman as 'a weak, obstinate and suspicious man'. Nevertheless
Sargent believed that the situation was not quite as bad as McNeil
had depicted. Sargent took heart in Truman's response to 'the
Jewish invasion of Egypt'. It indicated that the Americans at least
had some sense of conscience in restraining the Israelis. Sargent
also believed that the Jews in any case would stop at the international frontiers. With that in mind he made two forecasts which
are extremely interesting in view of what actually transpired. He
wrote to Bevin in mid-January 1949 about the cutting of losses
in a territorial sense:

The worst that we need consider is that the Jews should seize the whole of
Palestine up to the Jordan including Jerusalem, for I agree with the Minister
of State [McNeil] that the Jews are not going to invade Egypt or Transjordan
in order to annex any territory belonging to these countries.

His more favourable estimate left Jerusalem divided and King
Abdullah in control of part of Arab Palestine:

I am afraid things have gone too far for us to hope to secure what we want
for Transjordan in the Negeb. The best is likely to be a settlement whereby
the Jews get all Galilee, Jaffa, the Negeb (except Gaza and the Egyptian
frontier strip), a corridor to Jerusalem, the division of Jerusalem between

---

[9] Minute by McNeil, 14 Jan. 1949, FO 371/75337/E1881.
[10] Ibid.

Jews and Transjordan and in return Transjordan absorbs the rest of central Palestine.[11]

The latter calculation proved to be the more accurate, though Sir John Troutbeck was perhaps the most astute of all in foreseeing that the Israelis had merely postponed the conquest of 'central Palestine' and the rest of Jerusalem for a later day.

In the famous Parliamentary debate of the 26th of January 1949, Bevin came close to frankly admitting defeat, at least in the sense of failure to achieve any of the basic British aims. The goal in Palestine, he said, 'was to persuade Jews and Arabs to live together in one State as the Mandate charged us to do. We failed in this. The State of Israel is now a fact. . . . '[12] Bevin thus acknowledged the existence of the state of Israel, though according to Leo Amery he did so in a mood of 'sulky acquiescence'.[13] The debate was long and acrimonious. Bevin in his further remarks dwelt on the 'profound injustice to the Arabs' and made it clear that he believed that the historical record eventually would vindicate him in the effort to create a binational state. Churchill, in an excoriating reply, met that point by emphasizing the indecisiveness of the Labour government. 'After the war', he said, there could have been 'a partition scheme which would have been more favourable to the Arabs'.[14] And so the two fundamentally different solutions continued to be debated. By this stage everyone could emphatically agree with Churchill that the British 'Imperial' venture in Palestine had led to 'vast waste of money, to the repeated loss of British lives, [and] to humiliation of every kind'.[15]

In the course of the Parliamentary debate, Bevin made a comment with which it is appropriate to draw this chapter to a close because it touched on a matter of profound difference in the British and the American outlook. 'The tragic problem of Palestine', Bevin said, 'is to find some solution for these conflicting points of view without the Middle East sinking into chaos in the process.'[16] The British in 1948-9 believed that Israel might become a Communist state, if not a Russian satellite, and that the Middle East was on the verge of revolution. Sir Orme Sargent pessimistically forecast that the British would have to continue to give support to the Arabs because, for better or worse, they were Britain's only hope in the Middle East. He thought that point to be so important that he underscored it:

[11] Minute by Sargent, 17 Jan. 1949, FO 371/76336/E1273.
[12] *Parliamentary Debates* (Commons), 26 Jan. 1949, col. 931.
[13] *Selections from the Smuts Papers*, VII, p. 280.
[14] *Parliamentary Debates* (Commons), 26 Jan. 1949, col. 954.
[15] Ibid., col. 950.
[16] Ibid., col. 934.

We must in spite of all their shortcomings do what we can to maintain the present friendly regimes in the Arab States since with their disappearance we should be almost inevitably faced with petty dictatorships which would be violently anti-British and be forced to re-insure themselves with Russia.[17]

Bevin himself was explicit about the danger of a Communist Israel. According to an American report of one of the meetings in which the atmosphere was 'charged with anxiety':

'Within five years' Israel may be [a] Communist state. Bevin infers this from fact that new Jewish immigrants come largely from countries behind Iron Curtain where they have been exposed to Communist philosophy. There was no great exodus to Israel from the US and UK where democratic philosophy could have been absorbed.[18]

In retrospect that view clearly was misguided, but it was an apprehension quite consistent with British anxieties of the time. 'All the reinforcements to the Jews came from satellite countries', A. V. Alexander interjected during one of the discussions.[19] 'Another China', was the phrase Bevin used on several occasions to sum up his direst premonition about the Middle East.

The American reaction to the end of the Arab-Israeli war of 1948 was fundamentally different from the British not only in less pessimistic tone but also in more optimistic assessment of the long-range significance of a strong and stable Israeli state. The Americans made no secret about believing that the British had put their money on the wrong horse. Even if there were some truth in the view about the danger of Communism in Israel, it seemed to American officials to be much more important to try to win the Israelis on to the western side than to begin to take strategic precautions against them. The disagreement on this point became conspicuous in the discussions about the British scheme to secure the route through the Negev, which the Americans regarded as the height of strategic folly. According to Robert Lovett: 'If Israel were ill-disposed towards us these roads would have little value. . . . the major problem . . . was not on which side of the frontier the land route from Egypt to Transjordan and beyond lay, but rather to ensure as far as possible that Israel was a democratic State and to orientate it westwards.'[20] The main goal, which the Americans now put forward consistently and forcefully, should not be 'containing the Israelis' but 'to win

[17] Minute by Sargent, 17 Jan. 1949, FO 371/75336/E1273.
[18] Holmes to Lovett, Top Secret, 22 Dec. 1948, USSD 501.BB Palestine/12-2248 Box 2190; *Foreign Relations 1948*, V, pp. 1680-5.
[19] F. O. Record of a meeting of 20 Dec. 1948, FO 371/68512/E16134.
[20] As reported in Franks to Bevin, Top Secret, 13 Jan. 1949, FO 371/75334/E613.

the Israelis over into the Anglo-American camp and not to alienate them permanently'.[21]

After the Israeli victories over the Egyptian army, the American attitude became increasingly pro-Israeli. Even the Secretary of Defense now became 'most cordial', Eliahu Epstein wrote of Forrestal's change in outlook after the Americans had become convinced that the Israelis would not attempt to annex Egyptian territory.[22] It was encouraging to believe that the new Jewish state might emerge not only as a stabilizing and democratic force in the Middle East but also as an American ally. The following statement made by Robert Lovett to Sir Oliver Franks in mid-January 1949 appropriately summed up the American hope for the future. It also marked with ebullient words the close of one era and the beginning of another: 'It was clear, as indeed had been proved by recent events, that the State of Israel would be the most dynamic, efficient and vigorous Government in the Near East in the future.'[23]

---

[21] Franks to Bevin, Top Secret, 13 Jan. 1949, FO 371/75334/E614.
[22] Elath (Epstein) to Shertok, 24 Jan. 1949, ISA 93.01/2180/32.
[23] As reported in Franks to Bevin, Top Secret, 13 Jan. 1949, FO 371/75334/E614.

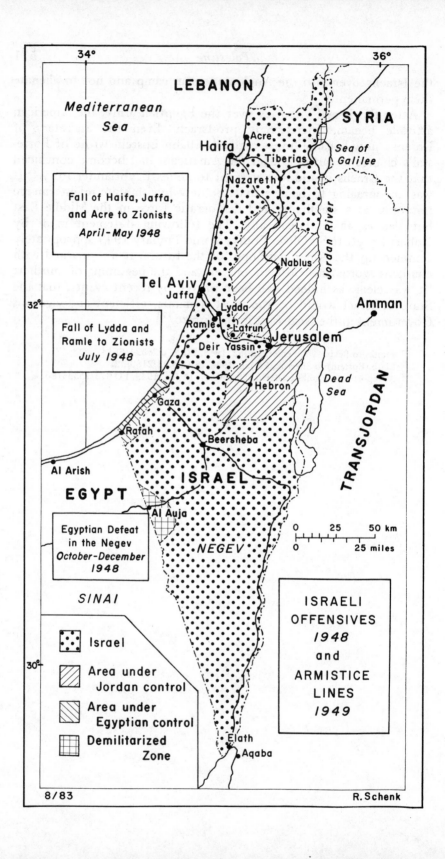

ISRAELI OFFENSIVES 1948 and ARMISTICE LINES 1949

PART V

THE MIDDLE EAST 1949–1951

PRELUDE: FROM DEIR YASSIN IN 1948
TO EGYPTIAN ABROGATION IN 1951

THE Deir Yassin massacre is a touchstone of historical controversy in the Middle East. In one way or another it must figure prominently in any discussion about British aims after 1948. To some British officials, though not to all by any means, the atrocity came as a revelation, though perhaps a belated one, about the nature of the new Jewish state. On the 9th of April 1948 Jewish irregular forces under the command of the Irgun killed 240 men, women, and children in Deir Yassin, an Arab village on the road to the western entrance to Jerusalem. The massacre helped to trigger the mass exodus of Arab refugees who by early 1949 numbered 726,000, or about seventy per cent of the population of Arab Palestine. To what extent were the Zionists responsible for the fear, panic, and confusion? What did the British make of that question at the time?

The High Commissioner in Palestine, General Sir Alan Cunningham, wrote three days after the massacre of 'that brutal Jewish attack on Deir Yassin where 250 Arab civilians were butchered, half being women and children'. He went on to explain to the Colonial Secretary, Arthur Creech Jones, the reasons why the British had not intervened:

> This village is still in the hands of the Jews as I write. I wanted the soldiers to attack it, if necessary with all the power they can produce and turn out the Jews. But I am told that they [the British Army] are not in a position to do so, or indeed do anything which may provoke a general conflict with either side as their troops are already fully committed. This is only one example out of many where the Civil Government has to stand idle while its authority is flouted in all directions.[1]

From the point of view of the High Commissioner, the tragedy of the massacre was matched by the calamity of British impotence during the last weeks of the mandate.

Those who seek the causes of the massacre, or for that matter answers to questions of responsibility for the precipitate flight of the refugees, will not discover conclusive evidence in the British

---

[1] Cunningham to Creech Jones, 'Private and Personal', 12 Apr. 1948, Cunningham Papers.

archives. Further detailed research will probably substantiate rather than alter the consensus based on the conclusions independently reached by Walid Khalidi and Erskine B. Childers in 1959–61.[2] In brief, Deir Yassin was not part of a systematic plan by the Haganah or the Jewish Agency to drive the Arabs out of Palestine. On the other hand the refugees did not, as Jewish officials claimed at the time, evacuate under orders from Arab leaders. In the words of one of the more balanced participants in this historic controversy, David Cairns (a writer sympathetic to the Zionists), 'what happened in 1947–48 . . . had no coherent pattern, but was a tangle of endless variation depending on the conflicting responses of Arab leaders and of local Haganah commanders, some of whom encouraged an exodus and waged psychological warfare to this end, others of whom opposed it. . . . Events were moving too fast for policy.'[3] And also too fast for reflective analysis on the British side until long afterwards. The realm of present controversy lies in the revelation of Deir Yassin as it was later perceived. The archives reveal two sets of attitudes that developed towards this issue, and the refugee question generally, which in turn are directly connected with Britain's quest for peace—some would say a faint-hearted quest—in 1949.

One pattern of response can be found in the elemental attitude of Sir John Troutbeck. It will be recalled that before the war Troutbeck had served in Czechoslovakia. He now believed that he was witnessing the spectacle of history repeating itself. He wrote in May 1948, four days after the end of the mandate and about five weeks after Deir Yassin: 'It is difficult to see that Zionist policy is anything else than unashamed aggression carried out by methods of deceit and brutality not unworthy of Hitler.' Troutbeck was examining the question 'Where does justice lie?' On the basis of his experience as head of the British Middle East Office in Cairo, he believed that he knew the faults of the Arabs as well as anyone. Indeed the key to his thought, as he sorted out his confused ideas about the Germans and the Czechs as well as the Arabs and the Jews, is that he was not so much an advocate for the Arabs as rather a quintessential Englishman with an outraged sense of justice:

---

[2] For this consensus see Howard M. Sachar, *Europe Leaves the Middle East, 1936–1954* (New York, 1972), pp. 548–54. For the original controversy, see Walid Khalidi, 'Why Did the Palestinians Leave?', *Middle East Forum*, XXXV, 7 (July 1959); and 'The Fall of Haifa', ibid., XXXV, 10 (Dec. 1959); Erskine B. Childers, 'The Other Exodus', *Spectator*, 12 May 1961, and correspondence in subsequent issues. See also Lucas Grollenberg, *Palestine Comes First* (London, 1980). For the refugees see Avi Plascov, *The Palestinian Refugees in Jordan 1948–1957* (London, 1981).

[3] David Cairns in the *Spectator*, 30 June 1961.

The Arabs may be silly, feckless people and one may resent their calm assumption that they alone have the right to determine the disposal of Palestine to whose liberation from the Turks they contributed very little. . . .

We should all support the Czechs if the Germans tried to put back a German population into the Sudetenland and make of it a German state, though that area is historically as German as Palestine is Jewish and the Czechs played as small a part in recovering it as the Arabs did in liberating Palestine. All in all there seems to be more justice in the Arab than in the Jewish cause.

Was it true, Troutbeck asked in making up his mind about a further point, that the Jews would make the desert 'flower like the rose', and that, by bringing with them capital, energy, technical knowledge, and 'modern ideas', the Jews would benefit the Arabs? 'That seems very speculative', he wrote in answer to his own question.

What is far more certain is that it would bring bitterness and unrest and, wherever the Jew was in control of an Arab population, the worst form of oppression. Deir Yassein is a warning of what a Jew will do to gain his purpose.[4]

In the mind of at least one ranking British official, Deir Yassin had thus become a symbol of ruthless Zionist determination to stop at nothing in order to achieve a Jewish state.

The other prevailing attitude towards Deir Yassin and the flight of the refugees can be identified in the robust response of Sir Hugh Dow. From his vantage point as Consul-General in Jerusalem, Dow tended to see the clash between the Arabs and the Jews from a pro-Arab perspective that resembled the ones of Sir Alec Kirkbride and Glubb Pasha in Amman (just as Troutbeck's pro-Egyptian outlook was virtually identical with the one coincidentally held by the Ambassador in Egypt, Sir Ronald Campbell).[5] Dow's reaction to the Arab-Jewish conflict was also influenced by his previous experience in India. He had been Governor of Sind. With the partition of India and Pakistan and the massacres of Hindus and Muslims fresh in mind, Deir Yassin and indeed the actual war between the Jews and the Arabs seemed to him to be of comparatively minor significance. He wrote to the end of hostilities in early 1949:

I am less pessimistic than Sir John Troutbeck. . . . Already in India, and in spite of the open war in Kashmir, the bitterness between Hindu and Muslim is much less than it was two years ago, and both in India and in Pakistan they are finding it possible to live side by side in peace and quietness. It is doubtful whether the division between Jew and Arab goes as deep as that between Hindu

[4] Troutbeck to Wright, Personal and Secret, 18 May 1948, FO 371/68386/E8738.
[5] See Campbell to Wright, 21 Mar. 1949, FO 371/75064 on the point that Campbell and Troutbeck held independent yet identical views.

and Muslim: there is far less blood spilt between them, and they are not so antithetic in religion.[6]

Though no less anti-Zionist than Troutbeck, Dow in short believed that in time Jew and Arab could live peacefully together, and, in any case, that the British should work towards a durable settlement between Israel and the neighbouring Arab states. Here then were the two contrasting views. Dow held that a lasting peace was possible. Troutbeck was more sceptical because of the way he perceived the nature of the Jewish state. Unlimited immigration would make it increasingly expansionist and therefore less inclined to exist within the artificial and 'unjust' frontiers that Troutbeck, and virtually all other British officials, believed that Israel had acquired as a result of the 1948 war.

It is essential to bear in mind the division of official opinion in order to understand the mood as well as the substance of the discussions that took place in the summer of 1949. In July Ernest Bevin summoned to London his representatives in the Middle East. The agenda of this conference included broad topics of economic development that might now commence after the cessation of hostilities. The conference itself will be discussed in the next chapter. Here the theme is the possibility of a lasting peace in the aftermath of the war. Bevin himself, though irrepressibly optimistic as usual, was still quite sore at the way he believed he had been maligned by the Zionists and abandoned by the Americans. Never again, he told the representatives at the conference, would Britain be involved politically, or deploy troops, 'in an area in which international Jewry disposed of such influence'. Far from accepting the armistice lines as the basis of permanent political frontiers, Bevin continued to speak of the Negev as 'a No Man's Land' with free communication between Egypt and Jordan, and between Israel and the Red Sea, and of Haifa as a 'free port' (or at least one under 'a joint Israeli–Arab Port Management Board'). He had in mind the partition of Jerusalem with the city itself 'under some form of loose international control'. He expected Israel to accept the return of some 200,000 to 300,000 refugees. He adhered to his basic idea of a political settlement: 'the Arab part of Palestine should be annexed to the Kingdom of Jordan'. Having outlined terms that the Israelis would not by any means have been disposed to accept collectively, Bevin left it to his Middle East hands to discuss specific proposals that might provide the basis for a durable peace. He emphasized one overriding political and military consideration: 'The settlement of the Palestine problem would clear

[6] Dow to Bevin, 8 Feb. 1949, FO 371/75054/E2478.

the way for our military plans for the Middle East, particularly Egypt.'[7]

With Egypt as the priority, a peace settlement in Palestine would have to take Egyptian opinion into account as a basic element. Bevin himself thus from the outset came down on the side of Troutbeck. There were powerful countervailing influences against the 'Jordan–Israel first' attitude urged by Dow and others, notably Sir Knox Helm, the new British Minister in Tel Aviv, and Kirkbride, who of course was at pains to explain King Abdullah's predicament. The transcript makes it clear that British policy acted as a brake on Jordan.[8] 'King Abdullah was personally anxious to come to agreement with Israel', Kirkbride stated, 'and in fact it was our restraining influence which had so far prevented him from doing so.' Knox Helm confirmed that the Israelis hoped to have a settlement with Jordan, and that they now genuinely wished to live peacefully within their frontiers, if only for economic reasons. He did not believe the economy of Israel would support an expansionist policy. At one stage in the discussions, 'Sir K. Helm repeated that he did not believe that Israel had aggressive intentions and . . . added however that the delay in the incorporation of Arab Palestine in the Jordan [state] was an invitation to Israel to expand'.[9] Sir Hugh Dow agreed with that interpretation. This was a complicated discussion, and it extended over several days as it touched on collateral points, but in essence it may be summed up by stating that Sir Ronald Campbell and Troutbeck disagreed fundamentally with Kirkbride, Dow, and Knox Helm.

Troutbeck maintained that British acquiescence in a permanent settlement between Israel and Jordan would be regarded by the Egyptians as appeasement of militant Zionism. The Egyptians continued to regard King Abdullah as no more than a British puppet. If the Egyptians were to conclude that the British had caved in to the Jews, a possible agreement about the Canal Zone would become even more remote—and there could be no doubt that, in terms of Britain's Imperial interests, an accommodation with the Egyptians over Suez was incomparably more important than a *modus vivendi* between Israel and Jordan. Any general settlement with Israel would have to satisfy minimal Egyptian aspirations. The transcript of the 1949 conference contains the following statement. It sums up the problem as viewed from the British position in Egypt.

Sir John Troutbeck said that in their hearts certain Arab governments [specifically Jordan] wished to conclude peace with Israel but all were afraid of

---

[7] Minutes of the Middle East Conference, 21 July 1949, FO 371/75012.
[8] On 2 June 1949 Transjordan was renamed 'The Hashemite Kingdom of Jordan'.
[9] Minutes of the Middle East Conference, 21 July 1949, FO 371/75012.

breaking the Arab front (aimed at the destruction of Israel), and that there was a danger of our incurring general Arab resentment if we encouraged any one State to act independently.[10]

The phrase 'general Arab resentment' touched on the heart of the matter. The British at any cost had to avoid Arab antagonism that would not only jeopardize their position in Suez but also their access to the oil reserves of the Middle East. Knox Helm, Dow, and Kirkbride (and everyone else as well) found Troutbeck's proposition (which was the same as Bevin's) to be unanswerable. They acquiesced in the argument that terms of peace between Israel and Jordan would have to command general Arab concurrence. Their general rejoinder to Troutbeck was that Britain should work gradually towards an improvement of relations between Israel and the Arab world. From that noble sentiment no one could dissent.

In August 1949 Bevin circulated a memorandum to the Cabinet that summed up the deliberations of the conference. The paragraphs about peace in the Middle East require quotation at length, not only because they represent British policy as shaped after highly secret and agonized discussions, but also because they reveal the conflicting and complex pressures on the British. These tensions were reconciled by the collective official mind with a deftness and sense of confidence worthy of British Imperialism in an earlier era. The line of thought would have been acceptable, for example, to statesmen of the First World War period such as Curzon or Milner. What emerges is a remarkable statement on the continuity of British policy in the Middle East:

> The developments in Palestine since the end of the Mandate, resulting in the emergence of the State of Israel, have been one of the most disturbing elements in Middle East policy. It is largely owing to them that the present review of our Middle East policy is being held. We must never under-rate the political and psychological preoccupation of all Arab Governments and peoples with the Palestine question. They will, for instance, refuse to respond to our guidance on social and economic matters if they find us differing too widely from them over Palestine.
>
> His Majesty's Government accept Israel as an established fact and intend to grant her *de jure* recognition at the earliest suitable moment. They regard it as

---

[10] Minutes of the Middle East Conference, 21 July 1949, FO 371/75012. This and other passages have been quoted in *The Times*, 24 Jan. 1983, in an article based on the research of Mr. Dore Gold, in order to support the argument that Britain 'blocked' a peace settlement in 1949. Within the context of the contemporary discussion, as will be seen, this is a misleading view. For comment on this issue in regard to Bevin's policy, see Bullock, *Bevin*, chap. 18 sect. 6. This part of the biography deals with Bevin and the reconciliation between Britain and Israel. By October 1949 the Israeli Ambassador could conclude that Bevin was not after all 'a sworn enemy'. This interpretation is consistent with the sentiment of the conference that relations between Britain and Israel, and between Israel and the Arab states, should be gradually improved.

a matter of high importance that she should be orientated towards the West and play her part in the defence of the Middle East against Communist penetration and Soviet aggression. For this purpose they will use their best endeavours to have friendly and mutually profitable relations with her.

At the same time they are bound to have regard to their existing friendships and alliances with the Arab States, particularly as the latter are at present more willing than Israel to commit themselves to the anti-Communist camp. It would be too high a price to pay for the friendship of Israel to jeopardise, by estranging the Arabs, either the base in Egypt or Middle Eastern oil.

Subject always to these interests being safeguarded, His Majesty's Government are anxious to promote not merely peace but friendly relations between Israel and the Arab States. They would see no objection to the development of normal trading relations between Israel and her Arab neighbours on a basis of complete independence.

But His Majesty's Government would not regard it as in their interest that Israel should acquire more Arab territory without a *quid pro quo* or that she should carry her economic exchanges with the Arab States to the point of dominating them economically and so politically, and thus perhaps imposing her own ideas of neutrality on the Arab world. They would not lend their assistance to the furtherance of any such ambitions and would indeed support the Arab States in resisting them.[11]

The British thus wished to see peace in the Middle East, but not a peace at any price. They would not pursue a policy of appeasement, or refuse to take into account what they believed to be Zionist expansionist policies that might result in the Arab states becoming economic and political satellites of Israel. The British would also stand vigilant against the dangers of Soviet penetration into the Middle East. Written in the aftermath of the Arab–Israeli war and at a critical stage of the cold war—the North Atlantic Treaty Organization had come into existence in April—this statement of British aims may have exaggerated the difficulties of a general peace settlement with Israel, but it nevertheless reaffirmed long-standing policy.

For the purpose of these prefatory remarks on the 1949–51 period, the principal point to be made about the 1949 policy is that it remained the same at least until the end of the Labour government. In 1951 there was a minor controversy among the Middle East hands of the Foreign Office that again reveals the continuity of British aims. In March of that year Sir Hugh Dow returned to the charge with proposals to ameliorate Israel–Jordan relations—even at the risk of antagonizing the other Arab countries. Dow was more on the fringe than in the centre of British policy-making in the Middle East, but, like a 'Colonel Blimp', he felt unrestrained in offering advice (it is useful to bear in mind that he had risen to the post of Governor in India). His views have the merit of putting issues into perspective

---

[11] Memorandum by Bevin, 'Middle East Policy', CP (49) 188, 25 Aug. 1949, CAB 129/36.

because they forced the officials of the Eastern Department to respond, thereby clarifying the actual British stand. Dow's comments in this case evoked remarks within the department as demonstrating 'strong anti-Israel and anti-Egyptian feelings' (to which might be added anti-American sentiment). Dow argued that the Israel–Jordan connection should be viewed as the key to a lasting peace in the Middle East. It was the same position he had held in 1949:

> Neither Israel nor the Arabs are going to be much use to us while they remain at daggers drawn with each other. It ought to be a cardinal point of our policy to heal the breach between them, and it is submitted that the best hope of doing this quickly is to concentrate on Israel and Jordan even if this means for a time some deterioration in our relations with other Arab states.[12]

Dow furthermore emphasized that Jordan was the only Arab country 'with real friendliness' towards the British, and 'the only one likely to be of any military value'. Unfortunately for the British, there was considerable truth in that view. A good political and military relationship with Jordan, however, was only part of the overall goal.

Dow received a friendly rebuke from Geoffrey Furlonge, the head of the Eastern Department. 'Dear Dow', he wrote in a personal and secret letter: 'I am afraid that we do not . . . share all of your conclusions.' The Eastern Department did not believe that the 'pace' could be forced in bringing about an accommodation between King Abdullah and the Israelis even though both parties desired a settlement:

> However much King Abdullah may want an accommodation, he does not seem to control his Government and subjects as he did in the past, and we imagine that he cannot afford to disregard the hostility which a premature settlement with Israel would arouse both among his own people and in the other Arab States.
>
> Similarly the Israel Government, however anxious for a settlement with Jordan, could hardly buy one at the price of concessions which Israel public opinion would regard as a surrender.

The two sides in other words were locked into positions for internal reasons. Any attempt by the British to press them into a general settlement would stir up the Iraqis and the Egyptians. Furlonge clarified the central issue:

> The strategic importance of the Canal Zone cannot be over-estimated, and our whole purpose in the current Anglo–Egyptian negotiations is to ensure that we retain that base on reasonable terms. We are seeking Egyptian goodwill, not for its own sake, but in order to secure facilities without which our strategy would be hamstrung.[13]

[12] Dow to Bevin, 3 Mar. 1951, FO 371/91184.
[13] Furlonge to Dow, 2 Apr. 1951, FO 371/91184/E1024.

The overriding concern of the British thus remained the Canal Zone. Furlonge stated the conclusions unequivocally, and they sum up the thrust of British policy in 1949–51: 'we feel unable either to force the pace in trying to reach an Israel–Jordan settlement, or to put all our eggs in the Jordan basket. So long as the Middle East as a whole is threatened with Russian aggression we cannot afford to disregard the susceptibilities of any of the component countries.'[14]

The Tripartite Declaration of May 1950

Assuming that Egypt as well as Jordan might eventually be reconciled with Israel, what type of general peace settlement were the British seeking in the Middle East? In both a political and a military sense the answer to that question could be summed up in the phrase 'regional security system' in which Israel as well as Jordan, and Turkey as well as Egypt, would be integrated. In May 1950 the Chiefs of Staff defined this 'Ultimate Aim' in these words: 'The ideal military arrangement in the Middle East would be a regional pact consisting of the United Kingdom, the Arab League States, Israel, Turkey, Persia and possibly Greece, in which Egypt, as a willing partner, would provide the base facilities required.'[15] Though the antecedents can be traced earlier, this was a significant beginning of the proposal for a 'Middle East Command'. As will be seen in the discussion about Iraq in the next section, and in the chapter about Egypt, the plans for a Middle East Command came to nothing. The only tangible achievement of a general nature in the 1949–51 period was the Tripartite Declaration of May 1950, the same month that the Chiefs of Staff defined their 'Ultimate Aim'. The tripartite declaration was negative in character, but a study of its origins and purpose throws light on the British aim to accommodate Israel as well as to stabilize the Arab countries in a pro-western alignment.

Although the 'Ultimate Aim' was a regional security system, the immediate aim was no more than the prevention of another round of the Palestine war. On that point both the British and the Americans could emphatically agree. The arms embargo had been lifted by the Security Council of the UN on the 11th of August 1949. The other source of direct anxiety was the uncertain status of Arab Palestine. The essence of the tripartite declaration of May 1950 was an attempt to regulate the flow of arms and to stabilize the territorial delimitation between Israel and Jordan.

If the Israelis and Arabs could not obtain arms from the West then

---

[14] Ibid.
[15] See Defence Committee, DO (50) 40, 19 May 1950, PREM 8/1359.

they would turn to the east. If the British armed the Arabs, and the Americans the Israelis, then the situation would revert to the implicit combination of the 1948 war. If however the British were to supply arms to Israel, then King Abdullah would regard it, in the contemporary phrase, as a 'stab in the back'. The Americans would face similar denunciation if it appeared that the military balance was shifting decisively in favour of the Arabs. Those possibilities were all unfortunately quite real. After long and exhausting discussions in the spring of 1950, the British and Americans finally made the best of bad choices by agreeing on the seemingly less dangerous formula of 'internal security'. Arms would be permitted in sufficient quantities to allow the Middle Eastern states to maintain internal security. The silent premiss of the formula was that the Arabs and Jews would be kept on the western side of the cold war. The point of importance that emerges from these intricate deliberations is the way in which Bevin kept his eye on Egypt as the central issue. 'I do not see how I can settle the question of arms', he wrote in early May, 'until I have an agreement regarding Egypt. The arms to them [the Egyptians] must be for Western purposes.' And he added that if there were to be a general formula he wished to bring in the French: 'If we do it, I prefer tripartite.'[16]

The significance of Bevin's cryptic minute becomes more clear if it is considered in the context of his remarks made at a Foreign Ministers meeting in May 1950 (at which time the British, Americans, and French were sorting out an array of problems in which the Middle East figured only occasionally). There was truth in the allegation, Bevin admitted candidly to Acheson and others, that in the past the British had treated the Egyptians 'rather shabbily' by providing them with 'junk' arms. The British and the Americans now required Egyptian co-operation in maintaining peace in the Middle East. But what could be expected of the Egyptians if they believed that their army was deliberately being kept inferior? It would be only a matter of time until the Egyptians would turn to the Russians. In Bevin's view it was imperative that the Egyptians be treated, eventually at least, as military equals. Egypt was the 'key point', he emphasized, in all of the Middle East.[17] If the Egyptians were convinced that

[16] Minute by Bevin, *c*.6 May 1950, FO 371/81910/E1023. For the tripartite declaration and the question of a 'Middle East Command' see J. C. Hurewitz, *Middle East Politics: The Military Dimension* (New York, 1969), chap. 5; and John C. Campbell, *Defense of the Middle East* (New York, 1958), chap. 2. For the tripartite declaration itself, see J. C. Hurewitz, *Diplomacy in the Near and Middle East: A Documentary Record* (Princeton, 1956), II, pp. 308-9.

[17] See Acheson to Acting Secretary of State, 11 May 1950, *Foreign Relations 1950*, V, pp. 158-60; and ibid., III, pp. 1027-31 for a record of the meeting of the same date.

Britain and the United States would wholeheartedly assist them in equipping their army, they would be more inclined to go along with western defence plans. Bevin had immense ability in turning difficult situations to advantage. By agreeing with the Americans that the supply of arms should be regulated on the principle of internal security, he also opened the way for the development of the Egyptian and other Middle Eastern military forces *for western purposes* (as he had written in his minute)—in other words, the eventual integration of Egypt into a 'Middle Eastern Command'.

If Bevin tended to emphasize the positive side of the problem, Acheson left no doubt about the nightmare of an arms race in which the British and the Americans—the stalwarts of NATO—might be aligned on opposite sides. What of the French? Until these issues were well on their way towards resolution between the British and the Americans, the French were not even brought into the discussions. The British among themselves were of divided opinion about the wisdom of including them, as if by the scruff of the neck. The French would certainly welcome the opportunity to participate in a great power declaration on the Middle East. It would be interpreted, in the Arab world at least, as an attempt to restore a concerted European dominance of the region. Precisely for that reason the officials of the Foreign Office were reluctant to go along with French participation until Bevin himself wrote in his minute, 'I prefer tripartite'. Here he agreed with Acheson's line of negative thought, in the latter's words, that the French 'were supplying arms to Syria and this loophole should be plugged'.[18]

In order to restrict the use of arms for purposes of 'internal stability', each of the Middle Eastern states pledged that arms shipments would not be used for 'aggressive' purposes. Collectively these declarations resembled the 'non-aggression pacts' of the 1930s, and it was recognized that their intrinsic value was worth about as much. These solemn declarations were necessary however because the violation of a 'non-aggression pact' would give the three powers the pretext to intervene. The corollary of 'arms for internal purposes' was thus elaborated as the 'opposition to the use of force'. The freezing of the status quo was the implicit purpose of the other part of the tripartite declaration.

No one wished to be associated with anything that implied a permanent settlement. But the upholding of the armistice lines seemed to be better than the risk of lapsing back into war. Thus the three powers declared that they would oppose any attempt to alter the armistice lines by force. The actual territorial issue being debated by the British

[18] Ibid.

and the Americans was the question of the West Bank. The longer the status of Arab Palestine remained indefinite, the greater would be the danger of an extremist independent Arab state led by the Mufti that would be hostile to Jews, British, and Americans alike. It would become, in the British view at least, a hotbed of Arab fanatical nationalism and irredentism. Both Britain and the United States therefore backed King Abdullah's annexation of the West Bank on the 24th of April 1950. Almost a month to the day later, on the 25th of May, the three powers issued the tripartite declaration. In that sense it served as a guarantee of Jordanian annexation.

'The US and the UK were basically after the same thing in this matter', observed one of the Middle East hands of the State Department, Raymond Hare, 'and it was purely a question of tactics.' Both the British and the Americans wished to prevent the deterioration of Arab Palestine, and, again in Hare's words, 'to let an explosive situation quiet down'.[19] Both the State Department and the Foreign Office viewed Jordan's annexation of the West Bank as a step towards stabilizing the region, and the Americans as well as the British saw one of the purposes of the tripartite declaration as a restraining influence on the Arab leaders who objected to the expansion of Abdullah's kingdom. When all is said the Americans were more inclined to accept the 1949 frontiers as a permanent demarcation than were the British. Nevertheless the talk about Jordan's 'corridor' through the Negev to the Mediterranean had long ago evaporated, not least because of American insistence that the Israelis simply could not be persuaded to relinquish any substantial piece of territory won in the 1948 war. The State Department now found itself tacitly if not openly supporting the territorial frontiers of Israel as they had been carved on the fields of battle, but it is equally important to emphasize that the American documents indicate a sensitivity to such issues as the sale of refugee property within territory under Israeli control. As for the upholding of the armistice lines rather than pushing on towards a general peace settlement, a statement made by Raymond Hare summed up the American view, which was remarkably similar to the British estimate: 'It is our belief that, motivated by his own personal interests, King Abdullah has gone as far as he could in attempting to reach an agreement with Israel.'[20]

The Foreign Office outlook generally continued to be anti-Zionist. In the context of the Anglo-American discussions about peace in the

---

[19] See memorandum of 24 Apr. 1950, *Foreign Relations 1950*, V, pp. 868–71. At this time Hare was Acting Assistant Secretary of State for Near Eastern, South Asian, and African Affairs.

[20] Memorandum by Hare, 8 Mar. 1950, ibid., V, pp. 787–8.

Middle East, the minutes of Bernard Burrows are particularly revealing. In January 1950 Burrows was transferred from his post as head
of the Eastern Department in London to a new assignment as the
Middle East expert at the Embassy in Washington. He had written
in the autumn of 1949 in a minute that reflected British bitterness
at the outcome of the war:

> We are still the major power in the Middle East which in its present state is
> a vacuum which will certainly be filled if we move out. Whatever our interests
> may be called, economic, political or strategic, they are all part of one interest,
> the survival of Western civilisation, to which Israel professes to belong.[21]

Burrows was sceptical whether Israel's need for 'neutrality'—in
view of the Jews in eastern Europe and the Soviet Union—would
permit Israeli leaders to work towards the type of regional security
pact that the British had in mind as the basis of peace in the Middle
East. Furthermore he believed that the Zionists basically misconceived
the Arab reaction to the territorial claims, and for that matter the
British ability to reconcile the Arabs to the new Jewish state:

> Israel's major need is peace with her Arab neighbours but she greatly under-
> estimates the difficulties in the way of securing it. It is a myth that the Arab
> peoples are not opposed to Zionism or that the idea of Arab unity is an artificial
> creation; Israel estimates of our own influence over Arab leaders are also largely
> mythical.[22]

It was the last point about British control of the Arabs that was
critical on the eve of the tripartite declaration. 'The influence of
the British Government upon King Abdullah', Burrows told his
American colleagues, 'was not unlimited and . . . the King seemed
definitely determined to go ahead with a formal proclamation of
union' with the West Bank. To prevent the 'disintegrating tendencies
of Arab Palestine', Burrows emphasized, 'the psychological stimulus
of formal incorporation [of the West Bank into Jordan] was
necessary'.[23] In that sense the tripartite declaration, by endorsing the
armistice lines, may be viewed as the best solution that could be
found at the time to the problem of the West Bank.

The tripartite declaration of course applied equally to the demilitarized area between Syria and Israel and the Gaza strip as well
as to the West Bank. These are problems beyond the scope of the
present discussion, as are those of the Palestine Conciliation Commission and the United Nations agencies that worked for the relief
of the refugees. Here, as in later sections, themes will be developed

---

[21] Minute by Burrows, 15 Sept. 1949, FO 371/75206/E8857.
[22] Ibid.
[23] See memorandum of 6 Apr. 1950, *Foreign Relations 1950*, V, pp. 844–7.

along lines closer to more immediate British concerns. Nevertheless a few words will be said about the Gaza strip because, like Deir Yassin, it had an important influence on British attitudes.

Troutbeck was one of the first civilian visitors to the Gaza strip after the cessation of hostilities. The experience reinforced his anti-Zionism. He reported that there were already at least 250,000 refugees (the United Nations figure was 180,000) in addition to the original population of 60,000. 'There is still time to save them', he wrote in June 1949, 'but the sands must be running out. It will be a tragedy if they are allowed to turn into a homeless and discontented proletariat.'[24] The plight of the refugees weighed heavily on Troutbeck's mind. Earlier he had pondered the fate of the refugees on the West Bank and in Jordan. In his reflective moods he meditated on what he believed to be the collective British guilt of the Balfour Declaration. If it had not been for the Balfour Declaration, there would have been no Deir Yassin and no Gaza strip. He once wrote about the refugees: 'After all it was we who created the situation in which they are now floundering and but for our action or inaction over the past thirty years there would not today be 700,000 odd refugees starving and shivering on the hillsides.'[25]

The tripartite declaration was issued exactly a month before the outbreak of the Korean war. The tide of American anti-colonialism was now definitely on the ebb. Whatever objections there might have been to the British Empire in the Middle East, the need for an ally now convinced most American critics of British imperialism that the expansionist aims of the Soviet Union and Communist China demanded a firm Anglo-American response. 'We fully agree that [the] UK is and should be [a] world power', one American official commented during the tripartite discussions, 'and "the more powerful and more worldly the better".'[26] The outbreak of the Korean war clarified the areas of British and American 'responsibility'. According to a Foreign Office minute of September 1950: 'because we have a base in Egypt we ought to take the initiative and bear the initial burden if any operation has to be undertaken in the Eastern Mediterranean similar to the Korean undertaking'.[27] The Korean war thus indirectly worked to their advantage as the British attempted to shore

[24] Troutbeck to Bevin, 16 June 1949, FO 371/75343/E7816.
[25] Troutbeck to Wright, Personal and Secret, 3 Mar. 1949, FO 371/75064. By 1952 a secret British estimate calculated the total number of refugees at 850,000 with the following breakdown: 460,000, Jordan; 200,000, Gaza; 104,000 Lebanon; 80,000, Syria; 4,000, Iraq; and 19,000 Israel. See memorandum entitled 'Palestine Refugees', 1952, FO 371/98254/E1056.
[26] A remark by Philip C. Jessup. 24 Apr. 1950, *Foreign Relations 1950*, III, p. 855.
[27] Minute by A. Rumbolt, 27 Sept. 1950, FO 371/81967/E1193/G.

up the British Empire in the Middle East. In the grand strategic view, the base at Suez now appeared as the anchor of western security in that part of the world. Nevertheless the British position of strength in the Canal Zone was also the point of greatest potential catastrophe.

The month following the tripartite declaration was not only the month of the Korean war but also the time that the British reopened discussions with the Egyptians about the future of the Canal Zone. The first problem was how best to convince the Egyptians that the purpose of the base was to defend Egypt itself, and, in a larger sense, the 'West'. Since the British had been using similar arguments for well over half a century, there was the apprehension that the Egyptians might regard the crisis of 'western civilization' as an excuse to prolong the occupation. Nevertheless the British plunged into these discussions with the conviction, in the words of a Chiefs of Staff paper, that in the event of a major war 'Egypt would certainly be singled out for early attack by the Russians'.[28] The Chief of the Imperial General Staff, Field-Marshal Sir William Slim, visited Cairo in June. He told King Farouk that the British wished to make 'a complete break with the past' and to put Anglo-Egyptian relations on a new footing. Slim's proposals included these points:

(a) The British should completely abandon any idea of the 'occupation' of Egypt.
(b) A complete new approach to defence based on equal alliance between Egypt and Britain on the lines of the Atlantic Defence Pact should be made.[29]

Bevin's ideas about integrating Egypt into a 'Middle Eastern Command' thus began to find concrete expression in the summer of 1950. The point is emphasized here because it was Egypt more than any other issue that continued to dominate British thought about the Middle East.

The other major question of course was oil. During the last two years of the Labour government the issues of the Canal Zone and Persian oil loomed so large that the British public tended to think of the Middle East in terms of the Empire's 'jugular vein' and its oleaginous lifeblood. There were also more general problems not so easily defined. In a broad sense they can be described as questions of economic viability and political stability. These themes will be developed in the next chapter, but unfortunately it is not feasible to pursue the consequences of the policies discussed in earlier chapters in all of the Middle Eastern territories, for example, Libya and Cyprus (not to mention countries of more peripheral British

[28] COS report, 'Co-Operation with Egypt', 19 May 1950, Defence Committee, DO (50) 40, PREM 8/1359.
[29] Copy of letter from Slim to King Farouk, 13 July 1950, PREM 8/1359.

concern such as Saudi Arabia).[30] The purpose of the last section of the present chapter will be to indicate the interconnection of the three themes of economic viability and political stability, oil, and defence, in the case of one of the more central Arab countries, Iraq.

Iraq as a Test Case of British Policy and Dilemmas, 1949–51

'Nuri knows in his heart of hearts', wrote Sir Alec Kirkbride in early 1949, 'that his own fate and prospects are inextricably identified with us.'[31] That shrewd observation offers the key to the inner thought of British officials who believed that collaboration with Nuri Pasha would be the best hope of achieving economic and social reform, and thereby averting revolution, in Iraq. Unfortunately for the British it was well known throughout the Middle East that they were equally dependent on Nuri. Nuri was by no means a British puppet in the same sense as King Abdullah, but the comparison was often made. In the words of Sir John Troutbeck, 'Nuri shares King Abdullah's reputation of being merely an instrument in British policy.'[32] During this period Nuri was Prime Minister from January to December 1949 and from September 1950 to July 1952 (an interval broken mainly by his rival Taufiq al-Suwaidi in 1950). Such was Nuri's ascendancy in Iraqi politics that without him there might have been the danger of victorious anti-British forces led by the 'Istiqlal' or 'Independence' party of the far right. So apprehensive were the British of Nuri having to yield 'to a reactionary, fanatical and anti-British government of the extreme right' that there was often a tone of relief in the official minutes that he remained such a stabilizing influence.[33] 'No Ataturk has yet emerged in Iraq', Troutbeck once wrote. 'Nuri Pasha, on the other hand, still has plenty of kick in him.'[34] During this time Nuri pursued economic and defence policies that were unpopular with the Iraqi public. His motives were debatable at the time, and his methods as well as his aims remain a subject of historical controversy.

[30] Anglo-American relations in Saudi Arabia will be touched on in the next section of this chapter, but the author regrets that the structure of this part of the book denies the opportunity to discuss in detail the birth of the Libyan state and the beginning of the trauma of Cyprus. They are historically rich subjects. James Griffiths, the Colonial Secretary in 1951, wrote for example about the latter: 'I am deeply concerned as to what we are to do about Cyprus politically. We cannot let it drift into another Palestine.' Minute by Griffiths, 11 Jan. 1951, CO 537/7463.

[31] Minute by Kirkbride, 29 Mar. 1949, FO 371/75064/E4691.

[32] Troutbeck to Bevin, 1 June 1949, FO 371/75550/E6770.

[33] 'Note on Political Forces in Iraq', attached to minute by Wright, 19 Mar. 1949, FO 371/75064/E3882.

[34] Troutbeck to Eden, 28 Nov. 1952, FO 371/98736/EQ1016/78.

Nuri's lack of initiative in domestic reform was a theme of British political reporting of the late 1940s. 'He . . . is more interested in international than internal affairs', according to a typical Foreign Office minute.[35] Troutbeck, one of the most astute observers of Iraqi politics, lamented Nuri's indifference to the low standard of 'honesty and efficiency' of the Iraqi government. To most British officials the question of 'corruption' remained acute. The following minute written in early 1949 may be taken as representative of British policy as well as an expression of traditional assumptions about Iraq:

> The fact is that the whole system of government in Iraq, from the Departments of State in the capital to the sub-divisions of the provinces, have always been by our standards inefficient and corrupt. . . . Our tactics, and they are practically the only ones open to us, are therefore to encourage the better elements among the relatively few leaders . . . to improve social and economic conditions, and by publicity and example to try gradually to inculcate feeling for higher standards in public administration and to show the younger men with progressive leanings that there is a possible alternative between reaction and communism.[36]

By about 1950 there were grounds for believing that this outlook had been vindicated. 'Inefficiency' rather than 'corruption' was now the word most frequently used to describe Iraqi government.[37] The phrase that Douglas Busk had invoked to describe Iraqi politics in 1948, *'hoffnungslos aber nicht ernst'* (hopeless but not serious), had given way to more optimistic views about progressive elements in Iraqi society. The 'old gang' continued to dominate the government, but this ruling élite (an interlocked miscellany numbering no more than about fifty men of the landed aristocracy, the civil service, the army, and the professions) now appeared to be more responsive to ideas about 'development'. This was about the time when Nuri began to acquire yet another reputation, this one as a statesman who devoted almost as much attention to economic planning as to international politics.[38] 1950 was the year of the Iraq Development Board.

In April 1950 the Iraqi Parliament established the Development

[35] Minute by P. A. Rhoads, 26 Sept. 1950, FO 371/82408/EQ1016/27.

[36] 'Note on Political Forces in Iraq', attached to minute by Wright, 19 Mar. 1949, FO 371/75064/E3882.

[37] E.g.: 'The main obstacle to the reform of government lies in the incompetence of Iraqi Civil Servants rather than in their widespread corruption.' Minute by the Chancery of the Baghdad Embassy enclosed in Mack to Furlonge, 15 Nov. 1950, FO 371/81922/E10213.

[38] Michael Ionides, a member of the Iraq Development Board, wrote later: 'Nuri was intensely interested in the Board's work. He never missed the main Board meeting every Saturday evening unless he was abroad. If some State function prevented his presence, which was rarely, he would postpone the meeting so that he could attend.' Michael Ionides, *Divide and Lose: The Arab Revolt of 1955-1958* (London, 1960), p. 125.

Board as an independent executive body responsible for the development of the country's resources. A British expert, and an American,
were among the members of the board. A portion of the Iraqi
government's oil revenues (eventually at seventy per cent) was
reserved to finance projects of capital development such as dams
and irrigation works, canal systems, roads and bridges, power stations,
and, later, hospitals and schools. The plans for this enlightened venture had been long in the making. The extent of the hopes aroused
by Iraq's economic development, and the implications for the
Middle East as a whole, may be gathered from a British Cabinet
paper of 1948. It assumed that Iraq had the greatest potential of all
Middle Eastern countries for rapid economic development because
of the anticipated oil boom. One source of inspiration, as cited by
Ernest Bevin, was the Tennessee Valley Authority.[39] According to
this forecast, the 'energetic' development of Iraq's resources would:

(a) enable Iraq to become a great food-producing country for the Middle
East, which is at present a net importer of cereals;
(b) enable Iraq to support a considerably larger population than her present
population of 4½ millions, which is, in fact, barely sufficient to maintain the
area already cultivated unless greater mechanisation is introduced;
(c) broaden the basis of Iraq's economic prosperity by enabling her to derive
profit, not only from her oil resources, but also from all her cultivable land;
(d) provide a unique opportunity in the Middle East not only for raising
the present very low standards of living of the labouring classes, but also for
introducing modern democratic forms of land ownership and management on
a large scale; and
(e) give Iraq the basis for that economic prosperity which will assist her to
achieve real political progress and stability, and thus provide the best possible
answer to subversive criticism of the present régime.[40]

Those aspirations, which in retrospect must strike one as extravagant,
were representative of the late 1940s. Economic development seemed
to offer the key to political stability as well as prosperity and the
improvement of the quality of life.

The history of the Development Board is beyond the scope of the
present discussion, but it should be mentioned that the investment of
the huge oil revenues into development projects encouraged the

[39] Memorandum by Bevin, CP (48) 114, 28 Apr. 1948, CAB 129/26; therein FO
memorandum dated April 1948 on 'The Economic Development of Iraq'. Bevin's imagination lit up whenever large development projects were discussed, especially those that involved hydroelectricity. The experts were sceptical about transplanting the experience of
the TVA to the Tigris–Euphrates valley. 'The TVA is not . . . considered a suitable prototype
by our experts since it is based largely on the principle of private land ownership and makes
no provision for the partnership of the labouring classes or for communal social services.
The Sudan Development Schemes are considered a far more suitable model.' 'The Economic
Development of Iraq'.
[40] Ibid.

British to believe that Iraq would justify their general Middle Eastern policy. The mistake lay in underestimating the time in which capital development projects could be brought to fruition (usually at a minimum of four years) and in underrating the human desire to realize benefits rather than to stand in awe, for example, at the construction of a power station or a refinery (which the poorer people believed would mainly make the rich even richer). Nevertheless all of the development works 'which had formerly been no more than dreams', including hospitals, schools, and local agricultural projects, 'seemed at last to be within Iraq's grasp', wrote Michael Ionides (a British engineer who served on the Development Board in its last years).[41]

The British who were responsible for creating the Development Board, and the Iraqis who supervised economic development, shared common assumptions. These may be summed up by stating that oil revenues should be wisely invested in long-term economic development. Social and political discontent would eventually be alleviated. The 'troublemakers' would be silenced by general prosperity. In fact, as became clear in the mid-1950s, the Development Board created 'strong and widespread resentment' at the way in which the new wealth was being spent.[42] Nuri believed that long-range development would bring prosperity to the common people, but at the same time he did not press ahead with economic and social reform that might have mitigated criticism. He did not wish to antagonize the large landowners.[43] As Majid Khadduri has written, there developed a race between development and revolution.[44]

After the revolution of 1958 Michael Ionides penned one of the more fair-minded assessments of Nuri. It is helpful in understanding Nuri's dominating personality and restless spirit that characterized his style of leadership during the oil crisis of 1950–1. Ionides wrote:

Despite his energy, he never found time enough to promote reforms which were getting more and more pressing. I do not mean only such things as land reform, springing from ideas of social advance, but also the kind of practical

[41] Ionides, *Divide and Lose*, p. vi.

[42] This was the celebrated phrase of Lord Salter, who played a central part in redirecting the priorities of the Development Board in the mid-1950s towards housing and other projects in order to ease some of the more pressing social problems. 'Here was a country', he lamented in his memoirs, 'which had not only rich undeveloped resources but ample capital from its own production of oil to develop them. . . . I had no premonition of the actual *coup d'état* of July 1958 but had long feared a revolution at some time which would frustrate the hopes of a few years before.' Lord Salter, *Memoirs of a Public Servant* (London, 1961), pp. 348–9.

[43] See Edith and E. F. Penrose, *Iraq: International Relations and National Development* (London, 1978), chap. 7.

[44] Majid Khadduri, *Arab Contemporaries: The Role of Personalities in Politics* (Baltimore, 1973), p. 37.

measures which were needed to bring all of the new projects we were building under efficient administrative control. I doubt if Nuri fully understood the need for these reforms. The complexity of affairs induced by this sudden economic expansion demanded a range of experience which he did not possess, and a concentration of thought and effort which he had no time to give. He wanted results—concrete results, completed projects which could be shown as evidence of economic progress. The rest had to look after itself.[45]

If only people would be patient, Nuri is reputed to have said shortly before his naked corpse was dragged through the streets of Baghdad in the summer of 1958, they would see how prosperous they would become from the investing of the oil revenues in long-range development projects.[46]

It is the controversy about the oil profits in 1950-1 that is the key issue for some of the main themes of the following chapters. Lord Curzon once stated that during the First World War the allied powers 'floated to victory on a wave of oil'. The metaphor is apt here not only because of the enduring importance of the Middle Eastern oil reserves at the time of the Korean war but also because, in the political ocean of oil, a crisis in the Gulf of Mexico eventually could contribute to a comparable crisis of tidal-wave proportion in the Persian Gulf. The antecedent of the Persian oil controversy of 1950-1 is to be found in the Venezuelan legislation that enacted the basis of fifty-fifty profit sharing in 1943. The oleaginous politics of Iraq were stirred by the subsequent cross-currents between Saudi Arabia and Iran.

The Iraq Petroleum Company (and its subsidiaries, the Basrah Petroleum Company and the Mosul Petroleum Company) held a virtual monopoly of oil concessions in Iraq. The shareholders of the Iraq Petroleum Company were as follows:

Anglo-Iranian Oil Company	23.75%
Royal Dutch–Shell Group	23.75%
Compagnie Française des Pétroles	23.75%
Standard Oil Company of New Jersey	11.875%
Socony Vacuum Oil Company (Mobil)	11.875%
Private interest (C. S. Gulbenkian)	5.00%[47]

[45] Ionides, *Divide and Lose*, p. 125.

[46] Khadduri, *Arab Contemporaries*, p. 34.

[47] Within Iraq the operation of the Naftkhana oilfield astride the Iran–Iraq border remained in the hands of the Khanaqin Oil Company and its marketing affiliate, the Rafidain Oil Company, both subsidiaries of the Anglo-Iranian Oil Company, until 1952, when the Iraqi government assumed control of refining and distribution functions. The map and table in Sachar, *Europe Leaves the Middle East*, pp. 396-7, are valuable guides to the holdings and structure of the Middle East oil companies.

As far as the British government was concerned, this was a satisfactory arrangement because the Anglo-Iranian Oil Company (known in the region affectionately or disaffectionately, depending on one's point of view, as 'Anglo-Iranian' or, even more affectionately or disaffectionately by its old name, 'Anglo-Persian') together with the Shell group (which was subject to British fiscal controls) possessed nearly fifty per cent of the shares. The British government itself in turn held over half the shares of 'Anglo-Persian'. It was the 'Anglo-Persian' involvement in the Iraq Petroleum Company that contributed to the latter company's sinister reputation. To Iraqi nationalists (as indeed to nationalists throughout the Middle East) 'Anglo-Persian' symbolized oppression and, in the words of the nationalist slogan of 1950–1, 'the colonial exploitation of the national heritage'. The intensity of nationalist enmity towards the Iraq Petroleum Company has to be understood within the context of the dominating and exploitative influence associated with the 'mother company' in Iran. 'Anglo-Iranian', according to Eric Berthoud (the Assistant Under-Secretary who supervised the Economic Relations Department of the Foreign Office) 'are particularly hated in Iraq because they are thought to be responsible for the stickiness of I. P. C.'[48]

By 'stickiness' Berthoud meant the refusal of the Iraq Petroleum Company to consider any alteration of the flat royalty rate in favour of profit sharing. In Iraq the public discussion about the 'fair' share of revenue that should be expected from the company took place against the completion of the network of pipelines from the company's main fields at Kirkuk to the Mediterranean in 1949–50 (the same time of the completion of the Trans-Arabian Pipeline, TAPLINE, from Saudi Arabia to the Mediterranean). In response to the developing crisis in Iran, the Iraq Petroleum Company in August 1950 finally acquiesced in a substantial increase in the royalty rate. Four months later the Arabian American Oil Company (Aramco) came to an agreement with the Saudi Arabian government that profits (as opposed to royalties) should be shared on a fifty–fifty basis. The new Iraqi agreement (and its counterpart in Iran, the 'Supplementary Oil Agreement') immediately became a dead letter. The Aramco–Saudi agreement of December 1950 signified as great a revolution in the economic affairs of the Middle East, as was recognized at the time, as the political transfer of power in India in 1947.

It is useful to bear in mind the realistic assessment made by the Office of Near Eastern and African Affairs in the State Department

[48] Minute by Berthoud reflecting the views of 'a reliable British informant', 22 Mar. 1951, FO 371/91244/E1531.

in September 1950 about the nature of the storm about to break in the Persian Gulf. The following points were made in a memorandum prepared for the Assistant Secretary, George McGhee:

> We have no doubt in our minds that Persian Gulf oil operations have been and continue to be *exceptionally profitable* from a commercial standpoint, particularly AIOC [Anglo-Iranian Oil Company] operations. It is sophistry to suggest oil companies can't pay and do much more. . . .
>
> The 50–50 sharing of profits agreement in Venezuela, wherein Venezuela earns three times total benefits to all Middle East states, is well known in Tehran. . . .
>
> Saudi Arabia has been earning over the past three years royalties now promised but not yet paid by AIOC. . . .
>
> The Korean war has already created shortages even with U. S., Venezuela, and Middle East production at record levels.[49]

In his discussions with the Iranians as well as the British, McGhee demonstrated a mastery of those issues in all of their ramifications.

McGhee played a critical part in the oil controversies of 1950–1. In British circles he was known as 'that infant prodigy'.[50] He was only thirty-eight in 1950, but he had behind him a successful education at Oxford (he had earned a D.Phil. as a Rhodes Scholar), a marriage into one of the prominent American oil families (his wife was the daughter of the geologist Dr. Everett DeGolyer, at one time chairman of the United States Petroleum Commission), and a close friendship with Dean Acheson (which made him invulnerable to British attempts to dislodge him). He had an almost unique capacity for irritating the British. He made no secret of his belief that the British had been in Iraq '30 years and had not developed it', and he was frankly contemptuous of British expertise.[51] He was not an Anglophobe. He merely wished to save the British from themselves, if only because their 'nineteenth century' attitude towards the oil question jeopardized the American position. As an independently wealthy oilman himself, he was acutely aware of the risks to which the oil companies were exposed in the Middle East. He frequently recited the history of the American oil ventures in Latin America, not least the Mexican expropriation of 1938. The advice that he persistently gave the British was 'to roll with the punches' and to find an 'imaginative' solution that would meet Persian and Arab nationalist aspirations. The Anglo-Iranian Oil Company, he once stated to the Middle East experts of the Foreign Office and representatives of the company itself, 'could not . . . merely stand on their own concession rights.

[49] Memorandum by Richard Funkhouser, 14 Sept. 1950, *Foreign Relations 1950*, V, pp. 97–9.

[50] See e.g. Houstoun-Boswall to Bowker, 'Personal and Secret', 29 Mar. 1951, FO 371/91184/E1024.

[51] Mack to Wright, 'Personal & Confidential', 13 Dec. 1949, FO 371/81950/E11345.

Nothing in the history of oil concessions indicated that they would be able to do so.'[52]

The solution fabricated by Aramco in the autumn of 1950 is known in oil lore as the 'golden gimmick'. Essentially it enabled the American company to deduct the amount of profits shared with the Saudi government from the amount due to the United States government as corporate taxes. It would be tempting to suspect collusion, but strictly speaking this was not the case. There was no advance arrangement made with the US Treasury, and McGhee, for example, refused to commit himself.[53] Yet there was the precedent of Venezuela (upheld under the Internal Revenue Act in favour of the oil companies during a comparable period of national emergency), and it was probable that the State Department and Department of Defense would support Aramco for strategic reasons (and coincidentally as a means of assisting an Arab 'ally' with minimal risk of antagonizing the Israeli lobby in the United States). In the words of Aramco's Vice-President, James Terry Duce, in November 1950, 'Aramco officials preferred retreating in this direction since it *might* involve no additional expense to the company.'[54] It was a gamble, but when the Internal Revenue Service audited Aramco's tax return in 1955, the tax credit was granted. To reduce the aftermath to its essentials, Saudi resentment against the royalty system had been diffused, and Aramco continued to prosper with the lucrative profits of the 1950s.[55]

The Aramco-Saudi '50–50' agreement bore the date of the 30th of December 1950. 'Neither we nor the British Oil Companies in the Middle East were warned or consulted', lamented a Foreign Office official.[56] Like an ocean storm, the Saudi danger gained momentum quickly and then blew over, but not without causing further major disturbances. Less than half a year later, on the 2nd of May 1951, Iran nationalized the oil industry. The precipitating element in these developments had been the visit of a Venezuelan diplomatic group

[52] Record of meeting in the Foreign Office, 2 Apr. 1951, FO 371/91244/EP1023/10/G.

[53] The best discussion of this point, and the entire question of the 'fifty–fifty' arrangement, is Irvine H. Anderson, *Aramco, The United States and Saudi Arabia: A Study of the Dynamics of Foreign Oil Policy, 1933–1950* (Princeton, 1981), chap. VI.

[54] *Foreign Relations 1950*, V, p. 107, emphasis added.

[55] Another happy outcome for the Americans of 1950–1 was the good political relationship that continued between Ibn Saud, Aramco, and the American government. The British, in what must be regarded as a tribute to Ibn Saud's political agility, persisted in believing that the King 'while recognising his dependence on oil revenues, resents any suggestion that he should take advice from the Americans and has more than once told the [British] Ambassador that he looks primarily to ourselves for advice and support in the political sphere'. Memorandum entitled 'Anglo-American Relations in Saudi Arabia' by L. A. C. Fry, 7 Feb. 1951, FO 371/91759.

[56] Ibid.

which, according to an American document of November 1950, had instilled in 'all Near Eastern officialdom' the 'concept of 50–50 sharing of profits'.[57] Why should the Middle Eastern states accept anything less than the more equitable and profitable Latin-American method of profit sharing? The circumstances of late 1950 were of course too complex to be reduced simply to the Latin-American influence, but it is certainly true that 'Venezuela' was on everyone's lips at the time. From the autumn of 1950 the prevailing wind blew in the direction of '50–50', and it was felt in all parts of the Middle East. The quick and decisive action by Aramco helped to solve one set of problems, but in doing so the Americans set off a chain of crises for the British, not only in Iran but also in Iraq, Kuwait, and Bahrain. ' "Nationalism" is not yet a force in the Persian Gulf', according to a Foreign Office document of April 1951, 'and it seems hardly conceivable that a serious demand for "nationalisation" of the local oil industry could arise for many years in so backward a place as Kuwait.'[58] Nevertheless within the year 1951 all of the major oil-producing states of the Middle East except Iran were brought into the fifty–fifty system of profit-sharing. The theme here is the way in which the Iraqis, from their point of view, managed to secure the best of the '50–50' arrangements.

The speed with which the Americans moved towards the fifty-fifty basis was possible in part because Aramco was an American company incorporated in the United States and subject to American tax laws that were far less rigid than the British. The Iraq Petroleum Company was on an entirely different footing, not only because of the international character of the company but also because of the British tax system. 'The Inland Revenue', according to Peter Ramsbotham (at that time on the oil desk of the Economic Relations Department of the Foreign Office) '. . . naturally favour a large royalty and a small tax element'—in other words, taxable royalties provided a lucrative source of revenue for the British Treasury that would be diluted or lost by shifting to a basis of profit-sharing in which taxes (or profits in lieu of taxes) were paid to the Iraqi government.[59] The British tax authorities had no inclination whatever to indulge in the liberal outlook permitted by the American system. There was the further complication of 'Anglo-Persian' in Iraq. The Iranians demanded a share of the company's profit not only in Iran but throughout the world, including of

---

[57] See *Foreign Relations 1950*, V, p. 109.

[58] Eastern Department memorandum, 'Iraq and Persian Gulf Oil', 2 Apr. 1951, FO 371/91244/E1531. For Kuwait and the new agreement of 1951, see Zuhayr Mikdashi, *A Financial Analysis of Middle Eastern Oil Concessions: 1901–65* (New York, 1966), chap. 5.

[59] Minute by Ramsbotham, 12 Apr. 1951, FO 371/91244/E1531.

course Iraq.[60] The cries of anguish from the Treasury were only beginning to mount to the level of a wail when suddenly they were cut short. In Ramsbotham's phrase the objections of the Treasury became 'irrelevant'. 'For better or worse this principle [of '50-50'] has come to stay', he wrote in April 1951.[61] The British companies had to accept the principle of the fifty-fifty split or run the risk of losing everything, and it was becoming apparent in Iran that even a belated offer of '50-50' might not save the day.

The critical development in Iraq occurred in April 1951. According to a Foreign Office minute:

> [The] Managing Director of Iraq Petroleum Company has promised that his Company will give Iraq terms 'comparable though not identical' with those granted by Aramco to the Saudi Arabian Government. Negotiations to that end will shortly begin but will take some time to complete, and meanwhile the Company are offering Iraq an immediate advance of £3,000,000 as an earnest of good faith.[62]

The phrase 'comparable but not identical' is significant. There was nothing sacrosanct about '50-50' in the company's view, but it could be endorsed as a general guide while hammering out the details of a new agreement. This grudging acquiescence nevertheless signified a volte-face on the part of the company. The reason for the sudden and generous impulse is to be found in the Iranian crisis. The Foreign Office and 'Anglo-Persian' were not only attempting to prevent the situation in Iraq from disintegrating into 'another Iran' but were also trying to demonstrate to the Iranians the advantages of a demonstrably 'fair' settlement, of which Nuri's government was quick to take advantage and to drive a hard bargain as well.

The '50-50' agreement between the Iraqi government and the Iraq Petroleum Company was not signed until the 3rd of February 1952, but it was retroactive to the 1st of January 1951. It differed from most of the other arrangements in the Middle East by offering even better terms than a split of the profits. For example there was a guarantee of a minimum level of payments of 25% to 35% of the seaboard value of exported oil as well as minimum levels of exports and annual production. The Iraqi government was also entitled to receive whatever quantity of crude oil it needed for local consumption, and to use up to 12½% of its oil in exchange for goods or

---

[60] 'The main difficulty as I see it', Berthoud wrote in emphasizing this point, 'in the case of Persia is that that country will not accept at all willingly the proposed sharing only of profits *within Persia*. They claim that all the outside activities of A. I. O. C. are based on profits earned on Persian oil and that they are entitled to half the global profits. This is a very serious point.' Minute by Berthoud, 4 Apr. 1951, FO 371/91244/E1531.

[61] Minute by Ramsbotham, 4 Apr. 1951, FO 371/91244/E1531.

[62] Minute by Fry, 6 Apr. 1951, FO 371/91244/E1531.

currency of certain countries.[63] One of the old regulations that fell by the wayside was the 'posted price' according to prices in the Gulf of Mexico. 'The fetish of charging the locals a price based on the Gulf of Mexico prices must really be broken once and for all', wrote Eric Berthoud during these deliberations.[64] 'Posted prices', in other words the retail value of crude oil at any particular place, would no longer be set arbitrarily by the companies but would be decided by mutual agreement.[65] In the case of the Iraq Petroleum Company, Iraqis would be appointed to the board of directors to establish these prices. This point reflected the nature of the new system. Peter Ramsbotham wrote in a minute that went to the heart of the matter:

> An inevitable corollary of a 50/50 arrangement is the granting of a right to the concessionary Government to appoint Directors to the Company's board, who would be entitled to look into such questions as production costs, prices and sales. Once they acquire a share in the profits, the concessionary Government will want to know how the profits are made.[66]

In Berthoud's view the admission into the directors' boardroom was the key 'psychological' difference between the new system and the old one of royalties, which the nationalists had invariably suspected of being rigged against them.[67]

The oil revenues of the Iraqi government increased from £7 million in 1950 to £15 million in 1951 to £34 million in 1952 and to over £50 million in 1953.[68] According to contemporary British judgement, Nuri was 'personally entitled to the greater part of the credit' for the new '50–50' arrangement and for the allocation of seventy per cent of the oil revenues for development projects.[69] If he miscalculated public tolerance for long-term development (as opposed to more modest yet more immediately gratifying and popular projects such as housing and water purification), this was an error of judgement for which the American and British development experts must be held accountable as well. The flaw in Nuri's character in contemporary eyes did not lie so much in the realm of development as in his obsession with grand strategy, which deflected his attention away from the economic and social grievances of the Iraqi public. It was in the 1950–1 period, against the background of

---

[63] These points are lucidly discussed by Mikdashi, *A Financial Analysis*, chap. 5.

[64] Minute by Berthoud, 4 Apr. 1951, FO 371/91244/E1531.

[65] For the 'posted prices' see especially Penrose, *Iraq*, chap. 6.

[66] Minute by Ramsbotham, 4 Apr. 1951, FO 371/91244/E1531.

[67] See minute by Berthoud, 4 Apr. 1951, FO 371/91244/E1531.

[68] S. H. Longrigg, *Oil in the Middle East* (Oxford, 1954), p. 196.

[69] See the assessment of Iraq enclosed in Ross to Bowker, 21 Nov. 1952, FO 371/98736/EQ1016/72.

the Korean war, that Nuri firmly established himself as a stalwart on the side of the British and the Americans in the cold war, yet at the same time as a traitor to the Arab cause.

Oil is a wasting asset. Its constructive use requires political stability. Nuri not only provided stability but enabled the British to nourish certain hopes. The oil revenues would not be squandered but wisely invested. Iraq would lead the way as the 'model' developing country.[70] As will be seen in the next chapter, it was utterly impossible for the British themselves to finance capital development projects. In 1950 Bevin himself agonized over the appointment of a single irrigation engineer from British funds.[71] In the summer of 1951, exactly at the time when the Iraqi oil revenues began to double (in part because of the drop in Iranian production), the British economy took a sharp turn for the worse. The chronic sterling dilemmas did much to damp down the jingo attitude that the Iranians, and later the Egyptians, somehow needed to be 'brought to their senses', if necessary by force. At this time the British could look upon Iraq, in large part because of Nuri, as one of the few places in the Middle East that offered hope for a stable and prosperous future (and one that would offer enormous benefits to the British economy). There were good reasons to respect Nuri's leadership. 'However wrong-headed Nuri may be in his strategic ideas', wrote Sir John Troutbeck, 'I think it should be borne in mind that he is firmly attached to co-operation with the West.' In paying tribute to Nuri's stabilizing influence, Troutbeck recorded his conviction that 'he is probably our firmest friend in the Arab world'.[72]

During the time that he served as head of the British Middle East Office in Cairo, one of Troutbeck's principal responsibilities had been the co-ordination of regional planning, both economic and strategic. When he became Ambassador in Baghdad in March 1951, he came into collision with Nuri on the latter point. Troutbeck's central idea, which he held in common with other planners both military and political, was the eventual creation of a (British) 'Supreme Middle East Command', in part to offset the American leadership of NATO.[73] If the Americans could be drawn into this

[70] For a discussion of these points in the critical postwar period of Iraqi development see especially Kathleen M. Langley, *The Industrialization of Iraq* (Cambridge, Mass., 1961), chap. 5; see also Fahim I. Qubain, *The Reconstruction of Iraq: 1950–1957* (New York, 1958).

[71] See e.g. minute by R. Barclay, 17 Oct. 1950, FO 371/82408.

[72] Troutbeck to Bowker, 4 Jan. 1952, FO 371/96919/JE1052/28.

[73] E.g. 'The creation of a command organisation under British supreme direction which we can represent politically as a counter-weight to the American position in the Atlantic. . . .' (Minute by H. A. Dudgeon, 29 May 1951, FO 371/91185/E1024/29/G.) The antecedents of the Middle East Defence Organisation thus may be traced to this period. For

grand strategy, perhaps by stationing troops in the Canal Zone and thus giving the venture an 'international' character, then the Egyptians might be more willing to sanction the project of a Middle Eastern 'alliance' under British leadership. Eventually the British were willing to make far-reaching concessions to both the Americans and the Egyptians about the nature and structure of the 'Middle East Command', but the essence of the 'Suez base' remained the same.

Nuri freely gave his advice to the British on these matters. With his military background and his fertile mind he indeed churned out so many and such conflicting ideas that the British might have had difficulty in keeping pace, if they had been so inclined. They did not in fact encourage Nuri to develop his 'half-baked plans' (Troutbeck's recurrent phrase), but it was clear what he had in mind. Nuri wished to play the honest broker between the Egyptians and the British. He believed himself to be in a good position to co-ordinate defence planning with Nahas Pasha (who returned to power in January 1950 as Egyptian Prime Minister). He thought the two of them could influence certain other parties, for example, the Syrians. Nuri's ideas were prolific, and there were many mutations, but in sum he held that the Egyptians could be persuaded to allow the RAF to remain in the Canal Zone if British combat forces were moved to Syria. Nuri together with Nahas would convince the Syrians of the wisdom of this plan (whether or not they hoped to persuade the French as well was not entirely clear). There is no reason to pursue Nuri's imaginative geopolitical schemes. Troutbeck patiently heard him out and did his utmost to discourage him.[74] Ultimately the significance of Nuri's military and strategic preoccupation, and his obsession with 'security' (internal as well as international), was the reinforcing of his association, especially in the public eye, with the status quo and the 'old gang'. 'Recently Nuri has tended to identify himself more and more with the old Sunni politicians', according to a report that anticipated Nuri's direction in the 1950s.[75] 'Feudalism' was one part of the revolutionary indictment against Nuri in 1958. In the eyes of his fellow nationalists, Nuri irrevocably tainted himself by his enthusiasm for 'defence' and thus by his apparent support of the British in their renewed quest for hegemony in the Middle East. 'Imperialism' was the other part of the revolutionary indictment against him.

scathing yet illuminating comment on the fruition of MEDO in 1955 as 'but another Portsmouth Treaty and worse', see Batatu, *The Old Social Classes*, p. 679.

[74] 'I trust that you expect me to listen to him with . . . sympathy even though I have to discourage some of his wilder ideas.' Troutbeck to Bowker, 4 Jan. 1952, FO 371/96919/ JE1052/28.

[75] Assessment enclosed in Ross to Bowker, 21 Nov. 1952, FO 371/98736.

Nuri's significance as the anchor of the British position in the Middle East is clear from the Foreign Office minutes about him in relation to the Persian oil crisis and the Egyptian move to oust the British from the Canal Zone in the autumn of 1951. The ballast was precarious. The assassination of King Abdullah (which will be discussed in the next chapter) left no doubt about Nuri's vulnerability. If Nuri 'were to be eliminated from the political scene', according to an appraisal of Iraq written after the tumultuous events of that year, 'a danger of [oil] nationalisation could not be ignored'.[76] The same held true in the realm of defence. If it had not been for Nuri, the British position would probably have deteriorated. When the Egyptians unilaterally dissolved the Anglo-Egyptian alliance in October 1951, Nuri stabilized Iraqi reaction by stating publicly that Iraq would expect terms as good as the Egyptians might receive in a new defence relationship (just as Iraq had demanded, and received, terms as good as others as a result of the oil crisis). Nationalist suspicion of Nuri would have been confirmed if it had been known that he was secretly telling the British that he had 'no intention' of terminating the Anglo-Iraq Treaty of Alliance.[77] In order to deal with the 'agitation' in Iraq as a result of the Egyptians 'acting very foolishly' in Nuri's own words, he would request an alteration of the treaty's terms, but the alliance itself would hold.[78] The British in the last major Middle Eastern crisis of the Labour government thus had good reason to be pleased with the response of their principal Arab collaborator. 'Considering the inflamed state of opinion in the Middle East', wrote Sir Willian Strang, 'Nuri's attitude . . . is not too bad.'[79]

---

[76] Ibid.

[77] 'Nuri went on to say that he, for his part, had no intention of abolishing [the] Anglo-Iraq alliance. . . . He felt that he had the army, police and tribes behind him and so need not fear opposition from other quarters though he wished to avoid all unnecessary difficulties with his public opinion.' Troutbeck to Morrison, 15 Oct. 1951, FO 371/91224/172G.

[78] Troutbeck to Morrison, 13 Oct. 1951, PREM 8/1463.

[79] Minute by Strang, 17 Oct. 1951, PREM 8/1463.

2

THE FUTURE OF THE MIDDLE EASTERN STATES: QUESTIONS OF ECONOMIC 'VIABILITY' AND POLITICAL STABILITY

IN JULY 1949 Ernest Bevin summoned his Middle Eastern officials to London to discuss the economic and social as well as the political problems of the Middle East. It was the first conference of this scope and importance in four years. In 1945, as will be recalled from an earlier chapter, Bevin had emphasized the overriding necessity of economic development in order to sustain Britain as the dominant power in the Middle East. In the meantime no other region in the world, he said in his introductory remarks to the conference, had caused him 'more frustration'. Mid-July 1949 could be regarded as the time for a fresh start. The Palestine dispute, he passionately hoped, now lay behind them. But the question of economic and social progress remained as acute as it had at the end of the war. He directed his remarks to the malaise of the Arab governments. The Palestine struggle had delayed economic development, and further stagnation would result in revolutionary conditions in which the Soviet Union would attempt to extinguish British influence. This passage of Bevin's speech is revealing about British thought in mid-1949:

> The old regimes, which we were forced to support, would not stand up to revolutionary conditions and would be swept away. These regimes were greedy and selfish and had not allowed any of the wealth which they have made out of the war and out of oil to benefit the poorer classes. If we continued to support them we should be blamed in the event of the Communists succeeding in turning the peoples of the Middle East against us.[1]

Bevin called upon his officials 'to co-ordinate our activities' and 'to demonstrate to the peoples of the Middle East the value of being associated with us'. He spoke of 'blue prints' for development. He advocated the formation of 'a great plan'—one which would 'appeal to the imagination'. This was Bevin's response to 'Point Four' of Truman's inaugural address earlier that year which pledged technical assistance to economically underdeveloped areas. Bevin in short wished to see formulated nothing less than a Marshall Plan for the Middle East.

[1] Conference minutes, 21 July 1949, FO 371/75072/E9043/G.

The agenda of the Foreign Office conference indicated the problems and aspirations of the British in what might be called the 'post-Palestine' era of the Labour government. No aspects of Middle Eastern affairs from pashas to postal rates were neglected. Economic development was foremost on the agenda. Political progress was the corollary. The prerequisite of economic development, however, was political stability. It is the interaction between economic planning and the British quest for stability in the Arab states and Israel that will form one of the main themes of this chapter.

Among the more important protagonists of this mundane but vital task of economic assistance were two officials whose minutes have been frequently quoted in earlier chapters—Sir John Troutbeck, the head of the Middle East Office in Cairo, and Michael Wright, the Assistant Under-Secretary at the Foreign Office who supervised Middle Eastern affairs. In early 1949 Wright took on, at Bevin's request, the further specific duties of overseeing economic development in the Middle East. Wright's job was to ensure that the drive did not slacken. This was a project that Bevin assigned priority. The frequency of his scrawls on minutes and reports indicates that he watched it closely. It is helpful to bear in mind that one of the memorable events of his last years in office was his journey to Ceylon in January 1950 to attend the Commonwealth Conference at Colombo which devoted much of its attention to the economic and social problems of Asia. The phrase 'Colombo Plan' became synonymous with economic development in the non-western world. Troutbeck and Wright were Bevin's lieutenants in the Middle Eastern part of this grand design. Their minutes reveal the hopes and the frustrations of the Middle East hands of the Foreign Office, but their thoughts should be read as part of the larger story of British decline in Asia—and the attempt to do something about it.

'The main obstacle', Wright had written in January 1949, 'has been and largely remains the shadow of Palestine.'[2] The Arab governments were demoralized and discredited. Their economies were in a downward spiral. It is important to note the way in which he linked this drift towards economic and political disintegration with wider trends. In a conversation with a representative of the International Bank, Wright stated:

During the recent weeks the Far East . . . had fallen to the Communists with a resounding crash and we were most anxious to prevent a similar course of events in the Middle East. Similar events were by no means improbable; the Communists, in association with the extreme Right-Wing, were already causing

[2] Minute by Wright, 29 Jan. 1949, FO 371/75083/E3030.

a great deal of trouble while the established Governments had lost much credit owing to the difficulties with Palestine.[3]

To prevent the disaster of China from reoccurring in the Middle East, the British would have to win the co-operation of the moderate nationalists in promoting economic development before the initative passed decisively to right-wing extremists or the Communists. Unfortunately for the British, at least according to their own reading of recent history, the Arab governments had been more interested in retaining power than in social and political progress. Wright and many of his colleagues now hoped that the 'moderate' Arabs would be jolted out of lethargy because of the defeat in the Israeli war and the menace of Communist take-overs. The time was therefore ripe, at least so it appeared to the British. Did it to the Arabs? The British were certain that they were dealing with 'unenlightened' governments. 'One of the most common accusations against us', Wright told the conference in July, 'was that we were supporting re-actionary regimes.' How far was it possible for the British to press for more liberal regimes? The irony was that the more paternal or 'reactionary' governments provided the stability necessary for economic development. Yet political repression would render 'development' futile. Wright had an elegant turn of phrase and he summed up the dilemma facing the British with a memorable paradox. It proved to be true for the 1949–51 era: 'If we intervened, we should be blamed for interference in internal affairs: if we did not, reaction would remain.'[4]

Sir John Troutbeck was sensitive to the political questions involved in economic development. 'It seems to me', he had written in April 1949, 'that the political side must march hand-in-hand with the economic side if progress is to be made on the latter.' He shared with Wright a belief that the Arabs had an unfortunate tradition 'of blaming us whenever things go wrong with them', but he thought that the shattering experience of defeat might now make the Arabs more eager to co-operate. In that sense the time might be right to push forward with economic development. Troutbeck's ideas reveal some of the British assumptions about the flaw in Arab society that made economic progress difficult:

I believe that to make real progress in economic and social development we may have to go deeper than we have as yet contemplated. Basically there is not much hope of progress until the Middle East peoples themselves have a burning desire for it (as the Jews for example have). It is that which we should try to

[3] As recorded in a minute by J. E. Chadwick, 29 Jan. 1949, FO 371/75083/E1771.
[4] Conference minutes, 21 July 1949, FO 371/75072/E9043.

instil in them. At present the very conception of good government has hardly penetrated the Middle East.[5]

He thus saw the problem essentially as one of instilling the idea of 'good and progressive government', and he believed that over the long haul this could be accomplished through education, administrative reform, and projects that would result in a more equitable distribution of national wealth. There was nothing profound in these ideas, but they are of interest because of Troutbeck's key position in attempting to realize them. He himself admitted to being 'rather nebulous' on the subject. But he had one definite proposal. He thought that the British should arm and train the Arab armies. 'We need to give practical proof that we want to see them strong and united.'[6] Assistance to the armed forces could be quick and effective —and in Troutbeck's view it was imperative because he believed it would only be a matter of time before the Jews made a bid for the hegemony of the Middle East.

At the conference in July, Troutbeck drove home the simple truth that economic development would be extremely difficult if all parties concerned were preparing for another round of war. He believed that the Israeli quest for domination was the source of the trouble. If the British themselves did not prepare for the eventual showdown, then the consequences might be expulsion from the Middle East. Troutbeck was gloomy, if not alarmist, on the danger of Israeli expansion:

It was Israeli policy to dominate the Arab world. We were in a position to control the Arab governments but not Israel. He foresaw that the Israelis might drag the Arab States into a neutral bloc and might even attempt to turn us out of Egypt.[7]

Troutbeck's views on economic development, in other words, were subordinate to his larger preoccupations with war and peace. But his prognosis of Israeli designs had important implications for Israeli economic development as well. Sir Knox Helm, the recently appointed Minister in Tel Aviv, flatly disagreed with Troutbeck's assessment. He thought that the Israelis could not afford to live in a state of perpetual war, nor would immigration trends allow them to do so. Militant Zionists might hope to pursue a course of expansion, but they would be checked by limited resources. The problem of Israeli development will be discussed later. Here the point is that outright controversy continued to exist in highest British circles about the

[5] Minute by Troutbeck, 12 Apr. 1949, FO 371/75085/E5082.
[6] Ibid.
[7] Conference minutes, 21 July 1949.

nature of the Israeli state and whether it would continue to expand.

Troutbeck also provoked controversy by reviving the project of 'Greater Syria' in regard to economic development. It certainly would have been more rational to be able to develop Jordan, Syria, Lebanon, and perhaps Iraq as a single unit. Nothing however could have been more calculated to stir up disagreement among the British themselves. The Arabs would have been greatly amused to have heard this discussion. The British Ambassador at Cairo remarked that it was well known that Nuri Pasha had 'aggressive designs on Syria'. HM Ambassador at Baghdad retorted that Nuri had rejected 'any idea of using force'. HM Ambassador at Damascus thought it important for the British to oppose plans for 'Greater Syria'. HM Ambassador at Amman thought that the 'Greater Syria' project 'would take time'. To Troutbeck himself here was the important point: 'Greater unity would prove a stronger safeguard against Israeli expansion.' As if the proceedings were becoming somewhat heated, HM Ambassador at Cairo remarked that 'the general effervescence caused by speculating on these subjects was unfortunate at a time when calm was necessary'.[8] 'Greater Syria' might have proved to be a more rational basis for economic planning, but it seldom led to rational discussion.

In dealing with the broader aspects of economic planning, Troutbeck raised one question that is fundamental to any discussion of the 'post-Palestine' period. He asked how the economic crisis in Britain would affect plans for development in the Middle East. The answer he received from the Treasury representative, Norman Young, was as straightforward as any contemporary comment on the British economic plight, or for that matter any subsequent historical account:

> Mr. Norman Young pointed out that high prices of British goods and the fear of devaluation of the £ sterling was causing Middle East countries to hold off purchasing and to postpone the overdue devaluation of their currency. His Majesty's Government had no intention of devaluing the pound at the present time. . . . It was, however, difficult to convince foreigners that we meant what we said.[9]

Two months later, in September 1949, the pound was devalued. The British were attempting to bring about an economic revolution in the Middle East at the same time that they themselves faced perpetual economic crisis.

It is important to bear in mind the temper of the times before

---

[8] Conference minutes, 21 July 1949.
[9] Conference minutes, 22 July 1949.

attempting to assess the British drive to make economic and political progress in the Middle East in 1949. As they now entered another phase of economic austerity, the men of the Labour government felt the strain of four years of office and the stress of worldwide burdens that would have tested the skill and perseverance of any men at any time. According to a perceptive American report written in the aftermath of devaluation, there was a general 'atmosphere of desperation' in London. These comments from the American vantage point are most useful in seeing the issues of 'economic development' in perspective:

> Having gone thru another economic crisis this year . . . Brit[ish] leaders feel that they are now fighting a last-stand battle for survival as a world power. They see themselves confronted by a host of life and death problems. They are trying simultaneously to maintain their Commonwealth and Empire and military commitments, balance their trade, modernize their industry, balance their budget, fight off inflation, and prevent a fall in their standard of living.
>
> Since there are no margins, even trivial things such as a battalion dispatched to Eritrea; a million pounds expenditure on this or that item; a million gained or lost in overseas trade; a penny rise in price of bread or a dime on the price of domestic coal become critical problems of major dimensions that require Cabinet attention.[10]

In studying the files of the Colombo Plan one is struck not only by the accuracy of those remarks but also the way in which they touched directly on the decisions that were being made about economic development in the Middle East and Asia. For example in November 1949 Attlee himself wrote a personal minute to the head of the committee preparing the economic surveys for Colombo, M. E. Dening, requesting him to be 'zealous' in making 'every practicable economy' and to do everything possible 'in preventing extravagance and encouraging thrift'.[11] It is therefore not surprising that the economic projects in the Middle East in retrospect strike one as small in scale—proposals for a dozen teachers for Egypt, a labour adviser for the Iraqi government, an agricultural project in Jordan —each consuming time and energy that often seemed disproportionate to the tangible result.

In contrast with the American 'drive and hustle' and the bounding belief 'that capitalism can provide as good a New Deal in Asia as could Communism', the British approach appeared to be not only cautious but staid. The words were those of Elizabeth Monroe, at that time on the staff of *The Economist*. In early 1950 she visited Washington to study 'Point Four' and the ways in which American aid would affect the Middle East. The origins and development of

[10] Holmes to Acheson, Secret, 7 Jan. 1950, *Foreign Relations 1950*, III, pp. 1599–1604.
[11] Minute by Attlee, 18 Nov. 1949, FO 371/76046/F18540.

the American economic assistance programmes are beyond the scope of the present discussion, but it is important to note the British reaction to them.[12] On her return to London, Miss Monroe presented a candid summary of her impressions to the 'Middle East Group' at the Royal Institute of International Affairs. Miss Monroe's later work set the trends of historical interpretation, and her contemporary comments about economic development are therefore of interest. 'When one is in . . . British offices', she told her audience, 'one gets an approach to every problem that is analytical, and competent and measured, and is based on a tremendous background of knowledge.' By contrast in American official circles 'one encounters an atmosphere of hustle, of much less background information, of much less basic knowledge of the facts, but seizure of a few essentials and of a greater readiness to act upon those essentials than one meets in British quarters'. She informed her listeners of the scope of American assistance: a modest $26.9 million as opposed to the $17 billion of the Marshall Plan, 'a very small sum indeed', and the emphasis on technical assistance: 'provided that that money pays for technical assistance by the right men, a small outlay could get reasonably good results'. The point of interest is her general impression:

I was extremely daunted by my visit . . . the over-confidence was terrifying. 'All we need is the dollars and a wrench, and we can change the face of Asia', was the attitude. . . . there seemed to be no conception that if assistance or loans are to be given to a Middle Eastern country there will be resistances to overcome, and that there will be more results if some strings are attached to the gift or loan.[13]

She added that the general attitude seemed to be that 'it would be an un-American activity to attach such conditions' or 'strings' to economic aid. Those were perceptive remarks, and one pauses to reflect what the British expected in return for assistance rendered from extremely scanty resources.

It is vital to recall that the question of economic development in the Middle East was part of the same problem that faced the British in Asia and Africa as well. If the Asian files of the Foreign Office on the Columbo Plan are studied in conjunction with those of the Middle Eastern Secretariat, then the overall design becomes much clearer. Above all one is struck not only with the scarcity of funds

[12] For the American side see Robert A. Pastor, *Congress and the Politics of U. S. Foreign Economic Policy* (Berkeley, 1980); and David A. Baldwin, *Economic Development and American Foreign Policy* (Chicago, 1966).

[13] Meeting of the Middle East Group, 28 Apr. 1950, RIIA. For discussion in Whitehall see especially the minutes of the meeting of the Committee on Colonial Development, CD (49) 4, 7 Apr. 1949, CAB 134/64. For Colonial Office discussion see the files in CO 537/5174 ff.

but also the awareness of limitations on the effectiveness of economic aid. Yet the meagre resources could be used to good effect in certain ways. Here follows an excerpt from an assessment by P. J. H. Stent, a former Indian Civil Service official now involved in economic planning. It realistically commented on the raising of living standards as well as on the use of economic assistance as a means of political influence:

Economic assistance . . . can be used as a most valuable incentive to induce governments to accept our advice in the strategic, political and social spheres, and, properly applied, may be a means of strengthening the position of existing anti-Communist governments, but it cannot, in the short-term, over the greater part of the region [of Asia] raise the general standard of living of the masses so as to make them 'immune to Communism'.[14]

Stent was primarily concerned with Asia, and it is worthwhile projecting his remarks into the Middle East. 'It might be possible by economic measures to raise the standard of living of the people within a period of, say, 10 years', Stent wrote, 'in small countries like Ceylon, Malaya, Borneo, Hong Kong and perhaps Siam'—as it would be in Jordan and perhaps Iraq. 'But it is idle to suppose that the utmost assistance the West could give, coupled with the most intense efforts of the Asian Governments, could in such a period bring about any significant rise in the standard of living of the millions of India, Pakistan, Indonesia and Indo-China.'[15] The same was true of Egypt, though the hydro-electric projects on the upper Nile made Egypt's future more rosy than that of most Asian countries.

Of all the 'blue prints' for economic development, Stent's was among the clearest in its unabashed proclamation of British rather than humanitarian goals. For the theorists of economic imperialism, this particular document would be of interest because it stripped the rhetoric of economic aid down to self-interest. The purpose of economic assistance above all would be 'to secure the good will and co-operation. . . . in our strategic and political aims', and 'to raise the standards of living in smaller countries, and [to] build up centres of prosperity as a bulwark against Communism'.[16] Economic aid was a means of sustaining British power. In Bevin's words to his advisers in December 1949, it was 'our one chance'. Yet any fair-minded reading of the evidence would reveal that more than self-interest was at stake. The civil servants of the Labour government, and above all Bevin himself, wished to see living standards raised in

[14] Memorandum by P. J. H. Stent, 21 Nov. 1949, FO 371/76046/F18509.
[15] Ibid.
[16] Ibid.

Africa, the Middle East, and Asia, and they believed it to be an ethical obligation for the richer nations to help the poorer ones. Technology might help to bridge the gap. Bevin was fascinated, for example, with the possibility of a breakthrough in electrification, which he thought might provide the jolt necessary for economic progress: 'the provision of such basic requirements as electricity', he told his advisers on the eve of the Columbo Conference, 'might quickly have an effect on the character of the people. He said there was evidence that this had occurred even in the most backward areas of the U.S.S.R'.[17]

The year 1949 was a turning point in the history of British economic aid to the Middle East not only because of the resolution of the Palestine problem, which made economic projects more feasible, but also because it had taken nearly four years to complete the economic surveys or 'blue prints' necessary to persuade the Arab governments to put plans into action. By then the United States, the International Bank, and the United Nations agencies had also begun to sponsor projects in the Middle East and elsewhere that the British alone could not have initiated. In other words the British sought the maintenance of their world position not merely through the Colonial Development and Welfare Act and the Colombo Plan, but also through international consortia. It was a prodigious effort that was sustained in the face of economic adversity. In 1949, at the time of devaluation, the Labour government had little over two years to run. Ministers of course did not know that their accomplishments in economic assistance would be associated with these two critical years. They believed that they were only getting under way. Yet ultimately it was the impact of economic aid in the actual region or country, not the debates in Whitehall or Parliament, by which the Labour government would be remembered. It is therefore useful briefly to survey the area as it was seen by the British themselves, at about the mid-way point of the two years, before passing on to more specific issues of economic growth and political controversy in Israel and the different Arab countries.

According to one of the principal inventories, circulated by Bevin to the Cabinet in October 1950, 'considerable progress' had been made. British experts, technicians, and teachers employed by the Middle Eastern governments now numbered over 500. In Egypt the planning for the Aswan hydro-electrical project was well advanced. Its costs was estimated at £10 million. In addition there were extensive irrigation projects being financed by the Egyptian government. In Iraq a 'Central Development Board' had been created. The

---

[17] Minutes of F. O. meeting, 20 Dec. 1949, FO 371/75092/E15181.

International Bank was sponsoring a flood-control project at the cost of $13 million, and another loan of $3 million, partly underwritten by the British, was helping to subsidize railway development. These of course were but examples of some of the more significant projects. Syria, Lebanon, and Jordan were sadder stories. 'Unfortunately, owing to shortage of funds and heavy calls for direct [refugee] relief, investment . . . has been much less than hoped.' There were plans for road construction, afforestation, irrigation, and housing projects— especially in Jordan, where the British acknowledged 'special interest and responsibilities'.[18] But all in all the 'considerable success' did not amount to much. Explanations of the shortages of funds—above all because of the dollar balances—were cold comfort. One could not have read the report without a sense of disappointment. Defeated expectation is a theme that runs through the 1945–51 files. 'I am disappointed', Bevin had scrawled on one of the first inventories submitted in January 1946.[19] 'In all this I am not sure that we are thinking on a big enough scale', Michael Wright had noted at the time of the great push in early 1949, and he continued with a comment that gives insight into the nature of the British achievement: 'One of the difficulties is that the obstacles to progress are not only financial.'[20] The problem was also one of recruitment, which met with some success. The 500 British experts in the field by late 1950 represented a breakthrough, perhaps small in scale but important in commitment. Elizabeth Monroe much later commented in a postscript to *Britain's Moment in the Middle East*: 'Yet Englishmen did good jobs in the fields at which they excel—on development, finance, dams, agriculture, drainage and other practical pursuits.'[21] The greatest achievement of the Labour government in the realm of economic development was the fielding of the 500 men.

Israeli 'Viability'

It is possible to argue that the solution of a binational state in Palestine, honourable in inspiration, would never have worked because the Jews and the Arabs were at different stages of economic development. All contemporary accounts agreed on the determination of the Jews to make the new state an economic as well as a

[18] Memorandum by T. E. Evans (head of the Middle East Secretariat), 31 Oct. 1950, CP (50), 264, CAB 129/43.

[19] Minute by Bevin on memorandum by Denis Greenhill, 15 Jan. 1946, FO 371/52318 (a key file on economic development).

[20] Minute by Wright, 29 Jan. 1949, FO 371/75083/E3030.

[21] Elizabeth Monroe, *Britain's Moment in the Middle East* (Baltimore, 1981 edn.), p. 219.

political success along western lines. For example, Richard Crossman, who visited Israel during the 1948–9 war, described how the Israeli government despite the military struggle had already launched housing projects and electrification schemes. There were projects for soil erosion and conservation as well as the irrigation of the desert. The buses ran. The postal, telephone, and other public utilities functioned. He reported from Tel Aviv to the *New Statesman*: 'With the removal of the Police State, into which the Mandate had degenerated, the nation has emerged equipped with civil and military administration; sea, road, and rail transport, and full-scale social services—the whole equipment of a Western European Socialist State.'[22] Crossman of course was enthusiastically pro-Zionist as well as intrigued with the experiment of Jewish socialism, but even the critics of the new state admitted that, in contrast with the Arabs, the Jews possessed the 'dynamism' that was essential to economic growth. The question was whether the Israeli state, small in size and dependent on foreign economic assistance, would prove to be 'viable'.

Sir John Troutbeck, for one, believed that the virtues of effervescence and discipline would not be sufficient. In a despatch that the Foreign Office considered to be so important that it was circulated to all Middle East posts and the Embassy in Washington, he wrote that 'dynamism, like patriotism, is not enough'. He saw the point about the two contrasting levels of economic development, and he drew a dire conclusion:

A country restricted within narrow territorial limits, with a population bursting with vitality, and surrounded by people of a medieval outlook, swollen also by immigrants for whom it has no room, is bound in any case to covet its neighbours' lands. The urge for more 'lebensraum' will be increased. . . .[23]

Was there, he asked, to be a 'manifest destiny' at Arab expense? Troutbeck's economic analysis is of interest among other reasons because he succeeded in giving it both an anti-Jewish and anti-American twist:

There may be some . . . Americans who would hope that with so greatly extended a promised land some of the Jews in the United States might be tempted to immigrate. But it seems doubtful if even the Americans are sufficiently dynamic for so clear-cut and drastic a solution. All one can predict is that the Israelis will be quickly aware of the anxiety of the United States Government to keep them within the Western fold and will not miss the opportunities for blackmail which this will afford them both in the financial and territorial spheres.[24]

[22] *New Statesman*, 15 Jan. 1949.
[23] Troutbeck to Bevin, Secret, 24 Jan. 1949, FO 371/75054/E3518.
[24] Ibid.

He had raised two vital questions on which the Foreign Office now solicited advice from the representatives in the Middle East and Washington. The first was the prospect of Israel as a viable state. The second, upon which the first seemed to depend, was the possibility of continued American economic assistance. Troutbeck in short doubted whether the United States would be prepared 'to maintain Israel as a more or less permanent pensioner' and that the Jewish state would therefore either collapse or be forced to expand.

The responses are historically interesting in the extreme, not only because of the issues at stake but also because of the contemporary British assumptions about economic development and political stability. According to Sir Hugh Dow in Jerusalem: 'It seems to me that excessive immigration is a greater danger to the viability of the Jewish State than the lack of outside financial backing, and would become likely to lead to economic collapse.'[25] The analysis by W. E. Houstoun-Boswall at Beirut was particularly outspoken and summarized many of the currents of thought about 'viability':

That Israel has given proof of an at least superficial dynamism and vigour cannot be denied. It should not be forgotten, however, that . . . the viability of Israel is a matter of considerable doubt. The poorness of its soil, its lack of raw materials and the high wages obtaining there make it uncertain whether Israel can ever hold its own as an industrial or agricultural country on purely economic grounds. . . .

Even in the commercial and financial fields it remains to be seen whether the Jews can compete with the Levantine merchants and bankers of, for example, Beirut. It may be that Israel will be able to carry on as a subsidised State. How long Jewry will go on paying the subsidies as an act of charity cannot be foreseen and whether it will be worth while for the United States Government to continue to do so . . . is also doubtful.[26]

On the question of American economic sponsoring of Israel, the Foreign Office of course listened especially to the advice of the Ambassador in Washington, Sir Oliver Franks.

Franks had the reputation, which his later career confirmed, of a shrewd political observer. Dean Acheson in his memoirs referred to his 'calm good judgment'.[27] Franks did not uncritically accept generalizations about Zionist expansion or American policy towards Israel. He did not believe that the pro-Jewish attitude on the part of the American people, which had characterized the public mood at the time of the creation of the Jewish state, would continue. In view of the credibility of Franks's political reporting, the reasons he

---

[25] Dow to Bevin, Secret, 8 Feb. 1949, FO 371/75054/E2478.

[26] Houstoun-Boswall to Bevin, Secret, 16 Feb. 1949, FO 371/75054/E2479.

[27] Acheson, *Present at the Creation*, p. 323.

gave for the more guarded response should be taken as a considered judgement:

> Anti-Semitism is strong in this country and it seems to be increasing. It is certainly fairly prevalent in Congress. Many Americans are irritated by the stridency of Zionist propaganda and this irritation might well come into the open as an influence on American policy if the policy of the State of Israel appeared to be leading to international difficulties or to constitute a clear threat to United States strategic or economic interests in the Middle East.[28]

Franks in other words was more optimistic than Troutbeck about American restraints on Zionist expansion. The reaction of the President at the time of the Israeli incursion across the Egyptian frontier—when the Israeli representative in Washington had described Truman as having an 'uneasy and sensitive state of mind' in January 1949—was a potent indication.[29] 'I do not believe', Franks wrote, 'that, once the frontiers of Israel had been established, the United States Government would readily . . . support further Israeli expansion at Arab expense.'[30] Franks thus disposed of the argument that the Americans would acquiesce in unlimited Israeli aggrandizement, at least beyond the frontiers of Palestine. Whether the lack of opportunities for territorial expansion would bring about the collapse of the Israeli state, as Troutbeck suggested, only time could tell, but Franks believed that 'viability' had more to do with the question of economic assistance and the problem of immigration.

Franks emphasized the average age and state of health of the immigrants, and he predicted that few would come from the United States. On the basis of information he was receiving indirectly from the American mission in Tel Aviv, he wrote that 'the proportion of young people is high and with the advantage of a good medical service, the birth rate also is likely to be high'. Franks granted that successive generations of virile Israelis might make more plausible the theory of the necessity of an expansionist state, but in the short term he believed that the critical factor in 'viability' was economic assistance rather than immigration. Writing from the American perspective, he anticipated that private funding of the Israeli state would diminish, and he admitted that it was impossible to predict over a period of years the level of official aid. He endorsed the belief that 'once the drama is taken out of the Palestine question, contributions from American Jewry will fall off'.[31] On the other hand, he

---

[28] Franks to Bevin, Top Secret, 17 Feb. 1949, FO 371/75054/E2480.
[29] Elath to Shertok, 5 Jan. 1949, ISA 130.09/2308/8.
[30] Franks to Bevin, 17 Feb. 1949, FO 371/75054/E2480.
[31] Ibid.

emphasized the importance of the amount of economic aid given by the American government during the first year of Israel's existence —$100 million.

The point of importance about the $100 million for the present discussion is that, to the British, it was a staggering amount. It was no less than all of the British economic assistance throughout the entire world.[32] The Colonial Development and Welfare Act of 1945 provided only £120 million for the ten-year period 1945–56, and the actual amount expended fell far short of expectations. There were of course other forms of British economic assistance, but the point here is one of scale in regard to Israel. It is now known that American aid in substantial amounts did continue, and continues today. One basic apprehension of the British in 1949 thus proved to be unfounded, at least in the sense that the new state would not prove to be viable because of lack of economic assistance.

As in the question of general aid to the region of the Middle East, it is the economic development in Israel rather than contemporary controversy in London that is ultimately important. To examine further the question of Israeli 'viability' in the two years 1949–51, a mid-way point, as in the previous section, will be chosen in order to establish the actual trends and dominating circumstances. The conclusions which the British drew from them are a matter perhaps of secondary importance but they are nevertheless of major relevance for the themes of this book. In both instances, factual and interpretative, the annual survey for the year 1950 prepared by the British mission in Tel Aviv provides an illuminating comment. A word needs to be said about the British annual surveys in order to understand the significance of this one. They were usually prepared by one member of the legation or embassy (in this instance by J. E. Chadwick, who had previously worked in the Eastern Department of the Foreign Office), but they nevertheless represented a collective estimate. Sometimes the report would be prefaced by a despatch written by the head of the mission in order to provide an additional conclusion or interpretation. In this case, as will be seen, the conclusion written by the Minister, Sir Knox Helm, was of exceptional interest. The annual reports were by no means perfunctory exercises. As before and during the war, some of the best British political and economic reporting found expression in these yearly estimates. In this one the point of convergence between

[32] This was the frequent comparison in 1949. For British economic development see D. J. Morgan, *The Official History of Colonial Development* (4 vols., London, 1980). This is the essential work on the subject, but see D. K. Fieldhouse's critical essay in the *English Historical Review*, XCVII (Apr. 1982).

political and economic analysis could be summed up in one word: immigration.

Conditions favourable to economic growth are usually determined by political circumstances, and in June 1950 the outbreak of the Korean war proved to be, in the words of the annual report, 'a landmark in Israel's domestic affairs'. The Israeli government endorsed the United Nations condemnation of North Korean aggression. Israel moved into alignment with the western powers in the ideological struggle against the Soviet Union. Previously the Israelis had pursued a course of 'non-identification' or 'independent judgement'. The annual report emphasized this point in part because it seemed to provide an answer to the question of Communism in Israel that had so preoccupied British observers. In 1950:

> The Israel Government endured stoically the wintry attitude of the Soviet Union, remembering always Russian help in the early days of Israel's existence and intent on doing nothing which might effectively close the Iron Curtain to the exit of Jews to Israel; but at the same time they took measures to restrict Communist activities based on Israel.[33]

The Israelis did not wish to nullify the possibility of further immigration from eastern Europe, but they had proved to be fiercely independent in managing the affairs of their own socialist state. The honeymoon with the Soviet Union had long been over.[34] The Korean war, according to the British interpretation, stimulated the Israelis into a recognition 'that their future survival was bound up with the West'.[35]

The transition in Israeli foreign affairs occurred in what might be called the era of heroic leadership of David Ben-Gurion. It is important to stress this point because the political stability of the Ben-Gurion regime greatly helped the Israelis to cope with their economic problems. There were many critics of Ben-Gurion, then and later, but in 1949–51 the British concluded that 'all persons of moderate views were ready to recognize the advantages of his strong rule'.[36] Ben-Gurion endorsed certain fundamentals of Israeli socialism that are important for the present discussion. These included the continuation of Jewish mass immigration, and the creation of full employment by the import of capital in order to finance the

---

[33] 'Israel: Annual Review for 1950', 24 Jan. 1951, FO 371/91705.

[34] See Arnold Krammer, *The Forgotten Friendship* (Urbana, 1974).

[35] Annual Review for 1950.

[36] The annual review also commented: 'The Israeli Government . . . were determined to run their Socialist economic policy without interference from abroad. Mr. Ben Gurion, indeed, would ill brook criticism from any source. As the year went on, his demeanour became more and more autocratic . . . some were disturbed by his apparent reliance on youthful advisers with more energy than judgement.'

immigrants' agricultural and other development projects. In this period the momentum in the building of Israeli industries and the drive for agricultural development went hand in hand with finding jobs for the masses of new immigrants. In 1950 alone there were 170,000 immigrants. In the 1949–51 period the Jewish population passed the one million mark, which must have astonished British observers, including Churchill, who believed that Palestine had only a severely limited 'economic absorptive capacity'.[37] But, to keep the problem in perspective, the total population of the new Jewish state in 1950 was only, in the words of the annual review, 'still less than half the Jewish population of New York City'.[38]

Virtually no controversy existed about continuing mass immigration. 'This was regarded by Government spokesmen both a sacred duty to oppressed co-religionists and as a means of strengthening the security of Israel.' The 170,000 immigrants in 1950 included 40,000 Yemeni Jews who were airlifted from Aden to the Israeli airfield at Lydda. 'The adjustment of these backward peoples to the pushful modernity of the new surroundings was tackled with great enthusiasm.' The accommodation of western Jews to oriental Jews, and vice versa, at this time generally was viewed with optimism. According to the annual review, one could not but admire the stamina and the perseverance of the new immigrants as they prepared inhospitable land for cultivation, endured hardships of inadequate housing, and suffered acute shortages of consumer goods. Limitation of immigration was 'politically unthinkable: the Jews fought the mandatory Government on this issue too long'. The expenses incurred in financing immigration and settlement, along with the fiscal burdens of defence, would have been impossible to manage had it not been for American economic assistance. With it, as the developments of 1949–51 proved, the new state would not disintegrate. According to a Foreign Office assessment made at the time of the fall of the Labour government in October 1951 about the future of Israel, 'the determination and discipline of her people, and the skill displayed by her rulers suggest . . . that she will somehow avoid collapse'.[39] Israel in short was a 'viable' state.

One cannot leave the 1950 estimate of Israeli affairs without noting

---

[37] Richard Crossman, in *A Nation Reborn* (London, 1960), pp. 99–101, almost gleefully emphasized this point, and his discussion of the early Israeli *Wirtschaftswunder* repays reading, e.g.: 'The only European state created under almost as unfavourable circumstances as Israel is Western Germany.'

[38] The population of New York City in 1950 was 7,891,957. Of that figure approximately 2,000,000 were Jews. The Jewish population of Israel in 1950 was about 1,000,000 (out of a total population of 1,170,000).

[39] Memorandum by G. Furlonge, 29 Oct. 1951, FO 371/91200.

the general conclusion of the Minister, Sir Knox Helm. It was by no means favourable, either in its assessment of the Israeli national character or in its outlook for the future:

> Israel. . . . Her greatest disability remains the more disagreeable features of the Jewish character, with an inability to realise that the obtaining of the last farthing does not necessarily mean the best bargain, that in an imperfect world unrelieved seriousness is not a virtue and, perhaps above all, that strength is not always best displayed through force.[40]

As if British optimism sprang eternal, Helm could not resist the further thought that 'even in these directions . . . there are grounds for hope'.

The Arab States

The question of 'viability' in 1949–51 arose in Syria, Iraq, and Jordan in both a political and in an economic sense, but it was the political part of the equation of stability that gave the region a sense of continuing crisis. It would be possible, as in the case of Israel, to devote detailed attention to particular problems of economic development. In Jordan for example the question of immigration also loomed large but for a different reason. One-third of the population now consisted of destitute refugees. In Iraq the 1949–51 era was critical for the development schemes for irrigation and flood control. It should be noted that in this period Nuri Pasha convinced the British that he was personally committed to the long-range projects of economic development that played such an important part in the country's history in the 1950s. Nevertheless, with the major exception of Iran and Egypt (which will also be discussed in later chapters) the last two years of the British Labour government were not marked with noteworthy progress in economic affairs in the Middle East. The impediment to development was summed up in a meeting in 1950: 'that obstacle was the provision of capital'.[41] The key to the question of 'viability' lay in the political realm, with two events at the beginning and towards the end of the 1949–51 period. In March 1949 Colonel Husni al-Zaim overthrew the civilian government in Damascus, the first of the post-Second World War military *coups d'état* in the Middle East. In July 1951 King Abdullah was assassinated, an event that shook one of the pillars of British rule.

As background to a discussion of political viability, it is useful to note the power of British stereotyped thought that prevailed just as much in the case of the Arabs as with the Jews. As has been seen in

[40] Helm's covering dispatch dated 17 Jan. 1951.
[41] Minutes of a meeting of 21 Sept. 1950, FO 371/81922.

the example of Sir Knox Helm and his assessment of the Jewish 'national character', the intellectual history of the British in the Middle East had a certain continuity. For the Arabs it is illuminating to dwell briefly on the ideas of the commander of the Arab Legion. Glubb was a man of straightforward and honest views. His assumptions about the Arabs are candidly revealing. He believed first and foremost that the grand design of Egyptian policy was to prevent the co-operation or union of the other Arab states so that Egypt might remain the leader of the Arab world. '"Divide and rule" summarizes her policy', he wrote. Here are his ideas about the Iraqis and Syrians as expressed in a top secret assessment of October 1949:

The Iraqis and the Syrians are very different people. The Iraqis are crude, coarse and over-bearing but more virile than the Syrians, who are on the other hand more cultured, suave and intellectual. Iraq has got away with a flying start by having a much better army, and thus is in a position to dominate the Syrians by force if 'union' were to take place. With ever increasing oil royalties, Iraq will become also far the wealthier of the two but it is unlikely that the Syrians would be contented with such a regime for long, though the wealthier and more virile Iraqis might continue to suppress them successfully.[42]

The question of 'union' to which he referred had been raised by the *coup d'état* in Damascus, which opened once again the issue of 'Greater Syria'.

Glubb believed that Syria was 'ripe for disintegration'. In one of his more exuberant moods (Sir Alex Kirkbride once noted that Glubb, like the Arabs, crested on waves of enthusiasm and defeatism), Glubb suggested the following as a step forward in the political problems of the Middle East:

A three-cornered loosely-knit federation of Iraq, Syria and Jordan would be a cautious step in a possibly beneficial direction, and quite within the realm of practical politics. Put another way, it might be called a little Arab League, with the sinister and selfish influence of Egypt excluded. The weakest aspect of such a solution is the internal chaos in Syria. . . .[43]

He identified the central problem in the Middle East at that time as the political and military crisis in Syria. 'The most burning question in the Arab countries today', he wrote, 'is that of the future of Syria.'

There are two points of general interest about the Syrian crisis of 1949. The first is that Bevin himself commented that Zaim's *coup d'état* merited attention because, as he rightly surmised, it might mark the beginning of a series of military governments in the Middle East. 'When a new type of regime emerged', he told the Foreign

[42] Memorandum by Glubb, Top Secret, 25 Oct. 1949, FO 371/75279.
[43] Ibid.

Office conference in July, 'we should decide our attitude and what we could do to help if we thought it was progressing along the right lines.' He emphasized that much could be done 'by suggestion'. In principle he did not oppose military governments. His socialist instinct led him to place more importance on the way governments were organized and the specific means of raising standards of living rather than on personalities or even political doctrine. 'The case of Syria', he continued, 'was particularly interesting as we might be faced with changes of regimes in other Arab countries.'[44]

The second reason why the crisis of 1949 is of absorbing interest is that the archives reveal the workings of the official mind in regard to Musa Alami. It has long been a matter of historical curiosity how the Foreign Office responded to his celebrated essay 'The Lesson of Palestine'.[45] Musa Alami was one of the powerful and respected spokesmen of the Palestinian Arab cause. A Foreign Office minute described him as 'the intellectual leader of the younger Arabs'.[46] He believed that the humiliating and demoralizing defeat made the goal of Arab unity not only desirable but imperative. He espoused the union of Syria, Jordan, and Iraq as the only answer to militant Zionism. This solution threw the Middle East experts of the Foreign Office into a dilemma that was at once painful and irresolvable. Any step that the British made either to encourage or discourage Arab unity among some Arab states would have unpalatable consequences in one or several of the others. In the end the Foreign Office had to settle for a formula 'that we do not support, and equally do not oppose, any spontaneous movement for unity'—hardly a reassurance that the British supported the Arab cause.[47]

It might be possible to argue that military dictatorship is an inevitable stage of Middle Eastern social and economic development, but in 1949 the British regarded it more as the result of the defeat in Palestine. The army became the catalyst of Syrian discontent. Colonel Zaim, the Chief of Staff, represented the 'soldier-reformer' at odds not only with the handling of the war in Palestine but also with the regime of Shukri al-Quwatli. It will be recalled from an earlier chapter that Quwatli championed the cause of independence against the French and the British in 1945. Since that time his

---

[44] Conference minutes, 21 July 1949, FO 371/75072.

[45] The essay was published in Arabic in March 1949 and summarized as 'The Lesson of Palestine', *Middle East Journal*, 3, 4 (October 1949).

[46] Minute by Lance Thirkell, 22 Oct. 1949, FO 371/75553/E12510.

[47] Minute by J. E. Chadwick, 19 Oct. 1949, FO 371/75553. The Eastern Department concluded in rather remorseful vein that the Arab 'intellectuals' were not helpful in resolving these dilemmas. 'The Department have great respect for Mousa Alami's undoubted position', wrote Lance Thirkell, but '. . . they have considerably less for Mousa Alami as a practical politician.' Minute by Thirkell, 22 Oct. 1949, FO 371/75553/E12510.

reputation as a statesman had diminished. His regime, in British eyes at least, had proved to be as corrupt and inefficient as Sir Terence Shone had anticipated. Nevertheless Quwatli cast a long shadow. 'You have taken over from Quwatli a wholly independent Syria', the Egyptian press warned Zaim, and he was further enjoined by the Egyptians to 'watch over that independence'.[48] The admonition was calculated to appeal to Zaim's sense of patriotism, which is the key to his moment in Syrian history.

Zaim's regime lasted for only four and a half months, but it had broad significance that the leaders of the other Arab states grasped just as keenly as the British. Zaim attempted to model himself on the image of Mustafa Kemal. The Ataturk tradition of modern Turkey would now be grafted onto Syria. 'By removing the corrupt and inefficient personal régime of ex-President Quwatly', wrote Lance Thirkell of the Eastern Department, Zaim 'opened up the way' for economic reform and social justice.[49] The British were not unduly distressed at the idea of military dictatorship in the Middle East. They held Syrian politicians in such low esteem that almost any type of regime short of the extreme anti-British right or left might be an improvement, especially if it could instil a sense of discipline necessary for economic and social progress. The head of the Eastern Department, Bernard Burrows, wrote:

> The regime is undemocratic—but so was that of Mustafa Kemal, on whom Colonel Zaim seems inclined to model himself, and that regime did incalculable good to Turkey.
>
> It has seemed clear for a long time that the present so called democratic regimes in most of the Arab States are not only not true democracies but are quite incapable of carrying out the necessary measures of social reform and economic development.[50]

During the brief period of Zaim's seizure of power he did restore the morale of the army. He also enacted by decree much useful social and economic legislation that had been shelved by his predecessors. He made improvements in the civil, criminal, and commercial codes. He removed deadwood from the civil service. He ratified agreements for the oil pipeline (TAPLINE) to pass through Syria. He imposed a control on food prices. Bakers who sold inferior bread were flogged in front of their shops. Literate women were given the right to vote. Like other dictators he seemed at first to represent new and vital forces of a society that had been dominated by a wealthy élite with

---

[48] Quoted in Patrick Seale, *The Struggle for Syria* (London, 1965), p. 52. Chap 4–6 of this work are an indispensable guide for Syrian political developments in the late 1940s and early 1950s.

[49] Minute by Thirkell, 19 Jan. 1950, FO 371/82782/E1011.

[50] Minute by Burrows, 14 Apr. 1949, FO 371/75534/E5062.

little sense of social conscience. Though in retrospect Zaim did not have a clearly defined programme of political and economic reform, his regime at the time seemed to represent a 'decisive new start in national life'.[51]

As if heralding things to come, Zaim's regime began with motor-cycle escorts and police sirens, and it ended with his execution. At the close of Zaim's first month, the British Minister in Damascus, P. M. Broadmead, expressed apprehension that the new 'man of the people' might be suffering delusions of grandeur:

> Colonel Zaim has been described . . . as a military adventurer, untrustworthy, a would-be Napoleon of the Middle East. There may be some truth in this: sight of his high-speed journeys through the town in the ex-President's car preceded by motor-cyclists with American police sirens and followed by a jeep carrying a tommy-gun bodyguard lends colour to this view.[52]

Nevertheless Broadmead and others still hoped that Zaim genuinely would work for social justice even though he might not prove capable of coherent economic reform. Broadmead wrote at the end of the second month:

> Colonel Zaim is, and indeed rather boasts of being, a man of the people. He is proud of being a poor man and he openly despises the politician who uses his position to make money: that is one of his main grievances against the old regime. . . . He is not an ascetic and is, I think, essentially a human man, wishing for the happiness of his fellow countrymen.[53]

Zaim stirred sympathy because he stood in protest, in a human and identifiable way, against the rich and corrupt. The significance of his short-lived regime is that it raised broad political hopes. In Broadmead's words, 'one is permitted to ask the question whether Colonel Zaim's regime is not the long-expected entry of the Arab middle-class into effective political life'.[54] Zaim's larger aspirations remained unfulfilled, but his motivation was not dissimilar from that of other military revolutionaries in the Middle East.

There were widespread suspicions throughout the Arab world that the British had put Zaim into power in order to have a more pliable regime in Damascus. In fact they had nothing to do with the *coup d'état* and had little subsequent influence over Zaim. Indeed their only indication that the putsch was in the making had come from one man, V. D. O'Harmar, the military attaché in Damascus. O'Harmar also gave the clearest warning that the ending of Zaim's regime would be abrupt and violent. Zaim made the mistake of alienating his fellow

---

[51] Alford Carleton, 'The Syrian Coups d'État of 1949', *Middle East Journal*, 4, 1 (1950), p. 5; and Seale, *Struggle for Syria*, chap. 7, which discusses these points at length.

[52] Broadmead to Bevin, Confidential, 25 Apr. 1949, FO 371/75535/E5336.

[53] Broadmead to Bevin, Confidential, 23 May 1949, FO 371/75536/E6555.

[54] Ibid.

army officers as well as the politicians. O'Harmar prognosticated in May 1949 that the reasons for Zaim's eventual fall would include:

> The economic distress of the country. The Arab mind seems incapable of realising that improvements are not made in a day. . . .
> Resentment at the many arrests that have been made, most of them without any apparent cause.
> The haughtiness of the Army. The Army has been so spoilt in the last six weeks with its long lists of promotions and increased allowances, that officers and other ranks are tending to treat civilians rather high-handedly.
> Husni Zaim's personal immorality. The fact that he has long had homosexual habits is widely known and, of course, used to turn public opinion against him.[55]

The nationalist army officers developed a personal revulsion against Zaim as well as a conviction that he had betrayed the reformist goals of his own revolution. He was tried and shot on the spot on the 14th of August 1949. So ended the first postwar military dictatorship in the Middle East.

It is beyond the present discussion to follow in detail the coup that deposed Zaim and the counter-coup in December, but it is important to establish the connection between the internal political situation in Syria and the project of 'Greater Syria' which so pre-occupied the British.[56] In the putsch against Zaim there is evidence of Iraqi complicity but no direct British involvement.[57] Nuri not only despised Zaim but also believed that Syria was in the process of becoming an Egyptian satellite. Here he misjudged Zaim's deter-mination to maintain the independence of Syria, though it is true that Egypt and Syria drew together. Zaim was candid in expressing his own fears of Iraqi ambition. 'As for Iraq', he stated in July, 'I am and shall remain categorically opposed to the establishment of a Greater Syria', in other words, union with Iraq. 'As for Jordan, which is and remains a Syrian province', he said on another occasion, 'she will sooner or later rejoin the mother country.'[58] But he denounced Abdullah's 'aggressiveness' and made it clear that 'Greater Syria' would not be realized in any form other than the eventual absorption by Syria of Jordan—presumably after Abdullah's demise. 'The Lords of Baghdad and Amman believed that I was about to

---

[55] O'Harmar to Lt. Col. W. W. Shaw (War Office), 16 May 1949, FO 371/75536/E6614/G.
[56] See Seale, *Struggle for Syria*, for a full discussion.
[57] See e.g. minute by J. E. Chadwick, 18 Aug. 1949, FO 371/75539/E10226: 'Nuri Pasha has admitted that he had foreknowledge that this coup was intended and even provided some fairly harmless facilities for it. It is possible, though not by any means certain, that King Abdullah and the Prime Minister of the Lebanon were also in the know. All of them at any rate must be relieved at the disappearance of Zaim from the scene.'
[58] Seale, *Struggle for Syria*, pp. 61 and 57.

offer them the crown of Syria on a silver platter', Zaim stated with finality, 'but they were disappointed.'[59]

The Foreign Office had not anticipated Zaim's *coup d'état*, but there was a remarkable grasp of the likelihood of the fate of the 'Greater Syria' project. In January 1949—three months before Zaim's seizure of power—M. T. Walker of the Eastern Department had written that the rulers of Syria would never subject themselves to the overlordship of a Hashemite king. They might favour closer military co-operation with the neighbouring Arab states in order to bolster their own prestige and security; but it was more probable that they would look towards Egypt and to Ibn Saud, as the rival of the Hashemites, rather than to Iraq or Jordan. According to Walker there were geographical and linguistic as well as economic and political patterns that would shape the outcome of the 'Greater Syria' question:

> There was always a complete separation between the two countries [Syria and Iraq] in Turkish days and the Turkish administrative divisions were based on several hundred years experience of geographical influences in that part of the world; the language spoken differs considerably. . . .
> Although the 500 miles of desert separating the two countries can now be crossed in a night by bus or a few hours by air, commercial intercourse is still comparatively slow and expensive; finally Baghdad and Damascus are historically rivals, and local interests are likely to continue this rivalry: it is just conceivable that a Hashemite King might sit on the throne of Syria but I am sure he would not also reign in Baghdad.[60]

Syrian anxiety about Hashemite domination proved to be even greater than Walker had apprehended. 'Greater Syria' in the form of union between Syria or Iraq or Syria and Jordan might have made better sense for the 'viability' of these countries, but no amount of rational argument at this time could shake the Syrians, Quwatli, Zaim, or their immediate successors, from the tradition of complete independence. Nevertheless the trend was clear. According to the British annual review for 1949, 'British stock tended to fall thanks to Zaim's loathing of the Hashimites, in particular Iraq'. As if noting an ominous development, the review observed that 'it was the anti-Hashimite *bloc* of Egypt and Saudi Arabia which won Syria's favour during Zaim's régime'.[61]

The general assessments of the complicated events of 1949 are helpful in understanding the problems of economic viability and political stability. Looking back at this turbulent period, Geoffrey

[59] Seale, *Struggle for Syria*, p. 56.
[60] Minute by Walker, *c*.30 Jan. 1949, FO 371/75077/E1152.
[61] Annual Review for 1949, FO 371/82782.

Furlonge, the new head of the Eastern Department who succeeded Bernard Burrows, reflected in 1950 that neither political instability nor chronic economic crisis had brought about the collapse of the Syrian state. As Terence Shone had predicted in 1945, the Syrian state would be able to 'rub along' with deplorably low administrative and political standards, and, barring a take-over by another Arab state, the Syrian government would probably continue to exist. One could not expect much of a state that had 'prematurely' achieved independence. According to Furlonge, pursuing the same line of thought five years later, the weakness of Syria 'lies in the notorious instability and fickleness of the population, and the absence of any outstanding statesmen'. There was no 'dominant power' in Syria, either internal or external. The French were hated as much as ever. 'We are held back by our pledge not to supplant France', Furlonge recorded.[62] This was a pledge Bevin had renewed to the French Foreign Minister, Robert Schuman, at the time of Zaim's *coup d'état*. 'I agreed with Schuman', Bevin had noted in an extremely important minute, '. . . that I had no intention of upsetting the status quo: that is Greater Syria was not being promoted by us. I have always argued this was a matter for the Arabs.'[63] This was a premiss of Bevin's Middle Eastern policy. Further European intervention in Syria would bring about further political instability, not only in Syria itself but throughout the region. So also would intervention by Iraq. As Furlonge later summed up the problem, an Iraqi bid for Syria would 'merely provoke counter-intervention by the Saudis or Egyptians which will increase the political chaos in Syria'.[64] As in 1945 the British preferred to live with 'chaos in Syria' even if it meant accepting an unsatisfactory status quo.

Nevertheless the British did not permanently rule out the possibility of 'Greater Syria'. Eventually they hoped to see a union between Syria and Iraq, or Syria and Jordan, and perhaps all three. Bevin approved a formula that was elaborately devised by Bernard Burrows, Michael Wright, and the new Permanent Under-Secretary, Sir William Strang. The British would not object to 'Greater Syria' provided it was not brought about by force. 'Greater Syria' would have to develop in Wright's words, 'naturally and organically, and without violent and abrupt action which might result in disorder or fighting'.[65] The Arabs, as Bevin had indicated, would have to devise their own solution. There was a negative corollary to this proposition.

[62] Minute by Furlonge, 14 June 1950, FO 371/82792/EY1025/2.
[63] Minute by Bevin, 15 Apr. 1949, FO 371/75534/E5062.
[64] Minute by Furlonge, 4 Dec. 1951, FO 371/91843/EY1015/52.
[65] See minute by Wright, 15 Apr. 1949, FO 371/75534/E5062.

Bevin stated it explicitly in one of his handwritten minutes, which, as usual, had to be deciphered for general consumption. It is of great interest because it indicates the persistence with which he adhered to one of the fundamentals of his Middle Eastern policy. As has been shown in earlier chapters, Bevin pursued a non-interventionist course. In the case of Syria, giving point to his general principle, he scrawled, 'We must not interfere in Syrian affairs.'[66]

Abdullah's Assassination

King Abdullah's lifelong amibition was to reign in Damascus. His murder on the 20th of July 1951 marked the close of one chapter of Hashemite ambition and with it the hopes for a 'Greater Syria'. It also raised in acute form the question of political viability. Jordan was the most artificial of the post-First World War experiments in state-building. As has been noted, Colonel Zaim and his colleagues continued to regard Jordan as a province of Syria. Jordan was totally dependent on the British in its economy and only to a lesser extent in its military and political structure. Abdullah had given the state a certain political stability, which, after the absorption of the west bank in 1949, seemed to be increasingly fragile. This was not a case, as in Syria, in which a state might continue to exist regardless of administrative incompetence or near bankruptcy. This was the case in which, after Abdullah's death, the state appeared to be on the verge of collapse. The central unifying force had vanished in an instant.

Abdullah died at the barrel of a British service revolver fired by an apprentice tailor. The assassin was shot instantly by the King's body-guard at the site of the murder in front of a mosque. Four accomplices were arrested, tried, and publicly executed. They were associated with the Muslim Brethren. 'Few of us in Amman did not believe that the Egyptian authorities were the real culprits in the crime', Sir Alec Kirkbride wrote later.[67] British views about the Muslim Brethren will be discussed later in the last chapter on Egypt. Here the issue is the British response to the assassination. The magnitude of the crisis can hardly be exaggerated. Abdullah had been Britain's most loyal ally in the Middle East. His son, Talal; was widely

[66] Minute by Bevin on F. O. to HM Ambassador in Paris, No. 1815, Secret, 17 June 1949, FO 371/75551. While the British thus pursued the policy of non-intervention, the period marked the beginning of CIA involvement in Syrian affairs. See in general Wilbur Crane Eveland, *Ropes of Sand: America's Failure in the Middle East* (New York, 1980), which is the most reliable (and certainly the most entertaining) of the CIA exposés.

[67] Sir Alec Kirkbride, *From the Wings: Amman Memoirs 1947-1951* (London, 1976), p. 138.

regarded as unbalanced and unfit for the succession. Support of Haj Amin, the Mufti, was substantial, especially among the refugees who believed Abdullah guilty of surrendering their patrimony to the Jews.

At the time of Abdullah's murder the 'Greater Syria' question had continued to be discussed as a possibility in the form of union between Jordan and Iraq (with the question of Syria itself left as a more remote goal). Within the Foreign Office there were sharply divided opinions, but a consensus eventually developed that the merger would have adverse consequences. Jordan would be an economic liability on Iraq, and conversely Iraqi interference in Jordan's internal affairs might have a destabilizing effect. After the assassination it seemed clear to Geoffrey Furlonge and the rest of the Eastern Department that any step towards union would be interpreted in the Middle East, and indeed throughout the world, as 'a snap decision taken in the confusion and excitement following on King Abdullah's murder'.[68] On the other hand the project of union between Jordan and Iraq—as a goal desirable in itself and as a solution to the crisis caused by the assassination—found a powerful champion in the foremost British advocate of the Arab cause at this time, Sir John Troutbeck.

Troutbeck had relinquished his duties as head of the British Middle East Office and had advanced to become Ambassador in Baghdad. No one was more passionately involved than he in the question of what course to pursue after the shattering event of the murder. In Troutbeck's judgement this was a time for bold action. He urged the merger of Jordan and Iraq. No matter that little attention had been given to 'the practical aspects of union'. He believed that these things would work themselves out. Troutbeck, who was incorrigible in his use of historical analogies, recalled that the British themselves in a time of crisis had proposed the 'Anglo-French union in 1940'.[69]

Troutbeck's principal apprehension was that the scaffolding of the Jordan state might 'crack'. He well knew that Glubb and Kirkbride provided military and political stability, but what might happen after their departure? 'Of course it is a wasting asset as none of us can go on forever', Troutbeck wrote. Here was his prognosis in anticipating the worst. He wrote of the crisis between Transjordan proper and 'Cis-Jordan', in other words the west bank.

It is of course not easy to predict what precisely would happen should Jordan start to crack. . . . But certain speculations may not be out of place. One must

---

[68] Minute by Furlonge, 1 Aug. 1951, FO 371/91797.
[69] Troutbeck to Furlonge, Secret, 15 Aug. 1951, FO 371/91798/ET10393/27.

first assume that the situation had got beyond the control of the Arab Legion or that the Legion had itself split into opposing factions.

I imagine that the initial situation should be one of confusion. One of the obvious dangers would then be that the country would split into Trans-Jordan and Cis-Jordan, with the Mufti, backed very possibly by Egypt and the Arab League Secretariat. . . . One can well imagine that Syria, with Saudi and perhaps Egyptian backing, might attempt to incorporate either the whole of Jordan or at any rate Transjordan into a Syrian Republic.[70]

'Greater Syria' might thus be realized after all, but not in any way favourable to the British. On the other hand all of those dire consequences could be averted by union with Iraq. Even economically it would be an improvement. Union, Troutbeck wrote, 'would surely be no worse in that respect than the present Kingdom of Jordan which is so uneconomic that we have to support it by large subsidies'.[71] Troutbeck in short believed that in any case and at any cost the British should ensure a 'friendly Jordan' and that if things began 'to crack' then immediate steps should be taken towards union with Iraq.

Kirkbride's response to Troutbeck's plea touched on the theme of 'viability'. His approach to Arab affairs was much more restrained, if perhaps more cynical, than Troutbeck's, though there is no doubt from his memoirs and other writings that he believed that a tragedy had occurred. Kirkbride thought that 'union' would never work simply because the Jordanians were increasingly opposed to it. They did not wish to fall under Iraqi domination. Kirkbride furthermore challenged Troutbeck on the proposition that Jordan was 'not viable economically'. The impression might be gained from Troutbeck, he wrote, that the British kept pouring money into Jordan without any return on the investment:

The facts are, however, that the subsidy provided by ourselves is used to support a division of troops which have a role assigned to them in our plans for the defence of the Middle East. . . . The Legion now costs eight million pounds a year but even if the annual cost was increased to ten million pounds, it would I imagine be very much less than that of a British division.[72]

Kirkbride did not wish to foretell the future of Jordan, but he did not think that it would include all the 'frightful possibilities' suggested by Troutbeck. Despite Abdullah's assassination, Kirkbride believed that Jordan would remain a 'viable' state. The Foreign Office supported his conclusion. In the long run Kirkbride's judgement about Jordan's future stability proved to be more accurate than

[70] Troutbeck to Furlonge, Secret, 15 Aug. 1951, FO 371/91798/ET10393/27.
[71] Ibid.
[72] Kirkbride to Furlonge, Secret, 25 Aug. 1951, FO 371/91798/ET10393/31.

Troutbeck's alarmist assessment. Nevertheless Troutbeck should be allowed to have the last word on the gravity of the crisis as it appeared after Abdullah's assassination:

> The principal prop has been eliminated. The sudden removal of King Abdullah upon whom we placed so great a reliance for our whole policy in the Arab world, is surely bound to have serious repercussions. . . . It is not merely "one Arab ruler" who has been eliminated, but the man who held his country together almost single-handed and was at the same time our staunchest supporter in the whole area.[73]

Who ultimately should be held responsible for the tragedy? In Troutbeck's view everything seemed to point towards the shadowy figure of the Mufti, whose terrorist activities were now directed from Cairo. Troutbeck probably spoke for his generation of British officials in the Middle East when he judged the Mufti to be 'an evil man'.[74]

---

[73] Troutbeck to Furlonge, Secret, 15 Aug. 1951, FO 371/91798/ET10393/27.

[74] Troutbeck in fact exaggerated Haj Amin's influence, which had declined after the 1948 war. In British eyes the Mufti remained a renegade because of his association with the Nazis. There was no direct contact with him, and therefore an element of distortion in the political reporting. The best assessment of the last stage of the Mufti's career is Majid Khadduri, *Arab Contemporaries* (Baltimore, 1973), pp. 83-7.

3

THE PERSIAN OIL CRISIS

IN EARLY 1949 Michael Wright commented that for a long time it had been clear that the situation of 'political stagnation' in Iran could not continue indefinitely. Either the Iranian government would have to come to grips with far-reaching economic and social reform or there would be a Communist revolution. As has been mentioned in the last chapter, Wright, in his capacity of Assistant Under-Secretary supervising Middle Eastern affairs, had been given an additional assignment of promoting economic progress. He attached particular importance to the part the Shah might play in this preliminary stage of economic development. There were however certain risks:

The Shah . . . is well disposed towards the West, has every desire to keep Persia from communist and Russian influence, and is anxious to press ahead with reforms. The danger is that he will act clumsily or over-eagerly, and by imposing or laying himself open to accusations of imposing a military dictatorship, precipitate a crisis in which he will fail to carry the country with him.[1]

Wright believed that 'handling the Shah' would be a critical problem in maintaining internal stability, which was the prerequisite of economic development. He argued that the Shah needed discreet assistance, especially as it might be rendered by the British Ambassador in Tehran.

Wright thought specifically that the British should help the Shah to select a 'strong' government that would be capable of enacting the economic and social measures the British believed to be necessary in order to avert a political and social revolution. At the same time the

[1] Minute by Wright, 9 Feb. 1949, FO 371/75464/E1723. It should be noted as a prelude to further discussion that Bevin initialled this minute. The books most useful for understanding the British response to Iranian nationalism are: Ervand Abrahamian, *Iran: Between Two Revolutions* (Princeton, 1982); Homa Katouzian, *The Political Economy of Iran, 1926–1979* (New York University Press, 1981); and Nikki R. Keddie, *Roots of Revolution: An Interpretive History of Modern Iran* (Yale University Press, 1981). See also James Alban Bill, *The Politics of Iran: Groups, Classes and Modernization* (Columbus, Ohio, 1972); Richard W. Cottam, *Nationalism in Iran* (University of Pittsburg Press, revised edn., 1979); George Lenczowski, ed., *Iran under the Pahlavis* (Stanford, 1978); Rouhollah K. Ramazani, *Iran's Foreign Policy 1941–1973* (University of Virginia Press, 1975); and Stepehr Zabih, *The Mossadegh Era: Roots of the Iranian Revolution* (Chicago, 1982). For the oil crisis see Alan W. Ford, *The Anglo-Iranian Oil Dispute of 1951–1952* (Berkeley, 1954); and L. P. Elwell-Sutton, *Persian Oil: A Study in Power Politics* (London, 1955). See also especially the chapters by Rose L. Greaves and Ronald W. Ferrier in Hossein Amirsadeghi, ed., *Twentieth-Century Iran* (New York, 1977).

Shah would have to be dissuaded from imposing a military dictatorship which might evolve into an anti-British regime. In this delicate
situation great tact would be necessary. Later in the year Wright had
an exchange with Bevin about the extent to which the British should
actively become the power behind the Shah. The ultimate issue, as
in similar cases that have been discussed in earlier chapters, was one
of intervention. In the history of the Persian oil crisis, as will be seen,
the question of intervention—which in the end meant the use of
force—became a test of the Labour government's determination to
uphold Britain's position in Iran. For reasons of ill health, Bevin
resigned as Foreign Secretary, and shortly thereafter died, in the
midst of the Persian oil controversy. His response to the question of
intervention in the early stages of the crisis is vital in keeping
perspective on later developments and indeed on the Labour government and the Middle East in its last 'post-Bevin' phase.

Towards the end of 1949 the Eastern Department of the Foreign
Office judged that the Iranian economy had degenerated into a state
of paralysis. Something more than 'friendly advice', according to one
strand of Foreign Office thought, would be necessary to induce the
Shah 'to accept and support a Prime Minister strong enough . . . to
enforce his authority in the country and to press on with urgent
measures of social amelioration'.[2] In analysing the situation the
Foreign Office officials, including Bevin himself, had followed and
approved the line taken in Tehran by Sir John Le Rougetel, the
Ambassador. Le Rougetel had an unvarnished contempt for the
political class of Iranians, but he believed that with sufficient 'guidance' they could be led to constructive efforts. The key to solving
the problem would be to select a 'strong' prime minister with whom
the Shah could work on such urgently needed reforms as more
equitable land distribution and taxation. In the past the Shah had
been disinclined to tolerate a prime minister who might overshadow
or eventually challenge him. In late 1949 the British warned the
Shah that the continued lack of an effective government would
undermine the Persian state and with it his own authority.

Le Rougetel couched this admonition in moderate and friendly
language. Bevin in fact endorsed the firm way in which the dangers
had been stated. According to Le Rougetel:

> I did my best to impress upon him [the Shah] . . . the importance of having a
> real Government led by a man of strong personality. He is still averse to this, I
> fancy, but the sands are running out with a vengeance now and I told him that
> the risk, if risk it were, of having too strong a Prime Minister was as nothing to
> that of the one who was too weak. . . .

[2] Minute by Alan Leavett, 29 Nov. 1949, FO 371/75468/E15087.

I said that . . . we wished Persia to be strong and independent, and therefore to improve social and economic conditions on the basis of a well conceived national plan.[3]

The question for the Foreign Office was whether Le Rougetel should be instructed to guide the Shah in the selection of a 'strong' leader of the Iranian government. Michael Wright believed that the British should play an active part in order to bring about social and economic reform as well as a stable 'Persia' (the words Persia and Iran continued to be used interchangeably). His recommendation triggered a response from Bevin which clarified the 'non-intervention policy' of the Labour government. It was thus an incident of magnitude, not least for one of the themes of this book.

Wright was convinced that the Shah should be prevented from 'appointing another "weak" Prime Minister'. He had confidence in the tact and persuasive powers of Le Rougetel not to alienate the Shah while bringing to power a suitable collaborator who would be amenable to British influence. Wright of course wrote with the knowledge that he was merely recommending the line the British had pursued in Egypt. He recognized the danger of putting the Shah in a position in which he could subsequently blame the British if the new Iranian government turned out to be no better than the old. Lord Curzon's famous dictum on the dangers of 'Cabinet-making in Persia' had left a permanent imprint on the official mind. Nevertheless Wright firmly held that 'the situation is extremely disquieting, and . . . that a strong Prime Minister is required'. He therefore urged that the Shah should be warned that the British would oppose any 'unsuitable' candidate and should take active steps towards 'the appointment of a suitable personality'. This unequivocal stand in favour of 'Cabinet-making in Persia' evoked a query from the Permanent Under-Secretary, Sir William Strang. 'How does this square', Strang asked, with the Foreign Secretary's 'policy of non-intervention?'[4]

The justification for intervention was based on the traditional and often unchallenged assumption that the British had the ethical as well as the political responsibility to ensure stability, social welfare, and economic development in Persia and throughout the Middle East as well as in their own colonial dependencies. Wright believed that this principle had been re-endorsed up to the hilt by the Foreign Office Conference of July 1949. 'The policy of non-intervention', he wrote, 'has never been interpreted as meaning that we are debarred from exercising our influence with Middle East Governments in

---

[3] Le Rougetel to Strang, 12 Nov. 1949, FO 371/75468/E14053.
[4] Minute by Wright, 2 Dec. 1949, FO 371/75468/E15087.

matters where their own welfare and progress is concerned.' He went on to quote one of the conclusions of the July conference, which Bevin had affirmed:

One of our principal tasks must be to use every possible means to encourage the emergence of progressive and honest governments and efficient administrations. Our means of carrying out this task are:
(a) Constant advice to Governments . . .[5]

Wright no doubt believed that he had rested his case on the side of the angels. He held that 'constant pressure' on all of the Middle Eastern governments was necessary in order to introduce financial reform, to balance budgets, and in this particular case to give 'advice' to the Shah 'in the interests of Persia herself'. Strang instructed that a telegram be drafted to Le Rougetel along those lines.

Bevin refused to endorse the telegram. 'I do not like this', he scrawled. 'I am not prepared to send the telegram.'[6] Wright had to be content with a private letter to Le Rougetel, which Wright himself now drafted, stating that the officials within the Foreign Office shared the anxieties about the lack of a strong and stable government in Persia. 'At the same time, the Secretary of State considers that we ought to act with great prudence.'[7] Here Bevin's attitude towards the question of intervention was consistent, as has been seen in earlier chapters, with his outlook in Greece, Egypt, and Syria as well as in Iran itself in 1946. It must be stated unequivocally that he never indicated that he would not be prepared to support a policy of intervention if it seemed appropriate at a particular time. What can be established with certainty is that he was not prepared to give a blank endorsement to a principle which had often been taken for granted, and that he persistently checked his permanent officials from pursuing a more active policy. He advised, as previously, 'great prudence' in the interference in the internal affairs of other countries, not least in Persia. As will be seen in the next chapter, he rejected just as adamantly the advice to fix the elections and meddle in other domestic affairs of Egypt, where the temptation to intervene must have been even greater. Pragmatism flavoured his outlook, but he remained convinced that 'Cabinet-making in Persia' would probably lead to unanticipated and undesirable consequences.

The decisions about intervention were made, as elsewhere in the Middle East, in the climate of political assassination. It was the murder of an Iranian minister, Abdul Hussain Hazhir, in November 1949 that had precipitated the discussion about installing a strong

[5] Minute by Wright, 3 Dec. 1949, FO 371/75468/E15087.
[6] Notation by Bevin on minute by Strang, 12 Dec. 1949, FO 371/75468/E15087.
[7] Strang to Le Rougetel (drafted by Wright), 17 Dec. 1947, FO 371/75468/E15087.

prime minister. At that time Bevin's inclination to proceed with caution was rewarded with as favourable a development as could have been expected. The Shah himself in June 1950—the same month as the outbreak of the war in Korea—appointed the Chief of Staff of the Army, General Ali Razmara, as Prime Minister. The Razmara regime lasted less than a year, but it held out hope of economic development and political progress, or, to put it in the popular phrase of the time, of the triumph of liberal nationalism. This was the time in which the Shah and a vigorous Prime Minister, together with a cabinet that included civil servants (with such backgrounds as banking, medicine, and education), attempted to move forward with a seven-year economic development plan. They raised expectations of far-reaching reform at all levels of Iranian society. It is arguable that the successful pursuit of their schemes for political decentralization and planned economic development might have averted the principal problem with which this chapter is concerned, the oil crisis. As it transpired, Razmara's regime was brief. He was assassinated in March 1951. Time and again there recurs in the British dispatches the theme that political stability is the prerequisite of economic development, without which there could be no social amelioration. It was difficult to expect economic progress and the easing of social tension in an atmosphere of political violence. The assassinations created a vicious economic and ideological circle which the British eventually despaired of breaking.

In February 1949 an attempt had been made to take the life of the Shah himself. He took it so well in stride that he increased his stature as a leader. The British Ambassador reported:

> The tension was already extreme when, on the afternoon of 4th February [1949] six shots were fired at the Shah at point-blank range as he was arriving at Tehran University. . . . there is little room for doubt that in addition to being an expert gunman he was both a member and an agent of the Tudeh [Communist] Party and that this outrage was intended to be the signal for serious disturbances. In the event it produced a spontaneous reaction in favour of the Shah, whose coolness and courage when attacked were matched by his refusal after the event to tolerate reprisals.[8]

As has been seen in an earlier chapter, the Shah in the immediate postwar period had appeared to the British as an almost inconsequential figure in comparison with the dominant politicians. By 1949–51 he was a personage to be reckoned with, not least as a willing collaborator. During the Razmara era he demonstrated an alacrity to turn to the British when he became irritated with the Americans. He was still young—age thirty in 1950—and commonly believed to

_____
[8] Le Rougetel to Bevin, 1 Jan. 1950, FO 371/82306/EP1011.

have potential as an enlightened ruler. The British thought that he did in fact have a genuine awareness of 'the wide-spread disillusionment among his people' and a real desire to bring about reforms that would raise the standard of living—if only because he was far-sighted enough to see that reform was necessary for his own survival.[9] In other words the Shah in 1949–51 was by no means the tyrant of later years, though the beginnings of the later regime can be traced to this era. For present purposes it is important to note that he had begun to consolidate his position by co-operating with the military and by introducing economic and social reform with the assistance of civil servants who possessed technical training.

It must be said at once that the British Ambassador at the time of the oil crisis, Sir Francis Shepherd (Le Rougetel's successor) did not place high hopes on the future of the Shah as a benevolent autocrat. Nor did Shepherd believe that the Shah possessed sufficient tenacity of purpose to pursue immediate and effective reform. The Shah did not 'hold out much promise of drastic action', he wrote in April 1950 shortly after his arrival.[10] Later in the year he penned a considered impression of the Shah which assessed the transitional period before the oil crisis:

> It is generally recognised that the Shah is somewhat weak and that he tends to be unduly influenced by the last comer. This weakness would however be easily forgiven if His Majesty did not intervene too frequently in the appointment of officials and if he did not show a tendency to consult with individual Ministers on matters of policy rather than doing so through his Prime Minister [Razmara]. The Royal Family are also considered to have intervened illegally and unnecessarily in public affairs. . . .
> These criticisms of the Shah have been supported by the clergy whose dislike of the dynasty has not been allowed entirely to die down and it must be confessed that the Shah and the Royal Family have not gone out of their way to placate the priesthood. They stand for a western way of life both the good and bad features of which can only be displeasing to a reactionary clergy.[11]

In general Shepherd's opinions were in line with American assessments. 'It might . . . be', the American Ambassador, John C. Wiley, wrote reflectively, that the Shah '. . . is a little too Westernized for an Oriental country.'[12]

Sir Francis Shepherd is of central importance for the present discussion because of his critical position as the British representative in Iran in time of crisis. He was a man of modest and stable intellect, and he possessed the British virtue of imperturbability. He has been

[9] Minute by Leavett, 10 Jan. 1950, FO 371/82310/EP106/2; and other minutes in subsequent files which substantiate this theme.

[10] Shepherd to Strang, Confidential, 6 Apr. 1950, FO 371/82311/EP1016/30.

[11] Shepherd to Bevin, Confidential, 17 Dec. 1950, FO 371/82313/EP1016/93.

[12] Wiley to Acheson, 30 Jan. 1950, *Foreign Relations 1950*, V, pp. 459–64.

described as 'a dispirited bachelor dominated by his widowed sister, [who] had been sent to Tehran for a rest after an arduous time elsewhere'.[13] The latter part of that assessment is certainly true. Shepherd had served in the Netherlands East Indies in the period immediately before independence. His previous service included the Belgian Congo. He had worked his way up in the consular service from Callao to the diplomatic pinnacle of Tehran (he subsequently retired after a tour of duty as Ambassador in Poland). His consular experiences in such places as Haiti had probably not led him to hold high expectations for the non-European world. Nevertheless he was sensitive to the need for reform in Iran. 'Something must be done, and done soon', he wrote in his early days in Tehran, 'to improve the lot of the common people, to cleanse the administration of a large number of parasites and to deal with corruption.'[14] He sensed a general dissatisfaction with 'the existing ruling clique' and a lack of public confidence in the plans for economic development. He held out only faint hope that the Iranian leadership would prove capable of meeting the challenge. Shepherd believed that there was a deficiency in the Persian national character which condemned even the most forward-looking nationalists to frustration and false expectation. Here he joined his predecessors, not least Sir Reader Bullard, in gloomy outlook about the unwarranted suspicion and lack of moral integrity of the Iranians:

> Anyone coming fresh to this country as I have done must be tempted to regard the cynicism and pessimism as a result of post-war difficulties and two years of bad harvests acting on the Oriental character. If this were the case, one might be justified in hoping that it might be possible to restore morale and to set things going again.
>
> I find, however, that Persian cynicism and pessimism, combined with a tendency to confess to their own shortcomings, is apparently less a passing phase than a permanent weakness.[15]

As if it were only to be expected, the nationalists now were attempting 'to squeeze more out of the Oil Company'. It was part of the same old story. Shepherd's views sometimes did not lack sophistication, but such blunt opinions placed him in a long line of British observers who had responded to Iranian nationalism in a similar way.

One of the most damning things ever written about the British in Iran was a judgement delivered by an American political scientist, Richard Cottam, in a classic work entitled *Nationalism in Iran*. 'The

[13] C. M. Woodhouse, *Something Ventured* (London, 1982), p. 109.
[14] Shepherd to Strang, Confidential, 6 Apr. 1950, FO 371/82311/EP1016/30.
[15] Ibid.

British', he wrote, ' . . . for practical and psychological reasons . . . persisted in their antiquarian conviction that the Iran of 1951 differed little from the Iran of 1901.'[16] It would be an insult to the intelligence and wisdom of Sir Reader Bullard and Sir Francis Shepherd uncritically to endorse that view, but there was a historical continuity in British outlook. In October 1951, shortly before the fall of the Labour government in Britain, Shepherd paused to reflect historically on the development of Iranian nationalism. He wrote in response to American criticism that the British had failed to understand the nature of Asian nationalism generally and therefore had been unable to come to terms with the Iranian nationalists. Shepherd took the line that Iranian nationalism flowed in a different channel from the main stream of Asian response to the West, and that it was important to make the distinction. His thoughts are helpful in understanding the British reaction to the crisis of 1951. His critique, entitled 'A Comparison between Persian and Asian Nationalism in General', spelled out certain assumptions that usually remained tacit in official minutes. It expressed commonly held British views on the origins and course of Iranian nationalism, and the reasons why the nationalist movement in Iran had failed to ripen into maturity as it had elsewhere in Asia. Here then is the testimony of Sir Francis Shepherd on the temper of Iranian nationalism—as a prelude to the oil crisis of 1951.

Shepherd's ideas about nationalism were clearly shaped by his recent experience in the Netherlands East Indies. He had been critical of the Dutch, but he also acknowledged their achievement as a colonial power. The Indonesian nationalists would not have had the opportunity to take over a viable political and economic state had it not been for the administrative apparatus created by the Dutch. Against the Dutch all Indonesian nationalists could unite, at least temporarily. In Iran there was no comparable unifying force. The Persian state had degenerated into 'Asiatic decadence' and had not been allowed to develop 'at the hands of a virile and civilised nation'. Geography and power politics had combined to exempt Persia from European colonial domination. This was a historical fact which Shepherd lamented. 'Persia . . . is now paying heavily for her immunity from tutelage', he wrote.[17] The Iranians in other words lacked the benefits of a nationalist movement which British imperialism might have inspired.

The arguments in favour of British colonial rule are today heard so

---

[16] Cottam, *Nationalism in Iran* (1964 edn.), p. 273.

[17] Shepherd, 'A Comparison between Persian and Asian Nationalism in General', 2 Oct. 1951, FO 371/91464/EP1015/361.

seldom that it is perhaps difficult to recall their wide acceptance in England in the postwar era. The point is important because Shepherd was merely articulating, perhaps rather simplistically, several basic assumptions about British and European imperialism that most Englishmen would probably have affirmed. European and British colonial rule provided the political stability for economic development and fostered a sense of national consciousness. In Africa nationalism had not existed before the advent of the Europeans. In Iran a period of European domination might have galvanized the Iranians into a national renaissance:

> The tragedy of the situation is that in the 20th century there is no country which either could or would undertake the education of Persia and its preparation for a *renaissance* which would bring it into equal relations with other Powers. But unless something is done the country is liable to sink further into corruption and to finish with a Communist revolution.[18]

Shepherd despaired of an alternative. There could be no 'national regeneration', he believed, because there did not exist a 'cadre of patriotic and comparatively honest individuals' which a British colonial regime, for example, might have nourished.

Shepherd doubted the existence of an authentic nationalist movement. He spoke rather in terms of 'waves of popular feeling' and the sentiments of the 'uneducated masses'. In the 1945–50 period 'nationalization of oil' became an Iranian obsession without any understanding of the essential issues. Shepherd summed up what he believed to be the crux of the matter:

> The nationalisation of oil has been in practice a move not in the right but in the wrong direction. The need for Persia is not to run the oil industry for herself (which she cannot do) but to profit from the technical ability of the West.
> This up till now she has been too suspicious to do. Persia is indeed rather like a man who knows very well that he ought to go to the dentist but is afraid of doing so and is annoyed with anybody who says that there is anything wrong with his teeth.[19]

In short the British, according to this interpretation, were not confronted as elsewhere with a genuine nationalist movement. 'It is a preliminary flicker', Shepherd concluded, 'but not yet the authentic flame.'

The Razmara Era and the 'Supplemental Oil Agreement'

'In Persia we face an emotional nationalism which is not primarily interested in the financial effects of the "nationalisation" that is

---

[18] Shepherd, 'A Comparison between Persian and Asian Nationalism in General', 2 Oct. 1951, FO 371/91464/EP1015/361.
[19] Ibid.

sought', wrote L. A. C. Fry of the Eastern Department.[20] It would be difficult to find a statement that more succinctly or accurately expressed the British perception of the problem. The Anglo-Iranian Oil Company (hereafter 'Anglo-Persian', as it was popularly called at the time) had become a symbol of foreign domination. The British now approached the crisis of an Iranian take-over. The only positive aspect of the situation was that popular discontent might subside under stable political leadership. In 1950 General Razmara offered that hope. The British wished to consummate an arrangement with the Iranian government that would rationally adjust the basis of the legitimate British oil industry and at the same time provide revenue for the economic development of Iran. The proposed agreement was known as the 'Supplemental Oil Agreement'—supplemental because it affirmed and augmented the original concession of 1933. In July 1949 representatives of Anglo-Persian and the Iranian government had signed the agreement. It now remained for Razmara to win its ratification by the Iranian Parliament, the Majlis. The supplemental oil agreement would have increased royalties from about fifteen to twenty per cent of the 1933 instrument up to a maximum of thirty per cent (though these provisions were couched in such dense legal jargon that they were obscure even to some of the experts).[21] There were great hopes pinned to this solution as an equitable arrangement that might provide a breakthrough in the economic development of Iran. No one on the British side doubted the urgency of the situation. The seven-year plan for economic development was dependent on the new arrangement for its revenue. Without the supplemental oil agreement the British feared that the Iranian state would crumble into Communist revolution. The stakes thus could not have been higher.

At first there was a tendency on the part of the British to distrust Razmara on grounds that he would probably attempt to establish a military dictatorship which might become anti-British. 'He is an able administrator but he is also a professional soldier without political experience', wrote Alan Leavett of the Eastern Department. He added that Razmara was 'notoriously intolerant of politicians and of the incompetence of the civil administration'.[22] Razmara temperamentally was at odds with the members of the Majlis. The politicians suspected that his proposed reforms in such areas as banking codes, along with his schemes to reduce unemployment

[20] Minute by Fry, 30 Mar. 1951, FO 371/91244.
[21] See especially Ford, *Anglo-Iranian Oil Dispute*, part II, for a lucid discussion of these points.
[22] Minute by Leavett, 5 June 1950, FO 371/82311/EP10116/45.

and raise the standard of living, might somehow adversely affect their own prosperity. 'General Razmara's methods', Sir Francis Shepherd reported, '. . . aroused obstinacy among the Deputies [of the Majlis] and this feeling was reinforced by a fear that the Prime Minister was likely to interfere with the sources of personal income.'[23] Razmara in other words was turning out to be the 'strong' type of reformist Prime Minister that Michael Wright and others had hoped for. Razmara had the makings of a strong Iranian nationalist. He furthermore recognized the necessity of British and American economic assistance. He favoured the supplemental oil agreement. The question was whether he could get it through the Majlis. In 1950 it remained within the realm of possibility that 'Anglo-Persian' and the Iranians might still find common ground.

In the literature of the oil crisis, 'Anglo-Persian' is usually indicted as an unenlightened and oppressive albatross hanging from the neck of the Foreign Office. In an earlier chapter it has been revealed that Bevin himself had pangs of conscience about the principle of nationalization. How could the British protest what they themselves were doing in England? Iranian oil was critical for the British economy (though it was not indispensable, as the Iranians learned to their regret). In the eyes of a socialist government, however, the company would also have to justify itself by contributing to the economic and social development of Iran. 'Anglo-Persian' was not only expected to contribute to postwar British recovery but also to demonstrate that it possessed a social conscience. This was no mean test of British capitalism, especially under the scrutiny of Ernest Bevin. The attitude of the Foreign Office towards the company has long been a matter of historical curiosity. It is also a matter of considerable political significance since a different British policy at this time might have altered the recent history of Iran. A more conciliatory or more aggressive British stance might have changed the course of events leading to the 'CIA coup' in 1953, or for that matter the Iranian revolution.

Bevin believed that the company had proved its case. This was a matter, in his own words, in which he took 'a personal interest'. 'Anglo-Persian', after long, arduous, and complex negotiations, had finally agreed to a settlement that would include a substantial increase of royalties and the payment of £20 million as a lump sum. This sum, together with the substantially increased annual income from the royalties, would finance the capital development of the seven-year plan. Bevin and his Foreign Office advisers regarded the offer as 'fair and reasonable'. The difficulty, in the Foreign Secretary's view,

[23] Sheperd to Bevin, Confidential, 17 Dec. 1950, FO 371/82313/EP1016/93.

did not lie with the company but with the Iranians. Razmara would not specify what the Iranians actually wanted in addition to the supplemental agreement. 'It was the bazaar method of negotiation', Bevin stated in August 1950. He was consistent and firm in his response to what he regarded as devious Persian tactics. 'We had made a good offer to Persia', he wrote, 'and I felt we should stick by it.' Bevin wanted to avoid giving the impression of 'weakness' that would lead 'to further demands'. 'The Persians must really make up their minds whether or not they were going to do business.'[24]

The head of the Eastern Department, Geoffrey Furlonge, believed that there should be a limit to British indulgence. Furlonge supervised the day-by-day Iranian business of the Foreign Office. He was an official of exceptional competence. Like most other civil servants he had no particular affection for 'Anglo-Persian', but he thought that the company had gone a long way in meeting Iranian demands that bordered on the unreasonable and even whimsical. 'We have consistently taken the line', he wrote in August 1950, '. . . that the agreement is a fair and indeed a generous one, and that we are not prepared to press the Company to make any further concessions.' Somewhere the line had to be drawn. If the company were to yield more, he continued, the Iranians would merely be encouraged 'to open their mouths wider and [further concessions] might decrease, rather than increase, the Prime Minister's [Razmara's] will to push it [the supplemental oil agreement] through the Majlis'. What were the Iranians really after? Did they themselves really know? Razmara himself spoke of 'Iranization' of the company. The British did not believe that this was the essential motive. There are frequent references in the Foreign Office minutes to the lamentable suspicion of the Iranians towards the British. This theme can be found on the British side as well. According to the officials of 'Anglo-Persian', beneath the talk of 'Iranization' was merely a determination to squeeze 'more money' out of the company.[25]

The historical records reveal a much greater flexibility on the part of the chairman of 'Anglo-Persian', Sir William Fraser, than is usually portrayed in the accounts of the oil crisis. Indeed he demonstrated a sensitivity to the mood of the Iranian nationalists, the danger of a breach, and the need to come to terms with Razmara. He regarded Razmara as distinctly a cut above the run-of-the-mill Iranian politician. Fraser was willing to discuss 'Iranization' and other measures, including more money, in order to salvage the supplemental oil agreement. He saw the need to give Razmara further aid in the

---

[24] Bevin to Franks, Secret, 12 Aug. 1950, FO 371/82375/EP1531/37.
[25] Minute by Furlonge, 11 Aug. 1950, FO 371/82375/EP1531/38.

battle against the 'xenophobe' Iranians who denounced 'Anglo-Persian', mistakenly in his view, as a repressive and exploitative force. Fraser was a figure of exceedingly strong personality. The Iranians were no doubt correct in regarding him as a symbol of British capitalism. He certainly was so regarded within the British government. His relations with the officials of the Foreign Office were not easy. He had a fire-eating contempt for civil servants.

By August 1950 the Foreign Office had become convinced that, unless Iran received economic assistance, the Razmara regime might be replaced with something far worse. 'The morale of the Persian people had dropped', according to a member of the Eastern Department, '. . . and money was needed to get the wheels of economic life in Persia turning, so that the standard of living could be raised.'[26] Sir William Fraser listened sympathetically to these arguments. But he maintained that it was best for 'Anglo-Persian' to stand firm. 'The Company wanted to help Persia', he stated at an important gathering in Whitehall. The meeting was attended by officials of the Treasury, the Ministry of Fuel and Power, and the Foreign Office, with Michael Wright in the chair. Fraser emphasized to them that the company was responsible to its stockholders. Here it is important to recall that the British government itself owned fifty-one per cent of the company's shares. This was ironic. By convention the government itself had no voice in the running of the company.[27] If the Foreign Office attempted to press 'Anglo-Persian' into providing funds to buoy up the Iranian government or to subsidize economic development beyond the amounts provided by royalties, there was certain to be protest by the shareholders. The Labour government may have introduced a new era of socialism in England, but the ethos of capitalism was alive and well. 'It was for Governments to lend money to Governments', Fraser stated emphatically, not oil companies. Why would the Iranians not sign the supplemental oil agreement—he asked rhetorically and somewhat disingenuously. 'Sir William Fraser complained that in Persia one always heard fine talk and saw paper plans, but no action.'[28] He believed that the Iranians had no financial or ethical grounds on which to refuse to ratify the supplemental oil agreement. From such statements it may fairly be deduced that the chairman of 'Anglo-Persian' had taken a firm and almost belligerent stand. His change of attitude two months later is thus all the more revealing.

[26] Minute by L. Barnett, 3 Aug. 1950, FO 371/82375/EP1531/40.
[27] See Ferrier, 'The Development of the Iranian Oil Industry', in Amirsadeghi, *Twentieth-Century Iran*, p. 96.
[28] Minutes of a meeting held at the F. O., 2 Aug. 1950, FO 371/82375/EP1531/40.

The financial deterioration of the Iranian government had reached such crisis proportions by October 1950 that the Foreign Office now saw no alternative but to admonish the company to make further concessions. Otherwise the Razmara regime might collapse. The oil concession itself might be in jeopardy. 'Nationalization' now appeared to be much more than a vague threat. Bevin continued to demonstrate a solicitude for the well-being of the company and at the same time a desire that 'Anglo-Persian' should make a determined effort to secure the supplemental oil agreement. 'Mr. Bevin hoped the Company would be able to find something to offer', Michael Wright wrote, 'even if it were somewhat painful, provided always it was not disastrous.'[29] Against the background of the Korean war, Bevin and other members of the Cabinet needed all the support they could get from British industry. Thus he gave the reassurance that the government would not push the company too far. He was also suspicious of Persian greed. In the words recorded earlier by the American Ambassador, Bevin did not want the Iranian government to 'run out of money', but he was well familiar with 'the Iranian propensity [to] keep opening their mouths wider'.[30] In any case on the 10th of October Bevin decided that the time had come to press the company to clinch the supplemental oil agreement. He repeated that he believed the agreement itself to be 'fair and even generous' but it was now imperative to make further concessions 'in the interests of the Company themselves.'[31]

It was Michael Wright who prepared the ground for the encounter with Sir William Fraser. In view of Wright's own overbearing personality it is amusing that he was intimidated by Fraser. 'Perhaps you would be prepared to see Sir W. Fraser with me', he wrote to the Permanent Under-Secretary, 'in view of the stake involved.'[32] When the meeting took place among the three of them, Wright recorded with considerable relief that Fraser 'responded in the most friendly manner'. They agreed that this was the psychological Iranian moment. The Shah had urged Razmara to consummate the supplemental oil agreement. Razmara himself wished to push it through the Majlis. To carry the vote he needed proof that he had won further concessions. Fraser, to the surprise of the others present, agreed that the company would have to yield a further substantial amount, and that it could not be, in his own words, a matter 'of half-crowns'. He had on his mind the recent raise in the royalties of the Iraq Petroleum

---

[29] Minute by Wright, 23 Oct. 1950, FO 371/82376/EP1531/70.
[30] Douglas to Acheson, 12 Aug. 1950, *Foreign Relations 1950*, V, pp. 580-1.
[31] Minute by Wright, 16 Oct. 1950, FO 371/82376/EP1531/69.
[32] Ibid.

Company to the Iraq government, which he believed 'Anglo-Persian' could match. 'He himself would not hesitate at finding further sums of even several million pounds if the right form and method could be devised.' This was a remarkable change of heart. Fraser mentioned possibilities of subsidizing the Iranian seven-year plan for economic development. He discussed the prospects of lowering prices of 'Anglo-Persian' products for sale in Iran.[33] His mental processes had definitely accelerated.

A few days later Fraser returned to the Foreign Office to say that he had been making calculations about the advantages to the Persians of the supplemental oil agreement. He now demonstrated a concern for Iranian economic welfare. The royalties would be substantially greater than he had formerly estimated because 'Anglo-Persian' had had a good year. The profits accruing to the Persian government would probably be closer to £30 million rather than the anticipated £20 million. Strang and Wright encouraged Fraser to expand further, and to dress up his proposals 'in the most attractive form'. He revealed a sensitive side to his character. He did not wish to offend Iranian susceptibilities. He also indicated an interest in Iranian social development. In what must be a remarkable entry in the annals of British capitalism, at least of the sort represented by Fraser, he now began to wax enthusiastic about Persian education. He mentioned a contribution to Tehran University of perhaps £1 million. Wright and Strang emphasized that technical training was greatly needed in Iran. Fraser said he would give thought to this and other points, and in great confidence said that he had something further 'up his sleeve' if it appeared to be necessary.[34] Clearly something was agitating the sudden and generous impulses of this captain of British industry.

Fraser was anticipating the consequences of the new Aramco agreement with the Saudis. This innovative arrangement would split the profits on a fifty–fifty basis. It represented a landmark in the economic affairs of the Middle East. There was a world of difference in the increase by 'Anglo-Persian' of *royalties* up to fifty per cent (as the supplemental oil agreement provided), and Aramco's fifty-fifty *profit-sharing*. Fraser would argue in vain that the difference was more apparent than real. There were psychological implications. A fifty–fifty share in the profits was a tangible concept. Nationalists could accept it as a fair basis without feeling that they were being bamboozled by intrigues in the calculations of royalties. Once this basic point became clear, the supplemental oil agreement was doomed. The Iranians learned of the new Aramco arrangement in the late

[33] Minute by Wright, 23 Oct. 1950, FO 371/82376/EP1531/70.
[34] Minute by Wright, 24 Oct. 1950, FO 371/82376/EP1551/71.

autumn of 1950, probably in October or early November at about the time of Fraser's desperate mental gyrations. Whatever he might have had 'up his sleeve' to salvage the supplemental oil agreement, nothing could match what appeared to be an across-the-board equity. As has been emphasized in the introductory section of this part of the book, the Aramco agreement of 1950 constituted an economic and political watershed no less significant for the Middle East than the transfer of power for India and Pakistan. Later in the Persian oil crisis Attlee himself used that analogy. But by then it was too late.

The Majlis forced the withdrawal of the supplemental oil agreement in December 1950. 'The heart of the matter', Sir Francis Shepherd reported at the time, 'is the Persian feeling that they have no control over their main source of revenue, once it is sold to the oil company.' 'Anglo-Persian' was generally denounced, Shepherd lamented, as ' "colonialism" in monopolising the Southern oil resources without considering national rights.'[35] In mid-January 1951 Bevin commented that there was 'dynamite' in these developments.[36] His failing health probably prevented him from devoting full-blooded attention to the developing crisis of 'nationalization'. It remains one of the great speculative questions of the Labour era how he might have responded. As a socialist Bevin had no objection in principle to the nationalization of an industry. On the other hand, as has been seen, he had a respect for the accomplishments of 'Anglo-Persian', which had invested huge sums of money in Iran. It possessed a legal concession with many years to run. 'Anglo-Persian' might be criticized on various grounds, but it had in good faith fulfilled its contract. Bevin believed its wages and working conditions to be reasonable. In comparison with other British overseas companies he judged 'Anglo-Persian' to have a good record, not least as a dollar-earner. On the other hand he knew that the future of the company would depend on the acceptance by the Iranians of what they, not the British, believed to be a fair settlement that would recognize Iranian national aspirations. It is arguable that a more decisive handling of the crisis, perhaps by Bevin, might have resulted in a more satisfactory outcome for the British.

In early 1951 the manager of 'Anglo-Persian' in Iran, V. J. Northcroft, returned to London to report on the company's response to impending nationalization. Speaking to high-ranking civil servants of the Treasury, the Ministry of Fuel and Power, and the Foreign Office, he said that he deplored the Aramco agreement. Nevertheless

[35] Shepherd to Bevin, Confidential, 31 Dec. 1950, FO 371/91521/EP153/7.
[36] Minute by Bevin on memorandum by Furlonge, 19 Jan. 1951, FO 371/91522/EP1531/32.

he could understand the reasons for its consummation. Aramco now stood a chance to reap even greater profits because of American tax laws. British companies could not expect such favourable treatment. The principle of profit-sharing itself would, in his opinion, be 'a disastrous one' for the Middle East. 'Anglo-Persian' simply 'could not afford' such an arrangement.[37] This typical response of the company struck the Middle East experts of the Foreign Office as neither bold nor imaginative.[38] 'Anglo-Persian' appeared to be preoccupied with short-term problems of finance, not with the long-range question of profit-sharing that would accommodate Iranian nationalism. The company in short was proving itself to be an anachronism. A Foreign Office minute summed up the problem by describing in bitter language one of the company's spokesmen in Iran. He seemed to represent all of the objectionable features of the British Empire in the Middle East that now needed drastically and immediately to be altered: 'with his monacle and indolent air, he creates the wrong atmosphere . . . and lends colour to suspicions that A. I. O. C. is still following a 19th century line'.[39]

It must not be assumed that all of the officials of 'Anglo-Persian' were obtuse, or for that matter, as most American comment has held, that the British in general regarded the protest against the company to be a sort of primitive response to western civilization. One example of sophisticated British interpretation is especially illuminating. It is an article that appeared anonymously in *The Times* in late March 1951 and was given circulation within the Foreign Office as an 'excellent' analysis of the 'internal' issues behind the oil demands.[40] The article called attention to the 'inner conflict' of Iranian society that had come to a head in the oil controversy. 'For many years', according to the article, 'Persian society has been in a state of disequilibrium.' Part of the cause of Iranian instability could be attributed to great power rivalry, but more fundamentally the disequilibrium originated with 'the stupidity, greed, and lack of judgement of the ruling classes in Persia'. Nepotism was rife. The government was parasitic. The huge civil service was underpaid and corrupt. There was uneven distribution of wealth that was concentrated in the hands of the land-owning class but was not restricted to it. These prosperous Iranians included merchants, the upper section of the bureaucracy, and the high ranks of the army. This is

[37] Minutes of 16 Jan. 1951, FO 371/91524.

[38] Northcroft did however convey one insight: 'The Company', he said, 'was now only at the beginning of its troubles.' Ibid.

[39] Minute by E. A. Berthoud, 18 Apr. 1951, FO 371/91527.

[40] *The Times*, 22 Mar. 1951, Minutes in FO 371/91454/EP10115/60. The anonymous author was Ann K. S. Lambton (private information).

not the place to deal with such analysis at length, but it also dwelt on the tensions between the urban and rural parts of the population, between the settled population and the tribes, and between the 'westernized' element and the masses. Such contemporary comment was in line with the trends of subsequent scholarly research.[41]

'The cumulative effect of the disequilibrium in Persia', *The Times* article continued, made life in Iran so intolerable that it appeared to many of those who wished to reform the economy and social order of Iran, including parts of the 'intelligentsia' and the professional as well as the working classes, that 'they were faced with a choice between revolutionary catastrophe and a royal enlightened despotism'. This tension between the rich and the corrupt and other segments of the Iranian population had become sublimated into the drive against external domination. 'Anglo-Persian' had become the scapegoat. The controversy of the oil agreement had served as a catalyst of Iranian discontent with the old social order, which was generally held to be supported by the British. This argument was put forward with considerable verve and perception. It concluded:

> There has been an unwillingness to accept personal responsibility and a tendency for years to simplify social disequilibrium by blaming the unresolved conflicting forces within society on personified scapegoats. This has been the part filled by the British Government for years. The corrupt ruling class was, and is, considered to be the creation of the British, and the belief was fostered that it was only the British Government which blocked internal reform. . . .
>
> The present crisis goes far deeper than the question of oil and cannot be solved by the nationalization of oil as certain irresponsible Persian politicians claim.[42]

The oil question was one on which Iranians from different backgrounds could unite in protest against the old order. The rich and corrupt themselves found it convenient to place the blame on the British. 'Anglo-Persian' had become the personification of the exploitative imperialism of the British Empire and the source of social and economic injustice. To the British public that followed Middle Eastern affairs it was undoubtedly ironic and unjust that Britain, the power that had traditionally maintained Persian independence against Russia, should now be pilloried for blocking internal reform.

Within 'Anglo-Persian' the official who possessed the greatest awareness of those larger issues, in the view of the Foreign Office, was Sir Frederick Leggett, the company's labour adviser. It will be recalled that Leggett had served on the Anglo-American Committee

---

[41] See e.g. Keddie, *Roots of Revolution*, chap. 6.
[42] *The Times*, 22 Mar. 1951.

of Inquiry on Palestine. He was one of Bevin's old associates in the British Labour movement. Bevin respected his work in labour relations. Leggett in turn was probably responsible more than anyone else for Bevin's favourable assessment of the company's record. Leggett now believed that the only hope of salvaging the situation in Iran was not only to affirm a fifty–fifty profit-sharing arrangement, but also to take the Iranians into actual partnership. What his colleagues in 'Anglo-Persian' did not appear to recognize, he explained to L. A. C. Fry of the Eastern Department in February 1951, was that 'it was not merely a question of the Supplemental Oil Agreement being dead but a question of Concessions being dead'. Leggett continued to unburden himself with a shrewd political diagnosis:

> The Company still seemed to be thinking in terms of offering a little money here and another sop there, but all this . . . was entirely beside the point. What was required was a fresh start, on the basis of equal partnership. Unless the Company realised that, and were sincerely prepared to go forward in that direction, they might sooner or later find themselves without any installations in Persia: even if the Russians did not come in, nationalisation might expropriate the Company.[43]

His colleagues in 'Anglo-Persian' did not share that view. For his part Leggett had no doubt at all that they were on the wrong side of history. He denounced them for their shortsightedness in uncompromising language: 'helpless, niggling, without an idea between them, confused, hide-bound, small-minded, blind' and 'generally ineffective'.[44]

It is worthwhile to dwell briefly on Leggett because he probably knew the actual conditions in the oilfields and working classes of Iran as well as any other Englishman. He also had friends in many walks of Iranian life. He had worked hard to raise the standard of living in Iran by increases of wages by 'Anglo-Persian', by the improvement of working conditions, and by the development of the company's programmes in health and education. 'Anglo-Persian' was not an arm of the British government, but it performed many of the functions of a colonial administration. Bevin himself, Leggett reminded Sir William Strang, had 'personally' been associated with the company's labour policy and Leggett's part in it. Now the

---

[43] As recounted in a minute by L. A. C. Fry, 6 Feb. 1951, FO 371/91522/EP1531/47.

[44] The members of the Eastern Department concurred in this harsh judgement: 'The views he [Leggett] expressed about the out-moded attitude of his Board coincide in general, I believe with our own impression . . . in our fairly frequent meetings with them, [they] have never appeared to be looking at this problem from a broad angle.' Fry's minute of 6 Feb. 1951, ibid.

achievement of many years threatened to come to an abrupt and disastrous end. Leggett believed that most Iranians remained 'entirely friendly to this country', but all of his acquaintances in Iran saw the necessity of changing the company's relationship to Iran in order 'to give greater recognition to Persian national dignity'. After Bevin had left the Foreign Office, Leggett wrote to the Permanent Under-Secretary in April 1951 in a heart-rending plea for action on the part of the British government:

Those in Persia who have pressed for Nationalisation have themselves been shocked by the weapon they have put into the hands of the most dangerous elements but they cannot rescue themselves unless there is such a gesture from our side of the kind I have suggested.[45]

Leggett in short recommended a fifty–fifty split of profits on a partnership basis. Unless such creative measures could be taken, he warned, then there could be no 'suppressing of the monster which has been created'.[46]

Musaddiq

After a brief period of confusion following the assassination of Razmara, Mohammed Musaddiq became Prime Minister of Iran in late April 1951. He enjoyed unprecedented popular support. He took an uncompromising stand on the issue of British imperialism. 'He is obsessed by a single idea', Sir Francis Shepherd reported from Tehran, 'the nationalization of oil and the elimination of what he considers the maleficent influence of the Oil Company from Persia.'[47] Some of Shepherd's initial reports possess an intrinsic importance in the study of the triumph of Iranian nationalism as well as the history of the decline of British influence. They are significant even though Shepherd himself decided that Musaddiq was a 'lunatic', a word that recurred in his despatches. The perception of Musaddiq as the British saw him is no less important for purposes of the present discussion than the Iranian interpretation of Musaddiq as a national hero. Shepherd's opinion was widely shared not only in official circles but also by the British public. It is essential to grasp the implications of that judgement, as Shepherd himself developed them.

[45] Leggett to Strang, 14 Apr. 1951, FO 371/91527/EP1531/202. Part of Strang's reply included this statement: 'One of the troubles, as you will be the first to appreciate, is that conceptions among Persians of what this national dignity demands vary from the reasonable to the almost fantastic, with the latter for the present in the ascendant.' Strang to Leggett, 7 May 1951, FO 371/91527/EP1531/202.

[46] Leggett to Strang, 14 Apr. 1951, FO 371/91527/EP1531/202.

[47] Shepherd to Furlonge, Confidential, 14 May 1951, FO 371/91535/EP1531/356.

'He is of course a demagogue', Shepherd wrote in restating a universal British impression of Musaddiq—a demagogue who had extraordinary gifts of captivating the masses by theatrical faintings as he would reach the climax of his denunciation of British imperialism. According to Shepherd, 'there is evidence that his fainting fits have been on more than one occasion completely bogus', but they helped to explain Musaddiq's hold over the public imagination. Here was a nationalist of some seventy years who so indignantly railed against foreign domination that he conveyed the impression of transcending his delicate state of health. In Shepherd's view the popular enthusiasm bordered on idolatry. In examining this phenomenon he made this comment in one of his initial descriptions of Musaddiq:

> We shall have to watch him carefully because he is both cunning and slippery and completely unscrupulous. . . . He is rather tall but has short and bandy legs so that he shambles like a bear, a trait which is generally associated with considerable physical strength. He looks rather like a cab horse and is slightly deaf so that he listens with a strained but otherwise expressionless look on his face. He conducts the conversation at a distance of about six inches at which range he diffuses a slight reek of opium. His remarks tend to prolixity and he gives the impression of being impervious to argument.[48]

Shepherd's letter containing this information was circulated within the Foreign Office and to the Chancellor of the Exchequer, the Minister of Fuel and Power, the Minister of Defence, and the Prime Minister. The point is important because the impressions of Musaddiq that the ministers in London received from Shepherd's letters were by no means flattering. Conducting business with a 'lunatic' would require patience and firmness.

Later in the month Shepherd reported on a trip to the Prime Minister's 'lair'. The interview was conducted in the apparel by which Musaddiq became renowned in western circles, his pyjamas. Shepherd wrote:

> I became aware of footsteps behind me and turning round found several unshaven types who were walking behind in a way that made me feel like Molotov scuttling into a conference in Paris. No doubt my face expressed my feelings because the secretary waved them away and they disappeared. Upstairs there was [an] ante-room containing four more thugs.
>
> I was then taken into a sort of board room occupied by three more [thugs]. Musaddiq's bed-room opened out of this. It was a small room with a French window looking out into a garden and contained two other doors, each of which was blocked by a wardrobe. The Prime Minister who was wearing two suits of pyjamas, one khaki and the other green, was stretched upon a bed in one corner. He is certainly in an unhealthy state and is not able to walk

[48] Shepherd to Furlonge, Confidential, 6 May 1951, FO 371/91459/EP1015/201.

much so that there is some excuse for his living near the scene of his labours, but the thugs and the blockage of wardrobes are certainly unnecessarily bizarre.[49]

In summing up his thoughts about the beginning of the Musaddiq era, Shepherd wrote that 'the situation in Persia . . . has been on the whole a good deal more lunatic than ever.'[50]

The assumption that Iranian politicians were irrational, and that Musaddiq was a 'lunatic' who personified the unfortunate situation in Iran, led to the alternatives of doing something about him, perhaps covertly, or waiting for events to take a turn for the better, in other words hoping that the Iranians themselves would dispose of him. During the period with which the rest of this chapter is concerned, from his advent to power in the spring until the evacuation of 'Anglo-Persian' in the autumn, the British found no redeeming virtues in Musaddiq's regime. During this time however he began to demonstrate his ability to manipulate the forces of 'disequilibrium' as well as his potential as a reformer. He managed to wrench control of the affairs of Iran from the hands of the large landowners, who as a class were allied with the wealthy merchants and members of the professional community, including the army and the civil service. Musaddiq had the support of the younger and 'westernized' nationalists against the rich and corrupt. He himself was a wealthy landowner, and it is arguable that his projected reforms in agriculture might have led to a more equitable distribution of wealth and land tenure.[51] The British in 1951 however could find no inspiration in Musaddiq's reformist impulses. They regarded him rather as obsessed with expropriating a British company, and by doing so bringing about the economic ruin of his own country.

The American assessment, at least initially, was drastically different. The American Ambassador in Iran was Henry F. Grady. It will be recalled from earlier chapters that Grady had participated in the mission to supervise the Greek elections and had been involved in the Palestine controversy. Previously, during the war, he had served as one of Roosevelt's 'trouble-shooters' in India. He had developed a substantial reputation in British circles for meddling in the affairs of the British Empire. He sympathized with nationalist aspirations. Immediately before his tour of duty in Iran he had served as ambassador in Greece. In Iran he thought that the nationalists had good reason to protest against the exploitation of 'Anglo-Persian'. He believed that the moderate nationalists had the potential to

---

[49] Shepherd to Bowker, Confidential, 28 May 1951, FO 371/91542/EP1531/547.
[50] Ibid.
[51] For a discussion of these issues see especially Keddie, *Roots of Revolution*, chap. 6.

modernize the economy and make Iran truly 'independent'. Shepherd wrote of him:

> He is intelligent and by no means unfriendly to us. But he is a vain man, he is desperately anxious to be the saviour of Persia in the same way that he believes himself to have been the saviour of Greece and, to a lesser extent, India. He is plagued with an inflated and rather mediocre staff who listen credulously to every bazaar rumour and are sometimes individually anti-British, and finally he is by temperament quite unsuited to dealing with Persian deviousness and intrigue which, he confesses, reduce him to '110% frustration'.[52]

There was a point of basic difference in outlook between Grady and Shepherd. Grady was willing to assume that Iranian politics were rational.

Throughout this stage of the oil crisis, from spring to autumn 1951, there were two fundamentally divergent reactions of the British and Americans. They were described, accurately and clearly, by Sir Francis Shepherd shortly after the evacuation by 'Anglo-Persian' in October. The first was that the Americans regarded Musaddiq as a rational and stable Iranian leader with whom a satisfactory agreement could be concluded. The Americans believed, in Shepherd's words, 'that Musaddiq is a sufficiently stable phenomenon . . . to come to an agreement . . . however unpalatable this may be for us'. Shepherd himself continued to deny Musaddiq's rationality as well as his stability. The second radically different assessment was the American view that Aramco's fifty–fifty profit-sharing precedent should be adopted in Iran and indeed in all of the Middle East. 'The Americans are quite prepared to sacrifice the Anglo-Iranian Oil Company for the sake of the 50/50 principle', Shepherd wrote.[53] In his view such a capitulation seemed to be neither compelling nor desirable. 'I do not believe it is necessary', he continued, 'to go so far as this.' Shepherd indeed took a patriotic pride in the company and thought it would be folly for the British government not to take a firm stand against Persian attempts to expropriate British property. His views coincided with those in London who favoured a strong British response. He explained his attitude and its rationale: 'I think we should fight for [the] retention by the Anglo-Iranian Oil Company, as far as possible, of the control of the industry they have built up. . . . The disappearance of the A. I. O. C. and its replacement by [an] international consortium would be a considerable blow to our prestige in this country.'[54] The extent to which the British could continue to hold

---

[52] Shepherd to Furlonge, Confidential, 14 May 1951, FO 371/91535/EP1531/356.
[53] Shepherd to Morrison, 23 Oct. 1951, FO 371/91606/EP1531/990.
[54] Ibid.

their own was a contentious issue in British circles. Here the point is the diametrically opposed American outlook. It held that, unless the British yielded on the principle of the fifty–fifty split, they would lose everything.

The champion of the American principle of equal profit-sharing was George C. McGhee, the Assistant Secretary of State for the Near East, South Asia, and Africa. McGhee, as has been pointed out, was a successful oil man who had the confidence of Acheson. He held robust opinions about the oil controversy. He left the British in no doubt whatever that he believed 'Anglo-Persian' to be niggardly and shortsighted.[55] In September 1950 he had warned the British of the 'repercussions' that the Aramco agreement would have throughout the Middle East. In straightforward and ominous language, 'he could not emphasize too strongly the impact that they would have'.[56] Some of these discussions became extremely technical because they involved problems of the sterling area and British taxes as well as the legal aspects of the concession. McGhee was quite unmoved by the fiscal and legal difficulties of 'Anglo-Persian' in matching the Aramco agreement. He believed that the Iranians had to be admitted as corporate partners and that it was imperative for the company to face these problems 'in an imaginative manner'. 'If we lost the day politically in Persia we would loose the oil anyway', he told Furlonge and others at a later meeting.[57]

By April 1951 McGhee was advising the British that they might have to accept 'nationalisation without compensation'—a phrase that apparently caused convulsions within the British Treasury.[58] Unless the company could find some way 'to satisfy Persia's national aspirations', then the British, in McGhee's characteristically blunt words, would be kicked out. He gave this advice generously, persistently, and, the British thought, arrogantly. They believed him to be anti-British, or at least so pro-Iranian that he was oblivious to British interests. In fact he despaired of the British grasping the basic point: if the company refused to yield on the fifty–fifty principle then the Americans as well as the British would stand to lose the oil reserves of Iran to the Soviet Union after the period of chaos following British withdrawal. What appeared to him to be a mandatory accommodation of not unreasonable demands, however, seemed to the British to be a sell-out at their expense. McGhee in British eyes stood guilty of a deadly sin of the postwar era—in Sir William

---

[55] See minutes in FO 371/82348 where these and other strong expressions are recorded.
[56] See *Foreign Relations 1950*, V, p. 596.
[57] Minutes of a meeting of 2 Apr. 1951, FO 371/91244/EP1023/10G.
[58] See minute by P. E. Ramsbotham, 13 Apr. 1951, FO 371/91527/EP1531/193.

Strang's judgement, 'appeasement'. McGhee was so outspoken on the need to yield to Iranian susceptibilities regardless of short-term British financial losses that the officials of the Foreign Office took steps towards lodging a formal complaint, only to discover that his views coincided with Acheson's.[59]

An analysis of American policy in Iran would be far beyond the scope of the present chapter, but it is necessary to comment briefly on Acheson's attitude in order to understand the British side of the crisis. The British were responding not only to developments in Iran but also to the American reaction to them. The local tension between Shepherd and Grady reflected wider discord. It is convenient to emphasize certain points made in Acheson's memoirs about this conflict in Anglo-American relations and his assessment of Musaddiq. Acheson had an acute grasp of the essentials of the crisis. His views about Musaddiq were also discerning: 'essentially a rich, reactionary, feudal-minded Persian inspired by a fanatical hatred of the British and a desire to expel them and all their works from the country regardless of the cost'. One might quarrel with parts of that description since Musaddiq believed himself to be a reformer and a demo-crat—and the genuineness of his conviction helps to explain his charisma—but Acheson was entirely right about Musaddiq's anti-British motivation. He summed up his impression of Musaddiq in the words of 'a neutral freebooter', which more or less corresponded with the Iranian concept of the 'negative equilibrium' and the British idea of the Persians fecklessly attempting to play off the great powers against each other. Acheson in other words did not under-estimate Musaddiq though he did, like most others, seriously ques-tion his comprehension of economic issues. Musaddiq in sum appeared to be 'a great actor and a great gambler', and Acheson accurately stated the case when he wrote that this 'unique character truly sowed the wind and reaped the whirlwind'.[60]

Acheson agreed with McGhee about the necessity for 'Anglo-Persian' to adjust its profits along the lines of a fifty–fifty split. On this point Acheson and McGhee were farsighted in anticipating that, once the Saudi government won this concession from Aramco, no other government in the Middle East eventually would accept any-thing less. Acheson found it incomprehensible that the company did not straightaway neutralize Iranian protest by yielding immediately on minor points such as the appointment of Iranians to its board of directors, the opening of the company's financial records to Iranian auditors, and the increasing of Iranian personnel. Such measures

[59] See e.g. C. E. Steel to Bowker, 30 Apr. 1951, FO 371/91531/EP1531/291.
[60] Dean Acheson, *Present at the Creation* (New York, 1969), pp. 503–7.

would have cost the company little, and they might to some extent have helped to satisfy the Iranian 'national dignity'. Acheson and McGhee were not alone in urging these reforms. These and many other measures were also advocated by Sir Frederick Leggett and by the Middle East experts of the Foreign Office.[61] What astounded Acheson was not so much that the British government appeared to have so little influence over a company in which it owned half the shares ('heterodox' was the word he used to describe the socialism of the Labour government), but the cretin attitude of the company towards its own long-term interests. 'Unusual and persistent stupidity' was the phrase he used to sum up the mentality of 'Anglo-Persian'.[62]

It is noteworthy that in his memoirs Acheson identified one of the sources of the British trouble as the assessments of Sir Francis Shepherd, who, as has been seen, tended to vindicate the company. 'This unimaginative disciple of the "whiff of grapeshot" school of diplomacy', Acheson commented, had arrived at an 'arbitrary and unyielding' appraisal of the situation in Iran that Acheson believed to be erroneous in interpretation and nefarious in its influence on the British government. Shepherd's assessments confirmed what the jingo elements wanted to believe. They were a root cause of the divergent British and American response to the crisis. Acheson's ultimate verdict on Shepherd and 'Anglo-Persian' should be borne in mind as the key to the general American attitude towards the British as the crisis reached a climax in the summer of 1951: 'Never had so few lost so much so stupidly and so fast.'[63]

The Question of Intervention

Effective intervention, whether overt or covert, requires firm and consistent political direction. The Middle East experts of the Foreign Office might possess a sophisticated knowledge of the social and economic structure of Iran as well as a shrewd appreciation of its political and religious leaders; but the overall British response to the 'nationalization' of the Anglo-Iranian Oil Company could be no better than the leadership at the time of the crisis. Herbert Morrison became Foreign Secretary at roughly the same time that Musaddiq ascended to power. When nationalization was proclaimed as Iranian law on the 2nd of May 1951, Musaddiq became one of the new Foreign Secretary's foremost anxieties. No one doubted Morrison's

---

[61] E.g. E. A. Berthoud wrote: 'I think that . . . A. I. O. C. . . . should . . . admit Persian Directors to the Board. This is a key psychological point which does not really cost anything.' Minute of 4 Apr. 1951, FO 371/91244/E1531/11.

[62] *Present at the Creation*, p. 501.

[63] Ibid., p. 503.

intellectual and political agility. His difficulty was that he found himself suddenly hurled into a controversy in which he had no background. The story of his struggle with the Persian oil crisis was one of frustration and indignation. His temperament would have led him to respond abrasively and perhaps belligerently. Instead he was compelled to take a more moderate line forced upon him by his colleagues in the Cabinet, not least Attlee. In one of the early Cabinet discussions on the subject, Morrison was told that he would be—in a remarkably strong phrase—'well advised' to avoid language 'which would give offence to the Persian Parliament and people' and not 'to stigmatize the new Prime Minister [Musaddiq] as an extremist'.[64]

It is worthwhile to inquire briefly into the motivation of the Labour government during the crisis. What was the basis of its knowledge? As has been noted, the American Secretary of State himself believed that the British Ambassador in Tehran conveyed a distorted impression in telegrams and despatches to London. The Eastern Department of the Foreign Office was well aware of the discrepancy between the American estimate of the situation and the conclusions drawn up by the British embassy. So great was the divergence that it troubled the head of the Eastern Department. In late April Furlonge returned from consultations in Washington to warn that the Americans were extremely sceptical about possible British intervention. They would probably give their blessing to overt intervention only in the event of an attempted Communist coup. They were not interested in salvaging the property of 'Anglo-Persian'. According to Furlonge, 'The Americans are above all preoccupied with the possibility that, by failing to accept some degree of "nationalisation", we may risk setting ourselves against a Nationalist force which in the last resort we shall not be able to oppose.'[65] What were the circumstances, to rephrase the question, within which the Labour government decided on a course of non-intervention? One important restraint was the uncertainty of American refusal to provide support, moral or otherwise, except in the event of a deteriorating situation in which the Shah might be swallowed up in a Communist revolution.

There was truth in the allegation that Sir Francis Shepherd might just as well have been writing at the turn of the century. Nevertheless his reports made a persuasive case, and, to those who took pride in the British Empire and the success of 'Anglo-Persian', a compelling one. To place Shepherd's response within the context of this book, it was the same as Lord Killearn's probably would have been, though

---

[64] Cabinet Minutes 32 (51), 30 Apr. 1951, CAB 128/19.
[65] Minute by Furlonge, 21 Apr. 1951, FO 371/91528/EP1531/215.

Killearn undoubtedly would have argued for intervention with considerably more vigour and intellectual substance. To rephrase one of Killearn's maxims, in the 'East' the knowledge that powder was in the gun was usually enough to be persuasive, provided the natives knew that the British had the will-power to pull the trigger if necessary. In Iran Shepherd's reaction to the crisis reflected the indignation of a considerable part of the British public who expected the Labour government to protect the property of British subjects as well as their lives, and generally to uphold British prestige in the 'East'. Shepherd was a linear descendant of Cromer and Curzon. He shared with Killearn a firm idea of the 'Imperial' tradition, and he thought it entirely justified to employ force to demonstrate that the British would not tolerate the illegal 'nationalisation' of a British company. 'Gunboat diplomacy' was not necessarily an anachronism. Herbert Morrison himself sympathized with those views. Nevertheless there was a clear recognition within the British Cabinet that the Iran of 1951 was not the Persia of 1901.

There were of course more subtle methods of intervention than 'gunboat diplomacy'. The origins of covert planning for the 1953 coup can be traced to the 1951 period. Here the historian treads on patchy ground. The British archives have been carefully 'weeded' in order to protect identities and indeed to obscure the truth about British complicity. Nevertheless enough fragmentary evidence exists to indicate the main progression of thought. In June 1951 E. A. Berthoud (an Assistant Under-Secretary who supervised economic affairs) discussed the crisis with Ann K. S. Lambton, who had served during the war as press attaché at the British Embassy in Tehran. She was now a Reader in Persian at the School of Oriental and African Studies at the University of London. Berthoud described her as an authority who had spent long periods of time in Iran and probably knew 'the language and mentality of its people better than anyone else in this country'. Miss Lambton was of the 'decided opinion' that it was not possible 'to do business' with Musaddiq. She thought it important not to make concessions to him except to the extent necessary to maintain order in southern Iran.[66]

Miss Lambton believed that it would be possible to undermine Musaddiq's position 'by *covert* means'. One way in which this could be done would be to give heart to the substantial body of Iranians who feared the risk of being denounced as traitors but whose idea of the Iranian national interest coincided with the British conception. She thought it might be possible through the public relations

[66] Minute by Berthoud, 15 June 1951, FO 371/91548/EP1531/674. Among Miss Lambton's works on Iran is *Landlord and Peasant in Persia* (London, 1953).

officer at the British Embassy in Tehran gradually to change the public mood and thus give the opportunity to intelligent Iranians who were well disposed to the British to speak out against Musaddiq. According to Berthoud's minute: 'Miss Lambton feels that without a campaign on the above lines it is not possible to create the sort of climate in Tehran which is necessary to change the régime.' With discreet efforts on the part of the British, it would be possible to co-operate with Iranians who knew that Musaddiq's programme of 'nationalisation' would probably lead to economic suicide on a national scale. There were plenty of Iranians who saw that what Iran needed was economic development, not a rupture with the British, and that the British could assist them in organizing Iranian finances and helping to raise the standard of living. Most educated or intelligent Iranians knew that 'Anglo-Persian' had been made the scapegoat for many problems which only they themselves could solve. What Miss Lambton was proposing was in effect a public relations and educational programme which she lamented that the company itself had not implemented.

She made one specific proposal which is of great historical interest. According to Berthoud, Miss Lambton suggested that Robin Zaehner, Lecturer in Persian (and later Professor of Eastern Religions) at Oxford, would be 'the ideal man' to conduct the covert pro-British campaign. Again according to Berthoud's minute:

> Dr. Zaehner was apparently extremely successful in covert propaganda in 1944 at the time that there was a serious threat that the Russians would take over Azerbaijan. He knows almost everyone who matters in Tehran and is a man of great subtlety. The line then was, of course, to mobilise public opinion from the bazaars upwards about the dangers of Russian penetration.[67]

In that minute may thus be found the origins of the 'Zaehner mission' and the beginnings of the 1953 coup.[68] For the purposes of the present discussion it is important to note Miss Lambton's insight into the manipulation of public opinion 'from the bazaars upwards'. The mobilization of public sentiment against the British was one of the key reasons for Musaddiq's success.

Since the archives, for better or worse, link Professor Lambton with the planning to undermine Musaddiq, it should be stated that her views were entirely in line with those of other British authorities on Iran. They believed that the situation was deteriorating so rapidly

---

[67] Minute by Berthoud, 15 June 1951, FO 371/91548/EP1531/674.

[68] See Woodhouse, *Something Ventured*, p. 111, whose account in general is of critical importance. It is the first to lift the veil of secrecy from the British side. For the dramatic American involvement see Kermit Roosevelt, *Countercoup: The Struggle for the Control of Iran* (New York, 1979). The best scholarly account is by Barry Rubin, *Paved with Good Intentions: The American Experience and Iran* (New York, 1980).

that firm and effective measures were necessary in order to offset the blunders of the company. From the British point of view the Musaddiq era was a tragedy, and not merely because of the fate of 'Anglo-Persian'. Musaddiq played on the xenophobe element in Iranian society in order to expel what he believed to be the parasite of British capitalism. In the process he poisoned the relations between the Iranian and British peoples. Miss Lambton herself later provided one of the soundest historical explanations of how Musaddiq succeeded in gaining such a hold over the masses. The discontent against the company, she argued subsequently, could best be understood in terms of the widespread dissatisfaction at the state of affairs in Iranian society and government. This 'negative factor of frustration' sprang from such diverse sources that only an appeal to extreme nationalism could galvanize it into a coherent movement. That was Musaddiq's achievement, and Miss Lambton identified a key element in the outburst of nationalism which he represented: 'it was not until the movement was interpreted by the religious classes in terms of Islam that it achieved widespread support.'[69]

Only over a long period of years has Iranian and western scholarship provided the full measure of Musaddiq and the reasons for his enduring reputation as a national hero. He was able to tap the nationalist energies of the shopkeepers and artisans of the bazaar as well as the members of trade unions and the intellectuals within the bureaucracy. When he spoke out for national independence and freedom from foreign economic exploitation, he articulated the sentiments of a large segment of the Iranian public which had a desire for social reform as well as a discontent with the old regime. In Nikki Keddie's words, 'Oppositionists of the most varying views —Marxists, leftists, liberals, and rightists, both secular and religious —invoked his name and example, cherished his picture, and found appropriate quotations from him to support their views.'[70] Such an interpretation helps to convey the richness of the era and offsets Sir Francis Shepherd's diagnosis of Musaddiq as a 'lunatic'. It should be borne in mind however that Shepherd's view, though influential, was not representative of sophisticated contemporary British analysis. The estimates by certain officials of the Eastern Department of the Foreign Office such as Geoffrey Furlonge, as well as those by Miss Lambton, flowed in the direction of subsequent scholarly interpretation. There was one element of general consensus. Musaddiq above all was an anti-imperialist nationalist.

[69] Ann K. S. Lambton, 'The Impact of the West on Persia', *International Affairs*, 33, 1 (Jan. 1957), p. 24.
[70] Keddie, *Roots of Revolution*, p. 141.

No one within the British Cabinet grasped that basic point more clearly than did the Prime Minister himself. Once 'nationalization' had been proclaimed, the British had to respond to Musaddiq by indicating how much of the principle they would accept. Here was an opportunity for endless legal and financial quibble. Attlee would have none of it. He expressed his own view vigorously and succinctly, and he did so bearing in mind his experiences with other nationalists. His broader outlook made a stark contrast with the more narrow legalistic and financial objections of the Foreign Office and Treasury. At the same time he made it clear that he did not have much hope for coming to terms with Musaddiq. Attlee's entire policy was based on the premiss that the moderate nationalists had to be accommodated before the initiative passed to the extremists. In his view Musaddiq was not only an extremist but a fanatic. Nevertheless he pursued the same principle as if trying to salvage a bad situation. Attlee's views were recorded in the form of an instruction to the Foreign Office over the telephone. They are of paramount importance in understanding the British response to Musaddiq and the question of intervention:

[W]e must, in view of the present highly charged atmosphere in Persia and in particular of the emotional state of the Persian Prime Minister (who appeared to be on the lunatic fringe), agree to accept the principle of nationalisation. It was no use making this a sticking point.

Attlee continued, and here he correlated his general political ideas about Dominion status with the issue of nationalisation in Iran:

It was . . . rather like trying to meet the term 'Dominion Status' in granting a country independence. In such a case it was the title and all that was implicit in it that was of overriding importance. It might well be that in negotiating an agreement in such a context a number of modifications would be introduced and that the resulting agreement would confer something that was in fact a good deal less than dominion status. . . . The great thing was to give Musaddiq an opportunity of saving face.[71]

According to Attlee's own precepts, it was already too late. The time to have negotiated a reasonable settlement would have been before Musaddiq. Now all one could do was to hope for the best. What were the circumstances in which the Labour government decided on a course of non-intervention? Part of the answer lies in Attlee's intuitive response, which probably was the same as Bevin's would have been.

Morrison was highly annoyed with Attlee's conciliatory attitude. It did not help him at all with the reaction of the British public and

[71] As recorded in a minute by M. R. Starkey, 14 May 1951, FO 371/91534/EP1531/321.

Parliament. 'Criticism might be severe', according to the Foreign Office minute that recorded Morrison's views, 'and he would have to answer it.'[72] His minutes give the impression that he was much more sensitive to 'Persian oil' as an inflammatory issue in British politics rather than as a critical lubricant in the economy or the source of volatile misunderstanding between the two countries. He was particularly disappointed in the lukewarm attitude of the Americans towards possible intervention. In his view they needed 'stiffening' against 'a largely non-existent Govt.' in Iran '& a PM who . . . fainted in the Majlis', as Morrison had heard the day before over the BBC.[73] He was contemptuous of Musaddiq. Nor did certain circumstances sooth Morrison's irritable disposition. In giving instructions to 'stiffen' the Americans he wrote at 5.30 a.m. on the 14th of May during Whitsuntide. The irritation of having to cancel a trip to Southampton because of Musaddiq crept through into his minutes. Such details are important. Morrison was not in his element in dealing with the oil crisis either temperamentally or by intellectual inclination. Nevertheless he was required to display vigilance because some sort of response to 'nationalisation' was necessary. He knew that the British position would be strengthened if the Americans would back him. To his chagrin however he discovered that his orders to 'stiffen' the Americans only resulted in a stiffening of their previous attitude. The British would only weaken their case, McGhee stated in response, if they gave the impression that the United States supported the claims of 'Anglo-Persian'.[74]

McGhee's blunt pronouncements on more than one occasion served as a catalyst for Morrison's anger at American policy. 'McGhee had not always been helpful', he commented. The Foreign Secretary failed to understand why the Americans in general disliked 'nationalisation' and believed it to be one of the root causes of British economic distress, yet nevertheless supported the principle in Iran. 'It was almost as if American opinion did not approve of nationalisation', according to Morrison's impression, 'excepting when it damaged British interests.' This grudging language represented Morrison's approach. 'It was open to us', according to him, 'to retaliate economically or militarily against Persia.'[75] Such bluster did not alter the American attitude. It merely confirmed doubts about Morrison's desire to work together towards a conciliatory solution. In such thoroughly bad moods Morrison would elaborate his solution to the

[72] Ibid.
[73] Minute by Morrison, 14 May 1951, FO 371/91534/EP1531/321.
[74] Franks to Morrison, Top Secret, 16 May 1951, FO 371/91534/EP1531/334/G.
[75] As conveyed in Bowker to Shepherd, Confidential, 5 May 1951, FO 371/91531/EP1513/294.

Iranian problem together with his conditions. According to a Foreign Office letter to Shepherd explaining the disposition of the new chief: 'Mr. Morrison's attitude in brief was that he was quite willing to let the Persians have a say in the oil industry and he was quite willing to negotiate some kind of compromise; but production must continue and there must be no unilateral action by the Persians.'[76] Such a firm stand may have been entirely rational, but Morrison's general outlook as well as his specific displeasure with McGhee (which was well known) confirmed American scepticism that there was not much difference, after all, between a Tory and a Labour approach to the problems of the Middle East.

Morrison accurately sensed that McGhee was a prime mover in American policy. McGhee himself, as has been noted, had genuine insight into the nature of the economic revolution in the Middle East as heralded by Aramco's fifty–fifty profit-sharing agreement. He was exasperated that Morrison appeared not to see Aramco's writing on the wall for 'Anglo-Persian'. Temperamentally McGhee would have preferred to see the British and the Iranians slug it out. They deserved each other. Such an encounter would have satisfied his sense of tragi-comedy, if not farce, had it not been for one overriding consideration. 'If it were not for the cold war', McGhee reflected much later, after tempers had cooled, 'there is no reason why we shouldn't let the British and the Iranians fight it out.' McGhee was touching on a central issue. Why, to rephrase the question about British non-intervention, did the Americans so persistently and strenuously object to the British defending their own interests? McGhee gave a clear and accurate summation when he reflected on the crisis three years later: 'It is only because we didn't want during the cold war to run the risk of losing Iran.'[77]

Morrison cheered on his permanent officials when they produced an important appreciation arguing that the occupation of southern Persia would not necessarily lead to Russian intervention. 'This is better', Morrison commented.[78] According to this calculation, the Soviet Union in the circumstances of the Korean war probably did not wish to risk the outbreak of a global war. If Russian troops did intervene in Iran they might occupy the northern part of the country without actually coming into contact with British forces. The oil-fields of 'Anglo-Persian' in southern Iran and the refinery at Abadan could be protected by the British and the flow of oil to the west

---

[76] Bowker to Shepherd, Confidential, 5 May 1951, FO 371/91531/EP1513/294.

[77] Transcript of the 'Princeton Seminars', 15–16 May 1954, p. 1691, Acheson Papers.

[78] Notation by Morrison on memorandum by Dixon of 18 May 1951, FO 371/91459/EP1015/308.

would continue. This argument gave heart to those who in 1946 would have preferred the creation of a British satellite in south-western Iran. It was the same line of thought that Bevin had emphatically rejected at the time of the Azerbaijan crisis. Its appeal in 1951 was one of pre-emption. By striking first the British would have consolidated their hold over the oilfields, but if they waited for the situation to deteriorate into one of a Communist revolution then the opportunity would be lost forever. It seemed to be an irrefutable case against the American argument that intervention should occur only in the event of impending revolution. 'If Persia by a communist coup passed into the Soviet orbit before the Western Powers had time to prevent this happening', according to this assessment, 'any subsequent Western intervention would be much more likely than before to provoke a major war with Russia.'[79] Unfortunately for those who were attracted to this 'pre-emptive' line of thought, the Americans decisively interpreted the situation in the opposite way. British intervention would increase the chances of an outbreak of world war. These calculations were taking place at the same time that American military authorities were assessing the risks of bombing bases in Manchuria. Would the Russians see that the British occupation was merely a prelude to the peaceful partition of Iran? The Americans feared not, quite apart from being sceptical about British political motivation. The larger strategic issues of the Korean war as well as the still vibrant strain of American anti-colonialism militated against British intervention.

It is not possible here to discuss the military ramifications of the problem, but it is important to bear in mind the question of British manpower. To occupy effectively the southern areas of Iran would have required the mobilization of reserves. Even with the clear intention of a limited military operation, it would have been extremely difficult if not impossible to dispel the impression that the British were mobilizing for world war. Against the background of Korea, Iran in 1951 differed from Suez in 1956, at least up to the time of Soviet intervention in Hungary.

It is also not possible here to go into the logistical and technical difficulties that the British might have faced, but here too it is important to bear in mind that the Chiefs of Staff foresaw immense problems. Sir John Slessor (Chief of the Air Staff), the principal advocate, in his own words, of 'a really bold and powerful strike', was greatly disappointed in the lack of military opportunity. Too few troops could be transported quickly enough to overcome Iranian resistance. Sir William Slim (Chief of the Imperial General Staff)

[79] Ibid.

throughout these discussions reminded his colleagues that it was all very well to speak of a 'tough' attitude but if the British found themselves unable to back it up with troops, 'it would indeed be disastrous'.[80] Ultimately this was the decisive point. In answer to the question about the reasons for British non-intervention, one must press beyond the ethos of the Labour government because some ministers, including Morrison, favoured a belligerent policy. This line of thought did not peter out, as will be seen, until the actual decision to evacuate in September, but it was curtailed by one overriding consideration that became apparent early on in all of the most searching discussions. The Labour government could not have mobilized the British nation for an indefinite military occupation of southern Iran. This was the time of the balance of payments crisis. There was neither the manpower, the economic resources, nor the sustained determination necessary for a successful 'Imperial' venture. There was a wistful and revealing tone of lament about one of the remarks made in a Chiefs of Staff meeting which serves as a most appropriate conclusion to the question of intervention: 'The military difficulty of mounting an operation in South West Persia nowadays was almost entirely due to our having been deprived of the use of the Indian Army.'[81]

The Meaning of 'Nationalisation' and Plans for the Seizure of Abadan

In the public debates about the consequences of Iranian 'nationalisation', one personality was conspicuous for clarity of thought and a grasp of essentials. His views are of considerable interest because of his part in a later era of the dissolution of the British Empire as well as in the summer of 1951, when he contributed substantially to clarifying a complex and emotional issue. This was Harold Macmillan, within a few months to become a member of the new Conservative government. In the great Middle East parliamentary debate of July 1951, Attlee commended him for rising above party politics. Macmillan's ideas revealed the conflict between passion and principle in the British response to the nationalization crisis. The public dimension of the debate is no less important than the discussions within the government, in part because the Labour government was especially sensitive to public sentiment at a time when a general election was in

---

[80] Confidential Annex to COS (51) 84, 21 May, 1951, DEFE 4/43; minutes in FO 371/91459/EP1015/202.
[81] Ibid.

the wind. The public mood was not yet jingoistic, and it could be argued that Macmillan and others who argued in the same vein prevented it from becoming so. He took a certain glee in seeing the Labour party hoist on its own socialist petard, but his main purpose was to urge restraint. He confronted the problem by asking 'What . . . does the British Government mean by "nationalisation"?'[82]

He assumed that the members of the Labour government were familiar with the concept. It was the basis of their political creed. His was definitely a Conservative approach to the problem:

> They have band[i]ed it [nationalization] about a good deal in the last 20 years. It is true that, like every epidemic, it has become a little less virulent at home. We are, perhaps, through the worst of it here. But the mischief is that this disease, like others, cannot be confined to one place. . . . One could have thought that the Government of a country which owns, or did own, more property abroad than any nation in the world would have realised the danger.[83]

What the Labour government should have anticipated, according to Macmillan, was that there were two types of nationalization. The first variety was one in which fair compensation would be given to the owners. The other was expropriation pure and simple. He now made a crucial point. He believed that it was vital to have a clear idea about the meaning of ownership:

> Persian oil is nationally owned. It has always been nationally owned. It is in the same position as coal in Britain became after it became the property of the nation. . . . The oil belongs to the Persians as does the mineral wealth . . . but the installations, the tanker fleet and the mass of other properties are, of course, the property of the Anglo-Iranian Oil Company.[84]

It was imperative to prevent the expropriation of British property and to continue the exploitation of the oil reserves for the benefit of both parties. Macmillan's answer to the problem was to persuade the Iranians of the desirability of 'partnership'. British thought was now moving in public as well as in government circles towards a solution along the lines of the Aramco arrangement with the Saudis.

What if the Iranians would not agree to 'partnership'? Macmillan gave a lucid answer. The British would have to rely on peaceful arbitration, perhaps through the international court of justice, or they would have to resort to force. If the Iranians flouted the decisions of the international court and unilaterally abrogated the company's concession, then the British would have the right to protest. Ultimately they might be led to a grave alternative. 'We may have to make a frightful choice: either another war, with all that we know

[82] *Parliamentary Debates* (Commons), 30 July 1951, col. 1056.
[83] Ibid.
[84] Ibid., col. 1057.

it means, or . . . surrender.'[85] In the meantime the British government would have to have faith in international arbitration even though there might be considerable insult to British 'prestige' in the process. He could hardly have put the case more clearly. He blamed the Labour government for not having had the foresight to avert an obvious crisis, but, now that the crisis was upon them, the British would have to bear with arbitration and only in the last resort contemplate war. His line of thought in fact followed the same pattern of agonized deliberations going on within the government. He also helped to clarify a general source of confusion, the word 'nationalization'. What was not at stake was the ownership of Iranian oil. It belonged to the Iranians. What was at stake was the property of the company, and perhaps the lives of British subjects. This was the short-term issue. The long-term question was whether the company would be allowed to continue to exploit the petroleum resources of Iran, or whether the company would be expelled. All of these issues came to a much more rapid head than was anticipated by Macmillan and his Conservative colleagues, by Attlee and the Labour government, and not least by the Anglo-Iranian Oil Company.

The decision not to intervene militarily in order to protect British property was taken on the 12th of July. This was a turning point. Morrison later observed that 'if military action was to be politically effective it should be quick'.[86] The eventual unsatisfactory outcome of the oil crisis gave great force to Morrison's comment. The failure to intervene effectively, either militarily or politically, undoubtedly became one of the root causes of the Suez crisis five years later. At the time however the balance of wisdom seemed clearly to lie on the side of restraint. According to the Cabinet minutes of the 12th of July: 'We had no legal right to interfere with Persian expropriation and operation of their oil industry.'[87] British intervention would flout the principles of the United Nations, and, in the words of the Foreign Office paper on which this opinion was based, 'we should not only alienate American and world opinion generally . . . but should run the risk of an eventual resolution in the United Nations calling on us to withdraw'. There was a further risk that weighed heavily on the minds of the Cabinet members—British subjects might be seized as hostages or perhaps even murdered. 'If force appeared to be about to threaten Persia', according to the same paper,

[85] Ibid., col. 1062. For his subsequent views on the crisis see Harold Macmillan, *Tides of Fortune* (London, 1969), pp. 341–50.

[86] Herbert Morrison, *An Autobiography* (London, 1960), p. 281.

[87] Cabinet Minutes 51 (51), 12 July 1951, CAB 128/20.

'our nationals in the oil fields might be placed in jeopardy before we could extricate them.'[88] Even on the best hypothesis that military intervention might be feasible and that British subjects would not be taken as hostages in the process, how long could the Anglo-Iranian Oil Company be maintained by British bayonets? One is tempted to be sarcastic about Morrison's insight. He reluctantly concluded that a military occupation 'would prejudice the Persians permanently against the Company'.[89] With a logic born of desperation the British hit upon one ingenious idea, or so it appeared to Sir Francis Shepherd, whose advice continued to be influential. The personnel of 'Anglo-Persian' would withdraw. The Iranians would quickly comprehend that they could not manage the oil industry themselves. They would come to terms and welcome the British back. In short, in Morrison's words, evacuation appeared to be 'the best means of bringing the Persians in general to their senses'.[90]

In the critical Cabinet discussions, in July while deciding not to intervene and in September when faced with eviction, it was Attlee who steadied nerves and guided his colleagues towards restraint. During this time of crisis he demonstrated genuine insight into the sources of Middle Eastern nationalism and the way in which British influence might be preserved. He not only believed in 'partnership' but saw the need of a real and not a superficial end to the old system of concessions. The minutes of the 12th of July record Attlee's estimate of Musaddiq as well as his general appraisal of the situation:

> Dr. Mussadiq had been able to form his Government owing to the support of Persians who were dissatisfied with former rule by a corrupt clique. We could not safely assume that if we succeeded in upsetting the present Government their successors would be less unsatisfactory, and we should risk identifying ourselves with support of an equally undemocratic régime.

Attlee then explained his views on nationalization, 'partnership', and the necessity to remain on good terms with the moderate nationalists:

> If negotiations could be resumed it would be wise to stress, not only our acceptance of the principle of nationalisation, but also our willingness to operate the oil industry, on behalf of the Persian Government, on a basis of friendly partnership: we must not alienate genuine nationalist feeling in Persia by clinging to the old technique of obtaining concessions and insisting upon exact compliance with their terms.[91]

In reading such comments one might reflect whether the crisis might have been averted had Attlee's ideas been applied earlier, or for that

[88] Memorandum by Morrison, 11 July 1951, CP (51) 200, CAB 129/46.
[89] Ibid.
[90] Ibid.
[91] Cabinet Minutes 51 (51), 12 July 1951, CAB 128/20.

matter whether it might have had a less disastrous outcome for the British had he been able to devote more sustained attention to it. He worked under great pressure, and he bore the burden of a Foreign Secretary whose views were neither inventive nor in line with his own. Attlee made mistakes. Two of the more salient in the oil crisis were his acquiescence in the idea to evacuate the personnel of 'Anglo-Persian' before he had thought through all of the consequences, and his endorsement of the appointment of the Lord Privy Seal, Richard Stokes, to negotiate a settlement with Musaddiq.

At this point it is important to stress the essential issues and to lament that it is not possible to discuss this stage of the crisis in its complexity. It lies beyond the present analysis to consider the case before the International Court of Justice (which had precipitated the Cabinet meeting of the 12th of July), or the Security Council of the United Nations. It is moreover not possible to discuss the broader economic dimension of the problem (though it is important to bear in mind that the balance of payments crisis was occurring simultaneously). It is also not feasible to consider the issue as seen from the points of view of the British Treasury, the Ministry of Fuel and Power, and the Ministry of Defence. Nor is it possible to pursue the various missions in the summer of 1951 including the 'Jackson Mission' of the Anglo-Iranian Oil Company, or the mission of President Truman's envoy, Averell Harriman. All of these subjects are important and no doubt will become the basis of different books by students of Iran's relations with Britain and the United States, and by those interested in the later stages of the crisis and the reorganization of the oil industry of Iran. Here these issues will be touched on only in relation to the theme of the Labour government's response to the question of intervention, in order to understand the outcome in October 1951.

'Phased withdrawal' was the term applied to the company's plan 'to bring the Persians to their senses'. According to Morrison during the Cabinet meeting of the 12th of July: 'Both the Company and His Majesty's Ambassador in Tehran were strongly in favour of adopting this course as the best method of demonstrating to the Persians our determination not to yield to their demands.' The danger of this scheme, as became immediately apparent once the withdrawal of the 'Anglo-Persian' staff began, was that it would be interpreted as a sign of British weakness. From the beginning it was highly debatable whether it would bring the Iranians 'to their senses'. When the American Secretary of State learned about it, his reaction was immediate and negative. He was not contemplating the fortunes of 'Anglo-Persian'. He feared that the chaos of withdrawal might lead to Communist revolution, the rule of the Tudeh Party, and eventually to a Russian take-over. 'He thinks this because he does not believe that . . . the suffering of great economic loss will deflect or modify the irrational headstrong course of Persian nationalism.'[92] At this time Acheson was putting forward proposals that Averell Harriman, who had acquired a considerable reputation of diplomatic skill in difficult situations, might be able to reconcile the British and the Iranians, especially since Musaddiq would probably welcome the idea of American intervention. If Harriman were to arrive in the midst of the confusion of British withdrawal, he could hardly be expected to bring Musaddiq to reason. Acheson was not unfriendly to the British cause, even though he was critical of their handling of the crisis. In his judgement, if the British left, they would never be given the opportunity to return.

Evacuation was also denounced widely and bitterly in Britain, especially by the Tories. Harold Macmillan, as has been seen, regarded the oil crisis as a national issue rather than one of party politics, yet he gave one of the sharpest warnings which was in line with some of the more jingoistic sentiments voiced by his Conservative colleagues:

> I confess that I do not understand the policy followed so far as regards evacuation. In my view, the day when the last British employee of the Anglo-Iranian Oil Company leaves Abadan will mark the end of the association of Britain with the development of Persian oil. It means, still more, the collapse of British power and prestige in the East.[93]

As a result of such pressure the Labour government began to change its mind. The criticism of Attlee is not so much that he supported the idea of 'phased withdrawal' in the first place but that he wobbled first in its execution and then in having second thoughts. He did not satisfy his critics when he responded to a question put by Macmillan, 'what about evacuation?' Attlee said on the 31st of July: 'There may have to be a withdrawal from the oil wells and there may have to be a withdrawal from some part of Abadan, but our intention is not to evacuate entirely.'[94] Part of the source of confusion was the need to rely on the company to withdraw its personnel in accordance with the danger of the situation in the oilfields. All of these developments were taking place against a background of possible anti-British violence in Iran as well as a continued deterioration of Anglo-Iranian relations. In late June deputies in the Majlis began to speak of 'treason' and the 'death sentence' for Iranians who continued to co-operate with the British. In early July the Iranian government

---

[92] Franks to Morrison, Top Secret, 5 July 1951, FO 371/91555/EP1531/804.

[93] *Parliamentary Debates* (Commons), 30 July 1951, col. 1059.

[94] Ibid., col. 1072.

rejected the International Court's order to do nothing to aggravate the dispute. 'Evacuation' was not merely a matter of protecting British subjects and 'bringing the Persians to their senses'. It involved the prestige of the British Empire and, as has been seen, the danger that withdrawal might be permanent. The wavering attitude of the Labour government can be explained in part by the conflicting impulses that arose from attempting to take everything into account.

'Anglo-Persian' itself was in two minds about 'phased withdrawal'. On the one hand it might help to bring the Persians to reason, but on the other hand who could predict what might happen if they did not 'come to their senses'? The general manager of the company in Iran, A. E. C. Drake, told the British Cabinet that evacuation 'would inevitably lower the morale of the staff . . . and would lead to final surrender of the Company's position in Persia'. The Chiefs of Staff however did not want to be drawn into the protection of the oil-fields (as opposed to the island of Abadan).[95] Thus there were conflicting views. The hesitancy in following one line consistently contributed to charges that the Labour government had a faulty grasp over the situation.

Attlee was under strong pressure from the Tories as well as from those within the government such as Morrison and Emmanuel Shinwell (now Minister of Defence) who wished to take a stronger line. Churchill told Attlee that he 'had never thought that the Persian oil fields could be held by force', but that 'Abadan Island was quite another matter'.[96] Here was the ultimate point of controversy within British circles, public and official. Should the island be held by military force? Part of the answer to the question lay in the military answer whether it *could* be held. It has been noted that on the 12th of July the Cabinet decided not to use force in order to defend the Company's property, including above all the refinery at Abadan. Part of the reason for this decision was the opinion of the Chiefs of Staff that the island would be extremely difficult to defend. The socialist virtues of not using force were reinforced by sound military arguments about the high risk of the operation. On the 20th of July, however, Morrison circulated a paper to the Cabinet explaining that the Chiefs of Staff had reversed themselves. They now believed that Abadan could be taken on short notice and could be held against Persian resistance. This was another turning point. From the 23rd of July, when the Cabinet discussed the issue again, until the decision

---

[95] Cabinet Minutes 48 (51), 2 July 1951, CAB 128/19.

[96] Notes of a meeting between Attlee, Churchill, Eden, and others, 27 June 1951, FO 371/91555.

to evacuate in September, the Labour government held open the option to seize Abadan. From now onwards this story of high political drama has an additional element—*temptation*.

There were two military plans. The purpose of operation MIDGET was the evacuation of British subjects from Abadan, which would be the withdrawal point from the mainland. Operation BUCCANEER would have held and defended Abadan indefinitely. Previously the Chiefs of Staff had calculated that it would take six weeks to prepare and execute the military seizure of Abadan. The planning involved in this operation was exceedingly complex, but in essence it involved not only the difficulties in manpower and transport but also the mobilization of the actual military equipment such as amphibious vehicles. The Labour government was not prepared for such a sophisticated operation. It would also necessitate the call-up of reservists who would not be acclimatized to the Persian summer. Seasoned troops would have to come from Egypt, but they would have to be replaced immediately in order to prevent the Egyptians from attempting to seize the Canal Zone. This was only the beginning of the difficulties and they are far too numerous to list here. Above all the Chiefs of Staff were sceptical that these preparations could be kept secret, and they emphasized the danger of a massacre as well as the seizing of hostages. Not least they were apprehensive about the 'fanatical' Persian opposition they would encounter. During the early planning stages there appeared to be little or no chance of success. In preparation for operation MIDGET, however, the Chiefs of Staff became more confident about operation BUCCANEER. By mid-July they believed that both these operations could be successful.

Much of the inspiration and hard work devoted to these projects can be traced to the Minister of Defence himself. Shinwell emerges historically as one of the toughest men of the Labour government. He had robust ideas about the significance of operation BUCCA-NEER. He told the Chiefs of Staff:

> Some of his colleagues in the Cabinet did not go so far as he did with regard to being prepared to take a really strong line with Persia. Nevertheless, he was convinced that we must in no circumstances throw up the sponge not only because of the direct consequences of the loss of Persian oil, but because of the effect which a diplomatic defeat in Persia would have on our prestige and on our whole position throughout the Middle East.
>
> If Persia was allowed to get away with it, Egypt and other Middle Eastern countries would be encouraged to think they could try things on: the next thing might be an attempt to nationalise the Suez Canal.
>
> The situation seemed to be rapidly developing where nobody 'cared a damn' about this country; this was quite intolerable; we must be prepared to show

that our tail could not be twisted interminably and that there was a limit to our willingness to have advantage taken of our good nature.[97]

There is something intoxicating about military planning, especially when it is imbibed with strong doses of patriotism. It has been emphasized previously that the British had neither the manpower, the economic resources, nor the tenacity of purpose to hold part of Iran indefinitely. In the long run this is certainly true. The proof of the point is that the Labour government itself decided in favour of non-intervention, in part because of an awareness of the danger of a full-blown confrontation with Iranian nationalism. At the same time it is equally true that Shinwell believed that an act of will could carry the British through their difficulties. This is indeed one theme that runs through the works of those who lament the decline and fall of the British Empire. Abadan island could have been held. The Iranians with proper tutelage could have been brought to their senses. Persian oil could have been developed for the benefit of both parties. Shinwell's full-blooded belief in those possibilities makes the ultimate decision of the Labour government all the more fascinating.

One of the reasons for the dramatic change in attitude, which was by no means confined to military circles, was the clarification of what could and could not be effectively accomplished by a military task force. After the proclamation of the Iranian nationalization law in May, the dominant assumption had been that the British, if they were to retaliate, would occupy the oilfields of south-western Iran. The military assessment made it obvious that this was an impossible assignment. The terrain, the climate, the logistics, the problems of manpower and transport, not to mention Iranian resistance, all pointed in the direction of a military fiasco. In the following weeks however the military planners devised operation BUCCANEER on the asumption that it would not be the oilfields on the mainland but the island of Abadan that could be seized and effectively held. Three brigades of airborne troops were flown to the base at Shaiba in Iraq. The Persian Gulf squadron was strengthened by three frigates and four destroyers from the Mediterranean. This was the force that has been referred to as the British 'Armada' in the Persian Gulf in the summer of 1951.[98] Attlee announced to the Cabinet in mid-July that the safety of British lives in Abadan could now be guaranteed and, moreover, that the island could be held 'even against Persian opposition'.[99] This was another turning point. 'Phased withdrawal'

[97] Confidential Annex to COS (51) 86, 23 May 1951, DEFE 4/43; minutes in FO 371/91460.
[98] Woodhouse, *Something Ventured*, p. 111.
[99] Cabinet Minutes 53 (51), 19 July 1951, CAB 128/20.

now made a great deal more sense, even to its critics. British subjects would be withdrawn to Abadan, where they could be effectively protected. Operation MIDGET (evacuation of British subjects if necessary) interlocked with the possibility of operation BUCCA-NEER (invasion and defence of Abadan). All in all this was a tangible and attractive military concept that easily appealed to the imagination.

Furthermore, in Morrison's view, military intervention would teach the Iranians a lesson. The presence of a task force might even bring about the fall of Musaddiq:

> Such an operation would have obvious advantages. . . . It would demonstrate once and for all to the Persians British determination not to allow the Anglo-Iranian Oil Company . . . to be evicted from Persia, and might well result in the downfall of the Mussadiq regime and its replacement by more reasonable elements prepared to negotiate a settlement.

An effective military operation would also have a wholesome effect on those who erroneously believed that the British Empire was in a state of decline:

> [I]t might be expected to produce a salutary effect throughout the Middle East and elsewhere, as evidence that the United Kingdom interests could not be recklessly molested with impunity. Indeed, failure to exhibit firmness in this matter may prejudice our interests throughout the Middle East.

And, finally but not least (perhaps above all in Morrison's view), intervention would serve the political purposes of the Labour Party: 'it would be warmly welcomed by those sections of public opinion in this country which have been criticising His Majesty's government's attitude over Persia as having hitherto been unduly weak'. In fairness to Morrison, he elaborated on objections to a forward policy just as fully, though there was no doubt that he favoured military intervention. There is one point on which his views are especially illuminating for the themes of this book. Morrison believed that the Arab states would respect a British show of force:

> It is arguable . . . that our use of force might produce violent nationalist reactions in the other oil producing countries in the Middle East. These countries are, however, all Arab, and the Arabs have little respect for the Persians. It seems, therefore, more likely that, while some ebullition of nationalist sentiment may be anticipated at first, the Arab peoples would be more likely to respect this display of determination on our part, and that they might therefore be deterred from taking action similar to Dr. Mussadiq's against British oil interests in their countries.[1]

Perhaps it was wishful thinking on his part, but Morrison believed that the Arabs were just as contemptuous of the Iranians as the

---

[1] Memorandum by Morrison, 20 July 1951, CP (51) 212, CAB 129/46.

British were themselves, and that British military intervention would command Arab respect.

Military intervention did not receive the endorsement of the Cabinet. Neither was it rejected. It was deferred.[2] The reasons will be discussed later in relation to British eviction, when action one way or the other became inevitable. Here the important point is that until the Cabinet made the decision to vacuate in September, military intervention remained an attractive and indeed tempting option.

The Labour government's restraint in late July must be viewed in the circumstances of Averell Harriman's arrival in Tehran. Harriman's mission followed Musaddiq's rupture with the Anglo-Iranian Oil Company. In June a representative of the company, Basil Jackson, had re-extended to Musaddiq the offer of the fifty–fifty split, and with it considerable advice which was not well received. Here was an example of the view held by Acheson and McGhee that the company was making conciliatory gestures too late (though probably not with too little, as will be seen). Iranian attitudes towards 'Anglo-Persian' had hardened to the extent that it is doubtful whether any offer made to Musaddiq at that time by the company would have been acceptable to his supporters. On the other hand Musaddiq could accept American mediation. It fitted into the Iranian concept of the 'negative equilibrium', or, as the British understood it in this case, playing off the Americans against themselves. Harriman did not find Musaddiq nearly so inflexible or irrational as did the British, though he found him exasperating enough. Harriman in fact developed an affection of sorts for him and referred to him as 'Mossie'. He persuaded 'Mossie' to accept a British delegation led by a senior minister of the Labour government. This became known, as has been mentioned, as the 'Stokes mission' led by the Lord Privy Seal, Richard Stokes, who arrived in Tehran in early August.

Harriman's liaison with the Labour government was through a personal friend, Hugh Gaitskell, who had replaced Cripps as Chancellor of the Exchequer in October 1950. The Harriman–Gaitskell connection is important because Gaitskell drove home to the Cabinet that Harriman was a reliable ally 'friendly and sympathetic to the United Kingdom Government'.[3] Gaitskell himself played a vital part in these discussions because he allied himself with Attlee against Morrison and Shinwell. Gaitskell indeed upheld the extreme principle that even economic pressure against Iran would be unwise 'since it would create in Persia economic disorders which might precipitate

---

[2] Cabinet Minutes 54 (51), 23 July 1951, CAB 128/20.

[3] CM 52 (51), 'No Circulation Record', 16 July 1951, CAB 128/21. See Philip M. Williams, *Hugh Gaitskell* (London, 1979), pp. 271-2.

a Communist revolution'.[4] In Gaitskell's conversations with Harriman, the latter made one off-hand remark that the British found profoundly disconcerting. 'His activities were being jealously watched by the American oil companies', according to Gaitskell. The British were not so much suspicious of Harriman's motives as those of his adviser on petroleum affairs who accompanied him, Walter Levy.[5] In late July Gaitskell reported to the Cabinet that Levy regarded the situation created by 'Anglo-Persian' to be so hopeless that the company itself would probably have to be liquidated or at least reconstituted. This was an extremely important point because it marked the beginning, as far as the British were concerned, of the international consortium that eventually replaced the Anglo-Iranian Oil Company. Gaitskell's verbatim words were: 'Mr. Levy considered that oil operations in Persia might have to be carried out by a new foreign company, jointly controlled by a number of oil companies, and that this company would not have the monopoly of the sale of Persian oil.'[6] This development was significant not only because of the fate of 'Anglo-Persian' but also because it created the impression during the summer of 1951 that the American oil companies were 'circling like vultures over Iran'.[7] Harriman himself appears to have been free from the suspicion of undermining 'Anglo-Persian'. Indeed the British were grateful to him at the time for persuading Musaddiq to accept the Stokes mission. 'No one could have done more than he has', Attlee wrote later to Truman about Harriman, 'to promote a settlement.'[8]

---

[4] Cabinet Minutes 35 (51), 10 May 1951, CAB 128/19.

[5] Levy's personal attitude towards the British was never in doubt. 'Levy ... 100% with us [and] has been magnificent', P. E. Ramsbotham of the Foreign Office wrote at the end of the Stokes mission (Ramsbotham to D. Logan, 20 Aug. 1951, FO 371/91580/EP1531/1391). It was Levy's proposed solution to the oil question that the British found disturbing. Levy made it clear from the outset, especially in his conversations with E. A. Berthoud, that he believed the only hope for the British to retain a stake in the Iranian oil would be to 'camouflage' the existence of 'Anglo–Persian' and 'dilute' the company into a consortium. Berthoud's minutes, which appear in abundance in the files of the Eastern Department, are of particular interest because he himself spent eight years in the employment of 'Anglo-Persian' before entering government service during the war. He thus was well qualified to respond to Levy's proposal, and he made it clear on several occasions that he regarded it as a disastrous 'mongrelisation' of an upright British company that had made mistakes but by no means deserved the fate overtaking it. Berthoud's minutes are also of interest because of his steadfast belief that 'the removal of Mr. Moussadek . . . [is] objective number one'. Minute of 21 June 1951, FO 371/91550/EP15331/713.

[6] Cabinet Minutes 56 (51), 30 July 1951, CAB 123/20.

[7] Woodhouse, *Something Ventured*, p. 110. These impressions were accentuated when a United States Congressman passed through Tehran in October 1951. 'I had a conversation last night with representative John Kennedy of Massachusetts', Shepherd telegraphed to Morrison. 'He asked whether I did not think if Anglo-Iranian Oil Company were unable to reach a settlement with the Persians it would be a good thing for American concerns to step into the breach.' Shepherd to Morrison, 10 Oct. 1951, FO 371/91599/EP1531/1837.

[8] As quoted in Morrison to Franks, 23 Aug. 1951, FO 371/91581.

There was a general British respect for Harriman which has to be taken into account in commenting briefly on the significance of the Stokes débâcle.

Stokes

Richard Stokes was a wealthy business man whose family industrial firm, Ransome and Rapier, had extensive and long-standing connections with the Middle East. During the 1930s he had offered to have his company's rearmament work done at cost price. In the circumstances of postwar England, he was probably one of the few Labour politicians who came within range of the American idea of a 'millionaire'. During the Palestine controversy he had acquired a reputation of being more pro-Arab than Ernest Bevin. In 1945 Attlee had regarded him as too erratic for political office, but in 1950 he was given a place in the Labour government as Minister of Works. He then became Lord Privy Seal and Minister of Materials, a key post in view of the government's rearmament policy. He had a reputation not only for efficiency but also as a man of ethical and religious principle. He espoused an eclectic brand of socialism that in effect amounted to a personal creed. This had a bearing, as will be seen, on his attitude towards the Anglo-Iranian Oil Company. He had a general demeanour of breezy goodwill. His business had enabled him to travel widely in the Middle East, and within Labour circles he was regarded as somewhat of an expert on the region. He now saw his goal, in his own words which acquired a renown of sorts, as putting before Musaddiq 'a jolly good offer'.

The offer in essence amounted to 'partnership' as had been discussed in Parliament as well as within Whitehall. What is of interest is the way in which the British saw certain principles at stake, and the extent to which Stokes was *not* prepared to go in yielding to Iranian 'national aspirations'. The Labour government, following Attlee's lead and his analogy of negotiating 'Dominion status', was willing to acknowledge the substance of the Iranian demands in the hope, as in parallel political questions, that some degree of economic dependence would be maintained in the actual agreement. The British in other words were prepared to change whatever terminology might be necessary in order to preserve as much as possible of their control over the production of Iranian oil. They still hoped to avoid 'nationalisation' in the sense of expropriation without compensation. They did not regard 'fifty–fifty' as a particularly sacrosanct principle, nor did they regard the example of Aramco as a subsidiary concession as an especially compelling one.

They were prepared however to uphold the fifty–fifty principle and to invoke the image of Aramco. By August 1951 the British were willing to go to substantial lengths to salvage the situation, if it would be done without wrecking the economic and political structure of the rest of the Middle East.

What the British could *not* do was to yield *more* than the fifty-fifty split. The Americans were so apprehensive on this point that McGhee warned Harriman that it would be disastrous for everyone concerned if the British attempted to offer more. As if anticipating that the British might become desperate, Walter Levy repeatedly emphasized to the British 'that his instructions were not to upset the 50/50 formula'.[9] The British had no intention of doing so. The key to their calculation was that the Iranian problem, however calamitous it might be in itself, could not be allowed adversely to influence oil production and profits elsewhere in the Middle East. This was a point that Stokes rationally attempted to impress on Musaddiq. There were limits to the concessions which the British could make. While willing to concede and correct the mistakes made by 'Anglo-Persian', the British would not be willing to establish further precedents in profit-sharing or to make sops to 'nationalisation' that would stir nationalist ambitions in Iraq or Egypt. At the same time they expected the Iranian government to honour contracts and demanded that Musaddiq himself bring 'national aspirations' down to 'a business-like agreement'. The British public would accept nothing less. Measured by British standards, it is easy to see why the Stokes mission ended in a depressing failure. Stokes made Musaddiq a 'jolly good' business offer comparable to the settlement that the Americans had concluded with the Saudis. Musaddiq, for reasons quite removed from the world of trade and commerce, rejected it.

Stokes's dealing with Musaddiq confirmed the British impression that they were dealing with an exceedingly clever buffoon (a variation of Shepherd's 'lunatic' theme). On several occasions Stokes found himself reduced to bizarre metaphors which were, he believed, the only effective method of communication. For example:

Dr. Mussadiq said that under the . . . nationalisation laws, the Persian Government had successfully divorced the Company. The Lord Privy Seal said that it was a curious statement for a man to divorce his wife and thus attempt to starve her to the point where she is obliged to kill him. Dr. Mussadiq very much enjoyed those humourous exchanges. . . .[10]

---

[9] As recorded in memorandum by P. E. Ramsbotham, 30 July 1951, FO 371/91575.
[10] Record of a meeting of 5 Aug. 1951, FO 371/91577/EP1531/1339.

It angered Stokes that Musaddiq refused to be pinned down to problems of management, markets, compensation, technicians, and an array of many other questions that urgently needed to be settled. In one of his parting sallies Stokes warned Musaddiq that 'no one ever got 100% of what they wanted', and, as if it were necessary to use animal metaphors to be understood, said that if Musaddiq continued in his obstinacy then the big bone he had 'got down the throat would tear open his stomach at the navel'.[11] From other accounts, it is fair to say that Stokes was not in his element in attempting Musaddiq's political idiom. It is also clear that, though Musaddiq derived a great deal of entertainment at Stokes's expense, he was deadly earnest. It will be recalled from an earlier chapter how Shukri al-Quwatli said that he would cut off his hand before he would sign an agreement with the French. Musaddiq now spoke of filling the oil wells with mud before he would come to terms with the British. In the volatile emotions of Iranian nationalist politics from Communist left to the xenophobe religious right, anti-British sentiment was one of Musaddiq's sources of strength and a sustaining negative inspiration.

Harriman, for one, believed that the theatrical attitude on Musaddiq's part was calculated, and that inveterate Iranian suspicion of the British lay at the root of the problem of communication. According to one of Harriman's asides, Musaddiq revealed his true motivation when he spoke of his belief that all of the problems of Iran, from low standards of living to a descent in world prominence, could all be attributed to the British. This was a genuine insight. Musaddiq believed that the British conspired against Iran. The 'machinations and craftiness of the British' were responsible for many of Iran's ills, political as well as economic. 'You do not know how crafty they are', he told Harriman, 'You do not know how evil they are. You do not know how they sully the things they touch.'[12] Harriman and other Americans recognized in Mussadiq, not a buffoon, but a man with a gifted intellect who was blinded by nationalist passion and a belief in a satanically inspired British conspiracy against the Iranian people. The divergence of Anglo-American outlook thus persisted through the episode of the Stokes mission. When all is said the American impression was certainly more accurate, though the reasons for the British stereotypes of Musaddiq as a 'buffoon' or 'lunatic' are easily comprehensible. By all accounts Musaddiq was oblivious to the long-range economic danger that Iran

---

[11] Note by Stokes, 22 Aug. 1951, FO 371/91583.
[12] Vernon A. Walters, *Silent Missions* (Garden City, NY, 1978), p. 247.

would face through the boycott of the oil industry. Nor could he bring his intellect to bear on the immediate economic crisis. In the words of an American scholar of Iran who has written with insight on Musaddiq and the crisis of 1951-3, 'Economic rationality models and cool financial reasoning made little sense in this climate of political upheaval and nationalist fervor.'[13]

It is debatable whether any Englishman, even of the stature of Mountbatten, could have successfully negotiated with Musaddiq. In any case Stokes was not a good choice. He assessed the situation in Iran with a sense of British outrage at corruption, inefficiency, and outright dishonesty. He expressed his contempt directly to the Shah and with it some advice about Musaddiq:

> I told him [the Shah] that one of the difficulties in making satisfactory arrangements with regard to management was the terrible dishonesty of his people. . . . He took this criticism of his fellow nationals without comment. He also asked me what I thought he ought to do and I said I thought he should get rid of Musaddiq and get a man of greater vision and one who was not himself a fanatic nor surrounded by people who were.[14]

Stokes did not believe that Musaddiq himself was worthy of much respect, or that he was the real cause of the trouble. He identified Musaddiq's 'fanatical' advisers as the source of anti-British Iranian discontent. In words that must surely strike one as a superficial remedy for the political and economic problems of Iran, Stokes recorded his opinion that probably the 'only solution' would be 'a strong Government under martial law and the bad boys in prison for two years or so'.[15]

Stokes broke off his relations with Musaddiq in late August 1951. He stood at variance with most of his colleagues in the Labour government in the belief that Musaddiq himself would be more amenable to a business-like agreement if the 'fanatics' who influenced him could be removed, perhaps by imprisonment, and that the situation could still be salvaged, perhaps by offering the Iranians more than the fifty–fifty split. On the latter point Stokes's views were shaped in part by his socialist principles. 'I have been very uneasy', he wrote to Attlee. On his return to England, Stokes collided with

[13] From a manuscript in progress on Iran and the United States by James A. Bill, which discusses all of these problems on the basis of Iranian as well as western sources.

[14] Note by Stokes, 22 Aug. 1951, FO 371/91583. Stokes's blunt statements about Iranian corruption disturbed Harriman, who later recalled an incident with Husain Ala, a former Ambassador to the United States and one of the most respected of Iranian statesmen: 'They were talking, and Ala and Stokes had had a few drinks—weren't intoxicated at all—and he [Stokes] . . . spoke very bitterly to Ala and said that Ala had to understand that the Iranians were all corrupt people and never could run any business and couldn't run their own government, let alone any [oil] business of this kind.' 'Princeton Seminars', 15-16 May 1954, p. 1624, Acheson Papers.

[15] Stokes to Morrison, 6 Sept. 1951, FO 371/91463/EP1015/311.

Sir William Fraser over the issue of legitimate profit. Fraser refused to divulge the company's financial details; but Stokes verified that there had been a profit of £170 million in 1950. 'For many years I have known that Iranian oil is the cheapest to produce in the world', he explained to the Prime Minister.[16] The cost of Iranian production, in Stokes's judgement, was so much less than in other oil-producing areas that there was no reason why the British should stick to the American formula of fifty–fifty if they could retain their access to Iranian oil by offering a more generous share of the profits. It would furthermore resolve an ethical question that Stokes believed to be significant. He had not been unresponsive to Iranian criticism that 'Anglo-Persian' existed as an exploitative enclave with little or no relation to the rest of the Iranian economy and that the company's profits were out of line with the ethos of socialist England. Stokes had a social conscience, and, despite his exasperation with Musaddiq, he thought it better to try to do business with him rather than the 'fanatical' entourage that was more extremist than Musaddiq himself. 'Getting rid of Mossadeq', according to Stokes, would not solve the problem. 'The fact of the matter is that he has tremendous influence in the country and the more we go for him the stronger his position gets.'[17] In the end, Stokes maintained, 'we shall have to negotiate with Mossadeq'.[18]

Attlee himself did not share those views, nor did Sir Donald Fergusson (the Permanent Under-Secretary at the Ministry of Fuel and Power), who had accompanied Stokes to Tehran. Fergusson is a significant figure in the oil crisis. In the last two months before the fall of the Labour government, Attlee increasingly relied on his judgement. After the company's evacuation, he was the Prime Minister's choice, along with Sir Oliver Franks, to continue discussing this delicate business with the Americans.[19] Fergusson's response to the crisis was in the mainstream of British reaction. He regarded Musaddiq as a principal obstacle to good relations between the two countries. He believed that the fifty–fifty principle should be upheld. He maintained that over time Musaddiq would fall from power and that a satisfactory oil agreement could then be reached with more moderate Iranian leaders. These were not hasty judgements. Fergusson had acquired knowledgeable economic views after long experience at the Treasury. He had firm ideas about the necessity to support principles of international law. He also had a genuine insight

[16] Quoted in Francis Williams, *A Prime Minister Remembers* (London, 1961), p. 249.

[17] Stokes to Younger, 24 Sept. 1951, FO 371/91591/EP1531/1641.

[18] Stokes to Morrison, 8 Oct. 1951, FO 371/91590/EP1531/1616.

[19] See Morrison's notation on a memorandum by Stokes, 25 Oct. 1951, FO 371/91607/EP1531/2029.

into the nature of the Iranian grievance against 'Anglo-Persian'. On the eve of British eviction he wrote a letter to Stokes that not only illuminates points of difference but also serves as an explanation of the logic behind the British response to Musaddiq, the rationale of disengagement, and the underlying reasons why the British hoped that economic boycott would eventually bring the Iranians to their senses.

Fergusson's first point was the impossibility of reaching an understanding with Musaddiq:

I feel absolutely sure that we cannot reach an agreement with Moussadec which would not have disastrous effects not only on all other British interests all over the world but on all other enterprises and trading activities in foreign countries on which the standard of living of the people of this country, and our ability to maintain our freedom and independence depend.

Persian oil is important, but it is not as important as all the rest of our foreign oil interests. And, apart from oil, it would be disastrous for the sake of a settlement of Persian oil to allow every foreign government, and foreigners generally, to feel that they can unilaterally repudiate contracts with British firms and companies and seize British assets in their countries on payment of such compensation as they themselves unilaterally decide to pay. This would strike a disastrous blow. . . .[20]

He meant that the unilateral abrogation of agreements would be a disastrous blow to international law which in turn would undermine the British Empire. 'I regard this as absolutely fundamental', he emphasized when he referred to the sanctity of treaties.

Fergusson was responding not only to Stokes's suggestion that the British should now attempt to resolve the crisis by offering the Iranians more than a fifty per cent share of the profits but also to the argument that the Persians were morally entitled to such a settlement. In this 'Personal & Private' letter to Stokes, Fergusson rejected that line of thought and released his pent-up intellectual energies as a dedicated but frustrated civil servant. He disagreed with some of the socialist assumptions of the Labour government, at least as Stokes was applying them to the oil crisis. Fergusson dealt with an issue that was widely discussed in England at the time, and it is easy in retrospect to forget how passionately many Englishmen felt about the accusation of 'exploitation'. 'It is worth remembering certain fundamentals', he wrote:

It was British enterprise, skill and effort which discovered oil under the soil of Persia, which has got the oil out, which has built the refinery, which has developed markets for Persian oil in 30 or 40 countries, with wharves, storage tanks and pumps, road and rail tanks and other distribution facilities, and also an immense fleet of tankers. This was done at a time when there was no easy

[20] Fergusson to Stokes, Top Secret, 'Private & Personal', 3 Oct. 1951, FO 371/91599.

outlet for Persian oil in competition with the vastly greater American oil industry.

None of these things would or could have been done by the Persian government or the Persian people. . . .

It has never been thought, least of all by the Labour Party, that owners of minerals who have done nothing to develop their minerals should receive a higher royalty per ton than the amount originally agreed because the people who produce and market the mineral greatly increase production and sales. . . .[21]

Fergusson now directed his remarks to a letter written by the Aga Khan, who as a Muslim spiritual leader had implored Stokes, for moral reasons of equity, to concede more than a fifty per cent share of the profits.[22] Fergusson continued:

I should like to point out to people that the Aga Khan, and the Egyptian, Persian and other ruling classes in Asia, who use the products of European and American skill and effort (e.g. motor cars, aeroplanes, oil, etc.) that they and their people have made no contribution to the invention or development of these things, and morally they have no claim to a share in the profits.

In the case of a mineral like oil they are of course morally entitled to a royalty. But to my mind the Asiatic idea as exemplified in the Aga Khan's letter that morally they are entitled to 50%, or, as he suggests, even more of the profits of enterprises to which they have made no contribution whatever, is bunk, and ought to be shown to be bunk.[23]

Those ideas still carried great force in postwar England.

Fergusson was convinced that the Americans did not base their enthusiasm for the fifty–fifty principle on ethical considerations but rather on ones of expediency and profit. On the other hand, Musaddiq's motivations, in his judgement, were psychological and emotional rather than economic. On these issues Fergusson demonstrated considerable insight:

[T]he Americans, for reasons of avoiding taxation, have started the idea of a 50/50 profit-sharing basis. There is no moral or any other sanctity about this, but Moussadec should not get better terms than this by breaking the contract embodied in the 1933 Agreement and repudiating the jurisdiction of the International Court of Justice. . . . It is not more money, but other objectives that he is really interested in. . . .

Since 1933 the Anglo-Iranian, by its huge development and present size, which in itself has been 'a good thing' has become in effect an imperium in imperio in Persia. Moussadec and other Persians object—it is a very natural feeling—to the existence in their country of this great foreign Company, which not only has revenues made, as they see it, out of Persian oil greatly in excess of the revenues of the Persian Government, but dominates the whole economic life of Persia, and therefore impairs her independence.

And Moussadec's real concern is not better financial terms but to get rid of

---

[21] Fergusson to Stokes, Top Secret, 'Private & Personal', 3 Oct. 1951, FO 371/91599.

[22] The letter is printed in Williams, *A Prime Minister Remembers*, pp. 251-4.

[23] Fergusson to Stokes, 3 Oct. 1951.

this foreign Company with its predominating influence out of Persia. He is quite ready to make heavy economic sacrifices, i.e. a greatly reduced oil industry in Persia, to free Persia from a great foreign organisation controlling Persia's economic life and destiny.[24]

For purposes of the present discussion Fergusson now came to his most important point, his assessment of the future of Iran and what should be done about Musaddiq. His views roughly coincided with the basis of British policy as it was being formulated in rapidly developing circumstances:

> I do not think Persia will go Communist, and I do not think Moussadec's Government will survive indefinitely with the oil industry at a virtual standstill.
> The right policy now seems to me, therefore, to be to wait and let Persia and other oil countries see the disastrous economic consequences to her of her action: to use any economic sanctions we can and prevent Persian oil being exported by Persia so far as we can. . . .[25]

Fergusson had in fact expressed some of the governing considerations at the time that the Cabinet decided on evacuation.

Fergusson's views epitomized the dominant thrust of British thought. He expressed ideas that were widely shared within the government and in Parliament, and by the British public. There was generally a consensus, and it included the scholarly authorities who were the most knowledgeable about Iran. The ideas of Ann Lambton at about the time of the fall of the Labour government are particularly striking, and they serve as an indication of the pervasive attitude, official as well as public, in the autumn of 1951: 'if only we keep steady Dr. Mussadiq will fall. There may be a period of chaos, but ultimately a government with which we can deal will come back.'[26] Stokes's view, that 'in the end we shall have to negotiate with Mossadeq', was definitely a minority opinion.

---

[24] Ibid.
[25] Ibid.
[26] As recorded in minute by Berthoud, 2 Nov. 1951, FO 371/91609/EP1531/2095. Anthony Eden, who was now Foreign Secretary, wrote: 'I agree with Miss Lambton. She has a remarkable first hand knowledge of Persians & their mentality.' (Minute by Eden on Strang to Bowker, 5 Nov. 1951, FO 371/91609/EP1531/20959.) It is a matter of considerable historical interest that Berthoud's minute also reported: 'our . . . unofficial efforts to undermine Dr. Mussadiq are making good progress' but that one of the problems, apparently, was American covert support of Mussadiq and the virulently anti-British religious leader, the Ayatullah Kashani. Again according to Miss Lambton, whose views were recorded indirectly in Berthoud's minute: 'Dr. Kashani has received large sums of money from somewhere. There is no evidence that it comes from the Russians. It is not impossible that there is an American source, not of course, State Department, but perhaps the U. S. brand of S. O. E. who may for some time have been supporting Dr. Mussadiq and Mr. Kashani as their answer to Communism.'

Eviction: October 1951

The immediate cause of the rupture between the British and Musaddiq was the issue of management and the future of the company's personnel. The Foreign Office believed that Stokes had blundered in becoming involved in an 'operational' question.[27] To Stokes it appeared to be a matter of efficiency and common sense to have a British manager of the new 'nationalized' company, and he held it to be imperative for the personnel to have contracts that would be honoured. To the Iranians however these were psychological questions as well as ones of principle. In the words of one of the first detailed accounts of the crisis, it seemed that the British, in return for their recognition of the principle of nationalization, believed that 'the Persian government should forego its insistence on that principle' (an assessment that was not far removed from Attlee's actual ideas on the subject).[28] According to Stokes himself, 'the reason why I decided to come home was simply that Dr. Mossadeq would not agree to any reasonable arrangement regarding the employment of British staff'.[29] The British suspended negotiations. There were allegations and counter-allegations about the British failure to respond to Musaddiq. On the 25th of September the Iranian government announced that the British staff in Abadan would be given seven days' notice to quit the country.

When the Cabinet met two days later, the British military strike-force was prepared to seize the island of Abadan, the site, it is important to remember, of the largest oil refinery in the world. Anthony Eden later wrote in his memoirs of the dilemma facing the Labour government: 'The temptation to intervene to reclaim this stolen property must have been strong. . . .'[30] It certainly was. It galled Morrison in particular to have to contemplate, in his own phrase, 'scuttle & surrender'.[31] As he himself later recalled, however, the time for intervention probably should have been in May at the time of 'nationalisation'. By September, especially after Musaddiq's ultimatum, there could be no possibility of a surprise attack, and the initiative within the Cabinet had definitely passed to those who opposed military intervention. Morrison nevertheless presented a powerful case. The British government, he stated to his colleagues, had acted 'with great reasonableness' in the face of 'much provocation'. If they allowed the remaining British staff to be thrown out,

[27] See memorandum by Makins, 23 Oct. 1951, FO 371/91607.

[28] Elwell-Sutton, *Persian Oil*, p. 210.

[29] Stokes to Eden, 11 Dec. 1951, FO 371/91619/EP1531/2348.

[30] Anthony Eden, *Full Circle* (Boston, 1960), p. 216.

[31] Minute by Morrison on memorandum by Furlonge, 5 Sept. 1951, FO 371/91587.

there would be repercussions throughout the world. Here was Morrison's main point:

> Egypt might be emboldened to take drastic action to end the military treaty and possibly to bring the Suez Canal under Egyptian control, and British legal rights in many other parts of the world would be placed in jeopardy. . . . the United Kingdom Government could not tolerate the expulsion of the remaining staff from Abadan. . . .[32]

Morrison was fully aware of the international difficulties that the British would face at the United Nations and elsewhere, but he clearly favoured whatever might be necessary to ensure that the British personnel in Abadan 'were not expelled'.

The arguments against military intervention were overwhelming, especially as they were presented by the Prime Minister. Attlee took the lead in taking a firm stand against the use of force at the beginning of the discussion, and he dominated the deliberations. Foremost among his objections to the possibility of military intervention was the attitude of the United States. 'In view of the attitude of the United States Government', he told his colleagues, he did not think it 'expedient' to use force to maintain the British staff in Abadan. The unwavering American opposition to military intervention, which Acheson had persistently made clear, presented an insurmountable obstacle. It would moreover be only the beginning of a difficult situation in which the international response, not least the Indian, would be less than delicate. 'If we attempted to find a solution by force', Attlee continued, 'we could not expect much support in the United Nations, where the South American Governments would follow the lead of the United States and Asiatic Governments would be hostile to us.'[33]

Attlee also dwelt on the internal situation in Iran. Here he was entirely consistent with his earlier views. In his estimation, military intervention might not topple the present government and might even strengthen Musaddiq's position. On the other hand, if the Iranians by their own mismanagement were to reduce the oil industry to chaos, then they might eventually recognize the desirability of British co-operation. Attlee was not especially sanguine about that prospect, but he held it to be the best that the British faced. He put these views forward with great force:

> [A]n occupation of Abadan island would not necessarily bring about a change in Persian Government and might well unite the Persian people against this country, and neither the oil wells nor the refinery could be worked without the assistance of Persian workers. . . .

[32] Cabinet Minutes 60 (51), 27 Sept. 1951, CAB 128/20.
[33] Ibid.

It would be humiliating to this country if the remaining British staff at Abadan were expelled, but this step would at least leave Dr. Mussadiq with the task of attempting to run the oil industry with inadequate facilities for refining oil and getting it away from Persia and he might then be driven to accept some form of agreement with this country.[34]

When Attlee used the word 'humiliating' he no doubt had partly in mind the British public and the impending general election. He had himself broken away from the Scottish Labour Conference to fly back to preside over the Cabinet meeting. 'Persian oil' was an election issue.

In these complex circumstances it is important to be clear about the governing consideration. There were international and economic complications (not least of which was the balance of payments problem). There was the question of how the local crisis might continue to arouse Iranian nationalism. There was also the advantage which the Tories might gain if the Labour government took a false step. Thus the inclination to punish the Iranians had to be weighed against a conflicting need for caution. What prevailed in the minds of those making the decisions? The Cabinet minutes are explicit on this point: 'It was . . . the general view of the Cabinet that, in the light of the United States attitude, . . . force could not be used to hold the refinery and maintain the British employees of the Anglo-Iranian Oil Company in Abadan. *We could not afford to break with the United States on an issue of this kind.*'[35]

Four years earlier when the British announced the decision to evacuate Palestine, they were greeted with almost univeral incredulity. The withdrawal from Iran was merely accepted as an indication of British weakness and decline. At the time of the Cabinet discussion the anticipated public reaction had agitated the collective ministerial mind. The minutes do not record Shinwell's contribution, but he was probably restrained by the appreciation of the Chiefs of Staff that the seizure of the island without the element of surprise would jeopardize British lives. 'The Chiefs of Staff', according to the minutes, 'had inclined to the view that military operations might endanger British lives, and from the strictly military point of view, they would prefer to postpone launching an operation until after the British employees had left Abadan.'[36] This was not a faint-hearted response. It merely gave emphasis to Shinwell's views that he had so forcefully impressed on the Chiefs of Staff. Such a situation should never have been allowed to develop; it should never be permitted to reoccur. In any case the British must never allow themselves again

[34] Ibid.
[35] Ibid., emphasis added.
[36] Ibid.

to be caught off guard. There was much to be learned from the Persian oil crisis, as will be seen in the next chapter on Egypt. The Chiefs of Staff were by no means alone in deploring the lamentable situation in Iran. The bitter word 'humiliation' ran throughout these discussions. There was a sense of indignation and frustration. There was also a definite public sentiment, shared in official circles, that the Iranians somehow needed to be taught a lesson. There was a latent jingoism within the Cabinet itself, which Attlee decisively and conspicuously kept under control. On that point one of the shrewdest of the contemporary participants in the Persian oil crisis delivered an emphatic judgement. 'To the great credit of the Labour Government', Dean Acheson wrote later, 'it stood against jingo pressures.'[37]

Despite the revelations of the secrets of the British archives, some of the most revealing insights into the nature of the British experience in Iran are to be found in books that have long been published. The episode of the evacuation from Abadan as told in the official history of the company puts the high-level Cabinet discussion into a dramatically different perspective:

> On the morning of October 4, 1951, the party assembled before the Gymkhana Club, the centre of so many of the lighter moments of their life in Persia, to embark for Basra in the British cruiser *Mauritius*. Some had dogs, though most had had to be destroyed; other carried tennis rackets and golf clubs; the hospital nurses and the indomitable Mrs. Flavell who ran the guest house and three days previously had intimidated a Persian tank commander with her parasol for driving over her lawn, were among the party, and the Rev. Tyrie had come sadly from locking up in the little church the records of those who had been born, baptised, or had died, in Abadan. . . .
> The ship's band, 'correct' to the end, struck up the Persian national anthem and the launches began their shuttle service. . . . The cruiser *Mauritius* steamed slowly away up the river with the band playing, the assembled company lining the rails and roaring in unison the less printable version of 'Colonel Bogey'. . . . The greatest single overseas enterprise in British commerce had ground to a standstill.[38]

During the crisis of evacuation Sir Francis Shepherd demonstrated great personal courage by having his chauffeur drive him through the streets of Tehran in an open car flying the Union Jack. And he persevered in his belief that Musaddiq essentially was a 'lunatic'.

[37] Acheson, *Present at the Creation*, p. 508.
[38] Henry Longhurst, *Adventure in Oil: The Story of British Petroleum* (London, 1959), pp. 143–4.

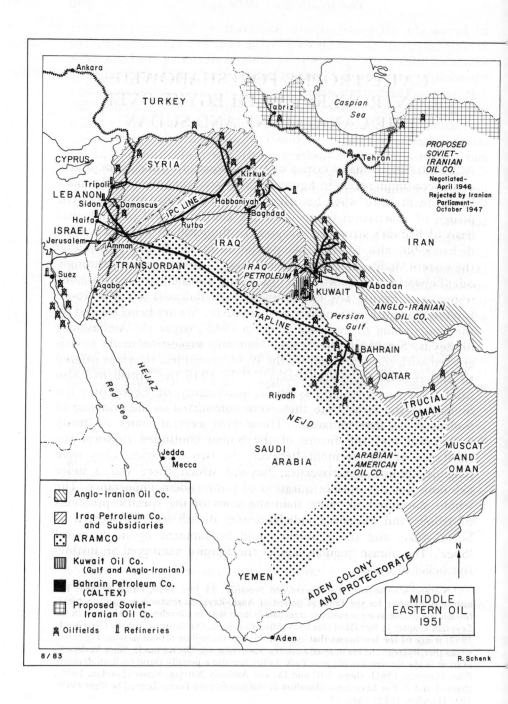

Anglo-Iranian Oil Co.

Iraq Petroleum Co.
and Subsidiaries

ARAMCO

Kuwait Oil Co.
(Gulf and Anglo-Iranian)

Bahrain Petroleum Co.
(CALTEX)

Proposed Soviet-
Iranian Oil Co.

⚒ Oilfields   🏭 Refineries

MIDDLE
EASTERN OIL
1951

R. Schenk

4

CATASTROPHE FORESHADOWED: CONTROVERSY WITH EGYPT OVER THE CANAL ZONE AND SUDAN

ACCORDING to many critics of the Labour government, the source of the continuing crisis in Egypt could be traced to the mistake made by Bevin in 1946 when he offered to withdraw British troops. The pledge of evacuation touched on the emotional and psychological basis of Britain's structure as a great or 'Imperial' power, not only to diehards but also to those who believed in the British presence in the eastern Mediterranean as a touchstone of British security throughout the world. The question of evacuation also shaped the nationalist response in Egypt. The commitment to withdrawal left little room for the moderate nationalists to manœuvre. 'We are being dogged by the undertaking to evacuate given in 1946', wrote the Ambassador in Egypt, Sir Ralph Stevenson, 'and any suggestion made now is greeted with the "How can we the Wafd, accept less than was offered to and rejected by Sidky Pasha?"'[1] In 1946 the British had also offered to recognize the symbolic sovereignty of Egypt over the Sudan. At the same time they were committed to the principle of Sudanese self-determination. Those two central issues of troop withdrawal and the future of the Sudan continued to form the substance of disagreement between the two countries. They were tangible, linked controversies, beyond which there was a more nebulous yet perceptible question of transcendent importance. The whole amounted to more than the sums of the specific problems of troops and Sudanese independence. British security seemed to be at stake, and the problem could be summed up in the word 'Suez'. The phrase 'jugular vein of the Empire' conveyed an instinctive belief of the era.

[1] Stevenson to Wright, 'Top Secret and Personal', 14 July 1950, PREM 8/1359. The historical literature for the 1949-51 period of Anglo-Egyptian relations is especially bleak, though the problems are sometimes trenchantly dealt with in the relevant works cited in the Egyptian chapter in Part III of this book. Miles Copeland, *The Game of Nations* (New York, 1969) is one of the few books that successfully lifts the veil of official secrecy. For recent works that deal with the era in relation to the Suez crisis, see Elie Kedourie, 'Suez Revisited', in *Islam in the Modern World* (New York, 1980). See also especially David Carlton, *Anthony Eden* (London, 1981), chaps. VIII and IX; and Anthony Nutting, *Nasser* (London, 1972), chaps. 1 and 2. For Egyptian nationalism at this juncture see Janice Terry, *The Wafd 1919–1952* (London, 1982), chap. 13.

On the question of the Sudan the British hoped that by playing for time—perhaps over a quarter of a century—the Sudanese themselves would resolve the issue of independence on terms in which the Egyptians would be compelled to acquiesce. The long-term cultivation of Sudanese nationalism provides an important clue to British tactics in the valley of the Nile. The question of troop withdrawal, however, demanded an immediate solution. The Egyptians had become prisoners of their own slogans. According to Stevenson, who related a conversation with one of the leading Egyptian politicians, Serag el Din Pasha:

In view of their repeated public adherence to the slogan of 'immediate and complete evacuation' . . . Serag el Din Pasha, the Minister of the Interior, went so far in conversation . . . as to say that the offer to evacuate was the greatest mistake we had made. We could not of course tell him at that time [in 1946] it was our intention to move lock stock and barrel to Palestine and that that was no longer practical.[2]

As will be recalled from earlier chapters, the situation in 1946 was more complicated than Stevenson implied. Bevin had hoped to prove the good faith of the Labour government by offering withdrawal as a means of negotiating a continued presence in the Canal Zone. It was true that in 1946 Palestine could still be regarded as a fallback position from Egypt, but the main thrust of British strategic planning had been to distribute British troops and eventually to establish an alternative base in Cyrenaica. The subsequent history of the subject had proved that there was no satisfactory substitute for Suez. In 1950 the Chief of the Imperial General Staff, Sir William Slim, wrote to King Farouk about the necessity of basing troops in the Canal Zone: 'It is no use locating this force in Cyprus, Malta or Cyrenaica. It is essential that it should be readily available, ready and on the spot.'[3]

Farouk himself needed no convincing. 'The impression I got from him', Slim wrote when the British reopened these negotiations in the summer of 1950, was the hope 'that British troops would remain for a very long period in his own interests.'[4] Farouk in other words played the part of a British collaborator who saw his own future bound up in the British presence. The British never let him forget, as Slim once bluntly reminded him, that there were 'no kings on the other side of the Iron Curtain'.[5] The subsequent story of Farouk's unhappy fate must not be allowed to obscure his relationship with

[2] Stevenson to Wright, 14 July 1950.
[3] Slim to Farouk, 13 July 1950, PREM 8/1359.
[4] Memorandum by Slim, 4 June 1950, PREM 8/1359.
[5] Memorandum by Slim, 4 Nov. 1949, FO 371/73505/J8847/G.

the British before his abdication. He gave them much astute advice about the psyche of the Egyptian nation. He emphasized that there was one thing that could never be forgotten. The British occupation of over six decades had shaped the temper of Egyptian nationalism. 'The memory of this occupation was very bitter with the mass of the people', he told Slim. Nevertheless Farouk held out hope that the problems between the British and the Egyptians could be resolved. One way in which this could be accomplished would be to disentangle the issue of the Sudan's future from the question of troop withdrawal. Another would be to convince the Egyptians that the British wished, in Farouk's own words, 'a complete break with the past'. There was nothing new in this suggestion, but those who wished to prevent a rupture still passionately, yet sceptically, hoped that reconciliation was possible. It is arguable that in the 1949–51 period the disastrous chain of events leading to the Suez crisis of 1956 might have been broken.

Part of the British problem had to be reckoned in terms of Farouk's personality. In the early postwar period those who knew him well, above all C. D. Quilliam of *The Times*, believed that he had the makings of 'a good king'. By about 1949 such assessments had become more pessimistic. 'The King's popularity . . . has been waning for some time', Quilliam wrote in August of that year.[6] This was the period of the scandal of Farouk's divorce and flamboyant public behaviour. The British were highly doubtful whether too close an association with him would inspire confidence in their own cause. At the time when the delicate discussions about Anglo-Egyptian relations entered into a critical phase in early 1951, Sir Ralph Stevenson wrote a balanced assessment of him that is useful to bear in mind while considering the problem of the Suez base and the question of the Sudan:

> King Farouk is passing through a difficult psychological and nervous phase. Fate, His Majesty thinks, is about to deal him a good hand but he does not quite trust the banker. Politically he is in a difficult position. . . . Psychologically King Farouk is uncertain of himself and he has been too prone to seek distraction in gambling and visiting night clubs. . . .
>
> Although there is much good in the King and although he is intelligent and shrewd, he is not an easy man to deal with. His overgrown inferiority complex makes him reluctant to accept any kind of information. He always tries to pretend he knows everything about any subject that may be mentioned. For instance, he even went so far in conversation . . . as to claim to be an authority on wines although he drinks no alcohol. Sometimes he is theatrical.[7]

---

[6] Quilliam to Ralph Deakin, 28 Aug. 1949, Quilliam Papers.

[7] Stevenson to Bevin, 'Secret and Personal', 28 Feb. 1951, FO 371/90110.

To give point to Farouk's inclination to melodrama, Stevenson mentioned a subject that recurred in their conversation. It was the humiliation inflicted on Farouk by Sir Miles Lampson (Lord Killearn) in 1942.

So painfully did the memory rankle that on one occasion Farouk produced a pistol from a drawer of his desk and exclaimed to Stevenson that 'it was always there ready loaded'.

He went on to say that it had been there on the 4th February, 1942 when Sir Miles Lampson faced him with an ultimatum at Abdin Palace, backed up by tanks in the courtyard. He said that although he would not have done anything to the soldiers who were present as he knew they were only carrying out orders, he assured me that Sir Miles had never been nearer death than on that day![8]

Farouk recalled the degradation of 1942 with 'bursts of cackling laughter'. The British not only had to deal with a monarch who nursed a lasting grudge against them but also had to anticipate that his behaviour might become increasingly unstable.

As in earlier periods, Egyptian politics could still be understood in terms of Killearn's description of the three-legged stool consisting of the monarch, the Wafd nationalists, and the British. To that structure had to be added the support given by the independent parties, which, if aligned with Farouk, might hold the Wafd in opposition. In this delicate balance the British might, as in the past, tilt the outcome of an election or place their weight discreetly behind certain leaders of the Wafd. After Nokrashi's murder in December 1948, officials in the Foreign Office had debated the desirability of attempting to persuade the Wafd to enter into an alliance with some of the independent parties in order to provide a stable government. This issue had caused profound soul-searching within the Foreign Office. The British in 1949 believed that they faced the possibility of Egyptian revolution. So sceptical were they of Farouk's grip over his part of the three-legged stool that they calculated that it might be best for the Wafd to remain outside the government in order not to be associated with the collapse of the monarchy. According to George Clutton, the head of the African Department (which had subsumed the Egyptian Department in early 1949):

Is it really to our advantage that the Wafd should enter the Government? There are many portents that the situation in Egypt is past remedy and that a revolution is inevitable. If this is so, it seems to me very doubtful whether the entry of the Wafd into the Government could alter matters.

All that would happen would be that when the revolution came, the Wafd would be as compromised as the other parties in the Government.

[8] Ibid.

If the revolution is inevitable, is it not to our advantage that there should be a party outside the Government which could step in and take control and thereby prevent the anarchy and chaos which would otherwise result and in which ample scope would be given to the Communists and other extreme elements to cease [sic] control?[9]

Michael Wright commented on that assessment. Though he often favoured interventionist policies, in this case he believed that there was much force in Clutton's argument. 'There may well be advantage', Wright wrote, 'in the Wafd remaining outside the Government until after the elections.'[10] His inclination to pursue an interventionist course had not diminished; he was merely pondering the desirability of harnessing the Wafd together with Farouk before the elections that would take place in January 1950.

Wright believed that the backing of certain politicians could be a powerful impetus towards social reform. They in turn could be expected to sustain British influence. The question in 1949 was whether or not the British should throw their support behind the Wafd in the elections to be held at the beginning of the next year. To Wright and others this appeared to be, in his words, 'a critical turning point both in Egypt itself and in relations between Egypt and the United Kingdom'. He could hardly have stated more cogently the Foreign Office's belief in the significance of the elections. A false step on Britain's part might accelerate what the Middle East experts believed to be an impending revolution; or it might lead in the opposite direction, in Wright's words, to 'a series of reactionary governments'. If the British did not act, in his judgement, 'an opportunity will have passed which might not recur for a very long time'.[11]

In general the Foreign Office officials who dealt with the Middle East regarded the Wafd as the only hope of bringing about an economic and political transformation of Egyptian society that might avert a revolution. Some of them, above all Wright, believed that opportunities for co-ordinating efforts with the principal Egyptian nationalist movement had been lost in the past. Wright is the case in point. He chafed under Bevin's restraint, though as a civil servant he faithfully executed the Foreign Secretary's policy with exceptional competence. Perhaps it is well to recall that in some circles he was regarded as the ablest Foreign Office official of his generation.[12] He now marshalled all of his arguments in favour of British intervention in the elections to the Wafd's advantage. So persuasive was the case

[9] Minute by Clutton, 3 Feb. 1949, FO 371/73463/J600/G.
[10] Minute by Wright, 7 Feb. 1949, FO 371/73463/J600/G.
[11] Minute by Wright, 28 June 1949, FO 371/73464/J5644.
[12] See *The Memoirs of Lord Chandos* (London, 1962), p. 245.

and so subtly tempting was the endorsement by the Permanent Under-Secretary that this example may be taken as one of the ultimate tests of Bevin's non-interventionist policy.

Wright feared that the palace would rig the elections to bring about the Wafd's defeat. Farouk hated Nahas. Farouk himself might exert a moderating influence on the more extremist wing of the Wafd, but the British could not rely on Farouk to carry out economic and social reform. They had to depend on Nahas's leadership and to hope that the Wafd would continue to represent the moderate mainstream of Egyptian nationalism, even though sometimes it might be vociferously anti-British. Here follow Wright's main points. He wrote in February 1949:

> The Wafd are certainly the party best equipped to introduce social reform. In spite of their anti-British utterances in opposition (which are common form in Egypt and mean relatively little), it might well prove again, as in the past, that the Wafd would be both more willing and more able to settle outstanding questions with Britain than any other party or combination of parties. . . . The fact that the Wafd have been out of power throughout the Palestine developments certainly puts them in a strong position.[13]

And in June of the same year:

> The Wafd . . . are probably the only party capable of carrying out the internal social and economic reforms which are so badly needed. . . . they are the party most friendly to Britain and are likely to be reasonable over the Sudan and Palestine.[14]

Wright was not proposing drastic intervention of the 1942 variety. He was urging that Farouk be discreetly but firmly told that he would not be allowed to place 'constitutional' barriers in the way of the Wafd's formation of a nationalist government in the event of victory following 'free' elections. The British at the same time would encourage the leaders of the Wafd to participate in the elections and would discourage the tactics of boycott. In other words the British would tilt the balance in favour of the Wafd, in part because they believed that Nahas and his associates would be willing to conclude lasting agreements about the Canal Zone and the Sudan.

In any historical account the issue of intervention must again become a matter of central importance because Bevin's response would help to determine, one way or another, Britain's relations with Egypt in the last years of the Labour government. Wright's recommendations were approved by the Permanent Under-Secretary, though not without a careful examination of the question of principle. 'Our policy', Strang wrote, 'is non-intervention in the internal

---

[13] Minute by Wright, 7 Feb. 1949, FO 371/73463/J600/G.
[14] Minute by Wright, 28 June 1949, FO 371/73464/J5644.

policies of Arab states.' Nevertheless he was aware, paradoxically, that non-intervention could amount to the same thing as intervention. As a result of his tour of the Middle East in May and June 1949 (which has been discussed in a previous chapter), he knew of the immense personal influence of the British representatives. 'They are often asked for advice', he wrote. He believed that the Arab governments wished to have a firm lead from the British. He deemed it 'legitimate' to try to work towards 'more public-spirited and less corrupt governmental regimes'. He held that the Foreign Office should not refrain from giving the Ambassador in Egypt 'a little encouragement' to work in that direction.[15] Strang's line of thought in other words flowed in the same direction as Wright's, though perhaps a little more cautiously. If Sir Ronald Campbell (the Ambassador who preceded Stevenson) were to remain silent on the question of elections, his reticence to give advice would be interpreted as support for Farouk's slate of palace stooges. On the other hand if the British endorsed 'free' elections then they would be denounced for intervention. Here truly was a dilemma that Bevin could not resolve merely by a straightforward formula of non-intervention.

On this occasion, as on so many others, Bevin's response (to the exasperation of the historian) consisted of a notation to the effect that he would deal orally with the matter. There can be no doubt however that he set Strang straight. Part of the substance of his reaction may be inferred from a later communication from him while abroad. His permanent officials again pressed on him, in ever more complex circumstances, the difficulty of remaining aloof from the Egyptian elections. Whatever Sir Ronald Campbell said, or did not say, would be exploited by one side or another. Campbell himself needed instructions. 'Free' elections would probably mean a return of the Wafd, while prior agreement about a coalition, or in other words 'rigged' elections, would probably lead to a palace regime. This was a dilemma that was not only painful but dangerous. 'The King's influence' Strang telegraphed to Bevin, 'is, of course, of great importance to us from the point of view of our strategic interests. On the other hand, 'we are inclined to think that the best line for us to take in private', Strang continued, 'is to favour free elections as being free from taint of intervention and at the same time perhaps carrying with it the better prospect of helping on our own policies' by indirectly assisting the Wafd.[16]

---

[15] Minute by Strang, 28 June 1949, FO 371/73464/J5644.
[16] Strang to Bevin, Top Secret, 28 Sept. 1949, FO 371/73465.

The pressures on Bevin for intervention were exquisitely subtle.[17]

Bevin's reply established once and for all the pre-eminence of his non-intervention policy:

We must firmly maintain our position that we cannot intervene in any way. If, however, Sir R. Campbell is pressed to give his personal opinion, he can say that the general policy of His Majesty's Government is to advocate free elections everywhere.[18]

Bevin thus remained consistent, though with a slight nod to the Wafd.

Since Michael Wright emerges from the historical records as the official who most conspicuously advocated an interventionist line, it would do him an injustice to leave this part of the story without indicating that he fully apprehended the risks of intervention, and that no one was more aware than Wright himself of the dangers of becoming entangled in internal Egyptian alliances. 'We clearly cannot be drawn into giving King Farouk any undertaking', he commented in November 1949, 'that we would support him in the event of revolution or coup d'etat.'[19] Nor was he less on guard about Nahas's machinations. Nevertheless there was an essential reason why Wright felt that discreet assistance to the Wafd would be worth the risk. He believed that the economic situation was becoming truly desperate. He had an abiding interest in questions of Egyptian welfare because of his supervision of plans for Middle Eastern economic development. His general impression of Egypt was of a country characterized by great economic hardship for the masses of the countryside and towns. The Wafd at least had an elaborate programme of reform based upon national unity and social justice which contained specific pledges to remove abuses. Wright no more than his colleagues held out much hope that the Wafd would make rapid or substantial progress with the reforms, but Nahas seemed to be a better bet than another palace regime. Wright's impatience with the slow pace of irrigation schemes, building programmes, industrialization, and social legislation explains his motivation as much as his wish for a satisfactory solution of the military problem for the British in the Canal Zone; but it is highly doubtful whether intervention in the election campaigns of 1949 would

---

[17] The flair for elegant analysis characterized the minutes of Wright rather than Strang, who expressed ideas with a sincerity reminiscent of Sir Edward Grey. For Strang's comments in retrospect on Egypt in 1949 see his autobiography, *Home and Abroad* (London, 1956), chap. IX.

[18] Bevin to Strang, 29 Sept. 1949, FO 371/73465/J1015/G.

[19] Minute by Wright, 8 Nov. 1949, FO 371/73505/J8847/G.

have benefited the British or the Egyptians in any of those areas.

Nahas and the Wafd won an overwhelming victory on the 3rd of January 1950. It is useful to pause briefly to reflect on the British and the Wafd at this time before addressing the question of break-down in 1950–1. Two of the old Egyptian hands of the Foreign Office recorded their thoughts about the Wafd at that time, the one in passing on the eve of the elections, the other pensively in his memoirs. Here follows a comment on Egyptian nationalism at this juncture by Sir Walter Smart and Sir Laurence Grafftey-Smith.

Smart, the former Oriental Counsellor in Cairo now in retire-ment, still occasionally gave advice to the Foreign Office. One can infer from his notes that he believed one of the dangers of a con-tinued palace regime to be the ultilization of 'Islamic fanaticism' as a weapon in the hands of the politicians who allied themselves with Farouk against the Wafd. He also held that the successfully 'cooked' elections by the palace were a source of popular discontent. At the same time he regarded 'lurid' corruption to be just as endemic in the Wafd as in the palace. He wrote of recent Egyptian history about two months before the election:

> The corruption of the Wafd Government [during the war] was more wide-spread but less deep than that of minority Governments. The majority Govern-ment had more hungry clients to satisfy than minority Governments, and its clients had been longer in the desert. Minority personalities, moreover, had more skill and knew better how to cover up their tracks. No one in Egypt would maintain for instance, that a Sidky was purer than a Nahas![20]

Or vice versa. No one who knew anything about Egypt deceived himself that the Wafd wished to attack the basic problem of a corrupt ruling élite.

In his memoirs Grafftey-Smith addressed himself to the question whether the British were allied with the right Egyptian leaders who might have dealt with fundamental reform. The answer that he gave was characteristically shrewd. He observed that in the 1950–2 period Egyptian politics were still dominated by the Turko-Egyptian palace élite, the landlord class, and the upper levels of the army and bureau-cracy. What of the *effendis*—'the brash young . . . mouthing politi-cal slogans, preaching change, menacing a paternalistic establish-ment'? What of the 'students, junior officials and others easily written-off as "half-baked" '? Above all what of the young army officers 'who found those pot-bellied and diabetic generals and

---

[20] Smart to George Kirk, 10 Nov. 1949, FO 371/73505. Smart was providing criticism of George Kirk's Chatham House manuscript which eventually appeared as *The Middle East in the War* (London, 1952).

time-serving politicians unacceptable'? The answer, Grafftey-Smith sorrowfully reflected, was that they were even more hostile to the British than they were to the pot-bellied pashas.[21] Nahas and his 'pasha government' in turn had to be just as anti-British as the younger nationalists. There lay one of the reasons for stalemate between the Wafd and the British in 1950-1.

The Sudan

'The Sudanese had a contempt for Egyptians as a less manly race', according to a British officer in the Sudan Political Service, and 'this contempt was reinforced by what Sudanese visiting Egypt saw of inefficiency and corruption in Government offices, and of the dishonesty of party politics.[22] It can be stated with certainty that whatever contempt the Sudanese may have had for the Egyptians, it was amplified many times by the British in the Sudan. The anti-Egyptian bias of the British administration in the Sudan must itself be reckoned as a determining force in the interplay of British and Egyptian efforts to reach agreement on the future of the Sudan. For purposes of the present discussion, there are two figures of particular interest. They are Sir Robert Howe, the Governor–General, and Sir James Robertson, the Civil Secretary of the Sudan administration.

Howe was Wright's predecessor as the Assistant Under-Secretary who supervised Middle Eastern affairs. In the wake of the Sudan crisis of 1946 that had been brought about by the 'Bevin–Sidky protocol', Howe, as Bevin's man, assumed the duties of Governor-General. Though he had previously served as Ambassador in Ethiopia and had a reputation as a Middle East hand, he had no experience in colonial administration. 'Howe . . . must have taken on the job from a strong sense of duty', according to one of Robertson's confidants.[23] The appointment received virtually no public notice at the time and has received little historical comment. It was a shrewd if intuitive assessment by Bevin of the man and the assignment. The future of the Sudan was a critical question of international importance that would help to shape world opinion on the dissolution of the British Empire. The Sudan was no less important as the first

[21] Laurence Grafftey-Smith, *Bright Levant* (London, 1970), p. 242.

[22] E. C. Haselden to Robertson, 28 Apr. 1946, Robertson Papers 523/10/1. For purposes of the present discussion the key work on Sudanese nationalism is Peter Woodward, *Condominium and Sudanese Nationalism* (London, 1979); see also especially M. O. Beshir, *Revolution and Nationalism in the Sudan* (London, 1972).

[23] Haselden to Robertson, 19 Mar. 1947, Robertson Papers 523/11/8.

British dependency to achieve independence in Africa. Not least it was an explosive issue in Anglo-Egyptian relations. Howe managed Sudanese affairs until his retirement in 1955 by becoming progressively, in a positive sense, no more than a figurehead. This achievement, with which it is not far-fetched to use the analogy of the smile of the Cheshire cat, can be understood in terms of his personality, his adherence to certain principles, and his reliance on Robertson. According to one of Howe's colleagues in the Sudan, he was 'a mystic of great erudition'.[24]

When Howe arrived in the Sudan, Robertson and other officials of the Sudan Political service suspected him of Foreign Office 'appeasement', in other words, the selling of the Sudan in order to conciliate the Egyptians. He was after all 'a Foreign Office man', in the words of his critics. Nothing could have been more misleading. He learned Arabic, kept himself open to all currents of Sudanese opinion, travelled widely within the Sudan, and from the beginning adhered steadfastly to the principle of Sudanese self-determination as the only way to resolve the Sudan's difficulties with Egypt. He believed that the Sudan should be prepared for independence as effectively and as quickly (though gradually) as possible, a goal which immediately set him at odds with British—and American —officials in Cairo who wished to placate the Egyptians by allowing them a wider hand in the affairs of the Sudan. 'We could not have had a more devoted supporter of the Sudan's right to self-determination than Sir Robert became', Robertson wrote later.[25]

The political collaboration that Howe embraced to achieve his goal was both controversial and dangerous. He wished to sustain the close relationship with the Sayed Abdel Rahman el Mahdi, the posthumous son of the founder of the Mahdist state extinguished by Kitchener at the battle of Omdurman half a century earlier. George Clutton, who played a key part in the development of British policy in 1949, wrote from his angle of vision as head of the African Department of the Foreign Office:

Our 'alliance' with S. A. R. [el Mahdi] always had its dangers, namely that this probably most powerful single influence in the Sudan would alienate other and probably steadier influences. . . . It is quite obvious that any question of a Kingship of the Sudan under S. A. R. would not merely wreck our relations with Egypt, but would also split the Sudan. A Mahdist régime would be bitterly opposed by large parts of the Arabic speaking country and it would be a disaster for the non-Moslem south.[26]

[24] J. S. R. Duncan, *The Sudan's Path to Independence* (London, 1957), p. 186.
[25] Sir James Robertson, *Transition in Africa: From Direct Rule to Independence* (London, 1974), p. 102.
[26] Minute by Clutton, 29 Jan. 1949, FO 371/73472/J343/G.

Howe had an important and influential ally in Clutton, who endorsed the policy of meeting Sudanese nationalist aspirations. Clutton encouraged Howe to advance at a steady pace and warned him of the dangers as they were perceived in London. The Foreign Office in a letter in early 1949 described the essential aim: 'to keep the ring until such time as the Sudanese are in a position to take over the control of their own country, and to decide for themselves their international status'.[27]

At this point it is vital to note some of the distinguishing characteristics of the officers who served under Howe and Robertson in the Sudan Political Service. Their ability, determination, and sense of duty has been a source of pride to many writers of British 'Imperial' history, yet their provincial outlook was a cause of concern to those in control of larger aspects of British policy. The British administration in the Sudan had no connection whatever with the Colonial Office. It functioned as an autonomous élite service with an extraordinarily high esprit de corps. In Robertson's words, which may be taken at face value, 'The British administrators' generally were 'imbued with a sense of service, knowing that we were there to administer the Sudan for the benefit of its peoples.'[28] At the same time the Sudan administration received much criticism within the British government. In the words of one Foreign Office official whose remarks caught Bevin's attention:

> We are too much at the mercy of the Sudan Civil Servant, who, with all his admirable qualities, has a rather limited and parochial public-school outlook. Nor do I like having to put our money on the Mahdist faction, which can hardly be said to represent the forces of moderation in the Sudan.[29]

Those remarks most certainly would have been endorsed by Sir Ronald Campbell in Cairo. He noted, in a long and indignant letter of complaint, that officers of the Sudan Service 'surpass many of the Sudanese leaders themselves in their championing of what they deem the rights of the Sudan, and in vilifying Egypt'. Campbell believed that the administration in the Sudan had set the country on a course towards 'premature' independence and that the root of the trouble could be located in the 'impertinent' and 'forceful' personality of Sir James Robertson.[30]

---

[27] Sargent to Howe (drafted by Clutton), 'Top Secret Personal', 18 Feb. 1949, FO 371/73472.

[28] Robertson, *Transition in Africa*, p. 162.

[29] Copy of a letter from Frank Roberts to Wright, 18 Apr. 1949, FO 371/73472/J4358. According to Strang, Bevin 'thinks there is a good deal of truth to the criticism of the Sudan Political Service'. Minute by Strang, 17 May 1949, ibid.

[30] Campbell to Wright, 'Personal and Secret', 14 May 1949, FO 371/73472/J4357.

Robertson proved to be an administrator of such outstanding ability that in 1955 he was appointed as Governor-General of Nigeria. In the late 1940s he appeared, in the eyes of his critics, especially those in Cairo, to be an arrogant and potentially dangerous bureaucrat who had usurped the functions of the Governor-General and who acted, in effect, as the 'Prime Minister' rather than the Civil Secretary of the Sudan government. There was some truth in that allegation. He differed temperamentally from Howe, who struck him as 'rather lonely' and 'solitary'.[31] Howe remained responsible for the overall affairs of the Sudan, but he allowed Robertson great latitude. It was Howe's success in maintaining friendly relations with Sudanese politicians, notably the future Prime Minister, Ismail el Azhari, that probably made the road to independence less rough than it might have been. Howe functioned as a quasi-Ambassador in an incipient nation-state. This is not to say that he did not act decisively in his ultimate command. He held the reins 'with the necessary velvet glove', Robertson wrote in his memoirs.[32] Nevertheless most of the inventive administrative steps were taken by Robertson.

This is not the place for an excursion into Sudanese political history, but it is important to note Robertson's part in the enactment of the ordinance of 1948 that set up a Legislative Council and an Executive Council (both of which were landmarks in Sudanese self-government) and his policy of bringing the southern part of the country—in his phrase, the African 'zoo'—into the mainstream of Sudanese politics. Not the least of the problems that tested Robertson's administrative genius was the prevention of the Sudan simply from splitting apart. 'The fear of the Southerners', he once wrote, militated against political progress because they believed that self-government 'would hand them over to the rule of the Northern Sudanese'. That was only part of the problem (though in the long run one of the most tragic). Robertson also emphasized the identical 'fear of the tribal leaders of the North against rule by the effendia of Khartoum and Omdurmàn'.[33] These tensions reflected the geographical, ethnic, and cultural divisions of the Sudan. There were also fundamental religious cleavages. At the time of the establishment of the Legislative Council, the Khatmia order of Sunni Muslims had boycotted the elections in protest against the political ambitions of the Sayed Abdel Rahman el Mahdi. The apprehension of the re-creation of a Mahdist state was a real and pervasive fear of a

---

[31] Robertson to R. C. Myall, 8 June 1948, 'Personal & Secret', Robertson Papers 522/1/56.
[32] Robertson, *Transition in Africa*, p. 161.
[33] Robertson to Bowker, 'Personal and Secret', 22 Jan. 1951, FO 371/90152/JE1052.

substantial part of the Sudanese population. The northern Sudan was roughly divided politically into the Khatmia and neo-Mahdist forces.

According to Howe, while on leave in London at an important meeting of the Middle East hands of the Foreign Office in August 1949, there was one 'sole reason' for the pro-Egyptian attitude of the Khatmia: 'They suffered under Mahdist rule 80 years ago and they fear that . . . the Sudan will become a Mahdist kingdom once again.'[34] The hereditary leader of the Khatmia order was the Sayid Ali el Mirghani, who in the postwar period increasingly gave cautious support to the nationalists who wished to see the Sudan allied with Egypt. It is possible to interpret the struggle for power in the Sudan in the late 1940s as a test between the Sayid Ali el Mirghani and the Khatmia, supported by Egypt, and the Sayid Abdel Rahman el Mahdi and his followers of the Ansar order, supported by Britain.

Until about 1951–2, as one authority on the Sudan has written, secular nationalism 'hardly deserves to be called "popular"; it was still the cult of the white collar *élite* rather than a genuine mass movement'.[35] Secular nationalism developed within the context of the Khatmia–Ansar conflict. The political party associated with the Khatmia was the 'Ashigga', and the political party of the Mahdi and the Ansar sect was the 'Umma'. The British archives reveal a sophisticated contemporary understanding of their religious foundations. British estimates were also particularly concerned to establish the extent of dominance of members of the two parties in the civil service and the penetration of political influence into the rural areas as well as the towns. According to British reports in the 1949–51 period, the Khatmia sect embraced 'about half the educated population of the North', and the Ashigga predominated among the 'Graduates', meaning those Sudanese who possessed at least a primary education in English. A survey by the Foreign Office Research Department gave this description of the principal political arm of the Khatmia:

The *Ashigga* (Brothers). This is the extremist party . . . standing for complete fusion of the Sudan with Egypt under the Egyptian Crown and the Egyptian Parliament. They would be prepared to accept a measure of local autonomy

[34] Minutes of F. O. meeting, 9 Aug. 1949, FO 371/73466.

[35] G. N. Sanderson, 'Sudanese Nationalism and the Independence of the Sudan', in ed. Michael Brett, *Northern Africa: Islam and Modernization* (London, 1973), p. 107. The other essential interpretative work with collaboration as the critical theme is Ronald Robinson, 'Non-European Foundations of European Imperialism: Sketch for a Theory of Collaboration', in eds. Roger Owen and Bob Sutcliffe, *Studies in the Theory of Imperialism* (London, 1972).

provided finance, foreign affairs and defence were controlled from Cairo. Its adherents, mostly civil servants and very often descended from an Egyptian parent or grand-parent, are mainly found in the larger towns of the Northern Sudan, few if any come from the rural areas.[36]

Egyptian propaganda and money had a significant influence in holding the allegiance of some members of the Ashigga, but among many there existed a genuine affinity for Egyptian culture, especially for those who regarded Cairo as their intellectual home. The Ashigga spoke of 'Dominion status', but with Egypt and not Britain, along the lines of 'an "India" rather than an "Australia" '.[37]

The Umma aimed at self-government and above all separation from Egypt. According to the Research Department's estimate:

> *The Umma* (People's Party). While not prepared . . . to commit itself to the eventual form of the Sudan state it welcomes . . . the right of the Sudanese to choose the future status of their country. The party envisages a Sudan either in close alliance with Great Britain, or with Egypt or with both. The party is neither pro-British nor anti-Egyptian but has cooperated with the Sudan Government during the past eight or nine years in the belief that it would thereby most speedily equip itself for self-government and independence of both co-domini. It is numerically the largest and most influential and progressive party in the country. It numbers members from both urban and rural districts; some are monarchists, some republicans and some would welcome the inclusion of an independent Sudan within the British Commonwealth.[38]

Members of the Umma also spoke of 'Dominion status' and they meant it in the true British sense of the Commonwealth. According to the minutes of a Foreign Office meeting of Middle East experts, at which Howe was present: the Umma party members 'have been greatly impressed by the example of India and when the Sudan becomes independent they say that they intend to seek membership of the British Commonwealth.[39] There was of course an element of political calculation in such Sudanese rhetoric. The Foreign Office officials did not attach so much importance to the title of the post-independence relationship as they did to the substance of the connection. In terms of broad Middle East politics, what the British hoped for at best was, in Howe's words, 'independence with some form of union with Egypt and a treaty of alliance with H. M. G.'[40]

The question of the Sudan is not only important for this chapter because of its central importance in Anglo-Egyptian relations and

[36] Foreign Office Research Department, December 1951, 'The Sudanese Parties and Sects', FO 371/90113/JE1017/51.
[37] Ibid.
[38] Ibid.
[39] Minutes of F. O. meeting, 9 Aug. 1949, FO 371/73466.
[40] Minute of F. O. conversation, 6 Oct. 1950, FO 371/80388/E1059.

the origins of the Suez crisis, but also because of the way it illuminates the dilemmas of British decolonization. According to Robertson, one unpalatable choice was 'either to continue to have the split in the political parties, which . . . plays into the hands of Egypt, or to risk the estrangement of the Tribal and Southern elements from ourselves and from the more politically conscious urban elements'.[41] In other words, what price independence? At the ethical risk of abandoning the southern Sudan? The Sudan as a whole was being propelled towards independence because of the crisis in Egypt. In studying the broader aspects of the problem it is important not to lose track of the British anguish aroused in anticipation of a 'premature' transfer of power and the consequences in the Sudan itself. According to Howe in September 1950:

> The Southern Sudan represents numerically some 30 per cent. of the total population of the country. Predominantly pagan and negroid, they are only now barely emerging from a primeval state to the appreciation of the benefits of fifty years of enlightened and Christian administration. They are already apprehensive of their future under a purely Sudanese Government. What would be their prospects under an Egyptian-dominated Sudanese Government? Given another twenty-five years of the present administration they might well be in a position to stand up against their Northern compatriots. . . .
>
> The Southerners *do not wish* progress towards a Sudanese Government to be too rapid and are opposed to ending the present régime too speedily. It would be wrong in my opinion to transfer power too soon to the Effendi class against the wishes of the tribal leaders and the great mass of the Sudanese.[42]

The minutes within the African Department of the Foreign Office on Howe's despatches make it clear that 'the Egyptian complication' preoccupied officials in the 1949–51 period, but that they had no doubt at all that over the long haul it would be 'the South which is likely to provide the most intractable problems in the Sudan'.[43]

Even if the Egyptians could be excluded from the eventual transfer of power, what of the prospects of Sudanese independence in only a few years when previously, before the acceleration brought about by the Egyptian emergency, at least a quarter of a century had been deemed the minimum amount of time necessary to integrate the north and the south? Contemplating the future of the Sudan as a whole was not much less melancholy than speculating on the fate of the southerners. One important aspect of the ethical dimension of the problem, as the British perceived it, was well brought out by a member of the African Department, Michael Stewart: 'I think . . . that in due course the educated Christian Southerner will prove to

[41] Robertson to Bowker, 22 Jan. 1951, FO 371/90152/J1052.
[42] Howe to Strang, Top Secret, 28 Sept. 1950, FO 371/80388.
[43] Minute by R. H. G. Edmonds, 21 Apr. 1951, FO 371/90111/JE1017/10.

have a stronger and more resourceful character than the Moslem townee of the North, whose politics and character will probably sink to the level of any other Arab Middle Eastern state when the hand of the British administration is removed.'[44]

Nahas, the Wafd, and the Question of Defence Planning at the Time of the Korean War

Shortly before Sir Ralph Stevenson assumed his duties in Cairo in the same month as the outbreak of the Korean war, in June 1950, he wrote himself an *aide-mémoire* on points about the Sudan to be borne in mind while talking to the Egyptians about other major issues such as the Canal Zone. The thing that impressed him above all during his briefings at the Foreign Office was the strong and unyielding attitude of the Egyptians. They still regarded themselves as co-masters of the Sudan, and technically they had an irrefutable case in international law because of the Anglo-Egyptian Condominium Agreement of 1899. If the British were to try to push them out of the Sudan, it would sour any effort to resolve issues of even more critical importance to the British, notably the defence of the Middle East and the question of the Suez Canal.

Howe (while in London for official consultations) together with Wright had also impressed on Stevenson that the Sudanese could now not be deflected from eventual independence. One of the points in Stevenson's *aide-mémoire* is of interest because of his assessment of the Ashigga in June 1950 and the way in which he foresaw possible developments:

The so-called pro-Egyptian elements in the Sudan are not so much pro-Egyptian as anti-Mahdi, and if the ever present fear of a Mahdist dynasty were removed there would be no obstacle to cooperation between the Khatmia and the Umma.[45]

That observation is significant because it was fundamentally right about the possible co-operation between the Khatmia and the Ansar, but quite oblivious to the consequences for the British. There was genuine apprehension in the Sudan about the danger of a neo-Mahdist state; but Stevenson left out of the equation the anti-British sentiment that was at least as important as the anti-Mahdist reaction. 'Nationalism' in this case is comprehensible as a struggle for the control of the Sudan. When the post-Farouk regime eventually recognized the right of the Sudanese to self-determination, the two Sayids and the Khatmia and Ansar uneasily yet decisively merged

[44] Minute by Stewart, 27 Apr. 1951, ibid.
[45] Minute by Stevenson, 31 May 1950, FO 371/80382/E1055.

into an independence movement that spelled the end of British rule. The British (in London at least) as well as the Egyptians were misreading the situation. It is perhaps debatable which side was more wrong than the other, but there can be no doubt that the officials of the Foreign Office believed that the Egyptians clung to the hope that the Sudanese, if left to themselves, would choose to unite with Egypt. In the words of a Foreign Office minute that went to the heart of other matters as well: 'The principal obstacle is . . . the general ignorance prevalent in Egypt . . . of the real state of affairs in the Sudan.'[46]

Michael Wright was responsible for formulating British policy to meet the two-pronged Egyptian challenge of 'evacuation' and 'unity of the Nile Valley'. The Sudan component may be dealt with briefly because, as he put it, the British wanted to keep it quiescent. It is important to bear in mind why they wished to work on the other part of the Wafd's formula. In May 1948 the Egyptian Foreign Minister, Ahmad Muhammad Khashaba, and Sir Ronald Campbell had agreed that an Anglo-Egyptian committee would be established to supervise Sudanese progress towards self-government. Khashaba, who was described by the Embassy in Cairo as a man of 'sincerity of purpose', had to suffer the humiliation of having his proposals rejected by the Egyptian Parliament because they did not enshrine the principle of 'the unity of the Nile Valley'.[47] Such was the power of this Nilotic cliché that Wright saw no hope of reconciling the divergent British and Egyptian positions. It would require an Egyptian statesman of extraordinary stature, in his judgement, to recast an essential element in the Egyptian national psyche. Wright therefore became keenly interested in reports after the advent of the Wafd that Nahas now felt that the fate of the Sudan should be determined by the Sudanese themselves.[48] Alas it proved to be merely part of the old story. Nahas, like most Egyptians, continued to believe that an exercise in self-determination would prove that the Sudanese wished to be united with Egypt. 'Until saner counsels regarding the Sudan prevail in Cairo', wrote a member of the African department, there could be no hope even of offering the Egyptians the face-saving device of participating in a committee (along the lines of the

[46] The minute continued along lines that restated the basic British assumption: the Egyptians 'have at the back of their minds the conviction that the fate which the majority of Sudanese, left to decide for themselves (i.e. without any British officials in Khartoum), would undoubtedly choose is union with Egypt'. Minute by R. H. G. Edmonds, 14 July 1950, FO 371/80382/JE1055/33.

[47] See the 'General Political Review—1948', enclosed in Campbell to Bevin, 7 June 1949, FO 371/73458/J4966. See Kirk, *The Middle East, 1945–1950*, pp. 138–43, for a discussion of the Campbell–Khashaba agreement and other points of controversy.

[48] Minute by Wright, 20 Mar. 1950, FO 371/80376/JE1051/22/G.

Khashaba–Campbell proposal) to supervise progress towards self-government. 'I intend to go very slow on the Sudan question', Stevenson wrote from Cairo in July 1950.[49] The issue was thus kept, in Wright's phrase, in 'cold storage'. Nevertheless it continued to be important, in a dormant sense, in relation to the other half of the equation, 'evacuation'. The British anticipated irrevocable stalemate. When it came, they preferred to see it over the Sudan. 'Morally our position is very strong', one official wrote in consolation about the Sudan on the eve of the actual deadlock in late 1950.[50]

As Wright pondered the question of the Egyptian demands for 'evacuation' he returned time and again to the root of the problem. It was the historic and continuing presence of British troops on Egyptian soil. 'The stumbling bloc', he wrote at the time of the Wafd's accession to power in January 1950, was psychological: 'The reluctance of any country to have foreign troops stationed in its territory, and the fact that in Egypt they may be regarded as a reminder and symbol of past occupation, are of course understandable.' The British justified the occupation of the Canal Zone on the basis of the 1936 treaty. They could also claim the right to defend Egypt, so ran the argument in international law and politics, by Britian's pre-eminence as the successor power to the Ottoman Empire. Here Wright demonstrated his powers of historical and psychological inquiry. His exercise in probing the roots of Egyptian anti-British sentiment is all the more striking because it originated in the mind of one of the most astute of the British civil servants. It serves as an example of the intellectual contortion in which the British found themselves in attempting to rationalize the continuing presence of British troops. Wright believed that the Egyptians saw 'a historical and psychological link' between the treaty of 1936 and the more vague yet undeniable fact that the British had succeeded the Turks by primitive force of arms, first by invasion in 1882 and then by military conquest during the First World War. Wright hoped that a 'public renouncement' of this 'link' would help to allay Egyptian resentment. He wished to break this 'link', the word he repeated, between the historical memory of the occupation and the present garrisoning of troops in the Canal Zone, the purpose of which was to defend Egypt and the Middle East generally.[51] Wright's argument may seem far-fetched and indeed preposterous in view of the obvious Egyptian rejoinder that occupation was occupation; but he was touching a key point on which the British had to remind

[49] Stevenson to Bevin, Secret, 7 July 1951, FO 371/80382/JE1055/33.
[50] Memorandum by Roger Allen, 8 Dec. 1950, FO 371/80381/JE1054/54.
[51] See e.g. Wright to Campbell, 'Personal and Top Secret', 24 Jan. 1950, FO 371/80375.

themselves at all times during these delicate discussions. The continuing British occupation of Egypt, even in the restricted area of the Canal Zone, needed some form of rationalization that would make it more acceptable to Egyptian nationalists.

Bevin met Nahas and other members of the Egyptian government in January 1950 on the return from the Colombo Conference. 'Exactly the right note had been struck', according to Sir Ronald Campbell, 'neither too little nor too much.'[52] Bevin drew out Nahas on the subject of economic development. Nahas stated that the Wafd 'had always set out to raise the standard of living of the Egyptian people'. The impression left in the minds of Bevin and his party was that Nahas and the Wafd would genuinely work for economic development and social reform, and that the Egyptians would prove to be responsive to the need for the general defence of the Middle East. Apart from economic questions, defence was the salient theme that Bevin developed in Cairo, and the one against which the Anglo-Egyptian conversations about 'evacuation' took place during the rest of the year. He spoke at length about the significance of the newly formed North Atlantic Treaty Organization. 'The Atlantic Pact', he told Nahas, 'had helped to steady the situation in the West', and it might now be possible to extend the line of defence from NATO to the Middle East. Bevin told the Egyptian Foreign Minister, Salah ed Din Bey, that there might be the possibility of 'some sort of triangular arrangement with the United States', Britain, and Egypt.[53] In this line of reasoning may be found the essential thrust of British thought about the Canal Zone and the defence of the Middle East in 1950. By bringing in the United States, the Egyptians would be more willing to tolerate a base in the Canal Zone, especially if they could be persuaded that they were being treated as equal partners in a major defence system.

Nahas was not unresponsive, but the concessions he could make within the constraints of the national slogan of 'evacuation' probably would not, in the Foreign Office's view, be sufficient to meet British requirements. What Nahas wished to be able to present to the Egyptian public was evidence, in his own words, that he had 'broken the link with the past'. Michael Wright had thus correctly identified the formula, according to Nahas's own preconceptions. Nahas even seemed to be moving along lines quite congenial to the Foreign Office and Chiefs of Staff, in other words, again in Nahas's own phrase, by making some 'token of concession'. The British were sceptical

[52] Campbell to R. E. Barclay, Confidential, 1 Feb. 1950, FO 371/80375.

[53] Record of conversation between Bevin and Nahas, and between Bevin and Salah ed Din Bey, 28 Jan. 1950, FO 371/80375/JE1051/11/G and 12/G.

whether this would be enough. They were willing to concede that Nahas might not have lost touch with reality (as his critics alleged), and that he possessed 'oriental cunning' as well as genuine patriotism. They simply did not believe that he had, among other things, the necessary charisma to mesmerize the Egyptian public into believing that 'token evacuation' would in fact be 'a break with the past'. This was going to be 'a very difficult game', Sir William Strang observed.[54] Roger Allen, who succeeded Clutton as head of the African Department in early 1950, at one stage of the discussions made a shrewd comment on the uncomfortable truth of the situation:

I think it boils down to this: if we could think up some device which allowed British troops to remain in Egypt, but provided the Egyptian Govt. with a really specious claim that we had evacuated, they would be delighted to accept it. Unfortunately our military requirements make this pretty well impossible— so the picture is gloomy.[55]

Whatever concessions Nahas might make, they would probably not be acceptable to the less moderate wing of his own party or even to the younger nationalists within the government. 'There were a number of younger members new to power', the Egyptian Ambassador told Wright, whom Nahas had to take into account. The conclusion that Wright drew from this and other exchanges was just as sobering as Allen's remark. Wright wrote to Bevin: 'One of the difficulties was that the Wafd had been out of power for six years, and were largely out of touch with the realities of the world situation.'[56]

'As for Nahas Pasha' and his difficulties with the moderate as well as the extreme nationalists, Sir Ralph Stevenson wrote shortly after his arrival in Cairo, Nahas along with his Foreign Minister 'both appear to be completely hamstrung by their slogans on "evacuation" and "unity of the Nile Valley" '. The two powerful expressions of Egyptian nationalism that had defeated Bevin and Sidky Pasha in 1946 continued to echo, plaguing Bevin in his last months of office and proving to be just as fatal for Nahas as they had been for Sidky. It must be said that the British did not view Nahas as a statesman capable of meeting the challenge. They suspected his failing ability at the time of his return to power and their apprehensions grew with time. Stevenson wrote in February 1951:

The Wafd Government continues to show up badly. Nahas himself does little or no work. Gallad Pasha, the newspaper proprietor, told me the other day that

---

[54] Minute by Strang, 20 Mar. 1950, FO 371/80376/JE1057/22/G.
[55] Minute by Allen, 27 July 1950, FO 371/80382/JE1055/33.
[56] Minute by Wright, 20 Mar. 1950, FO 371/80376/JE1057/22.

Nahas does not come down in the morning until half-past eleven or twelve o'clock and when he does, he appears powdered and scented, and as Gallad put it, 'dolled up like a village bridegroom' wearing grey silk gloves with his new cabochon emerald ring (bought on his last trip to Europe), worn outside the glove. He likes having his work done for him on the basis of rather woolly ideas which he expounds to chosen members of his Cabinet.[57]

And some months later:

The Prime Minister [Nahas] does very little work and seems to spend most of his day in the bathroom. He apparently sees people or reads from about 11.30 until 2 o'clock and from 7 until 9 in the evening. Apart from that he is said to pass the rest of the day in cleaning himself. This is probably an exaggeration but there is no doubt that he takes excessive care of his bodily health.[58]

There was of course much gossip about the rich and corrupt politicians who surrounded Nahas. For purposes of this chapter these circumstances might be dismissed as irrelevant were it not for growing British conviction that Nahas himself had deteriorated to the extent that he merely wished to remain in power.

Nahas was not the only one accused of losing his grip. After the British general election of February 1950, many of Bevin's critics believed that he should have resigned. He was increasingly handicapped by ill-health. Nevertheless the historical records do not reveal that his physical decline adversely influenced his policy. Like Roosevelt at Yalta, Bevin might have performed at greater capacity had he been in better health, but the assumption that his failing health affected his Egyptian policy, for example, cannot be proved.[59] There is no evidence of his slackening of control but rather the reverse. After his return from Colombo, Bevin instructed Wright to make detailed preparation for a possible 'comprehensive settlement of defence matters, and outstanding questions over Nile Waters, and possibly financial matters and the Sudan'.[60] As has been seen, Wright expeditiously performed this exacting task. By May 1950 Bevin was ready to move forward. He minuted on one of Wright's memoranda that he wanted '2 agreements'.[61] Sir Ralph Stevenson recorded Bevin's precise ideas. His minute indicates the continuity in Bevin's policy,

---

[57] Stevenson to Bevin, 'Secret and Personal', 28 Feb. 1951, FO 371/90110/JE1016/2/G.

[58] Stevenson to Morrison, 'Secret and Personal', 15 June 1951, FO 371/90110/JE1016/4/G.

[59] This is not to say that those who served under him were not alarmed at his state of health. For example Sir Ralph Stevenson wrote in his own hand in concluding a typewritten letter shortly before Bevin left the Foreign Office: 'I do hope that you are beginning to feel strong again now. Don't overdo it when you get back to the Office again.' Stevenson to Bevin 'Secret and Personal', 28 Feb. 1951, FO 371/90110/JE1016/2.

[60] Minute by Wright, 17 Feb. 1950, FO 371/80376/JE1057/18/G.

[61] Minute by Bevin on Wright's memorandum of 22 May 1950, FO 371/80382/E1055/20.

sustained by Bevin himself, as well as the direction of British efforts for the rest of the year:

The Secretary of State explained to me that what he had in mind was that we might avoid having a formal treaty, but that we might have an Anglo-Egyptian defence agreement of an intimate and specific character (it was conceivable that others, e.g. the Turks, might be brought in), and secondly that there should be a wider but much looser agreement which would bring in a number of other Middle Eastern Powers.[62]

The wider framework would include above all the United States. These were vigorous ideas that Bevin continued to pursue with a firm grip over detail as well as substance.

It is not proposed here to discuss the planning that might have integrated Egypt into a defence pact which in turn might have linked the Middle East with a chain of strategic alliances around the world. In the Middle East these extensive plans led only, in Dean Acheson's phrase, to a 'political stillbirth'.[63] Three points can be stated in summary about the Middle Eastern (and not merely the Egyptian), American, and British responses to the question of strategic planning. The debates about the defence of the Middle East and the future of the Canal Zone were taking place against the background of the Korean war. Sir John Troutbeck, in his former capacity as head of the Middle East Office in Cairo and now as Ambassador in Baghdad, had a gift for provoking his colleagues with comments that in retrospect often appear to have gone to the heart of the matter. In this case he called attention to a quotation from an Iraqi newspaper:

The call of the West finds no echo in our hearts. We do not understand them because we do not feel ourselves to be part of the so-called 'free world' which they say they are defending. We are part of the oppressed world which is struggling against them to achieve its freedom and throw off their yoke.[64]

That attitude, Troutbeck continued, should not be confused with Communism and did not imply identification with Moscow. It was merely a sense of not belonging to the 'West' any more than to Russia, and in that way it certainly expressed the sentiment of the Egyptians as well as other Arabs. No amount of effort could persuade the Wafd nationalists, who had been returned to power on the pledge to evict the British, that the occupation of Egypt by British troops was a matter of lesser importance than the 'defence of civilization'.

The point about the American attitude may be made in regard to George McGhee, whose duties as Assistant Secretary involved him

---

[62] Minute by Stevenson, 26 May 1950, FO 371/80382/JE1055/20.

[63] Acheson, *Present at the Creation*, p. 564.

[64] Quoted and discussed in Troutbeck to Morrison, Secret, 13 June 1951, FO 371/91185/E1024/35/G.

just as much in Anglo-Egyptian affairs as they had in those of Iran. McGhee struck the British as being so cocksure and overbearing that he seldom failed to irritate them—but not quite so much as in the case of Iran. In the Suez talks McGhee did not arouse the suspicion that he might be a catspaw of the American oil companies. 'One of the morals of the Korean war', as he would say to the British, was that one country might bear the responsibility for a particular area or territory—as the Americans had in Korea—but that it was 'extremely important' for the armed forces that might be engaged in an emergency to be of 'United Nations character'.[65] In other words the Far East would be primarily an American responsibility and the Middle East would be essentially a British area, though with an integrated 'international' command. This was exactly what the British wished to hear. McGhee on several occasions discussed in great detail various solutions to the impasse with Egypt, including the moving of the Suez base to the 'Gaza strip', and the greater distribution of British troops in Cyprus and Cyrenaica.[66] He was sceptical of British ability to maintain their position in the Canal Zone in the event of possible Egyptian obstruction such as the denial of labour or the cutting off of water supplies—circumstances in which the British would find it difficult to revert to force. He offered the British advice which had to be accepted as sound: 'He . . . thought it would pay us not to stand too rigidly on our treaty rights, but to meet the Egyptians half-way. . . . in our discussions with the Egyptians . . . they would swallow a multinational agreement like N. A. T. O. more easily than a bilateral one with us'.[67] This was a line that McGhee, and Acheson, consistently put forward, but not with much hope. When all was said the Americans as well as the British believed that there was no substitute for the Suez base. There was a general recognition that the presence of foreign troops on Egyptian soil, whether 'international' or British, would continue to arouse Egyptian nationalism. In these matters the United States, as Acheson accurately wrote in his memoirs, could play only a secondary and ameliorating part.[68] It was a matter in the end that had to be settled between the British and the Egyptians.

The British attitude, at least as expressed by the Chiefs of Staff, could be summed up in the belief that the Egyptians were being unreasonable in not seeing that they could not defend themselves. 'Egypt would certainly be singled out for early attack by the Russians',

[65] Furlonge to Barclay, Top Secret, 22 Sept. 1950, FO 371/81912. Bevin's minute on this letter is an example of the way in which he kept abreast of details of general policy.

[66] See e.g. *Foreign Relations 1950*, V, pp. 296-302.

[67] Minutes of F. O. meeting, 3 Apr. 1951, FO 371/90127/JE1024/1/G.

[68] Acheson, *Present at the Creation*, p. 567.

according to the C. O. S., ' . . . so they must have allies to assist them.'[69] On this 'delicate issue' the Defence Committee of the Cabinet approved instructions for the Chief of the Imperial General Staff, Sir William Slim, to emphasize the danger of Soviet aggression in talks with Farouk and other Egyptian leaders in June 1950. The results of these discussions were highly instructive. Farouk perceived the danger of continued occupation just as keenly as did Nahas and the other members of the government. When Slim drew the analogy between American troops in England and British forces in Egypt, Farouk replied that the two cases were not at all the same: 'It was a very different thing when a great nation occupied a small one.' When Slim produced the argument that the Dutch and the Belgians would be 'very happy' to have British forces in their countries, Farouk responded 'possibly so'—'but the situation in Egypt was quite different because none of these countries . . . had been occupied for sixty-five years'.[70] One must pause to reflect once again how permanently and irrevocably the British occupation had shaped Egyptian attitudes. Farouk expressed the indignation of all Egyptian patriots when he emphasized the phrase 'closed box', meaning the Canal Zone which the British operated as if it were an enclave in the heyday of late nineteenth century imperialism. The idea that this 'closed box' might eventually be converted into a 'United Nations' base met with considerable scepticism about what the British actually had in mind. On the basis of the Chiefs of Staff records, one must conclude that Egyptian suspicions were justified.

The magnitude of the problems facing the British may be conveyed with simple statistics. In late 1950 British forces in Egypt numbered over three times the amount of 10,000 allowed by the 1936 treaty. The 'Land Striking Force' accounted for 7,000; the Royal Air Force and army defence units, 10,000; and the personnel of General Headquarters and base troops, 13,000, plus some 8,000 Mauritian troops that guarded the base. Moreover the largest and most important military installation in the Middle East, the Tel-el-Kebir depot, was vulnerable to terrorist attacks. Any major shift in this military deployment, either to the 'Gaza strip', or to Cyprus or Cyrenaica, seemed to be grotesquely implausible. There were unimpeachable strategic as well as tactical reasons for the maintaining of British forces in Egypt, as summarized in the following lines from a memorandum circulated by Bevin to the Cabinet. The British force was even more essential than it had been a decade earlier:

[69] Report by COS, 19 May 1950, DO (50) 40, CAB 131/9.
[70] Memorandum by Slim, 4 June 1950, PREM 8/1359.

The strategic emphasis has in fact shifted since 1936, and our primary strategic requirement is now not so much the defence of the Suez Canal itself as the maintenance of a Base in Egypt capable of rapid expansion on the outbreak of war, in order to support a major campaign in the Middle East and the defence of the base against air attack.[71]

Whatever the necessity of the presence of the British forces, it is easy to comprehend, in view of the numbers that far exceeded the amount allowed by the 1936 treaty, why the British preferred to have a showdown over the Sudan.

In the event Nahas emphatically reaffirmed the unalterable bedrock-position of the Egyptian case. In a speech delivered at the opening of the Egyptian Parliament on the 16th of November 1950, he passionately declared the 1936 treaty to be null and void. He did not go so far as actually to suggest 'abrogation' in a formal sense, but his vehement denunciation of the British 'occupation' probably marked the turning point. 'Virtual deadlock has . . . been reached', Bevin wrote to members of the Cabinet.[72] Nahas had committed himself publicly to 'total and immediate evacuation' and had declared that the annulment of the 1936 treaty was 'inevitable'. In no less powerful language Nahas also emphasized Egypt's commitment to 'building the edifice of civilisation' in the valley of the Nile and 'the unity of Egypt and the Sudan under the Egyptian Crown'. In spite of Nahas's uncompromising statements Bevin expressed the hope in the House of Commons that he might still reconcile the differences between the two countries in the talks with the Egyptian Foreign Minister to be held shortly in London.[73]

The Anglo-Egyptian discussions of December 1950 are so important as a landmark on the road to the great Suez crisis six years later that it is useful to step back briefly to assess the significance of this juncture from a slightly more disinterested but nevertheless critical vantage point, the American. It is particularly illuminating to dwell momentarily on the ideas of the Ambassador in Cairo, Jefferson Caffery, who had served as the first postwar Ambassador to France and had the reputation as one of the most distinguished, and also most formidable, members of the United States Foreign Service. He certainly was well-informed, and on the whole well-disposed to the British—but more so to the British in Cairo than in Khartoum. In his judgement the situation had so deteriorated that the most important thing to be done was 'keeping [the] Egyptians talking' in order 'to ride out the storm'. There was still

[71] Memorandum by Bevin, CP (50) 283, 27 Nov. 1950, CAB 129/43.
[72] Ibid.
[73] *Parliamentary Debates* (Commons), 29 Nov. 1950, cols. 35–6.

a possibility, according to Caffery, that more time would enable both the British and the Americans to find something that the Wafd 'can sell to its clamorous clients'. He had in mind armaments, guarantees of Egyptian sovereignty, 'at least a facade of military consultation', and some sort of reassurance that the British and the Americans were at least informally aware of the danger of militant Zionism.[74] This was astute advice. On more long-range strategic planning— bearing in mind the year 1956 as the critical time of the expiration of the 1936 treaty—Caffery wrote that '*1952 is to be the critical year, in Mr. Bevin's thinking*', another shrewd and informed remark (and incidentally one that helps to dispel the myth that Bevin on the eve of the Anglo-Egyptian talks of December 1950 was losing his grip).[75] There was so little time left for bringing about a settlement in which the British (and the Americans) might stay on in Suez that Caffery saw the need to make the Egyptians a substantial offer. It is comprehensible in view of the broader strategic stakes of the Korean war. In Caffery's judgement a compromise with the Egyptians should be made in the Sudan if it would salvage the situation in Suez. For holding such a view Caffery was denounced by Sir James Robertson for 'selling the Sudan'.[76]

The American attitude towards the Sudan, especially as Caffery expressed it, differed in fundamental respects from the British. In the British view the Sudan was not necessarily a lesser priority, if regarded as a matter of principle. To some of those involved in the controversy such as Robertson, the British 'Imperial' mission in the Sudan was the transcendent issue. The Sudan part of the dispute was also a matter of practical politics. The British feared that the Egyptians would again haul them before the United Nations, where the growing anti-colonial sentiment would be vented against the obvious violations of the 1936 treaty because of the number of troops. By December 1950 the British, foreseeing deadlock, wished to appear in a favourable light in the Sudan in order to offset the criticism they would receive about the Canal Zone. There was also the question of domestic restraints. The British believed that Nahas and the Wafd were prisoners of their own political slogans, but 'self-determination' for the Sudan motivated the British in a similar way. Since 1946 British sentiment, as it could be perceived in the press and in Parliament, had hardened

---

[74] Caffery to Acheson, 25 Nov. 1950 and 11 Dec. 1950, *Foreign Relations 1950*, V, pp. 323-4 and 329-30.

[75] Caffery to Acheson, 31 Dec. 1950, ibid., pp. 332-4.

[76] Caffery was from the American South. Perhaps partly for that reason as well as for 'appeasement', Robertson in his memoirs denounced him, and by implication most other Americans, for not appreciating 'our concern for . . . "ten million bloody niggers"'. Robertson, *Transition in Africa*, p. 150.

against any concessions at all in the Sudan. There was now no question of Egyptian 'symbolic sovereignty'. The British public simply would not tolerate it. Nahas's renewed complaints had the effect of stiffening British attitudes in general. On the eve of the Anglo-Egyptian talks of December 1950 there was an acrimonious discussion in the House of Commons about the shipment of armaments to Egypt. The government was forced to give an assurance that sixteen tanks destined for Egypt would not leave British shores until Members of Parliament had an opportunity further to discuss the wider ramifications of the Egyptian crisis.[77] The talks of December 1950 thus opened under most inauspicious circumstances. Jefferson Caffery made an incisive comment when he wrote that they might 'set back the clock' rather than move the two sides forward.[78]

In December 1950 the British and the Egyptians became locked —deadlocked is not too strong a word—into their respective positions and managed to insult each other in the process. Under Bevin's leadership at the Foreign Office the British prided themselves on a pragmatic approach to international and 'Imperial' problems; but the phrase 'jugular vein of the Empire' evoked a passion that was practically as unyielding as the Egyptian cry for 'evacuation'. In the Sudan the British believed that they had an almost unassailable case by arguing that the Sudanese themselves should determine their own fate according to the formula of self-determination. The British in fact believed that the Sudanese, by being kept as immune as possible from corrupting Egyptian influence, would be more favourably disposed to the British cause. The Egyptians were no less the captives of their own 'Imperial' preconceptions. They had no doubt at all that the British by control of the Sudan had obstructed the historic 'unity of the Nile valley'. 'The official line here', C. D. Quilliam of *The Times* wrote confidentially from Cairo shortly after the conclusion of the talks, 'continues to be that 90% of the Sudanese are panting for unity with Egypt and that the British are planning to turn the Sudan into a British colony.'[79]

The results of these discussions may be briefly related because they have long been known. The Egyptians indignantly published the transcripts so that the truth might be known to all the world, which forced the British to publish their own version.[80] The

---

[77] See *Parliamentary Debates* (Commons), 22 Nov. 1950, cols. 424–68.

[78] Caffery to Acheson, 25 Nov. 1950, *Foreign Relations 1950*, V, pp. 323–4.

[79] Quilliam to Deakin, 2 Jan. 1951, Quilliam Papers.

[80] For the Egyptian documentation published by the Ministry of Foreign Affairs in Cairo, which is the fullest version, see *Records of Conversations, Notes and Papers Exchanged between the Royal Egyptian Government and the United Kingdom Government (March 1950–November 1951)*. For the British publication see Cmd. 8419, 'Egypt No. 2

protagonists were Bevin and the Egyptian Foreign Minister, Salah ed Din Bey. One of Bevin's opening remarks aimed at providing a more flexible basis for discussion than slogans. Salah ed Din retorted that 'evacuation' was no mere slogan: it was the demand of the Egyptian people and it should be completed within one year. Evacuation might be a 'slogan' to the British, he said, but sixty-five years of occupation gave it a real meaning to all Egyptians. Such a statement, Bevin admitted, had 'the advantage of clarity'. He could not find much else to say favourably about it. The only ray of hope in the talks about the Canal Zone was the assumption, which the Egyptians shared, that British troops would have the right of re-entry in the event of a world war. On almost all else the discussion was barren. Bevin wished to regard the past as a closed book and to talk about the future, but to Salah ed Din it was the history of the occupation that governed present circumstances. 'What Egypt asked for', he said, was 'the actual evacuation of Egyptian territory by British forces.' With words that carried a certain sting because of the presence of British troops in excess of the terms of the 1936 treaty, he emphasized that 'Words did not count in this connection. Actual facts were the only things that counted. . . . ' There is no point in relating the accusations and counter-accusations, but it is important to emphasize one theme of the conversations because it rankled then and later on the Egyptian side. Bevin said that he did not wish to disparage the Egyptian armed forces, but evacuation within a year, or even more, would be impossible because they lacked the technical expertise to run the base. He couched this remark about the deficiency of 'highly technical' and sophisticated knowledge in polite terms, and he no doubt meant it, but it was nevertheless supremely insulting to the Egyptians.

On the Sudan the conversation became even more pitched. Bevin expressed his opinions more emphatically because he believed that the British case to be stronger. Most informed western opinion on colonial affairs in 1951 would probably have concurred that the British were better 'guardians' of the Sudan than the Egyptians, which ultimately was the essence of one of the major questions in dispute. Nevertheless Salah ed Din scored some points that must have made Bevin at least temporarily uncomfortable. The Egyptian asked why the British had pursued, until recently, a policy of 'separation' for the southern part of the country which excluded northerners and Egyptian influence. Why had the British supported independence for Libya while dragging their feet in the Sudan? Why had they

(1951): Anglo-Egyptian Conversations on the Defence of the Suez Canal and on the Sudan. December 1950–November 1951'. For F.O. comment see FO 371/96924.

supported the union of Ethiopia and Eritrea under the Ethiopian crown and refused to recognize the Sudan under the Egyptian crown? Could anyone say that the ties between Eritrea and Ethiopia were as strong as the ties between Egypt and the Sudan? Bevin prudently did not respond to those questions without counsel from his Foreign Office advisers. The answers to the questions about Libya and Eritrea essentially concerned the exigencies of international politics, as will be recalled from an earlier chapter. The British were not without chinks in their imperial armour, but Bevin could state with considerable warmth that they had helped the Libyan people to determine their own future and in the case of Eritrea had concurred in a solution in which there was no better alternative.

It was on the question of the southern Sudan that Bevin responded with a definite tone of indignation. 'History had shown repeatedly', he said, 'that if primitive, indigenous cultures were to be preserved from extinction when they first came into contact with more advanced peoples, they had to be treated with the greatest care.'[81] He stated emphatically that the British administration of the Sudan was 'beyond reproach'. Here he was expressing a point on which the British public wholeheartedly would have agreed. British colonial rule in the African dependencies was a source of 'Imperial' pride. It should be borne in mind, however, that the Egyptians regarded themselves, historically and in international law, just as much the trustees of the Sudan as the British. It could be inferred from Bevin's remarks that the Egyptians were inferior guardians. In British circles the idea of Egyptian 'guardianship' even being compared with British trusteeship would not have been taken seriously. To Egyptians however it was no laughing matter. There was a historic and cultural connection between Egypt and the Sudan. The Egyptians had their own sense of an imperial mission. The implication that they were deficient as a civilizing power was an insult even greater than the one of lack of technical ability to run the Suez base.

Abrogation

Since the discussions about the Canal Zone were taking place in the midst of the Korean war, the Chiefs of Staff found a congenial atmosphere in which not to yield on the issue of evacuation. The more they studied the alternatives, the more they re-endorsed a fundamental premiss: Egypt was the only country that fulfilled the strategic requirements of housing a base capable of supporting a major campaign in the Middle East. Part of the purpose of the Suez

[81] Cmd. 8419, p. 21.

base was to enable British military forces to expand rapidly on the outbreak of war. Without the military installations in the Canal Zone the Chiefs of Staff believed that they would run the risk of losing the Middle East altogether. Bearing in mind that strategic concept, it is well to remember that to the military mind the Suez base had its own primeval justification. It commanded one of the supreme strategic positions in the entire world. Like the refinery at Abadan, it was a magnificent example of British resourcefulness and technological skill. In 'Imperial' splendour it was perhaps rivalled only by Singapore. It provided areas for year-round training and manœuvres for units of infantry, armour, and artillery as well as for fighter aircraft and heavy bombers. The Suez 'base' in fact consisted of no less than ten airfields, thirty-four military stations, railways, roads, ports, flying-boat stations, barracks, and a vast array of communication networks, including a local radio station. In 1951 there were 38,000 troops stationed at the 'Suez base'. It possessed all of the facilities that enabled an Englishman, as Churchill once remarked, to live in tropical climates without discomfort. The nature of the enclave, as well as the presence of British troops, helps to explain why the Suez 'base' was so resented by Egyptian nationalists.

In his memoirs Anthony Eden described a certain 'unimaginative mishandling' of the situation in Suez by the Labour government.[82] It was an astute remark, but it is important to distinguish the 'post-Bevin' era to which it applied. Bevin himself was sensitive to the Egyptian complaint about the enclave, but he was also sympathetic to the Chiefs of Staff's argument about the need to retain control over the most vital military installation in the Empire-Commonwealth. He shared the scepticism about Egyptian capabilities to take over and manage effectively such a sophisticated operation. Nevertheless he believed that the handover had to be made.[83]

In the last weeks before his death, Bevin continued to develop original ideas about the Suez problem.[84] His encounter with Salah ed

---

[82] Anthony Eden, *Full Circle* (Boston, 1960), p. 250.

[83] The critical despatch recording these views was dictated by Bevin on 8 Jan. 1951 (see FO 371/90129), when he recorded a conversation with the Egyptian Ambassador. Bevin expressed concern about 'the efficiency of the base during the present critical period', and made it quite clear that 'it was out of the question to hand over an intricate technical thing like a military base in the lighthearted way that some people had suggested'. The key to his policy then followed: 'there must be a properly organised transfer over a period of years'. The substance as well as the chronology is of interest because, like his Palestine policy, Bevin's ideas must be criticized in principle and in timing (in this case that he should have reacted this or another way, for example, in 1946) rather than on grounds of step-by-step development or overall coherence.

[84] 'I told Amr Pasha', the Egyptian Ambassador, Bevin wrote in one of his last despatches on Egypt two months before his death, 'that I had wished to assure him that in spite

Din had made him more responsive to the shift in international sentiment against the 'enclave' mentality. 'Occupation of territory by foreign troops', he told his colleagues in the Cabinet (he spoke in his capacity as Lord Privy Seal after he had resigned his duties as Foreign Secretary because of ill health) 'was increasingly out of line with world opinion.' He perceived that the British would have to leave Suez on Egyptian terms, but he believed that the situation might still be twisted to British advantage. He regarded the Egyptians as stubborn but not unreasonable people who would eventually recognize that 'evacuation' within one year was impossible. The bargain that he proposed was that the British would now undertake a commitment intensively to train Egyptian replacements. The British would move out as soon as possible, and in return for this tangible demonstration of sincerity and good faith, they could expect Egyptian military co-operation and the British right of re-entry in the event of war. Bevin believed that this crash programme of training the Egyptians was the only way to salvage the situation, and the scheme that he put before the Cabinet rang of genuine conviction and political inventiveness. He was in fact endorsing a set of proposals put forward by the Chiefs of Staff themselves, but with a much greater emphasis on the need for urgency and the development of 'cordiality' between the two military forces:

> The process of removing our troops would be gradual, and we should make every effort, by employing the best men for the purpose, to carry out our obligation to train the Egyptian forces. The proposals [of the C. O. S.] provided for our re-entry into Egypt in an emergency, and we should best be able to exercise this right if we had been able to build up in the meantime relations of real cordiality between the armed forces of the two countries.[85]

In Bevin's view the deadlock of December 1950 thus was only temporary. In his vision there could be a military transfer of power in Egypt that in the long run would be seen in the same light as the transformation of the Empire into Commonwealth.

One of the difficulties in promoting 'cordiality' was that the Chiefs of Staff did not have a high professional regard for the Egyptian army. In private they made no bones about the low potential of Egyptian troops, even as cannon fodder.[86] In the critical meeting of the Cabinet that formulated Egyptian policy—one of the last that Bevin attended—the Minister of Defence aligned himself with the new Foreign Secretary. In understanding the drift in British policy

of my illness I had been giving much thought to this problem and was most anxious to help to bring about a solution.' Record of conversation, 19 Feb. 1951, FO 371/90130.

[85] Cabinet Minutes 23 (51), 2 Apr. 1951, CAB 128/19.
[86] See e.g. memorandum by Allen, 5 June 1951, FO 371/90134.

during the spring and summer of 1951, it is important to bear in mind this meeting of minds between Shinwell and Morrison. The former made it clear that it would be essential 'to maintain the base in an efficient condition', and that he was much more interested in the 'protraction' of the talks with the Egyptians than he was in the withdrawal of troops. This was the military position. It held that over a long period of time it might be necessary to reduce the number of troops in the Canal Zone. The military mind was not entirely oblivious to the dangers of an enclave surrounded by a hostile native population. The immediate problem, as Shinwell expressed it, was to hang on in the hope that things might change for the better.[87] In the general discussion about this point the Cabinet minutes do not specify individual opinions, but it is certain that Shinwell and Morrison emphatically held the view that a firm British stand would buck up the Egyptians favourable to the British cause.[88]

The Cabinet discussions of April 1951 are exceedingly important because it might be argued that here was the last chance to adopt the policy suggested by Bevin of an all out, albeit last minute, effort to train the Egyptians to take over from the British and to begin the evacuation in a spirit of goodwill. These proceedings from time to time reveal shrewd insight into Egyptian nationalism—for example, in a general point that emerged, 'The anti-British bias of all political parties in Egypt might be due to a desire not to be outdone in patriotic fervour by political opponents rather than to any definite *animus* against this country.'[89] Nevertheless the thrust of the argument developed towards a stiffer line. When it came to the terms of reopening the talks with the Egyptians, the British formally made a number of demands that any Egyptian government would have found difficult to meet, not least one as committed to evacuation as was the Wafd regime. The British now spoke of 'phased withdrawal', but only after the conclusion of a new treaty. They simply rejected the Egyptian position on the Sudan. Moreover these new British views, when they were formally presented on the 11th of April, gave the Egyptians the impression of an *ultimatum*. With what must have been unprecedented speed for the Wafd government, or for that matter any other government of the time, the Egyptians flatly rejected the British proposals within two weeks—with 'deep regret and bitter disappointment'.[90]

Sir Ralph Stevenson must bear some of the responsibility for the

[87] Cabinet Minutes 23 (51), 5 Apr. 1951, CAB 128/19.
[88] Ibid.
[89] Ibid.
[90] See Cmd. 8419.

'ultimatum', but the abruptness and tendency to be abrasive was typical of Herbert Morrison. 'Foreign policy', Morrison once said to an American journalist, 'would be okay "except for the foreigners" '.[91] In this case he had in mind the 'wogs', the Egyptians. Intellectually and emotionally Morrison had much more sympathy with his Parliamentary critics than he did with the policy he had inherited from Bevin. Those who denounced British policy included some of his Labour friends. One of them, R. T. Paget, had been instrumental in the embargo of the sixteen 'Centurion' tanks. Morrison was perplexed with criticism that he should take a more aggressive line, especially since at heart he agreed. His minutes reveal that he was just as concerned, if not more so, with Parliamentary criticism of his policy as with the policy itself. He instructed his permanent officials not to 'under-estimate' the following lines written to him by Paget in April 1951:

> The M. E. is not an area in which it pays to reward your enemies and to neglect your friends. The governments of Egypt, having no social policy, are committed to competitive anti-Britishness. For purely internal reasons no Egyptian Government can be appeased. Evacuation will be followed by a demand to nationalise the Canal, for the Sudan and then for Uganda and the upper waters of the Nile. . . .
>
> This is not 1946. Since then Egypt has wasted her substance and our money on the maintenance of a system of social injustice that should have disappeared a century ago. . . .
>
> Surely it's time to get tough. We control the Nile water; we supply much of the money on which the Pasha Government live; we have an army and a navy![92]

Paget's lines were representative of increasing anti-Egyptian sentiment in Parliament and in the press. Morrison, for his part, might say publicly that he pursued the policy established by his predecessor, but privately he agreed with Paget. 'I wish I was Lord Palmerston', he once said to one of his assistants.[93]

Morrison took pride in intellectual agility, but this virtue of insight plus dexterity was not apparent in his short and unhappy career as Foreign Secretary, especially in Egyptian affairs. He found it frustrating to be able to devote only sporadic attention to Egypt, though there is no evidence that he found the subject intrinsically interesting. Nor did he find Iran any more gratifying, even though it took up much more of his time. In both cases there was a pattern to his responses, and it is important to identify his instinctive Egyptian impulses because the period before abrogation was a critical time in Anglo-Egyptian affairs. Morrison believed that yielding to Egyptian

[91] C. L. Sulzberger, *A Long Row of Candles* (New York, 1969), p. 658.
[92] Paget to Morrison, 9 Apr. 1951, FO 371/90133.
[93] Bernard Donoughue and G. W. Jones, *Herbert Morrison* (London, 1973), p. 498.

pressure would merely further weaken Britain's position in the Middle East. And he did not think that any concession should be made to the Egyptians in the Sudan. The reasons for his latter position did not derive from any particular ideas about the Sudan but rather from a conviction that 'appeasement' of Egyptian nationalism would lead to a deterioration of Britain's position as a world and 'Imperial' power. Beyond a distaste for doing business with the Egyptians, he had no ideas of substance and certainly no insight into the nature of the Egyptian protest either about the Canal Zone or the Sudan. He proposed merely, in his own words, 'to keep the discussions going'.[94] In the 'post-Bevin' era it is thus noteworthy that within the Cabinet the most radical criticism of this approach came from the Lord Privy Seal, Richard Stokes.

As will be recalled from the previous chapter, Stokes had business connections in the Middle East and frequently travelled to Egypt. His judgement was erratic, and was certainly so regarded by his colleagues, but on the question of Egypt he presented views to the Cabinet that in retrospect must strike one as perceptive. Stokes believed that the Egyptians were in dead earnest about 'evacuation' and that if the British continued merely to 'talk' about the Sudan it would inflame the question of the Canal Zone. Stokes confirmed to the Cabinet that the Egyptians had regarded the last set of proposals as an 'ultimatum'. The Cabinet minutes of the 31st of May 1951 relate Stokes's warning:

> *The Lord Privy Seal* said that, from his personal knowledge of conditions in Egypt, he was satisfied that no agreement could be reached with the Egyptian Government unless we were prepared to give an assurance that all combatant British troops would be removed from the Canal Zone within a reasonable period. . . .
> The proposals which His Majesty's Ambassador had put forward in pursuance of the Cabinet's decision of 5th April, had been regarded by the Egyptians as an ultimatum rather than a basis for negotiation; and he feared that no progress could be made unless we could satisfy the Egyptians that we were prepared to make some concession towards their point of view regarding the evacuation of combatant troops from the Canal Zone.

Here is the way in which Stokes quite accurately linked the talks about the Canal Zone with those of the Sudan:

> In these circumstances he saw no advantage in putting forward at this stage proposals regarding the future of the Sudan which would be equally unacceptable to the Egyptians. This was likely to exacerbate feelings still further and thus increase the difficulties of reaching any agreement on the Treaty [of 1936].[95]

---

[94] Cabinet Minutes 39 (51), 31 May 1951, CAB 128/19.
[95] Ibid.

Despite Stokes's clear and forcefully argued case about the danger of further Sudanese discussions, the Cabinet followed Morrison's lead in opening up another round which would make clear to the Egyptians, and if necessary to the world at large, Britain's morally superior position in the Sudan.

One must look beyond Morrison's own vague ideas to find the source of his inspiration. The Egyptian crisis had brought about something close to intellectual paralysis in the Foreign Office. 'We wish to avoid a break as long as possible', wrote Michael Stewart of the African Department, and in some of his briefs for Morrison may be found the key to the latter's thought. The basic British objective at this time was merely 'to play for time'. Part of the reason for this approach could be found in the calculation of the Egyptian 'national character' and climate. Nahas, who was playing 'a somewhat enigmatic part', would not wish to disturb his plans for a holiday in Europe in order to conduct serious business. Stewart took note that the Foreign Minister, Salah ed Din, might actually resign over the issue of evacuation, but this did not deter the Foreign Office from believing that 'the summer season in Egypt', which was 'a period of apathy', would deter undue nationalist exertion.[96] Such was the pattern of thought. Judged against the Foreign Office of Bevin (or perhaps that of any other Foreign Secretary in the twentieth century), the response of the permanent officials might be judged to have reached a sluggish bottom. That at least is one interpretation, though it is possible to argue, as will be seen, that the official mind was deliberately unresponsive. In any case, following the Foreign Office's lead, Morrison had proposed, to repeat his words, 'to keep the discussions going' about the Sudan, and the Cabinet had endorsed his suggestion rather than Stokes's. Doing something in a vague way appeared to be better than doing nothing, and far better than planning evacuation.[97]

Morrison managed to avert one potential personal catastrophe, which would have been the spectacle of himself discussing the complicated affairs of the Sudan with the Egyptian Foreign Minister in London. He firmly advised that any future talks should be held in Cairo. The focus in the summer of 1951 thus shifts from England to Egypt, and at this stage it is useful to assess briefly the ideas of Sir Ralph Stevenson. Before taking up his duties in Egypt, Stevenson had served for four years as Ambassador in China. Like Shepherd in Tehran (who had been in Indonesia), Stevenson thus had definite preconceptions about Asian nationalism. Stevenson was of greater

---

[96] Memorandum by Stewart, 7 May 1951, FO 371/90132.
[97] Cabinet Minutes 39 (51), 31 May 1951, CAB 129/19.

intellect than Shepherd, but it is useful to bear in mind their similar assumptions. The point of conspicuous importance to both of them was that the British troops in the Canal Zone served the same external function of 'scapegoat' as the British oil company did in Iran. Stevenson adamantly denied the premiss of the nationalist argument that the British occupation was the root cause of all Egyptian problems, and that the British should be held accountable for economic and social distress. In his view it was only a minority of government officials and newspaper editors 'who have founded their careers on the simple demand for "independence" or "evacuation" ' who, through demagoguery, distorted the true sentiments of the Egyptian people. Most Egyptians in other words were not Anglophobe but were lashed into anti-British sentiment by their leaders who wished to deflect attention from deep-seated economic and social problems. 'The Moslem Brotherhood,' Stevenson wrote, 'whose fire is really directed at the moral rottenness of their own countrymen, hang a Union Jack over their target, and other extremists do the same.'[98] Stevenson deplored the attempt by many Egyptian leaders to place the blame on the British for Egyptian poverty, ignorance, and disease, and he especially resented the accusation that the British were 'allies in corruption'. In these words he summed up what he thought to be the heart of the matter: 'I do not believe that the people feel any spontaneous indignation at the presence of our Base, but their bitter discontent with their lot in general can be easily focused on an "occupation" which their demagogues have for so long represented as the cause of all the country's ills.'[99]

There is one theme in Stevenson's thought that is of exceptional historical interest. He believed that the immediate cause of the unstable state of affairs in 1951 was the humiliation of defeat in the 1948 war against Israel. He thought that the rabble-rousing of the Wafd against British 'imperialism' in the Canal Zone was one way of attempting to redeem a sense of national pride, and that the Wafd leaders were playing with revolutionary fire. Their demagoguery might produce nothing less than 'an Egyptian Musaddeq', or perhaps an equally dangerous military equivalent. He believed that the Wafd leaders were shrewd enough to recognize that danger. Stevenson wrote in July 1951:

The Wafd are no less efficient rabble-rousers than the present Persian Government, and could, if they chose, unleash a popular movement for 'nationalisation' of our Base. . . . I doubt whether . . . the present leaders of the Wafd would be

[98] Stevenson to Morrison, Top Secret, 6 July 1951, FO 371/90134/JE1051/139/G.
[99] Ibid.

so ready to pull the house down on their own heads as Dr. Musaddeq apparently is. There are too many men in the Party and in the Administration now who understand the real causes of the discontent they might exploit and who realize that, though a mob movement would initially attack the 'Imperialists' it would most probably end by cutting the throats of the Pashas.

On the chances of 'an Egyptian Musaddeq', Stevenson reverted to the legacy of the 1948 war:

> It is important, I am sure, to do something now both to assist the morale of the Army and to remove its feeling—which has not lessened since the Palestine War—that we are the cause of its humiliation and frustration. . . .
>
> The Egyptian Army has a two-fold importance for the security of our position here: it is the ultimate Egyptian guarantee of law and order, and its officers could, in certain conceivable circumstances, make some gesture of despair which would be as little in our interests as any action to which either an Egyptian Musaddeq or the Communists could incite the people.[1]

Stevenson believed it to be of imperative importance to keep on as good terms as possible with the Egyptian army and to remove grievances about the 1948 war by supplies of weapons and other military equipment.

Stevenson's assessment aroused great interest within the Foreign Office, and the response is especially relevant to the themes of this book because the permanent officials again raised the question of intervention. The minutes also reveal some of the causes of the 'paralysis' of the official mind. The problems in the Middle East simply seemed to be impossible of resolution at that time. Roger Allen, the head of the African Department, wrote of a 'vicious circle'. Earlier Allen had served as liaison with the Chiefs of Staff. His observations about the Egyptian military thus carried particular weight within the Foreign Office. He concurred in the judgement that the army was the key to stability in Egypt and that 'in a strictly limited way' the army should be supported. His reservations were based on the obvious risk of supplying arms and equipment that might be used against British forces in the Canal Zone. Allen was by no means optimistic about the situation in Egypt:

> The truth of the matter is, that it suits the Egyptian Government very well to be able to go on abusing us and using us as the target of popular discontent. The only way of extricating ourselves from this position would be to reach an agreement with them; but as time goes on it becomes harder to reach an agreement and the Egyptian Government has less incentive to do so.
>
> This is the sort of vicious circle in which we are caught up; and our only hope of breaking out of it appears to be in the intervention of some *deus ex machina* in the form, for example, of an increased Soviet threat. . . .[2]

---

[1] Ibid.
[2] Minute by Allen, 25 July 1951, FO 371/90134/JE1051/139/G.

The immediate danger, in Allen's judgement, lay in Egyptian provocation.

If the Egyptians pushed the British too hard, either by attempting to force them out of the Canal Zone or by nationalizing the Canal, should the British intervene, perhaps covertly, to topple the Wafd government—as Allen put it, 'by rousing the mob ourselves'? The answer that he gave is of utmost significance in the history of the origins of the Suez crisis:

On the whole ... I think that, apart from moral scruples, this is too dangerous a solution to be contemplated at present, at any rate. The Egyptian Government, by their intransigence, might in the end force us to consider it seriously; but we should exhaust every legitimate means of reaching accommodation first.[3]

The British position thus could be summed up as sitting tight and continuing to look for a rational solution. Another of Allen's minutes offers further insight into the apparent British official lethargy in the summer of 1951. It states the ultimate rationale of the British response: 'we have studied the matter carefully, and do not consider that the Egyptians could make our position in Egypt untenable. ... there is a big difference between our position in Persia and our position in Egypt'.[4]

R. J. Bowker, who had replaced Wright as Assistant Under-Secretary supervising Middle Eastern affairs (the latter was now enjoying a Scandinavian interlude in his Middle Eastern career), elaborated on the 'scapegoat' interpretation. This minute reveals the workings of the official mind on the dynamics of the two crises and the belief that Egypt was less likely to boil over:

The fact is that the British 'occupation forces' are the scapegoat for the troubles in Egypt, just as the A[nglo]. I[ranian]. O[il]. C[ompany]. is the scapegoat for the troubles in Iran. In both countries, of course, the troubles are the result of government by a corrupt and irresponsible minority.

The difference is that the British forces in Egypt are much less vulnerable than the A. I. O. C. in Persia, and many influential Egyptians, including the King, appreciate that the presence of British forces on the Canal is one of the strongest safeguards of their own security. For these two reasons the Egyptian Government are less likely to bring things to a head than the Persians.[5]

Bowker expressed the salient theme of Foreign Office thought at this time when he wrote that the best thing to do would be 'to keep the atmosphere reasonably friendly'—in other words to keep on talking.

There were two further phases of the Anglo-Egyptian discussions,

---

[3] Minute by Allen, 25 July 1951, FO 371/90134/JE1051/139/G.
[4] Minute by Allen, 4 July 1951, FO 371/90134/JE1051/131/G.
[5] Minute by Bowker, 30 July 1951, FO 371/90134/JE1051/139/G.

one on the Sudan and the other on the Canal Zone, both of which will be dealt with here only briefly. In his discussion with Salah ed Din about the Sudan, Stevenson was handicapped by lack of intimate knowledge. It quickly became apparent that Salah ed Din was at least Stevenson's intellectual equal. The Egyptian Foreign Minister waxed vehemently eloquent on the subject of the historic connection between Egypt and the Sudan. He spoke of the Egypto-Sudanese 'Fatherland'. At one point Stevenson stated flatly that Salah ed Din's interpretation was 'not based on a thorough knowledge of affairs in the Sudan', which from a British point of view may have been true, but Salah ed Din demonstrated a thorough mastery of the Egyptian side of the case. The premiss of his argument was that Egypt and the Sudan had been linked together since time immemorial. The British, he told Stevenson, 'had nothing whatsoever to do with the Sudan before your occupation of Egypt'. Salah ed Din emphasized 'the ties which bind Egyptians and the Sudanese including ties of race, Arabism, language, by which I mean the Arabic language, and religion, by which I mean the Moslem religion'. He denounced British efforts to detach the southern part of the country, and he attacked the British justification of separation on 'racial' grounds as flying in the face of scientific evidence to the contrary. Stevenson retorted on that point: 'I cannot believe that the Egyptian Government seriously consider the primitive inhabitants of the Southern Sudan to be one people with the inhabitants of the Delta.' Salah ed Din did believe it. He was furthermore passionately convinced that the British had 'deliberately sought to isolate the south of the Sudan from the north and to prevent the inhabitants of the north from getting in touch with those of the south, thereby standing in the way of natural penetration and spreading of the Arabic language and the Moslem religion into the south'. The Egyptian 'civilizing mission' thus became quite comprehensible within the powerful and lucid line of thought pursued by Salah ed Din.[6]

So great was the cultural variance that Stevenson experienced genuine difficulty in persuading Salah ed Din of the moral rectitude of the British administration in the Sudan. 'You do not dispute the fact that we are trying to the best of our abilities to promote the welfare of the Sudanese?' Stevenson asked him. The Egyptian did dispute it. He believed that the British had attempted to convert the condominium of the Sudan into a sort of British colony and, if they were allowed to proceed with their plans for 'independence', would continue to try to achieve their aims indirectly. And so they

[6] The quotations are taken from Cmd. 8419, a reading of which is just as revealing and amusing as the archival records.

went round and round, as if in caricature of a debate at the United Nations on the evils of colonialism. There was one point that shook Stevenson from his affable efforts to keep the discussions under way. 'To us it is a question of life and death', Salah ed Din told him. Amiable 'talk' about the Sudan was not in fact possible. Richard Stokes had been quite right in warning the Cabinet that the Egyptians would only become more infuriated.

When the avenue of the Sudan came to a dead end, the British attempted to turn the discussions back to the Canal Zone. Morrison told C. L. Sulzberger of the *New York Times* about a 'vision'. It was to get the Egyptians in on the 'ground floor' of 'a Middle East treaty arrangement'.[7] This was merely an elaboration of the hope that an American involvement in the Canal Zone would make the British presence less objectionable to the Egyptians. It was the idea that Bevin had originally put forward, which Attlee now endorsed as a possible solution to prevent breakdown as well as to provide the basis of a long-range settlement. If the Prime Minister had been able to devote full attention to the project perhaps something might have come of it. Under Morrison's guidance the scheme seemed doomed to oblivion even within the Anglo–American context. On the 4th of September he announced to the Cabinet that the United States now took 'an interest' in Egyptian affairs: 'this was a welcome development even though the crudeness of American thinking had its embarrassments'. Morrison urged the creation of a new 'Allied Middle East Command' in which the British base would become an 'Allied base'. Egyptian troops would form part of the 'integrated Command'. Here is Morrison's rationale, which reveals his concern with his Parliamentary critics as well as his willingness to make a sop to the Egyptians, together with an illuminating response:

The Foreign Secretary said that . . . an offer on these lines . . . ought to satisfy not only Egyptian *amour propre* but also Parliamentary criticism in this country. . . .
The Chiefs of Staff said that this offer was at any rate a lesser evil than giving up the base in Egypt altogether.[8]

In its American, French, Turkish, and Commonwealth ramifications, the proposal for an 'Allied Command' became exceedingly complicated, but there is no point in discussing it here because, as Dean Acheson accurately remarked in his memoirs, the Egyptians merely regarded it as a camouflage of the continued occupation.[9]

The direst warning about the futility of the 'new approach' came

---

[7] Sulzberger, *Long Row of Candles*, p. 657.
[8] Cabinet Minutes 58 (51), 4 Sept. 1951, CAB 128/20.
[9] Acheson, *Present at the Creation*, p. 564.

from Stevenson in mid-August. If the British wanted an agreement with the Egyptians, he wrote, there was no way to get it other than to acknowledge the Egyptians' right to demand immediate evacuation of foreign troops. 'In no other way can we make them believe that the comparison between their position under the new arrangements and the position, say, of one of the participating countries of N. A. T. O. is a reality and not merely a hollow pretence.' As for the actual suggestions about the 'Allied Command', Stevenson continued, 'I know that we have not a chance of getting anything like those proposals across the Egyptians *in any circumstances*.'[10] When the British finally put forward the scheme for a 'Middle East Command' in October, the wave of Egyptian sentiment for abrogating the formal link between Britain and Egypt, the treaty of 1936, had already crested.

About a week before the fall of the Labour government in England in late October 1951, Sir Ralph Stevenson described the events that had led to the legislation that would, from the Egyptian point of view, annul the treaty of 1936 and the Condominium agreement of 1899. He believed that since early summer the Egyptians had become more and more convinced that 'our purpose was merely to drag out the conversations' while pushing ahead for constitutional changes in the Sudan that would make union with Egypt impossible. As in 1946 the Sudan remained the 'stone wall' that ultimately neither side could surmount in order to come to an agreement. Nor did the Egyptians seem any more hopeful about a resolution of the problem of the Canal Zone except by drastic measures. The Egyptian mood in other words was increasingly one of heroic gesture born of despair. According to Stevenson's reading of the newspapers and the speeches of the politicians, 'union' and 'evacuation' could only be achieved 'by bold, decisive, independent action on Egypt's part'. Those battle cries of the Wafd, he wrote, 'have been repeated so constantly and stridently that they have become a kind of patriotic creed to which everyone . . . has had to pay lip-service'. The slogans had become articles of faith. The key to all recent developments and the reasons for the demagogic tactics of Nahas and the other leaders of the Wafd government, Stevenson believed, could be understood only by their determination 'not to give up the leading rôle in the patriotic drama'. In attempting to preserve his reputation as a great Egyptian nationalist, Nahas had exploited the opportunity of using the British as a scapegoat. The 'scapegoat of British imperialism' served other functions as well. So corrupt was the Wafd regime that Stevenson judged that the leadership collectively had to be held

[10] Stevenson to Bowker, 'Top Secret & Personal', 14 Aug. 1951, FO 371/90136/179/G.

accountable. 'The temptation to try to cover up their all-too-obvious sins of corruption and misgovernment', he wrote, 'by some dramatic performance satisfying—although only temporarily—the emotions of the mob has always been difficult for them to resist.'[11]

Part of the story of Egyptian corruption concerned Nahas's wife and her notorious profiteering during the 1948 war that had contributed to Egyptian defeat because of the supply of deficient arms and ammunition. This sordid side of Egyptian politics is important to mention in passing because the full charge of this scandal, like a delayed time-bomb, threatened to explode at the same time that the agitation against the British was coming to a head. Nahas and his associates had good reason to try to cover their tracks by diverting attention to the repressive nature of the British 'occupation'. As will be seen in the next chapter, they met their nemesis early in the next year. Farouk dismissed the Wafd government after 'Black Saturday' of late January 1952, when mobs swept through Cairo killing, looting, and destroying one of the symbols of the British occupation by the burning of Shepheard's Hotel. As the British had apprehended, the Wafd government proved to be incapable of controlling its own demon of mass violence. The Wafd regime ended in disgrace, even though in the longer historical memory of the Egyptian people Nahas sustained his reputation as an Egyptian patriot. For purposes of the present discussion, however, the events of 1952 belong to another part of the drama, especially as far as the British were concerned, with Churchill and Eden as the protagonists. The point of significance here is the British lesson drawn from the episode of abrogation in the final days of the Labour government.

In applying one lesson to another, the moral of Britain's experience with the Wafd government, especially against the background of the crisis in Iran, appeared to be 'never again'. 'It was essential . . . ' Field Marshal Sir William Slim told the Chiefs of Staff, 'that we should not again fall into the same error as we have done in the case of Persia as a result of banking on the early removal of Mossadeq.'[12] A similar lesson could be drawn from events on a global scale. 'One thing leads to another or we wouldn't still be in Korea', an American admiral said to a member of the British military mission in Washington.[13] The necessity to stand firm whatever the cost was the emphatic theme of the telegrams from the Commander-in-Chief of British military forces in the Middle East, General Sir Brian Robertson.

[11] Stevenson to Morrison, Confidential, 16 Oct. 1951, FO 371/90144/JE1051/365.
[12] COS (51) 169, 23 Oct. 1951, DEFE 4/48.
[13] B. J. S. M. to Ministry of Defence, 16 Oct. 1951, copy in FO 371/90144/JE1051/361.

One of his messages at the time of the 'abrogation' crisis provides insight into the mental response of the British military:

> We have now entered the next phase in this struggle. I see no reason to suppose that it will be short and it will certainly have its tiresome features although our own position is impregnable. . . .
> There is no hope of agreement with the WAFD. Any attempt to conciliate the present Government will be interpreted as weakness and will prolong the struggle. Therefore we must bring about a complete collapse of the WAFD Government by making the Egyptian people realise that their Government has failed them and that the situation is hurting them much more than it hurts us.
> Probably the only foundation on which an alternative Government can be erected and satisfactory agreement concluded is represented by the King and his armed forces. Therefore we must be careful to avoid conflict with these elements. When the time comes we must be ready if necessary to go into the Delta with our troops in order to place them firmly in the saddle.[14]

With 38,000 troops in the Canal Zone the British could, in contrast with the circumstances of the Iranian crisis, respond from a position of strength. The danger however did not lie in direct military confrontation but in interference with British shipping in the Canal and the obstruction of base operations. Step by step the British might be led back into the occupation of Egypt. Or they might find themselves, as Robertson suggested, in a quasi-alliance with Farouk. The question of the nature of the British response to 'abrogation' and the long-range implications loomed large in the last days of the Labour government.

Even Herbert Morrison recognized the dangers of the intuitive British military reaction. 'He would not wish to hold back the Military authorities too tightly', he is recorded as saying on the 18th of October 1951, 'but . . . they must be able to prove very clearly that any action they took was reasonably necessary in order to preserve the security of British lives and property.'[15] Morrison had learned one principal lesson from the Iranian crisis. These delicate questions bordering on intervention were not for him. He now referred everything to the Prime Minister. Attlee himself chaired the sessions of the Chiefs of Staff when decisions were required on such matters as military control of the Canal, the protection of British shipping, and the removal of Egyptian troops. The effect of his presence may perhaps seem mundane, but it was highly significant: the military authorities in Egypt were instructed 'to refer each measure back for approval'.[16]

On that note of restraint the story of Britain and Egypt under the

[14] Robertson to C. I. G. S., 'Personal Top Secret', 23 Oct. 1951, copy in FO 371/90144/JE1051/368/G.
[15] Minute of 18 Oct. 1951, FO 371/90143.
[16] COS (51), 165, 18 Oct. 1951, DEFE 4/48.

Labour government comes to an end. Attlee no less than other British statesmen of the era responded instinctively to the threat to 'the jugular vein of the Empire', but, as the person ultimately responsible for British policy, he cannot be indicted for lack of control over the British military or for failing to uphold the principle solidly maintained by Bevin of non-intervention in the internal affairs of Egypt.

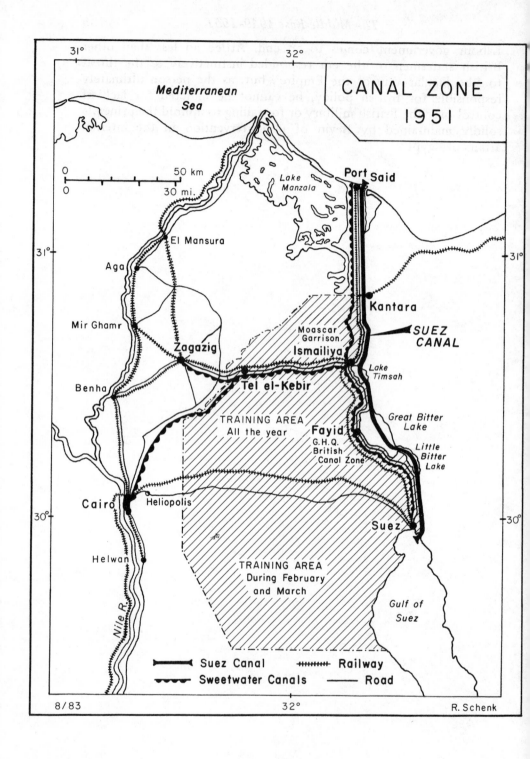

Mediterranean
Sea

CANAL ZONE
1951

Lake
Manzala

Port Said

El Mansura

Aga

Kantara

*SUEZ
CANAL*

Mir Ghamr

Moascar
Garrison

Zagazig

Ismailiya

Lake
Timsah

Benha

Tel el-Kebir

Great Bitter
Lake

TRAINING AREA
All the year

Fayid
G.H.Q.
British
Canal Zone

Little
Bitter
Lake

Cairo

Heliopolis

Suez

Helwan

TRAINING AREA
During February
and March

Gulf of
Suez

Nile R.

⊢━━━◄ Suez Canal	┼┼┼┼┼┼ Railway
⚬⚬⚬⚬ Sweetwater Canals	──── Road

8/83

R. Schenk

5

THE MIDDLE EAST AND THE FALL OF
THE LABOUR GOVERNMENT IN 1951:
THE END OF AN ERA

THE principle theme of this book has been Labour's 'grand strategy' of non-intervention and the conciliation of the moderate nationalists. The purpose was to preserve British power by preventing the initiative from passing to anti-British extremists. Throughout most of the period Ernest Bevin was the moving force. In Iran in 1946 he refused to sanction a breakaway state that might have secured the southwestern oilfields within the British equivalent of a Soviet satellite. He believed that interference with the Egyptian political system would eventually undermine rather than sustain British influence, and in 1948 he scotched plans to unseat the Prime Minister, Nokrashi. These and other episodes have been recounted in detail, but it is the underlying consistency of response, even more than the specific cases, that is significant. Bevin was sceptical whether political parties or individuals could be successfully manipulated, and he was exceedingly wary of being exposed in the event of a fiasco. In view of the opposition in the Labour party as well as in the United States to the old methods of British domination, there was good reason for restraint. Postwar circumstances required a fresh approach of attempting to deal with the Middle Eastern states as partners rather than dependants, but the goal was traditional: the preservation of Britain's status as a world power with a paramount position in the Middle East. This aim was pursued with dogged perseverance. It demanded just as great an 'act of will' to treat the Arabs as equals as it did to sit on them.

The explanation of postwar imperialism in the Middle East can be reduced to the level of power politics, but to do so would be to miss the *Zeitgeist* of the Labour era. Attlee, though dubious about an enduring British presence in the region, shared with Bevin and other Labour leaders an ethical commitment to the proposition that the peoples of the Middle East *should* be treated as equals. The Labour ethos held that there could be a harmony of interests. The Middle East could be 'developed', and defended, to the advantage of all concerned. This was an article of faith that was characteristic of the age, though affirmed less confidently by some, for example, who feared that the relative quiescence of the Palestine issue after the 1948 war was no more than a lull in the storm.

In the popular view Attlee had achieved an equilibrium in southern Asia while Bevin had failed in the Middle East. This point was made emphatically on the eve of the election in October 1951 by the *New Statesman*, which, though a socialist clarion, was an unrelenting critic of Labour's Middle East policy. The vindication of true Labour principles could be found in India:

> Mr. Attlee's greatest single service in Britain and the world was his post-war decision—for he played a strong personal part in the matter—that Britain should 'quit' India and Burma. As a result of our wise withdrawal, Britain has remained on excellent terms with the Governments and peoples of India, Pakistan and Burma, and British prestige has been immensely enhanced.[1]

Why had the Labour government not pursued a similar policy of disengagement in the Middle East? Again voicing a strongly held popular sentiment, the *New Statesman* believed that Bevin had been duped by the 'Foreign Office officials'. By resuscitating the myth of Bevin having fallen prey to a conspiracy of the mandarins of the Foreign Office, the *New Statesman* and others could argue that, while Bevin's policy had been misguided, a Tory line would have led to catastrophe, not only in the Middle East but throughout the world.

The stand of the *New Statesman* may be taken as representative of the general indictment against the Tories as well as the suspicion that if Churchill had been Prime Minister things indeed would have been different:

> If Mr. Churchill had been in power, and as bad as his word, we should have wasted our resources, our man-power and our credit on a war [in India and Asia generally] even more terrible, wrong and useless than the French struggle in Vietnam. India, like Vietnam, would now be in the hands of our bitter enemies; Indian nationalism, like that of Vietnam, would by now have turned to Communism.[2]

In Iran, when the nationalists demanded an equitable share of the oil revenues, 'the Tories talked about using troops'. Under Tory leadership, Abadan might have become 'the Sarajevo of 1951'. Those were typical accusations. 'The Tory still thinks in terms of Victorian imperialism', according to a Labour manifesto. 'Whose finger on the trigger?' asked the *Daily Mirror*. That became one of the provocative questions of the election. The extent to which such innuendo struck a sensitive nerve is apparent in a post-electoral analysis which indicated that twenty-one per-cent of all Tory speeches during the

[1] *New Statesman*, 13 Oct. 1951.
[2] Ibid.

campaign included a specific repudiation of the 'warmonger' charge.[3]

'The differences between parties in this island', Churchill stated after he had regained the office of Prime Minister, 'are not so great as the foreigner might think by listening to our abuse of one another.'[4] It was a disconcertingly true statement. Did the Tories generally believe that a 'whiff of grapeshot' would bring the Iranians to their senses?[5] Or did the policy of the Labour government in effect mask 'scuttle in slow motion'?[6] One drawback to the 'whiff of grapeshot', according to *The Economist* in an incisive comment on the element of truth in those clichés, was that Palmerstonian action would not only divide the British among themselves but would also cause 'an even wider rift between American and British opinion'.[7] There was also the difficulty that intervention might further arouse Iranian or Egyptian nationalism rather than quell it. 'Scuttle' was a different type of danger, one ostensibly encouraged by the leader of the radical left of the Labour party, Aneurin Bevan. Earlier in the year Bevan had resigned from the government on the issues of the budget and rearmament. During the campaign Attlee was taunted with the cry 'the end is Nye'. Churchill himself summed up Attlee's problems as 'the triple disasters of Aba*dan*, Su*dan*, and Bev*an*'. Nye Bevan came close to espousing the solution of unilateral disengagement, but this was not, as has been seen, the course favoured by Attlee and those shaping the policy of the Labour government.[8] In fact during the Iranian crisis Attlee and Morrison were in consultation with Churchill and Eden. There was more agreement than might

---

[3] D. E. Butler, *The British General Election of 1951* (London, 1952), p. 55.

[4] Ibid., p. 60.

[5] Some of them, it is true, apparently did: 'We have only for one moment to "stretch out a terrible right arm" ' Duff Cooper wrote to the *Daily Telegraph*, 'and we should hear no more from Persia but a scampering of timid feet. We are told that to take a strong line means to risk a world war. Sir, we have got to risk it. Let us have done with it.' Ibid., p. 122 n. 2.

[6] Or, to pose the question in an opposite way, was there any difference between Tory and Labour policy? One of the more bizzare spectacles of the campaign, in view of the secret Cabinet and Chiefs of Staff discussions, was Shinwell's masquerading as a prince of peace. 'We could easily have started another war by putting our troops in Abadan', he stated in one of his speeches. Ibid., p. 122.

[7] 4 Aug. 1951.

[8] Bevan actually did not pursue this issue positively during the campaign, but his position was inferred from his attacks on the Tories, e.g.: 'We believe when the Conservatives talk about using a stronger hand in Persia or in Egypt we are entitled to know what they mean. Do they mean war? If you send back a Conservative administration you will be declaring to the rest of the world that the people in this crowded island are prepared to run the risk of a third world war and this time an atom war.' (Butler, *British General Election*, p. 123.) His view of Churchill 'reverting to type' if given the opportunity, in other words as a 'warmonger', was quite consistent with his previously held positions. See Michael Foot, *Aneurin Bevan 1897–1945* (London, 1975), p. 485.

have been assumed from the public accusations. This consensus was not on 'whiff of grapeshot' or 'scuttle' but on the difficulty of punishing the Iranians. The balance-of-payments problem cast a long shadow over plans for offensive operations. 'How much would it cost?' was a frequent question in public as well as official circles. The Tory leadership as well as the Labour government acted responsibly during the crisis. 'There are underlying unities', Churchill said later, '. . . far greater than our differences.'[9]

It was the shading of past differences into nuances of similar outlook that helps to explain the year 1951 as a watershed in British Middle Eastern policy. One of the more important controversies in the past had been the tactical issue of how best to deal with the Egyptians in the confrontation over the Canal Zone. During the prelude to the election campaign, the *New Statesman* recalled that in 1946 Lord Stansgate, following Bevin's instructions, had offered to withdraw British troops from Egyptian soil. By 1951 this was an offer that the Labour government as well as the Tories wished to forget.[10] The proposal had been made in the hope that British generosity would be matched by an Egyptian invitation to stay on in a new defence relationship. Churchill at the time and consistently thereafter had denounced the Labour government for making a vital mistake, if only because moderate Egyptian nationalists as well as extremists would now demand total evacuation. The Iranian and Egyptian crises of 1951 seemed to prove that the Tories had been right on this one critical point: goodwill had not proved to be an adequate substitute for power. It was better to bargain from a position of strength.

To re-emphasize a most illuminating observation, Lord Milner, when he was Colonial Secretary after the First World War, stated that 'the real British "Empire" apart from the Dominions' could be described as 'that great sphere of British influence extending from the centre of East Africa, through the Sudan, Egypt, Arabia and the Persian Gulf to India. . . . '[11] Neither the disengagement from India nor the evacuation from Palestine necessarily invalidated that concept. Palestine was expendable. The cutting of losses in Palestine could be justified as a move towards stability, which was part of Bevin's vision. The only way in which Bevin essentially altered Milner's idea (at least when he was not making a similar statement about Africa) was to substitute the Middle East itself for India. 'My whole aim', he once wrote to Attlee, 'has been to develop the

---

[9] Butler, *British General Election*, p. 60.

[10] 'The Egyptians at least have not forgotten.' *New Statesman*, 11 Aug. 1951.

[11] In a letter to Lloyd George of May 1919 quoted in John Darwin, *Britain, Egypt and the Middle East* (London, 1981), p. 21.

Middle East as a producing area [in agriculture as well as oil] to help our own economy and take the place of India.'[12] Suez as the 'jugular vein of the Empire' did not lose its significance because of the loss of India. If anything it seemed more important than ever, especially after the withdrawal from Palestine. After 1947-8 the talk about an easy fallback position had come to an end. Cyrenaica and Cyprus simply did not offer satisfactory alternatives to the position at Suez. By 1950-1 the British were locked into the Canal Zone. To an Egyptian nationalist at this time there would have been no difference at all between the 'real' British Empire of Lord Milner and its latter-day version as re-endorsed by Bevin and Morrison. The Labour government might take pride in the doctrine of 'non-intervention', but to the Egyptians it was the presence of troops in the Canal Zone that counted. To most Egyptian nationalists the 'defence of the West' was merely an excuse for the continued occupation of Egyptian territory.

The hardening of attitude towards the Canal Zone had begun during the Palestine crisis, but it was the Korean war that dramatized the strategic foothold in Egypt as part of the world-wide emergency. R. J. Bowker (Michael Wright's successor as the Assistant Under-Secretary supervising Middle Eastern affairs) wrote in January 1951 in a minute in which he summarized the views of the Chiefs of Staff and explained the rationale of the British position:

Our Middle East Defence Plans aim at defending as much of the Middle East and of the Middle East oil as possible. . . . in the view of the Chiefs of Staff, Egypt, [i.e. the Canal Zone] still constitutes the only suitable wartime base from which to conduct the operations for this purpose.

For launching an attack on Russia, no doubt forward bases would be required, but so far as I know the Chiefs of Staff still regard Egypt as the best location for the necessary main base.

Apart from its oil, and the fact that it constitutes a platform from which to launch an attack against Russia's most vulnerable area (the Caucasus oil fields), the Middle East must be held as a barrier to Africa, and to deny to Russia Africa's rich resources. For this purpose again, Egypt remains the best base area.

Bowker also dealt with the enduring significance of the Suez Canal itself:

It is true . . . that the Suez Canal has not a vital wartime importance—it was rendered unusable in the last war. But Suez remains of vast importance as the back door to Egypt and will no doubt be of great importance in the next war in servicing the vital Australian and New Zealand, and also South African, contributions to Middle East defence. In a word, Egypt still remains the essential central point from which to defend the Middle East and all that the Middle East entails.[13]

[12] Bevin to Attlee, 9 Jan. 1947, FO 800/476/ME/47/4.
[13] Minute by Bowker, 10 Jan. 1951, FO 371/91219/E1192.

Bowker was convinced that the United States would continue to support the British as a stabilizing force in the eastern Mediterranean. 'The Americans are just as emphatic as we about the vital importance of defending the Middle East', he concluded, 'but regard it as a responsibility which should be borne primarily by the Commonwealth.'[14] In that view the 'British Supreme Command' in the Middle East would be the natural equivalent of American leadership in the Far East, or for that matter NATO.

Alas for the British, the judgement about American enthusiasm for a major Middle East base under British command proved to be too optimistic. The disillusionment can be traced to the summer of 1951 when the Iranian and Egyptian crises began to interact. Sir Pierson Dixon (the Deputy Under-Secretary who had been intimately involved in the shaping of Bevin's policy) wrote that it was 'depressing' that the Americans were 'not really interested in building up a Middle East Command based on the Canal Zone'.[15] He conveyed an accurate impression of American official sentiment. According to an assessment prepared for George McGhee (still Assistant Secretary of State for Near Eastern, South Asian, and African Affairs), the Egyptians were 'fully aware' of 'Iran's success vis-à-vis the British'. The abrogation of the 1936 treaty 'could touch off a powder keg'.[16] Later in the year a State Department official visited Egypt. He reported to his military and civilian colleagues: 'I found a terrible situation. The British are detested. The hatred against them is general and intense. It is shared by everyone in the country.'[17] The British Empire, or what was left of it, might offer certain strategic assets, but politically it was a liability. One assumption cherished by the British had been that the Korean war would increase the American need for a British or 'Commonwealth' ally in the Middle East. The British position would be reinforced. The British might withdraw from other parts of the world, but they would continue to be predominant in the Middle East. The Iranian and Egyptian crises of 1951 proved that American respect for the forces of Middle Eastern nationalism would be just as important as the alliance with the British. From the British vantage point it was becoming clear, to use the late Professor Gallagher's phrase, that 'One should not put one's trust in super-powers.'[18]

---

[14] Minute by Bowker, 10 Jan. 1951, FO 371/91219/E1192.

[15] Minute by Dixon, 21 Aug. 1951, FO 371/91223/E1192.

[16] See memorandum of 5 Oct. 1951, *Foreign Relations 1951*, V, pp. 203-5.

[17] Comments by Burton Y. Berry (Deputy Assistant Secretary) at a State-Joint Chiefs of Staff meeting, 12 Dec. 1951, *Foreign Relations 1951*, V, pp. 434-7.

[18] John Gallagher, *The Decline, Revival and Fall of the British Empire* (Cambridge, 1982), p. 150.

One of the dominant themes in the American response to the Iranian and Egyptian crises was the danger of being too closely associated with British 'imperialism'. Sir John Troutbeck, for one, believed that the Americans were attempting to curry favour with the nationalists by leaving the British in the lurch. It seemed obvious to him, and to others, that the cause of Arab (if not Iranian) nationalist 'effervescence' was the unsettled state of affairs in Palestine, for which the Americans bore a large responsibility. 'So far as Iraq is concerned at least', Troutbeck wrote, 'it is their connexion with the Jews, and with what is regarded here as the new imperialistic power of Israel, that appears to strike the Arabs . . . forcibly.' If the Americans believed that they could improve their standing in the Arab world by abandoning their British ally, Troutbeck thought that they would be rudely disillusioned. To the Arabs, he wrote, the 'West', above all the United States, was 'something alien and uncomprehending':

If to this fact is added the still unwaning resentment over Israel and the universal belief that the United States are responsible for its birth and survival, it will be seen that the policy, threatened apparently in some American circles, of shedding the British connection and 'going it alone' in the Middle East, would not be likely to produce the anticipated results, in Iraq at any rate.[19]

The Arab perception of the American–Israeli danger, according to Troutbeck's own letters, came as an unpalatable truth to his American friends, but he had no doubt himself that it was at the heart of unrest in the Middle East.

Troutbeck may have exaggerated. But it is undeniable that Palestine continued to poison the climate of the Middle East, and his point helps to explain one of the reasons for the failure of British policy. Arab nationalism could perhaps have been accommodated if it had been victorious in Palestine. Frustrated nationalism fed on British imperialism. He was correct in anticipating that it would eventually turn upon the American variety as well.

Troutbeck has been a prominent figure in this book, in part because of his key positions in Cairo and then in Baghdad, but above all because of his convictions. His sympathy for the Arab cause, his anti-Zionist sentiments, and his scepticism about the Americans often placed him in the centre of controversy. He had a philosophic cast of mind and a penchant for historical analogies. The danger of 'appeasement' as he had witnessed it in Czechoslovakia before the Second World War was prominent in his thought. He did not believe that 'the Musaddiqs and the Nahas Pashas' could be appeased. Some of his ideas in 1951 help to capture the spirit of the time, or, in

[19] Troutbeck to Morrison, 13 June 1951, FO 371/91185/E1024/G.

Elizabeth Monroe's phrase, 'Britain's Moment in the Middle East' at the close of the Labour era.

The time of the Korean war was also the period that nourished Arab and Asian 'neutralism'. 'This trend certainly exists in Iraq', Troutbeck wrote, 'and I should welcome any assistance the Americans can give in the task of checking and reversing it.' But he believed that the 'doctrinaires in the State Department' had only a 'superficial' appreciation of 'the true nature of the problem' because they equated 'neutralism' with sympathy for 'Communism' and the Soviet Union. The following excerpt from one of Troutbeck's despatches reveals his diagnosis of the causes of neutralism and the springs of Arab nationalism. He focused on the problem of Iraq as representative:

> Those Iraqis who have a political consciousness are tending more and more to identify themselves with the fledgling nations of Asia in their struggle against domination by the West and with the coloured races in their struggle against the whites.
>
> The truth, as I see it in Iraq, is that it would be surprising if the generality of politically conscious people *did* feel themselves to be involved in the conflict between Soviet Russia and the western world. . . .
>
> This attitude is not to be confused with communism and does not imply identification with Moscow. It is simply a sense of not belonging to the West (any more than to Russia), and it is this sense which lies at the root of Iraqi isolationism.[20]

Troutbeck thus believed that the Americans were profoundly wrong in associating 'neutralism' with 'Communism'. To the Iraqis no less than to the Iranians and the Egyptians it was the continued British presence, in one way or another, that represented—unjustifiably and unfortunately, in his view—oppression and exploitation while 'Communism' and the possibility of Soviet expansion remained little more than abstract dangers.[21] All the same Troutbeck was not alarmed about 'neutralism' causing a swing to the left. Iraq, he reflected later, 'will of course never be a very reliable factor but . . . we may hope that she will . . . at any rate remain something of a bastion against the inroads of communism'.[22]

[20] Troutbeck to Morrison, 13 June 1951, FO 371/91885/E1024/G.

[21] On Soviet aims and the Middle Eastern response, the Foreign Office at this time generally held that Islam would not be a sufficient barrier unless strengthened by social and economic reform. This minute by a member of the Research Department is representative: 'Although . . . the conservative Islamic community offers a glacis against Communism, this is not an effective defence against Soviet Communism which wants, not a Communist Arab world (except in the long-term sense) but unrest, political corruption, xenophobia, & social squalor. These will foster the growth of a well trained political core, which may be able to profit from a deteriorating or revolutionary situation and eventually seize power with the aid of the discontented unstable majority.' Minute by T. S. Tull, 1 June 1951, FO 371/91184/E1024/G.

[22] Troutbeck to Eden, 28 Nov. 1952, FO 371/98736/EQ1016/78. In the same month a Foreign Office assessment for the Chiefs of Staff concluded that 'Some sort of violent

Throughout the Middle East the British enclaves continued to be targets of nationalist resentment. During a mission to the Middle East during the Second World War, Oliver Harvey had recorded in his diary after arriving at one of the RAF bases in Iraq: 'a complete bit of England abroad. . . . football, cinema and a pack of hounds. All very Poona.'[23] The accounts of the evacuation at Abadan in 1951 reveal that the exclusive nature of British life in the enclaves still bore a similarity to Harvey's description.[24] Though not on the same scale as in Iran or Egypt, the two British areas in Iraq also offended nationalist sentiment. 'Although some Iraqis are aware of the Russian menace', a Foreign Office official lamented, 'it cannot be said that they feel compelled to seek our aid sufficiently to welcome the continued existence of our bases at Habbaniya and Shaiba.'[25] In the eyes of Iraqi nationalists, the two bases symbolized British 'imperialism', but in view of the danger of the cold war erupting into a third world war, the British were caught in the dilemma of weakening a link in strategic defence or continuing to antagonize the nationalists by maintaining the bases. The following minute was written by an official who was to play a leading part in the Middle Eastern controversies of the 1950s, Humphrey Trevelyan (at that time in the Embassy in Baghdad):

> Our Treaty with Iraq gives us bases in peacetime and a position in Iraq which materially helps us in peacetime to preserve the Middle East from Russian penetration. The bases will be required in wartime for initial delaying action, to give time to our Forces to be deployed behind Iraq territory against Russian attack.[26]

When weighed against such military considerations, nationalist clamour counted for little. Yet to an Iraqi no less than to an Egyptian, British troops were garrisoned in defiance of local opinion. This was true for the whole period of the Labour government. To an Iraqi no less than to an Egyptian or Iranian nationalist, the Labour

upheaval . . . [in Iraq] cannot be discounted, though there seems to be no *coherent* revolutionary movement.' See COS (52) 642, 24 Nov. 1952, DEFE 5/42.

[23] Diary entry of 4 Nov. 1943, British Library Add. MSS 56400.

[24] For the extreme indictment see L. P. Elwell-Sutton, *Persian Oil* (London, 1955), p. 200; 'Britain's greatest failure in her dealings with foreign peoples has been the inability of her diplomats, administrators and commercial representatives to "get inside" the people with whom they have to deal. They have been content to remain ensconced behind their embassy compound walls, or within the special European areas, and there to entertain the Europeanised aristocracy, or the wealthy merchants, or perhaps the unpaid clerk of a government ministry with the contents of some secret file to sell for a consideration. Of the people of the country, of their hopes, fears and aspirations, even of the way they live, they know and care nothing.'

[25] Minute by A. M. Williams, 30 Mar. 1950, FO 371/82414/EQ1051/3.

[26] Minute by Trevelyan, 20 June 1950, FO 371/82414/EQ1051/G. For his analysis of the later period see Humphrey Trevelyan, *The Middle East in Revolution* (London, 1970).

principle of 'non-intervention' meant little in view of the perpetuation of the enclaves.

Towards the end of his life Ernest Bevin had begun to think about vastly accelerating the training of Egyptian military personnel to permit the take-over of the installations in the Canal Zone. One of the themes in the last part of the book has been that the shift from royalties to profit sharing represented in the Middle East the economic counterpart of the transfer of power in India. The political and military matching part may be regarded as the Anglo-Egyptian agreement on British withdrawal from Suez—in Albert Hourani's words, 'the greatest change that had occurred in the Middle Eastern balance of power since 1923' when the former Ottoman Empire had been reduced to a rump Turkish state.[27] The agreement bore the date of the 19th of October 1954, three years to the month after the Egyptian unilateral abrogation of the 1936 treaty. The 1954 agreement embodied the transfer of the Canal Zone along the lines that Bevin had anticipated, including the right of British re-entry in the event of an attack on an Arab country or Turkey. Nevertheless it was too late to sustain the goodwill that he thought essential to an effective 'partnership'. Bevin's 'grand strategy' rested on the assumption of a harmony of interests (a notion that was shared, as has been seen, by other members of the Labour government). He believed that the British and the Egyptians could resolve their differences to mutual advantage. His overall plan may be reduced to the cold-blooded political calculation that the British had to yield in order to remain, but it was also an unfulfilled aspiration. The half-dozen years of the Labour government proved inadequate to dissipate the rancour generated by the seven decades of British occupation. Egyptian nationalists in 1951 saw the determination of the British to stay on, not the willingness to alter the basis of the relationship.

Indeed in early 1951 a glance at the map would have confirmed Milner's 'real' British Empire, not Bevin's 'partnership'. With the major (or minor, depending on one's point of view) exception of Palestine, not much had changed. It was true that the Ogaden and Eritrea had reverted to Ethiopia, and that the Italians were now back in the new guise of trusteeship in Somalia. Elsewhere the British appeared to be dug in more firmly than ever. In the Sudan the Egyptian pressure for 'unity of the Nile valley' helped to unite Sudanese political forces behind the British (temporarily, as would be seen). In Libya they were at last under way towards securing the strategic base in Cyrenaica (as would be conferred by the Anglo-

[27] Albert Hourani, 'The Anglo-Egyptian Agreement: Some Causes and Implications', *Middle East Journal*, 9, 3 (Summer 1955), p. 239.

Libyan agreement of July 1953). In Cyprus there was a mood building up not to yield to *Enosis* (and in 1954 a spokesman for the Conservative government would use the fateful word 'never' in response to a question about independence). In Jordan the British were secure (though King Abdullah's assassination in July would indicate the fragility of the Jordanian state as well as the British position). In Iraq the British grip seemed not only secure but also stable (though the Egyptian abrogation crisis would prove how quickly unrest in one Arab country might spread to another). The British had lost the naval base at Haifa and the air base at Lydda. They had withdrawn from Alexandria and the military installations in and around Cairo. Otherwise, from the British strategic vantage point, the Middle East remained essentially the same as it had been in 1945. There were military installations in the Sudan, Libya, Cyprus, and Jordan, there were the RAF bases in Iraq, and there were the naval bases in Aden and Bahrain. In the spring through the autumn of 1951 however this general picture began to change because of the crisis in the Persian oilfields and the emergency in the Canal Zone. The backbone of Milner's 'real' British Empire in the Middle East had finally begun to crack.

The disturbances in the Canal Zone precipitated riots elsewhere. On the 26th of January 1952—Black Saturday—clouds of smoke rose over the wealthy parts of Cairo as mobs unleashed their wrath against both the British and the Pashas by arson and murder. Shepheard's Hotel was burned to the ground and nine British subjects were murdered at the Turf Club, the symbol of British privilege in Cairo. This was the finale of the Labour government's crisis in the Canal Zone, now inherited by Churchill and the Conservative government. Churchill himself noted 'the degree of atrocity' and 'the murder and massacres' committed by the Egyptians:

> The horrible behaviour of the mob puts them lower than the most degraded savages now known. Unless the Egyptian Government can purge themselves . . . I doubt whether any relationship is possible with them. They cannot be classed as a civilized power until they have purged themselves.[28]

In his own inimitable way, Churchill was anticipating the Egyptian revolution the following July. In the 1940s the problem the British faced in the Middle East had been how to deal with the old regimes. In the 1950s it became a question of how to cope with the revolutionary Middle East.

---

[28] Churchill to Eden, 'Private and Personal', 30 Jan. 1952, PREM 11/91.

CHRONOLOGY

Commonwealth and World

5 July	British General Election
17 July–2 August	Potsdam Conference
27 July	Labour government—Prime Minister: Attlee Foreign Secretary: Bevin
6 August	Atomic bomb dropped on Hiroshima
14 August	Japan surrenders
21 August	Truman announces end of Lend-lease to Britain
6 December	American loan to Britain for $3.75 billion

Middle East

31 August	Truman urges British to admit 100,000 refugees into Palestine
14 September	Soviet Union demands trusteeship in Tripolitania
13 November	Anglo-American Committee of Inquiry on Palestine
20 December	Egyptians demand revision of 1936 treaty

1945

	27 December	Regent promises free elections in Iraq
1946		
	19 January	Iran complains to UN against Soviet Union
	2 March	Deadline for Soviet troop withdrawal from Iran
	5 March	Churchill denounces Soviet Union in 'Iron Curtain' speech
	22 March	Treaty of Alliance between Britain and Transjordan; Amir Abdullah assumes title of King
	31 March	Greek elections
	2 April	British Cabinet Mission to Egypt
	4 April	Soviet–Iranian Oil Agreement
	5 April	USS *Missouri* arrives in Istanbul
	15 April	French and British troops withdraw from Syria
	30 April	Anglo-American Committee of Inquiry Report on Palestine
	11 May	Attlee announces troop withdrawal from Egypt
	11 May	Soviet Union abandons claim to Tripolitania

	Middle East	Commonwealth and World
1946 *(cont.)*		
4 July	British troops evacuate Cairo	
22 July	Irgun blow up King David Hotel	
7 August	Soviet Union demands new regime at Straits	
15 August	Carrier *Franklin D. Roosevelt* reinforces US Mediterranean squadron	
4 October	Truman's 'Yom Kippur' statement calls for bridging of gap between British and Zionist proposals and the admission of 100,000 refugees into Palestine	
7 October		Creech Jones becomes Colonial Secretary
17–25 October	Bevin–Sidky discussions on Egypt and Sudan	
2 November	Riots in Khartoum	
9 December	Egyptian Prime Minister Sidky Pasha resigns	

11 December — Parliamentary statement about possible union of Cyprus with Greece: 'No such change is contemplated'

28 December — Weizmann defeated at Zionist Congress

1947

10 February — Signing of Italian Peace Treaty; Italy renounces sovereignty over African colonies

18 February — British announce referral of Palestine question to United Nations

21 February — British tell American government that economic and military assistance to Greece will end in late March

12 March — 'Truman Doctrine' of economic and military assistance to Greece and Turkey

10 March — Elections in Iraq

29 March — Saleh Jabr becomes first Shia Prime Minister of Iraq

13 May — United Nations Special Committee on Palestine

	Middle East		Commonwealth and World
1947 *(cont.)*		3 June	British announce plans for partition of India
		5 June	General Marshall proposes European Recovery Program
11 July	Egyptians submit anti-British case to United Nations	15 July	Sterling made convertible
18 July	*Exodus* Jews denied entry into Palestine		
30 July	Irgun hangs two British sergeants	15 August	Transfer of power in India and Pakistan
		20 August	Convertibility suspended
31 August	UNSCOP majority calls for partition of Palestine		
26 September	Britain announces intention to withdraw from Palestine		
22 October	Iranian Majlis rejects Soviet oil agreement		
29 November	UN General Assembly resolution on partition of Palestine		

1948

4 January	Burma rejects Commonwealth membership
15 January	Anglo-Iraqi 'Portsmouth' Treaty
16 January	Riots in Baghdad
4 February	Ceylon becomes a Dominion
25 February	Communist coup in Czechoslovakia
15 March	New Treaty of Alliance between Transjordan and Britain
9 April	Massacre at Deir Yassin
18 April	Setback for Communists in Italian national election
22 April	Jews capture Haifa
12 May	Jaffa surrenders to Jews
14 May	End of British Mandate in Palestine. Israel proclaims independence; US extends *de facto* recognition
17 May	Soviet recognition of Israel
11 June	1st truce
18 June	Soviet blockade of Berlin

	Commonwealth and World	
	28 June	Yugoslavia expelled from Cominform
	15 September	Italian peace treaty comes into force
	2 November	Truman elected President

Middle East		
1948 (*cont.*)		
11–12 July	Fall of Lydda and Ramle	
17 September	UN Mediator Bernadotte assassinated	
23 September	Ogaden reverts to Ethiopian control	
15–22 October	Israeli offensives in Negev	
27 December	Egyptian defeat at Al Auja	
28 December	Egyptian Prime Minister Nokrashi assassinated	
1949		
7 January	4 RAF Spitfires shot down in Negev. Egyptian–Israeli cease-fire	
29 January	British *de facto* recognition of Israel	
31 January	US *de jure* recognition of Israel and Transjordan	

24 February	Israel–Egypt armistice
23 March	Israel–Lebanon armistice
30 March	Zaim coup in Syria
3 April	Israel–Jordan armistice
4 April	North Atlantic Treaty signed
11 May	Israel admitted to UN
2 June	Transjordan renamed 'The Hashemite Kingdom of Jordan'
17 July	Anglo-Iranian Oil Company signs Supplemental Agreement with Iran
20 July	Israel–Syria armistice
11 August	Palestine Arms Embargo lifted
14 August	Zaim overthrown in Syria
18 September	Pound devalued from $4.03 to $2.80
22 September	US claims USSR has exploded atomic bomb
1 October	Chinese People's Republic proclaimed in Peking

Middle East		*Commonwealth and World*	
1949 *(cont.)*	21 November	UN calls for Libyan independence by 1 January 1952 and approves 10-year Italian trusteeship in Somalia	
		27 December	Indonesian independence
1950	3 January	Wafd election victory	
		9–14 January	Colombo Conference on economic development
		23 February	British General Election—Prime Minister: Attlee Foreign Secretary: Bevin
	11 April	Iraq Development Board	
	24 April	Jordan annexes West Bank	
	25 May	Tripartite Declaration on Arms and Palestine Armistice Lines	
	4 June	Britain and Egypt resume discussion on Canal Zone and Sudan	
		25 June	Outbreak of Korean War
	2 December	UN adopts plan for federation of Eritrea with Ethiopia	

	30 December	ARAMCO and Saudis agree on fifty-fifty split of profits
1951	7 March	Iranian Prime Minister Razmara assassinated
	9 March	Bevin resigns. Morrison becomes Foreign Secretary
	29 April	Musaddiq becomes Prime Minister of Iran
	2 May	Iran nationalizes oil industry
	8 July	Korean truce negotiations opened
	20 July	King Abdullah assassinated
	31 July	Abadan refinery halts operations
	5 August	Korean armistice talks broken off
	12 September	Iranian ultimatum to Anglo-Iranian Oil Company
	4 October	British evacuate Abadan
	8 October	Egypt denounces Treaty of 1936 and Sudan Agreement of 1899
	25 October	British General Election. Fall of Labour government

INDEX

Abadan, nature of the enclave, 8–9, 689; replacement of estimated at £120 million, 55; and the 1951 crisis, 671 ff., 686–9, 745

Abdul Aziz ibn Saud *see* Ibn Saud

Abdul Ilah *see* Regent of Iraq

Abdullah, King, criticized as a British stooge, 26; 'Mr. Bevin's Little King', 107, 346 n. 4; exasperating personality of, 117; and the Arab League, 129 ff.; and the Hashemite dynasty, 310; and 'Greater Syria', 314, 350 ff., 361 ff.; background and personality of, 346–7; his 'unswerving loyalty' to the British, 348; and 'appeasement' towards the Jews, 349; change in status from 'Amir' to 'King', 352; warns Attlee about Soviet aims in M.E., 357; his enthronement May 1946, 358; increasing isolation of, 359; his psychological make-up, 363; his 'monomania', 364; and the charge that 'he is prepared to sell Palestine', 365; and the Treaty of 1948, 366 ff.; negative assessment by Sargent, 370–1; assures Bevin that people of Jordan back the British alliance, 371; and the question of the 'rump Jewish state', 372 ff.; approaches a nervous breakdown in 1948, 374 n. 71; maintains his alliances with Nashashibis, 377; Crossman praises for statesmanship, 377; Troutbeck denounces as landgrabber, 378; Michael Wright defends for saving the 'dismal wreck of Arab Palestine', 379; and the question of partition of Palestine 1946, 450; his plan for Arab Palestine as described by Creech Jones to Shertok, 526; believed to hold the key to a general settlement in 1948, 545; his dilemma of being caught between the Zionist and Arab extremists, 546; and the question of an independent Arab state, 552; Arab antipathy towards during 1948 war, 553; the victim of appeasement and the Israeli victories, 563; his relations with Israel in 1949, 579; annexes West Bank April 1950, 586–7; compared with Nuri, 590; his assassination, 620, 628–31, 747

Abul-Huda, Taufiq *see* Taufiq Pasha

Acheson, Dean, his central position in Palestine controversy, 422, 479; and the Morrison-Grady proposals, 436–7; and the 'Yom Kippur statement', 440–1; on Sir Oliver Franks, 615; on Musaddiq, 656; identifies Sir Francis Shepherd as one of the causes of trouble in Iran, 657; fears that precipitate British withdrawal might plunge Iran into revolution, 670–1; on the Labour government withstanding jingo pressures, 689; on plans for the Middle East Command, 713, 731; believes that there is no substitute for the Suez base, 714.

Acre, 535, 538

Addis Ababa, 266, 289, 294

Aden, 10 n. 6, 30, 107, 213, 747

Afghanistan, 53, 489

Africa, as a replacement for India, viii; development of, 16; along with Middle East becomes mystique of British Empire, 16; dangers of nationalism believed to be remote, 108; and Soviet aims, 271; and the British civilizing mission in, 720.

Aga Khan, and the Persian oil crisis, 684

AKEL (Communist) Party in Cyprus, 214 ff.

Ala, Husain, and Richard Stokes, 681 n. 14

al-Alami, Musa, on Arab unity, 307 n. 1, 622

Al Auja, 564

Alexander, A. V., wishes to hold on to Cyprus for 'strategical' reasons, 217; alarmed at Soviet aims in Tripolitania, 271; on Montgomery and Palestine, 447; and the 1948 war, 535, 570

Alexandria, 247, 446, 747

Allen, Roger, and British strategic planning, 78–9; sees no alternative to continued British occupation of Canal Zone, 711; on possible intervention in Egypt 1951, 728–9

al-Quwatli, Shukri *see* Quwatli

al-Said, Nuri *see* Nuri Pasha

Alsop, Joseph, on the British being 'flicked on the raw by the self-righteousness of the American government' and its Palestine policy, 442 n. 3; (and Stewart) 'slick and poisonous' influence, 497 n. 2

Bevin, Ernest (*cont.*):
plans for a trusteeship regime, 521; and
localizing the conflict in Palestine, 522;
believes the Palestine conflict will spread
to inflame the entire Muslim world,
525 n. 31; suspected by Marshall of
duplicity, 526; expresses 'extreme displeasure' at United States recognition of
Israel, 528 n. 41; on American reckless
disregard for the consequences of a Jewish
state, 534; on minimal conditions for
settling with Jews during 1948 war, 535;
on the arms embargo, 536 n. 15; fed up
with Palestine, 542; on Abdullah during
the 1948 war, 546; endorses Bernadotte
plan, 551; believes he has persuaded
Marshall on necessity to limit Israeli
expansionism, 553; believes Arab Legion
to be in jeopardy, 557; and the RAF
incident of January 1949, 565; attitude
towards Truman's policy in the Negev,
567; admits defeat in Palestine, 569; on
the danger of a Communist Israel, 569–
70; his plans for the Middle East in
1949, 578–9; his formal statement of
Middle Eastern policy for the Cabinet
1949, 580–1; and the genesis of the tripartite declaration of May 1950, 584–5;
on the Tennessee Valley Authority, 592;
and scarcity of resources for economic
development, 601; and 'blue prints' for
development, 604; his attention to
details of development plans, 605; on
the stakes of economic development,
611; his fascination with electrification,
612; disappointed with progress in
development, 613; on Zaim's *coup
d'état*, 621–2; assurance to French not
to upset status quo in Syria, 627; will
not interfere in Syrian affairs, 628; his
non-intervention policy and Iran, 634;
his attitude towards non-intervention
consistent, 635; his views about 'Anglo-
Persian' and the question of nationalization, 642–3; on 'dynamite' in the Persian
oil negotiations, 647; his association
with Sir Francis Leggett, 650; refuses to
intervene in Egypt 1949–50 but tilts
towards Wafd, 697–8; meets with Nahas
January 1950 and discusses defence of
Middle East, 710; the question of his ill
health and his policy, 712; his ideas
about defence arrangements 1951, 712–
13, 718; does not believe Egyptians have
enough 'technical' knowledge to run the
base at Suez, 719; defends the British
civilizing mission in the Sudan, 720;

policies must be criticized on grounds of
timing rather than coherence, 721 n. 83;
continues to put forward inventive ideas
about Canal Zone near time of his death,
721–2; demonstrates 'act of will' by
treating Arabs as equals, 737; on the
development of the Middle East as a
replacement for India, 740–1
'Black Saturday' 1952, 733, 747
Bloom, Sol, 485
Bonesteel, Charles E., 301 n. 5
Bowker, R. J., contrasts British position in
Iran and Egypt 1951, 729; on the Middle
East as a barrier to Soviet penetration of
Africa, and on the enduring value of the
Suez Canal, 741
Brett, Michael, 268
Britain *see* Labour government, British
Empire, British Commonwealth, and
British public opinion
British Commonwealth, Bevin's views on, 4;
and an equivalent in the Middle East, 8;
and strategic assessment of 1946, 28 ff.;
loss of Jewish Palestine lamented, 42;
Greece as a potential member, 84;
question of India and Pakistan leaving
because of Palestine, 114; and Cyprus,
221–4; and the Sudan, 230, 705; and the
loss of Arab goodwill, 459; and the
transfer of power in India and Pakistan,
477; and the sterling crisis of 1949,
609; Attlee's use of the phrase 'Dominion
Status' in relation to the Iranian crisis,
662; Attlee's success with in 1947, 738
British Empire, preservation of in Middle
East, vii; and Ernest Bevin, viii; as a
beneficent force, 4; dependence on
Middle-Eastern oil, 8; and the multi-racial
Commonwealth, 8; economic causes of
decline, 14; and history of the period as
an unsuccessful attempt to convert from
formal rule to an informal basis, 15;
ascendancy of in strategic aims, 22;
preservation of as the British 'way of
life', 32; self-righteousness sharpens as
power wanes, 35; believed by Americans
to be in a state of dissolution, 45, 98;
bears initial brunt of possible Russian
expansion in Northern Tier, 53 ff.;
becoming economically and militarily
dependent on the United States, 87;
United States supports as the dominant
regional power in 1947, 102; manpower
resources, 106; defence of more difficult
because of air power and the erosion of
British sea power, 107; and pro-Muslim
sentiment, 113–14; and ensuing 'vacuum'

of Victor Gollancz and Left Book Club
with those of Labour government, 240

Dodecanese Islands, 208, 224

Donovan, Robert, on United Nations partition vote, 486; on Marshall's loyalty to
Truman, 515

Dorr, Goldthwaite, 434

Douglas, Lewis, and Ben Hecht's letter to the
'Terrorists of Palestine', 466; exchanges
of view with Bevin on American plans
for trusteeship regime in Palestine, 521;
records 'milestone' in British thought,
i.e. Arabs might be persuaded to accept
Jewish state, 535, 538; tells Truman that
the war in Palestine may cause a dangerous rift between Britain and the U.S.,
558; inquires whether there is a point
beyond which U.S. will *not* back Israeli
claims, 563

Dow, Sir Hugh, believes direction of Arab
League under Azzam's leadership to have
been 'uniformly calamitous for the
Arabs', 145; on the question of an independent Arab state in Palestine, 378,
552; on Zionist expansionism, 552;
applies his Indian knowledge to problem of war and peace in Middle East,
577–8; wishes to improve Israeli–Jordan
relations, 581–2; believes unlimited immigration to threat to Israeli 'viability',
615

Drake, A. E. C., and the Iranian crisis 1951,
672

Druzes, 364

Duce, James Terry, confidence in Arabs, 44;
believes Ibn Saud will not sever relations
with Aramco because of Palestine, 196;
predicts that war in Palestine will be 'a
cruel and bloody one' reminiscent of the
crusades, 202; buoyantly optimistic
about Aramco continuing to provide
ham and eggs, coffee, orange juice, and
hot cakes in air conditioned rooms, i.e.
the Americanization of Saudi Arabia,
203; and the 'Golden Gimmick', 597

Economic development, policies of the
British in the Middle East, vii–viii, 4, 8,
16, 20; difficulty in recruiting experts,
18 n. 21; paradox of economic dependency and British predominance, 21;
frustrated by instability, 50; and Saudi
Arabia, 180 ff.; and Cyprus, 206 ff.,
213 ff.; and Iraq, 309–10, 318, 592 ff.;
and Transjordan, 355 ff.; and the Tennessee Valley Authority as a model for
the Middle East, 405; the key to political

stability, 592; subsidized by Iraqi oil
revenues, 600 ff.; discussion of at the
1949 F.O. conference, 604 ff.

Economist, The, change in tone because of
Barbara Ward, 219 n. 39; on 'Greater
Syria', 362 n. 37; on the *Exodus* incident, 464; on anti-Semitism, 465, 476;
on the balance sheet of the British
experience in Palestine, 476; on the
'whiff of grapeshot' school of thought,
739

Eddy, William A., background as U.S. Minister in Saudi Arabia and consultant to
Aramco, 195; believes Ibn Saud ready to
die an honourable death on the battlefield of Palestine, 196

Eden, Anthony, pledges on Arab unity,
123–4; on intervention in Egypt in
1942, 124–5; and the disturbances in
Syria causing a threat to the security of
the whole of the Middle East, 147–8;
'Spears again!', 152; and the Syrian crisis
of May 1945, 168–9; on the 1936 Treaty
with Egypt as one of the few worthwhile settlements 'in that time of international lawlessness', 229 n. 6; and the
Parliamentary debate of May 1946, 238–
9; attitude towards intervention contrasted with Bevin's 256; pledge to the
Senusi in 1942, 267; on the Persian oil
crisis, 686

Edmonds, R. H. G., on African nationalism
and Sudanese independence, 262

Egypt, nationalist reaction to British troops
in Canal Zone, 10; sterling balances,
12–13; resources of, 16; question of
troop numbers, 17; military potential for
the British, 18; corruption, 19; and
regional defence schemes, 22 ff.; and
Soviet aims, 28 ff.; poses uncertainty for
Chiefs of Staff 1946, 31; General Marshall on British liquidation of position
in, 99; treaty relations in 1948, 105 ff.;
and 'unity of the Nile valley', 109, 126;
the key to British defence of Middle
East, 115; resentment towards British
condescending attitude, 121–2; and the
Arab League, 128 ff.; described by
Daniel Lascelles as suffering from 'an
acute inferiority complex', 141; Hankey
compares British enlightened policy in
and France's dark shadow in the Levant,
153; criticism of Saudi Arabia for becoming a satellite of U.S., 204; and Cyprus,
208 ff.; Killearn's historical analysis of,
226–7; occupation of by British in 1882
and slogan 'Egypt for the Egyptians',

French, 168; eloquent denunciation of the French bombardment of Damascus, 170; overthrown by Zaim, 622-3

RAF, and Egyptian Treaty of 1936, 230; incident with the Israelis January 1949, 565; and question of troops in the Canal Zone, 602
Rafah, 565
Rafidain Oil Company, 594 n. 47
Rahman, Sir Abdul, bias of during UNSCOP proceedings, 470 n. 17
Ramle, 547
Ramsbotham, Peter, on taxation of the oil companies, 598; on the principle of the fifty-fifty split, 599; on boards of directors, 600; on Walter Levy, 677 n. 5
Ras Tanura, 182
Rand, Ivan, and UNSCOP, 471-2
Rashid Ali, revolt of 1941, 311 ff.; regarded by British as a renegade, 313; his name invoked during 1948 crisis, 340, 343
Razmara, Ali, his background of 'liberal nationalism' and the climate of political violence, 636; and the Supplemental Oil Agreement, 640 ff.
Red Sea *see* Middle East *and* 107, 273, 300
refugees *see* Jewish refugees
Regent of Iraq (Abdul Ilah) assessed by British as a weak personality, 310-11; restored by British bayonets in 1941, 313; strengths of described by Stewart Perowne, 315-16; his precarious position, 317; and elections, 318 ff.; and defence arrangements with the British, 325 ff.; and the Treaty of 1948, 333 ff.; his ministers 'gibbering with fear' during 1948 crisis, 336; and the aftermath, 337 ff.; and Abdullah, 364
Renton, J. M. L., historical analysis of the Iraqi army, 323-4; and the future of the Iraqi air bases, 327; believes Regent managed to prevent revolution during 1948 crisis, 336; on British officials misunderstanding nature of Iraqi nationalism, 337
Reston, James, on Palestine controversy and Middle Eastern oil, 497 n. 2
Riches, D. M. H., on possibility of revolution in Egypt, 257
Riyadh, 176
Robertson, Sir Brian, and the need for a resolute stand at Suez, 733-4
Robertson, Sir James, on 'Nokkers' (Nokrashi) as 'an honest if misguided patriot', 261 n. 85; and Sir Robert Howe, 700-1; on the Sudan Political Service, 702; his

achievements with Legislative Council and the problem of the southern Sudan, 703; denounces Americans for 'selling the Sudan', 717
Robinson and Gallagher, debate about 'Imperialism of Free Trade' and the nature of imperialism (relevant passages in the book), vii, x; the imperial system to be sustained by other methods, i.e., the Commonwealth, 8; history of postwar period may be regarded an unsuccessful attempt at conversion to informal system, 15; British influence and 'development', 21; 'three-tier' explanation applied to evacuation of Palestine, 27; and to Libya, 265; Greece to be kept 'as a satellite in our own orbit', 84, 89, 91; 'official mind', 118-19; sustaining the informal empire by economic and social reform, 121; and the occupation of Egypt, 227 n. 1; in Transjordan nomenclature might change but business as usual, 354; 'sub-imperialism' in Transjordan, 362; use of the United Nations to maintain informal empire in Middle East, 460; Attlee on 'Dominion status' and 'independence', 662
Roosevelt, Eleanor, and Palestine policy in 1947, 483
Roosevelt, Elliot, and Bevin's reaction to *As He Saw It*, 37 n. 66
Roosevelt, Franklin D., his reputation as a pro-Zionist, 36-7; and 'full consultation' formula, 36 n. 65; assurances to Ibn Saud on question of Zionism, 36 n. 66, 174, 421; 'thrilled' with idea of developing the 'backward nation' of Iran, 64; believes that French cannot be trusted to fulfil promises of independence in the Levant, 165; on Saudi Arabia being 'a little far afield for us!', 184; assures Churchill that Americans are not making 'sheep's eyes' at British oil fields in Iran and Iraq, 188
Rostow, Eugene, on 'messianic globaloney', 65; on 'American hand-wringing, dithering, ineffectiveness' in Palestine, 102
Rowan, T. L., on Cyprus, 216 n. 33
Royal Dutch-Shell Group, 594
Rundall, F. B. A., on Dardanelles scare, 81
Rusk, Dean, and Palestine controversy, 500 ff.; irritated at British neutrality, 501; and proposals for a trusteeship regime in Palestine, 507; doubts that Truman will oppose the setting up of a Jewish state, 518; and the possibility of a truce, 523-4; on Jewish determination